A SHAKESPEAREAN GENEALOGY

This chart reflects Shakespeare's history plays and is thus not historically accurate. Many descendants of Henry II and Edward III are omitted. On occasion, Shakespeare combined or simply invented historical figures. These deviations from fact are explained in the notes.

In the chart, the names of Kings and Queens are printed in capitals, and the dates of their reigns are printed in bold. The names of characters appearing in the plays are underlined.

Henry
d. 1183

Edward, Prince of
Wales 1330–1376

RICHARD II
1367–1400
(**1377–99**)

William of
Hatfield

Lionel, Duke of
Clarence 1338–1368

Philippa
m. Edmund
Mortimer, Earl
of March

RICHARD I   Philip Faulconbridge*
1157–1199   (Richard Plantagenet)
(**1189–99**)

John of Gaunt,
Duke of Lancaster
1340–1399
m. Blanche of
Lancaster
m. Constance of
Castile
m. Katherine
Swynford

HENRY IV
1367–1413
(**1399–1413**)

Thomas Beaufort,
Duke of Exeter
1377–1427

Henry Beaufort,
Bishop of Winchester
1375–1447

HENRY II
1133–1189
(**1154–89**)
m. Eleanor
of Aquitaine
d. 1204

Geoffrey, d. 1186 Arthur
m. Constance   1187–1203
of Brittany

John Beaufort,
Earl of Somerset
1372–1409

Joan Beaufort
m. Ralph Neville,
Earl of
Westmoreland

JOHN 1167–1216 HENRY III   EDWARD I
(**1199–1216**)   1207–1272   1239–1307
                  (**1216–72**)   (**1272–1307**)

EDWARD II
1284–1327
(**1307–27**)

Edmund of Langley,
Duke of York
1341–1402

Edward, Duke of
Aumerle d. 1415

Richard, Earl
of Cambridge
d. 1415 m. Anne
Mortimer (above)

EDWARD III
1312–1377
(**1327–77**)
m. Philippa of
Hainault

Thomas of
Woodstock, Duke of
Gloucester 1355–1397

Anne

Eleanor   Blanche, d. 1252
m. Alfonso VIII,   m. Louis VIII
King of Castile   of France

William of
Windsor

*Philip Faulconbridge, the bastard son of Richard I, had no historical existence. Such a character appears in the play *The Life and Death of King John* and is referred to in passing in Holinshed's *Chronicles*.

† In the character of Edmund Mortimer, Shakespeare combines two historical figures. The Edmund Mortimer who married Catrin, daughter of Owain Glyndŵr, was the grandson of Lionel, Duke of Clarence, and the younger brother of Roger, Earl of March. He died in 1409. Shakespeare combines him with his nephew, the Edmund Mortimer recognized by Richard II as his heir (d. 1424). This second Edmund was the brother of Anne Mortimer and the uncle of Richard Plantagenet.

‡ The character of the Duke of Somerset combines Henry Beaufort with his younger brother Edmund (d. 1471), who succeeded him as Duke.

Elizabeth Mortimer ("Kate") m. Henry Percy ("Hotspur") 1364–1403 — Henry, Earl of Northumberland 1394–1455

EDWARD IV 1442–1483 (1461–83) m. Elizabeth Woodville d. 1492 — EDWARD V 1470–1483 (1483)
— Richard, Duke of York 1472–1483
— Elizabeth of York 1465–1503 m. HENRY VII (below)

— Edmund, Earl of Rutland 1443–1460

Edmund Mortimer†

— George, Duke of Clarence 1449–1478 m. Isabel Neville (below)

Anne Mortimer m. Richard, Earl of Cambridge (below) — Richard Plantagenet, Duke of York 1411–1460 m. Cicely Neville (below)

RICHARD III 1452–1485 (1483–85) m. Anne Neville (below) — Edward, Prince of Wales

HENRY V 1387–1422 (1413–22) m. Catherine 1401–1437

— HENRY VI 1421–1471 (1422–61) m. Margaret of Anjou d. 1482

— Edward, Prince of Wales 1453–1471 m. Anne Neville (below)

— Arthur m. Catherine of Aragon (below)

Thomas, Duke of Clarence d. 1421

— Margaret m. James IV of Scotland — James V of Scotland

Mary, Queen of Scots

John of Lancaster, Duke of Bedford 1389–1435

JAMES I 1566–1625 (1603–25)

Humphrey, Duke of Gloucester 1391–1447 m. Eleanor Cobham d. 1454

John Beaufort, Duke of Somerset 1403–1444

— Margaret Beaufort m. Edmund Tudor, Earl of Richmond

— HENRY VII 1457–1509 (1485–1509) m. Elizabeth of York (above)

HENRY VIII 1491–1547 (1509–47) m. Catherine of Aragon

— MARY I 1516–1558 (1553–58) m. Philip of Spain

Edmund Beaufort, Duke of Somerset 1406–1455

— Henry Beaufort, Duke of Somerset 1436–1464‡

m. Anne Boleyn

— ELIZABETH I 1533–1603 (1558–1603)

m. Jane Seymour

— Isabel Neville d. 1476 m. George, Duke of Clarence (above)

Richard Neville, Earl of Salisbury 1400–1460 — Richard Neville, Earl of Warwick 1428–1471

— EDWARD VI 1537–1553 (1547–53)

m. Anne of Cleves

— John Neville, Marquess of Montague d. 1471

— Anne Neville d. 1485 m. Edward, Prince of Wales (above)

m. RICHARD III (above)

m. Katherine Howard

m. Katherine Parr

Cicely Neville m. Richard Plantagenet, Duke of York (above)

— Mary m. Charles Brandon — Frances

Jane Grey 1537–1554

Humphrey, Duke of Buckingham 1402–1460 — Humphrey Stafford d. 1455 — Henry, Duke of Buckingham 1454?–1483 — Edward, Duke of Buckingham 1478–1521

RICHARD II, 1377–99   RICHARD was the eldest son of EDWARD THE BLACK PRINCE, himself the eldest son of KING EDWARD III, who ruled England from 1327 to 1377. When the BLACK PRINCE died in battle in France in 1376, RICHARD became the legitimate heir to the throne. He ruled from EDWARD's death in 1377 until he was deposed in 1399 by HENRY BOLINGBROKE, the eldest son of JOHN OF GAUNT, DUKE OF LANCASTER. Because he was the fourth son of EDWARD III, GAUNT and his Lancastrian descendants had weaker hereditary claims to the throne than did RICHARD. When deposed, RICHARD had no children to succeed him, but he recognized EDMUND MORTIMER, FIFTH EARL OF MARCH, as his heir presumptive. This MORTIMER was descended from LIONEL, DUKE OF CLARENCE, the third son of EDWARD III, and therefore also had stronger hereditary claims to the throne than did BOLINGBROKE. SHAKESPEARE combined this MORTIMER with his uncle EDMUND MORTIMER, who married OWAIN GLYNDŴR'S DAUGHTER.

HENRY IV, 1399–1413   HENRY BOLINGBROKE, eldest son of JOHN OF GAUNT, seized the throne from RICHARD II in 1399. When HENRY died in 1413, he was succeeded by his eldest son, PRINCE HAL, who became HENRY V.

HENRY V, 1413–22   HENRY V became king in 1413 and reigned until his death in 1422. He was succeeded by his son, HENRY VI.

HENRY VI, 1422–61   HENRY VI was less than one year old when he succeeded his father, HENRY V. In the young king's minority, his uncle HUMPHREY, DUKE OF GLOUCESTER, was named Lord Protector, and the kingdom was ruled by an aristocratic council. HENRY VI assumed personal authority in 1437. He was deposed in 1461 by his third cousin, who was crowned EDWARD IV. HENRY was murdered in 1471.

EDWARD IV, 1461–83   EDWARD, the eldest son of RICHARD, DUKE OF YORK, seized the throne from HENRY VI in 1461. His Yorkist claim to the throne derived from his grandmother, ANNE MORTIMER, who was descended from LIONEL, third son of EDWARD III, and was sister to that EDMUND MORTIMER recognized by RICHARD II as his heir presumptive; EDWARD IV's grandfather, RICHARD, EARL OF CAMBRIDGE, was the son of EDMUND OF LANGLEY, fifth son of EDWARD III. EDWARD IV reigned until his death in 1483. His heir was his eldest son (EDWARD), but the throne was usurped by his brother RICHARD, DUKE OF GLOUCESTER.

RICHARD III, 1483–85   RICHARD III was the youngeer brother of EDWARD IV. After the death of EDWARD IV in 1483, RICHARD prevented the coronation of EDWARD V with a claim of illegitimacy and succeeded to the throne himself. EDWARD and his younger brother, RICHARD, DUKE OF YORK, were murdered in the Tower of London. RICHARD III was killed at the Battle of Bosworth Field in 1485, and the kingdom fell to the victor, HENRY TUDOR, EARL OF RICHMOND.

HENRY VII, 1485–1509   HENRY TUDOR seized the throne from RICHARD III in 1485. He was descended from JOHN OF GAUNT by JOHN's third marriage, with CATHERINE SWYNFORD. He married ELIZABETH, daughter of EDWARD IV, uniting the houses of Lancaster and York. He died in 1509 and was succeeded by his son, HENRY VIII.

HENRY VIII, 1509–47   HENRY was the second son of HENRY VII. His older brother, ARTHUR, died in 1502. HENRY VIII's first wife was CATHERINE OF ARAGON, who bore his daughter MARY. His second wife, ANNE BOLEYN, was the mother of ELIZABETH. His third wife, JANE SEYMOUR, bore him a son, who succeeded to the throne as EDWARD VI after HENRY VIII died in 1547.

EDWARD VI, 1547–53   EDWARD VI was nine years old when he became king. From 1547 to 1549, the realm was governed by a Lord Protector, the DUKE OF SOMERSET; power then passed to JOHN DUDLEY, DUKE OF NORTHUMBERLAND. When EDWARD VI died in 1553, NORTHUMBERLAND attempted unsuccessfully to prevent the succession of MARY TUDOR by installing as queen his daughter-in-law, LADY JANE GREY, a great-granddaughter of HENRY VII.

MARY I, 1553–58   MARY, daughter of HENRY VIII and his first wife, CATHERINE OF ARAGON, came to the throne in 1553. She married KING PHILIP OF SPAIN but died childless. She was succeeded by her half sister, ELIZABETH.

ELIZABETH I, 1558–1603   ELIZABETH, the daughter of HENRY VIII and his second wife, ANNE BOLEYN, became queen after the death of her half sister, MARY, in 1558. She ruled until her death in 1603. She was succeeded by her cousin JAMES.

JAMES I, 1603–1625   JAMES VI OF SCOTLAND became JAMES I OF ENGLAND in 1603. His claim to the throne of England derived from his great-grandmother, MARGARET TUDOR, a daughter of HENRY VII who married JAMES IV OF SCOTLAND. JAMES ruled England and Scotland until his death in 1625; he was succeeded by his son, CHARLES I.

THE NORTON SHAKESPEARE

THIRD EDITION

Tragedies

THE NORTON
SHAKESPEARE

THIRD EDITION

Tragedies

Stephen Greenblatt, *General Editor*
HARVARD UNIVERSITY

Walter Cohen
UNIVERSITY OF MICHIGAN

Suzanne Gossett, *General Textual Editor*
LOYOLA UNIVERSITY CHICAGO (EMERITA)

Jean E. Howard
COLUMBIA UNIVERSITY

Katharine Eisaman Maus
UNIVERSITY OF VIRGINIA

Gordon McMullan, *General Textual Editor*
KING'S COLLEGE LONDON

W · W · NORTON & COMPANY · NEW YORK · LONDON

W. W. Norton & Company has been independent since its founding in 1923, when William Warder Norton and Mary D. Herter Norton first published lectures delivered at the People's Institute, the adult education division of New York City's Cooper Union. The firm soon expanded its program beyond the Institute, publishing books by celebrated academics from America and abroad. By mid-century, the two major pillars of Norton's publishing program—trade books and college texts—were firmly established. In the 1950s, the Norton family transferred control of the company to its employees, and today—with a staff of 400 and a comparable number of trade, college, and professional titles published each year—W. W. Norton & Company stands as the largest and oldest publishing house owned wholly by its employees.

Editor: Julia Reidhead
Managing Editor, College: Marian Johnson
Associate Editor: Emily Stuart
Manuscript Editors: Harry Haskell, Alice Vigliani
Media Editor: Carly Fraser Doria
Media Project Editor: Kristin Sheerin
Production Manager: Eric Pier-Hocking
Digital Production: Mateus Texeira, Colleen Caffrey
Marketing Manager, Literature: Kim Bowers
Photo Editor: Trish Marx
Composition: Westchester Book Company
Manufacturing: RR Donnelley

The Library of Congress has catalogued the full edition as follows:
Shakespeare, William, 1564–1616.
The Norton Shakespeare / Stephen Greenblatt, General Editor, Harvard University; Walter Cohen, University of Michigan; Suzanne Gossett, General Textual Editor, Loyola University Chicago (Emerita); Jean E. Howard, Columbia University; Katharine Eisaman Maus, University of Virginia; Gordon McMullan, General Textual Editor, King's College London.—Third edition.
pages cm
Includes bibliographical references and index.
ISBN 978-0-393-93499-1 (hardcover)
I. Greenblatt, Stephen, 1943– editor. II. Cohen, Walter, 1949– editor. III. Gossett, Suzanne, editor. IV. Howard, Jean E. (Jean Elizabeth), 1948– editor. V. Maus, Katharine Eisaman, 1955– editor. VI. McMullan, Gordon, 1962– editor. VII. Title.
PR2754.G74 2015
822.3'3—dc23

2015018869

This edition: ISBN 978-0-393-93860-9

W. W. Norton & Company, Inc., 500 Fifth Avenue, New York, NY 10110-0017
wwnorton.com

W. W. Norton & Company Ltd., Castle House, 75/76 Wells Street, London W1T 3QT

Contents

Additional works, media, contextual materials, and bibliographies
are available in the Digital Edition

TRAGEDIES

Appendices

DIGITAL EDITION

Shakespeare and His Works

Illustrations

Preface

This Third Edition of *The Norton Shakespeare* is both a continuation and a new beginning. Readers who have already found the format of the printed book and its editorial apparatus to their liking will get what they are looking for. The emphasis continues to be on the pleasure of reading, with a particular attention to undergraduates who may be encountering Shakespeare for the first time. "If then you do not like him," wrote Shakespeare's first editors almost four hundred years ago, "surely you are in some manifest danger not to understand him." We have from the start made every effort, through the glosses, notes, introductions, and other materials, to facilitate understanding and hence to enhance liking. We are careful not to overburden Shakespeare's words with explication or to crowd the page with distracting commentary. The clear, uncluttered, single-column format is designed to encourage absorption. But we try to offer enough help to allow the beauty and the luminous intelligence of these stupendous works to shine.

We have in this edition carefully revised each of our introductions (including the long General Introduction) and reviewed every one of our notes and glosses, altering and adding where appropriate. Our goal has been to hold onto what our readers have told us works well, but also to update the introductions, bibliographies, filmographies, and other materials to reflect current scholarship, shifting emphases, and newly released films. An entirely new feature of this edition is an illuminating Performance Note, by Brett Gamboa (Dartmouth College), that accompanies each of the plays. These notes describe the particular and recurrent theatrical challenges with which actors and directors have grappled in mounting any given work. The strategies devised over the centuries in response to these challenges are a fascinating point of entry into critical issues of interpretation. The notes are also an invaluable guide to what audiences should look for when they attend a new production.

From its inception, *The Norton Shakespeare* has paid exceptionally close attention to the accuracy as well as the accessibility of the texts and, in particular, to the challenge posed by those plays that exist in multiple substantive versions. For the Third Edition, all of Shakespeare's plays and poems have been newly edited, from scratch, by an international team of leading textual scholars. This hugely ambitious and complex undertaking has been based on the principle of single-text editing— that is, where more than one early authoritative text of a given play has survived, rather than merging them into one (as has been traditionally done), we have edited each text in its own right. We thereby offer the reader texts as close as possible to the original versions as read by Shakespeare's contemporaries. A lively and accessible new General Textual Introduction fully articulates this principle, explores the nature of the documents that have come down to us from Shakespeare's own time, and explains in detail the editorial practices on which this new text of the complete works is meticulously based.

Approximately half of Shakespeare's plays appeared both in small-format versions (quartos), printed in the playwright's own lifetime, and in the large-format First Folio (1623), published seven years after his death. As early as the eighteenth century, careful readers began to notice that there were differences, sometimes minor and sometimes quite significant, between these printings of the same plays. Starting with the landmark Shakespeare editions of Alexander Pope (1723) and Lewis Theobald (1733), editors initiated the practice of blending the different versions together, picking and choosing as their taste dictated or as they imagined that Shakespeare would have done, had he himself produced a definitive text. Hence, for example, the two distinct texts of *King Lear* were routinely fashioned into a single text, with editors combining lines that appear only in one or the other early version and choosing among hundreds of variant readings.

From its inception, *The Norton Shakespeare* rejected this editorial method (known as "conflation"). We have continued in the current print edition our hallmark practice of offering, on facing pages, the 1608 Quarto text of *King Lear* and the substantial revision of the play as printed in the First Folio (1623). While each version may be read independently—we have provided glosses and footnotes for each—the significant points of difference between the two are immediately apparent and available for comparison. It is thus possible to watch in extraordinarily sharp focus changes in the early modern text of one of Shakespeare's greatest plays. We recognize at the same time that a combined text, in one form or another, has long served as the *King Lear* upon which innumerable performances of the play have been based and on which a huge body of literary criticism has been written. Hence in addition to providing the Quarto and Folio texts, we wanted to offer readers a version of this great tragedy that combines the two without entirely erasing their differences. The solution that we provide in these pages is what in the first two editions of *The Norton Shakespeare* we used in the comparable case of *Hamlet*. We print the Folio text of *King Lear*, but we have moved the lines that are solely in the Quarto into the body of the play. In doing so, however, we did not want simply to produce a conflated version. We have therefore indented the Q-only passages, printed them in a slightly different typeface, and numbered them in such a way as to make clear their provenance. We call this a "scars-and-stitches" solution, since, though still eminently readable and enjoyable, it clearly marks the points of insertion and difference.

The Norton Shakespeare, then, includes three separate texts of *King Lear*. The reader can compare them, analyze the role of editors in constructing the texts we now call Shakespeare's, explore in detail the kinds of decisions that playwrights, editors, and printers make and remake, witness firsthand the historical transformation of what might at first glance seem fixed and unchanging. We offer extraordinary access to this supremely brilliant, difficult, compelling play.

Hamlet, the other great tragedy at the very center of Shakespeare's achievement, similarly exists in multiple versions: the 1604 Second Quarto (Q2), the longest of the early editions; the 1623 Folio text (F), which lacks some 200 lines found in Q2 but includes more than 70 lines not found there; and, casting a fascinating light on the more familiar version of the tragedy, the drastically different First Quarto (Q1, the so-called Bad Quarto). As in the case of *Lear*, editors for centuries have routinely conflated the Q2 and F *Hamlets*.

The realities of bookbinding—not to mention our recognition of the limited time in the typical undergraduate syllabus—preclude our offering in the print edition four *Hamlets* (Q1, Q2, F, and combined) to parallel the three *Lears*. What we have provided in these pages instead is a new incarnation of the solution we came up with in the first two editions of *The Norton Shakespeare*. While basing our *Hamlet* on the Q2 text, we have moved the Folio passages, among which are some of the tragedy's most famous lines, into the body of the play. But, as with the "scars-and-stitches" *Lear*, we have made it possible for readers who are interested to see what has been added.

The growing interest in the possibility of teaching the First Quarto of *Hamlet* has also led us to add that strange text, in fully glossed and annotated form, alongside the more familiar version of Shakespeare's most famous tragedy. Readers can wonder at a *Hamlet* in which the hero muses "To be, or not to be—ay, there's the point," and they can see how drastically one theater troupe in Shakespeare's own time probably cut the play for performance.

These and other changes all serve to keep *The Norton Shakespeare* fresh and current. But this Third Edition, as I have already suggested, is much more than a careful revision and updating. It is a thoroughgoing rethinking both of the entire Shakespeare corpus and of the whole way in which Shakespeare is experienced by contemporary readers. For the purposes of this preface, a single feature of the newly edited text should be emphasized: it was created not only for the print edition, but also for a new and exciting Digital Edition. From its inception the print edition featured both the Quarto and the Folio texts of *King Lear*, and we have now added the First Quarto of *Hamlet*. Our Digital Edition makes available fully glossed and annotated Quarto and Folio versions of the plays—fifteen in all—for which more than one early authoritative text exists, thereby offering the reader access to these plays as they were first experienced by Shakespeare's contemporaries. This means not only the two versions of *Lear*, which can be viewed in side-by-side scrolling format for comparison as well as individually, and not only the three versions of *Hamlet*. It also means multiple versions, with fascinating variants, of such beloved, centrally important plays as *Romeo and Juliet*, *Othello*, *Richard II*, *Richard III*, *Henry V*, *Love's Labor's Lost*, and *A Midsummer Night's Dream*. There are Quarto and Folio versions as well of 2 and 3 *Henry VI*, *Titus Andronicus*, 2 *Henry IV*, *The Merry Wives of Windsor*, and *Troilus and Cressida*. The Digital Edition also offers an appendix of selected scenes from a number of multiple-version plays, presented side-by-side so that they can easily be compared for teaching purposes. For anyone interested in Shakespeare's practices of composition and revision and in the fascinating process through which his plays, passing through the printing house, have managed to reach us, the digital *Norton Shakespeare* is an unprecedented resource.

Links to the widely respected *Norton Facsimile of the First Folio of Shakespeare*, edited by Charlton Hinman, and to quarto facsimile pages make it possible for readers to see for themselves the original materials with which the editors have been working to create this new text of the complete works.

In the digital *Norton Shakespeare* we also include for the first time an edition of the full text of *Sir Thomas More*, a multi-authored play, unpublished in the period, whose manuscript includes a section in Shakespeare's own hand, the only surviving one of its kind. We also include an edition of *Edward III*, another play of which Shakespeare appears to have been part-author. Both texts are interesting as examples of the collaborative nature of much Elizabethan and Jacobean theater, a collaboration reflected as well in the late plays *Pericles*, *Henry VIII*, *The Two Noble Kinsmen*, the lost *Cardenio*, and—more debatably—such works as 1 *Henry VI*, *Titus Andronicus*, and *Timon of Athens*.

This extraordinary wealth of texts, all complete with introductions, notes, and glosses, has been made possible by the vastness of the digital space. That space has allowed us to supplement the useful aids in the print edition—including maps, genealogies, a glossary, a short bibliography, a timeline, and a selection of key documents—with further resources. For the Digital Edition, the volume editors have created expanded bibliographies for the study of Shakespeare's works, and Misha Teramura (Harvard University), who edited and glossed the documents in the print text, has assembled and edited a larger archive of Tudor and Stuart documents relevant to Shakespeare and his theater world.

The remarkable expansion of texts is only the beginning. The resources of the Digital Edition have made possible innovations that were, until very recently, only a teacher's idle daydreams. Shakespeare scholars have long understood that the decisions editors make—for example, choosing one variant over another, or adding stage directions, or making consistent the multiple speech prefixes often used for a single character—can affect the meaning of the plays. But on the printed page it has been difficult to call attention to the significance of these decisions without interrupting the flow of the reading experience, while the long lists of textual variants printed at the ends of plays are so much raw data, rarely consulted or understood by anyone but experts. Now, by clicking a marginal icon, readers can summon illuminating Textual Comments for each play, written by the textual editor, that focus on textual-editing decision points influencing interpretation. It is possible for all interested readers now to understand textual cruxes and to see—and, for that matter, to call into question—key editorial choices.

Similarly, a crucially important dimension of Shakespeare's texts, as everyone grasps, is that they were originally intended for performance. Hence the brief discussion in the General Introduction of the theatrical scene Shakespeare encountered and helped to transform is now greatly enriched in "The Theater of Shakespeare's Time," a lively and original essay by Holger Schott Syme (University of Toronto). Syme conjures up a fiercely competitive world of multiple theater companies and rival venues, all scrambling for plays that will survive the attention of the government censor and lure crowds of spectators to part with their pennies.

Performance is obviously not only a matter of historical interest. It remains, for most of us and certainly for our students, central to the full experience of the plays. But, without overfreighting the page, it has been difficult to highlight this dimension in the printed book. Descriptions of famous performances, from Garrick to the present, rarely capture the significance of key interpretive choices by actors or directors. Now clicking on marginal icons keyed to particular moments in the texts allows one to read incisive and insightful Performance Comments that supplement the Performance Note preceding each play. These comments, by Brett Gamboa, highlight passages that are particularly famous challenges in performance and explore how a director or actor's interpretive choices affect meaning. Taken individually, the Performance Comments call attention to specific decisions that must be made in the realization of a play; taken together, they constitute a brilliant exploration of the performative dimensions of Shakespeare's art.

The performative dimension is enhanced by two further features of the Digital Edition. First, there are recordings of all of the songs—66 of them—in the plays, from the award-winning *Shakespeare's Songbook* audio companion by Ross Duffin. It is now possible for readers to take in fully the pervasive presence of music in Shakespeare's plays, something that the printed stage direction *"Music"* cannot hope to do. Second, there are over eight hours of spoken-word audio of key passages and scenes and those that pose particular challenges to readers. These have been specially recorded for the Digital Edition by the highly regarded company, Actors from the London Stage. With a simple click it is now possible for readers to hear the words on the page come alive in the voices of gifted actors.

The digital *Norton Shakespeare* brings together in one place an unparalleled array of resources for understanding and enjoying Shakespeare. These resources are not the primitive accumulation of materials, of dubious utility or reliability, which often makes the web an untrustworthy guide. Rather, each of the texts and other material has received the same careful scholarly and pedagogical attention that has made the print edition a success. But we are aware that different readers will have different interests and needs, often varying from time to time. The reading experience of the Digital Edition, including the visibility of icons, line numbers, glosses, and notes, can be easily customized, so that with a click readers can either "quiet" the page or access Norton's abundant reading help. The Digital Edition platform provides customizable highlighting, annotating, and comment-sharing tools that facilitate active reading.

The publisher also provides instructors with a wealth of free resources beyond the Digital Edition. An Instructor Resource Disc created for the new edition features the more than eight hours of spoken-word audio recorded by Actors from the London Stage, 150 songs, and over 100 images from the book in both JPEG and PowerPoint for easy classroom presentation. The images are available for download on the publisher's instructor resource page, wwnorton.com/instructors. In addition, the Norton Shakespeare YouTube channel brings together a carefully curated and regularly updated collection of the best of the web's Shakespeare video resources, allowing instructors to easily show clips from stage and film in class.

The extraordinary labor of love that has led to this new and revised edition of *The Norton Shakespeare* has involved a large number of collaborators. The volume editors owe a substantial debt of thanks to the readers of the earlier editions. Our readers have formed a large, engaged community, and their endorsements, observations, and suggestions for revision and expansion have proved invaluable. We have also profited from the highly detailed reviews of each individual feature of the edition commissioned by the publisher and performed with exemplary seriousness by many of our most esteemed professional colleagues.

At the very center of the Third Edition is the newly edited text of the Complete Works, an enormous, exhaustive, and exhausting enterprise. We wish to acknowledge with deepest gratitude the extraordinary labors of our gifted team of textual editors, listed on the title-page spread, led with an exemplary blend of discipline, patience, intellectual seriousness, and scholarly rigor by Gordon McMullan and Suzanne Gossett.

The *Norton Shakespeare* editors have had the valuable—indeed, indispensable—support of our publisher and a host of undergraduate and graduate research assistants, colleagues, friends, and family, whose names we gratefully note in the Acknowledgments that follow. All of these companions have helped us find in this long collective enterprise what the "Dedicatorie Epistle" to the First Folio promises to its readers: delight. We make the same promise to the readers of our edition and invite them to continue the great Shakespearean collaboration.

STEPHEN GREENBLATT
CAMBRIDGE, MASSACHUSETTS

Volume Editors' Acknowledgments

The creation of this edition has drawn heavily on the resources, experience, and skill of its remarkable publisher, W. W. Norton. Norton's record of success in academic publishing has sometimes made it seem like a giant, akin to the multinational corporations that dominate the publishing world, but it is in fact the only major publishing house that is employee-owned. Our principal guide has been our brilliant editor Julia Reidhead, whose calm intelligence, common sense, and steady focus have been essential in enabling us to reach our goal. With this Third Edition, we were blessed once again with the indispensable judgment and project-editorial expertise of Marian Johnson, managing editor, college department, as well as scrupulous manuscript editing by Alice Vigliani and Harry Haskell. Carly Fraser Doria, literature media editor, skillfully guided us through the new waters of the Digital Edition, following Cliff Landesman's innovative lead. Assistant editor Emily Stuart managed with remarkable skill and graciousness the complexities of manuscript preparation and review. Kim Yi, managing editor, digital media, and Kristin Sheerin, digital project editor, oversaw the monumental checking and proofing of files. In addition, we are deeply grateful to Cara Folkman, media assistant editor; JoAnn Simony and Elizabeth Audley, digital file coordinators; Eric Pier-Hocking, production manager; and Debra Morton Hoyt, corporate art director, who, along with designer Timothy Hsu, created our Ortelius-inspired cover design. Thanks also to Mary Jo Mecca for design and construction of the jester hat. For invaluable help in creating the Digital Edition, we would like to thank Jane Chu and Colleen Caffrey, digital designers, and Mateus Teixiera and Kristian Sanford, digital production.

The editors have, in addition, had the valuable—indeed, indispensable—support of a host of undergraduate and graduate research assistants, colleagues, friends, and family. Even a partial listing of those to whom we owe our heartfelt thanks is very long, but we are all fortunate enough to live in congenial and supportive environments, and the edition has been part of our lives for a long time. We owe special thanks for sustained dedication and learning to our colleagues, friends, and principal assistants:

Stephen Greenblatt wishes to thank his talented research assistants at Harvard, including Maria Devlin, Seth Herbst, Rhema Hokama, David Nee, Elizabeth Weckhurst, Benjamin Woodring, Catherine Woodring, and, above all, Misha Teramura. In addition, he is grateful for valuable assistance from Rebecca Cook and Aubrey Everett, along with advice and counsel from many friends, colleagues, and students. Thanks also go to C. Edward McGee (University of Waterloo), Barbara D. Palmer (late of the University of Mary Washington), Sylvia Thomas (the Yorkshire Archaeological Society), and John M. Wasson (late of Washington State University). He acknowledges a special and enduring debt to Ramie Targoff (Brandeis University).

Walter Cohen wishes to thank Marjorie Levinson (University of Michigan).

Jean Howard would like to acknowledge the help of each of her excellent research assistants at Columbia University: Bryan Lowrance, John Kuhn, Alexander Paulsson Lash, Chris McKeen, and especially Emily Shortslef, whose scholarly contributions have been indispensable and impeccable and whose good cheer is astonishingly unflagging.

We gratefully acknowledge the reviewers who provided thoughtful critiques for particular plays or of the project as a whole: Bernadette Andrea (University of Texas at San Antonio), John M. Archer (New York University), Oliver Arnold (University of California–Berkeley), Amanda Bailey (University of Connecticut), JoAnn D. Barbour

(Texas Woman's University), Catherine Belsey (Swansea University), Barbara Bono (University at Buffalo), Michael D. Bristol (McGill University), Karen Britland (University of Wisconsin–Madison), James C. Bulman (Allegheny College), William C. Carroll (Boston University), Kent Cartwright (University of Maryland, College Park), Joseph Cerami (Texas A&M University), Julie Crawford (Columbia University), Jonathan Crewe (Dartmouth College), Stephen Deng (Michigan State University), Christy Desmet (University of Georgia), Donald R. Dickson (Texas A&M University), Mario DiGangi (Graduate Center of the City University of New York), Tobias Doering (University of Munich), Frances Dolan (University of California–Davis), John Drakakis (University of Stirling), Heather Dubrow (Fordham University), Holly Dugan (George Washington University), Amy E. Earhart (Texas A&M University), Katherine E. Eggert (University of Colorado–Boulder), Lars D. Engle (University of Tulsa), Christopher John Fitter (Rutgers University), Mary Floyd-Wilson (University of North Carolina–Chapel Hill), Susan Caroline Frye (University of Wyoming), Brett Gamboa (Dartmouth College), Evelyn Gajowski (University of Nevada, Las Vegas), Hugh Hartridge Grady, Jr. (Arcadia University), Kenneth Gross (University of Rochester), Elizabeth Hanson (Queen's University), Jonathan Gil Harris (George Washington University), Michael Hattaway (New York University), Diana Henderson (Massachusetts Institute of Technology), Terence Allan Hoagwood (Texas A&M University), Lucia Kristina Hodgson (Texas A&M University), Peter Holbrook (The University of Queensland), Peter Holland (University of Notre Dame), John W. Huntington (University of Illinois at Chicago), Lorna Hutson (University of St. Andrews), Coppélia Kahn (Brown University), Jeffrey Knapp (University of California–Berkeley), Yu Jin Ko (Wellesley College), Paul A. Kottman (The New School), Bryon Lew (Trent University), Genevieve Love (Colorado College), Julia R. Lupton (University of California–Irvine), Ellen MacKay (Indiana University), Cristina Malcolmson (Bates College), Lawrence G. Manley (Yale University), Steven Mentz (St. John's University), Erin Minear (College of William and Mary), Arash Moradi (Shiraz University), Ian Moulton (Arizona State University), Steven Mullaney (University of Michigan), Cyrus Mulready (State University of New York–New Paltz), Karen Newman (Brown University), Mary A. O'Farrell (Texas A&M University), Laurie E. Osborne (Colby College), Simon Palfrey (Oxford University), Garry Partridge (Texas A&M University), Thomas Pendleton (Iona College), Peter G. Platt (Barnard College), Christopher Pye (Williams College), Phyllis R. Rackin (University of Pennsylvania), Sally Robinson (Texas A&M University), Mary Beth Rose (University of Illinois at Chicago), Suparna Roychoudhury (Mount Holyoke College), Elizabeth D. Samet (United States Military Academy at West Point), Melissa E. Sanchez (University of Pennsylvania), Michael Schoenfeldt (University of Michigan), Laurie J. Shannon (Northwestern University), Jyotsna Singh (Michigan State University), Elizabeth Spiller (Florida State University), Tiffany Stern (Oxford University), Richard Strier (University of Chicago), Ayanna Thompson (George Washington University), Douglas Trevor (University of Michigan), Henry S. Turner (Rutgers University), Brian Walsh (Yale University), Tiffany Jo Werth (Simon Fraser University), Adam Zucker (University of Massachusetts).

General Textual Editors' Acknowledgments

First and foremost, we are grateful to Stephen Greenblatt for inviting us to imagine, and then to create, a wholly new text of Shakespeare for the Third Edition of *The Norton Shakespeare*; to the volume editors—Jean Howard, Katharine Maus, and Walter Cohen—for working closely with us and for supporting the single text–editing principle we adopted; and to Julia Reidhead, the edition's publisher, for her gracious engagement and direction at every stage. And of course we are hugely grateful to the remarkable team of editors with whom we have worked, all of whom, without exception, accepted the invitation with alacrity, edited superbly, completed their work in timely fashion, and tolerated the necessary processes stemming from the need to ensure that each individual play functions both in its own right and as part of the edition as a whole. We want to thank and acknowledge them all. We also wish to thank Lacey Conley, who provided invaluable research assistance at crucial moments in the creation of the text. None of this would have been possible without the indefatigable work of the team at Norton. Marian Johnson, managing editor, college, provided invaluable wisdom and care for the newly edited text. Cliff Landesman's enthusiasm for the project and his willingness to explore—and help us understand—the digital possibilities were invaluable. Carly Fraser Doria and Emily Stuart responded with remarkable generosity, patience, and professionalism to our requests and anxieties. And we are particularly grateful to Norton's copy editors, Alice Vigliani and Harry Haskell, for their wonderfully precise work on the texts of the plays.

Editors tend to fight like cats in a sack over the choices they make when editing Shakespeare—they did this in the eighteenth century, and they try their best to keep up the tradition today—yet they also know that they are in fact highly mutually dependent, and it matters a great deal to us to note that we have had a second set of collaborators in the creation of this new text, none of whom has had actual direct involvement in *The Norton Shakespeare*, Third Edition—due in some cases to working on equivalent editions for other presses—but without whose textual and critical work we could not have acquired the knowledge we needed to create this edition. These include David Bevington, Peter Blayney, A. R. Braunmuller, R. A. Foakes, John Jowett, David Scott Kastan, Laurie Maguire, Sonia Massai, Eric Rasmussen, Tiffany Stern, Gary Taylor, Stanley Wells, and Martin Wiggins. And we would like in particular to acknowledge our considerable debt to Richard Proudfoot, who mentored us both in the fine art of editing and whose knowledge of the Shakespearean text and generosity with that knowledge are unsurpassed. We should acknowledge too certain key resources without which our editorial work would have been, practically speaking, impossible: these include the British Library's remarkable Shakespeare in Quarto website and the online text and facsimiles provided by the Internet Shakespeare Edition (a remarkable enterprise led by the generous and endlessly energetic Michael Best).

Finally, we should also note that any edition of Shakespeare is merely one in a very long line, and all modern Shakespearean editors are indebted to the extraordinary work of the earliest toilers in the field—from Shakespeare's friends Heminges and Condell assembling the First Folio and thus providing the crucial basis for all subsequent work on the Shakespeare canon, to the anonymous editors of the Second, Third, and Fourth Folios, to the crucial work of Rowe, Capell, Pope, Johnson, Theobald, and their successors in the eighteenth, nineteenth, and twentieth centuries. How they did any of it without word-processing software and the resources of the Internet we cannot for the life of us figure out.

Gordon McMullan and Suzanne Gossett

General Introduction

STEPHEN GREENBLATT

"He was not of an age, but for all time!"

There are writers whose greatness is recognized only long after they have vanished from the earth. There are writers championed by a coterie of devoted followers who tend the flame of admiration against the cold world's indifference. There are writers beloved in their native land but despised abroad, and others neglected at home yet celebrated on distant shores. Shakespeare is none of these. His genius was recognized almost immediately. The famous words with which we have begun were written by his friend and rival Ben Jonson. They have been echoed innumerable times, across the centuries, across national and linguistic boundaries, across the demarcation lines of race and class, religion and ideology. Shakespeare belongs not simply to a particular culture—English culture of the late sixteenth and early seventeenth centuries—but to world culture, the dense network of constraints and entitlements, dreams and practices that help to make us fully human. Indeed, so absolute is Shakespeare's achievement that he has himself come to seem like great creating nature. His works embody the imagination's power to transcend time-bound beliefs and assumptions, particular historical circumstances, and specific artistic conventions. If we should ever be asked as a species to bring forward one artist who has most fully expressed the human condition, we could with confidence elect Shakespeare to speak for us. As it is, when we do ask ourselves the most fundamental questions about life—about love and hatred, ambition, desire, and fear, the demand for justice and the longing for a second chance—we repeatedly turn to Shakespeare for the words we wish to hear.

The near-worship Shakespeare inspires is one of the salient facts about his art. But we must at the same time acknowledge that this art is the product of peculiar historical circumstances and specific conventions, four centuries distant from our own. The acknowledgment is important because Shakespeare the working dramatist did not typically lay claim to the transcendent, visionary truths attributed to him by his most fervent admirers; his characters more modestly say, in the words of the magician Prospero, that their project was "to please" (*The Tempest,* Epilogue, line 13). The starting point, and perhaps the ending point as well, in any encounter with Shakespeare is simply to enjoy him, to savor his imaginative richness, to take pleasure in his infinite delight in language.

"If then you do not like him," Shakespeare's first editors wrote in 1623, "surely you are in some manifest danger not to understand him." Over the years, accommodations have been devised to make liking Shakespeare easier for everyone. When aspects of his language began to seem difficult, texts were published with notes and glosses. When the historical events he depicted receded into obscurity, explanatory introductions were written. When the stage sank to melodrama and light opera, Shakespeare made his appearance in suitably revised dress. When the populace had a craving for hippodrama, plays performed entirely on horseback, *Hamlet* was dutifully rewritten and mounted. When audiences went mad for realism, live frogs croaked in productions of *A Midsummer Night's Dream.* When the stage was stripped

1

bare and given over to stark exhibitions of sadistic cruelty, Shakespeare was our contemporary. And when the theater ceded some of its cultural centrality to radio, film, and television, Shakespeare moved effortlessly to Hollywood and the sound stages of the BBC.

This virtually universal appeal is one of the most astonishing features of the Shakespeare phenomenon: plays that were performed before glittering courts thrive in junior high school auditoriums; enemies set on destroying one another laugh at the same jokes and weep at the same catastrophes; some of the richest and most complex English verse ever written migrates with spectacular success into German and Italian, Hindi, Swahili, and Japanese. Is there a single, stable, continuous object that underlies all of these migrations and metamorphoses? Certainly not. The global diffusion and long life of Shakespeare's works depend on their extraordinary malleability, their protean capacity to elude definition and escape secure possession. His art is the supreme manifestation of the mobility of culture. At the same time, this art is not without identifiable shared features: across centuries and continents, family resemblances link many of the wildly diverse manifestations of plays such as *Romeo and Juliet, Hamlet,* and *Twelfth Night.* Moreover, if there is no clear limit or end point, there is a reasonably clear beginning, the England of the late sixteenth and early seventeenth centuries, when the plays and poems collected in *The Norton Shakespeare* made their first appearance.

An art virtually without end or limit but with an identifiable, localized, historical origin: Shakespeare's achievement defies the facile opposition between transcendent and time-bound. It is not necessary to choose between an account of Shakespeare as the scion of a particular culture and an account of him as a universal genius who created works that continually renew themselves across national and generational boundaries. On the contrary: crucial clues to understanding his art's remarkable power to soar beyond the time and place of its origin lie in the very soil from which that art sprang.

Shakespeare's World

Life and Death

Life expectancy at birth in early modern England was exceedingly low by our standards: under thirty years, compared with over seventy today. Infant mortality rates were extraordinarily high, and it is estimated that in the poorer parishes of London only about half the children survived to the age of fifteen, while the children of aristocrats fared only a little better. In such circumstances, some parents must have developed a certain detachment—one of Shakespeare's contemporaries writes of losing "some three or four children"—but there are many expressions of intense grief, so that we cannot assume that the frequency of death hardened people to loss or made it routine.

Still, the spectacle of death, along with that other great threshold experience, birth, must have been far more familiar to Shakespeare and his contemporaries than to ourselves. There was no equivalent in early modern England to our hospitals, and most births and deaths occurred at home. Physical means for the alleviation of pain and suffering were extremely limited—alcohol might dull the terror, but it was hardly an effective anesthetic—and medical treatment was generally both expensive and worthless, more likely to intensify suffering than to lead to a cure. This was a world without a concept of antiseptics, with little actual understanding of disease, with few effective ways of treating earaches or venereal disease, let alone the more terrible instances of what Shakespeare calls "the thousand natural shocks that flesh is heir to."

The worst of these shocks was the bubonic plague, which repeatedly ravaged England, and particularly English towns, until the third quarter of the seventeenth

Bill recording plague deaths in London, 1609.

century. The plague was terrifyingly sudden in its onset, rapid in its spread, and almost invariably lethal. Physicians were helpless in the face of the epidemic, though they prescribed amulets, preservatives, and sweet-smelling substances (on the theory that the plague was carried by noxious vapors). In the plague-ridden year of 1564, the year of Shakespeare's birth, some 254 people died in his native Stratford-upon-Avon, out of a total population of 800. The year before, some 20,000 Londoners are thought to have died; in 1593, almost 15,000; in 1603, 36,000, or over a sixth of the city's inhabitants. The social effects of these horrible visitations were severe: looting, violence, and despair, along with an intensification of the age's perennial poverty, unemployment, and food shortages. The London plague regulations of 1583, reissued with modifications in later epidemics, ordered that the infected and their households should be locked in their homes for a month; that the streets should be kept clean; that vagrants should be expelled; and that funerals and plays (as occasions in which large numbers of people gathered and infection could be spread) should be restricted or banned entirely. Comparable restrictions were not placed on gatherings for religious observance, since it was hoped that God would heed the desperate prayers of his suffering people.

The plague, then, had a direct and immediate impact on Shakespeare's own profession. City officials kept records of the weekly number of plague deaths; when these surpassed a certain number, the theaters were peremptorily closed. The basic idea was not only to prevent contagion but also to avoid making an angry God still angrier with the spectacle of idleness. While restricting public assemblies may in fact have slowed the epidemic, other public policies in times of plague, such as killing the cats and dogs, may have made matters worse (since the disease was spread not by these animals but by the fleas that bred on the black rats that infested the poorer neighborhoods). Moreover, the playing companies, driven out of London by the closing of the theaters, may have carried plague to the provincial towns.

Even in good times, when the plague was dormant and the weather favorable for farming, the food supply in England was precarious. A few successive bad harvests, such as occurred in the mid-1590s, could cause serious hardship, even starvation. Not surprisingly, the poor bore the brunt of the burden: inflation, low wages, and rent increases left large numbers of people with very little cushion against disaster. Further, at its best, the diet of most people seems to have been seriously deficient. The lower classes then, as throughout most of history, subsisted on one or two foodstuffs, usually low in protein. The upper classes disdained green vegetables and milk and gorged themselves on meat. Illnesses that we now trace to vitamin deficiencies were rampant. Some but not much relief from pain was provided by the beer that Elizabethans, including children, drank almost incessantly. (Home brewing aside, enough beer was sold in England for every man, woman, and child to have consumed forty gallons a year.)

Wealth

Despite rampant disease, the population of England in Shakespeare's lifetime grew steadily, from approximately 3,060,000 in 1564 to 4,060,000 in 1600 and 4,510,000 in 1616. Though the death rate was more than twice what it is in England today, the birthrate was almost three times the current figure. London's population in particular soared, from 60,000 in 1520 to 120,000 in 1550, 200,000 in 1600, and 375,000 a half-century later, making it the largest and fastest-growing city not only in England but in all of Europe. Every year in the first half of the seventeenth century, about 10,000 people migrated to London from other parts of England—wages in London tended to be around 50 percent higher than in the rest of the country—and it is estimated that one in eight English people lived in London at some point in their lives. The economic viability of Shakespeare's profession was closely linked to this extraordinary demographic boom: between 1567 and 1642, theater historians have estimated, the London playhouses were paid anywhere between 50 and 75 million visits.

As these visits to the theater indicate, in the capital city and elsewhere a substantial number of English men and women, despite hardships that were never very distant, had money to spend. After the disorder and dynastic wars of the fifteenth century, England in the sixteenth and early seventeenth centuries was for the most part a nation at peace, and with peace came a measure of enterprise and prosperity: the landowning classes busied themselves building great houses, planting orchards and hop gardens, draining marshlands, bringing untilled acreage under cultivation. The artisans and laborers who actually accomplished these tasks, though they were generally paid very little, often managed to accumulate something, as did the small freeholding farmers, the yeomen, who are repeatedly celebrated in the period as the backbone of English national independence and well-being. William Harrison's *Description of Britain* (1577) lovingly itemizes the yeoman's precious possessions: "fair garnish of pewter on his cupboard, with so much more odd vessel going about the house, three or four featherbeds, so many coverlets and carpets of tapestry, a silver salt [cellar], a bowl for wine (if not a whole nest) and a dozen of spoons." There are comparable accounts of the hard-earned acquisitions of the city dwellers—masters and apprentices in small workshops, shipbuilders, wool merchants, cloth makers, chandlers, tradesmen, shopkeepers, along with lawyers, apothecaries, schoolteachers, scriveners, and the like—whose pennies from time to time enriched the coffers of the players.

The chief source of England's wealth in the sixteenth century was its textile industry, an industry that depended on a steady supply of wool. The market for English textiles was not only domestic. In 1565, woolen cloth alone made up more than three-fourths of England's exports. (The remainder consisted mostly of other textiles and raw wool, with some trade in lead, tin, grain, and skins.) The Company of Merchant Adventurers carried cloth not only to nearby countries like France, Holland, and Germany but also to distant ports on the Baltic and Mediterranean, establishing links with Russia and Morocco (each took about 2 percent of London's cloth in 1597–98). English lead and tin, as well as fabrics, were sold in Tuscany and Turkey, and merchants found a market for Newcastle coal on the island of Malta. In the latter half of the century, London, which handled more than 85 percent of all exports, regularly shipped abroad more than 100,000 woolen cloths a year, at a value of at least £750,000. This figure does not include the increasingly important and profitable trade in so-called New Draperies, including textiles that went by such exotic names as bombazines, callamancoes, damazellas, damizes, mockadoes, and virgenatoes. When the Earl of Kent in *King Lear* insults Oswald as a "filthy, worsted-stocking knave" (2.2.14–15) or when the aristocratic Biron in *Love's Labor's Lost* declares that he will give up "taffeta phrases, silken terms precise, / Three-piled hyperboles" and woo henceforth "in russet 'yeas,' and honest kersey 'noes'" (5.2.407–08, 414), Shakespeare is assuming that a substantial portion of his audience will be alert to the social significance of fabric.

There is amusing confirmation of this alertness from an unexpected source: the report of a visit made to the Fortune playhouse in London in 1614 by a foreigner, Father Orazio Busino, the chaplain of the Venetian embassy. Father Busino neglected to mention the name of the play he saw, but like many foreigners, he was powerfully struck by the presence of gorgeously dressed women in the audience. In Venice, there was a special gallery for courtesans, but socially respectable women would not have been permitted to attend plays, as they could in England. In London, not only could middle- and upper-class women go to the theater, but they could also wear masks and mingle freely with male spectators and women of ill repute. The bemused cleric was uncertain about the ambiguous social situation in which he found himself:

> These theaters are frequented by a number of respectable and handsome ladies, who come freely and seat themselves among the men without the slightest hesitation. On the evening in question his Excellency and the Secretary were pleased to play me a trick by placing me amongst a bevy of young women. Scarcely was I seated ere a very elegant dame, but in a mask, came and placed herself beside me. . . . She asked me for my address both in French and English; and, on my turning a deaf ear, she determined to honor me by showing me some fine diamonds on her fingers, repeatedly taking off not fewer than three gloves, which were worn one over the other. . . . This lady's bodice was of yellow satin richly embroidered, her petticoat of gold tissue with stripes, her robe of red velvet with a raised pile, lined with yellow muslin with broad stripes of pure gold. She wore an apron of point lace of various patterns: her head-tire was highly perfumed, and the collar of white satin beneath the delicately-wrought ruff struck me as extremely pretty.

Father Busino may have turned a deaf ear on this "elegant dame" but not a blind eye: his description of her dress is worthy of a fashion designer and conveys something of the virtual clothes cult that prevailed in England in the late sixteenth and early seventeenth centuries, a cult whose major shrine, outside the royal court, was the theater.

Imports, Patents, and Monopolies

England produced some luxury goods, but the clothing on the backs of the most fashionable theatergoers was likely to have come from abroad. By the late sixteenth century, the English were importing substantial quantities of silks, satins, velvets, embroidery, gold and silver lace, and other costly items to satisfy the extravagant tastes of the elite and of those who aspired to dress like the elite. The government tried to put a check on the sartorial ambitions of the upwardly mobile by passing sumptuary laws—that is, laws restricting to the ranks of the aristocracy the right to wear certain of the most precious fabrics. But the very existence of these laws, in practice almost impossible to enforce, only reveals the scope and significance of the perceived problem.

Sumptuary laws were in part a conservative attempt to protect the existing social order from upstarts. Social mobility was not widely viewed as a positive virtue, and moralists repeatedly urged people to stay in their place. Conspicuous consumption that was tolerated, even admired, in the aristocratic elite was denounced as sinful and monstrous in less exalted social circles. English authorities were also deeply concerned throughout the period about the effects of a taste for luxury goods on the balance of trade. One of the principal English imports was wine: the "sherris" whose virtues Falstaff extols in *2 Henry IV* came from Xeres in Spain; the malmsey in which poor Clarence is drowned in *Richard III* was probably made in Greece or in the Canary Islands (from whence came Sir Toby Belch's "cup of canary" in *Twelfth Night*); and the "flagon of rhenish" that Yorick in *Hamlet* had once poured on the Gravedigger's head came from the Rhine region of Germany. Other imports included canvas, linen, fish, olive oil, sugar, molasses, dates, oranges and lemons, figs, raisins, almonds, capers, indigo, ostrich feathers, and that increasingly popular drug tobacco.

Joint stock companies were established to import goods for the burgeoning English market. The Merchant Venturers of the City of Bristol (established in 1552) handled great shipments of Spanish sack, the light, dry wine that largely displaced the vintages of Bordeaux and Burgundy when trade with France was disrupted by war. The Muscovy Company (established in 1555) traded English cloth and manufactured goods for Russian furs, oil, and beeswax. The Venice Company and the Turkey Company— uniting in 1593 to form the wealthy Levant Company—brought silk and spices home from Aleppo and carpets from Constantinople. The East India Company (founded in 1600), with its agent at Bantam in Java, brought pepper, cloves, nutmeg, and other spices from East Asia, along with indigo, cotton textiles, sugar, and saltpeter from India. English privateers "imported" American products, especially sugar, fish, and hides, in huge quantities, along with more precious cargoes. In 1592, a privateering expedition principally funded by Sir Walter Ralegh captured a huge Portuguese carrack (sailing ship), the *Madre de Dios,* in the Azores and brought it back to Dartmouth. The ship, the largest that had ever entered any English port, held 536 tons of pepper, cloves, cinnamon, cochineal, mace, civet, musk, ambergris, and nutmeg, as well as jewels, gold, ebony, carpets, and silks. Before order could be established, the English seamen began to pillage this immensely rich prize, and witnesses said they could smell the spices on all the streets around the harbor. Such piratical expeditions were rarely officially sanctioned by the state, but the Queen had in fact privately invested £1,800, for which she received about £80,000.

In the years of war with Spain, 1586–1604, the goods captured by the privateers annually amounted to 10–15 percent of the total value of England's imports. But organized theft alone could not solve England's balance-of-trade problems. Statesmen were particularly worried that the nation's natural wealth was slipping away in exchange for unnecessary things. In his *Discourse of the Commonweal* (1549), the prominent humanist Sir Thomas Smith exclaims against the importation of such trifles as mirrors, paper, laces, gloves, pins, inkhorns, tennis balls, puppets, and playing cards. And more than a century later, the same fear that England was trading its riches for trifles and wasting away in idleness was expressed by the Bristol merchant John Cary. The solution, Cary argues in "An Essay on the State of England in Relation to Its Trade" (1695),

Forging a magnet, 1600. The metal on the anvil is aligned North/South (Septentrio/Auster). From *De Magnete* by William Gilbert.

is to expand productive domestic employment. "People are or may be the Wealth of a Nation," he writes, "yet it must be where you find Employment for them, else they are a Burden to it, as the Idle Drone is maintained by the Industry of the laborious Bee, so are all those who live by their Dependence on others, as Players, Ale-House Keepers, Common Fiddlers, and such like, but more particularly Beggars, who never set themselves to work."

Stage players, all too typically associated here with vagabonds and other idle drones, could have replied in their defense that they not only labored in their vocation but also exported their skills abroad: English actors routinely performed on the Continent. But their labor was not regarded as a productive contribution to the national wealth, and plays were in truth no solution to the trade imbalances that worried authorities.

The government attempted to stem the flow of gold overseas by establishing a patent system initially designed to encourage skilled foreigners to settle in England by granting them exclusive rights to produce particular wares by a patented method. Patents were granted for such things as the making of hard white soap (1561), ovens and furnaces (1563), window glass (1567), sailcloths (1574), drinking glasses (1574), sulfur, brimstone, and oil (1577), armor and horse harness (1587), starch (1588), white writing paper made from rags (1589), aqua vitae and vinegar (1594), playing cards (1598), and mathematical instruments (1598).

By the early seventeenth century, English men and women were working in a variety of new industries like soap making, pin making, knife making, and the brewing of alegar and beeregar (ale- and beer-based vinegar). But although the ostensible purpose of the government's economic policy was to increase the wealth of England, encourage technical innovation, and provide employment for the poor, the effect of patents was often the enrichment of a few and the hounding of poor competitors by wealthy monopolists, a group that soon extended well beyond foreign-born entrepreneurs to the favorites of the monarch who vied for the huge profits to be made. "If I had a monopoly out" on folly, the Fool in *King Lear* protests, glancing at the "lords and great men" around him, "they would have part in't." The passage appears only in the Quarto version of the play (*History of King Lear* 4.140–41); it may have been cut for political reasons from the Folio. For the issue of monopolies provoked bitter criticism and parliamentary debate for decades. In 1601, Elizabeth was prevailed upon to revoke a number of the most hated monopolies, including aqua vitae and vinegar, bottles, brushes, fish livers, the coarse sailcloth known as poldavis and mildernix, pots, salt, and starch. The whole system was revoked during the reign of James I by an act of Parliament.

Haves and Have-Nots

When in the 1560s Elizabeth's ambassador to France, Sir Thomas Smith, wrote a description of England, he saw the commonwealth as divided into four sorts of people: "gentlemen, citizens, yeomen artificers, and laborers." At the forefront of the class of gentlemen was the monarch, followed by a very small group of nobles—dukes, marquesses, earls, viscounts, and barons—who either inherited their exalted titles, as the eldest male heirs of their families, or were granted them by the monarch. Under Elizabeth, this aristocratic peerage numbered between 50 and 60 individuals; James's promotions increased the number to nearer 130. Strictly speaking, Smith notes, the younger sons of the nobility were only entitled to be called "esquires," but in common speech they were also called "lords."

Below this tiny cadre of aristocrats in the social hierarchy of gentry were the knights, a title of honor conferred by the monarch, and below them were the "simple gentlemen." Who was a gentleman? According to Smith, "whoever studieth the laws of the realm, who studieth in the universities, who professeth liberal sciences, and to be short, who can live idly and without manual labor, and will bear the port, charge and countenance of a gentleman, he shall be called master . . . and shall be taken for a gentleman." To "live idly and without manual labor": where in Spain, for example, the crucial mark of a gentleman was "blood," in England it was "idleness," in the sense of sufficient income to afford an education and to maintain a social position without having to work with one's hands.

For Smith, the class of gentlemen was far and away the most important in the kingdom. Below were two groups that had at least some social standing and claim to authority: the citizens, or burgesses, those who held positions of importance and responsibility in their cities, and yeomen, farmers with land and a measure of economic independence. At the bottom of the social order was what Smith calls "the fourth sort of men which do not rule." The great mass of ordinary people have, Smith writes, "no voice nor authority in our commonwealth, and no account is made of them but only to be ruled." Still, even they can bear some responsibility, he notes, since they serve on juries and are named to such positions as churchwarden and constable.

In everyday practice, as modern social historians have observed, the English tended to divide the population not into four distinct classes but into two: a very small empowered group—the "richer" or "wiser" or "better" sort—and all the rest who were without much social standing or power, the "poorer" or "ruder" or "meaner" sort. References to the "middle sort of people" remain relatively rare until after Shakespeare's lifetime; these people are absorbed into the rulers or the ruled, depending on speaker and context.

The source of wealth for most of the ruling class, and the essential measure of social status, was land ownership, and changes to the social structure in the sixteenth and seventeenth centuries were largely driven by the land market. The property that passed into private hands as the Tudors and early Stuarts sold off confiscated monastic estates and then their own crown lands for ready cash amounted to nearly a quarter of all the land in England. At the same time, the buying and selling of private estates was on the rise throughout the period. Land was bought up not only by established landowners seeking to enlarge their estates but also by successful merchants, manufacturers, and urban professionals; even if the taint of vulgar moneymaking lingered around such figures, their heirs would be taken for true gentlemen. The rate of turnover in land ownership was great; in many counties, well over half the gentle families in 1640 had appeared since the end of the fifteenth century. The class that Smith called "simple gentlemen" was expanding rapidly: in the fifteenth century, they had held no more than a quarter of the land in the country, but by the later seventeenth, they controlled almost half. Over the same period, the land held by the great aristocratic magnates held steady at 15–20 percent of the total.

Riot and Disorder

London was a violent place in the first half of Shakespeare's career. There were thirty-five riots in the city in the years 1581–1602, twelve of them in the volatile month of June 1595. These included protests against the deeply unpopular Lord Mayor Sir John Spencer, attempts to release prisoners, anti-alien riots, and incidents of "popular market regulation." There is an unforgettable depiction of a popular uprising in *Coriolanus*, along with many other glimpses in Shakespeare's works, including Jack Cade's grotesque rebellion in *2 Henry VI*, the plebeian violence in *Julius Caesar*, and Laertes' "riotous head" in *Hamlet*.

The London rioters were mostly drawn from the large mass of poor and discontented apprentices who typically chose as their scapegoats foreigners, prostitutes, and gentlemen's servingmen. Theaters were very often the site of the social confrontations that sparked disorder. For two days running in June 1584, disputes between apprentices and gentlemen triggered riots outside the Curtain Theater involving up to a thousand participants. On one occasion, a gentleman was said to have exclaimed that "the apprentice was but a rascal, and some there were little better than rogues that took upon them the name of gentlemen, and said the prentices were but the scum of the world." These occasions culminated in attacks by the apprentices on London's law schools, the Inns of Court.

The most notorious and predictable incidents of disorder came on Shrove Tuesday (the Tuesday before the beginning of Lent), a traditional day of misrule when apprentices ran riot. Shrove Tuesday disturbances involved attacks by mobs of young men on the brothels of the South Bank, in the vicinity of the Globe and other public theaters. The city authorities took precautions to keep these disturbances from getting completely out of control, but evidently did not regard them as serious threats to public order.

Of much greater concern throughout the Tudor and early Stuart years were the frequent incidents of rural rioting. Though in *The Winter's Tale* Shakespeare provides a richly comic portrayal of a rural sheepshearing festival, the increasingly intensive production of wool had its grim side. When a character in Thomas More's *Utopia* (1516) complains that "the sheep are eating the people," he is referring to the practice of enclosure: throughout the sixteenth and early seventeenth centuries, many acres of croplands once farmed in common by rural communities were fenced in by wealthy landowners and turned into pasturage. The ensuing misery, displacement, and food shortages led to repeated protests, some of them violent and bloody, along with a series of government proclamations, but the process of enclosure was not reversed. The protests were at their height during Shakespeare's career: in the years 1590–1610, the frequency of anti-enclosure rioting doubled from what it had been earlier in Elizabeth's reign.

Although they often became violent, anti-enclosure riots were usually directed not against individuals but against property. Villagers—sometimes several hundred, often fewer than a dozen—gathered to tear down newly planted hedges. The event often took place in a carnival atmosphere, with songs and drinking, that did not prevent the participants from acting with a good deal of political canniness and forethought. Especially in the Jacobean period, it was common for participants to establish a fund for legal defense before commencing their assault on the hedges. Women were frequently involved, and on a number of occasions wives alone participated in the destruction of the enclosure, since there was a widespread, though erroneous, belief that married women acting without the knowledge of their husbands were immune from prosecution. In fact, the powerful Court of Star Chamber consistently ruled that both the wives and their husbands should be punished.

Although Stratford was never the scene of serious rioting, enclosure controversies turned violent more than once in Shakespeare's lifetime. In January 1601, Shakespeare's friend Richard Quiney and others leveled the hedges of Sir Edward Greville, lord of Stratford manor. Quiney was elected bailiff of Stratford in September of that year but did not live to enjoy the office for long. He died from a blow to the head struck by one of Greville's men in a tavern brawl. Greville, responsible for the administration of justice, neglected to punish the murderer.

There was further violence in January 1615, when William Combe's men threw to the ground two local aldermen who were filling in a ditch by which Combe was enclosing common fields near Stratford. The task of filling in the offending ditch was completed the next day by the women and children of Stratford. Combe's enclosure scheme was eventually stopped in the courts. Though he owned land whose value would have been affected by this controversy, Shakespeare took no active role in it, since he had previously come to a private settlement with the enclosers insuring him against personal loss.

Most incidents of rural rioting were small, localized affairs, and with good reason: when confined to the village community, riot was a misdemeanor; when it spread outward to include multiple communities, it became treason, punishable by death. The greatest of

The Peddler. From Jost Amman, *The Book of Trades* (1568).

the anti-enclosure riots, those in which hundreds of individuals from a large area participated, commonly took place on the eve of full-scale regional rebellions. The largest of these disturbances, Kett's Rebellion, involved some 16,000 peasants, artisans, and townspeople who rose up in 1549 under the leadership of a Norfolk tanner and landowner, Robert Kett, to protest economic exploitation. The agrarian revolts in Shakespeare's lifetime were on a much smaller scale. In the abortive Oxfordshire Rebellion of 1596, a carpenter named Bartholomew Steer attempted to organize a rising against the hated enclosures. The optimistic Steer allegedly promised his followers that "it was but a month's work to overrun England" and informed them "that the commons long since in Spain did rise and kill all gentlemen . . . and since that time have lived merrily there." Steer expected several hundred men to join him on Enslow Hill on November 21, 1596, for the start of the rising; no more than twenty showed up. They were captured, imprisoned, and tortured. Several were executed, but Steer apparently cheated the hangman by dying in prison.

Rebellions, most often triggered by hunger and oppression, continued into the reign of James I. The Midland Revolt of 1607, which may be reflected in *Coriolanus,* consisted of a string of agrarian risings in the counties of Northamptonshire, Warwickshire, and Leicestershire, involving assemblies of up to five thousand rebels in various places. The best known of their leaders was John Reynolds, called "Captain Powch" because of the pouch he wore, whose magical contents were supposed to defend the rebels from harm. (According to the chronicler Edmund Howes, when Reynolds was captured and the pouch opened, it contained "only a piece of green cheese.") The rebels, who were called by themselves and others both "Levelers" and "Diggers," insisted that they had no quarrel with the King but only sought an end to injurious enclosures. But Robert Wilkinson, who preached a sermon against the leaders at their trial, credited them with the intention to "level all states as they leveled banks and ditches." Most of the rebels got off relatively lightly, but, along with other ringleaders, Captain Powch was executed.

The Legal Status of Women

English women were not under the full range of crushing constraints that afflicted women in some countries in Europe. Foreign visitors were struck by their relative freedom, as shown, for example, by the fact that respectable women could venture unchaperoned into the streets and attend the theater. Yet while England was ruled for over forty years by a powerful woman, the great majority of women in the kingdom had very restricted social, economic, and legal standing. To be sure, a tiny number of influential aristocratic women, such as the formidable Countess of Shrewsbury, Bess of Hardwick, wielded considerable power. But, these rare exceptions aside, women were denied any rightful claim to institutional authority or personal autonomy. When Sir Thomas Smith thinks of how he should describe his country's social order, he declares that "we do reject women, as those whom nature hath made to keep home and to nourish their family and children, and not to meddle with matters abroad, nor to bear office in a city or commonwealth." Then, with a kind of glance over his shoulder, he makes an exception of those few for whom "the blood is respected, not the age nor the sex": for example, the Queen.

Single women, whether widowed or unmarried, could, if they were of full age, inherit and administer land, make a will, sign a contract, possess property, sue and be sued, without a male guardian or proxy. But married women had no such rights under English common law, the system of law based on court decisions rather than on codified written laws. Early modern writings about women and the family constantly return to a political model of domination and submission, in which the husband and father justly rules over wife and children as the monarch rules over the state. The husband's dominance in the family was the justification for the common-law rule that prohibited married women from possessing property, administering land, signing contracts, or bringing lawsuits in their own names: married women were described as legally "covered" by their husbands. Yet this conception of a woman's role conveniently ignores the fact that a *majority* of the adult women at any time in Shakespeare's England were not married. They were either widows or spinsters (a term that was not yet pejorative), and thus for the most part managed their own affairs. Even within marriage, women typically had more control over certain spheres than moralizing writers on the family cared to admit. For example, village wives oversaw the production of eggs, cheese, and beer, and sold these goods in the market. As seamstresses, pawnbrokers, second-hand clothing dealers, peddlers and the like—activities not controlled by the all-male craft guilds–women managed to acquire some economic power of their own, and, of course, they participated as well in the unregulated, black-market economy of the age and in the underworld of thievery and prostitution.

Women were not in practice as bereft of property as, according to English common law, they should have been. Demographic studies indicate that the inheritance system called primogeniture, the orderly transmission of property from father to eldest male heir, was more often an unfulfilled wish than a reality. Some 40 percent of marriages failed to produce a son, and in such circumstances fathers often left their land to their daughters, rather than to brothers, nephews, or male cousins. In many families, the father died before his male heir was old enough to inherit property, leaving the land, at least temporarily, in the hands of the mother. And while they were less likely than their brothers to inherit land ("real property"), daughters normally inherited a substantial share of their parents' personal property (cash and movables).

In fact, the legal restrictions upon women, though severe in Shakespeare's time, actually worsened in subsequent decades. English common law was significantly less egalitarian in its approach to wives and daughters than were alternative legal codes (manorial, civil, and ecclesiastical) still in place in the late sixteenth century. The eventual triumph of common law stripped women of many traditional rights, slowly driving them out of economically productive trades and businesses.

Limited though it was, the economic freedom of Elizabethan and Jacobean women far exceeded their political and social freedom—the opportunity to receive a grammar school or university education, to hold office in church or state, to have a voice in public debates, or even simply to speak their mind fully and openly in ordinary conversation. Women who asserted their views too vigorously risked being perceived as shrewish and labeled "scolds." Both urban and rural communities had a horror of scolds. In the Elizabethan period, such women came to be regarded as a threat to public order, to be dealt with by the local authorities. The preferred methods of correction included public humiliation—of the sort Katherina endures in *The Taming of the Shrew*—and such physical abuse as slapping, bridling with a bit or muzzle, and half-drowning by means of a contraption called the "cucking stool" (or "ducking stool"). This latter punishment originated in the Middle Ages, but its use spread in the sixteenth century, when it became almost exclusively a punishment for women. From 1560 onward, cucking stools were built or renovated in many English provincial towns; between 1560 and 1600, the contraptions were installed by rivers or ponds in Norwich, Bridport, Shrewsbury, Kingston-upon-Thames, Marlborough, Devizes, Clitheroe, Thornbury, and Great Yarmouth.

Such punishment was usually intensified by a procession through the town to the sound of "rough music," the banging together of pots and pans. The same cruel festivity accompanied the "carting" or "riding" of those accused of being whores. In some parts of the country, villagers also took the law into their own hands, publicly shaming women who married men much younger than themselves or who beat or otherwise domineered over their husbands. One characteristic form of these charivaris, or rituals of shaming, was known in the West Country as the Skimmington Ride. Villagers would rouse the offending couple from bed with rough music and stage a raucous pageant in which a man, holding a distaff, would ride backward on a donkey, while his "wife" (another man dressed as a woman) struck him with a ladle. In these cases, the collective ridicule and indignation were evidently directed at least as much at the henpecked husband as at his transgressive wife.

Women and Print

Books published for a female audience surged in popularity in the late sixteenth century, reflecting an increase in female literacy. (It is striking how many of Shakespeare's women are shown reading.) This increase is probably linked to a Protestant longing for direct access to the Scriptures, and the new books marketed specifically for women included devotional manuals and works of religious instruction. But there were also practical guides to such subjects as female education (for example, Giovanni Bruto's *Necessary, Fit, and Convenient Education of a Young Gentlewoman*, 1598), midwifery (James Guillemeau's *Child-birth; or, the Happy Delivery of Women*, 1612), needlework (Federico di Vinciolo's *New and Singular Patterns and Works of Linen*, 1591), cooking (Thomas Dawson's *The Good Housewife's Jewel*, 1587), gardening (Pierre Erondelle's *The French Garden*, 1605), and married life (Patrick Hanney's *A Happy Husband; or, Directions for a Maid to Choose Her Mate*, 1619). As the authors' names suggest, many of these works were translations, and almost all were written by men.

Starting in the 1570s, writers and their publishers increasingly addressed works of recreational literature (romance, fiction, and poetry) partially or even exclusively to women. Some books, such as Robert Greene's *Mamillia, a Mirror or Looking-Glass for the Ladies of England* (1583), directly specified in the title their desired audience. Others, such as Sir Philip Sidney's influential and popular romance *Arcadia* (1590–93), solicited female readership in their dedicatory epistles. The ranks of Sidney's followers eventually included his own niece, Mary Wroth, whose romance *Urania* was published in 1621.

In the literature of Shakespeare's time, women readers were not only wooed but also frequently railed at, in a continuation of a popular polemical genre that had long inspired heated charges and countercharges. Both sides in the polemic generally agreed that it was the duty of women to be chaste, dutiful, and modest in demeanor; the argument was whether women fulfilled or fell short of this proper role. Ironically, then, a modern reader is more likely to find inspiring accounts of courageous women not in the books written in defense of female virtue but in attacks on those who refused to be silent and obedient.

The most famous English skirmish in this controversy took place in a rash of pamphlets at the end of Shakespeare's life. Joseph Swetnam's crude *Arraignment of Lewd, Idle, Froward, and Unconstant Women* (1615) provoked three fierce responses attributed to women: Rachel Speght's *A Muzzle for Melastomus*, Esther Sowernam's *Esther Hath Hang'd Haman*, and Constantia Munda's *Worming of a Mad Dog*, all in 1617. There was also an anonymous play, *Swetnam the Woman-Hater Arraigned by Women* (first performed around 1618), in which Swetnam, depicted as a braggart and a lecher, is put on trial by women and made to recant his misogynistic lies.

Prior to the Swetnam controversy, only one English woman, writing under the pseudonym "Jane Anger," had published a defense of women (*Jane Anger Her Protection for Women*, 1589). Learned women writers in the sixteenth century tended not to become involved in public debate but rather to undertake a project to which it was difficult for even obdurately chauvinistic males to object: the translation of devotional literature into English. Thomas More's daughter Margaret More Roper translated Erasmus (*A Devout Treatise upon the Pater Noster*, 1524); Francis Bacon's mother, Anne Cooke Bacon, translated Bishop John Jewel (*An Apology or Answer in Defence of the Church of England*, 1564); Anne Locke Prowse, a friend of John Knox, translated the *Sermons of John Calvin* in 1560; and Mary Sidney, the Countess of Pembroke, completed the metrical version of the Psalms that her brother Sir Philip

Sidney had begun. Elizabeth Tudor (the future queen) herself translated, at the age of eleven, Marguerite de Navarre's *Le Miroir de l'âme pécheresse* (*The Glass of the Sinful Soul,* 1544). The translation was dedicated to her stepmother, Katherine Parr, herself the author of a frequently reprinted book of prayers.

There was in the sixteenth and early seventeenth centuries a social stigma attached to print. Far from celebrating publication, authors, and particularly female authors, often apologized for exposing themselves to the public gaze. Nonetheless, a number of women ventured in print beyond pious translations. Some, including Elizabeth Tyrwhitt, Anne Dowriche, Isabella Whitney, Mary Sidney, and Aemilia Lanyer, composed and published their own poems. Aemilia Lanyer's *Salve Deus Rex Judaeorum,* published in 1611, is a poem in praise of virtuous women, from Eve and the Virgin Mary to her noble patron, the Countess of Cumberland. "A Description of Cookeham," appended to the poem, is one of the first English country house poems, a celebration in verse of an aristocrat's rural estate.

The first Tudor woman to translate a play was the learned Jane Lumley, who composed an English version of Euripides' *Iphigenia at Aulis* (ca. 1550). The first known original play in English by a woman was by Elizabeth Cary, Viscountess Falkland, whose *Tragedy of Mariam, the Fair Queen of Jewry* was published in 1613. This remarkable play, which was not intended to be performed, includes speeches in defense of women's equality, though the most powerful of these is spoken by the villainous Salome, who schemes to divorce her husband and marry her lover. Cary, who bore

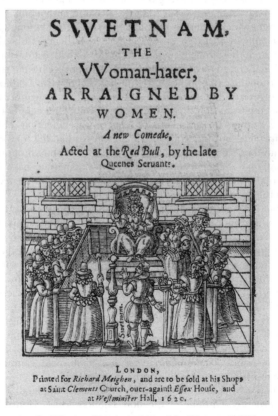

Title page of *Swetnam the Woman-Hater, Arraigned by Women* (1620), a play written in response to Joseph Swetnam's *The Arraignment of Lewd, Idle, Forward, and Unconstant Women* (1615); the woodcut depicts the trial of Swetnam in act 4.

eleven children, herself had a deeply troubled marriage, which effectively came to an end in 1625 when, defying her husband's staunchly Protestant family, she openly converted to Catholicism. Her biography was written by one of her four daughters, all of whom became nuns.

Henry VIII and the English Reformation

There had long been serious ideological and institutional tensions in the religious life of England, but officially, at least, England in the early sixteenth century had a single religion, Catholicism, whose acknowledged head was the pope in Rome. In 1517, drawing upon long-standing currents of dissent, Martin Luther, an Augustinian monk and professor of theology at the University of Wittenberg, challenged the authority of the pope and attacked several key doctrines of the Catholic Church. According to Luther, the Church, with its elaborate hierarchical structure centered in Rome, its rich monasteries and convents, and its enormous political influence, had become hopelessly corrupt, a conspiracy of venal priests who manipulated popular superstitions to enrich themselves and amass worldly power. Luther began by vehemently attacking the sale of indulgences—certificates promising the remission of punishments to be suffered in the afterlife by souls sent to purgatory to expiate their sins. These indulgences were a fraud, he argued; purgatory itself had no foundation in the Bible, which in his view was the only legitimate source of religious truth. Christians would be saved not by scrupulously following the ritual practices fostered by the Catholic Church—observing fast days, reciting the ancient Latin prayers, endowing chantries to say prayers for the dead, and so on—but by faith and faith alone.

This challenge, which came to be known as the Reformation, spread and gathered force, especially in northern Europe, where major leaders like the Swiss pastor Ulrich Zwingli and the French theologian John Calvin established institutional structures and elaborated various and sometimes conflicting doctrinal principles. Calvin, whose thought came to be particularly influential in England, emphasized the obligation of governments to implement God's will in the world. He advanced too the doctrine of predestination, by which, as he put it, "God adopts some to hope of life and sentences others to eternal death." God's "secret election" of the saved made Calvin uncomfortable, but his study of the Scriptures had led him to conclude that "only a small number, out of an incalculable multitude, should obtain salvation." It might seem that such a conclusion would lead to passivity or even despair, but for Calvin predestination was a mystery bound up with faith, confidence, and an active engagement in the fashioning of a Christian community.

The Reformation had a direct and powerful impact on those territories, especially in northern Europe, where it gained control. Monasteries, many of them fabulously wealthy, were sacked, their possessions and extensive landholdings seized by princes or sold off to the highest bidder; the monks and nuns, expelled from their cloisters, were encouraged to break their vows of chastity and find spouses, as Luther and his wife, a former nun, had done. In the great cathedrals and in hundreds of smaller churches and chapels, the elaborate altarpieces, bejeweled crucifixes, crystal reliquaries holding the bones of saints, and venerated statues and paintings were attacked as "idols" and often defaced or destroyed. Protestant congregations continued, for the most part, to celebrate the most sacred Christian ritual, the Eucharist, or Lord's Supper, but they did so in a profoundly different spirit from that of the Catholic Church—more as commemoration than as miracle—and they now prayed not in the ancient liturgical Latin but in the vernacular.

The Reformation was at first vigorously resisted in England. Indeed, with the support of his ardently Catholic chancellor, Thomas More, Henry VIII personally wrote (or at least lent his name to) a vehement, often scatological attack on Luther's character and views, an attack for which the pope granted him the honorific title "Defender of the Faith." Protestant writings, including translations of the Scriptures into English, were seized by officials of the church and state and burned. Protestants who made their views known were persecuted, driven to flee the country, or arrested, put on trial, and burned at the stake. But the situation changed drastically and decisively when in 1527 Henry decided to seek an annulment from his first wife, Catherine of Aragon, in order to marry Anne Boleyn.

Catherine had given birth to six children, but since only a daughter, Mary, survived infancy, Henry did not have the son he craved. Then as now, the Catholic Church did not ordinarily grant divorce, but Henry's lawyers argued on technical grounds that the marriage was invalid (and therefore, by extension, that Mary was illegitimate and hence unable to inherit the throne). Matters of this kind were far less doctrinal than diplomatic: Catherine, the daughter of Ferdinand of Aragon and Isabella of Castile, had powerful allies in Rome, and the pope ruled against Henry's petition. A series of momentous events followed, as England lurched away from the Church of Rome. In 1531, Henry charged the entire clergy of England with having usurped royal authority in the administration of canon law (the ecclesiastical law that governed faith, discipline, and morals, including such matters as divorce). Under extreme pressure, including the threat of mass confiscations and imprisonment, the Convocation of the Clergy begged for pardon, made a donation to the royal coffers of over £100,000, and admitted that the King was "supreme head of the English Church and clergy" (modified by the rider "as far as the law of Christ allows"). On May 15 of the next year, the convocation submitted to the demand that the King be the final arbiter of canon law; on the next day, Thomas More resigned his post.

In 1533, Henry's marriage to Catherine was officially declared null and void, and on June 1 Anne Boleyn was crowned queen (a coronation Shakespeare depicts in his late play *Henry VIII*). The King was promptly excommunicated by Pope Clement VII. In the following year, the parliamentary Act of Succession confirmed the effects of the annulment and required an oath from all adult male subjects confirming the new dynastic settlement. Thomas More and John Fisher, the Bishop of Rochester, were among the small number who refused. The Act of Supremacy, passed later in the year, formally declared the King to be "Supreme Head of the Church in England" and again required an oath to this effect. In 1535 and 1536, further acts made it treasonous to refuse the oath of royal supremacy or, as More had tried to do, to remain silent. The first victims were three Carthusian monks who rejected the oath—"How could the King, a layman," said one of them, "be Head of the Church of

The Pope as Antichrist riding the Beast of the Apocalypse. From *Fiery Trial of God's Saints* (1611; author unknown).

England?"—and in May 1535, they were duly hanged, drawn, and quartered. A few weeks later, Fisher and More were convicted and beheaded. Between 1536 and 1539, the monasteries were suppressed and their vast wealth seized by the crown.

Royal defiance of the authority of Rome was a key element in the Reformation but did not by itself constitute the establishment of Protestantism in England. On the contrary, in the same year that Fisher and More were martyred for their adherence to Roman Catholicism, twenty-five Protestants, members of a sect known as Anabaptists, were burned for heresy on a single day. Through most of his reign, Henry remained an equal-opportunity persecutor, ruthless to Catholics loyal to Rome but also hostile to some of those who espoused Reformation ideas, though many of these ideas gradually established themselves on English soil.

Even when Henry was eager to do so, it proved impossible to eradicate Protestantism, as it would later prove impossible for his successors to eradicate Catholicism. In large part this tenacity arose from the passionate, often suicidal heroism of men and women who felt that their souls' salvation depended on the precise character of their Christianity. It arose too from a mid-fifteenth-century technological innovation that made it almost impossible to suppress unwelcome ideas: the printing press. Early Protestants quickly grasped that with a few clandestine presses they could defy the Catholic authorities and flood the country with their texts. "How many printing presses there be in the world," wrote the Protestant polemicist John Foxe, "so many blockhouses there be against the high castle" of the pope in Rome, "so that either the pope must abolish knowledge and printing or printing at length will root him out." By the century's end, it was the Catholics who were using the clandestine press to propagate their beliefs in the face of Protestant persecution.

The greatest insurrection of the Tudor age was not over food, taxation, or land but over religion. On Sunday, October 1, 1536, stirred up by their vicar, the traditionalist parishioners of Louth in Lincolnshire, in the north of England, rose up in defiance of the ecclesiastical delegation sent to enforce royal supremacy. The rapidly spreading rebellion, which became known as the Pilgrimage of Grace, was led by the lawyer Robert Aske. The city of Lincoln fell to the rebels on October 6, and though it was soon retaken by royal forces, the rebels seized cities and fortifications throughout Yorkshire, Durham, Northumberland, Cumberland, Westmoreland, and northern Lancashire. Carlisle, Newcastle, and a few castles were all that were left to the King in the north. The Pilgrims soon numbered 40,000, led by some of the region's most prominent noblemen. The Duke of Norfolk, representing the crown, was forced to negotiate a truce, with a promise to support the rebels' demands that the King restore the monasteries, shore up the regional economy, suppress heresy, and dismiss his evil advisers. The Pilgrims kept the peace for the rest of 1536, on the naive assumption that their demands would be met. But Henry moved suddenly early in 1537 to impose order and capture the ringleaders; 130 people, including lords, knights, heads of religious houses, and, of course, Robert Aske, were executed.

In 1549, two years after the death of Henry VIII, the west and north of England were the sites of further unsuccessful risings for the restoration of Catholicism. The Western Rising is striking for its blend of Catholic universalism and intense regionalism among people who did not yet regard themselves as English. One of the rebels' articles, protesting against the imposition of the English Bible and religious service, declares, "We the Cornish men (whereof certain of us understand no English) utterly refuse this new English." The rebels besieged but failed to take the city of Exeter. As with almost all Tudor rebellions, the number of those executed in the aftermath of the failed rising was far greater than those killed in actual hostilities.

The Children of Henry VIII: Edward, Mary, and Elizabeth

Upon Henry's death in 1547, his ten-year-old son, Edward VI, came to the throne, with his maternal uncle Edward Seymour named as Duke of Somerset and Lord

Protector (regent while the King was still a minor). Both Edward and his uncle were staunch Protestants, and reformers hastened to transform the English church accordingly. During Edward's reign, Archbishop Thomas Cranmer formulated the forty-two articles of religion that became the core of Anglican orthodoxy and wrote the first Book of Common Prayer, which was officially adopted in 1549 as the basis of English worship services.

Somerset fell from power in 1549 and was replaced as Lord Protector by John Dudley, later Duke of Northumberland. When Edward fell seriously ill, probably of tuberculosis, Northumberland persuaded him to sign a will depriving his half-sisters Mary (the daughter of Catherine of Aragon) and Elizabeth (the daughter of Anne Boleyn) of their claim to royal succession. The Lord Protector was scheming to have his daughter-in-law, the Protestant Lady Jane Grey, a great-granddaughter of Henry VII, ascend to the throne. But when Edward died in 1553, Mary marshaled support, quickly secured the crown from Lady Jane (who had been titular queen for nine days), and had Lady Jane executed, along with her husband and Northumberland.

Queen Mary immediately took steps to return her kingdom to Roman Catholicism. Though she was unable to get Parliament to agree to return church lands seized under Henry VIII, she restored the Catholic Mass, once again affirmed the authority of the pope, and put down a rebellion that sought to depose her. Seconded by her ardently Catholic husband, Philip II, King of Spain, she initiated a series of religious persecutions that earned her (from her enemies) the name "Bloody Mary." Hundreds of Protestants took refuge abroad in cities such as Calvin's Geneva; almost three hundred less fortunate Protestants were condemned as heretics and burned at the stake.

Mary died childless in 1558, and her younger half-sister Elizabeth became queen. Elizabeth's succession had been by no means assured. For if Protestants regarded the marriage of Henry VIII to Catherine as invalid and hence deemed Mary illegitimate, so Catholics regarded his marriage to Anne Boleyn as invalid and deemed Elizabeth illegitimate. Henry VIII himself seemed to support both views, since only

The Family of Henry VIII: An Allegory of the Tudor Succession, by Lucas de Heere (ca. 1572). Henry, in the middle, is flanked by Mary to his right, and Edward and Elizabeth to his left.

three years after divorcing Catherine, he beheaded Anne Boleyn on charges of treason and adultery and urged Parliament to invalidate the marriage. Moreover, though
during her sister's reign Elizabeth outwardly complied with the official Catholic
religious observance, Mary and her advisers were deeply suspicious, and the young
princess's life was in grave danger. Poised and circumspect, Elizabeth warily evaded
the traps that were set for her. As she ascended the throne, her actions were scrutinized for some indication of the country's future course. During her coronation procession, when a girl in an allegorical pageant presented her with a Bible in English
translation—banned under Mary's reign—Elizabeth kissed the book, held it up reverently, and laid it to her breast; when the abbot and monks of Westminster Abbey
came to greet her in broad daylight with candles (a symbol of Catholic devotion) in
their hands, she briskly dismissed them with the telling words "Away with those
torches! We can see well enough." England had returned to the Reformation.

Many English men and women, of all classes, remained inwardly loyal to the old
Catholic faith; Shakespeare's father and mother may well have been among these.
But English authorities under Elizabeth moved steadily, if cautiously, toward ensuring at least an outward conformity to the official Protestant settlement. Recusants,
those who refused to attend regular Sunday services in their parish churches, were
fined heavily. Anyone who wished to receive a university degree, to be ordained as a
priest in the Church of England, or to be named as an officer of the state had to swear
an oath to the royal supremacy. Commissioners were sent throughout the land to
confirm that religious services were following the officially approved liturgy and to
investigate any reported backsliding into Catholic practice or, alternatively, any
attempts to introduce more radical reforms than the Queen and her bishops had chosen to embrace. For many of the Protestant exiles who streamed back to England
were eager not only to undo the damage Mary had done but to carry the Reformation
much further. They sought to dismantle the church hierarchy, to purge the calendar
of folk customs deemed pagan and the church service of ritual practices deemed
superstitious, to dress the clergy in simple garb, and, at the extreme edge, to smash
"idolatrous" statues, crucifixes, and altarpieces. Pressing for a stricter code of life
and a simplified system of worship, the religious radicals came to be called Puritans.
Throughout her long reign, however, Elizabeth herself remained cautiously conservative and determined to hold in check what she regarded as the religious zealotry of
Catholics, on the one side, and Puritans, on the other.

Shakespeare's plays tap into the ongoing confessional tensions: "sometimes," Maria
in *Twelfth Night* says of the sober, festivity-hating steward Malvolio, "he is a kind of
puritan" (2.3.129). But the plays tend to avoid the risks of direct engagement: "The devil
a puritan that he is, or anything constantly," Maria adds a moment later, "but a time-
pleaser" (2.3.135–36). *The Winter's Tale* features a statue that comes to life—exactly
the kind of magical image that Protestant polemicists excoriated as Catholic superstition and idolatry—but the play is set in the pre-Christian world of the Delphic Oracle.
And as if this careful distancing might not be enough, the play's ruler goes out of his
way to pronounce the wonder legitimate: "If this be magic, let it be an art / Lawful as
eating" (5.3.110–11).

In the space of a single lifetime, England had gone officially from Roman Catholicism, to Catholicism under the supreme headship of the English king, to a guarded
Protestantism, to a more radical Protestantism, to a renewed and aggressive Roman
Catholicism, and finally to Protestantism again. Each of these shifts was accompanied by danger, persecution, and death. It was enough to make some people wary. Or
skeptical. Or extremely agile.

The English Bible

Luther had undertaken a fundamental critique of the Catholic Church's sacramental
system, a critique founded on the twin principles of salvation by faith alone (*sola fide*)

and the absolute primacy of the Bible *(sola scriptura)*. *Sola fide* contrasted faith with "works," by which was meant primarily the whole elaborate system of rituals sanctified, conducted, or directed by the priests. Protestants proposed to modify or reinterpret many of these rituals or, as with the rituals associated with purgatory, to abolish them altogether. *Sola scriptura* required direct lay access to the Bible, which meant in practice the widespread availability of vernacular translations. The Roman Catholic Church had not always and everywhere opposed such translations, but it generally preferred that the populace encounter the Scriptures through the interpretations of the priests, trained to read the Latin translation known as the Vulgate. In times of great conflict, this preference for clerical mediation hardened into outright prohibition of vernacular translation and into persecution and book burning.

Zealous Protestants set out, in the teeth of fierce opposition, to put the Bible into the hands of the laity. A remarkable translation of the New Testament, by an English Lutheran named William Tyndale, was printed on the Continent and smuggled into England in 1525; Tyndale's translation of the Pentateuch, the first five books of the Hebrew Bible, followed in 1530. Many copies of these translations were seized and burned, as was the translator himself, but the printing press made it extremely difficult for authorities to eradicate books for which there was a passionate demand. The English Bible was a force that could not be suppressed, and it became, in its various forms, the single most important book of the sixteenth century.

Tyndale's translation was completed by an associate, Miles Coverdale, whose rendering of the Psalms proved to be particularly influential. Their joint labor was the basis for the Great Bible (1539), the first authorized version of the Bible in English, a copy of which was ordered to be placed in every church in the kingdom. With the accession of Edward VI, many editions of the Bible followed, but the process was sharply reversed when Mary came to the throne in 1553. Along with people condemned as heretics, English Bibles were burned in great bonfires.

Marian persecution was indirectly responsible for what would become the most popular as well as most scholarly English Bible, the translation known as the Geneva Bible (1560), prepared, with extensive, learned, and often fiercely polemical marginal notes, by English exiles in Calvin's Geneva and widely diffused in England after Elizabeth came to the throne. In addition, Elizabethan church authorities ordered a careful revision of the Great Bible, and this version, known as the Bishops' Bible (1568), was the one read in the churches. The success of the Geneva Bible in particular prompted those Elizabethan Catholics who now in turn found themselves in exile to bring out a vernacular translation of their own in order to counter the Protestant readings and glosses. This Catholic translation, the so-called Rheims Bible (1582), may have been known to Shakespeare, but he seems to have been far better acquainted with the Geneva Bible, and he would also have repeatedly heard the Bishops' Bible read aloud. Scholars have identified over three hundred references to the Bible in Shakespeare's work; in one version or another, the Scriptures had a powerful impact on his imagination.

A Female Monarch in a Male World

In the last year of Mary's reign, 1558, the Scottish Calvinist minister John Knox thundered against what he called "the monstrous regiment of women." When the Protestant Elizabeth came to the throne the following year, Knox and his religious brethren were less inclined to denounce female rulers, but in England as elsewhere in Europe there remained a widespread conviction that women were unsuited to wield power over men. Many men seem to have regarded the capacity for rational thought as exclusively male; women, they assumed, were led only by their passions. While gentlemen mastered the arts of rhetoric and warfare, gentlewomen were expected to display the virtues of silence and good housekeeping. Among upper-class males, the will to dominate others was acceptable and indeed admired; the same will in women was condemned as a grotesque and dangerous aberration.

The Armada portrait: note Elizabeth's hand on the globe.

Apologists for the Queen countered these prejudices by appealing to historical precedent and legal theory. History offered inspiring examples of just female rulers, notably Deborah, the biblical prophetess who judged Israel. In the legal sphere, crown lawyers advanced the theory of "the king's two bodies." As England's crowned head, Elizabeth's person was mystically divided between her mortal "body natural" and the immortal "body politic." While the queen's natural body was inevitably subject to the failings of human flesh, the body politic was timeless and perfect. In political terms, therefore, Elizabeth's sex was a matter of no consequence, a thing indifferent.

Elizabeth, who had received a fine humanist education and an extended, dangerous lesson in the art of survival, made it immediately clear that she intended to rule in more than name only. She assembled a group of trustworthy advisers, foremost among them William Cecil (later named Lord Burghley), but she insisted on making many of the crucial decisions herself. Like many Renaissance monarchs, Elizabeth was drawn to the idea of royal absolutism, the theory that ultimate power was properly concentrated in her person and indeed that God had appointed her to be his deputy in the kingdom. Opposition to her rule, in this view, was not only a political act but also a kind of impiety, a blasphemous grudging against the will of God. Apologists for absolutism contended that God commands obedience even to manifestly wicked rulers whom he has sent to punish the sinfulness of humankind. Such arguments were routinely made in speeches and political tracts and from the pulpits of churches, where they were incorporated into the Book of Homilies, which clergymen were required to read out to their congregations.

In reality, Elizabeth's power was not absolute. The government had a network of spies, informers, and agents provocateurs, but it lacked a standing army, a national police force, an efficient system of communication, and an extensive bureaucracy. Above all, the Queen had limited financial resources and needed to turn periodically to an independent and often recalcitrant Parliament, which by long tradition had the sole right to levy taxes and to grant subsidies. Members of the House of Commons were elected from their boroughs, not appointed by the monarch, and though the Queen had considerable influence over their decisions, she could by no means dictate policy. Under these constraints, Elizabeth ruled through a combination of adroit political maneuvering and imperious command, all the while enhancing her authority in the eyes of both court and country by means of an extraordinary cult of love.

"We all loved her," Elizabeth's godson Sir John Harington wrote, with just a touch of irony, a few years after the Queen's death, "for she said she loved us." Ambassadors, courtiers, and parliamentarians all submitted to Elizabeth's cult of love, in which the Queen's gender was transformed from a potential liability into a significant asset. Those who approached her generally did so on their knees and were expected to address her with extravagant compliments fashioned from the period's most passionate love poetry; she in turn spoke, when it suited her to do so, in the language of love poetry. The court moved in an atmosphere of romance, with music, dancing, plays, and the elaborate, fancy-dress entertainments called masques. The Queen adorned herself in gorgeous clothes and rich jewels. When she went on one of her summer "progresses," ceremonial journeys through her land, she looked like an exotic, sacred image in a religious cult of love, and her noble hosts virtually bankrupted themselves to lavish upon her the costliest pleasures. England's leading artists, such as the poet Edmund Spenser and the painter Nicholas Hilliard, enlisted themselves in the celebration of Elizabeth's mystery, likening her to the goddesses of classical mythology: Diana, Astraea, Phoebe, Flora. Her cult drew its power from cultural discourses that ranged from the secular (her courtiers could pine for her as a chaste, unattainable maiden) to the sacred (the veneration that under Catholicism had been due to the Virgin Mary could now be directed toward England's semidivine queen).

There was a sober, even grim aspect to these poetical fantasies: Elizabeth was brilliant at playing one dangerous faction off against another, now turning her gracious smiles on one favorite, now honoring his hated rival, now suddenly looking elsewhere and raising an obscure upstart to royal favor. And when she was disobeyed or when she felt that her prerogatives had been challenged, she was capable of an anger that, as Harington put it, "left no doubtings whose daughter she was." Thus when Sir Walter Ralegh, one of the Queen's glittering favorites, married without her knowledge or consent, he found himself promptly imprisoned in the Tower of London. And when the Protestant polemicist John Stubbs ventured to publish a pamphlet stridently denouncing the Queen's proposed marriage to the French Catholic Duke of Alençon, Stubbs and his publisher were arrested and had their right hands chopped off. (After receiving the blow, the now prudent Stubbs lifted his hat with his remaining hand and cried, "God save the Queen!")

The Queen's marriage negotiations were a particularly fraught issue. When she came to the throne at twenty-five years old, speculation about a suitable match, already widespread, intensified and remained for decades at a fever pitch, for the stakes were high. If Elizabeth died childless, the Tudor line would come to an end. The nearest heir was her cousin Mary, Queen of Scots, a Catholic whose claim was supported by France and by the papacy and whose penchant for sexual and political intrigue confirmed the worst fears of English Protestants. The obvious way to avert the nightmare was for Elizabeth to marry and produce an heir, and the pressure upon her to do so was intense.

More than the royal succession hinged on the question of the Queen's marriage; Elizabeth's perceived eligibility was a vital factor in the complex machinations of international diplomacy. A dynastic marriage between the Queen of England and a foreign ruler would forge an alliance powerful enough to alter the balance of power in Europe. The English court hosted a steady stream of ambassadors from kings and princes eager to win the hand of the royal maiden, and Elizabeth, who prided herself on speaking fluent French and Italian (and on reading Latin and Greek), played her romantic part with exemplary skill, sighing and spinning the negotiations out for months and even years. Most probably, she never meant to marry any of her numerous foreign (and domestic) suitors. Such a decisive act would have meant the end of her independence, as well as the end of the marriage game by which she played one power off against another. One day she would seem to be on the verge of accepting a proposal; the next, she would vow never to forsake her virginity. "She is a princess," the French ambassador remarked, "who can act any part she pleases."

The Kingdom in Danger

Beset by Catholic and Protestant extremists, Elizabeth contrived to forge a moderate compromise that enabled her realm to avert the massacres and civil wars that poisoned France and other countries on the Continent. But menace was never far off, and there were constant fears of conspiracy, rebellion, and assassination. Many of the fears swirled around Mary, Queen of Scots, who had been driven from her own kingdom in 1568 by a powerful faction of rebellious nobles and had taken refuge in England. Her presence, under a kind of house arrest, was a source of intense anxiety and helped generate continual rumors of plots. Some of these plots were real enough, others imaginary, still others traps set in motion by the secret agents of the government's intelligence service under the direction of Sir Francis Walsingham. The situation worsened greatly after Spanish imperial armies invaded the Netherlands in order to stamp out Protestant rebels (1567), after the St. Bartholomew's Day Massacre of Protestants (Huguenots) in France (1572), and after the assassination there of Europe's other major Protestant leader, William of Orange (1584).

The Queen's life seemed to be in even greater danger after the proclamation of Pope Gregory XIII in 1580 that the assassination of the great heretic Elizabeth (who had been excommunicated a decade before) would not constitute a mortal sin. The immediate effect of the proclamation was to make existence more difficult for English Catholics, most of whom were loyal to the Queen but who fell under grave suspicion. Suspicion was intensified by the clandestine presence of English Jesuits, trained at seminaries abroad and smuggled back into England to serve the Roman Catholic cause. When Elizabeth's spymaster Walsingham unearthed an assassination plot in the correspondence between the Queen of Scots and the Catholic Anthony Babington, the wretched Mary's fate was sealed. After vacillating, a very reluctant Elizabeth signed the death warrant in February 1587, and her cousin was beheaded.

The long-anticipated military confrontation with Catholic Spain was now unavoidable. Elizabeth learned that Philip II, her former brother-in-law and onetime suitor, was preparing to send an enormous fleet against her island realm. It was to sail to the Netherlands, where a Spanish army would be waiting to embark and invade England. Barring its way was England's small fleet of well-armed and highly maneuverable fighting vessels, backed up by ships from the merchant navy. The Invincible Armada reached English waters in July 1588, only to be routed in one of the most famous and decisive naval battles in European history. Then, in what many viewed as an act of God on behalf of Protestant England, the Spanish fleet was dispersed and all but destroyed by violent storms.

As England braced itself to withstand the invasion that never came, Elizabeth appeared in person to review a detachment of soldiers assembled at Tilbury. Dressed in a white gown and a silver breastplate, she declared that though some among her councillors had urged her not to appear before a large crowd of armed men, she would never fail to trust the loyalty of her faithful and loving subjects. Nor did she fear the Spanish armies. "I know I have the body of a weak and feeble woman," Elizabeth declared, "but I have the heart and stomach of a king, and of England too." In this celebrated speech, Elizabeth displayed many of her most memorable qualities: her self-consciously histrionic command of grand public occasion, her subtle blending of magniloquent rhetoric and the language of love, her strategic appropriation of traditionally masculine qualities, and her great personal courage. "We princes," she once remarked, "are set on stages in the sight and view of all the world."

The English and Otherness

Shakespeare's London had a large population of resident aliens, mainly artisans and merchants and their families, from Portugal, Italy, Spain, Germany, and above all France and the Netherlands. Many of these people were Protestant refugees, and they were accorded some legal and economic protection by the government. But they were not always welcomed by the local populace. Throughout the sixteenth century, London was the site of repeated demonstrations and, on occasion, bloody riots against the communities of foreign artisans, who were accused of taking jobs away from Englishmen. There was widespread hostility as well toward the Welsh, the Scots, and especially the Irish, whom the English had for centuries been struggling unsuccessfully to subdue. The kings of England claimed to be rulers of Ireland, but in reality they effectively controlled only a small area known as the Pale, extending north from Dublin. The great majority of the Irish people remained stubbornly Catholic and, despite endlessly reiterated English repression, burning of villages, destruction of crops, and massacres, incorrigibly independent.

Shakespeare's *Henry V* (1598–99) seems to invite the audience to celebrate the conjoined heroism of English, Welsh, Scots, and Irish soldiers all fighting together as a "band of brothers" against the French. But such a way of imagining the national community must be set against the tensions and conflicting interests that often set these brothers at each other's throats. As Shakespeare's King Henry realizes, a feared or hated foreign enemy helps at least to mask these tensions, and indeed, in the face of the Spanish Armada, even the bitter gulf between Catholic and Protestant Englishmen seemed to narrow significantly. But the patriotic alliance was only temporary.

Another way of partially masking the sharp differences in language, belief, and custom among the peoples of the British Isles was to group these people together in contrast to the Jews. Medieval England's Jewish population, the recurrent object of persecution, extortion, and massacre, had been officially expelled by King Edward I in 1290. Therefore few if any of Shakespeare's contemporaries would have encountered on English soil Jews who openly practiced their religion. Elizabethan England probably did, however, harbor a small number of so-called Marranos, Spanish or Portuguese Jews who had officially converted to Christianity but secretly continued to observe Jewish practices. One of those suspected to be Marranos was Elizabeth's own physician, Roderigo Lopez, who was tried in 1594 for an alleged plot to poison the Queen. Convicted and condemned to the hideous execution reserved for traitors, Lopez went to his death, in the words of the Elizabethan historian

A Jewish man depicted poisoning a well. From Pierre Boaistuau, *Certain Secret Wonders of Nature* (1569).

William Camden, "affirming that he loved the Queen as well as he loved Jesus Christ; which coming from a man of the Jewish profession moved no small laughter in the standers-by." It is difficult to gauge the meaning here of the phrase "the Jewish profession," used to describe a man who never as far as we know professed Judaism, just as it is difficult to gauge the meaning of the crowd's cruel laughter.

Elizabethans appear to have been fascinated by Jews and Judaism but quite uncertain whether the terms referred to a people, a foreign nation, a set of strange practices, a living faith, a defunct religion, a villainous conspiracy, or a messianic inheritance. Protestant reformers brooded deeply on the Hebraic origins of Christianity; government officials ordered the arrest of those "suspected to be Jews"; villagers paid pennies to itinerant fortune-tellers who claimed to be descended from Abraham or masters of cabalistic mysteries; and London playgoers, perhaps including some who laughed at Lopez on the scaffold, enjoyed the spectacle of the downfall of the wicked Barabas in Christopher Marlowe's *Jew of Malta* (ca. 1589) and the forced conversion of Shylock in Shakespeare's *Merchant of Venice* (1596–97). Jews were not officially permitted to resettle in England until the middle of the seventeenth century, and even then their legal status was ambiguous.

Shakespeare's England also had a small African population whose skin color was the subject of pseudo-scientific speculation and theological debate. Some Elizabethans believed that Africans' blackness resulted from the climate of the regions in which they lived, where, as one traveler put it, they were "so scorched and vexed with the heat of the sun, that in many places they curse it when it riseth." Others held that blackness was a curse inherited from their forefather Chus, the son of Ham, who had, according to Genesis, wickedly exposed the nakedness of the drunken Noah. George Best, a proponent of this theory of inherited skin color, reported that "I myself have seen an Ethiopian as black as coal brought into England, who taking a fair English woman to wife, begat a son in all respects as black as the father was, although England were his native country, and an English woman his mother: whereby it seemeth this blackness proceedeth rather of some natural infection of that man."

As the word "infection" suggests, Elizabethans frequently regarded blackness as a physical defect, though the blacks who lived in England and Scotland throughout the sixteenth century were also treated as exotic curiosities. At his marriage to Anne of Denmark, James I entertained his bride and her family by commanding four naked black youths to dance before him in the snow. (The youths died of exposure shortly afterward.) In 1594, in the festivities celebrating the baptism of James's son, a "Black-Moor" entered pulling an elabo-

pena, El rey delta tierra es muy podero-
so porque es señot de cincuenta y quatro
islas muy grádes y en cada vna destas ay
vn rey ⁊ todos son obedientes a el/en las
gles islas ay muchas maneras de gétes.

E n la india ay vna isla en la qual ay
y babitan vna manera de gétes las
quales son pequeñas de cuerpo y son de
miuv maliiada natura noioue ollac ni

Man with head beneath his shoulders. From a Spanish edition of Mandeville's *Travels*. See *Othello* 1.3.144–45: "and men whose heads / Grew beneath their shoulders." Such men were frequently reported by medieval travelers to the East.

rately decorated chariot that was, in the original plan, supposed to be drawn in by a lion. There was a black trumpeter in the courts of Henry VII and Henry VIII, while Elizabeth had at least two black servants, one an entertainer and the other a page. Africans became increasingly popular as servants in aristocratic and gentle households in the last decades of the sixteenth century.

Some of these Africans were almost certainly slaves, though the legal status of slavery in England was ambiguous. In Cartwright's Case (1569), the court ruled "that England was too Pure an Air for Slaves to breathe in," but there is evidence that black slaves were owned in Elizabethan and Jacobean England. Moreover, by the mid-sixteenth century, the English had become involved in the profitable trade that carried African slaves to the New World. In 1562, John Hawkins embarked on his first slaving voyage, transporting some three hundred blacks from the Guinea coast to Hispaniola, where they were sold for £10,000. Elizabeth is reported to have said of this venture that it was "detestable, and would call down the Vengeance of Heaven upon the Undertakers." Nevertheless, she invested in Hawkins's subsequent voyages and loaned him ships.

English men and women of the sixteenth century experienced an unprecedented increase in knowledge of the world beyond their island, for a number of reasons. Religious persecution compelled both Catholics and Protestants to live abroad; wealthy gentlemen (and, in at least a few cases, ladies) traveled in France and Italy to view the famous cultural monuments; merchants published accounts of distant lands such as Turkey, Morocco, and Russia; and military and trading ventures took English ships to still more distant shores. In 1496, a Venetian tradesman living in Bristol, John Cabot, was granted a license by Henry VII to sail on a voyage of exploration; with his son Sebastian, he discovered Newfoundland and Nova Scotia. Remarkable feats of seamanship and reconnaissance soon followed: on his ship the *Golden Hind,* Sir Francis Drake circumnavigated the globe in 1579 and laid claim to California on behalf of the Queen; a few years later, a ship commanded by Thomas Cavendish also completed a circumnavigation. Sir Martin Frobisher explored bleak Baffin Island in search of a Northwest Passage to the Orient; Sir John Davis explored the west coast of Greenland and discovered the Falkland Islands off the coast of Argentina; Sir Walter Ralegh ventured up the Orinoco Delta, in what is now Venezuela, in search of the mythical land of El Dorado. Accounts of these and other exploits were collected by a clergyman and promoter of empire, Richard Hakluyt, and published as *The Principal Navigations* (1589; expanded edition 1599).

"To seek new worlds for gold, for praise, for glory," as Ralegh characterized such enterprises, was not for the faint of heart: Drake, Cavendish, Frobisher, and Hawkins all died at sea, as did huge numbers of those who sailed under their command. Elizabethans sensible enough to stay at home could do more than read written accounts of their fellow countrymen's far-reaching voyages. Expeditions brought back native plants (including, most famously, tobacco), animals, cultural artifacts, and, on occasion, samples of the native peoples themselves, most often seized against their will. There were exhibitions in London of a kidnapped Eskimo with his kayak and of Native Virginians with their canoes. Most of these miserable captives, violently uprooted and vulnerable to European diseases, quickly perished, but even in death they were evidently valuable property: when the English will not give one small coin "to relieve a lame beggar," one of the characters in *The Tempest* wryly remarks, "they will lay out ten to see a dead Indian" (2.2.30–31).

Perhaps most nations learn to define what they are by defining what they are not. This negative self-definition is, in any case, what Elizabethans seemed constantly to be doing, in travel books, sermons, political speeches, civic pageants, public exhibitions, and theatrical spectacles of otherness. The extraordinary variety of these exercises (which include public executions and urban riots, as well as more benign forms of curiosity) suggests that the boundaries of national identity were by no means clear and unequivocal. Even peoples whom English writers routinely, viciously stigmatize

An Indian dance. From Thomas Hariot, *A Brief and True Report of the New Found Land of Virginia* (1590).

as irreducibly alien—Italians, Indians, Turks, and Jews—have a surprising instability in the Elizabethan imagination and may appear for brief, intense moments as powerful models to be admired and emulated before they resume their place as emblems of despised otherness.

James I and the Union of the Crowns

Though under great pressure to do so, the aging Elizabeth steadfastly refused to name her successor. It became increasingly apparent, however, that it would be James Stuart, the son of Mary, Queen of Scots, and by the time Elizabeth's health began to fail, several of her principal advisers, including her chief minister, Robert Cecil, had been for several years in secret correspondence with him in Edinburgh. Crowned King James VI of Scotland in 1567 when he was but one year old, Mary's son had been raised as a Protestant by his powerful guardians, and in 1589 he married a Protestant princess, Anne of Denmark. When Elizabeth died on March 24, 1603, English officials reported that on her deathbed the Queen had named James to succeed her.

Upon his accession, James—now styled James VI of Scotland and James I of England—made plain his intention to unite his two kingdoms. As he told Parliament in 1604, "What God hath conjoined then, let no man separate. I am the husband, and all of the whole isle is my lawful wife; I am the head and it is my body; I am the

Funeral procession of Queen Elizabeth. From a watercolor sketch by an unknown artist (1603).

shepherd and it is my flock." But the flock was less perfectly united than James optimistically envisioned: English and Scottish were sharply distinct identities, as were Welsh and Cornish and other peoples who were incorporated, with varying degrees of willingness, into the realm.

Fearing that to change the name of the kingdom would invalidate all laws and institutions established under the name of England, a fear that was partly real and partly a cover for anti-Scots prejudice, Parliament balked at James's desire to be called "King of Great Britain" and resisted the unionist legislation that would have made Great Britain a legal reality. Though the English initially rejoiced at the peaceful transition from Elizabeth to her successor, there was a rising tide of resentment against James's advancement of Scots friends and his creation of new knighthoods. Lower down the social ladder, English and Scots occasionally clashed violently on the streets: in July 1603, James issued a proclamation against Scottish "insolencies," and in April 1604, he ordered the arrest of "swaggerers" waylaying Scots in London. The ensuing years did not bring the amity and docile obedience for which James hoped, and, though the navy now flew the Union Jack, combining the Scottish cross of St. Andrew and the English cross of St. George, the unification of the kingdoms remained throughout his reign an unfulfilled ambition.

Unfulfilled as well were James's lifelong dreams of ruling as an absolute monarch. Crown lawyers throughout Europe had long argued that a king, by virtue of his power to make law, must necessarily be above law. But in England sovereignty was identified not with the king alone or with the people alone but with the "King in Parliament." Against his absolutist ambitions, James faced the crucial power to raise taxes that was vested not in the monarch but in the elected members of the Parliament. He faced as well a theory of republicanism that traced its roots back to ancient Rome and that prided itself on its steadfast and, if necessary, violent resistance to tyranny. Shakespeare's fascination with monarchy is apparent throughout his work, but in his Roman plays in particular, as well as in his long poem *The Rape of Lucrece*, he manifests an intense imaginative interest in the idea of a republic.

The Jacobean Court

With James as with Elizabeth, the royal court was the center of diplomacy, ambition, intrigue, and an intense jockeying for social position. As always in monarchies, proximity to the king's person was a central mark of favor, so that access to the royal bedchamber was one of the highest aims of the powerful, scheming lords who followed James from his sprawling London palace at Whitehall to the hunting lodges and country estates to which he loved to retreat. A coveted office, in the Jacobean as in the Tudor court, was the Groom of the Stool, the person who supervised the disposal of the king's wastes. The officeholder was close to the king at one of his most exposed and vulnerable moments and enjoyed the further privilege of sleeping on a pallet at the foot of the royal bed and assisting the monarch in putting on the royal undershirt. Another, slightly less privileged official, the Gentleman of the Robes, dressed the king in his doublet and outer garments.

The royal lifestyle was increasingly expensive. Unlike Elizabeth, James had to maintain separate households for his queen and for the heir apparent, Prince Henry. (Upon Henry's death at the age of eighteen in 1612, his younger brother, Prince Charles, became heir, eventually succeeding his father in 1625.) James was also extremely generous to his friends, amassing his own huge debts in the course of paying off theirs. As early as 1605, he told his principal adviser that "it is a horror to me to think of the height of my place, the greatness of my debts, and the smallness of my means." This smallness notwithstanding, James continued to lavish gifts upon handsome favorites such as the Earl of Somerset, Robert Carr, and the Duke of Buckingham, George Villiers.

The attachment James formed for these favorites was highly romantic. "God so love me," the King wrote to Buckingham, "as I desire only to live in the world for your sake, and that I had rather live banished in any part of the earth with you than live a sorrowful widow's life without you." Such sentiments, not surprisingly, gave rise to widespread rumors of homosexual activities at court. The rumors are certainly plausible, though the surviving evidence of same-sex relationships, at court or elsewhere, is extremely difficult to interpret. A statute of 1533 made "the detestable and abominable vice of buggery committed with mankind or beast" a felony punishable by death. (English law

declined to recognize or criminalize lesbian acts.) The effect of the draconian laws against sodomy seems to have been to reduce actual prosecutions to the barest minimum: for the next hundred years, there are no known cases of trials resulting in a death sentence for homosexual activity alone. If the legal record is therefore unreliable as an index of the extent of homosexual relations, the literary record (including, most famously, the majority of Shakespeare's sonnets) is equally opaque. Any poetic avowal of male-male love may simply be a formal expression of affection based on classical models, or, alternatively, it may be an expression of passionate physical and spiritual love. The interpretive difficulty is compounded by the absence in the period of any clear reference to a homosexual "identity," though there are many references to same-sex acts and feelings. What is clear is that male friendships at the court of James and elsewhere were suffused with eroticism, at once exciting and threatening, that subsequent periods policed more anxiously.

James I. Attributed to John De Critz the Elder (ca. 1606).

In addition to the extravagant expenditures on his favorites, James

Two Young Men. By Crispin van den Broeck.

was also the patron of ever more elaborate feasts and masques. Shakespeare's work provides a small glimpse of these in *The Tempest,* with its exotic banquet and its "majestic vision" of mythological goddesses and dancing nymphs and reapers. The actual Jacobean court masques, designed by the great architect, painter, and engineer Inigo Jones, were spectacular, fantastic, technically ingenious, and staggeringly costly celebrations of regal magnificence. With their exquisite costumes and their elegant blend of music, dancing, and poetry, the masques, generally performed by the noble lords and ladies of the court, were deliberately ephemeral exercises in conspicuous expenditure and consumption: by tradition, at the end of the performance, the private audience would rush forward and tear to pieces the gorgeous scenery. And though masques were enormously sophisticated entertainments, often on rather esoteric allegorical themes, they could on occasion collapse into grotesque excess. In a letter of 1606, Sir John Harington describes a masque in honor of the visiting Danish king in which the participants, no doubt toasting their royal majesties, had had too much to drink. A lady playing the part of the Queen of Sheba attempted to present precious gifts, "but, forgetting the steps arising to the canopy, overset her caskets into his Danish Majesty's lap. . . . His Majesty then got up and would dance with the Queen of Sheba; but he fell down and humbled himself before her, and was carried to an inner chamber and laid on a bed." Meanwhile, Harington writes, the masque continued with a pageant of Faith, Hope, and Charity, but Charity could barely keep her balance, while Hope and Faith "were both sick and spewing in the lower hall." This was, we can hope, not a typical occasion.

While the English seem initially to have welcomed James's free-spending ways as a change from the parsimoniousness of Queen Elizabeth, they were dismayed by its consequences. Elizabeth had died owing £400,000. In 1608, the royal debt had risen to £1,400,000 and was increasing by £140,000 a year. The money to pay off this debt, or at least to keep it under control, was raised by various means. These included customs farming (leasing the right to collect customs duties to private individuals); the highly unpopular impositions (duties on the import of nonnecessities, such as spices, silks, and currants); the sale of crown lands; the sale of baronetcies; and appeals to an increasingly grudging and recalcitrant Parliament. In 1614, Parliament demanded an end to impositions before it would relieve the King and was angrily dissolved without completing its business.

James's Religious Policy and the Persecution of Witches

Before his accession to the English throne, the King had made known his view of Puritans, the general name for a variety of Protestant sects that were agitating for a radical reform of the church, the overthrow of its conservative hierarchy of bishops, and the rejection of a large number of traditional rituals and practices. In a book he wrote, *Basilikon Doron* (1599), James denounced "brainsick and heady preachers" who were prepared "to let King, people, law and all be trod underfoot." Yet he was not entirely unwilling to consider religious reforms. In religion, as in foreign policy, he was above all concerned to maintain peace.

On his way south to claim the throne of England in 1603, James was presented with the Millenary Petition (signed by one thousand ministers), which urged him as "our physician" to heal the disease of lingering "popish" ceremonies. He responded by calling a conference on the ceremonies of the Church of England, which duly took place at Hampton Court Palace in January 1604. The delegates who spoke for reform were moderates, and there was little in the outcome to satisfy Puritans. Nevertheless, while the Church of England continued to cling to such remnants of the Catholic past as wedding rings, square caps, bishops, and Christmas, the conference did produce some reform in the area of ecclesiastical discipline. It also authorized a new English translation of the Bible, known as the King James Bible, which was printed in 1611, too late to have been extensively used by Shakespeare. Along with Shakespeare's works, the King James Bible has probably had the profoundest influence on the subsequent history of English literature.

Having arranged this compromise, James saw his main task as ensuring conformity. He promulgated the 1604 Canons (the first definitive code of canon law since the Reformation), which required all ministers to subscribe to three articles. The first affirmed royal supremacy; the second confirmed that there was nothing in the Book of Common Prayer "contrary to the Word of God" and required ministers to use only the authorized services; the third asserted that the central tenets of the Church of England

The "swimming" of a suspected witch.

were "agreeable to the Word of God." There were strong objections to the second and third articles from those of Puritan leanings inside and outside the House of Commons. In the end, many ministers refused to conform or subscribe to the articles, but only about ninety of them, or 1 percent of the clergy, were deprived of their livings. In its theology and composition, the Church of England was little changed from what it had been under Elizabeth. In hindsight, what is most striking are the ominous signs of growing religious divisions that would by the 1640s burst forth in civil war and the execution of James's son Charles.

James seems to have taken seriously the official claims to the sacredness of kingship, and he certainly took seriously his own theories of religion and politics, which he had printed for the edification of his people. He was convinced that Satan, perpetually warring against God and His representatives on earth, was continually plotting against him. James thought moreover that he possessed special insight into Satan's wicked agents, the witches, and in 1597, while King of Scotland, he published his *Demonology*, a learned exposition of their malign threat to his godly rule. Hundreds of witches, he believed, were involved in a 1589 conspiracy to kill him by raising storms at sea when he was sailing home from Denmark with his new bride.

In the 1590s, Scotland embarked on a virulent witch craze of the kind that had since the fifteenth century repeatedly afflicted France, Switzerland, and Germany, where many thousands of women (and a much smaller number of men) were caught in a nightmarish web of wild accusations. Tortured into making lurid confessions of infant cannibalism, night flying, and sexual intercourse with the devil at huge, orgiastic "witches' Sabbaths," the victims had little chance to defend themselves and were routinely burned at the stake.

In England too there were witchcraft prosecutions, though on a much smaller scale and with significant differences in the nature of the accusations and the judicial procedures. Witch trials began in England in the 1540s; statutes against witchcraft were enacted in 1542, 1563, and 1604. English law did not allow judicial torture, stipulated lesser punishments in cases of "white magic," and mandated jury trials. Juries acquitted more than half of the defendants in witchcraft trials; in Essex, where the judicial records are particularly extensive, some 24 percent of those accused were executed, while the remainder of those convicted were pilloried and imprisoned or sentenced and reprieved. The accused were generally charged with *maleficium*, an evil deed—usually harming neighbors, causing destructive storms, or killing farm animals—but not with worshipping Satan.

After 1603, when James came to the English throne, he somewhat moderated his enthusiasm for the judicial murder of witches, for the most part defenseless, poor women resented by their neighbors. Though he did nothing to mitigate the ferocity of the ongoing witch hunts in his native Scotland, he did not try to institute Scottish-style persecutions and trials in his new realm. This relative waning of persecutorial eagerness principally reflects the differences between England and Scotland, but it may also bespeak some small, nascent skepticism on James's part about the quality of evidence brought against the accused and about the reliability of the "confessions" extracted from them. It is sobering to reflect that plays like Shakespeare's *Macbeth* (1606), Thomas Middleton's *Witch* (before 1616), and Thomas Dekker, John Ford, and William Rowley's *Witch of Edmonton* (1621) seem to be less the allies of skepticism than the exploiters of fear.

The Playing Field

Cosmic Spectacles

The first permanent, freestanding public theaters in England date only from Shakespeare's own lifetime: a London playhouse, the Red Lion, is mentioned in 1567, and

James Burbage's playhouse, The Theatre, was built in 1576. (The innovative use of these new stages, crucial to a full understanding of Shakespeare's achievement, is discussed in a separate essay in this volume, by the theater historian Holger Schott Syme.) But it is quite misleading to identify English drama exclusively with these specially constructed playhouses, for in fact there was a rich and vital theatrical tradition in England stretching back for centuries. Many towns in late medieval England were the sites of annual festivals that mounted elaborate cycles of plays depicting the great biblical stories, from the creation of the world to Christ's Passion and its miraculous aftermath. Most of these plays have been lost, but the surviving cycles, such as those from York, are magnificent and complex works of art. They are sometimes called "mystery plays," either because they were performed by the guilds of various crafts (known as "mysteries") or, more likely, because they represented the mysteries of the faith. The cycles were most often performed on the annual feast day instituted in the early fourteenth century in honor of the Corpus Christi, the sacrament of the Lord's Supper, which is perhaps the greatest of these religious mysteries.

The Feast of Corpus Christi, celebrated on the Thursday following Trinity Sunday, helped give the play cycles their extraordinary cultural resonance, but it also contributed to their downfall. For along with the specifically liturgical plays traditionally performed by religious confraternities and the "saints' plays," which depicted miraculous events in the lives of individual holy men and women, the mystery cycles were closely identified with the Catholic Church. Protestant authorities in the sixteenth century, eager to eradicate all remnants of popular Catholic piety, moved to suppress the annual procession of the Host, with its gorgeous banners, pageant carts, and cycle of visionary plays. In 1548, the Feast of Corpus Christi was abolished. Towns that continued to perform the mysteries were under increasing pressure to abandon them. It is sometimes said that the cycles were already dying out from neglect, but recent research has shown that many towns and their guilds were extremely reluctant to give them up. Desperate offers to strip away any traces of Catholic doctrine and to submit the play scripts to the authorities for their approval met with unbending opposition from the government. In 1576, the courts gave York permission to perform its cycle but only if

> in the said play no pageant be used or set forth wherein the Majesty of God the Father, God the Son, or God the Holy Ghost or the administration of either the Sacraments of baptism or of the Lord's Supper be counterfeited or represented, or anything played which tend to the maintenance of superstition and idolatry or which be contrary to the laws of God . . . or of the realm.

Such "permission" was tantamount to an outright ban. The local officials in the city of Norwich, proud of their St. George and the Dragon play, asked if they could at least parade the dragon costume through the streets, but even this modest request was refused. It is likely that as a young man Shakespeare had seen some of these plays: when Hamlet says of a noisy, strutting theatrical performance that it "out-Herods Herod," he is alluding to the famously bombastic role of Herod of Jewry in the mystery plays. But by the century's end, the cycles were no longer performed by live actors in great civic celebrations. They survived, if at all, in the debased form of puppet shows.

Early English theater was by no means restricted to these civic and religious festivals. Payments to professional and amateur performers appear in early records of towns and aristocratic households, though the Latin terms—*ministralli, histriones, mimi, lusores,* and so forth—are not used with great consistency and make it difficult to distinguish among minstrels, jugglers, stage players, and other entertainers. Performers acted in town halls and the halls of guilds and aristocratic mansions, on scaffolds erected in town squares and marketplaces, on pageant wagons in the streets, and in inn yards. By the fifteenth century, and probably earlier, there were organized companies of players traveling under noble patronage. Such companies earned a living providing amusement, while enhancing the prestige of the patron.

Panorama of London, showing two theaters, both round and both flying flags: a flying flag indicated that a performance was in progress. The Globe is in the foreground, and the Hope, or Beargarden, is to the left.

A description of a provincial performance in the late sixteenth century, written by one R. Willis, provides a glimpse of what seems to have been the usual procedure:

> In the City of Gloucester the manner is (as I think it is in other like corporations) that when the Players of Interludes come to town, they first attend the Mayor to inform him what nobleman's servant they are, and so to get license for their public playing; and if the Mayor like the Actors, or would show respect to their Lord and Master, he appoints them to play their first play before himself and the Aldermen and common Council of the City and that is called the Mayor's play, where everyone that will come in without money, the Mayor giving the players a reward as he thinks fit to show respect unto them.

In addition to their take from this "first play," the players would almost certainly have supplemented their income by performing in halls and inn yards, where they could on some occasions charge an admission fee. It was no doubt a precarious existence.

The "Interludes" mentioned in Willis's description of the Gloucester performances are likely plays that were, in effect, staged dialogues on religious, moral, and political themes. Such works could, like the mysteries, be associated with Catholicism, but they were also used in the sixteenth century to convey polemical Protestant messages, and they reached outside the religious sphere to address secular concerns as well. Henry Medwall's *Fulgens and Lucrece* (ca. 1490–1501), for example, pits a wealthy but dissolute nobleman against a virtuous public servant of humble origins, while John Heywood's *Play of the Weather* (ca. 1525–33) stages a debate among social rivals, including a gentleman, a merchant, a forest ranger, and two millers. The structure of such plays reflects the training in argumentation that students received in Tudor schools and, in particular, the sustained practice in examining all sides of a difficult question. Some of Shakespeare's amazing ability to look at critical issues from multiple perspectives may be traced back to this practice and the dramatic interludes it helped to inspire.

Another major form of theater that flourished in England in the fifteenth century and continued on into the sixteenth was the morality play. Like the mysteries, moralities addressed questions of the ultimate fate of the soul. They did so, however, not by rehearsing scriptural stories but by dramatizing allegories of spiritual struggle. Typically, a person named Human or Mankind or Youth is faced with a choice between a pious life in the company of such associates as Mercy, Discretion, and Good Deeds and a dissolute life among riotous companions like Lust or Mischief. Plays like *Mankind* (ca. 1465–70) and *Everyman* (ca. 1495) show how powerful these unpromising-sounding dramas could be, in part because of the extraordinary comic vitality of the evil character, or the Vice, and in part because of the poignancy and terror of an individual's encounter with death. Shakespeare clearly grasped this power. The hunchbacked Duke of Gloucester in *Richard III* gleefully likens himself to "the formal Vice, Iniquity." And when Othello wavers between Desdemona and Iago (himself a Vice figure), his anguished dilemma echoes the fateful choice repeatedly faced by the troubled, vulnerable protagonists of the moralities.

If such plays sound a bit like sermons, it is because they were. Clerics and actors shared some of the same rhetorical skills. It would be misleading to regard church-going and playgoing as comparable entertainments, but in attacking the stage, ministers often seemed to regard the professional players as dangerous rivals. "To leave a Sermon to go to a Play," warned the preacher John Stoughton, "is to forsake the Church of God; to betake oneself to the Synagogue of Satan, to fall from Heaven to Hell." The players themselves were generally too discreet to rise to the challenge; it would have been foolhardy to present the theater as the church's direct competitor. Yet in its moral intensity and its command of impassioned language, the stage frequently emulates and outdoes the pulpit.

Music and Dance

Playacting took its place alongside other forms of public expression and entertainment as well. Perhaps the most important, from the perspective of the theater, were music and dance, since these were directly and repeatedly incorporated into plays. Many plays, comedies and tragedies alike, include occasions that call upon the characters to dance: hence Beatrice and Benedict join the other masked guests at the dance in *Much Ado About Nothing*; in *Twelfth Night*, the befuddled Sir Andrew, at the instigation of the drunken Sir Toby Belch, displays his skill, such as it is, in capering; Romeo and Juliet first see each other at the Capulet ball; the witches dance in a ring around the hideous caldron and perform an "antic round" to cheer Macbeth's spirits; and, in one of Shakespeare's strangest and most wonderful scenes, the drunken Antony in *Antony and Cleopatra* joins hands with Caesar, Enobarbus, Pompey, and others to dance "the Egyptian Bacchanals."

Moreover, virtually all plays in the period, including Shakespeare's, apparently ended with a dance. Brushing off the theatrical gore and changing their expressions from woe to pleasure, the actors in plays like *Romeo and Juliet* and *Julius Caesar* would presumably have received the audience's applause and then bid for a second round of applause by performing a stately pavane or a lively jig. The vogue may have begun to wane in the early seventeenth century, but only to give way to other post-play enter-tainments, such as the improvisation game known as "themes" where someone in the audience would shout out a theme or question (for example, "Why barks that dog?") and the actor would come up with an extempore response. (The clown Robert Armin, who played the Fool in *King Lear*, was apparently an expert at this game.) Jigs, with their comical leaping dance steps often accompanied by scurrilous ballads, remained popular enough to draw not only large crowds but also official disapproval. A court order of 1612 complained about the "cut-purses and other lewd and ill-disposed per-sons" who flocked to the theater at the end of every play to be entertained by "lewd jigs, songs, and dances." The players were warned to suppress these disreputable entertain-ments on pain of imprisonment.

The displays of dancing onstage clearly reflected a widespread popular interest in dancing outside the walls of the playhouse as well. Renaissance intellectuals con-jured up visions of the universe as a great cosmic dance, poets figured relations between men and women in terms of popular dance steps, stern moralists denounced dancing as an incitement to filthy lewdness, and, perhaps as significant, men of all classes evidently spent a great deal of time worrying about how shapely their legs looked in tights and how gracefully they could leap. Shakespeare assumes that his audience will be quite familiar with a variety of dances. "For, hear me, Hero," Beatrice tells her friend, "wooing, wedding, and repenting is as a Scotch jig, a measure, and a cinquepace" (*Much Ado About Nothing* 2.1.61–62). Her speech dwells on the comparison a bit, teasing out its implications, but it still does not make much sense if you do not already know something about the dances and perhaps occasionally venture to perform them yourself.

Closely linked to dancing and even more central to the stage was music, both instrumental and vocal. In the early sixteenth century, the Reformation had been disastrous for sacred music: many church organs were destroyed, choir schools were closed, the glorious polyphonic liturgies sung in the monasteries were suppressed. But by the latter part of the century, new perspectives were reinvigorating English music. Latin Masses were reset in English, and tunes were written for newly translated, metrical psalms. More important for the theater, styles of secular music were developed that emphasized music's link to humanist eloquence, its ability to heighten and to rival rhetorically powerful texts.

This link is particularly evident in vocal music, at which Elizabethan composers excelled. Renowned composers William Byrd, Thomas Morley, John Dowland, and others wrote a rich profusion of madrigals (part songs for two to eight voices unaccompanied) and ayres (songs for solo voice, generally accompanied by the lute). These works, along with hymns, popular ballads, rounds, catches, and other forms of song, enjoyed immense popularity, not only in the royal court, where musical skill was regarded as an important accomplishment, and in aristocratic households, where professional musicians were employed as entertainers, but also in less exalted social circles. In his *Plain and Easy Introduction to Practical Music* (1597), Morley tells a

Frans Hals, *The Clown with the Lute* (1625).

story of social humiliation at a failure to perform that suggests that a well-educated Elizabethan was expected to be able to sing at sight. Even if this is an exaggeration in the interest of book sales, there is evidence of impressively widespread musical literacy, reflected in a splendid array of music for the lute, viol, recorder, harp, and virginal, as well as the marvelous vocal music.

Whether it is the aristocratic Orsino luxuriating in the dying fall of an exquisite melody or bully Bottom craving "the tongs and the bones," Shakespeare's characters frequently call for music. They also repeatedly give voice to the age's conviction that there was a deep relation between musical harmony and the harmonies of the well-ordered individual and state. "The man that hath no music in himself," warns Lorenzo in *The Merchant of Venice*, "nor is not moved with concord of sweet sounds, / Is fit for treasons, stratagems, and spoils" (5.1.83–85). This conviction in turn reflects a still deeper link between musical harmony and the divinely created harmony of the cosmos. When Ulysses in *Troilus and Cressida* wishes to convey the image of universal chaos, he speaks of the untuning of a string (1.3.108–09).

The playing companies must have regularly employed trained musicians, and many actors (like the actor who in playing Pandarus in *Troilus and Cressida* is supposed to accompany himself on the lute) must have possessed musical skill. When Shakespeare's company began to use an indoor theater, the Blackfriars, as a second venue, it became famous for its orchestra, and, among other composers, the King's Musician, Robert Johnson, seems to have written songs for the actors to sing. Unfortunately, we possess the original settings for very few of Shakespeare's songs, possibly because many of them may have been set to popular tunes of the time that everyone knew and no one bothered to write down.

Alternative Entertainments

Plays, music, and dancing were by no means the only shows in town. There were jousts, tournaments, royal entries, religious processions, pageants in honor of newly installed civic officials or ambassadors arriving from abroad; wedding masques, court masques, and costumed entertainments known as "disguisings" or "mummings"; juggling acts, fortune-tellers, exhibitions of swordsmanship, mountebanks, folk healers, storytellers, magic shows; bearbaiting, bullbaiting, cockfighting, and other blood sports; folk festivals such as Maying, the Feast of Fools, Carnival, and Whitsun Ales. For several years, Elizabethan Londoners were delighted by a trained animal—Banks's Horse—that performed elaborate dance steps and could, it was thought, do arithmetic and answer questions. And there was always the grim but compelling spectacle of public shaming, mutilation, and execution.

Most English towns had stocks and whipping posts. Drunks, fraudulent merchants, adulterers, and quarrelers could be placed in carts or mounted backward on asses and paraded through the streets for crowds to jeer and throw refuse at. Women accused of being scolds, as we have already remarked, could be publicly muzzled by an iron device called a "brank" or tied to a cucking stool and dunked in the river. Convicted criminals could have their ears cut off, their noses slit, their foreheads branded. Public beheadings (generally reserved for the elite) and hangings were common. Those convicted of treason were sentenced to be "hanged by the neck, and being alive cut down, and your privy members to be cut off, and your bowels to be taken out of your belly and there burned, you being alive."

Shakespeare occasionally takes note of these alternative entertainments: at the end of *Macbeth*, for example, with his enemies closing in on him, the doomed tyrant declares, "They have tied me to a stake. I cannot fly, / But bearlike I must fight the course" (5.7.1–2). The audience is reminded then that it is witnessing the human equivalent of a popular spectacle—a bear chained to a stake and attacked by fierce dogs—that they could have paid to watch at an arena near the Globe. And when, a few moments later, Macduff enters carrying Macbeth's head, the audience is seeing the theatrical equiva-

An Elizabethan hanging.

lent of the execution of criminals and traitors that they could have also watched in the flesh, as it were, nearby. In a different key, the audiences who paid to see *A Midsummer Night's Dream* or *The Winter's Tale* got to enjoy the comic spectacle of a Maying and a Whitsun Pastoral, while the spectators of *The Tempest* could gawk at what the Folio list of characters calls a "savage and deformed slave" and to enjoy an aristocratic magician's wedding masque in honor of his daughter.

The Enemies of the Stage

In 1624, a touring company of players arrived in Norwich and requested permission to perform. Permission was denied, but the municipal authorities, "in regard of the honorable respect which this City beareth to the right honorable the Lord Chamberlain," gave the players twenty shillings to get out of town. Throughout the sixteenth and early seventeenth centuries, there are many similar records of civic officials prohibiting performances and then, to appease a powerful patron, paying the actors to take their skills elsewhere. As early as the 1570s, there is evidence that the London authorities, while mindful of the players' influential protectors, were energetically trying to drive the theater out of the city.

Why should what we now regard as one of the undisputed glories of the age have aroused so much hostility? One answer, curiously enough, is traffic: plays drew large audiences—the public theaters could accommodate thousands—and residents objected to the crowds, the noise, and the crush of carriages. Other, more serious concerns were public health and crime. It was thought that numerous diseases, including the dreaded bubonic plague, were spread by noxious odors, and the packed playhouses were obvious breeding grounds for infection. (Patrons often tried to protect themselves by sniffing nosegays or stuffing cloves into their nostrils.) The large crowds drew pickpockets, cutpurses, and other scoundrels. On more than one occasion, if Shakespeare's fellow actor Will Kemp may be believed, pickpockets, caught in the act during a performance, were tied to a post onstage "for all people to wonder at." The theater was, moreover, a well-known haunt of prostitutes and, it was alleged, a place where innocent

Syphilis victim in tub. Frontispiece to the play *Cornelianum Dolium* (1638), possibly written by Thomas Randolph. The tub inscription translates as "I sit on the throne of love, I suffer in the tub"; and the banner as "Farewell, O sexual pleasures and lusts."

maids were seduced and respectable matrons corrupted. It was darkly rumored that "chambers and secret places" adjoined the theater galleries, and in any case, taverns, disreputable inns, and whorehouses were close at hand.

There were other charges as well. Plays in the public, outdoor amphitheaters were performed in the afternoon and therefore drew people, especially the young, away from their work. They were schools of idleness, luring apprentices from their trades, law students from their studies, housewives from their kitchens, and potentially pious souls from the sober meditations to which they might otherwise devote themselves. Wasting their time and money on disreputable shows, citizens exposed themselves to sexual provocation and outright political sedition. Even when the content of plays was morally exemplary—and, of course, few plays were so gratifyingly highminded—the theater itself, in the eyes of most mayors and aldermen, was inherently disorderly.

The attack on the stage by civic officials was echoed and intensified by many of the age's moralists and religious leaders, especially those associated with Puritanism. While English Protestants earlier in the sixteenth century had attempted to counter the Catholic mystery cycles and saints' plays by mounting their own doctrinally correct dramas, by the century's end a fairly widespread consensus, even among those mildly sympathetic toward the theater, held that the stage and the pulpit were in tension with one another. After 1591, a ban on Sunday performances was strictly enforced, and in 1606, Parliament passed an act imposing a hefty fine of £10 on any person who shall "in any stage-play, interlude, show, May-game, or pageant, jestingly or profanely speak or use the holy name of God, or of Christ Jesus, or of the Holy Ghost, or of the Trinity (which are not to be spoken but with fear and reverence)." If changes in the printed texts are a reliable indication, the players seem to have complied at least to some degree with the ruling. The Folio (1623) text of *Richard III,* for example, omits the Quarto's (1597) four uses of "zounds" (for "God's wounds"), along with a mention of "Christ's dear blood shed for our grievous sins"; "God's my judge" in *The Merchant of Venice* becomes "well I know"; "By Jesu" in *Henry V* becomes a very proper "I say"; and in all the plays, "God" is from time to time metamorphosed to "Jove."

But for some of the theater's more extreme critics, these modest expurgations were tiny bandages on a gaping wound. In his huge book *Histriomastix* (1633), William Prynne regurgitates a half-century of frenzied attacks on the "sinful, heathenish, lewd, ungodly Spectacles." In the eyes of Prynne and his fellow antitheatricalists, stage plays were part of a demonic tangle of obscene practices proliferating like a cancer in the body of society. It is "manifest to all men's judgments," he writes, that effeminate mixed dancing, dicing, stage-plays, lascivious pictures, wanton fashions, face-painting, health-drinking, long hair, love-locks, periwigs, women's curling, powdering and cutting of their hair, bonfires, New-year's gifts, May-games, amorous pastorals, lascivious effeminate music, excessive laughter, luxurious disorderly Christmas-keeping, mummeries . . . [are] wicked, unchristian pastimes.

Given the anxious emphasis on effeminacy, it is not surprising that denunciations of this kind obsessively focused on the use of boy actors to play the female parts. The enemies of the stage charged that theatrical transvestism excited illicit sexual desires, both heterosexual and homosexual.

Since cross-dressing violated a biblical prohibition (Deuteronomy 22:5), religious antitheatricalists attacked it as wicked regardless of its erotic charge; indeed, they often seemed to consider any act of impersonation as inherently wicked. In their view, the theater itself was Satan's domain. Thus a Cambridge scholar, John Greene, reports the sad fate of "a Christian woman" who went to the theater to see a play: "She entered in well and sound, but she returned and came forth possessed of the devil. Whereupon certain godly brethren demanded Satan how he durst be so bold, as to enter into her a Christian. Whereto he answered, that *he found her in his own house,* and therefore took possession of her as his own" (italics in original). When the "godly brethren" came to power in the mid-seventeenth century, with the overthrow of Charles I, they saw to it that the playhouses, shut down in 1642 at the onset of the Civil War, remained closed. Public theater did not resume until the restoration of the monarchy in 1660.

Faced with enemies among civic officials and religious leaders, Elizabethan and Jacobean playing companies relied on the protection of their powerful patrons. As the liveried servants of aristocrats or of the monarch, the players could refute the charge that they were mere vagabonds, and they claimed, as a convenient legal fiction, that their public performances were necessary rehearsals in anticipation of those occasions when they would be called upon to entertain their noble masters. But harassment by the mayor and aldermen of the City of London—an area roughly one mile square, defined by the old Roman walls—continued unabated, and the players were forced to build their theaters outside the immediate jurisdiction of these authorities, either in the suburbs or in the areas known as the "liberties." A liberty was a piece of land within the City of London itself that was not directly subject to the authority of the Lord Mayor. The most significant liberty from the point of view of the theater was the area near St. Paul's Cathedral called "the Blackfriars," where, until the dissolution of the monasteries in 1538, there had been a Dominican priory. It was here that in 1608 Shakespeare's company, then called the King's Men, took over an indoor playhouse in which they performed during the winter months, reserving the open-air Globe in the suburb of Southwark for the warmer months.

Censorship and Regulation

In addition to those authorities who campaigned to shut down the theater, there were others whose task was to oversee, regulate, and censor it. Given the outright hostility of the former, the latter may have seemed to the London players equivocal allies rather than enemies. After all, plays that passed the censor were at least licensed to be performed and hence conceded to have some limited legitimacy. In April 1559, at the very start of her reign, Queen Elizabeth drafted a proposal that for the first time envisaged a system for the prior review and regulation of plays throughout her kingdom:

The Queen's Majesty doth straightly forbid all manner interludes to be played either openly or privately, except the same be notified beforehand, and licensed within any city or town corporate, by the mayor or other chief officers of the same, and within any shire, by such as shall be lieutenants for the Queen's Majesty in the same shire, or by two of the Justices of Peace inhabiting within that part of the shire where any shall be played. . . . And for instruction to every of the said officers, her Majesty doth likewise charge every of them, as they will answer: that they permit none to be played wherein either matters of religion or of the governance of the estate of the commonweal shall be handled or treated upon, but by men of authority, learning and wisdom, nor to be handled before any audience, but of grave and discreet persons.

This proposal, which may not have been formally enacted, makes an important distinction between those who are entitled to address sensitive issues of religion and politics—authors "of authority, learning and wisdom" addressing audiences "of grave and discreet persons"—and those who are forbidden to do so.

The London public theater, with its playwrights who were the sons of glovers, shoemakers, and bricklayers and its audiences in which the privileged classes mingled with rowdy apprentices, masked women, and servants, was clearly not a place to which the government wished to grant freedom of expression. In 1581, the Master of the Revels, an official in the Lord Chamberlain's department whose role had hitherto been to provide entertainment at court, was given an expanded commission. Sir Edmund Tilney, the functionary who held the office, was authorized

to warn, command, and appoint in all places within this our Realm of England, as well within franchises and liberties as without, all and every player or players with their playmakers, either belonging to any nobleman or otherwise . . . to appear before him with all such plays, tragedies, comedies, or shows as they shall in readiness or mean to set forth, and them to recite before our said Servant or his sufficient deputy, whom we ordain, appoint, and authorize by these presents of all such shows, plays, players, and playmakers, together with their playing places, to order and reform, authorize and put down, as shall be thought meet or unmeet unto himself or his said deputy in that behalf.

What emerged from this commission was in effect a national system of regulation and censorship. One of its consequences was to restrict virtually all licensed theater to the handful of authorized London-based playing companies. These companies would have to submit their plays for official scrutiny, but in return they received implicit, and on occasion explicit, protection against the continued fierce opposition of the local authorities. Plays reviewed and allowed by the Master of the Revels had been deemed fit to be performed before the monarch; how could mere aldermen legitimately claim that such plays should be banned as seditious?

The key question, of course, is how carefully the Master of the Revels scrutinized the plays brought before him either to hear or, more often from the 1590s onward, to peruse. What was Tilney, who served in the office until his death in 1610, or his successor, Sir George Buc, who served from 1610 to 1621, looking for? What did they insist be cut before they would release what was known as the "allowed copy," the only version licensed for performance? Unfortunately, the office books of the Master of the Revels in Shakespeare's time have been lost; what survives is a handful of scripts on which Tilney, Buc, and their assistants jotted their instructions. These suggest that the readings were rather painstaking, with careful attention paid to possible religious, political, and diplomatic repercussions. References, direct or strongly implied, to any living Christian prince or any important English nobleman, gentleman, or government official were particularly sensitive and likely to be struck. Renaissance political life was highly personalized; people in power were exceptionally alert to insult and zealously patrolled the boundaries of their prestige and reputation.

Moreover, the censors knew that audiences and readers were quite adept at applying theatrical representations distanced in time and space to their own world. At a time of riots against resident foreigners, Tilney read *Sir Thomas More,* a play in which Shakespeare probably had a hand, and instructed the players to cut scenes that, though set in

1517, might have had an uncomfortable contemporary resonance. "Leave out the insurrection wholly," Tilney's note reads, "and the cause thereof and begin with Sir Thomas More at the Mayor's sessions, with a report afterwards of his good service done being sheriff of London upon a mutiny against the Lombards only by a short report and not otherwise at your own perils. E. Tilney." Of course, as Tilney knew perfectly well, most plays succeed precisely by mirroring, if only obliquely, their own times, but this particular reflection evidently seemed to him too dangerous or provocative.

The topical significance of a play depends in large measure on the particular moment in which it is performed, and on certain features of the performance—for example, a striking resemblance between one of the characters and a well-known public figure—that the script itself will not necessarily disclose to us at this great distance, or even disclosed to the censor at the time. Hence the Master of the Revels noted angrily of one play performed in 1632 that "there were diverse personated so naturally, both of lords and others of the court, that I took it ill." Hence too a play that was deemed allowable when it was first written and performed could return, like a nightmare, to disturb a different place and time. The most famous instance of such a return involves Shakespeare, for on the day before the Earl of Essex's attempted coup against Queen Elizabeth in 1601, someone paid the Lord Chamberlain's Men (Shakespeare's company at the time) forty shillings to revive their old play about the deposition and murder of Richard II. "I am Richard II," the Queen declared. "Know ye not that?" However distressed she was by this performance, the Queen significantly did not take out her wrath on the players: neither the playwright nor his company was punished, nor was the Master of the Revels criticized for allowing the play in the first place. It was Essex and several of his key supporters, including the man who commissioned the performance, who lost their heads.

Evidence suggests that the Master of the Revels often regarded himself not as the strict censor of the theater but as its friendly guardian, charged with averting catastrophes. He was a bureaucrat concerned less with subversive ideas per se than with potential trouble. That is, there is no record of a dramatist being called to account for his heterodox beliefs; rather, plays were censored if they risked offending influential people, including important foreign allies, or if they threatened to cause public disorder by exacerbating religious or other controversies. The distinction is not a stable one, but it helps to explain the intellectual boldness, power, and freedom of a censored theater in a society in which the perceived enemies of the state were treated mercilessly. Shakespeare could have Lear articulate a searing indictment of social injustice—

> Robes and furred gowns hide all. Plate sins with gold,
> And the strong lance of justice hurtless breaks.
> Arm it in rags, a pigmy's straw does pierce it.
>   (4.5.159–61)

—and evidently neither the Master of the Revels nor the courtiers in their robes and furred gowns protested. But when the Spanish ambassador complained about Thomas Middleton's anti-Spanish allegory A Game at Chess, performed at the Globe in 1624, the whole theater was shut down, the players were arrested, and the King professed to be furious at his official for licensing the play in the first place and allowing it to be performed for nine consecutive days.

In addition to the system for the licensing of plays for performance, there was a system for the licensing of plays for publication. At the start of Shakespeare's career, such press licensing was the responsibility of the Court of High Commission, headed by the Archbishop of Canterbury and the Bishop of London. Their deputies, a panel of junior clerics, were supposed to review the manuscripts, granting licenses to those worthy of publication and rejecting any they deemed "heretical, seditious, or unseemly for Christian ears." Without a license, the Stationers' Company, the guild of the book trade, was not supposed to register a manuscript for publication. In practice, as various complaints and attempts to close loopholes attest, some playbooks were printed without a license. In 1607, the system was significantly revised when Sir George Buc began to license plays for the press. When Buc succeeded to the post of Master of the Revels in 1610, the powers to license plays for the stage and the page were vested in one man.

Theatrical Innovations

The theater continued to flourish under this system of regulation after Shakespeare's death in 1616; by the 1630s, as many as five playhouses were operating daily in London. When the theater reemerged in 1660 after the eighteen-year hiatus imposed by Puritan rule, it quickly resumed its cultural importance, but not without a number of significant changes. Major innovations in staging resulted principally from continental influences on the English artists who accompanied the court of Charles II into exile in France, where they supplied it with masques and other theatrical entertainments.

The institutional conditions and business practices of the two companies chartered by Charles after the Restoration in 1660 also differed from those of Shakespeare's theater. In place of the more collective practice of Shakespeare's company, the Restoration theaters were controlled by celebrated actor-managers who not only assigned themselves starring roles, in both comedy and tragedy, but also assumed sole responsibility for many business decisions, including the setting of their colleagues' salaries. At the same time, the power of the actor-manager, great as it was, was limited by the new importance of outside capital. No longer was the theater, with all of its properties from script to costumes, owned by the "sharers," that is, by those actors who held shares in the joint stock company. Instead, entrepreneurs would raise capital for increasingly fantastic sets and stage machinery that could cost as much as £3,000, an astronomical sum, for a single production. This investment in turn not only influenced the kinds of new plays written for the theater but helped to transform old plays that were revived, including Shakespeare's.

In his diary entry for August 24, 1661, Samuel Pepys notes that he has been "to the Opera, and there saw Hamlet, Prince of Denmark, done with scenes very well, but above all, Betterton did the prince's part beyond imagination." This is Thomas Betterton's first review, as it were, and it is typical of the enthusiasm he would inspire throughout his fifty-year career on the London stage. Pepys's brief and scattered remarks on the plays he voraciously attended in the 1660s are precious because they are among the few records from the period of concrete and immediate responses to theatrical performances. Modern readers might miss the significance of Pepys's phrase "done with scenes": this production of *Hamlet* was only the third play to use the movable sets first introduced to England by its producer, William Davenant. The central historical fact that makes the productions of this period so exciting is that public theater had been banned altogether for eighteen years until the Restoration of Charles II.

A brief discussion of theatrical developments in the Restoration period will enable us at least to glance longingly at a vast subject that lies outside the scope of this introduction: the rich performance history that extends from Shakespeare's time to our own, involving tens of thousands of productions and adaptations for theater, opera, dance, Broadway musicals, and of course films. The scale of this history is vast in space as well as time: already in the late sixteenth and early seventeenth centuries, troupes of English actors performed as far afield as Poland and Bohemia.

While producing masques at the court of Charles I, the poet William Davenant had become an expert on stage scenery, and when the theaters reopened, he set to work on converting an indoor tennis court into a new kind of theater. He designed a broad open platform like that of the Elizabethan stage, but at the back of this platform he added or expanded a space, framed by a proscenium arch, in which scenes could be displayed. These elaborately painted scenes could be moved on and off, using grooves on the floor. The perspectival effect for a spectator of one central painted panel with two "wings" on either side was that of three sides of a room. This effect anticipated that of the familiar "picture frame" stage, developed fully in the nineteenth century, and began a subtle shift in theater away from the elaborate verbal descriptions that are so central to Shakespeare and toward the evocative visual poetry of the set designer's art.

Another convention of Shakespeare's stage, the use of boy actors for female roles, gave way to the more complete illusion of women playing women's parts. The King issued a decree in 1662 forcefully permitting, if not requiring, the use of actresses. The royal decree is couched in the language of social and moral reform: the introduction of actresses will require the "reformation" of scurrilous and profane passages in plays, and this in turn will help forestall some of the objections that shut the theaters down in 1642. In reality, male theater audiences, composed of a narrower range of courtiers and aristocrats than in Shakespeare's time, met this intended reform with the assumption that the new actresses were fair game sexually; most actresses (with the partial exception of those who married male members of their troupes) were regarded as, or actually became, whores. But despite the social stigma, and the fact that their salaries were predictably lower than those of their male counterparts, the stage saw some formidable female stars by the 1680s.

The first recorded appearance of an actress was that of a Desdemona in December 1660. Betterton's Ophelia in 1661 was Mary Saunderson (ca. 1637–1712), who became Mrs. Betterton a year later. The most famous Ophelia of the period was Susanna Mountfort, who appeared in that role for the first time at the age of fifteen in 1705. The performance by Mountfort that became legendary occurred in 1720, after a disappointment in love, or so it was said, had driven her mad. Hearing that *Hamlet* was being performed, Mountfort escaped from her keepers and reached the theater, where she concealed herself until the scene in which Ophelia enters in her state of insanity. At this point, Mountfort rushed onto the stage and, in the words of a contemporary, "was in truth Ophelia herself, to the amazement of the performers and the astonishment of the audience."

David Garrick and George Anne Bellamy in a celebrated production of *Romeo and Juliet* at Drury Lane, London. Engraving after a painting by Benjamin Wilson (1753).

That the character Ophelia became increasingly and decisively identified with the mad scene owes something to this occurrence, but it is also a consequence of the text used for Restoration performances of *Hamlet*. Having received the performance rights to a good number of Shakespeare's plays, Davenant altered them for the stage in the 1660s, and many of these acting versions remained in use for generations. In the case of *Hamlet*, neither Davenant nor his successors did what they so often did with other plays by Shakespeare, that is, alter the plot radically and interpolate other material. But many of the lines were cut or "improved." The cuts included most of Ophelia's sane speeches, such as her spirited retort to Laertes' moralizing; what remained made her part almost entirely an emblem of "female love melancholy."

Thomas Betterton (1635–1710), the prototype of the actor-manager, who would be the dominant figure in Shakespeare interpretation and in the English theater generally through the nineteenth century, made Hamlet his premier role. A contemporary who saw his last performance in the part (at the age of seventy-four, a rather old Prince of Denmark) wrote that to *read* Shakespeare's play was to encounter "dry, incoherent, & broken sentences," but that to see Betterton was to "prove" that the play was written "correctly." Spectators especially admired his reaction to the Ghost's appearance in the Queen's bedchamber: "his Countenance . . . thro' the violent and sudden Emotions of Amazement and Horror, turn[ed] instantly on the Sight of his fathers Spirit, as pale as his Neckcloath, when every Article of his Body seem's affected with a Tremor inexpressible." A piece of stage business in this scene, Betterton's upsetting his chair on the Ghost's entrance, became so thoroughly identified with the part that later productions were censured if the actor left it out. This business could very well have been handed down from Richard Burbage, the star of Shakespeare's original production, for Davenant, who had coached Betterton in the role, had known the performances of Joseph Taylor, who had succeeded Burbage in it. It is strangely gratifying to notice that Hamlets on stage and screen still occasionally upset their chairs.

Shakespeare's Life and Art

Playwrights, even hugely successful playwrights, were not ordinarily the objects of popular curiosity in early modern England. Many plays in this period were issued without the name of the author—there was no equivalent to our copyright system, and publishers were not required to specify on their title pages who wrote the texts they printed. Only occasionally were there significant exceptions, motivated by the pursuit of profit. Though by 1597 seven of Shakespeare's plays had been printed, the title pages did not identify him as the author. Beginning in 1598 Shakespeare's name, spelled in various ways, began to appear, and indeed several plays almost certainly not written by him were printed with his name. His name—Shakespeare, Shake-speare, Shakspeare, Shaxberd, Shakespere, and the like—had evidently begun to sell plays. During his lifetime more published plays were attributed to Shakespeare than to any other contemporary dramatist.

But this marketplace interest did not extend to the details of his life. It is both revealing and frustrating that the First Folio editors, John Heminges and Henry Condell—who knew Shakespeare well—were virtually silent about their friend's personal history. Though they included the author's picture, they did not bother to include his birth and death dates, his marital status, the names of his surviving children, his intellectual and social affiliations, his endearing or annoying quirks of character, let alone anything more psychologically revealing, such as the "table talk" carefully recorded by followers of Martin Luther. Shakespeare may have been a very private man, but, as he was dead when the edition was produced, it is unlikely to have been his own wishes that dictated the omissions. The editors evidently assumed that the potential buyers of the book—and this was an expensive commercial venture—would not be particularly interested in what we would now regard as essential biographical details.

Such presumed indifference is, in all likelihood, chiefly a reflection of Shakespeare's modest origins. He flew below the radar of ordinary Elizabethan and Jacobean social curiosity. In the wake of the death of the poet Sir Philip Sidney, Fulke Greville wrote a fascinating biography of his friend, but Sidney was a dashing aristocrat, linked by birth and marriage to the great families of the realm, and he died tragically of a wound he received on the battlefield. Writers of a less exalted station did not excite the same interest, unless, like Ben Jonson, they cultivated an extravagant public persona, or, like another of Shakespeare's contemporaries, Christopher Marlowe, they ran afoul of the authorities and got themselves murdered. The fact that there are no police reports, Privy Council orders, indictments, or postmortem inquests about Shakespeare, as there are about Marlowe, tells us something significant about Shakespeare's life—he possessed a gift for staying out of trouble—but it is not the kind of detail on which biographers thrive.

Yet Elizabethan England was a record-keeping society, and centuries of archival labor have turned up a substantial number of traces of its greatest playwright and his family. By themselves the traces would have relatively little interest, but in the light of Shakespeare's plays and poems, they have come to seem like precious relics and manage to achieve a considerable resonance.

Shakespeare's Family

William Shakespeare's grandfather, Richard, farmed land by the village of Snitterfield, near the small, pleasant market town of Stratford-upon-Avon, about ninety-six miles northwest of London. The playwright's father, John, moved in the mid-sixteenth century to Stratford, where he became a successful glover, landowner, moneylender, and dealer in wool and other agricultural goods. In or about 1557, he married Mary Arden, the daughter of a prosperous and well-connected farmer from the same area, Robert Arden of Wilmcote.

John Shakespeare was evidently highly esteemed by his fellow townspeople, for he held a series of important posts in local government. In 1556, he was appointed ale taster, an office reserved for "able persons and discreet," in 1558 was sworn in as a constable, and in 1561 was elected as one of the town's fourteen burgesses. As burgess, John served as one of the two chamberlains, responsible for administering borough property and revenues. In 1567, he was elected bailiff, Stratford's highest elective office and the equivalent of mayor. Though John Shakespeare signed all official documents with a cross or other sign, it is likely, though not certain, that he knew how to read and write. Mary, who also signed documents only with her mark, is less likely to have been literate.

According to the parish registers, which recorded baptisms and burials, the Shakespeares had eight children, four daughters and four sons, beginning with a daughter, Joan, born in 1558. A second daughter, Margaret, was born in December 1562 and died a few months later. William Shakespeare ("Gulielmus, filius Johannes Shakespeare"), their first son, was baptized on April 26, 1564. Since there was usually a few days' lapse between birth and baptism, it is conventional to celebrate Shakespeare's birthday on April 23, which happens to coincide with the Feast of St. George, England's patron saint, and with the day of Shakespeare's death fifty-two years later.

William Shakespeare had three younger brothers, Gilbert, Richard, and Edmund, and two younger sisters, Joan and Anne. (It was often the custom to recycle a name, so the first-born Joan must have died before the birth in 1569 of another daughter christened Joan, the only one of the girls to survive childhood.) Gilbert, who died in his forty-fifth year in 1612, is described in legal records as a Stratford haberdasher; Edmund followed William to London and became a professional actor, though evidently of no

Southeast Prospect of Stratford-upon-Avon, 1746. From *Gentleman's Magazine* (December 1792).

particular repute. He was only twenty-eight when he died in 1607 and was given an expensive funeral, perhaps paid for by his successful older brother.

At the high point of his public career, John Shakespeare, the father of this substantial family, applied to the Herald's College for a coat of arms, which would have marked his (and his family's) elevation from the ranks of substantial middle-class citizenry to that of the gentry. But the application went nowhere, for soon after he initiated what would have been a costly petitioning process, John apparently fell on hard times. The decline must have begun when William was still living at home, a boy of twelve or thirteen. From 1576 onward, John Shakespeare stopped attending council meetings. He became caught up in costly lawsuits, started mortgaging his land, and incurred substantial debts. In 1586, he was finally replaced on the council; in 1592, he was one of nine Stratford men listed as absenting themselves from church out of fear of being arrested for debt.

The reason for the reversal in John Shakespeare's fortunes is unknown. Some have speculated that it may have stemmed from adherence to Catholicism, since those who remained loyal to the old faith were subject to increasingly vigorous and costly discrimination. But if John Shakespeare was a Catholic, as seems possible, it would not necessarily explain his decline, since other Catholics (and Puritans) in Elizabethan Stratford and elsewhere managed to hold on to their offices. In any case, his fall from prosperity and local power, whatever its cause, was not absolute. In 1601, the last year of his life, his name was included among those qualified to speak on behalf of Stratford's rights. And he was by that time entitled to bear a coat of arms, for in 1596, some twenty years after the application to the Herald's office had been initiated, it was successfully renewed. There is no record of who paid for the bureaucratic procedures that made the grant possible, but it is likely to have been John's oldest son, William, by that time a highly successful London playwright. By elevating his father, he would have made himself a gentleman as well.

Education

Stratford was a small provincial town, but it had long been the site of an excellent free school, originally established by the church in the thirteenth century. The main purpose of such schools in the Middle Ages had been to train prospective clerics; since many aristocrats could neither read nor write, literacy by itself conferred no special distinction and was not routinely viewed as desirable. But the situation began to change markedly in the sixteenth century. Protestantism placed a far greater emphasis upon lay literacy: for the sake of salvation, it was crucially important to be intimately acquainted with the Holy Book, and printing made that book readily available. Schools became less strictly bound up with training for the church and more linked to the general acquisition of "literature," in the sense both of literacy and of cultural knowledge. In keeping with this new emphasis on reading and with humanist educational reform, the school was reorganized during the reign of Edward VI (1547–53). School records from the period have not survived, but it is almost certain that William Shakespeare attended the King's New School, as it was renamed in Edward's honor.

Scholars have painstakingly reconstructed the curriculum of schools of this kind and have even turned up the names and rather impressive credentials of the schoolmasters who taught at the King's New School when Shakespeare was of school age. (The principal teacher at that time was Thomas Jenkins, an Oxford graduate, who received £20 a year and a rent-free house.) A child's education in Elizabethan England began at age four or five with two years at what was called the "petty school," attached to the main grammar school. The little scholars carried a "hornbook," a sheet of paper or parchment framed in wood and covered, for protection, with a transparent layer of horn. On the paper was written the alphabet and the Lord's Prayer, which were reproduced as well in the slightly more advanced *ABC with the Catechism,* a combination primer and rudimentary religious guide.

After students demonstrated some ability to read, education for most girls came to a halt, but boys could go on, at about age seven, to the grammar school. Shakespeare's images of the experience are not particularly cheerful. In his famous account of the Seven Ages of Man, Jaques in *As You Like It* describes

> the whining schoolboy with his satchel
> And shining morning face, creeping like snail
> Unwillingly to school.
>
> (2.7.145–47)

The schoolboy would have crept quite early: the day began at 6:00 A.M. in summer and 7:00 A.M. in winter and continued until 5:00 P.M., with very few breaks or holidays.

At the core of the curriculum was the study of Latin, the mastery of which was in effect a prolonged male puberty rite involving much discipline and pain as well as pleasure. A late sixteenth-century Dutchman (whose name fittingly was Batty)

The Cholmondeley Ladies (ca. 1600–1610). Artist unknown. This striking image brings to mind Shakespeare's fascination with twinship, both identical (notably in *The Comedy of Errors*) and fraternal (in *Twelfth Night*).

proposed that God had created the human buttocks so that they could be severely beaten without risking permanent injury. Such thoughts dominated the pedagogy of the age, so that even an able young scholar, as we might imagine Shakespeare to have been, could scarcely have escaped recurrent flogging.

Shakespeare evidently reaped some rewards for the miseries he probably endured: his works are laced with echoes of many of the great Latin texts taught in grammar schools. One of his earliest comedies, *The Comedy of Errors*, is a brilliant variation on a theme by the Roman playwright Plautus, whom Elizabethan schoolchildren often performed as well as read; and one of his earliest tragedies, *Titus Andronicus*, is heavily indebted to Seneca. These are among the most visible of the classical influences that are often more subtly and pervasively interfused in Shakespeare's works. He seems to have had a particular fondness for *Aesop's Fables,* Apuleius's *Golden Ass,* and above all Ovid's *Metamorphoses.* His learned contemporary Ben Jonson remarked that Shakespeare had "small Latin and less Greek," but from this distance what is striking is not the limits of Shakespeare's learning but rather the unpretentious ease, intelligence, and gusto with which he draws upon what he must have first encountered as laborious study.

Traces of a Life

In November 1582, William Shakespeare, at the age of eighteen, married twenty-six-year-old Anne Hathaway, who came from the village of Shottery near Stratford. Their first daughter, Susanna, was baptized six months later. This circumstance, along with the fact that Anne was eight years Will's senior, has given rise to a mountain of speculation, all the more lurid precisely because there is no further evidence. Shakespeare depicts in several plays situations in which marriage is precipitated by a pregnancy, but he also registers, in *Measure for Measure* (1.2.133ff), the Elizabethan belief that a "true contract" of marriage could be legitimately made and then consummated simply by the mutual vows of the couple in the presence of witnesses.

On February 2, 1585, the twins Hamnet and Judith Shakespeare were baptized in Stratford. Hamnet died at the age of eleven, when his father was already living for much of the year in London as a successful playwright. These are Shakespeare's only known children, though in the mid-seventeenth century the playwright and impresario William Davenant hinted that he was Shakespeare's bastard son. Since people did not ordinarily advertise their illegitimacy, the claim, though impossible to verify, at least suggests the unusual strength of Shakespeare's posthumous reputation.

William Shakespeare's father, John, died in 1601; his mother died seven years later. They would have had the satisfaction of witnessing their eldest son's prosperity, and not only from a distance, for in 1597 William purchased New Place, the second-largest house in Stratford. In 1607, the playwright's daughter Susanna married a successful and well-known physician, John Hall. The next year, the Halls had a daughter, Elizabeth, Shakespeare's first grandchild. In 1616, the year of Shakespeare's death, his daughter Judith married a vintner, Thomas Quiney, with whom she had three children. Shakespeare's widow, Anne, died in 1623, at the age of sixty-seven. His first-born, Susanna, died at the age of sixty-six in 1649, the year that King Charles I was beheaded by the parliamentary army. Judith lived through Cromwell's Protectorate and on to the Restoration of the monarchy; she died in February 1662, at the age of seventy-seven. By the end of the century, the line of Shakespeare's direct heirs was extinct.

Patient digging in the archives has turned up other traces of Shakespeare's life as a family man and a man of means: assessments, small fines, real estate deeds, minor actions in court to collect debts. In addition to his fine Stratford house and a large garden and cottage facing it, Shakespeare bought substantial parcels of land in the vicinity. When in *The Tempest* the wedding celebration conjures up a vision of "barns and garners never empty," Shakespeare could have been glancing at what the legal documents record as his own "tithes of corn, grain, blade, and hay" in the fields near

Stratford. At some point after 1610, Shakespeare seems to have begun to shift his attention from the London stage to his Stratford properties, though the term "retirement" implies a more decisive and definitive break than appears to have been the case. By 1613, when the Globe Theater burned down during a performance of Shakespeare and Fletcher's *Henry VIII,* Shakespeare was probably residing for the most part in Stratford, but he retained his financial interest in the rebuilt playhouse and probably continued to have some links to his theatrical colleagues. Still, by this point, his career as a playwright was substantially over. Legal documents from his last years show him concerned to protect his real estate interests in Stratford.

A half-century after Shakespeare's death, a Stratford vicar and physician, John Ward, noted in his diary that Shakespeare and his fellow poets Michael Drayton and Ben Jonson "had a merry meeting, and it seems drank too hard, for Shakespeare died of a fever there contracted." It is not inconceivable that Shakespeare's last illness was somehow linked, if only coincidentally, to the festivities on the occasion of the wedding in February 1616 of his daughter Judith (who was still alive when Ward made his diary entry). In any case, on March 25, 1616, Shakespeare revised his will, and on April 23 he died. Two days later, he was buried in the chancel of Holy Trinity Church beneath a stone bearing an epitaph he is said to have devised:

> Good friend for Jesus' sake forbear,
> To dig the dust enclosed here:
> Blest be the man that spares these stones,
> And curst be he that moves my bones.

The verses are hardly among Shakespeare's finest, but they seem to have been effective: though bones were routinely dug up to make room for others—a fate imagined with unforgettable intensity in the graveyard scene in *Hamlet*—his own remains were undisturbed. Like other vestiges of sixteenth- and early seventeenth-century Stratford, Shakespeare's grave has for centuries now been the object of a tourist industry that borders on a religious cult.

Shakespeare's will has been examined with an intensity befitting this cult; every provision and formulaic phrase, no matter how minor or conventional, has borne a heavy weight of interpretation, none more so than the sole bequest to his wife, Anne, of "my second-best bed." Scholars have pointed out that Anne would in any case have been provided for by custom and that the terms are not necessarily a deliberate slight, but the absence of the customary words "my loving wife" or "my well-beloved wife" is difficult to ignore.

Portrait of the Playwright as Young Provincial

The great problem with the surviving traces of Shakespeare's life is not that they are few but that they are unspectacular. Christopher Marlowe was a double or triple agent, accused of brawling, sodomy, and atheism. Ben Jonson, who somehow clambered up from bricklayer's apprentice to classical scholar, served in the army in Flanders, killed a fellow actor in a duel, converted to Catholicism in prison in 1598, and returned to the Church of England in 1610. Provincial real estate investments and the second-best bed cannot compete with such adventurous lives. Indeed, the relative ordinariness of Shakespeare's social background and life has contributed to a persistent current of speculation that the glover's son from Stratford-upon-Avon was not in fact the author of the plays attributed to him.

The anti-Stratfordians, as those who deny Shakespeare's authorship are sometimes called, almost always propose as the real author someone who came from a higher social class and received a more prestigious education. Francis Bacon, the Earl of Oxford, the Earl of Southampton, even Queen Elizabeth, have been advanced, among many others, as glamorous candidates for the role of clandestine playwright. Several famous people, including Mark Twain and Sigmund Freud, have espoused these theories, though very few scholars have joined them. Since Shakespeare was quite well known in his own time as the author of the plays that bear his name, there would need to have been an extraordinary conspiracy to conceal the identity of the real master who (the theory goes) disdained to appear in the vulgarity of print or on the public stage. Like many conspiracy theories, the extreme implausibility of this one seems only to increase the fervent conviction of its advocates.

To the charge that a middle-class author from a small town could not have imagined the lives of kings and nobles, one can respond by citing the exceptional qualities that Ben Jonson praised in Shakespeare: "excellent *Phantsie;* brave notions, and gentle expressions." Even in ordinary mortals, the human imagination is a strange faculty; in Shakespeare, it seems to have been uncannily powerful, working its mysterious, transforming effects on everything it touched. His imagination was intensely engaged by what he found in books. He seems throughout his life to have been an intense, voracious reader, and it is fascinating to witness his creative encounters with Raphael Holinshed's *Chronicles of England, Scotland, and Ireland,* Plutarch's *Lives of the Noble Grecians and Romans,* Ovid's *Metamorphoses,* Montaigne's *Essays,* and the Bible, to name only some of his favorite books. But books were clearly not the only objects of Shakespeare's attention; like most artists, he drew upon the whole range of his life experiences.

To those accustomed to instant telecommunication, photography, film, and digital media, that range might seem narrowly circumscribed, but in fact something like the opposite was the case. Though we inhabit a vast virtual world, our experiential world is deliberately reduced, carefully screened, and tightly delimited. Most of us are born, sicken, and die in special institutions set apart from everyday life. We have invented means to quiet toothaches, heal wounds, and put us to sleep through painful surgeries. Those we condemn as criminals are penned up and punished behind high, windowless walls. We scarcely ever see our political representatives in person, and when we vote, we enter small, private booths. We take our entertainments most often in the dark or in the privacy of our homes, and those homes are generally walled off from the homes of others. Our meat bears little or no visible relation to the animal from which it comes; the slaughtering and butchering is discretely done out of sight. Our wastes disappear down drains; our rubbish is collected and disposed of; we live and move about in a well-lit, heavily policed, massively controlled environment.

None of this was the case in Shakespeare's world. Virtually anyone who grew up in the late sixteenth century would have had occasion to hear the sharp cries of childbirth and the groans of dying. There were a small number of hospitals and lazar houses (for lepers), but for the most part the sick, the maimed, and the mad mingled with everyone else in the crowded, muddy streets. The sufferings attendant on ordinary life were inescapable, and very few palliatives were available. (There were limits to the oblivion that the strongest ale could bring.) Malefactors, as we have seen, were most often punished in public, often hideously. There was nothing remotely equivalent to our taste for privacy. Servants were ubiquitous, and it was a rare person who had the privilege or perhaps the inclination to escape into solitude. Guests at an inn would often find themselves sharing a room or even a bed with a complete stranger. Smells and tastes—in a world without flush toilets and refrigeration—were intense, and so too were colors, for Elizabethans of any means favored vividly dyed and elaborately worked clothing. There were no streetlights, and the days faded into nights that were pitch dark and often dangerous.

Nothing here is particular to Shakespeare's biography; these were the conditions in this period of everyone's life. And what would astonish or appall us, if we were suddenly carried back into the past, would simply have been taken for granted as the way things are by most of those born into that world. But Shakespeare seems precisely not to have taken anything for granted: he seems to have carefully noted everything, from the carter who urinates in the chimney and complains of his fleabites (*1 Henry IV* 2.1.19–20) to the mad beggar who sticks sprigs of rosemary into his numbed arms (*King Lear* 2.2.177–79) to the merchant who keeps his money locked up in a desk that is covered with a Turkish tapestry (*Comedy of Errors* 4.1.103–04).

Shakespeare may have begun this practice of noting quite early in his life. When he was a very young boy—not quite four years old—his father was chosen by the Stratford council as the town bailiff. The bailiff of an Elizabethan town was a significant position; he served the borough as a justice of the peace and performed a variety of other functions, including coroner and clerk of the market. He dealt routinely with an unusually wide spectrum of local society, for on the one hand he distributed alms and on the other he negotiated with the lord of the manor. More to the point, for our purposes, the office was attended with considerable ceremony. The bailiff and his deputy were entitled to appear in public in furred gowns, attended by sergeants bearing maces before them. On Rogation Days (three days of prayer for the harvest, before Ascension Day), they would solemnly pace out the parish boundaries, and they would similarly walk in processions on market and fair days. On Sundays, the sergeants would accompany the bailiff to church, where he would sit with his wife in a front pew, and he would have a comparable seat of honor at sermons in the Guild Chapel. On special occasions, there would also be plays in the Guildhall, at which the bailiff would be seated in the front row.

On a precocious child (or even, for that matter, on an ordinary child), this ceremony must have had a significant impact. It would have conveyed irresistibly the power of clothes (the ceremonial gown of office) and of symbols (the mace) to transform identity as if by magic. It would have invested the official in question—Shakespeare's own father—with immense power, distinction, and importance, awakening what we may call a lifelong dream of high station. And perhaps, pulling slightly against this dream, it would have provoked an odd feeling that the father's clothes do not fit, a perception that the office is not the same as the man, and an intimate, firsthand knowledge that when the robes are put off, their wearer is inevitably glimpsed in a far different, less exalted light.

The honoring of the bailiff was only one of the political rituals that Shakespeare could easily have witnessed as a young man growing up in the provinces. As we have seen, Queen Elizabeth was fond of going on what were known as "progresses," triumphant ceremonial journeys around her kingdom. In 1574—when Shakespeare was ten years old—one of these progresses took her to Warwick, near Stratford-upon-Avon. The crowds that gathered to watch were participating in an elaborate celebration of charismatic power: the courtiers in their gorgeous clothes, the nervous local officials bedecked in velvets and silks, and at the center, carried in a special litter like a bejeweled icon, the virgin queen. The Queen cultivated this charisma, taking over in effect some of the iconography associated with the worship of the Virgin Mary, but she was also paradoxically fond of calling attention to the fact that she was after all quite human. For example, on this occasion at Warwick, after the trembling Recorder, presumably a local civil official of high standing, had made his official welcoming speech, Elizabeth offered her hand to him to be kissed: "Come hither, little Recorder," she said. "It was told me that you would be afraid to look upon me or to speak boldly; but you were not so afraid of me as I was of you; and I now thank you for putting me in mind of my duty." Of course, the charm of this royal "confession" of nervousness depends on its manifest implausibility: it is, in effect, a theatrical performance of humility by someone with immense confidence in her own histrionic power.

A royal progress was not the only form of spectacular political activity that Shakespeare might well have seen in the 1570s; it is still more likely that he would have witnessed parliamentary elections, particularly since his father was qualified to vote. In 1571, 1572, 1575, and 1578, there were shire elections conducted in Warwick, elections that would certainly have attracted well over a thousand voters. These were often memorable events: large crowds came together; there was usually heavy drinking and carnivalesque festivity; and at the same time, there was enacted, in a very different register from that of the monarchy, a ritual of empowerment. The people, those entitled to vote by virtue of meeting the property and residence requirements, chose their own representatives by giving their votes—their voices—to candidates for office. Here, legislative sovereignty was conferred not by God but by the consent of the community, a consent marked by shouts and applause.

Recent cultural historians have been so fascinated by the evident links between the spectacles of the absolutist monarchy and the theater that they have largely ignored the significance of this alternative public arena, one that generated intense excitement throughout the country. A child who was a spectator at a parliamentary election in the 1570s might well have found the occasion enormously compelling. It is striking, in any case, how often the adult Shakespeare returns to scenes of mass consent, and striking too how much the theater depends on assembling crowds and soliciting popular acclamation.

The most frequent occasions for the gathering together of crowds were neither elections nor theatrical performances, but rather the religious services that all Eliza-bethans were expected to attend at least once a week. (Recurrent absences were noted and investigated.) Protestant spokesmen routinely condemned the Catholic Mass as a form of perverse theatrical performance: a "play of sacred miracles," a "wonderful pageant," a "devil Theater." The Catholic Mass, as it had been celebrated for centuries, was outlawed, and with it a range of other Catholic rites. On occasion those rites were still practiced in secret, at considerable danger, and it is possible that Shakespeare could have been among those present. He was certainly present at the services of the English Church, whose ceremonies led by berobed priests, guided by the resonant prose of the Book of Common Prayer, and held in settings whose mag-nificence continues to astonish us, had their own intense histrionic power.

The young Shakespeare, whether true believer or skeptic or something in between ("So have I heard, and do in part believe it," says Hamlet's friend Horatio [1.1.164]), might have carried away from such ceremonies several impressions: an intimation of immense, cosmic forces that may impinge upon human life; a heightened understand-ing of the power of language to form and exalt the spirit; an awareness of intense, even murderous competition and rivalry among competing rituals; and perhaps a sense of the longing to believe that may be awakened and shaped in large crowds.

I have placed Shakespeare himself in each of these scenes—which together sketch the root conditions of the Elizabethan theater—because some people have found it difficult to conceive how this one man, with his provincial origins and his restricted range of experience, could have so rapidly and completely mastered the central imagi-native themes of his times. Moreover, it is sometimes difficult to grasp how seeming abstractions such as market society, monarchical state, and theological doctrine were actually experienced directly by distinct individuals. Shakespeare's plays were social and collective events, but they also bore the stamp of a particular artist, one endowed with a remarkable capacity to craft lifelike illusions, a daring willingness to articulate an original vision, and a loving command, at once precise and generous, of language. These plays are stitched together from shared cultural experiences, inherited dra-matic devices, and the pungent vernacular of the day, but we should not lose sight of the extent to which they articulate an intensely personal vision, a bold shaping of the available materials. Four centuries of feverish biographical speculation, much of it foolish, bear witness to a basic intuition: the richness of these plays, their inexhaust-ible openness, is the consequence not only of the auspicious collective conditions of the culture but also of someone's exceptional skill, inventiveness, and courage at taking those conditions and making of them something rich and strange.

The Theater of the Nation

What precisely were the collective conditions disclosed by the spectacles that Shake-speare would likely have witnessed? First, the growth of Stratford-upon-Avon, the bustling market town of which John Shakespeare was bailiff, is a small version of a momentous sixteenth-century development that made Shakespeare's career possible: the making of an urban "public." That development obviously depended on adequate numbers; the period experienced a rapid and still unexplained growth in population. With it came an expansion and elaboration of market relations: markets became less periodic, more continuous, and more abstract—centered, that is, not on the familiar materiality of goods but on the liquidity of capital and goods. In practical terms, this meant that it was possible to conceive of the theater not only as festive entertainment for special events—Lord Mayor's pageants, visiting princes, seasonal festivals, and the like—but as a permanent, year-round business venture. The venture relied on revenues from admission—it was an innovation of this period to have money advanced in the expectation of pleasure rather than offered to servants afterward as a reward—and counted on habitual playgoing, with a concomitant demand for new plays from competing theater companies: "But that's all one, our play is done," sings the Clown at the end of *Twelfth Night* and adds a glance toward the next afternoon's proceeds: "And we'll strive to please you every day" (5.1.393–94).

Second, the royal progress is an instance of what the anthropologist Clifford Geertz has called the Theater State, a state that manifests its power and meaning in exemplary public performances. Professional companies of players, like the one Shakespeare belonged to, understood well that they existed in relation to this Theater State and would, if they were fortunate, be called upon to serve it. Unlike Ben Jonson, Shakespeare did not, as far as we know, write royal entertainments on commission, but his plays were frequently performed before Queen Elizabeth and then before King James and Queen Anne, along with their courtiers and privileged guests. There are many fascinating glimpses of these performances, including a letter from Walter Cope to Robert Cecil, early in James's reign. "Burbage is come," Cope writes, referring to the leading actor of Shakespeare's company, "and says there is no new play that the Queen hath not seen, but they have revived an old one, called *Love's Labor's Lost,* which for wit and mirth he says will please her exceedingly. And this is appointed to be played tomorrow night at my Lord of Southampton's." Not only would such theatrical performances have given great pleasure—evidently, the Queen had already exhausted the company's new offerings—but they conferred prestige upon those who commanded them and those in whose honor they were mounted.

Monarchical power in the period was deeply allied to spectacular manifestations of the ruler's glory and disciplinary authority. The symbology of power depended on regal magnificence, reward, punishment, and pardon, all of which were heavily theatricalized. Indeed, the conspicuous public display does not simply serve the interests of power; on many occasions in the period, power seemed to exist in order to make pageantry possible, as if the nation's identity were only fully realized in theatrical performance. It would be easy to exaggerate this perception: the subjects of Queen Elizabeth and King James were acutely aware of the distinction between shadow and substance. But they were fascinated by the political magic through which shadows could be taken for substantial realities, and the ruling elite was largely complicit in the formation and celebration of a charismatic absolutism. At the same time, the claims of the monarch who professes herself or himself to be not the representative of the nation but its embodiment were set against the counterclaims of the House of Commons. And this institution too, as we have glimpsed, had its own theatrical rituals, centered on the crowd whose shouts of approval, in heavily stage-managed elections, chose the individuals who would stand for the polity and participate in deliberations held in a hall whose resemblance to a theater did not escape contemporary notice.

Third, in outlawing the Catholic Mass and banning the medieval mystery plays, along with pilgrimages and other rituals associated with holy shrines and sacred images, English Protestant authorities hoped to hold a monopoly on religious observances. But they inevitably left some people, perhaps substantial numbers of them, mourning what they had lost. Playing companies could satisfy at least some of the popular longings and appropriate aspects of the social energy no longer allowed a theological outlet. That is, official attacks on certain Catholic practices made it more possible for the public theater to appropriate and exploit their allure. Hence, for example, the plays that celebrated the solemn miracle of the Catholic Mass were banned, along with the most elaborate church vestments, but in *The Winter's Tale* Dion can speak in awe of what he witnessed at Apollo's temple:

> I shall report,
> For most it caught me, the celestial habits—
> Methinks I so should term them—and the reverence
> Of the grave wearers. Oh, the sacrifice!
> How ceremonious, solemn, and unearthly
> It was i'th' off'ring!
>
> (3.1.3–8)

And at the play's end, the statue of the innocent mother breathes, comes to life, and embraces her child.

The theater in Shakespeare's time, then, is intimately bound up with all three crucial cultural formations: market society, the Theater State, and the church. But it is important to note that the institution is not *identified* with any of them. The theater may be a market phenomenon, but it is repeatedly and bitterly attacked as the enemy of diligent, sober, productive economic activity. Civic authorities generally regarded the theater as a pestilential nuisance, a parasite on the body of the commonwealth, a temptation to students, apprentices, housewives, even respectable merchants to leave their serious business and lapse into idleness and waste. That waste, it might be argued, could be partially recuperated if it went for the glorification of a guild or the entertainment of an important dignitary, but the only group regularly profiting from the theater were the players and their disreputable associates.

For his part, Shakespeare made a handsome profit from the commodification of theatrical entertainment, but he seems never to have written "city comedy"—plays set in London and more or less explicitly concerned with market relations—and his characters express deep reservations about the power of money and commerce: "That smooth-faced gentleman, tickling commodity," Philip the Bastard observes in *King John*, "wins of all, / Of kings, of beggars, old men, young men, maids" (2.1.569–73). We could argue that the smooth-faced gentleman is none other than Shakespeare himself, for his drama famously mingles kings and clowns, princesses and panderers. But the mingling is set against a romantic current of social conservatism: in *Twelfth Night*, the aristocratic heiress Olivia falls in love with someone who appears far beneath her in wealth and social station, but it is revealed that he (and his sister Viola) are of noble blood; in *The Winter's Tale*, Leontes' daughter Perdita is raised as a shepherdess, but her noble nature shines through her humble upbringing, and she marries the Prince of Bohemia; the strange island maiden with whom Ferdinand, son of the King of Naples, falls madly in love in *The Tempest* turns out to be the daughter of the rightful Duke of Milan. Shakespeare pushes against this conservative logic in *All's Well That Ends Well*, but the noble young Bertram violently resists the unequal match thrust upon him by the King, and the play's mood is notoriously uneasy.

Similarly, Shakespeare's theater may have been patronized and protected by the monarchy—after 1603, his company received a royal patent and was known as the King's Men—but the two institutions were by no means identical in their interests or their ethos. To be sure, *Richard III* and *Macbeth* incorporate aspects of royal propaganda, but given the realities of censorship, Shakespeare's plays, and the period's drama as a whole, are surprisingly independent and complex in their political vision. There is, in any case, a certain inherent tension between kings and player kings: Elizabeth and James may both have likened themselves to actors onstage, but they were loath to admit their dependence on the applause and money, freely given or freely withheld, of the audience. The charismatic monarch insists that the sacredness of authority resides in the body of the ruler, not in a costume that may be worn and then discarded by an actor. Kings are not *representations* of power—or do not admit that they are—but claim to be the thing itself. The government institution that was actually based on the idea of representation, Parliament, had theatrical elements, as we have seen, but it significantly excluded any audience from its deliberations. And Shakespeare's oblique portraits of parliamentary representatives, the ancient Roman tribunes Sicinius Velutus and Junius Brutus in *Coriolanus*, are anything but flattering.

Finally, the theater drew significant energy from the liturgy and rituals of the late medieval church, but as Shakespeare's contemporaries widely remarked, the playhouse and the church were scarcely natural allies. Not only did the theater represent a potential competitor to worship services, and not only did ministers rail against prostitution and other vices associated with playgoing, but theatrical representation itself, even when ostensibly pious, seemed to many to empty out whatever it presented, turning substance into mere show. The theater could and did use the period's deep currents of religious feeling, but it had to do so carefully and with an awareness of conflicting interests.

Shakespeare Comes to London

How did Shakespeare decide to turn his prodigious talents to the stage? When did he make his way to London? How did he get his start? Concerning these and similar questions we have a mountain of speculation but no secure answers. There is not a single surviving record of Shakespeare's existence from 1585, when his twins were baptized in Stratford church, until 1592, when a rival London playwright made an envious remark about him. In the late seventeenth century, the delightfully eccentric collector of gossip John Aubrey was informed that prior to moving to London the young Shakespeare had been a schoolteacher in the country. Aubrey also recorded a story that Shakespeare had been a rather unusual apprentice butcher: "When he killed a calf, he would do it in a high style, and make a speech."

These and other legends, including one that has Shakespeare whipped for poaching game, fill the void until the unmistakable reference in Robert Greene's *Groatsworth of Wit Bought with a Million of Repentance* (1592). An inspired hack writer with a university education, a penchant for self-dramatization, a taste for wild living, and a strong streak of resentment, Greene, in his early thirties, was dying in poverty when he penned his last farewell, piously urging his fellow dramatists Christopher Marlowe, Thomas Nashe, and George Peele to abandon the wicked stage before they were brought low, as he had been, by a new arrival: "For there is an upstart crow, beautified with our feathers, that with his 'Tiger's heart wrapped in player's hide' supposes he is as well able to bombast out a blank verse as the best of you, and, being an absolute *Johannes Factotum*, is in his own conceit the only Shake-scene in a country." If "Shake-scene" is not enough to identify the object of his attack, Greene parodies a line from Shakespeare's early play *3 Henry VI*: "O tiger's heart wrapped in a woman's hide" (1.4.137). Greene is accusing Shakespeare of being an upstart, a plagiarist, an egomaniacal jack-of-all-trades—and, above all perhaps, a popular success.

By 1592, then, Shakespeare had already arrived on the highly competitive London theatrical scene. He was successful enough to be attacked by Greene and, a few months later, defended by Henry Chettle, another hack writer who had seen Greene's manuscript through the press (or, some scholars speculate, had written the attack himself and passed it off as the dying Greene's). Chettle expresses his regret that he did not suppress Greene's diatribe and spare Shakespeare "because myself have seen his demeanor no less civil than he excellent in the quality he professes." Besides, Chettle adds, "divers of worship have reported his uprightness of dealing, which argues his honesty and his facetious [polished] grace in writing that approves his art." "Divers of worship": not only was Shakespeare established as an accomplished writer and actor, but he evidently had aroused the attention and the approbation of several socially prominent people. In Elizabethan England, aristocratic patronage, with the money, protection, and prestige it alone could provide, was probably a professional writer's most important asset.

This patronage, or at least Shakespeare's quest for it, is most visible in the dedications in 1593 and 1594 of his narrative poems *Venus and Adonis* and *The Rape of Lucrece* to the young nobleman Henry Wriothesley, Earl of Southampton. It may be glimpsed as well, perhaps, in the sonnets, with their extraordinary adoration of the fair youth, though the identity of that youth has never been determined. What return Shakespeare got for his exquisite offerings is likewise unknown. We do know that among wits and gallants, the narrative poems won Shakespeare a fine reputation as an immensely stylish and accomplished poet. An amateur play performed at Cambridge University at the end of the sixteenth century, *The Return from Parnassus,* makes fun of this vogue, as a foolish character effusively declares, "I'll worship sweet Mr. Shakespeare, and to honor him will lay his *Venus and Adonis* under my pillow." Many readers at the time may have done so: the poem went through sixteen editions before 1640, more than any other work by Shakespeare.

Patronage was crucially important not only for individual artists but also for the actors, playwrights, and investors who pooled their resources to form professional theater companies. The public playhouses had enemies, especially among civic and religious authorities, who wished greatly to curb performances or to ban them altogether. An Act of Parliament of 1572 included players among those classified as vagabonds, threatening them therefore with the horrible punishments meted out to those regarded as economic parasites. The players' escape route was to be nominally enrolled as apprentices in guilds, as if they were learning to be goldsmiths or grocers rather than actors. Alternatively, as we have noted, they could be officially listed as the servants of high-ranking noblemen.

When Shakespeare came to London, presumably in the late 1580s, there were more than a half-dozen of these companies operating under the patronage of various aristocrats. We do not know for which of these companies, several of which had toured in Stratford, he originally worked, nor whether he began, as legend has it, by holding gentlemen's horses outside the theater or by serving as a prompter's assistant and then graduated to acting and playwriting. Shakespeare is listed among the actors in Ben Jonson's *Every Man in His Humor* (performed in 1598) and *Sejanus* (performed in 1603), but we do not know for certain what roles he played, nor are there records of any of his other performances. Tradition has it that he played Adam in *As You Like It* and the Ghost in *Hamlet,* but he was clearly not one of the leading actors of the day.

Shakespeare may initially have been associated with the company of Ferdinando Stanley, Lord Strange; that company included actors with whom Shakespeare was later linked. Or he may have belonged to the Earl of Pembroke's Men, since there is evidence that they performed *The Taming of a Shrew* and a version of *3 Henry VI.* At any event, by 1594, Shakespeare was a member of the Chamberlain's Men, for his name, along with those of Will Kemp and Richard Burbage, appears on a record of those "servants to the Lord Chamberlain" paid for performance at the royal palace at Greenwich on December 26 and 28. Shakespeare stayed with this company, which during the reign of King James received royal patronage and became the King's Men, for the rest of his career.

Many playwrights in Shakespeare's time worked freelance, moving from company to company as opportunities arose, collaborating on projects, adding scenes to old plays, scrambling from one enterprise to another. But certain playwrights, among them the most successful, wrote for a single company, often agreeing contractually to give that company exclusive rights to their theatrical works. Shakespeare seems to have followed such a pattern. For the Chamberlain's Men, later the King's Men, he wrote an average of two plays per year. His company initially performed in The Theatre, a playhouse built in 1576 by an entrepreneurial actor and trained craftsman, James Burbage, the father of the actor Richard, who was to perform many of Shakespeare's greatest roles. When in 1597 their lease on this playhouse expired, the Chamberlain's Men passed through a difficult time, but they formed a joint stock company, raising sufficient capital to lease a site and put up a splendid new playhouse in the suburb of Southwark, on the south bank of the Thames. This playhouse, the Globe, opened in 1599. Shakespeare is listed in the legal agreement as one of the principal investors, and when the company began to use Blackfriars as their indoor playhouse around 1610, he was a major shareholder in that theater as well. The Chamberlain's Men dominated the theater scene, and the shares were quite valuable. Then as now, the theater was an extremely risky enterprise—most of those who wrote plays and performed in them made pathetically little money—but Shakespeare was a notable exception. The fine house in Stratford and the coat of arms he succeeded in acquiring were among the fruits of his multiple mastery, as actor, playwright, and investor of the London stage.

Edward Alleyn. Artist unknown. Alleyn was the great tragic actor of the Admiral's Men (the principal rival to Shakespeare's company). He was famous especially for playing the major characters of Christopher Marlowe.

The Shakespearean Trajectory

Though Shakespeare's England was in many ways a record-keeping society, no reliable record survives that details the performances, year by year, in the London theaters. Every play had to be licensed by the Master of the Revels, but the records kept by the relevant government officials from 1579 to 1621 have not survived. A major theatrical entrepreneur, Philip Henslowe, kept a careful account of his expenditures, including what he paid for the scripts he commissioned, but unfortunately Henslowe's main business was with the Rose and the Fortune theaters and not with the playhouses at which Shakespeare's company performed. A comparable ledger must have been kept by the shareholders of the Chamberlain's Men, but it has not survived. Shakespeare himself apparently did not undertake to preserve all his writings for posterity, let alone to clarify the chronology of his works or to specify which plays he wrote alone and which with collaborators.

The principal source for Shakespeare's works is the 1623 Folio volume of *Mr. William Shakespeares Comedies, Histories, & Tragedies*. The world owes this work,

IF YOV KNOW NOT ME,
You know no body.

OR,

The troubles of Queene ELIZABETH.

LONDON.
Printed by *B.A.* and *T.F.* for *Nathanaell Butter.* 1632.

Title page of *If You Know Not Me, You Know Nobody; or, the Troubles of Queen Elizabeth* (1632).

lovingly edited after his death by two of the playwright's friends, an incalculable debt: without it, nearly half of Shakespeare's plays, including many of his greatest masterpieces, would have been lost forever. The edition does not, however, include any of Shakespeare's nondramatic poems, and it omits four plays in which Shakespeare is now thought to have had a significant hand, *Edward III, Pericles, Cardenio,* and *The Two Noble Kinsmen,* along with his probable contribution to the multiauthored *Sir Thomas More.* (A number of other plays were attributed to Shakespeare, both before and after his death, but scholars have not generally accepted any of these into the established canon.) Moreover, the Folio edition does not print the plays in chronological order, nor does it attempt to establish a chronology. We do not know how much time would normally have elapsed between the writing of a play and its first performance, nor, with a few exceptions, do we know with any certainty the month or even the year of the first performance of any of Shakespeare's plays. The quarto editions of those plays that were published during Shakespeare's lifetime obviously establish a date by which we know a given play had been written, but they give us little more than an end point, because there was likely to be a substantial though indeterminate gap between the first performance of a play and its publication.

With enormous patience and ingenuity, however, scholars have gradually assembled a considerable archive of evidence, both external and internal, for dating the composition of the plays. Besides actual publication, the external evidence includes explicit reference to a play, a record of its performance, or (as in the case of Greene's attack on the "upstart crow") the quoting of a line, though all of these can be maddeningly ambiguous. The most important single piece of external evidence appears in 1598 in *Palladis Tamia,* a long book of jumbled reflections by the churchman Francis Meres that includes a survey of the contemporary literary scene. Meres finds that "the sweet, witty soul of Ovid lives in mellifluous and honey-tongued Shakespeare, witness his *Venus and Adonis,* his *Lucrece,* his sugared Sonnets among his private friends, etc." Meres goes on to list Shakespeare's accomplishments as a playwright as well:

> As Plautus and Seneca are accounted the best for Comedy and Tragedy among the Latins: so Shakespeare among the English is the most excellent in both kinds for the stage; for Comedy, witness his *Gentlemen of Verona,* his *Errors,* his *Love labors lost,* his *Love labors won,* his *Midsummers night dream,* & his *Merchant of Venice:* for Tragedy his *Richard the 2, Richard the 3, Henry the 4, King John, Titus Andronicus* and his *Romeo and Juliet.*

Meres thus provides a date by which twelve of Shakespeare's plays had definitely appeared (including one, *Love's Labor's Won,* that appears either to have been lost or to be known to us by a different title). Unfortunately, Meres provides no clues about the order of appearance of these plays, and there are no other comparable lists.

Faced with the limitations of the external evidence, scholars have turned to a bewildering array of internal evidence, ranging from datable sources and topical allusions on the one hand to evolving stylistic features (ratio of verse to prose, percentage of rhyme to blank verse, colloquialisms, use of extended similes, and the like) on the other. Thus, for example, a cluster of plays with a high percentage of rhymed verse may follow closely upon Shakespeare's writing of the rhymed poems *Venus and Adonis* and *The Rape of Lucrece* and therefore be datable to 1594–95. Similarly, vocabulary overlap probably indicates proximity in composition, so if four or five plays share relatively "rare" vocabulary, it is likely that they were written in roughly the same period. Again, there seems to be a pattern in Shakespeare's use of colloquialisms, with a steady increase from *As You Like It* (1599–1600) to *Coriolanus* (1608), followed in the late romances by a retreat from the colloquial.

Ongoing computer analysis should provide further guidance in the future, though the precise order of the plays, still very much in dispute, is never likely to be settled to universal satisfaction. Still, certain broad patterns are now widely accepted. These patterns can be readily grasped in *The Norton Shakespeare,* which presents the plays according to our best estimate of their chronological order.

Shakespeare began his career, probably in the early 1590s, by writing both comedies and history plays. The attack by Greene suggests that he made his mark with the series of theatrically vital, occasionally brilliant, and often crude plays based on the foreign and domestic broils that erupted during the unhappy reign of the Lancastrian Henry VI. Modern readers and audiences are more likely to find the first sustained evidence of unusual power in *Richard III* (ca. 1592), a play that combines a richly imagined central character, a dazzling command of histrionic rhetoric, and an overarching moral vision of English history.

At virtually the same time that he was setting his stamp on the genre of the history play, Shakespeare was writing his first—or first surviving—comedies. Here, there are even fewer signs than in the histories of an apprenticeship. *The Comedy of Errors,* one of his early works in this genre, already displays a rare command of the resources of comedy: mistaken identity, madcap confusion, and the threat of disaster, giving way in the end to reconciliation, recovery, and love. Shakespeare's other comedies from the first half of the 1590s, *The Two Gentlemen of Verona, The Taming of the Shrew,* and *Love's Labor's Lost,* are no less remarkable for their sophisticated variations on familiar comic themes, their inexhaustible rhetorical inventiveness, and their poignant intimation, in the midst of festive celebration, of loss.

Successful as are these early histories and comedies, and indicative of an extraordinary theatrical talent, Shakespeare's achievement in the later 1590s would still have been all but impossible to foresee. Starting with *A Midsummer Night's Dream* (1595–96), Shakespeare wrote an unprecedented series of romantic comedies—*The Merchant of Venice, Much Ado About Nothing, The Merry Wives of Windsor, As You Like It,* and *Twelfth Night* (1600–1601)—whose poetic richness and emotional complexity remain unmatched. In the same period, he wrote a sequence of profoundly searching and ambitious history plays—*Richard II, 1* and *2 Henry IV,* and *Henry V*—which together explore the death throes of feudal England and the birth of the modern nation-state ruled by a charismatic monarch. Both the comedies and histories of this period are marked by their capaciousness, their ability to absorb characters who press up against the outermost boundaries of the genre: the comedy *The Merchant of Venice* somehow contains the figure, at once nightmarish and poignant, of Shylock, while the *Henry IV* plays, with their somber vision of crisis in the family and the state, bring to the stage one of England's greatest comic characters, Falstaff.

If in the mid- to late 1590s Shakespeare reached the summit of his art in two major genres, he also manifested a lively interest in a third. As early as 1592–93, he wrote the crudely violent tragedy *Titus Andronicus,* the first of several plays on themes from Roman history, and a few years later, in *Richard II*, he created in the protagonist a figure who achieves by the play's close the stature of a tragic hero. In the same year that Shakespeare wrote the wonderfully farcical "Pyramus and Thisbe" scene in *A Midsummer Night's Dream*, he probably also wrote the deeply tragic realization of the same story in *Romeo and Juliet*. But once again, the lyric anguish of *Romeo and Juliet* and the tormented self-revelation of *Richard II*, extraordinary as they are, could not have led anyone to predict the next phase of Shakespeare's career, the great tragic dramas that poured forth in the early years of the seventeenth century: *Hamlet*, *Othello*, *King Lear*, *Macbeth*, *Antony and Cleopatra*, and *Coriolanus*. These plays, written between 1600 and 1608, seem to mark a major shift in sensibility, an existential and metaphysical darkening that many readers think must have drawn upon a deep personal anguish, perhaps caused by the decline and death of Shakespeare's father, John, in 1601.

Whatever the truth of these speculations—and we have no direct, personal testimony either to support or to undermine them—there appears to have occurred in the same period a shift as well in Shakespeare's comic sensibility. The comedies written between 1601 and 1607, *Troilus and Cressida*, *Measure for Measure*, and *All's Well That Ends Well*, are sufficiently different from the earlier comedies—more biting in tone, more uneasy with comic conventions, more ruthlessly questioning of the values of the characters and the resolutions of the plots—that they led many twentieth-century scholars to classify them as "problem plays" or "dark comedies." This category has recently begun to fall out of favor, since Shakespeare criticism is perfectly happy to demonstrate that *all* of the plays are "problem plays." But there is another group of plays, among the last Shakespeare wrote, that continue to constitute a distinct category. *Pericles*, *Cymbeline*, *The Winter's Tale*, and *The Tempest*—written between 1607 and 1611, when the playwright had developed a remarkably fluid, dreamlike sense of plot and a poetic style that could veer, apparently effortlessly, from the tortured to the ineffably sweet—have been known since the late nineteenth century as the "romances." These plays share an interest in the moral and emotional life less of the adolescents who dominate the earlier comedies than of their parents. The romances are deeply concerned with patterns of loss and recovery, suffering and redemption, despair and renewal. They have seemed to many critics to constitute a deliberate conclusion to a career that began in histories and comedies and passed through the dark and tormented tragedies.

One effect of the practice of printing Shakespeare's plays in a reconstructed chronological order, as this edition does, is to produce a kind of authorial plot, a progress from youthful exuberance and a heroic grappling with history, through psychological anguish and radical doubt, to a mature serenity built upon an understanding of loss. The ordering of Shakespeare's "complete works" in this way reconstitutes the figure of the author as the beloved hero of his own, lived romance. There are numerous reasons to treat this romance with considerable skepticism: the precise order of the plays remains in dispute, the obsessions of the earliest plays crisscross with those of the last, the drama is a collaborative art form, and the relation between authorial consciousness and theatrical representation is murky. Yet a longing to identify Shakespeare's personal trajectory, to chart his psychic and spiritual as well as professional progress, is all but irresistible.

The Fetishism of Dress

Whatever the personal resonance of Shakespeare's own life, his art is deeply enmeshed in the collective hopes, fears, and fantasies of his time. For example, throughout his plays, Shakespeare draws heavily upon his culture's investment in costume, symbols of authority, visible signs of status—the fetishism of dress he must have witnessed from early childhood. Disguise in his drama is often assumed to be incredibly effective: when Henry V borrows a cloak, when Portia dresses in a jurist's robes, when Viola puts on a young man's suit, it is as if each has become unrecognizable, as if identity resided in clothing. At the end of *Twelfth Night*, even though Viola's true identity has been disclosed, Orsino continues to call her Cesario; he will do so, he says, until she resumes her maid's garments, for only then will she be transformed into a woman:

> Cesario, come—
> For so you shall be while you are a man—
> But when in other habits you are seen,
> Orsino's mistress and his fancy's queen.
> (5.1.371–74)

The pinnacle of this fetishism of costume is the royal crown, for whose identity-conferring power men are willing to die, but the principle is everywhere, from the filthy blanket that transforms Edgar into Poor Tom to the coxcomb that is the badge of the licensed fool. Antonio, wishing to express his utter contempt, spits on Shylock's "Jewish gaberdine," as if the clothing were the essence of the man; Kent, pouring insults on the loathsome Oswald, calls him a "filthy worsted-stocking knave"; and innocent Imogen, learning that her husband has ordered her murder, thinks of herself as an expensive cast-off dress, destined to be ripped at the seams:

> Poor I am stale, a garment out of fashion,
> And for I am richer than to hang by th' walls,
> I must be ripped: to pieces with me.
> (*Cymbeline* 3.4.50–52)

What can be said, thought, felt in this culture seems deeply dependent on the clothes one wears—clothes that one is, in effect, *permitted* or *compelled* to wear, since there is little freedom in dress. Shakespearean drama occasionally represents something like such freedom: after all, Viola in *Twelfth Night* chooses to put off her "maiden weeds," as does Rosalind, who declares, "We'll have a swashing and a martial outside" (*As You Like It* 1.3.116). But these choices are characteristically made under the pressure of desperate circumstances, here shipwreck and exile. Part of the charm of Shakespeare's heroines is their ability to transform distress into an opportunity for self-fashioning, but the plays often suggest that there is less autonomy than meets the eye. What looks like an escape from cultural determinism may be only a deeper form of constraint. We may take, as an allegorical emblem of this constraint, the transformation of the beggar Christopher Sly in the playful Induction to *The Taming of the Shrew* into a nobleman. The transformation seems to suggest that you are free to make of yourself whatever you choose to be—the play begins with the drunken Sly claiming the dignity of his pedigree ("Look in the Chronicles" [Induction 1.3–4])—but in fact he is only the subject of the mischievous lord's experiment, designed to demonstrate the interwovenness of clothing and identity. "What think you," the lord asks his huntsman,

> if he were conveyed to bed,
> Wrapped in sweet clothes, rings put upon his fingers,
> A most delicious banquet by his bed,
> And brave attendants near him when he wakes—
> Would not the beggar then forget himself?

To which the huntsman replies, in words that underscore the powerlessness of the drunken beggar, "Believe me, lord, I think he cannot choose" (Induction 1.33–38).

Petruccio's taming of Katherina is similarly constructed around an imposition of identity, an imposition closely bound up with the right to wear certain articles of clothing. When the haberdasher arrives with a fashionable lady's hat, Petruccio refuses it over his wife's vehement objections: "This doth fit the time, / And gentlewomen wear such caps as these." "When you are gentle," Petruccio replies, "you shall have one, too, /

And not till then" (4.3.70–73). At the play's close, Petruccio demonstrates his authority by commanding his tamed wife to throw down her cap: "Off with that bauble; throw it underfoot" (5.2.122). Here as elsewhere in Shakespeare, acts of robing and disrobing are intensely charged, a charge that culminates in the trappings of monarchy. When Richard II, in a scene that was probably censored during the reign of Elizabeth from the stage as well as the printed text, is divested of his crown and scepter, he experiences the loss as the eradication of his name, the symbolic melting away of his identity:

> Alack the heavy day,
> That I have worn so many winters out
> And know not now what name to call myself.
> Oh, that I were a mockery king of snow,
> Standing before the sun of Bolingbroke
> To melt myself away in water-drops.
> (4.1.250–55)

When Lear tears off his regal "lendings" in order to reduce himself to the nakedness of the Bedlam beggar, he is expressing not only his radical loss of social identity but the breakdown of his psychic order as well, expressing therefore his reduction to the condition of the "poor bare forked animal" that is the primal form of undifferentiated existence. And when Cleopatra determines to kill herself in order to escape public humiliation in Rome, she magnificently affirms her essential being by arraying herself as she had once done to encounter Antony:

> Show me, my women, like a queen. Go, fetch
> My best attires. I am again for Cydnus
> To meet Mark Antony.
> (5.2.226–28)

Such scenes are a remarkable intensification of the everyday symbolic practice of Renaissance English culture, its characteristically deep and knowing commitment to illusion: "I know perfectly well that the woman in her crown and jewels and gorgeous gown is an aging, irascible, and fallible mortal—she herself virtually admits as much—yet I profess that she is the virgin queen, timelessly beautiful, wise, and just." Shakespeare understood how close this willed illusion was to the spirit of the theater, to the actors' ability to work on what the chorus in *Henry V* calls the "imaginary forces" of the audience. But there is throughout Shakespeare's works a counterintuition that, while it does not exactly overturn this illusion, renders it poignant, vulnerable, fraught. The "masculine usurp'd attire" that is donned by Viola, Rosalind, Portia, Jessica, and other Shakespeare heroines alters what they can say and do, reveals important aspects of their character, and changes their destiny, but it is, all the same, not theirs and not all of who they are. They have, the plays insist, natures that are neither transformed nor altogether concealed by their dress: "Pray God defend me," exclaims the frightened Viola. "A little thing would make me tell them how much I lack of a man" (*Twelfth Night* 3.4.271–72).

The Paradoxes of Identity

The gap between costume and identity is not simply a matter of what women supposedly lack; virtually all of Shakespeare's major characters, men and women, convey the sense of both a *self-division* and an *inward expansion*. The belief in a complex inward realm beyond costumes and status is a striking inversion of the clothes cult: we know perfectly well that the characters have no inner lives apart from what we see on the stage, and yet we believe that they continue to exist when we do not see them, that they exist apart from their represented words and actions, that they have hidden dimensions. How is this conviction aroused and sustained? In part, it is the effect of what the characters themselves say: "My grief lies all within," Richard II tells Bolingbroke,

> And these external manner of laments
> Are merely shadows to the unseen grief
> That swells with silence in the tortured soul.
>
> (4.1.288–91)

Similarly, Hamlet, dismissing the significance of his outward garments, declares, "I have that within which passes show— / These but the trappings and the suits of woe" (1.2.85–86). And the distinction between inward and outward is reinforced throughout this play and elsewhere by an unprecedented use of the aside and the soliloquy.

The soliloquy is a continual reminder in Shakespeare that the inner life is by no means transparent to one's surrounding world. Prince Hal seems open and easy with his mates in Eastcheap, but he has a hidden reservoir of disgust:

> I know you all, and will a while uphold
> The unyoked humor of your idleness.
> Yet herein will I imitate the sun,
> Who doth permit the base contagious clouds
> To smother up his beauty from the world,
> That, when he please again to be himself,
> Being wanted he may be more wondered at
> By breaking through the foul and ugly mists
> Of vapors that did seem to strangle him.
>
> (I Henry IV 1.2.170–78)

"When he please again to be himself": the line implies that identity is a matter of free choice—you decide how much of yourself you wish to disclose—but Shakespeare employs other devices that suggest more elusive and intractable layers of inwardness. There is a peculiar, recurrent lack of fit between costume and character, in fools as in princes, that is not simply a matter of disguise and disclosure. If Hal's true identity is partially "smothered" in the tavern, it is not completely revealed either in his soldier's armor or in his royal robes, nor do his asides reach the bedrock of unimpeachable self-understanding.

Identity in Shakespeare repeatedly slips away from the characters themselves, as it does from Richard II after the deposition scene and from Lear after he has given away his land and from Macbeth after he has gained the crown. The slippage does not mean that they retreat into silence; rather, they embark on an experimental, difficult fashioning of themselves and the world, most often through role-playing. "I cannot do it," says the deposed and imprisoned Richard II. "Yet I'll hammer't out" (5.5.5). This could serve as the motto for many Shakespearean characters: Viola becomes Cesario, Rosalind calls herself Ganymede, Kent becomes Caius, Edgar presents himself as Poor Tom, Hamlet plays the madman that he has partly become, Hal pretends that he is his father and a highwayman and Hotspur and even himself. Even in comedy, these ventures into alternate identities are rarely matters of choice; in tragedy, they are always undertaken under pressure and compulsion. And often enough it is not a matter of role-playing at all, but of a drastic transformation whose extreme emblem is the harrowing madness of Lear and of Leontes.

There is a moment in Richard II in which the deposed king asks for a mirror and then, after musing on his reflection, throws it to the ground. The shattering of the glass serves to remind us not only of the fragility of identity in Shakespeare but of its characteristic appearance in fragmentary mirror images. The plays continually generate alternative reflections, identities that intersect with, underscore, echo, or otherwise set off that of the principal character. Hence, Desdemona and Iago are not only important figures in Othello's world—they also seem to embody partially realized aspects of himself; Falstaff and Hotspur play a comparable role in relation to Prince Hal, Fortinbras and Horatio in relation to Hamlet, Gloucester and the Fool in relation to Lear, and so forth. In many of these plays, the complementary and contrasting characters figure in subplots, subtly interwoven with the play's main plot and illuminating its concerns. The note so conspicuously sounded by Fortinbras at the close of *Hamlet*—what the hero might have been, "had he been put on"—is heard repeatedly in Shakespeare and contributes to the overwhelming intensity, poignancy, and complexity of the characters. This is a world in which outward appearance is everything and nothing, in which individuation is at once sharply etched and continually blurred, in which the victims of fate are haunted by the ghosts of the possible, in which everything is simultaneously as it must be and as it need not have been.

Are these alternatives signs of a struggle between contradictory and irreconcilable perspectives in Shakespeare? In certain plays—notably, *Measure for Measure, All's Well That Ends Well, Coriolanus,* and *Troilus and Cressida*—the tension seems both high and entirely unresolved. But Shakespearean contradictions are more often reminiscent of the capacious spirit of Montaigne, who refused any systematic order that would betray his sense of reality. Thus, individual characters are immensely important in Shakespeare—he is justly celebrated for his unmatched skill in the invention of particular dramatic identities, marked with distinct speech patterns, manifested in social status, and confirmed by costume and gesture—but the principle of individuation is not the rock on which his theatrical art is founded. After the masks are stripped away, the pretenses exposed, the claims of the ego shattered, there is a mysterious remainder; as the shamed but irrepressible Paroles declares in *All's Well That Ends Well,* "Simply the thing I am / Shall make me live" (4.3.316–17). Again and again the audience is made to sense a deeper energy, a source of power that at once discharges itself in individual characters and seems to sweep right through them.

The Poet of Nature

In *The Birth of Tragedy,* Nietzsche called a comparable source of energy that he found in Greek tragedy "Dionysos." But the god's name, conjuring up Bacchic frenzy, does not seem appropriate to Shakespeare. In the late seventeenth and eighteenth centuries, it was more plausibly called Nature: "The world must be peopled," says the delightful Benedict in *Much Ado About Nothing* (2.3.213), and there are frequent invocations elsewhere of the happy, generative power that brings couples together—

> Jack shall have Jill,
> Naught shall go ill,
> The man shall have his mare again, and all shall be well.
> (*A Midsummer Night's Dream* 3.2.461–63)

—and the melancholy, destructive power that brings all living things to the grave: "Golden lads and girls all must, / As chimney-sweepers, come to dust" (*Cymbeline* 4.2.261–62).

But the celebration of Shakespeare as a poet of nature—often coupled with an inane celebration of his supposedly "natural" (that is, untutored) genius—has its distinct limitations. For Shakespearean art brilliantly interrogates the "natural," refusing to take for granted precisely what the celebrants think is most secure. His comedies are endlessly inventive in showing that love is not simply natural: the playful hint of bestiality in the line quoted above, "the man shall have his mare again" (from a play in which the Queen of the Fairies falls in love with an ass-headed laborer), lightly unsettles the boundaries between the natural and the perverse. These boundaries are called into question throughout Shakespeare's work, from the cross-dressing and erotic crosscurrents that deliciously complicate the lives of the characters in *Twelfth Night* and *As You Like It* to the terrifying violence that wells up from the heart of the family in *King Lear* or from the sweet intimacy of sexual desire in *Othello*. Even the boundary between life and death is not secure, as the ghosts in *Julius Caesar, Hamlet,* and *Macbeth* attest, while the principle of natural death (given its most eloquent articulation by old Hamlet's murderer, Claudius!) is repeatedly tainted and disrupted.

Disrupted too is the idea of order that constantly makes its claim, most insistently in the history plays. Scholars have observed the presence in Shakespeare's works of the so-called Tudor myth—the ideological justification of the ruling dynasty as a restoration of national order after a cycle of tragic violence. The violence, Tudor apologists claimed, was divine punishment unleashed after the deposition of the anointed king, Richard II, for God will not tolerate violations of the sanctified order. Traces of this propaganda certainly exist in the histories—Shakespeare may, for all we know, have personally subscribed to its premises—but a closer scrutiny of his plays has disclosed so many ironic reservations and qualifications and subversions as to call into question any straightforward adherence to a political line. The plays manifest a profound fascination with the monarchy and with the ambitions of the aristocracy, but the fascination is never simply endorsement. There is always at least the hint of a slippage between the great figures, whether admirable or monstrous, who stand at the pinnacle of authority and the vast, miscellaneous mass of soldiers, scriveners, ostlers, poets, whores, gardeners, thieves, weavers, shepherds, country gentlemen, sturdy beggars, and the like who make up the commonwealth. And the idea of order, though eloquently articulated (most memorably by Ulysses in *Troilus and Cressida*), is always shadowed by a relentless spirit of irony.

The Play of Language

If neither the individual nor nature nor order will serve, can we find a single comprehensive name for the underlying force in Shakespeare's work? Certainly not. The work is too protean and capacious. But much of the energy that surges through this astonishing body of plays and poems is closely linked to the power of language. Shakespeare was the supreme product of a rhetorical culture, a culture steeped in the arts of persuasion and verbal expressiveness. In 1512, the great Dutch humanist Erasmus published a work called *De copia* that taught its readers how to cultivate "copiousness," verbal richness, in discourse. (Erasmus obligingly provides, as a sample, a list of 144 different ways of saying "Thank you for your letter.") Recommended modes of variation include putting the subject of an argument into fictional form, as well as the use of synonym, substitution, paraphrase, metaphor, metonymy, synecdoche, hyperbole, diminution, and a host of other figures of speech. To change emotional tone, he suggests trying *ironia, interrogatio, admiratio, dubitatio, abominatio*—the possibilities seem infinite.

In Renaissance England, certain syntactic forms or patterns of words known as "figures" (also called "schemes") were shaped and repeated in order to confer beauty or heighten expressive power. Figures were usually known by their Greek and Latin names, though in an Elizabethan rhetorical manual, *The Art of English Poesy*, George Puttenham made a valiant if short-lived attempt to give them English equivalents, such as "*Hyperbole*, or the Overreacher," "*Ironia*, or the Dry Mock," and "*Ploce*, or the Doubler." Those who received a grammar school education throughout Europe at almost any point between the Roman Empire and the eighteenth century probably knew by heart the names of up to one hundred such figures, just as they knew by heart their multiplication tables. According to one scholar's count, Shakespeare knew and made use of about two hundred.

As certain grotesquely inflated Renaissance texts attest, lessons from *De copia* and similar rhetorical guides could encourage mere prolixity and verbal self-display. But though he shared his culture's delight in rhetorical complexity, Shakespeare always understood how to swoop from baroque sophistication to breathtaking simplicity. Moreover, he grasped early in his career how to use figures of speech, tone, and rhythm not only to provide emphasis and elegant variety but also to articulate the inner lives of his characters. Take, for example, these lines from *Othello*, where, as scholars have noted, Shakespeare deftly combines four common rhetorical figures— *anaphora, parison, isocolon,* and *epistrophe*—to depict with painful vividness Othello's psychological torment:

> By the world,
> I think my wife be honest, and think she is not;
> I think that thou art just, and think thou art not.
> I'll have some proof.

> (3.3.380–83)

Anaphora is simply the repetition of a word at the beginning of a sequence of sentences or clauses ("I/I"). *Parison* is the correspondence of word to word within adjacent sentences or clauses, either by direct repetition ("think/think") or by the matching of noun with noun, verb with verb ("wife/thou"; "be/art"). *Isocolon* gives exactly the same length to corresponding clauses ("and think she is not/and think thou art not"), and *epistrophe* is the mirror image of *anaphora*, in that it is the repetition of a word at the end of a sequence of sentences or clauses ("not/not"). Do we need to know the Greek names for these figures in order to grasp the effectiveness of Othello's lines? Of course not. But Shakespeare and his contemporaries, convinced that rhetoric provided the most natural and powerful means by which feelings could be conveyed to readers and listeners, were trained in an analytical language that helped at once to promote and to account for this effectiveness. In his 1593 edition of *The Garden of Eloquence,* Henry Peacham remarks that *epistrophe* "serveth to leave a word of importance in the end of a sentence, that it may the longer hold the sound in the mind of the hearer," and in *Directions for Speech and Style* (ca. 1599), John Hoskins notes that *anaphora* "beats upon one thing to cause the quicker feeling in the audience."

Shakespeare also shared with his contemporaries a keen understanding of the ways that rhetorical devices could be used not only to express powerful feelings but to hide them: after all, the artist who created Othello also created Iago, Richard III, and Lady Macbeth. He could deftly skewer the rhetorical affectations of Polonius in *Hamlet* or the pedant Holofernes in *Love's Labor's Lost*. He could deploy stylistic variations to mark the boundaries not of different individuals but of different social realms; in *A Midsummer Night's Dream*, for example, the blank verse of Duke Theseus is played off against the rhymed couplets of the well-born young lovers, and both in turn contrast with the prose spoken by the artisans. At the same time that he thus marks boundaries between both individuals and groups, Shakespeare shows a remarkable ability to establish unifying patterns of imagery that knit together the diverse strands of his plot and suggest subtle links among characters who may be scarcely aware of how much they share with one another.

One of the hidden links in Shakespeare's own works is the frequent use he makes of a somewhat unusual rhetorical figure called *hendiadys*. An example from the Roman poet Virgil is the phrase *pateris libamus et auro,* "we drink from cups and gold" (*Georgics* 2.192). Rather than serving as an adjective or a dependent noun, as in "golden cups" or "cups of gold," the word "gold" serves as a substantive joined to another substantive, "cups," by a conjunction, "and." Shakespeare uses the figure over three hundred times in all, and since it does not appear in ancient or medieval lists of tropes and schemes and is treated only briefly by English rhetoricians, he may have come upon it directly in Virgil. *Hendiadys* literally means "one through two," though Shakespeare's versions often make us quickly, perhaps only subliminally, aware of the complexity of what ordinarily passes for straightforward perceptions. When Othello, in his suicide speech, invokes the memory of "a malignant and a turbaned Turk," the figure of speech at once associates enmity with cultural difference and keeps them slightly apart. And when Macbeth speaks of his "strange and self-abuse," the *hendiadys* seems briefly to hold both "strange" and "self" up for scrutiny. It would be foolish to make too much of any single feature in Shakespeare's varied and diverse creative achievement, and yet this curious rhetorical scheme has something of the quality of a fingerprint.

But all of his immense rhetorical gifts, though rich, beautiful, and supremely useful, do not adequately convey Shakespeare's relation to language, which is less strictly functional than a total immersion in the arts of persuasion may imply. An Erasmian admiration for copiousness cannot fully explain Shakespeare's astonishing vocabulary of some 25,000 words. (His closest rival among the great English poets of the period was John Milton, with about 12,000 words, and most major writers, let alone ordinary people, have much smaller vocabularies.) This immense word hoard, it is worth noting, was not the result of scanning a dictionary; in the late sixteenth century, there were no large-scale English dictionaries of the kind to which we are now accustomed. Shakespeare seems to have absorbed new words from virtually every discursive realm he ever encountered, and he experimented boldly and tirelessly with them. These experiments were facilitated by a flexibility in grammar, orthography, and diction that the more orderly, regularized English of the later seventeenth and eighteenth centuries suppressed.

Owing in part to the number of dialects in London, pronunciation was variable, and there were many opportunities for phonetic association between words: the words "bear," "barn," "bier," "bourn" "born," and "barne" could all sound like one another. Homonyms were given greater scope by the fact that the same word could be spelled so many different ways—Christopher Marlowe's name appears in the records as Marlowe, Marloe, Marlen, Marlyne, Merlin, Marley, Marlye, Morley, and Morle—and by the fact that a word's grammatical function could easily shift, from noun to verb, verb to adjective, and so forth. Since grammar and punctuation did not insist on relations of coordination and subordination, loose, nonsyntactic sentences were common, and etymologies were used to forge surprising or playful relations between distant words.

It would seem inherently risky for a popular playwright to employ a vocabulary so far in excess of what most mortals could possibly possess, but Shakespeare evidently counted on his audience's linguistic curiosity and adventurousness, just as he counted on its general and broad-based rhetorical competence. He was also usually careful to provide a context that in effect explained or translated his more arcane terms. For example, when Macbeth reflects with horror on his murderous hands, he shudderingly imagines that even the sea could not wash away the blood; on the contrary, his bloodstained hand, he says, "will rather / The multitudinous seas incarnadine." The meaning of the unfamiliar word "incarnadine" is explained by the next line: "Making the green one red" (2.2.64–66).

What is most striking is not the abstruseness or novelty of Shakespeare's language but its extraordinary vitality, a quality that the playwright seemed to pursue with a kind of passionate recklessness. Perhaps Samuel Johnson was looking in the right direction when he complained that the "quibble," or pun, was "the fatal Cleopatra for which [Shakespeare] lost the world, and was content to lose it." For the power that continually discharges itself throughout the plays, at once constituting and unsettling everything it touches, is the polymorphous power of language, language that seems both costume and that which lies beneath the costume, personal identity and that which challenges the merely personal, nature and that which enables us to name nature and thereby distance ourselves from it.

Shakespeare's language has an overpowering exuberance and generosity that often resembles the experience of love. Consider, for example, Oberon's description in *A Midsummer Night's Dream* of the moment when he saw Cupid shoot his arrow at the fair vestal: "Thou rememberest," he asks Puck,

> Since once I sat upon a promontory
> And heard a mermaid on a dolphin's back
> Uttering such dulcet and harmonious breath
> That the rude sea grew civil at her song

And certain stars shot madly from their spheres
To hear the sea-maid's music?

(2.1.148–54)

Here, Oberon's composition of place, lightly alluding to a classical emblem, is infused with a fantastically lush verbal brilliance. This brilliance, the result of masterful alliterative and rhythmical technique, seems gratuitous; that is, it does not advance the plot, but rather exhibits a capacity for display and self-delight that extends from the fairies to the playwright who has created them. The rich music of Oberon's words imitates the "dulcet and harmonious breath" he is intent on recalling, breath that has, in his account, an oddly contradictory effect: it is at once a principle of order, so that the rude sea is becalmed like a lower-class mob made civil by a skilled orator, and a principle of disorder, so that celestial bodies in their fixed spheres are thrown into mad confusion. And this contradictory effect, so intimately bound up with an inexplicable, supererogatory, and intensely erotic verbal magic, is a key to *A Midsummer Night's Dream*, with its exquisite blend of confusion and discipline, lunacy and hierarchical ceremony.

The fairies in this comedy seem to embody a pervasive sense found throughout Shakespeare's work that there is something uncanny about language, something that is not quite human, at least in the conventional and circumscribed sense of the human that dominates waking experience. In the comedies, this intuition is alarming but ultimately benign: Oberon and his followers trip through the great house at the play's close, blessing the bride-beds and warding off the nightmares that lurk in marriage and parenthood. But there is in Shakespeare an alternative, darker vision of the uncanniness of language, a vision also embodied in creatures that test the limits of the human—not the fairies of *A Midsummer Night's Dream* but the weird sisters of *Macbeth*. When in the tragedy's opening scene the witches chant, "Fair is foul, and foul is fair," they unsettle through the simplest and most radical act of linguistic equation (x is y) the fundamental distinctions through which a moral order is established. And when Macbeth appears onstage a few minutes later, his first words unconsciously echo what we have just heard from the witches' mouths: "So foul and fair a day I have not seen" (1.3.39). What is the meaning of this linguistic "unconscious"? On the face of things, Macbeth presumably means only that the day of fair victory is also a day of foul weather, but the fact that he echoes the witches (something that we hear but that he cannot know) intimates an occult link between them, even before their direct encounter. It is difficult, perhaps impossible, to specify exactly what this link signifies—generations of emboldened critics have tried without notable success—but we can at least affirm that its secret lair is in the play's language, like a half-buried pun whose full articulation will entail the murder of Duncan, the ravaging of his kingdom, and Macbeth's own destruction.

Macbeth is haunted by half-buried puns, equivocations, and ambiguous grammatical constructions known as amphibologies. They manifest themselves most obviously in the words of the witches, from the opening exchanges to the fraudulent assurances that deceive Macbeth at the close, but they are also present in his most intimate and private reflections, as in his tortured broodings about his proposed act of treason:

If it were done when 'tis done, then 'twere well
It were done quickly. If th'assassination
Could trammel up the consequence and catch
With his surcease success—that but this blow
Might be the be-all and the end-all!—here,
But here, upon this bank and shoal of time,
We'd jump the life to come.

(1.7.1–7)

The dream is to reach a secure and decisive end, to catch as in a net (hence "trammel up") all of the slippery, unforeseen, and uncontrollable consequences of regicide, to hobble time as one might hobble a horse (another sense of "trammel up"), to stop the flow ("success") of events, to be, as Macbeth later puts it, "settled." But Macbeth's words themselves slip away from the closure he seeks; they slide into one another, trip over themselves, twist and double back and swerve into precisely the sickening uncertainties their speaker most wishes to avoid. And if we sense a barely discernible note of comedy in Macbeth's tortured language, a discordant playing with the senses of the word "done" and the hint of a childish tongue twister in the phrase "catch / With his surcease success," we are in touch with a dark pleasure to which Shakespeare was all his life addicted.

Look again at the couplet from *Cymbeline*: "Golden lads and girls all must, / As chimney-sweepers, come to dust." The playwright who insinuated a pun into the solemn dirge is the same playwright whose tragic heroine in *Antony and Cleopatra*, pulling the bleeding body of her dying lover into the pyramid, says, "Our strength is all gone into heaviness" (4.15.34). He is the playwright whose Juliet, finding herself alone on the stage, says, "My dismal scene I needs must act alone" (*Romeo and Juliet* 4.3.19), and the playwright who can follow the long, wrenching periodic sentence that Othello speaks, just before he stabs himself, with the remark "O bloody period!" (5.2.349). The point is not merely the presence of puns in the midst of tragedy (as there are stabs of pain in the midst of Shakespearean comedy); it is rather the streak of wildness that they so deliberately disclose, the sublimely indecorous linguistic energy of which Shakespeare was at once the towering master and the most obedient, worshipful servant.

From Page to Stage: Shakespeare at Work

Shakespeare's extraordinary imaginative and linguistic power left its mark, like a personal signature, on everything he wrote. But his plays became the property of the theatrical company in which he was a shareholder. The company could choose to sell its plays to printers who might hope to profit if the public was eager to read as well as to watch a popular hit. But relatively few plays excited that level of public interest. Moreover, playing companies did not always think it was in their interest to have their scripts circulating in print, at least while the plays were actively in repertory: players evidently feared competition from rival companies and thought that reading might dampen playgoing. Plays were on occasion printed quickly, in order to take advantage of their popularity, but they were most often sold to the printers when the theaters were temporarily closed by plague, or when the company was in need of capital (four of Shakespeare's plays were published in 1600, presumably to raise money to pay the debts incurred in building the new Globe), or when a play had grown too old to revive profitably. There is no conclusive evidence that Shakespeare disagreed with this professional caution. There was clearly a market for his plays in print as well as onstage, and he himself may have taken pride in what he wrote as suitable for reading as well as viewing. But unlike Jonson, who took the radical step of rewriting his own plays for publication in the 1616 folio of his *Works*, Shakespeare evidently never undertook to constitute his plays as a canon. If in the sonnets he imagines his verse achieving a symbolic immortality, this dream apparently did not extend to his plays, at least through the medium of print.

Moreover, there is no evidence that Shakespeare had an interest in asserting authorial rights over his scripts, or that he or any other working English playwright had a public "standing," legal or otherwise, from which to do so. (Jonson was ridiculed for his presumption.) There is no indication whatever that he could, for example, veto changes in his scripts or block interpolated scenes or withdraw a play from production if a particular interpretation, addition, or revision did not please him. To be sure, in his advice to the players, Hamlet urges that those who play the clowns "speak no more than is set down for them," but—apart from the question of whether the prince speaks for the playwright—the play-within-the-play in *Hamlet* is precisely an instance of a script altered to suit a particular occasion. It seems likely that Shakespeare would have routinely accepted the possibility of such alterations. Moreover, he would of necessity have routinely accepted the possibility, and in certain cases the virtual inevitability, of cuts in order to stage his plays in the two to two and one-half hours that was the normal performing time. There is an imaginative generosity in many of Shakespeare's scripts, as if he were deliberately offering his fellow actors more than they could use on any one occasion and hence giving them abundant materials with which to reconceive and revivify each play again and again, as they or their audiences liked it. The Elizabethan theater, like most theater in our own time, was a collaborative enterprise, and the collaboration almost certainly extended to decisions about selection, trimming, shifts of emphasis, and minor or major revision.

Writing for the theater for Shakespeare was never simply a matter of sitting alone at his desk and putting words on paper; it was a social process as well as individual act. We do not know the extent to which this process frustrated him; in Sonnet 66 he writes of "art made tongue-tied by authority." Shakespeare may have been forced on occasion to cut lines and even whole scenes to which he was attached; shifting political circumstances may have occasioned rewriting, possibly against his will; or his fellow players may have insisted that they could not successfully perform what he had written, compelling him to make changes he did not welcome. But compromise and collaboration are part of what it means to be in the theater, and Shakespeare was, supremely, a man of the theater.

As a man of the theater, Shakespeare understood that whatever he set down on paper was not the end of the story. It would inevitably be shaped by the words he spoke to his fellow actors and by their own ideas concerning emphasis, stage business, tone, pacing, possible cuts, and so forth. It could be modified too by the intervention of the government censor or by intimations that some powerful figure might take offense at something in the script. To the extent that the agreed-upon alterations were ever written down, they were recorded in the promptbook used for a particular performance, and that promptbook could in turn be modified for a subsequent performance in a different setting.

For many years, it was thought that Shakespeare himself did little or no revising. Some recent editors have argued persuasively that there are many signs of authorial revision, even wholesale rewriting. But there is no sign that Shakespeare sought through such revision to bring each of his plays to its "perfect," "final" form. On the contrary, many of the revisions seem to indicate that the scripts remained open texts that the playwright and his company expected to add to, cut, and rewrite as the occasion demanded.

Ralph Waldo Emerson once compared Shakespeare and his contemporary Francis Bacon in terms of the relative "finish" of their work. All of Bacon's work, wrote Emerson, "lies along the ground, a vast unfinished city." Each of Shakespeare's dramas, by contrast, "is perfect, hath an immortal integrity. To make Bacon's work complete, he must live to the end of the world." Recent scholarship suggests that Shakespeare was more like Bacon than Emerson thought. Neither the Folio nor the quarto texts of Shakespeare's plays bear the seal of final authorial intention, the mark of decisive closure that has served, at least ideally, as the guarantee of textual authenticity. We want to believe, as we read the text, "This is the play as Shakespeare himself wanted it read," but there is no license for such a reassuring sentiment. To be "not of an age, but for all time" means in Shakespeare's case not that the plays have achieved a static perfection, but that they are creatively, inexhaustibly unfinished.

The Status of the Artist

That we have been so eager to link certain admired scripts to a single known playwright is closely related to changes in the status of artists in the Renaissance, changes that led to a heightened interest in the hand of the individual creator. Like medieval painting, medieval drama gives us few clues as to the particular individuals who fashioned the objects we admire. We know something about the places in which these objects were made, the circumstances that enabled their creation, the spaces in which they were placed, but relatively little about the particular artists themselves. It is easy to imagine a wealthy patron or a civic authority in the late Middle Ages commissioning a play on a particular subject (appropriate, for example, to a seasonal ritual, a religious observance, or a political festivity) and specifying the date, place, and length of the performance, the number of actors, even the costumes to be used, but it is more difficult to imagine him specifying a particular playwright and still less insisting that the entire play be written by this dramatist alone. Only with the Renaissance do we find a growing insistence on the name of the maker, the signature that heightens the value and even the meaning of the work by implying that it is the emanation of a single, distinct shaping consciousness.

In the case of Renaissance painting, we know that this signature does not necessarily mean that every stroke was made by the master. Some of the work, possibly the greater part of it, may have been done by assistants, with only the faces and a few finishing touches from the hand of the illustrious artist to whom the work is confidently attributed. As the skill of individual masters became more explicitly valued, contracts began to specify how much was to come from the brush of the principal painter. Consider, for example, the Italian painter Luca Signorelli's contract of 1499 for frescoes in Orvieto Cathedral:

> The said master Luca is bound and promises to paint [1] all the figures to be done on the said vault, and [2] especially the faces and all the parts of the figures from the middle of each figure upwards, and [3] that no painting should be done on it without Luca himself being present. . . . And it is agreed [4] that all the mixing of colors should be done by the said master Luca himself.

Such a contract at once reflects a serious cash interest in the characteristic achievement of a particular artist and a conviction that this achievement is compatible with the presence of other hands, provided those hands are subordinate, in the finished work. For paintings on a smaller scale, it was more possible to commission an exclusive performance. Thus the contract for a small altarpiece by Signorelli's great teacher, Piero della Francesca, specifies that "no painter may put his hand to the brush other than Piero himself."

There is no record of any comparable concern for exclusivity in the English theater. Unfortunately, the contracts that Shakespeare and his fellow dramatists almost certainly signed have not, with one significant exception, survived. But plays written for the professional theater are by their nature an even more explicitly collective art form than paintings; they depend for their full realization on the collaboration of others, and that collaboration may well extend to the fashioning of the script. It seems that some authors may simply have been responsible for providing plots that others then dramatized; still others were hired to "mend" old plays or to supply prologues, epilogues, or songs. A particular playwright's name came to be attached to a certain identifiable style—a characteristic set of plot devices, a marked rhetorical range, a tonality of character—but this name may refer in effect more to a certain product associated with a particular playing company than to the individual artist who may or may not have written most of the script. The one contract whose details do survive, that entered into by Richard Brome and the actors and owners of the Salisbury Court Theater in 1635, does not stipulate that Brome's plays must be written by him alone or even that he must be responsible for a certain specifiable proportion of each script. Rather, it specifies that the playwright "should not nor would write any play or any part of a play to any other players or playhouse, but apply all his study and endeavors therein for the benefit of the said company of the said playhouse." The Salisbury Court players want rights to everything Brome writes for the stage; the issue is not that the plays associated with his name be exclusively *his* but rather that he be exclusively *theirs*.

Recent textual scholarship, then, has been moving steadily away from a conception of Shakespeare's plays as direct, unmediated emanations from the mind of the author and toward a conception of them as working scripts, composed and continually reshaped as part of a collaborative commercial enterprise in competition with other, similar enterprises. One consequence has been the progressive weakening of the idea of the solitary, inspired genius, in the sense fashioned by Romanticism and figured splendidly in the statue of Shakespeare in the public gardens in Germany's Weimar, the city of Goethe and Schiller: the poet, with his sensitive, expressive face and high domed forehead sitting alone and brooding, a skull at his feet, a long-stemmed rose in his crotch. In place of this projection of German Romanticism, we have now a playwright and sometime actor who is also (to his considerable financial advantage) a major shareholder in the company—the Chamberlain's Men, later the King's Men—to which he loyally supplies for most of his career an average of two plays per year.

As a shareholder Shakespeare had to concern himself with such matters as economic cycles, lists of plague deaths, the cost of costumes, government censorship, city ordinances, the hiring and firing of personnel, and innumerable other factors that affected his enterprise. Practical considerations did not merely affect the context of his writing for the stage; they also shaped the form of what he wrote. His plays were not monuments, fixed in every detail and immobilized forever. They were like living beings, destined to change as a condition for their very survival.

One of the very first biographical mentions of Shakespeare, in the Reverend Thomas Fuller's *History of the Worthies of England* (1662), seems to have grasped this principle of mobility. Fuller reports—or imagines—the "wit-combats" that Shakespeare and Jonson had at the Mermaid Tavern:

> which two I behold like a Spanish great galleon and an English man of war; Master Jonson (like the former) was built far higher in learning, solid but slow in his performances. Shakespeare, with the English man of war, lesser in bulk, but lighter in sailing, could turn with all tides, tack about, and take advantage of all winds by the quickness of his wit and invention.

The encounters Fuller describes may be apocryphal, but to "turn with all tides, tack about, and take advantage of all winds" is a canny description of the highly mobile texts that Shakespeare fashioned and bequeathed to posterity.

Conjuring Shakespeare

The Elizabethan and Jacobean public had an interest in reading plays as well as seeing them. There was a lively market in such texts, often rushed into print to catch public excitement, and there is even evidence that at certain performances it was possible for audiences at the playhouse to purchase a copy of the very play they were watching.

Shakespeare's attitude to this market is unclear. Unlike Ben Jonson, he never personally edited and oversaw the publication of his plays, either individually or as a collection, but he may, for all we know, have imagined some day doing so. Perhaps death simply overtook him before he reached that goal. Certainly the Folio editors, though they were themselves fellow actors, thought of his plays as literary works. In 1623, seven years after the playwright's death, Heminges and Condell believed they could sell copies of their expensive collection of Shakespeare's plays—"What euer you do," they urge their readers, "buy"—by insisting that their texts were "as he conceiued them."

"As he conceived them": potential readers in the early seventeenth century then were already interested in access to Shakespeare's "conceits"—his "wit," his imagination, and his creative power—and were willing to assign a high value to the products of his particular, identifiable skill, one distinguishable from that of his company and of his rival playwrights. After all, Jonson's dedicatory poem in the Folio praises Shakespeare not as the playwright of the incomparable King's Men but as the equal of Aeschylus, Sophocles, and Euripides. And if we now see Shakespeare's dramaturgy in the context of his contemporaries and of a collective artistic practice, readers continue to have little difficulty recognizing that most of the plays attached to his name tower over those of his rivals.

The First Folio included an engraving purporting to show what Shakespeare looked like, but in the little poem that accompanied this image Jonson urged the reader to "look / Not on his Picture, but his Book." The words on the page then should conjure up the author himself; they should ideally give the reader unmediated access to the astonishing forge of imaginative power that was the mind of the dramatist. Such is the vision—at its core closely related to the preservation of the divinely inspired text in the great scriptural religions—that has driven many of the great editors who have for centuries produced successive editions of Shakespeare's works. The vision was not yet fully formed in the First Folio, for Heminges and Condell still felt obliged to apologize to their noble patrons for dedicating to them a collection of mere "trifles." But by the eighteenth century, there were no longer any ritual apologies for Shakespeare; instead, there was growing recognition of the supreme artistic importance of his works.

At the same time, from the eighteenth century onward, there was growing recognition of the uncertain, conflicting, and in some cases corrupt state of the surviving texts. Every conceivable step, it was thought, must be undertaken to correct mistakes, strip away corruptions, and return the texts to their pure and unsullied form. Noticing that there were multiple texts of fully half of the plays and noticing too that these texts often contain significant variants, editors routinely conflated the distinct versions into a single text in an attempt to reconstruct the ideal, definitive, complete, and perfect copy that they imagined Shakespeare must have aspired to and eventually reached for each of his plays. In doing so they succeeded in producing something that Shakespeare himself never wrote.

Heminges and Condell, who knew the author and had access to at least some of his manuscripts, lamented the fact that Shakespeare did not live "to have set forth and overseen his own writings." But even had he done so—or, alternatively, even if a cache of his manuscripts were discovered in a Warwickshire attic tomorrow—all of the editorial problems would not be solved, though the textual landscape would change, nor would all of the levels of mediation be swept away. The written word has strange powers: it seems to hold onto something of the very life of the person who has written it, but it also seems to pry that life loose from the writer, exposing it to vagaries of history and chance quite independent of those to which the writer was personally subject. Moreover, with the passing of centuries, the language itself and the whole frame of reference within which language and symbols are understood have decisively changed. The most learned modern scholar still lives at a huge experiential remove from Shakespeare's world and, even holding a precious copy of the First Folio in hand, cannot escape having to read across a vast chasm of time what is, after all, an edited text. The rest of us cannot so much as indulge in the fantasy of direct access: our eyes inevitably wander to the glosses and the explanatory notes.

Abandoning the dream of direct access to Shakespeare's final and definitive intentions is not a cause for despair, nor should it lead us to throw our hands up and declare that one text is as good as another. What it does is to encourage us to be actively interested in the editorial principles that underlie the particular edition that we are using. It is said that the great artist Brueghel once told an inquisitive connoisseur who had come to his studio, "Keep your nose out of my paintings; the smell of the paint will poison you." In the case of Shakespeare, it is increasingly important to bring one's nose close to the page, as it were, and sniff the ink. More precisely, it is important to understand the rationale for the choices that the editors have made.

The rationale behind *The Norton Shakespeare* is described at length in the Textual Introduction to this volume. What should be stressed here is the fact that

Shakespeare was the master of the unfinished, the perpetually open. The notion of finding a perfectly fixed text of one of his plays, the copy that he directly handed over to the printer as his "final" version, goes against everything we know about his personal practice and about Elizabethan and Jacobean theater. Shakespeare wrote his plays to be performed by professional players in a range of different settings, at different times, and before different publics. The project required considerable flexibility. As a working playwright, he seems to have thought about the creation of "parts" or roles, often with specific actors in mind though always with the understanding that the personnel might change. Taken all together, of course, the parts made up a whole, but both the individual pieces and the larger structure they formed were and have remained open. The editors of *The Norton Shakespeare* have tried to record and preserve this openness.

Speaking only for myself, I will confess a further ambition: I would like to meet Shakespeare in person. I think that throughout his career Shakespeare produced in effect detachable parts of himself, parts that derived from his personhood (his social relationships, his acquired knowledge, his temperament, his memories, his inner life, and so forth) but that moved independently in the world. He created out of himself hundreds of secondary agents, his characters, some of whom seem even to float free of the particular narrative structures in which they perform their given roles and to take on an agency we ordinarily reserve for biological persons. As an artist he literally gave his life to these agents, transferring his personal energies to them.

I do not mean that Shakespeare's characters are all self-portraits in the sense of referring back to his individual existence (though some of them almost certainly do). I mean rather that Shakespeare's life is, in an unusually intense and vivid way, in his works. And therefore when I open the printed book or scroll through the Digital Edition, I feel his eerie presence and want to call out, with the words Ben Jonson wrote in his dedicatory poem to the First Folio, "My Shakespeare, rise!"

General Textual Introduction

GORDON McMULLAN AND SUZANNE GOSSETT

Most people read an edition of Shakespeare's plays and poems because they want to read the plays and poems, not because they wish to dwell on the material origins of the texts they are reading—where the texts came from, how the manuscripts looked, who printed them, for whom they were printed, how the publishing practices of the English Renaissance made them what they are. Yet attention to the text itself is, we believe, an integral part of understanding the meaning of Shakespeare's works, considerably enhancing the pleasure of the reading experience. Seeing Shakespeare in the theater, reading Shakespeare on the page: both can offer extraordinary, multiply layered experiences of entertainment and intellectual uplift, a sense of unparalleled access to the past, and often simply a great deal of fun. We have edited the text of Shakespeare with these pleasures, and the reader's choices, in mind, and we wish to share with you a sense of the further levels of engagement that close attention to the origins of the text itself can bring.

For us, first and foremost, the *textual* is inseparable from the *critical*. That is, the "themes" we locate in Shakespeare, the sense of the place of the plays and poems in Shakespeare's world and in our own, the ways in which these remarkable writings require us to reflect on being human, on being gendered, on living in community, on having an ethnicity and a class status, all have their foundation in the words we read—and if we don't know whether the words we are reading are the "right" ones, or if we don't have the tools to reflect on the challenges presented by the very idea of "right" words, then we may miss out on key aspects of the Shakespearean experience. The fantasies of the "anti-Stratfordians" (people who claim Shakespeare's works were written by one or another equally implausible candidate) serve to remind us of the obsession of our age with Shakespearean *authenticity,* with the urge to ensure that the Shakespeare we see performed, or that we read or study, is the *real* Shakespeare, the *authentic* Shakespeare. The primary question we address in our textual introduction is central to this debate—"How authentic is the text I am reading?"—and in order to do this we need to reflect on two things: on the nature of the Shakespearean text and on the complex idea of "authenticity." Once we have done that, we can begin to explain some of the decisions we made in editing the texts that together form *The Norton Shakespeare.*

The "Authentic" Shakespeare

For centuries, playgoers and readers had two questions answered for them in advance: which plays and poems to read as "Shakespeare's" (the reader logically assumed that if a play or poem was in the "complete works," then it was Shakespeare's, and if not, not), and, beyond that, which *text* of a given Shakespeare play or poem to read. This second question might seem odd. Surely there is only one *Hamlet* and that is the *Hamlet* Shakespeare wrote? Yet not only does more than one authoritative text of certain plays (above all, as it happens, of *Hamlet*) exist, some of which are very different from each other, but the word "authoritative" raises a third question—notably, "On what grounds do we decide that a printed text is close to what Shakespeare actually wrote?" Moreover, the first of these questions is itself not straightforward. The boundaries of the Shakespeare canon—those texts accepted as being written in whole or in part by Shakespeare—have always been porous. Neither *Pericles* nor *The Two Noble Kinsmen*, for instance, was included in the First Folio, yet both have long been attributed to Shakespeare (in each case, as it happens, to Shakespeare working jointly with another playwright, as pretty much all his fellow Elizabethan and Jacobean playwrights did), and both are now invariably included in "Complete Works" editions. Some plays have been considered part of the Shakespeare canon for far less time. *Edward III,* for instance, now appears in editions as a "Shakespeare and others" play, where a couple of decades ago it did not. Times change, evidence surfaces, and methods of attributing authorship develop. As a result, other plays continue to hover at the edges of the canon. At the time of writing, the newest contender for inclusion is a celebrated play by Thomas Kyd called *The Spanish Tragedy,* for which, it is suggested, Shakespeare supplied extra scenes, capitalizing on the play's success. *The Spanish Tragedy* does not appear in the present edition of *The Norton Shakespeare*, but if in due course we are sufficiently convinced by the arguments for its inclusion, then in it will come. What the French thinker Jacques Derrida called "the logic of the supplement" operates here: each time you add something to a volume called "Complete" you make it *more* complete, but the fact that you needed to add something to complete a volume already claiming to be "complete" has the effect of undermining the very possibility of completeness. For editors of Shakespeare, this is unavoidable—and to be celebrated, not resented.

It is not only the *external* borders of the Shakespeare canon that are fluid; the *internal* borders too—the choice of words within a given play or poem—have never, to the surprise of many readers, been firmly fixed. Shakespeare lovers are aware, perhaps, that Hamlet's flesh is too "solid," "sullied," or "sallied," depending on which version of the play one reads; they may also have wondered which of two "others"—"the base Judean" or "the base Indian"—is the one to which Othello really means to compare himself just before his suicide; but they may not realize that these celebrated instances of Shakespearean textual choice are part of a much broader canvas of instabilities, uncertainties, and options. This means that not only the choice of play, but the choice of *text* of that play, affects the reader's experience of Shakespeare.

The key question arising here is that of the "right" reading, the "authentic" reading, a status usually taken to require a direct relationship to the author. The mental adjustment needed is to accept that, quite often, there may be either *no* "right" reading or *more than one*. We cannot ever know exactly what Shakespeare wrote because (with one limited, debated exception) we do not have the holograph manuscript (a manuscript in his own handwriting) of any of his plays or poems. Shakespeare's own manuscripts of the plays in the First Folio or in the various quartos that predate the Folio have not survived, and so editors are unable to do the one thing they would most like to be able to do, which is to compare what Shakespeare actually wrote with what was printed. The apparent exception is the lines in the surviving manuscript of *Sir Thomas More* that are largely accepted as being in Shakespeare's hand—but, maddeningly, this is the one play in the Shakespeare canon as currently constituted that never found its way into print in the late sixteenth or early seventeenth century. So, even in the case of the one brief section of extant manuscript generally thought to be in Shakespeare's hand, we cannot make a direct comparison between what was written and what was printed.

It was long believed that Shakespeare never revised his texts (a myth prompted by the prefatory material to the First Folio) and therefore that there must have been one, and only one, lost master original from which all subsequent texts derive. But further complicating the notion of the "authentic Shakespeare" is the existence of short, variant quarto texts of several plays. Because certain of these are noticeably inferior to the Folio (or, sometimes, to a fuller quarto) text of the same play, they were traditionally referred to as "bad quartos." In recent years, scholars have sought to replace the unhelpful connotations of "bad" with neutral descriptive terms such as "short quartos," but the point of origin of these texts remains unclear. Are they "authentic"? One long-standing argument has it that they are "reported" texts, the product of "pirate" printers who sat a handful of actors down and persuaded them to recall not only their own lines but the entire play—this, it is claimed, explains the discrepancy in quality between the lines of certain characters in these quartos (e.g., Mercutio in the First Quarto of *Romeo and Juliet,* whose lines are nearly identical to those in the much fuller Second Quarto) and those of others. These quartos vary considerably, from the brief, highly problematic quarto of *The Merry Wives of Windsor* to the much more independent and interpretively convincing First Quarto of *Hamlet.* It has sometimes been proposed that these quartos may represent Shakespeare's early drafts. A further possibility, championed recently as a development of increasing editorial openness to the possibility that Shakespeare did occasionally revise his own work, is that the short quartos represent "theatrical" versions of the plays, whereas the lengthy Folio texts represent more overtly "literary" versions designed with readers in mind. It may be that we will never fully understand how these quartos came to be so different from the fuller, ostensibly more authoritative versions in the First Folio and elsewhere, but it seems essential to present them in all their intriguing difference. Our editorial principles and the technology we adopt in this edition allow us to include fully edited versions of all these quartos, so that the reader may understand the complexity of deciding what constitutes "authentic" Shakespeare.

The Text in the Print House

One reason it is hard to know what Shakespeare actually wrote is that all early modern printed texts include interpretations, adjustments, and misreadings of the manuscripts on which they are based (which may have been the author's own or a neater scribal copy), as well as mechanical errors made by the compositors in the process of setting the type for printing. Moreover, workers in the Renaissance print house did not simply transfer the words passively from writer to reader; they actively intervened in what they printed. There was no fixed way to spell words in Shakespeare's day—Shakespeare himself spelled his own name differently at different times when signing documents—and compositors made the most of this irregularity to even out or "justify" the line they were setting (for example, by adding or removing a final "e" on an individual word). Similarly, there was no sense that the printer's duty was to print exactly what he found in the manuscript with which he was working. On the contrary, since early modern play manuscripts typically included little or no punctuation, it was the job of the compositor setting the type to add punctuation so as to enable and enhance the reader's experience. One of the most misleading of Shakespearean myths, one prevalent among actors even today, is the claim that the punctuation in the First Folio expresses "Shakespeare's instructions to actors": those theater professionals who have carefully timed their pauses and breaths according to the arrangement of commas and semicolons in the First Folio may be sad to learn that they are almost certainly basing their practice on the habits of Compositor A or Compositor J (since we almost never know the names of the workers in the print houses, compositors are usually referred to by letter).

To understand how the printing process affected the texts we read, it helps to know how the two principal formats in which Shakespeare's plays were printed—folio and quarto—were put together. A folio is made up of standard-sized sheets of paper printed with two pages on each side, then folded in half and assembled with several other such folded sheets inserted inside each other to form a "gathering" or "quire"; these gatherings are then stitched together to form the book. A quarto is made of the same standard-sized sheets of paper but is printed with four pages on each side and then folded twice (so that it is a quarter the size of the original sheet and half the size of a folio); each set of four leaves is either stitched together with other sets or inserted into a number of others to form a gathering as with a folio; the gatherings are then sewn through the central fold to form a book (which is why, very occasionally, you might come across a book where some of the pages need cutting apart if the print is to be read; the folding of the sheet to form eight pages will always require two edges to be cut after binding). Try folding a sheet of paper and you will see how this works. If you write the page numbers from one to eight on the folded sheet and then unfold it again, you will see that pages 1, 4, 5, and 8 (the "outer forme") are on one side and 2, 3, 6, and 7 (the "inner forme") are on the other, and that only some pages on each side are printed consecutively. (Scholars in fact tend to specify locations in early printed texts not by page numbers, which are notoriously unreliable in books from Shakespeare's day, but by what are called "signatures," which express the physical construction of the book—that is, the number of leaves collected together as a gathering and the number of gatherings that make up the book. Thus B2, or B2r, signifies the front side—recto—of the second sheet in gathering B, while C3v means the reverse side—verso—of the third sheet in gathering C.) A compositor setting either an inner or an outer form was thus not setting the type in the order of the plot, and you can imagine the loss of understanding this might produce at moments of complication in the text, even in an experienced professional. And then of course there is the Elizabethan equivalent of the coffee break to consider: one compositor would at times take over from another and carry on setting the type, and you can see where this has happened because the new compositor has different habits—his own preferences for abbreviating speech prefixes, say—and in a context where there are two characters with similar names he might misunderstand the speech prefix for the one and set it as the other, thus attributing a speech to the wrong speaker—all of which makes it that much harder to determine the nature of the manuscript from which the compositors were working.

If you look at the illustration on the next page, you can see a visual summary of the print workers' tasks. In the right foreground a boy is examining a forme (the frame into which the type is locked for printing) that has been set with type; he seems to be doing a last check against the manuscript while waiting for the forme to be placed in the press. To the far left, a pair of compositors is setting type from typecases, with the manuscript copy from which they are working stuck to the wall in front of them; behind them, a worker is replacing used type into a typecase arranged alphabetically and vertically ("upper-case" letters, i.e., capitals, at the top, "lower-case" below); to his right, a bespectacled proofreader checks an as-yet-uncorrected sheet against copy; in the background, a figure who is just possibly a woman (there is evidence that women worked in, and sometimes even, as printers' widows, owned, print houses) is using absorbent, wool-stuffed leather balls to apply ink to the forme before it is placed on the bed of the press; and, finally, the pressman pulls the bar across to lower the central weight of the press onto the conjunction of inked type and blank paper and thus imprint the sheet.

The first sheet pulled would be handed to the proofreader for checking, and he would mark errors for correction; when he finished, the press would be stopped, the (now very inky) type adjusted to make the corrections, and the process would then continue. The pressman would, however, keep printing sheets during the twenty minutes it might take the proofreader to work through the proof, and those uncorrected sheets (a hundred or so) would be stacked together indiscriminately with the corrected ones in the overall print run (which was 1,200 or so copies in the case of the First Folio), not separated or discarded. The result is that early printed books are a blend of uncorrected and corrected sheets, and no individual copy of a book such

Unknown engraver, after Stradanus (Jan van der Straet), *Invention of Book Printing*,
from *Nova reperta* (New inventions and discoveries of modern times; ca. 1599–1603).

as the Folio is likely to be exactly the same as any other, given the random distribution of uncorrected sheets. If you look closely at the list of textual variants to this
edition, you will see that editors sometimes note when they have selected a corrected
reading from a copy of the base text other than the primary one from which they are
working.

One printing-house factor likely to affect the text was the need for print workers
to "cast off," that is, to work out how many lines of a given manuscript would fit on a
printed page, and to make pencil annotations in the manuscript to mark where page
breaks would fall in print. Occasionally mistakes would be made, and you can see in
the printed text where either a compositor has realized that he still has a lot of words
to set but little space to play with, and so keeps everything tight, or where he is, by
contrast, running out of words yet still has a fair amount of page to fill, and so
deploys white space, printers' ornaments, and the like. For examples of these composition strategies, see pages 80 and 81.

of Romeo and Iuliet.

On Thurſday next be married to the Countie.

   *Iu_: Tell me not Frier that thou hearſt of it,

Vnleſſe thou tell me how we may preuent it.

Giue me ſome ſudden counſell : els behold

Twixt my extreames and me, this bloodie Knife

Shall play the Vmpeere, arbitrating that

Which the Commiſsion of thy yeares and arte

Could to no iſſue of true honour bring.

Speake not, be briefe : for I deſire to die,

If what thou ſpeakſt, ſpeake not of remedie.

   Fr : Stay *Iuliet,* I doo ſpie a kinde of hope,

VVhich craues as deſperate an execution,

As that is deſperate we would preuent.

If rather than to marrie Countie *Paris*

Thou haſt the ſtrength or will to ſlay thy ſelfe,

Tis not vnlike that thou wilt vndertake

A thing like death to chyde away this ſhame,

That coapſt with death it ſelfe to flye from blame.

And if thou dooſt, Ile giue thee remedie.

   Iul : Oh bid me leape (rather than marrie *Paris*)

From off the battlements of yonder tower :

Or chaine me to ſome ſteepie mountaines top,

VVhere roaring Beares and ſauage Lions are :

Or ſhut me nightly in a Charnell-houſe,

VVith reekie ſhankes, and yeolow chaples ſculls :

Or lay me in tombe with one new dead :

Things that to heare them namde haue made me tremble ;

And I will doo it without feare or doubt,

To keep my ſelfe a faithfull vnſtaind VVife

To my deere Lord, my deereſt *Romeo.*

   Fr : Hold *Iuliet,* hie thee home, get thee to bed,

Let not thy Nurſe lye with thee in thy Chamber :

And when thou art alone, take thou this Violl,

And this diſtilled Liquor drinke thou off :

VVhen preſently through all thy veynes ſhall run

A dull and heauie ſlumber, which ſhall ſeaze

H 3

                                                  Each

Q1 *Romeo and Juliet,* H3r. An example of a "tight" page where the casting-off seems to have been efficient.

The excellent Tragedie

Each yitall spirit: for no Pulse shall keepe
His naturall progresse, but surcease to beate:
No signe of breath shall testifie thou liust,
And in this borrowed likenes of shrunke death,
Thou shalt remaine full two and fortie houres.
And when thou art laid in thy Kindreds Vault,
Ile send in hast to *Mantua* to thy Lord,
And he shall come and take thee from thy graue.

    Iul: Frier I goe, be sure thou send for my deare *Romeo.*
                              Exeunt.

Enter olde Capolet, his Wife, Nurse, and
Seruingman.

  Capo: Where are you sirra?
  Ser: Heere forsooth.
  Capo: Goe, prouide me twentie cunning Cookes.
  Ser: I warrant you Sir, let me alone for that, Ile knowe
them by licking their fingers.
  Capo: How canst thou know them so?
  Ser: Ah Sir, tis an ill Cooke cannot licke his owne fin-
gers.
  Capo: Well get you gone.

           Exit Seruingman.

But wheres this Head-strong?
  Moth: Shees gone (my Lord) to Frier *Laurence* Cell
To be confest.
  Capo: Ah, he may hap to doo some good of her,
A headstrong selfewild harlotrie it is.

                            Enter

Q1 *Romeo and Juliet,* H3v. An example of a "loose" page—note the white space and use of the ornament.

These moments of professional adjustment necessarily affect the texts we have inherited, and a close look at the early printed page may explain why lines that seem metrically regular have been set as prose, say, or as fragmented verse lines. Here from the First Quarto of *King Lear* is an example of verse lines that have been squeezed into prose in order to save space:

The Historie of King Lear.

like a riotous Inne;epicurifme,and luſt make more like a tauerne or brothell, then a great pallace; the ſhame it ſelfe doth ſpeake for inſtant remedie; be thou deſired by her, that elſe will take the thing ſhee begs, a little to diſquantitie your traine, and the remainder that ſhall ſtill depend, to bee ſuch men as may beſort your age, that know themſelues and you.

Lear. Darkenes,and Deuils! ſaddle my horſes, call my traine together; degenerate baſtard, ile not trouble thee; yet haue I left a daughter.

Gon. You ſtrike my people;and your diſordred rabble,make ſeruants of their betters,   *Enter Duke.*

Lear. We that too late repent. O ſir,are you come?is it your will that wee prepare any horſes?ingratitude!thou marble harted fiend, more hideous when thou ſheweſt thee in a child,then the Sea-monſter: deteſted kite, thou liſt my traine, and men of choiſe and rareſt parts, that all particulars of dutie knowe, and in the moſt exact regard, ſupport the worſhips of their name?O moſt ſmall fault, how vgly did'ſt thou in *Cordelia* ſhewe, that like an engine wrencht my frame of nature from the fixt place; drew from my heart all loue,and added to the gall.O *Lear!Lear!* beat at this gate that let thy folly in, and thy deere iudgement out;goe,goe, my people.

Duke, My Lord,I am giltles,as I am ignorant.

Lear. It may be ſo my Lord: harke *Nature,* heare deere Goddeſſe; ſuſpend thy purpoſe, if thou did'ſt intend to make this creature fruitful,into her wombe conuey ſterility; drie vp in hir the organs of increaſe,and from her derogate body neuer ſpring a babe to honour her; if ſhee muſt teeme, create her childe of ſpleene, that it may liue and bee a thourt diſſatur'd torment to her; let it ſtampe wrinckles in her brow of youth; with accent teares , fret channels in her cheeks;turne all her mothers paines and benefits to laughter and contempt, that ſhee may feele,that ſhe may feele, how ſharper then a ſerpents tooth it is, to haue a thankleſſe child; goe, goe, my people.

Duke. Now Gods that we adore, whereof comes this !

Gon. Neuer afflict your ſelfe to know the cauſe, but let his diſpoſition haue that ſcope that dotage giues it.

Lear. What,fiftie of my followers at a clap,within a fortnight?

D 2   *Duke.*

Q1 *King Lear*, D2r

And here from the First Quarto of *Henry V* is an example of prose that has been set as rough verse (notice how the first word of each line of Fluellen's speeches is capitalized) in order to stretch it out to fill the available space:

of Henry the fift.

So hath he sworne the like to me.

K. How think you *Flewellen*, is it lawfull he keep his oath?

Fl. And it please your maiesty, tis lawful he keep his vow.
If he be periur'd once, he is as arrant a beggerly knaue,
As treads vpon too blacke shues.

Kin. His enemy may be a gentleman of worth.

Flew. And if he be as good a gentleman as Lucifer
And Belzebub, and the diuel himselfe,
Tis meete he keepe his vowe.

Kin. Well sirrha keep your word.
Vnder what Captain serueft thou?

Soul. Vnder Captaine *Gower*.

Flew. Captaine *Gower* is a good Captaine
And hath good littrature in the warres.

Kin. Go call him hither.

Soul. I will my Lord.

Exit souldier.

Kin. Captain *Flewellen*, when *Alonson* and I was
Downe together, I tooke this gloue off from his helmet,
Here *Flewellen*, weare it. If any do challenge it,
He is a friend of *Alonsons*,
And an enemy to mee.

Fle. Your maieslie doth me as great a fauour
As can be desired in the harts of his subiects.
I would see that man now that should chalenge this gloue:
And it please God of his grace, I would but see him,
That is all.

Kin. *Flewellen* knowst thou Captaine *Gower*?

Fle. Captaine *Gower* is my friend.
And if it like your maieslie, I know him very well.

Kin. Go call him hither.

Flew. I will and it shall please your maieslie.

Kin. Follow *Flewellen* closely at the heeles,
The gloue he weares, it was the souldiers:

F 2

It

Q1 *Henry V*, F2r

Understanding these print-house procedures clarifies how at each stage of the printing process error and variety may be introduced: at the stage of "casting off," at the stage of setting the type from manuscript (especially if the writer had difficult handwriting), at the stages of proofreading and press correction, and in the assembly of corrected and uncorrected sheets into the book itself. Clearly, we need to be wary of assuming that the material features of the early texts unconditionally transmit "authorial intention."

What Kind of Edition Is This?

Editions always exist for readers. There is no more fundamental question for an editor than "For whom am I editing?" because the answer determines very substantially the nature of the edition produced. No edition can be designed for every imaginable reader; on the contrary, specific kinds of editing are done with specific sets of readers in mind. "Diplomatic" editions, for instance, are designed for scholars: they reproduce all the features of the original text without correction or alteration, but for most readers they would make for an unappealing reading experience. An "old-spelling" edition is another possibility: it is edited (that is, an editor has emended the text where error is apparent and included other aids to reading, such as stage directions), but it remains in the spelling (and, perhaps, the punctuation) of Shakespeare's day and is thus again likely to be difficult going for most contemporary readers. Modern-spelling editions are designed to make early modern texts as accessible as possible: the editor makes necessary corrections to the text, adds stage directions where they are needed to clarify the action, makes consistent certain variable features of the original, and modernizes the spelling and punctuation of those texts (while keeping a close eye on moments when the modernizing of spelling or punctuation might change the actual meaning). It is this latter course—the modern-spelling edition designed to offer maximum accessibility for contemporary readers—that *The Norton Shakespeare* adopts, but with certain developments and enhancements and with a specific set of principles for editorial choice.

We—the team of editors who together created this edition—have edited the works of Shakespeare—that is, the existing early texts—from scratch on the basis of a set of principles known as "single-text editing." The first two editions of *The Norton Shakespeare* were based on the text created in 1986 for Oxford University Press—a groundbreaking edition that transformed the modern editing of Shakespeare—but editorial practice has changed since that time, and Norton has created a new text for the present moment. This text is new both in its physical construction and in its theoretical underpinnings.

First, this, the Third Edition of *The Norton Shakespeare,* is "born digital." That is, we have taken the opportunity offered by the interactive ebook format to offer readers and classroom teachers an unprecedented set of options that will allow them to engage with, not just be passive recipients of, the words before them. The Digital Edition allows readers to open textual and performance comments by clicking on icons in the margin next to the line they are reading; to toggle from the text to a facsimile of the original printed folio or quarto; to hear all the songs scattered through the plays; and to listen to eight hours of selected scenes read by professional actors. In addition, readers can view the Quarto and Folio versions of *King Lear* side by side, scrolling as they choose; side-by-side viewing is also available for selected scenes from six plays and for two versions of a sonnet. Readers using the print and electronic editions in combination will be able to move between thumbing through the printed book and navigating the ebook not only for added portability but also in order to find additional versions of fifteen plays plus many enhancements, not least a selection of Textual Comments designed to underline the interconnections of textual decisions and the meaning of the plays.

Second, this edition adopts a new approach to the Shakespearean text, one made possible in part by the opportunities offered by the digital platform. Our underlying editorial principle has been, at its simplest, to edit the *text*, not the *work*. Let us explain what we mean by this with reference in particular to the plays (though there are similar issues with the sonnets). Shakespeare's plays exist in imperfect ways— none of them ideal, none of them perfectly representing what Shakespeare wrote or what his first audiences heard. Editors have always recognized that these surviving printed texts vary in their origins, though all must bear in some way "traces" of the original literary works that Shakespeare wrote out with quill and paper. Lying behind the surviving texts are, variously, authorial drafts, "fair" or scribal copies, theatrical promptbooks, and occasionally unfinished materials—often a mixture of more than one of these. One older editorial tradition sought to address the imperfections present in the texts as a result of this variable provenance by reconstructing, to a greater or lesser extent, an imagined original, creating an edition that—drawing on their professional knowledge of the writing habits of Shakespeare and his contemporaries, of Elizabethan handwriting, and of the printing process—the editors believed to be nearer to what Shakespeare and his audiences would have known or wanted than the actual surviving text with its flaws and imperfections. Of course editors need to correct many of those flaws and imperfections: to give readers a comprehensible reading experience, you must address errors and other distractions. But we believe it is not necessary or even desirable to try to reconstruct a "perfect" work that may never have existed in this form. Consequently, we have made the decision not to do what editors have normally done for centuries, which is to emend at will by merging the differing elements of distinct early texts of a given play, but rather to provide carefully considered editions of each of the early authoritative texts of works for which more than one such text survives. Similarly, in dealing with plays for which only one text survives, we have stayed as close as possible to that text when sense can be made of it, not adopting a traditional emendation if it appears to us to be the product of editorial preference rather than necessary for sense. In other words, we have chosen to edit the *texts* we actually have, not the *play* or the *poem* we do not, to accept uncertainty, and to exercise a certain skepticism toward earlier claims that sometimes made the editor seem a substitute for Shakespeare.

As we have noted, this edition was "born digital"—that is, we set out to invert the prior hierarchy of page and screen by creating an edition that would reach its fullest potential in digital form. Both the print and the digital editions are, in different ways, "complete works." The print volume includes all the poems, some of which exist in various manuscripts and others in print; there is usually only one form of each of these, though we include the entire *Passionate Pilgrim*, which was falsely ascribed to Shakespeare alone but does include some of his poems in variant forms. It—the print volume—includes all the plays too, providing one text for each play (except for *Hamlet*, for which we offer two editions, the First Quarto and a text merging the Second Quarto with materials from the Folio, and *King Lear*, for which we offer editions of the Quarto and the Folio, plus a merged text including all materials in both: for an account of the inclusion of these merged editions, or "conflations," in an edition based on single-text editing principles, see page 87, below. In deciding which of several texts to include in the bound volume we have used a pragmatic and flexible measure. Rather than (as has been done in the past) claiming to be able to determine and present the text that was Shakespeare's "original" version—or his "final" version, or the one that the company probably performed—we have in the case of plays that exist in significantly different texts printed the text that is most complete and apparently most finished. This often means the text in the First Folio, where about half the plays appear for the first time in the only text we have. But when—as, for example, in the case of *Romeo and Juliet* or of *1 Henry IV*—the Folio text is itself derived from a good quarto, we choose that earlier quarto as the base text from which our print edition is created.

We encourage readers to work with both versions, digital and print, to gain the most possible from *The Norton Shakespeare*. Editing Shakespeare digitally enables us to offer readers the opportunity to read, compare, and contrast the two (or, in the case of *Hamlet*, three) early texts of each of the plays for which multiple texts exist. Whether the plays exist in one substantive text or several, we have taken the same approach to the editing—modernizing spelling and punctuation on principles that are consistent across the edition, providing additional stage directions where they are required to clarify the action, and trusting the original text wherever possible, emending only where absolutely necessary and not "reconstructing" material in addition to that provided by the surviving texts.

The primary impact of these choices is, naturally, on those plays for which more than one early substantive text exists. For instance, we provide (in the Digital Edition) edited texts of Quarto *Othello* and Folio *Othello*—two different texts representing, we believe, two subtly different plays. Even when two separate early texts are nearly identical, the differences can be fascinating. Thus, in *Othello*, the female protagonist, Desdemona, infuriates her father by marrying an older man who is both black and a convert from Islam. Her father, who initially voices a series of racist reasons for assuming that Othello had brainwashed his daughter into eloping with him, sees her as shy and almost worryingly asexual (she has shown no interest in the eligible men he has introduced her to), but Othello's narrative of the process by which he wooed her suggests that she is more actively aware of her sexuality than her father believes: "My story being done, / She gave me for my pains a world of sighs. / [. . .] She thanked me / And bade me, if I had a friend that loved her, / I should but teach him how to tell my story, / And that would woo her" (Q 1.3.145–46, 150–53).

> She gaue me for my paines a world of sighes;
> She swore Ifaith twas strange,twas passing strange;
> Twas pittifull,twas wondrous pittifull;

Q1 *Othello*, C3v

So the Quarto. The slightly later Folio version of the play alters one key word: "My story being done, / She gave me for my pains a world of kisses" (F 1.3.158–59).

> She gaue me for my paines a world of kisses:
> She swore in faith 'twas strange :'twas passing strange,
> 'Twas pittifull:'twas wondrous pittifull.

F *Othello*, ss5v

Thus there are two equally coherent versions of the same line, different in one small but significant way. By providing editions of both texts, we avoid the necessity of preferring the one reading over the other (male editors have typically preferred "sighs," just as the editorial tradition seems generally to assume, in the phrasing of inserted stage directions, that men kiss women, not that women and men kiss each other), and we open up for our readers a degree of choice—to read the Quarto with its sighing Desdemona or the Folio with its more ardent, kissing Desdemona—and their decision about which version to read will impact the way they see the tragedy unfolding and thus their interpretation of the play. In this way, the study of the material features of the text and of the meaning of the play are inseparable.

This tiny difference between Quarto *Othello* and Folio *Othello* may represent revised authorial intention or some incidental external influence; we cannot know for certain. But there is a category of difference between Quarto and Folio that reminds us that when we read Shakespeare's plays we are dealing with the substantially collaborative process that is theatrical production—and thus with texts that have in various ways gone through the performance process. The severe reduction in Emilia's and Desdemona's parts in act 4 of Quarto *Othello*—the cutting, for instance, of the "Willow Song" that Desdemona sings before she goes to bed for the last time or of Emilia's wry lines about husbands—may be due not to authorial choice, a decision on Shakespeare's part to reduce the prominence of the women at this late stage of the play, but to theatrical necessity, that is, the presumed absence from the King's Men at one point of boy actors with sufficient singing ability or stamina. Often we can only guess at the reasons for such changes, but the point is that they are very often material and environmental, not intentional in the sense of being deliberate changes made for artistic reasons by the author. Yet they cannot be dismissed simply as "inauthentic," not only because we do not know Shakespeare's role at such moments but also because all staged plays are necessarily constructed through collaborative engagement between text and actor. Furthermore, for readers and playgoers across subsequent centuries, these renegotiated texts, offering evidence of multiple inputs for a range of practical reasons, were the "real" Shakespeare. Knowing about the practical processes of playwriting, performance, and printing enables the reader to gain a fuller understanding of the nature of the Shakespearean text as an expression of the highly socialized process of dramatic creativity.

We have noted in passing that, across the centuries, the borders of the Shakespeare canon have been fluid. For a century and a half, the *King Lear* that audiences saw in the theater was not Shakespeare's *King Lear* as we know it, but an adaptation of the play created by Irish poet and playwright Nahum Tate in the late seventeenth century that radically cut and altered the original, even providing a happy ending that suited the theatrical expectations of the day but looks to us bewilderingly inappropriate. Once the popularity of the Tate version had faded, the *King Lear* that audiences began to see reverted to "Shakespeare's *King Lear*"—or, rather, to a particular version of that play, one that editors (and directors) assembled from the two markedly different early texts, Quarto and Folio, by including as many of the different lines as possible from each and merging or "conflating" them into a play a few hundred lines longer than either of the early texts. The paradox is obvious—in the process of trying to present the reader with a "Shakespearean" text, editors produced a text different from either of the ones for which Shakespeare was responsible—yet for readers from the mid-nineteenth to the late twentieth centuries, this elongated version of *King Lear* was the one they read and grew to know and love as "Shakespeare's" play.

This history underpins the decision of *The Norton Shakespeare* to include, alongside editions of the early texts of *Hamlet* and *King Lear*, a further, "scars and stitches" conflated edition of each—that is, an edition of each play that, by way of indentation and a distinctive yet quiet difference in font, makes the process of conflation visible without intruding excessively on the pleasure of the reading experience. We provide these multiple options because they will enable readers to see how these texts changed, developed, and were remade across time. In the case of *King Lear*, it is very possible that Shakespeare was involved in reworking his tragedy a couple of years after he had first written it and it had gone into regular production, and readers can reflect on that dynamic process by comparing the two early versions; equally, they can choose to read the "scars and stitches" edition, which both replicates the experience of nineteenth- and twentieth-century readers who came to know the play through traditional conflated editions and makes visible the process through which that conflation was achieved. Thus in the Digital Edition we offer three versions of *King Lear*—and four of *Hamlet*—so as to enable readers to witness the dynamic and contingent processes that go into the bringing-into-the-present of Shakespeare's plays.

"Single-Text Editing" and the Treatment of Error

The Norton Shakespeare seeks to minimize intervention by the editor, but there are nonetheless occasions when the editor must assist the reader in making sense of the text and where it is not immediately obvious how to do so. In order to explain our decision making at such moments, we will offer some examples. Readers will see that for all texts in this edition, both print and digital, we offer in the Digital Edition a set of Textual Variants, compressed notes in which editors mark each moment where the edited version is in some way different from the "base text," that is, from the original quarto or folio text from which the edition is formed, specifying where the preferred word or other feature originates—from another early text, or from the editorial tradition, or from our own choice. No edition of a Shakespeare play can simply present the exact words of its base text, because no early text is free from error or complication. How many times, after all, reading a modern printed book, have you spotted errors, omissions, or typos? Even with the vast technological transformations since Shakespeare's death, the printing process remains flawed; so you would expect that any text printed in (or somewhat after) Shakespeare's day—created on a manually operated press using fiddly metal type set by hand in wooden frames, in often cramped conditions, using toxic ink, and always under pressure to speed up the process to keep the business afloat—would include a fair number of such errors. As we have noted, the print-house workers were actively involved in the creation of the Shakespearean text, an involvement that is by no means limited to error—but human error is inevitable and pervasive.

Consequently, editors working on the basis of single-text editing must always balance their commitment to the text against the possibility of error. Our basic premise is that the editor should not attempt to alter or "improve"—by following a different text, the editorial tradition, or her own informed invention—any reading that can make sense, even if that meaning seems a little strained. While such difficulties may arise from print-house errors, they may instead be signs of the semantic or syntactical differences between our current version of the English language and that of the late sixteenth and early seventeenth centuries. Single-text editing compels editors— and their readers—to make an effort to understand the given text, rather than to slide into something apparently more familiar. This is known as the principle of the "harder reading" (in Latin, *lectio difficilior*), and it expresses our urge not to risk obliterating the powerful specificity and difference of Shakespeare's works, even as it remains the editor's task to address error when it is undoubtedly present.

The multiplicity of early authoritative texts sometimes confronts the editor adhering to single-text-editing principles with difficult decisions. For example, at one point in the Folio text of *Troilus and Cressida,* Thersites is abusing Patroclus: "Let thy bloud be thy direction till thy death," he sneers, "then, if she that laies thee out sayes thou art a fair coarse [i.e., corpse], I'll be sworne and sworne upon't, she never shrowded any but Lazars." The earlier Quarto reads the central section as follows: "if she that layes thee out sayes thou art not a fair course," and it seems clear that the Folio corrects the Quarto reading, since the "not" makes nonsense of the meaning ("You'll be so ugly by the time you die that if the person laying out your corpse says you're beautiful then the only possible conclusion would be that the dead bodies she usually buries must all be lepers"). The editor therefore emends by removing the "not" from her Quarto edition on the grounds that while single-text editing normally requires her to maintain differences between cognate texts—that is, between texts of the same play that have reached us through different processes of transmission— she must not do this at the expense of sense.

By contrast, the two texts of *King Lear* provide a fine instance of the presence or absence of a word—again, as it happens, "not"—offering equal sense in two cognate texts. At the very end of the long first scene in the Folio, Lear's daughters Goneril and Regan talk together about their aging father's increasingly erratic behavior, and

Goneril notes that "the obseruation we haue made of it hath beene little"—an expression of regret for not taking notice of these mood swings before they led to the current crisis:

> *Gon.* You see how full of changes his age is, the obseruation we haue made of it hath beene little:he alwaies lou'd our Sister most,and with what poore iudgement he hath now cast her off,appeares too grossely.

In the Quarto, however, Goneril notes that "the obseruation we haue made of it hath *not* bin little" (our italics)—that is, that the sisters have in fact been aware of the problem for quite a while:

> *Gon.* You see how full of changes his age is the obseruation we haue made of it hath not bin little; hee alwaies loued our sister most, and with what poore iudgement hee hath now cast her off, appeares too grosse.

It is this earlier version that is invariably chosen by conflating editors and is thus the reading that those who already know *King Lear* will recognize. Yet it is not the only meaningful option. Both readings make sense, even if one is less familiar, and the advantage of single-text editing is that the editor is not forced to choose one option and thus to dilute the possibilities for meaning on both page and stage.

We briefly mentioned earlier one of the best-known cruxes in *Othello*, the moment at which the protagonist, just prior to his suicide, compares himself to a racial other who also failed to recognize the extraordinary value of what he had until he lost it. In the Quarto, the lines read "one whose hand, / Like the base *Indian*, threw a pearle away, / Richer then all his Tribe"; this has, marginally, been the version preferred by editors across time:

> Perplext in the extreame ; of one whose hand,
> Like the base *Indian*, threw a pearle away,
> Richer then all his Tribe : of one whose subdued eyes,

In the Folio, the lines read "one, whose hand / (Like the base Iudean) threw a Pearle away / Richer then all his Tribe"—the "Judean" here probably being associated with Christ's betrayer, Judas Iscariot, and thus, for Shakespeare's audiences, with Jews in general:

> Perplexed in the extreame : Of one, whose hand
> (Like the base Iudean) threw a Pearle away
> Richer then all his Tribe: Of one,whose subdu'd Eyes,

Note two elements here. First, the punctuation differs; neither version can be said to be either *better* or *more authorial* than the other in this regard (the parentheses in the Folio, for instance, are probably the preference of the King's company scribe, Ralph Crane, who transcribed several plays for inclusion in the Folio). Second, the difference between "*Indian*" and "*Iudean*" could be attributed to two kinds of easy error: a misreading of a scratchy secretary-hand "i" for "e" (or vice versa)—

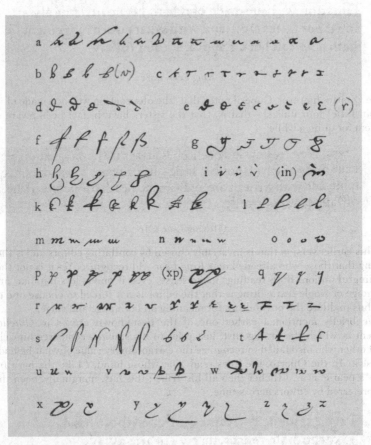

Sample minuscules in secretary hand from Ronald B. McKerrow, *An Introduction to Bibliography for Literary Students*, Oxford 1927.

—and an accidental inversion of the individual type "n" for "u" (or vice versa) by the compositor. The vice versas underline the impossibility of deciding which is "correct," and the presence in *The Norton Shakespeare* of editions of both early texts removes the need for the imposition of editorial preference.

Single-text editing thus seeks to minimize editorial intervention while remaining aware of the needs of the reader and offering clarification (e.g., in the form of expanded or inserted stage directions, which we mark with square brackets) of action, speaker, or other elements of the original that may delay the reader's progress through the play. For these pragmatic reasons, we have chosen to maintain certain traditional overarching elements that could be considered to run counter to the theory of single-text editing. An instance is our division of almost all play texts into acts and scenes, an editorial practice that dates back to the eighteenth century. Such neat divisions are by no means always present in the base texts—either in the Folio, which is not always consistent or precise in its divisions (*Love's Labor's Lost,* for instance, has two different acts marked "*Actus Quartus*"; Folio *Hamlet* stops marking act divisions after act 2), or in the various quartos, many of which either mark scene divisions only or offer no divisions or numbers at all. Act divisions only became fully formalized with the development of indoor playhouses, where the necessity of trimming the candles every half-hour or so required breaks in the action; they thus apply far less to Elizabethan plays than to Jacobean. Our working premise for this edition, however, is that many of our readers will wish to locate scholarly discussions of these plays by critics who, almost without exception, cite speeches by act and scene number; thus, we offer act and scene numbers for all main texts and reserve scene divisions only for a handful of quartos that do not fall into the usual divisions.

The single-text editor's task is not necessarily more straightforward when she is dealing with plays with only one early authoritative text. One of the key questions anyone editing on single-text-editing principles has to ask is when to emend and when to leave alone. An instance comes in *All's Well That Ends Well*, which opens (in our modernized version) with this stage direction:

> *Enter young* BERTRAM, *Count of Roussillon, his mother* [*the Dowager* COUNTESS], *and* HELEN, *Lord* LAFEU, *all in black.*

The "*and*" seems to be in an odd place here; that is, you might expect it to be positioned between "HELEN" and "*Lord*," completing the list. Yet it comes instead between "*Mother*" and "HELEN." Is this simply a mistake by the compositor? It could easily be. Often, editors simply move the "*and*" to what seems to be the logical place between "HELEN" and "*Lord*." But what if there is a different logic to its positioning? It might be that Shakespeare is using the conjunction to separate two pairs: to connect Bertram and his mother on the one hand, and Helen and Lafeu on the other. Equally, the "*and*" might serve to connect the Countess and Helen, a connection that proves particularly resilient in the action to follow. Rather than limit the possibilities, we leave the stage direction as it is in the Folio, simply modernizing and standardizing the names and clarifying (with "dowager") that the Countess is the widow of Bertram's father. A theater director might wish to think about the staging options this stage direction offers.

All of these editorial challenges inevitably require the creation of something hybrid, something impure, despite the earnest intentions of the regularizing editor. Editing is always negotiation, and it is always compromise. This does not mean it is slapdash or arbitrary; on the contrary, it must be exceptionally precise, requiring a level of patience and concentration that is not everyone's forte. The paradox for editors is that the outcome of good work—words or lines or stage directions that took a great deal of experience, research, and agonizing to establish—will be simply, and rightly, invisible to the reader. In this, the editor's lot is not so very different—structurally, if not creatively—from that of the collaborating playwright. Effective collaboration is about effacing the joins between the work of different contributors—we presume that Shakespeare and Fletcher, composing *Henry VIII* and *The Two Noble Kinsmen* together, would not have wanted audience members to register when the writing of a given scene switched from the one to the other—and the quiet collaboration across time that is the work of the editor ought by definition to be hidden, at least in the case of editions created for the general reader and the advanced student who do not want or need the intrusion of the mediator.

Shakespeare and the Multiplication of Meaning

Most people, reading a Shakespeare poem or play, have in mind the question "What did Shakespeare mean here?" as they reflect on the words, especially if the words are not easy to make sense of. Despite the profound ways in which the Romantic construction of authorship as a process of untrammeled, transcendent individual inspiration has been questioned and deconstructed over the last half-century, the general understanding of the processes of writing, as of all forms of creativity, remains firmly bound up with ideas of intention, of textual "ownership," of the creative artist as "author"— that is, as the sole source of "authority" in respect of the form and meaning of a given text. We have tried in this introduction to suggest that the meanings of Shakespeare's plays and poems have a wider range of starting points, emerge from a more complex, varied, and fascinating creative base, than simply what the poet himself "meant"—in other words, that Shakespearean "authenticity" is a multivalent concept, one that includes at its core what the author meant but also a range of other, contiguous collaborations, negotiations, and origins for meaning. The Shakespearean text is fluid and multiple, and the nature of the engagement of both editor and reader with that text should, we believe, follow suit. We have much to gain by being open to the increased possibilities this transformed understanding can bring. The very words themselves are, in so many ways, unfixed in their meanings; the ways through which they came into the public domain in Shakespeare's own day—in manuscript, on the stage, in the various print formats available to those seeking to profit from publication—are also multiple; and the ways in which the plays and poems have been presented and re-presented in subsequent centuries make "multiple" seem a gross understatement. Shakespeare seems to have re-thought and re-imagined his own writings; his colleagues in the King's Men negotiated and adapted his work to suit conditions; publishers printed it in a range of ways, official and unofficial, working with Shakespeare himself on the poems if not on the plays (we have no evidence that Shakespeare—unlike his friend and rival Ben Jonson—oversaw the printing of his plays, whereas he clearly did pay attention to the publication of his poems), and his former colleagues gathered most, though not all, of the plays into a single, rather grandiose Folio in 1623, initiating the long tradition of editing the works to make them available for the "great variety of readers." *The Norton Shakespeare* offers its readers a set of options for reading and understanding Shakespeare that makes the most both of the digital technologies and of the editorial practices of the present, giving the reader choices—of text, of taxonomy, of glossarial support—and in the process providing the means for a new generation actively to discover, engage with, learn from, and—above all—be thrilled and moved by these astonishing works in all their fabulous multiplicity.

The Theater of Shakespeare's Time

HOLGER SCHOTT SYME

Early modern London was a theatrical city like no other, as the travel writer Fynes Moryson proudly proclaimed: "as there be, in my opinion, more plays in London than in all parts of the world I have seen, so do these players or comedians excel all others in the world." Moryson wrote just after Shakespeare's death, around 1619, but the world of playacting he described had thrived in and around England's capital long before Shakespeare arrived there. The decades between 1567, when the first theater built in England since the Romans opened its doors, and 1642, when playacting was prohibited by Parliament, saw an unprecedented and still unparalleled flourishing of theatrical artistry. Moryson's account emphasizes not just the quality of London's actors, but also the sheer quantity of plays on offer: as far as he was concerned, there was more theater in the city than anywhere else in the world. The historical record bears out his impression. English acting companies, driven by a constant hunger for new work, kept dozens of dramatists busy writing a staggering number of plays—more than 2,500 works, of which just over 500 survive. Theaters sprang up all around London in the 1570s. Throughout Shakespeare's career, there were never fewer than four acting venues in operation; some years, up to nine theaters were competing for audiences. Different spaces and different companies catered to different tastes and income brackets: the tiny indoor location of the Boys of St. Paul's, an acting company of youths, could accommodate fewer than 100 of the wealthy courtiers and law students who were their typical spectators; the Swan Theater, on the other hand, the largest of the open-air venues that were the most common type of theater in Shakespeare's London, had room for over 3,000 people from all social backgrounds. The theater was rich and varied, an engine of artistic experiment and a place where traditions flourished; it was an art form both elite and popular; it provided entertainment for kings and queens even as their governments worried that it was difficult to control, attracting large and boisterous crowds and posing a threat to public health during plague outbreaks.

In London, theater was everywhere. But *what* was it? Who performed it, where, under what circumstances, using what methods and techniques, and for whom?

History

Before we can approach these questions, a few words about historical evidence are in order. Theater is a transitory art, not designed to leave behind lasting records or traces; it is, as Shakespeare never tired of noting, a kind of dream. In Shakespeare's time, it was a pursuit about which the government cared only intermittently, and was therefore rarely the subject of official recordkeeping. Much of what we know about playhouses and acting companies derives from squabbles over money and the lawsuits that followed. What information survives is just enough to make theater historians realize how much has been lost. For instance, with few exceptions, we do not know who performed which roles. We cannot name a single character Shakespeare played. Even for the most famous actors of the age, we can list at most a handful of parts. Nor do we know how popular most of Shakespeare's plays were. His history plays, more than his tragedies or comedies, sold well as books—but did they do as well on stage? We would like to think so, but without attendance records, we cannot know for sure. *Much Ado About Nothing* was never reprinted on its own after its initial publication in 1600. Does that mean it was a theatrical flop too? Probably not—else why print it at all? But we cannot be certain.

One extant document contains a tremendous amount of information: Philip Henslowe's business record, known as his *Diary*. Henslowe was a financier who owned three theaters and served as a financial manager of sorts for the acting companies that rented his venues. The *Diary* includes performance records from 1592 through 1597, mostly for the Lord Admiral's Men. It allows us to get a sense of this company's business practices, its repertory of plays, its inventory of props and costumes, and its dealings with playwrights and artisans. And the *Diary* makes us realize just how many plays have disappeared: it mentions about 280 titles, of which at most 31 survive.

This may all sound rather depressing, as if the story of Shakespeare's theater were ultimately irretrievable. But it is not. We can interpret archaeological discoveries; extrapolate from extant records such as Henslowe's or the accounts of court officials; trace contemporary responses to the theater in letters, diaries, satires, and polemics; and study plays and their stage directions to understand what features playwrights expected in playhouses and how they intended to use them. We can make the most of what survives to construct a tentative and careful, but not baseless, narrative of what this world may have been like.

Playhouses

Theater in Shakespeare's London was predominantly an outdoor activity. Most playhouses were open-air spaces much larger than the few indoor venues. The building simply called The Theatre, in the suburb of Shoreditch, north of the City of London, created a model in 1576 that many playhouses would follow for the next forty years. It was a fourteen-sided polygonal structure, nearly round, with an external diameter of about seventy-two feet; audiences stood in the open yard or sat in one of three galleries. There was probably a permanent stage, which thrust out into the yard, with the galleries behind it serving as a balcony over the performance area and, where they were walled off, providing a backstage area (the "tiring house" in early modern terminology). The Theatre may not have had a roof over its stage. The Rose Theater in Southwark, across the Thames from the City of London, was built without such a roof in 1587; one was added during renovations in 1592. The shape of the stage also changed over time: archaeological excavations have shown that the Rose's original stage was relatively shallow, not extending far into the yard. In 1592, the space was redesigned to allow the stage to thrust out farther, creating a deeper playing area surrounded by standing spectators on three sides. This model would be followed in later playhouses, but whereas the Rose's stage (and probably those of other early theaters as well) tapered toward the front, later ones were rectangular and thus quite large. Judging from the erosion around the stage area in the excavated Rose, audiences responded with enthusiasm to the new configuration, pressing as close to the action as possible.

This first generation of playhouses also included The Theatre's close neighbor in Shoreditch, the Curtain, built in 1577 and named not after a stage curtain, which these theaters did not have, but after its location, the "Curtain Estate." The Theatre, the Curtain, and the Rose resembled one another in size and shape and had room for 2,000–2,500 spectators. The next generation of theaters did not depart from the earlier model in shape, but anticipated larger crowds. The Swan (1595), the Globe (1599), and the last outdoor theater erected in London, the Hope (1613), had a capacity of about 3,000. They were impressive buildings not just because of their size but

This view of London's northern suburbs shows the Curtain playhouse (the three-story polygonal structure with the flag on the left). It aptly illustrates the almost rural location of these early theaters: the Curtain stands adjacent to farmhouses and windmills.

also because they were beautifully decorated, as foreign visitors reported. Johannes de Witt, a Dutchman, described the Swan in 1596 as an "amphitheater of obvious beauty," admiring its wooden columns painted to look like marble.

Although some of the later playhouses modified the formula set by The Theatre, all the open-air venues shared a common spatial and social logic. They all separated their audience into those standing in the yard (the "groundlings" or "understanders"), who paid a penny to enter the theater, and those who sat in one of the galleries, paying two pennies for the lower level or three for the upper levels, where the benches had cushions. The most exclusive seats, at sixpence, were in the "lords' rooms," probably located in the sections of the galleries closest to the stage, and possibly in the balcony over the stage. Fashionable gallants and wealthy show-offs could also sit on the stage itself, paying an additional sixpence for a stool. Neither the "lords' rooms" nor the stools onstage gave the best view of the play, but they provided unparalleled opportunities to put fancy clothes on display: these were seats for being seen. Stage-sitting was often satirized as a vain and foolish habit, and the groundlings evidently objected to the rich fops blocking their view. As Shakespeare's contemporary Thomas Dekker describes the scene at one of the outdoor theaters, the "scarecrows in the yard hoot at you, hiss at you, spit at you, yea, throw dirt even in your teeth: 'tis most Gentlemanlike patience to endure all this, and to laugh at the silly animals."

The theaters, though hierarchically structured, were unusually inclusive: audience members from all social spheres could gain admission and enjoy the same spectacles. Social hierarchies became dangerously porous in this shared space, as Dekker's stage-sitters experienced firsthand: the commoners in the yard could hurl abuse and even dirt at the gentle and noble audience members onstage. Lords had to suffer close proximity with their social inferiors. However, the playhouses' inclusiveness had limits, too: the poor and royalty were unlikely to enter a theater. Neither Queen Elizabeth I nor King James I ever did.

Purpose-built theaters were not the only places where plays were performed. From the mid-1570s on, four inns also regularly hosted acting companies: the Bell, the Bull, the Cross Keys, and the Bell Savage. Only one of them, the Bell, seems to have had an indoor hall for play performances; the others had yards in which a stage could be erected. These yards had open galleries to give guests access to rooms on the upper floors, so that the overall structure of the auditorium was similar to the theaters: an open yard surrounded by galleries, at least some of which would have had benches. Unlike the theaters, however, which stood in the suburbs surrounding London, the inns were within or just outside the city walls. This location made them favored acting sites in the winter, when the roads were unpredictable and the days

A Victorian photograph of the Elizabethan galleried yard of the White Hart Inn in Southwark, similar to the layout of the inns used for performing plays.

were short, making it difficult for audience members to return to the City before the gates were shut at nightfall. But the inns irked London authorities. No venues other than churches allowed for the assembly of as many people as inn yards did, and play performances could attract particularly unruly crowds. For the authorities, these places created a threat of public disorder right in the heart of the City, and for over two decades, Lord Mayors and aldermen made intermittent attempts to shut down acting at the inns. It seems they succeeded by 1596, since references to regular performances in those venues cease after that year.

No adult acting company regularly performed in an indoor space in London between 1576 and 1610. There were a number of such venues, though, notably a very small theater near St. Paul's Cathedral, with room for only a select few, and a somewhat larger space inside the former Blackfriars friary. Both were active in the 1570s and 1580s, when two children's companies used them—acting troupes made up of choirboys from the royal chapels and St. Paul's Cathedral. By the time Shakespeare arrived in London, however, the old Blackfriars had closed, and neither space was used during the 1590s. But the boys' companies started performing again around the turn of the century, acting exclusively indoors.

This reemergence lies behind the conversation between Rosencrantz and Hamlet about the "eyrie of children" that produce plays mocking "the common stages." Although the boys' companies could not seriously jeopardize the adult troupes' economic success, their reappearance around 1600 apparently made their grown-up competitors look unfashionable among the trendiest patrons. Exclusivity was the hallmark of these companies and their indoor theaters, which were referred to as "private" playhouses; unlike the "common" theaters, these venues kept the wider world out both architecturally and socially. Entrance fees were much higher, probably starting at sixpence (the price of the costliest seats in the open-air theaters) and going up to over two shillings.

The boys also performed less frequently than the adult companies. They made the most of their elite status, thriving on satirical plays and a willingness to court controversy that sometimes landed them in hot water with persons of influence. Their financial situation was as unstable as their favor with the authorities. When King James, in March 1608, shut down the children's company that was using a recently constructed theater inside the former Blackfriars monastery, he unwittingly made theater history. Soon thereafter, the decades-old division between outdoor adult and indoor boys' companies came to an end. In 1610, near the end of Shakespeare's career, the King's Men adopted the Blackfriars as a second venue. Even after that, however, most audiences would still have experienced plays in the outdoor playhouses that remained the most popular, accessible, and visible acting venues in and around London.

Companies and Repertories

What was an acting company in Shakespeare's time? Formally, a group of players serving a noble patron. A law of 1572 had forced performers to find official sponsors to avoid legal prosecution as "vagrants" and "masterless men." That is why the troupe with which Shakespeare was associated for most of his documented career was first known as the Lord Chamberlain's Servants, and after 1603 as the King's Servants: these actors were officially servants of the Lord Chamberlain (the member of the Privy Council in charge of the royal household), and later of King James I. (Modern scholars generally refer to these companies as the Lord Chamberlain's Men and the King's Men.) All companies resident in London for at least part of the year were associated with high-ranking noblemen. After 1603, most of these troupes came under royal patronage, formally serving the King, the Queen, or a member of their family.

In all likelihood, the connection between patrons and companies was fairly loose, although the players technically formed part of their patrons' households. Take the example of James's son-in-law, the Count Palatine: his troupe, the Palsgrave's Men, operated under that name from 1613 to 1632, although their supposed patron only lived in England for a few months from 1612 to 1613. Links may have been closer where companies were sponsored by nobles of lower rank, as was common throughout the kingdom. Dozens of these groups appear in contemporary records. They toured the towns, cities, and stately homes surrounding their lords' seats, returning at Christmas to entertain families and guests. Whether they visited London is unclear, as is the question of what plays they performed; but some of them were so active on the road that they probably traveled to the country's biggest city as well.

What most defined a company were its leading members: the actors who would typically take on all major roles and who jointly owned the troupe's stock of costumes, props, and, crucially, play scripts. There were between six and a dozen of these "sharers." They not only formed the heart of any acting company, but also had an immediate financial interest in its success, as they divided the weekly profits among themselves. But there was more to a troupe of actors than its sharers. When the King's Men received their royal patent, or license, in 1603, the document not only identified the nine sharers (Shakespeare among them) as "servants" of James I, but also recognized that those servants required further "associates" to stage plays. These hired actors could in some cases be as closely associated with a company as the sharers. John Sincklo, for example, was a member of the Chamberlain's Men for most of their existence and is mentioned by name in the stage directions to three of Shakespeare's plays. He was apparently an extraordinarily thin man and is often linked with very skinny characters—in 1 Henry IV he played the Beadle whom Doll Tearsheet calls a "thin man in a censer." Sincklo was a fixture of Chamberlain's Men productions for playwrights and audiences alike, and an integral part of their identity. Yet despite this status,

Sincklo continued to be an employee rather than an owner of the company for the rest of his recorded life.

The theatrical power of one other set of actors likewise outstripped their institutional power within the company: the male youths who played all female roles. These "boys"—in reality, adolescents who would not have started acting before they were twelve or thirteen and sometimes continued into their early twenties—were associated with the companies as sharers' apprentices. In effect, therefore, none of the actors who played Shakespeare's great female roles, from Tamora to Lady Macbeth to Hermione, were officially members of an acting troupe; rather, they belonged to a sharer's household. Each boy was contracted to serve his master for at least seven years, in return for instruction, room, and board. But officially, they would not have been in training as actors, since there was no guild for actors (and thus no official training available). Instead, they formally became apprentices in the trade governed by the guild to which their master belonged. For example, John Heminges, one of the leading sharers in Shakespeare's troupe, was a member of the Company of Grocers, the guild that oversaw that trade. Over thirty years, he had about ten apprentices. Since Heminges did not actually work as a grocer, these youths were probably boy actors, being trained as stage performers. If they completed their term, though, they could pay a fee and become "freemen" of the Company of Grocers and citizens of London—positions that came with many legal advantages and privileges. Although many boy actors did not become leading men, the social status they gained by formally completing an apprenticeship left them free to make their way in life after their careers as players had ended.

Although increasingly integrated into London's social life over the course of Shakespeare's career, most acting companies also spent part of the year touring market towns and stately homes. Acting was frowned upon if not strictly forbidden in London during Lent, the forty days or so before Easter, and companies had to go elsewhere to secure an income then; there was also a long-standing custom of traveling during the summer, when days were longer and roads more reliable (see the map of touring routes in the map appendix, below). Many companies only knew this itinerant existence, and it was their

Money was collected in small, round earthenware containers that had to be smashed after a performance. Many fragments of these were found during the excavation of the Rose playhouse.

work that the young Shakespeare may have seen in Stratford. But around the time he began working as a theater professional some companies had started to regard London as their home. By the 1590s, that group included Lord Strange's Men, the Admiral's Men, and the Earl of Pembroke's Men. They established long-term relationships with the owners of playhouses where they performed more or less permanently. The Admiral's Men became associated with the Rose and later the Fortune, both theaters belonging to Philip Henslowe. The Chamberlain's Men, founded in 1594, started at The Theatre, owned by James Burbage (whose son Richard would soon emerge as the troupe's young star). Pembroke's Men may have been the resident company at the Swan once that playhouse opened in 1595. A further troupe probably occupied the Curtain. By 1599 yet another company, the Earl of Derby's Men, took up residence at the Boar's Head. In fact, so many acting troupes performed in London that there were never fewer than four venues in operation during Shakespeare's career, and in some years the city sustained nine theaters.

The proprietors of most of those playhouses rented their buildings to the actors for a share of the revenues: half the takings from the galleries belonged to the landlord, while the sharers in the company retained all income from the yard and the other half of the takings from the galleries. Troupes and theater owners thus divided profits as well as risk: if a play flopped, the landlord also lost income, just as he gained from popular offerings. Some owners, Henslowe in particular, acted as the company's financial manager, keeping stock of belongings and conducting transactions on the actors' behalf.

Despite the great variety of playhouses and acting companies, or perhaps because of it, some venues developed specific profiles. This happened surprisingly early in the history of London theater. Writing in 1579, the antitheatrical polemicist Stephen Gosson excluded some plays from his general criticism, praising two "shown at the Bull"; two others "usually brought into the Theater"; and especially "the two prose books played at the Bell Savage, where you shall find never a word without wit, never a line without pith, never a letter placed in vain." Within a few years of opening, then, two of the inns and The Theatre were already known for specific plays one could expect to see there—whereas the four venues Gosson does not mention may have staged precisely the kinds of plays of which he disapproved.

All the same, few playhouses or acting companies were famous exclusively for a handful of titles or a particular kind of drama. The repertories of most troupes, including the Chamberlain's Men and King's Men, were inclusive in their approach to themes and genres and combined old favorites with new and potentially challenging material. The King's Men's 1603 patent describes them as performing not only "comedies, tragedies, histories"—the kinds of plays we might expect from Shakespeare's company—but also "interludes, morals, pastorals." Shakespeare's works do not represent all these categories, and they likely do not represent the full range of shows his troupe staged. If Henslowe's *Diary* is a reliable model, companies commissioned ten to twenty plays each year, and new plays dominated their repertory. If a play failed to draw crowds, it disappeared quickly. If it had staying power, it would remain in circulation for a while, but few became recognized classics destined to be revived every couple of years. In general, it seems that audiences enjoyed periodically reencountering older scripts, but had a more voracious appetite for fresh material—although old stories might frequently return in novel versions. Companies would produce their own take on plays from competing repertories: the Admiral's Men paid Ben Jonson in 1602 for a script about Richard III, for instance; and the Chamberlain's Men bought Jonson's *Every Man in His Humor* in 1598, probably hoping to capitalize on a 1597 hit at the Rose, George Chapman's *Comedy of Humors*. Even a single troupe's repertory might feature multiple plays drawn from the same stories or materials. The King's Men owned another *Richard II* play, which they staged at the Globe in April 1611—within weeks of performances of *Macbeth*, *Cymbeline*, and *The Winter's Tale*. Of those three Shakespearean offerings, the latter two were then still quite new; but *Macbeth* would have been a revival, an indication that it was a success when first performed.

The repertory system required daily turnover. Staging the same play for days at a time, let alone for weeks, was practically unheard of. The nine consecutive performances of Thomas Middleton's *A Game at Chess* at the Globe in 1624 were described as extraordinary at the time—nowadays, of course, a run of nine nights would be notable for its brevity. We can get a glimpse of what a typical selection of shows would have looked like in Shakespeare's company from Henslowe's *Diary*, which contains the only surviving sample of the Chamberlain's Men's repertory (staged in collaboration with the Admiral's Men in June 1594):

MON 3 June	*Hesther and Ahasuerus*
TUE 4 June	*The Jew of Malta*
WED 5 June	*Titus Andronicus*

THU 6 June	*Cutlack*
SAT 8 June	*Belin Dun*
SUN 9 June	*Hamlet*
MON 10 June	*Hesther and Ahasuerus*
TUE 11 June	*The Taming of a Shrew*
WED 12 June	*Titus Andronicus*
THU 13 June	*The Jew of Malta*

The two companies performed seven different plays in ten days. Of those, two were tragedies based on fictional plots (*The Jew of Malta* and *Titus Andronicus*), two were tragedies set in the distant northern European past (*Cutlack* and *Hamlet*—the latter not Shakespeare's version), one was a biblical drama (*Hesther and Ahasuerus*), one was a history or tragedy drawn from the English chronicles (*Belin Dun*, about a highwayman hanged by King Henry I), and one was a comedy (*The Taming of a Shrew*—again, not Shakespeare's). One play was brand-new (*Belin Dun*); one recent (*Titus Andronicus*, first performed in January 1594); two quite old (*The Jew of Malta* and *The Taming of a Shrew* were probably written before 1590); and we know nothing about the others.

The two companies' combined offerings constitute a representative mixture of old and new; of different geographical settings and historical periods; of tragic, heroic, moral, and comedic entertainments. Variety was a predictable feature of any company's stock of plays. Predictability, however, was not. For theatergoers keen to see a performance of *Titus* after its successful June 5 outing, finding out when the play was going to be mounted next was neither easy nor straightforward (we now know that their next chance would have come on June 12). They may have relied on word of mouth, as the actors commonly announced the next day's play at the end of a show; they might have encountered the players marching through the City in the morning hours, advertising that day's performance; or they may have read the news on one of the playbills posted daily all over the City to inform audiences what was being staged where. But would-be spectators had to keep their eyes peeled: while repertories responded to popular demand, they did not follow an easily foreseeable schedule. Since *Titus* did well, it would certainly be back onstage soon. But exactly when was uncertain.

Why Shakespeare's Company Was Different

The playhouse in which the Chamberlain's Men and the King's Men performed after 1599, the Globe, was a unique building project. In 1597 James Burbage's lease for the land on which The Theatre stood ran out, and a year later the Chamberlain's Men were forced to vacate the premises and move to the neighboring Curtain. The building itself, however, still belonged to Burbage, and after his death in 1597, to his sons Cuthbert and Richard, the latter Shakespeare's fellow sharer. The Burbages therefore took the extraordinary step of having a carpenter dismantle the structure and use the salvaged timber to build a new playhouse. This would be erected on a plot of land on the other side of London, south of the river and across the street from Henslowe's Rose Theater. This new theater, the Globe, would be significantly bigger than its predecessor. As archaeological digs have revealed, it was probably a sixteen-sided polygon with a diameter of about eighty-five feet, nearly fourteen feet more than The Theatre's. It was operational by September 1599, when the Swiss traveler Thomas Platter saw a performance of *Julius Caesar* at what he called "the straw-thatched house"—almost certainly the Globe, which had a thatched roof over the galleries and stage.

Opening a new playhouse right next to the small and aging Rose might look like an aggressive gesture on the Burbages' part, bringing the Chamberlain's Men into direct competition with the Admiral's Men. In such a turf-war narrative, Burbage and company look like history's winners: Henslowe and his son-in-law Edward Alleyn almost immediately started building a new playhouse elsewhere. The Admiral's Men abandoned the Rose in 1600 and moved into their new home, the Fortune, in Clerkenwell, northwest of the City and far away from the Globe. But there is no reason to think that a desire to ramp up competition motivated the Burbages' decision. For one thing, this kind of thinking would have been out of step with the general atmosphere of mutual respect among London's acting companies. For another, the very speed with which Henslowe and Alleyn acted supports a different story. In fact, the Burbages may have chosen the Southwark location because they knew that Henslowe had started to look for a suitable site for a new playhouse and that the Admiral's Men would soon leave their old home.

What made the Globe a remarkable project was neither its builders' allegedly aggressive approach to the theatrical marketplace nor its size or design, which were no more impressive than the Swan's. The Globe was unique for the way it was financed: it belonged not to a separate landlord, but to members of the acting company itself.

How did this come about? It may be that when the Burbages decided to move their playhouse in 1598, they did not have sufficient funds for that enterprise. In 1596, their father had spent the very large sum of £600 to transform a medieval hall inside the former Blackfriars monastery into a theater. The purpose of this investment is uncertain: the doomed lease negotiations for The Theatre had not yet begun, so James Burbage might have been trying to expand his activities as a theater owner rather than replace his old playhouse. He had only been his son's company's landlord for a little over a year when he bought the Blackfriars, and may very well have had another company in mind for the new space. Whatever the case, the new venue was the largest indoor performance space in London, and probably the first hall theater designed for an adult company. But the undertaking failed. Almost instantly, a group of wealthy inhabitants of the Blackfriars precinct successfully protested against the plan. The composition of that group is enlightening: it contained Lord Hunsdon, the patron of Shakespeare's company; and Hunsdon's recently deceased father had tried to buy part of the same property Burbage was after the year before. If the new playhouse was meant for the Chamberlain's Men, it is certainly strange that both these patrons of the company attempted to prevent its construction.

In any event, the property was not a viable alternative when Richard Burbage and his fellows lost The Theatre. Whether for financial reasons or because neither Cuthbert nor Richard Burbage wanted to play the role of theater owner and landlord, the brothers devised a solution that would for the first time put a venue mostly in actors' hands. Half the enterprise belonged to the Burbages (since they contributed the timber from The Theatre), but the remaining 50 percent was divided equally among five of the seven or eight remaining sharers in the Chamberlain's Men: John Heminges, William Kemp, Augustine Phillips, Thomas Pope, and William Shakespeare. At Christmas 1598, this consortium signed the lease for the plot of land in Southwark. They subsequently covered the construction costs of £700, exactly what The Theatre had cost to build in 1576.

Having a playhouse owned by the majority of the sharers in an acting company was a unique business model. These sharers now were responsible for the upkeep of the building, but they also, as landlords, received a portion of the entire revenue from every show (the Globe used the same rental agreement as the Rose, splitting performance income between landlords and actors). Beyond economics, the agreement created an unparalleled strong bond between these actors and their venue. It practically ensured that the Globe became their default home, and that its joint owners would remain members of the same acting company. The Globe was made for the Chamberlain's Men—but the Chamberlain's Men, in a sense, were also made by the Globe.

What happened to the Blackfriars property in the meantime? It stood empty for three years; and then, in 1600, it became an active theater after all. That year, Richard Burbage, clearly unwilling to adopt his father's or Henslowe's business model, leased

This section of Wenceslaus Hollar's 1647 "Long View" of London, drawn from South-wark, shows the Globe in its rebuilt state. The Globe is the round building in the middle, misidentified as a "Beere bayting" arena. The round building to its right, mislabeled "The Globe," is in fact the Hope playhouse, which by the 1620s was used exclusively as a bearbaiting venue.

the Blackfriars venue outright to the manager of a boys' acting company—for a flat annual fee of £40, and for twenty-one years. No revenue sharing, no managerial services: Burbage washed his hands of his father's failed endeavor. (The boys' company did not face the same opposition as the 1596 venture, perhaps because it performed as rarely as once a week, or because it represented a more up-market kind of playing.)

Eventually, the Blackfriars would become the King's Men's second venue: they probably started performing plays there sometime in 1610, at the very end of Shakespeare's career. But neither the company nor the Burbages were in any rush to move indoors. In 1604, the boys' company's manager tried to return the building to them and cut the twenty-one-year lease short, but the Burbages were uninterested. Only after the King forced out the children's troupe in 1608 did they agree to terminate the lease. The brothers owned the property and certainly had no financial incentive to search for investors. And yet the Burbages immediately turned the Blackfriars into another shared venture, splitting costs and revenues equally among themselves, one outsider, and four King's Men's sharers, including Shakespeare. The idea here was evidently not to maximize personal gain, but to enhance the company's profile—and its leaders' fortunes.

Within a decade, the Blackfriars turned into *the* place for new, fashionable plays. But during Shakespeare's lifetime, it never outshone the older outdoor space. For the first years of the new theater's existence, references to King's Men plays mention only the Globe; prominent audience members, including foreign princes, still visited the open-air venue; and in 1613, the company emphatically reaffirmed its commitment to its traditional playhouse. That year, the building's cost-effective thatched roof caught

Paulus wharfe

A different section of Hollar's panorama shows the Blackfriars precinct across the river from the Globe and Hope theaters. Just to the left of the center, next to the spire of St. Bride's Church, the long roof with two tall chimneys marks the probable location of the Blackfriars theater.

fire during the first performance of Shakespeare and Fletcher's *Henry VIII*. The Globe burned down, leaving the King's Men with only an indoor theater at their disposal. However, instead of redefining themselves as the Blackfriars company, they extended their lease on the Southwark plot, invested the enormous sum of £1,400, and rebuilt their playhouse—with decorations that made it, in the words of an eyewitness, "the fairest that ever was in England." This time, the galleries and stage had tiled roofs.

If the Chamberlain's/King's Men were unique in forming such a strong interconnection between actors and theaters, they also benefited from the unusual privilege of having an in-house playwright. No other company in the 1590s seems to have had a sharer who could also provide, on average, two plays a year. In addition, Shakespeare apparently performed other tasks for his company that would normally have been farmed out to hired dramatists, which included writing new scenes for old plays. The sheets in the *Sir Thomas More* manuscript that are probably in Shakespeare's handwriting are one example: there, he provided a long scene for a collaboratively authored text that needed major patching to be stageable. There is also evidence that additions to Thomas Kyd's *Spanish Tragedy* first printed in 1602 are by Shakespeare; if so, he wrote them for a Chamberlain's Men revival of this early classic (originally staged around 1587). The role of Hieronimo in the play was one of Richard Burbage's star turns, so we know the script found its way into the company's repertory at some point in the late 1590s or early 1600s.

Although the Chamberlain's Men were unusually fortunate to have Shakespeare as a sharer, we should not overestimate his place in their repertory. He was no Thomas Dekker, the dramatist who between 1597 and 1603 wrote or coauthored 41 new plays for a range of companies. Nor was Shakespeare as productive as Thomas Heywood, who claimed to have authored or cowritten more than 220 plays in a career spanning forty years. Given a need for at least ten fresh scripts a year, Shakespeare's contributions to his company's repertory were valuable, even indispensable—but they could never make up more than a fraction of the new material commissioned every year. Even if demand for new plays slowed in the 1620s, after the King's Men had accumulated a stock of reliably popular offerings, those of Shakespeare's works that had proved their lasting appeal would always be part of a much larger set of scripts. And the company treated Shakespeare's plays much like other authors' works, hiring playwrights to spruce up the old texts and make them newly exciting for audiences; in Shakespeare's case, it was Thomas Middleton who revised *Measure for Measure*, *Macbeth*, and possibly others.

At Court

Thinking of theater as a commercial enterprise taking place in venues accessible to all who paid the price of admission means leaving out one important aspect of early modern theater: private performances for aristocratic audiences. Companies were occasionally paid to stage their plays inside the London houses of noble clients, but such interactions with the highest social ranks were intermittent and unpredictable. The court, on the other hand, annually required actors to provide entertainments during lengthy revels between Christmas and Twelfth Night, and usually at Shrovetide (the three days before Ash Wednesday). Under Elizabeth I, there was only one court, her own, and theatrical activities were limited to those two holiday periods. With the ascension of James I, however, the number of royal courts multiplied—besides the King's own, Queen Anne, Prince Henry, and later Prince Charles also maintained courts with their own occasions for entertainment—and playing was no longer limited to holidays. The records show that the royally sponsored adult companies could be summoned to one of the palaces at any time. Officially, the courts' desire for theater justified the actors' need to play all year round in public venues, despite the City authorities' concerns: companies constantly had to rehearse and try out plays in front of live audiences so they could be ready to perform whenever a royal patron needed them.

The person in charge of organizing royal entertainments was the Master of the Revels, an officer who worked for the Lord Chamberlain. Under Elizabeth, the office was held by Sir Edmund Tilney. His job was not an easy one: he was responsible for choosing the appropriate companies and plays from the multitude available in London. In his early years, Tilney's approach seemed scattershot, with up to seven different troupes playing at court per season. The sheer complexity of keeping that many companies organized may have led to the foundation of an elite troupe under Elizabeth's own patronage, the Queen's Men, who dominated court entertainments for a few years after 1583. In 1594, the Master of the Revels apparently undertook a second effort to streamline holiday performances, this time relying not on a single troupe, but on a pair—and his superior, the Lord Chamberlain, adopted one of those companies as his own. For five years thereafter, Tilney could draw on two consistently excellent groups of actors, the Chamberlain's Men and the Admiral's Men.

As in 1583, though, this approach gave the Queen's revels a rather different complexion from the popular theaters. The Queen's Men were the leading company for about ten years after their creation, but other troupes eventually reappeared in the court season. Similarly, Shakespeare's company and their colleagues at the Rose were prominent but far from alone in London, and their competitors also turned up on Tilney's payroll again before long. Derby's Men, Worcester's Men, Hertford's Men, and the boys' companies all performed at court within a few years of the establishment of the Lord Chamberlain's troupe in 1594. Tilney's tenure as Master of the Revels was marked by repeated, ultimately futile efforts to limit actors' access to courtly employment—efforts seemingly designed to shut out the unrestrained variety of the public theatrical marketplace.

Under James I, the Lord Chamberlain's office finally acknowledged the size and diversity of London's theater world. Abandoning the model of a separate set of privileged companies with access to the court, the crown instead brought all major London companies gradually under royal patronage. By 1615, five adult troupes were being officially sponsored by members of James's family. Only those companies were asked to perform at court, but they were probably also the only acting outfits remaining in London: there were not enough playhouses to accommodate more than five permanent adult companies.

Even if the diversity of companies performing at court came to reflect the situation in the public playhouses over the course of Shakespeare's career, the repertory the actors drew on for their courtly performances remained distinct in surprising ways. We might expect that kings and queens, princes, ambassadors, and wealthy courtiers would have made for the most discerning and demanding audience imaginable, but the records tell a different story. Often, the plays staged at court were already several years old; by the 1610s, Revels playlists begin to feel like compilations of the classics that had their place in every company's repertory but could not normally compete with the appeal of new material. The court's, or the Master of the Revels', taste was broadly on the conservative side.

Though the records list almost no specific play titles from Elizabeth's reign, those surviving from James's time suggest that the King and his inner circle liked their Shakespeare well aged. In 1604, there were *A Midsummer Night's Dream*, nine years old; *The Merry Wives of Windsor*, seven years old; and *The Comedy of Errors*, over ten years old. The next year, we have recorded performances of *Henry V*, six or seven years after its first staging; and of *The Merchant of Venice*, at least seven years old, but performed twice within three days in James's presence in February 1605. These were the typical Shakespearean offerings. Exceptions occurred, including the still-new *Tempest* and *Winter's Tale* in November 1611, but for the most part, the Master of the Revels assembled an unadventurous repertory in which certain favorites often reappear. *Twelfth Night*, *The Winter's Tale*, *Othello*, and *1 Henry IV* show up every few years, as do some of Ben Jonson's plays (*Volpone* and *The Alchemist* in particular) and titles whose continued popularity at court now seems puzzling (such as the anonymous *Greene's Tu Quoque* and *The Merry Devil of Edmonton*). A company that performed for the royal households as often as did the King's Men must have adjusted to their courtly audience's expectations to some degree, and may therefore have been less quick to follow the latest artistic fashions than a company less in demand at court. But even so, Shakespeare and his fellows probably saw acting for their royal patrons as quite a different challenge from playing for London audiences. And in spite of the unquestionable importance of their connection to the royal household, the fact that they performed publicly far more frequently and depended on the income from those performances probably meant that their day-to-day activities were less influenced by the preferences of the court than we might imagine.

The Regulation of Playing and Its Failures

Organizing court entertainments was the most important aspect of the Master of the Revels' job, but he had another major responsibility: the licensing of new plays. Every script had to be submitted to him for approval, and only manuscripts bearing his license and signature were allowed to be performed. In their censorship activities, Tilney and his successors concentrated mainly on three concerns: no actual persons could be slandered or attacked; plays had to steer clear of incendiary topics and language; and, after a law banning profanity onstage had been passed in 1606, actors were no longer allowed to utter oaths using the name of God in any form. In the main, though, the Master of the Revels was not the acting companies' antagonist. For instance, Tilney did not simply reject *Sir Thomas More*, although he found the play objectionable on a number of counts; instead, he suggested changes that would enable him to give the players his license.

That relatively benign mode of control could quickly shift into an aggressive register when the players crossed a line. Companies that staged plays without first having them licensed, if discovered, were severely reprimanded. Stricter actions followed whenever a performance offended a person of high rank and influence. Playhouses were sometimes shut down as a consequence, and actors and playwrights found themselves in prison while under investigation. When these perceived transgressions happened (and they happened infrequently), the state was typically unable to explain what had gone wrong, especially if the play had been licensed. Playwrights would routinely offer the likeliest theory: the actors had ad-libbed, adding content the Master of the Revels had not seen and the author(s) had not written. There was certainly a kernel of truth to those defenses. Live performance is invariably different from the script on which it is based. But although that insight was not unknown to Shakespeare's contemporaries, it never seemed to affect the official system of licensing, which continued to operate unchanged throughout the early modern period.

Beyond the licensing requirements, there are few signs that the state took any sustained interest in regulating the theatrical marketplace, in London or elsewhere in the country. Nor were such efforts especially effective when they did occur. One of the most significant interventions took place in July 1597, apparently in response to a now-lost play, *The Isle of Dogs*, performed by Pembroke's Men at the Swan. This performance caused a massive scandal, landed some actors and the playwright Ben Jonson in jail under investigation for sedition, shut down all the theaters, and ruined Pembroke's Men financially. We do not know what made the play so offensive, but it must have been a serious trespass. The Privy Council's reaction to what it regarded as the players' "lewd and mutinous behaviour" was unprecedentedly severe; an order went out to stop all performances and have all playhouses demolished within three months. As telling as this order, though, is what happened next: almost nothing. The company was broken up, but no theaters were destroyed. Henslowe's *Diary* shows no signs that he was concerned about loss of income, and before long a new London-based company established itself in a new theater, the Boar's Head. For the next few years, the Privy Council attempted to control the number of troupes and playhouses in London, but every one of its annual letters to the local authorities expresses frustration about the inefficient implementation of the previous set of orders. No letters on the subject written after 1602 survive.

The Privy Council's general indifference to tightly regulating the theaters and its relatively hands-off attitude, even in the brief period when it adopted restrictive policies, did not align well with the wishes of the Lord Mayor and aldermen of the City, for whom the theaters posed a perennial challenge to public order. However, even the City authorities were not consistent in their opposition: they habitually relied on actors and playwrights for the annual civic entertainments, especially the Lord Mayor's pageants. Some aldermen befriended players, and actors participated in parish-level government (Shakespeare's colleagues Henry Condell and John Heminges were church wardens; Edward Alleyn and Philip Henslowe served as members of the vestry, or parish council, of St. Saviour's Church in Southwark). And although opposition to regular performances at the inns in the City was fairly consistent over twenty years, this policy may not have been the reason that all the large playhouses were built in the suburbs. Rather, high property prices and the scarcity of plots of land large enough for an amphitheater-style structure inside the densely packed City probably forced theater-builders to look beyond the city walls. Having large gathering places close to their gates but beyond their control vexed London authorities, but their anger may have been fueled by more than a simple desire to prohibit playacting: the theaters made a lot of money, and none of that income could be taxed by the City—despite the fact that the vast majority of playgoers would have been Londoners. The Mayor and his aldermen thus had many reasons for feeling aggrieved. Not only did they have to suffer the threat of riots and public disturbances sparked at the theaters, but they could not even collect fees and taxes in return.

The one cause that brought the interests of City and Privy Council together was also the single biggest economic threat to the acting companies, and the most frequent reason for playhouse closures: the plague. While the transmission of diseases was not well understood in early modern England, the authorities knew that crowds spread illness. Hence the government would order the theaters to shut whenever plague deaths reached a certain level (these figures had to be recorded and reported parish by parish every week). Sometimes, such closures were a precaution and did not last long. But on a number of occasions during Shakespeare's career, the theaters were closed for many months, with disastrous consequences for the London-based companies. A plague outbreak in 1593 halted performances for almost the entire year, forced all companies to tour, and caused a major reorganization of the theatrical landscape—out of which the Chamberlain's Men emerged as a new troupe formed from the fragments of its disbanded predecessors. At least as devastating was the horrific eruption of plague that shut down all playing in London from March 1603 to September 1604, and the less severe but longer episode that kept the theaters closed from August 1608 to the end of 1610. The first decade of James's reign was an especially chaotic and challenging time for the London companies, as there were lengthy plague closures even in the years when the playhouses were periodically open. If the world of London theater changed fundamentally after Shakespeare's retirement in 1613, the great watershed may not have been the introduction of multiple royal patrons or of new indoor performance venues, but instead the comparative stability offered by an extended period without plague outbreaks. In any case, it seems clear that the greatest threat to an acting company's fortunes was not the Privy Council, the censor, or local authorities, but a mysterious, unpredictable, and lethal disease.

Casting

We have already glimpsed some of the details of how an early modern acting company was put together: at its core were the sharers, the actors who jointly owned the troupe's assets; then there were a number of male youths, usually apprenticed to the sharers, who played women and children; and then there was a group of hired men, who had no financial stake in the group's success, as they were paid a set salary, although some (such as John Sincklo) stayed loyally with the same troupe. Beyond those actors, most London companies employed someone who functioned like a modern stage manager, the book-holder. That person was responsible for maintaining play scripts and organizing the backstage action during performances; he likely also acted as a prompter. Finally, there were employees who collected admission fees, cleaned the theater, and probably doubled as stagehands. Some of these workers were women, a female presence in an otherwise entirely male business.

Senior actors developed a degree of professional specialization. The most obvious experts were the clowns or fools, often among the most prominent members of any company. Richard Tarlton was the first of the great and famous Elizabethan clowns, and he was the Queen's Men's undisputed star until his death in 1588. Will Kemp, a sharer in the Chamberlain's Men as well as, for a short while, in the Globe, took over Tarlton's crown as the funniest man on English stages. After Kemp left the company in 1599, Robert Armin inherited his role as clown. The styles of these comedic performers differed, with Tarlton famed as an improviser and singer, Kemp known for his athleticism, and Armin for his subtler verbal wit, but they all had one thing in common: their responsibilities included the comic entertainments performed after plays

This portrait of Richard Tarlton, drawn by John Scottowe in or around 1588, shows Tarlton dressed as a jester, playing the tabor (a kind of drum) and pipe.

were done. Hence, they regularly appeared before audiences as themselves or as recognizable stage personae. They were certainly among the most readily identifiable faces of the company.

Unlike other roles, the clowns' parts in plays were often not fully scripted, and allowed for improvisation—the excessive use of which Hamlet criticizes when he tells the players to "let those that play your clowns speak no more than is set down for them." It is thus no coincidence that even as playwriting became a profession separate from acting, famous clowns still continued to be known as dramatists as well: Tarlton, Kemp, and Armin all wrote, as did John Shank, John Singer, and William Rowley. The line between the play and its performance, between the playwright's text and what the actors said and did, was particularly blurred in these performers' roles—and we should not assume that authors (or anyone else) found this especially troubling. It would be an error to read Hamlet's views as Shakespeare's, let alone the audience's: by all accounts, including Hamlet's, theatergoers enjoyed the clowns' ad-libbing and did not mind if such riffing delayed the progress of the play. We should, however, take seriously Hamlet's use of the plural "clowns." The company's specialist clown would never have been the only actor with comedic skills. *Hamlet* itself requires at least two clowns, the two gravediggers, even if Armin took on three of the plays' foolish roles and acted Polonius, Osric, and the first gravedigger (a casting choice the structure of the play allows). *Twelfth Night*, similarly, calls for a designated clown, but also needs another comically gifted actor as Sir Andrew Aguecheek. Shakespeare's company included a number of such performers. Thomas Pope, one of its founding sharers, had a reputation as a comedian, as did Richard Cowley, a hired man with the Chamberlain's Men who became a sharer in the King's Men.

If not all comic parts always went to the same performer, the same is true of dramatic leads. Two great tragic actors dominate all narratives of Shakespeare's stage: Edward Alleyn, the Admiral's Men's star, and Richard Burbage, the Chamberlain's and King's Men's leading player. Both rose to prominence in the 1590s. Alleyn, Burbage's senior by three years, gained fame first. However, although he led the longer life (Burbage died in 1619, Alleyn in 1626), his career as an actor lasted nowhere near as long as his colleague's: sometime before 1606, Alleyn retired from the stage to devote his attention to even more profitable ventures, whereas Burbage continued acting until his death. But even these two titans of the stage would not have taken the lead in every play: that is not how ensembles work. Alleyn certainly performed the title characters in Christopher Marlowe's *Tamburlaine* and *Doctor Faustus* and Barabas in *The Jew of Malta*, though he may not have originated those roles; beyond these, we know of five other parts in which he acted, four of them from lost plays. Burbage's list is not much longer. An elegy written shortly after his death laments that with him died characters that no other actor could bring to life as powerfully: "No more young Hamlet, old Hieronimo, / Kind Lear, the grievèd Moor." He was closely associated, then, with three of Shakespeare's plays and Kyd's *Spanish Tragedy*; notably, those works were at least ten years old when he died.

We might expect that Burbage, at the height of his fame, played all the largest parts, but the elegy suggests otherwise: Othello is a smaller role than Iago. What is more, when the Chamberlain's Men were established in 1594, Burbage was only twenty-five, the youngest sharer, and had not yet risen to the level of prominence he would later attain; and the company included other well-known actors: George Bryan, John Heminges, Augustine Phillips, and William Sly. Initially, Burbage's name would not have been the most recognizable among these, and even when his reputation ultimately eclipsed the others', he would—and could—not

A contemporary portrait of Richard Burbage. Burbage sometimes worked as a visual artist, and some scholars believe this painting to be a self-portrait.

have been the only choice for leads. Think of Shakespeare's plays from the mid-1590s: Burbage probably played Romeo, but what about *Richard II*? Would Burbage have been a better fit for the king or for the usurper Bolingbroke? In *The Merchant of Venice*, Shylock is the star turn nowadays, but Bassanio may have been the likelier role for Burbage, with older actors, like Bryan or Phillips, taking the roles of the other two male leads, Antonio and Shylock—or Thomas Pope, if Shylock was considered a comic part. Or take, as a final example, *Titus Andronicus*. Titus is the largest role, but Burbage may well have been a better fit for Aaron, a younger and more agile character.

Matching actors' ages to those of their characters, though, is a complicated business, and a casting consideration that was treated differently in Shakespeare's time from now. Burbage played Lear when he was no older than thirty-seven; and he was famous in the role of Hieronimo—an elderly father figure—by 1601, when he was just thirty-two. The same actor, then, might have acted the aged King Lear, "old Hieronimo," and "young Hamlet" within the span of a few days. And yet, despite this apparent disregard for verisimilitude, it was the supposedly lifelike quality of his acting that made Burbage famous. A writer in the 1660s reported on his ability to "wholly transfor[m] himself into his part, putting off himself with his clothes, as he never assumed himself again until the play was done." Part of Burbage's power was that he could seemingly become another person, even if that meant aging by decades. If the effect was a kind of make-believe, however, the means were an orator's, not those of modern psychological realism. What contemporary witnesses praise is Burbage's facility with speech, with finding the right vocal affect and the right quality of voice to express his character. As important was his aptitude at suiting his physical movement to the role, finding what were called the right "actions." That term probably referred to an elaborate arsenal of gestures and body positions that was systematic enough that audiences could read and make sense of actors' movements: putting a hand on the heart, holding one's face in one's hands, making a fist, and so on. Even if Burbage seemed able to go beyond conventions and give his actions an unusually personal or individual quality, though, it is clear that what seemed lifelike in Shakespeare's theater had little to do with a modern understanding of stage realism.

Burbage's specific talent may have been self-transformation; Alleyn, on the other hand, was known and remembered for his extraordinary stage presence. But both actors used a similar technical arsenal. Alleyn, like Burbage, was praised for his "excellent action"—as Thomas Nashe wrote in 1592, not even the greatest Roman actors "could ever perform more in action than famous Ned Alleyn." If Burbage disappeared into his roles, Alleyn was celebrated for the awe-inspiring quality he himself lent the characters he played. We do not know what his acting would have looked like onstage, but its outsized effect was not universally popular. Hamlet's criticism of players that "so strutted and bellowed" that "they imitated humanity so abominably" may refer to actors of Alleyn's ilk, perhaps an implicit statement that the Chamberlain's Men favored a different approach to performance. After Alleyn's death, in the reign of Charles I, the larger-than-life style associated with him was frowned upon by some writers and by spectators at some theaters. But there is no evidence that Burbage's brand of acting displaced Alleyn's within Shakespeare's lifetime. More probably, the two actors' particular aptitudes represented the pinnacles of two different but not incompatible acting techniques that in other players' work appeared in mixed forms. Both of these men were exceptional figures, after all. The Admiral's Men were not a company of many Alleyns, nor were the Chamberlain's Men a troupe of Burbages. What most performers and audiences probably understood "acting" (or "playing") to mean is captured vividly in these lines from *Richard III*:

> Come, cousin, canst thou quake, and change thy color,
> Murder thy breath in middle of a word,
> And then begin again, and stop again,
> As if thou wert distraught and mad with terror?

> (3.5.1–4)

What Richard is asking Buckingham here is whether he can act—and Buckingham replies that he can indeed "counterfeit the deep tragedian," in part because he can use the appropriate actions (looks, trembling, starts, smiles). Both characters describe a kind of performance that is highly codified, quite predictable, and not exactly lifelike; but both share the confidence that a talented actor can turn hackneyed gestures and tics into a convincing impression of reality.

If actors were capable of creating something like reality out of obvious fictions, and if those fictions could stretch to having an actor in his thirties play an old king one day and a young prince the next, then it cannot have been difficult for performers and audiences to come to terms with the widespread practice of doubling. All but the actors cast in the largest roles routinely played multiple characters, often leaving the stage as one person only to return shortly thereafter, wearing a new hat or a different cloak, as an entirely different character. Doubling meant that most early modern plays, although they may feature thirty or more characters, could be staged by around fourteen actors. In *The Merchant of Venice*, for example, the same player could take the parts of Old Gobbo, Tubal, the Jailer, and the Duke; or Morocco, Arragon, and the Duke—in either case, characters ranging widely in age and social status.

Like doubling, the casting of male youths in all female parts was a firmly established theatrical convention, though one that had less to do with pragmatic considerations than with a strong moral rationale. The idea of women putting their bodies on public display, even if fully clothed, was widely regarded as immoral and likened to prostitution. All-male casts were so deeply ingrained in English theatergoers' expectations that seeing actual women play female roles startled those who traveled abroad, where female actors were common. Some expressed their surprise that women could in fact act; others compared the Continental female performers critically to English boy players, whom they considered preferable not on moral but on artistic grounds. The women, these witnesses argued, played their characters too close to life, not artfully enough. A degree of artifice was as desirable in the boy actors' performances as in those delivered by the men. But as with the adult players, that artfulness did not diminish the potential impact of the show, as a famous account of a 1610 staging of *Othello* in Oxford attests. There, the scholar Henry Jackson recalls how Desdemona's death affected him: "although she always acted her whole part supremely well, yet when she was killed she was even more moving, for when she fell back upon the bed she implored the pity of the spectators by her very face." The boy player disappears behind the female pronouns, as if the artifice of the performance had become invisible. At the same time, Jackson registers that the body onstage, female or not, is not quite like a real corpse either; it responds to, and demands a response from, "the spectators." Yet, despite his recognition that the actor, or the character, is manipulating the audience's emotions, Jackson still responds emotionally and is in fact moved. The convention of using male youths for

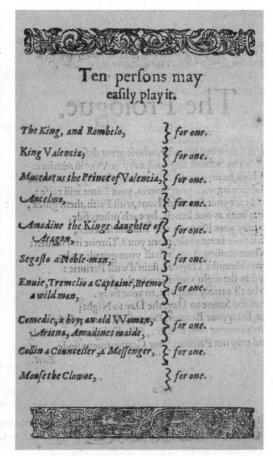

A chart from the second edition of the very popular anonymous play *Mucedorus* (1606), showing which actors can play more than one part.

female parts, then, was of a piece with the broader understanding of acting in Shakespeare's time as an art that deployed heightened artifice in order to create an affectively powerful semblance of real life.

Staging and Its Meanings

The staging of a new play in Shakespeare's time did not begin in a rehearsal room or in a theater, but in an actor's home. One of the first tasks of the company book-holder in readying a new script for performance was the preparation of the players' individual parts: each actor received only his own lines, along with the cues to which he was to respond and a handful of stage directions. Initially, then, most actors did not know who else was onstage with them, how many lines those other characters had, how much time passed between the scenes in which they appeared, or even who would give them their cues—nor what those characters said before the two or three words that made up the cue. Since companies performed together almost every day and actors often lived close to each other, informal discussions must have taken place to clarify relationships between characters, but any performer's primary duty would have been to learn

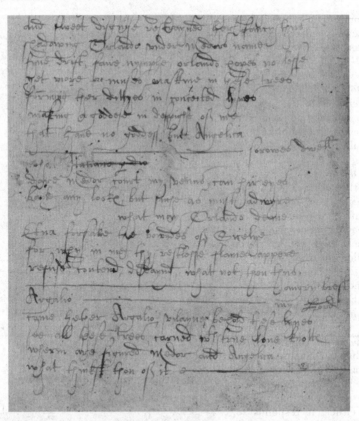

A section of Edward Alleyn's part for the role of Orlando in Robert Greene's *Orlando Furioso*. The long lines across the page mark breaks in Orlando's speech; at their end, the actor could find the cue for his next line.

his part in relative isolation, finding appropriate actions and intonations for his lines and memorizing cues. For leads, this was a formidable responsibility. Parts were written on strips of paper that were glued together to form a roll—which is why the terms "role" and "part" are synonymous. The scrolls for leads could reach remarkable length and heft. The one extant early modern part, Alleyn's copy of Orlando in Robert Greene's *Orlando Furioso*, is six inches wide and an impressive thirteen feet long, but its 530 lines probably did not overly tax an actor who had mastered more than 1,100 lines in *The Jew of Malta* and nearly 900 lines in the second part of *Tamburlaine*.

By Shakespeare's time, the solitary actor preparing his role could have predicted how the play would be staged with some certainty. The setup illustrated in the 1596 drawing of the Swan Theater is broadly representative of what a performer could expect in any venue: a rectangular, flat, largely empty stage; no sets in the modern sense, and few large furniture items; two pillars, probably set back from the edges of the stage by a few feet; at least two stage doors, and possibly a third in the center; and a balcony where scenes described as taking place "aloft" or "above" would be staged, though sections of it may also have offered additional audience seating, and part of it may have been used as a "music room." Even if there was no central stage door, there would have been an area between the two entrances that lay concealed behind an arras or a curtain that could be drawn to reveal pre-set tableaux, such as Hermione's statue in *The Winter's Tale*, Ferdinand and Miranda's chess game in *The Tempest*, or the caskets in *The Merchant of Venice*. There was also a trapdoor giving access to the space underneath the stage (sometimes called hell)—the place from which the ghost of Hamlet's father calls out to his son and his friends. In some theaters,

The interior of the Swan Theater, a sixteenth-century copy of a drawing by the Dutch traveler Johannes de Witt.

there was a pulley system that allowed objects, such as the figure of Jupiter in *Cymbeline*, to be lowered to the stage from the roof above it. That roof was often called the heavens, so that the stage as a whole represented a Christian microcosm, with hell, earth, and heaven enclosed in a round—*Hamlet*'s "distracted globe" or *Henry V*'s "wooden O."

This fairly stable, symbolically rich staging setup lent itself to an emblematic

The modern Globe on London's South Bank. This 1997 reconstruction is significantly larger than the original, but it captures the general idea of what an early modern theater may have looked like.

approach to performance. Figures appearing in the balcony are not always more powerful than those on the stage itself, but their position above could be dramatically exploited that way. When Tamora appears "aloft" alongside Saturninus in *Titus Andronicus*, for example, the staging suggests her elevation from prisoner of war to empress—a shift that officially does not take place until twenty lines later. The appearance of a prisoner and a foreigner in the location symbolically associated with supreme national power, however, also instantly signals how much of a topsy-turvy world Saturninus's Rome is about to become. This kind of visual logic of power returns in many plays that deal with the subjects of governance or rule: the descent of Richard II from the balcony to the stage when he surrenders to Bolingbroke is a particularly rich example. However, the emblematic use of the stage (where "above" means "powerful") could always be layered onto other modes of representation. In *Richard II*, the balcony also stands for an actual space "above," the battlements of Flint Castle; as the stage direction has it, Richard and his allies "enter on the walls." The stage to which he descends likewise is not simply "below" but also the "base court," the castle's lower court where Bolingbroke is waiting. From the perspective of the actor working with his part, the scene and its stage directions would have carried these various representational meanings—the text informed him both of Richard's movement from sun-like power to debasement before his enemy, and of the fact that the scene is taking place in two different locations in a castle. But the directions also had additional pragmatic value, as "on the walls" told the actor that he would have to enter on the balcony.

Stage directions such as these are explicit. Far more common are "internal" stage directions: textual references to actions characters perform. Often, these are straightforward: for instance, Bolingbroke's "there I throw my gage" in *Richard II*. But they can also be quite opaque. In *Hamlet*, when Polonius says, "Take this from this if this be otherwise," the line only tells the actor to perform some kind of gesture—he needs to indicate what "this" should be taken from what other "this" if Polonius is wrong. The most common interpretation is "my head from my shoulders" (indicated with appropriate gestures), but he may also be talking about his staff of office and his hand, or

A performance at the modern Globe.

his chain of office and his neck, or something else. The line requires actions to complete it, but it does not prescribe those actions.

Explicit and implicit stage directions allowed for a very short rehearsal period: they made it possible for the actor to conceive much of his performance alone. The text may not always tell him what to do, but it will often tell him when he needs to do *something*. However, there are also many cases where Shakespeare's plays seem to presuppose a good deal of back and forth between actors. For example, when Hamlet tells his mother to "leave wringing of your hands" in 3.4, the youth playing Gertrude would have needed to know to perform that action before Hamlet tells him to stop it—but there may have been no indication of this in his part. So while the part system allowed players to prepare for much, and while the established shape and features of playhouses by the 1590s made it possible for actors to anticipate many staging decisions before ever rehearsing a play, Shakespeare's texts also contain many instances where a successful performance depends on the players going beyond their individual parts.

Even if rehearsal periods were short, it is hard to imagine that the elaborate dumbshows, masques, and battle scenes featured in some plays were not carefully prepared. But rehearsal in the modern sense did not exist, mainly because the modern idea of character work did not exist. Renaissance actors did not spend long hours developing ideas about their characters' biographies, inner lives, or hidden feelings. Acting was primarily a physical and oratorical art and, in its conventionality, quite predetermined. What made any individual performance surprising and unpredictable were the specific effects achieved by bringing together a particular text with a conventionalized physical and vocal arsenal. But rehearsal also did not have to address many of the technological challenges that only came into being in the modern theater. In an outdoor venue without artificial lighting, actors do not need to hit their "marks"; an expansive stage lit only by sunlight allows for greater freedom of movement than one illuminated by an elaborate lighting design. Lastly, staging was determined in part by the architecture of the playhouses. Certain spots on stage worked especially well for certain set pieces. Soliloquies, for instance, were at their most powerful not when delivered front and center, but instead from a position farther away from the audience, off-center, and underneath the stage roof, which provided the greatest sense of acoustic intimacy. Therefore, an actor preparing a speech could predict with some certainty where onstage he would deliver it.

Of course there is more to staging a play than speaking lines and finding positions. Nowadays, sets are of paramount importance. In Shakespeare's time, they were all but nonexistent, except for some big-impact items: the Rose Theater owned a hell-mouth, probably covering the trapdoor, for devils to enter and exit in plays such as Marlowe's *Doctor Faustus*. Tombs, caves, and cages also appear in Henslowe's inventory, as do magical trees and severed heads. One other cost factor of modern productions, however, loomed similarly large in Shakespeare's time: costumes. Dresses in particular could be more expensive to commission than new plays, and companies maintained a rich stock of costumes; in 1598, the Admiral's Men owned at least eighty complete men's outfits. Most of these were generic items, but some were character-specific: "Harry the Fifth's velvet gown," "Longshanks' suit," or "Merlin's gown and cape."

What the actors wore was the most noteworthy visual aspect of staging. On a basic level, costumes identified characters. If the actor playing Tubal in *The Merchant of Venice* also played the jailor and the Duke, his three characters would have been distinguished initially and immediately by different garments. But costumes did more than facilitate identification. Dress signified social rank. It instantly allowed audiences to place characters, without having heard them speak or knowing anything else about them. More important, dress could set the scene: a nightgown signaled where and when an action took place; a forester's outfit told the audience to imagine a woodland setting; an innkeeper's costume moved the scene to a tavern. And dress denoted historical periods—as can be seen in Henry Peacham's famous illustration of *Titus Andronicus*. In this 1590s drawing, Titus's garments—Roman armor and a toga accessorized with a laurel wreath—immediately inform the viewer that this is a classical figure, and that the play is set in ancient Rome.

Yet Peacham's picture also shows that costume functioned in multiple registers on Shakespeare's stage. Titus wears Roman dress, and the short tunics of the three figures on the right also suggest quasiclassical costumes. But Tamora, on her knees in a flowing, embroidered gown and wearing a nonclassical crown, signifies less an ancient figure (Goth or Roman) than royalty. Her garments, unlike those of the characters beside her, are designed to situate her not in history, but in a particular social sphere. The outfits of the two leftmost characters follow a different logic yet again: they are Elizabethan soldiers, with breeches, halberds, and contemporary helmets. Their costume has no historical function; its sole purpose is to identify them as having a particular occupation. Dress, then, could signify in multiple, mutually contradictory ways at the same time on Shakespeare's stage. What Peacham's image

Henry Peacham's illustration of a scene from *Titus Andronicus* (ca. 1595).

suggests visually is that *Titus Andronicus*, while set in Rome, is also concerned with general questions of monarchic power and soldierly virtue. All three of those aspects of the play could be communicated through costume. If the picture portrays a kind of theater capable of sustaining anachronistic and logical contradictions in the pursuit of its thematic goals, it is representative of the broader, and pervasive, anachronism of Shakespearean drama, in which church bells ring and books rather than scrolls are read in *Julius Caesar's* Rome, while the title character wears that most Elizabethan of male garments, a doublet. No matter how far back in historical time these

Audience members seem to have consumed a wide range of foods at the theater. Archaeologists found oyster shells, remnants of crab, and a large quantity of nutshells and fruit seeds at the Rose Theater site.

plays were set, they also always took place in the present moment.

Impressive and expensive as the actors' costumes could be, their visual impact would necessarily have been lessened by the daylight playing conditions: performers were not isolated in space and light as they can be in modern theaters, but always competed for attention with the audience itself, with the equally splendid figures in the lords' rooms and on stage stools, and with whatever distracting things spectators chose to do while the play was in progress: play cards, smoke tobacco, solicit prostitutes (or johns). Aurally, too, Shakespeare's stage was not as insulated as a modern theater. Spectators were rowdier and more audibly present than audiences now. But the sounds of the city would also have infiltrated the open-air space: church bells, the noise of bears and hounds from the nearby bearbaiting arenas, the cries of street vendors, and perhaps even the sound of performances at neighboring playhouses might all have been heard. Going to a play in early modern London was never exclusively about the action and words onstage; it was always also about the theater itself, its temporary inhabitants, and the places where the theaters stood. Visually and aurally, the stage was in competition with the world, but it also found ways of integrating that world into its fictions.

Although the early modern theatrical experience was shaped by a host of immediate sensory perceptions, it equally depended on the audience's ability to refashion those impressions in their minds—even as plays insisted on drawing attention to the material reality of the stage. The Prologue to *Henry V* illustrates this condition perfectly. On the one hand, it mocks the apparent inadequacy of the theater, an "unworthy scaffold," a "cockpit" laughably ill suited to representing the "vasty fields of France"; it mercilessly reminds the audience where they are. At the same time, the Prologue also encourages the listeners to ignore all these carefully catalogued shortcomings and allow the play to work "on your imaginary forces," pleading with them to "piece out our imperfections with your thoughts." The Prologue seems to indulge in a risky game: it explains in detail why the theater should fail even as it dares the audience to make it work. But this risk lay at the heart of Shakespeare's theatrical art. We can detect it in the use of boy actors as much as in contradictory costuming choices and willful anachronisms. It found its most daring expression in the frequent use of narrative, seemingly the least theatrical form of writing. Antonio's tearful farewell to Bassanio in *The Merchant of Venice*; the deaths of the Dukes of Suffolk and York in *Henry V*; the reunion of Perdita and Leontes in *The Winter's Tale*; most remarkably, the death of as charismatic a character as Falstaff, in *Henry V*: again and again, Shakespeare chose to have events such as these reported by other characters rather than staging them before his spectators' eyes. In these scenes, the words and their demands on the audience's imagination do not just compete with what is visible, as they always did in the early modern playhouse. These narrations do more than that: they celebrate and rely on the power of words to take audiences out of the theater altogether, to transport them, without any visual aid whatsoever, to places and encounters that even the characters in the play itself only imagine.

And yet, despite placing such trust in language's capacity to transform reality, both the scenes and their author depended on their actors' ability to make audiences believe those words. If language's appeal to the imagination was meant to pull theatergoers out of their immediate sensory experience and into an engagement with a world of fiction, that goal could be achieved only by virtue of the very bodies, costumes, and props whose specific presence audiences were encouraged to transform into representations of an alternative reality. If a play worked, it enabled its viewers almost to forget the theaters whose splendor impressed so many visitors; allowed them to imagine for a moment that the words they heard did not come from a scroll of paper, that they had not been preapproved and licensed by a government official, purchased by a profit-hungry company, and written by a commercial playwright. Ultimately, then, in spite of the theater's undeniably powerful architectural, social, cultural, and visual presence in the lives of Shakespeare's contemporaries, its success in creating alternative, fictional worlds depended on an audience capable of understanding that all this splendor was not an end in itself. That is the marvelous paradox of Shakespeare's theater: it invested a great deal of goods, money, and physical labor in an effort to persuade people not to ignore those material realities altogether, but to use them as a means of accessing greater, still more wondrous, and wholly imaginary worlds beyond.

TRAGEDIES

Shakespearean Tragedy
by
STEPHEN GREENBLATT

Seven years after Shakespeare's death, two of his repertory company colleagues, John Heminges and Henry Condell, undertook to collect and print his plays in a single large volume, the First Folio. They chose not to present the plays in either chronological or alphabetical order, but rather to organize them in three large genres or literary categories: comedies, histories, and tragedies. In the latter category they included eleven plays: *Titus Andronicus, Romeo and Juliet, Julius Caesar, Hamlet, Othello, Timon of Athens, King Lear, Macbeth, Antony and Cleopatra, Coriolanus,* and *Cymbeline.* This last play, with a happy ending that resolves the dark dilemmas of a tangled plot, is now most often called a "romance," and it remains something of a surprise that the original editors did not include it with two roughly similar plays, *The Winter's Tale* and *The Tempest,* which they grouped with the comedies. The ten remaining plays in Heminges and Condell's tragedies category constitute the broadly accepted canon of Shakespearean tragedy. They are widely acknowledged to be the greatest outpouring of tragic art since the achievement in the fifth century B.C.E. of the ancient Greek dramatists Aeschylus, Sophocles, and Euripides.

The inclusion of *Cymbeline* among the Folio's tragedies signals that there is nothing fixed or absolute about the boundaries of Shakespearean genres. During Shakespeare's lifetime three of his other plays—*3 Henry VI, Richard III,* and *Richard II*—were published as tragedies. Almost all modern editors follow the Folio editors in renaming and reclassifying them as histories. The classification does not mean that Shakespeare's tragedies are necessarily less historical than his histories, nor that his histories are necessarily less tragic than his tragedies; it only means that the plays Heminges and Condell termed "histories" are all based on English history after the Norman Conquest of 1066. Many, though not all, of they plays they classified as tragedies are also based on historical sources—pre-Conquest British history, classical history, Danish and Scottish history. (*King Lear* had been published before the Folio as a "history," and *Hamlet* had been printed twice as a "tragical history.")

Generic boundaries were easily crossed, and there was ample room, then as now, for disagreement and bafflement. *Troilus and Cressida* was printed first as a history. The Folio editors had their doubts: they renamed the play *The Tragedy of Troilus and Cressida.* But this renaming did not solve the problem of a play that seemed to call all generic categories into question. Evidently perplexed and unable to come up with a solution, the editors decided not to list *Troilus and Cressida* in any of the categories of the Folio's title page, but instead simply to place it unheralded between the histories and the tragedies. Most modern editors now classify the play as a comedy, sometimes as a "problem comedy." But under enough pressure, all of Shakespeare's plays begin to seem like "problems." Generic compartments are convenient, but if you lean against them too hard they will splinter and break.

The challenge posed by tragedy in particular is not only categorical. It is the artistic form that has grappled strenuously with the most excruciatingly difficult, intractable elements of human experience: a seemingly accidental succession of circumstances that leads to a catastrophic end; a current of envy, anger, or unappeasable desire that undermines a psychic and moral framework built up over a lifetime; the terrible fragility of social and political relations, even those that seem most stable and secure; the sheer waste of what seems most precious—youth, innocence, love; and, looming over the guilty and the innocent alike, the certainty of death. Such dilemmas of existence have long preoccupied theologians and philosophers as well as artists, and the moral seriousness of the shared concern has served to confer upon tragedy, among all the forms of art, a particular dignity and weight. But there is also an unresolved strain: while theology and philosophy have repeatedly attempted to construct a systematic understanding of the human condition and to offer some resolution, in this world or the next, of its most painful problems, tragedy has tended to eschew consolation and to dwell in the realm of suffering. It is not surprising, perhaps, that many of the greatest philosophers—from Plato and Aristotle in the ancient world to Hegel and Nietzsche in the nineteenth century to Walter Benjamin, Jacques Derrida, and Stanley Cavell in our own times—have grappled with mingled admiration and resistance to the challenge posed by this strange and compelling art form.

More than two thousand years ago, in *The Poetics,* the Greek philosopher Aristotle, taking as his principal model Sophocles' *Oedipus Rex,* came up with some of the key terms for analyzing tragedy: the artful *imitation* of an action through the crafting of a plot of an appropriate scale; a fatal *blindness* or *defect* in character that brings the hero to destruction; a sudden *reversal* of fortune; a powerful moment of *recognition* in which ignorance gives way to a terrible knowledge; an intense emotional *catharsis* for the audience in the experience of pity and fear.

Each of these terms has some purchase on Shakespeare's tragedies, with their remarkable array of flawed heroes, their powerful plot twists and painful bursts of psychological and moral illumination, and their wrenching emotional effects. Yet the playwright's great achievement as a whole does not altogether comfortably fit the philosopher's influential descriptive account, and still less comfortably does it accord with the rules that Aristotle's followers attempted to deduce from this account. Even an early play like *Titus Andronicus,* though set in the ancient world and full of classical allusions, pulls sharply away from Aristotle's conception of tragedy. For Shakespeare the plot, the element central to *The Poetics,* is only a slender, fragile bark bobbing on an enormous, chaotic, destructive, and ecstatic sea of suffering and weird laughter. The elegantly chiseled structural design in which Aristotle was most interested may be glimpsed in Shakespeare—in the astonishing reversal of fortune brought about in *Julius Caesar* by Antony's funeral oration, for example, or in the blinded Gloucester's realization in *King Lear* that the son he trusted has betrayed him. Yet this design is often overshadowed by the sheer magnitude of events and passions not merely reported but directly represented on stage. The playwright who begins *Titus Andronicus* with the spectacle of an enraged father stabbing his son to death was in touch with energies in the tragic theater that the philosopher's analytical categories can only partially contain.

How did it happen? How did Shakespeare create a series of stupendous plays that continue to haunt audiences and readers? The answer certainly does not lie in any classical rules that he set out to follow, or in any well-defined collective understanding, shared with his contemporaries, of what constituted a successful tragedy. To be sure, in the late 1580s, Sir Philip Sidney drew on Aristotle's *Poetics* to pen an important attack on the tragedies currently being performed on the English stage. These native tragedies, Sidney complained, fail to observe the proper "unities of place and time." Instead of depicting only a single, well-demarcated place, the stage typically represents so many different places—Asia on one side and Africa on the other, as he puts it—that a performer when he enters has to begin by saying where he is, or the audience will be completely lost.

"Now ye shall have three ladies walk to gather flowers," Sidney writes, warming to his theme,

> and then we must believe the stage to be a garden. By and by we hear news of shipwreck in the same place, and then we are to blame if we accept it not for

a rock. . . . While in the meantime two armies fly in, represented with four swords and bucklers [shields], and then what hard heart will not receive it for a pitched [battle]field?

The same criticisms apply to the representation of time: in the course of the brief interval that the audience watches a play, a young prince and princess fall in love, marry, and have a child who grows up and himself falls in love, marries, and is ready to start a family of his own. "How absurd it is!" And to compound these errors, the aristocratic Sidney notes with disgust, English playwrights, by "mingling kings and clowns," do not even manage to write "right tragedies" or "right comedies." "Clowns"—country bumpkins fit only to laugh at—are thrust in "by head and shoulders, to play a part in majestical matters, with neither decency nor discretion, so as neither the admiration and commiseration, nor the right sportfulness, is by their mongrel tragicomedy obtained."

That Sidney, who was killed in battle in 1586, unwittingly describes important features of *King Lear, Antony and Cleopatra,* or *Cymbeline*—plays written years after his death—signals that Shakespeare was largely indifferent to the classical norms for tragedy. It signals, too, that Shakespearean tragedy (and comedy) did not come from nowhere. Shakespeare was drawing on native theatrical traditions that enabled him, when he wished, to use the bare stage to represent multiple places and variable stretches of time. The great medieval English "mystery cycles" had undertaken to stage the whole Christian vision of the world, from the creation to the Crucifixion to the Last Judgment, and the secular dramas that arose in the mid-sixteenth century entertained English audiences with sprawling stories drawn from the chronicles of both national and world history.

In Shakespeare the action shifts effortlessly in *Julius Caesar* from the Capitol in Rome to Sardis in western Turkey and then to the fateful battlefield near Philippi in Macedonia; *Othello* begins in Venice and moves to Cyprus, where the Venetian forces are bracing for a Turkish assault that never materializes; *Antony and Cleopatra* shuttles restlessly between Rome and Egypt, alighting as well in a bewildering array of army camps and ships moored off the Greek and Italian coasts. Time is comparably flexible: there are scenes—for example, the assassination of Duncan in *Macbeth*—in which the seconds seem to tick by with agonizing slowness; at other moments years pass without notice. And in one celebrated instance, *Othello*, time seems both short and long, so that events are at once precipitous and drawn out. The audience disorientation that worries Sidney seems to Shakespeare to be of no concern whatsoever: the playwright is altogether confident that he can give the audience exactly what information it needs, exactly when it needs it.

The aristocratic distaste for the mingling of kings and clowns is also entirely alien to Shakespeare, whose tragedies routinely bring together figures from the opposite ends of the social spectrum. Here again Shakespeare could draw upon the native theatrical tradition, with secular tales that interwove the lives of beggars and princes, and religious dramas that focused on often comic simple folk in the presence of transcendent suffering. It is not that Shakespeare is indifferent to social status: on the contrary, most of his tragedies center on the fate of charismatic monarchs, princes, and military heroes. (The most significant exception, *Romeo and Juliet*, concerns the sole heirs to two of the wealthiest and most socially prominent families in their city.) But some of his most powerful tragic effects arise in encounters such as those between the ruined Roman general Titus Andronicus and the poor, pigeon-bearing "clown"; Hamlet and the gravediggers; Lear and the Fool; or Cleopatra and the rustic who brings her the poisonous snakes with which she will commit suicide.

Sidney feared that encounters of this kind would undermine the "majestical" dignity of tragedy and leave in its stead "mongrel tragicomedy." Shakespeare seems to have enthusiastically embraced the mongrelization of genres. His comedies are shot through with pain and the fear of death; his tragedies, even the direst of them, echo with strange laughter. In a characteristically ghastly moment of a grisly play, Titus Andronicus is told that if he cuts off his hand and sends it to the emperor, the lives of his two sons will be spared. When a few moments later he gets back his severed hand, along with the heads of his sons, Shakespeare scripted for him this line: "Ha, ha, ha!" (3.1.263).

As this extreme example suggests, the laughter in Shakespearean tragedy is not only the incidental effect of the puns and antics of the clowns; it is pervasive and structural. The gulling of Othello—an older man (and an outlandish stranger) married to a beautiful young woman—is a traditional comic plot, as the conniving villain Iago understands. "It cannot be long that Desdemona should continue her love to the Moor," he confidently predicts; "she must change for youth" (1.3.331–38). So too in *King Lear,* old Lear and Gloucester attempt to block the desires of their children, exactly as the aged fathers always do in comedy. The illegitimate Edmond invites the audience to laugh at the cleverness with which he will topple his legitimate brother and deceive his foolish father:

> Well, then,
> Legitimate Edgar, I must have your land.
> Our father's love is to the bastard Edmond
> As to th' legitimate. Fine word: "legitimate"!
> Well, my legitimate, if this letter speed
> And my invention thrive, Edmond the base
> Shall to th' legitimate. I grow. I prosper.
> Now, gods, stand up for bastards!
> (*Tragedy* 1.2.15–22)

This is the stuff of comedy.

Yet *King Lear* and *Othello* are unmistakably tragedies; indeed, they are among the most searing, soul-searching tragedies ever written. The comic elements are real enough, but they serve only to enrich the human complexity, intensify the sense of irony, and highlight the suffering and loss that characterize these remarkable plays. Their impact derives not from any patrolling of generic boundaries but from an overwhelming emotional power.

Shakespeare's supreme confidence in his ability to wield this power seems bound up with the reckless daring with which he laces his tragedies with comedy. Near the end of *Hamlet,* with his fate closing in upon him, the prince has time to exchange witticisms with the gravediggers and to tease the fatuous courtier Osric. In *Antony and Cleopatra,* the despairing hero, rapidly bleeding to death, has time to bestow one farewell kiss on the Egyptian queen for whom he has given up the whole world. But Cleopatra, safely locked inside her monument, refuses to come down, for fear that she will be captured. Instead she and her women decide to pull Antony up—"Oh, quick," he gasps, "or I am gone!"—and as they struggle to do so, Cleopatra makes a joke: "Here's sport indeed. How heavy weighs my lord! / Our strength is all gone into heaviness" (4.16.32–34). The playwright who could at that charged moment call attention to his aging hero's bulk and insert a pun on "heaviness" (at once weight and sadness) was not playing by any conventional generic rules. There survives an intriguing trace of Shakespeare's critical reflection on how far he could go in the mingling of genres. In 1672, long after the playwright's death, the poet John Dryden remarked that "Shakespeare showed the best of his skill in his Mercutio, and he said himself, that he was forced to kill him in the third act, to prevent being killed by him." If the report that reached Dryden can be trusted, then Shakespeare registered the extent to which the mocking spirit of comedy, in the person of Mercutio, was threatening to subvert *Romeo and Juliet.*

What is perhaps most immediately striking about Shakespeare's tragedies, taken as a group, is how unlike one another they are. There is no sense of formula, and startlingly little repetition. As critics have often observed, the hero of any one of these plays, tormented by insoluble dilemmas, would have had no difficulty resolving the crises of another. Before the ghost had vanished from the ramparts, Macbeth would have unseamed Claudius from the nave to the chops, while Hamlet would in act 5 still be brooding on whether or not to kill Scotland's king. It is not simply that the heroes are remarkably different in their passions, their fears, and their longings; the world that each of them inhabits is utterly distinct and incommensurable. Romeo and Juliet's Verona seems to belong to an entirely different universe from Lear's Britain or Hamlet's Elsinore; Coriolanus and Brutus are both inhabitants of Rome, but neither would recognize the other's city.

The tragedies are, to be sure, demonstrably the works of the same person. Thus, for example, in *Antony and Cleopatra*, written fairly late in Shakespeare's career, we can identify themes that the play shares with some of the earlier tragedies:

- with *Romeo and Juliet*, a fascination with a passionate love that overwhelms traditional, deep-seated enmities before finally being overwhelmed by them.
- with *Julius Caesar*, a fascination with the lives of those who ruled the world, men and women who are fully aware of their historical significance, even as they grapple with the familiar desires and fears, the egotism, insecurity, and jealousy of ordinary mortals.
- with *Hamlet* and *Macbeth*, a fascination with ambiguity and an obsessive interest in the seductive, hidden power of female sexuality.
- with *King Lear*, a fascination with the loss of power attendant on aging, and an inquiry into the nature of service.
- with *Othello*, a fascination with the outsider, with the contrast of cultures, and with the exotic.

But the differences in the tragic territory marked off by *Antony and Cleopatra* are still more notable:

- The protagonists are decidedly not young lovers confined by their parents' choices for them.
- The possession of unlimited power is not finally the object of passion but gives way to something else.
- The collapse of categories is not, or not necessarily, a mark of evil, and the power of female sexuality is more celebrated than feared.
- Aging is a sign not of weakening but of a shift of interest and mood.
- The exoticism is not tamed or destroyed, but remains the object of longing.

The consequence is that this play feels entirely distinct, in its rhythms, its preoccupations, and its overarching mood, from anything that Shakespeare had written before. Even the deaths at the end seem radically different in spirit, so much so that critics have occasionally asked themselves whether *Antony and Cleopatra* should even be classified as a tragedy.

Shakespeare's tragedies all move toward an ending in death, just as his comedies move toward an ending in marriage. The death in question is principally, though usually not exclusively, the death of the hero; often there are others, on occasion many others, who in the course of the play accompany him on the path to destruction. Some of the corpses that litter the stage are of those—Iago's pawn Roderigo in *Othello*, Goneril's repellent steward Oswald in *King Lear*, the hateful Demetrius and Chiron in *Titus Andronicus*—who have willingly served the malevolent designs of the major villains. The villains themselves end up either dead or, like Aaron the Moor and Iago, on their way to a gruesome execution.

But it is not only the evil who join the heroes of the tragedies in the ranks of the dead. There are many entirely innocent victims, from the mutilated Lavinia to the loving Desdemona, from Cordelia to Lady Macduff and her sweet young children. These defenseless women and children are the objects of cunning plots and premeditated violence. There are others who simply find themselves at the wrong place at the wrong

Top: Woodcut *memento mori* (seventeenth century). *Bottom*: Printed form for recording mortalities and christenings in London and environs (1609).

time: the simple rustic who brings the emperor a gift of pigeons in *Titus*, the wet-nurse who carries Aaron's baby to him in that same play, Cinna the poet in *Julius Caesar*, and the grieving Paris in *Romeo and Juliet* who has come to strew flowers on Juliet's grave.

The heroes of several of Shakespeare's tragedies—Titus Andronicus, Macbeth, and Coriolanus—are virtual killing machines who are responsible for much of the mayhem around them and with whom the audience is nonetheless invited, even compelled, to be imaginatively invested. "I am in blood / Stepped in so far," says Macbeth halfway through the play, "that, should I wade no more, / Returning were as tedious as go o'er" (3.4.138–40). And the last words that Coriolanus hears, as the swords are thrust into his body, are the enraged cries of those he has irreparably harmed: "He killed my son!—My daughter!—He killed my cousin / Marcus!—He killed my father!" (5.6.120–21). Even those tragic heroes who are not professional killers very often cause, directly or indirectly, the deaths of those around them. The sword that Hamlet blindly thrusts through the arras, in the hope of killing his wicked uncle, is a fit emblem: Hamlet's blow kills not his uncle but rather Polonius, whose death in turn leads to the miserable end of his daughter Ophelia. Before the uncle is finally killed—both stabbed and poisoned by Hamlet—Ophelia's brother Laertes will also die, as will Hamlet's mother Gertrude and his school friends Rosencrantz and Guildenstern. Hamlet too is fatally wounded, and his best friend Horatio, determined to follow him to the grave, is stopped from suicide only by Hamlet's urgent plea:

Scenes from William Sampson's *The Vow Breaker* (1636).

> Absent thee from felicity awhile,
> And in this harsh world draw thy breath in pain
> To tell my story.

> (5.2.325–27)

Hamlet evidently views death, his own and that of others, as "felicity." In the course of the play he has somehow moved from tormented, anxious irresolution to a quiet acceptance of his own fate. "If it be," he tells Horatio,

> 'tis not to come; if it be not to come, it will be now; if it be not now, yet it will come; the readiness is all.

> (5.2.192–94)

But is the audience of Shakespeare's tragedies meant to share this view? In certain of the plays, the answer seems to be yes. At the end of *King Lear,* when the old man's heart finally fails, one of the bystanders tries desperately to revive him, but Kent, who has witnessed first-hand the whole course of Lear's atrocious sufferings, protests:

> Oh, let him pass! He hates him
> That would upon the rack of this tough world
> Stretch him out longer.

> (*Tragedy* 5.3.289–91)

If life is an instrument of torture, then death is the merciful cessation of pain. Something of the same could be said of Othello, for whom the only imaginable future is one of unendurable remorse, rage, and self-pity; or of Macbeth, whose life has become

> a tale
> Told by an idiot, full of sound and fury,
> Signifying nothing.
>
> (5.5.26–28)

So too Timon of Athens in his miserable cave at the end of his life feels only emptiness, contempt, and a longing for extinction. "Graves only be men's works," he declares in misanthropic disgust, "and death their gain" (5.2.107). And if, less despairing than these characters, Cleopatra can imagine a future, it is one in which she will be ruthlessly humiliated, paraded in the triumphal procession of her Roman conquerors, and given over to the vulgar amusement of the mob. "Bravest at the last," Caesar says admiringly of her suicide, "she leveled at our purposes"—that is, she understood the fate that was in store for her—"and, being royal, / Took her own way" (5.2.331–33).

But by no means all of Shakespeare's tragic protagonists welcome death. It is not even clear that Hamlet does. Ordering that the dead prince be lifted up "like a soldier," Fortinbras says that Hamlet was likely, "had he been put on"—that is, had he been put to the test—to have acted "most royal" (5.2.374–76). While we may doubt the assessment of Hamlet's military aptitude, Fortinbras' words remind us of the hero's thwarted ambition to succeed his father as king of Denmark, and remind us too of the hopes that have been cut off by his death and of all that remains to be said. "Oh, I could tell you," the dying Hamlet begins to say to his friend, only to realize that there is no time left: "But let it be. Horatio, I am dead" (5.2.315–16).

If in some of Shakespeare's tragedies death comes as a relief or a welcome release, in others it comes as a shattering interruption. In *Julius Caesar* Brutus, facing certain military defeat, chooses to end his life: "Our enemies have beat us to the pit," he acknowledges. "It is more worthy to leap in ourselves / Than tarry till they push us" (5.5.23–25). This end is neither the fulfillment of his deepest wish nor a release from his misery. It is the final, agonizing failure of his cherished dream to save the Roman republic. And Hamlet's resignation and Lear's exhaustion are entirely alien to Romeo and Juliet, who are only beginning to savor the joys of their passionate love, and whose death is precipitated, if not altogether caused, by a series of accidents.

There is then no typical form of "tragic death" in Shakespeare: no characteristic end, no consistent stance, and no single audience response. Not all kinds of death are represented: the death of the martyr, for example, sublimely fervent in religious belief, does not occur in Shakespearean tragedies, nor does the death of someone reduced to misery by abject poverty and illness. So too an entirely accidental end—the hero knocked down by a runaway horse or struck dead by lightning—is outside the range of ends regarded as tragic in the plays.

The deaths of the protagonists in these plays all bear a significant relation to everything that has come before, that is, to their choices, their suffering, their whole way of experiencing the world. Many of the heroes and heroines of Shakespearean tragedy actively choose death by committing suicide, and even when they do not kill themselves, they go to their deaths, like Macbeth or Coriolanus, as if they had chosen to do so. The principal figures seem to have a stake in "owning" their own deaths, as if they were determined to make their ends as expressive of their lives as all their other words and actions have been.

This determination does not preclude the sense of fatality that haunts many of the protagonists, from the "star-crossed lovers" Romeo and Juliet to Brutus, who senses Caesar's ghost haunting the battlefield at Philippi, to Macbeth, whose destiny in some obscure way is linked to the obscene connivance of the weird sisters. "The charm's wound up" (1.3.38), the weird sisters sing just before Macbeth makes

Antony displaying Caesar's wounds (mid to late nineteenth century). Alfred Krausse, printmaker; Heinrich Spiess, artist.

his first appearance: perhaps then the whole bloody sequence of events that follows is only the inexorable enactment of what they have predetermined and set in motion. That dismaying possibility is never laid to rest, and how could it be? After all, from a certain perspective, everything that happens in a Shakespearean tragedy has in reality been predetermined, set in motion by the master who has wound up the charm.

There are strange moments in these plays in which the principal characters seem to have an intimation of forces that are compelling them to act and react as they do, whether those forces are understood to be supernatural agents or some other invisible structural principle. "The time is out of joint," Hamlet cries, in the wake of his encounter with the ghost of his father; "oh, cursèd spite / That ever I was born to set it right" (1.5.189–90). "As flies to wanton boys are we to th' gods," says the despairing Gloucester in *King Lear*; "They kill us for their sport" (*Tragedy* 4.1.38–39). But however intense these intimations may be, Shakespeare's protagonists do not passively submit to their fate, as if they were sleepwalking toward death. (Though *Macbeth* includes a famous scene of sleepwalking, it is not about fatalism but about nightmarish guilt.) Hamlet spends much of the play trying to establish for himself what he should do and on what grounds he should do it. Gloucester—who has always had a tendency to blame the gods or the stars for whatever goes wrong—attempts to take his fate in his own hands by throwing himself off a cliff. And though at the end of his tragedy Macbeth grasps that he has been cunningly manipulated by the equivocations of witches

The death of Pyramus and Thisbe. Woodcut from Ovid's *Metamorphoses* (Venice, 1538).

who "palter with us in a double sense," he does not even then simply conclude that he is the passive instrument of a malevolent fate. "Be these juggling fiends no more believed," he says, and a moment later throws himself into a fight to the death: "Yet I will try the last" (5.7.49–50, 62).

None of these actions precludes the possibility of a predetermined end, of course, but the characters themselves cannot and do not live as if they had no agency at all. They suffer intensely from what Hamlet calls the "slings and arrows of outrageous fortune" (3.1.57), but they are never merely victims. They always contribute to the catastrophe that befalls them, if only by setting in motion through some irreversible action an uncontrollable chain of events that brings devastation in its wake. This contribution reflects to a considerable degree the fact that almost all of Shakespeare's tragic protagonists are socially important people whose inherited rank, office, and wealth accustom them to the exercise of power. The power, as they learn to their cost, is never absolute—"They told me I was everything," the ruined Lear says, shivering from cold and fever. "'Tis a lie, I am not ague-proof" (4.5.104–05). But they possess for the most part a quality that Kent, in disguise, claims to see in the face of Lear. "You have that in your countenance," Kent says, "which I would fain call master." "What's that?" Lear asks; and Kent's reply is a single word: "Authority" (*Tragedy* 1.4.25–28). The principal exceptions to this rule, Romeo and Juliet, do not possess such authority, and hence their fate seems more contingent than that of the other tragic heroes, but even here their determination to act upon their passion, whatever the cost, shapes their destiny.

Drawing upon Hegel, the critic A. C. Bradley, whose 1904 book *Shakespearean Tragedy* remains the best single study of the subject, observes that in almost all of Shakespeare's tragic heroes there is "a marked one-sidedness, a predisposition in some particular direction; a total incapacity, in certain circumstances, of resisting the force which draws in this direction; a fatal tendency to identify the whole being with one interest, object, passion, or habit of mind." The heroes, most of them at least, are driven to extremes, whether of love, ambition, generosity, anger, or some other intense emotion to which they devote the whole of their being.

"If there were reason for these miseries," cries Titus Andronicus, "then into limits could I bind my woes" (3.1.218–19). But there are no limits: "I am the sea" (3.1.224). "But come what sorrow can," Romeo tells Friar Laurence,

It cannot countervail the exchange of joy
That one short minute gives me in her sight.
Do thou but close our hands with holy words,
Then love-devouring death do what he dare—
It is enough I may but call her mine.

(2.5.3–8)

Friar Laurence tries to rein in Romeo's reckless passion: "Love moderately," he sagely advises. But such urgings of restraint, echoed in many of the plays, always fall on deaf ears.

The heroes are never figures of moderation; they are committed by nature and by choice to the experience of the absolute. "O my soul's joy," Othello exclaims when he is reunited with Desdemona,

If after every tempest come such calms,
May the winds blow till they have wakened death,
And let the laboring bark climb hills of seas
Olympus-high, and duck again as low
As hell's from heaven. If it were now to die
'Twere now to be most happy—for I fear
My soul hath her content so absolute
That not another comfort like to this
Succeeds in unknown fate.

(2.1.176–85)

Here as elsewhere Shakespeare's tragic heroes exist in a world of immense heights and immense depths, a world in which they are willing to hazard everything: "and when I love thee not, / Chaos is come again" (3.3.90–91).

As Bradley's many critics have observed, the chaos, when it comes, afflicts far more than the inner lives of the heroes. Shakespearean tragedies are political as well as psychological, the effect of brilliant plots as well as brilliant characters. They are concerned with dynastic struggles, as in *Hamlet, King Lear,* and *Macbeth*; with violent conflicts between social classes, as in *Coriolanus*; with world-historical events, as in *Julius Caesar*; with the clash of civilizations, as in *Antony and Cleopatra*. They are testing grounds for the nature and limits of fundamental human drives and values—love, hatred, revenge, generosity, the craving for power—and searching explorations of moral ambivalence.

The explorations center, of course, on the heroes whose inward experience Shakespeare represents with unrivaled mastery. But they are by no means limited to these heroes. Each play is a complex hall of mirrors, cunningly constructed to examine certain key questions from multiple perspectives. A son's fraught relationship to his father (and the memory of his father) is probed unforgettably in Hamlet's encounter with the ghost, but it is also explored in Laertes' and Fortinbras' dealings with their fathers. The mingled tyranny, gullibility, and suffering of Lear and his daughters are echoed in Gloucester and his sons. The political obsessions of Brutus are shared by Cassius, Casca, Trebonius, Decius, Metullus Cimber, and the other conspirators, all of whom, remarkably enough, are given just enough time to establish distinct individual identities as historical agents.

The plays are not monologues: they all involve multiple subjectivities, and Shakespeare's seemingly limitless imaginative generosity enabled him to grant at least a touch of life to virtually anyone he brought onstage. We cannot reduce the plays to their title characters alone, any more than we can reduce them to a list of tragic themes. But it is obviously not an accident that while almost all of the comedies have playfully general titles like *The Comedy of Errors, As You Like It, Much Ado About Nothing,* and *All's Well That Ends Well,* the titles of the tragedies all insist on dominant individuals. So too among the multiple and tangled concerns of the plays, it is possible to identify certain recurrent preoccupations, even obsessions.

This introduction has dwelt on one of these preoccupations, death, and anyone who reads the plays attentively can add others: an experience of radical vulnerability, an encounter with the intolerable, an ambivalent, destructive love, a seething hatred of beauty and goodness, a struggle against suicidal pessimism, a recognition of the strange, conjoined power and hollowness of language. Any worthwhile account of a Shakespearean tragedy will depend not on ballooning generalizations but on a particular, local richness of apprehension, a grasp of the boundless intelligence with which these preoccupations are explored, and above all, perhaps, a savoring of the playwright's inexhaustible poetic resources. At times Shakespeare draws upon those resources to make his characters speak in an exalted idiom far removed from the language of the everyday, as when Othello speaks of himself as

> one whose subdued eyes,
> Albeit unusèd to the melting mood,
> Drop tears as fast as the Arabian trees
> Their medicinable gum.
>
> (5.2.341–44)

At other times Shakespeare's characters, even when they are kings in a faraway land, speak in accents that are as familiar and terrible as one's own most intimate nightmares. Here is Shakespeare's excruciating vision, at the end of *King Lear,* of a distraught father holding in his arms his dead child. The language could not be simpler, nor could the suffering be more unbearably tragic:

> No, no, no life?
> Why should a dog, a horse, a rat have life,
> And thou no breath at all? Thou'lt come no more,
> Never, never, never, never, never!
>
> (*Tragedy* 5.3.281–84)

SELECTED BIBLIOGRAPHY

Bradley, A. C. *Shakespearean Tragedy: Lectures on "Hamlet," "Othello," "King Lear," "Macbeth."* 2nd ed. London: Macmillan, 1905. Presents an analysis centered on the tragic hero, understood as a great or sublime figure; posits that tragedy is a state of fundamental conflict between and especially within characters.

Cavell, Stanley. *Disowning Knowledge in Seven Plays of Shakespeare.* 2nd ed. Cambridge: Cambridge UP, 2003. Asserts that Shakespeare's tragedies respond to the early modern crisis of skepticism by dramatizing the limits of perception, especially perception of other people.

Dollimore, Jonathan. *Radical Tragedy: Religion, Ideology, and Power in the Drama of Shakespeare and His Contemporaries.* 2nd ed. Durham, NC: Duke UP, 1993. Argues that Renaissance tragedy contains a radical undercurrent of skepticism and secularism that subverts the ideologies of divine providence and human transcendence found both in the Renaissance context and in contemporary criticism.

Dutton, Richard, and Jean E. Howard, eds. *A Companion to Shakespeare's Works.* Vol. 1: *The Tragedies.* Malden, MA: Blackwell, 2003. Presents a collection of essays on individual plays, themes, and contexts, and film and performance history.

Frye, Northrop. *Fools of Time: Studies in Shakespearean Tragedy.* Toronto: U of Toronto P, 1967. Examines how tragedy is an experience of struggling against existence in time; and analyzes the plays as tragedies of order, or social crisis; of passion, or internal conflict; and of isolation, or search for individual identity.

Kottman, Paul A. *Tragic Conditions in Shakespeare: Disinheriting the Globe.* Baltimore, MD: Johns Hopkins UP, 2009. Asserts that by showing that we cannot control what we inherit or bequeath, tragedy reveals the radical contingency and fragility of familial and social bonds.

McEachern, Claire, ed. *The Cambridge Companion to Shakespearean Tragedy.* 2nd ed. Cambridge: Cambridge UP, 2013. Offers introductory essays on performance, cultural contexts, and key themes of Shakespeare's tragedies.

Miola, Robert S. *Shakespeare and Classical Tragedy: The Influence of Seneca.* Oxford: Clarendon P, 1992. Examines how Seneca is a key source for rhetorical style and themes of revenge, tyranny, and *furor* in Shakespeare's tragedies.

Neill, Michael. *Issues of Death: Mortality and Identity in English Renaissance Tragedy.* Oxford: Clarendon P, 1997. Draws on Renaissance science, art, and tragic drama to understand how Shakespeare's culture (re)imagined death in response to religious and cultural anxieties.

Smith, Emma, ed. *Shakespeare's Tragedies: A Guide to Criticism.* Malden, MA: Blackwell, 2004. Offers a history of the criticism of Shakespeare's tragedies, chiefly post-1900, broken down into topics of genre, character, language, gender and sexuality, history and politics, texts, and performance. Includes extracts of critical essays.

Titus Andronicus

Human sacrifice. Gang rape. Mutilation. Ritual butchery. Mother–son cannibalism. *Titus Andronicus* delighted audiences of the 1590s, and the memory of its enormous popular success was still alive more than twenty years later, when Shakespeare's contemporary, Ben Jonson, referred to it as a famous old crowd-pleaser in his comedy *Bartholomew Fair*. Several centuries of critics since then, however, have deplored the play's gratuitous violence. The late seventeenth-century playwright Edward Ravenscroft considered *Titus Andronicus* "a heap of rubbish"; the twentieth-century poet and critic T. S. Eliot called it "one of the stupidest and most uninspired plays ever written." Some have maintained that Shakespeare could not possibly have written *Titus Andronicus*, even though contemporaries testify to his authorship and the play inaugurates themes that will interest him again: he returns to the machiavellian villain in *Richard III*, to the urgency of revenge in *Hamlet*, to the old man unwisely relinquishing power in *Lear*, to questions of race and intermarriage in *Othello* and *The Tempest*, to important moments in Roman history in *The Rape of Lucrece*, *Julius Caesar*, *Coriolanus*, and *Antony and Cleopatra*.

Of course, Shakespeare himself, writing his first tragedy in 1592 (with, some scholars argue, the help of George Peele), could not have anticipated the reasons for which he would eventually be canonized. Moreover, the distinction between "high art" and "low entertainment" that often underlies complaints about *Titus Andronicus* would have been unfamiliar to Shakespeare and his audience: the contrast between popular and elite culture was drawn differently in early modern England than it has been in later centuries. Even by the standards of Shakespeare's contemporaries, however, *Titus Andronicus* is an extravagantly bloody play, often deliberately shocking or grotesque. It seems worth asking how it fits into an oeuvre in which many have been reluctant to grant it a place.

Generically speaking, *Titus Andronicus* is a tragedy of revenge, a very old form that originated in ancient Greece, flourished in ancient Rome, and was revived in the 1580s in England by Shakespeare's predecessor Thomas Kyd. English Renaissance revenge tragedies typically feature a man whose family members have been raped or murdered by a king, duke, or emperor. Because the administration of justice rests in the hands of the very person who has committed the outrage, no redress is obtainable through established institutions. As a result, the hero takes matters into his own hands. Ironically, as he struggles to impose a just order upon his world, he loses his own moral bearings and even his sanity: the commonsensical standards of "justice" upon which he has initially relied often come to seem either flawed or unreachable. In the final scenes, the revenger wreaks some appalling vengeance upon his enemies and then is killed or commits suicide himself. By staging the spectacle of a subject exterminating his "betters," Renaissance revenge tragedy taps into frustrations and ambivalences that must have accumulated in the hierarchical, deliberately inequitable social arrangements of early modern England. Spectators could experience a vicarious thrill of sympathy with the revenger and relish the atrocities represented onstage, even while, at the end of the play, acknowledging the moral unacceptability of revenge and the necessity for the revenger's death.

Titus Andronicus differs from roughly contemporary revenge tragedies in degree rather than in kind. Revengers typically begin as conscientious, law-abiding types:

otherwise their eventual descent into illegality would furnish little dramatic interest. In Titus's case, these traits are highly exaggerated: when offered the imperial diadem, his sense of propriety induces him to defer to Saturninus, the eldest son of the last emperor, even though in Rome the office of emperor was not necessarily an inherited one. Of course, the obligation that Saturninus thus incurs makes Titus's later suffering at the hands of the imperial family seem all the more galling. At the same time, Shakespeare complicates the action by giving Saturninus's wife, Tamora, an excellent reason for hating Titus: in the first scene, he has ignored her desperate pleas and sacrificed her eldest son. So, in fact, Titus's revenge is a response to Tamora's own vengeance. The doubling of reprisals in *Titus Andronicus* gives some pretext for the play's relentless bloodiness; but it is worth remembering too that bloodiness is an earmark of revenge tragedy then and now. One modern corollary to a play like *Titus Andronicus* is the movie thriller in which a rogue cop or ex-military officer brutally retaliates against those who have murdered his partners or loved ones: the kind of film, in other words, that is likely to attract a vast audience even while provoking condemnation of "media violence." *Titus* seems considerably less grotesque when it is compared with other plays of its kind rather than, say, *Romeo and Juliet*.

In its elaborately detailed antique setting, however, *Titus Andronicus* differs strikingly from most Renaissance revenge tragedies. The play is an early manifestation of Shakespeare's enduring interest in classical culture, a "Roman" play akin to *Julius Caesar, Coriolanus,* and *Antony and Cleopatra*. But in contrast to the later Roman plays, which are based on history and biography, the plot of *Titus Andronicus* is pure fiction. Unfettered by fact, Shakespeare is free to fabricate an extravagant nightmare universe that presses against the frontiers of plausibility. At the same time, he puts a great deal of emphasis on the play's "Roman-ness," making constant reference to classical myths, to legendary and historical figures, to imperial institutions, to the places and customs of ancient Rome.

Shakespeare creates what might be called a "Rome effect" by an eclectic process of extracting and combining motifs from a wide variety of classical stories. Titus as he appears in the opening scene, for instance—in his austere patriotism, his intolerance of dissent, his acute sense of personal and family honor, his traditional piety, and his ferocious commitment to patriarchal hierarchy—is a recurrent Roman personality type. Shakespeare could have found precedents for these traits in numerous figures from Roman history. After a victory in battle, Horatius killed his sister for lamenting her betrothed, a man of the enemy nation whom he himself had slain in combat; Gaius Mucius Scaevola deliberately burned off his right hand in the presence of an enemy king to demonstrate the resolution of the Romans; Titus Manlius Torquatus was a general so severe that he had his own son executed for eagerly anticipating an order to engage the enemy; Marcus Portius Cato's contempt for "softness" made him both an extraordinary military leader and an eloquent misogynist; Appius Claudius killed his daughter after her sexual honor was compromised. Most likely, Shakespeare had all these exemplary figures in mind, and probably more. Likewise, the career of Titus's son Lucius, a soldier who defends Rome bravely against external enemies but who finds himself persecuted by his own countrymen, recalls the experience of several historical figures: the brothers Publius Scipio Africanus and Lucius Scipio Asiaticus, who subdued much of North Africa and western Asia only to be falsely accused of embezzlement; or Caius Martius Coriolanus, who after his exile joined Rome's enemies and marched on his native city.

Similarly, Titus's daughter Lavinia has a number of classical precursors. The story of her rape and mutilation is loosely based on a story that, as retold in Ovid's *Metamorphoses,* was commonly assigned to Elizabethan boys in school. In this ancient legend, King Tereus rapes his sister-in-law Philomela and cuts out her tongue in order to prevent her from revealing his identity. Philomela, however, imparts the truth to her sister Procne, Tereus's wife, by weaving a tapestry that illustrates the crime. In revenge, Procne butchers her own son by Tereus and serves him to her husband as part of a

Procne serving Itys to Tereus. From Antonio Tempesta, *Ovid's "Metamorphoses"* (1606).

feast. The similarities between Lavinia's plight and Philomela's are often noted in *Titus Andronicus*, and Lavinia herself reveals the truth about the crime when she gets her stumps on a copy of the *Metamorphoses*.

But Philomela is not the only model for Lavinia. Shakespeare draws on the story of the rape of Lucretia, an ancient Roman matron violated by Tarquin, the king's son; she committed suicide after revealing the crime to her male relatives. Lucretia was revenged by a group of men who, like Lucius in *Titus Andronicus*, used the outrage as a pretext for overthrowing tyrannical power and setting up a new government. Shakespeare also incorporates into *Titus Andronicus* some features of the story of Appius and Virginia. Virginia was a young Roman woman who was sexually threatened by a powerful judge and killed by her father to prevent her rape; like Lucretia, she became the pretext for a revolutionary uprising. Lavinia's story, then, is an amalgam of classical rape narratives. Her terribly mutilated body condenses a long history of sporadic violence against women into a single, intensely imagined brutalization. Like Titus, Lavinia seems to sum up a whole tradition, one highly prestigious in an age that venerated the classics, and at the same time deeply disturbing.

This particular way of imagining "Rome," as an anthology of stories, reflects Shakespeare's education in sixteenth-century England. England had, of course, been a Roman territory, and marks of the Roman occupation persisted. Romans had built the road system still in use in Shakespeare's time; the remains of their fortifications were (and are) still visible in many locations. But England had been a remote outpost of the empire, not a place where the treasures of antiquity were commonly to be found. While Renaissance Italians could ground their knowledge of antiquity upon great architecture and statuary all around them, the English, few of whom traveled to Italy in the sixteenth century, imbibed the classical past through books, through a grammar school curriculum that emphasized a firm grounding in Latin literature and history. For Shakespeare and his compatriots, in other words, the Roman past had less to do with places or artifacts than with texts.

The influence of these texts echoes through *Titus Andronicus*: Ovid's *Metamorphoses*, a fantastic compilation of pagan myths; Virgil's *Aeneid*, which recounts the epic voyage of the Trojan prince Aeneas to Carthage and then Italy; the gory legends of vengeance dramatized by the tragedian Seneca; the histories of the Roman Republic and Empire, written by Livy, Plutarch, Tacitus, Sallust, and Suetonius. In *Titus Andronicus,* the sign of Rome's dominion often seems less a moral or political superiority than a kind of narrative ascendancy. Shakespeare's Goths and Africans apparently have no history, no myths, of their own: instead, they invoke and mimic examples provided by their conquerors, just as Renaissance Europeans revived the classical literary inheritance, testifying to its importance in the very acts of reading and imitating it.

All the characters in *Titus Andronicus* are acutely conscious of the glorious Roman past as it is enshrined in narrative. Their dependence on old stories means that their lives have a curiously derivative quality. The characters not only model their behavior on these stories, but consistently exceed the prototype. Whereas in the *Metamorphoses* one man rapes Philomela and cuts out her tongue afterward, in *Titus Andronicus* two men rape Lavinia and cut off not only her tongue but her hands as well. Whereas Procne cooks one child, Titus bakes two. "For worse than Philomel you used my daughter," Titus declares, "And worse than Procne I will be revenged" (5.2.193–94).* He both invokes and goes beyond his original example, intensifying the original crime in a way characteristic of revengers ancient and modern: "An act is not revenged," writes the ancient tragedian Seneca, "unless it is surpassed." Thus there is an interesting corollary between the spiraling ferocity typical of the revenge plot and the competitive way in which the characters in Shakespeare's revenge play fit themselves into a Roman tradition by exceeding its paradigms, enacting its stories "with a vengeance," as one says.

Of course, the oppressive weight of the past is a problem not merely for the characters of *Titus Andronicus* but also for its playwright. Like his characters, Shakespeare recycles the old stories with a difference, "surpassing" them just as the revenger surpasses the original crime. From our point of view, Shakespeare seems the world's preeminent dramatist, secure in the greatness that was already beginning to be accorded him at the time of his death. But in the early years of his career, Shakespeare might well have wondered whether and how it was possible to use, even while surpassing, the examples earlier writers had set for him. The notorious excesses of *Titus Andronicus* are one way of employing, even while going beyond, the examples he inherited.

If, in fact, Shakespeare worried about how he would measure up against his predecessors, and about whether the present and future would be able to compete with the past, it is interesting that he sets *Titus Andronicus* in the late fourth century C.E. At this point in history, Rome had dominated Europe, North Africa, and the Middle East for almost five hundred years. In both extent and duration, its empire was historically unprecedented and has never been achieved again. The Roman ritual that embodies and celebrates that rule is the "triumph" with which *Titus Andronicus* begins: a victory procession accorded to conquering Roman generals when they returned from the perimeters of the empire with barbarian chieftains in tow. By the fourth century, however, the long Roman dominion was drawing to a close. Shakespeare's sixteenth-century audience knows that although Titus may still be winning battles against the Goths, the time is near when the boundaries of the empire will crumble and invaders will sweep down from the north, annihilating Rome's power and bringing the era of classical civilization to an end.

In *Titus Andronicus,* then, Shakespeare portrays a society teetering on the verge of obsolescence: it has a long, long history but not much of a future. The signs of decadence, corruption, and loss of cultural confidence are everywhere. For instance, the difference between Roman and barbarian initially seems clearly, even absolutely, marked. Tamora and her sons are in chains, Titus and his sons conquering heroes. "Thou art a Roman; be not barbarous," Marcus advises Titus (1.1.381), as if the two

*All quotations are taken from the edited text of the Quarto, printed here. The Digital Edition includes edited texts of both the Quarto and the Folio.

Triumphal arch and its collapse. From Jan van der Noot, *A Theatre for Worldlings* (1569).

terms were necessarily incompatible. Even in the first scene, however, the Roman sense of superiority seems unwarranted. A quarrel over the imperial throne precedes Titus's victory celebration, suggesting the institutional instability that will ultimately subvert Rome from within even as uncouth armies threaten to overwhelm it from without. Moreover, the climax of Titus's victory celebration is his insistence on sacrificing Alarbus despite Tamora's maternal pleas: a case in which the traditional forms of piety that underlie Roman civilization seem to require the barbaric practice of human sacrifice. If Rome's conviction of racial and cultural supremacy—of *deserving* to rule the world—was once a workable notion, it is so no longer. The obsession with the past that pervades *Titus Andronicus* thus seems oddly empty. Even as inherited stories provide the only paradigms for action, they fail to nourish a fertile sense of tradition that might help Rome renew itself.

As traditional distinctions lose their prestige and plausibility, the social procedures that depend on such distinctions likewise begin to collapse. The play's first scene neatly exemplifies the problem. The brothers Saturninus and Bassianus quarrel first over the possession of the imperial throne and then over the possession of Lavinia, whom both wish to marry. In Shakespeare's England, the first dispute would have been settled according to the principle of "primogeniture," which gave priority in inheritance to the elder brother; the second would have been settled in favor of the younger brother, on the grounds of his preexisting betrothal to Lavinia. In Rome, however, it seems impossible to settle competing claims in an orderly way. In fact, Saturninus does eventually get the throne and Bassianus the woman, but not without a good deal of confusion and some lethal violence. The suggestion is that established methods of allocating property or privilege to one or another person may be quite arbitrary, but that the alternative to such methods is chaos.

In case the point is not sufficiently clear, Shakespeare immediately follows the quarrel between the two Roman brothers with another scene of sibling rivalry, this time between Tamora's sons, once again over sexual access to Lavinia. Unlike their Roman counterparts, these men are seeking not marriage but an adulterous relationship, and their villainous confidant Aaron has little difficulty massaging their illicit ambitions into plans for a rape. Adultery and rape seem the "opposites" of the marriage desired by the Roman men; and certainly the ferocity of the Gothic brothers' attack on Lavinia makes abundantly clear why such behavior is intolerable. At the same time, Shakespeare's juxtaposition of scenes suggests, subversively, the *similarities* between Roman marriage and rape. In neither case is Lavinia's consent at issue: she becomes the property of whoever happens to carry her off by force. Once again the distinction between legitimate and illegitimate behavior seems indispensable and at the same time remarkably indistinct.

The characters apparently best equipped to function in this world of collapsing distinctions are Aaron and Tamora, whose interracial adultery is perceived as particularly scandalous by both Romans and Goths. The classical account of racial difference, inherited by Shakespeare and his contemporaries, did not draw a binary distinction between "white" Europeans and "black" Africans; instead it contrasted the fair-skinned inhabitants of northern Europe on the one hand, and the dark-skinned inhabitants of Africa on the other, with the "temperate" natives of Mediterranean Europe (where, of course, this theory originated). Both Tamora and Aaron represent, in other words, outlandish extremes from a Roman point of view. Because Tamora and Aaron are outsiders, neither has much to gain by endorsing Rome's view of itself, which has relegated them to positions of servitude and powerlessness. They recognize from the outset the artificiality of the precepts by which Rome pretends to govern itself and the world, and understand that if they are ever to gain power, it must be by refusing to play by those rules. In a society in which women are treated as the sexual property of their male relatives, "good" women like Lavinia seem destined for passivity and victimization. In a few lines, then, Tamora—manipulative, ruthless, and cunning— transfers herself from the extreme of subjugation, as Titus's captive, to the apex of power as empress of Rome.

Aaron is a stage descendant of the "black men" of the medieval morality plays, which conflated traditional depictions of the devil with racist conceptions of "Moors" and "Africans." But at the same time that Shakespeare exploits to the full Aaron's capacity for gleeful villainy, he makes Aaron's point of view comprehensible, even at some points attractive, to the audience. Roman hierarchies would consign Aaron permanently to a subordinate position. Like Tamora, he sees no reason to accept the validity of that assignment. Why should he collaborate in his own oppression? It is no coincidence that Shakespeare's verse seems at its best in this play when Aaron is delivering a soliloquy. His view of the world is very close to what the play as a whole seems to endorse: that the assumptions upon which ethical behavior and social institutions depend represent fictions rather than facts.

For the dramatic technique of *Titus Andronicus*, like its villains, seems to insist that the "normal" or the "proper" is a mere construct, that apparently vivid distinctions are not as clear-cut as they seem, that moral opposites have a way of turning into one another. We have already seen Shakespeare setting the behavior of Bassianus and Saturninus beside the behavior of Chiron and Demetrius, as well as associating his white empress with his black slave. Such juxtapositions seem to be designed to induce a sort of evaluative vertigo, an effect that becomes most intense, perhaps, in the figure of the unnamed infant who results from Tamora's adultery with Aaron. In the view of most of the play's characters, this child physically embodies, and thus serves as both proof and symbol of, its parents' utter depravity. At the same time, Aaron's unexpectedly fierce solicitude for the child—which contrasts attractively with Titus's casual willingness to slaughter his own son—prevents the audience from taking at face value the rhetoric of disgust and fear discharged upon the little unfortunate from everyone else in the play. This is, after all, a baby. Every time it is brought onstage, the function it seems designed to serve in the play's symbolic economy powerfully conflicts with its intrinsic infant appeal.

In other cases, Shakespeare produces jarringly appropriate incongruities not by juxtaposing characters but by evoking apparently inappropriate dramatic genres. For instance, when Quintus and Martius find Bassianus's body, the audience knows they are being framed for murder, and one might expect a playwright to exploit the pathos of the situation, encouraging the audience to pity and sympathize with the innocent characters. Instead, the scene is played for laughs, as Titus's sons struggle farcically to pull one another out of a hole. Another jarring technique in *Titus Andronicus* is the deliberately awful play on words: "Mark, Marcus, mark" (3.1.143), cries Titus as they behold the ravished and mutilated Lavinia. In such cases, Shakespeare's humor shatters the norms of dramatic and moral suitability, implying the artificiality of what is conventionally considered "normal" or "proper."

Ethiopian soldier. From Cesare Vecellio, *De gli habiti antichi et moderni* (1590).

If the moral and social problem of *Titus* is that eventually nothing is taboo, the aesthetic problem of the play is that literary convention too comes to seem entirely artificial. Shakespeare's deliberate rule breaking in *Titus Andronicus* risks looking like, or simply being the equivalent of, tasteless incompetence. This is especially true when terrible suffering is at stake. Marcus's long, garishly metaphorical speech at the sight of his niece's bleeding body (2.4.13–57), for instance, seems grossly beside the point. Is Shakespeare merely being inept here—is he as out of control as Marcus seems to be? Or is he deliberately exploring the limits of his medium by unexpectedly violating its usual rules, in the manner of modern surrealists, absurdists, or postmodernists? The critical debate about *Titus Andronicus* has largely involved quarrels between those who claim the former and those who claim the latter.

Even if Shakespeare sometimes seems to share the heartlessness of Aaron and Tamora, he does not represent the Goth and the African as admirable characters. Rebelling against the principles of "civilization" puts them outside any moral community. At the end of the play, Lucius orders Aaron starved to death and Tamora's body thrown over the city walls, as if it were mere garbage. Their treatment indicates his conviction that their behavior has put themselves outside the classification of the human, so that when they are starving, no one has an obligation to relieve them, and when they are dead, no one need respect their remains. The final scene reasserts the difference between human society and what Titus calls "a wilderness of tigers," a difference that the revenge plot has come close to erasing. And despite the abundant evidence that Roman social organization is fundamentally flawed and soon to be toppled, it is not surprising that both Goths and Romans should greet Lucius's restoration of order at the end of the play with profound relief.

Titus Andronicus, then, suggests that the principles of Roman order are patently false and often arbitrarily oppressive; but it also suggests that acknowledging this arbitrariness or rebelling against this falsity and oppression will have disastrous consequences. What produces Roman "virtue" seems to be a delusion; but being undeluded, as Tamora and Aaron are and as Titus becomes, is even more terrible. In Shakespeare's later tragedies, the alternative to normality is often a visionary possibility that seems, if only it could be lived out, to improve upon the status quo: the loves of Romeo and Juliet, Antony and Cleopatra, Othello and Desdemona are examples of such "constructive rule breaking." In Titus Andronicus, however, traditional taboos, however cruel, brittle, or despotic they seem, are the sole guarantors of order. Once they are shattered, nothing can take their place, and sheer chaos ensues.

The pessimism, even nihilism, of this vision, combined with Shakespeare's almost playful emphasis on what most writers prefer to skirt or play down, is doubtless what has made Titus seem merely bad to so many readers since the late seventeenth century. From another point of view, however, Titus Andronicus is a daring experiment, one that Shakespeare did not repeat but that nonetheless provides fascinating insight into his development as a dramatist.

KATHARINE EISAMAN MAUS

SELECTED BIBLIOGRAPHY

Barker, Francis. "A Wilderness of Tigers: Titus Andronicus, Anthropology, and the Occlusion of Violence." The Culture of Violence: Tragedy and History. Chicago: U of Chicago P, 1993. 143–206. Shows how cultural anthropology and the history of criminal prosecution in early modern England illuminate Titus Andronicus, particularly the "Clown scene" (4.3).

Bartels, Emily. "Making More of the Moor: Aaron, Othello, and Renaissance Refashionings of Race." Shakespeare Quarterly 41 (1990): 433–54. Looks at Aaron in the context of other sixteenth-century English depictions of black Africans.

James, Heather. "Cultural Disintegration in Titus Andronicus: Mutilating Titus, Virgil, and Rome." Violence in Drama. Ed. James Redmond. New York: Cambridge UP, 1991. 123–40. Examines Shakespeare's debt to Virgil's Aeneid.

Kahn, Coppélia. "The Daughter's Seduction in Titus Andronicus; or, Writing Is the Best Revenge." The Roman Shakespeare: Warriors, Wounds, and Women. New York: Routledge, 1997. 46–76. Discusses Lavinia's role in the play.

Loomba, Ania. "Wilderness and Civilization in Titus Andronicus." Shakespeare, Race, and Colonialism. New York: Oxford UP, 2002. 75–90. Focuses on the alliance between Aaron and Tamora.

Palmer, D. J. "The Unspeakable in Pursuit of the Uneatable: Language and Action in Titus Andronicus." Critical Quarterly 14 (1972): 320–39. Analyzes the representation of suffering.

Rowe, Katherine. "Dismembering and Forgetting in Titus Andronicus." Shakespeare Quarterly 45 (1994): 279–303. Examines amputated hands and frustrated agency in the play.

Royster, Francesca. "White-Limed Walls: Whiteness and Gothic Extremism in Shakespeare's Titus Andronicus." Shakespeare Quarterly 51 (2000): 432–55. Looks at the play's presentation of racial difference in its Renaissance context.

Silverstone, Catherine. "'Honour the real thing': Gregory Doran's Titus Andronicus in South Africa." Shakespeare, Trauma and Contemporary Performance. New York: Routledge, 2011. 26–54. Discusses a 1995 production of Titus in South Africa as an exploration of violence, trauma, and national history.

Vickers, Brian. "Titus Andronicus with George Peele." Shakespeare, Co-Author: A Historical Study of Five Collaborative Plays. New York: Oxford UP, 2002. 148–243. Discusses the likelihood that Shakespeare and George Peele collaborated on Titus Andronicus.

FILMS

Titus Andronicus. 1985. Dir. Jane Howell. UK. 120 min. This production, stylized and self-consciously theatrical, is often considered one of the best of the BBC series and a major influence on Taymor's bigger-budget film (1999).

Titus. 1999. Dir. Julie Taymor. USA. 162 min. A visually stunning adaptation of Shakespeare's play, emphasizing its stomach-churning violence. The fine cast includes Anthony Hopkins as Titus and Jessica Lange as Tamora.

TEXTUAL INTRODUCTION

There are three quarto texts of *Titus Andronicus*: Q1 (1594), Q2 (1600), and Q3 (1611). There is only one surviving copy of Q1, *The Most Lamentable Roman Tragedy of Titus Andronicus*; it was purchased by Henry Clay Folger in 1905 following its discovery in Sweden in 1904. The Folger copy (Krafft) is necessarily the base text for any edition of Q1. Editors argue that there are several reasons to believe that Q1 was printed from a copy of Shakespeare's foul papers (working manuscript) or a scribal "fair copy," including variety in speech prefixes (e.g., "*Saturnine*," "*Emperour*," "*King*" are used variously for Saturninus), false starts (see Digital Edition TC 1), and the comparative lack of detail in stage directions in relation to the Folio text, *The Lamentable Tragedy of Titus Andronicus* (1623). Each of the quarto texts appears to have been printed from the preceding text.

F was printed from Q3 probably in conjunction with a theatrical prompt copy of Q1, Q2, or Q3, since F's stage directions are fuller; however, there is no conclusive evidence for the nature of the projected prompt copy. The compositor of Q2 made some corrections to Q1, including deleting the false start at 1.1.35–38; he is most likely the author of variant and new material, probably written in response to damage to the final (K) gathering of pages in the text from which he was working. Strikingly, he seems to have written new lines (5.3.163–67, 5.3.198–202) that were retained in Q3 and F, highlighting the role that compositors played in shaping the texts of Shakespeare's plays (see Digital Edition TC 9 and TC 10). The compositors of Q3 and F are generally regarded by editors as less experienced and less accurate than the compositors of Q1 and Q2. In particular, the compositor of Q3 omitted two lines (3.1.35, 4.4.102) and the compositor of F omitted five lines (2.1.102, 4.2.8, 4.2.76, 5.2.160, 5.3.51) and added two lines (1.1.398, 4.1.37); the *Norton Shakespeare* edition of F (available in the Digital Edition) has preserved these omissions and additions except where the deleted lines are judged necessary for sense (e.g., 2.1.102).

Most editors of *Titus Andronicus* use Q1 as the base text with the exception of 3.2 (the "fly-killing scene"), for which F is the earliest authority (see Digital Edition TC 4). Editors suggest that this scene was written after Q1 was printed, probably by Shakespeare for a revival of the play (it uses "*An.*" as the speech prefix for Titus, which is not used elsewhere in the text, suggesting a different date of composition). The scene was probably inserted into the prompt copy used by the compositor in preparing F. Editors also tend to replace and augment Q1's stage directions by way of those in F, which are generally taken to be closer to early modern theatrical practice.

The principles of single-text editing require that the *Norton Shakespeare* edition of Q1 does not contain scene 3.2. The phrasing and substance of Q1's stage directions are respected where possible. Nonetheless, some of Q1's stage directions have been augmented with information from F; others have been inserted from Q2, Q3, and F where this seems necessary to clarify the action. The false starts have been preserved in Q1 and F, and are marked by braces (curly brackets) to draw attention to the processes of authorship and printing. F retains the variant and new material introduced by the compositor of Q2 and reproduced in Q3 and F so as to draw further attention to the play's textual history and to the role of compositors in creating the text. Speech prefixes and variant spellings have been standardized between Q1 and F (e.g., "*Aaron*" for "*Moor*" in Q1 and F; "*Bassianus*" for "*Bascianus*" in Q1). F's "*Boy*" (named "*Young Lucius*" in stage directions) translates and replaces Q1's "*Puer.*" Titus's sons in 1.1 have been given proper names in preference to generic descriptions (e.g., "2. *Sonne*") in preparation for their further development in 2.3; these decisions draw attention to a key editorial crux and to the ways in which editors influence characterization (see Digital Edition TC 3). Duplicated speech prefixes have been deleted (e.g., 2.2.11 in Q1 and F). Missing speech prefixes have been added (e.g., 1.1.18 in Q1 and F) where the speaker is given in the preceding stage direction, and in cases where the text suggests that there is a shift in speaker (e.g., 1.1.476 in Q1); the latter identifies how editorial practice can affect meaning and characterization (see Digital Edition TC 5 and TC 8). Punctuation has been standardized across the two texts where the words are identical. Act and scene divisions accord with the editorial tradition for the play, following the Folio's act divisions (the Quarto offers no such divisions) and Nicholas Rowe's scene divisions in his 1709 edition, further subdivided by subsequent editors, Alexander Pope, Edward Capell, and Alexander Dyce. Lineation has also been standardized as much as possible in order to aid the reader who wishes to compare the two texts; the main corollary of this is that a number of F's pairs of short lines have been set as single lines.

CATHERINE SILVERSTONE

PERFORMANCE NOTE

Featuring a protagonist who vies for the opportunity to chop off his hand, debates the respect due to a swatted housefly, and cooks his guests' offspring into their meat pies, *Titus Andronicus* is a tragedy constantly inclining toward farce. It thus challenges theater companies to maintain pathos amid episodes almost certain to prompt laughter, causing many directors to reduce the text's gratuitous violence through adaptation, or to dodge grotesquerie by stylizing the blocking, using symbolic sounds, and rendering blood abstractly, as ribbons or cloth. Directors also earn their productions some dignity and complement the play's high rhetorical style by amplifying the ceremony around the first scene, solemnizing the subsequent violence by having it echo Titus's ritual sacrifice of Alarbus. Some directors aim for visceral representations of violence, using gruesome stage blood and hyperrealistic stray heads and hands, while others mount full-blown farces, provoking audiences to laughter that potentially deepens the shock and suddenness of events such as Lavinia's execution.

Whatever the balance struck between tragedy and dark comedy, directors make critical choices about *Titus*'s characters, especially Titus and Aaron. Titus, whose early onstage acts include denying all mercy to Tamora's son and murdering his own, does not easily invite sympathy; the villainous Aaron, meanwhile, inevitably attracts support with his charisma and compelling paternal instinct. Titus can appear reactionary or simply confused, his offenses owing to ego and spite or to misguided attempts at fealty. Aaron can be a motiveless fiend or justified in revenging himself on clear oppressors. Tamora, too, can emerge as a revenger or a savage, depending on whether the portrayal emphasizes her maternal dimension or her sensuousness and duplicity. Lavinia can participate actively in Tamora's flouting and Titus's revenge or simply transition from innocence to catatonia; Lucius can offer promise as a clear-sighted ruler or seem destined to renew the cycle of violence. Directors must also manage the contradictory staging demands in 1.1 (see Digital Edition TC 2); Quintus and Martius's fall into a "pit" (2.2); and Marcus's infamously challenging speech (2.4). And they must decide the extent of Titus's madness, the fate of Aaron's child, and whether Lavinia is complicit in her death.

BRETT GAMBOA

The Most Lamentable Roman Tragedy of Titus Andronicus

[THE PERSONS OF THE PLAY

SATURNINUS, eldest son to the late Emperor of Rome; later Emperor
BASSIANUS, younger brother to Saturninus
MARCUS Andronicus, tribune
PUBLIUS, son to Marcus
TITUS Andronicus, general, brother to Marcus
LAVINIA, daughter to Titus, betrothed to Bassianus
LUCIUS ⎫
QUINTUS ⎪
MARTIUS ⎬ sons to Titus
MUTIUS ⎭
BOY, Young Lucius, son to Lucius
Sempronius ⎫
Caius ⎬ kinsmen to Titus
Valentine ⎭
TRIBUNES
AEMILIUS
ROMAN LORD
CAPTAIN
NURSE
CLOWN
MESSENGER
Other ROMANS, including Senators, Soldiers, Judges, and Attendants

TAMORA, Queen of the Goths, later wife to Saturninus and Empress of Rome
Alarbus ⎫
DEMETRIUS ⎬ sons to Tamora
CHIRON ⎭
AARON, a Moor, lover of Tamora
Baby, son to Aaron and Tamora
FIRST GOTH
SECOND GOTH
THIRD GOTH
Army of GOTHS]

1.1 (F 1.1)

Enter the TRIBUNES *and Senators*[1] *aloft. And then
enter [below]* SATURNINUS *and his followers [and
Soldiers] at one door and* BASSIANUS *and his followers
[and Soldiers at the other], with drums° and trumpets.*   *drummer*

SATURNINUS [*to his followers*]   Noble patricians, patrons° of   *supporters*
   my right,
  Defend the justice of my cause with arms.
  And countrymen, my loving followers,
  Plead my successive title° with your swords.   *right to succeed*
5 I am his first-born son that was the last
  That wore the imperial diadem of Rome:
  Then let my father's honors live in me,
  Nor wrong mine age° with this indignity.   *seniority*
BASSIANUS [*to his followers*]   Romans, friends, followers,
   favorers of my right,
10 If ever Bassianus, Caesar's[2] son,
  Were gracious° in the eyes of royal Rome,   *Found favor*
  Keep° then this passage° to the Capitol,   *Defend / path*
  And suffer not dishonor to approach
  The imperial seat, to virtue consecrate,°   *consecrated*
15 To justice, continence, and nobility;
  But let desert[3] in pure election[4] shine,
  And, Romans, fight for freedom in your choice.
     [*Enter*] MARCUS *Andronicus, [aloft,] with the crown.*
MARCUS   Princes that strive by factions and by friends
  Ambitiously for rule and empery,°   *imperial rule*
20 Know that the people of Rome, for whom we stand
  A special party,[5] have by common voice
  In election for the Roman empery
  Chosen Andronicus, surnamèd Pius,[6]
  For many good and great deserts to Rome.
25 A nobler man, a braver warrior,
  Lives not this day within the city walls.
  He by the Senate is accited° home   *summoned*
  From weary wars against the barbarous Goths,
  That with his sons, a terror to our foes,
30 Hath yoked° a nation strong, trained up in arms.   *subdued*
  Ten years are spent since first he undertook
  This cause of Rome and chastised with arms
  Our enemies' pride. Five times he hath returned
  Bleeding to Rome, bearing his valiant sons
35 In coffins from the field; {and at this day[7]
  To the monument of the Andronici
  Done sacrifice of expiation,
  And slain the noblest prisoner of the Goths.}

1.1 Location: Before the Roman Capitol, represented by the upper stage ("aloft"). The tomb of the Andronicus family, a stage structure or a trapdoor, is accessible onstage.
1. Respectively, the representatives of the common people (plebeians) and the upper classes (patricians).
2. The previous Emperor (Bassianus is Saturninus's younger brother).
3. Merit (as opposed to birth order).
4. Free choice of the citizens.

5. A representative elected for a particular purpose.
6. Titus has been given the honorary title of "Dutiful."
7. TEXTUAL COMMENT The lines in curly brackets appear in Q1 but not in Q2 or Q3; they describe, in the past tense, the death of Alarbus, which actually occurs later in the scene. To modern editors, this inconsistency suggests that the Quarto was set from Shakespeare's foul papers, or working manuscript; see Digital Edition TC 1 (Quarto edited text).

40	And now, at last, laden with honor's spoils,
	Returns the good Andronicus to Rome,
	Renownèd Titus, flourishing in arms.
	Let us entreat, by honor of his° name

(the late Emperor's)

Whom worthily you would have now succeed,[8]
And in the Capitol and Senate's right,[9]
45 Whom you pretend° to honor and adore,   _claim_
That you withdraw you and abate your strength,
Dismiss your followers and, as suitors should,
Plead your deserts in peace and humbleness.
SATURNINUS How fair the tribune speaks to calm my thoughts.
50 BASSIANUS Marcus Andronicus, so I do affy°   _trust_
In thy uprightness and integrity,
And so I love and honor thee and thine,
Thy noble brother Titus and his sons
And her to whom my thoughts are humbled all,
55 Gracious Lavinia, Rome's rich ornament,
That I will here dismiss my loving friends
And to my fortunes and the people's favor
Commit my cause in balance to be weighed.
                              Exeunt [his] Soldiers [and followers].
SATURNINUS Friends that have been thus forward in my right,
60 I thank you all and here dismiss you all,
And to the love and favor of my country
Commit myself, my person, and the cause.
                        [Exeunt his Soldiers and followers.]
[_to the_ TRIBUNES _and Senators_] Rome, be as just and gracious
      unto me
As I am confident° and kind to thee.   _trusting_
65 Open the gates and let me in.
BASSIANUS Tribunes, and me, a poor competitor.°   _co-petitioner_
      [SATURNINUS _and_ BASSIANUS] _go up into the Senate_
      House.
            [_Exeunt aloft_ MARCUS, TRIBUNES, _and Senators._]
      Enter a CAPTAIN.
CAPTAIN Romans, make way. The good Andronicus,
Patron° of virtue, Rome's best champion,   _Representative; pattern_
Successful in the battles that he fights,
70 With honor and with fortune is returned
From where he circumscribèd° with his sword   _restrained_
And brought to yoke the enemies of Rome.
            Sound drums and trumpets, and then enter two of
            Titus' sons [LUCIUS _and_ MUTIUS], _and then men_
            bearing a coffin covered with black, then two other
            sons [MARTIUS _and_ QUINTUS], _then_ TITUS _Andronicus,_
            and then TAMORA _the Queen of Goths and her_ [_sons,_
            Alarbus,] CHIRON, _and_ DEMETRIUS, _with_ AARON _the_
            Moor,[1] _and others, as many as can be. Then set down_
            the coffin, and TITUS _speaks._

---

8. Whose place you want a worthy candidate to fill.
9. To choose a new emperor, traditionally an elected and not an inherited office.
1. "Moor" in classical times referred to an inhabitant of Mauretania, in northwest Africa; the term was later applied to Islamic Africans of Arab descent who conquered Spain in the Middle Ages. In Renaissance England, the word often was used of any black-skinned African.

TITUS Hail Rome, victorious in thy mourning weeds!° *garments*
Lo, as the bark° that hath discharged his fraught° *ship / its freight*
75 Returns with precious lading° to the bay *cargo*
From whence at first she weighed her anchorage,° *anchor*
Cometh Andronicus, bound with laurel boughs,[2]
To re-salute his country with his tears,
Tears of true joy for his return to Rome.
80 Thou great defender[3] of this Capitol,
Stand gracious to the rites that we intend.
Romans, of five-and-twenty valiant sons,
Half of the number that King Priam[4] had,
Behold the poor remains, alive and dead:
85 These that survive, let Rome reward with love;
These that I bring unto their latest° home, *last*
With burial amongst their ancestors.
Here Goths have given me leave[5] to sheathe my sword.
Titus, unkind[6] and careless of thine own,
90 Why suffer'st thou thy sons unburied yet
To hover on the dreadful shore of Styx?[7]
Make way to lay them by their brethren.
        They open the tomb.
There greet in silence, as the dead are wont,
And sleep in peace, slain in your country's wars.
95 O sacred receptacle of my joys,
Sweet cell of virtue and nobility,
How many sons hast thou of mine in store,
That thou wilt never render° to me more!° *return / again*
LUCIUS Give us the proudest prisoner of the Goths,
100 That we may hew his limbs and on a pile
Ad manes fratrum° sacrifice his flesh *To our brothers' shades (Latin)*
Before this earthy prison of their bones,
That so the shadows° be not unappeased, *spirits*
Nor we disturbed with prodigies° on earth. *evil happenings*
105 TITUS I give him you, the noblest that survives,
The eldest son of this distressèd Queen.
TAMORA [*kneeling*] Stay, Roman brethren! Gracious conqueror,
Victorious Titus, rue° the tears I shed— *pity*
A mother's tears in passion° for her son— *grief*
110 And if thy sons were ever dear to thee,
Oh, think my son to be as dear to me!
Sufficeth not that we are brought to Rome
To beautify thy triumphs° and return *triumphal processions*
Captive to thee and to thy Roman yoke?
115 But must my sons be slaughtered in the streets
For valiant doings in their country's cause?
Oh, if to fight for king and commonweal
Were piety in thine,° it is in these.° *(your sons) / (my sons)*
Andronicus, stain not thy tomb with blood.
120 Wilt thou draw near the nature of the gods?

---

2. Laurel wreath, symbol of victory.
3. Jupiter Capitolinus, king of the Roman gods, to whose shrine on the Capitol victorious generals brought their spoils.
4. King of Troy during the Trojan War.

5. Allowed me (ironic, since the Goths were defeated in battle).
6. Devoid of natural feeling; undutiful.
7. River surrounding the underworld; the dead could not cross it until they had been properly buried.

Draw near them, then, in being merciful:
Sweet mercy is nobility's true badge.
Thrice-noble Titus, spare my first-born son.
TITUS   Patient° yourself, madam, and pardon me.   *Calm*
125   These are their brethren whom your Goths beheld
Alive and dead, and for their brethren slain
Religiously° they ask a sacrifice.   *On religious grounds*
To this your son is marked, and die he must
T'appease their groaning shadows that are gone.
130   LUCIUS   Away with him, and make a fire straight,°   *immediately*
And with our swords upon a pile of wood
Let's hew his limbs till they be clean consumed.
        Exeunt Titus' sons [LUCIUS, QUINTUS, MARTIUS, *and*
                        MUTIUS] *with Alarbus.*
TAMORA [*rising*]   Oh, cruel irreligious piety!
CHIRON   Was never Scythia[8] half so barbarous!
135   DEMETRIUS   Oppose not Scythia to ambitious Rome.
Alarbus goes to rest and we survive
To tremble under Titus' threatening look.
Then, madam, stand resolved, but hope withal
The self-same gods that armed the Queen of Troy[9]
140   With opportunity of sharp revenge
Upon the Thracian tyrant in his tent
May favor Tamora the Queen of Goths—
When Goths were Goths and Tamora was Queen—
To quit° the bloody wrongs upon her foes.   *revenge*
        Enter the sons of Andronicus [LUCIUS, QUINTUS,
        MARTIUS, *and* MUTIUS] *again.*
145   LUCIUS   See, lord and father, how we have performed
Our Roman rites. Alarbus' limbs are lopped
And entrails feed the sacrificing fire,
Whose smoke like incense doth perfume the sky.
Remaineth naught but to inter our brethren
150   And with loud larums° welcome them to Rome.   *trumpet calls*
TITUS   Let it be so, and let Andronicus
Make this his latest° farewell to their souls.   *last*
        Sound trumpets and lay the coffin in the tomb.
In peace and honor rest you here, my sons;
Rome's readiest champions, repose you here in rest,
155   Secure from worldly chances and mishaps.
Here lurks no treason, here no envy° swells,   *malice*
Here grow no damnèd drugs,° here are no storms,   *poisons*
No noise, but silence and eternal sleep.
In peace and honor rest you here, my sons.
        Enter LAVINIA.
160   LAVINIA   In peace and honor live Lord Titus long;
My noble lord and father, live in fame.
Lo, at this tomb my tributary° tears   *tribute-bearing*
I render for my brethren's obsequies.°   *funeral rites*
[*She kneels.*] And at thy feet I kneel, with tears of joy
165   Shed on this earth, for thy return to Rome.

8. Uncivilized region north of the Black Sea.
9. In Ovid's *Metamorphoses* 13, Queen Hecuba, enslaved by the Greeks after the defeat of Troy, avenged her son Polydorus by killing the sons of his murderer, Polymnestor, tyrant of Thrace.

Oh, bless me here with thy victorious hand,
Whose fortunes Rome's best citizens applaud.
TITUS   Kind Rome, that hast thus lovingly reserved
The cordial° of mine age to glad my heart!   comfort
170   Lavinia, live, outlive thy father's days
And fame's eternal date for virtue's praise.[1]
[LAVINIA *rises. Enter aloft* TRIBUNES, *Senators,*
SATURNINUS, BASSIANUS, *and* MARCUS, *with a white
robe.*]
MARCUS   Long live Lord Titus, my belovèd brother,
Gracious triumpher in the eyes of Rome!
TITUS   Thanks, gentle tribune, noble brother Marcus.
175   MARCUS   And welcome, nephews, from successful wars,
You that survive and you that sleep in fame.
Fair lords, your fortunes are alike in all,
That in your country's service drew your swords.
But safer triumph is this funeral pomp
180   That hath aspired to Solon's happiness,[2]
And triumphs over chance in honor's bed.
Titus Andronicus, the people of Rome,
Whose friend in justice thou hast ever been,
Send thee by me, their tribune and their trust,
185   This palliament[3] of white and spotless hue,
And name thee in election for the empire
With these our late-deceasèd Emperor's sons.
Be *candidatus,*[4] then, and put it on,
And help to set a head on headless Rome.
190   TITUS   A better head her glorious body fits
Than his that shakes for age and feebleness.
What, should I don this robe and trouble you,
Be chosen with proclamations today,
Tomorrow yield up rule, resign my life,
195   And set abroad new business for you all?°   make you busy once again
Rome, I have been thy soldier forty years,
And led my country's strength successfully,
And buried one-and-twenty valiant sons,
Knighted in field, slain manfully in arms
200   In right° and service of their noble country.   the just cause
Give me a staff of honor for mine age,
But not a scepter to control the world.
Upright he held it, lords, that held it last.
MARCUS   Titus, thou shalt obtain and ask° the empery.   simply by asking
205   SATURNINUS   Proud and ambitious tribune, canst thou tell?°   how do you know
TITUS   Patience, Prince Saturninus.
SATURNINUS   Romans, do me right.
Patricians, draw your swords and sheathe them not
Till Saturninus be Rome's emperor.
Andronicus, would thou were shipped to hell,
210   Rather than rob me of the people's hearts!
LUCIUS   Proud Saturnine, interrupter of the good
That noble-minded Titus means to thee.

---

1. And may the praise of your virtue outlive eternity.
2. Solon, a Greek statesman, said, "Call no man happy until he is dead."
3. Ceremonial garment worn by aspirants to public office.
4. Candidate (literally, "one wearing the white toga").

TITUS   Content thee, Prince. I will restore to thee
 The people's hearts and wean them from themselves.
215 BASSIANUS   Andronicus, I do not flatter thee
 But honor thee and will do till I die.
 My faction if thou strengthen with thy friends
 I will most thankful be; and thanks to men
 Of noble minds is honorable meed.°   *reward*
220 TITUS   People of Rome, and people's tribunes here,
 I ask your voices and your suffrages.°   *votes*
 Will ye bestow them friendly on Andronicus?
 TRIBUNES   To gratify the good Andronicus
 And gratulate° his safe return to Rome,   *salute*
225 The people will accept whom he admits.°   *allows into office*
 TITUS   Tribunes, I thank you, and this suit I make,
 That you create° our emperor's eldest son,   *elect*
 Lord Saturnine, whose virtues will, I hope,
 Reflect on Rome as Titan's° rays on earth,   *the sun god*
230 And ripen justice in this commonweal.°   *community*
 Then if you will elect by my advice,
 Crown him and say, "Long live our emperor!"
 MARCUS   With voices and applause of every sort,
 Patricians and plebeians, we create
235 Lord Saturninus Rome's great emperor,
 And say, "Long live our emperor Saturnine!"
   [*A long flourish till* SATURNINUS, BASSIANUS, *and*
   MARCUS *come down.*][5]
 SATURNINUS   Titus Andronicus, for thy favors done
 To us in our election this day
240 I give thee thanks in part of thy deserts,[6]
 And will with deeds requite thy gentleness.° *pay back your kindness*
 And for an onset, Titus, to advance
 Thy name and honorable family,
 Lavinia will I make my empress,
 Rome's royal mistress, mistress of my heart,
245 And in the sacred Pantheon[7] her espouse.
 Tell me, Andronicus, doth this motion please thee?
 TITUS   It doth, my worthy lord, and in this match
 I hold me highly honored of your grace.
 And here in sight of Rome to Saturnine,
250 King and commander of our commonweal,
 The wide world's emperor, do I consecrate
 My sword, my chariot, and my prisoners,
 Presents well worthy Rome's imperious° lord.   *imperial*
 Receive them, then, the tribute that I owe,
255 Mine honor's ensigns° humbled at thy feet.   *symbols*
 SATURNINUS   Thanks, noble Titus, father of my life.
 How proud I am of thee and of thy gifts
 Rome shall record—and when I do forget
 The least of these unspeakable° deserts,   *inexpressible*

---

5. TEXTUAL COMMENT Most editors augment the
Quarto base text of *Titus Andronicus* with the fuller
stage directions from the Folio. *The Norton Shakespeare* follows this practice here, but the precise details

of the staging nonetheless remain ambiguous; see
Digital Edition TC 2 (Quarto edited text).
6. *in . . . deserts:* as part of what you deserve.
7. Roman temple dedicated to all the gods.

260   Romans, forget your fealty° to me.   *duty*
    TITUS [*to* TAMORA]   Now, madam, are you prisoner to an emperor,
      To him that for your honor and your state°   *royal dignity*
      Will use you nobly, and your followers.
    SATURNINUS [*aside*]   A goodly lady, trust me, of the hue°   *appearance; color*
265   That I would choose, were I to choose anew.
      —Clear up, fair Queen, that cloudy countenance.
      Though chance of war hath wrought this change of cheer,°   *expression*
      Thou com'st not to be made a scorn in Rome;
      Princely shall be thy usage every way.
270   Rest° on my word and let not discontent   *Rely*
      Daunt all your hopes. Madam, he comforts you
      Can° make you greater than the Queen of Goths.   *Who can*
      —Lavinia, you are not displeased with this?
    LAVINIA   Not I, my lord, sith° true nobility   *since*
275   Warrants° these words in princely courtesy.   *Justifies*
    SATURNINUS   Thanks, sweet Lavinia. —Romans, let us go.
      Ransomless here we set our prisoners free.
      Proclaim our honors, lords, with trump° and drum.   *trumpet*
          [*Flourish.* SATURNINUS, TAMORA, CHIRON, DEMETRIUS,
           and AARON *prepare to leave.*]
    BASSIANUS [*seizing* LAVINIA]   Lord Titus, by your leave, this
      maid is mine.
280   TITUS   How, sir? Are you in earnest, then, my lord?
    BASSIANUS   Ay, noble Titus, and resolved withal
      To do myself this reason and this right.
    MARCUS   *Suum cuique*° is our Roman justice.   *To each his own (Latin)*
      This prince in justice seizeth but his own.
285   LUCIUS   And that he will and shall, if Lucius live.
    TITUS   Traitors, avaunt!° Where is the Emperor's guard?   *be off*
      —Treason, my lord! Lavinia is surprised.
    SATURNINUS   Surprised? By whom?
    BASSIANUS   By him that justly may
      Bear his betrothed from all the world away.
          [*Exeunt* BASSIANUS, LAVINIA, *and* MARCUS.]
290   MUTIUS   Brothers, help to convey her hence away,
      And with my sword I'll keep this door safe.
          [*Exeunt* LUCIUS, QUINTUS, *and* MARTIUS.]
    TITUS   Follow, my lord, and I'll soon bring her back.
    MUTIUS   My lord, you pass not here.
    TITUS   What, villain boy,
      Barr'st me my way in Rome?
          [TITUS *attacks* MUTIUS.]
    MUTIUS   Help, Lucius, help!
         [TITUS *kills* MUTIUS.]
               [*Exeunt* SATURNINUS, TAMORA, CHIRON,
                     DEMETRIUS, *and* AARON.]
         [*Enter* LUCIUS.]
295   LUCIUS   My lord, you are unjust—and more than so:
      In wrongful quarrel you have slain your son.
    TITUS   Nor thou, nor he, are any sons of mine.
      My sons would never so dishonor me.
      Traitor, restore Lavinia to the Emperor.
300   LUCIUS   Dead, if you will, but not to be his wife
      That is another's lawful promised love.   [*Exit.*]

Enter aloft the Emperor [SATURNINUS] with TAMORA
and her two sons [CHIRON and DEMETRIUS], and
AARON the Moor.

SATURNINUS No, Titus, no. The Emperor needs her not,
Nor° her, nor thee, nor any of thy stock.   *Neither*
I'll trust by leisure° him that mocks me once,   *I'm in no hurry to trust*
305 Thee never, nor thy traitorous haughty sons,
Confederates all thus to dishonor me.
Was none in Rome to make a stale°   *laughingstock*
But Saturnine? Full well, Andronicus,
Agree these deeds with that proud brag of thine
310 That said'st I begged the empire at thy hands.
TITUS Oh, monstrous! What reproachful words are these?
SATURNINUS But go thy ways. Go give that changing piece°   *fickle wench*
To him that flourished for her with his sword.[8]
A valiant son-in-law thou shalt enjoy,
315 One fit to bandy° with thy lawless sons,   *brawl*
To ruffle° in the commonwealth of Rome.   *swagger*
TITUS These words are razors to my wounded heart.
SATURNINUS And therefore, lovely Tamora, Queen of Goths,
That like the stately Phoebe° 'mongst her nymphs   *Diana (the moon)*
320 Dost overshine the gallant'st dames of Rome,
If thou be pleased with this my sudden choice,
Behold, I choose thee, Tamora, for my bride,
And will create thee Empress of Rome.
Speak, Queen of Goths, dost thou applaud my choice?
325 And here I swear by all the Roman gods,
Sith priest and holy water are so near,
And tapers burn so bright and everything
In readiness for Hymenaeus° stand,   *god of marriage*
I will not re-salute the streets of Rome,
330 Or climb° my palace, till from forth this place   *ascend to*
I lead espoused my bride along with me.
TAMORA And here in sight of heaven to Rome I swear,
If Saturnine advance the Queen of Goths,
She will a handmaid be to his desires,
335 A loving nurse, a mother to his youth.°   *youthfulness*
SATURNINUS Ascend, fair Queen, Pantheon. Lords, accompany
Your noble emperor and his lovely bride,
Sent by the heavens for Prince Saturnine,
Whose wisdom[9] hath her fortune conquerèd.
340 There shall we consummate our spousal rites.
                                        Exeunt [all but TITUS].
TITUS I am not bid° to wait upon this bride.   *invited*
Titus, when wert thou wont to walk alone,
Dishonored thus and challengèd° of wrongs?   *accused*
                Enter MARCUS and Titus' sons [LUCIUS, QUINTUS,
                and MARTIUS].
MARCUS O Titus, see! Oh, see what thou hast done—
345 In a bad quarrel slain a virtuous son.
TITUS No, foolish tribune, no. No son of mine,
Nor thou, nor these, confederates in the deed

---

8. To him who brandished his sword to win her.   9. Wise consent to my proposal.

That hath dishonored all our family.
Unworthy brother and unworthy sons!

350 LUCIUS   But let us give him burial as becomes:°   *as is proper*
Give Mutius burial with our brethren.

TITUS   Traitors, away! He rests not in this tomb.
This monument five hundred years hath stood,
Which I have sumptuously re-edified.°   *rebuilt*

355 Here none but soldiers and Rome's servitors°   *defenders*
Repose in fame, none basely slain in brawls.
Bury him where you can; he comes not here.

MARCUS   My lord, this is impiety in you.
My nephew Mutius' deeds do plead for him.

360 He must be buried with his brethren.

QUINTUS *and* MARTIUS   And shall, or him we will accompany.[1]

TITUS   "And shall"? What villain was it spake that word?

MARTIUS   He that would vouch it° in any place but here.   *back it up*

TITUS   What, would you bury him in my despite?°   *in defiance of me*

365 MARCUS   No, noble Titus, but entreat of thee
To pardon Mutius and to bury him.

TITUS   Marcus, even thou hast struck upon my crest,
And with these boys mine honor thou hast wounded.
My foes I do repute° you every one,   *consider*

370 So trouble me no more but get you gone.

QUINTUS   He is not with° himself; let us withdraw.   *is beside*

MARTIUS   Not I, till Mutius' bones be buried.

The brother [MARCUS] *and the sons* [LUCIUS, QUINTUS,
and MARTIUS] *kneel.*

MARCUS   Brother, for in that name doth nature plead—

MARTIUS   Father, and in that name doth nature speak—

375 TITUS   Speak thou no more, if all the rest will speed.[2]

MARCUS   Renownèd Titus, more than half my soul—

LUCIUS   Dear father, soul, and substance of us all—

MARCUS   Suffer thy brother Marcus to inter
His noble nephew here in virtue's nest,

380 That died in honor and Lavinia's cause.
Thou art a Roman; be not barbarous.
The Greeks upon advice° did bury Ajax[3]   *deliberation*
That slew himself; and wise Laertes' son
Did graciously plead for his funerals.

385 Let not young Mutius, then, that was thy joy,
Be barred his entrance here.

TITUS   Rise, Marcus, rise.
The dismal'st day is this that e'er I saw,
To be dishonored by my sons in Rome.
Well, bury him, and bury me the next.

They put [*the body of* MUTIUS] *in the tomb.*

390 LUCIUS   There lie thy bones, sweet Mutius, with thy friends,
Till we with trophies° do adorn thy tomb.   *memorial tributes*

---

1. TEXTUAL COMMENT In this exchange between Titus and his sons, neither Q nor F supplies the sons' proper names, leaving it unclear who says what. See Digital Edition TC 3 (Quarto edited text) for a discussion of the ambiguities and how *The Norton Shakespeare* resolves them.

2. If the rest of you wish to meet with good fortune (that is, escape my anger).

3. In the Trojan War, after the Greek hero Ajax committed suicide, Odysseus ("wise Laertes' son") convinced Agamemnon, leader of the Greeks, to grant him honorable burial.

MARCUS, LUCIUS, QUINTUS, *and* MARTIUS *(kneeling)*   No man
    shed tears for noble Mutius:
    He lives in fame that died in virtue's cause.
       [They rise. Stand aside] all but MARCUS *and* TITUS.
  MARCUS   My lord, to step out of these dreary dumps,°   *melancholy*
395   How comes it that the subtle° Queen of Goths   *cunning*
    Is of a sudden thus advanced in Rome?
  TITUS   I know not, Marcus, but I know it is—
    Whether by device° or no, the heavens can tell.   *scheming*
    Is she not then beholden to the man
400   That brought her for this high good turn[4] so far?
       [Flourish.] Enter the Emperor [SATURNINUS], TAMORA
       and her two sons [CHIRON *and* DEMETRIUS], *with*
       [AARON] *the Moor at one door; enter at the other door*
       BASSIANUS *and* LAVINIA, *with others.*
  SATURNINUS   So, Bassianus, you have played your prize.°   *won your bout*
    God give you joy, sir, of your gallant bride.
  BASSIANUS   And you of yours, my lord. I say no more,
    Nor wish no less, and so I take my leave.
405 SATURNINUS   Traitor, if Rome have law, or we have power,
    Thou and thy faction shall repent this rape.°   *abduction*
  BASSIANUS   "Rape" call you it, my lord, to seize my own,
    My true betrothèd love and now my wife?
    But let the laws of Rome determine all.
410 Meanwhile am I possessed of that° is mine.   *what*
  SATURNINUS   'Tis good, sir; you are very short with us—
    But if we live we'll be as sharp with you.
  BASSIANUS   My lord, what I have done as best I may
    Answer I must, and shall do with my life.
415 Only thus much I give your grace to know:
    By all the duties that I owe to Rome,
    This noble gentleman, Lord Titus here,
    Is in opinion° and in honor wronged   *reputation*
    That, in the rescue of Lavinia,
420 With his own hand did slay his youngest son
    In zeal to you, and highly moved to wrath
    To be controlled° in that he frankly gave.[5]   *opposed*
    Receive him then to favor, Saturnine,
    That hath expressed himself in all his deeds
425 A father and a friend to thee and Rome.
  TITUS   Prince Bassianus, leave to plead° my deeds.   *stop defending*
    'Tis thou and those that have dishonored me.
    Rome and the righteous heavens be my judge
    How I have loved and honored Saturnine!
       [He kneels.]
430 TAMORA *[to* SATURNINUS]   My worthy lord, if ever Tamora
    Were gracious in those princely eyes of thine,
    Then hear me speak indifferently° for all;   *impartially*
    And at my suit, sweet, pardon what is past.
  SATURNINUS   What, madam, be dishonored openly
435 And basely put it up° without revenge?   *ignobly submit*

---

4. Recompense; "turn" was also slang for the sexual   5. Freely bestowed (by Lavinia upon Saturninus).
act.

TAMORA   Not so, my lord. The gods of Rome forfend°   *forbid*
    I should be author to dishonor⁶ you.
    But on mine honor dare I undertake°   *vouch*
    For good Lord Titus' innocence in all,
440   Whose fury not dissembled speaks his griefs.
    Then at my suit look graciously on him.
    Lose not so noble a friend on vain suppose,°   *idle conjecture*
    Nor with sour looks afflict his gentle heart.
    [*aside to* SATURNINUS] My lord, be ruled by me; be won at last;
445   Dissemble all your griefs and discontents.
    You are but newly planted in your throne;
    Lest, then, the people, and patricians too,
    Upon a just survey° take Titus' part   *examination*
    And so supplant you for ingratitude,
450   Which Rome reputes to be a heinous sin.
    Yield at entreats°—and then let me alone.   *to entreaty*
    I'll find a day to massacre them all,
    And raze their faction and their family—
    The cruel father and his traitorous sons,
455   To whom I sued for my dear son's life—
    And make them know what 'tis to let a queen
    Kneel in the streets and beg for grace in vain.
    —Come, come, sweet Emperor. —Come, Andronicus.°   *(Marcus)*
    —Take up° this good old man and cheer the heart   *Raise to his feet*
460   That dies in tempest of thy angry frown.
SATURNINUS   Rise, Titus, rise. My empress hath prevailed.
TITUS [*rising*]   I thank your majesty and her, my lord.
    These words, these looks, infuse new life in me.
TAMORA   Titus, I am incorporate in° Rome,   *made a part of*
465   A Roman now adopted happily,
    And must advise the Emperor for his good.
    This day all quarrels die, Andronicus.
    And let it be mine honor, good my lord,
    That I have reconciled your friends and you.
470   For you, Prince Bassianus, I have passed
    My word and promise to the Emperor
    That you will be more mild and tractable.
    And fear not, lords, and you, Lavinia;
    By my advice, all humbled on your knees,
475   You shall ask pardon of his majesty.
        [MARCUS, LAVINIA, LUCIUS, QUINTUS, *and* MARTIUS
        kneel.]
LUCIUS   We do, and vow to heaven and to his highness
    That what we did was mildly as we might,°   *possible*
    Tend'ring° our sister's honor and our own.   *Having regard for*
MARCUS   That on mine honor here do I protest.°   *solemnly declare*
480 SATURNINUS   Away, and talk not; trouble us no more.
TAMORA   Nay, nay, sweet Emperor, we must all be friends.
    The tribune and his nephews kneel for grace.
    I will not be denied. Sweetheart, look back.
SATURNINUS   Marcus, for thy sake and thy brother's here,
485   And at my lovely Tamora's entreats,

---

6. I should be responsible for dishonoring.

I do remit° these young men's heinous faults.   *forgive*
Stand up!
    [*They rise.*]
          Lavinia, though you left me like a churl,°   *boorishly*
I found a friend, and sure as death I swore
I would not part° a bachelor from the priest.   *depart*
490 Come: if the Emperor's court can feast two brides,
You are my guest, Lavinia, and your friends.
This day shall be a love-day,[7] Tamora.
TITUS Tomorrow, an° it please your majesty   *if*
To hunt the panther and the hart with me,
495 With horn and hound we'll give your grace *bonjour.*°   *good day (French)*
SATURNINUS Be it so, Titus, and gramercy,° too.   *Exeunt.*   *thank you*
    Sound trumpets. [AARON *the*] *Moor remains.*

2.1 (F 2.1)

AARON Now climbeth Tamora Olympus' top,[1]
Safe out of fortune's shot,° and sits aloft,   *range*
Secure of° thunder's crack or lightning flash,   *from*
Advanced above pale envy's° threat'ning reach.   *malice's*
5 As when the golden sun salutes the morn
And, having gilt the ocean with his beams,
Gallops° the zodiac in his glistering coach   *Gallops through*
And overlooks the highest-peering hills,
So Tamora.
10 Upon her wit° doth earthly honor wait,°   *intelligence / attend*
And virtue stoops and trembles at her frown.
Then, Aaron, arm thy heart and fit thy thoughts
To mount aloft with thy imperial mistress,
And mount her pitch[2] whom thou in triumph long
15 Hast prisoner held, fettered in amorous chains
And faster bound to Aaron's charming eyes
Than is Prometheus tied to Caucasus.[3]
Away with slavish weeds° and servile thoughts!   *clothes*
I will be bright, and shine in pearl and gold
20 To wait upon this new-made empress.
To wait, said I? To wanton° with this queen,   *play amorously*
This goddess, this Semiramis,[4] this nymph,
This siren[5] that will charm Rome's Saturnine
And see his shipwreck and his commonweal's.
    Enter CHIRON *and* DEMETRIUS, *braving.*°   *defying each other*
25 Hello! What storm is this?
DEMETRIUS Chiron, thy years wants° wit, thy wits wants edge°   *lack / sharpness*
And manners to intrude where I am graced,°   *favored*
And may, for aught thou knowest, affected° be.   *loved*
CHIRON Demetrius, thou dost overween° in all,   *behave presumptuously*
30 And so in this, to bear me down with braves.°   *threats*

---

7. Day for love; day appointed to settle disputes amicably.
2.1 Scene continues, but the tomb is no longer needed.
1. Mountain home of the Greek gods.
2. Rise to her height; a hawking term (sexually suggestive).
3. In Greek mythology, Zeus punished Prometheus by chaining him to a rock in the Caucasus Mountains; a vulture fed on his liver daily.
4. In Mesopotamian mythology, the Assyrian queen who founded and ruled Babylon, and who also had attributes of Ishtar, goddess associated with sexual lust.
5. In Greek mythology, sirens were female creatures who lured sailors to destruction.

'Tis not the difference of a year or two
Makes me less gracious or thee more fortunate.
I am as able and as fit as thou
To serve and to deserve my mistress' grace,
35 And that my sword upon thee shall approve°   prove
And plead my passions for Lavinia's love.
AARON [*aside*]   Clubs, clubs!⁶ These lovers will not keep the peace.
DEMETRIUS   Why, boy, although our mother, unadvised,°   rashly
Gave you a dancing-rapier° by your side,   ornamental sword
40 Are you so desperate grown to threat° your friends?   threaten
Go to. Have your lath⁷ glued within your sheath
Till you know better how to handle it.
CHIRON   Meanwhile, sir, with the little skill I have,
Full well shalt thou perceive how much I dare.
DEMETRIUS   Ay, boy, grow ye so brave?
                    They draw.
45 AARON   Why, how now, lords?
So near the Emperor's palace dare ye draw
And maintain such a quarrel openly?⁸
Full well I wot° the ground of all this grudge.°   know / quarrel
I would not for a million of gold
50 The cause were known to them it most concerns,
Nor would your noble mother for much more
Be so dishonored in the court of Rome.
For shame, put up.°   sheathe your swords
DEMETRIUS   Not I, till I have sheathed
My rapier in his bosom and withal
55 Thrust those reproachful speeches down his throat
That he hath breathed in my dishonor here.
CHIRON   For that I am prepared and full resolved,
Foul-spoken coward, that thund'rest with thy tongue,
And with thy weapon nothing dar'st perform.
60 AARON   Away, I say!
Now, by the gods that warlike Goths adore,
This petty brabble° will undo us all.   quarrel
Why, lords, and think you not how dangerous
It is to jet° upon a prince's right?   encroach
65 What, is Lavinia, then, become so loose,
Or Bassianus so degenerate,
That for her love such quarrels may be broached°   begun
Without controlment,° justice, or revenge?   restraint
Young lords, beware! And should the Empress know
70 This discord's ground,⁹ the music would not please.
CHIRON   I care not, I, knew she° and all the world.   if she knew
I love Lavinia more than all the world.
DEMETRIUS   Youngling, learn thou to make some meaner° choice;   lesser
Lavinia is thine elder brother's hope.
75 AARON   Why, are ye mad? Or know ye not in Rome
How furious and impatient they be
And cannot brook° competitors in love?   endure
I tell you, lords, you do but plot your deaths

6. Here's a brawl (a cry among London apprentices   8. In the Renaissance, it was illegal to draw a sword
to join or quell a fight).   in the presence of the sovereign or at court.
7. Wooden sword used in theatrical productions.   9. Basis; in music, the bass line.

By this device.

80 CHIRON   Aaron, a thousand deaths would I propose°   *face*
To achieve her whom I love.

AARON   To achieve her how?

DEMETRIUS   Why makes thou it so strange?
She is a woman, therefore may be wooed;
She is a woman, therefore may be won;
85 She is Lavinia, therefore must be loved.
What, man, more water glideth by the mill
Than wots the miller of, and easy it is
Of a cut loaf to steal a shive,° we know.   *slice*
Though Bassianus be the Emperor's brother,
90 Better than he have worn Vulcan's badge.[1]

AARON [*aside*]   Ay, and as good as Saturninus may.

DEMETRIUS   Then why should he despair that knows to court it°   *carry on a courtship*
With words, fair looks, and liberality?°   *generosity*
What, hast not thou full often struck° a doe   *struck dead*
95 And borne her cleanly° by the keeper's nose?   *deftly and unnoticed*

AARON   Why, then, it seems some certain snatch[2] or so
Would serve your turns.

CHIRON   Ay, so the turn were served.°   *(with sexual innuendo)*

DEMETRIUS   Aaron, thou hast hit it.

AARON   Would you had hit it,[3] too;
Then should not we be tired with this ado.°   *bothered with this fight*
100 Why, hark ye, hark ye, and are you such fools
To square° for this? Would it offend you, then,   *quarrel*
That both should speed?°   *succeed*

CHIRON   Faith, not me.

DEMETRIUS   Nor me, so° I were one.   *provided that*

AARON   For shame, be friends and join for that you jar.[4]
105 'Tis policy° and stratagem must do   *cunning*
That° you affect,° and so must you resolve   *What / desire*
That what you cannot as you would achieve
You must perforce accomplish as you may.
Take this of me: Lucrece[5] was not more chaste
110 Than this Lavinia, Bassianus' love.
A speedier course than lingering languishment°   *lovesickness*
Must we pursue, and I have found the path.
My lords, a solemn° hunting is in hand.   *ceremonial*
There will the lovely Roman ladies troop.°   *walk together*
115 The forest walks are wide and spacious,
And many unfrequented plots° there are,   *places*
Fitted by kind° for rape and villainy.   *nature*
Single° you thither, then, this dainty doe,   *Isolate*
And strike her home by force, if not by words.
120 This way, or not at all, stand you in hope.
Come, come: our empress, with her sacred wit
To villainy and vengeance consecrate,
Will we acquaint withal what we intend,

---

1. *worn Vulcan's badge*: been cuckolded, as the god
Vulcan was by Venus, the goddess of love.
2. Bite (with sexual innuendo).
3. Hit the nail on the head; "scored" sexually.
4. And join to get what you fight over.

5. Virtuous Roman matron raped by Tarquin, a member of the Roman royal family; after her suicide, her kin avenged her by overthrowing the king and establishing the Roman Republic. Shakespeare retells the story in *The Rape of Lucrece*.

And she shall file our engines° with advice, · sharpen our wits
125 That will not suffer you to square yourselves,° · be at odds
But to your wishes' height advance you both.
The Emperor's court is like the house of Fame,[6]
The palace full of tongues, of eyes and ears;
The woods are ruthless, dreadful, deaf, and dull.° · insensible
130 There speak and strike, brave boys, and take your turns.
There serve your lust, shadowed from heaven's eye,
And revel in Lavinia's treasury.
CHIRON   Thy counsel, lad, smells of no cowardice.
DEMETRIUS   Sit fas aut nefas,° till I find the stream · Be it right or wrong (Latin)
135 To cool this heat, a charm to calm these fits,
Per Stygia, per manes vehor.[7] · *Exeunt.*

2.2 (F 2.2)

Enter TITUS *Andronicus and his three sons* [LUCIUS,
QUINTUS, *and* MARTIUS], *making a noise with hounds
and horns*[, *and* MARCUS].

TITUS   The hunt is up, the moon is bright and gray,° · (used of dawn light)
The fields are fragrant, and the woods are green.
Uncouple[1] here, and let us make a bay° · deep barking
And wake the Emperor and his lovely bride,
5 And rouse the Prince, and ring° a hunter's peal, · sound
That all the court may echo with the noise.
Sons, let it be your charge, as it is ours,
To attend the Emperor's person carefully.
I have been troubled in my sleep this night,
10 But dawning day new comfort hath inspired.
Here a cry of hounds, and wind° *horns in a peal.* · blow
Then enter SATURNINUS, TAMORA, BASSIANUS,
LAVINIA, CHIRON, DEMETRIUS, *and their Attendants.*
Many good morrows to your majesty;
Madam, to you as many and as good.
I promised your grace a hunter's peal.
SATURNINUS   And you have rung it lustily,° my lords, · heartily
15 Somewhat too early for new-married ladies.
BASSIANUS   Lavinia, how say you?
LAVINIA   I say no.
I have been broad awake two hours and more.
SATURNINUS   Come on, then; horse and chariots let us have,
And to our sport. [*to* TAMORA] Madam, now shall ye see
Our Roman hunting.
20 MARCUS   I have dogs, my lord,
Will rouse the proudest panther in the chase° · hunting ground
And climb the highest promontory top.
TITUS   And I have horse will follow where the game
Makes way and runs like swallows o'er the plain.
25 DEMETRIUS [*aside*]   Chiron, we hunt not, we, with horse nor
hound,
But hope to pluck a dainty doe to ground. · *Exeunt.*

---

6. Rumor; the House of Fame is described by Ovid in *Metamorphoses* 12 and by Chaucer in *The House of Fame.*
7. I am carried through the underworld, through the

spirits (that is, I am in hell). Adapted from Seneca's *Hippolytus.*
2.2 Location: A forest near the Emperor's palace.
1. Unleash the hounds.

2.3 (F 2.3)
Enter AARON *alone [with a bag of gold].*

AARON   He that had wit would think that I had none,
To bury so much gold under a tree
And never after to inherit° it.   *possess*
Let him that thinks of me so abjectly
5   Know that this gold must coin a stratagem
Which, cunningly effected, will beget
A very excellent piece of villainy.
And so repose, sweet gold, for their unrest
That have their alms out of the Empress' chest.[1]
    [He hides the gold.]
    Enter TAMORA *alone to* [AARON] *the Moor.*
10   TAMORA   My lovely Aaron, wherefore lookest thou sad
When everything doth make a gleeful boast?°   *display*
The birds chant melody on every bush,
The snake lies rolled in the cheerful sun,
The green leaves quiver with the cooling wind
15   And make a checkered shadow on the ground.
Under their sweet shade, Aaron, let us sit,
And whilst the babbling echo mocks the hounds,
Replying shrilly to the well-tuned horns,
As if a double hunt were heard at once,
20   Let us sit down and mark their yellowing° noise.   *bellowing*
And after conflict such as was supposed
The wandering prince and Dido once enjoyed,[2]
When with a happy storm they were surprised
And curtained with a counsel-keeping° cave,   *secret-keeping*
25   We may, each wreathèd in the other's arms,
Our pastimes done, possess a golden slumber,
Whiles hounds and horns and sweet melodious birds
Be unto us as is a nurse's song
Of lullaby to bring her babe asleep.
30   AARON   Madam, though Venus govern your desires,
Saturn is dominator over mine.[3]
What signifies my deadly-standing° eye,   *murderously glaring*
My silence, and my cloudy° melancholy,   *gloomy*
My fleece of woolly hair that now uncurls
35   Even as an adder when she doth unroll
To do some fatal execution?
No, madam, these are no venereal[4] signs;
Vengeance is in my heart, death in my hand,
Blood and revenge are hammering in my head.
40   Hark, Tamora, the empress of my soul,
Which never hopes more heaven than rests in thee,
This is the day of doom for Bassianus.
His Philomel[5] must lose her tongue today;

2.3 Location: The forest.
1. *That . . . chest*: Who get this gold, which comes
from the Empress's treasury.
2. In Virgil's *Aeneid* 4, the Carthaginian queen Dido
and Aeneas, later founder of Rome, make love in a
cave where they have taken refuge. *conflict*: sexual
intercourse.
3. Those born when the planet Venus was ascendant

were supposed to be amorous; Saturn produced a
colder, gloomier temperament.
4. Sexual; derived from Venus.
5. In Greek mythology, an Athenian princess raped
by her brother-in-law Tereus; he cut out her tongue,
but she wove a tapestry incriminating him (see Introduction and Ovid, *Metamorphoses* 6).

Thy sons make pillage of her chastity
45 And wash their hands in Bassianus' blood.
Seest thou this letter? Take it up, I pray thee,
And give the King this fatal-plotted scroll.
Now question me no more.

Enter BASSIANUS *and* LAVINIA.

                                                We are espied.
Here comes a parcel° of our hopeful° booty,   part / hoped-for
50 Which dreads not yet their lives' destruction.
TAMORA Ah, my sweet Moor, sweeter to me than life!
AARON No more, great Empress; Bassianus comes.
Be cross with him and I'll go fetch thy sons
To back thy quarrels whatsoe'er they be.   [*Exit.*]
55 BASSIANUS Who have we here? Rome's royal empress,
Unfurnished of her well-beseeming troop?[6]
Or is it Dian,[7] habited° like her,   dressed
Who hath abandoned her holy groves
To see the general hunting in this forest?
60 TAMORA Saucy controller° of my private steps,   Insolent observer
Had I the power that some say Dian had,
Thy temples should be planted presently°   immediately
With horns, as was Actaeon's, and the hounds
Should drive° upon thy new-transformed limbs,   rush
65 Unmannerly intruder as thou art![8]
LAVINIA Under your patience, gentle Empress,
'Tis thought you have a goodly gift in horning,[9]
And to be doubted° that your Moor and you   suspected
Are singled forth° to try thy experiments.   drawn apart
70 Jove shield your husband from his hounds today!
'Tis pity they should take him for a stag.
BASSIANUS Believe me, Queen, your swarthy Cimmerian[1]
Doth make your honor of his body's hue,
Spotted, detested, and abominable.
75 Why are you sequestered from all your train,
Dismounted from your snow-white goodly steed,
And wandered hither to an obscure plot,
Accompanied but with a barbarous Moor,
If foul desire had not conducted you?
80 LAVINIA And being intercepted in your sport,
Great reason that my noble lord be rated°   scolded
For sauciness. [*to* BASSIANUS] I pray you, let us hence,
And let her joy° her raven-colored love.   enjoy
This valley fits the purpose passing well.
85 BASSIANUS The King, my brother, shall have notice of this.
LAVINIA Ay, for these slips have made him noted° long.   notorious
Good King, to be so mightily abused.°   deceived
TAMORA Why, I have patience to endure all this.

Enter CHIRON *and* DEMETRIUS.

DEMETRIUS How now, dear sovereign and our gracious mother,

---

6. *Unfurnished . . . troop:* Not accompanied by an appropriate escort.
7. Diana, chaste goddess of the hunt (sarcastic).
8. In Greek mythology, the hunter Actaeon came upon Diana naked; she turned him into a stag and his own

hounds tore him apart (see Ovid, *Metamorphoses* 3).
9. The husbands of unfaithful women were supposed to grow staglike horns.
1. The Cimmerians were a legendary people upon whom the sun never shone.

90   Why doth your highness look so pale and wan?
  TAMORA   Have I not reason, think you, to look pale?
        These two have 'ticed° me hither to this place.   *enticed*
        A barren detested vale you see it is:
        The trees, though summer, yet forlorn and lean,
95   Overcome° with moss and baleful² mistletoe;   *Overgrown*
        Here never shines the sun, here nothing breeds
        Unless the nightly owl or fatal° raven;   *ominous*
        And when they showed me this abhorrèd pit,
        They told me here at dead time of the night
100   A thousand fiends, a thousand hissing snakes,
        Ten thousand swelling toads, as many urchins,°   *goblins*
        Would make such fearful and confusèd cries
        As any mortal body hearing it
        Should straight fall mad, or else die suddenly.
105   No sooner had they told this hellish tale
        But straight they told me they would bind me here
        Unto the body of a dismal yew,³
        And leave me to this miserable death.
        And then they called me foul adulteress,
110   Lascivious Goth,⁴ and all the bitterest terms
        That ever ear did hear to such effect.
        And had you not by wondrous fortune come,
        This vengeance on me had they executed.
        Revenge it as you love your mother's life,
115   Or be ye not henceforth called my children.
  DEMETRIUS   This is a witness that I am thy son.
          [*He*] *stab*[*s* BASSIANUS].
  CHIRON   And this for me, struck home to show my strength.
          [*He stabs* BASSIANUS, *who dies.*]
  LAVINIA   Ay, come, Semiramis⁵—nay, barbarous Tamora,
        For no name fits thy nature but thy own.
120 TAMORA   Give me the poniard. You shall know, my boys,
        Your mother's hand shall right your mother's wrong.
  DEMETRIUS   Stay, madam, here is more belongs to her.
        First, thrash the corn, then after burn the straw.
        This minion stood° upon her chastity,   *hussy prided herself*
125   Upon her nuptial vow, her loyalty,
        And with that painted hope braves° your mightiness.   *defies*
        And shall she carry this unto her grave?
  CHIRON   An if° she do, I would I were an eunuch.   *An if = If*
        Drag hence her husband to some secret hole
130   And make his dead trunk pillow to our lust.
  TAMORA   But when ye have the honey we desire,
        Let not this wasp outlive us both to sting.
  CHIRON   I warrant you, madam, we will make that sure.
        Come, mistress, now perforce we will enjoy
135   That nice-preservèd honesty⁶ of yours.
  LAVINIA   O Tamora, thou bearest a woman's face—

---

2. Harmful (mistletoe is parasitic).   5. See note to 2.1.22.
3. The yew tree is associated with sadness.   6. Fastidiously guarded chastity.
4. Punning on "goat," a proverbially lustful animal.

TAMORA   I will not hear her speak. Away with her!

LAVINIA   Sweet lords, entreat her hear me but a word.

DEMETRIUS [to TAMORA]   Listen, fair madam, let it be your glory
140   To see her tears, but be your heart to them
    As unrelenting flint to drops of rain.

LAVINIA   When did the tiger's young ones teach the dam?°   mother
    Oh, do not learn her wrath! She taught it thee.
    The milk thou suck'st from her did turn to marble;
145   Even at thy teat thou hadst° thy tyranny.   took in
    Yet every mother breeds not sons alike:
    [to CHIRON] Do thou entreat her show a woman's pity.

CHIRON   What, wouldst thou have me prove myself a bastard?

LAVINIA   'Tis true the raven doth not hatch a lark.
150   Yet have I heard—oh, could I find it now—
    The lion moved with pity did endure
    To have his princely paws° pared all away.   claws
    Some say that ravens foster forlorn children°   abandoned baby birds
    The whilst their own birds famish in their nests.
155   Oh, be to me, though thy hard heart say no,
    Nothing so kind but something pitiful.[7]

TAMORA   I know not what it means. Away with her!

LAVINIA   Oh, let me teach thee for my father's sake
    That gave thee life when well he might have slain thee.
160   Be not obdurate; open thy deaf ears.

TAMORA   Hadst thou in person ne'er offended me,
    Even for his sake am I pitiless.
    Remember, boys, I poured forth tears in vain
    To save your brother from the sacrifice,
165   But fierce Andronicus would not relent.
    Therefore, away with her and use her as you will.
    The worse to her, the better loved of me.

LAVINIA   O Tamora, be called a gentle queen,
    And with thine own hands kill me in this place.
170   For 'tis not life that I have begged so long;
    Poor I was slain when Bassianus died.

TAMORA   What begg'st thou, then, fond° woman? Let me go!   foolish

LAVINIA   'Tis present° death I beg, and one thing more   immediate
    That womanhood denies° my tongue to tell:
175   Oh, keep me from their worse-than-killing lust,
    And tumble me into some loathsome pit
    Where never man's eye may behold my body.
    Do this, and be a charitable murderer.

TAMORA   So should I rob my sweet sons of their fee.
180   No, let them satisfy their lust on thee.

DEMETRIUS   Away, for thou hast stayed us here too long.

LAVINIA   No grace? No womanhood? Ah, beastly creature,
    The blot and enemy to our general name,°   the reputation of women
    Confusion° fall—   Destruction

CHIRON   Nay, then I'll stop your mouth.
185   [to DEMETRIUS] Bring thou her husband;
    This is the hole where Aaron bid us hide him.
        [DEMETRIUS throws Bassianus' body into the pit.]

---

7. Not so kind as the raven, but showing some pity.

[*Exeunt* CHIRON *and* DEMETRIUS, *dragging* LAVINIA.]

TAMORA   Farewell, my sons. See that you make her sure.[8]
    Ne'er let my heart know merry cheer indeed
    Till all the Andronici[9] be made away.°   *murdered*
190   Now will I hence to seek my lovely Moor,
    And let my spleenful° sons this trull° deflower.   [*Exit.*]   *lustful / whore*

    Enter AARON *with two of Titus' sons*[, QUINTUS *and*
    MARTIUS].

AARON   Come on, my lords, the better foot before.
    Straight will I bring you to the loathsome pit
    Where I espied the panther fast asleep.
195 QUINTUS   My sight is very dull, whate'er it bodes.[1]
MARTIUS   And mine, I promise you. Were it not for shame,
    Well could I leave our sport to sleep awhile.

    [MARTIUS *falls into the pit.*]

QUINTUS   What, art thou fallen? What subtle° hole is this,   *treacherous*
    Whose mouth is covered with rude-growing briars
200   Upon whose leaves are drops of new-shed blood
    As fresh as morning dew distilled on flowers?
    A very fatal° place it seems to me.   *ill-omened*
    Speak, brother. Hast thou hurt thee with the fall?
MARTIUS   O brother, with the dismal'st object hurt
205   That ever eye with sight made heart lament.
AARON [*aside*]   Now will I fetch the King to find them here,
    That he thereby may have a likely guess
    How these were they that made away his brother.   [*Exit.*]
MARTIUS   Why dost not comfort me and help me out
210   From this unhallow and blood-stained hole?
QUINTUS   I am surprisèd with an uncouth° fear;   *uncanny*
    A chilling sweat o'erruns my trembling joints.
    My heart suspects more than mine eye can see.
MARTIUS   To prove thou hast a true-divining heart,
215   Aaron and thou look down into this den,
    And see a fearful sight of blood and death.
QUINTUS   Aaron is gone, and my compassionate heart
    Will not permit mine eyes once to behold
    The thing whereat it trembles by surmise.°   *merely by imagining it*
220   Oh, tell me who it is, for ne'er till now
    Was I a child to fear I know not what.
MARTIUS   Lord Bassianus lies berayed° in blood,   *defiled*
    All on a heap, like to a slaughtered lamb,
    In this detested, dark, blood-drinking pit.
225 QUINTUS   If it be dark, how dost thou know 'tis he?
MARTIUS   Upon his bloody finger he doth wear
    A precious ring[2] that lightens all this hole,
    Which like a taper° in some monument   *candle*
    Doth shine upon the dead man's earthy° cheeks   *clay-colored*
230   And shows the ragged entrails° of this pit.   *rough interior*
    So pale did shine the moon on Pyramus[3]

---

8. Make sure of her, keep her from doing harm; kill
her.
9. Family of Andronicus.
1. Sleepiness was a bad omen.
2. Perhaps a carbuncle, thought to emit light.

3. In Ovid's version of a classical legend (*Metamorphoses* 4), Pyramus thinks his beloved Thisbe dead and kills himself; this is the subject of the mechanicals' play in *A Midsummer Night's Dream*.

When he by night lay bathed in maiden° blood.   *innocent*
O brother, help me with thy fainting hand—
If fear hath made thee faint, as me it hath—
235   Out of this fell° devouring receptacle,   *dreadful*
As hateful as Cocytus'° misty mouth.   *a river of hell*
QUINTUS   Reach me thy hand that I may help thee out
Or, wanting° strength to do thee so much good,   *lacking*
I may be plucked into the swallowing womb
240   Of this deep pit, poor Bassianus' grave.
I have no strength to pluck thee to the brink—
MARTIUS   Nor I no strength to climb without thy help.
QUINTUS   Thy hand once more; I will not loose again
Till thou art here aloft or I below.
245   Thou canst not come to me—I come to thee.
                [QUINTUS *falls into the pit.*]
                Enter the Emperor [SATURNINUS], [*with Attendants,*]
                and AARON *the Moor.*
SATURNINUS   Along with me; I'll see what hole is here
And what he is that now is leapt into it.
—Say, who art thou that lately didst descend
Into this gaping hollow of the earth?
250   MARTIUS   The unhappy sons of old Andronicus,
Brought hither in a most unlucky hour
To find thy brother Bassianus dead.
SATURNINUS   My brother dead? I know thou dost but jest.
He and his lady both are at the lodge
255   Upon the north side of this pleasant chase.°   *hunting ground*
'Tis not an hour since I left them there.
MARTIUS   We know not where you left them all alive,
But, out° alas, here have we found him dead!   *(emphatic)*
                Enter TAMORA, [TITUS] *Andronicus, and* LUCIUS.
TAMORA   Where is my lord the King?
260   SATURNINUS   Here, Tamora, though grieved with killing grief.
TAMORA   Where is thy brother Bassianus?
SATURNINUS   Now to the bottom dost thou search° my wound.   *probe*
Poor Bassianus here lies murderèd.
TAMORA   Then all too late I bring this fatal writ,°   *document*
265   The complot° of this timeless° tragedy,   *plot / untimely*
And wonder greatly that man's face can fold
In pleasing smiles such murderous tyranny.
                She giveth SATURNINUS *a letter.*
SATURNINUS (*read[ing] the letter*)
"An if we miss to meet him handsomely,°   *conveniently*
Sweet huntsman—Bassianus 'tis we mean—
270   Do thou so much as dig the grave for him.
Thou know'st our meaning. Look for thy reward
Among the nettles at the elder tree
Which overshades the mouth of that same pit
Where we decreed to bury Bassianus.
275   Do this and purchase us thy lasting friends."
O Tamora, was ever heard the like?
This is the pit, and this the elder tree.
—Look, sirs, if you can find the huntsman out
That should° have murdered Bassianus here.   *was to*
280   AARON   My gracious lord, here is the bag of gold.

SATURNINUS [*to* TITUS]   Two of thy whelps,° fell curs of bloody   *puppies; literally, sons*
   kind,°   *nature; breed*
  Have here bereft my brother of his life.
  —Sirs, drag them from the pit unto the prison.
  There let them bide until we have devised
285 Some never-heard-of torturing pain for them.
      [*Attendants drag* QUINTUS *and* MARTIUS *and*
      Bassianus' body from the pit.]
TAMORA   What, are they in this pit? Oh, wondrous thing!
  How easily murder is discoverèd!°   *revealed*
TITUS [*kneeling*]   High Emperor, upon my feeble knee
  I beg this boon with tears not lightly shed,
290 That this fell fault of my accursèd sons—
  Accursèd if the faults be proved in them—
SATURNINUS   If it be proved? You see it is apparent.°   *obvious*
  Who found this letter? Tamora, was it you?
TAMORA   Andronicus himself did take it up.
295 TITUS   I did, my lord, yet let me be their bail.
  For by my father's reverent tomb I vow
  They shall be ready at your highness' will
  To answer their suspicion[4] with their lives.
SATURNINUS   Thou shalt not bail them. See thou follow me.
300 Some bring the murdered body, some the murderers.
  Let them not speak a word; the guilt is plain.
  For by my soul, were there worse end than death,
  That end upon them should be executed.
TAMORA   Andronicus, I will entreat the King.
305 Fear not° thy sons; they shall do well enough.   *Fear not for*
TITUS [*rising*]   Come, Lucius, come. Stay not to talk with them.°   *(Quintus and Martius)*
                 [*Exeunt.*]

2.4 (F 2.4)

Enter the Empress' sons [CHIRON *and* DEMETRIUS],
with LAVINIA, *her hands cut off and her tongue cut*
out, and ravished.

DEMETRIUS   So, now go tell, an if thy tongue can speak,
  Who 'twas that cut thy tongue and ravished thee.
CHIRON   Write down thy mind, bewray° thy meaning so,   *reveal*
  An if thy stumps will let thee, play the scribe.
5 DEMETRIUS   See how with signs and tokens she can scrawl.
CHIRON   Go home; call for sweet° water; wash thy hands.   *perfumed*
DEMETRIUS   She hath no tongue to call, nor hands to wash,
  And so let's leave her to her silent walks.
CHIRON   An 'twere my cause,[1] I should go hang myself.
10 DEMETRIUS   If thou hadst hands to help thee knit° the cord.   *knot*
        Exeunt [CHIRON *and* DEMETRIUS].
    Enter MARCUS *from hunting.*
MARCUS   Who is this? My niece that flies away so fast?
  —Cousin,° a word. Where is your husband?   *Kinswoman*
      [LAVINIA *stops and turns.*]
  If I do dream, would all my wealth would wake me;[2]
  If I do wake, some planet strike me down

---

4. The suspicion they are under.
2.4 Location: Scene continues.

1. If I were in her position.
2. *would all . . . me:* I would give all I had to wake up.

15   That I may slumber an eternal sleep!
     Speak, gentle niece. What stern ungentle hands
     Hath lopped and hewed and made thy body bare
     Of her two branches, those sweet ornaments
     Whose circling shadows kings have sought to sleep in,
20   And might not gain so great a happiness
     As half thy love? Why dost not speak to me?
     Alas, a crimson river of warm blood,
     Like to a bubbling fountain stirred with wind,
     Doth rise and fall between thy rosèd lips,
25   Coming and going with thy honey breath.
     But sure some Tereus[3] hath deflowered thee
     And, lest thou shouldst detect° him, cut thy tongue.   *expose*
     Ah, now thou turn'st away thy face for shame,
     And notwithstanding all this loss of blood,
30   As from a conduit with three issuing spouts,
     Yet do thy cheeks look red as Titan's face,°   *(the sun)*
     Blushing to be encountered with a cloud.
     Shall I speak for thee? Shall I say 'tis so?[4]
     Oh, that I knew thy heart,° and knew the beast   *what is in thy heart*
35   That I might rail at him to ease my mind!
     Sorrow concealed, like an oven stopped,°   *stopped up*
     Doth burn the heart to cinders where it is.
     Fair Philomela—why, she but lost her tongue,
     And in a tedious sampler° sewed her mind;   *laborious tapestry*
40   But, lovely niece, that mean° is cut from thee.   *method*
     A craftier Tereus, cousin, hast thou met,
     And he hath cut those pretty fingers off
     That could have better sewed than Philomel.
     Oh, had the monster seen those lily hands
45   Tremble like aspen leaves upon a lute
     And make the silken strings delight to kiss them,
     He would not then have touched them for his life.
     Or, had he heard the heavenly harmony
     Which that sweet tongue hath made,
50   He would have dropped his knife and fell asleep,
     As Cerberus at the Thracian poet's feet.[5]
     Come, let us go and make thy father blind,
     For such a sight will blind a father's eye.
     One hour's storm will drown the fragrant meads;°   *meadows*
55   What will whole months of tears thy father's eyes?
     Do not draw back, for we will mourn with thee.
     Oh, could our mourning ease thy misery!   *Exeunt.*

3.1 (F 3.1)

Enter the Judges, [TRIBUNES,][1] *and Senators with
Titus' two sons* [QUINTUS *and* MARTIUS] *bound, passing
on the stage to the place of execution, and* TITUS *going
before, pleading.*

TITUS   Hear me, grave fathers! Noble tribunes, stay!
     For pity of mine age, whose youth was spent

---

3. See note to 2.3.43.
4. **PERFORMANCE COMMENT** Marcus's long, rhetorically elaborate speech presents difficulties in performance; for a discussion of the options, see Digital Edition PC 1.

5. The Thracian poet Orpheus, attempting to rescue his dead wife, Eurydice, used his music to lull to sleep Cerberus, the watchdog of the underworld.
3.1 Location: A Roman street.
1. Not including Marcus, who enters at line 58.

In dangerous wars whilst you securely slept;
For all my blood in Rome's great quarrel shed,
5   For all the frosty nights that I have watched,
And for these bitter tears which now you see
Filling the agèd wrinkles in my cheeks,
Be pitiful to my condemnèd sons,
Whose souls is not corrupted as 'tis thought.
10 For two-and-twenty sons I never wept,
Because they died in honor's lofty bed.
　　　　[TITUS] *Andronicus lieth down, and the Judges [and*
　　　　others] pass by him.
For these, tribunes, in the dust I write
My heart's deep languor° and my soul's sad tears.　　　　　　　*grief*
Let my tears staunch° the earth's dry appetite;　　　　　　　*satisfy*
15 My sons' sweet blood will make it shame° and blush.　　　*feel shame*
　　　　　　　　　　　[*Exeunt* TRIBUNES *and others.*]
O earth, I will befriend thee more with rain
That shall distill from these two ancient ruins°　　　　　　　*(his eyes)*
Than youthful April shall with all his showers.
In summer's drought I'll drop upon thee still;
20 In winter with warm tears I'll melt the snow
And keep eternal springtime on thy face,
So° thou refuse to drink my dear sons' blood.　　　　　　　*Provided that*
　　　　　Enter LUCIUS *with his weapon drawn.*
O reverend tribunes! O gentle agèd men!
Unbind my sons, reverse the doom of death,
25 And let me say, that never wept before,
My tears are now prevailing° orators.　　　　　　　　　　*persuasive*
LUCIUS　O noble father, you lament in vain.
　　The tribunes hear you not. No man is by,
　　And you recount your sorrows to a stone.
30 TITUS　Ah, Lucius, for thy brothers let me plead.
　　Grave tribunes, once more I entreat of you—
LUCIUS　My gracious lord, no tribune hears you speak.
TITUS　Why, 'tis no matter, man. If they did hear,
　　They would not mark° me; if they did mark,　　　　　　*attend to*
35 They would not pity me; yet plead I must,
　　{And bootless° unto them.}　　　　　　　　　　　　　*uselessly*
　　Therefore, I tell my sorrows to the stones
　　Who, though they cannot answer my distress,
　　Yet in some sort they are better than the tribunes
40 For that they will not intercept° my tale.　　　　　　　*interrupt*
　　When I do weep, they humbly at my feet
　　Receive my tears and seem to weep with me;
　　And were they but attired in grave weeds,°　　　　　*sober garments*
　　Rome could afford° no tribunes like to these.　　　　　*provide*
45 A stone is soft as wax, tribunes more hard than stones;
　　A stone is silent and offendeth not,
　　And tribunes with their tongues doom men to death.
　　But wherefore stand'st thou with thy weapon drawn?
LUCIUS　To rescue my two brothers from their death,
50 For which attempt the judges have pronounced
　　My everlasting doom of banishment.
TITUS　O happy man! They have befriended thee.
　　Why, foolish Lucius, dost thou not perceive
　　That Rome is but a wilderness of tigers?

55   Tigers must prey, and Rome affords no prey
        But me and mine. How happy art thou, then,
        From these devourers to be banishèd!
        But who comes with our brother Marcus here?
                Enter MARCUS *with* LAVINIA.
        MARCUS Titus, prepare thy agèd eyes to weep,
60   Or if not so, thy noble heart to break.
        I bring consuming sorrow to thine age.
        TITUS Will it consume me? Let me see it, then.
        MARCUS This was thy daughter.
        TITUS   Why, Marcus, so she is.
        LUCIUS [*falling to his knees*] Ay me, this object° kills me.   spectacle
65   TITUS Faint-hearted boy, arise and look upon her.
                [LUCIUS *rises.*]
        Speak, Lavinia, what accursèd hand
        Hath made thee handless in thy father's sight?
        What fool hath added water to the sea
        Or brought a faggot° to bright-burning Troy?[2]   piece of firewood
70   My grief was at the height before thou cam'st,
        And now, like Nilus, it disdaineth bounds.[3]
        Give me a sword! I'll chop off my hands too,
        For they have fought for Rome and all in vain;
        And they have nursed this woe in feeding life.[4]
75   In bootless° prayer have they been held up,   useless
        And they have served me to effectless° use.   fruitless
        Now all the service I require of them
        Is that the one will help to cut the other.
        'Tis well, Lavinia, that thou hast no hands,
80   For hands to do Rome service is but vain.
        LUCIUS Speak, gentle sister, who hath martyred° thee?   mutilated
        MARCUS Oh, that delightful engine° of her thoughts,   instrument (her tongue)
        That blabbed° them with such pleasing eloquence,   uttered
        Is torn from forth that pretty hollow cage
85   Where, like a sweet melodious bird, it sung
        Sweet varied notes, enchanting every ear.
        LUCIUS Oh, say thou for her, who hath done this deed?
        MARCUS Oh, thus I found her straying in the park,
        Seeking to hide herself, as doth the deer
90   That hath received some unrecuring° wound.   incurable
        TITUS It was my dear, and he that wounded her
        Hath hurt me more than had he killed me dead.
        For now I stand as one upon a rock
        Environed° with a wilderness of sea,   Surrounded
95   Who marks the waxing tide grow wave by wave,
        Expecting° ever when some envious° surge   Awaiting / malignant
        Will in his° brinish bowels swallow him.   its
        This way to death my wretched sons are gone;
        Here stands my other son, a banished man;
100   And here my brother weeping at my woes;
        But that which gives my soul the greatest spurn°   contemptuous blow

2. Troy was torched by the Greeks after their victory.
3. Before it was dammed, the river Nile flooded annually.
4. And by defending Rome, they have induced this
misery.

Is dear Lavinia, dearer than my soul.
—Had I but seen thy picture in this plight
It would have madded me.° What shall I do   *made me insane*
105 Now I behold thy lively° body so?   *living*
Thou hast no hands to wipe away thy tears,
Nor tongue to tell me who hath martyred thee;
Thy husband he is dead, and for his death
Thy brothers are condemned and dead by this.°   *this time*
110 —Look, Marcus! Ah, son Lucius, look on her!
When I did name her brothers, then fresh tears
Stood on her cheeks, as doth the honeydew
Upon a gathered lily almost withered.
MARCUS Perchance she weeps because they killed her husband;
115 Perchance because she knows them innocent.
TITUS [*to* LAVINIA] If they did kill thy husband, then be joyful,
Because the law hath ta'en revenge on them.
No, no, they would not do so foul a deed:
Witness the sorrow that their sister makes.
120 Gentle Lavinia, let me kiss thy lips,
Or make some sign how I may do thee ease.
Shall thy good uncle and thy brother Lucius
And thou and I sit round about some fountain,
Looking all downwards to behold our cheeks,
125 How they are stained like meadows yet not dry
With miry slime left on them by a flood?
And in the fountain shall we gaze so long
Till the fresh taste be taken from that clearness
And made a brine pit with our bitter tears?
130 Or shall we cut away our hands like thine?
Or shall we bite our tongues, and in dumb shows
Pass the remainder of our hateful days?
What shall we do? Let us that have our tongues
Plot some device° of further misery   *contrivance*
135 To make us wondered at in time to come.
LUCIUS Sweet father, cease your tears, for at your grief
See how my wretched sister sobs and weeps.
MARCUS Patience, dear niece. Good Titus, dry thine eyes.
TITUS Ah, Marcus, Marcus, brother, well I wot°   *know*
140 Thy napkin° cannot drink a tear of mine,   *handkerchief*
For thou, poor man, hast drowned it with thine own.
LUCIUS Ah, my Lavinia, I will wipe thy cheeks.
TITUS Mark, Marcus, mark. I understand her signs.
Had she a tongue to speak, now would she say
145 That to her brother which I said to thee.
His napkin with her true tears all bewet
Can do no service on her sorrowful cheeks.
Oh, what a sympathy° of woe is this,   *consensus*
As far from help as limbo[5] is from bliss!
         Enter AARON *the Moor alone.*
150 AARON Titus Andronicus, my lord the Emperor
Sends thee this word: that if thou love thy sons,

---

5. Region in hell dedicated to those denied entrance to heaven ("bliss") through no fault of their own: for instance, unbaptized infants, or virtuous people who lived before the advent of Christianity.

Let Marcus, Lucius, or thyself, old Titus,
Or any one of you, chop off your hand
And send it to the King. He for the same
155 Will send thee hither both thy sons alive,
And that shall be the ransom for their fault.
TITUS O gracious Emperor! O gentle Aaron!
Did ever raven sing so like a lark
That gives sweet tidings of the sun's uprise?
160 With all my heart I'll send the Emperor my hand.
Good Aaron, wilt thou help to chop it off?
LUCIUS Stay, father, for that noble hand of thine,
That hath thrown down so many enemies,
Shall not be sent. My hand will serve the turn.
165 My youth can better spare my blood than you,
And therefore mine shall save my brothers' lives.
MARCUS Which of your hands hath not defended Rome
And reared aloft the bloody battleax,
Writing destruction on the enemy's castle?
170 Oh, none of both but are of high desert.
My hand hath been but idle; let it serve
To ransom my two nephews from their death;
Then have I kept it to a worthy end.
AARON Nay, come, agree whose hand shall go along,
175 For fear they die before their pardon come.
MARCUS My hand shall go.
LUCIUS   By heaven, it shall not go.
TITUS Sirs, strive no more. Such withered herbs as these
Are meet° for plucking up, and therefore mine.   *proper*
LUCIUS Sweet father, if I shall be thought thy son,
180 Let me redeem my brothers both from death.
MARCUS And for our father's sake and mother's care,
Now let me show a brother's love to thee.
TITUS Agree between you. I will spare my hand.
LUCIUS Then I'll go fetch an ax.
MARCUS   But I will use the ax.
                    Exeunt [LUCIUS *and* MARCUS].
185 TITUS Come hither, Aaron. I'll deceive them both.
Lend me thy hand and I will give thee mine.
AARON [*aside*] If that be called deceit, I will be honest
And never whilst I live deceive men so.
But I'll deceive you in another sort,°   *way*
190 And that you'll say ere half an hour pass.
                    He cuts off Titus' hand.
                    Enter LUCIUS *and* MARCUS *again.*
TITUS Now stay your strife. What shall be is dispatched.
Good Aaron, give his majesty my hand.
Tell him it was a hand that warded° him   *defended*
From thousand dangers; bid him bury it.
195 More hath it merited; that° let it have.   *(burial)*
As for my sons, say I account of them
As jewels purchased at an easy price—
And yet dear too, because I bought mine own.
AARON I go, Andronicus, and for thy hand
200 Look by and by to have thy sons with thee.
[*aside*] Their heads, I mean! Oh, how this villainy

Doth fat° me with the very thoughts of it!   *feast*
Let fools do good and fair men call for grace,
Aaron will have his soul black like his face.   *Exit.*

205 TITUS   Oh, here I lift this one hand up to heaven
[*kneeling*] And bow this feeble ruin to the earth.
If any power pities wretched tears,
To that I call. [*to* LAVINIA, *who kneels*] What, wouldst thou
     kneel with me?
Do, then, dear heart. For heaven shall hear our prayers,
210 Or with our sighs we'll breathe the welkin dim°   *make the heavens misty*
And stain the sun with fog, as sometime° clouds   *sometimes do*
When they do hug him in their melting° bosoms.   *(with rain)*
MARCUS   O brother, speak with possibility°   *what is possible*
And do not break into these deep extremes.
215 TITUS   Is not my sorrow deep, having no bottom?
Then be my passions° bottomless with them.   *expression of suffering*
MARCUS   But yet let reason govern thy lament.
TITUS   If there were reason for these miseries,
Then into limits could I bind my woes.
220 When heaven doth weep, doth not the earth o'erflow?
If the winds rage, doth not the sea wax mad,
Threatening the welkin with his big-swoll'n face?
And wilt thou have a reason for this coil?°   *turmoil*
I am the sea. Hark how her sighs doth flow!
225 She is the weeping welkin, I the earth.
Then must my sea be movèd with° her sighs;   *by*
Then must my earth with her continual tears
Become a deluge, overflowed and drowned,
For why° my bowels[6] cannot hide her woes,   *Because*
230 But like a drunkard must I vomit them.
Then give me leave, for losers will have leave
To ease their stomachs[7] with their bitter tongues.
        Enter a MESSENGER *with two heads and a hand.*
MESSENGER   Worthy Andronicus, ill art thou repaid
For that good hand thou sent'st the Emperor.
235 Here are the heads of thy two noble sons,
And here's thy hand in scorn to thee sent back—
        [*He sets down the heads and hand.*]
Thy grief their sports, thy resolution mocked,
That° woe is me to think upon thy woes,   *So that*
More than remembrance of my father's death.   [*Exit.*]
240 MARCUS   Now let hot Etna° cool in Sicily   *volcano in Sicily*
And be my heart an ever-burning hell!
These miseries are more than may be borne.
To weep with them that weep doth ease some deal,°   *somewhat*
But sorrow flouted° at is double death.   *mocked*
245 LUCIUS   Ah, that this sight should make so deep a wound,
And yet detested life not shrink thereat.
That ever death should let life bear his name,°   *be called life*
Where life hath no more interest but to breathe![8]

6. The bowels were thought to be the seat of compas-   7. Resentments (with play on "vomit").
sion.   8. Where nothing is left of life but breathing.

[LAVINIA *kisses* TITUS.]

MARCUS   Alas, poor heart, that kiss is comfortless
250   As frozen water to a starvèd° snake.   *numb with cold*
    TITUS   When will this fearful slumber° have an end?   *nightmare*
    MARCUS   Now farewell, flattery.° Die, Andronicus.   *pleasing delusion*
  Thou dost not slumber. See thy two sons' heads,
  Thy warlike hand, thy mangled daughter here,
255   Thy other banished son with this dear sight
  Struck pale and bloodless, and thy brother, I,
  Even like a stony image, cold and numb.
  Ah, now no more will I control° thy griefs.   *try to restrain*
  Rent off thy silver hair, thy other hand
260   Gnawing with thy teeth, and be this dismal sight
  The closing up° of our most wretched eyes.   *(in death)*
  Now is a time to storm. Why art thou still?
    TITUS   Ha, ha, ha!
    MARCUS   Why dost thou laugh? It fits not with this hour.
265   TITUS   Why, I have not another tear to shed.
  Besides, this sorrow is an enemy
  And would usurp upon my watery eyes
  And make them blind with tributary[9] tears.
  Then which way shall I find Revenge's cave?
270   For these two heads do seem to speak to me
  And threat me I shall never come to bliss
  Till all these mischiefs° be returned° again   *calamities / turned back*
  Even in their throats that hath committed them.
  Come, let me see what task I have to do.
    [TITUS *and* LAVINIA *rise.*]
275   You heavy° people, circle me about,   *sad*
  That I may turn me to each one of you
  And swear unto my soul to right your wrongs.
    [LAVINIA, MARCUS, *and* LUCIUS *circle* TITUS. *He pledges*
    them.]
  The vow is made. Come, brother, take a head,
  And in this hand the other will I bear,
280   And, Lavinia, thou shalt be employèd in these arms.
  Bear thou my hand, sweet wench, between thy teeth.
  [*to* LUCIUS] As for thee, boy, go get thee from my sight.
  Thou art an exile and thou must not stay.
  Hie° to the Goths and raise an army there,   *Hurry*
285   And if ye love me, as I think you do,
  Let's kiss and part, for we have much to do.   *Exeunt.*
    [LUCIUS *remains.*]
    LUCIUS   Farewell, Andronicus, my noble father,
  The woefull'st man that ever lived in Rome.
  Farewell, proud Rome, till Lucius come again;
290   He loves his pledges[1] dearer than his life.
  Farewell, Lavinia, my noble sister;
  Oh, would thou wert as thou tofore° hast been!   *formerly*
  But now nor° Lucius nor Lavinia lives   *neither*
  But in oblivion and hateful griefs.
295   If Lucius live, he will requite your wrongs

---

9. Paying tribute (to sorrow, the enemy).
1. Vows; hostages (family members left behind in Rome).

And make proud Saturnine and his empress
Beg at the gates like Tarquin and his queen.[2]
Now will I to the Goths and raise a power°   *army*
To be revenged on Rome and Saturnine.   *Exit.*[3]

4.1 (F 4.1)

Enter Lucius' son [the BOY] *and* LAVINIA *running after
him, and the* BOY *flies from her with his books under
his arm. Enter* TITUS *and* MARCUS.

BOY Help, grandsire, help! My aunt Lavinia
Follows me everywhere, I know not why.
Good uncle Marcus, see how swift she comes.
Alas, sweet aunt, I know not what you mean.
 [*He drops his books.*]

5 MARCUS Stand by me, Lucius; do not fear thine aunt.

 TITUS She loves thee, boy, too well to do thee harm.

 BOY Ay, when my father was in Rome[1] she did.

 MARCUS What means my niece Lavinia by these signs?

 TITUS Fear her not, Lucius; somewhat° doth she mean. *something*

10 See, Lucius, see how much she makes of thee.[2]
Somewhither° would she have thee go with her. *Somewhere*
Ah, boy, Cornelia[3] never with more care
Read to her sons than she hath read to thee
Sweet poetry and Tully's[4] *Orator.*

15 Canst thou not guess wherefore she plies° thee thus? *importunes*

 BOY My lord, I know not, I, nor can I guess,
Unless some fit or frenzy do possess her;
For I have heard my grandsire say full oft
Extremity of griefs would make men mad,

20 And I have read that Hecuba of Troy[5]
Ran mad for sorrow: that made me to fear,
Although, my lord, I know my noble aunt
Loves me as dear as ever my mother did
And would not but in fury° fright my youth, *except in madness*

25 Which made me down to throw my books and fly—
Causeless, perhaps. —But pardon me, sweet aunt;
And, madam, if my uncle Marcus go,° *go with us*
I will most willingly attend your ladyship.

 MARCUS Lucius, I will.

30 TITUS How now, Lavinia? Marcus, what means this?
Some book there is that she desires to see.
Which is it, girl, of these? Open them, boy.
 [*to* LAVINIA] But thou art deeper read and better skilled;[6]
Come and take choice of all my library,

---

2. Tarquin and his family were banished from Rome after the rape of Lucrece; see note to 2.1.109.
3. TEXTUAL COMMENT The Folio text contains an additional scene here, the "fly-killing scene." While most modern editors use the Quarto as their base text and insert this one scene from F, the *Norton Shakespeare* text respects the integrity of the Quarto. Shakespeare probably wrote the fly-killing scene at a later date for a revival of the play; see Digital Edition TC 4 (Quarto edited text).
4.1 Location: Titus's garden.
1. That is, here to protect me.

2. TEXTUAL COMMENT Some editors reassign part of this speech to Marcus; for the rationale, see Digital Edition TC 5 (Quarto edited text).
3. Mother of the two Gracchi, famous tribunes; Cornelia was viewed as the ideal Roman mother because of her devotion to their education.
4. Cicero's; his *Orator* and *De oratore*, treatises on rhetoric written ca. 50 B.C.E., were both standard texts in Renaissance grammar schools.
5. See 1.1.139 and note.
6. Than to read schoolbooks.

35 And so beguile thy sorrow till the heavens
Reveal the damned contriver of this deed.
Why lifts she up her arms in sequence° thus?   *one after the other*
MARCUS I think she means that there were more than one
Confederate in the fact.° Ay, more there was,   *crime*
40 Or else to heaven she heaves them for revenge.
TITUS Lucius, what book is that she tosseth[7] so?
BOY Grandsire, 'tis Ovid's *Metamorphoses*;
My mother gave it me.
MARCUS   For love of her that's gone,
Perhaps, she culled° it from among the rest.   *picked*
45 TITUS Soft,° so busily she turns the leaves.   *Wait*
Help her. What would she find? Lavinia, shall I read?
This is the tragic tale of Philomel,
And treats of Tereus' treason and his rape[8]—
And rape, I fear, was root of thy annoy.°   *injury*
50 MARCUS See, brother, see. Note how she quotes° the leaves.   *examines*
TITUS Lavinia, wert thou thus surprised, sweet girl,
Ravished and wronged as Philomela was,
Forced in the ruthless, vast, and gloomy woods?
See, see!
55 Ay, such a place there is where we did hunt—
Oh, had we never, never hunted there!—
Patterned by° that the poet here describes,   *On the pattern of*
By nature made for murders and for rapes.
MARCUS Oh, why should nature build so foul a den,
60 Unless the gods delight in tragedies?
TITUS Give signs, sweet girl—for here are none but friends—
What Roman lord it was durst do the deed,
Or slunk not Saturnine,[9] as Tarquin erst,°   *once*
That left the camp to sin in Lucrece' bed?[1]
65 MARCUS Sit down, sweet niece. Brother, sit down by me.
Apollo, Pallas, Jove, or Mercury,[2]
Inspire me that I may this treason find.°   *discover the truth of*
My lord, look here. Look here, Lavinia.
   He writes his name with his staff, and guides it with
    feet and mouth.
This sandy plot is plain.° Guide, if thou canst,   *flat*
70 This after me. I have writ my name
Without the help of any hand at all.
Curst be that heart that forced us to this shift!°   *contrivance*
Write thou, good niece, and here display at last
What God will have discovered° for revenge.   *revealed*
75 Heaven guide thy pen to print thy sorrows plain
That we may know the traitors and the truth.
   She takes the staff in her mouth, and guides it with
    her stumps, and writes.[3]
Oh, do ye read, my lord, what she hath writ?

7. Clumsily turns the pages of.
8. See note to 2.3.43.
9. Was it Saturninus who slunk.
1. See note to 2.1.109.
2. Roman gods: Apollo was the god of prophecy, Pallas (Minerva) of wisdom, Mercury of hidden knowledge.

Jove (Jupiter), the king of the gods, was often imagined as all-knowing.
3. This action recalls Io in Ovid's *Metamorphoses* 1, who after her rape by Jove was turned into a heifer by Jove's jealous wife, Juno; she revealed her identity to her family by writing her story in the dust with her hoof.

TITUS "*Stuprum°*—Chiron—Demetrius."   *Defilement*

MARCUS What? What? The lustful sons of Tamora

80   Performers of this heinous bloody deed?

TITUS *Magni dominator poli,*

        Tam lentus audis scelera, tam lentus vides?[4]

MARCUS Oh, calm thee, gentle lord, although I know

        There is enough written upon this earth

85   To stir a mutiny in the mildest thoughts

        And arm the minds of infants to exclaims.°   *exclamations*

        My lord, kneel down with me. Lavinia, kneel.

        And kneel, sweet boy, the Roman Hector's[5] hope,

            [*All kneel.*]

        And swear with me—as, with the woeful fere°   *husband*

90   And father of that chaste dishonored dame,

        Lord Junius Brutus[6] swore for Lucrece' rape—

        That we will prosecute by good advice°   *after careful planning*

        Mortal revenge upon these traitorous Goths

        And see their blood or die with this reproach.°   *dishonor*

            [*They rise.*]

95 TITUS 'Tis sure enough, an° you knew how.   *if*

        But if you hunt these bear-whelps, then beware:

        The dam° will wake, and if she wind° ye once,   *mother / scent*

        She's with the lion deeply still in league

        And lulls him whilst she playeth on her back,

100   And when he sleeps will she do what she list.°   *pleases*

        You are a young huntsman, Marcus: let alone

        And come. I will go get a leaf° of brass   *sheet*

        And with a gad° of steel will write these words   *spike*

        And lay it by. The angry northern wind

105   Will blow these sands like Sibyl's leaves abroad,[7]

        And where's our lesson then? Boy, what say you?

BOY I say, my lord, that if I were a man

        Their mother's bedchamber should not be safe

        For these base bondmen to the yoke of Rome.

110 MARCUS Ay, that's my boy! Thy father hath full oft

        For his ungrateful country done the like.[8]

BOY And, uncle, so will I, an if I live.

TITUS Come, go with me into mine armory.

        Lucius, I'll fit° thee, and withal° my boy   *equip / in addition*

115   Shall carry from me to the Empress' sons

        Presents that I intend to send them both.

        Come, come; thou'lt do my message, wilt thou not?

BOY Ay, with my dagger in their bosoms, grandsire.

TITUS No, boy, not so. I'll teach thee another course.

120   Lavinia, come; Marcus, look to my house;

        Lucius and I'll go brave it° at the court.   *cut a fine figure*

        Ay, marry, will we, sir, and we'll be waited on.   *Exeunt.*

            [MARCUS *remains.*]

---

4. Ruler of the great heavens, are you so slow to hear
and see crimes? (adapted from Seneca's *Hippolytus*).
5. Lucius the elder, champion of Rome as Hector
was of Troy.
6. Leader of those who drove the Tarquins from Rome.

7. The Sybil of Cumae (in Italy) wrote prophecies on
leaves and placed them outside her cave; they sometimes blew away before they could be read.
8. That is, fought against the Goths.

MARCUS   O heavens, can you hear a good man groan
And not relent or not compassion° him?   *pity*
125   Marcus, attend him in his ecstasy°   *madness*
That hath more scars of sorrow in his heart
Than foemen's marks upon his battered shield,
But yet so just that he will not revenge.
Revenge the heavens[9] for old Andronicus!   *Exit.*

4.2 (F 4.2)

Enter AARON, CHIRON, *and* DEMETRIUS *at one door, and at*
the other door Young Lucius [the BOY] *and [an Attendant]*
with a bundle of weapons and verses writ upon them.

CHIRON   Demetrius, here's the son of Lucius.
He hath some message to deliver us.
AARON   Ay, some mad message from his mad grandfather.
BOY   My lords, with all the humbleness I may,
5   I greet your honors from Andronicus
[*aside*] And pray the Roman gods confound° you both.   *destroy*
DEMETRIUS   Gramercy,° lovely Lucius, what's the news?   *Thank you*
BOY [*aside*]   That you are both deciphered,° that's the news,   *detected*
For villains marked with rape. —May it please you,
10   My grandsire, well advised, hath sent by me
The goodliest weapons of his armory
To gratify° your honorable youth,   *grace*
The hope of Rome, for so he bid me say,
And so I do, and with his gifts present
15   Your lordships: whenever you have need,
You may be armèd and appointed° well.   *equipped*
And so I leave you both [*aside*] like bloody villains.
                         *Exeunt [*BOY *and Attendant].*
DEMETRIUS   What's here? A scroll, and written round about?
Let's see:
20   "Integer vitae, scelerisque purus,
    Non eget Mauri iaculis, nec arcu."[1]
CHIRON   Oh, 'tis a verse in Horace. I know it well:
I read it in the grammar long ago.
AARON   Ay, just° a verse in Horace; right you have it.   *exactly*
25   [*aside*] Now what a thing it is to be an ass!
Here's no sound° jest! The old man hath found their guilt   *wholesome*
And sends them weapons wrapped about with lines
That wound beyond their feeling to the quick.[2]
But were our witty° empress well afoot,°   *clever / up and about*
30   She would applaud Andronicus' conceit.°   *device*
But let her rest in her unrest[3] a while.
[*to* CHIRON *and* DEMETRIUS] And now, young lords, was't not
    a happy star
Led us to Rome strangers—and more than so,
Captives—to be advancèd to this height?
35   It did me good before the palace gate
To brave[4] the tribune in his brother's hearing.

---

9. May the heavens take revenge.
4.2 Location: The imperial palace.
1. "The man upright in life and free from crime needs
neither the Moorish javelin nor the bow" (Horace,
Odes 1.22.1–2); quoted in William Lily's Latin gram-

mar, standard in Elizabethan schools.
2. That pierce them deeply though they are too dull
to feel it.
3. Remain in her distress (Tamora is in childbirth).
4. To defy (not shown in the play).

DEMETRIUS   But me more good to see so great a lord
   Basely insinuate° and send us gifts.   *curry favor*
AARON   Had he not reason, Lord Demetrius?
40   Did you not use his daughter very friendly?
DEMETRIUS   I would we had a thousand Roman dames
   At such a bay,° by turn to serve our lust.   *Cornered like that*
CHIRON   A charitable wish and full of love.
AARON   Here lacks but your mother for to say amen.
45   CHIRON   And that would she for twenty thousand more.
DEMETRIUS   Come, let us go and pray to all the gods
   For our beloved mother in her pains.°   *(labor pains)*
AARON   Pray to the devils! The gods have given us over.
   Trumpets sound.
DEMETRIUS   Why do the Emperor's trumpets flourish thus?
50   CHIRON   Belike° for joy the Emperor hath a son.   *Probably*
DEMETRIUS   Soft, who comes here?
   Enter NURSE with a blackamoor child.
NURSE   Good morrow, lords.
   Oh, tell me, did you see Aaron the Moor?
AARON   Well, more° or less, or ne'er a whit at all.   *(punning on "Moor")*
   Here Aaron is, and what with Aaron now?
55   NURSE   O gentle Aaron, we are all undone.
   Now help or woe betide thee evermore!
AARON   Why, what a caterwauling dost thou keep!
   What dost thou wrap and fumble° in thy arms?   *bundle up*
NURSE   Oh, that which I would hide from heaven's eye:
60   Our Empress' shame and stately Rome's disgrace.
   She is delivered, lords, she is delivered!
AARON   To whom?
NURSE   I mean she is brought abed!°   *delivered of a child*
AARON   Well, God give her good rest! What hath he sent her?
NURSE   A devil.[5]
65   AARON   Why, then, she is the devil's dam; a joyful issue.°   *outcome; child*
NURSE   A joyless, dismal, black, and sorrowful issue.
   Here is the babe, as loathsome as a toad
   Amongst the fair-faced breeders of our clime.
   The Empress sends it thee, thy stamp, thy seal,[6]
70   And bids thee christen it with thy dagger's point.
AARON   Zounds,° ye whore! Is black so base a hue?   *God's wounds*
   [*to the baby*] Sweet blowse,° you are a beauteous blossom,   *red-cheeked wench*
     sure.
DEMETRIUS   Villain, what hast thou done?
AARON   That which thou canst not undo.
75   CHIRON   Thou hast undone our mother.
AARON   Villain, I have done° thy mother.   *used sexually*
DEMETRIUS   And therein, hellish dog, thou hast undone her.
   Woe to her chance and damned her loathèd choice,
   Accursed the offspring of so foul a fiend.
CHIRON   It shall not live.
80   AARON   It shall not die.
NURSE   Aaron, it must; the mother wills it so.

---

5. The devil was often imagined as black, and Afri-   6. *thy stamp, thy seal:* bearing your imprint.
cans as devils.

AARON What, must it, Nurse? Then let no man but I
    Do execution on my flesh and blood.
DEMETRIUS I'll broach° the tadpole on my rapier's point.   *impale*
85   Nurse, give it me; my sword shall soon dispatch it.
AARON Sooner this sword shall plow thy bowels up.
    [AARON *draws his sword.*]
    Stay, murderous villains! Will you kill your brother?
    Now, by the burning tapers of the sky
    That shone so brightly when this boy was got,°   *conceived*
90   He dies upon my scimitar's sharp point
    That touches this, my first-born son and heir.
    I tell you, younglings, not Enceladus,[7]
    With all his threatening band of Typhon's° brood,   *father of the Titans*
    Nor great Alcides,[8] nor the god of war
95   Shall seize this prey out of his father's hands.
    What, what, ye sanguine[9] shallow-hearted boys!
    Ye white-limed° walls, ye alehouse painted signs![1]   *whitewashed*
    Coal-black is better than another hue
    In that it scorns to bear another hue;
100   For all the water in the ocean
    Can never turn the swan's black legs to white,
    Although she lave° them hourly in the flood.[2]   *bathe*
    Tell the Empress from me I am of age
    To keep mine own, excuse it how she can.
105 DEMETRIUS Wilt thou betray thy noble mistress thus?
AARON My mistress is my mistress, this myself,
    The vigor and the picture of my youth.
    This before all the world do I prefer;
    This maugre° all the world will I keep safe,   *in spite of*
110   Or some of you shall smoke° for it in Rome.   *suffer*
DEMETRIUS By this our mother is forever shamed.
CHIRON Rome will despise her for this foul escape.°   *escapade*
NURSE The Emperor in his rage will doom° her death.   *decree*
CHIRON I blush to think upon this ignomy.°   *ignominy*
115 AARON Why, there's the privilege your beauty bears.
    Fie, treacherous hue, that will betray with blushing
    The close enacts° and counsels of thy heart.   *secret purposes*
    Here's a young lad framed of another leer.°   *complexion*
    Look how the black slave smiles upon the father,
120   As who should say, "Old lad, I am thine own."
    He is your brother, lords, sensibly° fed   *manifestly*
    Of that self° blood that first gave life to you,   *same*
    And from that womb where you imprisoned were
    He is enfranchisèd° and come to light.   *freed*
125   Nay, he is your brother by the surer side,°   *(the mother's)*
    Although my seal be stampèd in his face.
NURSE Aaron, what shall I say unto the Empress?
DEMETRIUS Advise thee,° Aaron, what is to be done,   *Consider*
    And we will all subscribe to° thy advice.   *follow*
130   Save thou the child, so° we may all be safe.   *provided that*

---

7. In Greek mythology, a Titan, or primeval deity,
who warred against the gods of Mount Olympus.
8. Hercules (literally, descendant of Alcaeus).
9. Ruddy (as opposed to black).

1. Cheap, garish images of men.
2. Stream; alluding to the proverb "One cannot wash
an Ethiop white."

AARON Then sit we down and let us all consult.
  My son and I will have the wind of you.[3]
  Keep there. Now talk at pleasure of your safety.
DEMETRIUS [*to the* NURSE] How many women saw this child of his?
135 AARON Why, so, brave lords, when we join in league
  I am a lamb—but if you brave the Moor,
  The chafèd° boar, the mountain lioness,   *enraged*
  The ocean swells not so as Aaron storms.
  [*to the* NURSE] But say again: how many saw the child?
140 NURSE Cornelia the midwife and myself,
  And no one else but the delivered Empress.
AARON The Empress, the midwife, and yourself.
  Two may keep counsel when the third's away.
  Go to the Empress; tell her this I said—
  He kills her.
145 "Wheek, wheek!"[4] So cries a pig preparèd to the spit.
DEMETRIUS What mean'st thou, Aaron? Wherefore didst thou this?
AARON O Lord, sir, 'tis a deed of policy.°   *prudence*
  Shall she live to betray this guilt of ours—
  A long-tongued babbling gossip? No, lords, no.
150 And now be it known to you my full intent.
  Not far, one Muliteus, my countryman,
  His wife[5] but yesternight was brought to bed.
  His child is like to° her, fair as you are.   *resembles*
  Go pack° with him and give the mother gold,   *conspire*
155 And tell them both the circumstance of all,°   *the full details*
  And how by this their child shall be advanced
  And be receivèd for the Emperor's heir,
  And substituted in the place of mine,
  To calm this tempest whirling in the court;
160 And let the Emperor dandle him for his own.
  Hark ye, lords, you see I have given her physic,°   *medicine*
  And you must needs bestow her funeral;
  The fields are near and you are gallant grooms.°   *fellows*
  This done, see that you take no longer days,°   *waste no time*
165 But send the midwife presently to me.
  The midwife and the nurse well made away,
  Then let the ladies tattle what they please.
CHIRON Aaron, I see thou wilt not trust the air with secrets.
DEMETRIUS For this care of Tamora,
170 Herself and hers are highly bound to thee.
                Exeunt [CHIRON *and* DEMETRIUS,
                carrying the Nurse's body].
AARON Now to the Goths, as swift as swallow flies,
  There to dispose° this treasure in mine arms   *bestow*
  And secretly to greet the Empress' friends.
  —Come on, you thick-lipped slave. I'll bear you hence,
175 For it is you that puts us to our shifts.°   *force us to scheme*
  I'll make you feed on berries and on roots,
  And feed on curds and whey, and suck the goat,
  And cabin in a cave, and bring you up
  To be a warrior and command a camp.°   *Exit.*   *an army*

---

3. Will keep downwind (as a wary hunter does when
stalking game).
4. Aaron imitates her death cry.

5. *one . . . wife:* the wife of a certain Muliteus, my
countryman.

4.3 (F 4.3)

Enter TITUS, *old* MARCUS, *Young Lucius [the* BOY], *and other*
gentlemen[, PUBLIUS, *Sempronius, and Caius,] with bows,*
and TITUS *bears the arrows with letters on the ends of them.*

TITUS   Come, Marcus, come; kinsmen, this is the way.
　　Sir boy, let me see your archery.
　　Look ye draw home° enough and 'tis there straight.°　　　　　*fully / immediately*
　　Terras Astraea reliquit.[1] Be you remembered,° Marcus,　　　　　*Remember*
5　She's gone, she's fled. Sirs, take you to your tools.
　　You, cousins, shall go sound the ocean
　　And cast your nets—
　　Happily° you may catch her in the sea,　　　　　*Perhaps*
　　Yet there's as little justice as at land.
10　No! Publius and Sempronius, you must do it;
　　'Tis you must dig with mattock and with spade
　　And pierce the inmost center of the earth.
　　Then, when you come to Pluto's region,[2]
　　I pray you deliver him this petition.
15　Tell him it is for justice and for aid,
　　And that it comes from old Andronicus,
　　Shaken with sorrows in ungrateful Rome.
　　Ah, Rome! Well, well, I made thee miserable
　　What time° I threw the people's suffrages°　　　　　*When / votes*
20　On him that thus doth tyrannize o'er me.
　　Go, get you gone, and pray be careful all,
　　And leave you not a man-of-war unsearched.
　　This wicked Emperor may have shipped her[3] hence,
　　And, kinsmen, then we may go pipe[4] for justice.
25　MARCUS   O Publius, is not this a heavy case°　　　　　*sad situation*
　　To see thy noble uncle thus distract?
　　PUBLIUS   Therefore, my lords, it highly us concerns
　　By day and night t'attend him carefully
　　And feed his humor° kindly as we may　　　　　*humor him*
30　Till time beget some careful° remedy.　　　　　*solicitous; laborious*
　　MARCUS   Kinsmen, his sorrows are past remedy.
　　But [　　　　　　　　　　　][5]
　　Join with the Goths and with revengeful war
　　Take wreak on° Rome for this ingratitude,　　　　　*Requite*
35　And vengeance on the traitor Saturnine.
　　TITUS   Publius, how now? How now, my masters?
　　What, have you met with her?
　　PUBLIUS   No, my good lord, but Pluto sends you word.
　　If you will have Revenge from hell, you shall.
40　Marry, for° Justice, she is so employed,　　　　　*as for*
　　He thinks, with Jove in heaven or somewhere else,
　　So that perforce you must needs stay a time.[6]
　　TITUS   He doth me wrong to feed me with delays.
　　I'll dive into the burning lake[7] below

4.3 Location: Outside the Emperor's palace.
1. Astraea (goddess of justice) has abandoned the
earth (Ovid, *Metamorphoses* 1.150).
2. The underworld, ruled by Pluto.
3. Astraea, whom the mad Titus imagines being
smuggled out of Rome in a war boat.

4. Whistle (that is, seek in vain).
5. TEXTUAL COMMENT A line or lines may be missing
here; see Digital Edition TC 6 (Quarto edited text).
6. So that by necessity ("perforce") you must wait a
while.
7. Phlegethon, river of fire of the underworld.

45 And pull her out of Acheron° by the heels. *river of the underworld*
Marcus, we are but shrubs, no cedars we,
No big-boned men, framed of the Cyclops'[8] size,
But metal, Marcus, steel to the very back,
Yet wrung with wrongs more than our backs can bear.
50 And sith° there's no justice in earth nor hell, *since*
We will solicit heaven and move the gods
To send down Justice for to wreak° our wrongs. *revenge*
Come, to this gear.° You are a good archer, Marcus. *business*
        He gives them the arrows.
"*Ad Jovem*," that's for you. Here, "*Ad Apollinem*."
55 "*Ad Martem*,"[9] that's for myself.
Here, boy, "To Pallas."° Here, "To Mercury." *Minerva*
"To Saturn,"° Caius, not to Saturnine! *father of Jove*
You were as good to° shoot against the wind. *might as well*
To it, boy! Marcus, loose° when I bid. *(the arrows)*
60 Of° my word, I have written to effect; *On*
There's not a god left unsolicited.
MARCUS Kinsmen, shoot all your shafts into the court.
We will afflict the Emperor in his pride.
TITUS Now, masters, draw. Oh, well said,° Lucius! *done*
65 Good boy, in Virgo's[1] lap! Give it Pallas!
MARCUS My lord, I aim a mile beyond the moon.[2]
Your letter is with Jupiter by this.
TITUS Ha, ha! Publius, Publius, what hast thou done?
See, see, thou hast shot off one of Taurus'[3] horns.
70 MARCUS This was the sport, my lord: when Publius shot,
The Bull, being galled,° gave Aries[4] such a knock *angered*
That down fell both the Ram's horns in the court,
And who should find them but the Empress' villain!° *servant; scoundrel*
She laughed and told the Moor he should not choose
75 But give them[5] to his master for a present.
TITUS Why, there it goes. God give his lordship joy!
        Enter the CLOWN° *with a basket and two pigeons in it.* *(rustic)*
News! News from heaven! Marcus, the post is come.
—Sirrah, what tidings? Have you any letters?
Shall I have justice? What says Jupiter?[6]
80 CLOWN Ho, the gibbet-maker?[7] He says that he hath taken
them down again, for the man must not be hanged till the
next week.
TITUS But what says Jupiter, I ask thee?
CLOWN Alas, sir, I know not Jubiter. I never drank with him
85 in all my life.
TITUS Why, villain, art not thou the carrier?
CLOWN Ay, of my pigeons, sir, nothing else.
TITUS Why, didst thou not come from heaven?

8. One-eyed giants of Greek legend.
9. "To Jove," "To Apollo," "To Mars"; Mars was the god
of war.
1. Constellation identified with Astraea after her
flight from earth.
2. Marcus, humoring Titus, expects him to take the
words literally; but they also mean "talk wildly, make
extravagant claims."

3. Constellation of the bull.
4. Constellation of the ram.
5. The horns, as the sign of the cuckold.
6. TEXTUAL COMMENT The Quarto misspells "Jupiter" in both Titus's speech and the Clown's; see Digital
Edition TC 7 (Quarto edited text) for the significance.
7. The Clown hears "Jupiter" as "gibbetter."

CLOWN From heaven? Alas, sir, I never came there. God for-
90   bid I should be so bold to press to heaven in my young days.
      Why, I am going with my pigeons to the tribunal plebs[8] to
      take up a matter of brawl betwixt my uncle and one of the
      Emperal's° men.   *(for "Emperor's")*
      {MARCUS [*to* TITUS] Why, sir, that is as fit as can be to serve for
95   your oration and let him deliver the pigeons to the Emperor
      from you.
      TITUS [*to the* CLOWN] Tell me, can you deliver an oration to
      the Emperor with a grace?
      CLOWN Nay, truly, sir, I could never say grace in all my life.}
100 TITUS Sirrah, come hither. Make no more ado
      But give your pigeons to the Emperor.
      By me thou shalt have justice at his hands.
      Hold, hold— [*He gives money.*] Meanwhile, here's money for
      thy charges.
      —Give me pen and ink.
105 —Sirrah, can you with a grace deliver up a supplication?
      CLOWN Ay, sir.
      TITUS Then here is a supplication for you. And when you
      come to him at the first approach, you must kneel, then kiss
      his foot, then deliver up your pigeons, and then look for your
110 reward. I'll be at hand, sir. See you do it bravely.°   *handsomely*
      CLOWN I warrant you, sir, let me alone.°   *leave it to me*
      TITUS Sirrah, hast thou a knife? Come, let me see it.
      —Here, Marcus, fold it in the oration.
      —For thou hast made it like an humble suppliant,
115 And when thou hast given it to the Emperor,
      Knock at my door and tell me what he says.
      CLOWN God be with you, sir; I will.   *Exit.*
      TITUS Come, Marcus, let us go. —Publius, follow me. *Exeunt.*

4.4 (F 4.4)

*Enter Emperor [*SATURNINUS*] and Empress [*TAMORA*]*
*and her two sons [*CHIRON *and* DEMETRIUS, *and*
Attendants]. The Emperor brings the arrows in his*
hand that TITUS *shot at him.*

SATURNINUS Why, lords, what wrongs are these? Was ever seen
      An emperor in Rome thus overborne,°   *insolently treated*
      Troubled, confronted thus, and for the extent
      Of equal justice[1] used in such contempt?
5   My lords, you know the mightful gods,
      However these disturbers of our peace
      Buzz in the people's ears; there naught hath passed
      But even with° law against the willful sons   *according to*
      Of old Andronicus. And what an if
10   His sorrows have so overwhelmed his wits?
      Shall we be thus afflicted in his wreaks,°   *vindictive deeds*
      His fits, his frenzy, and his bitterness?
      And now he writes to heaven for his redress.
      See, here's "To Jove," and this "To Mercury,"

---

8. *Tribunus plebis,* tribune of the common people.   1. *for . . . justice:* in return for exercising impartial
4.4 Location: The Emperor's palace.   justice.

15 This "To Apollo," this "To the God of War"—
Sweet scrolls to fly about the streets of Rome!
What's this but libeling against the Senate
And blazoning° our unjustice everywhere?   *proclaiming*
A goodly humor,° is it not, my lords?   *whim*
20 As who would° say, in Rome no justice were.   *As if one were to*
But, if I live, his feignèd ecstasies°   *pretended insanity*
Shall be no shelter to these outrages,
But he and his shall know that justice lives
In Saturninus' health whom, if he sleep,
25 He'll so awake[2] as he in fury shall
Cut off the proud'st conspirator that lives.
TAMORA   My gracious lord, my lovely Saturnine,
Lord of my life, commander of my thoughts,
Calm thee and bear the faults of Titus' age,
30 Th'effects of sorrow for his valiant sons,
Whose loss hath pierced him deep and scarred his heart;
And rather comfort his distressèd plight
Than prosecute the meanest or the best[3]
For these contempts. [*aside*] Why, thus it shall become
35 High-witted° Tamora to gloze° with all.   *Intelligent / delude*
But, Titus, I have touched thee to the quick,
Thy life blood out. If Aaron now be wise,
Then is all safe; the anchor in the port.
        Enter CLOWN.
—How now, good fellow? Wouldst thou speak with us?
40 CLOWN   Yea, forsooth, an° your mistress-ship be emperial.   *if*
TAMORA   Empress I am, but yonder sits the Emperor.
CLOWN   'Tis he. God and Saint Stephen give you good e'en.°   *good evening*
I have brought you a letter and a couple of pigeons here.
        [SATURNINUS] *reads the letter* [*and finds the knife
        within*].
SATURNINUS   Go, take him away and hang him presently.°   *instantly*
45 CLOWN   How much money must I° have?   *am I to*
TAMORA   Come, sirrah, you must be hanged.
CLOWN   Hanged, by'r Lady?[4] Then I have brought up a neck
to a fair end.   *Exit* [*with Attendants*].
SATURNINUS   Despiteful and intolerable wrongs!
50 Shall I endure this monstrous villainy?
I know from whence this same device proceeds.
May this be borne as if his traitorous sons,
That died by law for murder of our brother,
Have by my means been butchered wrongfully?
55 —Go, drag the villain hither by the hair.
Nor° age nor honor shall shape privilege.°   *Neither / afford immunity*
For this proud mock I'll be thy slaughterman,
Sly frantic wretch, that holp'st° to make me great   *helped*
In hope thyself should govern Rome and me.
        Enter a messenger, AEMILIUS.

2. *whom . . . awake:* A confusing passage. If the first
"he" (in line 24) refers to Titus, then the meaning is
"If Titus impairs Saturninus's health (tries to 'put him
to sleep'), then Saturninus will rouse himself angrily."
If the first "he" refers to Saturninus, then "Although

Saturninus seems not to respond now, he will awaken."
Some editors change the first and third (line 25) "he"s
to "she"s, making the phrase refer to justice.
3. Lowest- or highest-ranking.
4. By our Lady (the Virgin Mary).

60 SATURNINUS   What news with thee, Aemilius?
    AEMILIUS   Arm, my lords! Rome never had more cause.
        The Goths have gathered head° and with a power   *an army*
        Of high-resolvèd men bent to the spoil°   *eager to plunder*
        They hither march amain° under conduct°   *swiftly / command*
65   Of Lucius, son to old Andronicus,
        Who threats in course of this revenge to do
        As much as ever Coriolanus⁵ did.
    SATURNINUS   Is warlike Lucius general of the Goths?
        These tidings nip me, and I hang the head
70   As flowers with frost or grass beat down with storms.
        Ay, now begins our sorrows to approach.
        'Tis he the common people love so much.
        Myself hath often heard them say,
        When I have walkèd like a private man,⁶
75   That Lucius' banishment was wrongfully,°   *wrongfully imposed*
        And they have wished that Lucius were their emperor.
    TAMORA   Why should you fear? Is not your city strong?
    SATURNINUS   Ay, but the citizens favor Lucius
        And will revolt from me to succor him.
80 TAMORA   King, be thy thoughts imperious like thy name.
        Is the sun dimmed, that° gnats do fly in it?   *because*
        The eagle suffers little birds to sing
        And is not careful° what they mean thereby,   *troubled*
        Knowing that with the shadow of his wings
85   He can at pleasure stint° their melody: *stop*
        Even so mayst thou the giddy° men of Rome.   *fickle*
        Then cheer thy spirit—for know thou, Emperor,
        I will enchant the old Andronicus
        With words more sweet and yet more dangerous
90   Than baits to fish or honey-stalks⁷ to sheep,
        When as° the one is wounded with the bait,   *When*
        The other rotted⁸ with delicious seed.
    SATURNINUS   But he will not entreat his son for us.
    TAMORA   If Tamora entreat him, then he will.
95   For I can smooth° and fill his agèd ears   *flatter*
        With golden promises that, were his heart
        Almost impregnable, his old ears deaf,
        Yet should both ear and heart obey my tongue.
        [*to* AEMILIUS] Go thou before to be our ambassador.
100   Say that the Emperor requests a parley
        Of warlike Lucius, and appoint the meeting
        Even at his father's house, the old Andronicus.
    SATURNINUS   Aemilius, do this message honorably,
        And if he stand in hostage⁹ for his safety,
105   Bid him demand what pledge will please him best.
    AEMILIUS   Your bidding shall I do effectually.   *Exit.*
    TAMORA   Now will I to that old Andronicus
        And temper° him with all the art I have   *work on*
        To pluck proud Lucius from the warlike Goths.

---

5. Early Roman warrior who, after he was banished,
joined his former enemies and led an army against
Rome; the subject of Shakespeare's *Coriolanus*.
6. Disguised as an ordinary man.

7. Clover (large quantities make sheep ill).
8. Afflicted by the rot, a liver disease in sheep.
9. If he demand a hostage (to be killed if Titus is
threatened).

110 And now, sweet Emperor, be blithe again,
And bury all thy fear in my devices.
SATURNINUS Then go successantly° and plead to him. *Exeunt.*   *right away*

5.1 (F 5.1)

Enter LUCIUS *with an army of* GOTHS *with drums*°   *drummers*
and Soldiers.

LUCIUS Approvèd° warriors and my faithful friends,   *Proven*
I have received letters from great Rome
Which signifies what hate they bear their emperor
And how desirous of our sight they are.
5 Therefore, great lords, be, as your titles witness,
Imperious and impatient of your wrongs,
And wherein Rome hath done you any scathe°   *harm*
Let him make treble satisfaction.
FIRST GOTH Brave slip° sprung from the great Andronicus,   *offspring*
10 Whose name was once our terror, now our comfort,
Whose high exploits and honorable deeds
Ingrateful Rome requites with foul contempt,
Be bold° in us. We'll follow where thou lead'st,   *confident*
Like stinging bees in hottest summer's day
15 Led by their master[1] to the flowered fields,
And be avenged on cursèd Tamora.
ALL GOTHS And, as he saith, so say we all with him.
LUCIUS I humbly thank him, and I thank you all.
But who comes here, led by a lusty Goth?
Enter [SECOND] GOTH, *leading of* AARON *with his child*
in his arms.
20 SECOND GOTH Renownèd Lucius, from our troops I strayed
To gaze upon a ruinous monastery,
And as I earnestly did fix mine eye
Upon the wasted° building, suddenly   *ruined*
I heard a child cry underneath a wall.
25 I made unto the noise, when soon I heard
The crying babe controlled° with this discourse: *calmed*
"Peace, tawny slave,[2] half me and half thy dam.
Did not thy hue bewray° whose brat thou art,   *show*
Had nature lent thee but thy mother's look,
30 Villain, thou mightst have been an emperor.
But where the bull and cow are both milk-white,
They never do beget a coal-black calf.
Peace, villain, peace!"—even thus he rates° the babe—   *scolds*
"For I must bear thee to a trusty Goth
35 Who, when he knows thou art the Empress' babe,
Will hold thee dearly for thy mother's sake."
With this, my weapon drawn, I rushed upon him,
Surprised him suddenly, and brought him hither
To use as you think needful of° the man.   *appropriate to*
40 LUCIUS O worthy Goth, this is the incarnate devil
That robbed Andronicus of his good hand.
This is the pearl that pleased your Empress' eye,
And here's the base fruit of her burning lust.

5.1 Location: Outside Rome.   2. Used affectionately, like "brat" and "villain" below.
1. The queen bee was thought to be male.

[*to* AARON] Say, wall-eyed slave, whither wouldst thou convey
45   This growing image of thy fiend-like face?
   Why dost not speak? What, deaf? Not a word?
   A halter, soldiers! Hang him on this tree,
   And by his side his fruit of bastardy.
AARON   Touch not the boy; he is of royal blood.
50 LUCIUS   Too like the sire for ever being° good.   *ever to be*
   First, hang the child that he may see it sprawl:°   *twitch convulsively*
   A sight to vex the father's soul withal.
   Get me a ladder.
           [GOTHS *bring a ladder and force* AARON *to climb it.*]
AARON   Lucius, save the child
   And bear it from me to the Empress.
55   If thou do this, I'll show thee wondrous things
   That highly may advantage thee to hear.
   If thou wilt not, befall what may befall,
   I'll speak no more but "Vengeance rot you all!"
LUCIUS   Say on, an if it please me which thou speakest,
60   Thy child shall live and I will see it nourished.
AARON   An if it please thee? Why, assure thee, Lucius,
   'Twill vex thy soul to hear what I shall speak.
   For I must talk of murders, rapes, and massacres,
   Acts of black night, abominable deeds,
65   Complots° of mischief, treason, villainies,   *Conspiracies*
   Ruthful° to hear yet piteously[3] performed.   *Lamentable*
   And this shall all be buried in my death
   Unless thou swear to me my child shall live.
LUCIUS   Tell on thy mind. I say thy child shall live.
70 AARON   Swear that he shall and then I will begin.
LUCIUS   Who should I swear by? Thou believest no god.
   That granted, how canst thou believe an oath?
AARON   What if I do not?—As indeed I do not—
   Yet for I know thou art religious
75   And hast a thing within thee callèd conscience,
   With twenty popish tricks and ceremonies
   Which I have seen thee careful to observe,
   Therefore I urge° thy oath; for that I know   *insist on*
   An idiot holds his bauble° for a god,   *jester's stick*
80   And keeps the oath which by that god he swears,
   To that I'll urge him. Therefore thou shalt vow
   By that same god, what god so e'er it be
   That thou adorest and hast in reverence,
   To save my boy, to nourish and bring him up,
85   Or else I will discover naught to thee.
LUCIUS   Even by my god I swear to thee I will.
AARON   First know thou I begot him on the Empress.
LUCIUS   Oh, most insatiate and luxurious° woman!   *lascivious*
AARON   Tut, Lucius, this was but a deed of charity
90   To° that which thou shalt hear of me anon.   *Compared to*
   'Twas her two sons that murdered Bassianus;
   They cut thy sister's tongue, and ravished her,
   And cut her hands, and trimmed her as thou sawest.
LUCIUS   O detestable villain! Call'st thou that "trimming"?

---

3. In a way that would excite pity.

95	AARON Why, she was washed, and cut, and trimmed,	
	And 'twas trim° sport for them which had the doing of it.	*fine*
	LUCIUS Oh, barbarous beastly villains, like thyself!	
	AARON Indeed, I was their tutor to instruct them.	
	That codding° spirit had they from their mother,	*lustful*
100	As sure a card as ever won the set.°	*game*
	That bloody mind I think they learned of me,	
	As true a dog as ever fought at head.[4]	
	Well, let my deeds be witness of my worth.	
	I trained° thy brethren to that guileful hole	*lured*
105	Where the dead corpse of Bassianus lay.	
	I wrote the letter that thy father found,	
	And hid the gold within that letter mentioned,	
	Confederate with the Queen and her two sons.	
	And what not done that thou hast cause to rue	
110	Wherein I had no stroke of mischief in it?	
	I played the cheater[5] for thy father's hand,	
	And when I had it drew myself apart°	*went off alone*
	And almost broke my heart° with extreme laughter;	*died*
	I pried me° through the crevice of a wall	*I peered*
115	When for his hand he had his two sons' heads,	
	Beheld his tears, and laughed so heartily	
	That both mine eyes were rainy like to his;	
	And when I told the Empress of this sport,	
	She swoonèd almost at my pleasing tale	
120	And for my tidings gave me twenty kisses.	
	FIRST GOTH What, canst thou say all this and never blush?	
	AARON Ay, like a black dog, as the saying is.	
	LUCIUS Art thou not sorry for these heinous deeds?	
	AARON Ay, that I had not done a thousand more.	
125	Even now I curse the day—and yet I think	
	Few come within the compass of my curse—	
	Wherein I did not some notorious ill,	
	As kill a man or else devise his death,	
	Ravish a maid or plot the way to do it,	
130	Accuse some innocent and forswear myself,	
	Set deadly enmity between two friends,	
	Make poor men's cattle break their necks,	
	Set fire on barns and haystacks in the night,	
	And bid the owners quench them with their tears.	
135	Oft have I digged up dead men from their graves	
	And set them upright at their dear friends' door,	
	Even when their sorrows almost was forgot,	
	And on their skins, as on the bark of trees,	
	Have with my knife carved in Roman letters,	
140	"Let not your sorrow die though I am dead."	
	But I have done a thousand dreadful things	
	As willingly as one would kill a fly,	
	And nothing grieves me heartily indeed	
	But that I cannot do ten thousand more.	
145	LUCIUS Bring down the devil, for he must not die	
	So sweet a death as hanging presently.°	*immediately*

---

4. As ever went for the bull's head (in the sport of bullbaiting).

5. Swindler; escheator, an officer appointed to look after property forfeited to the crown.

[AARON *is brought down from the ladder.*]

AARON   If there be devils, would I were a devil,
　　To live and burn in everlasting fire,
　　So I might have your company in hell,
150　But to torment you with my bitter tongue.
LUCIUS   Sirs, stop his mouth and let him speak no more.
　　　　[AARON *is gagged.*]
　　　　Enter AEMILIUS.
THIRD GOTH   My lord, there is a messenger from Rome
　　Desires to be admitted to your presence.
LUCIUS   Let him come near.
155　—Welcome, Aemilius; what's the news from Rome?
AEMILIUS   Lord Lucius and you princes of the Goths,
　　The Roman Emperor greets you all by me.
　　And, for he understands you are in arms,
　　He craves a parley at your father's house,
160　Willing you to demand your hostages,
　　And they shall be immediately delivered.
FIRST GOTH   What says our general?
LUCIUS   Aemilius, let the Emperor give his pledges
　　Unto my father and my uncle Marcus,
165　And we will come. —March away.　　[*Flourish.*] [*Exeunt.*]

5.2 (F 5.2)

Enter TAMORA *and her two sons* [CHIRON *and*
DEMETRIUS], *disguised.*

TAMORA   Thus in this strange and sad habiliment°　　　　　*somber costume*
　　I will encounter with Andronicus
　　And say I am Revenge sent from below,
　　To join with him and right his heinous wrongs.
5　Knock at his study where they say he keeps°　　　　　*stays*
　　To ruminate strange plots of dire revenge.
　　Tell him Revenge is come to join with him
　　And work confusion on his enemies.
　　　　They knock, and TITUS[, *aloft,*] *opens his study door.*
TITUS   Who doth molest my contemplation?
10　Is it your trick to make me ope the door,
　　That so my sad decrees° may fly away　　　　　*solemn resolutions*
　　And all my study be to no effect?
　　You are deceived. For what I mean to do
　　See here in bloody lines I have set down,
15　And what is written shall be executed.
TAMORA   Titus, I am come to talk with thee.
TITUS   No, not a word. How can I grace my talk,
　　Wanting° a hand to give that accord?　　　　　*Lacking*
　　Thou hast the odds° of me; therefore no more.　　*advantage*
20　TAMORA   If thou didst know me, thou wouldst talk with me.
TITUS   I am not mad. I know thee well enough.
　　Witness this wretched stump, witness these crimson lines,
　　Witness these trenches° made by grief and care,　　*wrinkles*
　　Witness the tiring day and heavy night,
25　Witness all sorrow that I know thee well
　　For our proud empress, mighty Tamora.

5.2 Location: Titus's courtyard.

Is not thy coming for my other hand?

TAMORA   Know thou, sad man, I am not Tamora.
    She is thy enemy and I thy friend.

30   I am Revenge, sent from th'infernal kingdom
    To ease the gnawing vulture[1] of thy mind
    By working wreakful° vengeance on thy foes.   *vindictive*
    Come down and welcome me to this world's light.
    Confer with me of murder and of death.

35   There's not a hollow cave or lurking place,
    No vast obscurity° or misty vale   *dark wasteland*
    Where bloody murder or detested rape
    Can couch° for fear, but I will find them out,   *hide*
    And in their ears tell them my dreadful name,

40   Revenge, which makes the foul offender quake.

TITUS   Art thou Revenge? And art thou sent to me
    To be a torment to mine enemies?

TAMORA   I am. Therefore come down and welcome me.

TITUS   Do me some service ere I come to thee.

45   Lo, by thy side where Rape and Murder stands.
    Now give some surance° that thou art Revenge: *proof*
    Stab them or tear them on thy chariot wheels,
    And then I'll come and be thy wagoner,
    And whirl along with thee about the globes;

50   Provide thee two proper palfreys,° black as jet,   *handsome horses*
    To hale° thy vengeful wagon swift away   *draw*
    And find out murder in their guilty caves;
    And when thy car is loaden with their heads,
    I will dismount and by thy wagon wheel

55   Trot like a servile footman all day long,
    Even from Hyperion's° rising in the East   *the sun god*
    Until his very downfall in the sea;
    And day by day I'll do this heavy task,
    So° thou destroy Rapine and Murder there.   *Provided that*

60 TAMORA   These are my ministers and come with me.

TITUS   Are they thy ministers? What are they called?

TAMORA   Rape and Murder, therefore callèd so
    'Cause they take vengeance of such kind of men.

TITUS   Good Lord, how like the Empress' sons they are,
65   And you the Empress! But we worldly° men   *mortal*
    Have miserable, mad, mistaking eyes.
    O sweet Revenge, now do I come to thee,
    And if one arm's embracement will content thee,
    I will embrace thee in it by and by.   *[Exit aloft.]*

70 TAMORA *[to* CHIRON *and* DEMETRIUS*]*   This closing° with him   *agreeing*
    fits his lunacy.
    Whate'er I forge° to feed his brain-sick humors   *invent*
    Do you uphold and maintain in your speeches.
    For now he firmly takes me for Revenge,
    And being credulous in this mad thought,

75   I'll make him send for Lucius, his son.
    And whilst I at a banquet hold him sure,
    I'll find some cunning practice out of hand[2]

---

1. Alluding to the story of Prometheus; see note to   2. I'll find some scheme on the spur of the moment.
2.1.17.

To scatter and disperse the giddy Goths,
Or at the least make them his enemies.
　　　[*Enter* TITUS *below.*]
80　　See, here he comes, and I must ply my theme.°　　　*keep up the act*
　　TITUS　Long have I been forlorn, and all for thee.
　　　Welcome, dread Fury, to my woeful house;
　　　Rapine and Murder, you are welcome too.
　　　How like the Empress and her sons you are!
85　　Well are you fitted, had you but a Moor;
　　　Could not all hell afford you such a devil?
　　　For well I wot° the Empress never wags°　　　*know / stirs*
　　　But in her company there is a Moor,
　　　And would you represent our queen aright
90　　It were convenient° you had such a devil.　　　*fitting*
　　　But welcome as you are. What shall we do?
　　TAMORA　What wouldst thou have us do, Andronicus?
　　DEMETRIUS　Show me a murderer; I'll deal with him.
　　CHIRON　Show me a villain that hath done a rape,
95　　And I am sent to be revenged on him.
　　TAMORA　Show me a thousand that hath done thee wrong,
　　　And I will be revenged on them all.
　　TITUS [*to* DEMETRIUS]　Look round about the wicked streets of
　　　　Rome,
　　　And when thou find'st a man that's like thyself,
100　　Good Murder, stab him; he's a murderer.
　　　[*to* CHIRON] Go thou with him, and when it is thy hap°　　　*chance*
　　　To find another that is like to thee,
　　　Good Rapine, stab him; he is a ravisher.
　　　[*to* TAMORA] Go thou with them, and in the Emperor's court
105　　There is a queen attended by a Moor—
　　　Well shalt thou know her by thine own proportion,
　　　For up and down° she doth resemble thee.　　　*top to toe*
　　　I pray thee, do on them some violent death;
　　　They have been violent to me and mine.
110　　TAMORA　Well hast thou lessoned us; this shall we do.
　　　But would it please thee, good Andronicus,
　　　To send for Lucius, thy thrice-valiant son,
　　　Who leads toward Rome a band of warlike Goths,
　　　And bid him come and banquet at thy house?
115　　When he is here, even at thy solemn° feast,　　　*ceremonious*
　　　I will bring in the Empress and her sons,
　　　The Emperor himself, and all thy foes,
　　　And at thy mercy shall they stoop and kneel,
　　　And on them shalt thou ease thy angry heart.
120　　What says Andronicus to this device?
　　TITUS　—Marcus, my brother, 'tis sad Titus calls!
　　　　Enter MARCUS.
　　　Go, gentle Marcus, to thy nephew Lucius.
　　　Thou shalt inquire him out among the Goths.
　　　Bid him repair° to me and bring with him　　　*come*
125　　Some of the chiefest princes of the Goths.
　　　Bid him encamp his soldiers where they are.
　　　Tell him the Emperor and the Empress too
　　　Feast at my house and he shall feast with them.
　　　This do thou for my love and so let him,

130   As he regards his agèd father's life.
MARCUS   This will I do and soon return again.   [*Exit.*]
TAMORA   Now will I hence about thy business
       And take my ministers along with me.
TITUS   Nay, nay, let Rape and Murder stay with me,
135   Or else I'll call my brother back again
       And cleave to no revenge but Lucius.[3]
TAMORA [*aside to* CHIRON *and* DEMETRUS]   What say you, boys?
       Will you abide with him
       Whiles I go tell my lord, the Emperor,
       How I have governed our determined jest?[4]
140   Yield to his humor, smooth, and speak him fair,°   *flatter and humor him*
       And tarry with him till I turn° again.   *return*
TITUS [*aside*]   I knew them all, though they supposed me mad,
       And will o'erreach them in their own devices—
       A pair of cursèd hellhounds and their dam.
145   DEMETRIUS   Madam, depart at pleasure. Leave us here.
TAMORA   Farewell, Andronicus. Revenge now goes
       To lay a complot to betray thy foes.
TITUS   I know thou dost—and, sweet Revenge, farewell.
                                                            [*Exit* TAMORA.]
CHIRON   Tell us, old man, how shall we be employed?
150   TITUS   Tut, I have work enough for you to do.
       Publius, come hither! Caius and Valentine!
              [*Enter* PUBLIUS, *Valentine, and Caius.*]
PUBLIUS   What is your will?
TITUS   Know you these two?
PUBLIUS   The Empress' sons I take them:° Chiron, Demetrius.   *take them to be*
TITUS   Fie, Publius, fie! Thou art too much deceived.
155   The one is Murder, and Rape is the other's name—
       And therefore bind them, gentle Publius;
       Caius and Valentine, lay hands on them.
       Oft have you heard me wish for such an hour,
       And now I find it. Therefore bind them sure,
160   And stop their mouths if they begin to cry.   [*Exit.*]
CHIRON   Villains, forbear! We are the Empress' sons.
PUBLIUS   And therefore do we what we are commanded.
       —Stop close their mouths. Let them not speak a word.
       Is he sure° bound? Look that you bind them fast.   *securely*
              Enter TITUS *Andronicus with a knife and* LAVINIA *with*
              a basin.
165   TITUS   Come, come, Lavinia. Look: thy foes are bound.
       Sirs, stop their mouths. Let them not speak to me,
       But let them hear what fearful words I utter.
       O villains, Chiron and Demetrius!
       Here stands the spring whom you have stained with mud,
170   This goodly summer with your winter mixed.
       You killed her husband, and for that vile fault
       Two of her brothers were condemned to death,
       My hand cut off and made a merry jest,
       Both her sweet hands, her tongue, and that more dear
175   Than hands or tongue—her spotless chastity—

3. That is, depend on Lucius's invading army for   4. How have I managed the jest we planned.
revenge.

Inhuman traitors, you constrained and forced.
What would you say if I should let you speak?
Villains, for shame, you could not beg for grace.°   *mercy*
Hark, wretches, how I mean to martyr you.
180 This one hand yet is left to cut your throats,
Whiles that Lavinia 'tween her stumps doth hold
The basin that receives your guilty blood.
You know your mother means to feast with me,
And calls herself Revenge, and thinks me mad.
185 Hark, villains, I will grind your bones to dust,
And with your blood and it I'll make a paste,°   *dough*
And of the paste a coffin° I will rear,   *piecrust (with wordplay)*
And make two pasties of your shameful heads,
And bid that strumpet, your unhallowed dam,
190 Like to the earth swallow her own increase.°   *progeny*
This is the feast that I have bid her to,
And this the banquet she shall surfeit on.
For worse than Philomel you used my daughter,
And worse than Procne I will be revenged.[5]
195 And now prepare your throats. Lavinia, come,
Receive the blood, and when that they are dead,
Let me go grind their bones to powder small,
And with this hateful liquor temper° it,   *mix*
And in that paste let their vile heads be baked.
200 Come, come; be everyone officious°   *busy*
To make this banquet, which I wish may prove
More stern and bloody than the Centaurs' feast.[6]
        He cuts their throats.
So, now bring them in, for I'll play the cook,
And see them ready against° their mother comes.   *by the time*
        Exeunt [with the bodies].

5.3 (F 5.3)
Enter LUCIUS, MARCUS, *and the* GOTHS[, *with* AARON,
prisoner, and an Attendant with his child].
LUCIUS Uncle Marcus, since 'tis my father's mind
That I repair to Rome, I am content.
FIRST GOTH And ours with thine,[1] befall what fortune will.
LUCIUS Good uncle, take you in this barbarous Moor,
5 This ravenous tiger, this accursèd devil.
Let him receive no sustenance; fetter him
Till he be brought unto the Empress' face
For testimony of her foul proceedings.
And see the ambush° of our friends be strong.   *troops lying in wait*
10 I fear the Emperor means no good to us.
AARON Some devil whisper curses in my ear,
And prompt me that my tongue may utter forth
The venomous malice of my swelling heart.
LUCIUS Away, inhuman dog, unhallowed slave!
15 —Sirs, help our uncle to convey him in.

---

5. Philomela's sister, Procne, revenged herself on her
rapist husband, Tereus, by killing their son Itys and
serving his flesh in a meal (see Introduction).
6. In Greek legend, the wedding feast of Hippoda-
mia ended in a bloody battle when the Centaurs,

beings that were half human and half horse, tried to
carry off the bride and other women (see Ovid, *Metamorphoses* 12).
5.3 Location: Titus's courtyard.
1. Our minds accord with yours.

[*Exeunt* GOTHS *with* AARON *and the Attendant with his child.*]
    Sound trumpets.
  The trumpets show the Emperor is at hand.
    Enter Emperor [SATURNINUS] *and Empress* [TAMORA],
    with [AEMILIUS, ROMAN LORD,] TRIBUNES,
    [*Attendants,*] *and others.*

SATURNINUS What, hath the firmament more suns than one?
LUCIUS What boots° it thee to call thyself a sun?   *avails*
MARCUS Rome's emperor and nephew, break the parley:°   *stop the dispute*
20   These quarrels must be quietly debated.
    The feast is ready which the careful° Titus   *assiduous; troubled*
    Hath ordained to an honorable end,
    For peace, for love, for league, and good to Rome.
    Please you, therefore, draw nigh and take your places.
25 SATURNINUS Marcus, we will.
    Trumpets sounding. Enter TITUS [*dressed*] *like a cook,*
    placing the dishes, and LAVINIA *with a veil over her*
    face[, *and the* BOY].
TITUS Welcome, my lord; welcome, dread Queen;
    Welcome, ye warlike Goths; welcome, Lucius;
    And welcome, all. Although the cheer° be poor,   *refreshments*
    'Twill fill your stomachs. Please you, eat of it.
30 SATURNINUS Why art thou thus attired, Andronicus?
TITUS Because I would be sure to have all well
    To entertain your highness and your empress.
TAMORA We are beholden to you, good Andronicus.
TITUS An if your highness knew my heart, you were.
35   My lord the Emperor, resolve me this:
    Was it well done of rash Virginius[2]
    To slay his daughter with his own right hand
    Because she was enforced, stained, and deflowered?
SATURNINUS It was, Andronicus.
TITUS   Your reason, mighty lord?
40 SATURNINUS Because the girl should not survive her shame
    And by her presence still renew his sorrows.
TITUS A reason mighty, strong, and effectual.
    A pattern, precedent, and lively warrant
    For me, most wretched, to perform the like.
45   —Die, die, Lavinia, and thy shame with thee,
    And with thy shame thy father's sorrow die!
    [*He kills her.*]
SATURNINUS What hast thou done? Unnatural and unkind!
TITUS Killed her for whom my tears have made me blind.
    I am as woeful as Virginius was,
50   And have a thousand times more cause than he
    To do this outrage, and it now is done.
SATURNINUS What, was she ravished? Tell, who did the deed?
TITUS Will't please you eat? Will't please your highness feed?
TAMORA Why hast thou slain thine only daughter thus?
55 TITUS Not I; 'twas Chiron and Demetrius:
    They ravished her and cut away her tongue,
    And they, 'twas they, that did her all this wrong.
SATURNINUS Go, fetch them hither to us presently.°   *at once*

---

2. A Roman soldier who in some versions of the story killed his daughter to prevent her rape; in other versions, he killed her after the rape as Titus describes.

TITUS   Why, there they are, both bakèd in this pie,
60   Whereof their mother daintily hath fed,
     Eating the flesh that she herself hath bred.
     'Tis true, 'tis true; witness my knife's sharp point.
          He stabs the Empress [TAMORA].
SATURNINUS   Die, frantic° wretch, for this accursèd deed.   *deranged*
          [SATURNINUS *kills* TITUS.]
LUCIUS   Can the son's eye behold his father bleed?
65   There's meed for meed,° death for a deadly deed.   *measure for measure*
          [LUCIUS *kills* SATURNINUS. *Enter* GOTHS. LUCIUS,
          MARCUS, *and others go aloft.*]
MARCUS   You sad-faced men, people and sons of Rome,
     By uproars severed as a flight of fowl
     Scattered by winds and high tempestuous gusts,
     Oh, let me teach you how to knit again
70   This scattered corn° into one mutual° sheaf,   *grain / unified*
     These broken limbs again into one body.
ROMAN LORD   Let Rome herself be bane° unto herself,[3]   *destroyer*
     And she whom mighty kingdoms curtsy to,
     Like a forlorn and desperate castaway,
75   Do shameful execution on herself.
     But if my frosty signs and chaps° of age,   *white hair and wrinkles*
     Grave witnesses of true experience,
     Cannot induce you to attend my words,
     [*to* LUCIUS] Speak, Rome's dear friend, as erst° our ancestor,[4]   *once*
80   When with his solemn tongue he did discourse
     To lovesick Dido's sad-attending° ear   *seriously listening*
     The story of that baleful burning night
     When subtle Greeks surprised King Priam's Troy.
     Tell us what Sinon[5] hath bewitched our ears,
85   Or who hath brought the fatal engine[6] in
     That gives our Troy, our Rome, the civil° wound.   *incurred in civil war*
     My heart is not compact° of flint nor steel,   *composed*
     Nor can I utter all our bitter grief,
     But floods of tears will drown my oratory
90   And break° my utterance even in the time   *interrupt*
     When it should move ye to attend me most,
     And force you to commiseration.
     Here's Rome's young captain. Let him tell the tale,
     While I stand by and weep to hear him speak.
95 LUCIUS   Then, gracious auditory,° be it known to you   *audience*
     That Chiron and the damnèd Demetrius
     Were they that murderèd our emperor's brother,
     And they it were that ravishèd our sister.
     For their fell° faults our brothers were beheaded,   *cruel*
100   Our father's tears despised and basely cozened°   *cheated*
     Of that true hand that fought Rome's quarrel out°   *to the finish*
     And sent her enemies unto the grave;
     Lastly myself, unkindly° banishèd,   *unnaturally*
     The gates shut on me and turned, weeping, out

---

3. TEXTUAL COMMENT Q assigns this speech to an unnamed "*Romane Lord*"; F assigns it to a "*Goth*," although some phrases (e.g., "our Rome") suggest a Roman speaker. See Digital Edition TC 8 (Quarto edited text) for a fuller discussion of the editorial problem and the way modern editions have resolved it.
4. Aeneas, Trojan ancestor of the Roman people.
5. The Greek who persuaded the Trojans to admit the wooden horse full of soldiers.
6. Instrument (the wooden horse).

105　To beg relief among Rome's enemies,
　　　Who drowned their enmity in my true tears
　　　And oped their arms to embrace me as a friend.
　　　I am the turned-forth, be it known to you,
　　　That have preserved her° welfare in my blood,　　　　　　　(Rome's)
110　And from her bosom took the enemy's point,
　　　Sheathing the steel in my advent'rous body.
　　　Alas, you know, I am no vaunter,° I.　　　　　　　　　　　boaster
　　　My scars can witness, dumb although they are,
　　　That my report is just and full of truth.
115　But soft, methinks I do digress too much,
　　　Citing my worthless praise. Oh, pardon me,
　　　For when no friends are by, men praise themselves.
　　MARCUS　Now is my turn to speak. Behold the child.
　　　　　　[He points to Aaron's son.]
　　　Of this was Tamora deliverèd,
120　The issue of an irreligious Moor,
　　　Chief architect and plotter of these woes.
　　　The villain is alive in Titus' house,
　　　And as he is to witness, this is true.
　　　Now judge what cause had Titus to revenge
125　These wrongs, unspeakable past patience,°　　　　　　　　endurance
　　　Or more than any living man could bear.
　　　Now have you heard the truth, what say you, Romans?
　　　Have we done aught amiss? Show us wherein,
　　　And from the place where you behold us pleading,
130　The poor remainder of Andronici
　　　Will hand in hand all headless hurl ourselves,[7]
　　　And on the ragged stones beat forth our souls
　　　And make a mutual closure° of our house.°　　　　　　　end / family
　　　Speak, Romans, speak, and if you say we shall,
135　Lo, hand in hand, Lucius and I will fall.
　　AEMILIUS　Come, come, thou reverend man of Rome,
　　　And bring our emperor gently in thy hand—
　　　Lucius, our emperor, for well I know
　　　The common voice do cry it shall be so.
140　MARCUS　Lucius, all hail! Rome's royal emperor!
　　　[to Attendants] Go, go into old Titus' sorrowful house
　　　And hither hale that misbelieving Moor
　　　To be adjudged some direful slaught'ring death
　　　As punishment for his most wicked life.
　　　　　　　　　　　　　[Exeunt Attendants.]
　　　　　　[LUCIUS and MARCUS descend.]
145　—Lucius, all hail, Rome's gracious governor!
　　LUCIUS　Thanks, gentle Romans. May I govern so
　　　To heal Rome's harms and wipe away her woe.
　　　But, gentle people, give me aim° awhile,　　　　　　　encourage me
　　　For nature puts me to° a heavy task.　　　　　　　　　sets me
150　Stand all aloof, but, uncle, draw you near
　　　To shed obsequious° tears upon this trunk.　　　　　　mournful
　　　Oh, take this warm kiss on thy pale cold lips,
　　　　　　[He kisses TITUS.]

---

7. Traditionally, traitors were thrown from the Tarpeian Rock on the Capitoline Hill.

These sorrowful drops upon thy blood-stained face,
The last true duties of thy noble son.

155 MARCUS [*kissing* TITUS]   Tear for tear, and loving kiss for kiss,
Thy brother Marcus tenders on thy lips.
Oh, were the sum of these that I should pay
Countless and infinite, yet would I pay them.

LUCIUS [*to* BOY]   Come hither, boy; come, come, and learn of us
160 To melt in showers. Thy grandsire loved thee well.
Many a time he danced thee on his knee,
Sung thee asleep, his loving breast thy pillow.
Many a story hath he told to thee,[8]
And bid thee bear his pretty tales in mind,
165 And talk of them when he was dead and gone.

MARCUS   How many thousand times hath these poor lips,
When they were living, warmed themselves on thine!
Oh, now, sweet boy, give them their latest° kiss.   *last*
Bid him farewell. Commit him to the grave.
170 Do them° that kindness and take leave of them.   *(his lips)*

BOY   O grandsire, grandsire! Ev'n with all my heart
Would I were dead so° you did live again.   *provided that*
O Lord, I cannot speak to him for weeping.
My tears will choke me if I ope my mouth.

[*Enter Attendants with* AARON.]

175 ROMAN   You sad Andronici, have done with woes.
Give sentence on this execrable wretch
That hath been breeder of these dire events.

LUCIUS   Set him breast-deep in earth and famish him.
There let him stand, and rave, and cry for food.
180 If any one relieves or pities him,
For the offense he dies. This is our doom.°   *judgment*
Some stay to see him fastened in the earth.

AARON   Ah, why should wrath be mute and fury dumb?
I am no baby, I, that with base prayers
185 I should repent the evils I have done.
Ten thousand worse than ever yet I did
Would I perform if I might have my will.
If one good deed in all my life I did,
I do repent it from my very soul.

190 LUCIUS   Some loving friends convey the Emperor hence,
And give him burial in his father's grave.°   *ancestral tomb*
My father and Lavinia shall forthwith
Be closèd in our household's monument.
As for that ravenous tiger, Tamora,
195 No funeral rite, nor man in mourning weed,°   *garments*
No mournful bell shall ring her burial,
But throw her forth to beasts and birds to prey:°   *prey upon*
Her life was beastly and devoid of pity,
And, being dead, let birds on her take pity.[9]   *Exeunt.*

---

8. TEXTUAL COMMENT Variants between the Q and F texts at this point are likely due to a compositor (print house employee) of Q2 making up lines missing from his damaged copy of Q1. These lines were later incorporated into the Q3 and F texts. See Digital Edition TC 9 (Quarto edited text) for a fuller discussion.

9. TEXTUAL COMMENT The final lines of Q1 and F are different, probably because (as with lines 163–68) a compositor of Q2, likely working from a damaged copy of Q1, needed to "fill in the blanks": his changes were then reproduced in later texts of the play. See Digital Edition TC 10 (Quarto edited text).

Romeo and Juliet

Plato's dialogue *The Symposium* recounts a dinner party where the guests spent a long night in impassioned philosophical conversation about love. By daybreak, most of the guests had fallen asleep, but Socrates, who had spoken with particularly luminous intelligence, was still awake, trying to prove that a single playwright should be capable of writing both comedy and tragedy. As he clinched his case, his weary interlocutors nodded off. Thus we never learn Socrates' argument, and neither the ancient Greek nor the Roman world has left us an instance of that versatility. But we have its supreme embodiment in Shakespeare. The achievement is particularly striking in two plays probably written around 1595. Scholars have been unable to determine whether *Romeo and Juliet* was written before or after *A Midsummer Night's Dream*; one of Shakespeare's most delightful comedies and one of his most beloved tragedies appear to have been written at virtually the same time, using very similar materials.

In the entertainment performed for the newlyweds at the close of *A Midsummer Night's Dream*, the young lovers, Pyramus and Thisbe, are separated by a "vile wall." They attempt to elope together, but Pyramus, mistakenly thinking that Thisbe has been killed, rashly commits suicide, whereupon Thisbe in despair stabs herself. A strange way, it would seem, to celebrate festive nuptials, but Shakespeare's comedy continually triumphs over fears of rashness, mutability, and death by staging and laughing at them. The inept amateur actors call attention so crudely to the tragedy's artificiality and contrivance that it provokes derisive laughter: "This is the silliest stuff that ever I heard" (5.1.207).

In *Romeo and Juliet*, whose climax closely resembles that of Pyramus and Thisbe, Shakespeare does not shy away from artifice and contrivance. His tragedy is unusually dependent on coincidence, mischance, and accident to produce what the Chorus, in the sonnet that serves as the prologue, calls the lovers' "misadventured piteous overthrows."* Nor does he forswear the note of witty, wicked parody that transformed the woes of Pyramus and Thisbe into an occasion for mirth. Romeo's friend Mercutio gives voice to an irrepressible spirit of mockery, a spirit that seems to challenge the very possibility of romantic love or tragic destiny. But Shakespeare manages to make the story of his reckless, star-crossed lovers immensely moving, resistant at once to corrosive irony and to moralizing disapproval. He does so principally through his mastery of what the bumbling performers in *A Midsummer Night's Dream* conspicuously lack: the power of language to make and unmake the world.

It is this poetic power—"poetic" derives from the Greek word for "making"—that enables Shakespeare to transform his rather shopworn source materials into something rich and strange. The story of the ill-fated lovers from bitterly feuding families had been told many times in the sixteenth century by Italian and French writers and had already appeared more than once in English. Shakespeare's direct source is Arthur Brooke's *Tragical History of Romeus and Juliet* (1562), a long, leaden English poem based on a French prose version by Pierre Boiastuau (1559), who was in turn adapting an Italian version by Matteo Bandello (1554), who in turn based his narrative on Luigi da Porto's version (1525) of a tale by Masuccio Salernitano (1476).

---

*All quotations are taken from the edited text of the Second Quarto, printed here. The Digital Edition includes edited texts of both the Second Quarto and the First Quarto.

Though he follows the main outline of Brooke's narrative poem, Shakespeare makes many changes in the interests of theatrical compression and intensification. He telescopes the events that in Brooke take nine months into a few days. He brilliantly expands the figure of the vulgar, meddling, earthy Nurse and almost too brilliantly develops the character of Mercutio. (There is a seventeenth-century report—it doesn't date from the playwright's own lifetime—that Shakespeare remarked that he was forced to kill Mercutio in the third act to prevent being killed by him.) He depicts Juliet, eighteen years old in Bandello's version and sixteen in Brooke's, as only thirteen, a young girl suddenly awakening to passionate desires that set her against the will of her family. And at the end he deftly removes the consoling fantasies, conspicuous in the sources, that the dead lovers will be reunited in a happier afterlife. "Here, here will I remain," says Shakespeare's Romeo, in the tomb of his beloved, "With worms that are thy chambermaids" (5.3.108–109).

But it is principally by means of the incandescent brilliance of its language that *Romeo and Juliet* has earned its place as one of the greatest love stories in world literature. Shakespeare makes linguistic power figure thematically in the play by insisting on the crucial importance of naming and, more generally, by repeatedly calling attention to the force of verbal actions. This was by no means the playwright's private obsession. His play is the product of a rhetorical culture, a culture steeped in an awareness—in the philosopher J. L. Austin's phrase—of "how to do things with words." What are some of the things that characters do with words? For a start, they insult each other, a dangerous pastime of both servants and masters. They also invite one another (Capulet's favorite pastime); they confess (formally, to a priest; informally, to friends); they conjure; they curse; they make contracts; they vow; and, if they have the power of the prince, they banish. And through all of these verbal actions, no matter how serious or even deadly they may be, they constantly play with language.

Romeo and Juliet is saturated with language games: paradoxes, oxymorons, double entendres, rhyming tricks, verbal echoings, multiple puns. The obvious question is, why? One possible answer, proposed as early as the eighteenth century, is that Shakespeare could not resist: verbal wit was an addiction, an obsession, the object of an irrational passion. He could indulge this passion because a display of wit would appeal to those segments of the audience most attuned to rhetorical acrobatics. Another answer is that puns are a clarifying challenge, an assault on sentiments to test whether they are genuine or merely forced and empty. Hence Mercutio attempts to mock Romeo's passion with a set of ribald jests, jests that are reiterated unconsciously by the Nurse in such exclamations as "Stand up, stand up! Stand an you be a man!" (3.3.89). To survive the corrosive effect of such mockery is a measure of true love and a sign of authenticity: "He jests at scars that never felt a wound" (2.1.43).

But this explanation for the tragedy's pervasive wordplay is not wholly adequate, since at the height of both their love and their despair, Romeo and Juliet also pun. Romeo on the verge of suicide plays with the word "engrossing" (death as wholesaler; monopolist; lawyer); Juliet plays with the word "restorative" (the kiss as medicine; poison; death; resurrection); and both play with the Elizabethan "to die" as a term for "to have an orgasm." Here wordplay functions not to deflate but to cram into brief utterances more meanings than language would ordinarily hold and to force us to confront both unresolvable contradictions and hidden connections. That is, puns work to juxtapose or hold open possibilities that normally are viewed as mutually exclusive. Thus they may be said to reach both a psychological and a thematic level at which oppositions—pain and joy, loss and restoration, love and death, comedy and tragedy—are canceled.

Wordplay would be impossible in a language in which words were strictly bound to things in a perfect correspondence between naming and nature. Punning is possible only if there is some slippage in sound and meaning, so that one sign can refer to two or more objects or, as Mercutio wittily demonstrates in his Queen Mab speech, to nothing at all. Yet wordplay can also suggest surprising linkages and secret realities.

Two gallants fight a duel in the street.
From George Wither, *A Collection of Emblems* (1635).

Hence, for example, the punning in Romeo and Juliet's initial exchange at the Capulet ball derives its power from the lovers' conviction that there really is an essential relation between the touching of their hands and lips and a religious experience. This relation, invisible to the ordinary social world around them, is disclosed in the language game they spontaneously play, a game that takes the form of a shared sonnet.

Even to speak of this first exchange as a game, which it certainly is, is to risk diminishing its intense seriousness. For in the intertwining of these fourteen complexly rhymed lines, Romeo and Juliet, who do not yet so much as know each other's names, disclose a mutual longing in language whose formal elegance confers on physical desire a spiritual exaltation. The sonnet's blend of order and energy lends words the power of prayer. For Mercutio, by contrast, words are fantastic trifles in a world fit only for satire, sexual teasing, and make-believe. He is a young man in love with masks; indeed, as he readies himself for the masked ball, he seems to regard his own face as a mask: "Give me a case to put my visage in— / A visor for a visor" (1.4.27–28). The moment Romeo and Juliet meet, all masks seem to fall away, all prior emotions fade into nothingness, and all games become earnest. "Did my heart love till now?" asks Romeo (1.4.163), and Juliet, sending the Nurse to find out Romeo's name, declares, "If he be married, / My grave is like to be my wedding-bed" (1.4.245–46).

At some moments in *Romeo and Juliet,* then, wordplay reveals the arbitrariness of language; at other moments, it seems to reveal a hidden reality, even a sacred truth. These contradictory revelations are explored in the famous balcony scene in act 2. Mercutio's mockery gives way, after Romeo's abrupt, one-line dismissal, to incantatory language so intense as to create a new heaven and a new earth. A bare, daylit stage (as it would have been in the Elizabethan playhouse) becomes a dark garden above which Juliet appears like the sun. Visibility is canceled and then restored, by means of metaphor, to the "white upturnèd wond'ring eyes / Of mortals" (2.1.71–72).

Romeo's ecstatic words are the poetic record of a revelation, a vision of a creature unique, perfect, and infinitely beautiful.

The visionary moment turns into a moment of auditory revelation as well, as Romeo, in an intense, eroticized version of what audiences routinely do, overhears Juliet's soliloquy. He has entered into her most intimate thoughts and longings and has an overpowering proof of their authenticity, since she speaks with no awareness of his presence. The inner world his lyrical utterance has conjured up is miraculously united with her own. But her words at once offer a complete fulfillment of this union and a shattering of fulfillment: "O Romeo, Romeo, wherefore art thou Romeo?" (2.1.75). Only if Romeo's name is an arbitrary sign, to be stripped away, discarded, and replaced, can her love be realized. But in a world in which words are divorced from reality, what would be the status of a love made by language? In a world in which names are mere empty signs, how could language create a new reality?

If words are arbitrary, then Romeo and Juliet's love, woven of words, is wedded to nothingness. If they are not arbitrary, if they cannot float free of the body and society, then their love will be destroyed by the rage of feuding parents—the parents who have bestowed proper names on their offspring—and by the whole daylight world of social exchange that gives ordinary language its normal meanings. Against the magical, passionate, transformative language of Romeo and Juliet is set not only Mercutio's mockery but the Nurse's garrulous evocation of the inescapable life cycle: birth, weaning, sexual maturity, and death.

"Then I deny you, stars" (5.1.24). *Imagines Constellationum.*
From Ptolemy, *Almagest* (1541 ed.), after Dürer.

In the Nurse's view, all lives have a certain interchangeability. Juliet's value can be measured in gold coins—"I tell you, he that can lay hold of her / Shall have the chinks" (1.4.227–28)—and an exiled husband can be replaced: Paris is "a lovely gentleman!" she tells the grieving Juliet, "Romeo's a dishclout to him" (3.5.219–20). Romeo and Juliet insist by contrast on the absolute singularity of their love, on the stilling of cyclical time, and on the cancellation of the social network of form and compliment. For a moment on her balcony, Juliet regrets that Romeo has heard her declare her "true-love passion," but then she bids farewell to conventional restraint and boldly steps forward into the magical realm of reciprocal desire. This realm is not without its own solemn order: their love must be formally confirmed in honorable vows of holy matrimony spoken before the friar. But first in the garden, away from church and family and friends, the fullness of the lovers' matched longings finds expression in words that seem to possess mythic power, power to transform darkness into intense light and at the same time to block out the harsh, unforgiving light of the everyday.

The everyday has its own powerful resources, however, and forces its way back into the world that love has transformed. It does so through the ability of names like "Capulet" and "Montague" to conjure up bitter social rivalries. For, as *Romeo and Juliet* repeatedly discloses, words as we ordinarily use them are rarely wholly arbitrary or wholly mythic. They are social constructions, communal creations that are neither complete unto themselves nor empty and hence malleable by individuals. Both language as arbitrary and language as mythic are radical attempts to challenge this notion of words as shared creations carrying with them the tensions and resolutions present in communities, but the community in effect kills off the challenge—whether it comes from Mercutio, who tries to turn social hatred and love alike into a game about "nothing," or from Romeo and Juliet, who try to escape through darkness, subterfuge, and the language of love into a realm apart.

How does the communitarian spirit of language, and with it a sense of the inescapability of the social, manifest itself in *Romeo and Juliet*? It does so, first of all, through a series of characters such as those we glimpse in the opening moments of the play, when the Capulet servants, Samson and Gregory, provoke the absurd quarrel with the Montague servants, Abraham and Balthasar. The point is not only the foolishness of the social codes—"Do you bite your thumb at us, sir?" "I do bite my thumb, sir" (1.1.40–41)—but also their pervasiveness. In a tragedy memorable for its dreams of the most intense privacy—Juliet longs for Romeo to leap to her arms "untalked of and unseen" (3.2.7)—the bustling world makes its presence felt as insistently as the Nurse's voice calling again and again to Juliet as she stands at her window. Shakespeare is wonderfully resourceful in conveying this presence. There is, for example, the nameless servant whose inability to read the list of those invited to the Capulets' ball leads him to turn for assistance to Romeo and Benvolio, who chance at that moment to be walking by. The list itself deftly conjures up the social elite of Verona, with its network of kinship bonds:

> Signor Placentio and his lovely nieces;
> Mercutio and his brother Valentine;
> Mine uncle Capulet, his wife and daughters . . .

and so on through the whole "fair assembly" (1.2.68ff). At the ball itself, Shakespeare is careful to include a glimpse of the servants, hurrying to clear the dishes but finding time to put aside a piece of marzipan for themselves or arranging for a private party with Susan Grindstone and Nell. And, in the midst of the horror and lamenting, when Juliet's cold and stiff body is discovered on the morning she was to be married to Paris, Shakespeare turns our attention to the musicians who had been hired to entertain the wedding guests and who now stand around cracking lame jokes and hoping for a bit of dinner (as if—to invert a celebrated line from *Hamlet*—the marriage baked meats will coldly furnish forth the funeral table).

The city of Verona. From John Speed, *Prospect of the Most Famous Parts of the World* (1646).

There are, besides the servants, other social units that carry the glacial weight of the collective norms and ordinary interests against which Romeo and Juliet struggle. The exclusiveness and intensity of their love are clearly in tension with the bond that links Romeo to his friends, a bond affirmed in displays of masculine aggression and homosocial affection. An infatuation with this or that woman may on occasion seem to threaten the tight circle of friendship—as Romeo, mooning for Rosaline at the beginning of the play, has withdrawn by himself—but the threat is not a very serious one. No one in this world expects that love will seriously reconstitute personal identity or the social order. "Now art thou sociable," says Mercutio with evident relief, when Romeo briefly resumes the old mocking repartee; "now art thou Romeo" (2.3.81).

But from the moment they have encountered one another, neither Romeo nor Juliet is any longer the same person, and the passionate love that divides Romeo from his friends sets both lovers still more decisively against the values of their powerful families. Those values involve a complex intertwining of honor, dignity, love, will, and property, a blend that can manifest itself as gracious hospitality or as murderous feuding, as gentle nostalgia or as cold calculation, as a father's indulgent affection for his daughter or as blind rage when she attempts to thwart his will. Romeo and Juliet's love and clandestine marriage can find no place in this familial order of things, just as its absoluteness is incompatible with the familial sense of cyclical time.

Beyond the structure of the family in the society of Verona, though linked to that structure by ties of kinship, lies the state, embodied in the figure of Prince Escalus. Formally, *Romeo and Juliet* is built around the well-meaning ruler's attempt to stop the "civil brawls" (1.1.84) at the play's beginning, his banishment of Romeo at its midpoint, and his final inquiry, to "clear these ambiguities" (5.3.217), at its close. But this necessary principle of civic order, though it has important consequences, seems almost beside the point, as inadequate and irrelevant as the statues in pure gold that the grieving fathers propose to erect.

A much deeper social principle is figured in Friar Laurence, who embodies the collective wisdom and sanctity of the community. Though set apart, the friar is not a hermit or a recluse; he is an active agent in the community's affairs. His attempt to use Romeo and Juliet's love as a means to resolve the feud between the Montagues and the Capulets disastrously backfires, and with his sleeping potions, his elaborate plots, and, at the close, his fatal cowardice, he has some of the qualities of the stereotypical meddling friar of anticlerical satire. But Friar Laurence is a more complex figure, with a subtle grasp of the doubleness—both poison and medicine—of the natural world and a thoughtful advocacy of moderation. This advocacy draws on an ancient and powerful critique of extremes in passion, which the play's tragic outcome would seem to endorse.

Yet few readers or spectators come away from *Romeo and Juliet* with the conviction that it would be better to love moderately. The intensity of the lovers' passion seems to have its own compelling, self-justifying force, which quietly brushes away all social obstacles and moralizing warnings: "Think true love acted simple modesty" (3.2.16). And the play's incantatory language of love—braiding together the wildly fanciful and the exquisitely simple—has after four hundred years an unforgettable freshness:

> Come, gentle night; come, loving, black-browed night,
> Give me my Romeo; and, when I shall die,
> Take him and cut him out in little stars,
> And he will make the face of heaven so fine
> That all the world will be in love with night
> And pay no worship to the garish sun.
>
> (3.2.20–25)

If the society of the play will not tolerate such ecstatic desire, if the contingencies of the ordinary world manage to destroy it, *Romeo and Juliet* offers us the consoling realization that the lovers themselves have all along been in love with night.

STEPHEN GREENBLATT

SELECTED BIBLIOGRAPHY

Belsey, Catherine. "The Name of the Rose in *Romeo and Juliet*." *Yearbook of English Studies* 23 (1993): 126–42. Argues that *Romeo and Juliet* dramatizes both the desire to transcend the realm of signifiers into a metaphysical ideal and the impossibility of attaining it.

Callaghan, Dympna. "The Ideology of Romantic Love: The Case of *Romeo and Juliet*." *"Romeo and Juliet": Contemporary Critical Essays*. Ed. R. S. White. New York: Palgrave, 2001. 85–115. Proposes that rather than representing a timeless and universal love story, the play valorizes a particular construction of desire that emerged with the centralization of political power, the rise of bourgeois capitalism, and an assumption of patriarchal authority.

Kottman, Paul A. "Defying the Stars: Tragic Love as the Struggle for Freedom in *Romeo and Juliet*." *Shakespeare Quarterly* 63 (2012): 1–38. Asserts that the most important struggle in the play is not the one between lovers and a society hostile to their desires, but the struggle of Romeo and Juliet to realize their own distinct individuality.

Kristeva, Julia. "*Romeo and Juliet*: Love-Hatred in the Couple." *Shakespearean Tragedy*. Ed. John Drakakis. Harlow, Essex: Longman, 1992. 296–315. Offers a closer look, informed by Freud and Lacan, at the symptomatic (unconscious) response to transgressive and fantastic love as manifested in the characters, the playwright, and ourselves.

Nevo, Ruth. "Tragic Form in *Romeo and Juliet*." *Studies in English Literature* 9 (1969): 241–58. Argues that Shakespeare develops a distinctive style of tragedy, predicated on the heroic embodiment of opposing forces, the subversion of appearances, the presence of the uncanny, and the complex ideal of sexual love.

Porter, Joseph A. *Shakespeare's Mercutio: His History and Drama*. Chapel Hill: U of North Carolina P, 1988. Analyzes how, from a patchwork of sources, classical and contemporary, Shakespeare breathed life into the complex. subversive, homosexual Mercutio.

Snow, Edward. "Language and Sexual Difference in *Romeo and Juliet.*" *Shakespeare's "Rough Magic": Essays in Honor of C. L. Barber.* Ed. Peter Erickson and Coppélia Kahn. Newark: U of Delaware P, 1985. 168–92. Argues that, if the language of Juliet and Romeo articulates their profound interconnectedness, it also discloses ominous differences between them and suggests that gender difference is the tragedy's deepest dichotomy.

Snyder, Susan. "*Romeo and Juliet:* Comedy into Tragedy." *Essays in Criticism* 20 (1970): 391–402. Proposes that, at first possessing all the markings of a comedy, *Romeo and Juliet* morphs from one genre to another: the descent into tragedy becomes ineluctable upon the death of Mercutio.

Targoff, Ramie. "Mortal Love: Shakespeare's *Romeo and Juliet* and the Practice of Joint Burial." *Representations* 120 (2012): 17–38. Argues that whereas Shakespeare's sources imagine the lovers posthumously united in heaven, his own play rejects this consolation and gains its tragic power by insisting that love is mortal.

Watson, Robert N., and Stephen Dickey. "Wherefore Art Thou Tereu? Juliet and the Legacy of Rape." *Renaissance Quarterly* 58 (2005): 127–56. Proposes that *Romeo and Juliet*'s allusions to mythical perpetrators of rape make us aware of the specter of possible predatory sexuality that haunts the play, as well as Juliet's ultimate act of claiming her own erotic desire for herself.

FILMS

Romeo and Juliet. 1936. Dir. George Cukor. USA. 125 mins. A lavish, big-studio release, Cukor's film starred Leslie Howard, then forty-two, and Norma Shearer in the lead roles. John Barrymore played Mercutio.

West Side Story. 1961. Dir. Jerome Robbins and Robert Wise. USA. 152 mins. A musical, modernized adaptation of the play set in New York with rival ethnic gangs. Leonard Bernstein wrote the celebrated score.

Romeo and Juliet. 1968. Dir. Franco Zeffirelli. Italy. 138 mins. A flower-power, 1960s youth-culture interpretation of the play, featuring teenaged actors Leonard Whiting and Olivia Hussey in the title roles.

William Shakespeare's Romeo + Juliet. 1996. Dir. Baz Luhrmann. USA. 120 mins. Starring Leonardo DiCaprio and Claire Danes, Luhrmann's frenetic update, set in modern-day "Verona Beach," explains the family feud in terms of a gang conflict.

Qing ren jie (A Time to Love). 2005. Dir. Jianqi Huo. China. 113 mins. In this film, in Mandarin, set during the Cultural Revolution, two lovers read and watch versions of Shakespeare's play together, and enact the balcony scene.

TEXTUAL INTRODUCTION

The two earliest substantive versions of *Romeo and Juliet* are both quartos; they appeared in print two years apart, the first of them only two years or so after the play's first performance. The title page of the earlier quarto, of which five copies survive, reads: "AN EXCELLENT conceited Tragedie of Romeo and Iuliet, As it hath been often (with great applause) plaid publiquely, by the right Honourable the L. of *Hunsdon* his Seruants. LONDON, Printed by Iohn Danter. 1597." (A second printer, Edward Allde, was in fact responsible for printing slightly over half of the text.) This is now known as Q1, and has been, from the outset, both a revelation and a puzzle. It was not entered in the Stationers' Register, as was required of printed texts at this time. A second, lengthier quarto appeared two years later; its title page reads: "THE MOST EXcellent and lamentable Tragedie, of Romeo and Iuliet. *Newly corrected, augmented, and amended:* As it hath bene sundry times publiquely acted, by the right Honourable the Lord Chamberlaine his Seruants. LONDON Printed by Thomas Creede, for Cuthbert Burby, and are to be sold at his shop neare the Exchange. 1599." This, now known as Q2, is the source for all seventeenth-century editions of the play, including Q3, Q4, and the First Folio (which is why *The Norton Shakespeare* does not include an edition of the F version), and is the version familiar to modern readers and audiences.

Q2 may represent the *Romeo and Juliet* we know best, then, but Q1 has always interested editors and scholars, not only because of its intriguing differences from Q2 but also because, at times, its readings have seemed preferable to those of its better-known cousin. Furthermore, a section of Q2 (1.2.53–1.3.36) is in effect identical to that in Q1 (2.44–3.36) and appears to have been set not from Q2's primary manuscript source but from Q1 itself, perhaps because a page or two of the copy manuscript had been mislaid. A good instance of a generally preferred Q1 reading is Juliet's line about the prospect of marriage to Paris, "It is an honor that I dream not of" (Q1 3.59), which in Q2 reads, "It is an hour that I dream not of" (Q2 1.3.68). Editors have tended to choose the Q1 reading, presuming the "n" in "honour" (the original, also the modern British English, spelling) to have been accidentally omitted in Q2; thus one of the play's best-known lines derives from Q1, not Q2.

By and large, though, Q1 has been denigrated as one of the group of early Shake-speare quartos for which, at the beginning of the twentieth century, A. W. Pollard coined the term "Bad Quarto" and which have since come to be known more pro-saically as "short" quartos so as to avoid the inappropriate moral associations of "good" and "bad." Various theories have been put forward to account for the features of the short quartos — that they are Shakespeare's "first drafts"; that they are unofficial, "pirated" texts memorially reconstructed by actors who had played in them (certainly, there are strong indications of garbled recall at times in Q1); or that Shakespeare wrote two distinct versions of several of his plays, a "literary" version for publication and a shorter "acting" version. The latter theory has particular appeal in the case of *Romeo and Juliet*, given that the Prologue in both Q1 and Q2 claims that the play will last only two hours when performed.

The central issues in the complex textual history of *Romeo and Juliet* derive from the differences between Q1 and Q2, for which editors have consistently sought expla-nations. Q2 is a fuller, more authoritative text in most ways ("augmented, and amended"): it is a quarter or so (739 lines in this edition) longer than Q1; certain well-known passages in Q2 have no equivalent in Q1; lines attributed to one character in Q1 are spoken by another in Q2; lineation diverges frequently; and there are many differences at the level of the individual word. Certain features of Q2—e.g., words or lines that appear to have been added in the wrong place, or have been retained despite an attempt at deletion—strongly suggest that it was set from Shakespeare's "foul papers"—that is, from a draft of the play in the playwright's own hand, one that con-tains evidence of the creative process—as opposed to a "fair copy," a finished manu-script without insertions, deletions, or other afterthoughts.

The Norton Shakespeare provides editions of both Q1 and Q2 in the Digital Edition, with Q2 representing the play in the print edition. The differences make a fine starting point for critical reflection on the play. As is noted in the Textual Com-ments, Q1's prologue differs from that in Q2 in instructive ways: for Q2 the mutual hatred of the Montagues and Capulets is "ancient," habitual, a feud lasting genera-tions; Q1, by contrast, suggests that the two familes were close ("household friends") until they fell out. Key speeches, such as Mercutio's "Queen Mab" narrative, vary in intriguing ways, suggesting that the two quartos represent different stages of the com-position process. Characterization differs at times, too: the Nurse is more proactive, and more sympathetically engaged with Juliet's situation, in Q1 than in Q2; Friar Laurence's tendency to vacillate and fawn is more apparent in Q2. Both texts offer evidence of the practicalities of early staging, from movements between the upper and lower stage to possible doublings of minor roles.

Through the two texts of *Romeo and Juliet*, we gain access to the processes through which theatrical texts became printed texts, and we can develop a good, if by no means fully explained, sense of the variety of forms through which Shakespeare's plays, in their irresolvable multiplicity, came into being.

Gordon McMullan

PERFORMANCE NOTE

Productions of *Romeo and Juliet*—an archetypical story whose iconic leading characters dependably retain the capacity to disquiet and disarm—are dogged by expectations. The play is so familiar that directors often feel unusual pressure to reinvent it, with the result that casting the feuding households into contemporary analogues (Mafia families, old wealth vs. new money, Christians vs. Muslims), or activating subtextual sources of drama by playing characters against type (a sinister Friar Laurence, flamboyant Mercutio, or adulterous Lady Capulet) constitute minor performance traditions in themselves. Simultaneously, though, audiences tend to anticipate a simpler, more sympathetic pair of lovers than Shakespeare provides. Directors aiming to refresh a familiar plot must therefore take heed of the play's innate potential to alienate spectators expecting an idealized romance. Crucially in this respect, they must decide whether to stress or smooth over Romeo's rough edges: his fickleness in love; his attempt to bribe Rosaline to "ope her lap" (1.1.209) for him; his threat to strew the churchyard with Balthasar's limbs; his indiscriminate slaughter of Paris.

Casting the eponymous characters presents unique challenges, in line with the adage that actors experienced and versatile enough to play them are no longer young enough to do so. Romeo combines youthful impulsivity and Hamlet-like deliberation, equal parts melancholy versifier and man of action. Juliet is still more complex, tempering frankness with guile, trepidation with fierce resolve, innocence with raw sexuality. Actors can emphasize one set of characteristics over another, though the best performances seem to preserve paradoxes. Capulet, Friar Laurence, and Juliet's Nurse—respectively, a doting tyrant, faithful fraud, and loose-lipped confidante—likewise thrive by actors who can be convincingly inconsistent. Meanwhile, productions must decide whether Paris is innocuous or threatening, and whether Mercutio is primarily a tragic or comic figure, the answers helping to determine whether the play proceeds ominously toward its tragic end, or as a comedy spoiled at the last gasp. Other considerations include assigning the Prologue; managing passages of ostentatiously poetic dialogue; resolving difficult staging at the Capulets' ball (1.4) and tomb (5.3); and handling the famously challenging mourning scene that follows Juliet's death (4.4).

Brett Gamboa

The Most Lamentable Tragedy
of Romeo and Juliet

[THE PERSONS OF THE PLAY

CHORUS

PRINCE Escalus
MERCUTIO, kinsman to the Prince
County PARIS, kinsman to the Prince
Page to Mercutio
PAGE to Paris

CAPULET
CAPULET'S WIFE
JULIET, daughter to Capulet
TYBALT, nephew to Capulet's wife
CAPULET'S COUSIN
NURSE
PETER, servant to Nurse
PETRUCCIO, companion to Tybalt
Page to Tybalt
SAMSON, a Capulet retainer
GREGORY, a Capulet retainer
HEAD SERVINGMAN in the Capulet household
Three SERVINGMEN in the Capulet household

MONTAGUE
MONTAGUE'S WIFE
ROMEO, son to Montague
BENVOLIO, nephew to Montague
BALTHASAR, servant to Romeo
ABRAHAM, a Montague retainer
Servingmen

FRIAR LAURENCE
FRIAR JOHN

CHIEF WATCHMAN
WATCHMEN
OFFICER
CITIZENS of Verona
APOTHECARY
Three MUSICIANS
Masquers, Guests, Gentlewomen, Musicians, Attendants]

The Prologue[1]

[*Enter* CHORUS.]

CHORUS Two households, both alike in dignity,°   status
In fair Verona, where we lay our scene,
From ancient grudge break to new mutiny,°   wrangling
Where civil blood makes civil hands unclean.[2]
5   From forth the fatal° loins of these two foes,   ill-fated
A pair of star-crossed[3] lovers take their life,
Whose misadventured° piteous overthrows   unfortunate
Doth with their death bury their parents' strife.
The fearful passage of their death-marked love
10 And the continuance of their parents' rage—
Which, but their children's end, naught could remove—
Is now the two hours' traffic° of our stage;   business; movement
The which, if you with patient ears attend,
What here shall miss, our toil shall strive to mend.[4]   [*Exit.*]

1.1 (Q1 Scene 1)

Enter SAMSON *and* GREGORY *of the house of Capulet,*
with swords and bucklers.°   small round shields

SAMSON Gregory, on my word, we'll not carry coals.[1]
GREGORY No, for then we should be colliers.[2]
SAMSON I mean, an° we be in choler,° we'll draw.°   if / anger / draw swords
GREGORY Ay. While you live, draw your neck out of collar.°   a noose
5   SAMSON I strike quickly,° being moved.[3]   vigorously
GREGORY But thou art not quickly° moved to strike.   speedily
SAMSON A dog of the house of Montague moves me.
GREGORY To move is to stir, and to be valiant is to stand;[4]
therefore, if thou art moved, thou runn'st away.
10 SAMSON A dog of that house shall move me to stand. I will
take the wall of[5] any man or maid of Montague's.
GREGORY That shows thee a weak slave, for the weakest goes
to the wall.[6]
SAMSON 'Tis true—and therefore women, being the weaker
15 vessels,[7] are ever thrust to the wall;° therefore I will push Mon-   (sexually) assaulted
tague's men from the wall, and thrust his maids to the wall.
GREGORY The quarrel is between our masters and us their
men.
SAMSON 'Tis all one.° I will show myself a tyrant: when I have   the same
20 fought with the men, I will be civil with the maids—I will
cut off their heads.
GREGORY The heads of the maids?
SAMSON Ay, the heads of the maids—or their maidenheads;
take it in what sense thou wilt.
25 GREGORY They must take it in sense° that feel it.   through sensation

The Prologue

1. TEXTUAL COMMENT On the different versions of the Prologue in Q2 and Q1, see Digital Edition TC 1 (Second Quarto edited text). PERFORMANCE COMMENT On the directorial possibilities for representing the Chorus onstage, see Digital Edition PC 1.
2. Where citizens' hands are stained with the blood of their fellow citizens.
3. Thwarted by the adverse influence of the stars appearing at the time of their birth, which controlled their destinies.
4. *What . . . mend:* The actors will try to rectify

whatever is missing or ill told in the Prologue.
1.1 Location: A street or public place in Verona.
1. We'll not suffer humiliation.
2. Professional coal porters, proverbially sneaky.
3. Being roused to anger.
4. Stand firm against assault. Playing, as with "strike" and "stir," on sexual arousal.
5. I will assert superiority over. The sidewalk nearest the wall was cleaner than that nearer the street.
6. Proverbial: The weakest are always pushed aside.
7. Paul's description of women in 1 Peter 3:7.

SAMSON   Me they shall feel while I am able to stand, and 'tis
known I am a pretty piece of flesh.[8]

GREGORY   'Tis well thou art not fish; if thou hadst, thou hadst
been Poor John.[9]

    Enter [ABRAHAM and another Servingman
    of the Montagues].

30   Draw thy tool;[1] here comes of the house of Montagues.

SAMSON   My naked weapon is out. Quarrel; I will back thee.

GREGORY   How, turn thy back and run?

SAMSON   Fear me not.[2]

GREGORY   No, marry,[3] I fear thee!

35   SAMSON   Let us take the law of our sides; let them begin.

GREGORY   I will frown as I pass by, and let them take it as they
list.°   *like*

SAMSON   Nay, as they dare. I will bite my thumb at them,[4]
which is disgrace to them if they bear it.

    [*He bites his thumb.*]

40   ABRAHAM   Do you bite your thumb at us, sir?

SAMSON   I do bite my thumb, sir.

ABRAHAM   Do you bite your thumb at us, sir?

SAMSON [*aside to* GREGORY]   Is the law of our side if I say "Ay"?

GREGORY [*aside to* SAMSON]   No.

45   SAMSON   —No, sir, I do not bite my thumb at you, sir; but I
bite my thumb, sir.

GREGORY   Do you quarrel, sir?

ABRAHAM   Quarrel, sir? No, sir.

SAMSON   But if you do, sir, I am for you;[5] I serve as good a man

50   as you.

ABRAHAM   No better.

SAMSON   Well, sir.

    Enter BENVOLIO.

GREGORY [*aside to* SAMSON]   Say "better." Here comes one of
my master's kinsmen.

55   SAMSON [*to* ABRAHAM]   Yes, better, sir.

ABRAHAM   You lie.

SAMSON   Draw, if you be men. —Gregory, remember thy wash-
ing° blow.   *slashing; violent*

    They fight.

BENVOLIO [*drawing*]   Part, fools!

60   Put up your swords. You know not what you do.

    Enter TYBALT.

TYBALT   What, art thou drawn among these heartless hinds?[6]

    [*He draws.*] Turn thee, Benvolio; look upon thy death.

BENVOLIO   I do but keep the peace. Put up thy sword,
Or manage° it to part these men with me.   *wield*

65   TYBALT   What? Drawn, and talk of peace? I hate the word
As I hate hell, all Montagues, and thee.
Have at thee, coward.

    [*They fight.*]

---

8. An attractive fellow possessed of an impressive
member.
9. Dried salted hake, appropriate as a taunt because
shriveled and cheap. "Neither fish nor flesh" was proverbial for an uncategorizable oddity.
1. Weapon (and continuing the bawdy wordplay).
2. Do not doubt my fortitude; in the next line, Gregory takes it in the modern sense of "Do not be afraid

of me."
3. By the Virgin Mary, a mild oath with a meaning
similar to "indeed."
4. Flick the thumbnail from behind the upper teeth,
an insulting gesture.
5. I accept your invitation to fight.
6. These cowardly servants, punning on female deer
("hinds") unprotected by a stag ("hart/heart").

Enter three or four CITIZENS[*, including an* OFFICER,]
with clubs or partisans.°   *broad-tipped spears*

OFFICER   Clubs, bills,° and partisans! Strike! Beat them down!   *ax-bladed spears*
Down with the Capulets! Down with the Montagues!
Enter old CAPULET, *in his gown, and* [CAPULET'S] WIFE.

70 CAPULET   What noise is this? Give me my long sword, ho!
CAPULET'S WIFE   A crutch, a crutch! Why call you for a sword?
CAPULET   My sword, I say!
Enter old MONTAGUE *and* [MONTAGUE'S] WIFE.
                         Old Montague is come,
And flourishes his blade in spite° of me.   *defiance*
MONTAGUE   Thou villain Capulet!
[*to* MONTAGUE'S WIFE]   Hold me not: let me go!
75 MONTAGUE'S WIFE   Thou shalt not stir one foot to seek a foe.
Enter PRINCE *Escalus, with his train.*
PRINCE   Rebellious subjects, enemies to peace,
Profaners of this neighbor-stainèd steel[7]—
Will they not hear? —What ho, you men, you beasts
That quench the fire of your pernicious rage
80 With purple° fountains issuing from your veins!   *crimson*
On pain of torture, from those bloody hands
Throw your mistempered[8] weapons to the ground,
And hear the sentence of your movèd° prince.   *furious*
Three civil brawls, bred of an airy° word   *unsubstantial*
85 By thee, old Capulet, and Montague,
Have thrice disturbed the quiet of our streets
And made Verona's ancient° citizens   *elderly*
Cast by° their grave-beseeming ornaments[9]   *Cast away*
To wield old partisans in hands as old,
90 Cankered° with peace, to part your cankered° hate.   *Rusty / malignant*
If ever you disturb our streets again,
Your lives shall pay the forfeit° of the peace.   *ransom*
For this time, all the rest depart away!
—You, Capulet, shall go along with me;
95 —And Montague, come you this afternoon,
To know our farther pleasure in this case,
To old Freetown,[1] our common judgment-place.
Once more, on pain of death, all men depart!
                Exeunt [*all but* MONTAGUE, MONTAGUE'S WIFE,
                                    and BENVOLIO].
MONTAGUE   Who set this ancient quarrel new abroach?°   *open*
100 Speak, nephew. Were you by when it began?
BENVOLIO   Here were the servants of your adversary
And yours, close fighting ere I did approach.
I drew to part them. In the instant came
The fiery Tybalt, with his sword prepared,
105 Which, as he breathed° defiance to my ears,   *uttered*
He swung about his head and cut the winds
Who, nothing hurt withal,° hissed him in scorn.   *by that*
While we were interchanging thrusts and blows
Came more and more, and fought on part and part[2]

---

7. You who defile weapons with the stains of your neighbors' blood.
8. Badly shaped and hardened, as well as unnecessarily wrathful by disposition.
9. Attire and symbolic staffs appropriate to grave old

age. Possibly playing on the old men's proximity to the grave.
1. In the Italian source, the Capulet house is called Villa Franca, which Brooke translates as "Freetown."
2. Fought for one side and the other.

110 Till the Prince came, who parted either part.
MONTAGUE'S WIFE   Oh, where is Romeo? Saw you him today?
Right glad I am he was not at this fray.
BENVOLIO   Madam, an hour before the worshipped sun
Peered forth° the golden window of the East,   *out from*
115 A troubled mind drive° me to walk abroad   *drove*
Where, underneath the grove of sycamore[3]
That westward rooteth° from this city side,   *grows out*
So early walking did I see your son.
Towards him I made, but he was ware° of me   *wary*
120 And stole into the covert° of the wood.   *covering*
I, measuring his affections° by my own,   *inclination*
Which then most sought where most might not be found,[4]
Being one too many by my weary self,
Pursued my humor,° not pursuing his,   *mood*
125 And gladly shunned who gladly fled from me.[5]
MONTAGUE   Many a morning hath he there been seen,
With tears augmenting the fresh morning's dew,
Adding to clouds more clouds with his deep sighs;
But all so soon as the all-cheering sun
130 Should in the farthest East begin to draw
The shady curtains from Aurora's[6] bed,
Away from light steals home my heavy° son   *melancholy*
And private in his chamber pens himself,
Shuts up his windows, locks fair daylight out,
135 And makes himself an artificial night.
Black and portentous° must this humor[7] prove,   *ominous (of illness)*
Unless good counsel may the cause remove.
BENVOLIO   My noble uncle, do you know the cause?
MONTAGUE   I neither know it nor can learn of him.
140 BENVOLIO   Have you importuned him by any° means?   *all*
MONTAGUE   Both by myself and many other friends;
But he his own affection's counselor°   *confidant*
Is to himself—I will not say how true[8]—
But to himself so secret and so close,°   *discreet*
145 So far from sounding and discovery,°   *fathoming and revelation*
As is the bud bit with an envious worm°   *a spiteful grub (larva)*
Ere he can spread his sweet leaves° to the air   *petals*
Or dedicate his beauty to the same.
Could we but learn from whence his sorrows grow,
150 We would as willingly give cure as know.
          Enter ROMEO.
BENVOLIO   See where he comes. So please you,° step aside;   *please you = please*
I'll know his grievance or be much denied.
MONTAGUE   I would° thou wert so happy° by thy stay   *wish / fortunate*
To hear true shrift.° —Come, madam, let's away.   *confession*
          Exeunt [MONTAGUE *and* MONTAGUE'S WIFE].
BENVOLIO   Good morrow, cousin.

3. Associated with melancholy lovers, who are
"sick-amour."
4. *where . . . found*: in a place where I was unlikely to
have company.
5. TEXTUAL COMMENT Q1's briefer version of the
following exchange (lines 126–50) entails a direct juxtaposition between Romeo and Benvolio, whose melancholy here takes on darker connotations in light of
Q1's version of the final scene. See Digital Edition

TC 2 (Second Quarto edited text).
6. Goddess of the dawn in classical legend.
7. "Humors," essential bodily fluids, were considered
the basis of human beings' physical and psychological constitution. Too much black bile caused melancholy and a host of illnesses and derangements.
8. Loyal, but also invoking the proverbial wisdom
that only one who is "true to him- or herself" can be
upstanding in dealing with others.

155   ROMEO   Is the day so young?

      BENVOLIO   But new° struck nine.   *Only just*

      ROMEO   Ay me. Sad hours seem long.

Was that my father that went hence so fast?

      BENVOLIO   It was. What sadness lengthens Romeo's hours?

      ROMEO   Not having that which, having, makes them short.

160   BENVOLIO   In love?

      ROMEO   Out.

      BENVOLIO   Of love?

      ROMEO   Out of her favor where I am in love.

      BENVOLIO   Alas that Love, so gentle in his view,°   *appearance*

165   Should be so tyrannous and rough in proof.°   *experience*

      ROMEO   Alas that Love, whose view is muffled still,[9]

Should without eyes see pathways to his will.°   *intention; lust*

Where shall we dine?

      [*He sees signs of the brawl.*]

                        Oh, me! What fray was here?

Yet tell me not, for I have heard it all;

170   Here's much to do with hate, but more with love.

Why, then, O brawling love, O loving hate,

O anything of nothing first created,[1]

O heavy lightness, serious vanity,

Misshapen chaos of well-seeming forms,

175   Feather of lead, bright smoke, cold fire, sick health,

Still-waking° sleep that is not what it is—   *Always awake*

This love feel I, that feel no love in this.

Dost thou not laugh?

      BENVOLIO   No, coz,° I rather weep.   *cousin*

      ROMEO   Good heart, at what?

      BENVOLIO   At thy good heart's oppression.°   *affliction*

180   ROMEO   Why, such is love's transgression.

Griefs of mine own lie heavy in my breast,

Which thou wilt propagate° to have it pressed[2]   *multiply*

With more of thine: this love that thou hast shown

Doth add more grief to too much of mine own.

185   Love is a smoke made with the fume of sighs;

Being purged,° a fire sparkling in lovers' eyes;   *clarified*

Being vexed,° a sea nourished with loving tears.   *stirred up*

What is it else? A madness most discreet,°   *wise*

A choking gall, and a preserving sweet.

Farewell, my coz.

190   BENVOLIO   Soft;° I will go along.   *Wait*

An if° you leave me so, you do me wrong.   *An if = if*

      ROMEO   Tut, I have lost myself; I am not here.

This is not Romeo: he's some other where.

      BENVOLIO   Tell me, in sadness,[3] who is that you love?

195   ROMEO   What, shall I groan and tell thee?

      BENVOLIO   Groan? Why, no. But sadly tell me who.

      ROMEO   A sick man in sadness makes his will:

A word ill urged to one that is so ill.

In sadness, cousin, I do love a woman—

---

9. Who cannot see. Cupid was often depicted as blind or blindfolded.
1. Inverting the proverb "Nothing can come of nothing" and also recalling the doctrine that God made the world out of nothing. Romeo catalogues the "miraculous" paradoxes of love.
2. Burdened; embraced.
3. Seriousness, although Romeo plays on the sense "melancholy."

200 BENVOLIO I aimed so near when I supposed you loved.
ROMEO A right good mark,° man!—and she's fair I love.   *target; vulva*
BENVOLIO A right fair mark, fair coz, is soonest hit.
ROMEO Well, in that hit you miss; she'll not be hit
    With Cupid's arrow. She hath Dian's wit,[4]
205 And, in strong proof° of chastity well-armed,°   *tested armor / covered*
    From Love's weak childish bow she lives uncharmed.
    She will not stay° the siege of loving terms,   *undergo*
    Nor bide th'encounter of assailing eyes,[5]
    Nor ope her lap to saint-seducing gold.[6]
210 Oh, she is rich in beauty; only poor
    That, when she dies, with beauty dies her store.°   *wealth*
BENVOLIO Then she hath sworn that she will still° live chaste?   *always*
ROMEO She hath, and in that sparing° make huge waste: *refraining; thrift*
    For beauty starved with her severity
215 Cuts beauty off from all posterity.[7]
    She is too fair, too wise, wisely too fair,°   *just*
    To merit bliss° by making me despair.[8]   *heaven's blessing*
    She hath forsworn to love, and in that vow
    Do I live dead that live to tell it now.
220 BENVOLIO Be ruled by me: forget to think of her.
ROMEO Oh, teach me how I should forget to think!
BENVOLIO By giving liberty unto thine eyes.
    Examine other beauties.
ROMEO   'Tis the way
    To call hers, exquisite, in question more.[9]
225 These happy masks that kiss fair ladies' brows,
    Being black, puts us in mind they hide the fair.
    He that is strucken blind cannot forget
    The precious treasure of his eyesight lost.
    Show me a mistress that is passing° fair: *surpassingly*
230 What doth her beauty serve but as a note
    Where I may read who passed that passing fair?
    Farewell. Thou canst not teach me to forget.
BENVOLIO I'll pay° that doctrine, or else die in debt.[1] *Exeunt.*   *impart*

1.2 (Q1 Scene 2)
Enter CAPULET, *County*° PARIS, *and [a* SERVINGMAN].   *Count*

CAPULET But Montague is bound° as well as I,   *under oath*
    In penalty alike, and 'tis not hard, I think,
    For men so old as we to keep the peace.
PARIS Of honorable reckoning[1] are you both,
5   And pity 'tis you lived at odds so long.
    But now, my lord, what say you to my suit?
CAPULET But saying o'er what I have said before:
    My child is yet a stranger in the world;
    She hath not seen the change of fourteen years.
10 Let two more summers wither in their pride
    Ere we may think her ripe to be a bride.

---

4. The scruples and cleverness of Diana, the classical goddess of hunting and chastity.
5. *th'encounter of assailing eyes:* military metaphors for courtship conventionally used in Petrarchan love poetry.
6. To golden gifts that are irresistibly persuasive. Also, in classical legend, Jupiter descended upon Danaë as a shower of gold.

7. *For . . . posterity:* Since she will not have children, her beauty will die with her. *starved:* killed.
8. Despair of salvation, a grave sin.
9. *in question more:* more intensely to mind.
1. Die whatever the cost to me; die still owing you the doctrine of forgetfulness.
1.2 Location: A street or plaza in Verona.
1. Repute, with a play on "accounting."

PARIS   Younger than she are happy mothers made.

CAPULET   And too soon marred are those so early made.
Earth hath swallowed all my hopes but she;[2]
15   She's the hopeful lady of my earth.°   *body*
But woo her, gentle Paris; get her heart—
My will to her consent is but a part—
And, she agreed, within her scope of choice
Lies my consent and fair-according voice.
20   This night I hold an old-accustomed feast
Whereto I have invited many a guest,
Such as I love; and you among the store
One more, most welcome, makes my number more.
At my poor house look to behold this night
25   Earth-treading stars that make dark heaven light.
Such comfort as do lusty young men feel
When well-appareled April on the heel
Of limping winter treads, even such delight,
Among fresh fennel[3] buds, shall you this night
30   Inherit° at my house. Hear all, all see,   *Enjoy*
And like her most whose merit most shall be;
Which one more view, of many, mine being one,
May stand in number, though in reck'ning none.[4]
Come, go with me. [to SERVINGMAN] Go, sirrah;° trudge about   *(address to an inferior)*
35   Through fair Verona; find those persons out
Whose names are written there [*giving him a paper*], and to
     them say
My house and welcome on their pleasure stay.°   *wait*
                    Exeunt [CAPULET *and* PARIS].

SERVINGMAN   "Find them out whose names are written."
Here[5] it is written that the shoemaker should meddle with
40   his yard° and the tailor with his last,° the fisher with his   *yardstick / shoe form*
pencil° and the painter with his nets. But I am sent to find   *paintbrush*
those persons whose names are here writ, and can never
find° what names the writing person hath here writ. I must   *figure out*
to the learned.
                    Enter BENVOLIO *and* ROMEO.
45   In good time—

BENVOLIO   Tut, man, one fire burns out another's burning;
One pain is lessened by another's anguish;
Turn giddy,° and be holp° by backward turning;   *Turn until dizzy / helped*
One desperate grief cures with another's languish.[6]
50   Take thou some new infection[7] to thy eye,
And the rank poison of the old will die.

ROMEO   Your plantain leaf[8] is excellent for that.[9]

BENVOLIO   For what, I pray thee?

---

2. Many editors have felt that this and the following line, which are not present in Q1, were deleted by Shakespeare in the process of writing the scene.
3. A plant associated with weddings and brides.
4. *Which . . . none*: Upon another inspection of the many young women, my daughter may make a part of the gorgeous display, but be of no account by herself. "One" was proverbially "no number."
5. Editors sometimes change Q2's punctuation and move "Here" to the end of the previous sentence. In either case, the illiterate Servingman is exasperated.

6. *Cures . . . languish*: is displaced by the languishing pain of a new grief.
7. New object of passion, which causes a distortion of sight in the lover.
8. The ordinary plantain leaf, used to dress wounds or bruises and thought to have curative powers.
9. TEXTUAL COMMENT Lines 1.2.53–1.3.36 in Q2 are almost identical to those found in Q1, suggesting that Q2's printers relied not on a manuscript copy but on Q1 itself for this passage. See Digital Edition TC 3 (Second Quarto edited text).

ROMEO   For your broken° shin.   *gashed*
BENVOLIO   Why, Romeo, art thou mad?

55   ROMEO   Not mad, but bound more than a madman is:
      Shut up in prison, kept without my food,
      Whipped and tormented, and—
      [*to* SERVINGMAN]   Good e'en,° good fellow.   *evening (afternoon)*
      SERVINGMAN   God gi'° good e'en. I pray, sir, can you read?   *give you*
      ROMEO   Ay—mine own fortune in my misery.[1]
60   SERVINGMAN   Perhaps you have learned it without book.[2] But,
      I pray, can you read anything you see?
      ROMEO   Ay, if I know the letters and the language.
      SERVINGMAN   Ye say honestly. Rest you merry.[3]
      ROMEO   Stay, fellow. I can read.
            He reads the letter.
65   "Signor Martino and his wife and daughters;
      County Anselm and his beauteous sisters;
      The lady widow of Vitruvio;
      Signor Placentio and his lovely nieces;
      Mercutio and his brother Valentine;
70   Mine uncle Capulet, his wife and daughters;
      My fair niece Rosaline; Livia;
      Signor Valentio and his cousin Tybalt;
      Lucio and the lively Helena."
      A fair assembly! Whither should they come?
75   SERVINGMAN   Up.[4]
      ROMEO   Whither to supper?
      SERVINGMAN   To our house.
      ROMEO   Whose house?
      SERVINGMAN   My master's.
80   ROMEO   Indeed, I should have asked you that before.
      SERVINGMAN   Now I'll tell you without asking. My master is
      the great rich Capulet, and—if you be not of the house of
      Montagues—I pray come and crush° a cup of wine. Rest you   *drink*
      merry.   [*Exit.*]
85   BENVOLIO   At this same ancient° feast of Capulet's   *traditional*
      Sups the fair Rosaline, whom thou so loves,
      With all the admired beauties of Verona.
      Go thither, and with unattainted° eye   *unbiased*
      Compare her face with some that I shall show,
90   And I will make thee think thy swan a crow.
      ROMEO   When the devout religion° of mine eye   *pious belief*
      Maintains such falsehood, then turn tears to fire;
      And these° who, often drowned, could never die,   *these eyes*
      Transparent° heretics, be burnt for liars.   *Obvious; self-evident*
95   One fairer than my love? The all-seeing sun
      Ne'er saw her match since first the world begun.
      BENVOLIO   Tut, you saw her fair, none else being by,
      Herself poised with° herself in either eye;   *balanced against*
      But in that crystal scales let there be weighed
100   Your lady's love against some other maid

---

1. Romeo takes "read" to mean "understand" or "per-   3. A farewell. The Servingman takes Romeo to mean
ceive," as in "to read one's fortune."   "if only I knew the letters and the language."
2. *without book:* from memory or by ear, as well as   4. "Come up" is an expression of scorn.
through experience rather than education.

That I will show you shining at this feast,
And she shall scant show well that now seems best.

ROMEO   I'll go along no such sight to be shown,
But to rejoice in splendor of mine own.   [*Exeunt.*]

1.3 (Q1 Scene 3)

Enter CAPULET'S WIFE[1] *and* NURSE.

CAPULET'S WIFE   Nurse, where's my daughter? Call her forth
 to me.

NURSE   Now, by my maidenhead at twelve year old,[2]
I bade her come. —What,[3] lamb! What, ladybird!
God forbid[4]—where's this girl? What, Juliet!

  Enter JULIET.

5   JULIET   How now? Who calls?

NURSE   Your mother.

JULIET   Madam, I am here. What is your will?

CAPULET'S WIFE   This is the matter. —Nurse, give leave° a while;   excuse us
We must talk in secret.—Nurse, come back again;

10   I have remembered me. Thou's° hear our counsel.°   You shall / secrets
Thou knowest my daughter's of a pretty age.

NURSE   Faith, I can tell her age unto an hour.

CAPULET'S WIFE   She's not fourteen.

NURSE   I'll lay fourteen of my teeth—and yet, to my teen° be   sorrow

15   it spoken, I have but four—she's not fourteen. How long is
it now to Lammastide?[5]

CAPULET'S WIFE   A fortnight and odd days.

NURSE   Even or odd, of all days in the year,
Come Lammas Eve at night shall she be fourteen.

20   Susan[6] and she—God rest all Christian souls—
Were of an age. Well, Susan is with God;
She was too good for me. But, as I said,
On Lammas Eve at night shall she be fourteen—
That shall she, marry! I remember it well.

25   'Tis since the earthquake now eleven years,
And she was weaned—I never shall forget it—
Of all the days of the year upon that day;
For I had then laid wormwood[7] to my dug,°   on my nipple
Sitting in the sun under the dovehouse wall—

30   My lord and you were then at Mantua—
Nay, I do bear a brain°—but, as I said,   memory
When it did taste the wormwood on the nipple
Of my dug and felt it bitter, pretty fool°—   (an endearment)
To see it tetchy,° and fall out with the dug!   peevish

35   "Shake," quoth the dovehouse;[8] 'twas no need, I trow,
To bid me trudge.°   remove myself
And since that time it is eleven years,
For then she could stand high-lone°—nay, by th' rood,°   upright alone / cross
Her self poised with herself in either duck,

1.3 Location: Capulet's house.
1. TEXTUAL COMMENT On Lady Capulet's changing speech prefixes in Q2 and Q1, see Digital Edition TC 4 (Second Quarto edited text).
2. Presumably the latest date that the Nurse could swear by her virginity.
3. An expression of impatience.
4. Either an apology for the promiscuous connota-

tion of "ladybird" or fearing something amiss in Juliet's absence.
5. August 1, originally celebrated by the church as a harvest festival.
6. The Nurse evidently suckled Juliet after her own daughter died.
7. A proverbially bitter plant extract.
8. The dovehouse shook with the earthquake.

She could have run and waddled all about,
40 For, even the day before, she broke her brow,°   *cut her forehead*
And then my husband—God be with his soul;
'A° was a merry man—took up the child.   *He*
"Yea?" quoth he. "Dost thou fall upon thy face?
Thou wilt fall backward when thou hast more wit,°   *knowledge*
45 Wilt thou not, Jule?" And, by my holidam,°   *Holy Lady*
The pretty wretch left° crying, and said "Ay!"   *stopped*
To see now how a jest shall come about!°   *come true*
I warrant, an° I should live a thousand years,   *if*
I never should forget it. "Wilt thou not, Jule?" quoth he,
50 And, pretty fool, it stinted° and said "Ay!"   *she ceased*
CAPULET'S WIFE   Enough of this. I pray thee, hold thy peace.
NURSE   Yes, madam—yet I cannot choose but laugh
To think it should leave crying and say "Ay!"
And yet I warrant° it had upon it° brow   *assure you / its*
55 A bump as big as a young cock'rel's stone°—   *rooster's testicle*
A perilous knock—and it cried bitterly.
"Yea?" quoth my husband. "Fall'st upon thy face?
Thou wilt fall backward when thou comest to age,
Wilt thou not, Jule?" It stinted and said "Ay!"
60 JULIET   And stint thou too, I pray thee, Nurse, say I.
NURSE   Peace, I have done. God mark° thee to his grace,   *elect*
Thou wast the prettiest babe that e'er I nursed;
An° I might live to see thee married once,°   *If / one day*
I have my wish.
65 CAPULET'S WIFE   Marry,° that "marry" is the very theme   *Truly*
I came to talk of. —Tell me, daughter Juliet,
How stands your dispositions to be married?
JULIET   It is an hour that I dream not of.
NURSE   "An hour"! Were not I thine only nurse,
70 I would say thou hadst sucked wisdom from thy teat.[9]
CAPULET'S WIFE   Well, think of marriage now. Younger
   than you
Here in Verona, ladies of esteem,
Are made already mothers; by my count,
I was your mother much upon these years
75 That you are now a maid. Thus, then, in brief:
The valiant Paris seeks you for his love.
NURSE   A man, young lady! Lady, such a man
As all the world— Why, he's a man of wax![1]
CAPULET'S WIFE   Verona's summer hath not such a flower.
80 NURSE   Nay, he's a flower, in faith, a very flower!
CAPULET'S WIFE   What say you? Can you love the gentleman?
This night you shall behold him at our feast;
Read o'er the volume of young Paris' face,
And find delight writ there with beauty's pen;
85 Examine every married lineament,[2]
And see how one° another lends content;[3]   *one to*
And what obscured in this fair volume lies
Find written in the margin[4] of his eyes.

9. From the teat that nourished you.   3. Meaning; happiness.
1. Model of perfection, as if sculpted rather than born.   4. Glosses to difficult passages of text were set in the
2. Harmoniously composed feature; a joined line of   margin.
flowing handwriting.

This precious book of love, this unbound° lover,   *single; unrestrained*
90   To beautify him only lacks a cover.
The fish lives in the sea, and 'tis much pride
For fair without the fair within to hide;⁵
That book in many's eyes doth share the glory
That in gold clasps locks in the golden story.⁶
95   So shall you share all that he doth possess
By having him, making yourself no less.
NURSE   No less? Nay, bigger—women grow° by men!   *swell with child*
CAPULET'S WIFE   Speak briefly: can you like of Paris' love?
JULIET   I'll look° to like, if looking liking move;⁷   *expect; examine*
100   But no more deep will I endart mine eye⁸
Than your consent gives strength to make it fly.
    Enter a SERVINGMAN.⁹
SERVINGMAN   Madam, the guests are come; supper served up;
you called; my young lady asked for; the Nurse cursed in the
pantry; and everything in extremity.° I must hence to wait;°   *a terrible state / serve*
105   I beseech you follow straight.°   *immediately*
CAPULET'S WIFE   We follow thee.   [*Exit* SERVINGMAN.]
    —Juliet, the County stays.°   *the Count awaits*
NURSE   Go, girl! Seek happy nights to° happy days.   *Exeunt.*   *at the end of*

1.4 (Q1 Scene 4)

    Enter ROMEO, MERCUTIO, [*and*] BENVOLIO, *with five or*
    *six other Masquers,*¹ *torchbearers.*
ROMEO   What, shall this speech° be spoke for our excuse,   *prologue*
Or shall we on without apology?
BENVOLIO   The date is out of° such prolixity.   *past for*
We'll have no Cupid, hoodwinked² with a scarf,
5   Bearing a Tartar's painted bow of lath,³
Scaring the ladies like a crowkeeper.°   *scarecrow*
But let them measure° us by what they will,   *judge*
We'll measure° them a measure° and be gone.   *apportion / dance*
ROMEO   Give me a torch. I am not for this ambling;°   *dancing*
10   Being but heavy,° I will bear the light.   *melancholy*
MERCUTIO   Nay, gentle° Romeo, we must have you dance.   *noble; softhearted*
ROMEO   Not I, believe me. You have dancing shoes
With nimble soles; I have a soul of lead
So stakes me to the ground I cannot move.
15   MERCUTIO   You are a lover; borrow Cupid's wings,
And soar with them above a common bound.⁴
ROMEO   I am too sore° empiercèd with his shaft   *deeply*
To soar with his light° feathers, and, so bound,   *cheery; agile; wanton*
I cannot bound a pitch⁵ above dull woe;

---

5. *For fair . . . hide:* For a lovely setting (Juliet) to frame and enrich the fair Paris.
6. *That book . . . story:* Many esteem a book's golden binding as highly as the story it contains. The speech thoroughly confuses who is covering whom.
7. If looking can motivate liking.
8. Sink my eye like an arrow into its target; shoot glances that, like Cupid's arrows, inflame his passions.
9. TEXTUAL COMMENT On the roles of the Capulets' servingmen throughout the play, see Digital Edition TC 5 (Second Quarto edited text).
1.4 Location: Before Capulet's house.

1. Performers or participants in an aristocratic masked entertainment, consisting of dances and sometimes dumb shows and set speeches.
2. Blindfolded and foolish Cupid, a typical costume for the presenter of the masque's theme.
3. Short bow shaped like the upper lip, made of the thin wood used for theatrical properties. Tartars, a dark-skinned, supposedly savage people in Asia Minor, were famed for their archery.
4. A normal limit; an average dancer's leap.
5. Height from which a hawk stoops to kill.

20   Under love's heavy burden do I sink.

MERCUTIO   And to sink in it should you burden love:
Too great oppression for a tender thing.[6]

ROMEO   Is love a tender thing? It is too rough,
Too rude, too boist'rous, and it pricks like thorn.

25 MERCUTIO   If love be rough with you, be rough with love;
Prick° love for pricking, and you beat love down.[7]   *Stab; sexually penetrate*
Give me a case[8] to put my visage in—
A visor for a visor[9]—what care I
What curious eye doth quote° deformities?   *notice*
30 Here are the beetle brows° shall blush for me.   *protruding eyebrows*

BENVOLIO   Come, knock and enter—and, no sooner in,
But every man betake him to his legs.°   *to dancing; to flight*

ROMEO   A torch for me. Let wantons light of heart
Tickle the senseless rushes° with their heels,   *floor matting*
35 For I am proverbed with a grandsire° phrase: *an ancient*
I'll be a candleholder and look on.[1]
The game was ne'er so fair, and I am done.[2]

MERCUTIO   Tut, dun's the mouse[3]—the constable's own word.°   *phrase*
If thou art dun, we'll draw thee from the mire[4]
40 Or—save your reverence[5]—love wherein thou stickest
Up to the ears. Come; we burn daylight.° Ho!   *waste time*

ROMEO   Nay, that's not so.

MERCUTIO   I mean, sir, in delay
We waste our lights in vain, light lights by day.
Take our good meaning, for our judgment sits
45 Five times in that ere once in our fine wits.[6]

ROMEO   And we mean° well in going to this masque;   *intend*
But 'tis no wit° to go.   *intelligence*

MERCUTIO   Why, may one ask?

ROMEO   I dreamed a dream tonight.°   *last night*

MERCUTIO   And so did I.

ROMEO   Well, what was yours?

MERCUTIO   That dreamers often lie.

50 ROMEO   In bed asleep while they do dream things true.

MERCUTIO   Oh, then, I see Queen Mab[7] hath been with you.[8]
She is the fairies' midwife, and she comes
In shape no bigger than an agate stone[9]
On the forefinger of an alderman,
55 Drawn with a team of little atomi°   *atoms*
Over men's noses as they lie asleep,

6. Suggesting a pudendum.
7. *Prick . . . down*: Playing on the sense "satiate desire by fulfilling it."
8. Literally, "mask," but also slang for the vagina.
9. Mask for an ugly face. Proverbial: "A well-favored visor to hide an ill-favored face."
1. Proverbial: "A good candleholder proves a good gamester. A spectator loses nothing."
2. Proverbial: "When play is best, it is time to leave."
3. Proverbial: "Keep silent and unseen, like a mouse."
4. In the Christmas game "Dun Is in the Mire," players pantomimed drawing a log representing a horse out of a boggy road. Mercutio is suggesting that Romeo is a stick-in-the-mud.
5. An apology for crude language, here used mockingly.

6. *Take . . . wits*: Understand my intended good meaning using common sense ("judgment"), which is five times as trustworthy as witty ingenuity ("fine wits").
7. Possibly Celtic, but probably Shakespeare's invention. "Queen" suggested "quean," which meant "whore," and "Mab" was a stereotypical name for prostitutes.
8. PERFORMANCE COMMENT Mercutio's speech on Queen Mab can accommodate a range of styles and tones. For more about actors' varying interpretations of Mercutio and his relationship to Romeo, see Digital Edition PC 2. TEXTUAL COMMENT On the different versions of this speech in Q2 and Q1, see Digital Edition TC 6 (Second Quarto edited text).
9. A small human figure was often carved on agate stones set in seal rings.

Her wagon-spokes made of long spinners'° legs,   *spiders'*
The cover of the wings of grasshoppers,
Her traces of the smallest spider web,
60 Her collars of the moonshine's wat'ry beams,
Her whip of cricket's bone, the lash of film,°   *spider's-web thread*
Her wagoner° a small gray-coated gnat   *driver*
Not half so big as a round little worm
Pricked from the lazy finger of a maid.[1]
65 Her chariot is an empty hazelnut
Made by the joiner° squirrel or old grub[2]—   *carpenter*
Time out o'mind the fairies' coach-makers—
And in this state° she gallops night by night   *regal finery*
Through lovers' brains, and then they dream of love;
70 On courtiers' knees, that dream on curtsies straight;[3]
O'er lawyers' fingers, who straight dream on fees;
O'er ladies' lips, who straight on kisses dream,
Which oft the angry Mab with blisters plagues
Because their breath with sweetmeats° tainted are.   *candies*
75 Sometime she gallops o'er a courtier's nose,
And then dreams he of smelling out a suit;[4]
And sometime comes she with a tithe-pig's[5] tail,
Tickling a parson's nose as 'a° lies asleep—   *he*
Then he dreams of another benefice;[6]
80 Sometime she driveth o'er a soldier's neck,
And then dreams he of cutting foreign throats,
Of breaches, ambuscadoes, Spanish blades,[7]
Of healths five fathom deep[8]—and then anon°   *soon*
Drums in his ear, at which he starts and wakes
85 And, being thus frighted, swears a prayer or two
And sleeps again. This is that very Mab
That plaits° the manes of horses in the night,   *entangles*
And bakes the elflocks[9] in foul sluttish° hairs   *dirty*
Which, once untangled, much misfortune bodes.
90 This is the hag, when maids lie on their backs,
That presses them,[1] and learns° them first to bear,   *teaches*
Making them women of good carriage.[2]
This is she—
ROMEO   Peace, peace, Mercutio, peace!
Thou talk'st of nothing.°   *imaginings; a vagina*
MERCUTIO   True, I talk of dreams,
95 Which are the children of an idle brain,
Begot of nothing but vain fantasy,°   *empty imagination*
Which is as thin of substance as the air
And more inconstant than the wind, who woos

---

1. According to popular belief, worms generated in idle girls' fingers.
2. Grubs bore holes.
3. Dream of respectful bows immediately.
4. A petition at court, which the courtier could facilitate for a fee.
5. Pig paid as a tithe to the parish for the support of the priest.
6. Pluralism (holding multiple benefices simultaneously) was a common source of corruption in the early modern church.

7. *breaches:* burst fortifications. *ambuscadoes:* ambushes. *Spanish blades:* swords made in Toledo were famous for their quality.
8. Fantastically deep cups of liquor.
9. And hardens the tangles. According to folk legend, unknotting them would anger the malicious elves.
1. Evil spirits were supposed to be responsible for erotic dreams, taking the form of an illusory sexual partner.
2. Excellent deportment; the capacity for carrying the weight of a lover; childbearing.

Even now the frozen bosom of the North
100 And, being angered, puffs away from thence,
Turning his side to the dew-dropping South.
BENVOLIO   This wind you talk of blows us from ourselves;
Supper is done, and we shall come too late.
ROMEO   I fear too early, for my mind misgives°   *fears*
105 Some consequence yet hanging in the stars
Shall bitterly begin his fearful date°   *period*
With this night's revels and expire° the term   *finish*
Of a despisèd life closed in my breast
By some vile forfeit of untimely death.[3]
110 But He that hath the steerage of my course
Direct my suit. —On, lusty gentlemen!
BENVOLIO   Strike, drum!
> *They march about the stage, and* SERVINGMEN *come*
> *forth with napkins. Enter* [HEAD SERVINGMAN].
HEAD SERVINGMAN   Where's Potpan, that he helps not to take
away? He shift a trencher!° He scrape a trencher!   *wooden plate*
115 FIRST SERVINGMAN   When good manners shall lie all in one
or two men's hands—and they unwashed too—'tis a foul°   *bad; dirty*
thing.
HEAD SERVINGMAN   Away with the joint-stools![4] Remove the
court-cupboard!° Look to the plate!° —Good thou, save me   *sideboard / silverware*
120 a piece of marzipan, and, as thou loves me, let the porter let
in Susan Grindstone and Nell, Anthony, and Potpan.
SECOND SERVINGMAN   Ay, boy, ready.
HEAD SERVINGMAN   You are looked for and called for, asked
for and sought for, in the great chamber.
125 THIRD SERVINGMAN   We cannot be here and there too.
—Cheerly, boys! Be brisk a while, and the longer liver take
all.[5]   *Exeunt* [SERVINGMEN].
> *Enter* [CAPULET, CAPULET'S WIFE, JULIET, CAPULET'S
> COUSIN, PARIS,[6] TYBALT, NURSE, *a* SERVINGMAN,
> *Attendants, Tybalt's Page, Musicians, and*] *all the*
> *Guests and Gentlewomen to the Masquers.*
CAPULET   Welcome, gentlemen![7] Ladies that have their toes
Unplagued with corns will walk a bout° with you.   *dance a turn*
130 —Ah, my mistresses, which of you all
Will now deny to dance? She that makes dainty,°   *coyly demurs*
She I'll swear hath corns. Am I come near ye now?[8]
—Welcome, gentlemen! I have seen the day
That I have worn a visor, and could tell
135 A whispering tale in a fair lady's ear,
Such as would please: 'tis gone, 'tis gone, 'tis gone!
You are welcome, gentlemen! —Come, musicians, play.
> *Music plays, and they dance.*

---

3. As fate prematurely foreclosing on a mortgaged life.
4. Stools made by a furniture maker, commonly used for seating at large banquets.
5. Proverbial, meaning "Life is short."
6. PERFORMANCE COMMENT Although neither Paris nor Rosaline speaks in this scene, directors have

sometimes used the ball as an opportunity to develop their presence in the play. See Digital Edition PC 3.
7. TEXTUAL COMMENT On Capulet's rapid change of addressees, see Digital Edition TC 7 (Second Quarto edited text).
8. Does that strike home?

A hall,[9] a hall! Give room! —And foot it, girls!
[*to Attendants*] More light, you knaves! And turn the tables
up,[1]
140   And quench the fire; the room is grown too hot.
—Ah, sirrah,[2] this unlooked-for° sport comes well!   *unexpected*
—Nay, sit, nay, sit, good cousin° Capulet,   *kinsman*
For you and I are past our dancing days.
How long is't now since last yourself and I
Were in a masque?
145   CAPULET'S COUSIN   By'r Lady, thirty years.
CAPULET   What, man? 'Tis not so much, 'tis not so much;
'Tis since the nuptial of Lucentio—
Come Pentecost[3] as quickly as it will,
Some five-and-twenty years—and then we masqued.
150   CAPULET'S COUSIN   'Tis more, 'tis more! His son is elder, sir;
His son is thirty.
CAPULET   Will you tell me that?
His son was but a ward[4] two years ago.
ROMEO [*apart to a* SERVINGMAN]   What lady's that which doth
enrich the hand
Of yonder knight?
SERVINGMAN   I know not, sir.
155   ROMEO   Oh, she doth teach the torches to burn bright!
It seems she hangs upon the cheek of night
As a rich jewel in an Ethiop's ear:[5]
Beauty too rich for use, for earth too dear.[6]
So shows a snowy dove trooping° with crows   *flocking*
160   As yonder lady o'er her fellows shows.
The measure° done, I'll watch her place of stand[7]   *dance*
And, touching hers, make blessèd my rude hand.
Did my heart love till now? Forswear it, sight,
For I ne'er saw true beauty till this night.
165   TYBALT   This, by his voice, should be a Montague.
[*to his Page*] Fetch me my rapier, boy.   [*Exit Tybalt's Page.*]
What? Dares the slave
Come hither, covered with an antic face,[8]
To fleer° and scorn at our solemnity?°   *sneer / festivity*
Now, by the stock and honor of my kin,
170   To strike him dead I hold it not a sin.
CAPULET   Why, how now, kinsman? Wherefore storm you so?
TYBALT   Uncle, this is a Montague, our foe,
A villain° that is hither come in spite   *An ill-doer; a slave*
To scorn at our solemnity this night.
CAPULET   Young Romeo, is it?
175   TYBALT   'Tis he, that villain Romeo.
CAPULET   Content° thee, gentle coz. Let him alone.   *Calm*
'A bears him like a portly° gentleman,   *dignified*
And, to say truth, Verona brags of him

---

9. Make space in the hall.
1. Dismantle and stack the trestle tables.
2. TEXTUAL COMMENT For the implications of "sirrah" here, see Digital Edition TC 7 (Second Quarto edited text).
3. The seventh Sunday after Easter, a standard reference point in the medieval and Renaissance calendar.

4. Subject to a guardian; a minor.
5. In Romeo's image, a jewel shines brighter against an Ethiopian's proverbially dark skin.
6. Too precious for this world; too valuable to die and be buried in earth.
7. Where Juliet waits between dances.
8. A grotesque mask; a playful mask.

To be a virtuous and well-governed° youth;   *sensible*
180   I would not for the wealth of all this town
Here in my house do him disparagement.
Therefore, be patient; take no note of him.
It is my will, the which if thou respect,
Show a fair presence,° and put off these frowns,   *demeanor*
185   An ill-beseeming semblance° for a feast.   *expression*
TYBALT   It fits when such a villain is a guest;
I'll not endure him.
CAPULET   He shall be endured!
What, goodman[9] boy? I say he shall. Go to![1]
Am I the master here or you? Go to!
190   You'll "not endure him"? God shall mend my soul,
You'll make a mutiny° among my guests!   *brawl*
You will set cock-a-hoop![2] You'll be the man!
TYBALT   Why, uncle, 'tis a shame—
CAPULET   Go to, go to;
You are a saucy boy. Is't so, indeed?
195   This trick° may chance to scathe° you. I know what:[3]   *stupidity / harm*
You must contrary me—marry, 'tis time[4]—
        [*A dance ends, and* JULIET *moves to her place of
        stand, where* ROMEO *awaits.*]
[*to Masquers*] Well said,° my hearts! [*to* TYBALT] You are a   *done*
    princock.° Go.   *cheeky boy*
Be quiet, or— [*to Attendants*] More light! More light, for
    shame!
—I'll make you quiet. [*to Masquers*] What, cheerly, my hearts!
200   TYBALT [*aside*]   Patience perforce° with willful choler° meeting   *enforced / rash anger*
Makes my flesh tremble in their different° greeting.   *hostile*
I will withdraw, but this intrusion shall,
Now seeming sweet, convert to bitt'rest gall.   *Exit.*
ROMEO   If I profane with my unworthiest hand[5]
205   This holy shrine, the gentle sin is this:
My lips, two blushing pilgrims,[6] did ready stand
To smooth that rough touch with a tender kiss.
JULIET   Good pilgrim, you do wrong your hand too much,
Which mannerly° devotion shows in this;   *seemly*
210   For saints[7] have hands that pilgrims' hands do touch,
And palm to palm is holy palmers'° kiss.   *pilgrims'*
ROMEO   Have not saints lips, and holy palmers too?
JULIET   Ay, pilgrim, lips that they must use in prayer.
ROMEO   Oh, then, dear saint, let lips do what hands do:
215   They pray; grant thou, lest faith turn to despair.
JULIET   Saints do not move, though grant for prayer's sake.[8]

---

9. Courtesy title applied to a commoner (and thus an insult to the noble Tybalt).
1. An expression of impatience.
2. You will abandon restraint, like a drinker who removes the tap ("cock") from the barrel or like a boastfully crowing rooster.
3. I mean what I say.
4. Time to teach you a lesson; time that you became obedient.
5. Romeo and Juliet's first conversation takes the form of a shared sonnet.

6. John Florio's *World of Words* (1598) translates the Italian word *romeo* as "roamer," "wanderer," or "palmer" (pilgrim to the Holy Land).
7. Statues or pictures of saints, which attracted Catholic pilgrims. The Elizabethan Anglican Church held that the worship of such images was blasphemy; to an English audience, therefore, Romeo's description of his love could sound like idolatry.
8. Again identifying the saint with her image. As a statue she does not move, but as a saint in heaven she can intercede with God on behalf of the worshipper.

ROMEO   Then move not while my prayer's effect I take.
          [*He kisses her.*]
      Thus from my lips, by thine, my sin is purged.
JULIET   Then have my lips the sin that they have took.
220 ROMEO   Sin from my lips? Oh, trespass sweetly urged!⁹
      Give me my sin again.°   *back*
          [*He kisses her.*]
JULIET   You kiss by th' book.¹
NURSE   Madam, your mother craves a word with you.
          [*JULIET goes to speak with CAPULET'S WIFE.*]
ROMEO [*to* NURSE]   What is her mother?
NURSE   Marry, bachelor,°   *young man*
      Her mother is the lady of the house,
225 And a good lady, and a wise and virtuous.
      I nursed her daughter that you talked withal.°   *with*
      I tell you, he that can lay hold of her
      Shall have the chinks.°   *plenty of coins*
ROMEO [*aside*]   Is she a Capulet?
      Oh, dear account!° My life is my foe's debt.²   *costly reckoning*
230 BENVOLIO   Away! Begone! The sport is at the best.
ROMEO   Ay, so I fear; the more is my unrest.
          [*The Masquers prepare to depart.*]
CAPULET   Nay, gentlemen, prepare not to be gone!
      We have a trifling foolish banquet towards.³
          [*They whisper in his ear.*]
      Is it e'en so? Why, then I thank you all;
235 I thank you, honest gentlemen. Good night!
      —More torches here! —Come on, then: let's to bed.
      —Ah, sirrah, by my fay,° it waxes late!   *faith*
      I'll to my rest.
              [*Exeunt* CAPULET, CAPULET'S WIFE, *and* CAPULET'S
                COUSIN, *and* SERVINGMAN; *all others move toward
                the doors, and exeunt;* JULIET *and* NURSE *remain.*]
JULIET   Come hither, Nurse. What is yond gentleman?
240 NURSE   The son and heir of old Tiberio.
JULIET   What's he that now is going out of door?
NURSE   Marry, that, I think, be young Petruccio.
JULIET   What's he that follows here that would not dance?
NURSE   I know not.
JULIET   Go ask his name.   [*Exit* NURSE.]
245   If he be married,
      My grave is like° to be my wedding-bed.   *likely*
          [*Enter* NURSE.]
NURSE   His name is Romeo, and a Montague,
      The only son of your great enemy.
JULIET   My only love sprung from my only hate!
250 Too early seen unknown, and known too late!
      Prodigious° birth of love it is to me   *Monstrous; ominous*
      That I must love a loathèd enemy.
NURSE   What's tis?° What's tis?   *this (dialect pronunciation)*

---

9. Sweetly argued that the first kiss was a transgression, and sweetly advocated that the transgression of
a second kiss is needed to take away the sin of the
first.

1. According to the rules; implies "proficiently,"
"politely," or "with poetic flatteries."
2. A debt owing to my foe; in the power of my foe.
3. A paltry dessert coming.

JULIET   A rhyme I learned even now
 Of one I danced withal.
   One calls within, "Juliet!"
NURSE   Anon,° anon!   *Right away*
255 Come, let's away; the strangers all are gone. *Exeunt.*

2.0

 [*Enter* CHORUS.]
CHORUS Now old° desire doth in his deathbed lie, *Romeo's former*
 And young affection gapes° to be his heir;   *longs*
 That fair for which love groaned for and would die,
 With tender Juliet matched,° is now not fair.   *compared*
5 Now Romeo is beloved and loves again,° *in return; once more*
 Alike bewitchèd by the charm of looks;[1]
 But to his foe supposed° he must complain,[2]   *presumed*
 And she steal love's sweet bait from fearful° hooks. *fearsome*
 Being held a foe, he may not have access
10 To breathe such vows as lovers use° to swear, *are accustomed*
 And she as much in love, her means much less
 To meet her new belovèd anywhere.
 But passion lends them power, time means, to meet,
 Temp'ring extremities° with extreme sweet. [*Exit.*] *Mitigating dangers*

2.1 (Q1 Scene 5)

 Enter ROMEO *alone.*[1]
ROMEO Can I go forward when my heart is here?
 Turn back, dull earth,[2] and find thy center[3] out.
 [*He withdraws.*]
 Enter BENVOLIO *with* MERCUTIO.
BENVOLIO Romeo! My cousin Romeo! Romeo!
MERCUTIO He is wise and, on my life, hath stol'n him° home *himself*
 to bed.
5 BENVOLIO He ran this way, and leapt this orchard wall.
 Call, good Mercutio.
MERCUTIO   Nay, I'll conjure,° too. *summon as a spirit*
 Romeo! Humors![4] Madman! Passion! Lover!
 Appear thou in the likeness of a sigh;
 Speak but one rhyme, and I am satisfied;
10 Cry but "Ay me!"; pronounce but "love" and "dove";
 Speak to my gossip° Venus one fair word,   *crony*
 One nickname for her purblind° son and heir, *dim-sighted; blind*
 Young Abraham Cupid,[5] he that shot so true
 When King Cophetua loved the beggar maid.[6]
15 —He heareth not, he stirreth not, he moveth not:

2.0
1. Appearances; desirous glances.
2. Conventionally, make lovesick speeches.
2.1 Location: Outside Capulet's house.
1. The main stage represents the area outside the wall of Capulet's orchard and then the inside of the orchard below the window of Juliet's room. Romeo is imagined to leap over the garden wall when he withdraws at line 2.
2. Romeo's flesh, drawing on two traditional views of the human body: animated dust or clay, and a "microcosm," or little world, which mirrors the order of the

universe. Earth was the most sluggish and immobile element.
3. The point in the earth toward which everything falls; or Romeo's heart (metaphorically, Juliet).
4. Pure moods, not mixed together to form an even "temper."
5. Cupid, as Mercutio's nickname suggests, is at once a young boy and a patriarch, the oldest of the gods.
6. The story of a king who falls in love with a beggar and makes her his queen was the subject of a popular ballad.

The ape[7] is dead, and I must conjure him.
—I conjure thee by Rosaline's bright eyes,
By her high forehead and her scarlet lip,
By her fine foot, straight leg, and quivering thigh,
20 And the demesnes° that there adjacent lie,   *estates*
That in thy likeness thou appear to us!
BENVOLIO   An if he hear thee, thou wilt anger him.
MERCUTIO   This cannot anger him. 'Twould anger him
To raise a spirit[8] in his mistress' circle
25 Of some strange° nature, letting it there stand   *other person's*
Till she had laid it and conjured it down:
That were some spite. My invocation
Is fair and honest in his mistress' name;
I conjure only but to raise up him.
30 BENVOLIO   Come, he hath hid himself among these trees
To be consorted° with the humorous[9] night.   *in company*
Blind is his love, and best befits the dark.
MERCUTIO   If love be blind, love cannot hit the mark.°   *target; vulva*
Now will he sit under a medlar[1] tree
35 And wish his mistress were that kind of fruit
As maids call medlars when they laugh alone.
—O Romeo, that she were—oh, that she were—
An open-arse,° thou a popp'rin' pear![2]   *medlar*
Romeo, good night! —I'll to my truckle bed;[3]
40 This field bed[4] is too cold for me to sleep.
Come: shall we go?
BENVOLIO   Go, then; for 'tis in vain
To seek him here that means not to be found.
                    Exeunt [BENVOLIO *and* MERCUTIO].
             [ROMEO *comes forward.*]
ROMEO   He jests at scars that never felt a wound[5]—
But soft,° what light through yonder window breaks?   *wait; hush*
45 It is the East, and Juliet is the sun.
Arise, fair sun, and kill the envious moon,[6]
Who is already sick and pale with grief
That thou, her maid, art far more fair than she.
Be not her maid, since she is envious;
50 Her vestal° livery is but sick and green,[7]   *virginal*
And none but fools do wear it. Cast it off.
             [*Enter* JULIET *above.*]
It is my lady—oh, it is my love—
Oh, that she knew she were!
She speaks, yet she says nothing. What of that?
55 Her eye discourses; I will answer it.
I am too bold; 'tis not to me she speaks.

---

7. Foolish creature (a disrespectful endearment), or alluding to a magician's trick of "reviving" an ape that had been trained to play dead.
8. A word for "semen"; the entire speech is filled with obscene wordplay.
9. Damp; melancholy.
1. A fruit thought to resemble the female sex organs or the anus, with a play on "meddle" in the sense "have sexual intercourse with."
2. A pear from Poperinghe in Flanders, punning on "popper-in" or "pop her in."
3. Small bed, often for a child, that was stored under

a larger one.
4. A lying place in the open, and a soldier's portable bed.
5. Rhymes with "found." This line precedes a scene change in most editions, although the location remains the same if both the inside and the outside of the orchard are supposed to be visible onstage.
6. Emblem of Diana, goddess of chastity.
7. Unfulfilled sexual desire was thought to cause green sickness (anemia) in adolescent girls; also alluding to the moon's pallor.

Two of the fairest stars in all the heaven,
Having some business, do entreat her eyes
To twinkle in their spheres[8] till they return.
60 What if her eyes were there, they in her head?
The brightness of her cheek would shame those stars
As daylight doth a lamp; her eye in heaven
Would through the airy region° stream so bright   *ethereal sky*
That birds would sing and think it were not night.
65 See how she leans her cheek upon her hand—
Oh, that I were a glove upon that hand,
That I might touch that cheek!
JULIET   Ay me!
ROMEO [*aside*]   She speaks.
Oh, speak again, bright angel, for thou art
As glorious to this night, being o'er my head,
70 As is a wingèd messenger° of heaven   *angel*
Unto the white upturnèd[9] wond'ring eyes
Of mortals that fall back to gaze[1] on him
When he bestrides the lazy puffing clouds
And sails upon the bosom of the air.
75 JULIET   O Romeo, Romeo, wherefore° art thou Romeo?   *why*
Deny thy father and refuse thy name;
Or, if thou wilt not, be but sworn my love,
And I'll no longer be a Capulet.
ROMEO [*aside*]   Shall I hear more, or shall I speak at this?
80 JULIET   'Tis but thy name that is my enemy;
Thou art thyself, though° not a Montague.   *even if*
What's "Montague"? It is nor hand, nor foot,
Nor arm, nor face, nor any other part
Belonging to a man. Oh, be some other name!
85 What's in a name? That which we call a rose
By any other word would smell as sweet;
So Romeo would, were he not Romeo called,
Retain that dear perfection which he owes°   *owns*
Without that title. Romeo, doff° thy name,   *shed*
90 And, for thy name, which is no part of thee,
Take all myself.
ROMEO   I take thee at thy word.[2]
Call me but "love," and I'll be new baptized:[3]
Henceforth I never will be Romeo.
JULIET   What man art thou that, thus bescreened in night,
So stumblest on my counsel?°   *private thoughts*
95 ROMEO   By a name
I know not how to tell thee who I am.
My name, dear saint, is hateful to myself
Because it is an enemy to thee;
Had I it written, I would tear the word.
100 JULIET   My ears have yet not drunk a hundred words
Of thy tongue's uttering, yet I know the sound.
Art thou not Romeo, and a Montague?

---

8. In Ptolemaic astrology, crystalline spheres around the earth that carried the heavenly bodies in their rotations.
9. Turned up, revealing the whites at the bottoms.

1. Fall backward in gazing.
2. At face value; as you have asked me to.
3. Given a new name; born into a new persona.

ROMEO   Neither, fair maid, if either thee dislike.°   *displeases you*
JULIET   How camest thou hither, tell me—and wherefore?
105   The orchard walls are high and hard to climb,
    And the place death, considering who thou art,
    If any of my kinsmen find thee here.
ROMEO   With love's light wings did I o'erperch° these walls,   *fly over*
    For stony limits cannot hold love out,
110   And what love can do, that dares love attempt;
    Therefore thy kinsmen are no stop° to me.   *obstacle*
JULIET   If they do see thee, they will murder thee.
ROMEO   Alack, there lies more peril in thine eye
    Than twenty of their swords. Look thou but sweet,
115   And I am proof against° their enmity.   *impervious to*
JULIET   I would not for the world they saw thee here.
ROMEO   I have night's cloak to hide me from their eyes,
    And, but° thou love me, let them find me here: *unless*
    My life were better ended by their hate
120   Than death proroguèd,° wanting of° thy love.   *deferred / lacking*
JULIET   By whose direction found'st thou out this place?
ROMEO   By love, that first did prompt me to inquire.
    He lent me counsel, and I lent him eyes.
    I am no pilot, yet wert thou as far
125   As that vast shore washed with the farthest sea,
    I should adventure° for such merchandise.   *voyage*
JULIET   Thou knowest the mask of night is on my face,
    Else would a maiden blush bepaint my cheek
    For that which thou hast heard me speak tonight.
130   Fain° would I dwell on form°—fain, fain deny   *Gladly / propriety*
    What I have spoke—but farewell, compliment.°   *polite convention*
    Dost thou love me? I know thou wilt say "Ay,"
    And I will take thy word; yet, if thou swear'st,
    Thou mayst prove false. At lovers' perjuries
135   They say Jove laughs. O gentle Romeo,
    If thou dost love, pronounce° it faithfully,   *utter*
    Or if thou thinkest I am too quickly won,
    I'll frown and be perverse° and say thee nay   *contrary*
    So thou wilt woo—but else° not for the world.   *otherwise*
140   In truth, fair Montague, I am too fond,°   *infatuated*
    And therefore thou mayst think my behavior light.°   *loose*
    But trust me, gentleman, I'll prove more true
    Than those that have the coying° to be strange.°   *coyness / distant*
    I should have been more strange, I must confess,
145   But that thou overheard'st, ere I was ware,°   *aware*
    My true-love passion. Therefore pardon me,
    And not° impute this yielding to light love,   *do not*
    Which the dark night hath so discoverèd.°   *revealed*
ROMEO   Lady, by yonder blessèd moon I vow,
150   That tips with silver all these fruit-tree tops—
JULIET   Oh, swear not by the moon, th'inconstant moon
    That monthly changes in her circled orb,°   *orbital sphere*
    Lest that thy love prove likewise variable.
ROMEO   What shall I swear by?
JULIET   Do not swear at all,
155   Or, if thou wilt, swear by thy gracious self,

Which is the god of my idolatry,[4]
And I'll believe thee.

ROMEO　　　　　　If my heart's dear love—

JULIET　Well, do not swear. Although I joy in thee,
I have no joy of this contract° tonight;　　　　　　　　　　　*exchange of vows*
160　It is too rash, too unadvised,° too sudden,　　　　　　　　　*undeliberated*
Too like the lightning which doth cease to be
Ere one can say, "It lightens." Sweet, good night.
This bud of love by summer's ripening breath
May prove a beauteous flower when next we meet.
165　Good night, good night; as sweet repose and rest
Come to thy heart as that within my breast.

ROMEO　Oh, wilt thou leave me so unsatisfied?

JULIET　What satisfaction canst thou have tonight?

ROMEO　Th'exchange of thy love's faithful vow for mine.

170　JULIET　I gave thee mine before thou didst request it,
And yet I would it were° to give again.　　　　　　　　　　*were available*

ROMEO　Wouldst thou withdraw it? For what purpose, love?

JULIET　But to be frank° and give it thee again;　　　　　　　*generous; honest*
And yet I wish but for the thing I have.
175　My bounty is as boundless as the sea,
My love as deep; the more I give to thee,
The more I have, for both are infinite.
　　　　　[NURSE *calls within.*]
I hear some noise within! Dear love, adieu.
—Anon,° good Nurse! —Sweet Montague, be true.　　　　*One moment*
180　Stay but a little. I will come again.　　　　　　　[*Exit* JULIET.]

ROMEO　O blessèd, blessèd night! I am afeared,
Being in night, all this is but a dream,
Too flattering-sweet to be substantial.
　　　　　[*Enter* JULIET *above.*]

JULIET　Three words, dear Romeo, and good night indeed.
185　If that thy bent of love be honorable,
Thy purpose marriage, send me word tomorrow,
By one that I'll procure to come to thee,
Where and what time thou wilt perform the rite,
And all my fortunes at thy foot I'll lay,
190　And follow thee, my lord, throughout the world.

NURSE [*within*]　Madam!

JULIET　I come; anon! —But if thou meanest not well,
I do beseech thee—

NURSE [*within*]　　　　Madam!

JULIET　　　　　　By and by! I come!
—To cease thy strife,° and leave me to my grief.　　　　　*striving*
Tomorrow will I send.

195　ROMEO　　　　So thrive my soul.[5]

JULIET　A thousand times good night.　　　　　　　　[*Exit.*]

ROMEO　A thousand times the worse to want° thy light.　　　*lack*
Love goes toward love as schoolboys from their books,
But love from love toward school with heavy looks.
　　　　　Enter JULIET *again.*

---

4. Not only was loving a man more than God idolatrous, but so was swearing oaths by anything other
than God.
5. On peril of damnation.

200 JULIET Hist,° Romeo, hist! —Oh, for a falconer's voice (falconer's call)
     To lure this tercel-gentle[6] back again.
     Bondage[7] is hoarse and may not speak aloud,
     Else would I tear° the cave where Echo[8] lies split with cries
     And make her airy tongue more hoarse than mine
205 With repetition of my "Romeo."
     ROMEO It is my soul that calls upon my name.
     How silver-sweet sound lovers' tongues by night,
     Like softest music to attending ears.
     JULIET Romeo!
     ROMEO   Mine eyas?° young hawk
     JULIET   What o'clock tomorrow
     Shall I send to thee?
210 ROMEO   By the hour of nine.
     JULIET I will not fail. 'Tis twenty year till then.
     I have forgot why I did call thee back.
     ROMEO Let me stand here till thou remember it.
     JULIET I shall forget to have thee still° stand there, always
215 Rememb'ring how I love thy company.
     ROMEO And I'll still stay to have thee still forget,
     Forgetting any other home but this.
     JULIET 'Tis almost morning. I would have thee gone,
     And yet no farther than a wanton's° bird, spoiled child's
220 That lets it hop a little from his hand,
     Like a poor prisoner in his twisted gyves,° fetters
     And with a silken thread plucks it back again,
     So loving-jealous of his liberty.
     ROMEO I would° I were thy bird. wish
     JULIET   Sweet, so would I—
225 Yet I should kill thee with much cherishing.
     Good night, good night. Parting is such sweet sorrow
     That I shall say "good night" till it be morrow.
     ROMEO Sleep dwell upon thine eyes, peace in thy breast;
     Would I were sleep and peace, so sweet to rest.
                              [*Exit* JULIET.]
230 Hence will I to my ghostly° friar's close° cell spiritual / small; private
     His help to crave and my dear hap° to tell. *Exit*. fortune

2.2 (Q1 Scene 6)
Enter FRIAR LAURENCE *alone, with a basket.*

     FRIAR LAURENCE The gray°-eyed morn smiles on the pale blue
        frowning night,
     Check'ring the eastern clouds with streaks of light,
     And fleckled° darkness like a drunkard reels dappled
     From forth° day's path and Titan's[1] burning wheels.[2] Out of
5   Now ere the sun advance° his burning eye brings up

---

6. A male peregrine falcon. Literally, a noble ("gentle") hawk.
7. Confinement within her family's home; duty owed her family.
8. In classical legend, a woman who, scorned by Narcissus, wasted away with grief until only a voice remained to haunt empty caves.
2.2 Location: A street in Verona.

1. Helios, a classical sun god, was descended from the Titans. He traveled across the sky in a chariot.
2. TEXTUAL COMMENT In Q2, these four lines (2.2.1–4) appear twice, once spoken by Romeo at the end of the previous scene and again by Friar Laurence here, a textual redundancy that requires editorial intervention. See Digital Edition TC 8 (Second Quarto edited text).

The day to cheer and night's dank dew to dry,
I must upfill this osier cage° of ours   willow basket
With baleful weeds and precious-juicèd flowers.
The earth that's nature's mother is her tomb;
10   What is her burying grave, that is her womb,
And from her womb children of divers° kind   several; varied
We sucking on her natural bosom find:
Many for many virtues° excellent,   healthful properties
None but for some,³ and yet all different.
15   Oh, mickle° is the powerful grace° that lies   great / divine beneficence
In plants, herbs, stones, and their true qualities;
For naught° so vile that on the earth doth live   nothing is
But to the earth some special good doth give;
Nor aught so good but, strained° from that fair use,   twisted
20   Revolts from true birth, stumbling on abuse.⁴
Virtue itself turns vice, being misapplied,
And vice sometime by action dignified.
        Enter ROMEO.
Within the infant rind of this weak flower
Poison hath residence and medicine power:
25   For this, being smelled, with that part° cheers each part;°   act / bodily member
Being tasted, stays all senses with the heart.⁵
Two such opposèd kings encamp them still°   always
In man as well as herbs—grace and rude will—
And, where the worser is predominant,
30   Full soon the canker° death eats up that plant.   grub; cancer
ROMEO   Good morrow, Father.
FRIAR LAURENCE   *Benedicite.*°   God bless you (Latin)
What early tongue so sweet saluteth me?
Young son, it argues a distempered° head   disturbed
So soon to bid good morrow to thy bed.
35   Care keeps his watch in every old man's eye,
And, where care lodges, sleep will never lie;
But where unbruisèd° youth with unstuffed° brain   fresh / unanxious
Doth couch his limbs, there golden sleep doth reign.
Therefore thy earliness doth me assure
40   Thou art uproused with some distemp'rature—
Or, if not so, then here I hit it right:
Our Romeo hath not been in bed tonight.
ROMEO   That last is true; the sweeter rest was mine.
FRIAR LAURENCE   God pardon sin! Wast thou with Rosaline?
45   ROMEO   With Rosaline, my ghostly Father? No,
I have forgot that name and that name's woe.
FRIAR LAURENCE   That's my good son. But where hast thou
        been, then?
ROMEO   I'll tell thee ere thou ask it me again.
I have been feasting with mine enemy,
50   Where on a sudden one hath wounded me
That's by me wounded; both our remedies
Within thy help and holy physic° lies.   medicine
I bear no hatred, blessèd man, for, lo,

---

3. None that is not excellent for some use.
4. Turns from its intended benefits if it happens to
be misused.

5. *stays . . . heart*: paralyzes the heart, along with all
the senses.

My intercession° likewise steads° my foe.   *request / benefits*
55 FRIAR LAURENCE   Be plain, good son, and homely° in thy drift;   *direct*
Riddling confession finds but riddling shrift.°   *absolution*
ROMEO   Then plainly know my heart's dear love is set
On the fair daughter of rich Capulet.
As mine on hers, so hers is set on mine,
60 And all combined, save what thou must combine
By holy marriage. When, and where, and how
We met, we wooed, and made exchange of vow,
I'll tell thee as we pass; but this I pray,
That thou consent to marry us today.
65 FRIAR LAURENCE   Holy Saint Francis, what a change is here!
Is Rosaline, that thou didst love so dear,
So soon forsaken? Young men's love, then, lies
Not truly in their hearts but in their eyes.
Jesu Maria, what a deal of brine
70 Hath washed thy sallow° cheeks for Rosaline!   *yellowed*
How much salt water thrown away in waste
To season° love that of it doth not taste!   *preserve; flavor*
The sun not yet thy sighs[6] from heaven clears,
Thy old° groans yet ringing in mine ancient ears;   *former*
75 Lo, here upon thy cheek the stain doth sit
Of an old tear that is not washed off yet.
If ere thou wast thyself and these woes thine,
Thou and these woes were all for Rosaline—
And art thou changed? Pronounce this sentence,° then: *maxim; verdict*
80 Women may fall when there's no strength in men.
ROMEO   Thou chid'st me oft for loving Rosaline—
FRIAR LAURENCE   For doting, not for loving, pupil mine.
ROMEO   And bad'st me bury love.
FRIAR LAURENCE   Not in a grave
To lay one in, another out to have.
85 ROMEO   I pray thee, chide me not. Her I love now
Doth grace for grace and love for love allow;
The other did not so.
FRIAR LAURENCE   Oh, she knew well
Thy love did read by rote, that could not spell.[7]
But come, young waverer, come, go with me.
90 In one respect I'll thy assistant be,
For this alliance may so happy prove
To turn your households' rancor to pure love.
ROMEO   Oh, let us hence; I stand° on sudden haste.   *depend; insist*
FRIAR LAURENCE   Wisely and slow; they stumble that run fast.
Exeunt.

2.3 (Q1 Scene 7)
Enter BENVOLIO *and* MERCUTIO.

MERCUTIO   Where the devil should this Romeo be? Came he
not home tonight?°   *last night*

---

6. The mist Romeo's exhalations produced.
7. *did read . . . spell:* did recite the memorized
phrases of love poetry, without understanding or
meaning them.
2.3 Location: Scene continues.

BENVOLIO Not to his father's; I spoke with his man.

MERCUTIO Why, that same pale,° hard-hearted wench, that   *fair-skinned; frigid*
Rosaline,

5   Torments him so that he will sure run mad.

BENVOLIO Tybalt, the kinsman to old Capulet,
Hath sent a letter to his father's house.

MERCUTIO A challenge, on my life.

BENVOLIO Romeo will answer° it.   *accept*

10   MERCUTIO Any man that can write may answer a letter.

BENVOLIO Nay, he will answer the letter's master how he
dares, being dared.

MERCUTIO Alas, poor Romeo, he is already dead—stabbed with
a white wench's black eye, run through the ear with a love

15   song, the very pin[1] of his heart cleft with the blind bow-boy's
butt-shaft[2]—and is he a man to encounter Tybalt?

BENVOLIO Why, what is Tybalt?

MERCUTIO More than Prince of Cats.[3] Oh, he's the coura-
geous captain of compliments!° He fights as you sing prick-   *formalities of dueling*

20   song;[4] keeps time, distance,[5] and proportion;° he rests his   *harmony; form*
minim rests,[6] one, two—and the third in your bosom; the
very butcher of a silk button;[7] a duelist, a duelist; a gentleman of the very first house, of the first and second cause[8]—
ah, the immortal *passata,* the *punta riversa,* the *hai!*[9]

25   BENVOLIO The what?

MERCUTIO The pox of° such antic,° lisping, affecting° fanta-   *on / grotesque / affected*
sies,° these new tuners of accent.[1] "By Jesu, a very good   *bizarrely mannered men*
blade, a very tall° man, a very good whore!" Why,° is not   *valiant / Why, now*
this a lamentable thing, grandsire, that we should be thus

30   afflicted with these strange[2] flies, these fashionmongers,
these "pardon-me's,"[3] who stand so much on the new form
that they cannot sit at ease on the old bench?[4] Oh, their
bones, their bones![5]

Enter ROMEO.

BENVOLIO Here comes Romeo! Here comes Romeo!

35   MERCUTIO Without his roe, like a dried herring.[6] O flesh,
flesh, how art thou fishified![7] Now is he for the numbers°   *verses*

---

1. Peg in the center of an archery target.
2. Blunt practice arrow, fit for children and hence for Cupid.
3. Called Tybalt or Tibert in medieval stories of Rey-nard the fox. "Catso," from the Italian word for "penis," was also a slang term for a rogue.
4. Sung from sheet music and thus more precise and invariable than extempore or remembered music.
5. Musical intervals between notes; also, a set space to be kept between combatants.
6. Short musical rests, referring to the brief strategic pauses in a duel.
7. Alluding to the boast of an Italian fencing master in London that he could "hit any Englishman with a thrust upon any button."
8. *gentleman . . . cause:* superior practitioner of tak-ing up quarrels as duels. *first house:* the best fencing school. *cause:* a reason that according to the eti-quette of fencing would require an honorable gentle-man to seek a duel.
9. Italian fencing terms for, respectively, a lunging

sword thrust, backhanded thrust, and thrust that reaches through.
1. These faddishly novel speakers, such as those importing foreign phrases. A typical Renaissance English satire, here seemingly unaffected by the fact that Italian is the native tongue of Verona.
2. Newfangled; foreign.
3. *pardon-me's:* the fastidiously mannered, affecting the French *pardonnez-moi.*
4. *who . . . bench:* as if both Mercutio and Benvolio were elderly ("grandsire"), viewing the decline of the young. *stand:* insist. *form:* etiquette; fashion; bench.
5. *Oh . . . bones:* Aching on the austere furniture of their predecessors; infected with the "bone disease," syphilis.
6. Emaciated, since the roe is removed in curing. This leaves Romeo's name a mournful wail, "Me, O." He is also missing his roe deer (female, named Rosaline).
7. Gone pale and limp, turned into a herring. Fish, thought weak and relatively unnourishing, was the substitute for "flesh" (meat) during fasts.

that Petrarch[8] flowed in; Laura to° his lady was a kitchen   *compared to*
wench—marry, she had a better love to berhyme her—Dido[9]
a dowdy, Cleopatra a gypsy,[1] Helen and Hero[2] hildings° and   *hussies*
40 harlots, Thisbe[3] a gray-eye° or so. But not to the purpose.[4]   *blue-eyed*
Signor Romeo, *bonjour*: there's a French salutation to your
French slop.° You gave us the counterfeit fairly last night.   *loose breeches*

ROMEO   Good morrow to you both. What counterfeit did I
give you?

45 MERCUTIO   The slip,[5] sir, the slip—can you not conceive?°   *understand*

ROMEO   Pardon, good Mercutio. My business was great, and
in such a case as mine, a man may strain° courtesy.   *nearly abandon*

MERCUTIO   That's as much as to say such a case as yours constrains a man to bow in the hams.[6]

50 ROMEO   Meaning to curtsy?[7]

MERCUTIO   Thou hast most kindly hit it.[8]

ROMEO   A most courteous exposition.

MERCUTIO   Nay, I am the very pink° of courtesy.   *nonpareil; carnation*

ROMEO   Pink for flower?°   *dianthus; vulva*

55 MERCUTIO   Right.

ROMEO   Why, then, is my pump° well flowered.[9]   *shoe; penis*

MERCUTIO   Sure wit! Follow me° this jest now till thou hast   *Chase; respond to*
worn out thy pump, that when the single° sole of it is worn,   *thin*
the jest may remain after the wearing, solely singular.°   *utterly unique*

60 ROMEO   Oh, single-soled° jest, solely° singular for the   *shoddy / only*
singleness!°   *foolishness*

MERCUTIO   Come between us, good Benvolio; my wits faints.[1]

ROMEO   Switch and spurs,[2] switch and spurs, or I'll cry a
match!°   *claim a victory*

65 MERCUTIO   Nay, if our wits run the wild goose chase,[3] I am
done; for thou hast more of the wild goose° in one of thy   *folly*
wits than I am sure I have in my whole five.° Was I with° you   *(five senses) / even with*
there for the goose?

ROMEO   Thou wast never with me for anything when thou
70 wast not there for the goose.[4]

MERCUTIO   I will bite thee by the ear[5] for that jest.

ROMEO   Nay, good goose, bite not![6]

MERCUTIO   Thy wit is very bitter sweeting;° it is a most sharp   *apple*
sauce.°   *mockery*

75 ROMEO   And is it not, then, well served in to a sweet goose?

MERCUTIO   Oh, here's a wit of cheverel° that stretches from   *kid leather*
an inch narrow to an ell broad![7]

---

8. Petrarch's sonnets addressed to Laura were the model for an English love-sonnet craze.
9. The beautiful queen of Carthage who fell in love with Aeneas but was deserted by him in Virgil's *Aeneid*.
1. A term of abuse. Gypsies were supposed to have come from Egypt, where Cleopatra was queen and lover of Julius Caesar and Mark Antony.
2. Helen's abduction by Paris initiated the Trojan War. Hero was Leander's lover in a tragic legend.
3. Beloved of Pyramus in a classical legend that parallels *Romeo and Juliet*. The young lovers, coming from hostile families, die as a result of a missed meeting and misinterpreted evidence.
4. *to the purpose*: of consequence.
5. Counterfeit coin. To "give the slip" is to steal off.

6. Playing on "business" as "sexual intercourse" and "case" as "vagina." Mercutio suggests that Romeo is sexually exhausted and cannot stand up straight.
7. Pronounced the same as "courtesy."
8. Most truly guessed it; most truly sexually penetrated it.
9. Pinked, or decoratively perforated.
1. Treating the exchange of wit as a duel.
2. Flog your wits to a full gallop; continue.
3. A cross-country horse race in which the leader chose the course and the rest had to follow.
4. Silliness; whore's company.
5. Usually suggesting affectionate nibbling.
6. A proverbial cry for mercy, here used ironically.
7. That spreads itself very thin (an ell was 45 inches).

ROMEO I stretch it out for that word "broad," which, added to
the goose, proves thee far and wide a broad goose.[8]

80 MERCUTIO Why, is not this better now than groaning for love?
Now art thou sociable; now art thou Romeo; now art thou
what thou art by art° as well as by nature, for this driveling   *learning*
love is like a great natural° that runs lolling up and down to   *idiot*
hide his bauble[9] in a hole.

85 BENVOLIO Stop there! Stop there!

MERCUTIO Thou desirest me to stop in[1] my tale° against the hair.[2]   *story; penis ("tail")*

BENVOLIO Thou wouldst else have made thy tale large.

MERCUTIO Oh, thou art deceived! I would have made it short,
for I was come to the whole depth of my tale, and meant

90 indeed to occupy the argument° no longer.   *topic*

Enter NURSE *and her man*[, PETER].

ROMEO Here's goodly gear![3] A sail! A sail![4]

MERCUTIO Two, two: a shirt° and a smock.°   *man / woman*

NURSE Peter.

PETER Anon.°   *At your service*

95 NURSE My fan, Peter.

MERCUTIO Good Peter, to hide her face, for her fan's the
fairer face.

NURSE God ye° good morrow,° gentlemen.   *give you / morning*

MERCUTIO God ye good e'en,° fair gentlewoman.   *afternoon*

100 NURSE Is it good e'en?

MERCUTIO 'Tis no less, I tell ye, for the bawdy hand of the
dial is now upon the prick° of noon.   *mark; penis*

NURSE Out upon you![5] What° a man are you?   *What sort of*

ROMEO One, gentlewoman, that God hath made himself to

105 mar.[6]

NURSE By my troth, it is well said. "For himself to mar,"
quoth 'a?° —Gentlemen, can any of you tell me where I   *he*
may find the young Romeo?

ROMEO I can tell you, but young Romeo will be older when

110 you have found him than he was when you sought him. I am
the youngest of that name, for fault° of a worse.   *lack*

NURSE You say well.

MERCUTIO Yea, is the worst well? Very well took, i'faith; wisely,
wisely.

115 NURSE [*to* ROMEO] If you be he, sir, I desire some confidence
with you.

BENVOLIO She will indite[7] him to some supper.

MERCUTIO A bawd, a bawd, a bawd! So, ho![8]

ROMEO What hast thou found?°   *spotted; figured out*

120 MERCUTIO No hare,° sir, unless a hare, sir, in a lenten pie[9] that   *prostitute*

8. A gross idiot; a licentious fellow; a goose fattened
for the table.
9. *that ... bauble:* who runs to cover up a jester's
wand, grotesquely carved at one end; "bauble" also
suggests penis.
1. Cease; stuff in.
2. Against the grain; against the pubic hair.
3. Spoken ironically of Mercutio's witticisms or the
Nurse's voluminous appearance.
4. A sailor's cry upon sighting another ship.
5. An expression of indignation.
6. *One ... mar:* combines two proverbial expres-

sions. "It is his to make or mar" suggests that Mercutio has the free will to determine his own character.
"He is a man of God's making" places the blame for
Mercutio's character on God.
7. Deliberately substituted for "invite," to mock the
Nurse's erroneous use of "confidence" for "conference" in the line above.
8. The cry of a hunter who has spotted his quarry.
9. Meat illicitly eaten during Lent by disguising it in
a pie, just as the Nurse's unattractiveness hides whatever promiscuity she may practice.

is something stale and hoar ere it be spent.[1]
[*He walks by them and sings.*]
          An old hare hoar,
          And an old hare hoar
          Is very good meat in Lent;
125   But a hare that is hoar
          Is too much for a score[2]
          When it hoars° ere it be spent.   *turns moldy; whores*
Romeo, will you come to your father's? We'll to dinner thither.
ROMEO   I will follow you.
130 MERCUTIO   Farewell, ancient lady, farewell.
    [*Sings.*]   Lady, lady, lady![3]
               Exeunt [MERCUTIO *and* BENVOLIO].
NURSE   I pray you, sir, what saucy merchant° was this that   *commoner*
was so full of his ropery?°   *knavery*
ROMEO   A gentleman, Nurse, that loves to hear himself talk,
135 and will speak more in a minute than he will stand to° in a   *perform*
month.
NURSE   An 'a° speak anything against me, I'll take him down°   *If he / humble him*
an 'a were lustier[4] than he is, and twenty such jacks;° and, if   *scoundrels*
I cannot, I'll find those that shall. Scurvy knave! I am none
140 of his flirt-gills;° I am none of his skains mates.[5] [*She turns*   *loose women*
to PETER, *her man.*] And thou must stand by, too, and suffer
every knave to use me at his pleasure!
PETER   I saw no man use you at his pleasure; if I had, my
weapon should quickly have been out. I warrant you, I dare
145 draw as soon as another man if I see occasion in a good quarrel, and the law on my side.
NURSE   Now, afore God, I am so vexed that every part about
me quivers. Scurvy knave! [*to* ROMEO] Pray you, sir, a word;
and, as I told you, my young lady bid me inquire you out.
150 What she bid me say I will keep to myself; but first let me
tell ye, if ye should lead her in a fool's paradise, as they say,
it were a very gross° kind of behavior, as they say, for the   *outrageous*
gentlewoman is young, and therefore if you should deal
double° with her, truly it were an ill thing to be offered to   *falsely; forcefully*
155 any gentlewoman, and very weak° dealing.   *poor*
ROMEO   Nurse, commend me to thy lady and mistress. I pro-
test° unto thee—   *swear*
NURSE   Good heart—and i'faith I will tell her as much. Lord,
Lord, she will be a joyful woman!
160 ROMEO   What wilt thou tell her, Nurse? Thou dost not mark°   *pay attention to*
me.
NURSE   I will tell her, sir, that you do protest[6]—which, as I take
it, is a gentlemanlike offer.
ROMEO   Bid her devise some means to come to shrift this
     afternoon,
165 And there she shall, at Friar Laurence' cell,

---

1. Somewhat stale and moldy by the time the last of the rationed luxury is consumed.
2. Is too much to pay for.
3. Refrain to a ballad about a perfectly chaste woman, intended derisively.
4. Stronger; hornier.
5. Knife-wielding rogues.
6. The Nurse takes this as a marriage offer, probably confusing "protest" with "propose."

Be shrived° and married. [*He offers money.*] Here is for   *absolved after confession*
    thy pains.
NURSE   No, truly, sir, not a penny.
ROMEO   Go to—I say you shall.
NURSE   This afternoon, sir? Well, she shall be there.
170   ROMEO   And stay, good Nurse, behind the abbey wall.
    Within this hour my man shall be with thee
    And bring thee cords made like a tackled stair,°   *a knotted ladder*
    Which to the high topgallant[7] of my joy
    Must be my convoy° in the secret night.   *means of conveyance*
175   Farewell. Be trusty, and I'll quit° thy pains.   *repay*
    Farewell. Commend me to thy mistress.
NURSE   Now God in heaven bless thee! Hark you, sir.
ROMEO   What say'st thou, my dear Nurse?
NURSE   Is your man secret?° Did you ne'er hear say,   *discreet*
180   "Two may keep counsel, putting one away"?
ROMEO   Warrant thee, my man's as true as steel.
NURSE   Well, sir, my mistress is the sweetest lady. Lord, Lord,
    when 'twas a little prating thing— Oh, there is a nobleman
    in town, one Paris, that would fain lay knife aboard;[8] but she,
185   good soul, had as lief° see a toad, a very toad, as see him. I   *gladly*
    anger her sometimes, and tell her that Paris is the properer°   *more handsome*
    man; but, I'll warrant you, when I say so she looks as pale as
    any clout° in the versal° world. Doth not "rosemary"[9] and   *sheet / entire*
    "Romeo" begin both with a° letter?   *the same*
190   ROMEO   Ay, Nurse. What of that? Both with an "R."
NURSE   Ah, mocker, that's the dog's name![1] "R" is for the—no,
    I know it begins with some other letter; and she hath the
    prettiest sententious[2] of it—of you and rosemary—that it
    would do you good to hear it.
195   ROMEO   Commend me to thy lady.
NURSE   Ay, a thousand times. Peter!
PETER   Anon!
NURSE   Before,° and apace.°   *Exeunt.*   *Lead / quickly*

2.4 (Q1 Scene 8)

Enter JULIET.
JULIET   The clock struck nine when I did send the Nurse;
    In half an hour she promised to return.
    Perchance she cannot meet him— That's not so.
    Oh, she is lame! Love's heralds should be thoughts
5   Which ten times faster glides than the sun's beams,
    Driving back shadows over louring° hills.   *dark; threatening*
    Therefore do nimble-pinioned° doves draw Love;°   *winged / Venus*
    And therefore hath the wind-swift Cupid wings.
    Now is the sun upon the highmost hill°   *zenith*
10   Of this day's journey, and from nine till twelve
    Is three long hours, yet she is not come.
    Had she affections° and warm youthful blood,   *passions*

7. The highest platform on a mast, from which the topgallant sail was handled.
8. One claimed a place at dinner by laying one's personal knife on the table ("board").
9. A token of remembrance, between lovers and also of the dead.
1. "R"—the sound "arr"—was thought to resemble a dog's snarl.
2. Blunder for "sentences"; sayings.
2.4 Location: Capulet's orchard.

She would be as swift in motion as a ball;
My words would bandy° her to my sweet love,   *volley (as in tennis)*
15   And his to me.
But old folks: many feign° as they were dead,   *act*
Unwieldy, slow, heavy, and pale as lead.
          Enter NURSE [*and* PETER].
O God, she comes! O honey Nurse, what news?
Hast thou met with him? Send thy man away.
20   NURSE   Peter, stay° at the gate.   [*Exit* PETER.]   *wait*
JULIET   Now, good sweet Nurse— O Lord, why lookest thou
        sad?
Though news be sad, yet tell them merrily;
If good, thou shamest the music of sweet news
By playing it to me with so sour a face.
25   NURSE   I am a-weary; give me leave° a while.   *let me alone*
Fie, how my bones ache! What a jaunce° have I!   *trotting about*
JULIET   I would thou hadst my bones and I thy news.
Nay, come; I pray thee, speak. Good, good Nurse, speak.
NURSE   Jesu, what haste! Can you not stay a while?
30   Do you not see that I am out of breath?
JULIET   How art thou out of breath when thou hast breath
To say to me that thou art out of breath?
The excuse that thou dost make in this delay
Is longer than the tale thou dost excuse!
35   Is thy news good or bad? Answer to that—
Say either, and I'll stay° the circumstance.°   *wait for / full details*
Let me be satisfied: is't good or bad?
NURSE   Well, you have made a simple° choice. You know not   *foolish*
how to choose a man. Romeo? No, not he. Though his face
40   be better than any man's, yet his leg excels all men's; and for
a hand, and a foot, and a body, though they be not to be
talked on,° yet they are past compare. He is not the flower of   *worth mentioning*
courtesy, but I'll warrant him as gentle as a lamb. Go thy
ways,[1] wench; serve God. What, have you dined at home?
45   JULIET   No, no. But all this did I know before.
What says he of our marriage? What of that?
NURSE   Lord, how my head aches! What a head have I!
It beats as it would fall in twenty pieces.
My back!—O't' other side—ah, my back, my back![2]
50   Beshrew° your heart for sending me about   *Curse (mild oath)*
To catch my death with jauncing up and down.
JULIET   I'faith, I am sorry that thou art not well.
Sweet, sweet, sweet Nurse, tell me: what says my love?
NURSE   Your love says, like an honest gentleman,
55   And a courteous, and a kind, and a handsome,
And I warrant a virtuous— Where is your mother?
JULIET   Where is my mother? Why, she is within.
Where should she be? How oddly thou repliest:
"Your love says, like an honest° gentleman,   *honorable*
'Where is your mother?'"
60   NURSE   O God's Lady,° dear,   *Mary, Mother of God*

---

1. Off you go; do as you will do.
2. Perhaps the Nurse is giving Juliet directions to rub her back.

Are you so hot?° Marry, come up, I trow!³   *impatient; aroused*
Is this the poultice for my aching bones?
Henceforward do your messages yourself.
JULIET   Here's such a coil!° Come, what says Romeo?   *to-do*
65 NURSE   Have you got leave to go to shrift today?
JULIET   I have.
NURSE   Then hie° you hence to Friar Laurence' cell;   *hurry*
There stays a husband to make you a wife.
Now comes the wanton° blood up in your cheeks;   *fickle; lustful*
70 They'll be in scarlet straight° at any news.   *immediately*
Hie you to church. I must another way
To fetch a ladder by the which your love
Must climb a bird's nest soon when it is dark.
I am the drudge and toil in your delight,
75 But you shall bear the burden⁴ soon at night.
Go! I'll to dinner; hie you to the cell.
JULIET   Hie to high fortune! Honest Nurse, farewell.   *Exeunt.*

2.5 (Q1 Scene 9)
Enter FRIAR [LAURENCE] *and* ROMEO.
FRIAR LAURENCE   So smile the heavens upon this holy act
That after-hours with sorrow chide us not.
ROMEO   Amen, amen. But come what sorrow can,
It cannot countervail the exchange of joy
5 That one short minute gives me in her sight.
Do thou but close° our hands with holy words,   *join*
Then love-devouring death do what he dare—
It is enough I may but call her mine.
FRIAR LAURENCE   These violent° delights have violent ends   *sudden; intense*
10 And in their triumph die, like fire and powder¹
Which, as they kiss, consume. The sweetest honey
Is loathsome in his own deliciousness,
And in the taste confounds the appetite.²
Therefore love moderately: long love doth so;
15 Too swift arrives as tardy as too slow.
        Enter JULIET.
Here comes the lady. Oh, so light³ a foot
Will ne'er wear out the everlasting flint;⁴
A lover may bestride the gossamers°   *spiders' threads*
That idles in the wanton° summer air   *playful*
20 And yet not fall, so light is vanity.⁵
JULIET   Good even° to my ghostly° confessor.   *evening / spiritual*
FRIAR LAURENCE   Romeo shall thank thee, daughter, for us
   both.
        [ROMEO *kisses her.*]
JULIET   As much⁶ to him, else is his thanks too much.
        [JULIET *returns his kiss.*]
ROMEO   Ah, Juliet, if the measure° of thy joy   *measuring vessel*

---

3. *Marry . . . trow:* an expression of indignant or amused surprise and reproof.
4. Do the work; carry a lover; sing the theme of a duet, alluding to the sounds of lovemaking.
2.5 Location: Friar Laurence's cell.
1. Gunpowder. *triumph:* victory; celebration.
2. *The sweetest . . . appetite:* from the proverb "Too

much honey cloys the stomach." *his:* its. *confounds:* overwhelms.
3. Swift; dainty; free of care; sexually open.
4. Will never endure or subdue the hard road of life.
5. Temporary worldly pleasure.
6. An equal amount.

25   Be heaped like mine, and that thy skill be more
        To blazon° it, then sweeten with thy breath°   *describe; trumpet / speech*
        This neighbor air, and let rich music tongue
        Unfold the imagined° happiness that both   *unexpressed ideas of*
        Receive in either by this dear encounter.

30 JULIET   Conceit,° more rich in matter than in words,   *Imagination*
        Brags of his substance,[7] not of ornament.°   *rhetoric; form*
        They are but beggars that can count their worth,
        But my true love is grown to such excess,
        I cannot sum up sum of half my wealth.[8]

35 FRIAR LAURENCE   Come; come with me, and we will make short
            work.
        For, by your leaves, you shall not stay alone
        Till holy church incorporate two in one.[9]   [*Exeunt.*]

3.1 (Q1 Scene 10)

Enter MERCUTIO, BENVOLIO, [*Mercutio's Page,*] *and*
[*Montague's*] *Men.*

BENVOLIO   I pray thee, good Mercutio, let's retire.
    The day is hot, the Capels abroad,°   *about*
    And if we meet we shall not scape a brawl—
    For now, these hot days, is the mad blood stirring.

5   MERCUTIO   Thou art like one of these fellows that, when he
    enters the confines of a tavern, claps me° his sword upon the   *claps me = claps*
    table and says, "God send me no need of thee"—and, by
    the operation° of the second cup, draws him on the drawer[1]   *effect*
    when indeed there is no need.

10 BENVOLIO   Am I like such a fellow?

    MERCUTIO   Come, come, thou art as hot a jack° in thy mood   *rogue*
    as any in Italy, and as soon moved° to be moody,° and as   *provoked / angry*
    soon moody to be° moved.   *at being*

    BENVOLIO   And what to?

15 MERCUTIO   Nay, an there were two such, we should have none
    shortly, for one would kill the other. Thou—why, thou wilt
    quarrel with a man that hath a hair more or a hair less in his
    beard than thou hast. Thou wilt quarrel with a man for crack-
    ing nuts, having no other reason but because thou hast hazel
20 eyes. What eye but such an eye would spy out such a quarrel?
    Thy head is as full of quarrels as an egg is full of meat,° and   *foodstuff*
    yet thy head hath been beaten as addle° as an egg for quar-   *rotten; confused*
    reling. Thou hast quarreled with a man for coughing in the
    street, because he hath wakened thy dog that hath lain
25 asleep in the sun. Didst thou not fall out with a tailor for
    wearing his new doublet before Easter?[2] With another for
    tying his new shoes with old ribbon? And yet thou wilt tutor
    me from quarreling!

    BENVOLIO   An I were so apt to quarrel as thou art, any man
30 should buy the fee-simple[3] of my life for an hour and a
    quarter.

---

7. Wealth; content.
8. *I . . . wealth:* The amount is too large to be understood precisely.
9. Literally, put two into one body. Marriage mystically united man and woman in "one flesh" (Genesis
2:2).

3.1 Location: A street in Verona.
1. Draws his sword on the server.
2. New fashions came out at Easter, after the austere
penitence of Lent.
3. Outright possession of land, usually an inherited
right; here, the whole value of Benvolio's life.

MERCUTIO   The fee-simple? Oh, simple!°   *foolish*
   Enter TYBALT, PETRUCCIO, *and others*
   [*of Capulet's Men*].

BENVOLIO   By my head, here comes the Capulets.

MERCUTIO   By my heel, I care not.

35   TYBALT [*to* PETRUCCIO *and Capulets*]   Follow me close, for I will
   speak to them.
   [*to the Montagues*] Gentlemen, good e'en. A word with one
   of you.

MERCUTIO   And but one word with one of us? Couple it with
   something; make it a word and a blow.

TYBALT   You shall find me apt enough to that, sir, an you will
40   give me occasion.

MERCUTIO   Could you not take some occasion without giving?

TYBALT   Mercutio, thou consortest° with Romeo.   *associate*

MERCUTIO   "Consort"?° What, dost thou make us minstrels?   *Play in a band*
   An thou make minstrels of us, look to hear nothing but dis-
45   cords. Here's my fiddlestick;° here's that shall make you dance.   *(rapier)*
   Zounds!° "Consort"!   *By God's wounds*

BENVOLIO   We talk here in the public haunt° of men.   *gathering place*
   Either withdraw unto some private place,
   Or reason coldly° of your grievances,   *dispassionately*
50   Or else depart.° Here all eyes gaze on us.   *separate*

MERCUTIO   Men's eyes were made to look, and let them gaze.
   I will not budge for no man's pleasure, I.
      Enter ROMEO.

TYBALT   Well, peace be with you, sir; here comes my man.

MERCUTIO   But I'll be hanged, sir, if he wear your livery.[4]
55   Marry, go before to field, he'll be your follower;°   *servant; pursuer*
   Your worship in that sense may call him "man."

TYBALT   Romeo, the love I bear thee can afford
   No better term than this: thou art a villain.°   *base commoner; rogue*

ROMEO   Tybalt, the reason that I have to love thee
60   Doth much excuse the appertaining rage
   To[5] such a greeting. Villain am I none.
   Therefore, farewell. I see thou knowest me not.

TYBALT   Boy, this shall not excuse the injuries
   That thou hast done me; therefore turn and draw.

65   ROMEO   I do protest I never injuried thee,
   But love thee better than thou canst devise
   Till thou shalt know the reason of my love.
   And so, good Capulet—which name I tender°   *regard; love*
   As dearly as mine own—be satisfied.

70   MERCUTIO   Oh, calm, dishonorable, vile submission!
   Alla stoccata carries it away![6]
      [*He draws.*]
   Tybalt, you ratcatcher, will you walk?°   *withdraw to fight*

TYBALT   What wouldst thou have with me?

MERCUTIO   Good King of Cats, nothing but one of your nine
75   lives. That I mean to make bold withal° and, as you shall use   *be so bold as to take*
   me hereafter,[7] dry-beat° the rest of the eight. Will you pluck   *soundly thrash*

---

4. Mercutio obnoxiously mistakes Tybalt's "my man"   appropriate anger at.
for "personal servant."   6. The rapier thrust wins the day.
5. *Doth . . . To:* Permits me to put aside my otherwise   7. And, according to how you subsequently treat me.

your sword out of his pilcher° by the ears? Make haste, lest   *leather scabbard*
mine be about your ears ere it be out.

TYBALT [*drawing*] I am for you.

    [*They fight.*]

80 ROMEO   Gentle Mercutio, put thy rapier up!

MERCUTIO [*to* TYBALT]   Come, sir, your *passata!*°   *forward thrust*

ROMEO   Draw, Benvolio! Beat down their weapons.
Gentlemen, for shame, forbear this outrage.°   *criminal violence*
Tybalt! Mercutio! The Prince expressly hath
85 Forbid this bandying° in Verona streets.   *strife*
Hold, Tybalt! Good Mercutio—

    [TYBALT *under Romeo's arm thrusts* MERCUTIO *in.*]

PETRUCCIO   Away, Tybalt!

    [*Exeunt* TYBALT, PETRUCCIO, *and Capulet's Men.*]

MERCUTIO   I am hurt.
A plague o'both houses! I am sped.°   *finished*
Is he gone and hath nothing?

90 BENVOLIO   What, art thou hurt?

MERCUTIO   Ay, ay, a scratch, a scratch. Marry, 'tis enough.
Where is my page? —Go, villain: fetch a surgeon.

    [*Exit Page.*]

ROMEO   Courage, man; the hurt cannot be much.

MERCUTIO   No? 'Tis not so deep as a well, nor so wide as a
95 church door, but 'tis enough; 'twill serve. Ask for me tomorrow, and you shall find me a grave man: I am peppered,° I   *done for*
warrant, for this world. A plague o'both your houses! Zounds!
A dog, a rat, a mouse, a cat, to scratch a man to death—a
braggart, a rogue, a villain that fights by the book of arith-
100 metic.[8] Why the devil came you between us? I was hurt
under your arm.

ROMEO   I thought all for the best.

MERCUTIO   Help me into some house, Benvolio,
Or I shall faint. A plague o'both your houses!
105 They have made worms' meat of me;
I have it, and soundly, too. Your houses—

    Exeunt[9] [*all but* ROMEO].

ROMEO   This gentleman, the Prince's near ally,°   *relative*
My very° friend, hath got this mortal hurt   *true*
In my behalf, my reputation stained
110 With Tybalt's slander—Tybalt, that an hour
Hath been my cousin. O sweet Juliet,
Thy beauty hath made me effeminate,
And in my temper[1] softened valor's steel.

    Enter BENVOLIO.

BENVOLIO   O Romeo, Romeo, brave Mercutio is dead.
115 That gallant spirit hath aspired° the clouds,   *ascended to*
Which too untimely here did scorn the earth.

ROMEO   This day's black fate on more days doth depend;°   *hang over*
This but begins the woe others must end.

    [*Enter* TYBALT.]

---

8. By the numbers; according to a fencing manual.

9. PERFORMANCE COMMENT Directors have found widely differing ways to stage the duel scene and the death of Mercutio, with varying implications for the rest of the play. For more, see Digital Edition PC 4.

1. Emotional makeup, here suggesting the hardened character of a fighting man (*temper*: to harden steel). It was believed that too much time with or passion for women would cause a man to become effeminate.

BENVOLIO   Here comes the furious Tybalt back again.
120 ROMEO   He gan° in triumph, and Mercutio slain?   *going*
      Away to heaven, respective lenity,°   *respectful lenience*
      And fire and fury be my conduct° now!   *guide*
      —Now, Tybalt, take the "villain" back again
      That late thou gavest me, for Mercutio's soul
125   Is but a little way above our heads,
      Staying for thine to keep him company;
      Either thou, or I, or both, must go with him.
TYBALT   Thou, wretched boy, that didst consort° him here,   *accompany*
      Shalt with him hence.
ROMEO   This shall determine that.
      They fight; TYBALT *falls [and dies].*
130 BENVOLIO   Romeo, away; be gone!
      The citizens are up,° and Tybalt slain.   *up in arms*
      Stand not amazed;° the Prince will doom thee° death   *stupefied / sentence you to*
      If thou art taken. Hence! Be gone! Away!
ROMEO   Oh, I am fortune's fool.°   *dupe*
BENVOLIO   Why dost thou stay?
                                        Exit ROMEO.
      Enter CITIZENS.
135 CITIZEN   Which way ran he that killed Mercutio?
      Tybalt, that murderer—which way ran he?
BENVOLIO   There lies that Tybalt.
CITIZEN   Up, sir; go with me.
      I charge thee in the Prince's name obey.
            Enter PRINCE, *old* MONTAGUE, CAPULET[, MONTAGUE'S
            WIFE, CAPULET'S WIFE, *and Attendants*].
PRINCE   Where are the vile beginners of this fray?
140 BENVOLIO   O noble Prince, I can discover° all   *reveal*
      The unlucky manage° of this fatal brawl.   *handling*
      There lies the man, slain by young Romeo,
      That slew thy kinsman, brave Mercutio.
CAPULET'S WIFE   Tybalt, my cousin! O my brother's child!
145   O Prince, O cousin, husband! Oh, the blood is spilled
      Of my dear kinsman! Prince, as thou art true,
      For blood of ours shed blood of Montague.
      O cousin, cousin!
PRINCE   Benvolio, who began this bloody fray?
150 BENVOLIO   Tybalt here slain, whom Romeo's hand did slay—
      Romeo that spoke him° fair,° bid him bethink   *to him / courteously*
      How nice° the quarrel was, and urged withal°   *trivial / also*
      Your high displeasure. All this, utterèd
      With gentle breath, calm look, knees humbly bowed,
155   Could not take° truce with the unruly spleen°   *arrange / bitter mood*
      Of Tybalt, deaf to peace, but that he tilts
      With piercing steel at bold Mercutio's breast,
      Who, all as hot, turns deadly point to point,
      And, with a martial scorn, with one hand beats
160   Cold death aside,[2] and with the other sends
      It back to Tybalt, whose dexterity

---

2. *with . . . aside:* The two would have been fighting either with daggers in or cloaks rolled about their second
hand to ward off the other's weapon.

Retorts° it. Romeo he cries aloud,   *Returns*
"Hold, friends! Friends, part!" and, swifter than his tongue,
His agile arm beats down their fatal points,
165   And twixt them rushes—underneath whose arm
An envious° thrust from Tybalt hit the life   *A malicious*
Of stout° Mercutio. And then Tybalt fled—   *courageous*
But by and by comes back to Romeo,
Who had but newly entertained° revenge,   *considered*
170   And to't they go like lightning, for ere I
Could draw to part them was stout Tybalt slain
And, as he fell, did Romeo turn and fly.
This is the truth, or let Benvolio die.
CAPULET'S WIFE   He is a kinsman to the Montague:
175   Affection makes him false; he speaks not true.
Some twenty of them fought in this black strife,
And all those twenty could but kill one life.
I beg for justice—which thou, Prince, must give.
Romeo slew Tybalt; Romeo must not live.
180   PRINCE   Romeo slew him; he slew Mercutio;
Who now the price of his° dear blood doth owe?   *(Mercutio's)*
MONTAGUE   Not Romeo, Prince; he was Mercutio's friend.
His fault° concludes but what the law should end—   *offense*
The life of Tybalt.
PRINCE   And for that offense
185   Immediately we do exile him hence.
I have an interest in your hearts' proceeding;
My blood° for your rude brawls doth lie a-bleeding.   *kinsman*
But I'll amerce° you with so strong a fine   *penalize*
That you shall all repent the loss of mine:
190   It will be deaf to pleading and excuses.
Nor tears nor prayers shall purchase out° abuses;   *compensate for*
Therefore use none. Let Romeo hence in haste;
Else, when he is found, that hour is his last.
Bear hence this body, and attend our will.
195   Mercy but murders, pardoning those that kill.   *Exeunt.*

3.2 (Q1 Scene 11)

Enter JULIET *alone.*

JULIET   Gallop apace,° you fiery-footed steeds,   *quickly*
Towards Phoebus' lodging;[1] such a wagoner°   *charioteer*
As Phaëton[2] would whip you to the west,
And bring in cloudy night immediately.
5   Spread thy close° curtain, love-performing night,   *covering*
That runaways'[3] eyes may wink,° and Romeo   *close*
Leap to these arms, untalked of and unseen.
Lovers can see to do their amorous rites,
And by their own beauties; or, if love be blind,
10   It best agrees with night. Come, civil° night,   *solemn*
Thou sober-suited matron all in black,

3.2 Location: Capulet's house.
1. Under the world to the west, where the sun god
Phoebus Apollo was imagined to rest with his fiery
chariot at night.
2. The son of Apollo, who rashly attempted to steer

his father's chariot across the sky. To save the earth
from scorching, Jupiter struck him down with a lightning bolt.
3. Either the runaway horses of the sun or roving
and curious vagabonds.

And learn me how to lose a winning match,[4]
Played for a pair of stainless maidenhoods.
Hood my unmanned° blood, bating[5] in my cheeks, *untamed; virgin*
15   With thy black mantle, till strange° love grow bold; *shy*
Think true love acted simple° modesty. *mere; innocent*
Come, night; come, Romeo; come, thou day in night,
For thou wilt lie upon the wings of night
Whiter than new snow upon a raven's back.
20   Come, gentle night; come, loving, black-browed night,
Give me my Romeo; and, when I shall die,
Take him and cut him out in little stars,[6]
And he will make the face of heaven so fine
That all the world will be in love with night
25   And pay no worship to the garish sun.
Oh, I have bought the mansion of a love,
But not possessed it; and though I am sold,[7]
Not yet enjoyed. So tedious is this day
As is the night before some festival
30   To an impatient child that hath new robes
And may not wear them.
            Enter NURSE *with cords.*
                              Oh, here comes my nurse,
And she brings news, and every tongue that speaks
But Romeo's name speaks heavenly eloquence.
Now, Nurse, what news? What, hast thou there
The cords that Romeo bid thee fetch?
35   NURSE   Ay, ay, the cords.
JULIET   Ay me, what news? Why dost thou wring thy hands?
NURSE   Ah, welladay,° he's dead, he's dead, he's dead! *alas*
We are undone, lady; we are undone.
Alack the day—he's gone, he's killed, he's dead!
JULIET   Can heaven be so envious?° *spiteful; jealous*
40   NURSE   Romeo can,
Though heaven cannot. O Romeo, Romeo!
Whoever would have thought it? Romeo!
JULIET   What devil art thou that dost torment me thus?
This torture should be roared in dismal hell.
45   Hath Romeo slain himself? Say thou but "Ay,"
And that bare vowel "I" shall poison more
Than the death-darting eye of cockatrice;[8]
I am not I if there be such an "Ay,"
Or those eyes shut that makes thee answer "Ay."
50   If he be slain, say "Ay," or, if not, "No."
Brief sounds determine my weal° or woe. *welfare*
NURSE   I saw the wound—I saw it with mine eyes,
God save the mark[9]—here on his manly breast.
A piteous corpse, a bloody, piteous corpse,
55   Pale, pale as ashes, all bedaubed in blood,

---

4. *match:* competition. A husband and a marriage ("match") are won by surrendering.
5. Fluttering like a restless falcon before its eyes are covered with a "hood" to calm it.
6. *Take . . . stars:* an imagined transformation, based on those in Ovid's *Metamorphoses*, whereby Romeo also dies and is immortalized. Also, "die" could mean

"have an orgasm."
7. *Oh . . . sold:* The image is inverted: first Juliet buys the mansion, and then she becomes the "sold" house.
8. A mythical serpent that kills by merely looking.
9. An apology for mentioning something unpleasant, but also emphasizing the fatal "mark" of the rapier.

All in gore° blood; I swoonèd at the sight.   *clotted*

JULIET   O break, my heart; poor bankrupt, break at once!

To prison,[1] eyes; ne'er look on liberty.

Vile earth,[2] to earth resign; end motion° here;   *movement; emotion*

60   And thou and Romeo press[3] one heavy° bier.   *weighty; sad*

NURSE   O Tybalt, Tybalt, the best friend I had!

O courteous Tybalt, honest° gentleman,   *honorable*

That ever I should live to see thee dead!

JULIET   What storm is this that blows so contrary?

65   Is Romeo slaughtered, and is Tybalt dead,

My dearest cousin and my dearer lord?

Then, dreadful trumpet, sound the general doom,[4]

For who is living if those two are gone?

NURSE   Tybalt is gone, and Romeo banishèd;

70   Romeo, that killed him, he is banishèd.

JULIET   O God, did Romeo's hand shed Tybalt's blood?

NURSE   It did, it did, alas the day, it did!

JULIET   O serpent heart, hid with° a flow'ring° face!   *by / lovely; benign*

Did ever dragon keep° so fair a cave?   *guard*

75   Beautiful tyrant, fiend angelical,

Dove-feathered raven, wolvish-ravening lamb,

Despisèd substance of divinest show,°   *appearance*

Just opposite to what thou justly° seem'st,   *precisely; rightfully*

A damnèd saint, an honorable villain.

80   O nature, what hadst thou to do[5] in hell

When thou didst bower[6] the spirit of a fiend

In mortal paradise of such sweet flesh?

Was ever book containing such vile matter

So fairly bound? Oh, that deceit should dwell

In such a gorgeous palace.

85   NURSE   There's no trust,

No faith, no honesty in men: all perjured,

All forsworn, all naught,° all dissemblers.   *wicked*

Ah, where's my man? Give me some aqua vitae.°   *brandy*

These griefs, these woes, these sorrows, make me old.

Shame come to Romeo.

90   JULIET   Blistered be thy tongue

For such a wish! He was not born to shame;

Upon his brow shame is ashamed to sit,

For 'tis a throne where honor may be crowned

Sole monarch of the universal earth.

95   Oh, what a beast was I to chide at him!

NURSE   Will you speak well of him that killed your cousin?

JULIET   Shall I speak ill of him that is my husband?

Ah, poor my° lord, what tongue shall smooth° thy name   *my poor / praise*

When I, thy three hours' wife, have mangled it?

100   But wherefore, villain, didst thou kill my cousin?

That villain cousin would have killed my husband.

Back, foolish tears, back to your native spring;

Your tributary[7] drops belong to woe,

---

1. Bankruptcy—to "break" financially—was punishable by imprisonment.
2. The despised body, echoing Ecclesiastes 12:7: "Then shall the dust return to the earth as it was."
3. Burden; embrace.
4. The Last Judgment announced with angels' trumpets.
5. What were you doing.
6. Lodge or enclose, suggesting a surrounding garden.
7. Tribute-paying; in-flowing.

Which you, mistaking, offer up to joy.[8]
105 My husband lives that Tybalt would have slain,
And Tybalt's dead that would have slain my husband:
All this is comfort. Wherefore° weep I, then?   *Why*
Some word there was, worser than Tybalt's death,
That murdered me; I would forget it fain,°   *gladly*
110 But, oh, it presses to my memory
Like damnèd guilty deeds to sinners' minds:
Tybalt is dead and Romeo banishèd.
That "banishèd"—that one word, "banishèd"—
Hath slain ten thousand Tybalts. Tybalt's death
115 Was woe enough if it had ended there;
Or, if sour woe delights in fellowship,
And needly° will be ranked with[9] other griefs,   *necessarily*
Why followed not, when she said, "Tybalt's dead,"
"Thy father" or "Thy mother"—nay, or both—
120 Which modern° lamentation might have moved?°   *ordinary / produced*
But with a rearward[1] following "Tybalt's death,"
"Romeo is banishèd"—to speak that word
Is father, mother, Tybalt, Romeo, Juliet,
All slain, all dead. "Romeo is banishèd"—
125 There is no end, no limit, measure, bound,
In that word's death; no words can that woe sound.°   *utter; fathom*
—Where is my father and my mother, Nurse?
NURSE Weeping and wailing over Tybalt's corpse.
Will you go to them? I will bring you thither.
130 JULIET Wash they his wounds with tears? Mine shall be spent,
When theirs are dry, for Romeo's banishment.
Take up those cords. Poor ropes, you are beguiled°—   *cheated*
Both you and I—for Romeo is exiled;
He made you for a highway to my bed,
135 But I, a maid, die maiden-widowèd.
Come, cords; come, Nurse; I'll to my wedding bed,
And death, not Romeo, take my maidenhead.
NURSE Hie to your chamber. I'll find Romeo
To comfort you; I wot° well where he is.   *know*
140 Hark ye, your Romeo will be here at night.
I'll to him; he is hid at Laurence' cell.
JULIET Oh, find him! Give this ring to my true knight,
And bid him come to take his last farewell.   *Exeunt.*

3.3 (Q1 Scene 12)
Enter FRIAR [LAURENCE].
FRIAR LAURENCE Romeo, come forth, come forth, thou fear-
ful man.
Affliction is enamored of thy parts,°   *qualities*
And thou art wedded to calamity.
    [*Enter* ROMEO.]
ROMEO Father, what news? What is the Prince's doom?°   *sentence*
5 What sorrow craves acquaintance at my hand

---

8. Offer up to a joyful (and thus inappropriate)
occasion.
9. Will be accompanied by.

1. *rearward:* rearguard action, with a pun on
"afterword."
3.3 Location: Friar Laurence's cell.

That I yet know not?
FRIAR LAURENCE   Too familiar
   Is my dear son with such sour company.
   I bring thee tidings of the Prince's doom.
ROMEO   What less than doomsday is the Prince's doom?
10 FRIAR LAURENCE   A gentler judgment vanished° from his lips: escaped
   Not body's death, but body's banishment.
ROMEO   Ha? Banishment? Be merciful; say "death,"
   For exile hath more terror in his look,
   Much more than death. Do not say "banishment."
15 FRIAR LAURENCE   Here from Verona art thou banishèd.
   Be patient,° for the world is broad and wide.   able to endure
ROMEO   There is no world without° Verona walls   outside
   But purgatory, torture, hell itself;
   Hence banishèd is banished from the world,
20 And world's exile is death. Then "banishèd"
   Is death mis-termed: calling death "banishèd,"
   Thou cutt'st my head off with a golden ax,
   And smilest upon the stroke that murders me.
FRIAR LAURENCE   Oh, deadly° sin! Oh, rude unthankfulness!   damnable
25 Thy fault our law calls death,° but the kind Prince,   a capital offense
   Taking thy part, hath rushed° aside the law,   forced
   And turned that black word "death" to "banishment."
   This is dear mercy, and thou seest it not.
ROMEO   'Tis torture and not mercy! Heaven is here
30 Where Juliet lives—and every cat and dog
   And little mouse, every unworthy thing,
   Live here in heaven and may look on her,
   But Romeo may not. More validity,°   health
   More honorable state, more courtship,° lives   courtly state; wooing
35 In carrion flies than Romeo. They may seize
   On the white wonder of dear Juliet's hand,
   And steal immortal blessing from her lips,
   Who even in pure and vestal° modesty   virginal
   Still° blush, as thinking their own kisses[1] sin.   Always
40 This may flies do, when I from this must fly—
   And sayest thou yet that exile is not death?
   But Romeo may not; he is banishèd.
   Flies may do this, but I from this must fly;
   They are free men, but I am banishèd.
45 Hadst thou no poison mixed, no sharp-ground knife,
   No sudden mean° of death—though ne'er so mean°—   method / ignoble
   But "banishèd" to kill me? "Banishèd"?
   O Friar, the damnèd use that word in hell;[2]
   Howling attends it. How hast thou the heart,
50 Being a divine, a ghostly confessor,
   A sin-absolver, and my friend professed,
   To mangle me with that word "banishèd"?
FRIAR LAURENCE   Then, fond° madman, hear me a little speak.   foolish; infatuated
ROMEO   Oh, thou wilt speak again of banishment.
55 FRIAR LAURENCE   I'll give thee armor to keep off that word:
   Adversity's sweet milk, philosophy,

---

1. Their touching each other in closing.   2. Because they are banished from heaven.

To comfort thee, though thou art banishèd.

ROMEO   Yet "banishèd"? Hang up° philosophy!   *Hang up = Hang*
Unless philosophy can make a Juliet,

60   Displant° a town, reverse a prince's doom,   *Uproot*
It helps not, it prevails not. Talk no more.

FRIAR LAURENCE   Oh, then I see that madmen have no ears.

ROMEO   How should they, when that wise men have no eyes?

FRIAR LAURENCE   Let me dispute° with thee of thy estate.°   *discuss / position*

65   ROMEO   Thou canst not speak of that thou dost not feel.
Wert thou as young as I, Juliet thy love,
An hour but° married, Tybalt murderèd,   *Only an hour*
Doting like me, and like me banishèd,
Then mightst thou speak; then mightst thou tear thy hair

70   And fall upon the ground, as I do now,
Taking the measure of an unmade grave.
    NURSE *knocks* [*within*].

FRIAR LAURENCE   Arise! One knocks. Good Romeo, hide
thyself.

ROMEO   Not I, unless the breath of heartsick groans
Mistlike enfold me from the search of eyes.
    Knock [*within*].

75   FRIAR LAURENCE   Hark, how they knock! —Who's there?
    —Romeo, arise;
Thou wilt be taken! —Stay a while! —Stand up!
    [*Loud*] *knock* [*within*].
Run to my study. —By and by! —God's will,°   *By providence*
What simpleness° is this? —I come, I come!   *stupidity*
    Knock [*within*].
Who knocks so hard? Whence come you? What's your will?

80   NURSE [*within*]³   Let me come in, and you shall know my
errand.
I come from Lady Juliet.
    Enter NURSE.

FRIAR LAURENCE   Welcome, then.

NURSE   O holy Friar! Oh, tell me, holy Friar,
Where's my lady's lord? Where's Romeo?

FRIAR LAURENCE   There on the ground, with his own tears
made drunk.

85   NURSE   Oh, he is even° in my mistress' case,°   *exactly / condition; vagina*
Just in her case. Oh, woeful sympathy,
Piteous predicament! Even so lies she,
Blubb'ring and weeping, weeping and blubb'ring.
—Stand up, stand up! Stand an° you be a man!   *if*

90   For Juliet's sake, for her sake, rise and stand.
Why should you fall into so deep an O?°   *a groaning; a vagina*

ROMEO   Nurse—

NURSE   Ah, sir; ah, sir; death's the end of all.⁴

ROMEO   Spakest thou of Juliet? How is it with her?
Doth not she think me an old° murderer   *a practiced*

95   Now I have stained the childhood of our joy
With blood removed but little from her own?
Where is she? And how doth she? And what says

---

3. Behind one of the doors at the back of the stage,   4. A proverbial consolation.
representing the door of the cell.

My concealed lady° to our canceled° love?   *secret wife / invalidated*
NURSE   Oh, she says nothing, sir, but weeps and weeps,
100   And now falls on her bed, and then starts up,
        And Tybalt calls, and then on Romeo cries,
        And then down falls again.
ROMEO   As if that name,
        Shot from the deadly level° of a gun,   *aim*
        Did murder her, as that name's cursèd hand
105   Murdered her kinsman. Oh, tell me, Friar, tell me,
        In what vile part of this anatomy
        Doth my name lodge? Tell me, that I may sack
        The hateful mansion.
            [*He offers to stab himself.*]⁵
FRIAR LAURENCE   Hold° thy desperate hand!   *Restrain*
        Art thou a man? Thy form cries out thou art.
110   Thy tears are womanish; thy wild acts denote
        The unreasonable° fury of a beast: *incapable of reason*
        Unseemly° woman in a seeming man,   *Inappropriate; immodest*
        And ill-beseeming beast in seeming both⁶—
        Thou hast amazed me. By my holy order,
115   I thought thy disposition better tempered.
        Hast thou slain Tybalt? Wilt thou slay thyself?
        And slay thy lady, that in thy life lives,
        By doing damnèd° hate upon thyself?   *sinful*
        Why railest thou on thy birth, the heaven, and earth,
120   Since birth,° and heaven,° and earth,° all three, do meet   *nobility / soul / body*
        In thee at once, which thou at once wouldst lose?
        Fie, fie! Thou shamest thy shape, thy love, thy wit,
        Which like a usurer abound'st in all,
        And usest none in that true use indeed
125   Which should bedeck thy shape, thy love, thy wit.⁷
        Thy noble shape is but a form° of wax,   *figure*
        Digressing° from the valor of a man;   *If it deviates*
        Thy dear love sworn but hollow perjury,
        Killing that love which thou hast vowed to cherish;
130   Thy wit, that ornament° to shape and love,   *necessary accessory*
        Misshapen° in the conduct° of them both,   *Inept / management*
        Like powder in a skill-less soldier's flask,
        Is set afire by thine own ignorance,
        And thou dismembered with thine own defense.°   *weapon*
135   What, rouse thee, man! Thy Juliet is alive,
        For whose dear sake thou wast but lately dead;
        There art thou happy. Tybalt would kill thee,
        But thou slewest Tybalt; there art thou happy.
        The law that threatened death becomes thy friend
140   And turns it to exile; there art thou happy.
        A pack of blessings light upon thy back;
        Happiness courts thee in her best array;
        But, like a mishavèd° and sullen wench,   *misbehaved*
        Thou pouts upon thy fortune and thy love.

5. TEXTUAL COMMENT In Q1's version of this scene, a stage direction indicates that the Nurse "*snatches the dagger away*" from Romeo. See Digital Edition TC 9 (Second Quarto edited text).
6. An unnatural beast in seeming both man and unreasoning animal, or both man and woman.
7. *Thou shamest . . . wit:* You abound in looks, love, and intelligence ("wit"), but you do not use them judiciously and are therefore like a usurer who acquires money for its own sake, without putting it to good use.

145 Take heed, take heed, for such die miserable.
Go; get thee to thy love as was decreed;
Ascend her chamber; hence and comfort her.
But look thou stay not till the watch be set,[8]
For then thou canst not pass to Mantua,
150 Where thou shalt live till we can find a time
To blaze° your marriage, reconcile your friends,°   make public / kin
Beg pardon of the Prince, and call thee back
With twenty hundred thousand times more joy
Than thou went'st forth in lamentation.
155 —Go before, Nurse. Commend me to thy lady,
And bid her hasten all the house to bed,
Which heavy sorrow makes them apt unto.
Romeo is coming.
NURSE   O Lord, I could have stayed here all the night
160 To hear good counsel. Oh, what learning is!
My lord, I'll tell my lady you will come.
ROMEO   Do so, and bid my sweet prepare to chide.
NURSE   Here, sir: a ring she bid me give you, sir.
Hie you,° make haste, for it grows very late.   [Exit.]   Hurry
165 ROMEO   How well my comfort° is revived by this.   happiness
FRIAR LAURENCE   Go hence. Good night—and here stands°   and on this depends
all your state:
Either be gone before the watch be set,
Or, by the break of day, disguised from hence.
Sojourn in Mantua. I'll find out your man,
170 And he shall signify from time to time
Every good hap° to you that chances here.   event
Give me thy hand. 'Tis late. Farewell. Goodnight.
ROMEO   But that a joy past joy calls out on me,
It were a grief so brief° to part with thee.   hastily
175 Farewell.   Exeunt.

3.4 (Q1 Scene 13)
Enter old CAPULET, [CAPULET'S] WIFE, *and* PARIS.
CAPULET   Things have fall'n out, sir, so unluckily
That we have had no time to move° our daughter.   persuade
Look you, she loved her kinsman Tybalt dearly,
And so did I. Well, we were born to die.
5 'Tis very late; she'll not come down tonight.
I promise you, but for your company
I would have been abed an hour ago.
PARIS   These times of woe afford no times to woo.
—Madam, good night; commend me to your daughter.
10 CAPULET'S WIFE   I will, and know her mind early tomorrow.
Tonight she's mewed up to[1] her heaviness.°   sadness
CAPULET   Sir Paris, I will make a desperate tender°   reckless offer
Of my child's love. I think she will be ruled
In all respects by me; nay, more, I doubt it not.
15 —Wife, go you to her ere you go to bed,
Acquaint her here of my son Paris' love,
And bid her—mark you me?—on Wednesday next—

8. Until the guards take up their positions (at the
city gates).

3.4 Location: Capulet's house.
1. Shut in with. The "mews" are hawks' housing.

But soft, what day is this?

PARIS   Monday, my lord.

CAPULET   Monday? Ha, ha! Well, Wednesday is too soon;

20 O'Thursday let it be; o'Thursday, tell her,
She shall be married to this noble earl.
—Will you be ready? Do you like this haste?
We'll keep° no great ado—a friend or two—   celebrate with
For, hark you, Tybalt being slain so late,°   recently
25 It may be thought we held° him carelessly,°   regarded / indifferently
Being our kinsman, if we revel much.
Therefore we'll have some half a dozen friends,
And there an end. But what say you to Thursday?

PARIS   My lord, I would° that Thursday were tomorrow.   wish

30 CAPULET   Well, get you gone; o'Thursday be it, then.
[to CAPULET'S WIFE] Go you to Juliet ere you go to bed.
Prepare her, wife, against° this wedding day.   for
—Farewell, my lord. —Light to my chamber, ho!
—Afore me,² it is so very late
35 That we may call it early by and by!
Goodnight.   Exeunt.

3.5 (Q1 Scene 14)

Enter ROMEO *and* JULIET *aloft.*

JULIET   Wilt thou be gone? It is not yet near day.
It was the nightingale, and not the lark,
That pierced the fearful hollow of thine ear.
Nightly she sings on yond pom'granate tree.
5   Believe me, love: it was the nightingale.

ROMEO   It was the lark, the herald of the morn,
No nightingale. Look, love, what envious° streaks   spiteful
Do lace the severing° clouds in yonder East.   parting
Night's candles are burnt out, and jocund day
10 Stands tiptoe on the misty mountain tops.
I must be gone and live, or stay and die.

JULIET   Yond light is not daylight—I know it, I—
It is some meteor that the sun exhales¹
To be to thee this night a torchbearer
15 And light thee on thy way to Mantua.
Therefore stay yet; thou need'st not to be gone.

ROMEO   Let me be ta'en, let me be put to death;
I am content, so° thou wilt have it so.   as long as
I'll say yon gray is not the morning's eye—
20 'Tis but the pale reflex° of Cynthia's° brow—   reflection / the moon's
Nor that is not the lark whose notes do beat
The vaulty heaven so high above our heads.
I have more care° to stay than will to go.   desire
Come, death, and welcome: Juliet wills it so.
25 How is't, my soul? Let's talk; it is not day.

JULIET   It is, it is! Hie hence; be gone. Away!
It is the lark that sings so out of tune,

---

2. *Afore me:* A mild oath.
3.5 Location: The upper acting area represents
Juliet's window or balcony. The main stage represents
Capulet's orchard until line 59, then Juliet's bedroom

from line 64.
1. Breathes. Meteors were thought to be impure
vapors that the sun had drawn up from the earth and
ignited and were usually considered bad omens.

Straining° harsh discords and unpleasing sharps.[2]   *Distorting; tuning up*
Some say the lark makes sweet division;°   *variations on a melody*
30 This doth not so, for she divideth us.
Some say the lark and loathèd toad change eyes;[3]
Oh, now I would they had changed voices too,
Since arm from arm that voice doth us affray,°   *frighten*
Hunting thee hence with hunt's-up[4] to the day.
35 Oh, now be gone! More light and light it grows.
ROMEO   More light and light, more dark and dark our woes.
    Enter NURSE.
NURSE   Madam!
JULIET   Nurse?
NURSE   Your lady mother is coming to your chamber.
40 The day is broke; be wary; look about.   [*Exit.*]
JULIET   Then, window, let day in and let life out.
ROMEO   Farewell, farewell. One kiss, and I'll descend.
    [*He goeth down.*][5]
JULIET   Art thou gone so, love, lord—ay, husband, friend?°   *lover*
I must hear from thee every day in the hour,
45 For in a minute there are many days—
Oh, by this count I shall be much in years
Ere I again behold my Romeo!
ROMEO   Farewell.
I will omit no opportunity
50 That may convey my greetings, love, to thee.
JULIET   Oh, think'st thou we shall ever meet again?
ROMEO   I doubt it not, and all these woes shall serve
For sweet discourses° in our times to come.   *conversations*
JULIET   O God, I have an ill-divining° soul!   *a misfortune-predicting*
55 Methinks I see thee, now thou art so low,
As one dead in the bottom of a tomb;
Either my eyesight fails, or thou lookest pale.
ROMEO   And trust me, love, in my eye so do you;
Dry sorrow drinks our blood.[6] Adieu, adieu.   *Exit.*
60 JULIET   O Fortune, Fortune, all men call thee fickle;
If thou art fickle, what dost thou with him
That is renowned for faith?° Be fickle, Fortune,   *fidelity*
For then I hope thou wilt not keep him long,
But send him back.
    Enter [CAPULET'S WIFE *below*].
CAPULET'S WIFE   Ho, daughter, are you up?
65 JULIET   Who is't that calls? —It is my lady mother.
Is she not down° so late or up so early?   *in bed*
What unaccustomed cause procures° her hither?   *brings*
    [JULIET *goeth down and enters below.*][7]
CAPULET'S WIFE   Why, how now, Juliet?
JULIET   Madam, I am not well.
CAPULET'S WIFE   Evermore weeping for your cousin's death?

---

2. Harsh sounds, too-high tones.
3. A folk explanation for the supposed ugliness of the lark's eyes and the beauty of the toad's. *change:* exchange.
4. Morning song used to wake the bride after the wedding night.
5. Romeo descends using the ladder of cords men-

tioned earlier.
6. *Dry . . . blood:* Each sigh supposedly cost the heart a drop of blood. Thus, the lovers are pale. *Dry:* Thirsty.
7. TEXTUAL COMMENT On the representation of this scene's location changes in Q2 and Q1, see Digital Edition TC 10 (Second Quarto edited text).

70　What, wilt thou wash him from his grave with tears?
　　An if thou couldst, thou couldst not make him live;
　　Therefore have done. Some grief shows much of love,
　　But much of grief shows still° some want° of wit.　　　　*always / lack*
　JULIET　Yet let me weep for such a feeling° loss.　　　　　*profound*
75　CAPULET'S WIFE　So shall you feel° the loss, but not the friend°　*experience; touch / kin*
　　Which you weep for.
　JULIET　　　　　　　　　　Feeling so the loss,
　　I cannot choose but ever weep the friend.°　　　　　　　*lover*
　CAPULET'S WIFE　Well, girl, thou weep'st not so much for his
　　death
　　As that the villain lives which slaughtered him.
　JULIET　What villain, madam?
80　CAPULET'S WIFE　　　　　　　That same villain Romeo.
　JULIET [aside]　Villain and he be many miles asunder.
　　—God pardon; I do with all my heart,
　　And yet no man like° he doth grieve my heart.　　　　*so much as; resembling*
　CAPULET'S WIFE　That is because the traitor murderer lives.
85　JULIET　Ay, madam, from the reach of these my hands.
　　Would none but I might venge my cousin's death.
　CAPULET'S WIFE　We will have vengeance for it, fear thou not.
　　Then weep no more. I'll send to one in Mantua,
　　Where that same banished renegade doth live,
90　Shall give him such an unaccustomed dram
　　That he shall soon keep Tybalt company;
　　And then I hope thou wilt be satisfied.°　　　　　　*sufficiently avenged*
　JULIET　Indeed, I never shall be satisfied
　　With Romeo till I behold him—dead—
95　Is my poor heart[8] so for a kinsman vexed.
　　Madam, if you could find out but a man
　　To bear a poison, I would temper° it　　　　　　　　*mix; dilute*
　　That Romeo should, upon receipt thereof,
　　Soon sleep in quiet. Oh, how my heart abhors
100　To hear him named, and cannot come to him—
　　To wreak the love I bore my cousin
　　Upon his body that hath slaughtered him.
　CAPULET'S WIFE　Find thou the means, and I'll find such a man.
　　But now I'll tell thee joyful tidings, girl.
105　JULIET　And joy comes well in such a needy time.
　　What are they, beseech your ladyship?
　CAPULET'S WIFE　Well, well, thou hast a careful° father, child;　*solicitous*
　　One who, to put thee from thy heaviness,
　　Hath sorted out a sudden° day of joy　　　　　　*chosen an immediate*
110　That thou expects not, nor I looked not for.
　JULIET　Madam, in happy° time. What day is that?　　*at a fortunate*
　CAPULET'S WIFE　Marry, my child, early next Thursday morn,
　　The gallant, young, and noble gentleman,
　　The County Paris, at Saint Peter's Church
115　Shall happily make thee there a joyful bride!
　JULIET　Now, by Saint Peter's Church—and Peter, too—
　　He shall not make me there a joyful bride!
　　I wonder° at this haste, that I must wed　　　　　　*am astonished*

8. *till . . . heart:* Juliet allows her mother to understand that she will not be satisfied "till I behold him dead," while privately meaning that until she beholds him, "dead is my poor heart."

Ere he that should be husband comes to woo.
120 I pray you tell my lord and father, madam,
I will not marry yet—and when I do, I swear
It shall be Romeo, whom you know I hate,
Rather than Paris. These are news indeed!

CAPULET'S WIFE   Here comes your father; tell him so
yourself,
125 And see how he will take it at your hands.

Enter CAPULET *and* NURSE.

CAPULET   When the sun sets, the earth doth drizzle° dew;   *weep out*
But for the sunset of my brother's son
It rains downright.
How now? A conduit,° girl? What, still in tears?   *fountain*
130 Evermore show'ring? In one little body
Thou counterfeits a bark,° a sea, a wind—   *represent a ship*
For still thy eyes, which I may call the sea,
Do ebb and flow with tears; the bark thy body is,
Sailing in this salt flood, the winds thy sighs,
135 Who,° raging with thy tears and they with them,   *Which*
Without a sudden calm will overset
Thy tempest-tossèd body. —How now, wife,
Have you delivered to her our decree?

CAPULET'S WIFE   Ay, sir, but she will none,° she gives you   *not agree*
thanks.
140 I would the fool° were married to her grave.   *peevish child*

CAPULET   Soft! Take me with you;⁹ take me with you, wife.
How? Will she none? Doth she not give us thanks?
Is she not proud?° Doth she not count her blessed,   *gratified*
Unworthy as she is, that we have wrought°   *contrived for*
145 So worthy a gentleman to be her bride?°   *bridegroom*

JULIET   Not proud you have, but thankful that you have.
Proud can I never be of what I hate,
But thankful even for hate° that is meant love.°   *a hateful thing / as love*

CAPULET   How, how, how, how? Chopped logic?° What is this?   *Mere sophistry*
150 "Proud," and "I thank you," and "I thank you not,"
And yet "not proud," mistress minion,° you?   *spoiled child*
Thank me no thankings, nor proud me no prouds,
But fettle° your fine joints 'gainst° Thursday next   *prepare / for*
To go with Paris to Saint Peter's Church,
155 Or I will drag thee on a hurdle¹ thither.
Out,² you green-sickness carrion! Out, you baggage,
You tallow face!

CAPULET'S WIFE   Fie, fie! What, are you mad?

JULIET   Good father, I beseech you on my knees,
Hear me with patience but to speak a word.

160 CAPULET   Hang thee, young baggage, disobedient wretch!
I tell thee what: get thee to church o'Thursday,
Or never after look me in the face.
Speak not; reply not; do not answer me.
My fingers itch. —Wife, we scarce thought us blessed
165 That God had lent us but this only child,
But now I see this one is one too much,

---

9. Not so fast, let me understand you.
1. A sledge used to draw traitors through the streets   to execution.
2. An expression of disgust and impatience.

And that we have a curse in having her.
Out on her, hilding!°　　　　　　　　　　　　　　　　　　　　　　　*hussy*
NURSE　　　　　　　　　God in heaven bless her!
You are to blame, my lord, to rate° her so.　　　　　　　　*berate*
170　CAPULET　And why, my Lady Wisdom? Hold your tongue,
Good Prudence. Smatter° with your gossips.° Go!　　*Chatter / cronies*
NURSE　I speak no treason.
CAPULET　　　　　　　　　　Oh, God gi' good e'en!°　　　*(for God's sake)*
NURSE　May not one speak?
CAPULET　　　　　　　　　　Peace, you mumbling fool!
Utter your gravity° o'er a gossip's bowl,°　　*wisdom / drinking bowl*
For here we need it not.
175　CAPULET'S WIFE　　　　　You are too hot.°　　　*irascible; rash*
CAPULET　God's bread,° it makes me mad!　　*By the communion bread*
Day, night, hour, tide, time, work, play,
Alone, in company—still my care° hath been　　　　*business*
To have her matched; and, having now provided
180　A gentleman of noble parentage,
Of fair demesnes,° youthful, and nobly lined,°　*estates / descended*
Stuffed, as they say, with honorable parts,°　　　*qualities*
Proportioned as one's thought would wish a man,[3]
And then to have a wretched, puling fool,
185　A whining mammet° in her fortune's tender,[4]　　　*puppet*
To answer, "I'll not wed; I cannot love;
I am too young; I pray you, pardon me."
—But, an you will not wed, I'll pardon you:°　*excuse you (to leave)*
Graze where you will, you shall not house with me!
190　Look to't; think on't; I do not use° to jest.　*make it customary*
Thursday is near. Lay hand on heart;[5] advise.°　　　*consider*
An you be mine, I'll give you to my friend;
An you be not, hang, beg, starve, die in the streets—
For, by my soul, I'll ne'er acknowledge thee,
195　Nor what is mine shall never do thee good,
Trust to't. Bethink you; I'll not be forsworn.　　*Exit.*
JULIET　Is there no pity sitting in the clouds
That sees into the bottom of my grief?
O sweet my° mother, cast me not away!　　　　　　*my sweet*
200　Delay this marriage for a month, a week—
Or, if you do not, make the bridal bed
In that dim monument° where Tybalt lies.　　　*sepulcher*
CAPULET'S WIFE　Talk not to me, for I'll not speak a word.
Do as thou wilt, for I have done with thee.　　*Exit.*
205　JULIET　O God! O Nurse, how shall this be prevented?
My husband is on earth, my faith° in heaven.　*marriage vows*
How shall that faith return again to earth
Unless that husband send it me from heaven
By leaving earth?[6] Comfort me; counsel me!
210　Alack, alack, that heaven should practice stratagems
Upon so soft a subject as myself!
What say'st thou? Hast thou not a word of joy?

---

3. Shaped as handsomely as you can imagine.
4. When good fortune is offered her.
5. Ascertain your feelings.

6. *How . . . earth:* How can I swear marriage vows
again unless Romeo dies first, thus releasing me from
my vows to him?

Some comfort, Nurse!

NURSE   Faith, here it is.
Romeo is banished, and all the world to nothing⁷
215 That he dares ne'er come back to challenge° you;   *claim*
Or, if he do, it needs must be by stealth.
Then, since the case so stands as now it doth,
I think it best you married with the County.
Oh, he's a lovely gentleman!
220 Romeo's a dishclout° to him. An eagle, madam,   *dishcloth*
Hath not so green, so quick, so fair an eye
As Paris hath. Beshrew° my very heart,   *Curse*
I think you are happy° in this second match,   *lucky*
For it excels your first—or, if it did not,
225 Your first is dead, or 'twere as good he were
As living here and you no use of him.
JULIET   Speak'st thou from thy heart?
NURSE   And from my soul, too; else beshrew them both.
JULIET   Amen.
230 NURSE   What?
JULIET   Well, thou hast comforted me marvelous much.
Go in and tell my lady I am gone,
Having displeased my father, to Laurence' cell
To make confession and to be absolved.
235 NURSE   Marry, I will, and this is wisely done.   [*Exit.*]
JULIET   Ancient damnation!⁸ O most wicked fiend!
Is it more sin to wish me thus forsworn,
Or to dispraise my lord with that same tongue
Which she hath praised him with, above compare,
240 So many thousand times? Go, counselor;
Thou and my bosom° henceforth shall be twain.°   *heart's contents / divided*
I'll to the Friar to know his remedy.
If all else fail, myself have power to die.   *Exit.*

4.1 (Q1 Scene 15)
Enter FRIAR [LAURENCE] *and County* PARIS.

FRIAR LAURENCE   On Thursday, sir? The time is very short.
PARIS   My father Capulet will have it so,
And I am nothing slow¹ to slack his haste.
FRIAR LAURENCE   You say you do not know the lady's mind?
5 Uneven is the course;² I like it not.
PARIS   Immoderately she weeps for Tybalt's death,
And therefore have I little talk of love,
For Venus smiles not in a house of tears.
Now, sir, her father counts it dangerous
10 That she do give her sorrow so much sway,
And in his wisdom hastes our marriage
To stop the inundation of her tears,
Which, too much minded° by herself alone,   *brooded over*
May be put from her by society.°   *company*
15 Now do you know the reason of this haste.

7. *all . . . nothing*: it's a sure bet.
8. Damnable old woman (with a hint of "original sin").
4.1 Location: Friar Laurence's cell.

1. Not reluctant; not trying to drag behind him.
2. The plan is irregular; this is a tricky road to follow.

FRIAR LAURENCE [*aside*]   I would I knew not why it should be
    slowed.
            Enter JULIET.
    —Look, sir, here comes the lady toward my cell.
PARIS   Happily met, my lady and my wife.
JULIET   That may be, sir, when I may be a wife.
20 PARIS   That "may be" must be, love, on Thursday next.
JULIET   What must be shall be.
FRIAR LAURENCE   That's a certain text.
PARIS   Come you to make confession to this father?
JULIET   To answer that, I should confess to you.
PARIS   Do not deny to him that you love me.
25 JULIET   I will confess to you that I love him.
PARIS   So will ye, I am sure, that you love me.
JULIET   If I do so, it will be of more price°   value
    Being spoke behind your back than to your face.
PARIS   Poor soul, thy face is much abused with tears.
30 JULIET   The tears have got small victory by that,
    For it was bad enough before their spite.°   injury
PARIS   Thou wrong'st it more than tears with that report.
JULIET   That is no slander, sir, which is a truth;
    And what I spake, I spake it to my face.
35 PARIS   Thy face is mine, and thou hast slandered it.
JULIET   It may be so, for it is not mine own.[3]
    —Are you at leisure, holy Father, now,
    Or shall I come to you at evening mass?
FRIAR LAURENCE   My leisure serves me, pensive° daughter,   sorrowful
    now.
40 —My lord, we must entreat the time alone.
PARIS   God shield° I should disturb devotion.   forbid
    —Juliet, on Thursday early will I rouse ye;
    Till then, adieu, and keep this holy kiss.   *Exit.*
JULIET   Oh, shut the door, and, when thou hast done so,
45 Come weep with me—past hope, past care, past help.
FRIAR LAURENCE   O Juliet, I already know thy grief;°   grievous situation
    It strains me past the compass° of my wits.   limit
    I hear thou must—and nothing may prorogue° it—   postpone
    On Thursday next be married to this County.
50 JULIET   Tell me not, Friar, that thou hearest of this
    Unless thou tell me how I may prevent it.
    If in thy wisdom thou canst give no help,
    Do thou but call my resolution wise,
    And with this knife I'll help it presently.°   immediately
55 God joined my heart and Romeo's, thou our hands,
    And ere this hand, by thee to Romeo's sealed,
    Shall be the label[4] to another deed,
    Or my true heart with treacherous revolt
    Turn to another, this shall slay them both.
60 Therefore, out of thy long-experienced time,
    Give me some present counsel, or behold,
            [*She draws a knife.*]

3. Because it belongs to Romeo; also because Juliet,   4. Ribbon attaching a seal to a legal document (deed),
in her ambiguous replies, is not showing Paris her   and so a pledge confirming another marriage.
true face.

Twixt my extremes° and me, this bloody knife   *extreme difficulties*
Shall play the umpire, arbitrating that
Which the commission° of thy years and art°   *authority / learning*
65 Could to no issue of true honor bring.
Be not so long to speak; I long to die
If what thou speak'st speak not of remedy.
FRIAR LAURENCE Hold, daughter! I do spy a kind of hope,
Which craves as desperate° an execution⁵   *reckless*
70 As that is desperate° which we would prevent.   *hopeless*
If, rather than to marry County Paris,
Thou hast the strength of will to slay thyself,
Then is it likely thou wilt undertake
A thing like death to chide away this shame,
75 That cop'st° with death himself to scape from it.° *Who wrestles / (shame)*
An if thou darest, I'll give thee remedy.
JULIET Oh, bid me leap, rather than marry Paris,
From off the battlements of any tower,
Or walk in thievish° ways, or bid me lurk   *thief-infested*
80 Where serpents are; chain me with roaring bears;
Or hide me nightly in a charnel house,°   *burial vault*
O'ercovered quite with dead men's rattling bones,
With reeky° shanks and yellow chapless⁶ skulls;   *foully damp*
Or bid me go into a new-made grave,
85 And hide me with a dead man in his shroud—
Things that, to hear them told, have made me tremble—
And I will do it without fear or doubt°   *dread; hesitation*
To live an unstained wife to my sweet love.
FRIAR LAURENCE Hold, then. Go home; be merry; give consent
90 To marry Paris. Wednesday is tomorrow.
Tomorrow night look° that thou lie alone;   *be sure*
Let not the Nurse lie with thee in thy chamber.
Take thou this vial, being then in bed,
And this distilling° liquor drink thou off,   *permeating*
95 When presently through all thy veins shall run
A cold and drowsy humor°—for no pulse   *bodily fluid*
Shall keep his° native progress but surcease;°   *its / cease*
No warmth, no breath shall testify thou livest;
The roses in thy lips and cheeks shall fade
100 To wanny° ashes; thy eyes' windows° fall   *pale / lids*
Like death when he shuts up the day of life;
Each part, deprived of supple government,°   *control of movement*
Shall stiff and stark and cold appear, like death—
And in this borrowed likeness of shrunk death
105 Thou shalt continue two-and-forty hours,
And then awake as from a pleasant sleep.
Now, when the bridegroom in the morning comes
To rouse thee from thy bed, there art thou dead.
Then, as the manner of our country is,
110 In thy best robes, uncovered on the bier,
Be borne to burial in thy kindred's grave—
Thou shalt be borne to that same ancient vault
Where all the kindred of the Capulets lie.
In the meantime, against° thou shalt awake,   *in preparation for when*

---

5. A performance; a killing.   6. Without lower jaws.

115   Shall Romeo by my letters know our drift;°   *scheme*
    And hither shall he come, and he and I
    Will watch° thy waking, and that very night   *keep vigil for*
    Shall Romeo bear thee hence to Mantua,
    And this shall free thee from this present shame,
120   If no inconstant toy° nor womanish fear   *fickle whim*
    Abate thy valor in the acting it.
    JULIET   Give me, give me—oh, tell not me of fear!
    FRIAR LAURENCE   Hold! Get you gone; be strong and
       prosperous
    In this resolve. I'll send a friar with speed
125   To Mantua, with my letters° to thy lord.   *letter*
    JULIET   Love give me strength, and strength shall help afford.
    Farewell, dear Father.   *Exeunt.*

4.2 (Q1 Scene 16)

Enter Father CAPULET, [CAPULET'S WIFE,] NURSE,
and two or three SERVINGMEN.

    CAPULET [*to* FIRST SERVINGMAN, *giving him a paper*]   So many
      guests invite as here are writ.   [*Exit* FIRST SERVINGMAN.]
      [*to* SECOND SERVINGMAN] Sirrah, go hire me twenty cun-
      ning° cooks.   *skillful*
    SECOND SERVINGMAN   You shall have none ill, sir, for I'll try°   *test*
      if they can lick their fingers.
5   CAPULET   How, canst thou try them so?
    SECOND SERVINGMAN   Marry, sir, 'tis an ill cook that cannot
      lick his own fingers; therefore he that cannot lick his fingers
      goes not with me.
    CAPULET   Go! Be gone.
10   We shall be much unfurnished° for this time.   *unprepared*
                    [*Exit* SECOND SERVINGMAN.]
    —What, is my daughter gone to Friar Laurence?
    NURSE   Ay, forsooth.
    CAPULET   Well, he may chance to do some good on her.
    A peevish, self-willed harlotry it is.[1]
       Enter JULIET.
15   NURSE   See where she comes from shrift° with merry look.   *absolution*
    CAPULET   How now, my headstrong, where have you been
      gadding?
    JULIET   Where I have learnt me to repent the sin
    Of disobedient opposition
    To you and your behests, and am enjoined
20   By holy Laurence to fall prostrate here
    To beg your pardon.
           [*She kneels down.*]
               Pardon, I beseech you.
    Henceforward I am ever ruled by you.
    CAPULET   —Send for the County! Go tell him of this.
    I'll have this knot knit up tomorrow morning.
25   JULIET   I met the youthful lord at Laurence' cell,
    And gave him what becomèd° love I might,   *becoming; suitable*
    Not stepping o'er the bounds of modesty.
    CAPULET   Why, I am glad on't!° This is well. Stand up!   *of it*

4.2 Location: Capulet's house.   1. An obstinate, self-willed brat she is.

This is as't should be. —Let me see the County;
30   Ay, marry, go, I say, and fetch him hither.
      Now, afore God, this reverend holy friar—
      All our whole city is much bound to him.
JULIET   Nurse, will you go with me into my closet°   *chamber*
      To help me sort such needful ornaments
35   As you think fit to furnish me tomorrow?
CAPULET'S WIFE   No, not till Thursday; there is time enough.
CAPULET   Go, Nurse; go with her. We'll to church tomorrow.
                          Exeunt [JULIET *and* NURSE].
CAPULET'S WIFE   We shall be short in our provision:
      'Tis now near night.
CAPULET   Tush, I will stir about,
40   And all things shall be well, I warrant thee, wife.
      Go thou to Juliet; help to deck up her.
      I'll not to bed tonight. Let me alone;
      I'll play the housewife for this once. —What ho!
      —They are all forth. Well, I will walk myself
45   To County Paris to prepare up him
      Against tomorrow. My heart is wondrous light
      Since this same wayward girl is so reclaimed.[2]   *Exeunt.*

4.3 (Q1 Scene 17)

Enter JULIET *and* NURSE.
JULIET   Ay, those attires are best. But, gentle Nurse,
      I pray thee leave me to myself tonight,
      For I have need of many orisons°   *prayers*
      To move the heavens to smile upon my state,
5   Which, well thou knowest, is cross° and full of sin.   *adverse*
                Enter [CAPULET'S WIFE].
CAPULET'S WIFE   What, are you busy, ho? Need you my help?
JULIET   No, madam. We have culled such necessaries
      As are behooveful° for our state° tomorrow.   *needful / ceremony*
      So please° you, let me now be left alone,   *If it pleases*
10   And let the Nurse this night sit up with you,
      For I am sure you have your hands full all
      In this so sudden business.
CAPULET'S WIFE   Good night.
      Get thee to bed and rest, for thou hast need.
JULIET   Farewell.   *Exeunt* [CAPULET'S WIFE *and* NURSE].
      God knows when we shall meet again.
15   I have a faint cold fear thrills° through my veins,   *pierces*
      That almost freezes up the heat of life.
      I'll call them back again to comfort me.
      —Nurse! —What should she do here?
      My dismal° scene I needs must act alone.   *calamitous*
20   Come, vial.
      What if this mixture do not work at all?
      Shall I be married, then, tomorrow morning?
      No, no, this shall forbid it. [*She places a knife beside her.*] Lie
          thou there.
      What if it be a poison which the Friar

---

2. Reformed; claimed in marriage.   4.3 Location: Scene continues.

25 Subtly hath ministered to have me dead,
Lest in this marriage he should be dishonored
Because he married me before to Romeo?
I fear it is—and yet methinks it should not,°   *not be*
For he hath still° been tried° a holy man.   *always / proved*
30 How, if when I am laid into the tomb,
I wake before the time that Romeo
Come to redeem me? There's a fearful point!
Shall I not then be stifled in the vault,
To whose foul mouth no healthsome air breathes in,
35 And there die, strangled,° ere my Romeo comes?   *suffocated*
Or, if I live, is it not very like°   *likely*
The horrible conceit of death and night,
Together with the terror of the place,
As° in a vault, an ancient receptacle   *As it is*
40 Where, for this many hundred years, the bones
Of all my buried ancestors are packed—
Where bloody Tybalt, yet but green° in earth,   *newly*
Lies fest'ring in his shroud—where, as they say,
At some hours in the night spirits resort—
45 Alack, alack! Is it not like that I,
So early waking, what with loathsome smells
And shrieks like mandrakes[1] torn out of the earth
That living mortals, hearing them, run mad—
Oh, if I wake, shall I not be distraught,
50 Environèd with all these hideous fears,
And madly play with my forefathers' joints,
And pluck the mangled Tybalt from his shroud,
And, in this rage,° with some great kinsman's bone,   *insanity*
As with a club, dash out my desp'rate brains?
55 Oh, look! Methinks I see my cousin's ghost,
Seeking out Romeo that did spit his body
Upon a rapier's point. —Stay, Tybalt, stay!
—Romeo, Romeo, Romeo! Here's drink. I drink to thee.
[*She drinks from the vial and falls upon her bed
within the curtains.*]

4.4 (Q1 Scene 17 [continued])
Enter [CAPULET'S WIFE] *and* NURSE.
CAPULET'S WIFE   Hold! Take these keys and fetch more spices,
Nurse.
NURSE   They call for dates and quinces in the pastry.°   *pastry kitchen*
Enter old CAPULET.
CAPULET   Come, stir, stir, stir! The second cock hath crowed;
The curfew bell[1] hath rung; 'tis three o'clock!
5 Look to the baked meats, good Angelica;[2]
Spare not for cost.
NURSE   Go, you cotquean,° go!   *old housewife*
Get you to bed. Faith, you'll be sick tomorrow
For this night's watching.°   *wakefulness*

---

1. Plants with forked roots thought to resemble a
man. Popular belief held that they uttered a death- or
madness-producing shriek upon being pulled up.
4.4 Location: Scene continues.

1. Also rung at daybreak.
2. It is unclear whether Capulet refers to his wife or
the Nurse.

CAPULET   No, not a whit. What, I have watched ere now
10   All night for lesser cause, and ne'er been sick!
CAPULET'S WIFE   Ay, you have been a mouse-hunt° in your time,   *skirt chaser*
But I will watch° you from such watching now.   *guard*
                    Exeunt [CAPULET'S WIFE] *and* NURSE.
CAPULET   A jealous-hood,³ a jealous-hood!
          Enter three or four [SERVINGMEN] *with spits and logs
          and baskets.*
                              —Now, fellow, what is there?
FIRST SERVINGMAN   Things for the cook, sir, but I know not
     what.
CAPULET   Make haste, make haste!   [*Exit* FIRST SERVINGMAN.]
15   —Sirrah, fetch drier logs.
     Call Peter; he will show thee where they are.
SECOND SERVINGMAN   I have a head, sir, that will find out logs,⁴
     And never trouble Peter for the matter.
                              [*Exit* SECOND SERVINGMAN.]
CAPULET   Mass,° and well said! A merry whoreson,° ha!   *By the mass / rogue*
20   Thou shalt be loggerhead.° Good Father, 'tis day!   *wooden-headed*
     The County will be here with music straight,
     For so he said he would.
               Play music [*within*].
                    I hear him near!
     Nurse! Wife! What ho! What, Nurse, I say!
          Enter NURSE.
     Go waken Juliet; go and trim her up.
25   I'll go and chat with Paris. Hie, make haste,
     Make haste! The bridegroom, he is come already!
     Make haste, I say!
NURSE   Mistress! What, Mistress Juliet! —Fast,° I warrant   *Asleep*
     her, she—
     Why, lamb! Why, lady! Fie, you slug-a-bed!
30   Why, love, I say! Madam! Sweetheart! Why, bride!
     What, not a word? You take your pennyworth's° now;   *bits (of sleep)*
     Sleep for a week—for the next night, I warrant,
     The County Paris hath set up his rest⁵
     That you shall rest but little, God forgive me.
35   Marry, and amen! —How sound is she asleep!
     I needs must wake her. —Madam, madam, madam!
     Ay, let the County take° you in your bed: *catch; sexually possess*
     He'll fright you up, i'faith. Will it not be?
          [*She draws back the curtains.*]
     What, dressed and in your clothes, and down again?
40   I must needs wake you. Lady, lady, lady!
     Alas, alas! —Help, help! My lady's dead!
     Oh, welladay,° that ever I was born!   *alas*
     Some aqua vitae, ho! My lord! My lady!
          [*Enter* CAPULET'S WIFE.]
CAPULET'S WIFE   What noise is here?
NURSE   Oh, lamentable day!
CAPULET'S WIFE   What is the matter?
45 NURSE   Look! Look! Oh, heavy day!

---

3. Jealousy; jealous woman.
4. I have a good head for finding things, so I can
certainly find the logs; my head knows all about logs

(I am a blockhead).
5. *hath . . . rest*: has resolved (from staking everything in the card game primero), with bawdy pun.

CAPULET'S WIFE   O me, O me! —My child, my only life!
  Revive, look up, or I will die with thee!
  —Help, help! Call help!
      Enter [CAPULET].
CAPULET   For shame, bring Juliet forth! Her lord is come.
50 NURSE   She's dead, deceased; she's dead, alack the day!
CAPULET'S WIFE   Alack the day! She's dead, she's dead, she's
    dead!
CAPULET   Ha! Let me see her. Out,° alas, she's cold!   *Woe*
  Her blood is settled,° and her joints are stiff;   *motionless*
  Life and these lips have long been separated.
55 Death lies on her like an untimely frost
  Upon the sweetest flower of all the field.
NURSE   Oh, lamentable day!
CAPULET'S WIFE   Oh, woeful time!
CAPULET   Death, that hath ta'en her hence to make me wail,
  Ties up my tongue and will not let me speak.
      Enter FRIAR [LAURENCE] *and the County* [PARIS].
60 FRIAR LAURENCE   Come, is the bride ready to go to church?
CAPULET   Ready to go, but never to return.
  —O son, the night before thy wedding day
  Hath Death lain with thy wife. There she lies,
  Flower as she was, deflowered by him.
65 Death is my son-in-law; Death is my heir;
  My daughter he hath wedded. I will die
  And leave him all. Life, living,° all is Death's.   *property*
PARIS [*as to* JULIET]   Have I thought,° love, to see this   *expected*
    morning's face,
  And doth it give me such a sight as this?
70 CAPULET'S WIFE   Accursed, unhappy, wretched, hateful day!
  Most miserable hour that e'er time saw
  In lasting labor of his pilgrimage!
  But one, poor one, one poor and loving child,
  But one thing to rejoice and solace in—
75 And cruel death hath catched it from my sight.
NURSE   Oh, woe! Oh, woeful, woeful, woeful day!
  Most lamentable day! Most woeful day
  That ever, ever I did yet behold!
  Oh, day! Oh, day! Oh, day! Oh, hateful day!
80 Never was seen so black a day as this.
  Oh, woeful day! Oh, woeful day!
PARIS   Beguiled,° divorcèd, wrongèd, spited,° slain!   *Cheated / injured*
  Most detestable death, by thee beguiled,
  By cruel, cruel thee quite overthrown.
85 O love, O life—not life, but love in death.
CAPULET   Despised, distressed, hated, martyred, killed!
  Uncomfortable° time, why cam'st thou now   *Comfortless*
  To murder, murder our solemnity?°   *festivity*
  O child, O child, my soul and not my child,[6]
90 Dead art thou. Alack, my child is dead,
  And with my child my joys are burièd.
FRIAR LAURENCE   Peace, ho, for shame! Confusion's° care   *Destruction's*
    lives not

---

6. *not my child*: because dead and only a corpse.

In these confusions.° Heaven and yourself — *commotions*
Had part in this fair maid; now heaven hath all,
95 And all the better is it for the maid.
Your part in her you could not keep from death,
But heaven keeps his part in eternal life.
The most you sought was her promotion,° — *social advancement*
For 'twas your heaven° she should be advanced; — *highest ambition*
100 And weep ye now, seeing she is advanced
Above the clouds, as high as heaven itself?
Oh, in this love you love your child so ill
That you run mad, seeing that she is well.
She's not well married that lives married long,
105 But she's best married that dies married young.
Dry up your tears, and stick your rosemary⁷
On this fair corpse; and, as the custom is,
And in her best array, bear her to church.
For, though some nature° bids us all lament, — *affection*
110 Yet nature's tears are reason's merriment.° — *laughable idiocy*
CAPULET   All things that we ordainèd festival
Turn from their office° to black funeral: — *due function*
Our instruments to melancholy bells,
Our wedding cheer° to a sad burial feast, — *fare*
115 Our solemn° hymns to sullen° dirges change; — *ceremonial / mournful*
Our bridal flowers serve for a buried corpse,
And all things change them to the contrary.
FRIAR LAURENCE   Sir, go you in; and, madam, go with him;
And go, Sir Paris. Everyone prepare
120 To follow this fair corpse unto her grave.
The heavens do lour° upon you for some ill;° — *hang threatening / offense*
Move° them no more by crossing their high will. — *Anger*
Exeunt [all but the NURSE].
[Enter three MUSICIANS.]
FIRST MUSICIAN   Faith, we may put° up our pipes and be gone. — *pack*
NURSE   Honest good fellows—ah, put up, put up!
125 For well you know this is a pitiful case.
FIRST MUSICIAN   Ay, by my troth, the case may be amended.⁸
Exit [NURSE].
Enter [PETER].
PETER   Musicians! O musicians! "Heart's Ease"!° "Heart's — *(popular song)*
Ease"! Oh, an you will have me live, play "Heart's Ease"!
FIRST MUSICIAN   Why "Heart's Ease"?
130 PETER   O musicians, because my heart itself plays "My heart
is full." Oh, play me some merry dump° to comfort me. — *sad tune*
MUSICIANS   Not a dump, we! 'Tis no time to play now.
PETER   You will not, then?
FIRST MUSICIAN   No.
135 PETER   I will, then, give it you soundly.° — *thoroughly; in sound*
FIRST MUSICIAN   What will you give us?
PETER   No money, on my faith, but the gleek.⁹ I will give you
the minstrel.¹

---

7. Traditionally, a symbol of remembrance.
8. Things could be better; the instrument case can be repaired.

9. To "give the gleek" was to make a fool of or play a trick on.
1. I will insultingly call you a minstrel.

FIRST MUSICIAN   Then will I give you the serving-creature.

140 PETER   Then will I lay the serving-creature's dagger on your
pate. I will carry° no crotchets;[2] I'll re you, I'll fa you, do you   *bear; sing*
note° me?   *heed*

FIRST MUSICIAN   An you re us and fa us, you note° us.   *give notes to*

SECOND MUSICIAN   Pray you, put up your dagger, and put out°   *show; quench*
145 your wit.

PETER   Then have at you with my wit! I will dry-beat° you with   *thrash*
an iron° wit, and put up my iron dagger. Answer[3] me like men.   *a merciless*
[*Sings.*]   When griping griefs the heart doth wound,
Then music with her silver sound[4]—

150 Why "silver sound"? Why "music with her silver sound"?
What say you, Simon Catling?[5]

FIRST MUSICIAN   Marry, sir, because silver hath a sweet sound.

PETER   Prates!° What say you, Hugh Rebeck?[6]   *Chatter*

SECOND MUSICIAN   I say "silver sound," because musicians
155 sound for silver.

PETER   Prates, too! What say you, James Soundpost?[7]

THIRD MUSICIAN   Faith, I know not what to say.

PETER   Oh, I cry you mercy!° You are the singer; I will say for   *beg your pardon*
you. It is "music with her silver sound," because musicians
160 have no gold for sounding.[8]
[*Sings.*]   Then music with her silver sound
With speedy help doth lend redress.   *Exit.*

FIRST MUSICIAN   What a pestilent knave is this same!

SECOND MUSICIAN   Hang him, jack! Come, we'll in here, tarry
165 for the mourners, and stay° dinner.   *Exeunt.*   *await*

5.1 (Q1 Scene 18)

Enter ROMEO.

ROMEO   If I may trust the flattering° truth of sleep,   *encouraging*
My dreams presage some joyful news at hand.
My bosom's lord sits lightly in his throne,[1]
And all this day an unaccustomed spirit
5   Lifts me above the ground with cheerful thoughts.
I dreamt my lady came and found me dead—
Strange dream that gives a dead man leave to think—
And breathed such life with kisses in° my lips   *into*
That I revived and was an emperor.
10   Ah me, how sweet is love itself possessed°   *enjoyed in reality*
When but love's shadows° are so rich in joy!   *dreams; images*
Enter [BALTHASAR,] *Romeo's man.*[2]
News from Verona! How now, Balthasar?
Dost thou not bring me letters from the Friar?
How doth my lady? Is my father well?
15   How doth my lady Juliet? That I ask again,
For nothing can be ill if she be well.

BALTHASAR   Then she is well, and nothing can be ill.

---

2. Whimsy; quarter notes.
3. Defy; respond to.
4. Lines from the song "In Commendation of
Music," by Richard Edwardes, printed in *The Paradise of Dainty Devices* (1576).
5. *Catling*: catgut used for stringed instruments.
6. *Rebeck*: three-stringed instrument.
7. *Soundpost*: supporting peg fixed between the

sounding board and back of a stringed instrument.
8. Musicians are given no gold for playing; they are
poor and have no gold to jingle.
5.1 Location: A street in Mantua.
1. Love rules in the heart; the heart is at ease in the
chest.
2. In Q1, the stage direction indicates that Romeo's
man is "*booted*," as if he has just dismounted.

Her body sleeps in Capels' monument,
And her immortal part with angels lives.
20 I saw her laid low in her kindred's vault,
And presently° took post[3] to tell it you.   *immediately*
Oh, pardon me for bringing these ill news,
Since you did leave it for my office,° sir.   *duty*
ROMEO Is it e'en so? Then I deny° you, stars!   *repudiate*
25 —Thou knowest my lodging. Get me ink and paper,
And hire post-horses; I will hence tonight.
BALTHASAR I do beseech you, sir, have patience:
Your looks are pale and wild, and do import°   *signify*
Some misadventure.
ROMEO   Tush, thou art deceived.
30 Leave me, and do the thing I bid thee do.
Hast thou no letters to me from the Friar?
BALTHASAR No, my good lord.
ROMEO   No matter. Get thee gone,
And hire those horses. I'll be with thee straight.
                              Exit [BALTHASAR].
Well, Juliet, I will lie with thee tonight.
35 Let's see for means. O mischief, thou art swift
To enter in the thoughts of desperate men.
I do remember an apothecary,
And hereabouts 'a dwells, which late I noted,
In tattered weeds,° with overwhelming° brows,   *clothes / overhanging*
40 Culling of simples.° Meager were his looks;   *herbs*
Sharp misery had worn him to the bones;
And in his needy° shop a tortoise hung,   *poor*
An alligator stuffed, and other skins
Of ill-shaped fishes; and, about his shelves,
45 A beggarly account° of empty boxes,   *sparse collection*
Green earthen pots, bladders, and musty seeds,
Remnants of packthread,° and old cakes of roses[4]   *twine*
Were thinly scattered to make up a show.
Noting this penury, to myself I said,
50 "An if a man did need a poison now,
Whose sale is present death[5] in Mantua,
Here lives a caitiff° wretch would sell it him."   *pitiful*
Oh, this same thought did but forerun my need,
And this same needy man must sell it me.
55 As I remember, this should be the house.
Being holiday, the beggar's shop is shut.
—What ho, Apothecary!
          [*Enter* APOTHECARY.]
APOTHECARY   Who calls so loud?
ROMEO Come hither, man. I see that thou art poor.
Hold, there is forty ducats.[6] Let me have
60 A dram of poison, such soon-speeding gear[7]
As will disperse itself through all the veins
That the life-weary taker may fall dead,
And that the trunk° may be discharged of breath   *body*

3. Set out on post-horses.
4. Rose petals pressed into cake form and used as a sachet.
5. Punishable by immediate death.

6. Various gold coins used at times in much of Europe, and Shakespeare's usual currency for plays not set in England.
7. Quick-working stuff; quick-killing stuff.

As violently as hasty powder fired
65   Doth hurry from the fatal cannon's womb.
APOTHECARY   Such mortal drugs I have, but Mantua's law
    Is death to any he° that utters° them.   *man / offers to sell*
ROMEO   Art thou so bare° and full of wretchedness,   *destitute*
    And fearest to die? Famine is in thy cheeks;
70   Need and oppression starveth in thy eyes;
    Contempt and beggary hangs upon thy back.
    The world is not thy friend, nor the world's law;
    The world affords° no law to make thee rich;   *provides*
    Then be not poor, but break it, and take this.
75 APOTHECARY   My poverty, but not my will, consents.
ROMEO   I pay thy poverty and not thy will.
APOTHECARY   Put this in any liquid thing you will,
    And drink it off; and if you had the strength
    Of twenty men, it would dispatch you straight.°   *immediately*
80 ROMEO   There is thy gold—worse poison to men's souls,
    Doing more murder in this loathsome world
    Than these poor compounds that thou mayst not sell.
    I sell thee poison; thou hast sold me none.
    Farewell. Buy food, and get thyself in flesh.°   *grow fatter*

                          [*Exit* APOTHECARY.]

85   Come, cordial° and not poison, go with me   *restorative*
    To Juliet's grave, for there must I use thee.   *Exit.*

5.2 (Q1 Scene 19)

    Enter FRIAR JOHN.
FRIAR JOHN   Holy Franciscan Friar! Brother, ho!
    Enter FRIAR LAURENCE.
FRIAR LAURENCE   This same should be the voice of Friar John.
    —Welcome from Mantua! What says Romeo?
    Or, if his mind° be writ, give me his letter.   *thoughts*
5 FRIAR JOHN   Going to find a barefoot brother out,
    One of our order, to associate me,[1]
    Here in this city visiting the sick,
    And finding him, the searchers[2] of the town,
    Suspecting that we both were in a house
10   Where the infectious pestilence did reign,
    Sealed up the doors and would not let us forth,
    So that my speed to Mantua there was stayed.°   *stopped*
FRIAR LAURENCE   Who bare my letter, then, to Romeo?
FRIAR JOHN   I could not send it—here it is again—
15   Nor get a messenger to bring it thee,
    So fearful were they of infection.°   *contagion*
FRIAR LAURENCE   Unhappy fortune! By my brotherhood,
    The letter was not nice° but full of charge,°   *trivial / importance*
    Of dear import,° and the neglecting it   *serious consequence*
20   May do much danger. Friar John, go hence,
    Get me an iron crow,° and bring it straight   *crowbar*
    Unto my cell.
FRIAR JOHN   Brother, I'll go and bring it thee.   *Exit.*
FRIAR LAURENCE   Now must I to the monument alone.

5.2 Location: Friar Laurence's cell.   accompany.
1. Franciscan friars (barefoot because the order is   2. Health officers appointed to examine corpses and
sworn to poverty) traveled only in pairs. *associate:*   identify houses infected with the plague.

Within this three hours will fair Juliet wake;
25 She will beshrew° me much that Romeo   *curse*
Hath had no notice of these accidents,°   *events*
But I will write again to Mantua
And keep her at my cell till Romeo come.
Poor living corpse, closed in a dead man's tomb!   *Exit.*

5.3 (Q1 Scene 20)

Enter PARIS *and his* PAGE.

PARIS Give me thy torch, boy—hence, and stand aloof°—   *stay apart*
Yet put it out, for I would not be seen.
Under yond young trees lay thee all along,°   *stretched out*
Holding thy ear close to the hollow ground;
5 So shall no foot upon the churchyard tread,
Being° loose, unfirm with digging up of graves,   *The ground being*
But thou shalt hear it. Whistle then to me
As signal that thou hearest something approach.
Give me those flowers. Do as I bid thee. Go.
10 PAGE [*aside*] I am almost afraid to stand alone
Here in the churchyard, yet I will adventure.°   *risk it*
[*He retires.*]
PARIS [*as to* JULIET] Sweet flower, with flowers thy bridal bed
I strew—
Oh, woe, thy canopy° is dust and stones—   *covering; bed hangings*
Which with sweet° water nightly I will dew,   *perfumed*
15 Or, wanting that, with tears distilled by moans.
The obsequies° that I for thee will keep°   *funeral rites / perform*
Nightly shall be to strew thy grave and weep.
[PAGE *whistles.*]
The boy gives warning something doth approach.
What cursèd foot wanders this way tonight
20 To cross° my obsequies and true love's rite?   *thwart*
Enter ROMEO *and* [BALTHASAR].
What? With a torch? Muffle me, night, a while.
[*He retires.*]
ROMEO Give me that mattock° and the wrenching iron.   *pickax*
Hold; take this letter; early in the morning
See thou deliver it to my lord and father.
25 Give me the light. Upon thy life, I charge thee,
Whate'er thou hearest or seest, stand all aloof,
And do not interrupt me in my course.
Why I descend into this bed of death
Is partly to behold my lady's face,
30 But chiefly to take thence from her dead finger
A precious ring, a ring that I must use
In dear° employment. Therefore, hence; be gone.   *important; tender*
But if thou, jealous,° dost return to pry   *suspicious*
In what I farther shall intend to do,
35 By heaven, I will tear thee joint by joint
And strew this hungry churchyard with thy limbs!
The time and my intents are savage-wild,
More fierce and more inexorable far
Than empty° tigers or the roaring sea.   *hungry*

5.3 Location: The Capulet mausoleum.

40   BALTHASAR   I will be gone, sir, and not trouble ye.
    ROMEO   So shalt thou show me friendship. Take thou that.
        [*He gives* BALTHASAR *money.*]
    Live, and be prosperous; and farewell, good fellow.
    BALTHASAR [*aside*]   For all this same, I'll hide me here about.
    His looks I fear, and his intents I doubt.°   *suspect*
        [*He retires.*]
        [ROMEO *opens the tomb.*]
45   ROMEO   Thou detestable maw, thou womb[1] of death,
    Gorged with the dearest morsel of the earth,
    Thus I enforce thy rotten jaws to open,
    And, in despite,° I'll cram thee with more food.   *defiant ill will*
    PARIS [*apart*]   This is that banished haughty Montague
50   That murdered my love's cousin, with which grief
    It is supposèd the fair creature died,
    And here is come to do some villainous shame
    To the dead bodies. I will apprehend him.
        [*He steps forward.*]
    —Stop thy unhallowed° toil, vile Montague!   *unholy*
55   Can vengeance be pursued further than death?
    Condemnèd villain, I do apprehend thee.
    Obey and go with me, for thou must die.
    ROMEO   I must indeed, and therefore came I hither.
    Good gentle youth, tempt not a desp'rate° man;   *despairing; violent*
60   Fly hence and leave me. Think upon these gone;
    Let them affright thee. I beseech thee, youth,
    Put not another sin upon my head
    By urging me to fury. Oh, be gone!
    By heaven, I love thee better than myself,
65   For I come hither armed against myself.
    Stay not; be gone. Live, and hereafter say
    A madman's mercy bid thee run away.
    PARIS   I do defy thy conjuration,°   *entreaty*
    And apprehend thee for a felon here.
70   ROMEO   Wilt thou provoke me? Then have at thee, boy!
        [*They fight.*]
    PAGE   O Lord, they fight! I will go call the watch.   [*Exit.*]
    PARIS   Oh, I am slain! If thou be merciful,
    Open the tomb; lay me with Juliet.
        [*He dies.*]
    ROMEO   In faith, I will. —Let me peruse this face.
75   Mercutio's kinsman, noble County Paris!
    What said my man when my betossèd° soul   *storm-tossed*
    Did not attend° him as we rode? I think   *listen to*
    He told me Paris should have married Juliet.
    Said he not so? Or did I dream it so?
80   Or am I mad, hearing him talk of Juliet,
    To think it was so? —Oh, give me thy hand,
    One writ with me in sour misfortune's book.
    I'll bury thee in a triumphant° grave,   *magnificent*
    A grave—oh, no, a lantern,° slaughtered youth,   *lighthouse*
85   For here lies Juliet, and her beauty makes

---

1. Belly; also playing on the birthplace of Romeo's death.

This vault a feasting presence[2] full of light.
Death, lie thou there, by a dead man interred.
How oft when men are at the point of death
Have they been merry, which their keepers° call   *sick nurses; jailers*
90 A light'ning before death? Oh, how may I
Call this a light'ning? —O my love, my wife,
Death that hath sucked the honey of thy breath
Hath had no power yet upon thy beauty.
Thou art not conquered:° beauty's ensign° yet   *overpowered; seduced / flag*
95 Is crimson in thy lips and in thy cheeks,
And death's pale flag is not advancèd there.
—Tybalt, liest thou there in thy bloody sheet?
Oh, what more favor can I do to thee
Than with that hand that cut thy youth in twain
100 To sunder his° that was thine enemy?   *the youth of him*
Forgive me, cousin. —Ah, dear Juliet,
Why art thou yet so fair? Shall I believe
That unsubstantial° death is amorous,   *immaterial*
And that the lean abhorrèd monster keeps
105 Thee here in dark to be his paramour?
For fear of that I still will stay with thee,
And never from this pallet of dim night
Depart again. Here, here will I remain
With worms that are thy chambermaids; oh, here
110 Will I set up my everlasting rest,[3]
And shake the yoke of inauspicious stars
From this world-wearied flesh. Eyes, look your last;
Arms, take your last embrace; and lips—O you,
The doors of breath—seal with a righteous kiss
115 A dateless bargain° to engrossing[4] death.   *An eternal contract*
Come, bitter conduct;° come, unsavory guide,   *conductor; leader*
Thou desperate pilot, now at once run on
The dashing rocks thy seasick, weary bark!
Here's to my love. [*He drinks.*] O true apothecary,
120 Thy drugs are quick.° Thus, with a kiss, I die.[5]   *fast; vigorous*
    [*He falls and dies.*]
    Enter FRIAR [LAURENCE] *with lantern, crow,*
    and spade.
FRIAR LAURENCE   Saint Francis be my speed!° How oft tonight   *help*
Have my old feet stumbled at graves! —Who's there?
    [BALTHASAR *steps forward.*]
BALTHASAR   Here's one, a friend, and one that knows you
    well.
FRIAR   Bliss be upon you! Tell me, good my friend,
125 What torch is yond that vainly lends his light
To grubs and eyeless skulls? As I discern,
It burneth in the Capels' monument.
BALTHASAR   It doth so, holy sir, and there's my master,
One that you love.
FRIAR LAURENCE   Who is it?
BALTHASAR   Romeo.

---

2. Festive royal chamber for receiving guests.
3. Make my final determination.
4. Buying up in large quantities to monopolize; writing a legal document.

5. PERFORMANCE COMMENT On the different directorial possibilities for staging Romeo's death, see Digital Edition PC 5.

FRIAR LAURENCE   How long hath he been there?

130 BALTHASAR   Full half an hour.

FRIAR LAURENCE   Go with me to the vault.

BALTHASAR   I dare not, sir.
My master knows not but I am gone hence,
And fearfully° did menace me with death   *fearsomely*
If I did stay to look on his intents.

135 FRIAR LAURENCE   Stay, then. I'll go alone. Fear comes upon
         me.
Oh, much I fear some ill unthrifty° thing.   *unfortunate*

BALTHASAR   As I did sleep under this young tree here,
I dreamt my master and another fought,
And that my master slew him.
         [FRIAR LAURENCE *moves toward the vault.*]

FRIAR LAURENCE   Romeo!

140 Alack, alack, what blood is this which stains
The stony entrance of this sepulcher?
What mean these masterless and gory swords
To lie discolored by this place of peace?
Romeo! Oh, pale! Who else? What, Paris too?

145 And steeped in blood? Ah, what an unkind° hour   *an unnatural; a cruel*
Is guilty of this lamentable chance!°   *event*
         [JULIET *rises.*]
The lady stirs!

JULIET   O comfortable° Friar, where is my lord?   *solace-giving*
I do remember well where I should be,

150 And there I am. Where is my Romeo?

FRIAR LAURENCE   I hear some noise. —Lady, come from that
         nest
Of death, contagion, and unnatural sleep.
A greater power than we can contradict
Hath thwarted our intents. Come. Come away!

155 Thy husband in thy bosom there lies dead,
And Paris, too. Come—I'll dispose of thee
Among a sisterhood of holy nuns.
Stay not to question, for the watch is coming.
Come! Go, good Juliet! I dare no longer stay.

160 JULIET   Go, get thee hence, for I will not away.
                              Exit [FRIAR LAURENCE].
What's here? A cup closed in my true love's hand?
Poison I see hath been his timeless° end.   *untimely; lasting*
O churl,° drunk all, and left no friendly drop   *miser*
To help me after? I will kiss thy lips:

165 Haply° some poison yet doth hang on them   *Perhaps*
To make me die with a restorative.[6]
Thy lips are warm!
         Enter [PAGE *and* WATCHMEN].

CHIEF WATCHMAN   Lead, boy. Which way?

JULIET   Yea, noise? Then I'll be brief.
         [*She takes Romeo's dagger.*]
                                        O happy° dagger,   *fortunate*

170 This is thy sheath; there rust and let me die.
         [*She stabs herself and falls.*]

---

6. Both the kiss, which is healing, and the poison, which restores them to each other.

PAGE This is the place—there, where the torch doth burn.

CHIEF WATCHMAN The ground is bloody. Search about the
churchyard.

Go, some of you; whoe'er you find, attach.°   *arrest*
        [*Exeunt some of the watch.*]

Pitiful sight! Here lies the County, slain,

175 And Juliet, bleeding, warm, and newly dead,

Who here hath lain this two days buried.

Go tell the Prince! Run to the Capulets;

Raise up the Montagues! Some others, search.
        [*Exeunt others of the watch.*]

We see the ground° whereon these woes do lie,   *earth*

180 But the true ground° of all these piteous woes   *cause*

We cannot without circumstance° descry.   *a fuller account*
    Enter [SECOND WATCHMAN *with*] *Romeo's man*
    [BALTHASAR].

SECOND WATCHMAN Here's Romeo's man; we found him in
the churchyard.

CHIEF WATCHMAN Hold him in safety° till the Prince come   *securely*
hither.
    Enter [THIRD WATCHMAN *with* FRIAR LAURENCE].

THIRD WATCHMAN Here is a friar that trembles, sighs, and
weeps.

185 We took this mattock and this spade from him

As he was coming from this churchyard's side.[7]

CHIEF WATCHMAN A great suspicion! Stay° the Friar, too.   *Hold*
    Enter the PRINCE [*with Attendants*].

PRINCE What misadventure is so early up

That calls our person from our morning rest?
    Enter [CAPULET *and* CAPULET'S WIFE].

190 CAPULET What should it be that is so shrieked abroad?

CAPULET'S WIFE Oh, the people in the street cry "Romeo,"

Some "Juliet," and some "Paris," and all run

With open° outcry toward our monument!   *public; open-mouthed*

PRINCE What fear is this which startles° in your ears?   *bursts out*

195 CHIEF WATCHMAN Sovereign, here lies the County Paris slain,

And Romeo dead, and Juliet—dead before—

Warm, and new killed.

PRINCE Search, seek, and know how this foul murder comes.

CHIEF WATCHMAN Here is a friar, and slaughtered Romeo's
man,

200 With instruments upon them fit to open

These dead men's tombs.

CAPULET O heavens! O wife, look how our daughter bleeds!

This dagger hath mista'en, for lo, his house°   *scabbard*

Is empty on the back of Montague,

205 And it mis-sheathèd in my daughter's bosom.

CAPULET'S WIFE O me, this sight of death is as a bell

That warns° my old age to a sepulcher.   *summons*
    Enter MONTAGUE [*with Attendants*].

PRINCE Come, Montague, for thou art early up

To see thy son and heir now early down.

210 MONTAGUE Alas, my liege, my wife is dead tonight;

---

7. This side of the churchyard.

Grief of my son's exile hath stopped her breath.
What further woe conspires against mine age?
PRINCE   Look, and thou shalt see.
MONTAGUE [*as to* ROMEO]   O thou untaught! What manners is
    in this,
215   To press before° thy father to a grave?   *To shove ahead of*
PRINCE   Seal up the mouth of outrage[8] for a while,
    Till we can clear these ambiguities
    And know their spring, their head, their true descent;
    And then will I be general of your woes
220   And lead you even to death. Meantime, forbear,
    And let mischance be slave to° patience.   *overruled by*
    Bring forth the parties of suspicion.
FRIAR LAURENCE   I am the greatest,° able to do least,   *most suspect*
    Yet most suspected as the time and place
225   Doth make against me of this direful murder.
    And here I stand both to impeach and purge,
    Myself condemnèd and myself excused.[9]
PRINCE   Then say at once what thou dost know in this.
FRIAR   I will be brief, for my short date° of breath   *duration*
230   Is not so long as is a tedious tale.
    Romeo, there dead, was husband to that Juliet,
    And she, there dead—that's Romeo's faithful wife.
    I married them, and their stol'n marriage day
    Was Tybalt's doomsday, whose untimely death
235   Banished the new-made bridegroom from this city—
    For whom, and not for Tybalt, Juliet pined.
    —You, to remove that siege of grief from her,
    Betrothed and would have married her perforce°   *forcibly*
    To County Paris. Then comes she to me,
240   And, with wild looks, bid me devise some mean°   *method*
    To rid her from this second marriage,
    Or in my cell there would she kill herself.
    Then gave I her—so tutored by my art[1]—
    A sleeping potion, which so took effect
245   As I intended, for it wrought on her
    The form° of death. Meantime I writ to Romeo   *appearance*
    That he should hither come as this° dire night   *as this = this*
    To help to take her from her borrowed grave,
    Being the time the potion's force should cease.
250   But he which bore my letter, Friar John,
    Was stayed by accident, and yesternight
    Returned my letter back. Then, all alone,
    At the prefixèd° hour of her waking,   *prearranged*
    Came I to take her from her kindred's vault,
255   Meaning to keep her closely° at my cell   *secretly*
    Till I conveniently° could send to Romeo.   *befittingly*
    But when I came, some minute ere the time
    Of her awakening, here untimely lay
    The noble Paris and true Romeo, dead.
260   She wakes, and I entreated her come forth
    And bear this work of heaven with patience;

8. Of impassioned exclamation.
9. *to impeach . . . excused:* to accuse myself of what I
am guilty of and clear myself of what I am not.
1. As I knew through my medical study to do.

But then a noise did scare me from the tomb,
And she, too desperate, would not go with me,
But, as it seems, did violence on herself.
265 All this I know—and to the marriage
Her Nurse is privy; and, if aught in this
Miscarried by my fault, let my old life
Be sacrificed some hour before his° time   *its*
Unto the rigor of severest law.
270 PRINCE We still° have known thee for a holy man.   *always*
—Where's Romeo's man? What can he say to this?
BALTHASAR I brought my master news of Juliet's death,
And then in post° he came from Mantua   *haste*
To this same place, to this same monument.
275 This letter he early bid me give his father,
And threatened me with death, going in the vault,
If I departed not and left him there.
PRINCE Give me the letter; I will look on it.
Where is the County's page that raised the watch?
280 —Sirrah, what made° your master in this place?   *did*
PAGE He came with flowers to strew his lady's grave,
And bid me stand aloof, and so I did.
Anon° comes one with light to ope the tomb,   *Soon*
And by and by my master drew on him,
285 And then I ran away to call the watch.
PRINCE This letter doth make good the Friar's words—
Their course of love, the tidings of her death.
And here he writes that he did buy a poison
Of a poor 'pothecary, and therewithal
290 Came to this vault to die and lie with Juliet.
Where be these enemies? —Capulet, Montague:
See what a scourge is laid upon your hate,
That heaven finds means to kill your joys° with love,   *happiness; children*
And I, for winking at° your discords, too   *closing my eyes to*
295 Have lost a brace of kinsmen. All are punished.
CAPULET O brother Montague, give me thy hand.
This is my daughter's jointure,° for no more   *marriage portion*
Can I demand.
MONTAGUE   But I can give thee more;
For I will ray° her statue in pure gold,   *array (i.e., gild)*
300 That whiles Verona by that name is known
There shall no figure at such rate be set²
As that of true and faithful Juliet.
CAPULET As rich shall Romeo's by his lady's lie,
Poor sacrifices of our enmity.
305 PRINCE A glooming° peace this morning with it brings;   *frowning; dark*
The sun for sorrow will not show his head.
Go hence to have more talk of these sad things—
Some shall be pardoned, and some punishèd—
For never was a story of more woe
310 Than this of Juliet and her Romeo.   [*Exeunt.*]

---

2. No figure shall be so valued; no figure shall be erected at such a price.

Julius Caesar

In *Julius Caesar,* Shakespeare dramatizes incidents of world-historical significance. As the events of the play unfold, the characters are constantly aware that the eyes of the world are, and will remain, upon them. Indeed, one of the protagonists, Caius Cassius, eagerly anticipates his own impersonated presence on Shakespeare's stage:

> How many ages hence
> Shall this our lofty scene be acted over
> In states unborn and accents yet unknown!
> (3.1.112–14)

Cassius correctly forecasts that his own actions, although they will eventually become ancient history, will nonetheless remain compelling to people far removed in time, place, and language from the original events. Implicit in Cassius's prediction, moreover, may be a sly conjecture on Shakespeare's part about the power of his own drama to echo down the centuries. For most modern readers and playgoers, Shakespeare's vivid re-presentation of Julius Caesar's assassination has become much more familiar than the history that inspired it.

What was that history? By 44 B.C.E., an astonishing sequence of conquests had made Rome, once an unremarkable Italian town, the center of a vast empire that stretched from North Africa to Britain, from Babylon to Spain. Yet eventually Rome's outsized ambitions threatened to destroy it. For hundreds of years, Rome had been governed not by a king or a dictator, but by elected officers, and its republican traditions had been a source of fierce civic pride. Yet as the city's military endeavors grew increasingly ambitious, Rome's generals, with the might of their armies behind them, came to wield more power than the factionalized Senate to which they supposedly owed allegiance. Of these generals, the charismatic and enterprising Julius Caesar, who had subdued much of northwest Europe even while consolidating his popularity among the poorer classes at home, seemed particularly dangerous. When legal and military attempts to curb Caesar's growing power failed, a group of conspirators led by Caius Cassius and Marcus Brutus assassinated him. Yet the death of Caesar did not, as his killers had hoped, restore Rome to its tradition of republican government. Instead, civil war ensued, in which Caesar's friend Mark Antony and Caesar's adopted heir, Octavius, defeated the forces of the conspirators. Eventually, after a power struggle among the victors (recounted in Shakespeare's *Antony and Cleopatra*), Octavius was enthroned as the Emperor Augustus. His ascendancy, consolidating immense power in a single individual, completed the political transformation that Julius Caesar's assassins had tried to prevent.

Virtually from the moment the conspirators pulled their swords from Caesar's bleeding corpse, the events that Shakespeare treats in *Julius Caesar* were amply documented and their rationale debated. Different commentators from antiquity to the Renaissance, depending on their own political convictions, viewed the assassination as an act of heroism or villainy and celebrated or denounced its perpetrators accordingly. While Michelangelo and Milton idealize Brutus as a selfless defender of human liberty, Dante plunges him, with Cassius, into the deepest pit of hell. It is not surprising that Shakespeare, ever alive to the dramatic possibilities inherent in multiple, conflicting perspectives, should choose to stage an incident that had been provoking debate for more than sixteen hundred years.

Julius Caesar. From Plutarch, *The Lives of the Noble Grecians and Romans* (1595).

For Shakespeare's contemporaries, the questions raised by Caesar's career were not merely of antiquarian interest. Throughout early modern Europe, strong rulers were attempting, with varying degrees of success, to consolidate their power. In England, these efforts threatened the traditional prerogatives of the aristocracy and of elected representatives in the House of Commons. For thinkers and writers saturated by their classical education in the antique past, it was easy to see the shift toward strong monarchy as replaying the shift from republican to imperial Rome. In England in 1599, moreover, concerns over this general trend were exacerbated by more specific anxieties. Queen Elizabeth I had proven a remarkably durable and effective queen, but at sixty-six, she was an old woman by Renaissance standards. Since she had never begotten children nor named an heir, it was unclear who would succeed her or how the new monarch would be selected. Conceivably England would plunge, upon her death, into civil chaos. In a state in which censorship made direct commentary on contemporary political affairs virtually impossible, the story of Caesar's death and its calamitous aftermath provided an opportunity to reflect, at a suitably prudent distance, upon what might happen when accepted methods of allocating and transferring sovereign power disintegrated.

Although the consequences of Julius Caesar's assassination took years to unfold, the event is historically important because it seems to mark the end of one epoch and the beginning of another. Similarly, Shakespeare's *Julius Caesar*, first performed in 1599, marks a watershed in his career as a playwright. On the one hand, his foray into Roman history seems to look back to, and develop further, some of the central political concerns of the English history plays that Shakespeare had written in the 1590s. *Julius Caesar*, like the history plays, grapples with such questions as: Who constitutes a political community—everybody in the state, both rich and poor, or only the elite and powerful among them? What traits make a person fit to rule, and how is power conferred upon him or her? Are citizens allowed, or even obliged, to defend the rule of law by resorting to extralegal violence? When the demands of civic responsibility apparently conflict with those of personal loyalty, which ought to prevail? In *Julius Caesar*, these are questions not about individuals, but about the life of an entire society.

Yet in the English history plays, especially the "second tetralogy" consisting of *Richard II*, *1* and *2 Henry IV*, and *Henry V*, Shakespeare had dramatized political change in a way that highlighted the significance of individual characters. And in *Julius Caesar*, the problem of individual character figures even more profoundly. In the conflicted, articulate, highly self-conscious Brutus, Shakespeare invents a kind of hero who forecasts those of the tragedies that he will begin to write at the turn of the seventeenth century: the brooding Hamlet, the self-destructive Othello, the murderous but self-analytical Macbeth. Of course, distinctions between "personal" and "political" matters tend to be fuzzy and suspect, and, in a play about an assassination, are likely to be impossible to disentangle. Nonetheless, for all its acute analysis of human beings in groups, *Julius Caesar* turns on a question that seems more personal than social: What brings a man to destroy what he claims to love?

Shakespeare's source materials may well have encouraged this simultaneous attention to political dilemmas and psychological complexity. The most important sources for *Julius Caesar* were the biographies of Caesar and Brutus in Plutarch's *Lives of the Noble Grecians and Romans*, translated into English by Thomas North. Writing in the first century C.E., Plutarch had construed the biographer's task as inextricable from the historian's, since in his view history recorded the achievements of great men. Shakespeare followed Plutarch in stressing the decisive roles played by the acknowledged leaders of Roman society, rather than dwelling on the frictions among larger social groups. Not that he was unaware of the latter: the testiness of *Julius Caesar*'s opening scene makes the internal divisions in Roman society abundantly clear. But throughout the play, commoners are largely imagined from an upper-class perspective, as a politically unsophisticated mob. The capacity for conscious and reflective political decision making rests in the hands of a small elite.

Marc Antony. From Plutarch, *The Lives of the Noble Grecians and Romans* (1595).

Plutarch's "great man" view of history lends itself to compelling dramas involving a manageable number of psychologically complex characters. And Shakespeare's drastic condensation of narrative time frame in *Julius Caesar* has the effect of exaggerating Plutarch's emphases. In Plutarch, Caesar's triumph over Pompey's sons occurs in October, but Shakespeare makes it coincide with the mid-February festival of Lupercalia, so that the assassination on the Ides (15th) of March seems a direct response to a specific display of arrogance. Likewise, in Plutarch, Brutus and Cassius withdraw from Rome more than a year after Caesar's funeral, but in Shakespeare, their flight follows immediately upon Antony's brilliant incitement of the Roman mob. The effect is not only to escalate dramatic momentum but also to make the personal strengths and weaknesses of Rome's leaders seem matters of titanic consequence.

In the Roman Republic, Plutarch claimed, there was always more than one powerful person, but there were rarely more than a few. Shakespeare depicts the last days of the Republic in a drama that no single protagonist appropriates wholly to himself. Instead, *Julius Caesar* divides its attention among several characters, setting them off against one another, while the titular hero makes less claim upon the audience's attention than might be expected. Plutarch's biography emphasizes Caesar's military genius, his ruthless executive skill, and his astonishing capacity to rescue himself repeatedly from crushing adversity. Shakespeare's Caesar seems less outsized. His accomplishments are not shown or much alluded to, and much of what we do hear is filtered through the hostile reports of resentful observers. He wants supremacy less, apparently, because he has any particular vision for the Roman polity than because he yearns for the unqualified homage of others. His egotism seems a bit ridiculous: despite his physical frailties, he imagines himself as embodying a godlike permanence, "unshaked of motion" (3.1.71):

> I am constant as the Northern Star,
> Of whose true-fixed and resting quality
> There is no fellow in the firmament.
> (3.1.61–63)

Shakespeare loads this moment of self-description with dramatic irony: even as Caesar speaks these lines, the conspirators encircle him, daggers in hand. Yet Caesar's weaknesses also make the conspirators' fears seem less plausible. Deaf and epileptic, he seems an unlikely aspirant to tyrannical power.

Brutus, Caesar's friend and killer, is far more fully elaborated, and in fact the originality of Shakespeare's play lies in its concentration of attention on the complicated Brutus instead of upon the play's titular hero. Unlike the other characters, Brutus appears to us in several guises: as a public figure, a husband, a master of servants, a military leader. Thus he experiences painfully in his own person the value conflicts that are elsewhere dispersed among various antagonists. How is Brutus—and how are we—to reconcile his tender regard for his wife and servant with his willingness to commit political murder? Does Brutus's intimacy with Caesar make his decision to assassinate him truly noble, since it cannot be said to stem from self-interest? Or does it suggest a troubling insensitivity to the claims of friendship and to Caesar's genuinely exceptional character? Does he "love the name of honor" so much that he betrays it?

The soliloquies in which Brutus carefully deliberates upon his reasons for, and the possible consequences of, his actions provide abundant insight into his turbulent inner life. Yet the soliloquies raise as many questions about his motives as they resolve. They force the audience to wonder how Brutus's idealism and his commitment to principle are to be evaluated. Surely his habit of appealing to abstract moral and political tenets is an admirable trait, especially in a city in which selfishness seems the dominant passion. But repeatedly, this practice leads him to commit disastrous tactical errors. Concerned to minimize bloodshed, he refuses to countenance Cassius's suggestion that Antony be killed along with Caesar. Then—once again ignoring Cassius's advice—he permits Antony to deliver an unsupervised eulogy at Caesar's funeral, thereby losing the "spin" on Caesar's death and unleashing the rage of the crowd against himself and his allies. Later, his indignation at what he believes to be Cassius's corrupt practices seriously endangers their alliance.

In all these cases, Brutus tries to diminish the extent to which any of his actions might conceivably serve his own self-interested ends, even though by doing so he risks and eventually dooms the cause he is attempting to serve. Brutus shares Caesar's admiration for the Stoic virtue of "constancy," framing it, however, less in terms of power over others than in terms of personal self-control. By behaving according to immovable principles, he tries to give his life a stern but reassuring integrity. Like Caesar, Brutus ends up paying for this aspiration with his life, and even before he does so, the desire to be, in Caesar's words, "constant as the Northern Star" seems misplaced in a play in which character seems complex and highly mutable.

In comparison, the impulsive, unscrupulous Cassius is far more alert to the way the world really works, willingly stooping to expediency to get what he wants and what his cause needs. The contrast with Antony likewise clarifies the way in which Brutus's principles incapacitate him. Antony emerges as a formidable opponent not despite but because of traits that Brutus can see only as weaknesses: love of sensual indulgence, lack of principle, a tendency to live in the present without sufficient care for past or future. Antony's uninhibited, improvisatory nature suits him beautifully for swaying the plebeians. A marvelous actor, Antony exploits gestures, cunning rhetoric, props, and any other means that fully serve the particular moment in which he finds himself. In fact, his political astuteness seems to arise directly from his personal familiarity with passion, since much of politics is, as Brutus never quite realizes, a matter of assessing and responding to group desire. While Brutus naively believes that Caesar's death simply restores the Republic to its status quo ante, Antony immediately understands that the future of Rome and its institutions rests in the hands of Rome's populace and thus—since that populace is fickle and violent—ultimately in the hands of whoever can sway the populace to his will.

Even while Shakespeare vividly differentiates his characters, he shows clearly how they derive from the particular social and intellectual culture they inhabit. Shakespeare was no antiquarian: he imagines the characters of *Julius Caesar* wearing Elizabethan doublet and hose, and he notoriously equips ancient Rome with a medieval invention, the mechanical clock. Nonetheless, his Romans share a set of distinctive values, ideals, and assumptions. When Antony, at the end of the play, calls Brutus "the noblest Roman of them all," he is not simply praising Brutus as an individual. Instead, he is locating Brutus in a tradition of specifically "Roman" virtue, a virtue associated with the particular strengths of the republican form of government that Brutus died attempting to defend.

What does this virtue entail? Brutus's willingness to identify his abstract principles with the common good, as well as his intense suspicion of anyone who appears self-aggrandizing, is wholly characteristic of an ethos that distinguishes sharply between duty and pleasure, between public good and private self-enrichment. The heroes of the Roman Republic had always been celebrated for their incorruptibility and for their preference for public service, however thankless, over private goods such as marriage, friendship, sensual pleasure, and personal enrichment. Many of them adhered to a

Stoic code of personal conduct that mandated emotional self-control and self-sacrifice. At the same time, Rome was in fact a hotbed of nepotism and unscrupulousness, and its venality grew along with its power. Thus, pillars of the Roman Republic like Lucius Junius Brutus, Marcus Cato, Scipio Africanus, and Marcus Brutus himself were admired not merely because their civic-mindedness was socially valuable, but because such exemplars were rarer and more surprising than Romans liked to admit.

The sharp distinction that Roman culture made between public and private domains has important consequences in *Julius Caesar*. The public world is an all-male affair. Bonds and rivalries among men provide both the glue that holds the Roman Republic together and a competitive petulancy that ordinarily precludes a single individual's gaining too much power. We are given a vivid picture of this complex interpersonal dynamic in Cassius's account of his swimming contest with Caesar. In an incident of pure bravado, friends test their toughness against one another, and one ends up saving the other's life; but because all neediness is imagined to be shameful, what seems like generosity or charity is shot through with contempt. A similar rivalrous emotional intensity characterizes the highly charged quarrel and reconciliation between Brutus and Cassius in 4.2. For these men, loving someone does not preclude wanting to kill him.

Compared to the fraught ambivalence of the relationships between men, the heterosexual connections in the play seem rather pallid. Although Brutus is deeply attached to Portia, it does not occur to him to take her into his confidence until she struggles mightily for the privilege on the eve of the assassination; even then, all she requests is information, not permission to offer advice. Similarly, Decius easily shames Caesar into ignoring Calphurnia's foreboding dream:

> it were a mock
> Apt to be rendered, for someone to say,
> "Break up the Senate till another time
> When Caesar's wife shall meet with better dreams."
> (2.2.96–99)

Even the most powerful man in the Roman Empire, apparently, cannot risk being seen by other men to be influenced by a mere wife, no matter how intelligent or prescient she may be. Most telling, in what is perhaps a sign of textual corruption but more probably an instance of Shakespearean skill in delineating character, we are given two successive accounts of the way Brutus learns of Portia's suicide. In the first, Brutus divulges the loss himself to Cassius, expressing his grief in solitary conference with an old friend. Shortly thereafter, however, he tells his military subordinates that he has not received any news of Portia at all. Once informed that she has died "in strange manner," he affects a studied indifference, insisting that the tidings merely interfere with more important matters at hand. His apparent ability to sequester domestic concerns from public and military ones elicits the admiration of those around him: for true "Romans" are willing to incur huge emotional costs for what they imagine is the greater good.

Since honor, in this conceptual system, is supposed to involve fierce commitment to the public sphere, and since that sphere is exclusively the domain of men, the women in *Julius Caesar* are marginalized. Even within the confines of the household, they seem unable to cultivate an alternative form of social value. Maternity, for instance, is not a source of power here: Calphurnia is barren and Portia, too, is apparently childless. Their intuitive concern for their husbands has no practical effect. "Nobility" requires them to internalize values that for them have little use. Portia proves what she calls her masculine courage to her husband by the bizarre means of stabbing herself deliberately in the thigh, a gesture that suggests a self-castration, as if a woman were at best a slashed man. For the virtue that she claims to possess is not truly her own possession; rather, it is a quality reflected from her male relatives that makes her superior to ordinary women. "Think you I am no stronger than my sex, / Being so fathered and so husbanded?" (2.1.296–97). Portia kills herself, typically, in an exceptionally painful way, by swallowing hot coals. While the fabled hardihood of

Brutus falling on his sword. From Geffrey Whitney, A *Choice of Emblems* (1586).

Portia's father, Cato, or her husband, Brutus, has at least some military rationale, Portia's imitation of their fortitude seems pointlessly self-punishing, serving neither their ends nor her own.

The pressure of Roman values on the characters of *Julius Caesar* suggests that its protagonists are not entirely free to invent themselves; they are limited to the cultural materials at hand. Moreover the complexity of the situation in which they find themselves makes it difficult for them to know exactly why they behave as they do. Often in *Julius Caesar*, the same scene provides a character with a variety of motives, permitting alternative descriptions of a single action. Thus, when Brutus decides to participate in the conspiracy to kill Caesar, he believes that he has carefully sequestered his self-interest from his convictions about the common good. But Cassius has meanwhile been tossing flattering messages through his window, so the theater audience must consider the possibility that Brutus's appeal to principle is a rationalization, and that he is swayed by a personal ambition of which he may not be entirely aware.

Elsewhere, Shakespeare complicates his portraits by what might be called a technique of gradual release. By slowly making details available to the audience, he forces it to revise its previous impressions to take account of new information. For instance, Antony's bravura eulogy reaches a climax when he reads Caesar's will, thus harnessing the plebeians' greed to the end of revenging Caesar's death. A mere two scenes later, he is shown in conference with Lepidus and Octavius, giving brisk orders to minimize the cost of Caesar's generosity. The incongruity between the first scene and the second makes Antony's original celebration of his friend's magnanimity seem, in retrospect, less sincere or spontaneous. Nonetheless, the two scenes do not force the audience to a single obvious conclusion. Does Antony's later parsimony indicate that he was simply hypocritical when he used Caesar's will to provoke a riot? Perhaps, but not necessarily; he could simply have been caught up in a wave of loyalty to Caesar and in the pathos of the situation, or he could have had vaguely ambitious but not yet fully articulated plans. In such cases, Shakespeare's cunning dramatic presentation enhances the complexity of his characterizations. The realistic illusion depends as much on what he withholds from the audience as on what he provides it.

On other grounds, too, a reading focusing purely on character seems finally inadequate. In oft-cited lines, Cassius pronounces: "The fault, dear Brutus, is not in our stars, / But in ourselves, that we are underlings" (1.2.140–41). It is not at all clear, however, that he is right. Plutarch emphasizes how the fates of his biographical subjects fail to reflect their virtues. Caesar, who had miraculously survived so many strange adventures in hostile foreign lands, can be dispatched in a few minutes by his erstwhile friends just moments after leaving his own house. Cicero, whose oratory had held sway in Rome for so many years, is obliterated by Antony and Octavius practically as an afterthought. The gifted and honorable Brutus meets death after a military defeat that seems almost accidental. Cassius's suicide is even more haphazard. The inscrutable workings of fate play at least as great a role as personality does in determining the outcome of the action.

For this reason, virtually all the characters find it impossible to achieve a reliable perspective on events in which they are immersed. In the play's most literal case of limited vision, the "thick-sighted" Cassius misinterprets victory as defeat and kills himself moments before his triumphant soldiers arrive, hoping to congratulate him. Here and elsewhere, Shakespeare drums home the difference between the perspective of the theater audience, for whom the killing of Julius Caesar is an act centuries old, now replayed for its entertainment value, and the perspective of the characters within the play, for whom it is unfolding in the present moment, its consequences both dire and unknown. From our point of view, ironies are everywhere. Caesar pronounces upon his immovable constancy moments before being dispatched. His murderers, attempting to eliminate a potential tyrant, open the way for centuries of despotism. As Antony plots with Octavius to eliminate Lepidus, the audience knows, as Antony cannot, that the apparently modest, noncommittal Octavius will ultimately annihilate both his triumviral associates.

To be alive to such ironies, the characters would need to be able to look into the future. Struggling to understand their own place in history, they continually resort to augury, attempting—usually incorrectly—to comprehend the omens that shadow forth their fates. In *Julius Caesar,* omens are always telling, but they are rarely intelligible except in retrospect. No one knows what to make of the lions loose in the streets; the soothsayer arrives too late; Calphurnia's dream is misinterpreted; Cassius notices carrion birds on his standards but decides to disregard them. By emphasizing the analogies among personal, political, and natural forms of disruption, omens on the one hand intensify the significance of the play's characters: their decisions, quirks, and flaws affect the structure of the universe itself. They are indeed, as they have imagined themselves to be, persons of unprecedented and enormous significance. On the other hand, the reliability of omens challenges the notion that history is the product of personal effort. Augury implies restrictions on free will, suggesting that individuals are caught in the toils of a historical process they cannot possibly control or understand. Undergirding the other questions of authority and responsibility in *Julius Caesar* are two unanswerable questions: Who creates history? And what can that history possibly mean?

KATHARINE EISAMAN MAUS

SELECTED BIBLIOGRAPHY

Bloom, Harold, ed. *William Shakespeare's "Julius Caesar."* New York: Chelsea House, 1988. Anthology of critical essays.

Burckhardt, Sigurd. "How Not to Murder Caesar." *Shakespearean Meanings.* Princeton: Princeton UP, 1968. 3–21. Examines *Julius Caesar* and historical change.

Lucking, D. "Brutus' Reasons: *Julius Caesar* and the Mystery of Motive." *English Studies* 91 (2010): 119–32. Presents a detailed discussion of Brutus's enigmatic motives.

Miles, Gary B. "How Roman Are Shakespeare's 'Romans'?" *Shakespeare Quarterly* 40 (1989): 257–83. Analyzes Shakespeare's adaptation and revision of his classical sources.

Miola, Robert S. "*Julius Caesar* and the Tyrannicide Debate." *Renaissance Quarterly* 38 (1985): 271–89. Notes that Renaissance political theorists disagreed over whether the killing of a king was ever justified, and asserts that *Julius Caesar* shows Shakespeare's knowledge of this dispute.

Paster, Gail Kern. "'In the Spirit of Men There Is No Blood': Blood as a Trope of Gender in *Julius Caesar.*" *Shakespeare Quarterly* 40 (1989): 284–98. Looks at manliness and bloody bodies in the play.

Rebhorn, Wayne. "The Crisis of the Aristocracy in *Julius Caesar.*" *Renaissance Quarterly* 43 (1990): 75–111. Argues that Shakespeare's Romans resemble sixteenth-century English aristocrats in their desire for self-mastery and competitiveness with one another.

Visser, Nicholas. "Plebeian Politics in *Julius Caesar.*" *Shakespeare in Southern Africa* 7 (1994): 22–31. Looks at how contemporary South African performances offer insights into the play's concept of class relations and of the mob.

Wilson, Richard, ed. *Julius Caesar.* New York: Palgrave, 2002. Excellent collection of critical essays on the play.

Zander, Horst, ed. *Julius Caesar: New Critical Essays.* New York: Routledge, 2005. A collection of twenty-one essays on the politics, plot, and language of *Julius Caesar*, on current critical debates, and on the play's performance history.

FILMS

Julius Caesar. 1953. Dir. Joseph L. Mankiewicz. USA. 120 min. This black-and-white Hollywood production features James Mason as a brooding, intense Brutus, John Gielgud as Cassius, and the young Marlon Brando, in an Oscar-nominated performance, as a charismatic Antony.

Julius Caesar. 1970. Dir. Stuart Burge. UK. 117 min. A brisk production, enlivened by colorful street and battle scenes. Jason Robards plays Brutus, Charlton Heston is Antony, John Gielgud is Caesar, and Diana Rigg is Portia.

Julius Caesar. 1979. Dir. Herbert Wise. UK. 161 min. A BBC-TV production. Textually faithful but blandly acted. David Collings is, however, effective as Cassius.

TEXTUAL INTRODUCTION

Shakespeare's *Julius Caesar* exists in a single early version, that of the First Folio of 1623. The Folio entitles the play "The Tragedie of Ivlivs Caesar" (also calling it "The Life and death of Julius Caesar" in the "Catalogve," or Table of Contents) and divides it into five acts (without scene divisions). The play presents few textual difficulties. In fact, it is nearly free of the minor inconsistencies in names and confusions of speech attribution that typically occur in most early Shakespeare texts. Thus, whatever the exact nature of the manuscript that furnished copy for the printed version, it must have been quite clearly written out, although no editor has detected any of the usual signs that would suggest the involvement of a professional scribe in the process.

The relatively high number and unusual detail of the play's stage directions (e.g., *"Thunder and lightning. Enter Julius Caesar in his nightgown"* [2.2.0]) have suggested to some that the manuscript may have been based on performance practice. The frequent, but seemingly inconsistent, spelling of names as if they were Italian rather than Latin ("Antonio" for Antonius or Antony, "Octavio" rather than Octavius, etc.) may indicate Shakespearean preference. By the time of its publication in 1623, more than twenty years had passed since the play's probable first staging at the (then newly built) Globe in 1599, and there is no reason to doubt that it was in performance during those years, yet the printed text shows very few inconsistencies in roles or action that might signal alteration or revision. Some editors have questioned whether the double disclosure of Portia's death in 4.3 (4.3.146–57 and 4.3.180–94) might represent alternative versions of the scene, but most have retained both disclosure sequences as integral to a full portrayal of Brutus's character under the stress of the moment. In general, the Folio printers treated the text with some care, leaving very few typesetting errors such as misplaced or turned letters or obvious misspellings (a few examples of such errors remaining uncorrected by the Folio are noted at 2.1.267, 4.3.115, 4.3.271) and correcting three substantive errors on one page of text during the print run (at 5.3.97, 5.3.101, 5.5.23 SD).

The Folio text of the play is somewhat unusual in Shakespeare's canon for the high number of its short lines. Some of these are simply instances of the typesetters' typical interventions to avoid overrunning the margins (e.g., 1.1.31 appears arbitrarily divided in F as "Wherefore rejoice? / What conquest brings he home?"). Many appear as verse lines shared between speakers (e.g., 3.1.10, 3.1.85, 3.1.121, 3.1.144), while some occur within individual speeches that are otherwise lined as pentameter (e.g., at 1.3.71).

Subsequent early reprints of the First Folio text appear in the Second Folio (1632), Third Folio (1663), and Fourth Folio (1685), and these texts correct certain minor errors as noted in the Textual Variants. The play also appeared in six separately printed late seventeenth-century quarto versions derived from the Folio; two of these can be dated to 1684 and 1691.

James R. Siemon

PERFORMANCE NOTE

Julius Caesar tempts most directors to make stark choices: Is Rome a place of heroic ideals and grandeur, or of pettiness and infighting? Are the conspirators freedom fighters or jealous malcontents? Is Caesar a compassionate leader or a tyrant? The inclination to find answers for these questions helps explain a stage history largely split between productions that strive to make Caesar and Antony worthy of their generic statuses (one a more sympathetic tragic center for gaining psychological depth, the other a more welcome revenger for shedding callousness and opportunism), and those that place Caesar at the head of fascist versions of Rome that recall the regimes of Pinochet, Mugabe, and Mussolini—contemporary analogues that help to justify those who rebel against him. Yet a central challenge for directors is in fact to resist such dichotomies, since the text generates a great deal of its energy through a string of paradoxes. Caesar clearly is and is not ambitious; Brutus is eminently loyal, high-minded, *and* traitorous; Cassius alternates as the play's most sinister and most sensitive character; Antony weeps over Caesar one moment and orders the execution of a friend in the next. Casca, too, is sardonic and assured in 1.2, timid and superstitious in 1.3, while Portia is roundly hailed as a model of perseverance, yet kills herself soon after Brutus departs for battle.

Retaining such inconsistencies while taking both Caesar's and the conspirators' sides is a continuous challenge for productions, but the result can enrich a play built on a fundamental dissonance between the historical personages the audience has reason to expect and the ambivalent characters that Shakespeare delivers. Contemporary productions have increasingly moved away from heroism and nobility on either side, privileging the domestic dramas and internal turmoil and hesitation of the major players. Though the affect, interiority, and relationships of Brutus, Cassius, Antony, and Caesar are key concerns, productions must also consider the size and composition of the crowd of plebeians; the staging of the storm in 1.3 and the third-act assassinations of Caesar and Cinna; whether the play's engagement with the supernatural is sincere or superficial; the nature and extent of Caesar's infirmities; and the threat of anticlimax after Antony's funeral oration.

Brett Gamboa

The Tragedy of Julius Caesar

[THE PERSONS OF THE PLAY

Julius CAESAR
CALPHURNIA, wife to Caesar
SERVANT to them

Marcus BRUTUS
PORTIA, wife to Brutus
LUCIUS, servant to them

Caius CASSIUS ⎫
CASCA ⎪
CINNA ⎪
DECIUS Brutus ⎬ patricians who join with Brutus against Caesar
Caius LIGARIUS ⎪
METELLUS Cimber ⎪
TREBONIUS ⎭

CICERO ⎫
PUBLIUS ⎬ senators
POPILIUS Lena ⎭

FLAVIUS ⎫ tribunes
MURELLUS ⎭

Mark ANTONY ⎫
LEPIDUS ⎬ triumvirs who rule Rome after Caesar's death
OCTAVIUS ⎭

LUCILIUS ⎫
TITINIUS ⎪
MESSALA ⎪
VARRUS ⎪
CLAUDIO ⎪
Young CATO ⎬ officers and soldiers in the armies of Brutus and Cassius
STRATO ⎪
VOLUMNIUS ⎪
DARDANIUS ⎪
CLITUS ⎪
Flavius ⎭

CARPENTER
COBBLER
SOOTHSAYER
ARTEMIDORUS
PLEBEIANS
CINNA the Poet
Another POET
PINDARUS, slave to Cassius

288

MESSENGER
SOLDIERS
SERVANTS
Commoners]

1.1

Enter FLAVIUS, MURELLUS, *and certain Commoners*
[*including a* CARPENTER *and* COBBLER] *over the stage.*[1]

FLAVIUS   Hence! Home, you idle creatures, get you home!
 Is this a holiday? What, know you not,
 Being mechanical,° you ought not walk   *of the artisan class*
 Upon a laboring day without the sign°   *tools and garments*
5 Of your profession? —Speak, what trade art thou?
CARPENTER   Why, sir, a carpenter.
MURELLUS   Where is thy leather apron and thy rule?
 What dost thou with thy best apparel on?
 —You, sir, what trade are you?
10 COBBLER   Truly, sir, in respect of° a fine workman, I am but,   *in comparison with*
 as you would say, a cobbler.[2]
MURELLUS   But what trade art thou? Answer me directly.
COBBLER   A trade, sir, that I hope I may use with a safe con-
 science, which is indeed, sir, a mender of bad soles.°   *(punning on "souls")*
15 FLAVIUS   What trade, thou knave? Thou naughty° knave, what trade?   *wicked*
COBBLER   Nay, I beseech you, sir, be not out[3] with me. Yet if
 you be out, sir, I can mend you.
MURELLUS   What mean'st thou by that? Mend me, thou saucy fellow?
COBBLER   Why, sir, cobble you.
20 FLAVIUS   Thou art a cobbler, art thou?
COBBLER   Truly, sir, all that I live by is with the awl. I meddle
 with no tradesman's matters nor women's matters,° but withal[4]   *(a bawdy joke)*
 I am indeed, sir, a surgeon to old shoes: when they are in great
 danger, I recover° them. As proper° men as ever trod upon   *resole; cure / fine*
25 neat's leather° have gone° upon my handiwork.   *cowhide / walked*
FLAVIUS   But wherefore art not in thy shop today?
 Why dost thou lead these men about the streets?
COBBLER   Truly, sir, to wear out their shoes, to get myself into
 more work. But indeed, sir, we make holiday to see Caesar
30 and to rejoice in his triumph.[5]
MURELLUS   Wherefore rejoice? What conquest brings he home?
 What tributaries° follow him to Rome   *ransom payers*
 To grace in captive bonds his chariot wheels?[6]
 You blocks, you stones, you worse than senseless° things!   *inanimate*
35 O you hard hearts, you cruel men of Rome,
 Knew you not Pompey?[7] Many a time and oft
 Have you climbed up to walls and battlements,
 To towers and windows, yea, to chimney tops,
 Your infants in your arms, and there have sat

1.1 Location: A street in Rome.
1. PERFORMANCE COMMENT The crowd scenes in *Julius Caesar* are important for framing the political implications of the action. For a discussion of the performance options, see Digital Edition PC 1.
2. Mender of shoes; bungler (the sense Murellus understands).
3. Angry; worn out, like shoes.
4. Nevertheless; punning on "awl."

5. Triumphal procession in honor of victory (by Roman custom, over foreign enemies, but here over Caesar's political adversaries, Pompey's sons).
6. Captives were tied to their conquerors' chariots.
7. Pompey the Great, who had shared rule of Rome with Caesar and Crassus; he was defeated by Caesar after their alliance disintegrated and was later assassinated.

40   The livelong day with patient expectation
      To see great Pompey pass the streets of Rome.
      And when you saw his chariot but appear,
      Have you not made an universal shout,
      That Tiber[8] trembled underneath her banks
45   To hear the replication° of your sounds   *echo*
      Made in her concave shores?
      And do you now put on your best attire?
      And do you now cull out° a holiday?   *choose*
      And do you now strew flowers in his way
50   That comes in triumph over Pompey's blood?°   *offspring*
      Begone!
      Run to your houses, fall upon your knees,
      Pray to the gods to intermit[9] the plague
      That needs must light on this ingratitude.
55 FLAVIUS   Go, go, good countrymen, and for this fault
      Assemble all the poor men of your sort,°   *rank*
      Draw them to Tiber banks, and weep your tears
      Into the channel, till the lowest stream
      Do kiss the most exalted shores of all.°   *tops of the riverbanks*
               Exeunt all the Commoners.
60   See whe'er° their basest mettle be not moved.   *whether*
      They vanish tongue-tied in their guiltiness.
      Go you down that way towards the Capitol;[1]
      This way will I. Disrobe the images
      If you do find them decked with ceremonies.[2]
65 MURELLUS   May we do so?
      You know it is the Feast of Lupercal.[3]
    FLAVIUS   It is no matter. Let no images
      Be hung with Caesar's trophies.° I'll about   *ornaments*
      And drive away the vulgar° from the streets;   *commoners*
70   So do you too, where you perceive them thick.
      These growing feathers plucked from Caesar's wing
      Will make him fly an ordinary pitch,[4]
      Who else° would soar above the view of men   *otherwise*
      And keep us all in servile fearfulness.   *Exeunt.*

1.2

Enter CAESAR, ANTONY *for the course,*[1] CALPHURNIA,
PORTIA, DECIUS, CICERO, BRUTUS, CASSIUS, CASCA,
a SOOTHSAYER; *after them* MURELLUS *and* FLAVIUS.

CAESAR   Calphurnia.
CASCA   Peace ho, Caesar speaks.
CAESAR   Calphurnia.
CALPHURNIA   Here, my lord.
CAESAR   Stand you directly in Antonio's way
      When he doth run his course. —Antonio.

---

8. River that flows through Rome.
9. Withhold (plague was considered a divine punishment).
1. Hill on whose top was the Temple of Jupiter, where victorious generals in a triumph offered sacrifice.
2. Caesar's followers had put imperial crowns ("ceremonies") on his statues.

3. Lupercalia, a festival celebrated on February 15. Historically, Caesar's triumph took place in October.
4. At a medium height (an image from falconry).
1.2 Location: A public place in Rome.
1. During the Lupercalia, two celebrants ran naked through Rome, striking those they met with goatskin thongs.

5 ANTONY Caesar, my lord.
   CAESAR   Forget not in your speed, Antonio,
      To touch Calphurnia, for our elders say
      The barren touchèd in this holy chase
      Shake off their sterile curse.
   ANTONY   I shall remember.
10   When Caesar says, "Do this," it is performed.
   CAESAR   Set on° and leave no ceremony out.   *Proceed*
   SOOTHSAYER   Caesar.
   CAESAR   Ha? Who calls?
   CASCA   Bid every noise be still. Peace yet again.
15 CAESAR   Who is it in the press° that calls on me?   *crowd*
      I hear a tongue shriller than all the music
      Cry "Caesar." Speak, Caesar is turned to hear.
   SOOTHSAYER   Beware the Ides[2] of March.
   CAESAR   What man is that?
   BRUTUS   A soothsayer bids you beware the Ides of March.
20 CAESAR   Set him before me. Let me see his face.
   CASSIUS   Fellow, come from the throng. Look upon Caesar.
   CAESAR   What say'st thou to me now? Speak once again.
   SOOTHSAYER   Beware the Ides of March.[3]
   CAESAR   He is a dreamer; let us leave him. Pass.°   *Onward*
                Sennet.° *Exeunt all but* BRUTUS *and* CASSIUS.   *Trumpet flourish*
25 CASSIUS   Will you go see the order of the course?°   *running of the race*
   BRUTUS   Not I.
   CASSIUS   I pray you, do.
   BRUTUS   I am not gamesome.° I do lack some part   *fond of sport*
      Of that quick° spirit that is in Antony.   *lively*
30   Let me not hinder, Cassius, your desires;
      I'll leave you.
   CASSIUS   Brutus, I do observe you now of late.
      I have not from your eyes that gentleness
      And show of love as I was wont° to have.   *accustomed*
35   You bear too stubborn and too strange° a hand[4]   *unfriendly*
      Over your friend that loves you.
   BRUTUS   Cassius,
      Be not deceived. If I have veiled my look,°   *seemed less outgoing*
      I turn the trouble of my countenance°   *my troubled looks*
      Merely° upon myself. Vexèd I am   *Wholly*
40   Of late with passions of some difference,°   *conflicting kinds*
      Conceptions only proper° to myself,   *suitable*
      Which give some soil,° perhaps, to my behaviors;   *blemish*
      But let not therefore my good friends be grieved—
      Among which number, Cassius, be you one—
45   Nor construe any further° my neglect   *make any more of*
      Than that poor Brutus, with himself at war,
      Forgets the shows of love to other men.
   CASSIUS   Then, Brutus, I have much mistook your passion,°   *feelings*
      By means whereof[5] this breast of mine hath buried°   *concealed*

---

2. The ides marked roughly the midpoint of every Roman month (usually the 13th); in March, the 15th.
3. TEXTUAL COMMENT Short lines like this one, followed by complete iambic pentameter lines, may sometimes suggest a pause in performance, but Shake-speare uses short lines quite variously. See Digital Edition TC 1 for a fuller explanation.
4. Management of horse's reins (figurative).
5. In consequence of which mistake.

50   Thoughts of great value, worthy cogitations.
    Tell me, good Brutus, can you see your face?
    BRUTUS No, Cassius, for the eye sees not itself
    But by reflection, by some other things.
    CASSIUS 'Tis just,°   *true*
55   And it is very much lamented, Brutus,
    That you have no such mirrors as will turn
    Your hidden worthiness into your eye,
    That you might see your shadow.° I have heard   *reflection*
    Where many of the best respect° in Rome,   *repute*
60   Except immortal Caesar, speaking of Brutus
    And groaning underneath this age's yoke,
    Have wished that noble Brutus had his eyes.[6]
    BRUTUS Into what dangers would you lead me, Cassius,
    That you would have me seek into myself
65   For that which is not in me?
    CASSIUS Therefore,° good Brutus, be prepared to hear; *As to that*
    And since you know you cannot see yourself
    So well as by reflection, I, your glass,°   *mirror*
    Will modestly discover° to yourself   *reveal*
70   That of yourself which you yet know not of.
    And be not jealous on° me, gentle Brutus.   *suspicious of*
    Were I a common laughter,° or did use   *object of ridicule*
    To stale° with ordinary° oaths my love   *debase / cheap*
    To every new protester;° if you know   *declarer of friendship*
75   That I do fawn on men and hug them hard
    And after scandal° them; or if you know   *defame*
    That I profess myself° in banqueting   *declare friendship*
    To all the rout,° then hold me dangerous.   *mob*
        Flourish and shout.
    BRUTUS What means this shouting? I do fear the people
    Choose Caesar for their king.
80   CASSIUS   Ay, do you fear it?
    Then must I think you would not have it so.
    BRUTUS I would not, Cassius, yet I love him well.
    But wherefore do you hold me here so long?
    What is it that you would impart to me?
85   If it be aught toward the general good,
    Set honor in one eye and death i'th' other
    And I will look on both indifferently;°   *impartially*
    For let the gods so speed me as[7] I love
    The name of honor more than I fear death.
90   CASSIUS I know that virtue to be in you, Brutus,
    As well as I do know your outward favor.°   *appearance*
    Well, honor is the subject of my story.
    I cannot tell what you and other men
    Think of this life; but, for my single self,
95   I had as lief not be as° live to be   *I had rather be dead than*
    In awe of such a thing as I myself.
    I was born free as Caesar, so were you;
    We both have fed as well, and we can both
    Endure the winter's cold as well as he.

6. That is, could see properly.   7. Make me fortunate insofar as.

100	For once, upon a raw and gusty day,	
	The troubled Tiber chafing with° her shores,	*raging against*
	Caesar said to me, "Dar'st thou, Cassius, now	
	Leap in with me into this angry flood	
	And swim to yonder point?"° Upon the word,	*promontory*
105	Accoutered° as I was, I plungèd in	*Fully dressed*
	And bade him follow; so indeed he did.	
	The torrent roared, and we did buffet it	
	With lusty sinews, throwing it aside	
	And stemming° it with hearts of controversy.°	*confronting / rivalry*
110	But ere we could arrive° the point proposed,	*reach*
	Caesar cried, "Help me, Cassius, or I sink!"	
	I, as Aeneas,[8] our great ancestor,	
	Did from the flames of Troy upon his shoulder	
	The old Anchises bear, so from the waves of Tiber	
115	Did I the tired Caesar; and this man	
	Is now become a god, and Cassius is	
	A wretched creature and must bend his body°	*must bow*
	If Caesar carelessly but nod on him.	
	He had a fever when he was in Spain,	
120	And when the fit was on him, I did mark	
	How he did shake. 'Tis true, this god did shake.	
	His coward lips did from their color fly,[9]	
	And that same eye whose bend° doth awe the world	*glance*
	Did lose his° luster. I did hear him groan.	*its*
125	Ay, and that tongue of his that bade the Romans	
	Mark him and write his speeches in their books,	
	"Alas," it cried, "Give me some drink, Titinius,"	
	As a sick girl. Ye gods, it doth amaze me	
	A man of such a feeble temper° should	*constitution*
130	So get the start of° the majestic world	*advantage over*
	And bear the palm° alone.	*be victor*

Shout. Flourish.

BRUTUS Another general shout?
I do believe that these applauses are
For some new honors that are heaped on Caesar.

135 CASSIUS Why, man, he doth bestride the narrow world
Like a Colossus,[1] and we petty men
Walk under his huge legs and peep about
To find ourselves dishonorable graves.
Men at some time are masters of their fates.
140 The fault, dear Brutus, is not in our stars,
But in ourselves, that we are underlings.
"Brutus" and "Caesar"—what should be in that "Caesar"?
Why should that name be sounded more than yours?
Write them together, yours is as fair a name;
145 Sound them, it doth become the mouth as well;
Weigh them, it is as heavy; conjure with 'em,
"Brutus" will start[2] a spirit as soon as "Caesar."

---

8. Legendary Trojan warrior and founder of Rome; when the Greeks burned Troy, he carried his father, Anchises, out on his back.
9. Did turn pale; did desert their flag (Caesar suffered epileptic seizures).

1. Giant statue of Apollo, which straddled the harbor of Rhodes.
2. Raise (only the names of the gods were thought to be able to raise the dead).

Now, in the names of all the gods at once,
Upon what meat° doth this our Caesar feed   *food*
150   That he is grown so great? Age, thou art shamed!
Rome, thou hast lost the breed of noble bloods!
When went there by an age, since the great flood,³
But it was famed with° more than with one man?   *renowned for*
When could they say, till now, that talked of Rome,
155   That her wide walks encompassed but one man?
Now is it Rome indeed, and room° enough,   *(pronounced like "Rome")*
When there is in it but one only man.
Oh, you and I have heard our fathers say
There was a Brutus once⁴ that would have brooked°   *endured*
160   Th'eternal devil to keep his state° in Rome   *hold court*
As easily as a king.
BRUTUS   That you do love me, I am nothing jealous.°   *not at all uncertain*
What you would work° me to, I have some aim.°   *persuade / idea*
How I have thought of this, and of these times,
165   I shall recount hereafter. For this present,°   *present time*
I would not, so with love° I might entreat you,   *if in friendship*
Be any further moved.° What you have said,   *persuaded*
I will consider; what you have to say,
I will with patience hear, and find a time
170   Both meet° to hear and answer such high things.   *Fitting both*
Till then, my noble friend, chew upon this:
Brutus had rather be a villager
Than to repute himself a son of Rome
Under these hard conditions as this time
175   Is like to lay upon us.
CASSIUS   I am glad that my weak words
Have struck but thus much show of fire from Brutus.
             Enter CAESAR and his train.°   *retinue*
BRUTUS   The games are done, and Caesar is returning.
CASSIUS   As they pass by, pluck Casca by the sleeve,⁵
180   And he will, after his sour fashion, tell you
What hath proceeded worthy° note today.   *worthy of*
BRUTUS   I will do so. But look you, Cassius,
The angry spot doth glow on Caesar's brow,
And all the rest look like a chidden° train: *scolded*
185   Calphurnia's cheek is pale, and Cicero
Looks with such ferret⁶ and such fiery eyes
As we have seen him in the Capitol,
Being crossed in conference° by some senators.   *opposed in debate*
CASSIUS   Casca will tell us what the matter is.
190   CAESAR   Antonio.
ANTONY   Caesar.
CAESAR   Let me have men about me that are fat,
Sleek-headed men, and such as sleep a-nights.
Yond Cassius has a lean and hungry look.
195   He thinks too much; such men are dangerous.

---

3. A great flood was recorded in classical as well as
biblical accounts.
4. Lucius Junius Brutus, an ancestor of Marcus Brutus and a founder of the Roman Republic, famed for
his role in expelling the Tarquins, who had ruled Rome

as kings.
5. Like "cloak" (line 215), "doublet" (line 261), and
"unbraced" (1.3.48), this suggests a performance in
Elizabethan dress.
6. Ferretlike (red and darting).

ANTONY   Fear him not, Caesar; he's not dangerous.

He is a noble Roman and well given.°   *well disposed*

CAESAR   Would he were fatter! But I fear him not.

Yet if my name[7] were liable to fear,

200   I do not know the man I should avoid

So soon as that spare Cassius. He reads much,

He is a great observer, and he looks

Quite through[8] the deeds of men. He loves no plays,

As thou dost, Antony; he hears no music.[9]

205   Seldom he smiles, and smiles in such a sort°   *manner*

As if he mocked himself and scorned his spirit

That could be moved to smile at anything.

Such men as he be never at heart's ease

Whiles they behold a greater than themselves,

210   And therefore are they very dangerous.

I rather tell thee what is to be feared

Than what I fear; for always I am Caesar.

Come on my right hand, for this ear is deaf,

And tell me truly what thou think'st of him.

             Sennet. Exeunt CAESAR *and his train*

                  [*leaving* CASCA *behind*].

215 CASCA   You pulled me by the cloak.° Would you speak with me?   *pulled me aside*

BRUTUS   Ay, Casca. Tell us what hath chanced today

That Caesar looks so sad.°   *serious*

CASCA   Why, you were with him, were you not?

BRUTUS   I should not then ask Casca what had chanced.

220 CASCA   Why, there was a crown offered him; and being offered

him, he put it by with the back of his hand, thus, and then

the people fell a-shouting.

BRUTUS   What was the second noise for?

CASCA   Why, for that, too.

225 CASSIUS   They shouted thrice. What was the last cry for?

CASCA   Why, for that, too.

BRUTUS   Was the crown offered him thrice?

CASCA   Ay, marry,° was't, and he put it by thrice, every time   *indeed*

gentler than other; and at every putting-by, mine honest°   *(sarcastic)*

230 neighbors shouted.

CASSIUS   Who offered him the crown?

CASCA   Why, Antony.

BRUTUS   Tell us the manner of it, gentle° Casca.   *noble*

CASCA   I can as well be hanged as tell the manner of it. It was

235 mere foolery;° I did not mark it. I saw Mark Antony offer him   *utter absurdity*

a crown—yet 'twas not a crown neither, 'twas one of these

coronets—and, as I told you, he put it by once; but for all that,

to my thinking, he would fain° have had it. Then he offered it   *gladly*

to him again; then he put it by again; but to my thinking, he

240 was very loath to lay his fingers off it. And then he offered it

the third time; he put it the third time by, and still° as he   *continually*

refused it the rabblement hooted and clapped their chopped°   *chapped*

hands, and threw up their sweaty nightcaps,[1] and uttered such

---

7. One of my name (that is, myself).

8. Completely into the motives of.

9. Dislike of music was regarded as a sign of wicked-

ness; see *The Merchant of Venice*.

1. Artisans wore felt hats on holidays.

a deal of stinking breath because Caesar refused the crown
245   that it had—almost—choked Caesar, for he swooned and fell
down at it; and for mine own part, I durst not laugh for fear of
opening my lips and receiving the bad air.

CASSIUS But soft, I pray you. What, did Caesar swoon?

CASCA He fell down in the marketplace, and foamed at mouth,
250   and was speechless.

BRUTUS 'Tis very like; he hath the falling sickness.[2]

CASSIUS No, Caesar hath it not, but you and I,
And honest Casca, we have the falling sickness.

CASCA I know not what you mean by that, but I am sure Cae-
255   sar fell down. If the tag-rag people° did not clap him and   *riffraff*
hiss him, according as he pleased and displeased them, as
they use° to do the players in the theater, I am no true man.   *are accustomed*

BRUTUS What said he when he came unto himself?

CASCA Marry, before he fell down, when he perceived the
260   common herd was glad he refused the crown, he plucked me
ope[3] his doublet° and offered them his throat to cut; an° I had   *jacket / if*
been a man of any occupation,° if I would not have taken him   *workingman*
at a° word, I would I might go to hell among the rogues. And   *his*
so he fell. When he came to himself again, he said if he had
265   done or said anything amiss, he desired their worships to
think it was his infirmity. Three or four wenches where I
stood cried, "Alas, good soul!" and forgave him with all their
hearts. But there's no heed to be taken of them; if Caesar
had stabbed their mothers, they would have done no less.

270 BRUTUS And after that, he came thus sad away?

CASCA Ay.

CASSIUS Did Cicero say anything?

CASCA Ay, he spoke Greek.

CASSIUS To what effect?
275 CASCA Nay, an I tell you that, I'll ne'er look you i'th' face again.
But those that understood him smiled at one another and
shook their heads; but, for mine own part, it was Greek to me.
I could tell you more news, too: Murellus and Flavius, for
pulling scarves[4] off Caesar's images, are put to silence.° Fare   *deprived of office*
280   you well. There was more foolery yet, if I could remember it.

CASSIUS Will you sup with me tonight, Casca?

CASCA No, I am promised forth.°   *elsewhere*

CASSIUS Will you dine with me tomorrow?

CASCA Ay, if I be alive, and your mind hold,° and your dinner   *does not change*
285   worth the eating.

CASSIUS Good. I will expect you.

CASCA Do so. Farewell both.   *Exit.*

BRUTUS What a blunt fellow is this grown to be!
He was quick mettle° when he went to school.   *of energetic spirit*
290 CASSIUS So is he now in execution
Of any bold or noble enterprise,
However he puts on this tardy form.[5]
This rudeness° is a sauce to his good wit,°   *harshness / intelligence*

---

2. Epilepsy (Cassius then puns on "collapse from power").
3. Pulled open ("me" is colloquial).
4. Decorations (see 1.1.63–64).
5. Although he feigns this indolent manner.

Which gives men stomach° to digest his words   *relish*
295   With better appetite.
   BRUTUS   And so it is. For this time I will leave you.
    Tomorrow, if you please to speak with me,
    I will come home to you; or, if you will,
    Come home to me, and I will wait for you.
300 CASSIUS   I will do so. Till then, think of the world.°   *Exit* BRUTUS.   *state of affairs*
    Well, Brutus, thou art noble. Yet I see
    Thy honorable mettle may be wrought
    From that it is disposed.⁶ Therefore it is meet°   *fitting*
    That noble minds keep ever with their likes;
305   For who so firm that cannot be seduced?
    Caesar doth bear me hard,° but he loves Brutus.   *ill will*
    If I were Brutus now, and he were Cassius,
    He should not humor° me. I will this night   *influence*
    In several hands° in at his windows throw,   *various handwritings*
310   As if they came from several citizens,
    Writings, all tending to° the great opinion   *intimating*
    That Rome holds of his name, wherein obscurely°   *cryptically*
    Caesar's ambition shall be glancèd° at.   *hinted*
    And after this, let Caesar seat him sure,⁷
315   For we will shake him or worse days endure.   *Exit.*

1.3
Thunder and lightning. Enter CASCA *and* CICERO.
  CICERO   Good even,° Casca. Brought° you Caesar home?   *evening / Escorted*
    Why are you breathless? And why stare you so?
  CASCA   Are not you moved, when all the sway° of earth   *realm*
    Shakes like a thing unfirm? O Cicero,
5   I have seen tempests when the scolding winds
    Have rived° the knotty oaks, and I have seen   *split*
    Th'ambitious ocean swell, and rage, and foam
    To be exalted with° the threat'ning clouds;   *raised as high as*
    But never till tonight, never till now,
10   Did I go through a tempest dropping fire.
    Either there is a civil strife in heaven,
    Or else the world, too saucy° with the gods,   *insolent*
    Incenses them to send destruction.
  CICERO   Why, saw you anything more° wonderful?   *else*
15 CASCA   A common slave—you know him well by sight—
    Held up his left hand, which did flame and burn
    Like twenty torches joined; and yet his hand,
    Not sensible of° fire, remained unscorched.   *Not feeling*
    Besides—I ha' not since put up° my sword—   *sheathed*
20   Against° the Capitol I met a lion,¹   *Next to*
    Who glazed° upon me and went surly by   *stared*
    Without annoying° me. And there were drawn   *harming*
    Upon a heap² a hundred ghastly° women   *terrified*

---

6. *wrought . . . disposed:* changed from its natural property (alluding to the alchemical transmutation of metals).
7. Establish himself securely.
1.3 Location: A street in Rome.
1. African beasts were brought to Rome in large quan-

tities for display and for spectacular staged games; kept in an enclosure outside the city, they occasionally escaped. Casca's encounter is thus unusual but not impossible.
2. Huddled in a crowd.

Transformèd with their fear, who swore they saw
25   Men all in fire walk up and down the streets.
And yesterday the bird of night° did sit   screech owl
Even at noonday upon the marketplace,
Hooting and shrieking. When these prodigies°   abnormalities
Do so conjointly meet,° let not men say,   happen together
30   "These are their reasons, they are natural,"
For I believe they are portentous things
Unto the climate° that they point upon.   region
CICERO   Indeed, it is a strange-disposèd time;
But men may construe things after their fashion,°   in their own way
35   Clean° from the purpose of the things themselves.   Completely different
Comes Caesar to the Capitol tomorrow?
CASCA   He doth; for he did bid Antonio
Send word to you he would be there tomorrow.
CICERO   Good night then, Casca. This disturbèd sky
Is not to walk in.
40   CASCA   Farewell, Cicero.   *Exit* CICERO.
              Enter CASSIUS.
CASSIUS   Who's there?
CASCA   A Roman.
CASSIUS   Casca, by your voice.
CASCA   Your ear is good. Cassius, what night is this?
CASSIUS   A very pleasing night to honest men.
CASCA   Who ever knew the heavens menace so?
45   CASSIUS   Those that have known the earth so full of faults.
For my part, I have walked about the streets,
Submitting me unto the perilous night,
And thus unbracèd,° Casca, as you see,   with open doublet
Have bared my bosom to the thunder-stone;°   thunderbolt
50   And when the cross° blue lightning seemed to open   forked; hostile
The breast of heaven, I did present myself
Even° in the aim and very flash of it.   Exactly
CASCA   But wherefore did you so much tempt the heavens?
It is the part of men to fear and tremble
55   When the most mighty gods by tokens° send   signs
Such dreadful heralds to astonish° us.   dismay
CASSIUS   You are dull, Casca, and those sparks of life
That should be in a Roman you do want,°   lack
Or else you use not. You look pale, and gaze,
60   And put on fear, and cast yourself in wonder
To see the strange impatience of the heavens.
But if you would consider the true cause
Why all these fires, why all these gliding ghosts,
Why birds and beasts from quality and kind,[3]
65   Why old men, fools, and children calculate,°   prophesy
Why all these things change from their ordinance,°   usual order
Their natures, and pre-formèd faculties,
To monstrous° quality—why, you shall find   unnatural
That heaven hath infused them with these spirits
70   To make them instruments of fear and warning

---

3. *from quality and kind:* behaving contrary to their nature.

Unto some monstrous state.[4]
Now could I, Casca, name to thee a man
Most like this dreadful night
That thunders, lightens, opens graves, and roars
75 As doth the lion in the Capitol;[5]
A man no mightier than thyself or me
In personal action, yet prodigious° grown,   *ominous*
And fearful,° as these strange eruptions° are.   *terrifying / upheavals*
CASCA   'Tis Caesar that you mean, is it not, Cassius?
80 CASSIUS   Let it be who it is; for Romans now
Have thews° and limbs like to their ancestors,   *sinews*
But, woe the while,° our fathers' minds are dead,   *alas for these times*
And we are governed with our mothers' spirits.
Our yoke and sufferance° show us womanish.   *servitude and patience*
85 CASCA   Indeed, they say the senators tomorrow
Mean to establish Caesar as a king,
And he shall wear his crown by sea and land
In every place save here in Italy.
CASSIUS   I know where I will wear this dagger then;
90 Cassius from bondage will deliver Cassius.
Therein, ye gods, you make the weak most strong;
Therein, ye gods, you tyrants do defeat.
Nor stony tower, nor walls of beaten brass,
Nor airless dungeon, nor strong links of iron,
95 Can be retentive to° the strength of spirit;   *Can imprison*
But life, being weary of these worldly bars,°   *hindrances*
Never lacks power to dismiss itself.
If I know this, know all the world besides,
That part of tyranny that I do bear
I can shake off at pleasure.
Thunder still.
100 CASCA   So can I.
So every bondman in his own hand bears
The power to cancel his captivity.
CASSIUS   And why should Caesar be a tyrant then?
Poor man, I know he would not be a wolf
105 But that he sees the Romans are but sheep;
He were no lion, were not Romans hinds.°   *female deer; servants*
Those that with haste will make a mighty fire
Begin it with weak straws. What trash is Rome!
What rubbish and what offal,° when it serves   *waste product*
110 For the base° matter to illuminate   *underlying; despicable*
So vile a thing as Caesar! But, O grief,
Where hast thou led me? I perhaps speak this
Before a willing bondman; then I know
My answer must be made.[6] But I am armed,°   *(physically and morally)*
115 And dangers are to me indifferent.°   *insignificant*
CASCA   You speak to Casca, and to such a man
That is no fleering° telltale. Hold.° My hand.   *sneering / Enough*
Be factious° for redress of all these griefs,   *Form a group*

---

4. Abnormal situation; atrocious government.
5. Possibly the lion of line 20; or Shakespeare may
imagine that the Romans kept a live lion or two at the

Capitol as the English did at the Tower of London,
where they were a popular attraction.
6. I must pay the penalty.

And I will set this foot of mine as far
As who° goes farthest.   *whoever*

120 CASSIUS   There's a bargain made.
Now know you, Casca, I have moved° already   *persuaded*
Some certain of the noblest-minded Romans
To undergo° with me an enterprise   *undertake*
Of honorable, dangerous consequence;
125 And I do know by this° they stay° for me   *this time / wait*
In Pompey's Porch.[7] For now, this fearful night,
There is no stir or walking in the streets;
And the complexion of the element°   *disposition of the sky*
In favor's° like the work we have in hand,   *In appearance is*
130 Most bloody, fiery, and most terrible.

Enter CINNA.

CASCA   Stand close° awhile, for here comes one in haste.   *concealed*
CASSIUS   'Tis Cinna; I do know him by his gait.
He is a friend. —Cinna, where haste you so?
CINNA   To find out you. Who's that? Metellus Cimber?
135 CASSIUS   No, it is Casca, one incorporate°   *a party*
To our attempts. Am I not stayed for,° Cinna?   *awaited*
CINNA   I am glad on't.[8] What a fearful night is this!
There's two or three of us have seen strange sights.
CASSIUS   Am I not stayed for? Tell me.
140 CINNA   Yes, you are. O Cassius, if you could
But win the noble Brutus to our party—
CASSIUS   Be you content. Good Cinna, take this paper,
And look you lay it in the praetor's[9] chair,
Where Brutus may but° find it; and throw this   *must surely*
145 In at his window; set this up with wax
Upon old Brutus'° statue. All this done,   *Lucius Junius Brutus's*
Repair° to Pompey's Porch, where you shall find us.   *Proceed*
Is Decius Brutus and Trebonius there?
CINNA   All but Metellus Cimber, and he's gone
150 To seek you at your house. Well, I will hie°   *hasten*
And so bestow these papers as you bade me.
CASSIUS   That done, repair to Pompey's Theater.

Exit CINNA.

Come, Casca, you and I will yet ere day
See Brutus at his house. Three parts° of him   *quarters*
155 Is ours already, and the man entire
Upon the next encounter yields him ours.
CASCA   Oh, he sits high in all the people's hearts;
And that which would appear offense in us,
His countenance, like richest alchemy,[1]
160 Will change to virtue and to worthiness.
CASSIUS   Him, and his worth, and our great need of him,
You have right well conceited.° Let us go,   *understood*
For it is after midnight, and ere day
We will awake him and be sure of him.   *Exeunt.*

---

7. Portico of a theater commissioned by Pompey.
8. Cinna is responding to Cassius's information about Casca.
9. Brutus was one of sixteen praetors, or chief magistrates, subordinate only to the two consuls.
1. Alchemy attempted to change base metals into gold. *countenance:* approval; noble appearance.

2.1

Enter BRUTUS *in his orchard.*

BRUTUS What, Lucius, ho!
　—I cannot by the progress of the stars
　Give guess how near to day. —Lucius, I say!
　—I would it were my fault to sleep so soundly.

5　—When, Lucius, when?° Awake, I say. What, Lucius!　　*(expressing impatience)*
　　　Enter LUCIUS.

LUCIUS Called you, my lord?

BRUTUS Get me a taper° in my study, Lucius.　　*candle*
　When it is lighted, come and call me here.

LUCIUS I will, my lord.　　　　　　　　　*Exit.*

10　BRUTUS It must be by his° death; and for my part　　*(Caesar's)*
　I know no personal cause to spurn° at him　　*kick*
　But for the general.° He would be crowned:　　*common good*
　How that might change his nature, there's the question.
　It is the bright day that brings forth the adder,

15　And that craves° wary walking. Crown him that,　　*calls for*
　And then I grant we put a sting in him
　That at his will he may do danger with.
　Th'abuse of greatness is when it disjoins
　Remorse° from power; and to speak truth of Caesar,　　*Conscience*

20　I have not known when his affections swayed°　　*passions ruled*
　More than his reason. But 'tis a common proof°　　*experience*
　That lowliness° is young ambition's ladder,　　*humility*
　Whereto the climber upward turns his face;
　But when he once attains the upmost round°　　*rung*

25　He then unto the ladder turns his back,
　Looks in the clouds, scorning the base degrees[1]
　By which he did ascend. So Caesar may;
　Then, lest he may, prevent. And since the quarrel
　Will bear no color for the thing he is,[2]

30　Fashion° it thus: that what he is, augmented,　　*Describe*
　Would run to these and these extremities.
　And therefore think him as a serpent's egg
　Which, hatched, would as his kind° grow mischievous,°　　*by its nature / harmful*
　And kill him in the shell.
　　　Enter LUCIUS.

35　LUCIUS The taper burneth in your closet,° sir.　　*private room*
　Searching the window for a flint, I found
　This paper, thus sealed up, and I am sure
　It did not lie there when I went to bed.
　　　[He] gives him the letter.

BRUTUS Get you to bed again; it is not day.

40　Is not tomorrow, boy, the first of March?[3]

LUCIUS I know not, sir.

BRUTUS Look in the calendar and bring me word.

LUCIUS I will, sir.　　　　　　　　　　*Exit.*

BRUTUS The exhalations° whizzing in the air　　*meteors*

45　Give so much light that I may read by them.

2.1 Location: Outside Brutus's house.
1. Low rungs; contemptible means; lowly social ranks.
2. Will find no plausible pretext in his conduct so far.

3. TEXTUAL COMMENT Some editors emend "first" to "Ides." For the rationale behind retaining the Folio "first," see Digital Edition TC 2.

[He] opens the letter and reads.
"Brutus, thou sleep'st. Awake, and see thyself.
Shall Rome, et cetera?⁴ Speak, strike, redress!"
"Brutus, thou sleep'st. Awake."
Such instigations have been often dropped
50   Where I have took them up.
"Shall Rome, et cetera?" Thus must I piece it out:
Shall Rome stand under one man's awe? What, Rome?
My ancestors did from the streets of Rome
The Tarquin drive when he was called a king.⁵
55   "Speak, strike, redress!" Am I entreated
To speak and strike? O Rome, I make thee promise,
If the redress will follow,⁶ thou receivest
Thy full petition at the hand of Brutus.
                Enter LUCIUS.
       LUCIUS   Sir, March is wasted fifteen days.
                Knock within.
60   BRUTUS   'Tis good. Go to the gate; somebody knocks.
                                    [Exit LUCIUS.*]*
Since Cassius first did whet° me against Caesar,   incite
I have not slept.
Between the acting of a dreadful thing
And the first motion,° all the interim is   impulse
65   Like a phantasma° or a hideous dream: nightmare
The genius° and the mortal instruments⁷   immortal spirit
Are then in council, and the state of man,
Like to a little kingdom, suffers then
The nature of an insurrection.⁸
                Enter LUCIUS.
70   LUCIUS   Sir, 'tis your brother Cassius⁹ at the door,
Who doth desire to see you.
       BRUTUS   Is he alone?
       LUCIUS   No, sir, there are more with him.
       BRUTUS   Do you know them?
       LUCIUS   No, sir. Their hats are plucked about their ears,
And half their faces buried in their cloaks,
75   That by no means I may discover° them   identify
By any mark of favor.°   distinctive feature
       BRUTUS   Let 'em enter.   *[Exit* LUCIUS.*]*
They are the faction. O conspiracy,
Sham'st thou to show thy dang'rous brow by night
When evils are most free?° Oh, then, by day   uninhibited
80   Where wilt thou find a cavern dark enough
To mask thy monstrous visage? Seek none, conspiracy.
Hide it in smiles and affability;
For if thou path, thy native semblance on,°   walk undisguised

---

4. TEXTUAL COMMENT "Et cetera" might be a word
in the note Brutus is reading, or it might indicate
that he is not bothering to read the entire note
because he knows its contents in advance. Digital
Edition TC 3 explains why the first possibility is the
more likely: the note implies rather than states a
dangerous proposition.

5. See note to 1.2.159.
6. That is, if killing Caesar will restore the Republic.
7. Bodily powers.
8. *the state . . . insurrection:* referring to a commonplace analogy between disorder in man, in the body
politic, and in nature.
9. Cassius was married to Brutus's sister.

Not Erebus° itself were dim enough   *dark underworld region*
85   To hide thee from prevention.[1]
                Enter the conspirators, CASSIUS, CASCA, DECIUS,
                    CINNA, METELLUS, *and* TREBONIUS.
      CASSIUS I think we are too bold[2] upon your rest.
          Good morrow, Brutus. Do we trouble you?
      BRUTUS I have been up this hour, awake all night.
          Know I these men that come along with you?
90   CASSIUS Yes, every man of them; and no man here
          But honors you; and every one doth wish
          You had but that opinion of yourself
          Which every noble Roman bears of you.
          This is Trebonius.
      BRUTUS   He is welcome hither.
      CASSIUS This, Decius Brutus.
95   BRUTUS   He is welcome too.
      CASSIUS This, Casca; this, Cinna; and this, Metellus Cimber.
      BRUTUS They are all welcome.
          What watchful° cares do interpose themselves   *sleep-preventing*
          Betwixt your eyes and night?
      CASSIUS   Shall I entreat a word?
                They whisper.
100   DECIUS Here lies the east. Doth not the day break here?
      CASCA No.
      CINNA Oh, pardon, sir, it doth; and yon gray lines
          That fret° the clouds are messengers of day.   *interlace*
      CASCA You shall confess that you are both deceived.
105   Here, as I point my sword, the sun arises,
          Which is a great way growing° on the south,   *encroaching*
          Weighing° the youthful season of the year.   *On account of*
          Some two months hence up higher toward the north
          He first presents his fire, and the high° east   *due*
110   Stands, as the Capitol, directly here.
      BRUTUS Give me your hands all over, one by one.
      CASCA And let us swear our resolution.
      BRUTUS No, not an oath. If not the face° of men,   *(grave) expressions*
          The sufferance° of our souls, the time's abuse[3]—   *suffering*
115   If these be motives weak, break off betimes,°   *at once*
          And every man hence to his idle° bed.   *unused; lazy*
          So let high-sighted° tyranny range on   *arrogant*
          Till each man drop by lottery.[4] But if these,°   *these reasons*
          As I am sure they do, bear fire enough
120   To kindle cowards and to steel with valor
          The melting spirits of women, then, countrymen,
          What need we any spur but our own cause
          To prick us to redress? What other bond
          Than secret Romans[5] that have spoke the word
125   And will not palter?° And what other oath   *equivocate*
          Than honesty° to honesty engaged   *integrity*
          That this shall be or we will fall for it?

1. From being recognized and thwarted.
2. We intrude too presumptuously.
3. The corruption of the present time.
4. Chance (the tyrant's caprice).
5. Than that we are Romans capable of secrecy.

Swear° priests and cowards and men cautelous,°   *Let swear / crafty; wary*
Old feeble carrions,° and such suffering souls   *corpselike men*
130 That welcome wrongs.[6] Unto bad causes swear
Such creatures as men doubt,° but do not stain   *suspect*
The even° virtue of our enterprise,   *just; straightforward*
Nor th'insuppressive° mettle of our spirits,   *the indomitable*
To think that or° our cause or our performance   *either*
135 Did need an oath, when every drop of blood
That every Roman bears, and nobly bears,
Is guilty of a several bastardy[7]
If he do break the smallest particle
Of any promise that hath passed from him.

140 CASSIUS   But what of Cicero? Shall we sound him?°   *find out his thoughts*
I think he will stand very strong with us.

CASCA   Let us not leave him out.

CINNA   No, by no means.

METELLUS   Oh, let us have him, for his silver hairs
Will purchase us a good opinion°   *reputation*
145 And buy men's voices to commend our deeds.
It shall be said his judgment ruled our hands;
Our youths and wildness shall no whit appear,
But all be buried in his gravity.

BRUTUS   Oh, name him not. Let us not break with° him,   *disclose our plans to*
150 For he will never follow anything
That other men begin.

CASSIUS   Then leave him out.

CASCA   Indeed, he is not fit.

DECIUS   Shall no man else be touched, but only Caesar?

155 CASSIUS   Decius, well urged.° I think it is not meet°   *suggested / proper*
Mark Antony, so well beloved of Caesar,
Should outlive Caesar. We shall find of him
A shrewd° contriver; and you know, his means,   *malicious*
If he improve° them, may well stretch so far   *make the most of*
160 As to annoy° us all. Which to prevent,   *harm*
Let Antony and Caesar fall together.

BRUTUS   Our course[8] will seem too bloody, Caius Cassius,
To cut the head off and then hack the limbs,
Like wrath in death and envy° afterwards;   *malice*
165 For Antony is but a limb of Caesar.
Let's be sacrificers, but not butchers, Caius.
We all stand up against the spirit of Caesar,
And in the spirit of men there is no blood.
Oh, that we then could come by° Caesar's spirit   *obtain*
170 And not dismember Caesar! But, alas,
Caesar must bleed for it. And, gentle friends,
Let's kill him boldly, but not wrathfully;
Let's carve him as a dish fit for the gods,
Not hew him as a carcass fit for hounds.
175 And let our hearts, as subtle° masters do,   *cunning*
Stir up their servants° to an act of rage   *(that is, our hands)*
And after seem to chide 'em. This shall make
Our purpose necessary and not envious,°   *malicious*

---

6. That gladly submit to oppression.   non-Roman blood.
7. Will show itself individually to be adulterated by   8. Punning on "corse," meaning "corpse."

Which so appearing to the common eyes,
180 We shall be called purgers,° not murderers. *purifiers*
And for Mark Antony, think not of him,
For he can do no more than Caesar's arm
When Caesar's head is off.
CASSIUS   Yet I fear him,
For in the engrafted° love he bears to Caesar— *deep-rooted*
185 BRUTUS Alas, good Cassius, do not think of him.
If he love Caesar, all that he can do
Is to himself: take thought° and die for Caesar. *succumb to melancholy*
And that were much he should,⁹ for he is given
To sports, to wildness, and much company.
190 TREBONIUS There is no fear° in him; let him not die, *nothing to fear*
For he will live and laugh at this hereafter.
            Clock strikes.
BRUTUS Peace, count the clock.¹
CASSIUS   The clock hath stricken three.
TREBONIUS 'Tis time to part.
CASSIUS   But it is doubtful yet
Whether Caesar will come forth today or no,
195 For he is superstitious grown of late,
Quite from the main° opinion he held once *Contrary to the strong*
Of fantasy, of dreams, and ceremonies.
It may be these apparent° prodigies, *manifest*
The unaccustomed terror of this night,
200 And the persuasion of his augurers²
May hold him from the Capitol today.
DECIUS Never fear that. If he be so resolved,
I can o'ersway° him. For he loves to hear *prevail upon*
That unicorns may be betrayed with trees,³
205 And bears with glasses,⁴ elephants with holes,° *pits*
Lions with toils,° and men with flatterers; *nets*
But when I tell him he hates flatterers,
He says he does, being then most flattered.
Let me work,
210 For I can give his humor the true bent,⁵
And I will bring him to the Capitol.
CASSIUS Nay, we will all of us be there to fetch him.
BRUTUS By the eighth hour. Is that the uttermost?° *latest*
CINNA Be that the uttermost, and fail not then.
215 METELLUS Caius Ligarius doth bear Caesar hard,° *ill will*
Who rated° him for speaking well of Pompey; *rebuked*
I wonder none of you have thought of him.
BRUTUS Now, good Metellus, go along by him.° *to his house*
He loves me well, and I have given him reasons;
220 Send him but hither and I'll fashion° him. *work upon*
CASSIUS The morning comes upon's. We'll leave you, Brutus.
And, friends, disperse yourselves; but all remember
What you have said, and show yourselves true Romans.
BRUTUS Good gentlemen, look fresh and merrily.

---

9. And that is more than he is likely to do.
1. The clock is an anachronism, like sleeves and doublets.
2. Priests who interpreted "auguries," or omens.

3. The unicorn could supposedly be caught by tricking it into impaling its horn on a tree.
4. Mirrors (imagined to bewilder bears).
5. Give his disposition the right direction.

225   Let not our looks put on° our purposes,   *display*
        But bear it as our Roman actors do,
        With untired spirits and formal constancy.°   *decorous self-possession*
        And so good morrow to you every one.

                     Exeunt all but BRUTUS.
        Boy! Lucius! Fast asleep? It is no matter.
230   Enjoy the honey-heavy dew of slumber.
        Thou hast no figures° nor no fantasies   *imaginings*
        Which busy care draws in the brains of men;
        Therefore thou sleep'st so sound.

              Enter PORTIA.
PORTIA   Brutus, my lord.
BRUTUS   Portia, what mean you? Wherefore rise you now?
235   It is not for° your health thus to commit   *good for*
        Your weak condition to the raw cold morning.
PORTIA   Nor for yours neither. You've ungently,° Brutus,   *unkindly*
        Stole from my bed. And yesternight at supper
        You suddenly arose and walked about,
240   Musing and sighing, with your arms across;[6]
        And when I asked you what the matter was,
        You stared upon me with ungentle looks.
        I urged you further; then you scratched your head
        And too impatiently stamped with your foot.
245   Yet I insisted; yet you answered not,
        But with an angry wafture° of your hand   *gesture*
        Gave sign for me to leave you. So I did,
        Fearing to strengthen that impatience
        Which seemed too much enkindled, and withal°   *besides*
250   Hoping it was but an effect of humor,°   *moodiness*
        Which sometime hath his° hour with every man.   *its*
        It will not let you eat, nor talk, nor sleep;
        And could it work so much upon your shape
        As it hath much prevailed on your condition,°   *disposition*
255   I should not know you[7] Brutus. Dear my lord,
        Make me acquainted with your cause of grief.
BRUTUS   I am not well in health, and that is all.
PORTIA   Brutus is wise, and were he not in health,
        He would embrace the means to come by it.
260 BRUTUS   Why, so I do. Good Portia, go to bed.
PORTIA   Is Brutus sick? And is it physical°   *curative*
        To walk unbracèd° and suck up the humors[8]   *with open doublet*
        Of the dank morning? What, is Brutus sick,
        And will he steal out of his wholesome bed
265   To dare the vile contagion of the night,
        And tempt the rheumy and unpurgèd° air   *moist and impure*
        To add unto his sickness? No, my Brutus,
        You have some sick offense° within your mind,   *disturbance*
        Which by the right and virtue° of my place°   *prerogative / (as a wife)*

---

6. Crossed (a sign of melancholy).
7. "know you": recognize you as. TEXTUAL COMMENT
There is no comma in the Folio text between "you" and
"Brutus," indicating that the name is the object of
"know." In his behavior, in other words, Brutus lives up
to the reputation for wisdom that he has already established for himself. For this way of using names in
Julius Caesar, see Digital Edition TC 4.
8. Inhale the mists.

270   I ought to know of. And upon my knees
I charm° you, by my once-commended beauty,   *conjure*
By all your vows of love, and that great vow
Which did incorporate and make us one,
That you unfold to me, your self, your half,
275   Why you are heavy,° and what men tonight   *dejected*
Have had resort to you; for here have been
Some six or seven who did hide their faces
Even from darkness.
BRUTUS   Kneel not, gentle Portia.
PORTIA   I should not need, if you were gentle Brutus.
280   Within the bond of marriage, tell me, Brutus,
Is it excepted[9] I should know no secrets
That appertain to you? Am I your self
But, as it were, in sort or limitation?[1]
To keep with you at meals, comfort your bed,
285   And talk to you sometimes? Dwell I but in the suburbs[2]
Of your good pleasure? If it be no more,
Portia is Brutus' harlot, not his wife.
BRUTUS   You are my true and honorable wife,
As dear to me as are the ruddy drops
290   That visit° my sad heart.   *afflict; come to*
PORTIA   If this were true, then should I know this secret.
I grant I am a woman, but withal°   *still*
A woman that Lord Brutus took to wife.
I grant I am a woman, but withal
295   A woman well reputed, Cato's daughter.[3]
Think you I am no stronger than my sex,
Being so fathered and so husbanded?
Tell me your counsels;° I will not disclose 'em.   *secrets*
I have made strong proof of my constancy,
300   Giving myself a voluntary wound
Here, in the thigh. Can I bear that with patience
And not my husband's secrets?
BRUTUS   O ye gods,
Render me worthy of this noble wife!
         Knock.
Hark, hark, one knocks. Portia, go in awhile,
305   And by and by thy bosom shall partake
The secrets of my heart.
All my engagements° I will construe° to thee,   *commitments / explain*
All the character[4] of my sad brows.
Leave me with haste.   *Exit* PORTIA.
        Enter LUCIUS *and* LIGARIUS.
            Lucius, who's that knocks?
310   LUCIUS   Here is a sick man that would speak with you.
BRUTUS   Caius Ligarius, that Metellus spake of.
Boy, stand aside. —Caius Ligarius, how?°   *how are you*
LIGARIUS   Vouchsafe° good morrow from a feeble tongue.   *Deign to accept*

---

9. Is it stipulated as a qualification that.
1. *in sort or limitation*: after a fashion or with restrictions (like "excepted," "limited" is a legal term).
2. Outlying areas (where brothels were located in Shakespeare's time).

3. Marcus Portius Cato was renowned for his strict moral integrity; after Caesar's victory over Pompey, he killed himself rather than submit to Caesar's rule.
4. Handwriting (the lines of care "inscribed" on his forehead).

BRUTUS   Oh, what a time have you chose out, brave Caius,
315   To wear a kerchief![5] Would you were not sick!
LIGARIUS   I am not sick, if Brutus have in hand
   Any exploit worthy the name of honor.
BRUTUS   Such an exploit have I in hand, Ligarius,
   Had you a healthful ear to hear of it.
320 LIGARIUS   By all the gods that Romans bow before,
   I here discard my sickness. Soul of Rome,
   Brave son derived from honorable loins,
   Thou like an exorcist° hast conjured up   *a magician*
   My mortifièd° spirit. Now bid me run,   *deadened*
325   And I will strive with things impossible,
   Yea, get the better of them. What's to do?
BRUTUS   A piece of work that will make sick men whole.°   *healthy*
LIGARIUS   But are not some whole that we must make sick?
BRUTUS   That must we also. What it is, my Caius,
330   I shall unfold to thee as we are going
   To whom it must be done.
LIGARIUS   Set on° your foot,   *Advance*
   And with a heart new fired I follow you
   To do I know not what; but it sufficeth
   That Brutus leads me on.
            Thunder.
BRUTUS   Follow me then.   *Exeunt.*

2.2

*Thunder and lightning. Enter Julius CAESAR in his
nightgown.°*   *dressing gown*
CAESAR   Nor heaven nor earth have been at peace tonight.
   Thrice hath Calphurnia in her sleep cried out,
   "Help ho, they murder Caesar!" —Who's within?
      Enter a SERVANT.
SERVANT   My lord.
5 CAESAR   Go bid the priests do present° sacrifice,   *immediate*
   And bring me their opinions of success.[1]
SERVANT   I will, my lord.   *Exit.*
      Enter CALPHURNIA.
CALPHURNIA   What mean you, Caesar? Think you to walk forth?
   You shall not stir out of your house today.
10 CAESAR   Caesar shall forth. The things that threatened me
   Ne'er looked but on my back. When they shall see
   The face of Caesar, they are vanishèd.
CALPHURNIA   Caesar, I never stood on ceremonies,°   *heeded omens*
   Yet now they fright me. There is one within,
15   Besides the things that we have heard and seen,
   Recounts most horrid sights seen by the watch.[2]
   A lioness hath whelpèd in the streets,
   And graves have yawned and yielded up their dead.
   Fierce fiery warriors fight[3] upon the clouds

---

5. Kerchiefs were commonly worn by the sick in Elizabethan England.
2.2 Location: Caesar's house.
1. Of the outcome (good or bad), as determined by
reading the entrails of the sacrificial animals.
2. Night watchmen (another anachronism).

3. TEXTUAL COMMENT Some editors change Folio's
"fight" to "fought," but between lines 13 and 26, past
and present tenses are variable, suggesting perhaps
Calphurnia's panic and trepidation. See Digital Edition TC 5 for a fuller explanation.

20 In ranks and squadrons and right form of war,°   *regular battle formation*
Which drizzled blood upon the Capitol.
The noise of battle hurtled in the air;
Horses do neigh, and dying men did groan,
And ghosts did shriek and squeal about the streets.
25 O Caesar, these things are beyond all use,°   *all normal experience*
And I do fear them.
CAESAR   What can be avoided
Whose end is purposed by the mighty gods?
Yet Caesar shall go forth, for these predictions
Are to° the world in general as to Caesar.   *Are as applicable to*
30 CALPHURNIA   When beggars die there are no comets seen;
The heavens themselves blaze forth° the death of princes.   *flame out; proclaim*
CAESAR   Cowards die many times before their deaths;
The valiant never taste of death but once.
Of all the wonders that I yet have heard,
35 It seems to me most strange that men should fear,
Seeing that death, a necessary end,
Will come when it will come.
Enter a SERVANT.
                          What say the augurers?
SERVANT   They would not have you to stir forth today.
Plucking the entrails of an offering forth,
40 They could not find a heart within the beast.
CAESAR   The gods do this in shame of cowardice.°   *to put cowardice to shame*
Caesar should be a beast without a heart
If he should stay at home today for fear.
No, Caesar shall not. Danger knows full well
45 That Caesar is more dangerous than he.
We are two lions littered in one day,
And I the elder and more terrible;
And Caesar shall go forth.
CALPHURNIA   Alas, my lord,
Your wisdom is consumed in confidence.°   *overconfidence*
50 Do not go forth today. Call it my fear
That keeps you in the house, and not your own.
We'll send Mark Antony to the Senate House,
And he shall say you are not well today.
Let me upon my knee prevail in this.
55 CAESAR   Mark Antony shall say I am not well,
And for thy humor° I will stay at home.   *whim*
Enter DECIUS.
Here's Decius Brutus. He shall tell them so.
DECIUS   Caesar, all hail! Good morrow, worthy Caesar.
I come to fetch you to the Senate House.
60 CAESAR   And you are come in very happy° time   *opportune*
To bear my greeting to the senators
And tell them that I will not come today.
Cannot is false; and that I dare not, falser;
I will not come today. Tell them so, Decius.
CALPHURNIA   Say he is sick.
65 CAESAR   Shall Caesar send a lie?
Have I in conquest stretched mine arm so far
To be afeard to tell graybeards the truth?
Decius, go tell them Caesar will not come.

DECIUS   Most mighty Caesar, let me know some cause,
70   Lest I be laughed at when I tell them so.
CAESAR   The cause is in my will: I will not come.
         That is enough to satisfy the Senate.
         But for your private satisfaction,
         Because I love you, I will let you know.
75   Calphurnia here, my wife, stays° me at home.   *keeps*
         She dreamt tonight° she saw my statue,   *last night*
         Which, like a fountain with an hundred spouts,
         Did run pure blood; and many lusty° Romans   *joyful*
         Came smiling and did bathe their hands in it.
80   And these does she apply° for warnings and portents   *interpret*
         And evils imminent, and on her knee
         Hath begged that I will stay at home today.
DECIUS   This dream is all amiss interpreted;
         It was a vision fair and fortunate.
85   Your statue spouting blood in many pipes,
         In which so many smiling Romans bathed,
         Signifies that from you great Rome shall suck
         Reviving blood, and that great men shall press
         For tinctures, stains, relics, and cognizance.[4]
90   This by Calphurnia's dream is signified.
CAESAR   And this way have you well expounded it.
DECIUS   I have, when you have heard what I can say,
         And know it now: the Senate have concluded
         To give this day a crown to mighty Caesar.
95   If you shall send them word you will not come,
         Their minds may change. Besides, it were a mock
         Apt to be rendered,[5] for someone to say,
         "Break up the Senate till another time
         When Caesar's wife shall meet with better dreams."
100   If Caesar hide himself, shall they not whisper,
         "Lo, Caesar is afraid"?
         Pardon me, Caesar, for my dear dear love
         To your proceeding° bids me tell you this,   *advancement*
         And reason to my love is liable.[6]
105 CAESAR   How foolish do your fears seem now, Calphurnia!
         I am ashamèd I did yield to them.
         Give me my robe, for I will go.
              Enter BRUTUS, LIGARIUS, METELLUS, CASCA,
                 TREBONIUS, CINNA, *and* PUBLIUS.
         And look where Publius is come to fetch me.
PUBLIUS   Good morrow, Caesar.
CAESAR   Welcome, Publius.
110   —What, Brutus, are you stirred so early too?
         —Good morrow, Casca. —Caius Ligarius,
         Caesar was ne'er so much your enemy
         As that same ague° which hath made you lean.   *fever*
         What is't o'clock?
BRUTUS   Caesar, 'tis strucken eight.

---

4. Heraldic colors and emblems ("tinctures," "stains,"   5. *a mock . . . rendered:* a sarcastic reply likely to be
and "cognizance"); venerated properties of saints   made.
("tinctures," "stains," and "relics").   6. And prudence is subordinate to my affection.

115 CAESAR   I thank you for your pains and courtesy.
        Enter ANTONY.
    See, Antony that revels long a-nights
    Is notwithstanding up. —Good morrow, Antony.
ANTONY   So to most noble Caesar.
CAESAR   Bid them prepare within.
120   —I am to blame to be thus waited for.
    —Now, Cinna. —Now, Metellus. —What, Trebonius,
    I have an hour's talk in store for you.
    Remember that you call on me today;
    Be near me that I may remember you.
125 TREBONIUS   Caesar, I will. [*aside*] And so near will I be
    That your best friends shall wish I had been further.
CAESAR   Good friends, go in and taste some wine with me,
    And we, like[7] friends, will straightway go together.
BRUTUS [*aside*]   That every like is not the same, O Caesar,
130   The heart of Brutus earns° to think upon.   *Exeunt.*   grieves

2.3

Enter ARTEMIDORUS [*reading*].
ARTEMIDORUS   "Caesar, beware of Brutus, take heed of Cassius,
    come not near Casca, have an eye to Cinna, trust not Trebo-
    nius, mark well Metellus Cimber. Decius Brutus loves thee
    not. Thou hast wronged Caius Ligarius. There is but one mind
5   in all these men, and it is bent against Caesar. If thou beest
    not immortal, look about you. Security gives way to° conspir-   Overconfidence permits
    acy. The mighty gods defend thee. Thy lover,° Artemidorus."   friend
    Here will I stand till Caesar pass along,
    And as a suitor° will I give him this.   petitioner
10   My heart laments that virtue cannot live
    Out of the teeth of emulation.[1]
    If thou read this, O Caesar, thou mayest live;
    If not, the fates with traitors do contrive.°   *Exit.*   conspire

2.4

Enter PORTIA *and* LUCIUS.
PORTIA   I prithee, boy, run to the Senate House.
    Stay not to answer me, but get thee gone.
    Why dost thou stay?
LUCIUS   To know my errand, madam.
PORTIA   I would have had thee there and here again
5   Ere I can tell thee what thou shouldst do there.
    [*aside*] O constancy, be strong upon my side;
    Set a huge mountain 'tween my heart and tongue.
    I have a man's mind but a woman's might;
    How hard it is for women to keep counsel.°   a secret
    —Art thou here yet?
10 LUCIUS   Madam, what should I do?
    Run to the Capitol, and nothing else?
    And so return to you, and nothing else?

---

7. As becomes (but Brutus plays on the senses "resembling" and "equal to").
2.3 Location: A street near the Capitol.

1. Beyond the danger of ambitious envy.
2.4 Location: Brutus's house.

PORTIA   Yes, bring me word, boy, if thy lord look well;
For he went sickly forth. And take good note
15   What Caesar doth, what suitors press to him.
Hark, boy, what noise is that?
LUCIUS   I hear none, madam.
PORTIA   Prithee, listen well.
I heard a bustling rumor° like a fray,   *disturbed clamor*
And the wind brings it from the Capitol.
20   LUCIUS   Sooth,° madam, I hear nothing.   *In truth*
        Enter the SOOTHSAYER.
PORTIA   Come hither, fellow. Which way hast thou been?
SOOTHSAYER   At mine own house, good lady.
PORTIA   What is't o'clock?
SOOTHSAYER   About the ninth hour, lady.
25   PORTIA   Is Caesar yet gone to the Capitol?
SOOTHSAYER   Madam, not yet. I go to take my stand
    To see him pass on to the Capitol.
PORTIA   Thou hast some suit to Caesar, hast thou not?
SOOTHSAYER   That I have, lady, if it will please Caesar
30   To be so good to Caesar as to hear me:
    I shall beseech him to befriend himself.
PORTIA   Why, know'st thou any harms intended towards him?
SOOTHSAYER   None that I know will be, much that I fear may chance.
    Good morrow to you. —Here the street is narrow.
35   The throng that follows Caesar at the heels,
    Of senators, of praetors, common suitors,
    Will crowd a feeble man almost to death.
    I'll get me to a place more void° and there   *empty*
    Speak to great Caesar as he comes along.   *Exit.*
40   PORTIA   I must go in. Ay me! How weak a thing
    The heart of woman is! O Brutus,
    The heavens speed thee in thine enterprise!
    Sure the boy heard me. —Brutus hath a suit
    That Caesar will not grant. —Oh, I grow faint.
45   —Run, Lucius, and commend me to my lord.
    Say I am merry.° Come to me again   *in good spirits*
    And bring me word what he doth say to thee.   *Exeunt.*

3.1

Flourish. Enter CAESAR, BRUTUS, CASSIUS, CASCA,
DECIUS, METELLUS, TREBONIUS, CINNA, ANTONY,
LEPIDUS, ARTEMIDORUS, PUBLIUS, [POPILIUS,] *and*
the SOOTHSAYER.

CAESAR   The Ides of March are come.
SOOTHSAYER   Ay, Caesar, but not gone.
ARTEMIDORUS   Hail, Caesar. Read this schedule.°   *document*
DECIUS   Trebonius doth desire you to o'erread,
5   At your best leisure, this his humble suit.
ARTEMIDORUS   O Caesar, read mine first, for mine's a suit
    That touches° Caesar nearer. Read it, great Caesar.   *concerns*
CAESAR   What touches us ourself shall be last served.°   *attended to*
ARTEMIDORUS   Delay not, Caesar; read it instantly.

3.1 Location: At the Capitol.

CAESAR   What, is the fellow mad?

10 PUBLIUS   Sirrah, give place.

CASSIUS   What, urge you your petitions in the street?
Come to the Capitol.

[CAESAR *moves away, others following.*]

POPILIUS [*to* CASSIUS]   I wish your enterprise today may thrive.

CASSIUS   What enterprise, Popilius?

15 POPILIUS   Fare you well.

BRUTUS   What said Popilius Lena?

CASSIUS   He wished today our enterprise might thrive.
I fear our purpose is discoverèd.

BRUTUS   Look how he makes to° Caesar. Mark him.   *goes toward*

20 CASSIUS   Casca, be sudden,° for we fear prevention.   *swift*
—Brutus, what shall be done? If this be known,
Cassius or Caesar never shall turn back,°   *return alive*
For I will slay myself.

BRUTUS   Cassius, be constant.°   *resolute*
Popilius Lena speaks not of our purposes:

25 For look, he smiles, and Caesar doth not change.

CASSIUS   Trebonius knows his time, for look you, Brutus,
He draws Mark Antony out of the way.

[*Exeunt* TREBONIUS *and* ANTONY.]

DECIUS   Where is Metellus Cimber? Let him go
And presently prefer° his suit to Caesar.   *at once present*

30 BRUTUS   He is addressed.° Press near and second him.   *ready*

CINNA   Casca, you are the first that rears your hand.

CAESAR   Are we all ready? What is now amiss
That Caesar and his Senate must redress?

METELLUS   Most high, most mighty, and most puissant° Caesar,   *powerful*

35 Metellus Cimber throws before thy seat
An humble heart.

CAESAR   I must prevent° thee, Cimber: *thwart*
These couchings° and these lowly courtesies°   *stoopings / bows*
Might fire the blood° of ordinary men,   *passions*
And turn preordinance and first decree[1]

40 Into the lune of children.[2] Be not fond[3]
To think that Caesar bears such rebel° blood   *lawless*
That will be thawed from the true quality°   *proper constancy*
With that which melteth fools—I mean sweet words,
Low-crookèd° curtsies, and base spaniel fawning.   *Obsequious; dishonest*

45 Thy brother by decree is banishèd.[4]
If thou dost bend and pray and fawn for him,
I spurn thee like a cur out of my way.
Know, Caesar doth not wrong, nor without cause
Will he be satisfied.

50 METELLUS   Is there no voice more worthy than my own
To sound more sweetly in great Caesar's ear
For the repealing of my banished brother?

---

1. Established precedent and original rulings.
2. TEXTUAL COMMENT "Lane" in Folio, emended to "lune" (whim or caprice) in this and other modern editions. For the rationale behind this change, see

Digital Edition TC 6.
3. Do not be so foolish as.
4. Shakespeare's sources do not indicate why Publius Cimber was banished.

BRUTUS   I kiss thy hand, but not in flattery, Caesar,
    Desiring thee that Publius Cimber may
55 Have an immediate freedom of repeal.°   *release from banishment*
CAESAR   What, Brutus?
CASSIUS   Pardon, Caesar; Caesar, pardon.
    As low as to thy foot doth Cassius fall
    To beg enfranchisement° for Publius Cimber.   *liberation*
CAESAR   I could be well moved, if I were as you;
60 If I could pray to move,° prayers would move me.   *make pleas*
    But I am constant as the Northern Star,°   *polestar*
    Of whose true-fixed and resting° quality   *stationary*
    There is no fellow° in the firmament.   *equal*
    The skies are painted with unnumbered sparks;
65 They are all fire, and every one doth shine.
    But there's but one in all doth hold his place.
    So in the world: 'tis furnished well with men,
    And men are flesh and blood, and apprehensive;°   *capable of understanding*
    Yet in the number I do know but one
70 That unassailable holds on his rank,°   *maintains his place*
    Unshaked of motion;[5] and that I am he
    Let me a little show it, even in this:
    That I was constant° Cimber should be banished   *resolute*
    And constant do remain to keep him so.
CINNA   O Caesar—
75 CAESAR   Hence. Wilt thou lift up Olympus?[6]
DECIUS   Great Caesar—
CAESAR   Doth not Brutus bootless° kneel?   *in vain*
CASCA   Speak, hands, for me.[7]
          They stab CAESAR.[8]
CAESAR   *Et tu, Brutè?*[9] —Then fall, Caesar.
    [*He*] *dies.*
CINNA   Liberty! Freedom! Tyranny is dead!
80 Run hence, proclaim, cry it about the streets.
CASSIUS   Some to the common pulpits° and cry out,   *public platforms (rostra)*
    "Liberty, freedom, and enfranchisement."
BRUTUS   People and senators, be not affrighted.
    Fly not, stand still. Ambition's debt is paid.
CASCA   Go to the pulpit, Brutus.
85 DECIUS   And Cassius too.
BRUTUS   Where's Publius?°   *(an elderly senator)*
CINNA   Here, quite confounded° with this mutiny.°   *confused / tumult*
METELLUS   Stand fast together, lest some friend of Caesar's
    Should chance—
90 BRUTUS   Talk not of standing. —Publius, good cheer.
    There is no harm intended to your person,
    Nor to no Roman else. So tell them, Publius.
CASSIUS   And leave us, Publius, lest that the people
    Rushing on us should do your age some mischief.°   *injury*

---

5. Completely steady; unmoved by persuasion.
6. High mountain in Greece where the gods were
supposed to dwell.
7. Let my hands beseech in prayer; let violent action
take over where speech has failed.
8. PERFORMANCE COMMENT Caesar's assassination
can be staged as a quasi-ritual "sacrifice" or as a
bloody slaughter, and there are a variety of options

for the actors who play Brutus and Caesar. See Digital Edition PC 2 for a discussion of how the staging
of Caesar's death affects an audience's understanding of the play.
9. Latin: You too, Brutus? According to the historian
Suetonius, Caesar spoke these words in Greek and
stopped defending himself when he saw Brutus among
the conspirators, saying, in Greek, "You too, child?"

95 BRUTUS Do so, and let no man abide° this deed   *pay the penalty for*
    But we the doers.
          Enter TREBONIUS.
  CASSIUS Where is Antony?
  TREBONIUS   Fled to his house amazed.
    Men, wives, and children stare, cry out, and run
    As° it were doomsday.   *As if*
  BRUTUS   Fates, we will know your pleasures.
100   That we shall die, we know; 'tis but the time
    And drawing days out that men stand upon.[1]
  CASCA Why, he that cuts off twenty years of life
    Cuts off so many years of fearing death.
  BRUTUS Grant that, and then is death a benefit:
105   So are we Caesar's friends, that have abridged
    His time of fearing death. Stoop, Romans, stoop,
    And let us bathe our hands in Caesar's blood
    Up to the elbows and besmear our swords.
    Then walk we forth, even to the marketplace,°   *the Roman Forum*
110   And, waving our red weapons o'er our heads,
    Let's all cry, "Peace, freedom, and liberty!"
  CASSIUS Stoop then, and wash. How many ages hence
    Shall this our lofty scene be acted over
    In states unborn and accents° yet unknown!   *languages*
115 BRUTUS How many times shall Caesar bleed in sport,°   *for entertainment*
    That now on Pompey's basis lies along[2]
    No worthier than the dust!
  CASSIUS So oft as that shall be,
    So often shall the knot° of us be called   *group*
120   The men that gave their country liberty.
  DECIUS What, shall we forth?
  CASSIUS   Ay, every man away.
    Brutus shall lead, and we will grace° his heels   *honor*
    With the most boldest and best hearts of Rome.
          Enter a SERVANT.
  BRUTUS Soft,° who comes here? A friend of Antony's.   *Wait*
125 SERVANT [*kneeling*] Thus, Brutus, did my master bid me kneel.
    Thus did Mark Antony bid me fall down,
    And, being prostrate, thus he bade me say:
    "Brutus is noble, wise, valiant, and honest;°   *honorable*
    Caesar was mighty, bold, royal, and loving.
130   Say, I love Brutus, and I honor him;
    Say, I feared Caesar, honored him, and loved him.
    If Brutus will vouchsafe that Antony
    May safely come to him and be resolved°   *learn for certain*
    How Caesar hath deserved to lie in death,
135   Mark Antony shall not love Caesar dead
    So well as Brutus living, but will follow
    The fortunes and affairs of noble Brutus
    Thorough° the hazards of this untrod state[3]   *Through*
    With all true faith." So says my master Antony.
140 BRUTUS Thy master is a wise and valiant Roman.

---

1. *'tis . . . upon:* it is but the specific time of death and the possibility of extending their lives with which men concern themselves.

2. Lies stretched out on the pedestal ("basis") of Pompey's statue.
3. These unprecedented circumstances.

I never thought him worse.
Tell him, so° please him come unto this place,   *if it should*
He shall be satisfied and, by my honor,
Depart untouched.
SERVANT   I'll fetch him presently.°   *Exit.*   *at once*
145   BRUTUS   I know that we shall have him well to friend.°   *as a friend*
     CASSIUS   I wish we may, but yet have I a mind
That fears him much; and my misgiving still
Falls shrewdly to the purpose.[4]
           Enter ANTONY.
     BRUTUS   But here comes Antony. —Welcome, Mark Antony.
150   ANTONY   O mighty Caesar! Dost thou lie so low?
Are all thy conquests, glories, triumphs, spoils,
Shrunk to this little measure? Fare thee well.
—I know not, gentlemen, what you intend,
Who else must be let blood, who else is rank.[5]
155   If I myself, there is no hour so fit
As Caesar's death's hour, nor no instrument
Of half that worth as those your swords, made rich
With the most noble blood of all this world.
I do beseech ye, if you bear me hard,°   *bear me ill will*
160   Now, whilst your purpled° hands do reek° and smoke,   *bloody / steam*
Fulfill your pleasure. Live° a thousand years,   *If I live*
I shall not find myself so apt° to die.   *ready*
No place will please me so, no mean° of death,   *manner*
As here by Caesar and by you cut off,
165   The choice° and master spirits of this age.   *most select*
     BRUTUS   O Antony! Beg not your death of us.
Though now we must appear bloody and cruel,
As by our hands and this our present act
You see we do, yet see you but our hands
170   And this the bleeding business they have done.
Our hearts you see not. They are pitiful;°   *full of pity*
And pity to the general wrong of Rome—
As fire drives out fire, so pity pity[6]—
Hath done this deed on Caesar. For your part,°   *As for you*
175   To you our swords have leaden° points, Mark Antony.   *blunt*
Our arms in strength of malice[7] and our hearts
Of brothers' temper,° do receive you in   *disposition*
With all kind love, good thoughts, and reverence.
     CASSIUS   Your voice° shall be as strong as any man's   *opinion*
180   In the disposing of new dignities.[8]
     BRUTUS   Only be patient till we have appeased°   *calmed*
The multitude, beside themselves with fear,
And then we will deliver you the cause
Why I, that did love Caesar when I struck him,
Have thus proceeded.
185   ANTONY   I doubt not of your wisdom.
Let each man render me his bloody hand.

---

4. *my . . . purpose:* my suspicions always turn out to be unfortunately pertinent.
5. Festering with disease; overgrown. *let blood:* have blood drawn off medically (but here, killed).

6. That is, pity for the state has driven out pity for Caesar.
7. Although strong in their apparent enmity.
8. Conferring new offices of state.

First, Marcus Brutus, will I shake with you;
—Next, Caius Cassius, do I take your hand;
—Now, Decius Brutus, yours; —now yours, Metellus;
190 —Yours, Cinna; —and, my valiant Casca, yours;
—Though last, not least in love, yours, good Trebonius.
Gentlemen all, alas, what shall I say?
My credit° now stands on such slippery ground   *credibility*
That one of two bad ways you must conceit° me: *judge*
195 Either a coward or a flatterer.
—That I did love thee, Caesar, oh, 'tis true.
If then thy spirit look upon us now,
Shall it not grieve thee dearer° than thy death   *more keenly*
To see thy Antony making his peace,
200 Shaking the bloody fingers of thy foes,
Most noble, in the presence of thy corpse?
Had I as many eyes as thou hast wounds,
Weeping as fast as they stream forth thy blood,
It would become me better than to close°   *agree*
205 In terms of friendship with thine enemies.
Pardon me, Julius. Here wast thou bayed,° brave hart,[9]   *brought to bay*
Here didst thou fall, and here thy hunters stand
Signed° in thy spoil° and crimsoned in thy Lethe.[1]   *Marked / slaughter*
O world! Thou wast the forest to this hart,
210 And this indeed, O world, the heart of thee.
How like a deer strucken by many princes
Dost thou here lie!
CASSIUS   Mark Antony—
ANTONY   Pardon me, Caius Cassius.
The enemies of Caesar shall say this;
215 Then, in a friend, it is cold modesty.°   *moderation*
CASSIUS   I blame you not for praising Caesar so,
But what compact° mean you to have with us?   *agreement*
Will you be pricked in number of° our friends,   *be counted among*
Or shall we on° and not depend on you?   *proceed*
220 ANTONY   Therefore I took your hands, but was indeed
Swayed from the point by looking down on Caesar.
Friends am I with you all and love you all,
Upon this hope, that you shall give me reasons
Why and wherein Caesar was dangerous.
225 BRUTUS   Or else were this a savage spectacle.
Our reasons are so full of good regard°   *sound considerations*
That were you, Antony, the son of Caesar,
You should be satisfied.
ANTONY   That's all I seek;
And am, moreover, suitor° that I may   *petitioner*
230 Produce° his body to the marketplace   *Bring out*
And in the pulpit,° as becomes a friend,   *rostrum*
Speak in the order° of his funeral.   *ceremony*
BRUTUS   You shall, Mark Antony.
CASSIUS   Brutus, a word with you.

---

9. Stag (punning on "heart").
1. Lost lifeblood (Lethe was the river of forgetfulness in the classical underworld).

[*aside to* BRUTUS] You know not what you do. Do not consent
235 That Antony speak in his funeral.
Know you how much the people may be moved
By that which he will utter?
BRUTUS [*aside to* CASSIUS]   By your pardon:°   *With your permission*
I will myself into the pulpit first
And show the reason of our Caesar's death.
240 What Antony shall speak I will protest°   *proclaim*
He speaks by leave and by permission,
And that we are contented Caesar shall
Have all true° rites and lawful ceremonies.   *proper*
It shall advantage° more than do us wrong.   *benefit*
245 CASSIUS [*aside to* BRUTUS]   I know not what may fall.° I like it not.   *happen*
BRUTUS   Mark Antony, here, take you Caesar's body.
You shall not in your funeral speech blame us,
But speak all good you can devise of Caesar
And say you do't by our permission,
250 Else shall you not have any hand at all
About° his funeral. And you shall speak   *In*
In the same pulpit whereto I am going,
After my speech is ended.
ANTONY   Be it so.
I do desire no more.
255 BRUTUS   Prepare the body, then, and follow us.
                              Exeunt all but ANTONY.
ANTONY   O pardon me, thou bleeding piece of earth,
That I am meek and gentle with these butchers.
Thou art the ruins of the noblest man
That ever livèd in the tide of times.°   *flow of history*
260 Woe to the hand that shed this costly° blood.   *precious*
Over thy wounds now do I prophesy,
Which like dumb mouths do ope their ruby lips
To beg the voice and utterance of my tongue,
A curse shall light upon the limbs of men;
265 Domestic fury and fierce civil strife
Shall cumber° all the parts of Italy;   *oppress*
Blood and destruction shall be so in use°   *so customary*
And dreadful objects so familiar
That mothers shall but smile when they behold
270 Their infants quartered° with the hands of war,   *cut in pieces*
All pity choked with custom of fell° deeds;   *familiarity with cruel*
And Caesar's spirit, ranging° for revenge,   *roving like a wild beast*
With Ate° by his side come hot from hell,   *goddess of discord*
Shall in these confines° with a monarch's voice   *regions*
275 Cry havoc² and let slip° the dogs of war,   *unleash*
That this foul deed shall smell above the earth
With carrion men groaning for burial.
                    Enter Octavius' SERVANT.
You serve Octavius Caesar, do you not?
SERVANT   I do, Mark Antony.
280 ANTONY   Caesar did write for him to come to Rome.

---

2. Military order for slaughter and pillage.

SERVANT He did receive his letters and is coming,
  And bid me say to you by word of mouth—
  O Caesar!
ANTONY Thy heart is big.° Get thee apart and weep.   swollen with grief
285 Passion,° I see, is catching, for mine eyes,   Sorrow
  Seeing those beads of sorrow stand in thine,
  Began to water. Is thy master coming?
SERVANT He lies° tonight within seven leagues° of Rome.   stays / twenty miles
ANTONY Post° back with speed and tell him what hath chanced.   Ride quickly
290 Here is a mourning Rome, a dangerous Rome,
  No Rome of safety for Octavius yet.
  Hie° hence and tell him so. Yet stay awhile;   Hasten
  Thou shalt not back till I have borne this corpse
  Into the marketplace. There shall I try°   test
295 In my oration how the people take
  The cruel issue° of these bloody men;   deed
  According to the which thou shalt discourse
  To young Octavius of the state of things.
  Lend me your hand.   *Exeunt [with Caesar's body].*

3.2

Enter BRUTUS *and goes into the pulpit, and* CASSIUS,
with the PLEBEIANS.

PLEBEIANS We will be satisfied!° Let us be satisfied!   given an explanation
BRUTUS Then follow me, and give me audience, friends.
  Cassius, go you into the other street
  And part the numbers.°   divide the multitude
5 —Those that will hear me speak, let 'em stay here;
  Those that will follow Cassius, go with him;
  And public reasons shall be renderèd
  Of Caesar's death.
FIRST PLEBEIAN   I will hear Brutus speak.
SECOND PLEBEIAN I will hear Cassius and compare their reasons
10 When severally° we hear them renderèd.   separately
          [*Exit* CASSIUS, *with some* PLEBEIANS.]
THIRD PLEBEIAN The noble Brutus is ascended. Silence.
BRUTUS Be patient till the last.°   end of my address
  Romans, countrymen, and lovers,° hear me for my cause, and   dear friends
  be silent that you may hear. Believe me for° mine honor, and   on account of
15 have respect to° mine honor that you may believe. Censure°   regard for / Judge
  me in your wisdom, and awake your senses° that you may the   understanding
  better judge. If there be any in this assembly, any dear friend
  of Caesar's, to him I say that Brutus' love to Caesar was no
  less than his. If then that friend demand why Brutus rose
20 against Caesar, this is my answer: not that I loved Caesar less,
  but that I loved Rome more. Had you rather Caesar were living and die all slaves, than that Caesar were dead, to live all
  freemen? As Caesar loved me, I weep for him; as he was fortunate, I rejoice at it; as he was valiant, I honor him; but, as
25 he was ambitious, I slew him. There is tears for his love; joy
  for his fortune; honor for his valor; and death for his ambition. Who is here so base that would be a bondman? If any,

3.2 Location: The Forum.

speak, for him have I offended.° Who is here so rude° that   *wronged / barbarous*
would not be a Roman? If any, speak, for him have I offended.
30 Who is here so vile that will not love his country? If any,
speak, for him have I offended. I pause for a reply.

ALL   None, Brutus, none.

BRUTUS   Then none have I offended. I have done no more to
Caesar than you shall do[1] to Brutus. The question of° his   *reasons for*
35 death is enrolled° in the Capitol, his glory not extenuated°   *recorded / diminished*
wherein he was worthy, nor his offenses enforced° for which   *unduly stressed*
he suffered death.

     Enter MARK ANTONY [*and others*] *with Caesar's body.*
Here comes his body, mourned by Mark Antony, who, though
he had no hand in his death, shall receive the benefit of his
40 dying—a place in the commonwealth—as which of you shall
not? With this I depart, that, as I slew my best lover° for the   *friend*
good of Rome, I have the same dagger for myself when it shall
please my country to need my death.

ALL   Live, Brutus, live, live.

45 FIRST PLEBEIAN   Bring him with triumph home unto his house.

SECOND PLEBEIAN   Give him a statue with his ancestors.

THIRD PLEBEIAN   Let him be Caesar.

FOURTH PLEBEIAN   Caesar's better parts°   *qualities*
Shall be crowned in Brutus.

FIRST PLEBEIAN   We'll bring him to his house with shouts and
clamors.

BRUTUS   My countrymen—

50 SECOND PLEBEIAN   Peace, silence! Brutus speaks.

FIRST PLEBEIAN   Peace, ho!

BRUTUS   Good countrymen, let me depart alone,
And, for my sake, stay here with Antony.
Do grace° to Caesar's corpse and grace[2] his speech   *Pay respect*
55 Tending° to Caesar's glories, which Mark Antony—   *Relating*
By our permission—is allowed to make.
I do entreat you, not a man depart,
Save I alone, till Antony have spoke.   *Exit.*

FIRST PLEBEIAN   Stay, ho, and let us hear Mark Antony.

60 THIRD PLEBEIAN   Let him go up into the public chair.
We'll hear him. —Noble Antony, go up.
     [ANTONY *ascends to the pulpit.*]

ANTONY   For Brutus' sake, I am beholden to you.

FOURTH PLEBEIAN   What does he say of Brutus?

THIRD PLEBEIAN   He says for Brutus' sake
65 He finds himself beholden to us all.

FOURTH PLEBEIAN   'Twere best he speak no harm of Brutus here.

FIRST PLEBEIAN   This Caesar was a tyrant.

THIRD PLEBEIAN   Nay, that's certain.
We are blest that Rome is rid of him.

SECOND PLEBEIAN   Peace, let us hear what Antony can say.

ANTONY   You gentle Romans—

70 ALL   Peace, ho! Let us hear him.

ANTONY   Friends, Romans, countrymen, lend me your ears.[3]

---

1. Should do (in such circumstances).
2. Courteously hear.
3. PERFORMANCE COMMENT Antony's bravura funeral
oration can be played as a sincerely mournful funeral
eulogy of a dead friend, as a deliberate attempt to
instigate violence against Caesar's assassins, or as
something in between. For a discussion of the possibilities, see Digital Edition PC 3.

I come to bury Caesar, not to praise him.
The evil that men do lives after them;
The good is oft interrèd with their bones.
75 So let it be with Caesar. The noble Brutus
Hath told you Caesar was ambitious.
If it were so, it was a grievous fault,
And grievously hath Caesar answered° it.   paid the penalty for
Here, under leave° of Brutus and the rest—   by permission
80 For Brutus is an honorable man;
So are they all, all honorable men—
Come I to speak in Caesar's funeral.
He was my friend, faithful and just to me;
But Brutus says he was ambitious,
85 And Brutus is an honorable man.
He hath brought many captives home to Rome,
Whose ransoms did the general coffers° fill.   public treasury
Did this in Caesar seem ambitious?
When that the poor have cried, Caesar hath wept;
90 Ambition should be made of sterner stuff.
Yet Brutus says he was ambitious,
And Brutus is an honorable man.
You all did see that on the Lupercal
I thrice presented him a kingly crown,
95 Which he did thrice refuse. Was this ambition?
Yet Brutus says he was ambitious,
And sure he is an honorable man.
I speak not to disprove what Brutus spoke,
But here I am to speak what I do know.
100 You all did love him once, not without cause.
What cause withholds you, then, to mourn for him?
—O judgment! Thou art fled to brutish beasts,
And men have lost their reason. —Bear with me;
My heart is in the coffin there with Caesar,
105 And I must pause till it come back to me.
FIRST PLEBEIAN Methinks there is much reason in his sayings.
SECOND PLEBEIAN If thou consider rightly of the matter,
    Caesar has had great wrong.
THIRD PLEBEIAN   Has he, masters?
    I fear there will a worse come in his place.
110 FOURTH PLEBEIAN Marked ye his words? He would not take the
    crown;
    Therefore 'tis certain he was not ambitious.
FIRST PLEBEIAN If it be found so, some will dear abide° it.   pay dearly for
SECOND PLEBEIAN Poor soul, his eyes are red as fire with
    weeping.
THIRD PLEBEIAN There's not a nobler man in Rome than Antony.
115 FOURTH PLEBEIAN Now mark him. He begins again to speak.
ANTONY But° yesterday the word of Caesar might   Only
    Have stood against the world. Now lies he there,
    And none so poor to do him reverence.[4]
    O masters! If I were disposed to stir
120 Your hearts and minds to mutiny° and rage,   rebellion

_____

4. And no one is so lowly as to owe obeisance to him.

I should do Brutus wrong and Cassius wrong,
Who, you all know, are honorable men.
I will not do them wrong; I rather choose
To wrong the dead, to wrong myself and you,
125   Than I will wrong such honorable men.
But here's a parchment with the seal of Caesar;
I found it in his closet.° 'Tis his will.   study
Let but the commons° hear this testament—   commoners
Which, pardon me, I do not mean to read—
130   And they would go and kiss dead Caesar's wounds
And dip their napkins⁵ in his sacred blood,
Yea, beg a hair of him for memory,
And, dying, mention it within their wills,
Bequeathing it as a rich legacy
135   Unto their issue.°   children
FOURTH PLEBEIAN   We'll hear the will. Read it, Mark Antony.
ALL   The will, the will! We will hear Caesar's will.
ANTONY   Have patience, gentle friends: I must not read it.
It is not meet° you know how Caesar loved you.   fitting
140   You are not wood, you are not stones, but men;
And being men, hearing the will of Caesar,
It will inflame you, it will make you mad.
'Tis good you know not that you are his heirs,
For if you should, oh, what would come of it?
145   FOURTH PLEBEIAN   Read the will! We'll hear it, Antony.
You shall read us the will, Caesar's will.
ANTONY   Will you be patient? Will you stay awhile?
I have o'ershot myself⁶ to tell you of it.
I fear I wrong the honorable men
150   Whose daggers have stabbed Caesar; I do fear it.
FOURTH PLEBEIAN   They were traitors. "Honorable men"!
ALL   The will! The testament!
SECOND PLEBEIAN   They were villains, murderers. The will! Read
the will!
155   ANTONY   You will compel me then to read the will?
Then make a ring about the corpse of Caesar,
And let me show you him that made the will.
Shall I descend? And will you give me leave?
ALL   Come down.
160   SECOND PLEBEIAN   Descend.
THIRD PLEBEIAN   You shall have leave.
              [ANTONY comes down.]
FOURTH PLEBEIAN   A ring; stand round.
FIRST PLEBEIAN   Stand from the hearse.° Stand from the body.   bier
SECOND PLEBEIAN   Room for Antony, most noble Antony.
165   ANTONY   Nay, press not so upon me. Stand far° off.   farther
ALL   Stand back! Room! Bear back!
ANTONY   If you have tears, prepare to shed them now.
You all do know this mantle. I remember
The first time ever Caesar put it on:
170   'Twas on a summer's evening in his tent,

---

5. Handkerchiefs (implying that Caesar is a martyr   6. I have gone too far (an image from archery).
whose bloody relics should be regarded as holy).

That day he overcame the Nervii.[7]
Look, in this place ran Cassius' dagger through.
See what a rent the envious° Casca made.   *spiteful*
Through this the well-belovèd Brutus stabbed,
175 And as he plucked his cursèd steel away,
Mark how the blood of Caesar followed it,
As° rushing out of doors to be resolved[8]   *As if*
If Brutus so unkindly° knocked or no;   *cruelly; unnaturally*
For Brutus, as you know, was Caesar's angel.[9]
180 Judge, O you gods, how dearly Caesar loved him!
This was the most unkindest cut of all;
For when the noble Caesar saw him stab,
Ingratitude, more strong than traitors' arms,
Quite vanquished him. Then burst his mighty heart,
185 And in his mantle muffling up his face,
Even at the base of Pompey's statue,
Which all the while ran blood, great Caesar fell.
Oh, what a fall was there, my countrymen!
Then I, and you, and all of us fell down,
190 Whilst bloody treason flourished[1] over us.
Oh, now you weep, and I perceive you feel
The dint° of pity. These are gracious drops.   *impression*
Kind souls, what, weep you when you but behold
Our Caesar's vesture° wounded? Look you here,   *garment*
195 Here is himself, marred as you see with traitors.
      [ANTONY *lifts Caesar's mantle.*]
FIRST PLEBEIAN O piteous spectacle!
SECOND PLEBEIAN O noble Caesar!
THIRD PLEBEIAN O woeful day!
FOURTH PLEBEIAN O traitors, villains!
200 FIRST PLEBEIAN O most bloody sight!
SECOND PLEBEIAN We will be revenged!
ALL Revenge! About!° Seek! Burn! Fire! Kill! Slay! Let not a   *To work*
    traitor live!
ANTONY Stay, countrymen.
205 FIRST PLEBEIAN Peace there! Hear the noble Antony.
SECOND PLEBEIAN We'll hear him, we'll follow him, we'll die
    with him!
ANTONY Good friends, sweet friends, let me not stir you up
    To such a sudden flood of mutiny.
210 They that have done this deed are honorable.
What private griefs° they have, alas, I know not,   *personal grievances*
That made them do it. They are wise and honorable,
And will no doubt with reasons answer you.
I come not, friends, to steal away your hearts.
215 I am no orator, as Brutus is,
But, as you know me all, a plain blunt man
That love my friend, and that they know full well
That gave me public leave to speak[2] of him.

---

7. Gallic tribe conquered by Caesar in 57 B.C.E.; it
was an important victory, extravagantly celebrated in
Rome.
8. To find out for sure.
9. Attendant spirit (that is, dearest friend).
1. Shook its sword; triumphed.
2. Permission to speak in public.

For I have neither wit,° nor words, nor worth,°   *intelligence / stature*
220   Action,° nor utterance, nor the power of speech   *Gesture*
To stir men's blood. I only speak right on.°   *straightforwardly*
I tell you that which you yourselves do know,
Show you sweet Caesar's wounds, poor poor dumb mouths,
And bid them speak for me. But were I Brutus,
225   And Brutus Antony, there were an Antony
Would ruffle° up your spirits and put a tongue   *stir*
In every wound of Caesar that should move
The stones of Rome to rise and mutiny.°   *riot*
ALL   We'll mutiny.
FIRST PLEBEIAN   We'll burn the house of Brutus.
230   THIRD PLEBEIAN   Away, then. Come, seek the conspirators.
ANTONY   Yet hear me, countrymen; yet hear me speak.
ALL   Peace, ho! Hear Antony, most noble Antony.
ANTONY   Why, friends, you go to do you know not what.
Wherein hath Caesar thus deserved your loves?
235   Alas, you know not. I must tell you then.
You have forgot the will I told you of.
ALL   Most true, the will! Let's stay and hear the will.
ANTONY   Here is the will, and under Caesar's seal:
To every Roman citizen he gives,
240   To every several° man, seventy-five drachmas.[3]   *individual*
SECOND PLEBEIAN   Most noble Caesar! We'll revenge his death.
THIRD PLEBEIAN   O royal Caesar!
ANTONY   Hear me with patience.
ALL   Peace,° ho!   *Silence*
245   ANTONY   Moreover, he hath left you all his walks,
His private arbors, and new-planted orchards,°   *gardens*
On this side Tiber. He hath left them you,
And to your heirs forever: common pleasures°   *public parks*
To walk abroad and recreate yourselves.
250   Here was a Caesar! When comes such another?
FIRST PLEBEIAN   Never, never! —Come, away, away!
We'll burn his body in the holy place
And with the brands fire the traitors' houses.
Take up the body.
255   SECOND PLEBEIAN   Go fetch fire.
THIRD PLEBEIAN   Pluck down benches.
FOURTH PLEBEIAN   Pluck down forms,° windows,° anything.   *benches / shutters*
Exeunt PLEBEIANS [*with the body*].
ANTONY   Now let it work. Mischief, thou art afoot;
Take thou what course thou wilt.
Enter SERVANT.
How now, fellow?
260   SERVANT   Sir, Octavius is already come to Rome.
ANTONY   Where is he?
SERVANT   He and Lepidus are at Caesar's house.
ANTONY   And thither will I straight° to visit him.   *at once*
He comes upon a wish.° Fortune is merry   *just as I wished*
265   And in this mood will give us anything.

3. Greek silver coins.

SERVANT I heard him say Brutus and Cassius
 Are rid° like madmen through the gates of Rome.   *Have ridden*
ANTONY Belike° they had some notice° of the people,   *Probably / warning*
 How I had moved them. Bring me to Octavius.   *Exeunt.*

3.3

Enter CINNA *the poet, and after him the* PLEBEIANS.

CINNA I dreamt tonight° that I did feast with Caesar,   *last night*
 And things unluckily charge my fantasy.¹
 I have no will to wander forth of doors,
 Yet something leads me forth.
5 FIRST PLEBEIAN What is your name?
 SECOND PLEBEIAN Whither are you going?
 THIRD PLEBEIAN Where do you dwell?
 FOURTH PLEBEIAN Are you a married man or a bachelor?
 SECOND PLEBEIAN Answer every man directly.²
10 FIRST PLEBEIAN Ay, and briefly.
 FOURTH PLEBEIAN Ay, and wisely.
 THIRD PLEBEIAN Ay, and truly, you were best.°   *you'd better*
 CINNA What is my name? Whither am I going? Where do I
  dwell? Am I a married man or a bachelor? Then to answer
15   every man directly and briefly, wisely and truly: wisely I say,
  I am a bachelor.
 SECOND PLEBEIAN That's as much as to say they are fools that
  marry. You'll bear me a bang° for that, I fear. Proceed directly. *get a blow from me*
 CINNA Directly, I am going to Caesar's funeral.
20 FIRST PLEBEIAN As a friend or an enemy?
 CINNA As a friend.
 SECOND PLEBEIAN That matter is answered directly.
 FOURTH PLEBEIAN For your dwelling—briefly.
 CINNA Briefly, I dwell by the Capitol.
25 THIRD PLEBEIAN Your name, sir, truly.
 CINNA Truly, my name is Cinna.
 FIRST PLEBEIAN Tear him to pieces! He's a conspirator.
 CINNA I am Cinna the poet, I am Cinna the poet!
 FOURTH PLEBEIAN Tear him for his bad verses, tear him for his
30 bad verses!
 CINNA I am not Cinna the conspirator.
 FOURTH PLEBEIAN It is no matter, his name's Cinna. Pluck
  but his name out of his heart, and turn him going.°   *send him packing*
 THIRD PLEBEIAN Tear him, tear him! Come, brands, ho, fire-
35 brands! To Brutus', to Cassius', burn all! Some to Decius'
  house, and some to Casca's, some to Ligarius'. Away, go!
    Exeunt all the PLEBEIANS [*carrying off* CINNA].

4.1

Enter ANTONY, OCTAVIUS, *and* LEPIDUS.

ANTONY These many, then, shall die; their names are pricked.°   *marked down*
OCTAVIUS Your brother too must die. Consent you, Lepidus?
LEPIDUS I do consent.

3.3 Location: A street in Rome.
1. And bad omens oppress my imagination.

2. At once; speaking straightforwardly.
4.1 Location: Antony's house in Rome.

OCTAVIUS   Prick him down, Antony.

LEPIDUS   Upon condition° Publius shall not live,   *Provided that*

5   Who is your sister's son, Mark Antony.

ANTONY   He shall not live; look, with a spot I damn him.[1]

But, Lepidus, go you to Caesar's house;

Fetch the will hither, and we shall determine

How to cut off some charge in legacies.[2]

10 LEPIDUS   What, shall I find you here?

OCTAVIUS   Or° here, or at the Capitol.   *Exit* LEPIDUS.   *Either*

ANTONY   This is a slight unmeritable° man,   *undeserving*

Meet° to be sent on errands. Is it fit,   *Fit*

The threefold world divided,[3] he should stand

One of the three to share it?

15 OCTAVIUS   So you thought him

And took his voice° who should be pricked to die   *accepted his opinion*

In our black° sentence and proscription.[4]   *death*

ANTONY   Octavius, I have seen more days than you,

And though we lay these honors on this man

20   To ease ourselves of divers sland'rous loads,°   *burdens of reproach*

He shall but bear them as the ass bears gold,

To groan and sweat under the business,

Either led or driven as we point the way;

And having brought our treasure where we will,

25   Then take we down his load and turn him off,

Like to the empty° ass, to shake his ears   *unladen*

And graze in commons.[5]

OCTAVIUS   You may do your will,

But he's a tried and valiant soldier.

ANTONY   So is my horse, Octavius, and for that

30   I do appoint° him store of provender.   *provide*

It is a creature that I teach to fight,

To wind,° to stop, to run directly on,   *turn*

His corporal° motion governed by my spirit;   *bodily*

And in some taste° is Lepidus but so.   *measure*

35   He must be taught and trained and bid go forth—

A barren-spirited fellow, one that feeds

On objects, arts, and imitations[6]

Which, out of use and staled° by other men,   *made uninteresting*

Begin his fashion.[7] Do not talk of him

40   But as a property.° And now, Octavius,   *tool*

Listen° great things. Brutus and Cassius   *Give ear to*

Are levying powers.° We must straight make head.[8] *armies*

Therefore let our alliance be combined,

Our best friends made,° our means stretched;[9]   *mustered*

45   And let us presently go sit in council

How covert matters° may be best disclosed   *dangers*

---

1. With a mark I condemn him to death.
2. Reduce the amount paid out to beneficiaries of Caesar's will.
3. Antony, Octavius, and Lepidus, in the second triumvirate, or joint rule of three, parceled out rule of Rome's empire among themselves.
4. A "proscribed" person had a price on his head, his property was confiscated, and his children were prevented from holding office.
5. In the public pasture; among the common people.
6. On curiosities, contrivances, and counterfeits.
7. He then takes up as fashionable.
8. We must raise an army at once.
9. Our bands of followers augmented.

And open perils surest answerèd.°   *most safely confronted*
OCTAVIUS   Let us do so, for we are at the stake[1]
    And bayed about with many enemies;
50   And some that smile have in their hearts, I fear,
    Millions of mischiefs.°   *Exeunt.*   *evils*

4.2

Drum. Enter BRUTUS, LUCILIUS, [LUCIUS,] *and the army.*
TITINIUS *and* PINDARUS *meet them.*   *Halt*
BRUTUS   Stand ho!°
LUCILIUS   Give the word, ho, and stand![1]
BRUTUS   What now, Lucilius, is Cassius near?
LUCILIUS   He is at hand, and Pindarus is come
5   To do you salutation from his master.
BRUTUS   He greets me well.° Your master, Pindarus,   *with a worthy man*
    In his own change or by ill officers,[2]
    Hath given me some worthy° cause to wish   *justifiable*
    Things done, undone; but if he be at hand
    I shall be satisfied.[3]
10 PINDARUS   I do not doubt
    But that my noble master will appear
    Such as he is, full of regard[4] and honor.
BRUTUS   He is not doubted.
         [BRUTUS *and* LUCILIUS *speak apart.*]
         A word, Lucilius,
    How he received you: let me be resolved.°   *informed*
15 LUCILIUS   With courtesy and with respect enough,
    But not with such familiar instances°   *tokens of friendship*
    Nor with such free and friendly conference°   *conversation*
    As he hath used of old.
BRUTUS   Thou hast described
    A hot friend cooling. Ever note, Lucilius,
20   When love begins to sicken and decay
    It useth an enforcèd ceremony.°   *a strained formality*
    There are no tricks° in plain and simple faith,   *artifices*
    But hollow° men, like horses hot at hand,[5]   *insincere*
    Make gallant show and promise of their mettle;
         Low march[6] *within.*
25   But when they should endure the bloody spur,
    They fall their crests° and like deceitful jades°   *lower their necks / nags*
    Sink° in the trial. Comes his army on?   *Fail*
LUCILIUS   They mean this night in Sardis to be quartered.
    The greater part, the horse in general,°   *all the cavalry*
    Are come with Cassius.
         Enter CASSIUS *and his powers.*°   *armies*
30 BRUTUS   Hark, he is arrived.
    March gently° on to meet him.   *slowly*
CASSIUS   Stand ho!

---

1. That is, like bears in the sport of bearbaiting, tied to a stake and surrounded by baying hounds.
4.2 Location: Sardis, in what is now western Turkey. Outside Brutus's tent in his army's camp.
1. Pass the word, and halt.
2. By his own altered feelings or through the actions of bad subordinates.
3. I shall receive a full explanation.
4. Respect for you; renown (for his own abilities).
5. Eager at the outset.
6. Soft drumbeat (as from a distance; the sound becomes louder as the army enters).

BRUTUS   Stand ho! Speak the word along.
FIRST SOLDIER   Stand!
35 SECOND SOLDIER   Stand!
THIRD SOLDIER   Stand!
CASSIUS   Most noble brother, you have done me wrong.
BRUTUS   Judge me, you gods! Wrong I mine enemies?
And if not so, how should I wrong a brother?
40 CASSIUS   Brutus, this sober form of yours hides wrongs,
And when you do them—
BRUTUS   Cassius, be content.°   *keep calm*
Speak your griefs° softly. I do know you well.   *grievances*
Before the eyes of both our armies here,
Which should perceive nothing but love from us,
45 Let us not wrangle. Bid them move away;
Then in my tent, Cassius, enlarge° your griefs,   *express fully*
And I will give you audience.
CASSIUS   Pindarus,
Bid our commanders lead their charges° off   *troops*
A little from this ground.
50 BRUTUS   Lucilius, do you the like, and let no man
Come to our tent till we have done our conference.
Let Lucius and Titinius guard our door.

                    Exeunt all but BRUTUS *and* CASSIUS.

4.3

CASSIUS   That you have wronged me doth appear in this:
You have condemned and noted° Lucius Pella   *publicly disgraced*
For taking bribes here of the Sardians,
Wherein my letters, praying on his side
5   Because I knew the man, was slighted off.°   *contemptuously ignored*
BRUTUS   You wronged yourself to write in such a case.
CASSIUS   In such a time as this it is not meet°   *appropriate*
That every nice° offense should bear his comment.°   *trivial / be criticized*
BRUTUS   Let me tell you, Cassius, you yourself
10   Are much condemned to have° an itching palm,   *for having*
To sell and mart° your offices for gold   *traffic in*
To undeservers.
CASSIUS   I, an itching palm?
You know that you are Brutus that speaks this,
Or, by the gods, this speech were else° your last.   *otherwise*
15 BRUTUS   The name of Cassius honors this corruption,[1]
And chastisement doth therefore hide his head.
CASSIUS   Chastisement?
BRUTUS   Remember March, the Ides of March remember:
Did not great Julius bleed for justice' sake?
20   What villain touched his body that did stab
And not for justice?[2] What, shall one of us
That struck the foremost man of all this world
But for supporting robbers,[3] shall we now
Contaminate our fingers with base bribes,

4.3 Location: Sardis, in what is now western Turkey.
Scene continues in Brutus's tent.
1. Makes this corruption appear honorable.
2. *What . . . justice?*: Who was so villainous as to

stab Caesar for any motive other than justice?
3. Caesar was accused of permitting, even encouraging, corruption among his subordinates.

25	And sell the mighty space of our large honors°	*impressive reputations*
	For so much trash° as may be graspèd thus?	*money (contemptuous)*
	I had rather be a dog and bay° the moon	*howl at*
	Than such a Roman.	
	CASSIUS Brutus, bait° not me.	*howl at; harass*
	I'll not endure it. You forget yourself	
30	To hedge me in.° I am a soldier, I,	*limit my authority*
	Older in practice, abler than yourself	
	To make conditions.°	*manage affairs*
	BRUTUS Go to! You are not, Cassius.	
	CASSIUS I am.	
	BRUTUS I say you are not.	
35	CASSIUS Urge° me no more; I shall forget myself.	*Provoke*
	Have mind upon your health. Tempt me no farther.	
	BRUTUS Away, slight man.	
	CASSIUS Is't possible?	
	BRUTUS Hear me, for I will speak.	
	Must I give way and room to your rash choler?[4]	
40	Shall I be frighted when a madman stares?	
	CASSIUS O ye gods, ye gods! Must I endure all this?	
	BRUTUS All this? Ay, more. Fret till your proud heart break.	
	Go show your slaves how choleric° you are	*enraged*
	And make your bondmen tremble. Must I budge?°	*flinch*
45	Must I observe° you? Must I stand and crouch°	*defer to / cringe*
	Under your testy humor?° By the gods,	*irritable temper*
	You shall digest[5] the venom of your spleen°	*anger*
	Though it do split you; for, from this day forth,	
	I'll use you for my mirth, yea, for my laughter,	
	When you are waspish.	
50	CASSIUS Is it come to this?	
	BRUTUS You say you are a better soldier.	
	Let it appear so; make your vaunting° true,	*boasting*
	And it shall please me well. For mine own part,	
	I shall be glad to learn of° noble men.	*from*
55	CASSIUS You wrong me every way; you wrong me, Brutus.	
	I said an elder soldier, not a better.	
	Did I say "better"?	
	BRUTUS If you did, I care not.	
	CASSIUS When Caesar lived he durst not thus have moved° me.	*angered*
	BRUTUS Peace, peace, you durst not so have tempted him.	
60	CASSIUS I durst not?	
	BRUTUS No.	
	CASSIUS What, durst not tempt him?	
	BRUTUS For your life you durst not.	
	CASSIUS Do not presume too much upon my love;	
	I may do that I shall be sorry for.	
65	BRUTUS You have done that you should be sorry for.	
	There is no terror, Cassius, in your threats,	
	For I am armed so strong in honesty°	*rectitude*
	That they pass by me as the idle wind,	
	Which I respect not.° I did send to you	*pay no attention to*
70	For certain sums of gold, which you denied me;	

---

4. Must I allow free passage to your rash anger?   5. Swallow (not give vent to).

For I can raise no money by vile means.
By heaven, I had rather coin my heart
And drop my blood for drachmas than to wring
From the hard hands of peasants their vile trash
75 By any indirection.° I did send   *devious means*
To you for gold to pay my legions,
Which you denied me. Was that done like Cassius?
Should I have answered Caius Cassius so?
When Marcus Brutus grows so covetous
80 To lock such rascal counters from his friends,
Be ready, gods, with all your thunderbolts;
Dash him to pieces!
CASSIUS   I denied you not.
BRUTUS You did.
CASSIUS   I did not. He was but a fool
That brought my answer back. Brutus hath rived° my heart. *broken*
85 A friend should bear his friend's infirmities,
But Brutus makes mine greater than they are.
BRUTUS I do not, till you practice them on me.
CASSIUS You love me not.
BRUTUS   I do not like your faults.
CASSIUS A friendly eye could never see such faults.
90 BRUTUS A flatterer's would not, though they do appear
As huge as high Olympus.
CASSIUS Come, Antony, and young Octavius, come,
Revenge yourselves alone on Cassius,
For Cassius is aweary of the world:
95 Hated by one he loves, braved° by his brother,   *defied*
Checked° like a bondman, all his faults observed,   *Rebuked*
Set in a notebook, learned, and conned by rote°   *memorized*
To cast into my teeth. Oh, I could weep
My spirit from mine eyes! There is my dagger,
100 And here my naked breast; within, a heart
Dearer° than Pluto's[6] mine, richer than gold.   *More valuable*
If that thou beest a Roman, take it forth.
I that denied thee gold will give my heart.
Strike as thou didst at Caesar; for I know,
105 When thou didst hate him worst, thou loved'st him better
Than ever thou loved'st Cassius.
BRUTUS   Sheathe your dagger.
Be angry when you will, it shall have scope;°   *room for exercise*
Do what you will, dishonor shall be humor.[7]
O Cassius, you are yokèd° with a lamb   *allied*
110 That carries anger as the flint bears fire,
Who, much enforcèd,° shows a hasty spark   *struck*
And straight° is cold again.   *immediately*
CASSIUS   Hath Cassius lived
To be but mirth and laughter to his Brutus
When grief and blood ill-tempered[8] vexeth him?
115 BRUTUS When I spoke that, I was ill-tempered too.

---

6. Roman god of riches (Plutus; often conflated with Pluto, god of the underworld).
7. Dishonorable actions shall be ascribed to moodiness.
8. Literally, badly mixed blood (thought to produce anger and melancholy).

CASSIUS Do you confess so much? Give me your hand.
BRUTUS And my heart, too.
CASSIUS   O Brutus!
BRUTUS   What's the matter?
CASSIUS Have not you love enough to bear with me
  When that rash humor° which my mother gave me   *temperament*
  Makes me forgetful?
120 BRUTUS   Yes, Cassius, and from henceforth
  When you are over-earnest with your Brutus,
  He'll think your mother chides and leave you so.°   *let you alone*
    Enter a POET [*with* LUCILIUS *and* TITINIUS].
POET Let me go in to see the generals.
  There is some grudge between 'em; 'tis not meet
  They be alone.
125 LUCILIUS   You shall not come to them.
POET Nothing but death shall stay me.
CASSIUS How now? What's the matter?
POET For shame, you generals; what do you mean?
  Love and be friends, as two such men should be;
130 For I have seen more years, I'm sure, than ye.
CASSIUS Ha, ha, how vilely doth this cynic[9] rhyme!
BRUTUS Get you hence, sirrah.° Saucy fellow, hence!   *(contemptuous address)*
CASSIUS Bear with him, Brutus. 'Tis his fashion.
BRUTUS I'll know his humor when he knows his time:[1]
135 What should the wars do with these jigging° fools?   *incompetently versifying*
  —Companion,° hence!   *(contemptuous)*
CASSIUS   Away, away, be gone.   *Exit* POET.
BRUTUS Lucilius and Titinius, bid the commanders
  Prepare to lodge their companies tonight.
CASSIUS And come yourselves, and bring Messala with you
140 Immediately to us.   [*Exeunt* LUCILIUS *and* TITINIUS.]
BRUTUS [*calls*] Lucius, a bowl of wine.
CASSIUS I did not think you could have been so angry.
BRUTUS O Cassius, I am sick of° many griefs.   *suffering from*
CASSIUS Of your philosophy you make no use
145 If you give place to accidental evils.[2]
BRUTUS No man bears sorrow better. Portia is dead.
CASSIUS Ha? Portia?
BRUTUS She is dead.
CASSIUS How scaped I killing° when I crossed you so?   *being killed*
150 O insupportable and touching loss!
  Upon what sickness?
BRUTUS   Impatient of° my absence,   *Inability to tolerate*
  And grief that young Octavius with Mark Antony
  Have made themselves so strong—for with° her death   *with the news of*
  That tidings came—with this she fell distract
155 And, her attendants absent, swallowed fire.[3]
CASSIUS And died so?

9. Member of a philosophical school that refused to respect differences in social class.
1. I'll tolerate his eccentricity when he finds an appropriate time for it.
2. Brutus admired the Stoics, who taught that the wise man should remain unaffected by circumstances outside himself. *evils:* misfortunes.
3. Portia committed suicide by swallowing live embers.

BRUTUS　　　　　　　　　Even so.

CASSIUS　　　　　　　　　O ye immortal gods!

　　　　Enter LUCIUS *with wine and tapers.*°　　　　　　　*candles*

BRUTUS　Speak no more of her. —Give me a bowl of wine.

　—In this I bury all unkindness, Cassius.

　　[*He*] *drinks.*

CASSIUS　My heart is thirsty for that noble pledge.

160　—Fill, Lucius, till the wine o'erswell° the cup.　　　　　*overflow*

　I cannot drink too much of Brutus' love.　　　[*Exit* LUCIUS.]

　　　Enter TITINIUS *and* MESSALA.

BRUTUS　Come in, Titinius. —Welcome, good Messala.

　Now sit we close about this taper here

　And call in question° our necessities.　　　　　　　　　*discuss*

CASSIUS　Portia, art thou gone?

165　BRUTUS　　　　　　　　　No more, I pray you.

　—Messala, I have here receivèd letters

　That young Octavius and Mark Antony

　Come down upon us with a mighty power,

　Bending their expedition° toward Philippi.[4]　　　*Pressing hastily*

170　MESSALA　Myself have letters of the selfsame tenor.

BRUTUS　With what addition?

MESSALA　That by proscription[5] and bills of outlawry

　Octavius, Antony, and Lepidus

　Have put to death an hundred senators.

175　BRUTUS　Therein our letters do not well agree:

　Mine speak of seventy senators that died

　By their proscriptions, Cicero being one.

CASSIUS　Cicero one?

MESSALA　　　　　　　　Cicero is dead,

　And by that order of proscription.

180　Had you your letters from your wife, my lord?

BRUTUS　No, Messala.

MESSALA　Nor nothing in your letters writ of her?

BRUTUS　Nothing, Messala.

MESSALA　　　　　　　　That methinks is strange.

BRUTUS　Why ask you? Hear you aught of her in yours?

185　MESSALA　No, my lord.

BRUTUS　Now, as you are a Roman, tell me true.

MESSALA　Then like a Roman bear the truth I tell,

　For certain she is dead, and by strange manner.

BRUTUS　Why, farewell, Portia.[6] We must die, Messala.

190　With meditating that she must die once,°　　　　　*at some time*

　I have the patience to endure it now.

MESSALA　Even so great men great losses should endure.

CASSIUS　I have as much of this in art[7] as you,

　But yet my nature could not bear it so.

195　BRUTUS　Well, to our work alive.[8] What do you think

　Of marching to Philippi presently?°　　　　　　　　　　*at once*

CASSIUS　I do not think it good.

BRUTUS　Your reason?

---

4. City in northeastern Greece.
5. See note to 4.1.17.
6. Brutus claims not to have heard any news of Portia, though earlier (lines 146–55) he describes her

death to Cassius; see the Introduction for a discussion of this conflict.
7. I have learned as much of this philosophy.
8. *alive:* of concern to those now living.

CASSIUS　This it is:
200　'Tis better that the enemy seek us.
　　So shall he waste his means, weary his soldiers,
　　Doing himself offense, whilst we, lying still,
　　Are full of rest, defense, and nimbleness.
BRUTUS　Good reasons must of force° give place to better:　　　　*of necessity*
205　The people twixt Philippi and this ground
　　Do stand but in a forced affection,
　　For they have grudged us contribution.[9]
　　The enemy, marching along by them,
　　By them shall make a fuller number up,
210　Come on refreshed, new-added,° and encouraged;　　　　*reinforced*
　　From which advantage shall we cut him off
　　If at Philippi we do face him there,
　　These people at our back.
CASSIUS　　　　　　　　　Hear me, good brother.
BRUTUS　Under your pardon.° You must note beside　　　*Allow me to continue*
215　That we have tried the utmost of our friends;
　　Our legions are brimful, our cause is ripe.
　　The enemy increaseth every day;
　　We, at the height, are ready to decline.
　　There is a tide in the affairs of men
220　Which, taken at the flood, leads on to fortune;
　　Omitted,° all the voyage of their life　　　　*Once missed*
　　Is bound in° shallows and in miseries.　　　*confined to*
　　On such a full sea are we now afloat,
　　And we must take the current when it serves
　　Or lose our ventures.[1]
225　CASSIUS　　　　　　　Then, with your will,° go on.　　*as you wish*
　　We'll along ourselves and meet them at Philippi.
BRUTUS　The deep of night is crept upon our talk,
　　And nature must obey necessity,
　　Which we will niggard° with a little rest.　　　*stint*
　　There is no more to say.
230　CASSIUS　　　　　　No more. Good night.
　　Early tomorrow will we rise and hence.°　　　*depart*
BRUTUS　Lucius.
　　　　　[*Enter* LUCIUS.]
　　　　　My gown.°　　　　　[*Exit* LUCIUS.]　　*dressing gown*
　　　　　Farewell, good Messala.
　　—Good night, Titinius. —Noble, noble Cassius,
　　Good night, and good repose.
CASSIUS　　　　　　　O my dear brother,
235　This was an ill beginning of the night.
　　Never come such division tween our souls!
　　Let it not, Brutus.
　　　　　Enter LUCIUS *with the gown.*
BRUTUS　Everything is well.
CASSIUS　Good night, my lord.
240　BRUTUS　Good night, good brother.
TITINIUS *and* MESSALA　Good night, Lord Brutus.
BRUTUS　Farewell, everyone.

---

9. Money to support the army.　　　　　1. Investments (in trading voyages).

Exeunt [all but BRUTUS *and* LUCIUS].

Give me the gown. Where is thy instrument?° *(probably a lute)*

LUCIUS　Here in the tent.

BRUTUS　　　　　　　　　What, thou speak'st drowsily?

245 Poor knave,° I blame thee not; thou art o'erwatched.[2]　　　*lad*
Call Claudio and some other of my men;
I'll have them sleep on cushions in my tent.

LUCIUS　Varrus and Claudio.

Enter VARRUS *and* CLAUDIO.

VARRUS　Calls my lord?

250 BRUTUS　I pray you, sirs, lie in my tent and sleep.
It may be I shall raise you° by and by　　　　　　*get you up*
On business to my brother Cassius.

VARRUS　So please you, we will stand and watch your pleasure.[3]

BRUTUS　I will not have it so. Lie down, good sirs.

255 It may be I shall otherwise bethink me.°　　　　*change my mind*
—Look, Lucius, here's the book I sought for so;
I put it in the pocket of my gown.

LUCIUS　I was sure your lordship did not give it me.

BRUTUS　Bear with me, good boy, I am much forgetful.

260 Canst thou hold up thy heavy eyes awhile
And touch thy instrument a strain or two?

LUCIUS　Ay, my lord, an't° please you.　　　　　　　　*if it*

BRUTUS　　　　　　　　　It does, my boy.
I trouble thee too much, but thou art willing.

LUCIUS　It is my duty, sir.

265 BRUTUS　I should not urge thy duty past thy might;
I know young bloods° look for a time of rest.　　*youthful spirits*

LUCIUS　I have slept, my lord, already.

BRUTUS　It was well done, and thou shalt sleep again;
I will not hold thee long. If I do live,

270 I will be good to thee.

Music and a song.

This is a sleepy tune. —O murd'rous slumber!
Layest thou thy leaden mace° upon my boy　　*heavy staff of office*
That plays thee music? —Gentle knave, good night;
I will not do thee so much wrong to wake thee.

275 If thou dost nod, thou break'st thy instrument;
I'll take it from thee and, good boy, good night.
Let me see, let me see; is not the leaf turned down
Where I left reading? Here it is, I think.

Enter the GHOST OF CAESAR.

How ill this taper burns.[4] Ha! Who comes here?

280 I think it is the weakness of mine eyes
That shapes this monstrous apparition.
It comes upon° me. —Art thou any thing?　　　　　*toward*
Art thou some god, some angel, or some devil,
That mak'st my blood cold and my hair to stare?°　*stand on end*

285 Speak to me what thou art.

GHOST OF CAESAR　Thy evil spirit, Brutus.

BRUTUS　　　　　　　　　Why com'st thou?

---

2. You have stayed up too long.
3. And stay awake to attend to your wishes.

4. The dimming of a flame was held to indicate a ghost's presence.

GHOST OF CAESAR   To tell thee thou shalt see me at Philippi.
BRUTUS   Well, then I shall see thee again?
GHOST OF CAESAR   Ay, at Philippi.
290 BRUTUS   Why, I will see thee at Philippi, then.

[*Exit* GHOST OF CAESAR.]

Now I have taken heart, thou vanishest.
Ill spirit, I would hold more talk with thee.
—Boy, Lucius! —Varrus, Claudio, sirs, awake!
Claudio!
295 LUCIUS   The strings, my lord, are false.°   *out of tune*
BRUTUS   He thinks he still is at his instrument.
Lucius, awake.
LUCIUS   My lord.
BRUTUS   Didst thou dream, Lucius, that thou so cried'st out?
300 LUCIUS   My lord, I do not know that I did cry.
BRUTUS   Yes, that thou didst. Didst thou see anything?
LUCIUS   Nothing, my lord.
BRUTUS   Sleep again, Lucius. —Sirrah Claudio.
[*to* VARRUS] Fellow, thou, awake.
305 VARRUS   My lord.
CLAUDIO   My lord.
BRUTUS   Why did you so cry out, sirs, in your sleep?
BOTH   Did we, my lord?
BRUTUS   Ay. Saw you anything?
VARRUS   No, my lord, I saw nothing.
CLAUDIO   Nor I, my lord.
310 BRUTUS   Go and commend me° to my brother Cassius.   *send my regards*
Bid him set on his powers betimes before,[5]
And we will follow.
BOTH   It shall be done, my lord.   *Exeunt.*

5.1

Enter OCTAVIUS, ANTONY, *and their army.*

OCTAVIUS   Now, Antony, our hopes are answerèd.
You said the enemy would not come down
But keep the hills and upper regions.
It proves not so: their battles° are at hand;   *forces*
5 They mean to warn° us at Philippi here,   *challenge*
Answering before we do demand of them.
ANTONY   Tut, I am in their bosoms,[1] and I know
Wherefore they do it: they could be content
To visit other places° and come down   *To go elsewhere*
10 With fearful bravery,[2] thinking by this face°   *pretense; defiance*
To fasten in our thoughts that they have courage;
But 'tis not so.

Enter a MESSENGER.

MESSENGER   Prepare you, generals.
The enemy comes on in gallant show.
Their bloody sign° of battle is hung out,   *red flag*
15 And something to° be done immediately.   *is to*
ANTONY   Octavius, lead your battle softly° on   *your army warily*

---

5. March off with his army before me.
5.1 Location: The remainder of the play takes place on the battlefield near Philippi.

1. I know their secret thoughts.
2. With a show of courage that conceals fear; with a terrifying display.

Upon the left hand of the even field.
OCTAVIUS Upon the right hand, I. Keep thou the left.
ANTONY Why do you cross° me in this exigent?°   *thwart / critical moment*
20 OCTAVIUS I do not cross you,[3] but I will do so.
    March.
    Drum. Enter BRUTUS, CASSIUS, *and their army*
    [*including* LUCILIUS, TITINIUS, *and* MESSALA].
BRUTUS They stand and would have parley.
CASSIUS Stand fast, Titinius. We must out° and talk.   *go forward*
OCTAVIUS Mark Antony, shall we give sign of battle?
ANTONY No, Caesar, we will answer on their charge.[4]
25 Make forth.° The generals would have some words.   *Go forward*
OCTAVIUS [*to his officers*] Stir not until the signal.
    [*The generals step toward one another.*]
BRUTUS Words before blows. Is it so, countrymen?
OCTAVIUS Not that we love words better, as you do.
BRUTUS Good words are better than bad strokes, Octavius.
30 ANTONY In your° bad strokes, Brutus, you give good words.   *As you deliver*
Witness the hole you made in Caesar's heart,
Crying, "Long live! Hail, Caesar."
CASSIUS   Antony,
The posture° of your blows are yet unknown;   *quality*
But for your words, they rob the Hybla[5] bees
And leave them honeyless.
35 ANTONY   Not stingless too?
BRUTUS Oh, yes, and soundless too,
For you have stol'n their buzzing, Antony,
And very wisely threat before you sting.
ANTONY Villains, you did not so when your vile daggers
40 Hacked one another in the sides of Caesar.
You showed your teeth like apes,° and fawned like hounds,   *You pretended to smile*
And bowed like bondmen, kissing Caesar's feet,
Whilst damnèd Casca, like a cur, behind
Struck Caesar on the neck. O you flatterers!
45 CASSIUS Flatterers? —Now, Brutus, thank yourself.
This tongue had not offended so today
If Cassius might have ruled.°   *had his way*
OCTAVIUS Come, come, the cause.° If arguing make us sweat,   *matter in hand*
The proof° of it will turn to redder drops: *testing*
50 Look, I draw a sword against conspirators.
    [*He draws.*]
When think you that the sword goes up again?
Never, till Caesar's three-and-thirty wounds
Be well avenged, or till another Caesar[6]
Have added slaughter to[7] the sword of traitors.
55 BRUTUS Caesar, thou canst not die by traitors' hands
Unless thou bring'st them with thee.°   *(Unless by your hand)*
OCTAVIUS   So I hope.
I was not born to die on Brutus' sword.
BRUTUS Oh, if thou wert the noblest of thy strain,°   *family*

---

3. March on the right side; dispute with you in the
future.
4. We will meet them when they attack.

5. Sicilian town famous for honey.
6. That is, Octavius Caesar himself.
7. Has increased the slaughter committed by.

Young man, thou couldst not die more honorable.
60 CASSIUS A peevish° schoolboy, worthless of such honor,   silly
Joined with a masquer and a reveler.[8]
ANTONY Old Cassius still.
OCTAVIUS   Come, Antony, away.
—Defiance, traitors, hurl we in your teeth.
If you dare fight today, come to the field;
65 If not, when you have stomachs.°   inclination; courage
        Exeunt OCTAVIUS, ANTONY, *and* [*their*] *army.*
CASSIUS Why now, blow wind, swell billow, and swim bark!°   ship
The storm is up, and all is on the hazard.°   at risk
BRUTUS Ho, Lucilius! Hark, a word with you.
        LUCILIUS *and* MESSALA *stand forth.*°   come forward
LUCILIUS My lord.
        [BRUTUS *and* LUCILIUS *step aside together.*]
70 CASSIUS Messala.
MESSALA What says my general?
CASSIUS Messala,
This is my birthday, as° this very day   on
Was Cassius born. Give me thy hand, Messala.
75 Be thou my witness that against my will,
As Pompey was, am I compelled to set
Upon one battle all our liberties.
You know that I held Epicurus strong
And his opinion.[9] Now I change my mind
80 And partly credit things that do presage.
Coming from Sardis, on our former ensign°   foremost banner
Two mighty eagles fell,° and there they perched,   alighted
Gorging and feeding from our soldiers' hands,
Who to Philippi here consorted° us.   accompanied
85 This morning are they fled away and gone,
And in their steads do ravens, crows, and kites[1]
Fly o'er our heads and downward look on us
As° we were sickly prey. Their shadows seem   As if
A canopy most fatal,° under which   ominous
90 Our army lies, ready to give up the ghost.
MESSALA Believe not so.
CASSIUS   I but believe it partly,
For I am fresh of spirit and resolved
To meet all perils very constantly.°   resolutely
BRUTUS Even so, Lucilius.
        [*He rejoins* CASSIUS.]
95 CASSIUS Now, most noble Brutus,
The gods° today stand friendly that we may,   May the gods
Lovers° in peace, lead on our days to age.   Close friends
But since the affairs of men rests still° incertain,   always remain
Let's reason with° the worst that may befall.   consider
100 If we do lose this battle, then is this
The very last time we shall speak together.
What are you then determinèd to do?

---

8. That is, Antony, who was noted for his love of extravagant entertainments and banquets.
9. Epicurus, a Greek philosopher, thought the gods indifferent to human affairs and therefore disbelieved omens.
1. These are all scavenger birds, considered bad omens.

BRUTUS   Even by the rule of that philosophy[2]
    By which I did blame Cato[3] for the death
105   Which he did give himself—I know not how,
    But I do find it cowardly and vile,
    For fear of what might fall,° so to prevent°   *happen / anticipate*
    The time° of life—arming myself with patience   *natural limit*
    To stay° the providence of some high powers   *await*
110   That govern us below.
CASSIUS   Then, if we lose this battle,
    You are contented to be led in triumph[4]
    Thorough° the streets of Rome?   *Through*
BRUTUS   No, Cassius, no. Think not, thou noble Roman,
115   That ever Brutus will go bound to Rome;
    He bears too great a mind. But this same day
    Must end that work the Ides of March begun,
    And whether we shall meet again, I know not.
    Therefore our everlasting farewell take:
120   Forever and forever farewell, Cassius.
    If we do meet again, why, we shall smile;
    If not, why then this parting was well made.
CASSIUS   Forever and forever farewell, Brutus.
    If we do meet again, we'll smile indeed;
125   If not, 'tis true this parting was well made.
BRUTUS   Why, then, lead on. Oh, that a man might know
    The end of this day's business ere it come.
    But it sufficeth that the day will end,
    And then the end is known. —Come, ho, away.   *Exeunt.*

5.2

    Alarum.° Enter BRUTUS *and* MESSALA.   *Offstage call to battle*
BRUTUS   Ride, ride, Messala, ride, and give these bills°   *written orders*
    Unto the legions on the other side.°   *(Cassius's wing)*
    Loud alarum.
    Let them set on° at once; for I perceive   *advance*
    But cold demeanor° in Octavio's wing,   *lack of fighting spirit*
5   And sudden push gives them the overthrow.
    Ride, ride, Messala! Let them all come down.   *Exeunt.*

5.3

    Alarums. Enter CASSIUS *[carrying a standard°] and*   *a banner*
    TITINIUS.
CASSIUS   Oh, look, Titinius, look, the villains° fly!   *(Cassius's own men)*
    —Myself have to mine own turned enemy.
    This ensign° here of mine was turning back;   *standard-bearer*
    I slew the coward and did take it° from him.   *(the standard)*
5 TITINIUS   O Cassius, Brutus gave the word too early,
    Who having some advantage on Octavius,
    Took it too eagerly. His soldiers fell to spoil,°   *looting*
    Whilst we by Antony are all enclosed.
    Enter PINDARUS.
PINDARUS   Fly further off, my lord, fly further off!

---

2. Brutus admired Plato, who rejected suicide.
3. See note to 2.1.295.

4. As a captive in a triumphal procession; see note to
1.1.30.

10 Mark Antony is in your tents, my lord.
Fly therefore, noble Cassius, fly far off.
CASSIUS   This hill is far enough. —Look, look, Titinius,
Are those my tents where I perceive the fire?
TITINIUS   They are, my lord.
CASSIUS   Titinius, if thou lovest me,
15 Mount thou my horse and hide thy spurs in him
Till he have brought thee up to yonder troops
And here again, that I may rest assured
Whether yond troops are friend or enemy.
TITINIUS   I will be here again even with° a thought.   *Exit.*   *as fast as*
20 CASSIUS   Go, Pindarus, get higher on that hill.
My sight was ever thick.° Regard Titinius,   *dim*
And tell me what thou not'st about the field.
—This day I breathèd first. Time is come round,
And where I did begin, there shall I end.
25 My life is run his compass.° —Sirrah, what news?   *its circuit*
PINDARUS (*above*°)   O my lord!   *(on the stage balcony)*
CASSIUS   What news?
PINDARUS   Titinius is enclosèd round about
With horsemen that make to him on the spur,[1]
30 Yet he spurs on. Now they are almost on him.
Now, Titinius! Now some light.° Oh, he lights too.   *alight*
He's ta'en.° (*Shout.*) And hark, they shout for joy.   *taken*
CASSIUS   Come down, behold no more.
—O coward that I am, to live so long
35 To see my best friend ta'en before my face.
        Enter PINDARUS.
—Come hither, sirrah.
In Parthia° did I take thee prisoner,   *(modern Iran)*
And then I swore thee, saving of[2] thy life,
That whatsoever I did bid thee do,
40 Thou shouldst attempt it. Come now, keep thine oath.
Now be a freeman, and with this good sword
That ran through Caesar's bowels, search° this bosom.   *penetrate*
Stand° not to answer. Here, take thou the hilts,°   *Delay / sword handle*
And when my face is covered, as 'tis now,
45 Guide thou the sword. —Caesar, thou art revenged,
Even with the sword that killed thee.
        [*He dies.*]
PINDARUS   So, I am free, yet would not so have been
Durst° I have done my will. —O Cassius,   *Dared*
Far from this country Pindarus shall run,
50 Where never Roman shall take note of him.   [*Exit.*]
        Enter TITINIUS *and* MESSALA.
MESSALA   It is but change,° Titinius; for Octavius   *an even exchange*
Is overthrown by noble Brutus' power,
As Cassius' legions are by Antony.
TITINIUS   These tidings will well comfort Cassius.
MESSALA   Where did you leave him?
55 TITINIUS   All disconsolate,

5.3
1. Who approach him at a gallop.

2. I made you swear, when I spared.

With Pindarus his bondman on this hill.

MESSALA   Is not that he that lies upon the ground?

TITINIUS   He lies not like the living. O my heart!

MESSALA   Is not that he?

TITINIUS   No, this was he, Messala,

60   But Cassius is no more. O setting sun,
As in thy red rays thou dost sink to night,
So in his red blood Cassius' day is set.
The sun of Rome is set. Our day is gone.
Clouds, dews, and dangers come; our deeds are done.

65   Mistrust of my success³ hath done this deed.

MESSALA   Mistrust of good success hath done this deed.
O hateful Error, Melancholy's child,⁴
Why dost thou show to the apt° thoughts of men   impressionable
The things that are not? O Error, soon conceived,

70   Thou never com'st unto a happy birth
But kill'st the mother° that engendered thee.   (the melancholy person)

TITINIUS   What, Pindarus! Where art thou, Pindarus?

MESSALA   Seek him, Titinius, whilst I go to meet
The noble Brutus, thrusting this report

75   Into his ears. I may say "thrusting" it,
For piercing steel and darts° envenomèd   spears
Shall be as welcome to the ears of Brutus
As tidings of this sight.

TITINIUS   Hie you, Messala,
And I will seek for Pindarus the while.   [Exit MESSALA.]

80   Why didst thou send me forth, brave Cassius?
Did I not meet thy friends, and did not they
Put on my brows this wreath of victory
And bid me give it thee? Didst thou not hear their shouts?
Alas, thou hast misconstrued everything.

85   But hold thee, take this garland on thy brow.
Thy Brutus bid me give it thee, and I
Will do his bidding. —Brutus, come apace,°   quickly
And see how I regarded° Caius Cassius.   esteemed
—By your leave, gods. This is a Roman's part.

90   —Come, Cassius' sword, and find Titinius' heart.
         [He] dies.
         Alarum. Enter BRUTUS, MESSALA, young CATO,⁵
         STRATO, VOLUMNIUS, and LUCILIUS.

BRUTUS   Where, where, Messala, doth his body lie?

MESSALA   Lo, yonder, and Titinius mourning it.

BRUTUS   Titinius' face is upward.

CATO   He is slain.

BRUTUS   O Julius Caesar, thou art mighty yet;

95   Thy spirit walks abroad and turns our swords
In our own proper° entrails.   our very own
         Low° alarums.   Soft

CATO   Brave Titinius!
—Look whe'er° he have not crowned dead Cassius.   whether

BRUTUS   Are yet two Romans living such as these?

---

3. Doubt about the outcome of my mission.   5. The son of Marcus Portius Cato.
4. That is, bred from melancholy thoughts.

The last of all the Romans, fare thee well!
100 It is impossible that ever Rome
Should breed thy fellow. —Friends, I owe more tears
To this dead man than you shall see me pay.
—I shall find time, Cassius; I shall find time.
—Come therefore, and to Thasos° send his body.   *an island near Philippi*
105 His funerals shall not be in our camp,
Lest it discomfort° us. —Lucilius, come.   *dishearten*
—And come, young Cato, let us to the field.
Labio and Flavio set our battles° on.   *forces*
'Tis three o'clock, and, Romans, yet ere night
110 We shall try fortune in a second fight.   *Exeunt.*

5.4

Alarum. Enter BRUTUS, MESSALA, [*young*] CATO,
LUCILIUS, *and Flavius.*

BRUTUS Yet, countrymen, oh, yet hold up your heads.
            [*Exeunt* BRUTUS, MESSALA, *and Flavius.*]
CATO What bastard° doth not? Who will go with me?   *untrue Roman*
    I will proclaim my name about the field.
    I am the son of Marcus Cato, ho!
5   A foe to tyrants and my country's friend.
    I am the son of Marcus Cato, ho!
        Enter SOLDIERS, *and fight.*
LUCILIUS And I am Brutus, Marcus Brutus, I!
    Brutus, my country's friend! Know me for Brutus!
    O young and noble Cato, art thou down?
10 Why now thou diest as bravely as Titinius
    And mayst be honored, being Cato's son.
FIRST SOLDIER Yield, or thou diest.
LUCILIUS   Only I yield to die.[1]
    There is so much[2] that thou wilt kill me straight;°   *immediately*
    Kill Brutus and be honored in his death.
15 FIRST SOLDIER We must not. A noble prisoner.
SECOND SOLDIER Room, ho! Tell Antony, Brutus is ta'en.
FIRST SOLDIER I'll tell the news.
        Enter ANTONY.
                        Here comes the general.
    —Brutus is ta'en, Brutus is ta'en, my lord.
ANTONY Where is he?
20 LUCILIUS Safe, Antony, Brutus is safe enough.
    I dare assure thee that no enemy
    Shall ever take alive the noble Brutus.
    The gods defend him from so great a shame!
    When you do find him, or° alive or dead,   *either*
25 He will be found like Brutus, like himself.°   *true to his noble nature*
ANTONY [*to* FIRST SOLDIER] This is not Brutus, friend,
        but I assure you,
    A prize no less in worth. Keep this man safe;
    Give him all kindness. I had rather have
    Such men my friends than enemies. —Go on,
30 And see whe'er Brutus be alive or dead;

5.4
1. I yield only so that I may die.

2. There is enough inducement.

And bring us word unto Octavius' tent
How everything is chanced.°   *has happened*

Exeunt [in different directions].

5.5

Enter BRUTUS, DARDANIUS, CLITUS, STRATO, *and*
VOLUMNIUS.

BRUTUS   Come, poor remains of friends, rest on this rock.
CLITUS   Statilius[1] showed the torchlight, but, my lord,
He came not back: he is or ta'en° or slain.   *either captured*
BRUTUS   Sit thee down, Clitus. Slaying is the word;
5   It is a deed in fashion. Hark thee, Clitus.
        [He whispers.]
CLITUS   What, I, my lord? No, not for all the world.
BRUTUS   Peace then, no words.
CLITUS   I'll rather kill myself.
BRUTUS   Hark thee, Dardanius.
        [He whispers.]
DARDANIUS   Shall I do such a deed?
CLITUS   O Dardanius!
10   DARDANIUS   O Clitus!
CLITUS   What ill request did Brutus make to thee?
DARDANIUS   To kill him, Clitus. Look, he meditates.
CLITUS   Now is that noble vessel full of grief,
    That it runs over even at his eyes.
15   BRUTUS   Come hither, good Volumnius. List° a word.   *Listen to*
VOLUMNIUS   What says my lord?
BRUTUS   Why this, Volumnius:
    The ghost of Caesar hath appeared to me
    Two several° times by night—at Sardis once,   *different*
    And this last night here in Philippi fields.
    I know my hour is come.
20   VOLUMNIUS   Not so, my lord.
BRUTUS   Nay, I am sure it is, Volumnius.
    Thou seest the world, Volumnius, how it goes:
    Our enemies have beat° us to the pit.[2]   *driven*
      Low alarums.
    It is more worthy to leap in ourselves
25   Than tarry till they push us. Good Volumnius,
    Thou know'st that we two went to school together;
    Even for that our love of old, I prithee,
    Hold thou my sword hilts whilst I run on it.
VOLUMNIUS   That's not an office for a friend, my lord.
      Alarum still.
30   CLITUS   Fly, fly, my lord! There is no tarrying here.
BRUTUS   Farewell to you, —and you, —and you, Volumnius.
    —Strato, thou hast been all this while asleep.
    Farewell to thee too, Strato. —Countrymen,
    My heart doth joy that yet in all my life
35   I found no man but he was true to me.
    I shall have glory by this losing day
    More than Octavius and Mark Antony

5.5
1. A soldier sent ahead with instructions to signal by   torchlight if all is well.
    2. Animal trap; grave.

By this vile conquest shall attain unto.
So fare you well at once, for Brutus' tongue
40   Hath almost ended his life's history.
Night hangs upon mine eyes; my bones would rest,
That have but labored³ to attain this hour.
         Alarum. Cry within, "Fly, fly, fly!"
CLITUS   Fly, my lord, fly!
BRUTUS   Hence, I will follow.
         [*Exeunt* CLITUS, DARDANIUS, *and* VOLUMNIUS.]
I prithee, Strato, stay thou by thy lord.
45   Thou art a fellow of a good respect;°   reputation
Thy life hath had some smatch° of honor in it.   relish
Hold, then, my sword and turn away thy face
While I do run upon it. Wilt thou, Strato?
STRATO   Give me your hand first. Fare you well, my lord.
50   BRUTUS   Farewell, good Strato.
         [*He runs on his sword.*]
                     —Caesar, now be still.
I killed not thee with half so good a will.
         [*He*] *dies.*
         *Alarum. Retreat.*⁴ Enter ANTONY, OCTAVIUS, MESSALA,
         LUCILIUS, *and the army.*
OCTAVIUS   What man is that?
MESSALA   My master's man. —Strato, where is thy master?
STRATO   Free from the bondage you are in, Messala.
55   The conquerors can but make a fire of him,°   burn his body
For Brutus only overcame himself,⁵
And no man else hath honor by his death.
LUCILIUS   So Brutus should be found. —I thank thee, Brutus,
That thou hast proved Lucilius' saying true.
60   OCTAVIUS   All that served Brutus, I will entertain them.°   take them into service
—Fellow, wilt thou bestow° thy time with me?   spend
STRATO   Ay, if Messala will prefer° me to you.   recommend
OCTAVIUS   Do so, good Messala.
MESSALA   How died my master, Strato?
65   STRATO   I held the sword, and he did run on it.
MESSALA   Octavius, then take him to follow° thee,   serve
That did the latest° service to my master.   last
ANTONY   This was the noblest Roman of them all.
All the conspirators save only he
70   Did that° they did in envy of great Caesar;   what
He only in a general honest thought⁶
And common good to all⁷ made one of them.
His life was gentle,° and the elements⁸   noble
So mixed in him that Nature might stand up
75   And say to all the world, "This was a man."
OCTAVIUS   According to° his virtue, let us use him   In accordance with
With all respect and rites of burial.
Within my tent his bones tonight shall lie,
Most like a soldier, ordered° honorably.   treated
80   So call the field to rest, and let's away
To part° the glories of this happy day.   *Exeunt all.*   share

---

3. Labored for no other purpose than.
4. Trumpet signal to cease pursuit.
5. For only Brutus conquered Brutus.
6. With a virtuous, principled conviction.

7. And desire for the common good.
8. The four bodily humors, different combinations of which supposedly affected temperament; in the ideal individual, no single humor predominated.

Hamlet

"Who's there?" Shakespeare's most famous play begins. The question, turned back on the tragedy itself, has haunted actors, audiences, and readers for centuries. *Hamlet* is an enigma. Mountains of feverish speculation have only deepened the interlocking mysteries: Why does Hamlet delay avenging the murder of his father by Claudius, his father's brother? How much guilt does Hamlet's mother, Gertrude, who has since married Claudius, bear in this crime? How trustworthy is the Ghost of Hamlet's father, who has returned from the grave to demand that Hamlet avenge his murder? Is vengeance morally justifiable in this play, or is it to be condemned? What exactly *is* the Ghost, and where has it come from? Why is the Ghost, visible to everyone in the first act, visible only to Hamlet in act 3? Is Hamlet's madness feigned or true, a strategy masquerading as a reality or a reality masquerading as a strategy? Does Hamlet, who once loved Ophelia, continue to love her in spite of his apparent cruelty? Does Ophelia, crushed by that cruelty and driven mad by Hamlet's murder of her father, Polonius, actually intend to drown herself, or does she die accidentally? What enables Hamlet to pass from thoughts of suicide to faith in God's providence, from "To be or not to be" to "Let be"? What is Hamlet trying to say before death stops his speech at the close?

It is tempting to think that when *Hamlet* was first performed at the Globe around 1600, the audiences possessed answers to many of these questions and that our perplexities result principally from the passage of time. Yet the play seems designed to provoke bafflement. "What art thou?" Horatio asks the Ghost, and the question, unanswered, is echoed again and again until it seems to touch on everything: "Is it not like the King?" (1.1.57);* "Why seems it so particular with thee?" (1.2.75); "What does this mean, my lord?" (1.4.7); "Whither wilt thou lead me?" (1.5.1); "What's Hecuba to him or he to her / That he should weep for her?" (2.2.478–79); "Why wouldst thou be a breeder of sinners?" (3.1.119–20); "What should such fellows as I do crawling between earth and heaven?" (3.1.125–26); "Do you see nothing there?" (3.4.131); "What is it you would see?" (5.2.340). The dream of getting answers to such questions tantalizes many of the play's characters and drives them to scrutinize one another. But the task is maddeningly difficult. When Hamlet repeatedly asks Guildenstern, one of the school friends whom his uncle has set to spy on him, to play the recorder, Guildenstern protests that he does not know how. "[Y]ou would play upon me," Hamlet returns, "you would seem to know my stops, you would pluck out the heart of my mystery. . . . [D]o you think I am easier to be played on than a pipe?" (3.2.339–44).

Hamlet at once invites and resists interrogation. He is, more than any theatrical character before and perhaps since, a figure constructed around an unseen or secret core. Such a figure in the theater is something of a paradox, since all that exists of any character onstage is what is seen and heard there. But from his place onstage at the center of a courtly world in which he is "the observed of all observers" and hence a person allowed virtually no privacy, Hamlet insists that he has "that within which passes show" (1.2.85). What is it that he has "within"? In the nineteenth century, following a suggestion by the German poet Johann Wolfgang von Goethe, critics frequently argued that Hamlet has within him the soul of a poet, too sensitive, delicate,

---

*All quotations are taken from the edited text of the Second Quarto with additions from the Folio (the "combined text"). The print edition also includes the edited First Quarto text. The Digital Edition includes both these texts plus the edited Second Quarto and Folio texts.

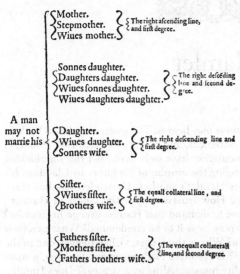

A man may not marrie his		
Mother. Stepmother. Wiues mother.	The right afcending line, and firft degree.	
Sonnes daughter. Daughters daughter. Wiues fonnes daughter. Wiues daughters daughter.	The right defcēding line and fecond degree.	
Daughter. Wiues daughter. Sonnes wife.	The right defcending line and firft degree.	
Sifter. Wiues fifter. Brothers wife.	The eqnall collaterall line, and firft degree.	
Fathers fifter. Mothers fifter. Fathers brothers wife.	The vnequall collaterall line, and fecond degree.	

30 Therfore fhall ye keepe mine ordinances, that ye doe not any of the abhominable cuftomes, which haue been done before you.

Table of prohibited marriages. From William Clerke, *The Trial of Bastardy* (London, 1594).

and complex to endure the cruel pressures of a coarse world. In the twentieth century, following a suggestion by the founder of psychoanalysis, Sigmund Freud, many critics have speculated that Hamlet has within him an unresolved Oedipus complex, a sexual desire for his mother that prevents him from taking decisive action against the man who has done in reality the thing that Hamlet unconsciously desires to do: kill his father and marry his mother. On occasion, this psychological speculation has been challenged by a political one: Hamlet hides within himself a spirit of political resistance, a subversive challenge to a corrupt, illegitimate regime shored up by lies, spies, and treachery.

These recurrent attempts to pluck out the heart of Hamlet's mystery are a modern continuation of an interpretive activity that goes on throughout the play itself. Attempting to solve the riddle of Hamlet's strange behavior, Polonius speculates that the Prince is desperately lovesick for his daughter, but Claudius concludes, after spying on Hamlet's conversation with Ophelia, that his "affections do not that way tend" (3.1.159). Rosencrantz and Guildenstern propose that Hamlet is suffering from ambition—after all, though Denmark is an elective monarchy, the Prince could have hoped to succeed his father on the throne—but Hamlet vehemently refutes the charge: "O God, I could be bounded in a nutshell and count myself a king of infinite space, were it not that I have bad dreams" (2.2.231.15–17). Claudius doubts that Hamlet is mad and, though he never directly articulates this suspicion, seems to fear that the Prince somehow knows of his secret crime, but Hamlet's painful interiority, his melancholy insistence that he has something "within," is already clear from his first appearance, before the Ghost's revelation. Gertrude therefore seems wiser to argue that her son's distemper at least originates in "[h]is father's death and our hasty marriage" (2.2.57).

As we first encounter him, Hamlet is a young man in deep mourning, which his mother and uncle both urge him to cease. The death of fathers is natural and inevitable, they point out, and while it is customary to grieve, it is unreasonable to persist obstinately in sorrow. Hamlet responds that his grief is not a theatrical performance, a mere costume to be put on and then discarded. When he is alone onstage a few moments later, he discloses, in the first of his famous soliloquies, a near-suicidal despair and a corrosive bitterness centered on the haste with which his mother has remarried. This bitterness is intensified by Hamlet's idealized image of his father and by painful memories of what had seemed to him his parents' perfect mutual love. Like any adolescent whose family has undergone unexpected and traumatic changes, Hamlet finds himself caught up in the painful process of reassessing his image of his parents and of himself, a process that spills over into his relationship with a new, unwelcome stepparent and with his peers. As he broods on the brief time between his father's death and his mother's remarriage, Hamlet's mind convulsively shortens the interval: "two months," "nay, not so much, not two," "within a month."

At such moments—and there are many in this play—the audience seems to have direct access to the protagonist's tormented inner life. That life appears startlingly raw and unscripted, but the impression is actually the consequence of Shakespeare's sophisticated poetic skills. Hamlet's soliloquies are carefully crafted rhetorical performances. Thus, for example, the celebrated lines that begin "To be or not to be: that is the question" (3.1.55ff) have the structure of a formal academic debate on the subject of suicide: prudently considering both sides of the question and rehearsing venerable commonplaces, Hamlet does not once use the words "I" or "me." Yet here and elsewhere his words manage with astonishing vividness to convey the spontaneous rhythms of a mind in motion. Shakespeare had anticipated this achievement in such plays as *Richard II, 1 Henry IV,* and *Julius Caesar*: King Richard, Prince Hal, and Brutus all have intimate moments in which they seem to disclose the troubled faces that are normally hidden behind expressionless social masks. But in its moral complexity, psychological depth, and philosophical power, *Hamlet* seems to mark an epochal shift not only in Shakespeare's own career but in Western drama; it is as if the play were giving birth to a whole new kind of literary subjectivity.

This subjectivity—the sense of being inside a character's psyche and following its twists and turns—is to a large degree an effect of language, the product of dramatic poetry and prose of unprecedented intensity. In order to convey a traumatized mind struggling to articulate perceptions of a shattered world, Shakespeare developed a complex syntax and a remarkably expanded diction. Take the moment, for example, in which Hamlet broods on the spectacle of Fortinbras's army marching off to fight to the death for a worthless piece of ground. Hamlet is struck by the absurd waste of lives and wealth, but then his agonized consciousness of his failure to act more quickly to avenge his father's death begins to transform his thinking:

> Rightly to be great
> Is not to stir without great argument
> But greatly to find quarrel in a straw
> When honor's at the stake.
> (4.1.52–55)

The strain in the syntax reflects the strain of a mind queasily in motion. For the sentence to be made fully coherent, we would need to add a missing "not" or otherwise change the wording, but the point is not coherence. Such strange twists in meaning, along with a host of words used in new or unfamiliar ways, give us intimate access to the vortex of moral principle and psychological compulsion that constitutes Hamlet's inner life. The innovative inwardness is not restricted to scenes in which Hamlet is alone onstage, nor is it restricted to the Prince himself; indeed, many of the deepest psychic revelations in the play are conveyed not in moments of isolation but in disturbing exchanges, intimate encounters in which love and poison are intertwined.

These innovations are not called for by the story itself. In *Hamlet,* as in so many of his plays, Shakespeare was recycling narratives long in circulation. The legendary tale of Hamlet (Amleth) had already been recounted at length in the late twelfth-century *Danish History* compiled in Latin by Saxo the Grammarian. (The tale was retold in French in François de Belleforest's 1570 collection *Histoires Tragiques.*) In Saxo's version the unscrupulous Feng ambushes and kills his brother Horwendil and marries Horwendil's wife, Gerutha. Horwendil and Gerutha had a son, Amleth, who undertakes to avenge his father. In doing so, the son suffers no pangs of conscience, since in pre-Christian Denmark revenge was not a violation of the moral or religious law but a filial obligation. And he needs no ghost to inform him of what happened and experiences no sickening uncertainty about his uncle's guilt, since the murder is public knowledge. Amleth's problem is survival: young and surrounded by Feng's henchmen, he finds his every move carefully watched. In order to avert suspicion and buy time, the cunning avenger pretends to be feebleminded. His strategy works: with the active assistance of his mother, Amleth eventually succeeds in killing his uncle, along with the uncle's followers, and is enthusiastically proclaimed King of Denmark. Amleth suffers no doubt about his uncle's guilt and no pangs of conscience over killing him.

This is the rough outline of the story Shakespeare inherited, along, it seems, with at least one other version about which we know tantalizingly little: by 1589, English audiences had evidently seen a play, now lost, on the theme of Hamlet. Apparently, this play—which scholars call the Ur (original)-*Hamlet*—featured a ghost who cried, "Hamlet, revenge!" On the basis of the barest shreds of contemporary evidence, scholars have constructed elaborate theories about this supposed source play, but there is little agreement among them. Assuming that there was an Elizabethan staging of the story that preceded Shakespeare's, its author remains unknown.

Shakespeare probably wrote *Hamlet* in 1600 (shortly after *Julius Caesar*, to which Polonius seems to allude at 3.2.94–95), but the precise date of composition is uncertain, and this uncertainty is compounded by the complex state of the text: Shakespeare's most famous tragedy is a monument of world literature, but it is a monument built on shifting sands. The two fullest early texts of the play are found in a quarto dated 1604–05 (the Second Quarto, Q2) and in the First Folio of 1623 (F). However, these texts differ in important ways, each including passages not found in the other. The edition of the play printed in *The Norton Shakespeare* is based on the Second Quarto text; lines that appear only in the Folio are also included but are made visually distinct, so that readers will be able to assess the major variations between the two. Those who want to read these early texts in their original forms can find fully edited versions of both the Second Quarto and the Folio texts in the Digital Edition of *The Norton Shakespeare*, which also offers side-by-side comparisons of selected scenes.

To further complicate the textual situation, there is yet a third version of *Hamlet*. This earliest known text appeared in 1603 and is therefore called the First Quarto (Q1). Much shorter and less reliable than either the Second Quarto or the Folio texts, it was long known as the "bad quarto" of *Hamlet*. (The Prince's celebrated soliloquy, for example, begins "To be, or not to be—ay, there's the point.") The First Quarto is nevertheless a fascinating document, theatrically effective in its own right, with valuable clues about what a severely cut and reshaped *Hamlet* might have looked like on the Elizabethan stage. For these reasons, a fully edited version of this earliest text is presented in *The Norton Shakespeare*—both print and digital—for the first time.

These early published texts, along with numerous early references to the play, suggest that *Hamlet* was a success from the beginning. The play may well have seemed radically innovative to its first audiences—after four hundred years it still seems startlingly fresh—but it also spoke to contemporary theatrical interests. One of the most successful and enduring Elizabethan plays was *The Spanish Tragedy* (ca. 1587), written by Thomas Kyd, who is a prime candidate for authorship of the lost Ur-*Hamlet*. *The Spanish Tragedy* itself has features that strikingly anticipate Shakespeare's tragedy, including a ghost impatient for revenge, a secret crime, a hero tormented by uncertainty and self-reproach, the strategic feigning of a madness that seems disturbingly close to real, a woman who goes mad from grief and commits suicide, a play-within-the-play, and a final slaughter that wipes out much of the royal family and court, along with the avenger himself. Kyd's play is entirely structured around the problem of revenge—"wild justice," in Francis Bacon's haunting phrase—and gave rise to a whole genre of revenge plays in which *Hamlet* participates.

These plays generally share certain conventional assumptions. First, revenge is an individual response to an intolerable wrong or a public insult. It is an unauthorized, violent action in a world whose institutions seem unable or unwilling to satisfy a craving for justice. Second, since institutional channels are closed and since the criminal is usually either hidden or well protected, revenge almost always follows a devious path toward its violent end. Third, the revenger is in the grip of an inner compulsion: his course of action may be motivated by institutional failure—for example, the mechanisms of justice are in the hands of the criminals themselves—but even if these mechanisms were operating perfectly, they would not allow the psychic satisfactions of revenge. Fourth, revengers generally need their victims to know what is happening and why: satisfaction depends on a moment of declaration and vindication. And fifth, revenge is a universal imperative more powerful than the pious injunctions of any particular belief system, including Christianity itself.

Shakespeare had already produced a sensationally violent version of these conventions in *Titus Andronicus*. In *Hamlet,* he at once reproduces them and calls them into question. The audience knows for certain—from Claudius's tortured attempt to pray in act 3—that there has been a "foul murder," a fratricide successfully covered over by the story that a serpent stung the sleeping King. But Hamlet does not overhear Claudius's confession and has only the questionable testimony of the Ghost. That testimony is open to question because the nature of the Ghost is open to question. The Ghost speaks as if he were condemned to a term of suffering in the realm Catholics called purgatory:

> Doomed for a certain term to walk the night
> And for the day confined to fast in fires
> Till the foul crimes done in my days of nature
> Are burnt and purged away.
>
> (1.5.10–13)

But Protestant theologians vehemently denied that purgatory existed and argued that spirits thought to be ghosts were in fact devils sent to lure humans into sinful actions. Hamlet responds at first as if he believes the Ghost to be the authentic spirit of his father returned from the dead. But he subsequently expresses serious doubts— "The spirit that I have seen / May be a dev'l" (2.2.517–18)—and in the play's most famous soliloquy he speaks of death as "[t]he undiscovered country from whose bourn / No traveler returns" (3.1.78–79).

The theatrical test Hamlet devises to authenticate the Ghost's accusation— carefully watching the reaction of his uncle to *The Mousetrap*—appears to resolve any doubts: "I'll take the Ghost's word," Hamlet exults, after the King has stormed out in a rage, "for a thousand pound" (3.2.265–66). Yet even here Shakespeare introduces an occasion for uncertainty: after all, the murderer in the play-within-the play is "one Lucianus, nephew to the King" (3.2.226). Claudius's anger could have arisen from the spectacle of the player-nephew killing his player-uncle and not from the spectacle of his own hidden crime. The effect on the audience is not so much to cast doubt on the Ghost's word as to uncouple Hamlet's inner life once again from the external world, even at the moment that he himself thinks they are at last securely linked.

This uncoupling, this sense of inward thoughts and feelings painfully cut off from the world around him, haunts virtually all of Hamlet's relationships. When he speaks with his old school friends Rosencrantz and Guildenstern, with the courtier Osric or with Polonius, he is deliberately evasive, but his exchanges with Ophelia are equally oblique and baffling. Even with his intimate friend Horatio, there is some gap across which Hamlet struggles to speak: "There are more things in heaven and earth, Horatio," Hamlet says after his first encounter with the Ghost, "[t]han are dreamt of in your philosophy" (1.5.168–69). When Hamlet directly confronts his mother with the charge of murder, she reacts with astonishment. The painful words that follow, Hamlet's weird, tormented admonition to his mother to shun her husband's bed, do indeed seem to strike home: "These words like daggers," Gertrude exclaims, "enter in mine ears" (3.4.95). But the Ghost's sudden reappearance, visible this time only to Hamlet (and, of course, to the audience), convinces his mother that her son is mad. "Do you see nothing there?" asks Hamlet, to which his mother, certain that her son is hallucinating, replies steadfastly, "Nothing at all, yet all that is I see" (3.4.131–32).

Ironically, the distance between what Hamlet sees and what those around him see is smallest in the case of Claudius, since both share a knowledge of the secret crime that has poisoned the kingdom, and each maneuvers against the other throughout the play. But their fatal opposition never rises to full, open view until the final

The man in prayer. By Mair von Landshut (1499).

violent seconds, nor does Hamlet ever establish unequivocal, unambiguous public confirmation of his uncle's guilt. It would have been easy for Shakespeare to provide such confirmation, for example in a last speech by the mortally wounded usurper, but he chooses instead to leave what Horatio calls "th' yet unknowing world" (5.2.357) in the dark. Until the explosion of treason and murder, the horrified bystanders know only a court in which the loving Claudius appeals to Hamlet as his "son" and wagers on his skill in fencing. Hamlet begins an explanation—"oh, I could tell you" (5.2.315)—but he is cut short by death. The effect is to extend Hamlet's tragic isolation, his gnawing inward pain, all the way to his final silence.

What would it take to get rid of this pain? The possibility of cleansing, definitive action at once continually tantalizes and eludes the Prince. Such action is embodied in the soldier Fortinbras, but if Hamlet finds some way of easing his mental anguish, it is not through any comparable martial exploit, nor is it through the secret plotting undertaken by Laertes. The fact that both Fortinbras and Laertes are also attempting to avenge the deaths of fathers only intensifies the contrast with Hamlet's spiritual journey. The calm to which he gives voice near the play's close—"There is special providence in the fall of a sparrow. If it be, 'tis not to come; if it be not to come, it will be now; if it be not now, yet it will come; the readiness is all" (5.2.191–94)—descends upon him *before,* not as a result of, his revenge. The act of revenge itself happens in a flash of rage, without planning, without any self-vindicating declaration by Hamlet to Claudius, and without any public confession of guilt by the usurper. Revenge leaves the Prince not with inner satisfaction but with intense anxiety over his "wounded name."

Swordsmen. From *Vincentio Saviolo his Practise* (London, 1595).

Standing on a stage littered with corpses, Horatio promises to fulfill Hamlet's dying request to tell his story, but his account of "carnal, bloody, and unnatural acts," though it may be accurate, must be inadequate to the play we have just witnessed. For *Hamlet* situates the need for revenge in a context that goes beyond any crime, however heinous, and that seems resistant to violent solutions. Before the Ghost disclosed his uncle's villainy, Hamlet was suffering from the traumas of mortality: the searing pain of his father's death, a troubled recognition of his mother's sexuality, a sickening awareness of the vulnerability and corruptibility of the flesh. There was a time, the play implies, when Hamlet embodied all the hopes and aspirations of his age and his own vision of human possibility was unbounded—"What piece of work is a man"—but that vision has given way to bitter disillusionment: "and yet to me what is this quintessence of dust?" (2.2.264–65, 268–69).

Renaissance psychologists had a word for Hamlet's condition: melancholy, a state of spiritual desolation akin to madness but also to literary and artistic genius. In Hamlet's melancholy consciousness, human existence has been reduced to dust at its dustiest. Though Claudius's secret crime is a political act that has poisoned the public sphere, the roots of Hamlet's despair seem to lie in a more intractably inward place, a place perhaps less consonant with revenge than with suicide. If there were only the evil usurper to depose, Hamlet might compass a straightforward course of action, but his soul-sickness has receding layers: beyond political corruption, there is the time-serving shallowness of his friends Rosencrantz and Guildenstern, and beyond this there is Ophelia's dismayingly compliant obedience to her father, and beyond this there is his mother's disturbing carnality, and beyond this there is the ongoing, endlessly transformative, morally indifferent cycle of life itself. For Hamlet, the quintessence of dust is not only the cold, inert matter produced by the nauseating triumph of death—the flesh of Alexander the Great metamorphosed into a plug of dirt stopping up a beer barrel—but also living matter pullulating with tenacious, meaningless vitality, produced by the equally nauseating triumph of life. "We fat all creatures else to fat us," Hamlet tells Claudius, "and we fat ourselves for maggots" (3.6.21–22).

In a world pervaded by decay, the process of natural renewal has come to seem grotesque and disgusting:

> 'tis an unweeded garden
> That grows to seed; things rank and gross in nature
> Possess it merely.
>
> (1.2.135–37)

These lines immediately give way to bitter reflections on his mother's sexual appetite: in Hamlet's diseased consciousness, the spectacle of nature run riot, of uncontrolled breeding and feeding, centers on the body of woman. His bitterness at his mother's remarriage spreads like a stain to touch all women, including the woman he had once ardently courted. "Get thee to a nunnery!" Hamlet urges Ophelia, as if the only virtuous course of action were renunciation of the flesh. "Why wouldst thou be a breeder of sinners?" (3.1.119–20). Even this desperate advice seems to be undermined by Hamlet's obsessive sense of rampant female sexuality and of his own corruption, since in Elizabethan slang "nunnery" could also be a term for "brothel."

Even before her father's murder causes her complete mental collapse, the fragile Ophelia begins to crack under the strain of Hamlet's misogynistic revulsion. Set up as a decoy to enable her father and the King to spy on Hamlet, she is treated humiliatingly by the Prince who had once passionately wooed her and now showers her with a blend of disgust and self-loathing. Gertrude, who also takes the full brunt of this misogyny, does not lose her wits, but when confronted alone by her son, she fears for her life. Both women sense the violence and despair seething in Hamlet beneath what he calls his "antic disposition" (1.5.173). That disposition, manifested in his disordered dress and in the "wild and whirling words" (1.5.135) that he begins to speak after encountering the Ghost, casts Hamlet in the strange role of jester in the court in which he is the mourning son and the heir apparent. Of all Shakespeare's tragic heroes, he is at once the saddest and the funniest. His blend of sarcasm, riddling, and sly wordplay initially strikes those around him as folly, but this first impression continually gives way to an uneasy awareness of hidden meanings: Claudius, alert to danger, notes that "[t]here's something in his soul / O'er which his melancholy sits on brood" (3.1.161–62). The "something" Claudius senses is in part the murderous design of the revenger, but it is also the philosophical meditation on life and death that haunts Hamlet throughout the play. This meditation reaches a climax in the graveyard, where Hamlet, trading zany quibbles with one of the gravediggers, directly confronts the corruption and decay that had obsessed him ever since his father's death. If there is any release for Hamlet from this obsession—and it is not clear that there is—it comes from an unflinching gaze at a skull, the skull of the jester Yorick, but also, by extension, his father's skull and his own.

STEPHEN GREENBLATT

SELECTED BIBLIOGRAPHY

Adelman, Janet. "Man and His Wife Is One Flesh: *Hamlet* and the Confrontation with the Maternal Body." *Suffocating Mothers: Fantasies of Maternal Origin in Shakespeare's Plays, "Hamlet" to "The Tempest."* New York: Routledge, 1992. 11–37. Argues that for Shakespeare, fully realized female sexuality (in the form of Gertrude) gives birth not only to fallen and contaminated man, but also to tragedy itself.

Bradley, A. C. *Shakespearean Tragedy: Lectures on "Hamlet," "Othello," "King Lear," "Macbeth."* 1904. 3rd ed. Basingstoke: Macmillan, 1992. Discusses how Hamlet's character—at the center of the tragedy that bears his name—is dominated by a morbid melancholy that weakens his ability to love and impedes his ability to act.

Cavell, Stanley. "Hamlet's Burden of Proof." *Disowning Knowledge in Seven Plays of Shakespeare.* Cambridge: Cambridge UP, 2003. 179–91. Explores how the play-within-the-play, interpreted with Freud's concept of the "primal scene," can be seen as a dreamlike expression of Hamlet's refusal to confront the burden of his own existence.

de Grazia, Margreta. *"Hamlet" without Hamlet.* Cambridge: Cambridge UP, 2007. Argues that the elusiveness of Hamlet's inner life is a largely modern critical invention, obscuring the dispossession that Renaissance audiences would have seen as the tragedy's central crisis.

Eliot, T. S. "Hamlet and His Problems." *The Sacred Wood: Essays on Poetry and Criticism.* London: Methuen, 1920. 87–94. Asserts that *Hamlet* proves deficient as a work of art: Hamlet's disproportionate confusion about his condition reflects Shakespeare's own confusion concerning the proper assembly of his diverse literary materials.

Garber, Marjorie. *"Hamlet:* Giving Up the Ghost." *Shakespeare's Ghost Writers: Literature as Uncanny Causality.* New York: Methuen, 1987. 124–76. Discusses how, simultaneously constituting and dissolving the self, the Ghost haunts the unstable relationship between action and memory, and argues that Shakespeare himself has a similarly haunting purchase on the modern imagination.

Greenblatt, Stephen. *Hamlet in Purgatory.* Princeton, NJ: Princeton UP, 2001. Examines how *Hamlet* exploits and transforms into theatrical ritual the fears and desires generated by the Catholic cult of purgatory, a cult banned by Tudor Protestantism.

Maguire, Laurie. "'Actions that a man might play': Mourning, Memory, Editing." *Performance Research* 7 (2002): 66–76. Argues that editors of Shakespeare searching for one "true" text of the play should take a hint from Hamlet himself: single viewpoints (whether ontological or editorial) ultimately bow to the daunting yet rich reality of multiplicity.

McGee, Arthur. *The Elizabethan Hamlet.* New Haven, CT: Yale UP, 1987. Sees Hamlet emerging as a sophisticated manifestation of Vice from the medieval morality-play tradition.

Showalter, Elaine. "Representing Ophelia: Women, Madness, and the Responsibilities of Feminist Criticism." *Shakespeare and the Question of Theory.* Ed. Patricia Parker and Geoffrey Hartman. New York: Methuen, 1985. 77–94. Surveys shifting cultural attitudes toward the representation of Ophelia and notes how they serve as a barometer of ideological conflict and contribute to the evolving discourse of feminist criticism.

Wilson, J. Dover. *What Happens in "Hamlet."* 3rd ed. Cambridge: Cambridge UP, 1951. Argues that in grappling with the play's dramatic difficulties, especially the problematic *Mousetrap* scene, we more nearly approach "the secret of Hamlet's character."

See also the creative uses of *Hamlet* in Johann Wolfgang von Goethe's *Wilhelm Meister's Apprenticeship* (1796), James Joyce's *Ulysses* (1922), Tom Stoppard's *Rosencrantz and Guildenstern Are Dead* (1967), Heiner Müller's *Hamletmachine* (1978), and John Updike's *Gertrude and Claudius* (2000).

FILMS

Hamlet. 1948. Dir. Laurence Olivier. UK. 155 min. Olivier's Hamlet is an oedipal prince, tormented by a desire to kill his father and sleep with his mother (played in the film by an actress only two years older than Olivier).

Gamlet. 1963. Dir. Grigori Kozintsev. USSR. 148 min. A powerful, black-and-white Cold War *Hamlet*, in Russian, set in a prisonlike Elsinore.

Hamlet. 1990. Dir. Franco Zeffirelli. UK. 135 min. Naturalistic medieval scenes, with Glenn Close's strong Gertrude in an oedipally charged relationship with Mel Gibson's Hamlet.

Hamlet. 1996. Dir. Kenneth Branagh. UK. 242 min. (cut version 150 min.). Opulent full-text epic rendered in the mirrored halls of a palatial nineteenth-century Austrian court.

Hamlet. 2000. Dir. Michael Almereyda. USA. 112 min. Inspired by director Akira Kurosawa, Almereyda updates the play to modern New York and draws on communications technologies such as video cameras and computers.

TEXTUAL INTRODUCTION

The textual situation of *Hamlet* is unusually intricate. The play survives in three distinct early versions: the First Quarto (Q1, 1603), the Second Quarto (Q2, 1604–05), and the Folio (F, 1623). The dates of publication are, however, misleading if we are trying to understand the provenance of the various texts; the different versions were not composed in the order in which they were printed. Most scholars now agree that the Q2 version predates that in F, which in turn preceded Q1. But we can't be sure. (Three other quartos, based closely on the second and hence without independent authority, were printed in 1611, ca. 1621, and 1637; Restoration quartos, emended and marked with cuts, also had no textual authority.)

There are many substantive differences between these early texts, and while there is general agreement among scholars about the outlines of the relations between them, there are many areas of disagreement, making it difficult to say anything definitive about the various tangles. Here is what most, though certainly not all, scholars believe: Somewhere around 1600–1601, Shakespeare wrote a play about Hamlet; a few years later, his manuscript, or a copy of it, served as the basis for Q2. In the period between the initial composing of the play and its printing in 1604–05, the text underwent a number of important transformations. It was streamlined somewhat, undergoing several cuts, probably with performance in mind, and at the same time many verbal substitutions and other minor revisions were made. It is likely, though by no means definite, that Shakespeare himself, perhaps in consultation with his theatrical colleagues, was responsible for most of these changes. A copy of this somewhat shorter and in many small ways different text may have served as the "playbook" used in performance, or at least a playbook was derived from it, perhaps having been further reduced. Much later, in 1623, this initial playbook manuscript, no doubt changed in various ways over the intervening years, became the basis for the text printed in F.

Meanwhile, back in 1601 or 1602, a radically cut and restructured version, based on the playhouse text that became F rather than on the authorial manuscript that became Q2, was put together, possibly for touring performance, by either Shakespeare's company or some smaller troupe of provincial players. In 1603 this much shorter text was made available by one or two of the players to the London publishers Nicholas Ling and John Trundle, and was printed as Q1. This text seems to have been reconstructed at least partially from memory by an actor working with a scribe; the man responsible appears to have doubled as Marcellus and Lucianus, and possibly played Voltemand as well, since those roles closely match the roles as they appear in Q2/F. A year later, Ling hired a different printer to produce a text (Q2) that he described on the title page as "enlarged to almost as much againe as it was, according to the true and perfect Coppie." This implies that Ling knew his initial offering (Q1) was defective and that he somehow had got hold of a much more complete and authoritative manuscript.

First Quarto

There are no act or scene divisions in Q1. Editors have usually divided the play into separate scenes, numbered consecutively, and this edition has adopted that policy.

The division is based on the usual Elizabethan practice of beginning a new scene after the stage is completely cleared and a new character or set of characters enters. The text is very short—not much more than half the length of Q2. The title page declares that it was acted by "his Highnesse seruants" (i.e., Shakespeare's company) in London, Oxford, Cambridge, "and else-where." How true this is we don't know, but many scholars believe that the text was at some point prepared for a London-based company, likely for a provincial tour, and later reconstructed for presentation to a publisher. A noteworthy feature of Q1 is that it frequently accords with F where the latter differs from Q2 (though, to complicate matters, it sometimes agrees with Q2 against F). This affinity between the two texts suggests that the Q1 manuscript was probably based on the manuscript that after further transcription became the basis for F, while Q2 derives from a different stem. F shows a closer relationship to the theater than does Q2, so perhaps some of the players, having acted in a version similar to F, used that as the basis for a shorter text they could take on tour.

However we explain its puzzling origins, we can appreciate that Q1 is a revenge drama, which, missing much of the speculation and philosophizing usually associated with *Hamlet*, has been shown to work remarkably well onstage. Though parts of it read like a garbled version of the play that we are used to (see, e.g., Q1 Textual Comment 4), other parts are coherent and effective (and some bits, notably in the first few scenes, are almost exactly the same as their counterparts in F). Whoever devised it knew something about theatrical value. For example, the complicated interweaving of themes and plots in 2.2 in Q2/F (the longest scene in the play) is simplified by separating the Ophelia plot from the business with the players. Thus the "To be or not to be" speech and the "nunnery scene" come earlier in Q1, before the arrival of the players; in this more "rational" scenario, Hamlet's enthusiastic decision to make the play the thing that will catch the conscience of the King *follows* rather than precedes the anomie of the "To be" soliloquy. (Because the order of events and interweaving of plots in Q1 differs so much from that in the other texts, *The Norton Shakespeare* does not give cross-references from scenes between Q1 and F or Q2.) A second example is the appearance of an entirely new scene (14) that firmly establishes the Queen's alliance with her son (clearing up an ambiguity in the longer versions and making her a more sympathetic character), and skillfully compresses information from several different scenes in the longer texts (see Q1 Textual Comments 6 and 8). Such adaptations allow the play to move more quickly and make it more immediately accessible to an audience.

Second Quarto and Folio

Except for some sections of act 1 where the compositor probably had recourse to a copy of Q1, Q2, scholars agree, was printed from Shakespeare's "foul papers" (a draft in his hand), or perhaps a copy of them. There are many signs that the underlying manuscript was difficult to read; there are numerous instances of what seem to be characteristically Shakespearean spellings; and, tellingly, there is an example of a "false start," an authorial second thought or revision of a passage where apparently unrevised text is printed beside revised:

> For women fear too much even as they love,
> And women's fear and love hold quantity:
> Either none, in neither aught or in extremity.
> (3.2.150–52)

The second line immediately revises the first (which is left without a corresponding rhyme line), and "in neither aught" revises "Either none"; but the compositor failed to note any deletion marks there may have been. F omits both "false starts." These features of Q2 suggest that it is based on Shakespeare's foul papers.

There is more debate about the provenance of F, though most scholars allow that it derives from a separate manuscript from that behind Q2 and, further, that that manuscript had some connection to performance. Most likely, a fair copy was made of the foul papers and that copy was then subjected to theatrical modification. F's stage directions are normally fuller and more precise than Q2's; its apparent cuts from Q2 seem aimed at speeding up the action; and many of its verbal substitutions help clarify obscurity. There has been debate about whether the many changes indicate theatrical "corruption" (for example, the phrase "Oh, vengeance!" in Hamlet's second soliloquy may well be an actorly interpolation) or whether they represent attempts at improvement in which Shakespeare may have taken an active part. No doubt both factors played a part.

Q2 contains some 220 lines that have no counterpart in F and which seem mostly to have been cut for performance. In act 1, Horatio's scholarly disquisition on portents and omens (Q2 1.111–24) and Hamlet's analysis of how a single blemish can poison the whole organism (Q2 4.17–38) are excised, doubtless because they distract from the growing excitement around the Ghost's appearances. Hamlet's extended attack on his mother in the "closet scene" is reduced by a total of 27 lines; almost the whole of 4.1 disappears, including Hamlet's final soliloquy (see F Textual Comment 7); 27 lines go from 4.3; and two passages (around 40 lines) from 5.2 disappear in the course of revision (see F Textual Comment 10). Conversely, Q2 lacks about 70 lines found in F, mostly in three extended passages. One of these is likely a deliberate addition, while the other two are more uncertain (see combined text Textual Comments 10 and 4).

There are puzzles and ambiguities associated with all these texts, and for that reason this Norton edition provides the reader with four different edited versions, Q2 and F in digital form and Q1 and a fourth, combined text in both digital and print editions. This fourth edition is based on the Q2 text, augmented by passages from F of a line or more; the latter are presented in a different typeface to indicate their addition. Yet this "scars-and-stitches" edition is *not* a conflated edition in the tradition of Shakespearean editing as it was practiced throughout the twentieth century— that is, one in which the editor chose, word by word, from the surviving texts, according to a view of which was better, and then as much as possible hid the joins between elements of text from different sources. Rather, this edition is a hybrid designed to do two things: to provide as many as possible of the lines readers expect to find in *Hamlet* (for example, the long passage about the "eyrie of children" in 2.2, which is present only in F) and to demonstrate what most nineteenth- and twentieth-century readers understood to be *Hamlet*. Thus the edition gives the reader more *Hamlet* than any one of the early texts does, but, by making the seams obvious, reminds the reader that the conflation represents a *Hamlet* that never in fact existed in this form.

Two Notes on Editorial Procedure

Character names. For the three original texts, *The Norton Shakespeare* spells the names of the characters as they are most frequently spelled in the originals. However, for the Q2/F version, the proper names have been regularized so that they match the usual spellings in other modern editions.

Act and scene numbers. Q1 and Q2 have no act or scene designations. F marks only act 1, scenes 1–3 and both scenes in act 2. Editors have supplied the other act and scene numbers, but where act 3 should end has proven controversial. The traditional 3.4 ends with Hamlet "tugging" Polonius out, leaving his mother onstage to face a worried Claudius, who enters immediately. Gertrude does not leave the stage (none of the texts has an exit for her, though Q2 mistakenly includes her in the stage direction for the king's entry), and thus what follows is not a new scene. Commentators since the eighteenth century have noted the anomaly, though most editors have, for ease of reference, retained the traditional divisions that have been in place since 1676. This edition takes note of the continuous nature of the traditional 3.4 and 4.1

by running them together as a single scene, ending with Claudius's command to Rosencrantz and Guildenstern to find Hamlet and bring him to the King. The next two scenes (traditional 4.2 and 4.3) follow directly from that and therefore belong in the same act. So traditional 4.2 and 4.3 become 3.5 and 3.6. The next scene (Fortinbras, the Captain, and, in Q2 only, Hamlet and his guard) takes place sometime later and in a different location. It therefore seems a suitable place to begin a new act, so traditional 4.4 becomes in this edition 4.1, and the other scenes in what remains of traditional act 4 are renumbered accordingly.

ANTHONY B. DAWSON

PERFORMANCE NOTE

Perhaps the foremost concern for directors of *Hamlet* is assembling a text for performance. Most companies cut the play substantially, as a full combination of the two primary sources (Q2 and F) can easily run four hours or longer. Cutting can help determine whether the tragedy takes on a more political or domestic character, and whether espionage, madness, theater, militarism, and the supernatural surface as dominant or momentary themes. Besides Hamlet (the longest role in Shakespeare) the more frequent targets of editing or elision are Fortinbras, Reynaldo, *The Mousetrap,* and Hamlet's final soliloquy ("How all occasions . . ."), though cutting is also employed to confer unity on the characters and plot, making Claudius a purer villain, for example, or Denmark a more palpably corrupt state.

There are at least as many approaches to the role of Hamlet as there are to the text, though most actors fall somewhere within the traditions of either the prince or the rebel. In one tradition (greatly simplified), Hamlet is a noble and capable successor to his father, slow to his revenge not from fear but prudence, using his soliloquies primarily to renew his commitment to the task at hand. In the other, Hamlet is an outcast, a disaffected student who scorns the politics at court yet likely would struggle to succeed there. This Hamlet is often a cynic and joker, indulging in playacting to escape the despair that pervades solitary moments. Within these broad contours, myriad further choices present themselves: Hamlet can loathe Gertrude or regard her with oedipal fascination; heap abuse on Ophelia or treat her with pity and restraint; condescend to Horatio or seem, admirably, without pretension. These and other choices can inform whether the production works to deliver a markedly sympathetic character or one whose theatrical appeal is complicated or undercut by moral deficiencies.

The portrayals of the supporting cast critically affect the audience's reception of Hamlet and the degree to which he dominates their awareness at play's end. Claudius can be the "bloat king" Hamlet describes or a respected ruler; Gertrude, an oversexed newlywed or a concerned mother; Polonius, a cunning politician or bumbling fool; Rosencrantz and Guildenstern, caring friends or sinister mercenaries; Laertes, a loyal brother and son or self-satisfied favorite; and Ophelia, a clever upstart or model of naïve obedience. Other dramaturgical considerations include representing the Ghost (see Digital Edition PC 1); determining Gertrude's complicity in the murder of King Hamlet and her awareness of Claudius's intentions for her son; placing "To be or not to be" and deciding on its audience; cultivating attention for some extremely familiar set pieces; clarifying Hamlet's awareness or ignorance of being watched in 3.1 (Digital Edition PC 5); sorting out textual confusion regarding the ship for England and the pirates; and determining whether Laertes' (and Fortinbras') return to Denmark is a private matter or a coup.

BRETT GAMBOA

The Tragedy of Hamlet, Prince of Denmark

COMBINED TEXT*

[THE PERSONS OF THE PLAY

HAMLET, Prince of Denmark
KING Claudius of Denmark, brother to former King Hamlet
QUEEN Gertrude of Denmark, mother to Hamlet
GHOST of Hamlet, former King of Denmark and father to Prince Hamlet
POLONIUS, a royal counselor
OPHELIA, daughter to Polonius
LAERTES, son to Polonius
REYNALDO, servant to Polonius
FOLLOWERS of Laertes
HORATIO, companion to Hamlet
ROSENCRANTZ ⎫
GUILDENSTERN ⎭ school friends to Hamlet
CORNELIUS ⎫
VOLTEMAND ⎭ Danish ambassadors
English AMBASSADORS
FRANCISCO ⎫
BARNARDO ⎬ sentries
MARCELLUS ⎭
FIRST PLAYER, leader of the troupe
PLAYERS, playing roles of PROLOGUE, PLAYER KING, PLAYER QUEEN, and LUCIANUS
FORTINBRAS, Prince of Norway
Norwegian CAPTAIN
Soldiers in the Norwegian army
GRAVEDIGGER
SECOND MAN, his companion
PRIEST
OSRIC, a courtier
GENTLEMAN
LORDS
SAILORS
MESSENGER
Attendants, Officers, Servants]

1.1

Enter BARNARDO *and* FRANCISCO, *two sentinels.*

BARNARDO   Who's there?
FRANCISCO   Nay, answer me!¹ Stand and unfold° yourself.   *identify*
BARNARDO   Long live the King.
FRANCISCO   Barnardo?
BARNARDO   He.
FRANCISCO   You come most carefully° upon your hour.   *dutifully; cautiously*

---

*Text based on the Second Quarto, with interpolated
lines, passages, and scenes from the Folio.
1.1 Location: A guard platform at Elsinore Castle,
Denmark.
1. Francisco, as sentry on duty, is responsible for
challenging anyone who appears.

5 BARNARDO 'Tis now struck twelve—get thee to bed, Francisco.

FRANCISCO For this relief much thanks. 'Tis bitter cold,
And I am sick at heart.

BARNARDO Have you had quiet guard?

FRANCISCO   Not a mouse stirring.

BARNARDO Well, good night.

10   If you do meet Horatio and Marcellus,
The rivals° of my watch, bid them make haste.   *partners*

     Enter HORATIO *and* MARCELLUS.

FRANCISCO I think I hear them. —Stand ho! Who is there?

HORATIO Friends to this ground.°   *country*

MARCELLUS   And liegemen° to the Dane.[2]   *sworn servants*

FRANCISCO Give° you good night.   *God give*

15 MARCELLUS Oh, farewell, honest soldier. Who hath relieved
you?

FRANCISCO Barnardo hath my place. Give you good night.

                        Exit.

MARCELLUS Holla, Barnardo!

BARNARDO Say, what, is Horatio there?

HORATIO   A piece of him.

BARNARDO Welcome, Horatio; welcome, good Marcellus.

20 HORATIO What, has this thing appeared again tonight?

BARNARDO I have seen nothing.

MARCELLUS Horatio says 'tis but our fantasy
And will not let belief take hold of him
Touching° this dreaded sight twice seen of us.   *Concerning*

25   Therefore I have entreated him along
With us to watch the minutes of this night,
That if again this apparition come
He may approve° our eyes and speak to it.[3]   *verify the evidence of*

HORATIO Tush, tush, 'twill not appear.

BARNARDO   Sit down awhile,

30   And let us once again assail your ears
That are so fortified against our story
What we have two nights seen.

HORATIO   Well, sit we down,
And let us hear Barnardo speak of this.

BARNARDO Last night of all,°   *Just last night*

35   When yond same star that's westward from the pole°   *polestar*
Had made his° course t'illume that part of heaven   *its*
Where now it burns, Marcellus and myself,
The bell then beating one—

     Enter GHOST.[4]

MARCELLUS Peace, break thee off—look where it comes
again!

40 BARNARDO In the same figure like the King that's dead.

MARCELLUS Thou art a scholar: speak to it, Horatio.

BARNARDO Looks 'a° not like the King? Mark it, Horatio!   *he*

HORATIO Most like; it harrows me with fear and wonder.

---

2. King of Denmark.
3. A ghost was believed to speak only when spoken
to. As a precaution, the experiment will be conducted
by an educated man (Horatio; see line 41) who knows
Latin (the language effective for exorcising demonic
spirits).

4. PERFORMANCE COMMENT Productions range widely
in how they choose to represent the Ghost, whether as
a figure who arouses terror or one who evokes pity; a
spectral image or a full-fleshed person; a radical alternative to Claudius or his uncanny double. For the
implications of these choices, see Digital Edition PC 1.

BARNARDO   It would° be spoke to.   *wishes to*

MARCELLUS   Speak to it, Horatio!

45   HORATIO   What art thou that usurp'st⁵ this time of night
Together with that fair and warlike form
In which the majesty of buried Denmark°   *the buried King*
Did sometimes° march? By heaven, I charge thee, speak!   *formerly*

MARCELLUS   It is offended.

BARNARDO   See, it stalks away.

50   HORATIO   Stay! Speak, speak, I charge thee, speak!

Exit GHOST.

MARCELLUS   'Tis gone and will not answer.

BARNARDO   How now, Horatio? You tremble and look pale:
Is not this something more than fantasy?
What think you on't?°   *of it*

55   HORATIO   Before my God, I might not this believe
Without the sensible° and true avouch°   *sensory / testimony*
Of mine own eyes.

MARCELLUS   Is it not like the King?

HORATIO   As thou art to thyself.
Such was the very armor he had on

60   When he the ambitious Norway° combated;   *King of Norway*
So frowned he once, when in an angry parle°   *encounter*
He smote the sledded Polacks⁶ on the ice.
'Tis strange.

MARCELLUS   Thus twice before, and jump° at this dead hour,   *precisely*

65   With martial stalk° hath he gone by our watch.   *gait*

HORATIO   In what particular thought to work,⁷ I know not,
But in the gross and scope of mine opinion⁸
This bodes some strange eruption° to our state.   *calamity*

MARCELLUS   Good now,° sit down, and tell me he that knows,   *(an entreaty: Good sir, now)*

70   Why this same strict and most observant watch
So nightly toils the subject of the land,⁹
And with such daily cost of brazen cannon
And foreign mart° for implements of war—   *trade*
Why such impress° of shipwrights whose sore task   *drafting*

75   Does not divide the Sunday from the week?
What might be toward° that this sweaty haste   *impending*
Doth make the night joint laborer with the day—
Who is't that can inform me?

HORATIO   That can I.
At least the whisper goes so: our last king,

80   Whose image even but now appeared to us,
Was, as you know, by Fortinbras of Norway,
Thereto pricked° on by a most emulate° pride,   *spurred / rivalrous*
Dared to the combat, in which our valiant Hamlet—
For so this side of our known world esteemed him—

85   Did slay this Fortinbras, who, by a sealed compact¹
Well ratified by law and heraldry,²
Did forfeit with his life all these his lands

---

5. Wrongfully seize (both the night and the shape of the King). The familiar "thou" would be an inappropriate form of address for a real king.
6. Poles who traveled by sled.
7. *In . . . work:* What precise theory to follow.
8. But in my general opinion.

9. *So . . . land:* Requires the country's subjects to toil every night.
1. A mutually agreed-upon contract ("compact") to which each set his seal.
2. Properly ratified in accordance with civil law and the law of arms.

	Which he stood seized of° to the conqueror;	*held possession of*
	Against the which a moiety competent°	*an equal portion*
90	Was gagèd° by our king, which had return[3]	*staked*
	To the inheritance° of Fortinbras	*ownership*
	Had he been vanquisher—as by the same co-mart[4]	
	And carriage of the article designed[5]	
	His fell to Hamlet. Now, sir, young Fortinbras,	
95	Of unimprovèd° mettle hot and full,	*untested; untrained*
	Hath in the skirts° of Norway here and there	*outlying parts*
	Sharked up a list[6] of lawless[7] resolutes	
	For food and diet to some enterprise	
	That hath a stomach in't,[8] which is no other,	
100	As it doth well° appear unto our state,	*obviously*
	But to recover of us by strong hand[9]	
	And terms compulsatory° those foresaid lands	*compulsory*
	So by his father lost. And this, I take it,	
	Is the main motive of our preparations,	
105	The source of this our watch, and the chief head°	*source*
	Of this post-haste and rummage[1] in the land.[2]	

BARNARDO   I think it be no other, but e'en so.

	Well may it sort° that this portentous figure	*be fitting*
	Comes armèd through our watch so like the King	
110	That was and is the question° of these wars.	*cause*

HORATIO   A mote° it is to trouble the mind's eye.   *speck of dust*

	In the most high and palmy° state of Rome,	*flourishing*
	A little ere the mightiest Julius[3] fell,	
	The graves stood tenantless and the sheeted° dead	*shrouded*
115	Did squeak and gibber in the Roman streets.	
	As stars with trains of fire and dews of blood,	
	Disasters[4] in the sun; and the moist star,[5]	
	Upon whose influence Neptune's empire stands,°	*depends*
	Was sick almost to doomsday with eclipse.[6]	
120	And even the like precurse° of feared events,	*forerunner*
	As harbingers preceding still° the fates	*always*
	And prologue to the omen° coming on,	*disastrous event*
	Have heaven and earth together demonstrated	
	Unto our climatures° and countrymen.	*regions*

Enter GHOST.

125	But soft,° behold: lo, where it comes again!	*hush*
	I'll cross[7] it though it blast° me. —Stay, illusion!	*wither*

It spreads his arms.

If thou hast any sound or use of voice,
Speak to me!

---

3. Which would have gone. *return:* returned.
4. Covenant. Q2's use of "co-mart" is unattested elsewhere.
5. And execution of the contract's provision.
6. Gathered together indiscriminately (as a shark takes prey) a band ("list").
7. F uses "landless," providing a more specific motive for their enlistment.
8. *For . . . in't:* The men will "feed" his enterprise; they are fed in return for their service. *stomach:* courageous action; challenge to the pride (of both the Prince and his men).
9. By main force (punning on the name "Fortinbras," literally "strong arm").

1. Of this feverish activity and commotion.
2. The following passage, lines 107–24, is omitted in F.
3. Julius Caesar, whose assassination Shakespeare dramatized in his play of that name.
4. Malevolent influences (astrological term).
5. The moon, thought to control tides by drawing water out of the sea ("Neptune's empire," line 118).
6. Eclipses of sun and moon would accompany Christ's return to earth on Judgment Day (see Revelation 6:12).
7. Confront, cross its path; also, make the sign of the cross (to counter its evil influence).

If there be any good thing to be done
130   That may to thee do ease and grace to me,
Speak to me!
If thou art privy to thy country's fate
Which happily° foreknowing may avoid,   *perhaps; fortunately*
Oh, speak!
135   Or if thou hast uphoarded in thy life
Extorted treasure in the womb of earth,
For which they say your spirits oft walk in death,
Speak of it.

         The cock crows.

        Stay and speak! Stop it, Marcellus!
MARCELLUS   Shall I strike it with my partisan?°   *spear-handled blade*
HORATIO   Do, if it will not stand.
BARNARDO   'Tis here.
140   HORATIO   'Tis here.
                      [Exit GHOST.*]*

MARCELLUS   'Tis gone.
We do it wrong, being so majestical,
To offer it the show of violence,
For it is as the air, invulnerable,
145   And our vain blows malicious mockery.
BARNARDO   It was about to speak when the cock crew.
HORATIO   And then it started like a guilty thing
Upon a fearful summons. I have heard
The cock that is the trumpet to the morn
150   Doth with his lofty and shrill-sounding throat
Awake the god of day,[8] and at his warning,
Whether in sea or fire, in earth or air,
Th'extravagant and erring[9] spirit hies°   *hurries*
To his confine°—and of the truth herein   *enclosure*
155   This present object° made probation.°   *example / proof*
MARCELLUS   It faded on the crowing of the cock.
Some say that ever 'gainst° that season comes   *always when*
Wherein our Savior's birth is celebrated,
This bird of dawning singeth all night long,
160   And then, they say, no spirit dare stir abroad,
The nights are wholesome, then no planets strike,[1]
No fairy takes,° nor witch hath power to charm,   *bewitches*
So hallowed and so gracious° is that time.   *full of God's grace*
HORATIO   So have I heard and do in part believe it.
165   But look, the morn in russet mantle clad[2]
Walks o'er the dew of yon high eastward hill.
Break we our watch up and, by my advice,
Let us impart what we have seen tonight
Unto young Hamlet, for upon my life
170   This spirit, dumb to us, will speak to him.
Do you consent we shall acquaint him with it
As needful in our loves,[3] fitting our duty?
MARCELLUS   Let's do't, I pray, and I this morning know
Where we shall find him most convenient.   *Exeunt.*

---

8. The sun god, Phoebus Apollo.
9. Wandering out of its boundaries.
1. When they were in certain unfavorable astrological positions, heavenly bodies were thought to exercise a negative influence on earthly events.
2. Dressed in a reddish-brown cloak.
3. As necessary because of the love we have for him.

1.2

Flourish. Enter Claudius, KING *of Denmark, Gertrude
the* QUEEN, *Council [members, such] as* POLONIUS *and
his son* LAERTES, HAMLET, *with others[, including*
VOLTEMAND *and* CORNELIUS].

KING   Though yet of Hamlet our¹ dear brother's death
        The memory be green, and that it us befitted
        To bear our hearts in grief and our whole kingdom
        To be contracted in one brow of woe,²
5   Yet so far hath discretion fought with nature°   *natural love*
        That we with wisest sorrow think on him
        Together with remembrance of ourselves.³
        Therefore our sometime° sister, now our queen,⁴   *former*
        Th'imperial jointress to° this warlike state,   *joint possessor of*
10   Have we as 'twere with a defeated joy,
        With an auspicious and a dropping eye,⁵
        With mirth in funeral and with dirge in marriage,
        In equal scale weighing delight and dole,°   *sorrow*
        Taken to wife. Nor have we herein barred°   *excluded; contradicted*
15   Your better wisdoms, which have freely gone
        With this affair along—for all, our thanks.
        Now follows that you know:° young Fortinbras,   *that which you should know*
        Holding a weak supposal° of our worth   *poor opinion*
        Or thinking by our late dear brother's death
20   Our state to be disjoint° and out of frame,°   *fractured / order*
        Co-leaguèd with this dream of his advantage,⁶
        He hath not failed to pester us with message
        Importing° the surrender of those lands   *Concerning*
        Lost by his father, with all bands° of law,   *obligations*
25   To our most valiant brother. So much for him.
        Now for ourself and for this time of meeting,
        Thus much the business is: we have here writ
        To Norway, uncle of young Fortinbras,
        Who, impotent and bedrid, scarcely hears
30   Of this his nephew's purpose, to suppress
        His further gait° herein, in that the levies,   *progress*
        The lists, and full proportions are all made
        Out of his subject;⁷ and we here dispatch
        You, good Cornelius, and you, Voltemand,
35   For bearers of this greeting to old Norway,
        Giving to you no further personal power
        To business with the King more than the scope
        Of these delated° articles allow.   *spelled out; specific*

1.2 Location: The castle.
1. My. (Kings often referred to themselves in the plural, the royal "we," although in the lines that follow, Claudius may also be talking about Danes in general.)
2. To be drawn together into a collective expression of mourning (playing on the expression "the frowning brow of a mourner").
3. *we . . . ourselves:* "He is not wise that is not wise for himself" was proverbial.
4. English canon law forbade marriage between a former brother- and sister-in-law (Leviticus 18:16; Book of Common Prayer); it was on this ground that

Henry VIII annulled his marriage to his brother's widow and married Anne Boleyn, Queen Elizabeth's mother. The relationship between Claudius and Gertrude could thus be regarded as incestuous. In some early Germanic societies, however, a new king customarily married the late king's widow.
5. One eye looking hopefully, the other downcast, or "dropping" tears.
6. Reinforced by this illusion of his own advantageous position.
7. *in that . . . subject:* since the moneys, enlistments, and forces are made up of his (the King of Norway's) subjects.

Farewell, and let your haste commend your duty.[8]

40 CORNELIUS *and* VOLTEMAND In that and all things will we
 show our duty.
 KING We doubt it nothing;° heartily farewell. *not at all*
 [*Exeunt* VOLTEMAND *and* CORNELIUS.]
 And now, Laertes, what's the news with you?
 You told us of some suit°—what is't, Laertes? *petition; request*
 You cannot speak of reason to the Dane° *the Danish King*
45 And lose your voice. What wouldst thou beg, Laertes,
 That shall not be my offer, not thy asking?[9]
 The head is not more native[1] to the heart,
 The hand more instrumental to the mouth,
 Than is the throne of Denmark to thy father.
 What wouldst thou have, Laertes?
50 LAERTES My dread° lord, *revered*
 Your leave° and favor° to return to France, *permission / approval*
 From whence, though willingly I came to Denmark
 To show my duty in your coronation,
 Yet now I must confess, that duty done,
55 My thoughts and wishes bend again toward France
 And bow them to your gracious leave and pardon.[2]
 KING Have you your father's leave? —What says Polonius?
 POLONIUS He hath, my lord, wrung from me my slow leave
 By laborsome petition, and at last
60 Upon his will° I sealed my hard° consent. *desire / reluctant*
 I do beseech you give him leave to go.
 KING Take thy fair hour,[3] Laertes; time be thine
 And thy best graces spend it at thy will.[4]
 But now, my cousin[5] Hamlet, and my son—
65 HAMLET A little more than kin and less than kind.[6]
 KING How is it that the clouds still hang on you?
 HAMLET Not so much, my lord; I am too much in the sun.[7]
 QUEEN Good Hamlet, cast thy nighted color[8] off
 And let thine eye look like a friend on Denmark.[9]
70 Do not forever with thy veilèd lids° *downcast eyes*
 Seek for thy noble father in the dust—
 Thou know'st 'tis common, all that lives must die,
 Passing through nature to eternity.
 HAMLET Ay, madam, it is common.[1]
 QUEEN If it be,
75 Why seems it so particular° with thee? *personal*
 HAMLET "Seems," madam? Nay, it is. I know not "seems."
 'Tis not alone my inky cloak, cold mother,
 Nor customary suits of solemn black,
 Nor windy suspiration° of forced breath, *sigh*

---

8. Let your swift departure (rather than elaborate speeches) show your loyalty.
9. *What wouldst . . . asking:* What could you ask of me that I would not offer before you asked?
1. Naturally connected; an allusion to the "body politic," headed by the King and having as its heart the King's council.
2. And humbly ask you to grant permission to depart.
3. Opportunity (while you are young).
4. *time . . . will:* your time is your own; use it in accordance with your best qualities.
5. Kinsman (outside one's immediate family).
6. "The nearer in kin the less in kindness" was pro-

verbial. Hamlet's riddling comment indicates first that there is little warmth in their new, only nominally closer relationship. Playing on "kind" in the sense of natural type or offspring, however, he also refers to the incestuousness of the marriage that has produced their unnatural kinship.
7. In the sunshine of Claudius's favor; also, punning on "son."
8. Black mourning garments and melancholic behavior.
9. Both the King of Denmark and the country.
1. Commonplace; crude (?).

80 No, nor the fruitful° river in the eye,
Nor the dejected 'havior° of the visage,
Together with all forms, moods, shapes of grief
That can denote me truly. These indeed seem,
For they are actions that a man might play,
85 But I have that within which passes show—
These but the trappings and the suits of woe.
KING 'Tis sweet and commendable in your nature, Hamlet,
To give these mourning duties to your father,
But you must know your father lost a father,
90 That father lost, lost his, and the survivor bound
In filial obligation for some term
To do obsequious sorrow;[2] but to persever
In obstinate condolement° is a course   *lamenting*
Of impious stubbornness—'tis unmanly grief;
95 It shows a will most incorrect° to heaven,   *unsubmissive*
A heart unfortified or mind impatient,[3]
An understanding simple° and unschooled—   *childish*
For what we know must be and is as common
As any the most vulgar thing to sense,[4]
100 Why should we in our peevish opposition
Take it to heart? Fie, 'tis a fault to heaven,
A fault against the dead, a fault to nature,
To reason most absurd, whose common theme
Is death of fathers and who still° hath cried   *always*
105 From the first corpse[5] till he that died today,
"This must be so." We pray you throw to earth
This unprevailing° woe and think of us   *unavailing*
As of a father, for let the world take note
You are the most immediate° to our throne,   *next in succession*
110 And with no less nobility° of love   *purity; generosity*
Than that which dearest father bears his son
Do I impart toward you. For your intent
In going back to school in Wittenberg,[6]
It is most retrograde° to our desire,   *contrary*
115 And we beseech you bend you° to remain   *yield; agree*
Here in the cheer and comfort of our eye,
Our chiefest courtier, cousin, and our son.
QUEEN Let not thy mother lose her prayers, Hamlet:
I pray thee stay with us; go not to Wittenberg.
120 HAMLET I shall in all my best obey you, madam.
KING Why, 'tis a loving and a fair reply.[7]
Be as ourself in Denmark. —Madam, come;
This gentle and unforced accord of Hamlet
Sits smiling to° my heart, in grace° whereof   *Pleases / honor*
125 No jocund health° that Denmark° drinks today   *toast / the King*
But the great cannon to the clouds shall tell,°   *sound*
And the King's rouse[8] the heaven shall bruit again,°   *loudly echo*

2. To mourn as befits obsequies, or funeral ceremonies.
3. A heart not strengthened (against emotion or misfortune), a mind unprepared to suffer.
4. As the most obvious and ordinary thing we perceive using our senses.
5. That of Abel, the first human to die, murdered by his brother, Cain.
6. The birthplace of Protestantism, the university of Luther and Faustus; many Danes studied there.
7. PERFORMANCE COMMENT Whether the King's behavior merits the insult implicit in Hamlet's "loving" reply is a critical question for productions, which must decide how to depict the relationships in this scene. For discussion of the range of options, see Digital Edition PC 2.
8. Bout of drinking.

Re-speaking earthly thunder. Come away.
Flourish. Exeunt all but HAMLET.
HAMLET   Oh, that this too, too sallied[9] flesh would melt,
130   Thaw, and resolve° itself into a dew,   dissolve
Or that the Everlasting had not fixed
His canon° 'gainst self-slaughter. O God, God,   law
How weary, stale, flat, and unprofitable
Seem to me all the uses° of this world.   customs; business
135   Fie on't, ah, fie, 'tis an unweeded garden
That grows to seed; things rank and gross in nature
Possess it merely.° That it should come thus: entirely
But two months dead—nay, not so much, not two—
So excellent a king, that was to this
140   Hyperion to a satyr,[1] so loving to my mother
That he might not beteem° the winds of heaven   permit
Visit her face too roughly—heaven and earth,
Must I remember? Why, she would hang on him
As if increase of appetite had grown
145   By what it fed on. And yet within a month—
Let me not think on't—Frailty, thy name is woman—
A little month, or e'er° those shoes were old   before
With which she followed my poor father's body,
Like Niobe all tears,[2] why, she—
150   O God, a beast that wants discourse of reason[3]
Would have mourned longer—married with my uncle,
My father's brother, but no more like my father
Than I to Hercules.[4] Within a month,
Ere yet the salt of most unrighteous tears
155   Had left the flushing in her gallèd° eyes,   irritated
She married. Oh, most wicked speed, to post°   hurry
With such dexterity to incestuous sheets—
It is not, nor it cannot come to good.
But break, my heart, for I must hold my tongue.
Enter HORATIO, MARCELLUS, *and* BARNARDO.
HORATIO   Hail to your lordship!
160   HAMLET   I am glad to see you well—
Horatio, or I do forget myself.
HORATIO   The same, my lord, and your poor servant ever.
HAMLET   Sir, my good friend, I'll change° that name with   exchange
you.
And what make you from[5] Wittenberg, Horatio?
165   —Marcellus!
MARCELLUS   My good lord.
HAMLET   I am very glad to see you. [*to* BARNARDO] Good
even, sir.
[*to* HORATIO] But what in faith make you from Wittenberg?

9. TEXTUAL COMMENT Q1 and Q2 read "sallied,"
while F reads "solid." "Solid" fits with the imagery of
thawing, but "sallied" (meaning "assailed" or "sullied") also works well, evoking the themes of oppression and pollution that Hamlet explores elsewhere in
the play. See Digital Edition TC 1 (combined text).
1. *So . . . satyr:* That king was to this as the sun god
(Hyperion, a Titan) is to a lustful half goat (mythological companion of the wine god, Bacchus).

2. Niobe's fourteen children were killed by Apollo
and Artemis to punish her for boasting about them.
She continued to weep bitterly even after she was
turned to stone.
3. That lacks the faculty of rational thought.
4. In Greek and Roman mythology, a powerful demigod renowned for his strength, as exemplified in his
twelve famous "labors."
5. What are you doing away from.

HORATIO   A truant disposition, good my lord.

170 HAMLET   I would not hear your enemy say so,
Nor shall you do my ear that violence
To make it truster° of your own report   *believer*
Against yourself. I know you are no truant.
But what is your affair in Elsinore?

175 We'll teach you for to° drink ere you depart.   *for to = to*

HORATIO   My lord, I came to see your father's funeral.

HAMLET   I prithee° do not mock me, fellow student,   *pray thee*
I think it was to see my mother's wedding.

HORATIO   Indeed, my lord, it followed hard upon.°   *quickly thereafter*

180 HAMLET   Thrift, thrift, Horatio: the funeral baked meats°   *meat pies and pastries*
Did coldly° furnish forth the marriage tables.   *when cold*
Would I had met my dearest° foe in heaven   *most hated*
Or ever° I had seen that day, Horatio.   *Before*
My father—methinks I see my father.

HORATIO   Where, my lord?

185 HAMLET   In my mind's eye, Horatio.

HORATIO   I saw him once; 'a° was a goodly king.   *he*

HAMLET   'A was a man, take him for all in all;
I shall not look upon his like again.

HORATIO   My lord, I think I saw him yesternight.

HAMLET   Saw? Who?

190 HORATIO   My lord, the King your father.

HAMLET   The King my father?

HORATIO   Season° your admiration° for a while   *Moderate / amazement*
With an attent° ear till I may deliver,   *attentive*
Upon the witness of these gentlemen,
This marvel to you.

195 HAMLET   For God's love let me hear!

HORATIO   Two nights together had these gentlemen,
Marcellus and Barnardo, on their watch
In the dead waste° and middle of the night,   *bleak stillness*
Been thus encountered: a figure like your father

200 Armed at point° exactly, cap-à-pie,°   *in readiness / head to foot*
Appears before them and with solemn march
Goes slow and stately by them. Thrice he walked
By their oppressed and fear-surprisèd eyes
Within his truncheon's[6] length, whilst they, distilled°   *dissolved*

205 Almost to jelly with the act° of fear,   *effect*
Stand dumb and speak not to him. This to me
In dreadful secrecy impart they did,
And I with them the third night kept the watch
Where, as they had delivered,° both in time,   *reported*

210 Form of the thing, each word made true and good,
The apparition comes. I knew your father:
These hands are not more like.[7]

HAMLET   But where was this?

MARCELLUS   My lord, upon the platform where we watch.

HAMLET   Did you not speak to it?

HORATIO   My lord, I did,

215 But answer made it none; yet once methought

6. Officer's baton.
7. These hands are not more like each other than the apparition was like King Hamlet.

It lifted up it° head and did address   *its*
Itself to motion like as it would speak.[8]
But even° then the morning cock crew loud,   *just*
And at the sound it shrunk in haste away
And vanished from our sight.
220 HAMLET   'Tis very strange.
HORATIO   As I do live, my honored lord, 'tis true,
And we did think it writ down° in our duty   *prescribed*
To let you know of it.
HAMLET   Indeed, sirs, but this troubles me—
Hold you the watch tonight?
225 BARNARDO *and* MARCELLUS   We do, my lord.
HAMLET   Armed, say you?
HORATIO, BARNARDO, *and* MARCELLUS   Armed, my lord.
HAMLET   From top to toe?
HORATIO, BARNARDO, *and* MARCELLUS   My lord, from head to foot.
HAMLET   Then saw you not his face.
HORATIO   Oh, yes, my lord, he wore his beaver° up.   *helmet's faceguard*
230 HAMLET   What, looked he frowningly?
HORATIO   A countenance more in sorrow than in anger.
HAMLET   Pale or red?
HORATIO   Nay, very pale.
HAMLET   And fixed his eyes upon you?
HORATIO   Most constantly.
HAMLET   I would I had been there.
235 HORATIO   It would have much amazed you.
HAMLET   Very like; stayed it long?
HORATIO   While one with moderate haste might tell° a   *count*
   hundred.
BARNARDO *and* MARCELLUS   Longer, longer.
HORATIO   Not when I saw't.
HAMLET   His beard was grizzled,° no?   *gray*
240 HORATIO   It was as I have seen it in his life,
A sable silvered.[9]
HAMLET   I will watch tonight;
Perchance 'twill walk again.
HORATIO   I warr'nt° it will.   *guarantee*
HAMLET   If it assume my noble father's person,
I'll speak to it though hell itself should gape
245 And bid me hold my peace. I pray you all,
If you have hitherto concealed this sight,
Let it be tenable[1] in your silence still;
And whatsomever° else shall hap° tonight   *whatever / occur*
Give it an understanding but no tongue.
250 I will requite your loves. So fare you well.
Upon the platform twixt eleven and twelve
I'll visit you.
HORATIO, BARNARDO, *and* MARCELLUS   Our duty to your honor.
HAMLET   Your loves, as mine to you; farewell.
                  Exeunt [HORATIO, BARNARDO, *and* MARCELLUS].
My father's spirit in arms! All is not well:

---

8. *address . . . speak:* start to move as though it wished   9. Black sprinkled with white.
to speak.   1. That is, able to be held. F's reading is "treble."

255   I doubt° some foul play. Would the night were come!   *suspect*
       Till then sit still, my soul. Foul deeds will rise,
       Though all the earth o'erwhelm them, to men's eyes.   *Exit.*

1.3

Enter LAERTES *and* OPHELIA, *his sister.*

LAERTES   My necessaries are embarked.° Farewell.   *aboard ship*
       And, sister, as the winds give benefit
       And convey is assistant,[1] do not sleep
       But let me hear from you.

OPHELIA   Do you doubt that?

5 LAERTES   For Hamlet and the trifling of his favor,
       Hold it a fashion and a toy in blood,
       A violet in the youth of primy nature,
       Forward,[2] not permanent, sweet, not lasting,
       The perfume and suppliance° of a minute,   *diversion*
       No more.

OPHELIA   No more but so?

10 LAERTES   Think it no more.
       For nature crescent° does not grow alone   *growing*
       In thews° and bulks, but as this temple° waxes,   *muscles / body*
       The inward service° of the mind and soul   *responsibility*
       Grows wide withal.° Perhaps he loves you now,   *along with it*
15   And now no soil° nor cautel° doth besmirch   *stain / deception*
       The virtue of his will.° But you must fear,   *intentions; desires*
       His greatness weighed,[3] his will is not his own:
       He may not, as unvalued° persons do,   *common*
       Carve for himself,[4] for on his choice depends
20   The safety and health of this whole state.
       And therefore must his choice be circumscribed
       Unto the voice° and yielding° of that body[5]   *vote / consent*
       Whereof he is the head. Then if he says he loves you,
       It fits° your wisdom so far to believe it   *befits*
25   As he in his particular act and place[6]
       May give his saying deed,[7] which is no further
       Than the main° voice of Denmark goes withal.   *collective*
       Then weigh what loss your honor may sustain
       If with too credent° ear you list° his songs,   *trusting / listen to*
30   Or lose your heart, or your chaste treasure open
       To his unmastered° importunity.   *uncontrolled*
       Fear it, Ophelia, fear it, my dear sister,
       And keep you in the rear of your affection[8]
       Out of the shot and danger of desire.
35   The chariest° maid is prodigal enough   *most careful; modest*
       If she unmask her beauty to the moon.[9]

1.3 Location: Polonius's apartments in the castle.
1. And means of transport is available.
2. *a toy . . . Forward:* a passing sexual fancy, a flower of his natural impulses in their prime, early blooming ("forward").
3. When his high rank is considered.
4. Help himself to his own choice of the roast (proverbially, to choose for himself).
5. Body politic; nation.
6. His power of action and social position.

7. May act on his promise.
8. And be restrained, despite the forward march of your feelings.
9. *prodigal . . . moon:* risk-taking enough if she exposes herself to the moon. (The suggestion here is that a maid can never be too cautious. Upper-class women wore masks to screen their complexions from the sun. The moon was classically figured as chaste, while the sun was traditionally associated with passion.)

Virtue itself scapes not calumnious strokes,
The canker galls the infants[1] of the spring
Too oft before their buttons be disclosed,°   *buds are open*
40 And in the morn and liquid dew of youth
Contagious blastments° are most imminent.   *blights*
Be wary, then: best safety lies in fear.
Youth to itself rebels, though none else near.[2]
OPHELIA   I shall the effect of this good lesson keep
45 As watchman to my heart. But, good my brother,
Do not as some ungracious° pastors do   *ungodly*
Show me the steep and thorny way to heaven
Whiles, a puffed° and reckless libertine,   *proud*
Himself the primrose path of dalliance treads
And recks° not his own rede.°   *heeds / advice*
50 LAERTES   Oh, fear me not.°   *fear not for me*

Enter POLONIUS.

I stay too long—but here my father comes.
A double blessing is a double grace;
Occasion smiles upon a second leave.[3]
POLONIUS   Yet here, Laertes? Aboard, aboard for shame!
55 The wind sits in the shoulder° of your sail   *at the back*
And you are stayed° for. There, my blessing with thee,   *waited*
And these few precepts in thy memory
Look thou character:° give thy thoughts no tongue   *inscribe*
Nor any unproportioned° thought his act;   *unruly*
60 Be thou familiar but by no means vulgar;[4]
Those friends thou hast, and their adoption tried,[5]
Grapple them unto thy soul with hoops of steel,
But do not dull° thy palm with entertainment[6]   *callous*
Of each new-hatched, unfledged courage;° beware   *comrade*
65 Of entrance to a quarrel but, being in,
Bear't° that th'opposèd may beware of thee;   *Manage it so*
Give every man thy ear but few thy voice;
Take each man's censure,° but reserve thy judgment;   *opinion*
Costly thy habit° as thy purse can buy   *dress*
70 But not expressed in fancy,° rich not gaudy—   *showiness*
For the apparel oft proclaims the man,
And they in France of the best rank and station
Are of a most select and generous chief in that.[7]
Neither a borrower nor a lender be,
75 For loan oft loses both itself and friend,
And borrowing dulleth th'edge of husbandry.°   *economy*
This above all: to thine own self be true,
And it must follow as the night the day
Thou canst not then be false to any man.
80 Farewell, my blessing season° this in thee.   *mature*
LAERTES   Most humbly do I take my leave, my lord.
POLONIUS   The time invests° you—go, your servants tend.°   *presses / wait*
LAERTES   Farewell, Ophelia, and remember well

---

1. The cankerworm injures the shoots.
2. Young people are naturally rebellious, even without provocation.
3. Favorable circumstances provide us with a second farewell.
4. *Be . . . vulgar:* Be friendly but by no means indiscriminately social.
5. *Those . . . tried:* Those friends of yours who have proven true and reliable.
6. Greeting (handshaking).
7. Are of all people the most adept at displaying rank in fine appearance.

What I have said to you.

OPHELIA   'Tis in my memory locked,
85   And you yourself shall keep the key of it.

LAERTES   Farewell.   *Exit.*

POLONIUS   What is't, Ophelia, he hath said to you?

OPHELIA   So please you, something touching the Lord Hamlet.

POLONIUS   Marry,[8] well bethought.
90   'Tis told me he hath very oft of late
Given private time to you, and you yourself
Have of your audience° been most free and bounteous.   *attention*
If it be so, as so 'tis put on° me—   *suggested to*
And that in way of caution—I must tell you
95   You do not understand yourself so clearly
As it behooves my daughter and your honor.
What is between you? Give me up the truth.

OPHELIA   He hath, my lord, of late made many tenders°   *offers*
Of his affection to me.

100   POLONIUS   Affection! Pooh! You speak like a green girl
Unsifted° in such perilous circumstance.   *Inexperienced*
Do you believe his "tenders,"[9] as you call them?

OPHELIA   I do not know, my lord, what I should think.

POLONIUS   Marry, I will teach you: think yourself a baby
105   That you have ta'en these tenders for true pay
Which are not sterling.[1] Tender° yourself more dearly   *Value; protect*
Or—not to crack the wind of the poor phrase
Wronging it thus[2]—you'll tender me a fool.[3]

OPHELIA   My lord, he hath importuned me with love
110   In honorable fashion—

POLONIUS   Ay, "fashion"° you may call it. Go to,[4] go to!   *conventional flattery*

OPHELIA   And hath given countenance° to his speech,   *authority*
My lord, with almost all the holy vows of heaven.

POLONIUS   Ay, springes to catch woodcocks.[5] I do know
115   When the blood burns how prodigal° the soul   *lavishly*
Lends the tongue vows; these blazes, daughter,
Giving more light than heat, extinct° in both   *extinguished*
Even in their promise as it is a-making,
You must not take for fire. From this time
120   Be something scanter of your maiden presence;
Set your entreatments at a higher rate
Than a command to parle.[6] For Lord Hamlet,
Believe so much in° him that he is young,   *concerning*
And with a larger tether may he walk
125   Than may be given you. In few,° Ophelia,   *brief*
Do not believe his vows, for they are brokers°   *go-betweens*
Not of that dye which their investments° show   *clerical vestments*
But mere implorators° of unholy suits,   *solicitors*
Breathing° like sanctified and pious bonds°   *Speaking / promises*
130   The better to beguile. This is for all:
I would not, in plain terms, from this time forth

---

8. By the Virgin Mary, a mild oath.
9. *tenders*: offers of payment in compensation for something.
1. Genuine currency.
2. *crack . . . thus*: ruin the phrase with overworking (like a "broken-winded" horse).

3. A multiple pun: make me look foolish; seem yourself a fool; show me a baby (idiomatically, a "fool").
4. That's enough; come, come.
5. Traps for proverbially gullible birds.
6. *Set . . . parle*: Do not negotiate a surrender (of your chastity) just because he asks to speak with you.

'ou so slander° any moment leisure   *disgrace*
ive words or talk with the Lord Hamlet.
.. ..o't, I charge you. Come your ways.°   *Come along*
155 OPHELIA   I shall obey, my lord.   *Exeunt.*

1.4

Enter HAMLET, HORATIO, *and* MARCELLUS.

HAMLET   The air bites shrewdly;° it is very cold.   *sharply*
HORATIO   It is nipping and an eager° air.   *a bitter*
HAMLET   What hour now?
HORATIO   I think it lacks of twelve.
MARCELLUS   No, it is struck.
HORATIO   Indeed? I heard it not—
5   It then draws near the season°   *time*
     Wherein the spirit held his wont° to walk.   *was accustomed*
          A *flourish of trumpets and two pieces*° [*go*] *off.*   *cannons*
     What does this mean, my lord?
HAMLET   The King doth wake tonight and takes his rouse,
     Keeps wassail and the swaggering upspring reels,[1]
10   And as he drains his drafts of Rhenish° down   *Rhine wine*
     The kettledrum and trumpet thus bray out
     The triumph of his pledge.[2]
HORATIO   Is it a custom?
HAMLET   Ay, marry, is't,
     But to my mind, though I am native here
15   And to the manner° born, it is a custom   *custom*
     More honored in the breach than the observance.[3]
     This heavy-headed revel east and west
     Makes us traduced and taxed of other nations:
     They clepe° us drunkards and with swinish phrase   *call*
20   Soil our addition,° and indeed it takes   *reputation*
     From our achievements, though performed at height,°   *excellently*
     The pith° and marrow of our attribute.°   *heart / attributed glory*
     So oft it chances in particular men
     That for some vicious mole of nature[4] in them,
25   As in their birth° wherein they are not guilty—   *parentage*
     Since nature cannot choose his° origin—   *its*
     By their o'er-growth of some complexion[5]
     Oft breaking down the pales° and forts of reason,   *fences; boundaries*
     Or by some habit that too much o'er-leavens
30   The form of plausive manners[6]—that these men,
     Carrying, I say, the stamp of one defect—
     Being nature's livery or fortune's star[7]—
     His virtues else, be they as pure as grace,
     As infinite as man may undergo,°   *sustain*
35   Shall in the general censure° take corruption   *the public opinion*

1.4 Location: The castle's battlements.
1. *The King . . . reels:* The King revels and carouses
rather than sleeping, has a drinking party ("wassail"),
and staggers ("reels") through a wild German dance.
2. His success in draining his cup upon making a
toast.
3. Which is more honored in being broken than in
being observed. The following passage, lines 17–38,
is omitted in F.
4. Natural blemish that tends to vice.

5. By the disproportionate amount of one humor
(see note to 2.2.280–81), and thus an unbalanced
personality.
6. *o'er-leavens . . . manners:* changes the whole effect
of otherwise pleasing ("plausive") manners for the
worse (as too much yeast ruins a batch of bread).
7. Being a congenital defect (the "livery," or clothing,
given by nature) or a blemish caused by fortune (the
influence of chance astrological events).

From that particular fault: the dram of eale
Doth all the noble substance of a doubt
To his own scandal[8]—
    Enter GHOST.

HORATIO   Look, my lord, it comes.

HAMLET   Angels and ministers of grace defend us!

40   Be thou a spirit of health or goblin° damned,   *demon*
Bring with thee airs° from heaven or blasts[9] from hell,   *gentle breezes*
Be thy intents wicked or charitable,
Thou com'st in such a questionable shape
That I will speak to thee: I'll call thee Hamlet,

45   King, father, royal Dane. Oh, answer me!
Let me not burst in ignorance, but tell
Why thy canonized° bones, hearsed° in death,   *consecrated / coffined*
Have burst their cerements,° why the sepulcher   *grave clothes*
Wherein we saw thee quietly interred°   *entombed*

50   Hath oped his ponderous and marble jaws
To cast thee up again. What may this mean
That thou, dead corpse, again in complete steel°   *armor*
Revisits thus the glimpses of the moon,[1]
Making night hideous and we fools of nature[2]

55   So horridly to shake our disposition°   *mental foundations*
With thoughts beyond the reaches of our souls?
Say, why is this? Wherefore? What should we do?
    [*The* GHOST] *beckons.*

HORATIO   It beckons you to go away with it
As if it some impartment° did desire   *communication*
To you alone.

60 MARCELLUS   Look with what courteous action
It waves° you to a more removèd ground—   *beckons*
But do not go with it.

HORATIO   No, by no means.

HAMLET   It will not speak; then I will follow it.

HORATIO   Do not, my lord.

HAMLET   Why, what should be the fear?

65   I do not set my life at a pin's fee,°   *value*
And for my soul, what can it do to that,
Being a thing immortal as itself?
It waves me forth again; I'll follow it.

HORATIO   What if it tempt you toward the flood,° my lord,   *sea*

70   Or to the dreadful summit of the cliff
That beetles o'er° his base into the sea,   *overhangs*
And there assume some other horrible form
Which might deprive your sovereignty of reason
And draw you into madness? Think of it:[3]

75   The very place puts toys of desperation,[4]
Without more motive,° into every brain   *cause*
That looks so many fathoms to the sea
And hears it roar beneath.

8. *dram:* tiny amount (eighth of an ounce). *scandal:* shame. TEXTUAL COMMENT *the dram . . . scandal:* These famously obscure lines, absent from Q1 and F, are plagued by uncertain syntax and opaque words and phrases. See Digital Edition TC 2 (combined text).
9. Pestilent gusts.

1. *glimpses of the moon:* (earth lit by) flickering moonlight.
2. Mere mortals (terrified by encounters with the supernatural).
3. The following passage, lines 75–78, is omitted in F.
4. Imaginings of despair and suicide.

HAMLET   It waves me still. —Go on, I'll follow thee.

MARCELLUS   You shall not go, my lord.

80 HAMLET   Hold off your hands.

HORATIO   Be ruled; you shall not go.

HAMLET   My fate cries out

And makes each petty art'ry° in this body   *artery*

As hardy as the Nemean lion's⁵ nerve.

[GHOST *beckons.*] Still am I called—unhand me, gentlemen!

85 By heaven, I'll make a ghost of him that lets me.°   *gets in my way*

I say, away! —Go on, I'll follow thee.

                          Exeunt GHOST *and* HAMLET.

HORATIO   He waxes desperate with imagination.

MARCELLUS   Let's follow. 'Tis not fit thus to obey him.

HORATIO   Have after.° To what issue° will this come?   *Go on / end*

90 MARCELLUS   Something is rotten in the state of Denmark.

HORATIO   Heaven will direct it.

MARCELLUS   Nay, let's follow him.

                          Exeunt.

1.5

          Enter GHOST *and* HAMLET.

HAMLET   Whither wilt thou lead me? Speak! I'll go no

     further.

GHOST   Mark me.

HAMLET   I will.

GHOST   My hour is almost come

     When I to sulf'rous and tormenting flames

     Must render up myself.

HAMLET   Alas, poor ghost.

5 GHOST   Pity me not, but lend thy serious hearing

     To what I shall unfold.

HAMLET   Speak, I am bound to hear.

GHOST   So art thou to revenge, when thou shalt hear.

HAMLET   What?

GHOST   I am thy father's spirit,

10   Doomed for a certain term to walk the night

     And for the day confined to fast° in fires   *do penance*

     Till the foul crimes done in my days of nature°   *my natural life*

     Are burnt and purged away. But that I am forbid

     To tell the secrets of my prison house,

15   I could a tale unfold whose lightest word

     Would harrow up° thy soul, freeze thy young blood,   *torment*

     Make thy two eyes like stars start from their spheres,

     Thy knotted and combinèd locks to part,

     And each particular hair to stand on end

20   Like quills upon the fearful porcupine.

     But this eternal blazon¹ must not be

     To ears of flesh and blood. List,° list, oh, list.   *Listen*

     If thou didst ever thy dear father love—

HAMLET   O God!

25 GHOST   Revenge his foul and most unnatural murder.

---

5. A ferocious beast killed by Hercules.   1. Catalogue or display of the afterlife's mysteries.
1.5 Location: Scene continues.

HAMLET   Murder?

GHOST   Murder most foul, as in the best it is,
But this most foul, strange, and unnatural.

HAMLET   Haste me to know't, that I with wings as swift
30   As meditation or the thoughts of love
May sweep to my revenge.

GHOST   I find thee apt,
And duller shouldst thou be than the fat° weed   *gross*
That roots itself[2] in ease on Lethe wharf,[3]
Wouldst thou not stir in this. Now, Hamlet, hear:
35   'Tis given out° that, sleeping in my orchard,   *It's being said*
A serpent stung me; so the whole ear of Denmark
Is by a forgèd process° of my death   *fabricated account*
Rankly abused.° But know, thou noble youth,   *deceived*
The serpent that did sting thy father's life
40   Now wears his crown.

HAMLET   Oh, my prophetic soul! My uncle!

GHOST   Ay, that incestuous, that adulterate° beast,   *adulterous*
With witchcraft of his wits, with traitorous gifts°—   *abilities; presents*
Oh, wicked wit and gifts that have the power
45   So to seduce!—won to his shameful lust
The will of my most seeming-virtuous queen.
O Hamlet, what falling off was there,
From me whose love was of that dignity
That it went hand in hand even with the vow
50   I made to her in marriage, and to decline°   *sink down*
Upon a wretch whose natural gifts were poor
To° those of mine.   *Compared to*
But virtue, as it never will be moved
Though lewdness court it in a shape of heaven,
55   So lust, though to a radiant angel linked,
Will sate itself[4] in a celestial bed
And prey on garbage.
But soft,[5] methinks I scent the morning air.
Brief let me be: sleeping within my orchard—
60   My custom always of the afternoon—
Upon my secure hour thy uncle stole
With juice of cursed hebona[6] in a vial
And in the porches° of my ears did pour   *entranceways*
The leprous distilment,[7] whose effect
65   Holds such an enmity with blood of man
That swift as quicksilver[8] it courses through
The natural gates and alleys of the body,
And with a sudden vigor it doth possess
And curd, like eager° droppings into milk,   *acid (like vinegar)*
70   The thin and wholesome blood. So did it mine,
And a most instant tetter° barked about,[9]   *scaly rash*
Most lazar-like,° with vile and loathsome crust   *leper-like*

---

2. F prints "rots itself," or decays under its own excessive growth.
3. In classical mythology, Lethe was the river of forgetfulness in Hades.
4. Will become satiated (and unable to find further pleasure).
5. The Ghost urges himself quickly to wrap up his speech.
6. A poison, possibly henbane.
7. Distillation causing skin to become scaly (as in leprosy, a disease familiar in Elizabethan England).
8. Liquid mercury, noted for its capacity for rapid motion.
9. Covered the body like bark.

All my smooth body.
Thus was I, sleeping, by a brother's hand

75   Of life, of crown, of queen at once dispatched,°   *deprived*
Cut off even in the blossoms of my sin,[1]
Unhouseled, disappointed, unaneled,[2]
No reck'ning made, but sent to my account
With all my imperfections on my head.[3]

80   Oh, horrible, oh, horrible, most horrible!
If thou hast nature° in thee, bear it° not;   *natural feeling* / *(this injustice)*
Let not the royal bed of Denmark be
A couch for luxury° and damnèd incest.   *lechery*
But howsomever° thou pursuest this act,   *however*

85   Taint not thy mind,[4] nor let thy soul contrive
Against thy mother aught;° leave her to heaven   *any (punishment)*
And to those thorns that in her bosom lodge
To prick and sting her. Fare thee well at once—
The glowworm shows the matin° to be near   *morning*

90   And 'gins° to pale his uneffectual fire.   *begins*
Adieu, adieu, adieu: remember me.   [*Exit.*]
HAMLET   O all you host of heaven! O earth! What else?
And shall I couple° hell? Oh, fie! Hold, hold, my heart,   *add*
And you, my sinews, grow not instant old,

95   But bear me swiftly up. Remember thee?
Ay, thou poor ghost, whiles memory holds a seat
In this distracted globe.[5] Remember thee?
Yea, from the table° of my memory   *tablet; book*
I'll wipe away all trivial fond° records,   *foolish*

100   All saws of books, all forms, all pressures past[6]
That youth and observation copied there,
And thy commandment all alone shall live
Within the book and volume of my brain
Unmixed with baser matter. Yes, by heaven!

105   O most pernicious woman!
O villain, villain, smiling damnèd villain—
My tables![7] Meet it is I set it down
That one may smile and smile and be a villain—
At least I am sure it may be so in Denmark.
          [*He writes.*]

110   So, uncle, there you are. Now to my word:°   *watchword; motto*
It is "Adieu, adieu, remember me."
I have sworn't.
          Enter HORATIO *and* MARCELLUS.
HORATIO   My lord, my lord!
MARCELLUS   Lord Hamlet!
HORATIO   Heavens secure him.
HAMLET   So be it.

115   MARCELLUS   Illo, ho, ho, my lord!

---

1. Cut off when my sins were full-blown, flourishing.
2. Without the sacrament of the Eucharist, without deathbed confession and absolution, and without extreme unction, the ritual anointing of those who are close to death.
3. *No . . . head:* Without having made restitution for my sins, but sent to the Last Judgment liable for all my faults.
4. Do not let yourself be corrupted.
5. Confused head; disordered world; often also taken as a reference to the Globe Theater and the audience.
6. All adages from books, all images or customs, all past impressions.
7. Scholars and others might carry two writing tablets hinged together, as a notebook.

HAMLET Hillo, ho, ho, boy, come and come![8]
MARCELLUS How is't, my noble lord?
HORATIO What news, my lord?
HAMLET Oh, wonderful!
120 HORATIO Good my lord, tell it.
HAMLET No, you will reveal it.
HORATIO Not I, my lord, by heaven.
MARCELLUS   Nor I, my lord.
HAMLET How say you, then, would heart of man once
    think it—
    But you'll be secret?
HORATIO *and* MARCELLUS Ay, by heaven.
125 HAMLET There's never a villain dwelling in all Denmark   *a complete*
    But he's an arrant° knave.
HORATIO There needs no ghost, my lord, come from the grave
    To tell us this.
HAMLET   Why, right, you are in the right,
    And so without more circumstance° at all   *elaborate speech*
130 I hold it fit that we shake hands and part,
    You as your business and desire shall point you—
    For every man hath business and desire,
    Such as it is. And for my own poor part,
    I will go pray.
135 HORATIO These are but wild and whirling words, my lord.
HAMLET I am sorry they offend you. Heartily,
    Yes, faith, heartily.
HORATIO   There's no offense, my lord.
HAMLET Yes, by Saint Patrick,[9] but there is, Horatio,   *Concerning*
    And much offense too. Touching° this vision here,   *a reliable; a genuine*
140 It is an honest° ghost, that let me tell you.
    For your desire to know what is between us,
    O'ermaster't as you may. And now, good friends,
    As you are friends, scholars, and soldiers,
    Give me one poor request.
145 HORATIO What is't, my lord? We will.
HAMLET Never make known what you have seen tonight.
HORATIO *and* MARCELLUS My lord, we will not.
HAMLET Nay, but swear't.
HORATIO   In faith, my lord, not I.[1]
MARCELLUS Nor I, my lord, in faith.
HAMLET   Upon my sword.[2]
150 MARCELLUS We have sworn, my lord, already.
HAMLET Indeed, upon my sword, indeed.
GHOST (*cries under the stage*) Swear.
HAMLET Ha, ha, boy, say'st thou so? Art thou there,
    truepenny?°   *trusty fellow*
    Come on, you hear this fellow in the cellarage.°   *cellars*
    Consent to swear.
155 HORATIO   Propose the oath, my lord.
HAMLET Never to speak of this that you have seen:
    Swear by my sword.

---

8. Hamlet parodies a falconer's call.
9. Perhaps because St. Patrick was thought to be keeper
of purgatory.

1. I will indeed not reveal it.
2. Swearing on a sword was a fairly common practice
because the hilt and blade form a cross.

[*under the stage*]   Swear.

T   *Hic et ubique?*[3] Then we'll shift our ground.

e hither, gentlemen, and lay your hands

Again upon my sword. Swear by my sword

Never to speak of this that you have heard.

GHOST [*under the stage*]   Swear by his sword.

HAMLET   Well said, old mole: canst work i'th' earth so fast?

165   A worthy pioneer![4] —Once more remove,° good friends.   *move*

HORATIO   O day and night, but this is wondrous strange.

HAMLET   And therefore as a stranger give it welcome.[5]

There are more things in heaven and earth, Horatio,

Than are dreamt of in your philosophy.[6] But come,

170   Here, as before, never, so help you mercy,

How strange or odd some'er° I bear myself—   *so ever*

As I perchance hereafter shall think meet

To put an antic disposition on[7]—

That you at such times seeing me, never shall

175   With arms encumbered° thus, or this head-shake,   *folded*

Or by pronouncing of some doubtful° phrase,   *ambiguous*

As "Well, well, we know," or "We could an if° we would,"   *an if = if*

Or "If we list° to speak," or "There be an if they might,"[8]   *liked*

Or such ambiguous giving out, to note

180   That you know aught° of me[9]   *anything*

180.1   —*This not to do,*

So grace and mercy at your most need help you,

181.1   *Swear.*

GHOST [*under the stage*]   Swear.

          [*They swear.*]

HAMLET   Rest, rest, perturbèd spirit. —So, gentlemen,

With all my love I do commend me to you,

185   And what so poor a man as Hamlet is

May do t'express his love and friending° to you,   *friendship*

God willing shall not lack.° Let us go in together—   *be left undone*

And still° your fingers on your lips, I pray.   *always*

The time is out of joint:° oh, cursèd spite   *dislocated; disordered*

190   That ever I was born to set it right.

Nay, come,[1] let's go together.   *Exeunt.*

2.1

Enter old POLONIUS, *with his man* [REYNALDO] *or two.*

POLONIUS   Give him this money and these notes, Reynaldo.

REYNALDO   I will, my lord.

POLONIUS   You shall do marv'lous wisely, good Reynaldo,

Before you visit him, to make inquire

Of his behavior.

5   REYNALDO   My lord, I did intend it.

POLONIUS   Marry, well said, very well said. Look you, sir:

Inquire me° first what Danskers° are in Paris,   *for me / Danes*

---

3. Here and everywhere (Latin).
4. Army trench digger.
5. As if it had a guest's right to courteous hospitality.
6. Human speculative knowledge; science. F prints "our philosophy."
7. To assume the behavior of a madman.
8. There are those who would speak if they were

allowed.
9. Lines 180.1 and 181.1 are found only in F. Q2 reads: "This do swear, / So grace and mercy . . . ."
1. The others are politely waiting for Hamlet, the Prince, to lead the way; he insists on informality.
2.1 Location: Polonius's apartments in the castle.

And how, and who, what means,° and where they keep,°   *wealth; inc[*
What company, at what expense, and finding
10   By this encompassment and drift of question[1]
That they do know my son, come you more nearer
Than your particular demands will touch it.[2]
Take you° as 'twere some distant knowledge of him,   *Pretend*
As thus, "I know his father and his friends
15   And in part him." Do you mark this, Reynaldo?
REYNALDO   Ay, very well, my lord.
POLONIUS   "And in part him, but," you may say, "not well;
But if't be he I mean, he's very wild,
Addicted so and so," and there put on him°   *attribute to him*
20   What forgeries° you please—marry, none so rank[3]   *made-up tales*
As may dishonor him, take heed of that—
But, sir, such wanton,° wild, and usual slips   *unrestrained*
As are companions noted and most known
To youth and liberty.
REYNALDO   As gaming, my lord?
25   POLONIUS   Ay, or drinking, fencing, swearing,
Quarreling, drabbing°—you may go so far.   *whoring*
REYNALDO   My lord, that would dishonor him.
POLONIUS   Faith, as you may season° it in the charge.   *mitigate*
You must not put another scandal on him
30   That he is open° to incontinency;°   *inclined / sexual excess*
That's not my meaning. But breathe his faults so quaintly
That they may seem the taints of liberty,[4]
The flash and outbreak of a fiery mind,
A savageness in unreclaimèd° blood   *unchecked*
Of general assault.[5]
35   REYNALDO   But my good lord—
POLONIUS   Wherefore should you do this?
REYNALDO   Ay, my lord,
I would know that.
POLONIUS   Marry, sir, here's my drift—
And I believe it is a fetch of wit[6]—
You laying these slight sallies on my son,
40   As 'twere a thing a little soiled with working,[7]
Mark you, your party° in converse, him you would sound,°   *partner / sound out*
Having° ever seen in the prenominate crimes[8]   *If he has*
The youth you breathe of guilty, be assured
He closes° with you in this consequence:[9]   *confides*
45   "Good sir," or so, or "Friend," or "Gentleman,"
According to the phrase° or the addition[1]   *expression*
Of man and country—
REYNALDO   Very good, my lord.
POLONIUS   And then, sir, does 'a° this: 'a does—   *he*
What was I about to say? By the mass, I was about to say

1. By this roundabout and indirect way of inquiry.
2. *come . . . it:* you will come closer to the truth than
by direct questions.
3. Excessive; foul.
4. Faults resulting from freedom of action.
5. That afflicts all young men.
6. *fetch of wit:* clever scheme. F has "fetch of war-

rant," or justifiable trick.
7. Stained by education in the ways of the world,
"shop soiled."
8. Aforesaid faults.
9. To the following effect.
1. Title of address.

50 something—where did I leave?[2]

REYNALDO At "closes in the consequence."

POLONIUS At "closes in the consequence"—ay, marry.
    He closes thus: "I know the gentleman,
    I saw him yesterday"—or "th'other day,"
55 Or then, or then, with such or such°—"and as you say,   *such and such*
    There was 'a gaming, there o'ertook in 's rouse,
    There falling out° at tennis," or perchance   *quarreling*
    "I saw him enter such a house of sale,"
    Videlicet,° a brothel, or so forth. See you now,   *That is to say (Latin)*
60 Your bait of falsehood take this carp of truth,
    And thus do we of wisdom and of reach°   *wide understanding*
    With windlasses and with assays of bias[3]
    By indirections find directions° out.   *real tendencies*
    So by my former° lecture and advice   *preceding*
65 Shall you my son.[4] You have me,[5] have you not?

REYNALDO My lord, I have.

POLONIUS   God b'wi'ye, fare ye well.

REYNALDO Good my lord.

POLONIUS Observe his inclination in° yourself.   *for*

REYNALDO I shall, my lord.

POLONIUS   And let him ply° his music.   *work at*

70 REYNALDO Well, my lord.

POLONIUS Farewell.   *Exit* REYNALDO.
      Enter OPHELIA.
              How now, Ophelia, what's the matter?

OPHELIA O my lord, my lord, I have been so affrighted!

POLONIUS With what, i'th' name of God?

OPHELIA My lord, as I was sewing in my closet,°   *private chamber*
75 Lord Hamlet, with his doublet all unbraced,°   *jacket all unfastened*
    No hat upon his head, his stockings fouled,
    Ungartered, and down-gyvèd to his ankle,[6]
    Pale as his shirt, his knees knocking each other,
    And with a look so piteous in purport
80 As if he had been loosèd out of hell
    To speak of horrors, he comes before me.

POLONIUS Mad for thy love?

OPHELIA   My lord, I do not know,
    But truly I do fear it.

POLONIUS   What said he?

OPHELIA He took me by the wrist and held me hard,
85 Then goes he to the length of all his arm
    And with his other hand thus o'er his brow,
    He falls to such perusal of my face
    As 'a° would draw it. Long stayed he so;   *As if he*
    At last, a little shaking of mine arm
90 And thrice his head thus waving up and down,
    He raised a sigh so piteous and profound
    As it did seem to shatter all his bulk

---

2. PERFORMANCE COMMENT Productions can indicate quite different reasons for Polonius's forgetfulness, affecting the reception of the character and, sometimes, the stability of the dramatic experience. See Digital Edition PC 3.
3. And with indirect tests, like the curved line, or "bias," that a weighted bowling ball describes. *wind-*lasses: roundabout paths (a hunter's circuit to intercept game).
4. And so shall you figure out what my son has been doing.
5. You get my meaning.
6. Fallen round his ankles, like a prisoner's fetters, or "gyves."

And end his being. That done, he lets me go,
And with his head over his shoulder turned
95 He seemed to find his way without his eyes,
For out o'doors he went without their helps,
And to the last bended their light[7] on me.
POLONIUS Come, go with me; I will go seek the King.
This is the very ecstasy° of love,   *insanity*
100 Whose violent property fordoes° itself   *nature destroys*
And leads the will to desperate undertakings
As oft as any passions under heaven
That does afflict our natures. I am sorry—
What, have you given him any hard words of late?
105 OPHELIA No, my good lord, but as you did command
I did repel his letters and denied
His access to me.
POLONIUS   That hath made him mad.
I am sorry that with better heed and judgment
I had not quoted° him. I feared he did but trifle   *observed*
110 And meant to wrack thee.[8] But beshrew my jealousy!°   *curse my suspicion*
By heaven it is as proper to our age
To cast beyond ourselves in our opinions,
As it is common for the younger sort
To lack discretion. Come, go we to the King.
115 This must be known which, being kept close, might move
More grief to hide than hate to utter love.[9]
Come.   *Exeunt.*

2.2

Flourish. Enter KING *and* QUEEN, ROSENCRANTZ *and*
GUILDENSTERN[1] [*with Attendants*].
KING Welcome, dear Rosencrantz and Guildenstern.
Moreover° that we much did long to see you,   *Beyond the fact*
The need we have to use you did provoke
Our hasty sending.° Something have you heard   *summons*
5 Of Hamlet's transformation—so call it,
Sith° nor th'exterior nor the inward man   *Since*
Resembles that° it was. What it should be,   *what*
More than his father's death, that thus hath put him
So much from th'understanding of himself
10 I cannot dream of. I entreat you both
That, being of so young days[2] brought up with him,
And sith so neighbored° to his youth and 'havior,   *familiar*
That you vouchsafe your rest[3] here in our court
Some little time, so by your companies
15 To draw him on to pleasures and to gather
So much as from occasion° you may glean   *opportunity*
Whether aught to us unknown afflicts him thus,
That, opened,° lies within our remedy.   *if disclosed*

---

7. Sight was thought to result from both sending light out and taking it in through the eyes.
8. To ruin you through seduction.
9. *which . . . love:* we may incur hatred by revealing (Hamlet's) love, but to conceal it may cause greater suffering. *close:* secret.
2.2 Location: A stateroom in the castle.

1. Shakespeare may have thought of these names as characteristically Danish. For example, an English ambassador dispatched to Elsinore in 1588 sent back a list of Danish statesmen that included one "Rosenkrantz" and two men named "Guldenstern."
2. From such an early age.
3. That you agree to stay.

QUEEN   Good gentlemen, he hath much talked of you,
20   And sure I am two men there is not living
      To whom he more adheres.[4] If it will please you
      To show us so much gentry° and goodwill   *courtesy*
      As to expend your time with us awhile
      For the supply and profit of our hope,[5]
25   Your visitation shall receive such thanks
      As fits a king's remembrance.
ROSENCRANTZ   Both your majesties
      Might by the sovereign power you have of° us   *over*
      Put your dread° pleasures more into command   *reverend*
      Than to entreaty.
GUILDENSTERN   But we both obey,
30   And here give up ourselves in the full bent[6]
      To lay our service freely at your feet
      To be commanded.
KING   Thanks, Rosencrantz and gentle Guildenstern.
QUEEN   Thanks, Guildenstern and gentle Rosencrantz.
35   And I beseech you instantly to visit
      My too-much-changèd son. —Go, some of you,
      And bring these gentlemen where Hamlet is.
GUILDENSTERN   Heavens make our presence and our
        practices
      Pleasant and helpful to him.
QUEEN   Ay, amen.

              Exeunt ROSENCRANTZ *and* GUILDENSTERN
               [*with some Attendants*].
      Enter POLONIUS.
40 POLONIUS   Th'ambassadors from Norway, my good lord,
      Are joyfully returned.
KING   Thou still° hast been the father of good news.   *always*
POLONIUS   Have I, my lord? I assure my good liege
      I hold my duty as I hold my soul
45   Both to my God and to my gracious king.
      And I do think, or else this brain of mine
      Hunts not the trail of policy° so sure   *cleverness*
      As it hath used to do, that I have found
      The very cause of Hamlet's lunacy.
50 KING   Oh, speak of that, that do I long to hear!
POLONIUS   Give first admittance to th'ambassadors;
      My news shall be the fruit° to that great feast.   *dessert*
KING   Thyself do grace to them and bring them in.
                    [*Exit* POLONIUS.]
      He tells me, my dear Gertrude, he hath found
55   The head° and source of all your son's distemper. *origin; chief part*
QUEEN   I doubt[7] it is no other but the main,°   *main matter*
      His father's death and our hasty marriage.
KING   Well, we shall sift him.°   *interrogate (Polonius)*

      Enter [POLONIUS, *with the*] *Ambassadors* [VOLTEMAND
      and CORNELIUS].
                Welcome, my good friends.

---

4. To whom he is more attached.
5. *For . . . hope:* To provide support for and further-
ance of our hope.

6. To the fullest extent (like an archer's bow, fully
drawn).
7. Fear, suspect. *distemper:* unbalanced mind.

Say, Voltemand, what from our brother° Norway?   *fellow monarch*
60   VOLTEMAND   Most fair return of greetings and desires.°   *good wishes*
     Upon our first,[8] he sent out to suppress
     His nephew's levies,° which to him appeared   *raising of troops*
     To be a preparation 'gainst the Polack,°   *King of Poland*
     But, better looked into, he truly found
65   It was against your highness; whereat, grieved
     That so his sickness, age, and impotence
     Was falsely borne in hand,[9] sends out arrests
     On Fortinbras,[1] which he in brief obeys,
     Receives rebuke from Norway, and, in fine,°   *in the end*
70   Makes vow before his uncle never more
     To give th'assay of arms[2] against your majesty.
     Whereon old Norway, overcome with joy,
     Gives him threescore thousand crowns in annual fee°   *income*
     And his commission to employ those soldiers,
75   So levied as before, against the Polack,
     With an entreaty herein further shown
     That it might please you to give quiet pass
     Through your dominions for this enterprise
     On such regards of safety and allowance[3]
     As therein are set down.
80   KING   It likes° us well,   *pleases*
     And at our more considered° time we'll read,   *suitable for thought*
     Answer, and think upon this business.
     Meantime, we thank you for your well-took labor.
     Go to your rest; at night we'll feast together.
     Most welcome home.
          Exeunt Ambassadors [VOLTEMAND *and* CORNELIUS].
85   POLONIUS   This business is well ended.
     My liege and madam, to expostulate°   *discuss; dilate*
     What majesty should be, what duty is,
     Why day is day, night night, and time is time,
     Were nothing but to waste night, day, and time;
90   Therefore brevity is the soul of wit
     And tediousness the limbs and outward flourishes.°   *rhetorical devices*
     I will be brief. Your noble son is mad—
     Mad call I it, for to define true madness,
     What is't but to be nothing else but mad?
     But let that go.
95   QUEEN   More matter with less art.
  POLONIUS   Madam, I swear I use no art at all.
     That he's mad 'tis true; 'tis true, 'tis pity,
     And pity 'tis 'tis true—a foolish figure,°   *figure of speech*
     But farewell it, for I will use no art.
100   Mad let us grant him, then, and now remains
     That we find out the cause of this effect—
     Or rather say the cause of this defect,
     For this effect defective[4] comes by cause.

8. When we first raised the matter.
9. Disloyally taken advantage of; tricked.
1. *arrests / On Fortinbras:* orders commanding Fortinbras to stop his preparations and (presumably) present himself to explain them.

2. To mount a military challenge.
3. *On . . . allowance:* Following conditions regarding your realm's safety, subject to your approval.
4. This consequence shows a lack of something (Hamlet's reason).

Thus it remains, and the remainder thus:

Perpend.°   *Consider*

I have a daughter—have while she is mine°—   *until she marries*

Who in her duty and obedience, mark,

Hath given me this. Now gather and surmise:

[*Reads.*] "To the celestial and my soul's idol, the most beauti-

110 fied Ophelia"—that's an ill phrase, a vile phrase—"beautified"

is a vile phrase. But you shall hear—thus: "in her excellent

white bosom, these—" etc.

QUEEN   Came this from Hamlet to her?

POLONIUS   Good madam, stay° awhile; I will be faithful.[5]   *wait*

115 [*Reads.*] "Doubt thou the stars are fire,

    Doubt that the sun doth move,

    Doubt° truth to be a liar,   *Suspect*

    But never doubt I love.

O dear Ophelia, I am ill at these numbers.[6] I have not art to

120 reckon my groans,[7] but that I love thee best—oh, most best—

believe it. Adieu. Thine evermore, most dear lady, whilst this

machine is° to him, Hamlet."   *this body belongs*

This in obedience hath my daughter shown me,

And, more above,° hath his solicitings   *in addition*

125 As they fell out° by time, by means, and place,   *occurred*

All given to mine ear.

KING   But how hath she

Received his love?

POLONIUS   What do you think of me?

KING   As of a man faithful and honorable.

POLONIUS   I would fain° prove so. But what might you think,   *be glad to*

130 When I had seen this hot love on the wing—

As I perceived it (I must tell you that)

Before my daughter told me—what might you

Or my dear majesty, your queen here, think,

If I had played the desk or table-book,[8]

135 Or given my heart a working mute and dumb,[9]

Or looked upon this love with idle sight—

What might you think? No, I went round° to work,   *directly*

And my young mistress thus I did bespeak:°   *address*

"Lord Hamlet is a prince out of thy star.°   *above your sphere*

140 This must not be." And then I prescripts° gave her   *instructions*

That she should lock herself from his resort,°   *visits*

Admit no messengers, receive no tokens.

Which done, she took the fruits of my advice

And he, repelled—a short tale to make—

145 Fell into a sadness, then into a fast,

Thence to a watch,° thence into a weakness,   *an insomnia*

Thence to lightness,° and by this declension°   *dizziness / decline*

Into the madness wherein now he raves

And all we° mourn for.   *of us*

KING   Do you think this?

150 QUEEN   It may be, very like.

---

5. I will accurately read out the letter's contents.
6. I.e., I am inept at writing verse.
7. Count my groans; also, number my groans metrically.

8. If I had recorded the perception (in my memory) but kept it hidden.
9. Or made my heart effectively silent.

POLONIUS   Hath there been such a time—I would fain know
    that—
  That I have positively said, "'Tis so"
  When it proved otherwise?
KING   Not that I know.
POLONIUS [*indicating his head and torso*]   Take this from this,
    if this be otherwise.
155 If circumstances lead me, I will find
  Where truth is hid, though it were hid indeed
  Within the center.°   *middle of the earth*
KING   How may we try° it further?   *test*
POLONIUS   You know sometimes he walks four hours together
  Here in the lobby.
QUEEN   So he does indeed.
160 POLONIUS   At such a time, I'll loose my daughter to him.
  Be you and I behind an arras;° then   *a wall tapestry*
  Mark the encounter—if he love her not
  And be not from his reason fallen thereon,°   *on that account*
  Let me be no assistant for a state
  But keep a farm and carters.°   *wagon drivers*
165 KING   We will try it.
        Enter HAMLET.
QUEEN   But look where sadly° the poor wretch comes   *gravely*
  reading.
POLONIUS   Away, I do beseech you both, away.
  I'll board him presently;° oh, give me leave.[1]   *accost him immediately*
        Exeunt KING *and* QUEEN [*and Attendants*].
  How does my good lord Hamlet?
170 HAMLET   Well, God ha' mercy.[2]
POLONIUS   Do you know me, my lord?
HAMLET   Excellent well—you are a fishmonger.
POLONIUS   Not I, my lord.
HAMLET   Then I would you were so honest a man.
175 POLONIUS   Honest, my lord?
HAMLET   Ay, sir, to be honest as this world goes is to be one
  man picked out of ten thousand.
POLONIUS   That's very true, my lord.
HAMLET   For if the sun breed maggots in a dead dog, being a
180 good kissing carrion[3]—have you a daughter?
POLONIUS   I have, my lord.
HAMLET   Let her not walk i'th' sun.[4] Conception[5] is a blessing,
  but as your daughter may conceive, friend—look to't.°   *take care*
POLONIUS [*aside*]   How say you by that? Still harping on my
185 daughter. Yet he knew me not at first: 'a° said I was a fishmon-   *he*
  ger. 'A is far gone—and truly in my youth I suffered much
  extremity for love, very near this. I'll speak to him again.
  —What do you read, my lord?
HAMLET   Words, words, words.
190 POLONIUS   What is the matter,[6] my lord?
HAMLET   Between who?

1. Excuse me (politely asking the King and Queen to leave).
2. Thank you (used with inferiors).
3. Piece of flesh good for kissing. Dead matter was thought to breed maggots, especially in sunlight.
4. Walk out in public.
5. The ability to form ideas; pregnancy.
6. Content, although Hamlet deliberately takes it as "subject of a quarrel."

POLONIUS   I mean the matter that you read, my lord.

HAMLET   Slanders, sir, for the satirical rogue says here that
old men have gray beards, that their faces are wrinkled, their
195   eyes purging° thick amber° and plumtree gum, and that they   *discharging / resin*
have a plentiful lack of wit° together with most weak hams.°   *intellect / thighs*
All which, sir, though I most powerfully and potently believe,[7]
yet I hold it not honesty° to have it thus set down. For your-   *honorable*
self, sir, shall grow old as I am, if like a crab you could go
200   backward.

POLONIUS   [*aside*]   Though this be madness, yet there is
method in't. —Will you walk out of the air,[8] my lord?

HAMLET   Into my grave.

POLONIUS   Indeed, that's out of the air. [*aside*] How pregnant°   *meaningful*
205   sometimes his replies are—a happiness° that often madness   *an appropriateness*
hits on, which reason and sanctity[9] could not so prosperously°   *successfully*
be delivered of. I will leave him and[1]
207.1   *suddenly*° *contrive the means of meeting between him*   *immediately*
and
my daughter. —My lord, I will take my leave of you.

HAMLET   You cannot take from me anything that I will not
210   more willingly part withal°—except my life, except my life,   *with*
except my life.

POLONIUS   Fare you well, my lord.

HAMLET   These tedious old fools.

Enter GUILDENSTERN *and* ROSENCRANTZ.

POLONIUS   You go to seek the Lord Hamlet? There he is.

215 ROSENCRANTZ   [*to* POLONIUS]   God save you, sir.

[*Exit* POLONIUS.]

GUILDENSTERN   My honored lord.

ROSENCRANTZ   My most dear lord.

HAMLET   My excellent good friends! How dost thou, Guildenstern? Ah, Rosencrantz! Good lads, how do you both?

220 ROSENCRANTZ   As the indifferent° children of the earth.   *ordinary*

GUILDENSTERN   Happy° in that we are not ever° happy—   *Fortunate / perpetually*
on Fortune's cap we are not the very button.°   *highest point*

HAMLET   Nor the soles of her shoe.

ROSENCRANTZ   Neither, my lord.

225 HAMLET   Then you live about her waist or in the middle of her
favors.

GUILDENSTERN   Faith, her privates[2] we.

HAMLET   In the secret parts of Fortune? Oh, most true, she is
a strumpet.° What news?   *whore*

230 ROSENCRANTZ   None, my lord, but the world's grown honest.

HAMLET   Then is doomsday near—but your news is not true.[3]

231.1   *Let me question more in particular: what have you, my*
good friends, deserved at the hands of Fortune that she
sends you to prison hither?

GUILDENSTERN   *Prison, my lord?*

231.5   HAMLET   *Denmark's a prison.*

---

7. TEXTUAL COMMENT Q1 7.216 reads "believe not,"
which covers the sarcasm with superficial politeness.
See Digital Edition TC 3 (combined text).
8. Outdoor air was regarded as a hazard for the sick;
Polonius may mean "out of the drafts," since the
scene seems to be set indoors.
9. *sanctity*: virtue. F has "sanity."
1. F has the following lines, 207.1–207.2, not found

in Q2.
2. A triple pun: private persons holding no office;
intimate friends; private parts, genitalia.
3. TEXTUAL COMMENT The following passage (231.1–
231.30) occurs only in F. Its denigration of Denmark
leads some to believe that it is a missed cut rather than
an addition. See Digital Edition TC 4 (combined text).

ROSENCRANTZ *Then is the world one.*

HAMLET *A goodly[4] one, in which there are many confines,°*
wards,° and dungeons, Denmark being one o'th' worst.   enclosures / cells

ROSENCRANTZ *We think not so, my lord.*

231.10 HAMLET *Why, then 'tis none to you, for there is nothing*
either good or bad but thinking makes it so. To me it is a
prison.

ROSENCRANTZ *Why, then your ambition makes it one—*
'tis too narrow for your mind.

231.15 HAMLET *O God, I could be bounded in a nutshell and*
count myself a king of infinite space, were it not that I
have bad dreams.

GUILDENSTERN *Which dreams indeed are ambition: for*
the very substance of the ambitious is merely the shadow
231.20 *of a dream.*

HAMLET *A dream itself is but a shadow.*

ROSENCRANTZ *Truly, and I hold ambition of so airy and*
light a quality that it is but a shadow's shadow.

HAMLET *Then are our beggars bodies, and our monarchs*
231.25 *and outstretched heroes the beggars' shadows.[5] Shall*
we to th' court? For, by my fay,° I cannot reason.   faith

ROSENCRANTZ *and* GUILDENSTERN *We'll wait upon° you.*   accompany

HAMLET *No such matter.° I will not sort° you with the*   Certainly not / class
rest of my servants, for, to speak to you like an honest
231.30 *man, I am most dreadfully attended.°*   waited upon

But in the beaten way[6] of friendship, what make you° at   are you doing
Elsinore?

ROSENCRANTZ To visit you, my lord, no other occasion.

235 HAMLET Beggar that I am, I am ever poor in thanks, but I
thank you, and sure, dear friends, my thanks are too dear a
halfpenny.[7] Were you not sent for? Is it your own inclining?
Is it a free° visitation? Come, come, deal justly with me.   voluntary
Come, come, nay, speak.

240 GUILDENSTERN What should we say, my lord?

HAMLET Anything, but to th' purpose: you were sent for, and
there is a kind of confession in your looks which your mod-
esties[8] have not craft enough to color.° I know the good King   disguise
and Queen have sent for you.

245 ROSENCRANTZ To what end, my lord?

HAMLET That you must teach me. But let me conjure° you, by   solemnly request
the rights of our fellowship, by the consonancy° of our youth,   harmonious friendship
by the obligation of our ever-preserved love, and by what more
dear a better proposer can charge you withal, be even° and   level
250 direct with me whether you were sent for or no.

ROSENCRANTZ [*to* GUILDENSTERN] What say you?

HAMLET [*aside*] Nay, then, I have an eye of° you. —If you love   on
me, hold not off.

GUILDENSTERN My lord, we were sent for.

255 HAMLET I will tell you why—so shall my anticipation pre-

---

4. Spacious; fine.
5. *Then . . . shadows:* Then beggars, being without ambition, are not shadows but have substance; if monarchs and heroes (who ambitiously "stretch" too far) are shadows and only substantial bodies can cast shadows, they must be the beggars' shadows.

6. Well-worn track (plain words).
7. Too expensive at a halfpenny (not worth a half-penny); perhaps also, too expensive by a halfpenny for me to give in return for such worthless information.
8. Senses of decency.

vent° your discovery and your secrecy to the King and   *forestall*
Queen molt no feather.[9] I have of late, but wherefore I
know not, lost all my mirth, forgone all custom of exercises,
and indeed it goes so heavily with my disposition[1] that this
260   goodly frame,° the earth, seems to me a sterile promontory;   *structure*
this most excellent canopy, the air, look you, this brave
o'erhanging firmament,[2] this majestical roof fretted° with   *adorned*
golden fire—why, it appeareth nothing to me but a foul and
pestilent congregation° of vapors. What piece of work is a   *mass*
265   man—how noble in reason, how infinite in faculties,° in form   *natural powers*
and moving how express[3] and admirable, in action how like
an angel, in apprehension how like a god, the beauty of the
world, the paragon of animals—and yet to me what is this
quintessence of dust?[4] Man delights not me—nor women
270   neither, though by your smiling you seem to say so.

ROSENCRANTZ   My lord, there was no such stuff in my thoughts.

HAMLET   Why did ye laugh, then, when I said man delights
not me?

ROSENCRANTZ   To think, my lord, if you delight not in man,
275   what lenten entertainment[5] the players shall receive from
you. We coted° them on the way, and hither are they coming   *passed*
to offer you service.

HAMLET   He that plays the King shall be welcome—his majesty shall have tribute on me. The adventurous Knight shall
280   use his foil° and target,° the lover shall not sigh gratis,° the   *sword / shield / for free*
Humorous Man shall end his part in peace,[6]
281.1   *the Clown shall make those laugh whose lungs are tick-*
led o'th' sear,[7]
and the Lady shall say her mind freely or the blank verse
shall halt for't.[8] What players are they?

ROSENCRANTZ   Even those you were wont to take such delight
285   in, the tragedians° of the city.   *actors*

HAMLET   How chances it they travel? Their residence° both in   *(in the city)*
reputation and profit was better both ways.

ROSENCRANTZ   I think their inhibition comes by the means of
the late innovation.[9]

290   HAMLET   Do they hold the same estimation° they did when I   *esteem*
was in the city? Are they so followed?

ROSENCRANTZ   No, indeed are they not.[1]

292.1   HAMLET   *How comes it? Do they grow rusty?*

9. Remain unimpaired. To pull the feathers off a
reputation meant to detract from it.
1. *it goes . . . disposition:* I am so heavy with melancholy.
2. This splendid heavens overhead. The image may
refer to the "heavens," the roof overhanging the Elizabethan stage, which was decorated with stars.
3. Precise; expressive.
4. It was thought that the heavenly bodies were composed of a fifth element ("quintessence"), superior to
the other four (earth, air, fire, and water) and also the
purest distillation of earthly objects. Hamlet thinks
of humanity as dust at its dustiest.
5. Welcome. Lent was a period of penitence and fasting (when London theaters were closed).
6. *the Humorous . . . peace:* the eccentric (governed by
excess of one humor, or mood-influencing bodily fluid)
should be allowed to rant on without disturbance. F

has the following line, 281.1–281.2, not found in Q2.
7. Whose lungs are primed to laugh. (The "sear" is
the part of a gun holding back the hammer until the
trigger releases it.)
8. *and the Lady . . . for't:* if the Lady is not allowed to
speak all her part, the poetry will "halt," or limp (fail
to scan).
9. Comes from recent fashion (probably the rage for
companies of boy actors). An "inhibition" could be
either a hindrance or an official prohibition. (Elizabethan theaters were commonly closed at signs of
political instability.)
1. TEXTUAL COMMENT With the exception of six lines
that appear in Q1, the following passage (292.1–292.26)
occurs only in F. These lines on the "War of the Theaters" seem to be a purposeful addition tacked on for
a performance after the original play had already been
written. See Digital Edition TC 4 (combined text).

ROSENCRANTZ   *Nay, their endeavor keeps° in the wonted°*   continues / accustomed
pace; but there is, sir, an eyrie of children, little eyases,[2]
that cry out on the top of question[3] and are most tyran-
292.5   *nically° clapped for't. These are now the fashion and so*   outrageously
berattled° the common stages[4]—so they call them—that   noisily abused
many wearing rapiers are afraid of goose-quills[5] and dare
scarce come thither.

HAMLET   *What, are they children? Who maintains 'em?*
292.10   *How are they escoted?° Will they pursue the quality° no*   provided for / profession
longer than they can sing?[6] Will they not say afterwards,
if they should grow themselves to common players—as it
is most like° if their means° are not better—their writers   likely / financial options
do them wrong to make them exclaim against their own
292.15   *succession?°*   later employment

ROSENCRANTZ   *Faith, there has been much to-do on both*
sides, and the nation° holds it no sin to tar° them to   populace / goad
controversy. There was for awhile no money bid for
argument unless the poet and the player went to cuffs in
292.20   *the question.[7]*

HAMLET   *Is't possible?*

GUILDENSTERN   *Oh, there has been much throwing about*
of brains.[8]

HAMLET   *Do the boys carry it° away?*   (the victory)
292.25   ROSENCRANTZ   *Ay, that they do, my lord, Hercules and his*
load too.[9]

HAMLET   It is not very strange, for my uncle is King of Denmark, and those that would make mouths° at him while my   grimaces
295   father lived give twenty, forty, fifty, a hundred ducats apiece
for his picture in little.° 'Sblood,[1] there is something in this   miniature
more than natural if philosophy could find it out.
A flourish.[2]

GUILDENSTERN   There are the players.

HAMLET   Gentlemen, you are welcome to Elsinore. Your hands,
300   come then: th'appurtenance° of welcome is fashion and cere-   fitting accompaniment
mony; let me comply with you in this garb,[3] lest my extent° to   offering (of welcome)
the players, which I tell you must show fairly° outwards,   courteously
should more appear like entertainment° than yours. You are   (warm) welcome
welcome, but my uncle-father and aunt-mother are deceived.
305   GUILDENSTERN   In what, my dear lord?

HAMLET   I am but mad north-northwest;[4] when the wind is
southerly, I know a hawk from a handsaw.[5]
Enter POLONIUS.

POLONIUS   Well be with you, gentlemen.

HAMLET   Hark you, Guildenstern, and you too—at each ear a

2. Young hawks. A company of boy actors flourished at the private Blackfriars Theater, leased from the Burbages, from 1600 to 1608. *eyrie:* nest for a bird of prey.
3. That yell over their critics' voices.
4. Public theaters (such as the Globe).
5. That gentlemen are afraid of the poet's satirical pen.
6. Only until their voices break.
7. *no money . . . question:* nothing offered for the plot (or draft) of a play unless it added to the dispute between the children's dramatists and the public theater companies. *went to cuffs:* came to blows.
8. A great battle of wits.
9. In the course of one of his labors, Hercules held up the world on his shoulders while Atlas (its usual support) ran an errand; Hercules bearing the world was the sign of the Globe.
1. By God's blood.
2. Trumpet flourishes often heralded dramatic performances.
3. Let me follow accepted forms in this recognized manner (by shaking hands).
4. The smallest compass point away from true north, and thus not far from sane; or possibly, only mad on occasions when the wind blows from the north-northwest.
5. A small saw, and possibly a variant of "heronshaw" (heron).

310   hearer. That great baby you see there is not yet out of his
    swaddling clouts.°   *clothes*

ROSENCRANTZ   Happily° he is the second time come to them,   *Perhaps*
    for they say an old man is twice a child.

HAMLET   I will prophesy he comes to tell me of the players;
315   mark it. —You say right, sir, o'Monday morning, 'twas then
    indeed.

POLONIUS   My lord, I have news to tell you.

HAMLET   My lord, I have news to tell you: when Roscius[6] was
    an actor in Rome—

320 POLONIUS   The actors are come hither, my lord.

HAMLET   Buzz, buzz.[7]

POLONIUS   Upon my honor—

HAMLET   Then came each actor on his ass—

POLONIUS   The best actors in the world, either for tragedy, com-
325   edy, history, pastoral, pastoral-comical, historical-pastoral,[8]
325.1   *tragical-historical, tragical-comical-historical-pastoral,*
    scene individable[9] or poem unlimited.[1] Seneca cannot be
    too heavy, nor Plautus too light.[2] For the law of writ and the
    liberty,[3] these are the only men.

HAMLET   O Jephthah, judge of Israel, what a treasure hadst
330   thou![4]

POLONIUS   What a treasure had he, my lord?

HAMLET   Why,
[*Sings.*]   One fair daughter and no more,
           The which he lovèd passing° well.   *surpassingly*
335 POLONIUS [*aside*]   Still on my daughter.

HAMLET   Am I not i'th' right, old Jephthah?

POLONIUS   If you call me Jephthah, my lord, I have a daughter
    that I love passing well.

HAMLET   Nay, that follows not.[5]

340 POLONIUS   What follows then, my lord?

HAMLET   Why,
        As by lot,° God wot.°   *chance / knows*
  And then you know
        It came to pass, as most like° it was—   *probable*
345 The first row° of the pious chanson° will show you more, for   *stanza / ballad*
    look where my abridgment[6] comes.
        Enter the PLAYERS.
    You are welcome, masters, welcome all. I am glad to see thee
    well. Welcome, good friends; O old friend, why, thy face is
    valanced[7] since I saw thee last. Com'st thou to beard° me in   *defy*
350 Denmark? What, my young lady and mistress![8] By'r Lady,
    your ladyship is nearer to heaven than when I saw you last by

---

6. The most famous ancient Roman actor, a rather dated news item.
7. A response to stale news.
8. F has the following line, 325.1, not found in Q2.
9. Probably, play with no breaks in performance, or play observing the unity of place (and presumably the other classical unities). Shakespeare parodies the classifications of contemporary dramatic theorists.
1. (Dramatic) poem unrestricted by classical rules.
2. The best-known Roman playwrights, masters of tragedy and comedy, respectively.
3. For plays where classical rules are either observed

or abandoned.
4. Jephthah vowed that if he defeated the Ammonites, he would sacrifice the first living thing he saw on his return. He won, and his daughter became the sacrificial victim (Judges 11). *Jephthah, Judge of Israel* was the title of a popular ballad, the "pious chanson" from which Hamlet subsequently sings.
5. Polonius's having a daughter is not a logical consequence of Hamlet's calling him Jephthah.
6. Those who cut me short; also, entertainment.
7. Fringed (with beard).
8. The boy who played female roles.

the altitude of a chopine;° pray God your voice, like a piece of   *high platform shoe*
uncurrent gold, be not cracked within the ring.[9] Masters,
you are all welcome. We'll e'en to't like French falconers,[1] fly
355   at anything we see. We'll have a speech straight°—come, give   *right away*
us a taste of your quality.° Come, a passionate speech.   *professional skill*

FIRST PLAYER   What speech, my good lord?

HAMLET   I heard thee speak me a speech once, but it was
never acted, or if it was, not above once, for the play I
360   remember pleased not the million—'twas caviar to the general;° but it was, as I received it, and others whose judgments   *populace*
in such matters cried in the top of[2] mine, an excellent play,
well digested° in the scenes, set down with as much mod-   *organized*
esty° as cunning. I remember one said there were no salads[3]   *restraint*
365   in the lines to make the matter savory, nor no matter in the
phrase that might indict the author of affection,° but called it   *affectedness*
an honest method, as wholesome as sweet, and by very much
more handsome than fine.[4] One speech in't I chiefly loved:
'twas Aeneas' talk to Dido, and thereabout of it especially
370   when he speaks of Priam's slaughter.[5] If it live in your memory, begin at this line—let me see, let me see,
   "The rugged° Pyrrhus[6] like th' Hyrcanian beast"°—   *savage / tiger*
'Tis not so. It begins with Pyrrhus—
   "The rugged Pyrrhus, he whose sable° arms,   *black*
375   Black as his purpose, did the night resemble
When he lay couchèd° in th'ominous horse,[7]   *hidden*
Hath now this dread and black complexion° smeared   *appearance*
With heraldry° more dismal: head to foot   *heraldic colors*
Now is he total gules,° horridly tricked°   *all red / inked over*
380   With blood of fathers, mothers, daughters, sons,
Baked and impasted with° the parching° streets   *encrusted by / fiery*
That lend a tyrannous and a damnèd light
To their lord's murder. Roasted in wrath and fire
And thus o'ersizèd[8] with coagulate gore,
385   With eyes like carbuncles,[9] the hellish Pyrrhus
Old grandsire Priam seeks."
So, proceed you.

POLONIUS   Fore God, my lord, well spoken, with good accent
and good discretion.

390   FIRST PLAYER   "Anon° he finds him,   *Soon*
Striking too short at Greeks. His antique sword,
Rebellious to his arm, lies where it falls,
Repugnant° to command. Unequal matched,   *Resistant*
Pyrrhus at Priam drives, in rage strikes wide,
395   But with the whiff and wind of his fell° sword   *fierce*
Th'unnervèd° father falls. Then senseless Ilium,[1]   *strengthless*

---

9. A coin was no longer legal tender if the circle or
ring enclosing the monarch's head was broken (by
"clipping," or trimming off small amounts of gold).
1. We'll go to work at once. (French falconers seem to
have been regarded as experts, willing to try any
potential prey.)
2. *cried . . . of:* outweighed.
3. Seasoned dishes. I.e., deliberate attempts to vary
or embellish the style in order to make the lines more
pleasing ("savory").
4. Beautifully crafted rather than showy.
5. The murder of the Trojan king Priam, at the end

of the Trojan War; adapted from Virgil's *Aeneid*, possibly via Christopher Marlowe's *Dido, Queen of Carthage*. Aeneas recounts the story of Priam's slaughter
to his beloved, Dido.
6. Also known as Neoptolemus, he came to Troy to
avenge the death of his father, the Greek hero
Achilles.
7. The Trojan horse, full of Greek warriors.
8. As though coated with sizing, the thick liquid
used to prepare a canvas for painting.
9. Gems supposed to glow with their own light.
1. The citadel of Troy.

Seeming to feel this blow, with flaming top
Stoops to his° base and with a hideous crash   *its*
Takes prisoner Pyrrhus' ear: for lo, his sword,
400 Which was declining° on the milky° head   *descending / white*
Of reverend Priam, seemed i'th' air to stick.
So as a painted tyrant[2] Pyrrhus stood
Like a neutral to his will and matter,[3]
Did nothing.
405 But as we often see against° some storm   *before*
A silence in the heavens, the rack° stand still,   *cloud banks*
The bold winds speechless, and the orb° below   *earth*
As hush as death, anon the dreadful thunder
Doth rend the region,° so after Pyrrhus' pause   *sky*
410 A rousèd vengeance sets him new a-work,
And never did the Cyclops'[4] hammers fall
On Mars's armor, forged for proof eterne,[5]
With less remorse° than Pyrrhus' bleeding sword   *pity; hesitation*
Now falls on Priam.
415 Out, out, thou strumpet Fortune! All you gods
In general synod, take away her power,
Break all the spokes and fellies from her wheel[6]
And bowl the round nave° down the hill of heaven°   *wheel hub / Mount Olympus*
As low as to the fiends."
420 POLONIUS This is too long.
HAMLET It shall to the barber's with your beard.° —Prithee   *It shall be cut short*
   say on; he's for a jig[7] or a tale of bawdry, or he sleeps. Say on;
   come to Hecuba.
FIRST PLAYER "But who, ah woe, had seen the mobled°   *veiled; muffled*
   Queen—"
425 HAMLET "The mobled Queen"!
POLONIUS That's good.
FIRST PLAYER "—Run barefoot up and down, threat'ning the
   flames
With bisson rheum,° a clout° upon that head   *blinding tears / cloth*
Where late the diadem stood, and for a robe
430 About her lank and all-o'erteemèd[8] loins
A blanket in the alarm of fear caught up—
Who this had seen, with tongue in venom steeped,
'Gainst Fortune's state° would treason have pronounced.   *rule*
But if the gods themselves did see her then,
435 When she saw Pyrrhus make malicious sport
In mincing with his sword her husband limbs,
The instant burst of clamor that she made,
Unless things mortal move them not at all,
Would have made milch° the burning eyes of heaven   *milky; moist*
440 And passion° in the gods."   *suffering; pity*
POLONIUS Look where° he has not turned his color and has   *whether*
   tears in 's eyes! —Prithee, no more.

---

2. Tyrant depicted in a painting and so incapable of
moving.
3. As one indifferent toward his intention and the
action at hand.
4. The three one-eyed giants who served as armorers
to the classical gods and heroes.
5. To remain impenetrable forever.
6. The power of Fortune's ever-turning wheel, raising and lowering men in succession, was proverbial.
fellies: curved sections of a wooden wheel rim.
7. A ridiculous piece of poetry, or the dance that followed many plays (unrelated to the drama).
8. Completely worn out with childbearing. (Hecuba
was supposed to have borne seventeen or more
children.)

HAMLET [*to* FIRST PLAYER]   'Tis well. I'll have thee speak out
   the rest of this soon. [*to* POLONIUS] Good my lord, will you
445   see the players well bestowed?° Do you hear, let them be   *lodged*
   well used,° for they are the abstract° and brief chronicles of   *treated / summary*
   the time; after your death you were better have a bad epi-
   taph than their ill report while you live.
POLONIUS   My lord, I will use them according to their desert.
450 HAMLET   God's bodkin,° man, much better! Use every man   *By God's dear body*
   after° his desert and who shall scape whipping? Use them   *according to*
   after your own honor and dignity—the less they deserve the
   more merit is in your bounty. Take them in.
POLONIUS   Come, sirs.
455 HAMLET   Follow him, friends; we'll hear a play tomorrow.
       [*As* POLONIUS *leads the* PLAYERS *off,* HAMLET *speaks*
       aside to the FIRST PLAYER.]
   Dost thou hear me, old friend—can you play *The Murder of*
   Gonzago?
FIRST PLAYER   Ay, my lord.
HAMLET   We'll ha't° tomorrow night. You could, for need,°   *have it / if necessary*
460   study a speech of some dozen lines or sixteen lines which I
   would set down and insert in't, could you not?
FIRST PLAYER   Ay, my lord.
HAMLET   Very well. Follow that lord, and look you mock
   him not.   [*Exit* FIRST PLAYER.]
465 [*to* ROSENCRANTZ *and* GUILDENSTERN] My good friends, I'll
   leave you till night. You are welcome to Elsinore.
ROSENCRANTZ   Good my lord.
HAMLET   Ay so, good-bye to you.
        Exeunt [ROSENCRANTZ *and* GUILDENSTERN].
   Now I am alone.
   Oh, what a rogue and peasant slave am I!
470   Is it not monstrous that this player here,
   But° in a fiction, in a dream of passion,   *Merely*
   Could force his soul so to his own conceit[9]
   That from her° working all the° visage wanned,°   *(the soul's) / his / grew pale*
   Tears in his eyes, distraction in his aspect,
475   A broken voice, and his whole function suiting
   With forms to his conceit?[1] And all for nothing!
   For Hecuba!
   What's Hecuba to him or he to her
   That he should weep for her? What would he do
480   Had he the motive and that for passion
   That I have? He would drown the stage with tears
   And cleave the general ear[2] with horrid speech,
   Make mad the guilty and appall the free,°   *innocent*
   Confound the ignorant and amaze° indeed   *bewilder*
485   The very faculties of eyes and ears. Yet I,
   A dull and muddy-mettled° rascal, peak°   *dull-spirited / mope*
   Like John-a-dreams,° unpregnant of[3] my cause,   *a sleepy idler*
   And can say nothing—no, not for a King

---

9. Could make his innermost being conform so well
with his imagined situation.
1. *his whole . . . conceit:* the action of his whole body

in outward accord with his imagination.
2. The ears of people generally.
3. Not quickened into action by.

	Upon whose property° and most dear life	*rightful sovereignty*
490	A damned defeat[4] was made. Am I a coward?	
	Who calls me villain, breaks my pate° across,	*head*
	Plucks off my beard and blows it in my face,	
	Tweaks me by the nose, gives me the lie i'th' throat	
	As deep as to the lungs?[5] Who does me this?	
495	Ha? 'Swounds,° I should take it, for it cannot be	*By God's wounds*
	But I am pigeon-livered and lack gall[6]	
	To make oppression bitter, or ere this	
	I should've fatted all the region kites[7]	
	With this slave's offal. Bloody, bawdy villain!	
500	Remorseless, treacherous, lecherous, kindless° villain![8]	*unnatural*
500.1	*Oh, vengeance!*	
	Why, what an ass am I! This is most brave,°	*fine*
	That I, the son of a dear murdered,°	*the dear murdered man*
	Prompted to my revenge by heaven and hell,	
	Must like a whore unpack my heart with words	
505	And fall a-cursing like a very drab,°	*whore*
	A stallion![9] Fie upon't, foh!	
	About,° my brains! Hmm—I have heard	*Into action*
	That guilty creatures sitting at a play	
	Have by the very cunning° of the scene	*artfulness*
510	Been struck so to the soul that presently°	*immediately*
	They have proclaimed their malefactions.	
	For murder, though it have no tongue, will speak	
	With most miraculous organ. I'll have these players	
	Play something like the murder of my father	
515	Before mine uncle. I'll observe his looks;	
	I'll tent° him to the quick. If 'a° do blench,	*probe (a wound) / he*
	I know my course. The spirit that I have seen	
	May be a dev'l, and the dev'l hath power	
	T'assume a pleasing shape; yea, and perhaps	
520	Out of my weakness and my melancholy,	
	As he is very potent with such spirits,[1]	
	Abuses° me to damn me. I'll have grounds	*Deceives*
	More relative° than this. The play's the thing	*relevant*
	Wherein I'll catch the conscience of the King. *Exit.*	

3.1

Enter KING, QUEEN, POLONIUS, OPHELIA,
ROSENCRANTZ, [*and*] GUILDENSTERN.[1]

KING   And can you by no drift of conference[2]
    Get from him why he puts on this confusion,
    Grating so harshly all his days of quiet
    With turbulent and dangerous lunacy?

---

4. An act of overthrow worthy of damnation.
5. *gives . . . lungs:* calls me a thoroughgoing liar.
6. Pigeons were thought not to secrete gall, a bitter fluid produced by the liver and the supposed source of anger.
7. All the kites (birds of prey) in the sky ("region").
8. F has the following line, 500.1, not found in Q2.
9. *stallion:* a male prostitute. F has "scullion," a menial kitchen servant.
1. *Out of . . . spirits:* It was thought that those afflicted with too much black bile, a humor (fluid) or "spirit" (distillation), became melancholy and subject to hallu-

cinations, which in turn made them easily tricked by the devil. *potent with:* powerful over.
3.1 Location: The castle.
1. TEXTUAL COMMENT We have cut the entry of the "*Lords*" originally specified in F and Q2. There is no reasonable moment in the scene for the Lords to exit (unless it is with Rosencrantz and Guildenstern or the Queen), and the King's plans to spy on Hamlet are presumably meant to be secretive. See Digital Edition TC 5 (combined text).
2. By no carefully directed conversation.

5 ROSENCRANTZ He does confess he feels himself distracted,°   *confused; agitated*
But from what cause 'a will by no means speak.
GUILDENSTERN Nor do we find him forward° to be sounded,°   *eager / probed*
But with a crafty madness keeps aloof
When we would bring him on to some confession
10 Of his true state.
QUEEN   Did he receive you well?
ROSENCRANTZ Most like a gentleman—
GUILDENSTERN But with much forcing of his disposition.°   *mood*
ROSENCRANTZ Niggard of question,³ but of° our demands   *to*
Most free in his reply.
15 QUEEN Did you assay° him to any pastime?   *try to persuade*
ROSENCRANTZ Madam, it so fell out that certain players
We o'erraught° on the way; of these we told him,   *passed*
And there did seem in him a kind of joy
To hear of it. They are here about the court
20 And, as I think, they have already order
This night to play before him.
POLONIUS   'Tis most true,
And he beseeched me to entreat your majesties
To hear and see the matter.
KING With all my heart! And it doth much content me
25 To hear him so inclined.
Good gentlemen, give him a further edge,°   *stimulus; appetite*
And drive his purpose into these delights.
ROSENCRANTZ We shall, my lord.
                Exeunt ROSENCRANTZ *and* GUILDENSTERN.
KING   Sweet Gertrude, leave us too,
For we have closely° sent for Hamlet hither,   *privately*
30 That he, as 'twere by accident, may here
Affront° Ophelia. Her father and myself,   *Confront*
We'll so bestow ourselves that, seeing unseen,
We may of their encounter frankly judge
And gather by him as he is behaved
35 If't be th'affliction of his love or no
That thus he suffers for.
QUEEN   I shall obey you.
And for your part, Ophelia, I do wish
That your good beauties be the happy cause
Of Hamlet's wildness; so shall I hope your virtues
40 Will bring him to his wonted° way again   *customary*
To both your honors.
OPHELIA   Madam, I wish it may. [*Exit* QUEEN.]
POLONIUS Ophelia, walk you here. [*to the* KING] Gracious,° so   *Your grace*
    please you,
We will bestow ourselves. [*to* OPHELIA] Read on this book
That show of such an exercise may color
45 Your lowliness.⁴ We are oft to blame in this:
'Tis too much proved° that with devotion's visage   *true in experience*
And pious action we do sugar o'er
The devil himself.
KING   Oh, 'tis too true.

---

3. Reluctant to offer conversation.
4. *may . . . lowliness:* may show your humility, and

also give it a virtuous or pious look. The "book" is a
prayer book or devotional text.

'de] How smart° a lash that speech doth give my   *sharp*
conscience.
50 The harlot's cheek, beautied with plast'ring° art,   *cosmetic*
Is not more ugly to the thing that helps it[5]
Than is my deed to my most painted word.
Oh, heavy burden!
ᴘᴏʟᴏɴɪᴜs   I hear him coming—withdraw, my lord.
    [ᴋɪɴɢ *and* ᴘᴏʟᴏɴɪᴜs *withdraw and hide.*]
    Enter ʜᴀᴍʟᴇᴛ.
55 ʜᴀᴍʟᴇᴛ   To be or not to be: that is the question.[6]
Whether 'tis nobler in the mind to suffer
The slings and arrows of outrageous fortune
Or to take arms against a sea of troubles
And by opposing end them. To die, to sleep,
60 No more, and by a sleep to say we end
The heartache and the thousand natural shocks
That flesh is heir to—'tis a consummation
Devoutly to be wished. To die, to sleep;
To sleep, perchance to dream—ay, there's the rub:[7]
65 For in that sleep of death what dreams may come
When we have shuffled° off this mortal coil°   *cast / turmoil; flesh*
Must give us pause. There's the respect°   *consideration*
That makes calamity of so long life:[8]
For who would bear the whips and scorns of time,
70 Th'oppressor's wrong, the proud man's contumely,°   *scornful abuse*
The pangs of despised° love, the law's delay,   *scorned*
The insolence of office,° and the spurns°   *bureaucrats / kicks; insults*
That patient merit of th'unworthy takes,[9]
When he himself might his quietus make[1]
75 With a bare bodkin?° Who would fardels° bear   *mere dagger / burdens*
To grunt and sweat under a weary life
But that the dread of something after death,
The undiscovered country from whose bourn°   *border*
No traveler returns, puzzles the will
80 And makes us rather bear those ills we have
Than fly to others that we know not of?
Thus conscience[2] does make cowards,
And thus the native hue° of resolution   *ruddy complexion*
Is sicklied o'er with the pale cast° of thought,   *tint*
85 And enterprises of great pitch and moment[3]
With this regard° their currents turn awry   *consideration*
And lose the name of action. Soft you now,[4]
The fair Ophelia! —Nymph, in thy orisons°   *prayers*
Be all my sins remembered.
ᴏᴘʜᴇʟɪᴀ   Good my lord,
90 How does your honor for this many a day?

---

5. *to . . . it:* compared to the artificially beautiful surface that covers it.
6. Pᴇʀꜰᴏʀᴍᴀɴᴄᴇ Cᴏᴍᴍᴇɴᴛ Productions must decide
whether Ophelia overhears some or all of this celebrated soliloquy, whose familiarity to many playgoers
poses a challenge to actors seeking to make it fresh
and compelling. See Digital Edition PC 4.
7. Obstacle in the game of bowls, an impediment to
the ball's intended path.
8. Makes adversity so long-lived (as opposed to quickly
ended in suicide).

9. That the deserving has to accept patiently from
the unworthy.
1. A paid-off account was marked "Quietus est"
(Latin: "It is laid to rest").
2. Both consciousness (introspective knowledge)
and moral conscience.
3. Of great height and importance. "Pitch" refers to
"height" in the context of a falcon's flight. F gives
"pith," or profundity.
4. Wait a moment (an expression of surprise).

HAMLET   I humbly thank you, well.

OPHELIA   My lord, I have remembrances of yours
That I have longèd long to redeliver;
I pray you now receive them.

95   HAMLET   No, not I. I never gave you aught.

OPHELIA   My honored lord, you know right well you did,
And with them words of so sweet breath composed
As made these things more rich. Their perfume lost,
Take these again, for to the noble mind

100   Rich gifts wax° poor when givers prove unkind.   *grow*
There, my lord.

HAMLET   Ha, ha! Are you honest?°   *chaste; truthful*

OPHELIA   My lord?

HAMLET   Are you fair?

105   OPHELIA   What means your lordship?

HAMLET   That if you be honest and fair, you should admit no
discourse to[5] your beauty.

OPHELIA   Could beauty, my lord, have better commerce° than   *dealings*
with honesty?

110   HAMLET   Ay, truly, for the power of beauty will sooner transform honesty from what it is to a bawd than the force of hon-
esty can translate beauty into his° likeness. This was sometime   *its (honesty's)*
a paradox, but now the time[6] gives it proof. I did love you once.

OPHELIA   Indeed, my lord, you made me believe so.

115   HAMLET   You should not have believed me, for virtue cannot
so inoculate our old stock but we shall relish of it.[7] I loved
you not.

OPHELIA   I was the more deceived.

HAMLET   Get thee to a nunnery![8] Why wouldst thou be a

120   breeder of sinners? I am myself indifferent honest,° but yet I   *moderately virtuous*
could accuse me of such things that it were better my mother
had not borne me. I am very proud, revengeful, ambitious,
with more offenses at my beck° than I have thoughts to put   *command*
them in, imagination to give them shape, or time to act them

125   in. What should such fellows as I do crawling between earth
and heaven? We are arrant° knaves—believe none of us. Go   *complete*
thy ways to a nunnery. Where's your father?

OPHELIA   At home, my lord.

HAMLET   Let the doors be shut upon him that he may play the

130   fool nowhere but in 's own house. Farewell.[9]

OPHELIA   O help him, you sweet heavens!

HAMLET   If thou dost marry, I'll give thee this plague for thy
dowry: be thou as chaste as ice, as pure as snow, thou shalt
not escape calumny. Get thee to a nunnery. Farewell. Or if

135   thou wilt needs marry, marry a fool, for wise men know well
enough what monsters[1] you° make of them. To a nunnery   *you women*
go, and quickly too. Farewell.

---

5. No familiar conversation with.
6. This was formerly an uncredited opinion, but now the present age.
7. *virtue . . . it*: virtue grafted onto fallen human nature cannot eradicate completely the taste ("relish") of original sin.
8. By entering a nunnery, Ophelia will take a vow of lifelong chastity. But in Elizabethan slang, "nunnery" could also mean "brothel."

9. PERFORMANCE COMMENT Some productions of this scene make Hamlet aware, or at least suspicious, that he is being watched. Others emphasize his emotional instability and his apparently unprovoked cruelty to Ophelia. See Digital Edition PC 5.
1. Alluding to the belief that cuckolds grew horns, but Hamlet may mean a more spiritual or psychological transformation as well.

OPHELIA   Heavenly powers restore him!

HAMLET   I have heard of your paintings° well enough. God   *cosmetics*
140   hath given you one face and you make yourselves another;
you jig and amble and you lisp,² you nickname God's crea-
tures³ and make your wantonness ignorance.⁴ Go to, I'll no
more on't°—it hath made me mad. I say we will have no   *of it*
more marriage. Those that are married already—all but
145   one—shall live; the rest shall keep as they are. To a nunnery, go.   *Exit.*

OPHELIA   Oh, what a noble mind is here o'erthrown!
The courtier's, soldier's, scholar's eye, tongue, sword,
Th'expectation° and rose of the fair state,   *The hope*
150   The glass° of fashion and the mold of form,⁵   *mirror image*
Th'observed of all observers, quite, quite down!
And I, of ladies most deject and wretched,
That sucked the honey of his musicked vows,
Now see what noble and most sovereign reason
155   Like sweet bells jangled out of time and harsh—
That unmatched form and stature of blown° youth,   *fully blossoming*
Blasted° with ecstasy.° Oh, woe is me   *Withered / madness*
T'have seen what I have seen, see what I see!
        KING *and* POLONIUS [*come forward*].

KING   Love? His affections° do not that way tend,   *emotions*
160   Nor what he spake, though it lacked form a little,
Was not like madness. There's something in his soul
O'er which his melancholy sits on brood,
And I do doubt° the hatch and the disclose⁶   *fear*
Will be some danger—which for to prevent
165   I have in quick determination
Thus set it down:° he shall with speed to England   *resolved it*
For the demand of our neglected tribute.⁷
Haply° the seas and countries different   *Perhaps; with luck*
With variable objects⁸ shall expel
170   This something-settled° matter in his heart,   *somewhat rooted*
Whereon his brains still° beating puts him thus   *constantly*
From fashion of himself.⁹ What think you on't?

POLONIUS   It shall do well. But yet do I believe
The origin and commencement of his grief
175   Sprung from neglected° love. How now, Ophelia?   *unrequited*
You need not tell us what Lord Hamlet said—
We heard it all. My lord, do as you please,
But if you hold it fit, after the play
Let his queen-mother all alone entreat him
180   To show his grief. Let her be round° with him,   *blunt*
And I'll be placed, so please you, in the ear°   *within earshot*
Of all their conference. If she find him not,¹
To England send him, or confine him where

---

2. *you jig . . . lisp:* you dance (or sing), walk with an
affectedly easy gait, and speak artificially.
3. Use new and fashionable names instead of the
God-given ones.
4. *make . . . ignorance:* "play dumb" to excuse your
(seductive) affectations.
5. Pattern of decorum.

6. Public disclosure.
7. Although the play is set in a Renaissance world,
Claudius's words invoke a distant medieval past,
when England paid tribute to Denmark.
8. With different sights or interests.
9. *puts . . . himself:* makes him unlike his normal self.
1. If she fails to discover his secret.

Your wisdom best shall think.

KING   It shall be so.

185   Madness in great ones must not unmatched go.[2]   *Exeunt.*

3.2

Enter HAMLET *and three of the* PLAYERS.

HAMLET   Speak the speech, I pray you, as I pronounced it to
you, trippingly on the tongue. But if you mouth it[1] as many of
our players do, I had as lief° the town crier spoke my lines.   *willingly*
Nor do not saw the air too much with your hand thus, but
5   use all gently, for in the very torrent, tempest, and, as I may
say, whirlwind of your passion, you must acquire and beget a
temperance that may give it smoothness. Oh, it offends me
to the soul to hear a robustious° periwig-pated° fellow tear a   *bombastic / wig-wearing*
passion to tatters, to very rags, to split the ears of the ground-
10   lings,[2] who for the most part are capable of nothing but inexplicable dumb shows[3] and noise. I would have such a fellow
whipped for o'erdoing Termagant—it out-Herods Herod.[4]
Pray you avoid it.

PLAYER   I warrant your honor.[5]

15   HAMLET   Be not too tame neither, but let your own discretion
be your tutor. Suit the action to the word, the word to the
action, with this special observance: that you o'erstep not
the modesty° of nature. For anything so o'erdone is from°   *moderation / opposed to*
the purpose of playing, whose end both at the first and now
20   was and is to hold as 'twere the mirror up to nature, to
show virtue her feature, scorn her own image, and the very
age and body of the time his form and pressure.[6] Now this
overdone, or come tardy° off, though it makes the unskill-   *faultily*
ful° laugh, cannot but make the judicious grieve, the cen-   *undiscriminating*
25   sure of which one[7] must in your allowance o'erweigh a whole
theater of others. Oh, there be players that I have seen play,
and heard others praised, and that highly, not to speak it
profanely,[8] that neither having th'accent of Christians nor
the gait of Christian, pagan, nor man, have so strutted and
30   bellowed that I have thought some of nature's journeymen[9]
had made men, and not made them well, they imitated humanity so abominably.

PLAYER   I hope we have reformed that indifferently° with us.   *moderately well*

HAMLET   Oh, reform it altogether. And let those that play your
35   clowns speak no more than is set down for them; for there be
of° them that will themselves laugh to set° on some quantity   *some of / urge*
of barren° spectators to laugh too, though in the meantime   *unthinking*
some necessary question of the play be then to be consid-

2. Madness in great ones should not be left alone, or
unopposed.
3.2 Location: A stateroom of the castle.
1. If you speak exaggeratedly.
2. Spectators standing on the ground before the stage
(the cheapest area).
3. Pantomimes, featuring gestures without words.
By Shakespeare's time, this once-common device
was out of fashion.
4. It surpasses the excesses of Herod, who, as a character in medieval cycle plays, was famous for his
ranting. Termagant, an imaginary deity supposedly

worshipped by Muslims, takes the form of a violent
speaking idol in medieval drama.
5. I assure your honor (that we will avoid it).
6. *the very . . . pressure:* the true state of things at
present, in shape ("form") and likeness (as a stamp
pressed in wax).
7. The judgment of one of whom (judicious persons).
8. Meaning no blasphemy (by implying as he goes on
to do that some humans were not created by God).
9. Hirelings, those who have completed their apprenticeship but are not yet "masters" of their trade.

ered. That's villainous and shows a most pitiful ambition in
40   the fool that uses it. Go, make you ready.
            [*Exeunt* PLAYERS.]
    Enter POLONIUS, GUILDENSTERN, *and* ROSENCRANTZ.
How now, my lord, will the King hear this piece of work?
POLONIUS And the Queen too, and that presently.°   *immediately*
HAMLET Bid the players make haste.   [*Exit* POLONIUS.]
Will you two help to hasten them?
ROSENCRANTZ   Ay, my lord.
     Exeunt [GUILDENSTERN *and* ROSENCRANTZ].
45   HAMLET What ho, Horatio!
    Enter HORATIO.
HORATIO Here, sweet lord, at your service.
HAMLET Horatio, thou art e'en as just° a man   *honest; balanced*
As e'er my conversation coped withal.[1]
HORATIO O my dear lord—
HAMLET   Nay, do not think I flatter,
50   For what advancement° may I hope from thee   *political favors*
That no revenue hast but thy good spirits
To feed and clothe thee? Why should the poor be flattered?
No, let the candied° tongue lick absurd pomp   *flattering*
And crook the pregnant° hinges of the knee   *ready (to bow)*
55   Where thrift° may follow° fawning. Dost thou hear? *prosperity / follow from*
Since my dear soul was mistress of her choice
And could of° men distinguish her election,   *between*
Sh'ath sealed thee for herself.[2] For thou hast been
As one in suff'ring all that suffers nothing,
60   A man that Fortune's buffets and rewards
Hast ta'en with equal thanks; and blest are those
Whose blood° and judgment are so well co-meddled° *passion / mixed*
That they are not a pipe for Fortune's finger
To sound what stop° she please. Give me that man *finger hole; note*
65   That is not passion's slave and I will wear him
In my heart's core—ay, in my heart of heart—
As I do thee. Something too much of this.
There is a play tonight before the King.
One scene of it comes near the circumstance
70   Which I have told thee of my father's death.
I prithee, when thou seest that act afoot,
Even with the very comment of thy soul[3]
Observe my uncle: if his occulted° guilt   *hidden*
Do not itself unkennel in one speech,
75   It is a damnèd ghost that we have seen,
And my imaginations are as foul
As Vulcan's stithy.[4] Give him heedful note,
For I mine eyes will rivet to his face,
And after we will both our judgments join
In censure of his seeming.[5]
80   HORATIO   Well, my lord,
If 'a° steal aught the whilst this play is playing   *he*

---

1. As I ever encountered in my dealings with men.
2. She has marked you as her own (on a document, a legal sign of possession).
3. With your utmost critical faculty.

4. Smithy, or forge, of Vulcan, the Roman blacksmith god.
5. In assessing his outward reaction.

And scape detected, I will pay the theft.[6]

Enter trumpets and kettledrums, KING, QUEEN,
POLONIUS, OPHELIA[, ROSENCRANTZ, GUILDENSTERN,
and other LORDS *attendant with the King's guard*
carrying torches. Danish march. Sound a flourish].

HAMLET They are coming to the play. I must be idle.° Get you   *mad; unoccupied*
a place.

85   KING How fares[7] our cousin° Hamlet?   *kinsman*

HAMLET Excellent, i'faith. Of the chameleon's dish: I eat the
air, promise-crammed.[8] You cannot feed capons[9] so.

KING I have nothing with this answer, Hamlet; these words
are not mine.

90   HAMLET No, nor mine now, my lord. [*to* POLONIUS] You played
once i'th' university, you say?

POLONIUS That did I, my lord, and was accounted a good actor.

HAMLET What did you enact?

POLONIUS I did enact Julius Caesar. I was killed i'th' Capitol[1]—
95   Brutus killed me.

HAMLET It was a brute part of him to kill so capital a calf°   *such a prize fool*
there. —Be the players ready?

ROSENCRANTZ Ay, my lord, they stay° upon your patience.   *wait*

QUEEN Come hither, my dear Hamlet, sit by me.

100 HAMLET No, good mother, here's mettle[2] more attractive.

POLONIUS [*aside to* KING] Oh ho, do you mark that?

HAMLET Lady, shall I lie in your lap?

OPHELIA No, my lord.[3]

103.1   HAMLET *I mean my head upon your lap.*
           OPHELIA *Ay, my lord.*

HAMLET Do you think I meant country matters?[4]

105 OPHELIA I think nothing, my lord.

HAMLET That's a fair thought to lie between maids' legs.

OPHELIA What is, my lord?

HAMLET Nothing.

OPHELIA You are merry, my lord.

110 HAMLET Who, I?

OPHELIA Ay, my lord.

HAMLET O God, your only jig-maker.[5] What should a man do
but be merry? For look you how cheerfully my mother looks,
and my father died within's° two hours.   *within these*

115 OPHELIA Nay, 'tis twice two months, my lord.

HAMLET So long? Nay, then let the devil wear black, for I'll
have a suit of sables.[6] O heavens, die two months ago and
not forgotten yet! Then there's hope a great man's memory

6. *If . . . theft*: If he so much as secretly sighs or glances
without my noticing, you can hold me accountable.
7. How does; Hamlet's response puns on "fare" as
food and drink.
8. The chameleon was supposed to live on air. Hamlet puns on "heir," referring to Claudius's insubstantial promise of the succession.
9. Castrated cocks, crammed or fattened for the table
(and a term for a fool).
1. Perhaps an allusion to Shakespeare's own *Julius
Caesar*; the actor who first played Polonius may also
have played the part of Caesar.
2. A disposition (punning on magnetically attractive
"metal").

3. F has the following passage, lines 103.1–103.2,
not found in Q2.
4. Rustic doings (with an obscene pun on "cunt").
The punning continues in the following lines, where
"nothing" suggests the female genitals (often linked
to the shape of a zero), and "thing" the male genitals.
5. The leading comic actor often devised and performed the farcical song and dance concluding a play.
only: unrivaled.
6. Sable is both an expensive fur for cloaks and trim
and the heraldic term for "black"; Hamlet simultaneously forswears his ascetic mourning and vows to
continue it.

may outlive his life half a year—but by'r Lady, 'a must build
churches then, or else shall 'a suffer not thinking on,[7] with
the hobbyhorse whose epitaph is "For oh! For oh! The hobbyhorse is forgot."[8]

The trumpets sounds. Dumb show follows.
Enter a [PLAYER] KING *and a* [PLAYER] QUEEN, *the*
QUEEN *embracing him and he her.* [*She kneels and*
makes show of protestation unto him.] *He takes her*
up and declines° his head upon her neck. He lies him   leans
down upon a bank of flowers; she, seeing him asleep,
leaves him. Anon come in another man, takes off his
crown, kisses it, pours poison in the sleeper's ears, and
leaves him. The QUEEN *returns, finds the* KING *dead,*
makes passionate action. The poisoner with some
three or four come in again, seem to condole with her.
The dead body is carried away. The poisoner woos the
QUEEN *with gifts. She seems harsh awhile but in the*
end accepts love.   [*Exeunt.*]

OPHELIA   What means this, my lord?
HAMLET   Marry, this miching mallico?° It means mischief.   *sneaking wrongdoing*
OPHELIA   Belike this show imports the argument° of the play.   *plot*
Enter PROLOGUE.
HAMLET   We shall know by this fellow. The players cannot
keep counsel°—they'll tell all.   *a secret*
OPHELIA   Will 'a tell us what this show meant?
HAMLET   Ay, or any show that you will show him. Be not you
ashamed to show, he'll not shame to tell you what it means.
OPHELIA   You are naught,° you are naught. I'll mark the play.   *indecent*
PROLOGUE   For us and for our tragedy
    Here stooping to your clemency,
    We beg your hearing patiently.   [*Exit.*]
HAMLET   Is this a prologue or the posy of a ring?[9]
OPHELIA   'Tis brief, my lord.
HAMLET   As woman's love.
Enter [PLAYER] KING *and* [PLAYER] QUEEN.
PLAYER KING   Full thirty times hath Phoebus' cart[1] gone round
Neptune's salt wash and Tellus' orbèd ground[2]
And thirty dozen moons with borrowed sheen°   *reflected light*
About the world have times twelve thirties been
Since love our hearts and Hymen° did our hands   *god of marriage*
Unite commutual in most sacred bands.
PLAYER QUEEN   So many journeys may the sun and moon
Make us again count o'er ere love be done.
But woe is me, you are so sick of late,
So far from cheer and from our former state,
That I distrust° you. Yet though I distrust,   *am worried about*
Discomfort° you, my lord, it nothing must.[3]   *Sadden*
For women fear too much even as they love,
And women's fear and love hold quantity°   *are in equal proportions*

---

7. He shall have to endure being forgotten.
8. The hobbyhorse, a man with a mock horse's body
strapped round his waist, was a figure in May Day
morris dances (under attack in Shakespeare's time by
religious reformers). "The hobbyhorse is forgot"
seems to have been a ballad refrain.

9. The motto engraved in a ring.
1. Apollo's chariot (the sun).
2. *Neptune's . . . ground:* The salty flood of the sea
god and the round foundation of Tellus (the earth).
3. The following line, 150, is omitted in F.

Either none, in neither aught or in extremity.[4]
Now what my love is, proof° hath made you know,
And as my love is sized,° my fear is so.[5]
155 Where love is great, the littlest doubts are fear;
Where little fears grow great, great love grows there.
PLAYER KING   Faith, I must leave thee, love, and shortly too.
My operant° powers their functions leave° to do,   *vital / cease*
And thou shalt live in this fair world behind,
160 Honored, beloved; and haply° one as kind   *perhaps*
For husband shalt thou—
PLAYER QUEEN   Oh, confound the rest!
Such love must needs be treason in my breast.
In second husband let me be accurst:
None wed the second but who killed the first.
165 HAMLET   That's wormwood.[6]
PLAYER QUEEN   The instances° that second marriage move°   *motives / prompt*
Are base respects of thrift° but none of love.   *economic considerations*
A second time I kill my husband dead
When second husband kisses me in bed.
170 PLAYER KING   I do believe you think what now you speak,
But what we do determine, oft we break.
Purpose is but the slave to[7] memory,
Of violent birth but poor validity,°   *enduring strength*
Which now like fruit unripe sticks on the tree
175 But fall unshaken when they mellow be.
Most necessary 'tis that we forget
To pay ourselves what to ourselves is debt;[8]
What to ourselves in passion we propose,
The passion ending, doth the purpose lose.
180 The violence of either grief or joy
Their own enactures with themselves destroy.[9]
Where joy most revels grief doth most lament,
Grief joys, joy grieves, on slender accident.[1]
This world is not for aye,° nor 'tis not strange   *eternity*
185 That even our loves should with our fortunes change—
For 'tis a question left us yet to prove
Whether love lead fortune or else fortune love.
The great man down, you mark his favorite flies;
The poor advanced° makes friends of enemies.   *promoted*
190 And hitherto° doth love on fortune tend,°   *to this extent / attend*
For who not needs shall never lack a friend,
And who in want a hollow friend doth try°   *test*
Directly seasons him[2] his enemy.
But orderly to end where I begun,
195 Our wills and fates do so contrary run[3]
That our devices still° are overthrown—   *our plans always*

---

4. *Either . . . extremity:* Either love and fear are both absent, or both are extremely strong.
5. The following couplet, lines 155–56, is omitted in F.
6. A bitter herb taken medicinally (hence, "a bitter pill to swallow").
7. *Purpose . . . slave to:* Our intentions serve and depend on.
8. *Most . . . debt:* It is inevitable (or necessary for our well-being) that we neglect to fulfill those promises made to ourselves.
9. *The violence . . . destroy:* Extreme grief and joy destroy themselves, and the motive for action vanishes with them.
1. On account of a small, unforeseen event.
2. Immediately hardens him, as timber is seasoned for use.
3. What we desire and what is destined to happen are so opposed.

Our thoughts are ours, their ends° none of our own.   *results*
So think thou wilt no second husband wed,
But die thy thoughts when thy first lord is dead.
200   PLAYER QUEEN   Nor earth to me give food nor heaven light,
Sport and repose lock from me day and night,[4]
To desperation turn my trust and hope,
And anchors' cheer[5] in prison be my scope,°   *extent (of good)*
Each opposite[6] that blanks° the face of joy   *makes pale*
205   Meet what I would have well and it destroy,
Both here and hence pursue me lasting strife,
If once I be a widow ever I be a wife.
HAMLET   If she should break it now!
PLAYER KING   'Tis deeply sworn. Sweet, leave me here awhile;
210   My spirits grow dull and fain° I would beguile   *gladly*
The tedious day with sleep.
                                [*He sleeps.*]
PLAYER QUEEN   Sleep rock thy brain,
And never come mischance between us twain.   [*Exit.*]
HAMLET   Madam, how like you this play?
QUEEN   The lady doth protest too much, methinks.
215   HAMLET   Oh, but she'll keep her word.
KING   Have you heard the argument?° Is there no offense in't?   *plot*
HAMLET   No, no, they do but jest, poison in jest. No offense
i'th' world.
KING   What do you call the play?
220   HAMLET   *The Mousetrap*—marry, how tropically![7] This play is
the image of a murder done in Vienna. Gonzago is the Duke's
name, his wife Baptista.[8] You shall see anon. 'Tis a knavish
piece of work, but what of that? Your majesty and we that
have free° souls—it touches[9] us not. Let the galled jade wince;   *guiltless*
225   our withers are unwrung.[1]
            Enter LUCIANUS.
This is one Lucianus, nephew to the King.
OPHELIA   You are as good as a chorus,[2] my lord.
HAMLET   I could interpret between you and your love if I could
see the puppets dallying.[3]
230   OPHELIA   You are keen,° my lord, you are keen.   *sharply satirical*
HAMLET   It would cost you a groaning to take off mine edge.[4]
OPHELIA   Still better and worse.[5]
HAMLET   So you mistake your husbands.[6] —Begin, murderer.
Leave thy damnable° faces and begin. Come, the croaking   *grimacing*
235   raven doth bellow for revenge.[7]

---

4. The following couplet, lines 202–03, is omitted in F.
5. Food for anchorites (ascetic religious hermits).
6. Each adverse force.
7. As a trope, or rhetorical figure (perhaps punning
on "trap").
8. That is, the Player King and Queen (called "Duke"
and "Duchess" throughout Q1). Shakespeare seems
to base *The Mousetrap* on an extremely muddled version of the Duke of Urbino's alleged murder by Luigi
Gonzaga in 1538.
9. Wounds; concerns.
1. Let the chafed horse wince; our shoulders are not
rubbed sore.
2. The chorus explained the forthcoming action. In
puppet shows, a choric narrator, or "interpreter,"
announced the characters' names and spoke the
dialogue.
3. Flirting. Hamlet uses "interpret" here in the
sense of acting as the go-between, or pander, for two
lovers.
4. To satisfy my sexual appetite (leading to groaning
in either sexual intercourse or childbirth).
5. Wittier, and more obscene.
6. With these false promises ("for better and for
worse"), you take your husbands in marriage and
cheat on them.
7. Misquoted from *The True Tragedy of Richard III*
(ca. 1591; not to be confused with Shakespeare's own
Richard III).

LUCIANUS   Thoughts black, hands apt, drugs fit, and time
          agreeing,
     Considerate° season, else no creature seeing,   *Amenable*
     Thou mixture rank° of midnight weeds collected,   *foul*
     With Hecate's ban[8] thrice blasted, thrice infected,
240 Thy natural magic and dire property°   *quality*
     On wholesome life usurps immediately.
          [*He pours the poison in the Player King's ears.*]
HAMLET   'A poisons him i'th' garden for his estate.° His name's   *position; state*
     Gonzago, the story is extant and written in very choice Ital-
     ian. You shall see anon how the murderer gets the love of
245 Gonzago's wife.
OPHELIA   The King rises.[9]
246.1   HAMLET   *What, frighted with false fire?*[1]
QUEEN [*to* KING]   How fares my lord?
POLONIUS   Give o'er the play.
KING   Give me some light, away.
250 POLONIUS   Lights, lights, lights![2]
                         Exeunt all but HAMLET *and* HORATIO.
HAMLET   "Why, let the stricken deer go weep,[3]
     The hart ungallèd° play,   *unafflicted*
     For some must watch° while some must sleep—   *stay awake*
     Thus runs the world away."[4]
255 Would not this,° sir, and a forest of feathers,[5] if the rest of my   *(The Mousetrap)*
     fortunes turn Turk° with me, with provincial roses on my   *renegade*
     razed[6] shoes, get me a fellowship in a cry of players?[7]
HORATIO   Half a share.
HAMLET   A whole one, I.
260 "For thou dost know, O Damon[8] dear,
     This realm dismantled° was   *deprived*
     Of Jove himself, and now reigns here
     A very, very—" pajock.[9]
HORATIO   You might have rhymed.
265 HAMLET   O good Horatio, I'll take the Ghost's word for a thou-
     sand pound. Didst perceive?
HORATIO   Very well, my lord.
HAMLET   Upon the talk of the poisoning?
HORATIO   I did very well note him.
270 HAMLET   Ah ha! [*He calls offstage.*] Come, some music! Come,
     the recorders!
     "For if the King like not the comedy,
     Why then belike he likes it not, perdie."°   *indeed (pardieu)*
     Come, some music!
          Enter ROSENCRANTZ *and* GUILDENSTERN.

---

8. Curse by the goddess of witchcraft.
9. PERFORMANCE COMMENT Productions must decide how attentive Claudius and Gertrude are to the play presented at court and when—and how fully—they grasp its implications. See Digital Edition PC 6.
1. F has this line, 246.1, but it is not found in Q2. *false fire*: fireworks or blank cartridges.
2. In F, this line is spoken by "*All.*"
3. A deer was thought to weep when mortally wounded. Lines 251–54 are probably from a lost ballad.
4. That's the way of the world.

5. Plumes, worn often onstage.
6. Decorated with slashes. *provincial roses*: large rosettes concealing shoelaces.
7. *a fellowship . . . players*: a profit-sharing partnership in a pack ("cry") of actors (such as Shakespeare had in the Lord Chamberlain's Men).
8. Damon and Pythias were legendary ideals of friendship.
9. "Patchock" (rare, meaning something like "oaf"), or "peacock," emblem of the sin of pride. (The expected rhyme word would be "ass.")

275 GUILDENSTERN Good my lord, vouchsafe me a word with you.
HAMLET Sir, a whole history.
GUILDENSTERN The King, sir—
HAMLET Ay, sir, what of him?
GUILDENSTERN Is in his retirement° marvelous distempered. *withdrawal*
280 HAMLET With drink, sir?
GUILDENSTERN No, my lord, with choler.[1]
HAMLET Your wisdom should show itself more richer° to sig- *resourceful*
nify this to the doctor, for for me to put him to his purgation[2]
would perhaps plunge him into more choler.
285 GUILDENSTERN Good my lord, your discourse into some
frame° and start° not so wildly from my affair. *order / jump away*
HAMLET I am tame, sir. Pronounce.
GUILDENSTERN The Queen your mother, in most great affliction of spirit, hath sent me to you.
290 HAMLET You are welcome.
GUILDENSTERN Nay, good my lord, this courtesy is not of the
right breed.° If it shall please you to make me a wholesome° *kind; nobility / sane*
answer, I will do your mother's commandment. If not, your
pardon° and my return shall be the end of business. *permission to go*
295 HAMLET Sir, I cannot.
ROSENCRANTZ What, my lord?
HAMLET Make you a wholesome answer: my wit's diseased.
But sir, such answer as I can make, you shall command, or
rather, as you say, my mother. Therefore no more, but to the
300 matter. My mother, you say?
ROSENCRANTZ Then thus she says: your behavior hath struck
her into amazement and admiration.° *bewilderment*
HAMLET Oh, wonderful son that can so 'stonish a mother! But
is there no sequel at the heels of this mother's admiration?
305 Impart.° *Do tell*
ROSENCRANTZ She desires to speak with you in her closet° ere *private chamber*
you go to bed.
HAMLET We shall obey, were she ten times our mother. Have
you any further trade with us?
310 ROSENCRANTZ My lord, you once did love me.
HAMLET And do still, by these pickers and stealers.[3]
ROSENCRANTZ Good my lord, what is your cause of distemper? You do surely° bar the door upon your own liberty if *securely*
you deny your griefs to your friend.
315 HAMLET Sir, I lack advancement.
ROSENCRANTZ How can that be when you have the voice of
the King himself for your succession in Denmark?
Enter the PLAYERS *with recorders.*
HAMLET Ay, sir, but while the grass grows[4]—the proverb is
something° musty. —Oh, the recorders! Let me see one. *somewhat*
320 —To withdraw° with you: why do you go about to recover *speak privately*
the wind of me as if you would drive me into a toil?[5]

1. Both anger (Guildenstern's meaning) and indiges-
tion (Hamlet's). In Renaissance medical psychology,
each was a symptom of too much yellow bile—an
imbalance ("distemper") of the bodily fluids (humors).
2. A complicated pun: bloodletting; spiritual purging
(confession and absolution); legal purging (clearing
oneself of a crime).
3. Hands. (The catechism in the Book of Common

Prayer includes a promise to "keep my hands from
picking and stealing, and my tongue from evil speaking, lying, and slandering.")
4. "While the grass grows, the horse starves."
5. *go . . . toil:* contrive to get windward of me as if
you were hunters cunningly driving me toward a trap
("toil").

GUILDENSTERN   O my lord, if my duty be too bold, my love is
    too unmannerly.[6]
HAMLET   I do not well understand that. Will you play upon
325   this pipe?
GUILDENSTERN   My lord, I cannot.
HAMLET   I pray you.
GUILDENSTERN   Believe me, I cannot.
HAMLET   I do beseech you.
330 GUILDENSTERN   I know no touch of it, my lord.
HAMLET   It is as easy as lying. Govern these ventages° with   *finger holes*
    your fingers and thumb, give it breath with your mouth, and
    it will discourse most eloquent music. Look you, these are
    the stops.°   *finger holes; notes*
335 GUILDENSTERN   But these cannot I command to any utterance
    of harmony. I have not the skill.
HAMLET   Why, look you now how unworthy a thing you make
    of me: you would play upon me, you would seem to know my
    stops, you would pluck out the heart of my mystery, you
340   would sound° me from my lowest note to my compass,° and   *fathom; play on / limit*
    there is much music, excellent voice, in this little organ,° yet   *musical instrument*
    cannot you make it speak. 'Sblood, do you think I am easier
    to be played on than a pipe? Call me what instrument you
    will, though you fret[7] me, you cannot play upon me.
        Enter POLONIUS.
345 God bless you, sir.
POLONIUS   My lord, the Queen would speak with you, and
    presently.
HAMLET   Do you see yonder cloud that's almost in shape of a
    camel?
350 POLONIUS   By th' mass, and 'tis like a camel indeed.
HAMLET   Methinks it is like a weasel.
POLONIUS   It is backed like a weasel.
HAMLET   Or like a whale.
POLONIUS   Very like a whale.
355 HAMLET   Then I will come to my mother by and by. [*aside*]
    They fool me to the top of my bent.[8] —I will come by and by.
    [*to* ROSENCRANTZ *and* GUILDENSTERN] Leave me, friends. [*to*
    POLONIUS] I will—say so. "By and by" is easily said.
                      [*Exeunt all but* HAMLET.]
    'Tis now the very witching time of night
360   When churchyards yawn and hell itself breaks out
    Contagion to this world. Now could I drink hot blood
    And do such business as the bitter day
    Would quake to look on. Soft, now to my mother.
    O heart, lose not thy nature,° let not ever   *natural affection*
365   The soul of Nero[9] enter this firm° bosom—   *resolved*
    Let me be cruel, not unnatural.
    I will speak daggers to her but use none.
    My tongue and soul in this be hypocrites:[1]

---

6. If I have been discourteous in pursuing what is my
duty, my love for you is to blame.
7. Irritate, punning on frets of stringed instruments,
which regulate fingering and pitch.
8. They go along with my foolishness to its limit, or

to the limit of my endurance.
9. The Roman emperor Nero reputedly murdered his
mother, in one account, by cutting open her womb.
1. Let me appear and speak as if I intended violence
(though I do not).

How in my words somever² she be shent,°   rebuked
370   To give them seals³ never my soul consent.   *Exit.*

3.3

Enter KING, ROSENCRANTZ, *and* GUILDENSTERN.

KING   I like him not, nor stands it safe with us
To let his madness range. Therefore prepare you:
I your commission will forthwith dispatch
And he to England shall along with you.
5   The terms of our estate¹ may not endure
Hazard so near us as doth hourly grow
Out of his brows.²

GUILDENSTERN   We will ourselves provide.
Most holy and religious fear° it is   care
To keep those many many bodies safe
10   That live and feed upon your majesty.

ROSENCRANTZ   The single° and peculiar° life is bound   individual / private
With all the strength and armor of the mind
To keep itself from noyance,° but much more   harm
That spirit upon whose weal° depends and rests   well-being
15   The lives of many. The cease° of majesty   decease
Dies not alone but like a gulf° doth draw   whirlpool
What's near it with it, or it is a massy° wheel   massive
Fixed on the summit of the highest mount
To whose huge spokes ten thousand lesser things
20   Are mortised° and adjoined, which° when it falls   affixed / so that
Each small annexment, petty consequence,
Attends° the boist'rous ruin. Never alone   Accompanies
Did the king sigh, but with a general groan.

KING   Arm° you, I pray you, to this speedy voyage,   Prepare
25   For we will fetters put about this fear
Which now goes too free-footed.

ROSENCRANTZ   We will haste us.
Exeunt [ROSENCRANTZ *and* GUILDENSTERN].
Enter POLONIUS.

POLONIUS   My lord, he's going to his mother's closet.
Behind the arras° I'll convey myself   wall tapestry
To hear the process.° I'll warrant she'll tax him home,³   proceedings
30   And as you said—and wisely was it said—
'Tis meet° that some more audience than a mother,   fitting
Since nature makes them partial, should o'erhear
The speech of vantage.° Fare you well, my liege.   in addition
I'll call upon you ere you go to bed
And tell you what I know.
35   KING   Thanks, dear my lord.
Exit [POLONIUS].

Oh, my offense is rank, it smells to heaven;
It hath the primal eldest curse⁴ upon't—

---

2. However much by my words.
3. To confirm them with visible deeds.
3.3 Location: The castle.
1. The responsibilities of our position.
2. An ambiguous term suggesting "brain," "expres-

sions," or "effrontery." Instead of "brows," F has
"lunacies."
3. I'm sure she will rebuke him thoroughly.
4. The first, oldest curse (God's curse on Cain for
murdering his brother, Abel; see Genesis 4:10–12).

A brother's murder. Pray can I not:
Though inclination be as sharp as will,[5]
40 My stronger guilt defeats my strong intent
And like a man to double business bound[6]
I stand in pause where I shall first begin,
And both neglect. What if this cursèd hand
Were thicker than itself with brother's blood[7]—
45 Is there not rain enough in the sweet heavens
To wash it white as snow?[8] Whereto serves mercy
But to confront the visage of offense?[9]
And what's in prayer but this twofold force:
To be forestalled° ere we come to fall   *prevented*
50 Or pardoned, being down? Then I'll look up.
My fault is past, but, oh, what form of prayer
Can serve my turn? Forgive me my foul murder?
That cannot be, since I am still possessed
Of those effects for which I did the murder—
55 My crown, mine own ambition, and my queen.
May one be pardoned and retain th'offense?[1]
In the corrupted currents of this world
Offense's gilded° hand may shove by justice,   *bribing*
And oft 'tis seen the wicked prize[2] itself
60 Buys out the law, but 'tis not so above.
There is no shuffling,° there the action lies   *evasion*
In his true nature,[3] and we ourselves compelled
Even to the teeth and forehead of[4] our faults
To give in evidence.[5] What then? What rests?°   *remains to be done*
65 Try what repentance can—what can it not?
Yet what can it when one cannot repent?
Oh, wretched state; oh, bosom black as death;
Oh, limèd[6] soul that struggling to be free
Art more engaged!° Help, angels! Make assay°—   *entangled / some attempt*
70 Bow, stubborn knees, and heart with strings of steel,
Be soft as sinews of the newborn babe.
All may be well.
        Enter HAMLET [*behind him*].
HAMLET Now might I do it, but now 'a° is a-praying.   *he*
And now I'll do't! [*He draws his sword.*] And so 'a goes to
        heaven,
75 And so am I revenged—that would be scanned:[7]
A villain kills my father, and for that
I, his sole son, do this same villain send
To heaven.
Why, this is base and silly, not revenge.

---

5. Though my desire (to pray) is as strong as my determination to do so.
6. Committed to two different goals.
7. Were covered with a layer of brother's blood deeper than the hand's thickness.
8. Compare Isaiah 1:15–18: "And though ye make many prayers, I will not hear: for your hands are full of blood. Wash you, make you clean; take away the evil of your works from before mine eyes. . . . though your sins were as crimson, they shall be made white as snow."
9. *Whereto . . . offense:* What purpose has mercy if not to oppose sin face to face?

1. And keep what was gained from the crime.
2. The profits from wickedness.
3. *the action . . . nature:* the deed appears in its true form; legal proceedings are properly conducted.
4. *Even . . . of:* Even face to face with. (English law provided for the confrontation of the accused and the witnesses.)
5. To testify. In English law, one cannot be forced to give evidence against oneself; heavenly justice is different.
6. Caught as if in birdlime, a sticky substance smeared on twigs to catch birds.
7. That needs careful evaluation.

80 'A took my father grossly, full of bread,[8]
With all his crimes broad blown,[9] as flush° as May—   *vigorously thriving*
And how his audit° stands, who knows save heaven?   *spiritual account*
But in our circumstance and course of thought[1]
'Tis heavy with him. And am I then revenged
85 To take him in the purging of his soul
When he is fit and seasoned° for his passage?   *made ready*
No.
      [*He sheathes his sword.*]
Up, sword, and know thou a more horrid hent[2]—
When he is drunk asleep, or in his rage,
90 Or in th'incestuous pleasure of his bed,
At game, a-swearing, or about some act
That has no relish° of salvation in't.   *trace*
Then trip him that his heels may kick at heaven
And that his soul may be as damned and black
95 As hell whereto it goes. My mother stays°—   *waits*
This physic[3] but prolongs thy sickly days.   *Exit.*
KING My words fly up, my thoughts remain below;
Words without thoughts never to heaven go.   *Exit.*

3.4

Enter QUEEN *and* POLONIUS.

POLONIUS 'A will come straight.° Look you lay home to him:[1]   *immediately*
Tell him his pranks have been too broad° to bear with   *outrageous*
And that your grace hath screened and stood between
Much heat and him. I'll silence me even here.
5 Pray you be round.[2]
5.1   HAMLET (*within*) *Mother, mother, mother.*
QUEEN I'll warr'nt you, fear° me not.   *doubt*
Withdraw, I hear him coming.
      [POLONIUS *hides behind an arras.*]
      Enter HAMLET.
HAMLET Now, mother, what's the matter?
QUEEN Hamlet, thou hast thy father much offended.
10 HAMLET Mother, you have my father much offended.
QUEEN Come, come, you answer with an idle tongue.
HAMLET Go, go, you question with a wicked tongue.
QUEEN Why, how now,° Hamlet?   *what's this*
HAMLET   What's the matter now?
QUEEN Have you forgot me?[3]
HAMLET   No, by the rood,° not so: *cross of Christ*
15 You are the Queen, your husband's brother's wife,
And, would it were not so, you are my mother.
QUEEN Nay, then I'll set those to you that can speak.[4]
HAMLET Come, come and sit you down, you shall not budge;

---

8. Not spiritually prepared. Compare Ezekiel 16:49: "Behold, this was the iniquity of thy sister Sodom, pride, fullness of bread, and abundance of idleness."
9. With all his sins in full bloom.
1. But in our indirect and limited way of knowing on earth.
2. Design. Or, occasion (if "hent" is taken from "hint").
3. Medicine (both Claudius's prayer and Hamlet's

postponement of the revenge).
3.4 Location: The Queen's private chamber.
1. Be sure to rebuke him thoroughly.
2. F has the following line, 5.1, omitted in Q2. *round*: blunt.
3. Forgotten the respect you owe to me as your mother.
4. *that can speak*: who can deal with someone as impossibly rude as you.

You go not till I set you up a glass°
20   Where you may see the inmost part of you.
    QUEEN What wilt thou do? Thou wilt not murder me?
    Help, ho!
    POLONIUS [*behind the arras*] What ho! Help!
    HAMLET How now, a rat?
    [*He stabs through the arras and kills* POLONIUS.]
                 Dead for a ducat, dead.[5]
    POLONIUS Oh, I am slain!
25   QUEEN   O me, what hast thou done?
    HAMLET Nay, I know not. Is it the King?
    [*He parts the arras, discovering* POLONIUS.]
    QUEEN Oh, what a rash and bloody deed is this!
    HAMLET A bloody deed—almost as bad, good mother,
    As kill a king and marry with his brother.
    QUEEN As kill a king?
30   HAMLET   Ay, lady, it was my word.
    [*to* POLONIUS] Thou wretched, rash, intruding fool,
       farewell.
    I took thee for thy better. Take thy fortune.
    Thou find'st to be too busy° is some danger.   *nosy*
    —Leave wringing of your hands. Peace, sit you down
35   And let me wring your heart, for so I shall
    If it be made of penetrable stuff,
    If damnèd custom° have not brazed it so   *sinful habit*
    That it be proof and bulwark against sense.[6]
    QUEEN What have I done that thou dar'st wag thy tongue
    In noise so rude against me?
40   HAMLET   Such an act
    That blurs the grace and blush of modesty,
    Calls virtue hypocrite, takes off the rose
    From the fair forehead of an innocent love
    And sets a blister there,[7] makes marriage vows
45   As false as dicers' oaths—oh, such a deed
    As from the body of contraction° plucks   *marriage contract*
    The very soul, and sweet religion makes
    A rhapsody[8] of words. Heaven's face does glow°   *blush*
    O'er this solidity and compound mass[9]
50   With heated visage as against the doom,[1]
    Is thought-sick at the act—
    QUEEN   Ay me, what act
    That roars so loud and thunders in the index?[2]
    HAMLET Look here upon this picture, and on this—
    The counterfeit presentment° of two brothers.   *painted portrayal*
55   See what a grace was seated on this brow,
    Hyperion's° curls, the front° of Jove himself,   *The sun god's / forehead*
    An eye like Mars° to threaten and command,   *Roman god of war*
    A station like the herald Mercury[3]
    New lighted° on a heaven-kissing hill,   *Newly alighted*

---

5. I bet a ducat I have killed it.
6. *brazed . . . sense:* made it so brazen that it is impenetrably fortified against natural feeling ("sense").
7. Prostitutes, among other criminals, were branded on the forehead during the sixteenth and seventeenth centuries.

8. Meaningless jumble.
9. Solid earth (a compound of the four elements).
1. As if preparing for the Last Judgment.
2. Table of contents; preface.
3. A stance like the winged herald of the gods.

60 A combination and a form indeed
    Where every god did seem to set his seal
    To give the world assurance of a man.
    This was your husband. Look you now what follows:
    Here is your husband, like a mildewed ear°   *ear of grain*
65 Blasting° his wholesome brother. Have you eyes?   *Infecting*
    Could you on this fair mountain leave° to feed   *cease*
    And batten on this moor?⁴ Ha, have you eyes?
    You cannot call it love, for at your age
    The heyday in the blood⁵ is tame, it's humble
70 And waits° upon the judgment, and what judgment   *follows*
    Would step from this to this?⁶ Sense⁷ sure you have,
    Else could you not have motion, but sure that sense
    Is apoplexed,° for madness would not err   *paralyzed*
    Nor sense to ecstasy was ne'er so thralled
75 But it reserved some quantity of choice
    To serve in such a difference.⁸ What devil was't
    That thus hath cozened you at hoodman-blind?⁹
    Eyes without feeling, feeling without sight,
    Ears without hands or eyes, smelling sans all,¹
80 Or but a sickly part of one true sense
    Could not so mope.² O shame, where is thy blush?
    Rebellious hell,
    If thou canst mutine° in a matron's bones,   *mutiny*
    To flaming youth let virtue be as wax
85 And melt in her° own fire. Proclaim no shame   *(youth's)*
    When the compulsive ardor gives the charge,°   *order to attack*
    Since frost itself as actively doth burn,
    And reason pardons will.³
QUEEN   O Hamlet, speak no more!
    Thou turn'st my very eyes into my soul,
90 And there I see such black and grievèd° spots   *diseased*
    As will leave there their tinct.°   *color*
HAMLET   Nay, but to live
    In the rank sweat of an enseamèd° bed,   *a greasy*
    Stewed in corruption, honeying and making love
    Over the nasty sty—
QUEEN   Oh, speak to me no more!
95 These words like daggers enter in my ears.
    No more, sweet Hamlet.
HAMLET   A murderer and a villain,
    A slave that is not twentieth part the kith°   *likeness; kin*
    Of your precedent° lord, a vice⁴ of kings,   *previous*
    A cutpurse° of the empire and the rule,   *pickpocket*

---

4. And glut yourself on this poor pastureland (possibly punning on "blackamoor").
5. The excitement of sexual passion.
6. The following passage (to line 81) appears in Q2, where F simply reads: "What devil was't / That thus hath cozened you at hoodman-blind? / O shame, where is thy blush?"
7. Sensation; the five senses (sight, smell, hearing, taste, and touch).
8. *ne'er . . . difference:* never so enslaved by madness that it did not retain some ability to choose between such different men ("sense" connoting "reason").

9. That in this way has cheated you in blindman's buff (as if her second husband had been put in her way while she was groping blindfolded).
1. *sans all:* without any other sense. Cf. Psalm 115:5–6 on idolaters: "Eyes have they, but they see not: They have ears but they hear not: noses have they, but they smell not."
2. Could not be so obtuse.
3. And mature reason abets lust (rather than restraining it).
4. In morality plays, the Vice was the buffoon who personified evil.

100   That from a shelf the precious diadem stole
And put it in his pocket—

QUEEN   No more!

HAMLET   A king of shreds and patches[5]—

        Enter GHOST.[6]

Save me and hover o'er me with your wings,
You heavenly guards! —What would your gracious figure?

105 QUEEN   Alas, he's mad.

HAMLET   Do you not come your tardy son to chide
That, lapsed in time and passion,[7] lets go by
Th'important° acting of your dread command?   *The urgent*
Oh, say.

GHOST   Do not forget. This visitation

110   Is but to whet thy almost blunted purpose.
But look, amazement on thy mother sits.
Oh, step between her and her fighting soul—
Conceit° in weakest bodies strongest works.   *Imagination*
Speak to her, Hamlet.

HAMLET   How is it with you, lady?

115 QUEEN   Alas, how is't with you
That you do bend your eye on vacancy
And with th'incorporal° air do hold discourse?   *bodiless*
Forth at your eyes your spirits wildly peep,
And as the sleeping soldiers in th'alarm°   *the call to arms*

120   Your bedded hair like life in excrements[8]
Start up and stand on end. O gentle son,
Upon the heat and flame of thy distemper°   *unbalanced mind*
Sprinkle cool patience. Whereon do you look?

HAMLET   On him, on him! Look you how pale he glares;

125   His form and cause conjoined,[9] preaching to stones,
Would make them capable. [*to* GHOST] Do not look
    upon me
Lest with this piteous action you convert°   *change (to mercy)*
My stern effects°—then what I have to do   *intended acts*
Will want true color,[1] tears perchance° for blood.   *perhaps*

130 QUEEN   To whom do you speak this?

HAMLET   Do you see nothing there?

QUEEN   Nothing at all, yet all that is I see.

HAMLET   Nor did you nothing hear?

QUEEN   No, nothing but ourselves.

135 HAMLET   Why, look you there, look how it steals away—
My father in his habit[2] as° he lived!   *when; as if*
Look where he goes even now out at the portal.°   *door*

        Exit GHOST.

QUEEN   This is the very coinage of your brain:
This bodiless creation ecstasy

140   Is very cunning in.[3]

---

5. *shreds and patches:* motley, the costume of a jester.
6. Q1 specifies that the Ghost enters in his nightgown; Q2 and F leave open the possibility that the Ghost is appearing again in his armor.
7. *lapsed . . . passion:* having allowed time to pass and passionate dedication (to revenge) to fade.
8. In insensate outgrowths (used of nails and hair). *bedded:* (formerly) flat and inert.

9. His appearance joined with his reason for appearing.
1. Will not be as it should (since he cries colorless tears instead of shedding red blood).
2. Dress and bearing.
3. *This bodiless . . . in:* This type of hallucination is a particular skill ("cunning") of madness.

HAMLET   My pulse as yours doth temperately keep time
  And makes as healthful music. It is not madness
  That I have uttered. Bring me to the test
  And I the matter will reword,° which madness   *repeat exactly*
145 Would gambol° from. Mother, for love of grace,   *skitter away*
  Lay not that flattering unction⁴ to your soul
  That not your trespass but my madness speaks.
  It will but skin° and film the ulcerous place   *cover*
  Whiles rank corruption, mining° all within,   *undermining*
150 Infects unseen. Confess yourself to heaven,
  Repent what's past, avoid what is to come,
  And do not spread the compost on the weeds
  To make them ranker. Forgive me this my virtue,° *virtuous exhortation*
  For in the fatness° of these pursy° times   *grossness / flabby*
155 Virtue itself of vice must pardon beg,
  Yea, curb° and woo for leave° to do him good.   *bow / permission*
QUEEN   O Hamlet, thou hast cleft my heart in twain.
HAMLET   Oh, throw away the worser part of it
  And live the purer with the other half.
160 Good night. But go not to my uncle's bed—
  Assume° a virtue if you have it not.⁵   *Put on (actions of)*
  That monster custom, who all sense doth eat,
  Of habits devil,° is angel yet in this,   *devilish*
  That to the use° of actions fair and good   *habitual practice*
165 He likewise gives a frock or livery
  That aptly° is put on. Refrain tonight,   *quickly*
  And that shall lend a kind of easiness
  To the next abstinence, the next more easy.
  For use almost can change the stamp of nature,
170 And either lodge the devil, or throw him out⁶
  With wondrous potency. Once more good night,
  And when you are desirous to be blessed,
  I'll blessing beg of you. For this same lord
  I do repent. But heaven hath pleased it so
175 To punish me with this and this with me,
  That I must be their scourge and minister.⁷
  I will bestow° him and will answer well⁸   *dispose of*
  The death I gave him. So again, good night.
  I must be cruel only to be kind.
180 This bad begins and worse remains behind.°   *to follow*
  One word more, good lady.
QUEEN   What shall I do?
HAMLET   Not this, by no means that I bid you do:
  Let the bloat King tempt you again to bed,
  Pinch wanton on your cheek, call you his mouse,
185 And let him for a pair of reechy° kisses,   *filthy*
  Or paddling° in your neck with his damned fingers, *fondly fingering*
  Make you to ravel° all this matter out   *disclose*
  That I essentially am not in madness

---

4. Do not apply an ointment that relieves pain but does not heal (contrasted to a sacramental unction that blesses the soul).
5. Lines 162–71 represent Q2's version of the passage, which is considerably shorter in F.
6. Textual Comment Q2's version of this line (which begins "And either the deuill") is clearly defective, and supplying a verb meant to contrast with "throwing out" seems the most sensible solution. See Digital Edition TC 6 (combined text).
7. Heaven's agent of punishment.
8. Will take responsibility for.

But mad in craft.° 'Twere good you let him know,   *cunning*
190 For who that's but° a queen, fair, sober, wise,   *only*
Would from a paddock,° from a bat, a gib,°   *toad / tomcat*
Such dear concernings° hide? Who would do so?   *vital affairs*
No, in despite of sense and secrecy,
Unpeg the basket on the house's top,
195 Let the birds fly and, like the famous ape,
To try conclusions, in the basket creep
And break your own neck down.[9]
QUEEN   Be thou assured, if words be made of breath
And breath of life, I have no life to breathe
200 What thou hast said to me.
HAMLET   I must to England, you know that.
QUEEN   Alack,
I had forgot; 'tis so concluded on.[1]
HAMLET   There's letters sealed and my two schoolfellows,
Whom I will trust as I will adders fanged,
205 They bear the mandate. They must sweep my way
And marshal me to knavery.[2] Let it work,°   *proceed*
For 'tis the sport to have the enginer[3]
Hoist with his own petard[4]—and't shall go hard
But I will delve one yard below their mines°   *military tunnels*
210 And blow them at the moon. Oh, 'tis most sweet
When in one line two crafts directly meet.[5]
[*He indicates* POLONIUS.] This man shall set me packing—
I'll lug the guts into the neighbor room.
Mother, good night indeed. This counselor
215 Is now most still, most secret, and most grave,
Who was in life a most foolish prating knave.
—Come, sir, to draw toward an end with you.[6]
—Good night, mother.   *Exit* [*with Polonius' body*].
          Enter KING *with* ROSENCRANTZ *and* GUILDENSTERN.
KING   There's matter in these sighs; these profound heaves
220 You must translate—'tis fit we understand them.
Where is your son?
QUEEN   Bestow this place on us a little while.
            [*Exeunt* ROSENCRANTZ *and* GUILDENSTERN.]
Ah, mine own lord, what have I seen tonight!
KING   What, Gertrude? How does Hamlet?
225 QUEEN   Mad as the sea and wind when both contend
Which is the mightier: in his lawless fit,
Behind the arras hearing something stir,
Whips out his rapier, cries, "A rat, a rat,"
And in this brainish apprehension° kills   *brain-sick notion*
The unseen good old man.
230 KING   Oh, heavy deed!
It had been so with us° had we been there.   *me (royal "we")*

---

9. *like . . . down:* A tale presumably involving an ape who opened a wicker cage full of birds and released them from the rooftop; after climbing into the basket, he tried to imitate their flight to freedom but died in the fall. *try conclusions:* test the results.
1. The following passage, lines 203–11, is omitted in F.
2. *sweep . . . knavery:* prepare my path and escort me into a trap (also, and provoke me to crime).

3. Designer and builder of "engines" (military devices).
4. Blown skyward by his own bomb (for breaching enemy fortifications).
5. That is, when two devious plots ("crafts") meet along the same path of tunneling (a standard technique in siege warfare).
6. To conclude my dealings with you (punning on "draw" as "drag").

His liberty is full of threats to all,
To you yourself, to us, to everyone.
Alas, how shall this bloody deed be answered?°   *accounted for*
235   It will be laid to° us whose providence°   *blamed on / foresight*
Should have kept short,° restrained, and out of haunt[7]   *closely tethered*
This mad young man. But so much was our love
We would not understand what was most fit,
But like the owner° of a foul disease,   *victim*
240   To keep it from divulging,° let it feed   *being seen*
Even on the pith of life. Where is he gone?
QUEEN   To draw apart the body he hath killed,
    O'er whom his very madness, like some ore°   *vein of gold*
    Among a mineral° of metals base,   *mine*
245   Shows itself pure: 'a° weeps for what is done.   *he*
KING   O Gertrude, come away.
    The sun no sooner shall the mountains touch
    But we will ship him hence, and this vile deed
    We must with all our majesty and skill
250   Both countenance° and excuse. Ho, Guildenstern!   *condone*
        Enter ROSENCRANTZ *and* GUILDENSTERN.
    Friends both, go join you with some further aid.
    Hamlet in madness hath Polonius slain,
    And from his mother's closet hath he dragged him.
    Go seek him out, speak fair, and bring the body
255   Into the chapel. I pray you haste in this.
        [*Exeunt* ROSENCRANTZ *and* GUILDENSTERN.]
    Come, Gertrude, we'll call up our wisest friends
    And let them know both what we mean to do
    And what's untimely done[8]—
    Whose whisper[9] o'er the world's diameter,°   *whole extent*
260   As level as the cannon to his blank[1]
    Transports his poisoned shot, may miss our name
    And hit the woundless° air. Oh, come away,   *invulnerable*
    My soul is full of discord and dismay.   *Exeunt.*

3.5

    Enter HAMLET.
HAMLET   Safely stowed.
    [*Shouts within, "Hamlet!"*]
    But soft, what noise? Who calls on Hamlet? Oh, here they
    come.
        Enter ROSENCRANTZ, [GUILDENSTERN,] *and others.*
ROSENCRANTZ   What have you done, my lord, with the dead
5   body?
HAMLET   Compound° it with dust whereto 'tis kin.   *Mix*
ROSENCRANTZ   Tell us where 'tis that we may take it thence
    and bear it to the chapel.
HAMLET   Do not believe it.
10   ROSENCRANTZ   Believe what?

---

7. Public gatherings.
8. The following passage, lines 259–62, is omitted in F.
9. The subject of "whisper" is unclear. Scholars have conjectured that the passage is defective, perhaps lacking a line that establishes "slander" as the subject

of "whisper."
1. As straight as the cannon at a target at point-blank range. (The cannon would be tilted to aim at a distant target.)
3.5 Location: Scene continues.

HAMLET   That I can keep your counsel and not mine own.[1]
   Besides, to be demanded of° a sponge, what replication°   *questioned by / reply*
   should be made by the son of a king?
ROSENCRANTZ   Take you me for a sponge, my lord?
15 HAMLET   Ay, sir, that soaks up the King's countenance,° his   *favor*
   rewards, his authorities. But such officers do the King best
   service in the end. He keeps them like an ape in the corner
   of his jaw—first mouthed to be last swallowed. When he
   needs what you have gleaned, it is but squeezing you and,
20   sponge, you shall be dry again.
ROSENCRANTZ   I understand you not, my lord.
HAMLET   I am glad of it. A knavish speech sleeps in a foolish
   ear.[2]
ROSENCRANTZ   My lord, you must tell us where the body is
25   and go with us to the King.
HAMLET   The body is with the King, but the King is not with
   the body.[3] The King is a thing—
GUILDENSTERN   A thing, my lord?
HAMLET   Of nothing. Bring me to him.   *Exeunt.*

3.6

Enter KING *and two or three.*[1]
KING   I have sent to seek him and to find the body.
   How dangerous is it that this man goes loose!
   Yet must not we put the strong law on him—
   He's loved of° the distracted° multitude,   *by / unreasonable*
5   Who like not in their judgment but their eyes,[2]
   And where 'tis so, th'offender's scourge° is weighed   *punishment*
   But never the offense. To bear° all smooth and even,   *manage*
   This sudden sending him away must seem
   Deliberate pause.° Diseases desperate grown   *Careful planning*
10   By desperate appliance° are relieved   *remedy*
   Or not at all.
      Enter ROSENCRANTZ[, GUILDENSTERN,] *and all*
      the rest.
   How now, what hath befallen?
ROSENCRANTZ   Where the dead body is bestowed, my lord,
   We cannot get from him.
KING   But where is he?
ROSENCRANTZ   Without,° my lord, guarded, to know your   *Outside*
   pleasure.
KING   Bring him before us.
15 ROSENCRANTZ   —Ho! Bring in the lord.
      Enter [HAMLET, *guarded*].
KING   Now, Hamlet, where's Polonius?
HAMLET   At supper.

---

1. Hamlet plays on two senses of "counsel": that I
can follow your advice and not keep my secret.
2. An insulting remark is not perceived by a fool.
3. A riddle. Hamlet may mean that Polonius is gone
to the afterlife with King Hamlet but Claudius is still
alive; or he may refer to the legal theory of the "king's
two bodies" (one the king's natural body, the other
the immortal abstract body of the state).
3.6 Location: Scene continues.
1. TEXTUAL COMMENT F's version of this stage direc-

tion, which has the King enter alone and speak his
opening lines as a soliloquy, makes better theatrical
sense than Q2's, which has the King enter with *"two
or three"* attendants. This and other confusions in this
scene's stage directions corroborate the view that Q2
was printed from Shakespeare's "foul papers." See
Digital Edition TC 7 (combined text).
2. Who choose not by reason but by external
appearance.

KING   At supper? Where?

HAMLET   Not where he eats, but where 'a is eaten:[3] a certain
20   convocation of politic° worms are e'en° at him. Your worm is   *cunning / now*
    your only emperor for diet.[4] We fat all creatures else° to fat   *besides ourselves*
    us, and we fat ourselves for maggots. Your fat king and your
    lean beggar is but variable service,° two dishes but to one   *different courses*
    table. That's the end.

25   KING   Alas, alas.

HAMLET   A man may fish with the worm that hath ate of a
    king and eat of the fish that hath fed of that worm.

KING   What dost thou mean by this?

HAMLET   Nothing but to show you how a king may go a prog-
30   ress° through the guts of a beggar.   *royal journey*

KING   Where is Polonius?

HAMLET   In heaven. Send thither to see; if your messenger
    find him not there, seek him i'th' other place yourself. But if
    indeed you find him not within this month, you shall nose
35   him as you go up the stairs into the lobby.

KING [to Attendants]   Go seek him there.

HAMLET   'A will stay till you come.   [Exeunt Attendants.]

KING   Hamlet, this deed, for thine especial safety,
    Which we do tender° as we dearly grieve   *value*
40   For that which thou hast done, must send thee hence.
    Therefore prepare thyself:
    The bark° is ready and the wind at help,   *ship*
    The associates tend,° and everything is bent°   *companions wait / poised*
    For England.

HAMLET   For England?

KING   Ay, Hamlet.

HAMLET   Good.

45   KING   So is it if thou knew'st our purposes.

HAMLET   I see a cherub[5] that sees them. But come, for
        England.
    Farewell, dear mother.

KING   Thy loving father, Hamlet.

HAMLET   My mother: father and mother is man and wife,
    Man and wife is one flesh,[6] so my mother.
50   Come, for England.   *Exit.*

KING   Follow him at foot,° tempt him with speed aboard.   *his heel*
    Delay it not—I'll have him hence tonight.
    Away, for everything is sealed and done
    That else leans° on th'affair. Pray you make haste.   *bears*
        [Exeunt all but KING.]

55   And England,[7] if my love thou hold'st at aught°—   *any value*
    As my great power thereof may give thee sense,[8]
    Since yet thy cicatrice° looks raw and red   *scar*
    After the Danish sword, and thy free awe[9]

---

3. Possibly an allusion to the Eucharist (Lord's Supper), in which the body of Christ is consumed in the
form of bread.
4. *Your worm . . . diet:* The average worm is the only
creature with a diet superior to a king's. The Diet
(Council) of Emperor Charles V at Worms in 1521
called on Martin Luther to defend his new Protestant
doctrine. A scholar at Hamlet's university at Wittenberg, Luther maintained that faith alone, rather than

sacramental ritual, was the basis of salvation.
5. The keen-sighted second order of angels, cherubim symbolized heavenly knowledge.
6. As stated in Genesis 2:23–24 and the marriage
rite of the Book of Common Prayer.
7. King of England.
8. May give you a reason to feel the value of that love.
9. Your respect unconstrained (by an army of occupation).

Pays homage to us—thou mayst not coldly set°   *indifferently,*
60 Our sovereign process, which imports at full,[1]
By letters congruing to° that effect,   *according with*
The present° death of Hamlet. Do it, England,   *immediate*
For like the hectic° in my blood he rages   *fever*
And thou must cure me. Till I know 'tis done,
65 Howe'er my haps,° my joys will ne'er begin.   *Exit.*   *fortunes*

4.1

Enter FORTINBRAS [*and a* CAPTAIN] *with his army*
over the stage.

FORTINBRAS   Go, Captain, from me greet the Danish King.
Tell him that by his license° Fortinbras   *permission*
Craves the conveyance of° a promised march   *escort for*
Over his kingdom. You know the rendezvous.
5 If that his majesty would aught with us,
We shall express our duty in his eye°—   *presence*
And let him know so.
CAPTAIN   I will do't, my lord.
FORTINBRAS   Go softly° on.[1]   *slowly; circumspectly*
[*Exeunt* FORTINBRAS *and his army.*
The CAPTAIN *remains.*]

Enter HAMLET, ROSENCRANTZ[, GUILDENSTERN,
and others].

HAMLET   Good sir, whose powers° are these?   *forces*
CAPTAIN   They are of Norway, sir.
10 HAMLET   How purposed, sir, I pray you?
CAPTAIN   Against some part of Poland.
HAMLET   Who commands them, sir?
CAPTAIN   The nephew to old Norway, Fortinbras.
HAMLET   Goes it against the main° of Poland, sir,   *heart*
15 Or for some frontier?
CAPTAIN   Truly to speak, and with no addition,°   *exaggeration*
We go to gain a little patch of ground
That hath in it no profit but the name.
To pay five ducats—five—I would not farm° it,   *lease*
20 Nor will it yield to Norway or the Pole
A ranker rate should it be sold in fee.[2]
HAMLET   Why, then, the Polack never will defend it.
CAPTAIN   Yes, it is already garrisoned.
HAMLET   Two thousand souls and twenty thousand ducats
25 Will now debate the question of this straw.°   *trifle*
This is th'impostume° of much wealth and peace   *the abscess*
That inward breaks and shows no cause without[3]
Why the man dies. I humbly thank you, sir.
CAPTAIN   God b'wi'you, sir.   [*Exit* CAPTAIN.]
ROSENCRANTZ   Will't please you go, my lord?
30 HAMLET   I'll be with you straight. Go a little before.
[ROSENCRANTZ, GUILDENSTERN, *and the others*
move aside.]

---

1. Our sovereign command, which signifies in detailed
instructions.
4.1 Location: The Danish coast.
1. The rest of the scene, lines 8–65, is omitted in F.

2. Sold outright as a freehold. *ranker rate:* more generous return.
3. That ruptures internally without external symptom.

◆

)ccasions do inform against° me   *accuse*
my dull revenge. What is a man
ef good and market° of his time   *profit*
sleep and feed? A beast, no more.
that made us with such large discourse,°   *reasoning faculty*
Looking before and after,[4] gave us not
That capability° and godlike reason   *intelligence*
To fust° in us unused. Now, whether it be   *grow moldy*
Bestial oblivion[5] or some craven scruple
40   Of thinking too precisely on th'event—
A thought which quartered hath but one part wisdom
And ever three parts coward—I do not know
Why yet I live to say this thing's to do,
Sith° I have cause and will and strength and means   *Since*
45   To do't. Examples gross as earth exhort me:
Witness this army of such mass and charge,°   *cost*
Led by a delicate and tender° prince,   *young*
Whose spirit with divine ambition puffed°   *inspired*
Makes mouths at the invisible event,[6]
50   Exposing what is mortal and unsure
To all that fortune, death, and danger dare,
Even for an eggshell. Rightly to be great
Is not to stir without great argument
But greatly to find quarrel in a straw
55   When honor's at the stake.[7] How stand I, then,
That have a father killed, a mother stained,
Excitements° of my reason and my blood,   *Urgings*
And let all sleep, while to my shame I see
The imminent death of twenty thousand men
60   That, for a fantasy and trick° of fame,   *fragile trifle*
Go to their graves like beds, fight for a plot
Whereon the numbers cannot try the cause,[8]
Which is not tomb enough and continent°   *container*
To hide the slain? Oh, from this time forth,
65   My thoughts be bloody or be nothing worth.

                             Exit [with the others].

4.2

Enter HORATIO, [QUEEN,] *and a* GENTLEMAN.

QUEEN   I will not speak with her.
GENTLEMAN[1]   She is importunate—indeed distract:°   *deranged; mad*
Her mood will needs be pitied.
QUEEN   What would she have?
GENTLEMAN   She speaks much of her father, says she hears
5   There's tricks i'th' world, and hems and beats her heart,
Spurns enviously at straws,[2] speaks things in doubt°   *obscurely*
That carry but half sense. Her speech is nothing,
Yet the unshaped use° of it doth move   *incoherent manner*
The hearers to collection:° they yawn° at it   *inference / gape*

---

4. Able to see past and future.
5. Animal-like inability to remember.
6. Shows a scornful face to unforeseeable outcomes.
7. *Rightly . . . stake:* These lines, syntactically ambiguous, seem to mean that true greatness lies not in rational restraint but in noble action. *the stake:* post to which a bull or bear was fastened for baiting.

8. That is not big enough for the armies to fight on.
4.2 Location: A public room of the castle.
1. In F, lines 2–3 and 4–13 are spoken by Horatio, while Gertrude comments on them in lines 14–15 (assigned in Q2 to Horatio).
2. Kicks bitterly (takes offense) at the slightest thing.

10 And botch° the words up fit to° their own thoughts patch / to match
Which,° as her winks and nods and gestures yield them, (words)
Indeed would make one think there might be thought,
Though nothing sure, yet much unhappily.³
HORATIO 'Twere good she were spoken with, for she may strew
15 Dangerous conjectures in ill-breeding minds.
QUEEN Let her come in.   [Exit GENTLEMAN.]
[aside] To my sick soul, as sin's true nature is,
Each toy° seems prologue to some great amiss.° triviality / calamity
So full of artless jealousy° is guilt, uncontrolled suspicion
20 It spills itself in fearing to be spilt.
        Enter OPHELIA.
OPHELIA Where is the beauteous majesty of Denmark?
QUEEN How now,° Ophelia? What's this
OPHELIA (sings) How should I your true love know
                From another one?
25   By his cockle hat and staff
                And his sandal shoon.⁴
QUEEN Alas, sweet lady, what imports° this song? means
OPHELIA Say you? Nay, pray you mark:° listen
    (Sings.)   He is dead and gone, lady,
30   He is dead and gone;
                At his head a grass-green turf,
                At his heels a stone.
Oh, oh!
QUEEN Nay, but Ophelia—
35 OPHELIA Pray you, mark:
    (Sings.)   White his shroud as the mountain snow—
            Enter KING.
QUEEN Alas, look here, my lord.
OPHELIA   Larded° all with sweet flowers, Garnished
            Which bewept to the ground did not⁵ go
40   With true love showers.° tears
KING How do you, pretty lady?
OPHELIA Well, good dild° you. They say the owl was a baker's God yield (reward)
daughter.⁶ Lord, we know what we are, but know not what
we may be. God be at your table.
45 KING Conceit° upon her father. Brooding imagination
OPHELIA Pray let's have no words of this, but when they ask
you what it means, say you this:
    (Sings.)   Tomorrow is Saint Valentine's day,
            All in the morning betime,° early
50   And I a maid at your window
                To be your valentine.

            Then up he rose and donned his clothes
            And dupped° the chamber door, unlatched
            Let in the maid that out a maid
55   Never departed more.

---

3. Though they reveal nothing for certain, her words provoke disturbing inferences.
4. Shoes. *cockle hat:* a cockleshell badge worn in the hat was a pilgrim's memento of St. James's shrine at Compostela in Spain.
5. By adding "not," Ophelia changes the song's words and meter to fit the circumstances of Polonius's

burial (see lines 82–83).
6. Referring to a folktale wherein Jesus visits a baker's shop asking for bread. The shop's mistress puts a generous piece in the oven but is reprimanded by her daughter, who is later turned into an owl for her stinginess.

KING   Pretty Ophelia—

OPHELIA   Indeed, without an oath I'll make an end on't:° *of it*

[*Sings.*]   By Gis° and by Saint Charity, *Jesus*
                 Alack and fie for shame,
60   Young men will do't if they come to't,
                 By Cock[7] they are to blame.

                 Quoth she, "Before you tumbled me
                 You promised me to wed."

He answers:

65   "So would I ha' done by yonder sun
                 An° thou hadst not come to my bed." *If*

KING   How long hath she been thus?

OPHELIA   I hope all will be well. We must be patient. But I can-
          not choose but weep to think they would lay him i'th' cold
70   ground. My brother shall know of it. And so I thank you for
          your good counsel. Come, my coach! Good night, ladies, good
          night, sweet ladies, good night, good night.   [*Exit.*]

KING [*to* HORATIO]   Follow her close. Give her good watch, I
          pray you.   [*Exit* HORATIO.]
          Oh, this is the poison of deep grief. It springs
75   All from her father's death—and now behold!
          O Gertrude, Gertrude,
          When sorrows come, they come not single spies° *scouts*
          But in battalions: first her father slain;
          Next your son gone, and he most violent author
80   Of his own just remove; the people muddied,° *confused*
          Thick and unwholesome in thoughts and whispers
          For good Polonius' death—and we have done but greenly° *naively*
          In hugger-mugger° to inter him; poor Ophelia, *secrecy*
          Divided from herself and her fair judgment,
85   Without the which we are pictures or mere beasts;
          Last, and as much containing° as all these, *and as important*
          Her brother is in secret come from France,
          Feeds on this wonder, keeps himself in clouds,° *his intentions obscure*
          And wants° not buzzers° to infect his ear *lacks / scandalmongers*
90   With pestilent speeches of his father's death,
          Wherein necessity, of matter beggared,
          Will nothing stick our person to arraign
          In ear and ear.[8] O my dear Gertrude, this,
          Like to a murdering piece,[9] in many places
95   Gives me superfluous° death. *redundant*
                 A noise within.[1]

95.1   QUEEN   *Alack, what noise is this?*

KING   Attend!
          Where is my Switzers?[2] Let them guard the door.
                 Enter a MESSENGER.
          What is the matter?

MESSENGER   Save yourself, my lord.

---

7. A corruption of "God" in very mild swearing (playing on "penis").
8. *Wherein . . . ear*: In which affair, because they
have no real information and need to give some
account, they will not hesitate to whisper accusations
against us.
9. Small cannon that fired shrapnel.
1. F has the following line, 95.1, not found in Q2.
2. Company of Swiss mercenaries (employed as royal
bodyguards in many European countries).

The ocean, overpeering of his list,[3]

100 Eats not the flats with more impiteous[4] haste
Than young Laertes in a riotous head°   *insurrection; tidal wave*
O'erbears your officers. The rabble call him lord
And, as° the world were now but° to begin,   *as if / only now*
Antiquity forgot, custom not known—

105 The ratifiers and props of every word[5]—
They cry, "Choose we: Laertes shall be king!"
Caps, hands, and tongues applaud it to the clouds,
"Laertes shall be king, Laertes king!"
      A *noise within.*
QUEEN   How cheerfully on the false trail they cry![6]

110 Oh, this is counter,[7] you false Danish dogs!
KING   The doors are broke.
      Enter LAERTES *with* [FOLLOWERS].
LAERTES   Where is this King? Sirs, stand you all without.
FOLLOWERS   No, let's come in.
LAERTES   I pray you give me leave.
FOLLOWERS   We will, we will.
LAERTES   I thank you. Keep° the door.   [*Exeunt* FOLLOWERS.]   *Guard*

115   O thou vile King,
Give me my father.
QUEEN [*restraining him*]   Calmly, good Laertes.
LAERTES   That drop of blood that's calm proclaims me
      bastard,
Cries "Cuckold!" to my father, brands the harlot
Even here between the chaste unsmirchèd brow
Of my true mother.

120 KING   What is the cause, Laertes,
That thy rebellion looks so giant-like?
—Let him go, Gertrude. Do not fear° our person: *fear for*
There's such divinity doth hedge a king
That treason can but peep to what it would,[8]

125 Acts little of his will. —Tell me, Laertes,
Why thou art thus incensed. —Let him go, Gertrude.
—Speak, man.
LAERTES   Where is my father?
KING   Dead.
QUEEN   But not by him.°   *(the King)*
KING   Let him demand his fill.

130 LAERTES   How came he dead? I'll not be juggled with.°   *deceived*
To hell allegiance, vows to the blackest devil,
Conscience and grace to the profoundest pit!
I dare damnation. To this point° I stand,   *resolve*
That both the worlds I give to negligence.[9]

135 Let come what comes, only I'll be revenged
Most throughly° for my father.   *thoroughly*

---

3. Rising over its boundary at the shore.
4. Probably meaning "merciless" as well as "rash." *flats:* low-lying countryside.
5. *Antiquity . . . word:* Ignoring history and traditional precedents, which give meaning, order, and stability to society by fixing the agreed-upon meaning of political contracts (and of any truth expressed in language).
6. How enthusiastically they run after the wrong scent (like a pack of hounds hunting the murderer of Polonius).
7. This is following the quarry's trail, but in the wrong direction.
8. That treason can only glance furtively at what it would like to do.
9. That both this world and the next do not matter to me.

KING   Who shall stay° you?   *prevent*

LAERTES   My will, not all the world's.
And for my means I'll husband them so well
They shall go far with little.

KING   Good Laertes,
140 If you desire to know the certainty
Of your dear father,[1] is't writ in your revenge
That, sweepstake,[2] you will draw° both friend and foe,   *take from*
Winner and loser?

LAERTES   None but his enemies.

KING   Will you know them, then?
145 LAERTES   To his good friends thus wide I'll ope my arms
And, like the kind life-rend'ring pelican,
Repast them with my blood.[3]

KING   Why, now you speak
Like a good child and a true gentleman.
That I am guiltless of your father's death
150 And am most sensibly° in grief for it,   *sympathetically*
It shall as level° to your judgment 'pear   *directly*
As day does to your eye.

A noise within. [OPHELIA *is heard singing.*]
[*to an Attendant*]   Let her come in.

LAERTES   How now, what noise is that?

Enter OPHELIA.

Oh, heat dry up my brains, tears seven times salt
155 Burn out the sense and virtue° of mine eye!   *natural power*
By heaven, thy madness shall be paid with weight
Till our scale turn the beam.[4] O rose of May,
Dear maid, kind sister, sweet Ophelia!
O Heavens, is't possible a young maid's wits
160 Should be as mortal as a poor man's life?[5]
160.1   *Nature is fine in love, and where 'tis fine*
             It sends some precious instance of itself
             After the thing it loves.[6]

OPHELIA (*sings*)   They bore him bare-faced on the bier[7]
161.1   *Hey non nonny, nonny, hey nonny,*
                  And in his grave rained many a tear.
Fare you well, my dove.

LAERTES   Hadst thou thy wits and didst persuade° revenge,   *argue for*
165 It could not move thus.

OPHELIA   You must sing "a-down a-down" —and you "call him
a-down-a." Oh, how the wheel[8] becomes it. It is the false
steward that stole his master's daughter.[9]

LAERTES   This nothing's more than matter.[1]

---

1. That is, of his death.
2. Indiscriminately. (The winner of a sweepstake gained the stakes of all other players.)
3. The female pelican was supposed to feed, and even revive, its young with blood from a wound it pecked in its own breast. *Repast:* Feed.
4. *shall . . . beam:* shall be atoned for until vengeance outweighs the injury of madness (thus tilting the "scale" of justice).
5. F has the following passage, lines 160.1–160.3, not found in Q2.
6. *Nature . . . loves:* Human nature is made most ethe-

really pure by love and sends a precious token ("instance") of itself after the object of its love. Laertes struggles to say that because of Ophelia's great love for her father, her sanity departed with him.
7. F has the following line of verse, 161.1, not found in Q2.
8. Probably refrain, although possibly spinning wheel (at which women sang ballads) or Fortune's wheel. "A-down a-down" resembles the refrain of ballads of the period.
9. *false . . . daughter:* The tale is unknown.
1. This nonsense signifies more than coherent speech.

170 OPHELIA   There's rosemary: that's for remembrance. Pray you,
          love, remember. And there is pansies: that's for thoughts.[2]
      LAERTES   A document° in madness: thoughts and remembrance   *An object lesson*
          fitted.
      OPHELIA   There's fennel for you and columbines;[3] there's rue
175   for you, and here's some for me. We may call it herb of grace
          o'Sundays. You may wear your rue with a difference.[4] There's
          a daisy. I would give you some violets,[5] but they withered all
          when my father died. They say 'a made a good end.
          [*Sings.*]   For bonny sweet Robin is all my joy.
180 LAERTES   Thought and afflictions, passion, hell itself
          She turns to favor° and to prettiness.   *beauty*
      OPHELIA (*sings*)   And will 'a not come again,
                          And will 'a not come again?
                          No, no, he is dead.
185   Go to thy deathbed.
                          He never will come again.

                          His beard was as white as snow,
                          Flaxen° was his poll.°   *White / head*
                          He is gone, he is gone,
190   And we cast away moan.
                          God ha' mercy on his soul—
          and of all Christians' souls. God b'wi'you.   [*Exit.*]
      LAERTES   Do you see this, O God?
      KING   Laertes, I must commune with your grief
195   Or you deny me right. Go but apart,
          Make choice of whom° your wisest friends you will,   *whichever of*
          And they shall hear and judge twixt you and me:
          If by direct or by collateral° hand   *an agent's*
          They find us touched,° we will our kingdom give,   *involved in guilt*
200   Our crown, our life, and all that we call ours
          To you in satisfaction;° but if not,   *recompense*
          Be you content to lend your patience to us
          And we shall jointly labor with your soul
          To give it due content.
      LAERTES   Let this be so.
205   His means of death, his obscure funeral—
          No trophy, sword, nor hatchment[6] o'er his bones,
          No noble rite, nor formal ostentation°—   *rite of grief*
          Cry to be heard as 'twere from heaven to earth
          That I must call't in question.[7]
      KING   So you shall.
210   And where th'offense is, let the great ax fall.
          I pray you go with me.   *Exeunt.*

---

2. *There's . . . thoughts:* Ophelia, recalling the flowers'
symbolic significance, distributes them to Laertes,
Gertrude, and Claudius.
3. Columbines were associated with ingratitude or
marital infidelity, fennel with flattery.
4. In heraldry, minor branches of a family were distinguished by a "difference," a variation or an addition
to the coat of arms. Ophelia probably means "for a
different reason." Rue is associated with repentance,
and Ophelia identifies it with the "herb of grace"

(wormwood), since penitence depended on and enabled
God's blessing.
5. Representing faithfulness; daisies could symbolize dissembling seduction.
6. Lozenge-shaped tablet bearing a coat of arms,
carried in funeral processions and deposited near the
tomb. *trophy:* memorial (often consisting of real or
symbolic weapons and armor).
7. I must demand an explanation of it.

4.3

Enter HORATIO *and* [*a* GENTLEMAN].

HORATIO   What are they that would speak with me?

GENTLEMAN   Seafaring men, sir. They say they have letters
for you.

HORATIO   Let them come in.   [*Exit* GENTLEMAN.]

5   I do not know from what part of the world I should be
greeted, if not from Lord Hamlet.

                    Enter SAILORS.

SAILOR   God bless you, sir.

HORATIO   Let Him bless thee too.

SAILOR   'A shall, sir, an° please Him. There's a letter for you, sir.   *if it*

10   It came from th'ambassador that was bound for England—if
your name be Horatio, as I am let to know it is.

HORATIO   [*reads the letter*]   "Horatio, when thou shalt have
overlooked° this, give these fellows some means° to the King: *read / access*
they have letters for him. Ere we were two days old at sea, a

15   pirate of very warlike appointment° gave us chase. Finding   *equipment*
ourselves too slow of sail, we put on a compelled valor and in
the grapple I boarded them. On the instant, they got clear of
our ship, so I alone became their prisoner. They have dealt
with me like thieves of mercy, but they knew what they did:[1]

20   I am to do a turn for them. Let the King have the letters I
have sent and repair thou° to me with as much speed as thou   *come*
wouldst fly death. I have words to speak in thine ear will
make thee dumb, yet are they much too light for the bore° of   *caliber; size*
the matter. These good fellows will bring thee where I am.

25   Rosencrantz and Guildenstern hold their course for England.
Of them I have much to tell thee. Farewell.

He that thou knowest thine,   Hamlet."

Come, I will give you way° for these your letters,   *means of delivery*
And do't the speedier that you may direct me

30   To him from whom you brought them.   *Exeunt.*

4.4

Enter KING *and* LAERTES.

KING   Now must your conscience my acquittance seal,[1]
And you must put me in your heart for friend
Sith° you have heard, and with a knowing ear,   *Since*
That he which hath your noble father slain
Pursued my life.

5   LAERTES   It well appears. But tell me
Why you proceed not against these feats,°   *acts*
So criminal and so capital° in nature,   *punishable by death*
As by your safety, greatness, wisdom, all things else,
You mainly° were stirred up.   *greatly*

KING   Oh, for two special reasons,

10   Which may to you perhaps seem much unsinewed,°   *uncompelling*

4.3 Location: The castle.
1. *They have . . . did:* They have been merciful, but
with the expectation of a return. Hamlet recalls the
thieves crucified next to Christ (one of whom he
blessed) and Christ's plea of forgiveness for those

who "know not what they do" (Luke 23:34–43).
4.4 Location: Claudius's private apartments.
1. *my acquittance seal:* affirm my innocence (of Polonius's death).

But yet to me they're strong. The Queen his mother
Lives almost by his looks and, for myself—
My virtue or my plague, be it either which—
She is so conjunct to my life and soul

15 That as the star moves not but in his sphere[2]
I could not but by her. The other motive
Why to a public count° I might not go   *accounting*
Is the great love the general gender° bear him,   *common people*
Who, dipping all his faults in their affection,

20 Work like the spring that turneth wood to stone,[3]
Convert his gyves° to graces; so that my arrows,   *shortcomings (lit. fetters)*
Too slightly timbered for so loud a wind,
Would have reverted to my bow again
But not where I have aimed them.

25 LAERTES   And so have I a noble father lost,
A sister driven into desperate terms,
Whose worth, if praises may go back again,[4]
Stood challenger on mount of all the age
For her perfections.[5] But my revenge will come.

30 KING   Break not your sleeps for that. You must not think
That we are made of stuff so flat and dull
That we can let our beard be shook with danger[6]
And think it pastime. You shortly shall hear more.
I loved your father, and we love ourself,

35 And that, I hope, will teach you to imagine[7]—
            Enter a MESSENGER *with letters.*
35.1   *How now, what news?*
    MESSENGER   *Letters, my lord, from Hamlet;*
These to your majesty, this to the Queen.
    KING   From Hamlet? Who brought them?
    MESSENGER   Sailors, my lord, they say—I saw them not.
They were given me by Claudio; he received them
Of him that brought them.

40 KING   Laertes, you shall hear them.
—Leave us.   [*Exit* MESSENGER.]
[*He reads.*] "High and mighty, you shall know I am set naked°   *destitute*
on your kingdom. Tomorrow shall I beg leave to see your
kingly eyes, when I shall, first asking you pardon,° thereunto   *permission*

45 recount the occasion of my sudden return."
What should this mean? Are all the rest come back,
Or is it some abuse° and no such thing?   *deception*
    LAERTES   Know you the hand?
    KING   'Tis Hamlet's character.°   *handwriting*
"Naked"?

50 And in a postscript here he says "alone."
Can you devise° me?   *direct*
    LAERTES   I am lost in it, my lord—but let him come.

---

2. According to Ptolemaic astronomy, heavenly bodies moved in hollow spheres. *conjunct* (line 14): closely united (as two planets were said astronomically to be "in conjunction" when they appeared close).
3. In limestone-rich areas (such as south Warwickshire), concentrations in spring water may be great enough to petrify absorbent objects.

4. May refer to what was (but is no longer).
5. *Stood . . . perfections:* Conspicuously challenged the world to match her perfections.
6. That I can allow anyone to endanger me with contemptuous behavior.
7. F has the following passage, lines 35.1–35.2, not found in Q2.

It warms the very sickness in my heart
That I live and tell him to his teeth,
"Thus didst thou."[8]

55 KING   If it be so, Laertes—
As how should it be so, how otherwise?[9]—
Will you be ruled by me?

LAERTES   Ay, my lord,
So° you will not o'errule me to a peace.   *Provided that*

KING   To thine own peace. If he be now returned
60 As checking at[1] his voyage and that he means
No more to undertake it, I will work him
To an exploit now ripe in my device,°   *planning*
Under the which he shall not choose but fall.
And for his death no wind of blame shall breathe
65 But even his mother shall uncharge° the practice°   *not accuse / connivance*
And call it accident.[2]

LAERTES   My lord, I will be ruled
The rather if you could devise it so
That I might be the organ.°   *agent*

KING   It falls right.
You have been talked of since your travel much,
70 And that in Hamlet's hearing, for a quality
Wherein they say you shine. Your sum of parts°   *abilities*
Did not together pluck such envy from him
As did that one, and that in my regard
Of the unworthiest siege.°   *lowest rank*

75 LAERTES   What part is that, my lord?

KING   A very ribbon in the cap of youth—
Yet needful too, for youth no less becomes°   *is suited by*
The light and careless livery that it wears
Than settled age his sables and his weeds
80 Importing health and graveness.[3] Two months since
Here was a gentleman of Normandy.
I have seen myself, and served against, the French,
And they can well° on horseback, but this gallant   *are skilled*
Had witchcraft in't; he grew unto his seat
85 And to such wondrous doing brought his horse
As had he been incorpsed and demi-natured[4]
With the brave beast. So far he topped,° methought,   *surpassed*
That I in forgery of shapes and tricks[5]
Come short of what he did.

LAERTES   A Norman, was't?

90 KING   A Norman.

LAERTES   Upon my life, Lamord!

KING   The very same.

LAERTES   I know him well—he is the brooch° indeed   *ornament*
And gem of all the nation.

KING   He made confession° of you   *testimonial*

---

8. This which I do now to you, you did to my father.
9. *As . . . otherwise:* How could Hamlet be returning, and yet how else could he have sent this letter?
1. As one who has been diverted from ("checking at" is a term from falconry).
2. The following passage, lines 66–80, is omitted in F.

3. *his sables . . . graveness:* its rich gowns trimmed with sable, garments ("weeds") signifying concern for prosperity and dignity.
4. As if he had been in the same body and had half the nature of (the image of a centaur).
5. That I in my very imagination ("forgery") of figures and skillful feats of horsemanship.

95 And gave you such a masterly report
For art and exercise in your defense,
And for your rapier most especial,
That he cried out 'twould be a sight indeed
If one could match you. The scrimers° of their nation   *fencers*
100 He swore had neither motion, guard, nor eye,
If you opposed them. Sir, this report of his
Did Hamlet so envenom with his envy
That he could nothing do but wish and beg
Your sudden° coming o'er to play with you.   *immediate*
Now out of this—
105 LAERTES   What out of this, my lord?
KING   Laertes, was your father dear to you?
Or are you like the painting of a sorrow,
A face without a heart?
LAERTES   Why ask you this?
KING   Not that I think you did not love your father,
110 But that I know love is begun by time°   *circumstance*
And that I see in passages of proof[6]
Time qualifies° the spark and fire of it.[7]   *moderates*
There lives within the very flame of love
A kind of wick or snuff[8] that will abate it,
115 And nothing is at a like° goodness still°—   *an equal / always*
For goodness growing to a pleurisy[9]
Dies in his own too much.° That we would do   *overabundance*
We should do when we would: for this "would" changes
And hath abatements and delays as many
120 As there are tongues, are hands, are accidents,
And then this "should" is like a spendthrift's sigh
That hurts by easing.[1] But to the quick° of th'ulcer—   *center*
Hamlet comes back. What would you undertake
To show yourself indeed your father's son
More than in words?
125 LAERTES   To cut his throat i'th' church.
KING   No place indeed should murder sanctuarize;[2]
Revenge should have no bounds. But, good Laertes,
Will you do this: keep close within your chamber;
Hamlet, returned, shall know you are come home.
130 We'll put on those shall[3] praise your excellence
And set a double varnish on the fame
The Frenchman gave you, bring you in fine° together   *conclusion*
And wager o'er your heads. He being remiss,°   *unwary*
Most generous° and free from all contriving,   *noble*
135 Will not peruse the foils, so that with ease,
Or with a little shuffling, you may choose
A sword unbated, and in a pass of practice[4]
Requite him for your father.

6. From experiences that have tested this.
7. The following passage, lines 113–22, is omitted in F.
8. Burned part of the wick (which causes smoke and reduces light if not removed).
9. A chest inflammation, metaphorically like a fire in the heart; thought to take its name from the Latin for "more" (*plus*) and to be caused by an excess of humors (and so playing on "excess").

1. A sigh was thought to use up a drop of blood.
2. Give sanctuary to a murderer. In English tradition, a criminal remained temporarily (and in some cases, permanently) safe from arrest for most crimes (save sacrilege and treason) as long as he took refuge in a church.
3. *We'll . . . shall:* I shall incite some people to.
4. In a treacherous thrust. *unbated:* unblunted (recreational or practice foils were typically blunted).

LAERTES   I will do't,
And for purpose I'll anoint my sword.
140   I bought an unction° of a mountebank°   *ointment / quack*
So mortal that, but dip a knife in it,
Where it draws blood no cataplasm° so rare,   *poultice*
Collected from all simples° that have virtue°   *herbs / potency*
Under the moon, can save the thing from death
145   That is but scratched withal.° I'll touch my point   *with it*
With this contagion that if I gall° him slightly   *prick*
It may be death.
KING   Let's further think of this—
Weigh what convenience both of time and means
May fit us to our shape.⁵ If this should fail
150   And that our drift look° through our bad performance,   *our intention be seen*
'Twere better not essayed. Therefore this project
Should have a back or second⁶ that might hold
If this did blast in proof.⁷ Soft, let me see,
We'll make a solemn wager on your cunnings°—   *skills*
155   I ha't:
When in your motion° you are hot and dry,   *exercise*
As make your bouts more violent to that end,
And that he calls for drink, I'll have prepared him
A chalice for the nonce° whereon but sipping,   *occasion*
160   If he by chance escape your venomed stuck,°   *thrust*
Our purpose may hold there. But stay, what noise?
            Enter QUEEN.
QUEEN   One woe doth tread upon another's heel,
So fast they follow. Your sister's drowned, Laertes.
LAERTES   Drowned? Oh, where?
165   QUEEN   There is a willow grows askant° the brook   *aslant*
That shows his hoary leaves⁸ in the glassy stream;
Therewith fantastic garlands did she make
Of crowflowers, nettles, daisies, and long purples⁹
That liberal shepherds give a grosser¹ name
170   But our cold° maids do dead men's fingers call them.   *chaste*
There on the pendant boughs her crownet° weeds   *garlanded*
Clamb'ring to hang,² an envious sliver° broke,   *a malicious twig*
When down her weedy trophies and herself
Fell in the weeping brook. Her clothes spread wide
175   And mermaid-like awhile they bore her up,
Which time she chanted snatches of old lauds°   *hymns*
As one incapable° of her own distress,   *uncomprehending*
Or like a creature native and endued
Unto that element.³ But long it could not be
180   Till that her garments, heavy with their drink,
Pulled the poor wretch from her melodious lay°   *song*

5. May make us ready to put into effect our plot and to assume the roles we are to play.
6. Should have something in reserve (military metaphor for the plotting).
7. Should blow up in our faces when put to the test (like a cannon).
8. The willow leaf is gray-white ("hoary") on the underside (reflected from below by the water). The willow was an emblem of mourning and of forsaken love.
9. Early purple orchids. *crowflowers*: common name

for several wildflowers, including Ragged Robin and bluebells (often appearing beside long purples in woodland and sharing their association with fertility).
1. More indecent. Among the recorded names for the purple orchis are "priest's-pintle" (penis), "dog's cullions" (testicles), "goat's cullions," and "fool's ballochs." *liberal*: free-spoken.
2. Deserted lovers proverbially hung garlands on willows.
3. *native . . . element*: naturally fit to live in water.

To muddy death.

LAERTES   Alas, then she is drowned.

QUEEN   Drowned, drowned.

LAERTES   Too much of water hast thou, poor Ophelia,

185   And therefore I forbid my tears. But yet
It is our trick°—nature her custom holds,   *characteristic way*
Let shame say what it will. [*He weeps.*] When these are
      gone
The woman will be out.[4] Adieu, my lord.
I have a speech o'fire that fain° would blaze   *gladly*
But that this folly drowns it.   *Exit.*

190   KING   Let's follow, Gertrude.
How much I had to do to calm his rage!
Now fear I this will give it start again.
Therefore let's follow.   *Exeunt.*

5.1

Enter two Clowns°[, *a* GRAVEDIGGER *and a*   *rustics; peasants*
SECOND MAN].

GRAVEDIGGER   Is she to be buried in Christian burial when
she willfully seeks her own salvation?[1]

SECOND MAN   I tell thee she is. Therefore make her grave
straight.° The crowner hath sat on her[2] and finds it Chris-   *right away*

5   tian burial.[3]

GRAVEDIGGER   How can that be, unless she drowned herself
in her own defense?

SECOND MAN   Why, 'tis found so.

GRAVEDIGGER   It must be "so offended";[4] it cannot be else, for

10   here lies the point: if I drown myself wittingly, it argues an
act, and an act hath three branches—it is to act, to do, to
perform. Argal,[5] she drowned herself wittingly.

SECOND MAN   Nay, but hear you, goodman delver[6]—

GRAVEDIGGER   Give me leave. Here lies the water, good; here

15   stands the man, good. If the man go to this water and drown
himself, it is, willy-nilly, he goes, mark you that. But if the
water come to him and drown him, he drowns not himself.
Argal, he that is not guilty of his own death shortens not his
own life.

20   SECOND MAN   But is this law?

GRAVEDIGGER   Ay, marry is't, crowner's 'quest° law.   *inquest*

SECOND MAN   Will you ha' the truth on't? If this had not been
a gentlewoman, she should have been buried out o' Christian burial.

25   GRAVEDIGGER   Why, there thou say'st,° and the more pity that   *how right you are*
great folk should have countenance° in this world to drown   *privilege*

---

4. *When . . . out:* When I have cried my tears, the
feminine side of my nature will be gone with them.
5.1 Location: A churchyard.
1. Probably the Gravedigger's mistake for "damnation"; suicide was a mortal sin. Ordinarily, suicides
would not receive a "Christian burial" (in consecrated ground with the church's blessing and ritual).
2. Conducted an inquest on the cause of her death.
crowner: coroner.
3. And has given the verdict that she is eligible for a
Christian burial (in effect, a decision that Ophelia

did not drown herself).
4. A mangled version of *se defendendo*, the legal term
for "killing in self-defense."
5. For "ergo," or "therefore." The argument parodies
a famous law case of 1554 concerning suicide by
drowning, in which the act was said to have three
parts: imagination, resolution, and perfection (accomplishment).
6. Master Digger ("Goodman" was the ordinary title
in addressing a man by his occupation).

or hang themselves more than their even°-Christian. Come,   *fellow*
my spade. There is no ancient gentlemen but gardeners,
ditchers, and gravemakers: they hold up° Adam's profession.   *carry on*

30 SECOND MAN   Was he a gentleman?

GRAVEDIGGER   'A was the first that ever bore arms.[7]

31.1   SECOND MAN   *Why, he had none.*

GRAVEDIGGER   *What, art a heathen? How doth thou understand the Scripture? The Scripture says Adam digged. Could he dig without arms?*

I'll put another question to thee. If thou answerest me not to the purpose, confess thyself.[8]

SECOND MAN   Go to.[9]

35 GRAVEDIGGER   What is he that builds stronger than either the mason, the shipwright, or the carpenter?

SECOND MAN   The gallowsmaker, for that outlives a thousand tenants.

GRAVEDIGGER   I like thy wit well, in good faith. The gallows
40 does° well, but how does it well? It does well to those that do   *serves*
ill. Now, thou dost ill to say the gallows is built stronger
than the church. Argal, the gallows may do well to thee. To't
again, come.

SECOND MAN   Who builds stronger than a mason, a shipwright,
45 or a carpenter?

GRAVEDIGGER   Ay, tell me that and unyoke.[1]

SECOND MAN   Marry, now I can tell—

GRAVEDIGGER   To't.

SECOND MAN   Mass,° I cannot tell.   *By the mass*

50 GRAVEDIGGER   Cudgel thy brains no more about it, for your
dull ass will not mend° his pace with beating; and when you   *improve*
are asked this question next, say "a gravemaker"—the houses
he makes lasts till doomsday. Go get thee in and fetch me a
stoup° of liquor.   [*Exit* SECOND MAN.]   *flagon*
[*He digs and sings.*]

        Song.
55   In youth when I did love, did love,
      Methought it was very sweet
      To contract°-a the time for-a my behove,°   *shorten / advantage*
      Oh, methought there a-was nothing a-meet.[2]

    Enter HAMLET *and* HORATIO.

HAMLET   Has this fellow no feeling of his business? 'A sings in
60 gravemaking.

HORATIO   Custom hath made it in him a property of easiness.[3]

HAMLET   'Tis e'en so, the hand of little employment hath the
daintier sense.[4]

GRAVEDIGGER (*sings*)   But age with his stealing steps
65   Hath clawed me in his clutch
      And hath shipped me into the land°   *earth*
      As if I had never been such.
  [*He tosses up a skull.*]

HAMLET   That skull had a tongue in it and could sing once.

---

7. Those bearing a family coat of arms were officially recognized as gentlemen; playing on "limbs."
8. "Confess thyself and be hanged" was proverbial.
9. An expression of impatience.
1. Rest your wits from work (like draft animals).
2. *meet:* suitable. The Gravedigger sings garbled snatches of Thomas Lord Vaux's poem "The Aged

Lover Renounceth Love," printed in *Tottel's Miscellany* (1557). The extrametrical "a"s are probably grunts while digging.
3. *a property of easiness:* something he can do without distress.
4. Has more delicate feeling (because not hardened by callouses).

How the knave jowls° it to the ground as if 'twere Cain's *slams*
70   jawbone that did the first murder. This might be the pate of
  a politician which this ass now o'erreaches⁵—one that would
  circumvent God, might it not?

HORATIO   It might, my lord.

HAMLET   Or of a courtier which could say, "Good morrow,
75   sweet lord, how dost thou, sweet lord?" This might be my
  lord Such-a-one that praised my lord Such-a-one's horse
  when 'a went to beg it, might it not?

HORATIO   Ay, my lord.

HAMLET   Why, e'en so, and now my lady Worm's, chopless° and *lacking a lower jaw*
80   knocked about the mazard° with a sexton's spade—here's fine *head*
  revolution⁶ an° we had the trick° to see't. Did these bones cost *if / ability*
  no more the breeding but to play at loggets with them?⁷ Mine
  ache to think on't.

GRAVEDIGGER *(sings)*   A pickax and a spade, a spade,
85   For and° a shrouding sheet, *And also*
              Oh, a pit of clay for to be made
              For such a guest is meet.

    [He tosses up another skull.]

HAMLET   There's another. Why, may not that be the skull of a
  lawyer? Where be his quiddities⁸ now, his quillets,° his *quibbles*
90   cases, his tenures,° and his tricks? Why does he suffer this *property titles*
  mad knave now to knock him about the sconce° with a dirty *head*
  shovel, and will not tell him of his action of battery?⁹ Hmm,
  this fellow might be in 's time a great buyer of land, with his
  statutes, his recognizances, his fines, his double vouchers,
95   his recoveries,¹ to have his fine° pate full of fine° dirt. Will *subtle / fine-grained*
  vouchers vouch° him no more of his purchases and dou- *guarantee*
  bles° than the length and breadth of a pair of indentures?² *(duplicate purchases)*
  The very conveyances° of his lands will scarcely lie in this *deeds*
  box,° and must th'inheritor° himself have no more, ha? *deed box; coffin / owner*
100 HORATIO   Not a jot more, my lord.

HAMLET   Is not parchment made of sheepskins?

HORATIO   Ay, my lord, and of calves' skins too.

HAMLET   They are sheep and calves° which seek out assur- *simpletons and fools*
  ance³ in that. I will speak to this fellow. —Whose grave's
105   this, sirrah?⁴

GRAVEDIGGER   Mine, sir.

    [Sings.]   Oh, a pit of clay for to be made⁵
107.1   *For such a guest is meet.*

HAMLET   I think it be thine indeed, for thou liest in't.

GRAVEDIGGER   You lie out on't, sir, and therefore 'tis not yours.
110   For my part I do not lie in't, yet it is mine.

---

5. *o'erreaches*: reaches over or overtakes. In Elizabethan England, a "politician" was a schemer for political advantage.
6. Reversal of fortune (literally, the turning of Fortune's wheel).
7. Was it so inexpensive and easy to bring these bones to maturity that they can be treated as loggets (small wooden clubs thrown at a stake)?
8. Subtle distinctions.
9. Legal prosecution for assault.
1. Fines and recoveries were both kinds of lawsuits brought to make legal an agreement to transfer land ownership. The "double voucher" summoned two wit-

nesses to attest to the land's ownership in these cases. *statutes*: mortgages on land, often linked with "recognizances" (bonds acknowledging a particular debt).
2. The two copies of a document (written on one sheet and separated by an irregular cut so that they could later be proved to be part of one transaction). The dead man's property (his grave) is hardly bigger than these elaborate papers.
3. Security, playing on the legal conveyance of a property title.
4. An address used with inferiors.
5. F has the following line of verse, 107.1, not found in Q2.

HAMLET   Thou dost lie in't to be in't and say it is thine—'tis
for the dead, not for the quick.° Therefore thou liest.   *living*
GRAVEDIGGER   'Tis a quick° lie, sir, 'twill away again from me   *nimble*
to you.
115   HAMLET   What man dost thou dig it for?
GRAVEDIGGER   For no man, sir.
HAMLET   What woman, then?
GRAVEDIGGER   For none neither.
HAMLET   Who is to be buried in't?
120   GRAVEDIGGER   One that was a woman, sir, but rest her soul,
she's dead.
HAMLET   How absolute° the knave is! We must speak by the   *precise*
card[6] or equivocation will undo us. By the Lord, Horatio,
this three years I have took note of it, the age is grown so
125   picked° that the toe of the peasant comes so near the heel of   *punctilious*
the courtier, he galls his kibe.° —How long hast thou been   *chafes his heel sore*
gravemaker?
GRAVEDIGGER   Of the days i'th' year, I came to't that day that
our last King Hamlet overcame Fortinbras.
130   HAMLET   How long is that since?
GRAVEDIGGER   Cannot you tell that? Every fool can tell that.
It was that very day that young Hamlet was born—he that is
mad and sent into England.
HAMLET   Ay, marry, why was he sent into England?
135   GRAVEDIGGER   Why, because 'a was mad. 'A shall recover his
wits there, or, if 'a do not, 'tis no great matter there.
HAMLET   Why?
GRAVEDIGGER   'Twill not be seen in him there—there the men
are as mad as he.
140   HAMLET   How came he mad?
GRAVEDIGGER   Very strangely, they say.
HAMLET   How, "strangely"?
GRAVEDIGGER   Faith, e'en with losing his wits.
HAMLET   Upon what ground?[7]
145   GRAVEDIGGER   Why, here in Denmark. I have been sexton
here, man and boy, thirty years.
HAMLET   How long will a man lie i'th' earth ere he rot?
GRAVEDIGGER   Faith, if 'a be not rotten before 'a die—as we
have many pocky corpses that will scarce hold the laying
150   in[8]—'a will last you some eight year or nine year. A tanner
will last you nine year.
HAMLET   Why he more than another?
GRAVEDIGGER   Why, sir, his hide is so tanned with his trade
that 'a will keep out water a great while, and your water is a
155   sore decayer of your whoreson° dead body. Here's a skull   *vile*
now hath lain you i'th' earth twenty-three years.
HAMLET   Whose was it?
GRAVEDIGGER   A whoreson mad fellow's it was—whose do you
think it was?
160   HAMLET   Nay, I know not.

---

6. With precisely defined meanings (literally, by the
directions marked on a mariner's compass card).
7. From what cause? (The Gravedigger takes him to
mean "In what country?")

8. *pocky . . . in*: bodies riddled with venereal disease
that hardly keep from disintegrating during their
burial rites.

GRAVEDIGGER   A pestilence on him for a mad rogue. 'A poured
a flagon of Rhenish° on my head once. This same skull, sir,   *Rhine wine*
was, sir, Yorick's skull, the King's jester.
HAMLET *[taking the skull]*   This?
165   GRAVEDIGGER   E'en that.
HAMLET   Alas, poor Yorick. I knew him, Horatio—a fellow of
infinite jest, of most excellent fancy. He hath bore me on his
back a thousand times and now how abhorred° in my imagi-   *disgusting*
nation it is. My gorge rises at it. Here hung those lips that I
170   have kissed I know not how oft. —Where be your gibes now,
your gambols, your songs, your flashes of merriment that
were wont to set the table on a roar? Not one now to mock
your own grinning? Quite chapfallen?⁹ Now get you to my
lady's table and tell her, let her paint an inch thick, to this
175   favor° she must come—make her laugh at that. Prithee,   *appearance*
Horatio, tell me one thing.
HORATIO   What's that, my lord?
HAMLET   Dost thou think Alexander looked o'this fashion i'th'
earth?
180   HORATIO   E'en so.
HAMLET   And smelt so? Pah!
        [He puts down the skull.]
HORATIO   E'en so, my lord.
HAMLET   To what base uses we may return, Horatio. Why may
not imagination trace the noble dust of Alexander till 'a find
185   it stopping a bunghole?°   *opening of a cask*
HORATIO   'Twere to consider too curiously° to consider so.   *oversubtly*
HAMLET   No, faith, not a jot. But to follow him thither with
modesty° enough and likelihood to lead it: Alexander died,   *reasonable speculation*
Alexander was buried, Alexander returneth to dust, the dust
190   is earth, of earth we make loam,¹ and why of that loam
whereto he was converted might they not stop a beer barrel?
Imperious Caesar, dead and turned to clay,
Might stop a hole to keep the wind away.
Oh, that that earth which kept the world in awe
195   Should patch a wall t'expel the water's flaw.°   *squall*
But soft, but soft awhile—
        Enter KING, QUEEN, LAERTES, *and the corpse [of*
        Ophelia, with other LORDS *and a* PRIEST].
                            here comes the King,
The Queen, the courtiers; who is this they follow,
And with such maimèd rites?² This doth betoken
The corpse they follow did with desperate hand
200   Fordo it° own life. 'Twas of some estate.³   *Bring down its*
Couch we° awhile and mark.   *Let's lie low*
        *[*HAMLET *and* HORATIO *stand aside.]*
LAERTES   What ceremony else?⁴
HAMLET *[to* HORATIO*]*   That is Laertes, a very noble youth—
mark.
LAERTES   What ceremony else?
205   PRIEST   Her obsequies have been as far enlarged

---

9. Dejected; also, with a dropped or lost lower jaw.
1. A mix of clay and straw used as plaster.
2. Truncated ceremonies; curtailed rituals.
3. Someone of importance.
4. Laertes insists upon further funeral rites.

As we have warranty.° Her death was doubtful,[5]   *proper sanction*
And, but that great command o'ersways the order,[6]
She should in ground unsanctified been lodged
Till the last trumpet. For° charitable prayers,   *Rather than*
210 Flints and pebbles should be thrown on her,
Yet here she is allowed her virgin crants,[7]
Her maiden strewments,[8] and the bringing home
Of bell and burial.[9]

LAERTES Must there no more be done?

PRIEST   No more be done.
215 We should profane the service of the dead
To sing a requiem and such rest to her
As to peace-parted° souls.   *peacefully deceased*

LAERTES   Lay her i'th' earth,
And from her fair and unpolluted flesh
May violets spring. I tell thee, churlish priest,
220 A minist'ring angel shall my sister be
When thou liest howling.°   *(in hell)*
      [*Ophelia's body is laid in the grave.*]

HAMLET [*aside*]   What, the fair Ophelia?

QUEEN [*scattering flowers on the grave*]   Sweets to the sweet.
      Farewell.
I hoped thou shouldst have been my Hamlet's wife—
I thought thy bride-bed to have decked, sweet maid,
And not have strewed thy grave.

225 LAERTES   Oh, treble woe
Fall ten times double on that cursèd head
Whose wicked deed thy most ingenious sense[1]
Deprived thee of. Hold off the earth awhile[2]
Till I have caught her once more in mine arms.
      [*He leaps into the grave.*]
230 Now pile your dust upon the quick and dead
Till of this flat a mountain you have made
T'o'ertop old Pelion or the skyish head
Of blue Olympus.[3]

HAMLET [*coming forward*]   What is he whose grief
Bears such an emphasis,[4] whose phrase° of sorrow   *rhetoric*
235 Conjures the wand'ring stars° and makes them stand   *planets*
Like wonder-wounded° hearers? This is I,   *awestruck*
Hamlet the Dane.[5]

LAERTES The devil take thy soul!
      [*He grapples with* HAMLET.][6]

---

5. That is, possibly suicide.
6. And if royal authority had not prevailed over the usual ecclesiastical procedure.
7. TEXTUAL COMMENT F has "Shardes" additionally strewn on Ophelia, while substituting "Rites" for Q2's "Crants." See Digital Edition TC 8 (combined text).
8. Flowers strewed over the casket or grave. Throughout northern Europe, funerary flowers of an unmarried girl often included a special wreath that was sometimes afterward hung in the church. *crants:* garlands.
9. *the bringing . . . burial:* the taking her to her resting place with the ritual passing bells and funeral service.
1. Quick, perceptive intelligence.

2. Stop filling the grave for a moment.
3. In Greek mythology, giants piled Pelion (a mountain in Thessaly) on top of Mount Ossa in an attempt to climb Mount Olympus.
4. A violent expression.
5. Normally the title of the king of Denmark.
6. TEXTUAL COMMENT The stage directions of F and Q1 make clear that Laertes jumps into the grave, whereas in Q2 the jump is only implied through a later line. But only Q1 specifies that Hamlet jumps into the grave after him. We omit any specific staging direction concerning whether Hamlet jumps, or how the ensuing fight takes place, because the scene's ambiguities admit multiple possible arrangements. See Digital Edition TC 9 (combined text).

HAMLET   Thou pray'st not well.
    I prithee take thy fingers from my throat,

240   For though I am not splenative° and rash,   *quick-tempered*
    Yet have I in me something dangerous
    Which let thy wisdom fear. Hold off thy hand.

KING   Pluck them asunder.

QUEEN   Hamlet, Hamlet!

LORDS   Gentlemen!

HORATIO [*to* HAMLET]   Good my lord, be quiet.

245 HAMLET   Why, I will fight with him upon this theme
    Until my eyelids will no longer wag.°   *blink*

QUEEN   O my son, what theme?

HAMLET   I loved Ophelia. Forty thousand brothers
    Could not with all their quantity of love

250   Make up my sum. What wilt thou do for her?

KING   Oh, he is mad, Laertes.

QUEEN   For love of God, forbear him.°   *let him alone*

HAMLET   'Swounds,° show me what thou'lt do—   *By Christ's wounds*
    Wilt weep, wilt fight, wilt fast, wilt tear thyself,

255   Wilt drink up eisel,° eat a crocodile?   *vinegar*
    I'll do't. Dost come here to whine,
    To outface me with leaping in her grave?
    Be buried quick° with her and so will I.   *alive*
    And if thou prate of mountains, let them throw

260   Millions of acres on us till our ground,
    Singeing his pate° against the burning zone,°   *head / sun's sphere*
    Make Ossa[7] like a wart. Nay, an° thou'lt mouth,° *if / speak excessively*
    I'll rant as well as thou.

QUEEN   This is mere madness—
    And thus awhile the fit will work on him;

265   Anon,° as patient as the female dove   *Soon*
    When that her golden couplets are disclosed,°   *chicks are hatched*
    His silence will sit drooping.

HAMLET   Hear you, sir,
    What is the reason that you use me thus?
    I loved you ever—but it is no matter.

270   Let Hercules himself do what he may,
    The cat will mew and dog will have his day.[8]   *Exit.*

KING   I pray thee, good Horatio, wait upon him.

                                Exit HORATIO.

    [*aside to* LAERTES] Strengthen your patience in° our last   *with*
      night's speech—
    We'll put the matter to the present push.°   *the test immediately*

275   —Good Gertrude, set some watch over your son.
    —This grave shall have a living monument.[9]
    An hour of quiet thereby shall we see;
    Till then in patience our proceeding be.   *Exeunt.*

5.2

Enter HAMLET *and* HORATIO.

HAMLET   So much for this, sir. Now shall you see the other:°   *other matter*
    You do remember all the circumstance?°   *state of things then*

---

7. Greek mountain (see note to line 233).
8. *Let . . . day:* Despite Laertes' Herculean ranting, my day will come.

9. A lasting memorial; hinting that Hamlet, now "living," will soon be sacrificed to Ophelia's memory.
5.2 Location: A stateroom of the castle.

HORATIO   Remember it, my lord?

HAMLET   Sir, in my heart there was a kind of fighting
5   That would not let me sleep; methought I lay
Worse than the mutines in the bilbo.[1] Rashly°—   *Impulsively*
And praised be rashness for it—let us know°   *acknowledge*
Our indiscretion° sometime serves us well   *unreasoned action*
When our deep plots do fall,[2] and that should learn us
10   There's a divinity that shapes our ends,
Rough-hew them° how we will.   *Form them roughly*

HORATIO   That is most certain.

HAMLET   Up from my cabin,
My sea-gown scarfed about me, in the dark
Groped I to find out them, had my desire,
15   Fingered° their packet, and in fine° withdrew   *Stole / finally*
To mine own room again, making so bold—
My fears forgetting manners—to unfold
Their grand commission; where I found, Horatio,
A royal knavery: an exact command,
20   Larded° with many several° sorts of reasons   *Elaborated / different*
Importing° Denmark's health and England's too,   *Concerning*
With—ho!—such bugs and goblins in my life[3]
That on the supervise,° no leisure bated°—   *reading / allowed*
No, not to stay° the grinding of the ax—   *await*
My head should be struck off.

25   HORATIO   Is't possible?

HAMLET   Here's the commission: read it at more leisure.
But wilt thou hear now how I did proceed?

HORATIO   I beseech you.

HAMLET   Being thus benetted round with villains—
30   Ere I could make a prologue to my brains
They had begun the play[4]—I sat me down,
Devised a new commission, wrote it fair.[5]
I once did hold it as our statists° do   *statesmen*
A baseness to write fair and labored much
35   How to forget that learning,[6] but, sir, now
It did me yeoman's service.[7] Wilt thou know
Th'effect of what I wrote?

HORATIO   Ay, good my lord.

HAMLET   An earnest conjuration° from the King,   *appeal*
As England was his faithful tributary,
40   As love between them like the palm might flourish,
As peace should still her wheaten garland[8] wear
And stand a comma[9] 'tween their amities,
And many suchlike "as," sir, of great charge,[1]
That on the view and knowing of these contents,

1. Worse than the mutineers in the ankle fetters.
2. When our best-laid plans fail.
3. Such fanciful horrors that would result were I to remain alive. *bugs:* bugbears.
4. *Ere . . . play:* Hamlet's brains "acted" before he consciously thought out a plan.
5. In the professional handwriting of finished (published) documents.
6. *I once . . . learning:* In the sixteenth century, the upper echelons of government became increasingly professionalized; Hamlet implies that these newly elevated officials are prone to snobbish pretensions,
covering up their education as common clerks, and he confesses that he once shared their snobbery.
7. It served me valiantly. English yeomen (free landholders) were famous for military strength, supposedly because they fought for their national interest rather than for base pay.
8. The wheaten garland, like the palm tree, is an emblem of peace and prosperity.
9. And hold their interests separate but still connected (unlike a period, which would cut off "amity").
1. Weighty clauses beginning with "as."

45   Without debatement further more or less,
      He should those bearers put to sudden death,
      Not shriving time[2] allowed.

HORATIO   How was this sealed?

HAMLET   Why, even in that was heaven ordinant;°   *guiding*
      I had my father's signet in my purse,
50   Which was the model of that Danish seal;
      Folded the writ up in the form of th'other,
      Subscribed° it, gave't th'impression,° placed it safely,   *Signed / the seal (in wax)*
      The changeling[3] never known. Now, the next day
      Was our sea fight, and what to this was sequent°   *subsequent*
55   Thou knowest already.

HORATIO   So Guildenstern and Rosencrantz go to't.[4]

56.1   HAMLET   *Why, man, they did make love to this employment.*
      They are not near my conscience; their defeat°   *destruction*
      Does by their own insinuation grow.
      'Tis dangerous when the baser nature comes
60   Between the pass and fell incensèd points[5]
      Of mighty opposites.°   *opponents*

HORATIO   Why, what a king is this!

HAMLET   Does it not, think thee, stand me now upon[6]—
      He that hath killed my king and whored my mother,
65   Popped in between th'election and my hopes,
      Thrown out his angle° for my proper° life,   *fishhook / own*
      And with such coz'nage°— is't not perfect conscience[7]   *trickery*

67.1   *To quit° him with this arm? And is't not to be damned*   *requite*
      To let this canker° of our nature come   *cancerous sore*
      In° further evil?   *Into*

      HORATIO   *It must be shortly known to him from England*
67.5   *What is the issue° of the business there.*   *result*

      HAMLET   *It will be short; the interim's mine,*
      And a man's life's no more than to say "one."[8]
      But I am very sorry, good Horatio,
      That to Laertes I forgot myself,
67.10   *For by the image° of my cause I see*   *mirror's reflection*
      The portraiture of his. I'll court his favors.
      But sure the bravery° of his grief did put me   *ostentation*
      Into a tow'ring passion.

          *Enter [*OSRIC,*] a courtier.*

      HORATIO   *Peace, who comes here?*

OSRIC   Your lordship is right welcome back to Denmark.

HAMLET   I humbly thank you, sir. [*aside to* HORATIO] Dost
70   know this water fly?

HORATIO   No, my good lord.

HAMLET   Thy state is the more gracious,° for 'tis a vice to know   *blessed*
    him. He hath much land, and fertile. Let a beast be lord of

---

2. Time for final confession and absolution, a part of the state ritual of legal executions.
3. A malicious elf child substituted for an infant, as Hamlet swaps his counterfeit letter for their authentic one.
4. F has the following line, 56.1, not found in Q2.
5. *the pass . . . points*: fencing language; the thrust ("pass") and fiercely angry ("fell") rapiers.
6. Rest incumbent upon me.
7. TEXTUAL COMMENT F has the following passage,

lines 67.1–67.13, omitted in Q2. There is a similar passage in Q1 but not in Q2. These lines, combined with F's omission of Hamlet's mean-spirited exchange with Ostrick of Q2 (5.2.96–117), evoke a more sympathetic protagonist who does not need Q2's subsequent reminders of princely duty (5.2.178–80). See Digital Edition TC 10 (combined text).
8. And life lasts no longer than it takes to pronounce ("say") the monosyllable "one."

beasts and his crib shall stand at the king's mess.[9] 'Tis a
75   chough° but, as I say, spacious in the possession of dirt.   *rich boor; jackdaw*
OSRIC   Sweet lord, if your lordship were at leisure, I should
impart a thing to you from his majesty.
HAMLET   I will receive it, sir, with all diligence of spirit. Your
bonnet° to his right use—'tis for the head.   *hat*
80   OSRIC   I thank your lordship, it is very hot.
HAMLET   No, believe me, 'tis very cold: the wind is northerly.
OSRIC   It is indifferent° cold, my lord, indeed.   *rather*
HAMLET   But yet methinks it is very sultry and hot, or my
complexion°—   *constitution*
85   OSRIC   Exceedingly, my lord, it is very sultry, as 'twere—I can-
not tell how. My lord, his majesty bade me signify to you
that 'a° has laid a great wager on your head. Sir, this is the   *he*
matter.
HAMLET   I beseech you, remember.[1]
[*He gestures to* OSRIC *to put on his hat.*]
90   OSRIC   Nay, good my lord, for my ease, in good faith.[2] Sir,
here is newly come to court Laertes—believe me, an abso-
lute gentleman full of most excellent differences,° of very   *superior qualities*
soft° society and great showing.° Indeed, to speak feel-   *pleasing / appearance*
ingly° of him, he is the card or calendar of gentry,[3] for you   *appreciatively*
95   shall find in him the continent of what part[4] a gentleman
would see.
HAMLET   Sir, his definement suffers no perdition in you,[5]
though I know to divide him inventorially would dozy°   *dizzy*
th'arithmetic of memory, and yet but yaw neither in respect
100   of his quick sail;[6] but in the verity of extolment,° I take   *in truthful praise*
him to be a soul of great article[7] and his infusion° of such   *inborn essence*
dearth° and rareness as, to make true diction[8] of him, his   *preciousness*
semblable° is his mirror, and who else would trace him,   *likeness*
his umbrage, nothing more.[9]
105   OSRIC   Your lordship speaks most infallibly of him.
HAMLET   The concernancy,° sir—why do we wrap the gentle-   *relevance (to us)*
man in our more rawer breath?[1]
OSRIC   Sir?
HORATIO   Is't not possible to understand in another tongue?
110   You will to't, sir, really.[2]
HAMLET   What imports the nomination° of this gentleman?   *mention*
OSRIC   Of Laertes?
HORATIO   His purse is empty already—all 's golden words are
spent.
115   HAMLET   Of him, sir.
OSRIC   I know you are not ignorant—

9. *Let . . . mess:* If an animal owned enough herds, even
it might find a place at the king's table. *crib:* manger.
1. "Remember your courtesy," the conventional expression inviting a subordinate to put his hat back on.
2. A conventional expression declining Hamlet's
invitation. After "faith," the following passage, lines
91–118, is omitted in F.
3. The model of gentlemanly behavior. *card:* chart or
map. *calendar:* account book, directory.
4. Attribute or quality, playing on "region" (to which
Laertes is the "card"). *continent:* embodiment, continuing the geographical pun.
5. Your picture of him ("definement") loses none of
the man's real excellence.

6. *to divide . . . sail:* to list his qualities individually
would confuse the memory's reckoning up (through
recounting vast numbers), and yet only steer errati-
cally ("yaw") around Laertes' skills—that is, the
description would only approximate his virtues.
7. An obscure phrase. Possibly, large scope; excellent
quality.
8. To speak truly.
9. And whoever imitates him is like his shadow
("umbrage"), not the real thing at all.
1. Our less refined words (since we are so much inferior to Laertes).
2. *Is't . . . really:* Can't he understand his words in
another man's mouth? You will have your joke, sir, truly.

HAMLET I would you did, sir. Yet, in faith, if you did, it would
not much approve° me. Well, sir?   *commend*

OSRIC You are not ignorant of what excellence Laertes is.

120   HAMLET I dare not confess that, lest I should compare with
him in excellence.[3] But to know a man well were to know
himself.[4]

OSRIC I mean, sir, for his weapon; but in the imputation laid
on him by them in his meed,° he's unfellowed.°   *merit / unmatched*

125   HAMLET What's his weapon?

OSRIC Rapier and dagger.

HAMLET That's two of his weapons, but well.

OSRIC The King, sir, hath wagered with him six Barbary
horses, against the which he has impawned,° as I take it, six   *staked*

130   French rapiers and poniards with their assigns,° as girdle,°   *accessories / sword belt*
hanger,[5] and so. Three of the carriages, in faith, are very dear
to fancy, very responsive to the hilts, most delicate carriages
and of very liberal conceit.[6]

HAMLET What call you the carriages?[7]

135   HORATIO I knew you must be edified by the margin[8] ere you
had done.

OSRIC The carriages, sir, are the hangers.

HAMLET The phrase would be more germane to the matter if
we could carry a cannon by our sides;[9] I would it might be

140   "hangers" till then. But on: six Barbary horses against six
French swords, their assigns, and three liberal-conceited
carriages—that's the French bet against the Danish. Why, is
this all you call it?

OSRIC The King, sir, hath laid,° sir, that in a dozen passes   *placed his bet*

145   between yourself and him, he shall not exceed you three
hits.[1] He hath laid on twelve for nine,[2] and it would come to
immediate trial if your lordship would vouchsafe the answer.[3]

HAMLET How if I answer no?

OSRIC I mean, my lord, the opposition of your person in trial.

150   HAMLET Sir, I will walk here in the hall. If it please his majesty, it is the breathing° time of day with me—let the foils   *exercising*
be brought. The gentleman willing and the King hold his
purpose, I will win for him an° I can; if not, I will gain noth-   *if*
ing but my shame and the odd hits.

155   OSRIC Shall I deliver you so?

HAMLET To this effect, sir, after what flourish your nature will.

OSRIC I commend my duty° to your lordship.   *dedicate my service*

HAMLET Yours.   [*Exit* OSRIC.]

'A does well to commend° it himself; there are no tongues   *recommend*

160   else for 's turn.°   *purpose*

---

3. Claim to match him (since, proverbially, only excellence recognizes excellence).

4. For in order to know another man truly, one must know oneself.

5. Attaching straps.

6. *are . . . conceit:* capture the imagination ("fancy") and match or echo ("responsive to") the ornamentation on the rapiers' hilts; further, they are finely wrought ("delicate") and of an elaborate ("liberal") design.

7. Osric's inflated term for "hangers," or straps.

8. Must be informed by an explanatory note (from the margin of a book). F omits Horatio's line.

9. A common definition of "carriage" at the time was a mount for a cannon.

1. Laertes must score three more "hits" than Hamlet out of twelve bouts of swordplay to win the wager.

2. If "he" is Laertes, Osric may mean "He has bet twelve passes for nine hits" (a greater challenge than the King's terms, by which he would only need eight hits to win).

3. Would accept the challenge (Osric's meaning, and the only honorable response). In the next line, Hamlet deliberately misunderstands "answer" as "(any) reply."

HORATIO   This lapwing runs away with the shell on his head.[4]

HAMLET   'A did so, sir, with his dug[5] before 'a sucked it. Thus
has he, and many more of the same breed that I know the
drossy° age dotes on, only got the tune of the time,[6] and out   *worthless*
165   of an habit of encounter, a kind of yeasty collection,[7] which
carries them through and through the most profane and
winnowed opinions[8]—and do but blow them to their trial,
the bubbles are out.[9]

                    Enter a LORD.

LORD   My lord, his majesty commended him to you by young
170   Osric, who brings back to him that you attend him in the
hall. He sends to know if your pleasure hold to play with
Laertes or that you will take longer time?

HAMLET   I am constant to my purposes. They follow the
King's pleasure; if his fitness speaks, mine is ready—now or
175   whensoever, provided I be so able as now.

LORD   The King and Queen and all are coming down.

HAMLET   In happy time.

LORD   The Queen desires you to use some gentle entertainment[1] to Laertes before you fall to play.

180   HAMLET   She well instructs me.   [*Exit* LORD.]

HORATIO   You will lose, my lord.

HAMLET   I do not think so. Since he went into France I have
been in continual practice. I shall win at the odds. Thou
wouldst not think how ill all's here about my heart, but it is
185   no matter.

HORATIO   Nay, good my lord.

HAMLET   It is but foolery, but it is such a kind of gaingiving°   *misgiving*
as would perhaps trouble a woman.

HORATIO   If your mind dislike anything, obey it. I will fore-
190   stall their repair° hither and say you are not fit.   *coming*

HAMLET   Not a whit. We defy augury. There is special providence[2] in the fall of a sparrow. If it be, 'tis not to come; if it
be not to come, it will be now; if it be not now, yet it will
come; the readiness is all. Since no man, of aught he leaves,
195   knows, what is't to leave betimes?[3] Let be.

                    A table prepared. [*Enter*] *trumpets, drums, and*
                    Officers with cushions, foils, [*and*] *daggers.* [*Then*
                    enter] KING, QUEEN, LAERTES, [OSRIC, LORDS,] *and*
                    all the state.

KING   Come, Hamlet, come and take this hand from me.
                    [*He puts Laertes' hand in Hamlet's.*]

---

4. The newly hatched chicks of the plover ("lapwing") were supposed to scurry about still wearing
their eggshells, a reference to the bonnet that Osric
has finally put back on, as well as to the courtier's
brainless chirping.
5. *'A did . . . dug:* He did the same to his mother's
breast. Obscure in Q2, the line in F—"He did comply
with his dug"—mocks Osric's obsequiousness.
6. *the tune of the time:* the fashionable turns of speech.
7. *and out . . . collection:* and from the formulas
("habit") of courteous conversation ("encounter")
they make a frothy and inflated repertoire of speech
and behavior ("yeasty collection").
8. *which . . . opinions:* their empty clichés get them
through or pass for the most carefully considered
wisdom (which is "winnowed" like wheat separated

from chaff during threshing).
9. And if you test them by blowing on them—as
Hamlet does by speaking to Osric—they pop and dissolve. The following passage, lines 169–80, is omitted in F.
1. To behave with conciliatory courtesy.
2. God's direction for a specific event (over and
above "general providence," the whole shape of God's
design). Compare Matthew 10:29: "Are not two sparrows sold for a farthing? and one of them shall not
fall on the ground without your Father."
3. Since no man fully understands what he's leaving
behind him, why does it matter to leave it early
("betimes")? F reads: "Since no man has aught of what
he leaves, what is't to leave betimes?"

HAMLET [*to* LAERTES]   Give me your pardon, sir. I have done
  you wrong,
But pardon't as you are a gentleman.
This presence° knows, and you must needs have heard,   roy⎦   ⎦ny
200 How I am punished with a sore distraction.°   agitation; insanity
What I have done
That might your nature, honor, and exception°   disapproval
Roughly awake, I here proclaim was madness.
Was't Hamlet wronged Laertes? Never Hamlet.
205 If Hamlet from himself be ta'en away,
And when he's not himself does wrong Laertes,
Then Hamlet does it not; Hamlet denies it.
Who does it then? His madness. If't be so,
Hamlet is of the faction that is wronged—
210 His madness is poor Hamlet's enemy.[4]
210.1   *Sir, in this audience,*
Let my disclaiming from a purposed evil[5]
Free me so far in your most generous thoughts
That I have shot my arrow o'er the house
And hurt my brother.[6]
215 LAERTES   I am satisfied in nature,
Whose motive in this case should stir me most
To my revenge. But in my terms of honor[7]
I stand aloof and will no reconcilement
Till by some elder masters of known honor
220 I have a voice and precedent of peace[8]
To keep my name ungored.° But all that time   my reputation intact
I do receive your offered love like love
And will not wrong it.
HAMLET   I embrace it freely
And will this brothers' wager frankly° play.   freely
  —Give us the foils.
225 LAERTES   Come, one for me.
HAMLET   I'll be your foil,[9] Laertes. In mine ignorance
Your skill shall like a star i'th' darkest night
Stick° fiery off indeed.   Sparkle; jab
LAERTES   You mock me, sir.
HAMLET   No, by this hand.
230 KING   Give them the foils, young Osric. Cousin Hamlet,
You know the wager.
HAMLET   Very well, my lord.
Your grace has laid the odds o'th' weaker side.
KING   I do not fear it. I have seen you both.
But since he is better,° we have therefore odds.°   favored / handicapping
235 LAERTES   This is too heavy—let me see another.
HAMLET   This likes° me well. These foils have all a° length?   pleases / the same
OSRIC   Ay, my good lord.
    [*They prepare to play. Enter Servants with flagons
    of wine.*]

4. F has the following line, 210.1, not found in Q2.
5. Let my disavowal of evil intention.
6. F's reading is "mother."
7. But where my social standing as a man of honor is concerned.
8. *Till . . . peace:* Until the consensus of men of

authoritative standing, judging by the standards of tradition (precedent), holds that I can make an honorable peace.
9. Flattering contrast. Jewels were often set with a piece of metal foil under them to increase their glitter.

KING   Set me the stoups° of wine upon that table.   *flagons*
    If Hamlet give the first or second hit,
240 Or quit in answer of the third exchange,[1]
    Let all the battlements their ordnance° fire.   *cannons*
    The King shall drink to Hamlet's better breath°   *energy*
    And in the cup an union[2] shall he throw
    Richer than that which four successive kings
245 In Denmark's crown have worn. Give me the cups,
    And let the kettle° to the trumpet speak,   *kettledrum*
    The trumpet to the cannoneer without,
    The cannons to the heavens, the heaven to earth:
    Now the King drinks to Hamlet. Come, begin.
            Trumpets the while.
250 And you the judges bear a wary eye.
HAMLET   Come on, sir.
LAERTES   Come, my lord.
            [*They play.*]
HAMLET   One.
LAERTES   No.
255 HAMLET   Judgment!
OSRIC   A hit, a very palpable hit.
            Flourish. Drum [and] trumpets. A piece° goes off.   *cannon*
LAERTES   Well, again.
KING   Stay,° give me drink. Hamlet, this pearl is thine.   *Stop*
            [*He drops the pearl in the cup.*]
    Here's to thy health. Give him the cup.
260 HAMLET   I'll play this bout first; set it by awhile.
    —Come.
            [*They play again.*]
            Another hit. What say you?
LAERTES   I do confess't.
KING   Our son shall win.
QUEEN   He's fat° and scant of breath.   *sweaty*
    Here, Hamlet, take my napkin,° rub thy brows.   *handkerchief*
265 The Queen carouses to thy fortune, Hamlet.
HAMLET   Good madam.
KING   Gertrude, do not drink.
QUEEN   I will, my lord. I pray you pardon me.
            [*She drinks and offers the cup to* HAMLET.]
KING [*aside*]   It is the poisoned cup; it is too late!
270 HAMLET   I dare not drink yet, madam—by and by.
QUEEN   Come, let me wipe thy face.
LAERTES [*aside to* KING]   My lord, I'll hit him now.
KING   I do not think't.
LAERTES [*aside*]   And yet it is almost against my conscience.
HAMLET   Come for the third, Laertes, you do but dally.
275 I pray you pass° with your best violence—   *thrust*
    I am sure you make a wanton° of me.   *spoiled child*
LAERTES   Say you so? Come on.
            [*They play.*]
OSRIC   Nothing neither way.

---

1. Or repay Laertes' victories by winning the third bout.
2. A pearl of exceptional quality, possibly poisoned.

Claudius is perhaps proposing to dissolve the gem, as Cleopatra did in a much-repeated legend. We follow F's "union" here.

LAERTES   Have at you now.
          [LAERTES *wounds* HAMLET.]
          [*In scuffling they change rapiers,*[3] *and* HAMLET
          wounds LAERTES.]

KING   Part them—they are incensed.

280   HAMLET   Nay, come again.
          [QUEEN *falls down.*][4]

OSRIC   Look to the Queen there, ho!

HORATIO   They bleed on both sides. [*to* HAMLET] How is it, my
   lord?
          [LAERTES *falls down.*]

OSRIC   How is't, Laertes?

285   LAERTES   Why, as a woodcock to mine own springe,° Osric.   *snare*
   I am justly killed with mine own treachery.

HAMLET   How does the Queen?

KING   She swoons to see them bleed.

QUEEN   No, no, the drink, the drink! O my dear Hamlet,
   The drink, the drink—I am poisoned.
          [*The* QUEEN *dies.*]

290   HAMLET   Oh, villainy! Ho! Let the door be locked.
   Treachery! Seek it out.   [*Exit* OSRIC.]

LAERTES   It is here, Hamlet. Thou art slain.
   No med'cine in the world can do thee good;
   In thee there is not half an hour's life.

295   The treacherous instrument is in thy hand,
   Unbated° and envenomed. The foul practice   *Not blunted*
   Hath turned itself on me: lo, here I lie
   Never to rise again. Thy mother's poisoned—
   I can no more. The King, the King's to blame.

300   HAMLET   The point envenomed too? Then, venom, to thy work!
          [*He hurts the* KING.]

LORDS   Treason! Treason!

KING   Oh, yet defend me, friends; I am but hurt.

HAMLET   Here, thou incestuous damnèd Dane,
   Drink of this potion.
          [*He forces the drink down the King's throat.*]
                    Is thy union[5] here?
   Follow my mother.
          [*The* KING *dies.*]

305   LAERTES   He is justly served:
   It is a poison tempered° by himself.   *mixed*
   Exchange forgiveness with me, noble Hamlet.
   Mine and my father's death come not upon thee,[6]
   Nor thine on me.
          [*He dies.*]

310   HAMLET   Heaven make thee free of it. I follow thee.
   I am dead, Horatio. Wretched Queen, adieu.

---

3. *In . . . rapiers:* from F. Q2 lacks any stage direction
here. Performances often have Hamlet and Laertes
drop their swords during the duel and then pick up
their opponent's. However, Q1 has "They catch one
another's rapiers," suggesting that each combatant is
trying to disarm the other with his free hand. If the
duelists were fighting with both foils and daggers (line
126), the latter would presumably have been dropped
so that each man would have a free hand.
4. This stage direction and the one at line 289 are
taken from Q1.
5. Referring to both the pearl and his incestuous
marriage to Gertrude.
6. May your soul not be judged accountable for our
murders.

You that look pale and tremble at this chance,
That are but mutes° or audience to this act,   *nonspeaking actors*
Had I but time—as this fell sergeant,[7] Death,
315 Is strict in his arrest—oh, I could tell you—
But let it be. Horatio, I am dead.
Thou livest: report me and my cause aright
To the unsatisfied.
HORATIO   Never believe it:
I am more an antique Roman than a Dane;[8]
Here's yet some liquor left—
320 HAMLET   As thou'rt a man,
Give me the cup. Let go—by heaven I'll ha't!
O God, Horatio, what a wounded name,
Things standing thus unknown, shall I leave behind me!
If thou didst ever hold me in thy heart,
325 Absent thee from felicity awhile
And in this harsh world draw thy breath in pain
To tell my story.
          A march afar off.
          Enter OSRIC.
                    What warlike noise is this?
OSRIC Young Fortinbras, with conquest come from Poland,
To th'ambassadors of England gives this warlike volley.°   *military salute*
330 HAMLET Oh, I die, Horatio—
The potent poison quite o'ercrows[9] my spirit.
I cannot live to hear the news from England,
But I do prophesy th'election lights
On Fortinbras—he has my dying voice.[1]
335 So tell him, with th'occurrents° more and less   *events*
Which have solicited[2]—the rest is silence.
336.1   *Oh, oh, oh, oh.*[3]
          [*He dies.*]
HORATIO Now cracks a noble heart. Good night, sweet prince,
And flights of angels sing thee to thy rest.
          [*Drums sound within.*]
Why does the drum come hither?
          Enter FORTINBRAS *with* [*his train and*] *the* [*English*]
          AMBASSADORS.
FORTINBRAS Where is this sight?
340 HORATIO   What is it you would see?
If aught of woe or wonder, cease your search.
FORTINBRAS This quarry cries on havoc.[4] O proud Death,
What feast is toward° in thine eternal cell   *preparing*
That thou so many princes at a shot
So bloodily hast struck?
345 AMBASSADOR   The sight is dismal,

---

7. As this fierce sheriff's officer.
8. Ancient ("antique") Romans generally regarded
suicide as preferable to dishonor; in particular, they
believed that servants or retainers should not outlive
their master's overthrow.
9. Announces triumph over, like the victorious rooster
in a cockfight.
1. Vote. Because Denmark is an elective monarchy,
Fortinbras can only become king by receiving the
"voice," or vote, of electors like Hamlet.

2. Some editors assume that the sentence is gram-
matically incomplete, broken off by death. Hamlet
seems to refer to the events that have moved ("solicited") him to have his story told and to give his support to Fortinbras.
3. These exclamations, which appear in F but not Q2,
might be suggestive stage directions for death throes,
rather than scripted cries.
4. All this slaughtered game ("quarry") proclaims a
massacre.

And our affairs from England come too late.
The ears are senseless that should give us hearing
To tell him° his commandment is fulfilled   *(Claudius)*
That Rosencrantz and Guildenstern are dead.
Where should we have our thanks?
350 HORATIO [*indicating* KING]   Not from his mouth,
Had it th'ability of life to thank you:
He never gave commandment for their death.
But since so jump° upon this bloody question°   *immediately / matter*
You from the Polack wars and you from England
355 Are here arrived, give order that these bodies
High on a stage be placèd to the view,
And let me speak to th' yet unknowing world
How these things came about. So shall you hear
Of carnal, bloody, and unnatural acts,
360 Of accidental judgments,° casual° slaughters,   *retributions / chance*
Of deaths put on° by cunning and for no cause,   *instigated*
And in this upshot purposes mistook
Fall'n on th'inventors' heads. All this can I
Truly deliver.
FORTINBRAS   Let us haste to hear it—
365 And call the noblest to the audience.
For° me, with sorrow I embrace my fortune.   *As for*
I have some rights of memory[5] in this kingdom,
Which now to claim my vantage° doth invite me.   *favorable opportunity*
HORATIO   Of that I shall have also cause to speak,
370 And from his mouth whose voice will draw no more.
But let this same be presently performed
Even while men's minds are wild, lest more mischance
On° plots and errors happen.   *On top of*
FORTINBRAS   Let four captains
Bear Hamlet like a soldier to the stage,
375 For he was likely, had he been put on,°   *put to the test*
To have proved° most royal. And for his passage   *shown himself; acted*
The soldier's music and the rite of war
Speak loudly for him.
Take up the bodies. Such a sight as this
380 Becomes the field[6] but here shows° much amiss.   *appears*
Go, bid the soldiers shoot.   *Exeunt.*

---

5. *of memory*: unforgotten; traditional.   6. Is most appropriate to a battlefield.

1603 HAMLET

In 1823 a British army officer and antiquary, Sir Henry Bunbury, found in a closet in his country estate a volume that, he thought, must have been acquired by his grandfather, an ardent collector of old dramas. The volume, which bound together twelve Shakespeare quartos, had a curious feature: the quarto of *Hamlet* that it contained did not correspond to any that Shakespeare scholars had previously known. The title page was dated 1603, and the text differed in crucial ways from both that printed in a quarto of 1604–05 (Q2) and that included in the 1623 First Folio (F). Bunbury exchanged his volume of quartos with a bookseller for books worth £180. In 1856 a second copy of the strange 1603 quarto of *Hamlet*, lacking the title page, was bought from a student for one shilling by a Dublin bookdealer, who turned a tidy profit by selling it for £70. The first of these copies is in the Huntington Library in California, the second in the British Library in London. Immensely valuable, they are the only two known surviving copies of what is called the First Quarto (Q1) of *Hamlet*.

The first and most striking difference between the 1603 Q1 and the other early texts of *Hamlet* is its length. The title page of the 1604–05 Q2 announced accurately that it was "[n]ewly imprinted" and that it was "enlarged to almost as much againe as it was" (that is, it was almost twice as long). With a further glance back at Q1, the Q2 title page advertised that it was printed from "the true and perfect Coppie," and, though there is no way to verify this claim (or even fully to understand what it means), the text of Q1 certainly has many moments of incoherence, awkwardness, and confusion.

When Q1 returned to circulation in the nineteenth century, many of its readers thought that they were encountering Shakespeare's first draft of his tragedy. They believed, for example, that he had initially written "To be, or not to be—ay, there's the point" (as the soliloquy begins in Q1), and then made the inspired revision that resulted in the version with which everyone is familiar. They assumed he had started with "Corambis" and "Montano" and then changed the names to "Polonius" and "Reynaldo." Or they thought he had first depicted Gertrude as Hamlet's ally in the plot against Claudius—for so she is in several scenes of Q1—and then decided to make the extent of her knowledge and her allegiance far more ambiguous.

But gradually another theory was advanced and gained ascendency. Q1, it was said, was one of those "stolen and surreptitious copies" that the Folio editors denounced, copies that were "maimed and deformed by the frauds and stealths of injurious impostors." It was a "bad quarto"—as A. W. Pollard termed it in 1909—defective, the theory went, because it had been pirated, possibly by an audience member good at shorthand, or more probably by one or more of the actors who had been paid to reconstruct from memory the whole script. Careful examination even seemed to reveal the principal culprit: the actor who played Marcellus. Hence the scenes in which Marcellus appears are relatively close in Q1 to those same scenes in Q2 and F; the further Marcellus gets from the stage, the more distorted the memorial reconstruction. But what of the *Mousetrap* scene in Q1, a scene without Marcellus and yet also fairly close to the other versions? The answer, it was proposed, lay in doubling: the performer who played Marcellus also played one or more of the minor characters elsewhere in the play.

Most (though not all) contemporary scholars accept some presence of memorial reconstruction in the Q1 *Hamlet*. But it is difficult to attribute all of the features of the text to the vagaries and inadequacies of memory. Whoever helped put together the text may have forgotten some lines, but the brevity and the rearrangement of several scenes seem to have at least as much to do with the exigencies of performance on the Elizabethan and Jacobean public stage. That is, both the "good" texts of *Hamlet*—the massive Q2 and even the somewhat shorter version printed in F—were too long to be performed in the ordinary circumstances of the times: an open-air stage without artificial lighting where in some seasons it begins to get dark by midafternoon. They would have had to be cut, and it is possible that the shape of Q1 reflects, in some way or other, one such theatrical abridgment.

This possibility would make Q1 a particularly fascinating trace, a trace not of Shakespeare's own manuscript but rather of a contemporary theater company's way of handling the play. (The title page calls attention to performance, claiming that it has been "diverse times acted by his Highnesse seruants in the City of London, as also in the two universities of Cambridge and Oxford, and else-where.") Since its recovery, Q1 has served as the basis for a number of productions, and its theatrical viability—its pace and momentum and compression—has found adherents. And even when Q1 is regarded as nothing but an interesting oddity, most productions of *Hamlet* have mined it for hints for performance. Thus Q2 brings on the mad Ophelia with the stage direction *"Enter Ophelia,"* while Q1 says *"Enter Ofelia playing on a lute, and her hair down, singing."* So too in the closet scene between Hamlet and his mother: Q2 and F have *"Enter Ghost,"* while Q1 tells us *"Enter the Ghost in his nightgown."* The nightgown—a striking change from the full armor of his initial appearance—seems to mark a crucial transformation in the Ghost's status.

STEPHEN GREENBLATT

SELECTED BIBLIOGRAPHY

Clayton, Thomas, ed. *The Hamlet First Published (Q1, 1603): Origins, Form, Intertextualities.* Newark: U of Delaware P; London and Toronto: Associated UP, 1992. How and why was the First Quarto composed, and what is its value? The twelve essays in this collection address these questions in wide-ranging and sometimes conflicting ways.

Craig, Hardin. *A New Look at Shakespeare's Quartos.* Stanford: Stanford UP, 1961. Shakespeare's "bad quartos" are not reconstructions by actors, but rather revisions or early versions made by the playwright himself.

Egan, Gabriel. *The Struggle for Shakespeare's Text: Twentieth-Century Editorial Theory and Practice.* Cambridge: Cambridge UP, 2010. Egan traces the twentieth-century debate between the New Bibliographers, with their author-centered approach, and the New Textualists, who focused instead on the socialized text, taking the side of the New Bibliographers.

Lesser, Zachary. *Hamlet after Q1.* Philadelphia: U of Pennsylvania P, 2015. A study of the reevaluation of *Hamlet* in text and performance after the 1823 discovery of Q1, which is consequently both the earliest and the latest text.

Maguire, Laurie E. *Shakespearean Suspect Texts: The "Bad" Quartos and Their Context.* Cambridge: Cambridge UP, 1996. Based on the examination of forty-one "suspect texts," Maguire argues that a case for memorial reconstruction can be made for only a few of the supposed "bad quartos," including Q1 of *Hamlet.*

Menzer, Paul. *The Hamlets: Cues, Qs, and Remembered Texts.* Newark: U of Delaware P, 2008. On the basis of an analysis of the cues, Menzer argues that Q1 was not intended as a memorial reconstruction of Shakespeare's *Hamlet* but rather as a separate project cobbled together out of a range of recollected *Hamlet* materials.

Sams, Eric. "Shakespeare's Hand in the Copy for the 1603 First Quarto of *Hamlet.*" *Hamlet Studies* 20 (1998): 80–88. An orthographical analysis of the Q1 and Q2 editions of *Hamlet* suggests that the First Quarto is a revision of an earlier Shakespearean text rather than a memorial reconstruction.

The Tragical History of Hamlet, Prince of Denmark

FIRST QUARTO

[THE PERSONS OF THE PLAY

HAMLET, Prince of Denmark
KING of Denmark and stepfather to Prince Hamlet
Gertred, QUEEN of Denmark
GHOST of Hamlet, former King of Denmark and father to Prince Hamlet
CORAMBIS, a royal counselor
OFELIA, daughter to Corambis
LEARTES, son to Corambis
MONTANO, servant to Corambis
BARNARDO ⎱ sentries
MARCELLUS ⎰
FIRST SENTINEL
HORATIO, friend to Hamlet
ROSSENCRAFT ⎱ school friends to Hamlet
GILDERSTONE ⎰
CORNELIUS ⎱ Danish ambassadors
VOLTEMAR ⎰
English AMBASSADORS
FIRST PLAYER, leader of the troupe
PLAYERS, who take on the roles of PROLOGUE, DUKE, DUCHESS, and LUCIANUS
FORTENBRASSE, Prince of Norway
FIRST CLOWN, a gravedigger
SECOND CLOWN, companion to First Clown
PRIEST
Braggart GENTLEMAN
Lords, Norwegian Captain, Soldiers in the Norwegian army, Attendants]

Scene 1

Enter [FIRST SENTINEL *and* BARNARDO].

FIRST SENTINEL   Stand! Who is that?

BARNARDO   'Tis I.

FIRST SENTINEL   Oh, you come most carefully° upon your   *dutifully; cautiously*
   watch.

BARNARDO   An if° you meet Marcellus and Horatio,   *An if = If*
5   The partners of my watch, bid them make haste.

FIRST SENTINEL   I will. See, who goes there?

Enter HORATIO *and* MARCELLUS.

HORATIO   Friends to this ground.°   *country*

MARCELLUS   And liegemen° to the Dane.[1]   *sworn servants*
   [*to* FIRST SENTINEL] Oh, farewell, honest soldier; who hath
   relieved you?

Scene 1 Location: A guard platform at Elsinore Castle, Denmark.
1. King of Denmark.

451

FIRST SENTINEL Barnardo hath my place. Give° you good
   night.   [Exit.]   *God give*

MARCELLUS Holla, Barnardo!

10 BARNARDO   Say, is Horatio there?

HORATIO A piece of him.

BARNARDO Welcome, Horatio; welcome, good Marcellus.

MARCELLUS What, hath this thing appeared again tonight?

BARNARDO I have seen nothing.

15 MARCELLUS Horatio says 'tis but our fantasy
   And will not let belief take hold of him
   Touching this dreaded sight twice seen by us.
   Therefore I have entreated him along
   With us to watch the minutes of this night,
20   That if again this apparition come
   He may approve° our eyes and speak to it.[2]   *verify the evidence of*

HORATIO Tut, 'twill not appear.

BARNARDO Sit down, I pray, and let us once again
   Assail your ears that are so fortified
   What we have two nights seen.

25 HORATIO   Well, sit we down,
   And let us hear Barnardo speak of this.

BARNARDO Last night of all,°   *Just last night*
   When yonder star that's westward from the pole°   *polestar*
   Had made his° course to illumine that part of heaven   *its*
30   Where now it burns, the bell then tolling one—
          Enter GHOST.

MARCELLUS Break off your talk, see where it comes again!

BARNARDO In the same figure like the King that's dead.

MARCELLUS Thou art a scholar: speak to it, Horatio.

BARNARDO Looks it not like the King?

35 HORATIO Most like: it horrors[3] me with fear and wonder.

BARNARDO It would° be spoke to.   *wishes to*

MARCELLUS   Question it, Horatio.

HORATIO What art thou[4] that thus usurps the state°   *shape; nature*
   In which the majesty of buried Denmark°   *the buried King*
   Did sometimes° walk? By heaven, I charge thee, speak!   *formerly*

MARCELLUS It is offended.   *Exit* GHOST.

40 BARNARDO   See, it stalks away.

HORATIO Stay! Speak, speak! By heaven, I charge thee,
   speak!

MARCELLUS 'Tis gone and makes no answer.

BARNARDO How now, Horatio? You tremble and look pale:
   Is not this something more than fantasy?
45   What think you on't?°   *of it*

HORATIO Afore my God,° I might not this believe   *By God*
   Without the sensible° and true avouch°   *sensory / testimony*
   Of my own eyes.

MARCELLUS   Is it not like the King?

---

2. A ghost was believed to speak only when spoken to. As a precaution, the experiment will be conducted by an educated man (Horatio; see line 33) who knows Latin (the language ostensibly effective for exorcising demonic spirits).

3. Horrifies, or possibly harrows, as suggested in Q2 and F.

4. The familiar "thou" would be an inappropriate form of address for a real king.

HORATIO   As thou art to thyself.

50   Such was the very armor he had on
    When he the ambitious Norway° combated;   *King of Norway*
    So frowned he once, when in an angry parle°   *encounter*
    He smote the sledded Polacks[5] on the ice.
    'Tis strange.

55 MARCELLUS   Thus twice before, and jump° at this dead hour,   *precisely*
    With martial stalk° he passèd through our watch.   *gait*

HORATIO   In what particular to work,[6] I know not,
    But in the thought and scope of my opinion,
    This bodes some strange eruption° to the state.   *calamity*

60 MARCELLUS   Good now,[7] sit down and tell me he that knows
    Why this same strict and most observant watch
    So nightly toils the subject of the land,[8]
    And why such daily cost° of brazen cannon   *expenditure*
    And foreign mart° for implements of war—   *trade*

65   Why such impress° of shipwrights, whose sore task   *drafting*
    Does not divide the Sunday from the week?
    What might be toward° that this sweaty watch[9]   *impending*
    Doth make the night joint laborer with the day—
    Who is't that can inform me?

HORATIO   Marry,[1] that can I.

70   At least the whisper goes so: our late king
    Who, as you know, was by Fortenbrasse of Norway,
    Thereto pricked° on by a most emulous° cause,   *spurred / rivalrous*
    Dared to the combat, in which our valiant Hamlet—
    For so this side of our known world esteemed him—

75   Did slay this Fortenbrasse, who by a sealed compact[2]
    Well ratified by law and heraldry,[3]
    Did forfeit with his life all those his lands
    Which he stood seized of° by the conqueror;   *held possession of*
    Against the which a moiety competent°   *an equal portion*

80   Was gagèd° by our king. Now, sir, young Fortenbrasse,   *staked*
    Of unapprovèd° mettle hot and full,   *untested; untrained*
    Hath in the skirts° of Norway here and there   *outlying parts*
    Sharked up[4] a sight of lawless resolutes
    For food and diet to some enterprise

85   That hath a stomach in't.[5] And this, I take it,
    Is the chief head° and ground of this our watch.   *source*

      Enter the GHOST.

    But lo, behold, see where it comes again!
    I'll cross[6] it though it blast° me. —Stay, illusion!   *wither*
    If there be any good thing to be done

90   That may do ease to thee and grace to me,

---

5. Poles who traveled by sled.
6. As far as what he is attempting to do.
7. An entreaty: Good sir, now.
8. *So . . . land:* Requires the country's subjects to toil every night.
9. TEXTUAL COMMENT We have emended Q1's "march" to "watch," as "watch" better fits the activity being described—staying awake for military preparations. See Digital Edition TC 1 (First Quarto edited text).
1. By the Virgin Mary (a mild oath).
2. A mutually agreed-upon contract ("compact") to

which each set his seal.
3. Properly ratified in accordance with civil law and the law of arms.
4. Gathered together indiscriminately (as a shark takes prey).
5. *For . . . in't:* The men will "feed" his enterprise; they are fed in return for their service. *stomach:* courageous action; challenge to the pride (of both the Prince and his men).
6. Confront, cross its path; also, make the sign of the cross (to counter its evil influence).

Speak to me!
If thou art privy to thy country's fate,
Which happily° foreknowing may prevent,   *perhaps; fortunately*
Oh, speak to me!
95   Or if thou hast extorted in thy life
Or hoarded treasure in the womb of earth,
For which they say you spirits oft walk in death,
Speak to me, stay and speak! Speak!
        [*The cock crows.*]
Stop it, Marcellus—

BARNARDO   'Tis here.

HORATIO   'Tis here.   *Exit* GHOST.

MARCELLUS   'Tis gone.
100   Oh, we do it wrong, being so majestical,
To offer it the show of violence,
For it is as the air invulnerable,
And our vain blows malicious mockery.

BARNARDO   It was about to speak when the cock crew.

105   HORATIO   And then it faded like a guilty thing
Upon a fearful summons. I have heard
The cock, that is the trumpet to the morning,
Doth with his early and shrill-crowing throat
Awake the god of day,[7] and at his sound,
110   Whether in earth or air, in sea or fire,
The extravagant and erring[8] spirit hies°   *hurries*
To his confines°—and of the truth hereof   *enclosure*
This present object° made probation.°   *example / proof*

MARCELLUS   It faded on the crowing of the cock.
115   Some say that ever 'gainst° that season comes   *always when*
Wherein our Savior's birth is celebrated,
The bird of dawning singeth all night long;
And then, they say, no spirit dare walk abroad,
The nights are wholesome, then no planet strikes,[9]
120   No fairy takes,° nor witch hath power to charm,   *bewitches*
So gracious° and so hallowed is that time.   *full of God's grace*

HORATIO   So have I heard and do in part believe it.
But see, the sun in russet mantle clad[1]
Walks o'er the dew of yon high mountaintop.
125   Break we our watch up and, by my advice,
Let us impart what we have seen tonight
Unto young Hamlet, for upon my life
This spirit, dumb to us, will speak to him.
Do you consent we shall acquaint him with it,
130   As needful in our love,[2] fitting our duty?

MARCELLUS   Let's do't, I pray, and I this morning know
Where we shall find him most conveniently.   [*Exeunt.*]

---

7. The sun god, Phoebus Apollo.
8. Wandering out of its boundaries.
9. When they were in certain unfavorable astrological positions, heavenly bodies were thought to exercise a negative influence on earthly events.
1. Dressed in a reddish-brown cloak.
2. As necessary because of the love we have for him.

Scene 2

Enter KING, QUEEN, HAMLET, LEARTES, CORAMBIS, *and*
the two Ambassadors [CORNELIUS *and* VOLTEMAR],
with Attendants.

KING   Lords, we here have writ to Fortenbrasse,
    Nephew to old Norway, who, impotent
    And bedrid, scarcely hears of this his
    Nephew's purpose. And we here dispatch
5   You, good Cornelius, and you, Voltemar,
    For bearers of these greetings to old Norway,
    Giving to you no further personal power
    To business with the King
    Than those related articles do show.
10   Farewell, and let your haste commend your duty.
CORNELIUS *and* VOLTEMAR   In this and all things will we
    show our duty.
KING   We doubt it nothing;° heartily farewell.   *not at all*
            [*Exeunt* CORNELIUS *and* VOLTEMAR.]
    And now, Leartes, what's the news with you?
    You said you had a suit°—what is't, Leartes?   *petition; request*
15 LEARTES   My gracious lord, your favorable license,
    Now that the funeral rites are all performed,
    I may have leave° to go again to France;   *permission*
    For though the favor of your grace might stay me,
    Yet something is there whispers in my heart
20   Which makes my mind and spirits bend all for France.
KING   Have you your father's leave, Leartes?
CORAMBIS   He hath, my lord, wrung from me a forced grant,°   *concession*
    And I beeseech you grant your highness' leave.
KING   With all our heart, Leartes, fare thee well.
25 LEARTES   I in all love and duty take my leave.   *Exit.*
KING   And now, princely son Hamlet,
    What means these sad and melancholy moods?
    For° your intent going to Wittenberg,[1]   *As for*
    We hold it most unmeet° and unconvenient,   *unsuitable*
30   Being the joy and half-heart° of your mother.   *darling*
    Therefore let me entreat you stay in court,
    All Denmark's hope, our cousin[2] and dearest son.
HAMLET   My lord, 'tis not the sable° suit I wear,   *black*
    No, nor the tears that still stand in my eyes,
35   Nor the distracted 'havior° in the visage,   *expression*
    Nor all together mixed with outward semblance,
    Is equal to the sorrow of my heart.
    Him have I lost I must of force forgo,
    These but the ornaments and suits° of woe.   *trappings*
40 KING   This shows a loving care in you, son Hamlet,
    But you must think your father lost a father,
    That father dead lost his, and so shall be
    Until the general ending.°   *apocalypse*
    Therefore cease laments. It is a fault
45   'Gainst heaven, fault 'gainst the dead, a fault 'gainst nature,

---

Scene 2 Location: The castle.
1. The birthplace of Protestantism, the university of
Luther and Faustus; many Danes studied there.

Hamlet intends to resume his studies at the university in Wittenberg.
2. Kinsman (outside one's immediate family).

And in reason's common course most certain
None lives on earth but he is born to die.
QUEEN   Let not thy mother lose her prayers, Hamlet—
Stay here with us, go not to Wittenberg.
50   HAMLET   I shall in all my best obey you, madam.
KING   Spoke like a kind and a most loving son.
And there's no health° the King shall drink today   *toast*
But° the great cannon to the clouds shall tell°   *Unless / sound*
The rouse° the King shall drink unto Prince Hamlet.   *large cup of drink*

Exeunt all but HAMLET.

55   HAMLET   Oh, that this too much grieved and sallied³ flesh
Would melt to nothing, or that the universal
Globe of heaven would turn all to a chaos!
O God, within two months—no, not two—married
Mine uncle—oh, let me not think of it—
60   My father's brother, but no more like
My father than I to Hercules.⁴
Within two months, ere° yet the salt of most   *before*
Unrighteous tears had left their flushing
In her galled° eyes, she married. O God, a beast   *distressed*
65   Devoid of reason would not have made
Such speed! Frailty, thy name is woman!
Why, she would hang on him as if increase
Of appetite had grown by what it looked on.
Oh, wicked, wicked speed, to make such
70   Dexterity to incestuous sheets!
Ere yet the shoes were old
With which she followed my dead father's corpse
Like Niobe, all tears⁵—married! Well, it is not,
Nor it cannot come to good.
75   But break, my heart, for I must hold my tongue.

Enter HORATIO, MARCELLUS[, *and* BARNARDO].

HORATIO   Health to your lordship!
HAMLET   I am very glad to see you—
Horatio, or I much forget myself.
HORATIO   The same, my lord, and your poor servant ever.
80   HAMLET   O my good friend, I change° that name with you.   *exchange*
But what make you from⁶ Wittenberg, Horatio?
—Marcellus!
MARCELLUS   My good lord.
HAMLET   I am very glad to see you. Good even, sirs!
85   [*to* HORATIO] But what is your affair in Elsinore?
We'll teach you to drink deep ere you depart.
HORATIO   A truant disposition, my good lord.
HAMLET   Nor shall you make me truster°   *believer*
Of your own report against yourself—
90   Sir, I know you are no truant.
But what is your affair in Elsinore?

---

3. "Sallied" is a possible spelling of "sullied." Editors have seen wordplay on "sallied," assailed, or, alternatively, salty, tear-soaked (salting was a method of preserving meat), and "sullied," or contaminated, ill-used. F has "solid."
4. In Greek and Roman mythology, a powerful demigod renowned for his strength, as exemplified in his twelve famous "labors."
5. Niobe's fourteen children were killed by Apollo and Artemis to punish her for boasting about them. She continued to weep bitterly even after she was turned to stone.
6. What are you doing away from.

HORATIO   My good lord, I came to see your father's funeral.
HAMLET   Oh, I prithee do not mock me, fellow student,
   I think it was to see my mother's wedding.
95   HORATIO   Indeed, my lord, it followed hard upon.°   *quickly thereafter*
HAMLET   Thrift, thrift, Horatio: the funeral baked meats°   *meat pies and pastries*
   Did coldly° furnish forth the marriage tables.   *when cold*
   Would I had met my dearest° foe in heaven   *most hated*
   Ere ever I had seen that day, Horatio.
100   Oh, my father, my father, methinks I see my father.
HORATIO   Where, my lord?
HAMLET   Why, in my mind's eye, Horatio.
HORATIO   I saw him once: he was a gallant king.
HAMLET   He was a man, take him for all in all;
105   I shall not look upon his like again.
HORATIO   My lord, I think I saw him yesternight.
HAMLET   Saw? Who?
HORATIO   My lord, the King your father.
HAMLET   Ha! Ha! The King my father, kee° you?   *say*
HORATIO   Season° your admiration° for awhile   *Moderate / amazement*
110   With an attentive ear till I may deliver,
   Upon the witness of these gentlemen,
   This wonder to you.
HAMLET   For God's love let me hear it!
HORATIO   Two nights together had these gentlemen,
115   Marcellus and Barnardo, on their watch
   In the dead vast° and middle of the night,   *stillness*
   Been thus encountered by a figure like your father,
   Armed to point,[7] exactly, cap-à-pie,°   *head to foot*
   Appears before them. Thrice he walks
120   Before their weak and fear-oppressèd eyes
   Within his truncheon's[8] length while they, distilled°   *dissolved*
   Almost to jelly with the act° of fear,   *effect*
   Stand dumb and speak not to him. This to me
   In dreadful secrecy impart they did,
125   And I with them the third night kept the watch
   Where, as they had delivered°—form° of the thing,   *reported / the form*
   Each part made true and good—
   The apparition comes. I knew your father:
   These hands are not more like.[9]
HAMLET   'Tis very strange.
130   HORATIO   As I do live, my honored lord, 'tis true,
   And we did think it right done° in our duty   *prescribed*
   To let you know it.
HAMLET   Where was this?
MARCELLUS   My lord, upon the platform where we watched.
HAMLET   Did you not speak to it?
135   HORATIO   My lord, we did, but answer made it none;
   Yet once methought it was about to speak,
   And lifted up his head to motion
   Like as he would speak, but even° then   *just*
   The morning cock crew loud, and in all haste

7. Armed in each point or detail.   9. These hands are not more like each other than the
8. Officer's baton.   apparition was like King Hamlet.

140   It shrunk in haste away, and vanishèd° our sight.   *vanished from*
    HAMLET   Indeed, indeed, sirs—but this troubles me.
       Hold you the watch tonight?
    BARNARDO *and* MARCELLUS   We do, my lord.
    HAMLET   Armed, say ye?
    HORATIO, BARNARDO, *and* MARCELLUS   Armed, my good lord.
145   HAMLET   From top to toe?
    HORATIO, BARNARDO, *and* MARCELLUS   My good lord, from
       head to foot.
    HAMLET   Why, then, saw you not his face?
    HORATIO   Oh, yes, my lord, he wore his beaver° up.   *helmet's faceguard*
    HAMLET   How looked he—frowningly?
150   HORATIO   A countenance more in sorrow than in anger.
    HAMLET   Pale, or red?
    HORATIO   Nay, very pale.
    HAMLET   And fixed his eyes upon you?
    HORATIO   Most constantly.
    HAMLET   I would I had been there.
    HORATIO   It would've much amazed you.
155   HAMLET   Yea, very like, very like—stayed it long?
    HORATIO   While one with moderate pace might tell° a   *count*
       hundred.
    MARCELLUS   Oh, longer, longer.
    HAMLET   His beard was grizzled,° no?   *gray*
    HORATIO   It was as I have seen it in his life,
       A sable silver.[1]
    HAMLET   I will watch tonight;
       Perchance 'twill walk again.
160   HORATIO   I warrant° it will.   *guarantee*
    HAMLET   If it assume my noble father's person,
       I'll speak to it, if hell itself should gape
       And bid me hold my peace. Gentlemen,
       If you have hitherto concealed this sight,
165   Let it be tenable° in your silence still;   *held*
       And whatsoever else shall chance tonight
       Give it an understanding but no tongue.
       I will requite your loves. So fare you well.
       Upon the platform twixt eleven and twelve
       I'll visit you.
170   ALL   Our duties to your honor.
    HAMLET   Oh, your loves, your loves, as mine to you. Farewell.
           Exeunt [HORATIO, MARCELLUS, *and* BARNARDO].
       My father's spirit in arms! Well, all's not well:
       I doubt° some foul play. Would the night were come!   *suspect*
       Till then, sit still my soul. Foul deeds will rise,
175   Though all the world o'erwhelm them, to men's eyes.   *Exit.*

Scene 3
Enter LEARTES *and* OFELIA.

    LEARTES   My necessaries are embarked°—I must aboard.   *on the ship*
       But, ere I part, mark what I say to thee:

---

1. Black sprinkled with white.
Scene 3 Location: Corambis's apartments in the castle.

I see Prince Hamlet makes a show of love—
Beware, Ofelia, do not trust his vows.
5 Perhaps he loves you now, and now his tongue
Speaks from his heart, but yet take heed, my sister:
The chariest° maid is prodigal enough   *most careful; modest*
If she unmask her beauty to the moon.[1]
Virtue itself scapes not calumnious thoughts—
10 Believe't, Ofelia—therefore keep aloof
Lest that he trip° thy honor and thy fame.°   *bring down / reputation*
OFELIA Brother, to this I have lent attentive ear
And doubt not but to keep my honor firm.
But, my dear brother, do not you,
15 Like to a cunning sophister,[2]
Teach me the path and ready way to heaven,
While you, forgetting what is said to me,
Yourself, like to a careless libertine,
Doth give his heart his appetite at full
20 And little recks° how that his honor dies.   *notices; cares*
LEARTES No, fear it not,° my dear Ofelia.   *fear not for me*
Here comes my father:
Occasion smiles upon a second leave.[3]
    Enter CORAMBIS.
CORAMBIS Yet here, Leartes? Aboard, aboard, for shame,
25 The wind sits in the shoulder° of your sail   *at the back*
And you are stayed° for. There [*laying his hand on Leartes'*   *waited*
    head], my blessing with thee,
And these few precepts in thy memory:
Be thou familiar but by no means vulgar;[4]
Those friends thou hast, and their adoptions tried,[5]
30 Grapple them to thee with a hoop of steel,
But do not dull° the palm with entertain°   *callous / the greeting (handshaking)*
Of every new unfledged courage;[6]
Beware of entrance into a quarrel, but, being in,
Bear it° that the opposed may beware of thee;   *Manage it so*
35 Costly thy apparel as thy purse can buy,
But not expressed in fashion°—   *showiness*
For the apparel oft proclaims the man,
And they of France, of the chief rank and station,
Are of a most select and general chief in that.
40 This above all: to thy own self be true,
And it must follow as the night the day
Thou canst not then be false to anyone.
Farewell, my blessing with thee.
LEARTES I humbly take my leave. Farewell, Ofelia,
45 And remember well what I have said to you.

---

1. *prodigal . . . moon:* risk-taking enough if she exposes herself to the moon. (Upper-class women wore masks to screen their complexions from the sun.) The moon was classically figured as chaste, while the sun was traditionally associated with passion. The suggestion here is that a maid can never be too cautious.
2. *cunning sophister:* one using speech in a deceptive or suspect manner.
3. Favorable circumstances provide us with a second farewell.
4. *Be . . . vulgar:* Be friendly but by no means indiscriminately social.
5. *Those . . . tried:* Those friends of yours who have proven true and reliable.
6. *Of . . . courage:* Of any given untried (and thus not fully trusted) acquaintance. "Courage," meaning heart or spirit here, is a synecdoche for a person, like "soul" in "you must not tell a soul."

OFELIA   It is already locked within my heart,
    And you yourself shall keep the key of it.   *Exit* [LEARTES].
CORAMBIS   What is't, Ofelia, he hath said to you?
OFELIA   Something touching the Prince Hamlet.
50   CORAMBIS   Marry, well thought on; 'tis given me to
    understand
    That you have been too prodigal of your
    Maiden presence unto Prince Hamlet.
    If it be so—as so 'tis given to° me,   *suggested to*
    And that in way of caution—I must tell you,
55   You do not understand yourself so well
    As befits my honor and your credit.°   *reputation*
OFELIA   My lord, he hath made many tenders° of   *offers*
    His love to me—
CORAMBIS   "Tenders"? Ay, ay, "tenders"[7] you may call them—
60   OFELIA   And withal° such earnest vows—   *also*
CORAMBIS   Springes to catch woodcocks.[8]
    What, do not I know, when the blood doth burn,
    How prodigal° the heart lends the tongue vows?   *lavishly*
    In brief, be more scanter of your maiden presence,
65   Or, tendering thus, you'll tender me a fool.[9]
OFELIA   I shall obey, my lord, in all I may.
CORAMBIS   Ofelia, receive none of his letters,
    For lovers' lines are snares to entrap the heart;
    Refuse his tokens: both of them° are keys   *(lines and tokens)*
70   To unlock chastity unto desire.
    Come in, Ofelia. Such men often prove
    Great in their words but little in their love.
OFELIA   I will, my lord.   *Exeunt.*

Scene 4
Enter HAMLET, HORATIO, *and* MARCELLUS.
HAMLET   The air bites shrewd;°   *sharply*
    It is an eager° and a nipping wind.   *a bitter*
    What hour is't?
HORATIO   I think it lacks of twelve.
MARCELLUS   No, 'tis struck.
HORATIO   Indeed? I heard it not.
    Sound trumpets[, drums, and cannon].
5   What doth this mean, my lord?
HAMLET   Oh, the King doth wake tonight and takes his
    rouse,
    Keeps wassail and the swaggering upspring reels,[1]
    And as he drains his draughts of Rhenish° down   *Rhine wine*
    The kettledrum and trumpet thus bray out
10   The triumphs of his pledge.[2]
HORATIO   Is it a custom here?
HAMLET   Ay, marry, is't, and though I am

---

7. *tenders:* offers of payment in compensation for something.
8. Traps for proverbially gullible birds.
9. A multiple pun: make me look foolish; seem yourself a fool; show me a baby (idiomatically, a "fool").
Scene 4 Location: The castle's battlements.

1. *the King . . . reels:* the King revels and carouses, has a drinking party ("wassail"), and staggers ("reels") through a wild German dance.
2. His success in draining his cup upon making a toast.

Native here and to the manner° born,   *custom*
It is a custom more honored in the breach
Than in the observance.[3]
    Enter the GHOST.
15 HORATIO   Look, my lord, it comes.
  HAMLET   Angels and ministers of grace defend us!
Be thou a spirit of health or goblin° damned,   *demon*
Bring with thee airs° from heaven or blasts[4] from hell,   *gentle breezes*
Be thy intents wicked or charitable,
20 Thou comest in such questionable shape
That I will speak to thee. I'll call thee Hamlet,
King, father, royal Dane. Oh, answer me!
Let me not burst in ignorance, but say
Why thy canonized° bones, hearsed° in death,   *consecrated / coffined*
25 Have burst their ceremonies,[5] why thy sepulcher
In which we saw thee quietly interred
Hath burst his° ponderous and marble jaws   *its*
To cast thee up again. What may this mean
That thou, dead corpse, again in complete steel°   *armor*
30 Revisits thus the glimpses of the moon,[6]
Making night hideous and we fools of nature[7]
So horridly to shake our disposition°   *mental foundations*
With thoughts beyond the reaches of our souls?
Say, speak: wherefore? What may this mean?
35 HORATIO   It beckons you, as though it had something
To impart to you alone.
  MARCELLUS   Look with what courteous action
It waves you to a more removèd ground—
But do not go with it.
  HORATIO   No, by no means, my lord.
40 HAMLET   It will not speak—then will I follow it.
  HORATIO   What if it tempt you toward the flood,° my lord,   *sea*
That beckles[8] o'er his base into the sea,
And there assume some other horrible shape
Which might deprive your sovereignty of reason
45 And drive you into madness? Think of it.
  HAMLET   Still am I called. —Go on, I'll follow thee.
  HORATIO   My lord, you shall not go.
  HAMLET   Why, what should be the fear?
I do not set my life at a pin's fee,°   *worth*
And for my soul, what can it do to that,
50 Being a thing immortal like itself?
—Go on, I'll follow thee.
  MARCELLUS   My lord, be ruled, you shall not go.
  HAMLET   My fate cries out and makes each petty artery
As hardy as the Nemean lion's[9] nerve.
55 Still am I called—unhand me, gentlemen!

---

3. Which is more honored in being broken than in being observed.
4. Pestilent gusts.
5. Funeral ceremonies more generally, or perhaps Q2 and F's "cerements," grave clothes.
6. *glimpses of the moon:* (earth lit by) flickering moonlight.

7. Mere mortals (terrified by encounters with the supernatural).
8. "Beckles" is unattested in the *OED*. Q2 and F have "bettles" and "beetles," suggesting a protruding or overhanging into the sea.
9. A ferocious beast killed by Hercules.

By heaven I'll make a ghost of him that lets° me.   hinders
Away, I say! —Go on, I'll follow thee.

                             [*Exeunt* GHOST *and* HAMLET.]

HORATIO   He waxeth desperate with imagination.
MARCELLUS   Something is rotten in the state of Denmark.
60   HORATIO   Have after!° To what issue° will this sort?   *Go on / end*
MARCELLUS   Let's follow; 'tis not fit thus to obey him.

                                       Exeunt.

Scene 5

Enter GHOST *and* HAMLET.

HAMLET   I'll go no farther. Whither wilt thou lead me?
GHOST   Mark me.
HAMLET   I will.
GHOST   I am thy father's spirit,
    Doomed for a time to walk the night
    And all the day confined in flaming fire
5   Till the foul crimes done in my days of nature°   *my natural life*
    Are purged and burnt away.
HAMLET   Alas, poor ghost.
GHOST   Nay, pity me not, but to my unfolding
    Lend thy listening ear: but that I am forbid
    To tell the secrets of my prison house,
10   I would a tale unfold whose lightest word
    Would harrow up° thy soul, freeze thy young blood,   *vex*
    Make thy two eyes like stars start from their spheres,
    Thy knotted and combinèd locks to part,
    And each particular hair to stand on end
15   Like quills upon the fretful porcupine.
    But this same blazon[1] must not be to ears
    Of flesh and blood. Hamlet,
    If ever thou didst thy dear father love—
HAMLET   O God!
20   GHOST   Revenge his foul and most unnatural murder.
HAMLET   Murder?
GHOST   Yea, murder in the highest degree—
    As in the least 'tis bad, but mine most foul,
    Beastly, and unnatural.
HAMLET   Haste me to know it,
    That with wings as swift as meditation,
25   Or the thought of it, may sweep to my revenge.
GHOST   Oh, I find thee apt, and duller shouldst thou be
    Than the fat° weed which roots itself in ease   *gross*
    On Lethe wharf.[2] Brief let me be:
    'Tis given out° that, sleeping in my orchard,   *It's being said*
30   A serpent stung me; so the whole ear of Denmark
    Is with a forgèd process° of my death   *a fabricated account*
    Rankly abused.° But know, thou noble youth,   *deceived*
    He that did sting thy father's heart now wears
    His crown.
HAMLET   Oh, my prophetic soul, my uncle!

Scene 5 Location: Scene continues.
1. Catalogue or display of the afterlife's mysteries.
2. In classical mythology, Lethe was the river of forgetfulness in Hades. The comparison as it stands
seems incomplete, as it is missing the "Wouldst thou
not stir in this" from Q2 and F.

35   My uncle!
        GHOST   Yea, he!
        That incestuous wretch won to his will with gifts°—   *abilities; presents*
        Oh, wicked will and gifts that have the power
        So to seduce—my most seeming-virtuous queen.
40   But virtue, as it never will be moved
        Though lewdness court it in a shape of heaven,
        So lust, though to a radiant angel linked,
        Would sate itself[3] from a celestial bed
        And prey on garbage.
45   But soft,[4] methinks I scent the morning's air.
        Brief let me be: sleeping within my orchard—
        My custom always in the afternoon—
        Upon my secure hour thy uncle came
        With juice of hebona[5] in a vial
50   And through the porches° of my ears did pour   *entranceways*
        The leprous distilment,[6] whose effect
        Holds such an enmity with blood of man
        That swift as quicksilver[7] it posteth° through   *speeds*
        The natural gates and alleys of the body
55   And turns the thin and wholesome blood
        Like eager° droppings into milk,   *acid (like wine)*
        And all my smooth body barked and tettered[8] over.
        Thus was I, sleeping, by a brother's hand
        Of crown, of queen, of life, of dignity
60   At once deprived, no reckoning made of,
        But sent unto my grave with all my accounts
        And sins upon my head.[9] Oh, horrible, most horrible!
        HAMLET   O God!
        GHOST   If thou hast nature° in thee, bear it° not—   *natural feeling / (this injustice)*
65   But, howsoever, let not thy heart conspire
        Against thy mother aught;° leave her to heaven   *any (punishment)*
        And to the burden that her conscience bears.
        I must be gone:
        The glowworm shows the matin° to be near   *morning*
70   And 'gins° to pale his uneffectual fire.   *begins*
        Hamlet, adieu! Adieu, adieu, remember me!   *Exit.*
        HAMLET   O all you host of heaven! O earth! What else?
        And shall I couple° hell? Remember thee?   *add*
        Yes, thou poor ghost,
75   From the tables° of my memory I'll wipe away   *tablet; book*
        All saws of books, all trivial fond° conceits   *foolish*
        That ever youth or else observance noted,
        And thy remembrance all alone shall sit.
        Yes, yes, by heaven, a damned pernicious villain,
80   Murderous, bawdy, smiling, damnèd villain!

---

3. Will become satiated (and unable to find further pleasure).
4. The Ghost urges himself quickly to wrap up his speech.
5. A poison, possibly henbane.
6. Distillation causing skin to become scaly (as in leprosy, a disease familiar in Elizabethan England).
7. Liquid mercury, noted for its capacity for rapid motion.
8. *barked and tettered*: covered in a scaly barklike rash.
9. *no . . . head*: without having made restitution for my sins, but sent to the Last Judgment liable for all my faults.

My tables[1]—[*He takes out his table-book and writes.*] Meet°   *Appropriate*
   it is I set it down
That one may smile and smile and be a villain—
At least I am sure it may be so in Denmark.
So, uncle, there you are, there you are.

85   Now to the words: it is "Adieu, adieu,
Remember me." So, 'tis enough, I have sworn.
          Enter HORATIO *and* MARCELLUS.
HORATIO   My lord, my lord!
MARCELLUS   Lord Hamlet!
HORATIO   Illo, lo, ho, ho!
90   MARCELLUS   Illo, lo, so, ho, so, come, boy, come![2]
HORATIO   Heavens secure him.
MARCELLUS   How is't, my noble lord?
HORATIO   What news, my lord?
HAMLET   Oh, wonderful, wonderful!
95   HORATIO   Good my lord, tell it.
HAMLET   No, not I, you'll reveal it.
HORATIO   Not I, my lord, by heaven.
MARCELLUS   Nor I, my lord.
HAMLET   How say you, then—would heart of man once
   think it—
But you'll be secret?
100   HORATIO *and* MARCELLUS   Ay, by heaven, my lord.
HAMLET   There's never a villain dwelling in all Denmark
But he's an arrant° knave.   *a complete*
HORATIO   There need no ghost
Come from the grave to tell you this.
HAMLET   Right, you are in the right; and therefore
105   I hold it meet, without more circumstance° at all,   *elaborate speech*
We shake hands and part, you as your business
And desires shall lead you—for, look you,
Every man hath business and desires
Such as it is—and, for my own poor part,
110   I'll go pray.
HORATIO   These are but wild and whirling words, my lord.
HAMLET   I am sorry they offend you. Heartily,
Yes, faith, heartily.
HORATIO   There's no offense, my lord.
HAMLET   Yes, by Saint Patrick,[3] but there is, Horatio,
115   And much offense too. Touching° this vision,   *Concerning*
It is an honest° ghost, that let me tell you.   *a reliable; a genuine*
For your desires to know what is between us,
O'ermaster it as you may. And now, kind friends,
As you are friends, scholars, and gentlemen,
Grant me one poor request.
120   HORATIO *and* MARCELLUS   What is't, my lord?
HAMLET   Never make known what you have seen tonight.
HORATIO *and* MARCELLUS   My lord, we will not.
HAMLET   Nay, but swear.
HORATIO   In faith, my lord, not I.[4]

---

1. Scholars and others might carry two writing tab-   3. Perhaps because St. Patrick was thought to be
lets hinged together, as a notebook.   keeper of purgatory.
2. Marcellus parodies a falconer's call.   4. I will indeed not reveal it.

MARCELLUS   Nor I, my lord, in faith.
125 HAMLET   Nay, upon my sword;[5] indeed, upon my sword.
            The GHOST *[calls out] under the stage.*
      GHOST   Swear.
      HAMLET   Ha, ha! Come, you hear this fellow in the
            cellarage:°   *cellar*
      Here consent to swear.[6]
      HORATIO   Propose the oath, my lord.
130 HAMLET   Never to speak what you have seen tonight,
      Swear by my sword.
      GHOST   Swear.
      HAMLET   *Hic et ubique?*[7] Nay then, we'll shift our ground.
      Come hither, gentlemen, and lay your hands
135 Again upon this sword. Never to speak
      Of that which you have seen, swear by my sword.
      GHOST   Swear.
      HAMLET   Well said, old mole: canst work in the earth so fast?
      A worthy pioneer![8] —Once more remove.°   *move*
140 HORATIO   Day and night, but this is wondrous strange.
      HAMLET   And therefore as a stranger give it welcome:[9]
      There are more things in heaven and earth, Horatio,
      Than are dreamt of in your philosophy.[1]
      But come here: as before, you never shall,
145 How strange or odd soe'er I bear myself—
      As I perchance hereafter shall think meet
      To put an antic disposition on[2]—
      That you at such times seeing me never shall
      With arms encumbered° thus, or this head-shake,   *folded*
150 Or by pronouncing some undoubtful[3] phrase
      As "Well, well, we know," or "We could an if° we would,"   *an if = if*
      Or "There be an if they might,"[4] or such ambiguous
      Giving out, to note that you know aught° of me—   *anything*
      This not to do, so grace and mercy
155 At your most need help you, swear.
      GHOST   Swear.
            [*They swear.*]
      HAMLET   Rest, rest, perturbèd spirit. —So, gentlemen,
      In all my love I do commend me to you,
      And what so poor a man as Hamlet may
160 To pleasure you, God willing, shall not want.°   *be left undone*
      Nay, come, let's go together.
      But still° your fingers on your lips, I pray.   *always*
      The time is out of joint:° oh, cursèd spite,   *dislocated; disordered*
      That ever I was born to set it right.
165 Nay, come,[5] let's go together.   *Exeunt.*

5. Swearing on a sword was a fairly common practice because the hilt and blade form a cross.
6. TEXTUAL COMMENT This moment—exactly whom Hamlet is addressing and what he is saying—is treated differently in Q2 and F and admits multiple interpretations. See Digital Edition TC 2 (First Quarto edited text).
7. Here and everywhere (Latin).
8. Army trench digger.

9. As if it had a guest's right to courteous hospitality.
1. Human speculative knowledge; science.
2. To assume the behavior of a madman.
3. Q2 and F read "doubtfull."
4. There are those who would speak if they were allowed.
5. The others are politely waiting for Hamlet, the Prince, to lead the way; he insists on informality.

Scene 6

Enter CORAMBIS *and* MONTANO.

CORAMBIS Montano, here, these letters to my son
And this same money with my blessing to him,
And bid him ply° his learning, good Montano. *work at*

MONTANO I will, my lord.

5   CORAMBIS You shall do very well, Montano, to say thus: "I
knew the gentleman," or "know his father"; to inquire the
manner of his life, as thus: being amongst his acquaintance,[1]
you may say you saw him at such a time, mark you me, at
game, or drinking, swearing, or drabbing°—you may go so *whoring*

10 far.

MONTANO My lord, that will impeach his reputation.

CORAMBIS I'faith, not a whit, no, not a whit. Now, happily, he
closeth° with you in the consequence[2]—as you may bridle it, *confides*
not disparage him a jot—What was I about to say?

15 MONTANO "He closeth with him in the consequence."

CORAMBIS Ay, you say right, he closeth with him° thus: this *(you)*
will he say—let me see what he will say—marry, this: "I saw
him yesterday," or t'other day, or then, or at such a time,
"a-dicing" or "at tennis," ay, or "drinking drunk" or "entering

20 of a house of lightness"—*videlicet*,° brothel. Thus, sir, do we *that is to say*
that know the world, being men of reach,° by indirections *wide understanding*
find directions° forth, and so shall you my son[3]—you ha' *real tendencies*
me,° ha' you not? *my meaning*

MONTANO I have, my lord.

25 CORAMBIS Well, fare you well: commend me to him.

MONTANO I will, my lord.

CORAMBIS And bid him ply his music.

MONTANO My lord, I will.

CORAMBIS Farewell.   *Exit* [MONTANO].

Enter OFELIA.

30 How now, Ofelia? What's the news with you?

OFELIA O my dear father, such a change in nature,
So great an alteration in a prince,
So pitiful to him, fearful to me,
A maiden's eye ne'er looked on.

35 CORAMBIS Why, what's the matter, my Ofelia?

OFELIA Oh, young Prince Hamlet, the only flower of
Denmark,
He is bereft of all the wealth he had.
The jewel that adorned his feature most
Is filched and stolen away: his wit's bereft him.

40 He found me walking in the gallery all alone—
There comes he to me with a distracted° look, *deranged; mad*
His garters lagging down, his shoes untied,
And fixed his eyes so steadfast on my face
As if they had vowed this is their latest object.

45 Small while he stood, but grips me by the wrist
And there he holds my pulse till, with a sigh,

Scene 6 Location: Corambis's apartments in the
castle.
1. His acquaintances.

2. To the following effect.
3. And so shall you figure out what my son has been
doing.

He doth unclasp his hold and parts away,°   *departs*
Silent as is the mid-time of the night.
And as he went, his eye was still on me,
50   For thus his head over his shoulder looked.
He seemed to find the way without his eyes,
For out of doors he went without their help,
And so did leave me.
CORAMBIS   Mad for thy love.
What, have you given him any cross words of late?
55   OFELIA   I did repel his letters, deny his gifts,
As you did charge me.
CORAMBIS   Why, that hath made him mad.
By heav'n, 'tis as proper for our age to cast
Beyond ourselves as 'tis for the younger sort
To love their wantonness. Well, I am sorry
60   That I was so rash. But what remedy?
Let's to the King. This madness may prove,
Though wild awhile, yet more true to thy love.   *Exeunt.*

Scene 7
Enter KING, QUEEN, ROSSENCRAFT, *and* GILDERSTONE.
KING   Right noble friends, that our dear cousin Hamlet
Hath lost the very heart of all his sense
It is most right,° and we most sorry for him.   *true*
Therefore we do desire, even as you tender
5   Our care to him and our great love to you,
That you will labor but to wring from him
The cause and ground of his distemperance.
Do this, the King of Denmark shall be thankful.
ROSSENCRAFT   My lord, whatsoever lies within our power.
10   Your majesty may more command in words
Than use persuasions to your liegemen, bound
By love, by duty, and obedience.
GILDERSTONE   What we may do for both your majesties
To know the grief troubles the Prince your son,
15   We will endeavor all the best we may.
So, in all duty, do we take our leave.
KING   Thanks, Gilderstone and gentle Rossencraft.
QUEEN   Thanks, Rossencraft and gentle Gilderstone.
                    [*Exeunt* ROSSENCRAFT *and* GILDERSTONE.]
            Enter CORAMBIS *and* OFELIA.
CORAMBIS   My lord, the ambassadors are joyfully
20   Returned from Norway.
KING   Thou still° hast been the father of good news.   *always*
CORAMBIS   Have I, my lord? I assure your grace
I hold my duty as I hold my life
Both to my God and to my sovereign king.
25   And I believe—or else this brain of mine
Hunts not the train of policy° so well   *cleverness*
As it had wont to do¹—but I have found
The very depth of Hamlet's lunacy.

Scene 7 Location: A stateroom in the castle.   1. As it had in the past.

QUEEN God grant he hath.
   Enter the Ambassadors [VOLTEMAR *and* CORNELIUS].

30 KING Now, Voltemar, what from our brother° Norway?   *fellow monarch*
VOLTEMAR Most fair returns of greetings and desires.°   *good wishes*
 Upon our first,[2] he sent forth to suppress
 His nephew's levies,° which to him appeared   *raising of troops*
 To be a preparation 'gainst the Polack,°   *King of Poland*
35 But, better looked into, he truly found
 It was against your highness; whereat, grieved
 That so his sickness, age, and impotence
 Was falsely borne in hand,[3] sends out arrests
 On Fortenbrasse,[4] which he in brief obeys,
40 Receives rebuke from Norway, and, in fine,°   *conclusion*
 Makes vow before his uncle never more
 To give the assay of arms[5] against your majesty.
 Whereon old Norway, overcome with joy,
 Gives him three thousand crowns in annual fee°   *income*
45 And his commission to employ those soldiers,
 So levied as before, against the Polack—
 With an entreaty herein further shown
 That it would please you to give quiet pass
 Through your dominions for that enterprise
50 On such regards of safety and allowances[6]
 As therein are set down.
KING It likes° us well, and at fit time and leisure   *pleases*
 We'll read and answer these his articles.
 Meantime, we thank you for your well-took labor.
55 Go to your rest; at night we'll feast together.
 Right welcome home!
    Exeunt Ambassadors [VOLTEMAR *and* CORNELIUS].
CORAMBIS This business is very well dispatched.
 Now, my lord, touching the young Prince Hamlet,
 Certain it is that he is mad; mad let us grant him, then.
60 Now, to know the cause of this effect—
 Or else to say the cause of this defect,
 For this effect defective[7] comes by cause—
QUEEN Good my lord, be brief.
CORAMBIS   Madam, I will.
 My lord, I have a daughter—have while she's mine°—   *until she marries*
65 For that we think is surest we often lose.
 Now, to the Prince: my lord, but note this letter,
 The which my daughter in obedience
 Delivered to my hands.
KING   Read it, my lord.
CORAMBIS Mark, my lord:
70 [*Reads.*] "Doubt that in earth is fire,
    Doubt that the stars do move,
    Doubt° truth to be a liar,   *Suspect*
    But do not doubt I love.

---

2. When we first raised the matter.
3. Disloyally taken advantage of; tricked.
4. *arrests / On Fortenbrasse:* orders commanding Fortenbrasse to stop his preparations and (presumably) present himself to explain them.

5. To mount a military challenge.
6. *On . . . allowances:* Following conditions regarding your realm's safety, subject to your approval.
7. This consequence shows a lack of something (Hamlet's reason).

To the beautiful Ofelia: thine ever, the most unhappy Prince
75   Hamlet."
My lord, what do you think of me?
Ay, or what might you think when I saw this?
KING   As of a true friend and a most loving subject.
CORAMBIS   I would be glad to prove so.
80   Now, when I saw this letter, thus I bespake my maiden:
"Lord Hamlet is a prince out of your star°   *above your sphere*
And one that is unequal° for your love."   *not proper*
Therefore I did command her refuse his letters,
Deny his tokens, and to absent herself.
85   She, as my child, obediently obeyed me.
Now, since which time, seeing his love thus crossed—
Which I took to be idle and but sport—
He straightway grew into a melancholy,
From that unto a fast, then unto a distraction,
90   Then into a sadness, from that unto a madness,
And so, by continuance and weakness of the brain,
Into this frenzy which now possesseth him.
An if this be not true, take this from this.
       [*He points to his head and shoulders.*]
KING   Think you 'tis so?
95   CORAMBIS   How? So? My lord, I would very fain know
That thing that I have said 'tis so, positively,
And it hath fallen out otherwise.
Nay, if circumstances lead me on
I'll find it out, if it were hid as deep
100   As the center of the earth.
KING   How should we try° this same?   *test*
CORAMBIS   Marry, my good lord, thus:
The Prince's walk is here in the gallery—
There let Ofelia walk until he comes.
105   Yourself and I will stand close in the study:
There shall you hear the effect° of all his heart,   *purpose; drift*
And if it prove any otherwise than love,
Then let my censure fail another time.
KING   See where he comes, poring upon a book.
       Enter HAMLET.
110   CORAMBIS   Madam, will it please your grace to leave us here?
QUEEN   With all my heart.   *Exit.*
CORAMBIS   And here, Ofelia, read you on this book
And walk aloof.° The King shall be unseen.   *at a distance*
       [KING *and* CORAMBIS *retire.*]
HAMLET[8]   To be, or not to be—ay, there's the point.°   *issue to debate*
115   To die, to sleep, is that all? Ay, all.
No, to sleep, to dream—ay, marry,[9] there it goes[1]—
For in that dream of death, when we awake

---

8. TEXTUAL COMMENT Hamlet's famous soliloquy
here seems to be recomposed from memory. This
process evidently caused some confusions and inconsistencies, but it also led to a more accessible and
distilled version than its rendering in Q2 and F. See
Digital Edition TC 3 (First Quarto edited text).
9. *marry*: used for emphasis, expressing astonish-

ment or outrage.
1. *there it goes*: the "point" or question "goes" toward
the potentially problematic consideration that dreams
by necessity accompany sleep. The line is confusing
because, unlike in Q2 and F, Hamlet does not subsequently explain why the question should pivot on
dreams.

And borne before an everlasting judge,
From whence no passenger ever returned,
120   The undiscovered country, at whose sight
The happy smile and the accursèd damned—
But for this, the joyful hope of this,
Who'd bear the scorns and flattery of the world—
Scorned by the right° rich (the rich cursed of the poor),   *downright*
125   The widow being oppressed, the orphan wronged,
The taste of hunger or a tyrant's reign,
And thousand more calamities besides—
To grunt and sweat under this weary life
When that he may his full quietus make[2]
130   With a bare bodkin?° Who would this endure,   *mere dagger*
But for a hope of something after death,
Which puzzles the brain and doth confound the sense,
Which makes us rather bear those evils we have
Than fly to others that we know not of?
135   Ay, that—oh, this conscience[3] makes cowards of us all.
—Lady, in thy orisons° be all my sins remembered.   *prayers*

OFELIA   My lord, I have sought opportunity, which now I
have, to redeliver to your worthy hands a small remembrance: such tokens which I have received of you.

140   HAMLET   Are you fair?

OFELIA   My lord?

HAMLET   Are you honest?°   *chaste; truthful*

OFELIA   What means my lord?

HAMLET   That if you be fair and honest, your beauty should
145   admit no discourse to[4] your honesty.

OFELIA   My lord, can beauty have better privilege than with
honesty?

HAMLET   Yea, marry, may it, for beauty may sooner transform
honesty from what she was into a bawd than honesty can
150   transform beauty. This was sometimes° a paradox, but now   *formerly*
the time gives it scope.[5] I never gave you nothing.

OFELIA   My lord, you know right well you did, and with them
such earnest vows of love as would have moved the stoniest
breast alive.
155   But now too true I find
Rich gifts wax° poor when givers grow unkind.   *grow*

HAMLET   I never loved you.

OFELIA   You made me believe you did.

HAMLET   Oh, thou shouldst not ha' believed me! Go to a nun-
160   nery,[6] go! Why shouldst thou be a breeder of sinners? I am
myself indifferent honest,° but I could accuse myself of such   *moderately virtuous*
crimes it had been better my mother had ne'er borne me.
Oh, I am very proud, ambitious, disdainful, with more sins
at my beck° than I have thoughts to put them in. What   *command*
165   should such fellows as I do, crawling between heaven and

---

earth? To a nunnery, go! We are arrant° knaves all—believe   *complete*
none of us. To a nunnery, go!

OFELIA   Oh, heavens secure him!

HAMLET   Where's thy father?

170   OFELIA   At home, my lord.

HAMLET   For God's sake, let the doors be shut on him. He
may play the fool nowhere but in his own house. To a nunnery, go!

OFELIA   Help him, good God!

175   HAMLET   If thou dost marry, I'll give thee this plague to thy
dowry:
Be thou as chaste as ice, as pure as snow,
Thou shalt not scape calumny. To a nunnery, go!

OFELIA   Alas, what change is this!

180   HAMLET   But if thou wilt needs marry, marry a fool, for wise
men know well enough what monsters[7] you° make of them.   *you women*
To a nunnery, go!

OFELIA   Pray God restore him!

HAMLET   Nay, I have heard of your paintings° too: God hath   *cosmetics*
185   given you one face and you make yourselves another. You
fig[8] and you amble and you nickname God's creatures,[9]
making your wantonness your ignorance.[1] A pox,[2] 'tis scurvy!
I'll no more of it—it hath made me mad. I'll no more marriages. All that are married, but one, shall live, the rest shall
190   keep as they are. To a nunnery, go. To a nunnery, go!   *Exit.*

OFELIA   Great God of heaven, what a quick change is this!
The courtier, scholar, soldier—all in him,
All dashed and splintered thence. Oh, woe is me,
To ha' seen what I have seen, see what I see.   *Exit.*
     KING *and* CORAMBIS [*come forward*].

195   KING   Love? No, no, that's not the cause:
Some deeper thing it is that troubles him.

CORAMBIS   Well, something it is. My lord, content you
     awhile,
I will myself go feel him. Let me work,
I'll try him every way.
     Enter HAMLET.
                 See where he comes—

200   Send you those gentlemen. Let me alone
To find the depth of this—away, be gone.   *Exit* KING.
—Now, my good lord, do you know me?

HAMLET   Yea, very well, you're a fishmonger.

CORAMBIS   Not I, my lord.

205   HAMLET   Then, sir, I would you were so honest a man, for to
be honest as this age goes[3] is one man to be picked out of
ten thousand.

CORAMBIS   What do you read, my lord?

HAMLET   Words, words.

---

7. Alluding to the belief that cuckolds grew horns,
but Hamlet may mean a more spiritual or psychological transformation as well.
8. TEXTUAL COMMENT "Fig" is more obscene than
Q2's "gig" and F's "gidge." See Digital Edition TC 4
(First Quarto edited text).

9. Use new and fashionable names instead of the
God-given ones. *amble:* dance.
1. *making . . . ignorance:* "playing dumb" to excuse
your (seductive) affectations.
2. (An oath.)
3. These days.

210 CORAMBIS What's the matter,[4] my lord?

HAMLET Between who?

CORAMBIS I mean the matter you read, my lord.

HAMLET Marry, most vile heresy: for here the satirical satyr
writes that old men have hollow eyes, weak backs, gray
215 beards, pitiful weak hams,° gouty legs—all which, sir, I   *thighs*
most potently believe not.[5] For, sir, yourself shall be old as I
am if, like a crab, you could go backward.

CORAMBIS [*aside*] How pregnant° his replies are, and full of   *meaningful*
wit. Yet at first he took me for a fishmonger. All this comes
220 by love, the vehemency of love. And when I was young, I was
very idle and suffered much ecstasy in love, very near this.
—Will you walk out of the air,[6] my lord?

HAMLET Into my grave.

CORAMBIS By the mass, that's out of the air indeed. [*aside*]
225 Very shrewd answers! —My lord, I will take my leave of you.

HAMLET You can take nothing from me, sir, I will more will-
ingly part withal.° [*aside*] Old doting fool!   *with*

Enter GILDERSTONE *and* ROSSENCRAFT.

CORAMBIS You seek Prince Hamlet—see, there he is. *Exit.*

GILDERSTONE Health to your lordship!

230 HAMLET What, Gilderstone and Rossencraft! Welcome, kind
schoolfellows, to Elsinore.

GILDERSTONE We thank your grace and would be very glad
you were as when we were at Wittenberg.

HAMLET I thank you. But is this visitation free° of yourselves,   *voluntary*
235 or were you not sent for? Tell me true. Come, I know the
good King and Queen sent for you. There is a kind of confession in your eye: come, I know you were sent for.

GILDERSTONE What say you?

HAMLET Nay then, I see how the wind sits: come, you were
240 sent for.

ROSSENCRAFT My lord, we were—and willingly. If we might
know the cause and ground of your discontent—

HAMLET Why, I want preferment.[7]

ROSSENCRAFT I think not so, my lord.

245 HAMLET Yes, faith, this great world you see contents me not—
no, nor the spangled heavens, nor earth, nor sea, no, nor man
that is so glorious a creature, contents not me—no, nor
woman too, though you laugh.

GILDERSTONE My lord, we laugh not at that.

250 HAMLET Why did you laugh then, when I said man did not
content me?

GILDERSTONE My lord, we laughed when you said man did
not content you, what entertainment the players shall have.
We boarded° them o'the way; they are coming to you.   *passed by*

255 HAMLET Players? What players be they?

ROSSENCRAFT My lord, the tragedians° of the city, those that   *actors*
you took delight to see so often.

---

4. Content, although Hamlet deliberately takes it as
"subject of a quarrel."
5. TEXTUAL COMMENT The "not," at once polite and
sarcastic, is absent from Q2 and F. See Digital Edi-

tion TC 5 (First Quarto edited text).
6. Outdoor air was regarded as a hazard for the sick.
7. I'm lacking a promotion; I'm being deprived of an
office.

HAMLET   How comes it that they travel? Do they grow resty?[8]
GILDERSTONE   No, my lord, their reputation holds as it was
260   wont.°   *accustomed*
HAMLET   How then?
GILDERSTONE   I'faith, my lord, novelty carries it away,[9] for the
   principal public audience that came to them are turned to
   private plays[1] and to the humor of children.[2]
265 HAMLET   I do not greatly wonder of it, for those that would
   make mops and mows° at my uncle when my father lived   *grimaces*
   now give a hundred, two hundred, pounds for his picture.
   But they shall be welcome: he that plays the King shall have
   tribute of me, the venturous Knight shall use his foil° and   *sword*
270   target,° the Lover shall sigh gratis,° the Clown shall make   *shield / for free*
   them laugh that are tickled in the lungs,[3] and the Lady shall
   have leave to speak her mind freely, or the blank verse shall
   halt° for't.   *limp*
       The trumpets sound. Enter CORAMBIS.
   Do you see yonder great baby? He is not yet out of his swad-
275   dling clouts.°   *clothes*
GILDERSTONE   That may be, for they say an old man is twice a
   child.
HAMLET   I'll prophesy to you he comes to tell me o'the players.
   —You say true, o'Monday last, 'twas so indeed.
280 CORAMBIS   My lord, I have news to tell you.
HAMLET   My lord, I have news to tell you: when Roscius[4] was
   an actor in Rome—
CORAMBIS   The actors are come hither, my lord.
HAMLET   Buzz, buzz.[5]
285 CORAMBIS   The best actors in Christendom, either for comedy, tragedy, history, pastoral, pastoral-historical, historical-
   comical, comical-historical-pastoral, tragedy historical.[6]
   Seneca cannot be too heavy, nor Plautus too light.[7] For the
   law hath writ those are the only men.[8]
290 HAMLET   O Jephthah, judge of Israel, what a treasure hadst
   thou![9]
CORAMBIS   Why, what a treasure had he, my lord?
HAMLET   Why,
   One fair daughter and no more,
295   The which he lovèd passing° well.   *surpassingly*
CORAMBIS [*aside*]   Ah, still harping o'my daughter! —Well, my
   lord, if you call me Jephthah, I have a daughter that I love
   passing well.
HAMLET   Nay, that follows not.[1]

---

8. Lazy, rusty; or perhaps restless.
9. *carries it away:* carries the day, proves victorious.
1. Private playhouses were smaller and more expensive venues than the large open theaters on the out-
skirts of the city.
2. Children's acting companies surged in popularity
at the turn of the seventeenth century.
3. Whose lungs are primed to laugh.
4. The most famous ancient Roman actor, a rather
dated news item.
5. A response to stale news.
6. Shakespeare parodies the classifications of contemporary dramatic theorists.

7. The best-known Roman playwrights, masters of
tragedy and comedy, respectively.
8. I.e. it's widely recognized that these are the superior playwrights.
9. Jephthah vowed that if he defeated the Ammonites, he would sacrifice the first living thing he saw
on his return. He won, and his daughter became the
sacrificial victim (Judges 11). *Jephthah, Judge of Israel*
was the title of a popular ballad, the "godly ballad"
from which Hamlet subsequently quotes or sings.
1. Corambis's having a daughter is not a logical consequence of Hamlet's calling him Jephthah.

300 CORAMBIS   What follows then, my lord?

HAMLET   Why, "By lot"° or "God wot"° or "As it came to pass,   *chance / knows*
and so it was"—the first verse of the godly ballad[2] will tell
you all, for look you where my abridgment[3] comes.

Enter PLAYERS.

Welcome masters, welcome all! What, my old friend, thy
305 face is valanced° since I saw thee last. Com'st thou to   *fringed (with beard)*
beard° me in Denmark? My young lady and mistress,[4] by'r   *defy*
Lady but your ladyship is grown by the altitude of a chopine°   *high platform shoe*
higher than you were. Pray God, sir, your voice, like a piece
of uncurrent gold, be not cracked in the ring.[5] Come on,
310 masters, we'll even to't like French falconers,[6] fly at anything we see. Come, a taste of your quality°—a speech, a   *professional skill*
passionate speech.

FIRST PLAYER   What speech, my good lord?

HAMLET   I heard thee speak a speech once, but it was never
315 acted, or if it were, never above twice. For, as I remember, it
pleased not the vulgar—it was caviar to the million.° But to   *general population*
me (and others that received it in the like kind cried in the
top of[7] their judgments) an excellent play, set down with as
great modesty° as cunning. One said there was no salads[8] in   *restraint*
320 the lines to make them savory but called it an honest method,
as wholesome as sweet. Come, a speech in it I chiefly remember was Aeneas' tale to Dido, and then especially where he
talks of Priam's slaughter.[9] If it live in thy memory begin at
this line—let me see,
325   "The rugged° Pyrrhus,[1] like th' Hyrcanian beast°—"   *savage / tiger*
No 'tis not so, it begins with Pyrrhus—oh, I have it—
"The rugged Pyrrhus, he whose sable° arms,   *black*
Black as his purpose, did the night resemble
When he lay couchèd° in the ominous horse,[2]   *hidden*
330 Hath now his black and grim complexion° smeared   *appearance*
With heraldry° more dismal: head to foot   *heraldic colors*
Now is he total gules,° horridly tricked°   *all red / inked over*
With blood of fathers, mothers, daughters, sons,
Backed and imparched in coagulate gore,[3]
335 Rifted in earth and fire—old grandsire Priam seeks."
So, go on.

CORAMBIS   Afore God, my lord, well spoke and with good accent.

FIRST PLAYER   "Anon° he finds him, striking too short at Greeks: *Soon*
His antique sword, rebellious to his arm,
340 Lies where it falls, unable to resist.
Pyrrhus at Priam drives, but all in rage

---

2. Religious song or verse.
3. Those who cut me short; also, entertainments.
4. The boy who played female roles.
5. A coin was no longer legal tender if the circle or ring enclosing the monarch's head was broken (by "clipping," or trimming off small amounts of gold).
6. We'll go to work at once. (French falconers seem to have been regarded as experts, willing to try any potential prey.)
7. *cried . . . of:* outweighed.
8. Seasoned dishes. I.e., deliberate attempts to vary or embellish the style in order to make the lines more pleasing ("savory").

9. The murder of the Trojan king Priam, at the end of the Trojan War; adapted from Virgil's *Aeneid*, possibly via Christopher Marlowe's *Dido, Queen of Carthage*. Aeneas recounts the story of Priam's slaughter to his beloved, Dido.
1. Also known as Neoptolemus, he came to Troy to avenge the death of his father, the Greek hero Achilles.
2. The Trojan horse, full of Greek warriors.
3. His back is fully covered and dried out by clinging gore. "Baked" is also possible here, suggesting a similar but less localized image.

Strikes wide; but with the whiff and wind
Of his fell° sword, th'unnervèd° father falls."

fierce / strengthless

CORAMBIS Enough, my friend, 'tis too long.

345 HAMLET It shall to the barber's with your beard°—a pox, he's
for a jig⁴ or a tale of bawdry,° or else he sleeps. Come on: to
Hecuba,⁵ come.

It shall be cut short
obscenity

FIRST PLAYER "But who, oh, who had seen the moblèd°
queen—"

veiled; muffled

CORAMBIS "Moblèd queen" is good, faith, very good—

350 FIRST PLAYER "All in the alarum and fear of death rose up,
And o'er her weak and all o'er-teeming⁶ loins
A blanket, and a kercher° on that head
Where late the diadem stood—who this had seen,
With tongue-envenomed speech would treason
have pronounced.

kerchief

355 For if the gods themselves had seen her then,
When she saw Pyrrhus with malicious strokes
Mincing her husband's limbs, it would have made milch°
The burning eyes of heaven and passion° in the gods."

milky; moist
suffering; pity

CORAMBIS Look, my lord, if he hath not changed his color
360 and hath tears in his eyes. —No more, good heart, no more.

HAMLET 'Tis well, 'tis very well. I pray, my lord, will you see
the players well bestowed?° I tell you they are the chronicles
and brief abstracts° of the time. After your death, I can tell
you, you were better have a bad epitaph than their ill report
365 while you live.

lodged
summaries

CORAMBIS My lord, I will use them according to their deserts.

HAMLET Oh, far better, man! Use every man after° his deserts,
then who should scape whipping? Use them after your own
370 honor and dignity: the less they deserve, the greater credit's
yours.

according to

CORAMBIS Welcome, my good fellows.   [*He begins to*] *exit.*

HAMLET Come hither, masters. Can you not play *The Murder
of Gonzago?*

FIRST PLAYER Yes, my lord.

375 HAMLET And couldst not thou, for a need,° study me some
dozen or sixteen lines which I would set down and insert?

if necessary

FIRST PLAYER Yes, very easily, my good lord.

HAMLET 'Tis well, I thank you. Follow that lord—and do you
hear, sirs, take heed you mock him not!

[Exeunt PLAYERS, following CORAMBIS.]

380 [*to* ROSSENCRAFT *and* GILDERSTONE] Gentlemen, for your
kindness I thank you, and for a time I would desire you
leave me.

GILDERSTONE Our love and duty is at your command.

Exeunt [ROSSENCRAFT and GILDERSTONE].

HAMLET Why, what a dunghill idiot slave am I!
385 Why, these players here draw water from eyes—
For Hecuba! Why, what is Hecuba to him,
Or he to Hecuba?

---

4. A ridiculous piece of poetry, or the dance that followed many plays (unrelated to the drama).
5. In Greek mythology, the wife of King Priam of
Troy, mother of Hector and Cassandra.

6. Completely worn out with childbearing. (Hecuba
was supposed to have borne seventeen or more
children.)

What would he do an if° he had my loss—   *an if = if*
His father murdered and a crown bereft him?
390 He would turn all his tears to drops of blood,
Amaze the standers-by with his laments,
Strike more than wonder in the judicial ears,
Confound the ignorant, and make mute the wise—
Indeed, his passion would be general.°   *felt by all*
395 Yet I, like to an ass and John-a-dreams,°   *a sleepy idler*
Having my father murdered by a villain,
Stand still and let it pass! Why, sure I am a coward!
Who plucks me by the beard or twits° my nose,   *taunts; makes fun of*
Gives me the lie i'th' throat down to the lungs?[7]
400 Sure I should take it. Or else I have no gall,[8]
Or by this I should've fatted all the region kites[9]
With this slave's offal—this damnèd villain,
Treacherous, bawdy, murderous villain!
Why, this is brave,° that I, the son of my dear father,   *fine*
405 Should like a scullion,° like a very drab,°   *kitchen servant / whore*
Thus rail in words! About,° my brain!   *Into action*
I have heard that guilty creatures sitting at a play
Hath by the very cunning° of the scene   *artfulness*
Confessed a murder committed long before.
410 This spirit that I have seen may be the devil,
And out of[1] my weakness and my melancholy,
As he is very potent with[2] such men,
Doth seek to damn me.
I will have sounder proofs: the play's the thing
415 Wherein I'll catch the conscience of the King.   *Exit.*

Scene 8
Enter the KING, QUEEN, *and Lords* [CORAMBIS,
ROSSENCRAFT, *and* GILDERSTONE].

KING Lords, can you by no means find
The cause of our son Hamlet's lunacy?
You, being so near in love even from his youth,
Methinks should gain more than a stranger should.
5 GILDERSTONE My lord, we have done all the best we could
To wring from him the cause of all his grief,
But still he puts us off and by no means
Would make an answer to that we exposed.[1]
ROSSENCRAFT Yet was he something more inclined to mirth
10 Before we left him, and I take it
He hath given order for a play tonight,
At which he craves your highness' company.
KING With all our heart: it likes us very well.
Gentlemen, seek still to increase his mirth.
15 Spare for no cost: our coffers shall be open,
And we unto yourselves will still be thankful.

---

7. *Gives . . . lungs:* Calls me a thoroughgoing liar.
8. A bitter fluid produced by the liver; the supposed source of anger.
9. All the kites (birds of prey) in the sky ("region").
1. *out of:* capitalizing upon.

2. *potent with:* powerful over.
Scene 8 Location: The castle.
1. "Exposed" functions here like a (now obsolete) use of "expostulate": to demand, question.

GILDERSTONE *and* ROSSENCRAFT   In all we can, be sure you
    shall command.
QUEEN   Thanks, gentlemen, and what the Queen of
    Denmark
    May pleasure you, be sure you shall not want.[2]
20 GILDERSTONE   We'll once again unto the noble Prince.
    KING   Thanks to you both.
                [*Exeunt* ROSSENCRAFT *and* GILDERSTONE.]
                Gertred, you'll see this play?
QUEEN   My lord, I will, and it joys me at the soul
    He is inclined to any kind of mirth.
CORAMBIS   Madam, I pray be ruled by me,
25 And, my good sovereign, give me leave to speak:
    We cannot yet find out the very ground
    Of his distemperance; therefore I hold it meet,
    If so it please you—else they shall not meet—and thus it is—
    KING   What is't, Corambis?
CORAMBIS   Marry, my good lord, this:
30 Soon when the sports° are done,   *entertainments*
    Madam, send you in haste to speak with him,
    And I myself will stand behind the arras.[3]
    There question you the cause of all his grief
    And then, in love and nature unto you,°   *natural feeling toward you*
35 He'll tell you all. My lord, how think you on't?
    KING   It likes us well.° Gertred, what say you?   *It pleases me*
QUEEN   With all my heart! Soon will I send for him.
CORAMBIS   Myself will be that happy messenger
    Who hopes his grief will be revealed to her.   *Exeunt.*

Scene 9
Enter HAMLET *and the* PLAYERS.

HAMLET   Pronounce me this speech trippingly o'the tongue
    as I taught thee. Marry, an you mouth it[1] as a many of your
    players do, I'd rather hear a town bull[2] bellow than such a
    fellow speak my lines. Nor do not saw the air thus with your
5 hands, but give everything his action with temperance. Oh,
    it offends me to the soul to hear a robustious° periwigged° *bombastic / wig-wearing*
    fellow to tear a passion in tatters, into very rags, to split the
    ears of the ignorant, who for the most part are capable of
    nothing but dumb shows[3] and noises. I would have such a fel-
10 low whipped for o'erdoing Termagant—it out-Herods Herod.[4]
FIRST PLAYER   My lord, we have indifferently° reformed that *moderately well*
    among us.
HAMLET   The better, the better. Mend it altogether. There be
    fellows that I have seen play—and heard others commend
15 them, and that highly too—that, having neither the gait of
    Christian, pagan, nor Turk, have so strutted and bellowed

---

2. *what . . . want:* you will not be lacking in anything
that the Queen may do for you.
3. A hanging screen of tapestry fabric placed around
the walls of a room.
Scene 9 Location: A stateroom of the castle.
1. If you speak exaggeratedly.
2. A bull shared in common by a village's cow-keepers.

3. Pantomimes, featuring gestures without words.
4. It surpasses the excesses of Herod, who, as a character in medieval cycle plays, was famous for his
ranting. Termagant, an imaginary deity supposedly
worshipped by Muslims, takes the form of a violent
speaking idol in medieval drama.

that you would've thought some of nature's journeymen[5]
had made men, and not made them well, they imitated
humanity so abominably. Take heed, avoid it.

20 FIRST PLAYER   I warrant° you, my lord.   *assure*

HAMLET   And do you hear? Let not your clown speak more
than is set down. There be of° them, I can tell you, that will   *some of*
laugh themselves to set° on some quantity of barren° specta-   *urge / unthinking*
tors to laugh with them, albeit there is some necessary point

25 in the play then to be observed. Oh, 'tis vile and shows a
pitiful ambition in the fool that useth it. And then you have
some again that keeps one suit of jests, as a man is known
by one suit of apparel, and gentlemen quotes his jests down
in their tables before they come to the play, as thus: "Cannot

30 you stay till I eat my porridge?" and "You owe me a quarter's
wages" and "My coat wants a cullison"° and "Your beer is   *badge*
sour" and, blabbering with his lips and thus keeping in his
cinquepace[6] of jests, when, God knows, the warm° clown   *warmed up; practiced*
cannot make a jest unless by chance, as the blind man

35 catcheth a hare. Masters, tell him of it.

FIRST PLAYER   We will, my lord.

HAMLET   Well, go make you ready.   *Exeunt* PLAYERS.

        [*Enter* HORATIO.]

HORATIO   Here, my lord.

HAMLET   Horatio, thou art even as just° a man   *honest; balanced*

40 As e'er my conversation coped withal.[7]

HORATIO   O my lord!

HAMLET   Nay, why should I flatter thee?
Why should the poor be flattered?
What gain should I receive by flattering thee
That nothing hath but thy good mind?

45 Let flattery sit on those time-pleasing[8] tongues,
To gloze° with them that loves to hear their praise,   *flatter*
And not with such as thou, Horatio.
There is a play tonight wherein one scene they have
Comes very near the murder of my father.

50 When thou shalt see that act afoot,
Mark thou the King; do but observe his looks,
For I mine eyes will rivet to his face.
And if he do not bleach° and change at that,   *lose color*
It is a damnèd ghost that we have seen.

55 Horatio, have a care, observe him well.

HORATIO   My lord, mine eyes shall still° be on his face   *always*
And not the smallest alteration
That shall appear in him but I shall note it.

HAMLET   Hark, they come.

        Enter KING, QUEEN, CORAMBIS[, OFELIA,
        ROSSENCRAFT, GILDERSTONE], *and other Lords.*

60 KING   How now, son Hamlet, how fare you? Shall we have a
play?

HAMLET   I'faith, the chameleon's dish—not capon-crammed,

---

5. Hirelings, those who have completed their apprenticeship but are not yet "master" of their trade.
6. A lively five-step dance.

7. As I ever encountered in my dealings with men.
8. Fawning upon whomever is powerful or popular at
the time.

feed o'the air.[9] Ay, father. [*to* CORAMBIS] My lord, you played
in the university?

65 CORAMBIS That I did, my lord, and I was counted a good
actor.

HAMLET What did you enact there?

CORAMBIS My lord, I did act Julius Caesar. I was killed in the
Capitol:[1] Brutus killed me.

70 HAMLET It was a brute part of him to kill so capital a calf.°   *such a prize fool*
Come, be these players ready?

QUEEN Hamlet, come sit down by me.

HAMLET No, by my faith, mother, here's a mettle[2] more
attractive. [*to* OFELIA] Lady, will you give me leave, and so
75 forth, to lay my head in your lap?

OFELIA No, my lord.

HAMLET Upon your lap. What do you think I meant, contrary
matters?[3]

> *Enter in a dumb show the* [DUKE] *and the* [DUCHESS].
> *He sits down in an arbor; she leaves him.*
> *Then enters* LUCIANUS *with poison in a vial and*
> *pours it in his ears and goes away. Then the*
> [DUCHESS] *cometh and finds him dead, and goes*
> *away with the other.*
> [*The* PLAYERS *retire.*]

OFELIA What means this, my lord?

80 HAMLET This is miching mallico°—that means mischief.   *sneaking wrongdoing*

> *Enter the* PROLOGUE.

OFELIA What doth this mean, my lord?

HAMLET You shall hear anon—this fellow will tell you all.

OFELIA Will he tell us what this show means?

HAMLET Ay, or any show you'll show him. Be not afraid to
85 show, he'll not be afraid to tell. Oh, these players cannot
keep counsel:° they'll tell all.   *a secret*

PROLOGUE For us and for our tragedy,
Here stooping to your clemency,
We beg your hearing patiently.   [*Exit.*]

90 HAMLET Is't a prologue or a posy for a ring?[4]

OFELIA 'Tis short, my lord.

HAMLET As women's love.

> *Enter the* DUKE *and* DUCHESS.

DUKE Full forty years are past, their date is gone,
Since happy time joined both our hearts as one.
95 And now the blood that filled my youthful veins
Runs weakly in their pipes, and all the strains
Of music which whilom° pleased mine ear   *at one time*
Is now a burden that age cannot bear—
And therefore, sweet, nature must pay his due:

---

9. Hamlet is addressing the King's first question,
"how fare you?" by punning on "fare." The chameleon
was supposed to live on air. Hamlet also puns on
"heir," referring to the King's insubstantial promise of
the succession. All of this he contrasts with the eating
habits of the capon, a castrated cock, crammed or fattened for the table (and a term for a fool).
1. Perhaps an allusion to Shakespeare's own *Julius*

Caesar; the actor who first played Corambis may also
have played the part of Caesar.
2. A disposition (punning on magnetically attractive
"metal").
3. F and Q2 have "country matters" (i.e., coarse or
rustic, with an obscene pun on "cunt").
4. The motto engraved in a ring.

100   To heaven must I and leave the earth with you.
    DUCHESS Oh, say not so, lest that you kill my heart;
      When death takes you, let life from me depart.
    DUKE   Content thyself. When ended is my date,
      Thou mayst perchance have a more noble mate,
105   More wise, more youthful, and one—
    DUCHESS Oh, speak no more, for then I am accursed:
      None weds the second but she kills the first.
      A second time I kill my lord that's dead
      When second husband kisses me in bed.
110   HAMLET [*aside*] Oh, wormwood,[5] wormwood!
    DUKE   I do believe you, sweet, what now you speak,
      But what we do determine oft we break,
      For our devices still are overthrown.
      Our thoughts are ours, their ends° none of our own.   *results*
115   So think you will no second husband wed,
      But die thy thoughts when thy first lord is dead.
    DUCHESS Both here and there pursue me lasting strife
      If, once a widow, ever I be wife.
    HAMLET   If she should break now—
120   DUKE   'Tis deeply sworn. Sweet, leave me here awhile:
      My spirits grow dull and fain° I would beguile   *gladly*
      The tedious time with sleep.
    DUCHESS   Sleep rock thy brain,
      And never come mischance between us twain.

                              Exit [DUCHESS].

    HAMLET   Madam, how do you like this play?
125   QUEEN   The lady protests too much.
    HAMLET   Oh, but she'll keep her word.
    KING   Have you heard the argument?° Is there no offense   *plot*
      in it?
    HAMLET   No offense in the world—poison in jest, poison in
130   jest.
    KING   What do you call the name of the play?
    HAMLET   *Mousetrap.* Marry, how? Trapically.[6] This play is the
      image of a murder done in Guyana. Albertus was the Duke's
      name, his wife Baptista.[7] Father, it is a knavish piece o'work,
135   but what o'that, it toucheth not us—you and I that have
      free° souls. Let the galled jade[8] wince.   *guiltless*
         [*Enter* LUCIANUS.]
      This is one Lucianus, nephew to the king.[9]
    OFELIA   You're as good as a chorus,[1] my lord.
    HAMLET   I could interpret the love you bear, if I saw the poop-
140   ies[2] dallying.
    OFELIA   You're very pleasant, my lord.
    HAMLET   Who, I? Your only° jig-maker! Why, what should a   *preeminent*

---

5. A bitter herb taken medicinally (hence, "a bitter
pill to swallow").
6. Punning on "tropically": figuratively.
7. Shakespeare seems to base *The Mousetrap* on an
extremely muddled version of the Duke of Urbino's
alleged murder by Luigi Gonzaga in 1538.
8. *galled jade*: chafed horse.
9. King = the Duke.

1. The chorus explained the forthcoming action. In
puppet shows, a choric narrator, or "interpreter,"
announced the characters' names and spoke the
dialogue.
2. Q2 and F have "puppets." "Poopies" could also
mean puppet (though the *OED* does not have it
attested before 1659) or a promiscuous woman.

man do but be merry? For look how cheerfully my mother
looks—my father died within these two hours.

145 OFELIA Nay, 'tis twice two months, my lord.

HAMLET Two months? Nay then, let the devil wear black, for
I'll have a suit of sables.[3] Jesus, two months dead and not
forgotten yet? Nay, then, there's some likelihood a gentleman's death may outlive memory. But, by my faith, he must

150 build churches then, or else he must follow the old epithet:
"With ho, with ho, the hobbyhorse is forgot."[4]

OFELIA Your jests are keen,° my lord.   *sharp*

HAMLET It would cost you a groaning to take them off.[5]

OFELIA Still better and worse.[6]

155 HAMLET So you must take your husband.[7] —Begin, murderer,
begin! A pox, leave thy damnable° faces and begin. Come: *grimacing*
"The croaking raven doth bellow for revenge."[8]

LUCIANUS Thoughts black, hands apt, drugs fit, and time
agreeing,
Confederate° season else no creature seeing.   *Complicit*

160 Thou mixture rank° of midnight weeds collected,   *foul*
With Hecate's bane[9] thrice blasted, thrice infected,
Thy natural magic and dire property°   *quality*
One wholesome life usurps immediately.
        [He pours poison in the Duke's ear and] exit.

HAMLET He poisons him for his estate.°   *position; state*

165 KING Lights! I will to bed.

CORAMBIS The King rises! Lights, ho!
        Exeunt [all but HAMLET *and* HORATIO].

HAMLET What, frighted with false fires?[1]
Then let the stricken deer go weep,[2]
The hart ungallèd° play,   *unafflicted*

170 For some must laugh, while some must weep,
Thus runs the world away.[3]

HORATIO The King is moved,° my lord.   *vexed*

HAMLET Ay, Horatio, I'll take the Ghost's word for more than
all the coin in Denmark.
        Enter ROSSENCRAFT *and* GILDERSTONE.

175 ROSSENCRAFT Now, my lord, how is't with you?

HAMLET An if° the King like not the tragedy,   *An if = If*
Why then, belike he likes it not, perdie.°   *indeed (pardieu)*

ROSSENCRAFT We are very glad to see your grace so pleasant.
My good lord, let us again entreat to know of you the ground

180 and cause of your distemperature.

GILDERSTONE My lord, your mother craves to speak with you.

HAMLET We shall obey, were she ten times our mother.

---

3. Sable is both an expensive fur for cloaks and trim
and the heraldic term for "black"; Hamlet simultaneously forswears his ascetic mourning and vows to
continue it.
4. The hobbyhorse, a man with a mock horse's body
strapped around his waist, was a figure in May Day
morris dances (under attack in Shakespeare's time by
religious reformers). "The hobbyhorse is forgot" seems
to have been a ballad refrain.
5. To satisfy my sexual appetite (leading to groaning
in either sexual intercourse or childbirth).

6. Wittier, and more obscene.
7. The marriage vow compels one to take a husband
"for better and for worse."
8. Misquoted from *The True Tragedy of Richard III*
(ca. 1591; not to be confused with Shakespeare's own
Richard III).
9. Poison from the goddess of witchcraft.
1. Fireworks or blank cartridges.
2. A deer was thought to weep when mortally wounded.
These four lines are probably from a lost ballad.
3. That's the way of the world.

ROSSENCRAFT But, my good lord, shall I entreat thus much?

HAMLET I pray, will you play upon this pipe?[4]

185 ROSSENCRAFT Alas, my lord, I cannot.

HAMLET [to GILDERSTONE] Pray, will you?

GILDERSTONE I have no skill, my lord.

HAMLET Why, look, it is a thing of nothing: 'tis but stopping
of these holes and, with a little breath from your lips, it will

190 give most delicate music.

GILDERSTONE But this cannot we do, my lord.

HAMLET Pray now, pray—heartily I beseech you.

ROSSENCRAFT My lord, we cannot.

HAMLET Why, how unworthy a thing would you make of me?

195 You would seem to know my stops,[5] you would play upon
me, you would search the very inward part of my heart and
dive into the secret of my soul. Zounds,[6] do you think I am
easier to be played on than a pipe? Call me what instrument
you will, though you can fret[7] me, yet you cannot play upon

200 me. Besides, to be demanded by a sponge—

ROSSENCRAFT How? A sponge, my lord?

HAMLET Ay, sir, a sponge that soaks up the King's countenance, favors, and rewards, that makes his liberality your
storehouse. But such as you do the King in the end best ser-

205 vice: for he doth keep you as an ape doth nuts, in the corner
of his jaw: first mouths you, then swallows you. So, when he
hath need of you, 'tis but squeezing of you and, sponge, you
shall be dry again—you shall.

ROSSENCRAFT Well, my lord, we'll take our leave.

210 HAMLET Farewell, farewell, God bless you.

                    [Exeunt] ROSSENCRAFT and GILDERSTONE.
                Enter CORAMBIS.

CORAMBIS My lord, the Queen would speak with you.

HAMLET Do you see yonder cloud in the shape of a camel?

CORAMBIS 'Tis like a camel indeed.

HAMLET Now methinks it's like a weasel.

215 CORAMBIS 'Tis backed like a weasel.

HAMLET Or like a whale.

CORAMBIS Very like a whale.

HAMLET Why, then, tell my mother I'll come by and by.

                                        Exit CORAMBIS.

Good night, Horatio.

220 HORATIO Good night unto your lordship.   Exit HORATIO.

HAMLET My mother she hath sent to speak with me.
O God, let ne'er the heart of Nero[8] enter
This soft bosom.
Let me be cruel, not unnatural.

225 I will speak daggers—those sharp words being spent,
To do her wrong my soul shall ne'er consent.   Exit.

---

4. Hamlet appears to present them with a recorder.
5. Finger holes; notes.
6. By God's wounds, an oath.
7. Irritate, punning on frets of stringed instruments,
which regulate fingering and pitch.
8. The Roman emperor Nero reputedly murdered his
mother, in one account, by cutting open her womb.

Scene 10

Enter the KING.

KING   Oh, that this wet° that falls upon my face   *these tears*
    Would wash the crime clear from my conscience!
    When I look up to heaven I see my trespass.
    The earth doth still cry out upon my fact:°   *act*
5   Pay me the murder of a brother and a king
    And the adulterous fault I have committed.
    Oh, these are sins that are unpardonable.
    Why, say thy sins were blacker than is jet,[1]
    Yet may contrition make them as white as snow.[2]
10 Ay, but still to persever in a sin,
    It is an act 'gainst the universal power.
    Most wretched man, stoop, bend thee to thy prayer,
    Ask grace of heaven to keep thee from despair.
          He kneels. Enter HAMLET.

HAMLET   Ay, so. [*He draws his sword.*] Come forth and work
    thy last—
15 And thus he dies, and so am I revenged.
    No, not so:
    He took my father sleeping, his sins brimful,°   *overflowing*
    And how his soul stood to the state of heaven,
    Who knows save the immortal powers? And shall
20 I kill him now, when he is purging of his soul,
    Making his way for heaven?
    This is a benefit and not revenge.
    No, get thee up again. [*He sheathes his sword.*] When he's at
    game,
    Swearing, taking his carouse, drinking drunk,
25 Or in the incestuous pleasure of his bed,
    Or at some act
    That hath no relish° of salvation in't,   *trace*
    Then trip him that his heels may kick at heaven
    And fall as low as hell. My mother stays,°   *waits*
30 This physic° but prolongs thy weary days.   *Exit.*   *medicine*
KING   My words fly up, my sins remain below.
    No king on earth is safe if God's his foe.   *Exit.*

Scene 11

Enter QUEEN *and* CORAMBIS.

CORAMBIS   Madam, I hear young Hamlet coming: I'll shroud
    myself behind the arras.
QUEEN   Do so, my lord.
    CORAMBIS [*hides behind the arras*].
HAMLET [*within*]   Mother, mother!
    [*Enter* HAMLET.]
5 Oh, are you here? How is't with you, mother?
QUEEN   How is't with you?
HAMLET   I'll tell you, but first we'll make all safe.[1]

Scene 10 Location: The castle.
1. A glossy black stone.
2. Compare Isaiah 1:15–18: "And though ye make
many prayers, I will not hear: for your hands are full
of blood. Wash you, make you clean; take away the
evil of your works from before mine eyes . . . though

your sins were as crimson, they shall be made white
as snow."
Scene 11 Location: The Queen's private chamber.
1. Hamlet looks for a private ("safe") conversation
with his mother.

QUEEN Hamlet, thou hast thy father much offended.

HAMLET Mother, you have my father much offended.

QUEEN How now,° boy?   *What's this*

10 HAMLET   How now, mother?
     Come here. Sit down, for you shall hear me speak.

QUEEN What wilt thou do? Thou wilt not murder me?
     Help, ho!

CORAMBIS [*behind the arras*] Help for the Queen!

HAMLET   Ay, a rat!
     [*He stabs* CORAMBIS *through the arras.*]
     Dead for a ducat!² [*He looks behind the arras.*] Rash
        intruding fool,

15   Farewell. I took thee for thy better.

QUEEN Hamlet, what hast thou done?

HAMLET Not so much harm, good mother,
     As to kill a king and marry with his brother.

QUEEN How? Kill a king?

20 HAMLET Ay, a king. Nay, sit you down, and ere you part,
     If you be made of penetrable stuff,
     I'll make your eyes look down into your heart
     And see how horrid there and black it shows.

QUEEN Hamlet, what mean'st thou by these killing words?

25 HAMLET Why, this I mean: see here, behold this picture.
     It is the portraiture of your deceased husband.
     See here a face to outface Mars° himself,   *the Roman god of war*
     An eye at which his foes did tremble at,
     A front° wherein all virtues are set down   *forehead*

30   For to adorn a king and gild his crown,
     Whose heart went hand in hand even with that vow
     He made to you in marriage. And he is dead—
     Murdered, damnably murdered! This was your husband.
     Look you now:

35   Here is your husband, with a face like Vulcan,³
     A look fit for a murder and a rape,
     A dull, dead, hanging look, and a hell-bred eye
     To affright children and amaze the world.
     And this same have you left to change with this.

40   What devil thus hath cozened you at hob-man blind?⁴
     Ah! Have you eyes, and can you look on him
     That slew my father and your dear husband,
     To live in the incestuous pleasure of his bed?

QUEEN O Hamlet, speak no more.

45 HAMLET To leave him that bare a monarch's mind
     For a king of clouts, of very shreds!⁵

QUEEN Sweet Hamlet, cease.

HAMLET Nay, but still to persist and dwell in sin,
     To sweat under the yoke of infamy,

50   To make increase of shame, to seal damnation—

QUEEN Hamlet, no more!

---

2. I bet a ducat I have killed it.
3. The Roman god of fire and metalworking.
4. In this way has cheated you in blindman's buff (as if her second husband had been put in her way while

she was groping blindfolded).
5. *clouts . . . shreds:* a king of tattered clothing, possibly suggesting the costume of a jester.

HAMLET   Why, appetite with you is in the wane,
    Your blood runs backward now from whence it came.
    Who'll chide hot blood within a virgin's heart
55   When lust shall dwell within a matron's breast?
QUEEN   Hamlet, thou cleav'st my heart in twain.
HAMLET   Oh, throw away the worser part of it
    And keep the better.
         Enter the GHOST *in his nightgown.*
    Save me, save me, you gracious powers above,
60   And hover over me with your celestial wings!
    —Do you not come your tardy son to chide
    That I thus long have let revenge slip by?
    Oh, do not glare with looks so pitiful,
    Lest that my heart of stone yield to compassion
65   And every part that should assist revenge
    Forgo their proper powers and fall to pity.
GHOST   Hamlet, I once again appear to thee
    To put thee in remembrance of my death.
    Do not neglect nor long time put it off.
70   But I perceive by her distracted° looks   *distressed*
    Thy mother's fearful, and she stands amazed.
    Speak to her, Hamlet, for her sex is weak;
    Comfort thy mother, Hamlet. Think on me.
HAMLET   How is't with you, lady?
QUEEN   Nay, how is't with you
75   That thus you bend your eyes on vacancy
    And hold discourse with nothing but with air?
HAMLET   Why, do you nothing hear?
QUEEN   Not I.
HAMLET   Nor do you nothing see?
QUEEN   No, neither.
HAMLET   No?
    Why, see, the King, my father—
80   My father in the habit[6] as° he lived!   *when; as if*
    Look you how pale he looks—
    See how he steals away out of the portal!°   *door*
    Look, there he goes.   *Exit* GHOST.
QUEEN   Alas, it is the weakness of thy brain
85   Which makes thy tongue to blazon° thy heart's grief.   *describe in detail*
    But, as I have a soul, I swear by heaven
    I never knew of this most horrid murder.
    But, Hamlet, this is only fantasy,
    And for my love forget these idle° fits.   *delirious*
90 HAMLET   Idle? No, mother, my pulse doth beat like yours.
    It is not madness that possesseth Hamlet.
    O mother, if ever you did my dear father love,
    Forbear the adulterous bed tonight,
    And win yourself by little as you may.[7]
95   In time it may be you will loathe him quite.
    And mother, but assist me in revenge
    And in his death your infamy shall die.

---

6. Dress and bearing.
7. Wean yourself (i.e., away from sex with the King) and recover your virtue.

QUEEN[8]   Hamlet, I vow by that Majesty
            That knows our thoughts and looks into our hearts,
100   I will conceal, consent, and do my best,
            What stratagem soe'er thou shalt devise.
HAMLET   It is enough. Mother, good night.
            —Come, sir, I'll provide for you a grave,
            Who was in life a foolish prating knave.

> *Exit* HAMLET *with the dead body.*
> *Enter the* KING *and* [ROSSENCRAFT *and*
> GILDERSTONE].

105   KING   Now, Gertred, what says our son? How do you find him?
      QUEEN   Alas, my lord, as raging as the sea.
            Whenas° he came, I first bespake him fair,   *When*
            But then he throws and tosses me about
            As one forgetting that I was his mother.
110   At last I called for help and, as I cried,
            Corambis called, which Hamlet no sooner heard
            But whips me out his rapier and cries,
            "A rat, a rat!"
            And in his rage the good old man he kills.
115   KING   Why, this his madness will undo our state.
            Lords, go to him: inquire the body out.
      GILDERSTONE   We will, my lord.

> *Exeunt* [ROSSENCRAFT *and* GILDERSTONE].

      KING   Gertred, your son shall presently to England.
            His shipping is already furnished,
120   And we have sent by Rossencraft and Gilderstone
            Our letters to our dear brother of England
            For Hamlet's welfare and his happiness:
            Haply the air and climate of the country
            May please him better than his native home.
125   See where he comes.

> *Enter* HAMLET *and the Lords* [ROSSENCRAFT *and*
> GILDERSTONE].

      GILDERSTONE   My lord, we can by no means know of him
            Where the body is.
      KING   Now, son Hamlet, where is this dead body?
      HAMLET   At supper—not where he is eating, but where he is
130   eaten.[9] A certain company of politic° worms are even now at   *cunning*
      him. Father, your fat king and your lean beggar are but vari-
      able services,° two dishes to one mess.° Look you, a man   *different courses / meal*
      may fish with that worm that hath eaten of a king, and a
      beggar eat that fish which that worm hath caught.
135   KING   What of this?
      HAMLET   Nothing, father, but to tell you how a king may go a
      progress° through the guts of a beggar.   *royal journey*
      KING   But, son Hamlet, where is this body?
      HAMLET   In heav'n. If you chance to miss him there, father,
140   you had best look in the other parts below for him, and if you
      cannot find him there, you may chance to nose him as you
      go up the lobby.

8. TEXTUAL COMMENT Gertred's lines here, unique to Q1, make her pledge to support Hamlet far more concrete and explicit than in Q2 or F. See Digital Edition TC 6 (First Quarto edited text).

9. Possibly an allusion to the Eucharist (Lord's Supper), in which the body of Christ is consumed in the form of bread.

KING [*to* ROSSENCRAFT *and* GILDERSTONE] Make haste and
find him out.

145 HAMLET Nay, do you hear? Do not make too much haste—I'll
warrant you he'll stay till you come.

                    [*Exeunt* ROSSENCRAFT *and* GILDERSTONE.]

KING Well, son Hamlet,
We, in care of you, but specially
In tender preservation of your health—

150 The which we prize even as our proper self[1]—
It is our mind° you forthwith go for England.   *intention*
The wind sits fair; you shall aboard tonight.
Lord Rossencraft and Gilderstone shall go
Along with you.

155 HAMLET Oh, with all my heart. Farewell, mother.

KING Your loving father, Hamlet.

HAMLET My mother, I say: you married my mother, my
mother is your wife, man and wife is one flesh[2]—and so, my
mother. Farewell. For England, ho!   [*Exit.*][3]

160 KING Gertred, leave me, and take your leave of Hamlet.

                        [*Exit* QUEEN.]

To England is he gone, ne'er to return.
Our letters are unto the King of England
That on the sight of them, on his allegiance,
He presently,° without demanding why—   *immediately*

165 That Hamlet lose his head. For he must die:
There's more in him than shallow eyes can see.
He once being dead, why then our state is free.   *Exit.*

Scene 12

Enter FORTENBRASSE, [*Captain,*] *Drum,*° *and*   *Drummer*
Soldiers.

FORTENBRASSE Captain, from us go greet the King of
Denmark.
Tell him that Fortenbrasse, nephew to old Norway,
Craves a free pass and conduct over his land
According to the articles agreed on.

5 You know our rendezvous, go. —March away!   *Exeunt.*

Scene 13

Enter KING *and* QUEEN.

KING Hamlet is shipped for England. Fare him well!
I hope to hear good news from thence ere long,
If everything fall out to our content,
As I do make no doubt but so it shall.

5 QUEEN God grant it may. Heav'ns keep my Hamlet safe!
But this mischance of old Corambis' death
Hath piercèd so the young Ofelia's heart
That she, poor maid, is quite bereft her wits.

KING Alas, dear heart! And on the other side,

---

1. Which we prize as much as our own health.
2. As stated in Genesis 2:23 and the marriage rite of
the Book of Common Prayer.
3. TEXTUAL COMMENT We have emended the stage
direction to account for the dramatic needs of the
scene. The "*Lordes*" (possibly Rossencraft and Gil-

derstone) would conceivably seek the dead body as a
unit, leaving the disturbed Hamlet to exit the stage
alone. See Digital Edition TC 7 (First Quarto edited
text).
Scene 12 Location: The Danish coast.
Scene 13 Location: A public room of the castle.

10   We understand her brother's come from France,
             And he hath half the heart of all our land,
             And hardly he'll forget his father's death
             Unless by some means he be pacified.
       QUEEN   Oh, see where the young Ofelia is!
             Enter OFELIA *playing on a lute, and her hair down,*
             singing.

15   OFELIA   How should I your true love know
                      From another man?
                      By his cockle hat, and his staff,
                      And his sandal shoon.[1]

                      White his shroud as mountain snow,
20   Larded° with sweet flowers,   *Garnished*
                      That bewept to the grave did not[2] go
                      With true lovers' showers.°   *tears*

                      He is dead and gone, lady,
                      He is dead and gone:
25   At his head a grass green turf,
                      At his heels a stone.
      KING   How is't with you, sweet Ofelia?
    OFELIA   Well, God yield° you. It grieves me to see how they   *God reward*
       laid him in the cold ground—I could not choose but weep.
30   [*Sings.*]   And will he not come again?
                      And will he not come again?
                      No, no, he is gone,
                      And we cast away moan,
                      And he never will come again.

35   His beard as white as snow,
                      All flaxen° was his poll,°   *white / head*
                      He is dead, he is gone,
                      And we cast away moan:
                      God ha' mercy on his soul.
40   And of all Christian souls, I pray God. God be with you,
       ladies, God be with you!   *Exit* OFELIA.
      KING   A pretty wretch! This is a change indeed.
       O Time, how swiftly runs our joys away!
       Content° on earth was never certain bred: *Contentment*
45   Today we laugh and live, tomorrow dead.
             A noise within.
       How now? What noise is that?
             Enter LEARTES.
    LEARTES   [*to his followers offstage*]   Stay there until I come.
       —O thou vile king, give me my father! Speak! Say, where's
       my father?
50   KING   Dead.
    LEARTES   Who hath murdered him? Speak! I'll not be juggled
       with°—for he is murdered.   *deceived*
       QUEEN   True, but not by him.°   *(the King)*

---

1. Shoes. *cockle hat:* a cockleshell badge worn in the hat was a pilgrim's memento of St. James's shrine at Compostela in Spain.

2. By adding "not," Ofelia changes the song's words and meter to fit the circumstances of Corambis's burial.

LEARTES   By whom? By heav'n, I'll be resolved.

55   KING   Let him go, Gertred. Away, I fear him not.
There's such divinity doth wall a king
That treason dares not look on.
Let him go, Gertred. —That your father is murdered
'Tis true, and we most sorry for it,
60   Being the chiefest pillar of our state.
Therefore, will you, like a most desperate gamester,
Swoopstake-like,³ draw at° friend and foe and all?   *prepare to attack*

LEARTES   To his good friends thus wide I'll ope mine arms
And lock them in my heart, but to his foes
65   I will no reconcilement but by blood.

KING   Why, now you speak like a most loving son.
And that in soul we sorrow for his death,
Yourself ere long shall be a witness.
Meanwhile, be patient and content yourself.
        Enter OFELIA *as before.*

70   LEARTES   Who's this? Ofelia? O my dear sister!
Is't possible a young maid's life
Should be as mortal as an old man's saw?⁴
O heav'ns themselves! How now, Ofelia?

OFELIA   Well, God ha' mercy. I ha' been gathering of flowers:
75   here, here is rue for you: you may call it herb o'grace o'Sundays.
Here's some for me too. You must wear your rue with a differ-
ence.⁵ There's a daisy.⁶ Here, love, there's rosemary for
you—for remembrance. I pray, love, remember. And there's
pansy for thoughts.⁷

80   LEARTES   A document° in madness! Thoughts, remembrance!   *An object lesson*
O God, God!

OFELIA   There is fennel for you: I would ha' giv'n you some
violets,⁸ but they all withered when my father died. Alas,
they say the owl was a baker's daughter.⁹ We see what we
85   are, but cannot tell what we shall be.
    [*Sings.*]   For bonny sweet Robin is all my joy.

LEARTES   Thoughts and afflictions—torments worse than
        hell!

OFELIA   Nay, love, I pray you make no words of this now. I
pray now, you shall sing "a-down" and you "a-down-a." 'Tis
90   o'the king's daughter and the false steward¹—and if anybody
ask you of anything, say you this:
    [*Sings.*]   Tomorrow is Saint Valentine's day,
                All in the morning betime,°   *early*
                And a maid at your window
95   To be your valentine.

---

3. Indiscriminately. (The winner of a sweepstake gained the stakes of all other players.)
4. Is it possible a young maid's life can be as dead as a worn-out saying?
5. In heraldry, minor branches of a family were distinguished by a "difference," a variation or an addition to the coat of arms. Ofelia probably means "for a different reason." Rue is associated with repentance, and Ofelia identifies it with the "herb of grace" (wormwood), since penitence depended on and enabled God's blessing.

6. Daisies could symbolize dissembling seduction.
7. *there's . . . thoughts:* Ofelia, recalling the flowers' symbolic significance, distributes them to Leartes, Gertred, and the King.
8. Representing faithfulness.
9. Referring to a folktale wherein Jesus visits a baker's shop asking for bread. The shop's mistress puts a generous piece in the oven but is reprimanded by her daughter, who is later turned into an owl for her stinginess.
1. The tale is unknown.

The young man rose and donned his clothes
And dupped° the chamber door,   *unlatched*
Let in the maid that out a maid
Never departed more.
100   Nay, I pray, mark now:
By Gis° and by Saint Charity,   *Jesus*
Away, and fie for shame!
Young men will do't when they come to't,
By Cock,[2] they are to blame.

105   Quoth she, "Before you tumbled me,
You promised me to wed."
"So would I ha' done, by yonder sun,
If thou hadst not come to my bed."
So God be with you all, God b'wi'y', ladies. God b'wi'you,
110   love.   *Exeunt* OFELIA [*and* QUEEN].
LEARTES   Grief upon grief:
My father murdered, my sister thus distracted.
Cursed be his soul that wrought this wicked act!
KING   Content you, good Leartes, for a time,
115   Although I know your grief is as a flood,
Brimful of sorrow; but forbear awhile
And think already the revenge is done
On him that makes you such a hapless son.
LEARTES   You have prevailed, my lord. Awhile I'll strive
120   To bury grief within a tomb of wrath
Which, once unhearsed, then the world shall hear
Leartes had a father he held dear.
KING   No more of that. Ere many days be done,
You shall hear that° you do not dream upon.   *Exeunt.*   *that which*

Scene 14[1]
Enter HORATIO *and the* QUEEN.

HORATIO   Madam, your son is safe arrived in Denmark.
This letter I even° now received of him   *just*
Whereas he writes how he escaped the danger
And subtle treason that the King had plotted.
5   Being crossed by the contention of the winds,
He found the packet sent to the King of England,
Wherein he saw himself betrayed to death—
As at his next conversing with your grace
He will relate the circumstance at full.
10   QUEEN   Then I perceive there's treason in his° looks   *(the King's)*
That seemed to sugar o'er his villainy.
But I will soothe and please him for a time,
For murderous minds are always jealous.
But know not you, Horatio, where he° is?   *(Hamlet)*
15   HORATIO   Yes, madam, and he hath appointed me
To meet him on the east side of the city

2. A corruption of "God" in very mild swearing (playing on "penis").
Scene 14 Location: The castle.
1. TEXTUAL COMMENT Q1 here condenses material concerning Hamlet's adventures treated elsewhere in Q2 and F. It also differs from Q2 and F by having Gertred explicitly ally herself with Hamlet and plan to deceive her husband. See Digital Edition TC 8 (First Quarto edited text).

Tomorrow morning.

QUEEN   Oh, fail not, good Horatio.
And withal° commend me a mother's care to him;   *also*
Bid him awhile be wary of his presence
20   Lest that he fail in that he goes about.
HORATIO   Madam, never make doubt of that. I think by this
The news be come to court he is arrived:
Observe the King and you shall quickly find,
Hamlet being here, things fell not to his mind.
25 QUEEN   But what became of Gilderstone and Rossencraft?
HORATIO   He being set ashore,² they went for England
And in the packet there writ down that doom
To be performed on them 'pointed for him.
And by great chance° he had his father's seal,   *luck*
30   So all was done without discovery.³
QUEEN   Thanks be to heaven for blessing of the Prince!⁴
Horatio, once again I take my leave,
With thousand mother's blessings to my son.
HORATIO   Madam, adieu.   [*Exeunt separately.*]

Scene 15
Enter KING *and* LEARTES.

KING   Hamlet from England! Is it possible?
What chance is this—they are gone and he come home?
LEARTES   Oh, he is welcome—by my soul, he is.
At it my jocund heart doth leap for joy
5   That I shall live to tell him, thus he dies.
KING   Leartes, content yourself. Be ruled by me,
And you shall have no let° for your revenge.   *hindrance*
LEARTES   My will, not all the world.¹
KING   Nay, but Leartes, mark the plot I have laid:
10   I have heard him often with a greedy wish,
Upon some praise that he hath heard of you
Touching° your weapon, wish with all his heart   *Concerning*
He might be once tasked for to try your cunning.
LEARTES   And how for this?²
15 KING   Marry, Leartes, thus: I'll lay a wager—
Shall be on Hamlet's side and you shall give the odds
(The which will draw him with a more desire
To try the mastery)—that in twelve venies
You gain not three of him.³ Now, this being granted,
20   When you are hot in midst of all your play,
Among the foils shall a keen rapier lie
Steeped in a mixture of deadly poison
That, if it draws but the least dram of blood
In any part of him, he cannot live.
25   This being done will free you from suspicion,

---

2. Hamlet is ultimately set ashore on account of the "contention of the winds" in line 5.
3. By editing the letter and giving it his father's official stamp, Hamlet transfers his "doom" (death sentence) to Gilderstone and Rossencraft.
4 Thanks be to heaven for saving the prince.
Scene 15 Location: The King's private apartments.

1. By my will, not all the world combined could hinder me.
2. Leartes is essentially asking, "What has this got to do with my revenge?"
3. In twelve venies, or rounds, of fencing, you do not top him by three.

And not the dearest friend that Hamlet loved
Will ever have Leartes in suspect.
LEARTES   My lord, I like it well.
But say Lord Hamlet should refuse this match?
30 KING   I'll warrant you, we'll put on you
Such a report of singularity°   *exceptional skill*
Will bring him on, although against his will.
And lest that all should miss,
I'll have a potion that shall ready stand,
35 In all his heat when that he calls for drink,
Shall be his period° and our happiness.   *end*
LEARTES   'Tis excellent. Oh, would the time were come!
          Enter the QUEEN.
Here comes the Queen.
KING   How now, Gertred? Why look you heavily?
40 QUEEN   O my lord, the young Ofelia,
Having made a garland of sundry sorts of flowers,
Sitting upon a willow by a brook,
The envious° sprig broke—into the brook she fell   *evil*
And for awhile her clothes, spread wide abroad,
45 Bore the young lady up. And there she sat
Smiling, even mermaid-like, twixt heaven and earth,
Chanting old sundry tunes—uncapable,°   *uncomprehending*
As it were, of her distress; but long it could not be
Till that her clothes, being heavy with their drink,
Dragged the sweet wretch to death.
50 LEARTES   So, she is drowned.
Too much of water hast thou, Ofelia—
Therefore I will not drown thee in my tears.
Revenge it is must yield this heart relief,
For woe begets woe, and grief hangs on grief.   *Exeunt.*

Scene 16
          Enter [FIRST *and* SECOND CLOWNS].°   *rustics; peasants*
FIRST CLOWN   I say no, she ought not to be buried in Chris-
tian burial.[1]
SECOND CLOWN   Why, sir?
FIRST CLOWN   Marry, because she's drowned.
5 SECOND CLOWN   But she did not drown herself.
FIRST CLOWN   No, that's certain, the water drowned her.
SECOND CLOWN   Yea, but it was against her will.
FIRST CLOWN   No, I deny that, for look you, sir—I stand here:
if the water come to me, I drown not myself, but if I go to
10 the water and am there drowned, ergo,[2] I am guilty of my
own death. You're gone,[3] go, you're gone, sir.
SECOND CLOWN   Ay, but see, she hath Christian burial because
she is a great° woman.   *important; powerful*
FIRST CLOWN   Marry, more's the pity that great folk should
15 have more authority to hang or drown themselves more than
other people. Go fetch me a stoup° of drink. But before thou   *flagon*

Scene 16 Location: A churchyard.   blessing and ritual).
1. Ordinarily, suicides would not receive a "Chris-   2. Therefore (Latin).
tian burial" (in consecrated ground with the church's 3. You lose.

goest, tell me one thing: who builds strongest of[4] a mason, a
shipwright, or a carpenter?

SECOND CLOWN Why, a mason, for he builds all of stone and
20   will endure long.

FIRST CLOWN That's pretty! To't again, to't again.[5]

SECOND CLOWN Why then, a carpenter, for he builds the gallows and that brings many a one to his long home.

FIRST CLOWN Pretty again! The gallows doth° well—marry,   *serves*
25   how does it well? The gallows does well to them that do ill.
Go, get thee gone. And if anyone ask thee hereafter, say a
gravemaker, for the houses he builds last till doomsday.
Fetch me a stoup of beer, go.   [*Exit* SECOND CLOWN.]
      Enter HAMLET *and* HORATIO [*apart*].

   [*Sings.*]   A pick-ax and a spade, a spade,
30   For and° a winding sheet,   *And also*
                  Most fit it is, for 'twill be made
                  For such a guest most meet.
      He throws up a [*skull*].

HAMLET Hath this fellow any feeling of himself that is thus
merry in making of a grave? See how the slave jowls° their   *slams*
35   heads against the earth.

HORATIO My lord, custom hath made it in him seem
nothing.

FIRST CLOWN [*sings*] A pickax and a spade, a spade,
                  For and a winding sheet,
40   Most fit it is for to be made,
                For such a guest most meet.
      [*He throws up another skull.*]

HAMLET Look you, there's another, Horatio. Why, may't not
be the skull of some lawyer? Methinks he should indict that
fellow of an action of battery[6] for knocking him about the
45   pate° with 's shovel. Now, where is your quirks and quillets°   *head / quibbles*
now, your vouchers and double vouchers,[7] your leases and
freehold and tenements?[8] Why, that same box° there will   *deed box; coffin*
scarce hold the conveyance° of his land, and must his honor   *deed*
lie there? Oh, pitiful transformance! I prithee tell me, Hora-
50   tio, is parchment made of sheepskins?

HORATIO Ay, my lord, and of calves' skins too.

HAMLET I'faith, they prove themselves sheep and calves° that   *simpletons and fools*
deal with them or put their trust in them.°   *(lawyers)*
      [FIRST CLOWN *throws up another skull.*]
There's another—why, may not that be Such-a-one's skull
55   that praised my lord Such-a-one's horse when he meant to
beg him? Horatio, I prithee let's question yonder fellow.
—Now, my friend, whose grave is this?

FIRST CLOWN Mine, sir.

HAMLET But who must lie in it?

60   FIRST CLOWN If I should say I should, I should lie in my
throat, sir.

---

4. The "of" functions something like a colon here,
introducing the three types of men to be compared.
5. That's not bad, but try again.
6. Legal prosecution for assault.
7. "Vouchers" summoned witnesses to attest to a

piece of land's ownership. A "double voucher" required
two such witnesses.
8. *freehold*: a land or property held permanently with
full rights of disposal. *tenements*: an umbrella term
for properties in freehold (i.e., beyond land).

HAMLET   What man must be buried here?

FIRST CLOWN   No man, sir.

HAMLET   What woman?

65   FIRST CLOWN   No woman neither, sir—but indeed one that
was a woman.

HAMLET   An excellent fellow, by the Lord, Horatio. This seven
years have I noted it: the toe of the peasant comes so near
the heel of the courtier that he galls his kibe.° [to FIRST   *chafes his heel sore*
70   CLOWN] I prithee tell me one thing: how long will a man lie
in the ground before he rots?

FIRST CLOWN   I'faith, sir, if he be not rotten before he be laid
in—as we have many pocky° corpses—he will last you eight   *pox-riddled*
years. A tanner will last you eight years full out, or nine.

75   HAMLET   And why a tanner?

FIRST CLOWN   Why, his hide is so tanned with his trade that it
will hold out water—that's a parlous° devourer of your dead   *dangerous; awful*
body, a great soaker. Look you, here's a skull hath been here
this dozen year—let me see, ay, ever since our last King
80   Hamlet slew Fortenbrasse in combat—young Hamlet's
father, he that's mad.

HAMLET   Ay, marry—how came he mad?

FIRST CLOWN   I'faith, very strangely—by losing of his wits.

HAMLET   Upon what ground?[9]

85   FIRST CLOWN   O'this ground, in Denmark.

HAMLET   Where is he now?

FIRST CLOWN   Why, now they sent him to England.

HAMLET   To England? Wherefore?

FIRST CLOWN   Why, they say he shall have his wits there or, if
90   he have not, 'tis no great matter there—it will not be seen
there.

HAMLET   Why not there?

FIRST CLOWN   Why, there they say the men are as mad as he.

HAMLET   Whose skull was this?

95   FIRST CLOWN   This? A plague on him, a mad rogue's it was—
he poured once a whole flagon of Rhenish° on my head.   *Rhine wine*
Why, do not you know him? This was one Yorick's skull.

HAMLET   Was this? I prithee let me see it.
        [*He takes the skull.*]
Alas, poor Yorick. I knew him, Horatio—a fellow of infinite
100   mirth. He hath carried me twenty times upon his back.
Here hung those lips that I have kissed a hundred times,
and, to see now, they abhor° me. Where's your jests now,   *disgust; frighten*
Yorick, your flashes of merriment? Now go to my lady's
chamber and bid her paint herself an inch thick, to this she
105   must come, Yorick. Horatio, I prithee tell me one thing: dost
thou think that Alexander looked thus?

HORATIO   Even so, my lord.

HAMLET   And smelt thus?

HORATIO   Ay, my lord, no otherwise.

110   HAMLET   No. Why might not imagination work, as thus, of
Alexander: Alexander died, Alexander was buried, Alexander became earth, of earth we make clay, and Alexander

---

9. From what cause? (The Clown takes him to mean "In what country?")

being but clay, why might not time bring to pass that he
might stop the bung-hole° of a beer barrel?   *opening*
115   Imperious Caesar, dead and turned to clay,
Might stop a hole to keep the wind away.

> *Enter* KING *and* QUEEN, LEARTES, *and other Lords,*
> *with a* PRIEST *after* [*Ofelia's*] *coffin.*

HAMLET   What funeral's this that all the court laments?
It shows to be some noble parentage.
Stand by awhile.
120   LEARTES   What ceremony else?[1] Say, what ceremony else?
PRIEST   My lord, we have done all that lies in us,
And more than well the church can tolerate.
She hath had a dirge sung for her maiden soul
And, but for favor of the King and you,
125   She had been° buried in the open fields,   *would have been*
Where° now she is allowed Christian burial.   *Whereas (instead)*
LEARTES   So! I tell thee, churlish priest,
A minist'ring angel shall my sister be
When thou liest howling.°   *(in hell)*
HAMLET [*aside*][2]   The fair Ofelia dead!
130   QUEEN [*scattering flowers*]   Sweets to the sweet. Farewell.
I had thought to adorn thy bridal bed, fair maid,
And not to follow thee unto thy grave.
LEARTES   Forbear the earth a while.[3] Sister, farewell!

>   LEARTES *leaps into the grave.*

Now pour your earth on, Olympus-high,
135   And make a hill to o'ertop old Pelion.[4]

>   HAMLET *leaps in after* LEARTES.[5]

HAMLET   What's he that conjures so? Behold, 'tis I,
Hamlet the Dane.[6]
LEARTES   The devil take thy soul!
HAMLET   Oh, thou prayest not well.
I prithee take thy hand from off my throat,
140   For there is something in me dangerous
Which let thy wisdom fear. Hold off thy hand!
I loved Ofelia as dear as twenty brothers could.
Show me what thou wilt do for her:
Wilt° fight? Wilt fast? Wilt pray?   *Wilt (thou)*
145   Wilt drink up vessels? Eat a crocodile?
I'll do't. Com'st thou here to whine?
And where thou talk'st of burying thee alive,
Here let us stand and let them throw on us
Whole hills of earth till with the height thereof
150   Make Ossa[7] as a wart.
KING   Forbear, Leartes. Now is he mad as is the sea,
Anon° as mild and gentle as a dove.   *Soon*

---

1. Leartes insists upon further funeral rites.
2. TEXTUAL COMMENT We have chosen to cast this line as an aside rather than as a comment to Horatio, in order to convey Hamlet's inward shock of grief. See Digital Edition TC 9 (First Quarto edited text).
3. Stop filling the grave for a moment.
4. In Greek mythology, giants piled Pelion (a mountain in Thessaly) on top of Mount Ossa in an attempt to climb Mount Olympus.

5. TEXTUAL COMMENT Q1 is the only edition to direct specifically what form Hamlet's reaction to Leartes' grieving should take. This active decision of leaping into the grave after Leartes possibly squares with earlier cultural conceptions of Hamlet's character. See Digital Edition TC 10 (First Quarto edited text).
6. Normally the title of the King of Denmark.
7. Greek mountain (see note to line 135).

Therefore awhile give his wild humor scope.[8]

HAMLET   What is the reason, sir, that you wrong me thus?
155   I never gave you cause. But stand away,
       A cat will mew, a dog will have a day.[9]
                                  Exeunt HAMLET *and* HORATIO.
QUEEN   Alas, it is his madness makes him thus
       And not his heart, Leartes.
KING   My lord, 'tis so. [*aside to* LEARTES] But we'll no longer
       trifle—
160   This very day shall Hamlet drink his last,
       For presently we mean to send to him.
       Therefore, Leartes, be in readiness.
LEARTES [*aside to* KING]   My lord, till then my soul will not
       be quiet.
KING   Come, Gertred, we'll have Leartes and our son
165   Made friends and lovers, as befits them both,
       Even as they tender° us and love their country.   care for
QUEEN   God grant they may.   *Exeunt.*

Scene 17
Enter HAMLET *and* HORATIO.
HAMLET   Believe me, it grieves me much, Horatio,
       That to Leartes I forgot myself.
       For by myself methinks I feel his grief,
       Though there's a difference in each other's wrong.
                  Enter a braggart GENTLEMAN.
5   Horatio, but mark yon water fly:
       The court knows him, but he knows not the court.
GENTLEMAN   Now God save thee, sweet Prince Hamlet.
HAMLET   And you, sir. [*aside to* HORATIO] Foh, how the musk-
       cod[1] smells!
10   GENTLEMAN   I come with an embassage from his majesty to
       you.
HAMLET   I shall, sir, give you attention. By my troth, methinks
       'tis very cold.
GENTLEMAN   It is indeed very rawish cold.
15   HAMLET   'Tis hot methinks.
GENTLEMAN   Very sweltery hot. The King, sweet Prince, hath
       laid a wager on your side: six Barbary horse against six
       French rapiers, with all their accoutrements, too, and the
       carriages—in good faith, they are very curiously wrought.
20   HAMLET   The carriages,[2] sir? I do not know what you mean.
GENTLEMAN   The girdles and hangers,[3] sir, and suchlike.
HAMLET   The word had been more cousin-german° to the   related; appropriate
       phrase if he could have carried the cannon by his side.[4] And
       how's the wager? I understand you now.
25   GENTLEMAN   Marry, sir, that young Leartes, in twelve venies at
       rapier and dagger, do not get three odds of you,[5] and on your
       side the King hath laid and desires you to be in readiness.

8. Let his temper run its course.
9. Despite Leartes' ranting, my day will come.
Scene 17 Location: A stateroom of the castle.
1. An excessively perfumed gentleman.
2. The Gentleman's inflated term for "hangers," or
straps.

3. Attaching straps.
4. A common definition of "carriage" at the time was
a mount for a cannon.
5. Leartes must score three more "hits" than Hamlet
out of twelve bouts of swordplay to win the wager.

HAMLET Very well. If the King dare venture his wager, I dare
venture my skill. When must this be?

30 GENTLEMAN My lord, presently—the King and her majesty,
with the rest of the best judgment in the court, are coming
down into the outward palace.

HAMLET Go tell his majesty I will attend him.

GENTLEMAN I shall deliver your most sweet answer. *Exit.*

35 HAMLET You may, sir, none better, for you're spiced°—else he   *fragrant*
had a bad nose could not smell a fool!

HORATIO He will disclose himself without inquiry.

HAMLET Believe me, Horatio, my heart is on the sudden very
sore all hereabout.

40 HORATIO My lord, forbear the challenge then.

HAMLET No, Horatio, not I. If danger be now, why, then, it is
not to come. There's a predestinate providence[6] in the fall of
a sparrow. Here comes the King.

　　　Enter KING, QUEEN, LEARTES, [*and*] *Lords.*

KING Now, son Hamlet, we have laid upon your head[7]

45 And make no question but to have the best.[8]

HAMLET Your majesty hath laid o'the weaker side.

KING We doubt it not.[9] —Deliver them the foils.

HAMLET First, Leartes, here's my hand and love,
Protesting° that I never wronged Leartes.   *Declaring*

50 If Hamlet in his madness did amiss,
That was not Hamlet but his madness did it.
And all the wrong I e'er did to Leartes
I here proclaim was madness.
Therefore let's be at peace and think I have shot

55 Mine arrow o'er the house and hurt my brother.

LEARTES Sir, I am satisfied in nature, but
In terms of honor I'll stand aloof and will
No reconcilement till by some elder masters
Of our time[1] I may be satisfied.

KING Give them the foils.

60 HAMLET　　　　　　　　　I'll be your foil,[2] Leartes.
These foils have all a° length? [*He chooses a foil.*] Come   *the same*
on, sir.
　　　Here they play.
A hit!

LEARTES No, none!

HAMLET Judgment?

65 GENTLEMAN A hit, a most palpable hit.

LEARTES Well, come again.
　　　They play again.

HAMLET Another! Judgment?

LEARTES Ay, I grant—a touch, a touch.

KING Here, Hamlet, the King doth drink a health to thee.[3]

---

6. God's direction for a specific event (over and
above "general providence," the whole shape of God's
design). Compare Matthew 10:29: "Are not two sparrows sold for a farthing? and one of them shall not
fall on the ground without your Father."
7. *we . . . head:* we have cast our bet on your side.
8. *but . . . best:* that we've picked the best.
9. We're not fearful of that being true.

1. *till . . . time:* until the consensus of men of authoritative standing holds that I can accept Hamlet's
apology.
2. Flattering contrast. Jewels were often set with a
piece of metal foil under them to increase their
glitter.
3. Here in Q2 and F, the King drops a poisoned pearl
into Hamlet's cup.

70 QUEEN   Here, Hamlet, take my napkin,° wipe thy face.   *handkerchief*
   KING   Give him the wine.
   HAMLET   Set it by. I'll have another bout first. I'll drink anon.°   *shortly*
   QUEEN   Here, Hamlet, thy mother drinks to thee.
      She drinks.
   KING   Do not drink, Gertred. [*aside*] Oh, 'tis the poisoned cup!
75 HAMLET   Leartes, come, you dally with me. I pray you pass°   *thrust*
   with your most cunning'st play.
   LEARTES   Ay, say you so? Have at you! I'll hit you now, my
   lord. [*aside*] And yet it goes almost against my conscience.
   HAMLET   Come on, sir.
      They catch one another's rapiers and both are
      wounded.
      LEARTES *falls down; the* QUEEN *falls down.*
80 KING   Look to the Queen.
   QUEEN   Oh, the drink, the drink! Hamlet, the drink!
      [*She*] *dies.*
   HAMLET   Treason, ho! Keep the gates!
   GENTLEMAN   How is't, my lord Leartes?
   LEARTES   Even as a coxcomb should[4]—foolishly slain with my
85 own weapon.
   Hamlet,
   Thou hast not in thee half an hour of life.
   The fatal instrument is in thy hand,
   Unbated° and envenomed. Thy mother's poisoned—   *Not blunted*
90 That drink was made for thee.
   HAMLET   The poisoned instrument within my hand?
   Then venom to thy venom: die, damned villain!
      [*He stabs the* KING.]
   Come, drink: here lies thy union—here!
      [*He pours the drink down the King's throat and*] *the*
      KING *dies.*
   LEARTES   Oh, he is justly served.
95 Hamlet, before I die, here take my hand
   And withal° my love: I do forgive thee.   *with it*
      LEARTES *dies.*
   HAMLET   And I thee.
   Oh, I am dead, Horatio; fare thee well.
   HORATIO   No, I am more an antique Roman
100 Than a Dane[5]—here is some poison left.
   HAMLET   Upon my love I charge thee, let it go.
   Oh fie, Horatio—an if° thou shouldst die,   *an if = if*
   What a scandal wouldst thou leave behind!
   What tongue should tell the story of our deaths
105 If not from thee? Oh, my heart sinks, Horatio,
   Mine eyes have lost their sight, my tongue his use.
   Farewell, Horatio: heaven receive my soul.
      HAMLET *dies.*

4. *Even . . . should:* Just like a coxcomb; in the manner of a coxcomb.
5. Ancient ("antique") Romans generally regarded
suicide as preferable to dishonor; in particular, they
believed that servants or retainers should not outlive
their master's overthrow.

Enter VOLTEMAR *and the* AMBASSADORS *from England.*
Enter [through a different door] FORTENBRASSE *with*
his train.

FORTENBRASSE   Where is this bloody sight?
HORATIO   If aught of woe or wonder you'd behold,
110   Then look upon this tragic spectacle.
FORTENBRASSE   O imperious Death, how many princes
  Hast thou at one draft° bloodily shot to death?   *draw of the bow*
AMBASSADOR   Our embassy that we have brought from
    England—
  Where be these princes that should hear us speak?
115   Oh, most unlooked-for time! Unhappy country!
HORATIO   Content yourselves. I'll show to all the ground,
  The first beginning of this tragedy.
  Let there a scaffold be reared up in the marketplace,
  And let the state of the world be there,
120   Where you shall hear such a sad story told
  That never mortal man could more unfold.
FORTENBRASSE   I have some rights of memory⁶ to this
    kingdom,
  Which now to claim my leisure doth invite me.
  Let four of our chiefest captains
125   Bear Hamlet like a soldier to his grave,
  For he was likely, had he lived,
  To've proved° most royal.   *shown himself; acted*
  Take up the body; such a sight as this
  Becomes the fields,⁷ but here doth much amiss.   [*Exeunt.*]

---

6. *of memory:* unforgotten; traditional.   7. Is most appropriate to a battlefield.

Othello

Othello (ca. 1601–03) has always been popular in performance, although—or per-haps, paradoxically, because—it is excruciating to watch. We look on helplessly as Iago tricks Othello into believing that Desdemona, Othello's beloved and loving wife, has committed adultery. We see the villain cunningly stage-manage appearances to "prove" her guilt. We witness Othello's psychic degeneration into insane jealousy. As mere spectators, we can say nothing to warn or exonerate her. We then watch Othello kill the innocent Desdemona, and finally we watch him, tormented with bafflement and remorse, kill himself.

Massive, collective, transhistorical forces—racism, ancient gender stereotypes, deep-rooted sexual and religious anxieties—conspire against Othello and Desdemona. These forces have by no means vanished from our own world. But Shakespeare depicts them in a highly specific form, shaped by the culture of the Venetian Republic and its outpost, Cyprus, at a moment of historical conflict with the Ottoman Turks. So too the central characters grapple with universal passions, but the passions are only set in fatal motion by circumstances particular to their place and time. *Othello* in consequence is a play that is at once utterly alien and utterly familiar.

Racism's persistence today offers an accessible path into *Othello*; at the same time, some of the play's racial markers are now unfamiliar and hence easily overlooked. The First Folio calls Othello "the Moor of Venice." In the Renaissance, the term "Moor" could designate an African (north or south of the Sahara), a Muslim, or even a South Asian Indian. While *Othello*'s Moorish protagonist, and much of its plot, derive from Giovanbattista Giraldi Cinthio's *De gli hecatommithi* (Hundred Tales, 1565), Shake-speare gives race far more attention than Cinthio does, and explores the issue in sustained and unsettling fashion.

How, then, does race function in *Othello*? Roderigo, who lusts after Desdemona, incites horror of miscegenation when, goaded by Iago, he informs Desdemona's father, Brabanzio, that "an old black ram / Is tupping [copulating with] your white ewe" (1.1.86–87).* Iago adds: "you'll have your daughter covered with a Barbary [Arab, North African] horse" (1.1.108–09). These comments register Elizabethan prejudice toward black Africans resident in England and reflect the growing European participation in the African slave trade that had long been dominated by Arab merchants. Such racially charged language recurs throughout the play, reinforced by the conventional association of blackness with evil. Othello considers his "best judgment collied" (darkened; 2.3.185) by anger; Iago speaks of "the blackest sins," vowing to "turn" Desdemona's "virtue into pitch" (sticky black resin; 2.3.322, 331). But when Brabanzio accuses Othello of seducing his daughter by magic, Iago recognizes that the charges will fall on deaf ears: Venice needs Othello to repel the Turkish navy that has invaded Cyprus. And practical necessity is not the only mitigating factor. The Sen-ate's acceptance of his courtship of Desdemonda projects overtones of Christian universalism and the positive view of interracial love in the Song of Songs. As the Duke tells Brabanzio, in a backhanded compliment, "Your son-in-law is far more fair than black" (1.3.287).

The racist attack on Othello falters partly because the play initially obeys the logic of romantic comedy—nighttime encounters, an old but ineffectual father blocking

---

*Except where noted, all quotations are taken from the edited text of the Folio, printed here. The Digital Edition includes edited texts of both the Folio and the Quarto.

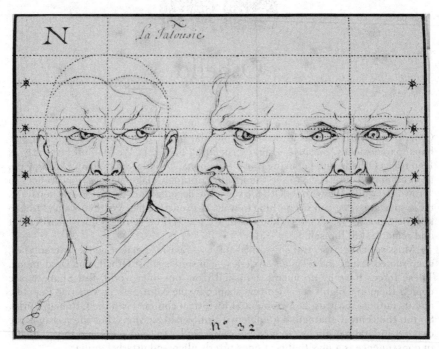

Jealousy. Charles Le Brun (1619–1690).

his daughter's marriage, and official ratification of the couple's marriage. It then modulates into romance, a form in which, characteristically, virtuous lovers are parted and face perilous adventures before happily reuniting. Here, Desdemona and Othello separately sail for Cyprus through bad weather to confront the Turks. But they arrive safely and a storm disperses the enemy fleet. Hence, the obstacles seem to have been overcome.

As the plot unfolds, however, less familiar racial discourses emerge, coincident with a generic shift to domestic tragedy—a wife's alleged adultery and her husband's response. Since we know that Desdemona is innocent, Othello's rush toward violence is horrific. Shakespeare offers various, sometimes incompatible, motivations for that swiftness. His portrait of Othello draws on a stereotype of African men's extreme jealousy that he likely took from *A Geographical History of Africa* (trans. 1600) by Leo Africanus, a Moroccan Muslim who converted to Catholicism after being captured by Christian pirates. The play owes a further debt to geohumoralism, a theory linking psychology ("humors") to geography or climate. For geohumoralists, Africans (unlike Italians) were not naturally jealous but, once provoked, responded fiercely. When Iago's wife Emilia comments on Othello's jealousy, Desdemona replies: "Who, he? I think the sun where he was born / Drew all such humors from him" (3.4.27–28). And Othello ultimately sees himself as "one not easily jealous but, being wrought, / Perplexed in the extreme" (5.2.338–39).

Iago invokes another racial stereotype—that of African naïveté—when he observes that Othello

> is of a free and open nature
> That thinks men honest that but seem to be so,
> And will as tenderly be led by th' nose
> As asses are.
>
> (1.3.377–80)

This gullibility went hand in hand, in European eyes, with the propensity of "uncivilized" Africans to fetishize—to overvalue or even attribute magical powers to—trivial objects. Thus, in act 3, Shakespeare has Othello chastise Desdemona for failing to produce the handkerchief he gave to her. (Iago planted it on Cassio, Othello's lieutenant, to suggest that he and Desdemona were lovers.) Othello explains that an Egyptian presented the handkerchief to his mother.

> To lose't or give't away were such perdition
> As nothing else could match. . . .
>   There's magic in the web of it.
> . . . .
> And it was dyed in mummy, which the skillful
> Conserved of maidens' hearts.
>   (3.4.64–72)

In short, *Othello* attributes Othello's susceptibility to Iago to multiple facets of his blackness and Africanness. As social mores have changed, so have interpretations of blackness in the play. Well into the twentieth century, audiences and critics often agreed with Brabanzio that Othello's barbaric African essence triumphs over his civilized European surface. Those who defended his nobility tended to argue that he was not black at all, but white, Oriental, or Arab. Historic performances by black actors have often seemed blows for freedom—for example, in Europe following the 1848 revolutions, in czarist Russia just before the liberation of the serfs, after the emancipation of American slaves in 1863, in World War II America, and in the final years of South African apartheid. Although commentators of African descent have sometimes worried that casting a black actor as Othello risks reinforcing racism, recent years have seen a return to the pre-1800 conviction that Othello is black. Directors have avoided casting white performers in the part, lest they conjure images of the blackface minstrel-shows that figured in nineteenth-century burlesques of the play—the charge made against Laurence Olivier's 1965 film portrayal. Additionally, the intertwining of race with gender and sexuality, especially the killing of a young white woman, has inspired adaptations of *Othello* by novelists of African descent—notably, the American Richard Wright in *Native Son* (1940) and the Sudanese Tayeb Salih in the Arabic-language *Season of Migration to the North* (1966).

Although race is an important issue in *Othello*, it does not solely drive the plot. Roderigo calls Othello an "old black ram" to highlight disparities not only of skin color but also of age. The allusion is to the farcical January–May marriage between an old man and a young woman who, sexually unsatisfied by her husband, looks elsewhere for gratification. In Venice, Iago says, such women "let heaven see the pranks / They dare not show their husbands" (3.3.200–201). Venice's reputation as a center of sexual license was a commonplace of Shakespeare's England, for instance in Thomas Coryat's *Coryat's Crudities* (1611). Coryat estimated that there were at least twenty thousand courtesans in Venice, "whereof many are esteemed so loose," as he put it, "that they are said to open their quivers to every arrow." And as in Venice, so in Cyprus. Once the storm scatters the Turks, the island loses its garrison status, recovering instead a traditional association with Venus, the classical goddess of love.

Othello registers Desdemona's threatening allure when they are reunited there: "If it were now to die, / 'Twere now to be most happy," where "to die" also means to have an orgasm (2.1.181–82). Christian doctrine sometimes considered excessive marital sexual pleasure a form of adultery, and Shakespeare hints that Othello experiences his own desire as adulterous, projecting this desire onto Cassio. Sex also connects with violence in the handkerchief, "[s]potted with strawberries" (3.3.431), that may evoke the blood Desdemona loses with her virginity. Othello anticipates that her "bed, lust-stained, shall with lust's blood be spotted" (5.1.36). Yet even as he prepares to murder his sleeping wife, he cannot resist kissing her. He recalls this necrophilic perversity at his own death: "I kissed thee ere I killed thee. No way but this: / Killing myself, to die upon a kiss" (5.2.351–52), where "die" again connotes sexual pleasure. Romance's reunion of long-separated lovers becomes postmortem embrace.

Desdemona seems entirely unaware of this dangerous current of male sexual anxiety. At the beginning of the play, she is frank and forthright about her own desires, declaring that she will "trumpet" her love for Othello "to the world" (1.3.247). At the end, Shakespeare emphasizes her innocent victimization, dramatizing her submission to Othello.

> DESDEMONA   Oh, falsely, falsely murdered!
> . . . .
>   A guiltless death I die.
> EMILIA   Oh, who hath done this deed?
> DESDEMONA   Nobody. I myself. Farewell.
>   Commend me to my kind lord. Oh, farewell!
>   (5.2.115–22)

Desdemona's last words may indicate a submissiveness bordering on suicide, normally a mortal sin for Christians but here more like Christlike self-sacrifice. Her speech also increases Othello's guilt, underscoring the mistreatment of women that is seen as well in Iago's relationship with Emilia and Cassio's with Bianca, the courtesan who loves him.

In addition to racial and sexual anxieties, *Othello* is woven through with religious concerns. Iago's pleasure in the sport of destroying Othello descends from the earlier English morality plays' Vice figure, a semi-secularized devil out to damn the virtuous. Tellingly, Othello refers to his scheming ensign as "that demi-devil" who "hath thus ensnared my soul and body" (5.2.294–95). On the verge of stabbing his antagonist, he declares, "If that thou beest a devil, I cannot kill thee." To which Iago rejoins, "I bleed, sir, but not killed" (5.2.280–81).From a Christian perspective, Othello reenacts the Fall in repudiating Desdemona, his good "angel" (5.2.128), and succumbing to demonic temptation. Desdemona, by contrast, commends herself to her "kind lord"—Othello, but also God. The word "lord" runs through the final scene, as does religious language more generally, especially references to heaven. Iago is damned and Desdemona saved, but what of Othello? He believes that killing Desdemona protects her immortal "soul," is a "sacrifice," is "merciful" (5.2.32, 66, 86). Once disabused, however, he reverses himself: "This look of thine [Desdemona's] will hurl my soul from heaven, / And fiends will snatch at it" (5.2.268–69). In murdering his innocent wife, he has committed a mortal sin, and in committing suicide—another mortal sin—he compounds his damnation.

Othello's final act calls up another tension that has been present throughout the play: that between the Europeans and the Turks, whose ethnic difference underlies the political, military, and religious threats to Cyprus and beyond. For this material, absent from Cinthio, Shakespeare may have drawn on Richard Knolles's *General History of the Turks* (1603), which could have provided various details, along with an international resonance. Shakespeare borrows the storm in act 1 of *Othello*, which completes the fictitious defeat of the Turks, from England's destruction of the Spanish Armada in 1588. When Othello breaks up Cassio's fight, he asks,

> Are we turned Turks, and to ourselves do that
> Which heaven hath forbid the Ottomites?
> For Christian shame, put by this barbarous brawl.
>   (2.3.149–51)

Othello speaks as the Christian he is. Although the passage refers to the providential storm that saves Christian Cyprus, "turning Turk" usually referred to captives of Muslim pirates who renounced Christianity for Islam. This fear seems remote until

Othello's final speech, in which he partially identifies with the non-Christian world. In the Quarto, Othello is culpably ignorant, "like the base Indian" who "threw a pearl away / Richer than all his tribe" (Q 5.2.319–20). But the Folio reads "base Judean" (F 5.2.340), perhaps alluding to Judas, betrayer of Christ, or to Herod the Great, jealous murderer of his wife.

In act 1, Othello leads Venice against the Turks—Muslims with whom Moors were linked. At the end of the play, he recalls his service in defending the Republic against "a malignant and a turbaned Turk" who "[b]eat a Venetian and traduced the state" (5.2.346–47). The deed divides him into agent and object of justice, servant and enemy of the Christian state. A "base Judean" and "circumcisèd dog" (5.2.348), he is both Jew and Turk. Othello internalizes the military conflict, half assuming ethnic and religious otherness

The manner of Turkish tyrannie over Christian flaves.

Woodcut, from F. Knight, *A Relation of Seven Years Slavery under the Turks of Argeire . . .* (1640). See Othello's speech before he kills himself (5.2.331–49).

to exorcise his guilt. Hence, the uneasy ending, with responsibility located both within and beyond Europe. But the last word on Othello's death is Cassio's: "This did I fear . . . / For he was great of heart" (5.2.353–54). The allusion to classical Roman suicide, rendered by Shakespeare earlier in *Julius Caesar* (1599), emphasizes Othello's nobility despite his damnation.

These social and cultural forces suggest why *Othello might* end tragically. But *must* it? Since it would take little to unmask Iago, we long for a happy ending. Yet audiences feel a helpless sense of inevitability. These contradictory perspectives coexist because *Othello* presents a world of guesswork misunderstood as proof, dramatizing characters who are driven by imperfect information, conjecture, and (im)probability. Yet what gives these considerations of likelihood, on which ordinary life depends, such destructive consequences? The answer seems to lie in the villain.

Iago wittily speaks to, not just before, the audience, and he speaks a lot, uttering two hundred more lines than Othello—more than any other Shakespearean character except Hamlet and Richard III. His verbal dominance is all the more evident in a play that deploys the smallest cast in Shakespearean tragedy and that, after the first act, almost conforms to the Aristotelian unities of time, place, and action, a convention that Shakespeare normally ignores but here turns to claustrophobic effect. Iago's verboseness is far from harmless. Indeed, destruction ensues in part because of Iago's ability to turn Othello's and Desdemona's noblest traits against them. Having invoked Othello's "constant, loving, noble nature" (2.1.272), he explains:

> 'tis most easy
> Th'inclining Desdemona to subdue

> In any honest suit: she's framed as fruitful
> As the free elements. And then for her
> To win the Moor . . .
> . . . .
> His soul is so enfettered to her love
> That she may make, unmake, do what she list.
>
> (2.3.310–17)

Othello's trustfulness and Desdemona's support of Cassio's "honest suit"—her persistent efforts to get Cassio reinstated after Othello dismisses him following a drunken brawl—thus become grist for "Honest Iago['s]" mill (1.3.291). And Iago seems honest to others because his blunt speech conceals his varied, impenetrable motives. Poet and critic Samuel Taylor Coleridge accordingly spoke of Iago's "motiveless malignity." That impenetrability persists even when it cannot help him. Captured, Iago refuses to explain himself—perhaps because he cannot—thereby leaving behind a sense of the mystery of things.

Othello also hurtles toward tragedy because Iago can manipulate other characters' belief in the debased cultural clichés by which he and they live. His sexual jealousy rests on the surmise that Emilia has committed adultery with Othello:

> I know not if't be true,
> But I, for mere suspicion in that kind,
> Will do as if for surety.
>
> (1.3.366–68)

"Suspicion" functions as "surety," a destructive substitution. It is a dangerous surmise based on the clichéd fear of the adulterous wife. Iago must then convince Othello to share his belief in Desdemona's adultery with Cassio. The rhetorician par excellence, he repeats a commonplace—Brabanzio's warning that Desdemona "has deceived her father, and may thee" (1.3.290)—in order to persuade Othello to internalize the stereotype of the unfaithful woman:

> She did deceive her father, marrying you;
> And when she seemed to shake and fear your looks,
> She loved them most.
>
> (3.3.204–06)

The same appeal to likelihood underpins Iago's presentation of "proof" in the form of "the fleers [sneers], the jibes, and notable scorns / That dwell in every region of his [Cassio's] face" (4.1.79–80). Similarly, to explain Desdemona's alleged betrayal, Othello echoes Roderigo's "old black ram":

> Haply, for I am black
> And have not those soft parts of conversation
> That chamberers have, or for I am declined
> Into the vale of years. . . .
>
> (3.3.261–64)

And after Iago considers Cassio and Desdemona "as prime as goats, as hot as monkeys" (3.3.400), Othello parrots his very words: "Goats and monkeys!" (4.1.250).

The play constantly warns against mere plausibility. Characters, as unstable as their own suspicions, are not what they seem. Iago confesses, "Were I the Moor, I would not be Iago" (1.1.55)—perhaps indicating a preference for Othello's lofty status, but also acknowledging their differences in character. In the same speech, he declares more elusively, "I am not what I am" (1.1.63). This reversal of God's words in Exodus—"I am what I am"—suggests Iago's psychic disunity. His self-presentation is not what he is, or he is not what he seems. Iago's explanation of Othello's jealousy is similar:

He's that he is . . . .
What he might be—if what he might, he is not—
I would to heaven he were.

(4.1.257–59)

The meaningless statement of psychic unity is promptly undermined as Iago seems to have it both ways: if Othello is not sane, I wish he were; on the other hand, if Othello is not insane, I wish he were (since that would explain his behavior). This duality returns at the end:

LODOVICO   Where is this rash and most unfortunate man?
OTHELLO   That's he that was Othello: here I am."

(5.2.276–77)

Othello considers his former, third-person self "this rash and most unfortunate man"; the first-person Othello is someone else. And when Iago is asked for his own motives, he replies: "What you know, you know" (5.2.296). Self-identity reveals nothing; self-division reveals something, but what?

As the play demonstrates again and again, to act on suspicion is dangerous. The Duke is dismissive of Brabanzio's claims that Othello must have used witchcraft to win Desdemona:

To vouch this is no proof
Without more wider and more overt test
Than these thin habits and poor likelihoods
Of modern seeming do prefer against him.

(1.3.106–09)

Emilia likewise repudiates Othello's charges against Desdemona, demanding evidence: "Why should he call her 'whore?' Who keeps her company? / What place, what time, what form, what likelihood?" (4.2.136–37). These challenges to surmise encourage in the audience a position of anguished superiority. But Shakespeare undermines this superiority by asking us to accept the plot's improbabilities. These include the love marriage of the older black foreigner to the young white woman, unlikely in Shakespeare's day; Iago's inconsistent motives, most opaque at the end; the lapses of memory and plausibility concerning the handkerchief; and the play's double time, in which events hurry forward, perhaps within a week, while Othello asserts that Desdemona "with Cassio hath the act of shame / A thousand times committed" (5.2.206–07). In seeing *Othello*, we impose reason on the incomprehensible, replicating the characters' behavior. We, too, operate via best guesses. This is the way of the world.

In *Othello*, however, Shakespeare makes us believe not that such behavior *may* lead to tragedy but that it *must*. It *must* because of the debased prejudices prevalent in society, Iago's remarkable skill in deploying them, and Desdemona's and Othello's equally remarkable nobility of soul and love for each other. It is a tragedy wrought of prejudice and of guesswork, and, most dangerously, of the two combined. Unable to intervene, we experience an overwhelming sense of loss at the destruction of something precious and rare. It is this that makes *Othello* so painfully moving.

WALTER COHEN

SELECTED BIBLIOGRAPHY

Altman, Joel. *The Improbability of Othello: Rhetorical Anthropology and Shakespearean Selfhood.* Chicago: U of Chicago P, 2010. Sees, especially in Iago and Othello, a classical and humanist exploration of probability, where a rhetorically multiple self (a dramatis persona) periodically coalesces into a dialectically fixed subject (a specific character).

Floyd-Wilson, Mary. *English Ethnicity and Race in Early Modern Drama.* Cambridge: Cambridge UP, 2003. Draws on classical geohumoral theory (linking character to climate and geography) to see Italian Iago as naturally jealous and African Othello as naturally calm—a theory modified by early racism, deployed by Iago to corrupt Othello.

Greenblatt, Stephen. *Renaissance Self-Fashioning: From More to Shakespeare.* Chicago: U of Chicago P, 1980. 222–54. Examines Othello's narrative self-fashioning and its subversion by Desdemona's submission and Iago's malice; a central essay for modern *Othello* scholarship and for New Historicist criticism generally.

Hall, Kim F. *Othello, the Moor of Venice: Texts and Contexts.* Boston: Bedford/St. Martin's, 2007. Presents a text of the play; contemporary primary sources on race and religion, cultural geography, marriage and the household, masculinity and military life, and passions; and critical and artistic responses from the past three centuries.

Korda, Natasha. *Shakespeare's Domestic Economies: Gender and Property in Early Modern England.* Philadelphia: U of Pennsylvania P, 2002. Links Othello's jealousy, focused on Desdemona's handkerchief, to contradictory discourses of private property manipulated by Iago—African fetishistic overvaluation of trifling objects, English household discipline, and European female extravagance.

Lupton, Julia Reinhard. "Othello Circumcised: Shakespeare and the Pauline Discourse of Nations." *Representations* 57 (Winter 1997): 73–89. Views Othello through the prism of St. Paul's distinction between pagans and Jews, seeing the Moor as both ex-barbarian and ex-Muslim, positions to which he partly returns.

Neill, Michael, ed. *Othello, the Moor of Venice.* Oxford: Oxford UP, 2006. Outstanding scholarly edition with a book-length critical introduction.

Orlin, Lena Cowen, ed. *Othello.* New York: Palgrave Macmillan, 2004. Collects leading essays since 1990, mostly on gender and marriage (Berger, Bristol, Sinfield) or race and reception (Bartels, Singh, Hodgdon, Albanese).

Vaughan, Virginia Mason. *Performing Blackness on English Stages, 1500–1800.* Cambridge: Cambridge UP, 2005. Reviews *Othello*'s stage and screen history, arguing that the text metatheatrically refers to blackface performance—a tradition that emphasizes the actor's artifice and raises ideological problems opposite to those of a black actor's apparently authentic impersonation.

Vitkus, Daniel. *Turning Turk: English Theater and the Multicultural Mediterranean, 1570–1630.* New York: Palgrave Macmillan, 2003. Argues for a Turkish Othello, emblematic of the Ottoman threat to Christian Europe, associated with unbridled sexuality and to some extent racial otherness—a position undermined early in the play but subsequently confirmed and resulting in Othello's damnation.

FILMS

Othello. 1952. Dir. Orson Welles. USA. 93 min. This black-and-white film stars Welles as Othello. Famous for its innovative and disorienting camera work more than for its acting.

Othello. 1965. Dir. Stuart Burge and John Dexter. UK. 165 min. Film of a stage performance, with Laurence Olivier as Othello and Maggie Smith as Desdemona.

Notable not only for the white actor's effort fully to impersonate a black African—seen at the time as both troubling and moving—but also for Smith's spirited Desdemona, a break with the prior stage tradition of representing the character as a passive victim.

Othello. 1988. Dir. Janet Suzman. South Africa/UK. 187 min. Film of the controversial South African stage performance (the first with a black African actor and a white actress) that became a form of anti-apartheid protest.

Othello. 1995. Dir. Oliver Parker. USA/UK. 123 min. First version made for film with an African American, Laurence Fishburne, as Othello. Kenneth Branagh as Iago dominates the play (as often happens with Iago). Ironically, racial issues are muted.

O. 2001. Dir. Tim Blake Nelson. USA. 95 min. Set in a contemporary high school, centered on a basketball player, Odin (Mekhi Phifer), in love with Desi (Julia Stiles), undone by Hugo (Josh Hartnett); also with Martin Sheen.

TEXTUAL INTRODUCTION

Othello's uncertain textual history shows the fluid processes by which a play moved between stage and printed page. *Othello* was written ca. 1601–03, and its first recorded performance was at court on November 1, 1604. Despite at least two revivals, at Oxford in 1610 and at court in 1612–13, *Othello* was not published during Shakespeare's lifetime. Twenty years after its composition, however, it was printed in swift succession in two distinct forms. It was entered in the Stationers' Register (the list of plays to be printed) on October 6, 1621, by the bookseller and publisher Thomas Walkley, who brought it out the following year. The play survives in two printed versions: Walkley's 1622 Quarto and the First Folio of 1623. No manuscript survives, and editors have expended considerable effort in trying to establish the relationships between the printed texts and whatever lost manuscripts may lie behind them, as well as their sequence of composition.

Othello's two early texts differ in ways that cumulatively seem significant. Perhaps the most obvious difference is found in 4.3. In the Folio, 4.3 contains dialogue, the "Willow Song," and Emilia's speech on husbands, all of which are missing from the Quarto. There has been speculation that the song was cut from the Quarto because when that text was solidified, the company lacked an actor—Desdemona was probably played by an adolescent male—capable of singing the part. (This casting issue has been used to support a proposed date of composition in 1602 rather than later [Honigmann 346–50]). The Folio's other unique passages include Desdemona's protestation of her innocence at 4.2.150–63 and Roderigo's account of Othello and Desdemona's elopement, when he famously describes Othello as "an extravagant and wheeling stranger" (1.1.132).

Most of the thousands of differences, though, are small. They are found at the most basic level: punctuation (the Quarto uses commas and colons, while the Folio favors periods); oaths (the Quarto is peppered with them, the Folio has few); and some seemingly arbitrary alternative choices (e.g., the Quarto's *coloquintida* is "acerb" [1.3.324–25], while the Folio's, less colorfully, is "bitter" [1.3.337–38]). These small differences slowly build to create two subtly different plays. So, for instance, when Othello describes at F 1.3.159 the "world of kisses" Desdemona gives him, she is characterized as more sexually active than the woman who offers him "a world of sighs" (Q 1.3.146). In all, the Folio has around 160 lines not in the Quarto; the Quarto, in its turn, has several unique lines.

Uncertainty about the history and nature of the two texts continues; each suggests a different relationship to the playhouse and to Shakespeare, and these differences may also reveal that while the two were published close in time, they derive from different periods in the play's life. The Folio, it has been argued, comes from a scribe's transcription of Shakespeare's own "fair copy" (Honigmann 1). Unique passages in the Folio, such as Othello's speech at 3.3.447–54, are thought to preserve Shakespeare's "second thoughts," though filtered by the work of a scribe who made changes of his own (Honigmann 58–76). When precisely these changes were made is unclear.

There is even less agreement about the history of the Quarto. The Quarto has much fuller stage directions than does the Folio, which suggests that it is at least partly the product of the early modern theater. Scott McMillin proposes that the Quarto derives from a scribe's transcription of a prompt book from a later Jacobean revival—even possibly after Shakespeare's death—and that the missing sections were cut to meet the constraints of performance (7–8). Following this logic, differences such as the Quarto's "muttering" (3.3.67) for the Folio's rare "mammering" (3.3.68) might be actors' adaptations. This would bring the Quarto very close to the stage indeed, although as Lukas Erne argues, the Quarto still might retain more of the play than just what was performed (183–84). Other scholars, while agreeing that the Quarto is a scribal copy, instead propose that it derives from Shakespeare's own draft manuscript or "foul papers"—not necessarily the same manuscript that gave us the Folio (Honigmann 1)—thereby drawing the Quarto closer to Shakespeare and in fact suggesting that the text it contains is earlier—not, as is normally assumed, later—than that of the Folio. One theory enshrines the author, the other collaborative theater: neither is watertight.

The differing history of the two texts may, in part, explain their differences in lineation. The Quarto's lineation has often been criticized as substandard. However, it has many more short lines that can be read as shared lines than does the Folio. McMillin proposes that these short lines, many clearly misplaced in the middle of speeches, are the result of a listening scribe mistakenly anticipating the end of an actor's speech. Nevertheless, the Folio also has lineation problems, sometimes making odd divisions between verse and prose. The Folio sets Iago's misogynistic proverbs at 2.1.108–11 as prose, though they fall neatly enough into slightly irregular iambic pentameter lines; in *The Norton Shakespeare* they are set as verse. The Quarto, too, also sometimes mistakes the shift between prose and verse, as in Cassio's lament over his "reputation" at 2.3.242–44. Here the Quarto mistakenly continues the verse form of the previous passage before belatedly shifting into prose at line 245; in *The Norton Shakespeare* the speech is all set as prose.

The two distinct forms of *Othello* reflect different moments in the play's development, and each has a coherent logic. Most editors use the Folio as their base text, drawing from the Quarto when the Folio seems corrupt or inadequate. The Folio apparently preserves more of the play and is probably closer to Shakespeare's final thoughts. The Quarto, however, may transmit a version that was seen on the stage in Shakespeare's time. Consequently, *The Norton Shakespeare* offers an edition of the Folio in the print volume and editions of both texts in the Digital Edition, in each case preserving distinctive features wherever possible.

CLARE MCMANUS

TEXTUAL BIBLIOGRAPHY

Erne, Lukas. *Shakespeare as a Literary Dramatist*. Cambridge: Cambridge UP, 2003.
Honigmann, E. A. J. *The Texts of "Othello" and Shakespearian Revision*. London: Routledge, 1996.
McMillin, Scott, ed. *The First Quarto of "Othello."* Cambridge: Cambridge UP, 2001.

PERFORMANCE NOTE

Directors of *Othello* make critical decisions respecting the protagonist's assimilation and acceptance in Venice. Through choices of accent, expression, costume, and bearing, Othello can appear a well-acclimated emigrant or an insecure outsider; a dignified general or a repressed brute; a sincere Christian or a heathen—and the Venetians can treat the Moor with earnest respect, grudging tolerance, or contempt. Race is often (but not always) a major factor: Othello can appear suspicious or confrontational because of perceived slights over his skin color, or basically indifferent to them; Iago and Brabanzio can be conspicuous bigots or voices of the majority. Productions must further decide whether Cyprus is an extension of a palpably racist Venice or a refuge of civility, and whether the Venetian military represents a shield from Turkish invaders or a violent occupation in its own right.

Another prominent consideration in performance is Iago's motivation for villainy. Productions regularly implicate envy of Cassio, racism, homoerotic desire, or psychotic ambition; some, though, obscure his motives altogether, thus harnessing uncertainties that deepen the tragic outcome. Whatever the choice, Iago is consistently a favorite of audiences, who are teasingly made complicit in his treachery through his use of direct address and uncanny blend of humor, improvisation, and menace. Productions therefore face the challenge of facilitating his unique theatrical power without sidelining Othello and (effectively) his tragedy. Creating genuine sexual chemistry between Othello and Desdemona, thereby raising the stakes of what is lost, and exhibiting Othello's extremes of character (brutality and heroism, jealousy and tenderness, impulsiveness and eloquence) without qualifications, can help the Moor emerge as the clear star of the final acts. Desdemona must likewise maintain theatrical interest alongside Emilia, another audience favorite. Actors are challenged to portray the "fair warrior" who stands up to her father and banters with Iago, then convincingly sustain the persona despite her naïveté and apparent willing subjection to her persecutor in the late acts.

Emilia, for her part, can variously balance roles as wife, waiting woman, and confidante; treat Desdemona with sisterly tenderness or a rival's jealousy; suspect Iago from the beginning or seem desperate for his affection. Cassio can be an entitled intellectual or a modest soldier; Roderigo, a fop or a site of unexpected pathos; Brabanzio, comic in his ranting or gravely prophetic; Bianca, a savvy prostitute or an unfortunate innocent, a Venetian who chases the soldiers to Cypress or a Cypriot preyed upon by them. Other considerations in performance include Othello's race and religion (Digital Edition PC 1); managing the play's "double" time schemes; fixing the point at which Othello is convinced of the supposed adultery; motivating Emilia's participation in Iago's deception (PC 6); and solving problems posed by Desdemona's bed and Othello's third weapon (PC 7).

BRETT GAMBOA

The Tragedy of Othello, the Moor of Venice

THE PERSONS OF THE PLAY

OTHELLO, the Moor
BRABANZIO, father to Desdemona
DESDEMONA, wife to Othello
IAGO, a villain
EMILIA, wife to Iago
RODERIGO, a gulled gentleman
DUKE of Venice
MONTANO, Governor of Cyprus
Michael CASSIO, an honorable lieutenant
BIANCA, a courtesan
LODOVICO
GRAZIANO } two noble Venetians
FIRST SENATOR
SECOND SENATOR
OFFICERS
SAILOR
MESSENGERS
GENTLEMEN of Cyprus
HERALD
MUSICIANS
CLOWN
Servants, Attendants

1.1 (Q 1.1)

Enter RODERIGO *and* IAGO.[1]

RODERIGO   Never tell me!° I take it much unkindly   *(annoyance; disbelief)*
  That thou, Iago, who hast had my purse
  As if the strings were thine, shouldst know of this.
IAGO   But you'll not hear me. If ever I did dream
  Of such a matter, abhor me.
5 RODERIGO   Thou told'st me
  Thou didst hold him in thy hate.
IAGO   Despise me[2]
  If I do not. Three great ones of the city,
  In personal suit to make me his lieutenant,
  Off-capped° to him—and, by the faith of man,   *Took off their caps*
10 I know my price: I am worth no worse a place—
  But he, as loving his own pride and purposes,
  Evades them with a bombast circumstance[3]
  Horribly stuffed with epithets of war;°   *military jargon*

1.1 Location: A street in Venice.
1. Iago's name may be related to Santiago Matamoros, St. James the Moor Slayer, the patron saint of Spain. The potential irony lies in having a character with a foreign-sounding name express hatred for foreigners on behalf of Venice.
2. *abhor, hate, Despise* (lines 4–6): The language of

animosity here, largely undirected toward particular objects or persons, may suggest something about Iago or even the world of the play.
3. With an inflated circumlocution. *bombast:* cotton padding in clothes, a metaphor running through "stuffed" (line 13), and possibly "suit" (line 8) and "Nonsuits" (line 14).

Nonsuits° my mediators. For, "Certes,"° says he,   *Denies / Certainly*
15   "I have already chose my officer."
  And what was he?
  Forsooth, a great arithmetician:[4]
  One Michael Cassio, a Florentine,°   *(hence, a foreigner)*
  A fellow almost damned in a fair wife,[5]
20   That° never set a squadron in the field,   *Who*
  Nor the division° of a battle° knows   *ordering / battalion*
  More than a spinster°—unless the bookish theoric,°   *housewife / learning*
  Wherein the tonguèd consuls can propose[6]
  As masterly as he! Mere prattle without practice
25   Is all his soldiership. But he, sir, had th'election
  And I—of whom his° eyes had seen the proof   *(Othello's)*
  At Rhodes, at Cyprus, and on others' grounds,
  Christened and heathen—must be be-leed° and calmed°   *without wind / becalmed*
  By debitor and creditor. This counter-caster,[7]
30   He, in good time,° must his lieutenant be   *in timely fashion (ironic)*
  And I, bless the mark,° his moorship's ensign.[8]   *God help us*
RODERIGO   By heaven, I rather would have been his hangman!
IAGO   Why, there's no remedy. 'Tis the curse of service:
  Preferment goes by letter and affection[9]
35   And not by old gradation,° where each second   *traditional seniority*
  Stood heir to th' first. Now, sir, be judge yourself
  Whether I in any just term am affined°   *am bound in any just way*
  To love the Moor.[1]
RODERIGO   I would not follow him, then.
IAGO   O sir, content you!°   *be content*
40   I follow him to serve my turn upon him.°   *serve my own interests*
  We cannot all be masters, nor all masters
  Cannot be truly followed. You shall mark
  Many a duteous and knee-crooking° knave   *(servilely) knee-bending*
  That, doting on his own obsequious bondage,
45   Wears out his time,° much like his master's ass,   *Spends his years serving*
  For naught but provender,° and when he's old—cashiered.°   *animal feed / fired*
  Whip me° such honest knaves! Others there are   *I'd have whipped*
  Who, trimmed° in forms and visages of duty,   *outwardly decorated*
  Keep yet their hearts attending on themselves
50   And, throwing but shows of service on their lords,
  Do well thrive by them° and, when they have lined their°   *("shows," "lords") / (own)*
    coats,
  Do themselves homage. These fellows have some soul
  And such a one do I profess myself. For, sir,
  It is as sure as you are Roderigo,
55   Were I the Moor, I would not be Iago:[2]

---

4. Implying that Cassio's knowledge of war is purely theoretical.
5. Obscure. Cassio has not yet met Bianca and is unmarried, although in Shakespeare's source he is. Perhaps Shakespeare's error, a reference to Cassio as a ladies' man, or an oblique, debatable anticipation of the main plot.
6. In which the talkative political leaders (of ancient Rome, but referring to modern Italy) can debate.
7. *debitor and creditor, counter-caster:* pejorative terms for an accountant (Cassio).
8. As "ensign," Iago is something like a standard-bearer or third-in-command, ranking below "lieuten-ant" Cassio, the second-in-command. "His moorship": the first indication of whom Iago is complaining about.
9. Promotion comes through connections and favoritism.
1. TEXTUAL COMMENT For possible meanings of "Moor," see Digital Edition TC 1 (Folio edited text).
2. If I could have Othello's status, I would not want my own position. Or: if I were a person of Othello's (nobler) character—but occupied my current rank—I would not behave so self-servingly. The line perhaps also suggests both a deeper self-loathing and identification with Othello.

In following him, I follow but myself.
Heaven is my judge: not I for° love and duty,   *I am not driven by*
But seeming so for my peculiar° end.   *personal*
For when my outward action doth demonstrate
60   The native act and figure[3] of my heart
In complement extern,° 'tis not long after   *outward appearance*
But I will wear my heart upon my sleeve
For daws° to peck at. I am not what I am.[4]   *crowlike birds*

RODERIGO   What a full fortune does the thicklips owe°   *own*
If he can carry't thus?°   *succeed*
65   IAGO   Call up her° father: *(Desdemona's)*
Rouse him,[5] make after° him, poison his delight,   *hound*
Proclaim° him in the streets, incense her kinsmen,   *criminally accuse*
And, though he in a fertile climate dwell,
Plague him with flies. Though that his joy be joy,[6]
70   Yet throw such chances of vexation on't
As it may lose some color.[7]

RODERIGO   Here is her father's house. I'll call aloud.

IAGO   Do, with like timorous accent° and dire yell   *frightening tone*
As when, by night and negligence, the fire
75   Is spied in populous cities.

RODERIGO   What ho, Brabanzio! Signor Brabanzio, ho!

IAGO   Awake! What ho, Brabanzio! Thieves! Thieves!
Look to your house, your daughter, and your bags!
Thieves! Thieves!

[*Enter*] BRABANZIO *above.*

80   BRABANZIO   What is the reason of this terrible summons?
What is the matter there?

RODERIGO   Signor, is all your family within?

IAGO   Are your doors locked?

BRABANZIO   Why? Wherefore ask you this?

IAGO   Sir, you're robbed. For shame, put on your gown.
85   Your heart is burst; you have lost half your soul:
Even now, now, very now, an old black ram[8]
Is tupping° your white ewe. Arise! Arise!   *copulating with*
Awake the snorting° citizens with the bell,   *snoring*
Or else the devil will make a grandsire of you.
Arise, I say!

90   BRABANZIO   What, have you lost your wits?

RODERIGO   Most reverend signor, do you know my voice?

BRABANZIO   Not I. What are you?

RODERIGO   My name is Roderigo.

BRABANZIO   The worser welcome.
I have charged thee not to haunt about my doors:

---

3. The internal operation (or motivation) and shape (or nature).
4. Probably: I am not in essence what I seem in appearance, or the opposite, though it comes to the same thing: I am not in appearance what I am in essence. Either way, the language reverses God's "I am what I am" (Exodus 3:14), while perhaps indicating Iago's divided self. See also 1.1.55 and n., 4.1.257–59 and n., 5.2.277, 5.2.296 and n., and Introduction.
5. *him, his, he* (lines 66–69): The pronouns can refer

either to Brabanzio, Desdemona's father, or to Othello, seemingly moving from the former to the latter as the passage proceeds.
6. Though his joy is real; also consistent with Iago's evocation of false equivalences (lines 55, 63).
7. Basis, plausibility, rationale, sign of good health; but perhaps more literally anticipating "old black ram" (line 86).
8. Connoting animalistic, monstrous, diabolical (horned) sexuality.

95 In honest plainness thou hast heard me say
   My daughter is not for thee, and now in madness,
   Being full of supper and distempering draughts,°   *inebriating beverages*
   Upon malicious knavery dost thou come
   To start° my quiet?   *upset*
RODERIGO   Sir! Sir! Sir!
BRABANZIO   But thou must needs be sure:
100 My spirits and my place° have in their power   *rank*
   To make this bitter to thee.
RODERIGO   Patience, good sir.
BRABANZIO   What, tell'st thou me of robbing?
   This is Venice: my house is not a grange.°   *country house*
RODERIGO   Most grave Brabanzio,
105 In simple and pure soul I come to you—
IAGO   Sir, you are one of those that will not serve God if the
   devil bid you! Because we come to do you service and you
   think we are ruffians, you'll have your daughter covered with a
   Barbary horse;[9] you'll have your nephews° neigh to you; you'll   *grandsons*
110 have coursers for cousins and jennets for germans.[1]
BRABANZIO   What profane wretch art thou?
IAGO   I am one, sir, that comes to tell you your daughter and
   the Moor are making the beast with two backs.°   *copulating*
BRABANZIO   Thou art a villain!
IAGO   You are a senator.[2]
115 BRABANZIO   —This thou shalt answer:° I know thee, Roderigo.   *answer for*
RODERIGO   Sir, I will answer anything. But, I beseech you,
   If't be your pleasure and most wise consent[3]
   —As partly I find it is—that your fair daughter
   At this odd even° and dull° watch o'th' night   *(near midnight) / sleepy*
120 Transported with no worse nor better guard
   But with a knave of common° hire, a gondolier,   *public*
   To the gross clasps of a lascivious Moor—
   If this be known to you and your allowance,°   *allowed by you*
   We then have done you bold and saucy° wrongs.   *impudent*
125 But if you know not this, my manners tell me
   We have your wrong rebuke. Do not believe
   That, from° the sense of all civility,   *in opposition to*
   I thus would play and trifle with your reverence.
   Your daughter—if you have not given her leave,
130 I say again—hath made a gross° revolt,   *foul; brazen*
   Tying her duty, beauty, wit, and fortunes
   In an extravagant° and wheeling° stranger   *vagrant / resltess*
   Of here and everywhere. Straight° satisfy yourself: *Immediately*
   If she be in her chamber or your house,
135 Let loose on me the justice of the state
   For thus deluding you.
BRABANZIO [*to Servants within*]   Strike on the tinder,° ho!   *A light*
   Give me a taper!° Call up all my people!   *candle*

---

9. Horse from northwest coastal Africa; an Arab; suggesting Berbers or barbarians; *covered:* (sexually). 1. *coursers:* strong horses. *cousins:* kinsmen. *jennets:* small Spanish horses. *germans:* close relatives.

2. *villain:* criminal; peasant. *senator:* ironically respectful, but perhaps also suggesting that both attributions are accurate.
3. Lines 117–33 do not appear in Q.

[*aside*] This accident° is not unlike my dream; — event
Belief of it oppresses me already.
—Light, I say! Light! — *Exit* [*above*].

140 IAGO [*to* RODERIGO]   Farewell, for I must leave you.
It seems not meet° nor wholesome to my place — proper
To be produced°—as, if I stay, I shall— — presented as witness
Against the Moor. For I do know the state,
However this may gall him with some check,° — reprimand
145 Cannot with safety cast° him: for he's embarked° — dismiss / committed
With such loud reason° to the Cyprus wars, — vociferous, just support
Which even now stand in act° that, for° their souls, — are taking place / to save
Another of his fathom° they have none — caliber
To lead their business. In which regard,
150 Though I do hate him as I do hell pains,
Yet, for necessity of present life,° — livelihood
I must show out a flag and sign of love,
Which is indeed but sign. That you shall surely find him,
Lead to the Sagittary⁴ the raisèd search,° — awakened searchers
155 And there will I be with him. So, farewell. — *Exit.*
    Enter BRABANZIO *with Servants and torches.*
BRABANZIO   It is too true an evil: gone she is,
And what's to come of my despisèd time° — lifetime
Is naught but bitterness. Now, Roderigo,
Where didst thou see her? —O unhappy girl!
160 —With the Moor, say'st thou? —Who would be a father?
—How didst thou know 'twas she? —Oh, she deceives me
Past thought! —What said she to you? [*to Servants*] Get more
    tapers!
Raise all my kindred! —Are they married, think you?
RODERIGO   Truly, I think they are.
BRABANZIO   O heaven!
165 How got she out? Oh, treason of the blood!
Fathers, from hence trust not your daughters' minds
By what you see them act. Is there not charms° — magic
By which the property° of youth and maidhood° — nature / virginity
May be abused? Have you not read, Roderigo,
Of some such thing?
170 RODERIGO   Yes, sir, I have indeed.
BRABANZIO [*to Servants*]   Call up my brother! —Oh, would you
    had had her!
[*to Servants*] Some one way, some another. —Do you know
Where we may apprehend her and the Moor?
RODERIGO   I think I can discover him, if you please
175 To get good guard and go along with me.
BRABANZIO   Pray you, lead on. At every house I'll call:
I may command° at most.° [*to Servants*] Get — demand help / most of them
    weapons, ho!
And raise some special officers of might.
—On, good Roderigo: I will deserve° your pains.   *Exeunt.* — reward

---

4. Perhaps indicating an inn named for the astrological sign Sagittarius, where Othello and Desdemona are staying. It may also suggest Othello himself, since Sagittarius is depicted as a centaur (a mythological being part man, part horse), and Iago has already likened Othello to a "Barbary horse."

1.2 (Q 1.2)

Enter OTHELLO, IAGO, [*and*] *Attendants with torches.*

IAGO   Though in the trade of war I have slain men,
  Yet do I hold it very stuff° o'th' conscience   *essence*
  To do no contrived° murder. I lack iniquity   *premeditated*
  Sometime to do me service: nine or ten times
5   I had thought t'have yerked° him here under the ribs.   *struck with a dagger*
OTHELLO   'Tis better as it is.
IAGO   Nay, but he prated
  And spoke such scurvy and provoking terms
  Against your honor
  That, with the little godliness I have,
10   I did full hard forbear him.[1] But I pray you, sir,
  Are you fast° married? Be assured of this: *legitimately*
  That the magnifico° is much beloved,   *(Brabanzio)*
  And hath in his effect a voice potential°   *powerful*
  As double as the Duke's.[2] He will divorce you,
15   Or put upon you what restraint or grievance
  The law, with all his might to enforce it on,
  Will give him cable.°   *rope; scope*
OTHELLO   Let him do his spite:[3]
  My services which I have done the signory°   *Venetian government*
  Shall out-tongue his complaints. 'Tis yet to know°—   *It has never been shown*
20   Which, when I know that boasting is an honor,
  I shall promulgate—I fetch my life and being
  From men of royal siege,° and my demerits°   *rank / deserts*
  May speak unbonneted° to as proud a fortune   *with(out?) deference*
  As this that I have reached. For know, Iago,
25   But that° I love the gentle Desdemona,   *But for the fact that*
  I would not my unhousèd° free condition   *unconfined*
  Put into circumscription and confine
  For the sea's worth—

Enter CASSIO [*and* OFFICERS] *with torches.*

              But look, what lights come yond?°   *yonder*
IAGO   Those are the raisèd father and his friends.
  You were best go in.
30 OTHELLO   Not I: I must be found.
  My parts,° my title, and my perfect soul[4]   *qualities*
  Shall manifest me rightly. Is it they?
IAGO   By Janus,° I think no.   *two-faced Roman god*
OTHELLO   The servants of the Duke's? And my lieutenant?
35   —The goodness of the night upon you, friends.
  What is the news?
CASSIO   The Duke does greet you, general,
  And he requires your haste-post-haste appearance
  Even on the instant.
OTHELLO   What is the matter, think you?
CASSIO   Something from Cyprus, as I may divine.
40   It is a business of some heat:° the galleys   *urgency*
  Have sent a dozen sequent° messengers   *successive*

1.2 Location: Another street in Venice, before Othello's lodgings.
1. I barely restrained myself from attacking him.
2. Like the Duke's, Brabanzio's influence is twice as great as that of any other senator.

3. PERFORMANCE COMMENT For the importance of Othello's physical appearance in this, his first, scene, as well as multiple options open to directors, see Digital Edition PC 1.
4. My clear conscience.

This very night at one another's heels,
And many of the consuls, raised and met,
Are at the Duke's already. You have been hotly called for:
45   When, being not at your lodging to be found,
The Senate hath sent about three several quests
To search you out.[5]

OTHELLO   'Tis well I am found by you.
I will but spend a word here in the house,
And go with you.   [*Exit.*]

CASSIO   Ensign, what makes he here?
50   IAGO   Faith, he tonight hath boarded a land carrack:°   *large merchant ship*
If it prove lawful prize, he's made for ever.

CASSIO   I do not understand.

IAGO   He's married.

CASSIO   To who?

IAGO   Marry,° to—   *By Mary (wordplay)*
        [*Enter* OTHELLO.]
    [*to* OTHELLO]   Come, captain, will you go?

OTHELLO   Have with you.°   *Let's go*
    Enter BRABANZIO, RODERIGO, *with* OFFICERS
    and torches.

CASSIO   Here comes another troop to seek for you.
55   IAGO   It is Brabanzio. —General, be advised:
He comes to bad intent.

OTHELLO [*to* BRABANZIO *and* RODERIGO]   Holla, stand there!

RODERIGO   Signor, it is the Moor.

BRABANZIO   Down with him, thief!

IAGO [*drawing*]   You, Roderigo! Come, sir, I am for you.

OTHELLO   Keep up° your bright swords, for the dew will rust   *Put away*
    them.
60   [*to* BRABANZIO] Good signor, you shall more command with
        years
Than with your weapons.

BRABANZIO   O thou foul° thief! Where hast thou stowed my   *(ethically); (in color)*
        daughter?
Damned as thou art, thou hast enchanted her:
For I'll refer me to all things of sense,[6]
65   If she in chains of magic were not bound,
Whether a maid, so tender, fair, and happy,
So opposite to marriage that she shunned
The wealthy curlèd darling° of our nation,   *darlings*
Would ever have, t'incur a general mock,
70   Run from her guardage to the sooty bosom
Of such a thing as thou—to fear, not to delight.
Judge me the world if 'tis not gross in sense[7]
That thou hast practiced on her with foul charms,
Abused her delicate youth with drugs or minerals
75   That waken motion.[8] I'll have't disputed on:°   *argued; looked into*
'Tis probable, and palpable to thinking.

---

5. Cassio's speech suggests that the issue of Cyprus is a surprise to him and apparently to the Senate and Othello as well. But Iago (1.1.143–49) has already acknowledged that Othello is crucial to Venice's dealings with Cyprus. Either the point here is the immediacy of the danger or, more likely, the two passages are not fully harmonized.
6. For I'll refer the matter to all rational beings.
7. Let the world judge me if it is not patently obvious. Lines 72–77 do not appear in Q.
8. Mental agitation.

I therefore apprehend and do attach° thee   *arrest*
For an abuser of the world, a practicer
Of arts inhibited and out of warrant.°   *prohibited and illegal*
80 [*to* OFFICERS] Lay hold upon him. If he do resist,
 Subdue him at his peril.
OTHELLO   Hold your hands,
 Both you of my inclining° and the rest!   *following*
 Were it my cue to fight, I should have known it
 Without a prompter. [*to* BRABANZIO] Whither will you that I go
 To answer this your charge?
85 BRABANZIO   To prison, till fit time
 Of law and course of direct session°   *court session*
 Call thee to answer.
OTHELLO   What if I do obey?
 How may the Duke be therewith satisfied,
 Whose messengers are here about my side
90 Upon some present business of the state
 To bring me to him?
OFFICER   'Tis true, most worthy signor:
 The Duke's in council, and your noble self,
 I am sure, is sent for.
BRABANZIO   How? The Duke in council?
 In this time of the night? Bring him away!°   *along*
95 Mine's not an idle cause. The Duke himself,
 Or any of my brothers of the state,
 Cannot but feel this wrong as 'twere their own:
 For if such actions may have passage free,
 Bondslaves and pagans[9] shall our statesmen be.   *Exeunt.*

1.3 (Q 1.3)
Enter DUKE, [FIRST *and* SECOND] SENATORS,
and OFFICERS.

DUKE There's no composition in this news
 That gives them credit.[1]
FIRST SENATOR   Indeed, they are disproportioned:°   *inconsistent*
 My letters say a hundred and seven galleys—
DUKE And mine a hundred forty—
SECOND SENATOR   And mine two hundred.
5 But though they jump not on a just account°—   *don't exactly agree*
 As in these cases where the aim reports,
 'Tis oft with difference[2]—yet do they all confirm
 A Turkish fleet, and bearing up to Cyprus.
DUKE Nay, it is possible enough to judgment:°   *if one judges rationally*
10 I do not so secure me in the error
 But the main article I do approve
 In fearful sense.[3]
SAILOR (*within*)   What ho! What ho! What ho!
    Enter SAILOR.
OFFICER A messenger from the galleys.

---

9. Implicitly accusing Othello of being both slave and non-Christian, though he is neither.
1.3 Location: A Venetian council room.
1. *There is . . . credit:* The reports lack the consistency that would make them believable.

2. *where . . . difference:* where the reports are estimates, there are often discrepancies among them.
3. *I do not . . . sense:* I am not so reassured by the discrepancies as to dismiss the main concern—the approach of the Turkish fleet.

DUKE   —Now, what's the business?

SAILOR   The Turkish preparation° makes for Rhodes: *battle-ready fleet*
15   So was I bid report here to the state
        By Signor Angelo.[4]

DUKE [*to* SENATORS]   How say you by this change?

FIRST SENATOR   This cannot be
        By no assay° of reason: 'tis a pageant   *test*
        To keep us in false gaze. When we consider
20   Th'importancy of Cyprus to the Turk,
        And let ourselves again but understand
        That as it more concerns the Turk than Rhodes,
        So may he with more facile question bear it,[5]
        For that it stands not in such warlike brace,
25   But altogether lacks th'abilities
        That Rhodes is dressed in. If we make thought of this,
        We must not think the Turk is so unskillful
        To leave that latest° which concerns him first,   *last*
        Neglecting an attempt of ease and gain
30   To wake and wage° a danger profitless.   *risk*

DUKE   Nay, in all confidence, he's not for Rhodes.

OFFICER   Here is more news.
                Enter a MESSENGER.

MESSENGER   The Ottomites,° reverend and gracious,°   *Turks / (the Senators)*
        Steering with due course toward the isle of Rhodes,
35   Have there injointed them with an after° fleet.   *joined with another*

FIRST SENATOR   Ay, so I thought. How many, as you guess?

MESSENGER   Of thirty sail. And now they do restem°   *retrace*
        Their backward course, bearing with frank appearance
        Their purposes toward Cyprus. Signor Montano,
40   Your trusty and most valiant servitor,
        With his free duty recommends you thus,[6]
        And prays you to believe him.

DUKE   'Tis certain, then, for Cyprus.
        Marcus Luccicos,[7] is not he in town?

45 FIRST SENATOR   He's now in Florence.

DUKE   Write from us to him, post-post-haste.—Dispatch!
                [*Exeunt* MESSENGER *and* SAILOR.]

FIRST SENATOR   Here comes Brabanzio and the valiant Moor.
                Enter BRABANZIO, OTHELLO, CASSIO, IAGO, RODERIGO,
                and OFFICERS.

DUKE   Valiant Othello, we must straight° employ you   *immediately*
        Against the general enemy° Ottoman.   *(of all Christendom)*
50   [*to* BRABANZIO] I did not see you. Welcome, gentle° signor;   *noble*
        We lacked your counsel and your help tonight.

BRABANZIO   So did I yours. Good your grace, pardon me:
        Neither my place° nor aught I heard of business   *official duty*
        Hath raised me from my bed; nor doth the general care
55   Take hold on me, for my particular grief
        Is of so floodgate° and o'er-bearing nature   *drenching*
        That it engluts and swallows other sorrows,

---

4. Not mentioned elsewhere in the play, Angelus Sorianus was a Venetian sea captain who received the Venetian ambassador bearing from Constantinople the Turkish ultimatum to surrender Cyprus shortly before its capture by the Turks in 1571.

5. So also can the Turkish fleet more easily win it. Lines 24–30 are not in Q.
6. With his freely given loyalty reports to you thus.
7. Not mentioned elsewhere in the play.

And it is still itself.[8]

DUKE   Why, what's the matter?

BRABANZIO   My daughter! Oh, my daughter!

FIRST *and* SECOND SENATORS   Dead?

BRABANZIO   Ay—to me.

60   She is abused,° stol'n from me, and corrupted°   deluded / harmed bodily
      By spells and medicines bought of mountebanks:°   quacks
      For nature so preposterously° to err,   monstrously
      Being not deficient, blind, or lame of sense,
      Sans° witchcraft could not.   Without

65   DUKE   Whoe'er he be that in this foul proceeding
      Hath thus beguiled your daughter of herself
      And you of her, the bloody book of law
      You shall yourself read in the bitter letter
      After your own sense, yea, though our proper son
70   Stood in your action.[9]

BRABANZIO   Humbly I thank your grace.
      Here is the man: this Moor, whom now it seems
      Your special mandate for the state affairs
      Hath hither brought.

FIRST *and* SECOND SENATORS   We are very sorry for't.

DUKE [*to* OTHELLO]   What in your own part can you say to this?

75   BRABANZIO   Nothing, but this is so.

OTHELLO   Most potent, grave, and reverend signors,
      My very noble and approved° good masters: proven; experienced
      That I have ta'en away this old man's daughter,
      It is most true; true I have married her.
80   The very head and front° of my offending   height and breadth
      Hath this extent, no more. Rude° am I in my speech,   Unpolished
      And little blessed with the soft phrase of peace
      For, since these arms of mine had seven years' pith°   strength
      Till now some nine moons wasted,° they have used   nine months ago
85   Their dearest° action in the tented° field,   most valued / military
      And little of this great world can I speak
      More than pertains to feats of broils° and battle;   combats
      And, therefore, little shall I grace my cause
      In speaking for myself. Yet, by your gracious patience,
90   I will a round° unvarnished tale deliver   plain
      Of my whole course of love: what° drugs, what charms,   with what
      What conjuration, and what mighty magic—
      For such proceeding I am charged withal°—   with
      I won his daughter.

BRABANZIO   A maiden never bold,
95   Of spirit so still and quiet that her motion
      Blushed at herself;[1] and she, in spite of nature,
      Of years, of country, credit,° everything,   reputation
      To fall in love with what she feared to look on?
      It is a judgment maimed and most imperfect
100   That will confess perfection so could err
      Against all rules of nature, and must° be driven   (we therefore) must

---

8. *That . . . itself*: That my "grief" can incorporate
other "sorrows" without being affected.
9. *You shall . . . action*: You yourself shall interpret
the law as you see fit even if you are accusing my

own son.
1. *her . . . herself*: she blushed at her slightest display
of emotion.

To find out practices of cunning hell
Why this should be. I therefore vouch again
That with some mixtures powerful o'er the blood,°   passions
105 Or with some dram conjured° to this effect,   enchanted dose
He wrought upon her.
DUKE   To vouch this is no proof
Without more wider and more overt test
Than these thin habits and poor likelihoods
Of modern seeming do prefer against him.[2]
110 FIRST SENATOR   But, Othello, speak.
Did you by indirect and forcèd courses°   means
Subdue and poison this young maid's affections?
Or came it by request and such fair question°   conversation
As soul to soul affordeth?
OTHELLO   I do beseech you,
115 Send for the lady to the Sagittary,°   (see 1.1.154 and note)
And let her speak of me before her father.
If you do find me foul in her report,
The trust, the office I do hold of you,
Not only take away, but let your sentence
120 Even fall upon my life.
DUKE [to OFFICERS]   Fetch Desdemona hither.
OTHELLO   Ensign, conduct them: you best know the place.
                    [Exeunt IAGO and OFFICERS.]
—And till she come, as truly as to heaven
I do confess the vices of my blood,°   sins of passion
125 So justly to your grave ears I'll present
How I did thrive in this fair lady's love
And she in mine.
DUKE   Say it, Othello.
OTHELLO   Her father loved me, oft invited me,
Still° questioned me the story of my life   Constantly
130 From year to year: the battles, sieges, fortune,
That I have passed.
I ran it through, even from my boyish days
To th' very moment that he bade me tell it,
Wherein I spoke of most disastrous chances;°   events
135 Of moving accidents° by flood and field;   events
Of hairbreadth scapes i'th' imminent deadly breach;[3]
Of being taken by the insolent foe
And sold to slavery; of my redemption thence,
And portance° in my traveler's history;   conduct
140 Wherein of antres° vast and deserts idle,   caves
Rough quarries, rocks, hills whose head touch heaven,
It was my hint° to speak—such was my process°—   occasion / story
And of the cannibals that each other eat—
The Anthropophagi[4]—and men whose heads
145 Grew beneath their shoulders. These things to hear

---

2. *Without . . . him*: Without fuller and more direct testimony than mere appearances and conjecture based on current, shallow popular beliefs tell against him.
3. In the deadly gaps in a fortification.
4. Man-eaters. The term is from the ancient Roman writer Pliny the Elder. Shakespeare was also indebted to the travel literature of the Middle Ages (*Mandeville's Travels*) and the Renaissance (Hakluyt's *Principal Navigations*, among others), as well as to John Pory's English description of Leo Africanus's life in his translation of Leo's *Geographical History* (see the Introduction).

Would Desdemona seriously incline;°   *eagerly lean (listen)*
But still the house affairs would draw her hence,
Which ever as° she could with haste dispatch,   *Whenever*
She'd come again, and with a greedy ear
150   Devour up my discourse. Which I, observing,
Took once a pliant° hour, and found good means   *convenient*
To draw from her a prayer of earnest heart
That I would all my pilgrimage dilate°   *relate*
Whereof by parcels she had something heard
155   But not instinctively.° I did consent,   *naturally*
And often did beguile her of her tears
When I did speak of some distressful stroke
That my youth suffered. My story being done,
She gave me for my pains a world of kisses.[5]
160   She swore, "In faith, 'twas strange, 'twas passing° strange.   *exceptionally*
'Twas pitiful, 'twas wondrous pitiful."
She wished she had not heard it, yet she wished
That heaven had made her such a man.[6] She thanked me
And bade me, if I had a friend that loved her,
165   I should but teach him how to tell my story,
And that would woo her. Upon this hint,° I spake.   *opportunity; suggestion*
She loved me for the dangers I had passed,
And I loved her that she did pity them.
This only is the witchcraft I have used.

        Enter DESDEMONA, IAGO, [*and*] *Attendants.*

170   Here comes the lady. Let her witness it.
DUKE   I think this tale would win my daughter too.
    —Good Brabanzio, take up this mangled matter at the best:°   *as well as you can*
Men do their broken weapons rather use
Than their bare hands.
BRABANZIO   I pray you hear her speak.
175   If she confess that she was half the wooer,
Destruction° on my head if my bad blame   *May destruction fall*
Light on the man. [*to* DESDEMONA] Come hither, gentle
    mistress:
Do you perceive in all this noble company
Where most you owe obedience?
DESDEMONA   My noble father,
180   I do perceive here a divided duty.
To you I am bound for life and education;
My life and education both do learn° me   *teach*
How to respect you. You are the lord of duty;
I am, hitherto, your daughter. But here's my husband,
185   And so much duty as my mother showed
To you, preferring you before her father,
So much I challenge° that I may profess   *assert*
Due to the Moor my lord.
BRABANZIO   God be with you. I have done.
190   [*to* DUKE] Please it, your grace, on to the state affairs.
I had rather to adopt a child than get° it.   *beget*
    [*to* OTHELLO] Come hither, Moor.

---

5. F reads "kisses," Q "sighs." It is hard to explain "kisses" as a textual error.

6. Made such a man for her; made her into such a man.

I here do give thee that with all my heart
Which, but° thou hast already, with all my heart   *except that*
195   I would keep from thee. [*to* DESDEMONA] For your sake, jewel,
I am glad at soul I have no other child,
For thy escape would teach me tyranny,
To hang clogs[7] on them. [*to* DUKE] I have done, my lord.
    DUKE   Let me speak like yourself, and lay a sentence°   *draw a moral*
200   Which as a grece° or step may help these lovers.   *flight of stairs*
"When remedies are past, the griefs are ended
By seeing the worst, which late on hopes depended.[8]
To mourn a mischief that is past and gone
Is the next way to draw new mischief on.
205   What cannot be preserved, when Fortune takes,
Patience her injury a mockery makes.[9]
The robbed that smiles steals something from the thief;
He robs himself that spends a bootless° grief."   *pointless*
    BRABANZIO   So let the Turk of Cyprus us beguile:
210   We lose it not so long as we can smile.
He bears the sentence° well that nothing bears   *saying; judgment*
But the free comfort which from thence he hears;
But he bears both the sentence and the sorrow
That, to pay grief, must of poor patience borrow.
215   These sentences, to sugar or to gall,°   *both sweet and bitter*
Being strong on both sides, are equivocal.°   *equally apt*
But words are words: I never yet did hear
That the bruised heart was piercèd[1] through the ears.
I humbly beseech you, proceed to th'affairs of state.
220   DUKE   The Turk with a most mighty preparation makes for
Cyprus. Othello, the fortitude° of the place is best known to   *military layout*
you, and, though we have there a substitute of most allowed
sufficiency,° yet opinion, a more sovereign mistress of effects,   *known ability*
throws a more safer voice on you.[2] You must therefore be con-
225   tent to slubber° the gloss of your new fortunes with this more   *soil*
stubborn° and boisterous expedition.   *rougher*
    OTHELLO   The tyrant custom, most grave senators,
Hath made the flinty and steel coach° of war   *captain's quarters*
My thrice-driven° bed of down. I do agnize°   *sifted / acknowledge*
230   A natural and prompt alacrity
I find in hardness,° and do undertake   *hardship*
This present war against the Ottomites.
Most humbly, therefore, bending to your state,°   *authority*
I crave fit disposition for my wife,
235   Due reference of place and exhibition[3]
With such accommodation and besort°   *suitable attendance*
As levels with° her breeding.   *fits*
    DUKE   Why, at her father's.
    BRABANZIO   I will not have it so.
    OTHELLO   Nor I.
    DESDEMONA   Nor would I there reside

---

7. Blocks of wood tied to criminals' legs to keep them from escaping.
8. By seeing those things come to pass that caused grief in anticipation, "griefs are ended." The Duke paints the moral in rhyming couplets, to which Brabanzio replies in kind.
9. Patience laughs at what cannot be helped (and thus reduces the "injury").
1. Surgically lanced (and presumably cured).
2. *opinion . . . you:* public opinion, which determines what gets done, finds greater security with you.
3. Proper accommodation and maintenance.

240 To put my father in impatient thoughts
By being in his eye. —Most gracious Duke,
To my unfolding° lend your prosperous° ear,   *proposal / receptive*
And let me find a charter° in your voice   *an authorization*
T'assist my simpleness.
DUKE   What would you, Desdemona?
245 DESDEMONA   That I love the Moor to live with him
My downright violence and storm of fortunes[4]
May trumpet to the world. My heart's subdued
Even to the very quality of my lord.[5]
I saw Othello's visage in his mind,[6]
250 And to his honors and his valiant parts°   *qualities*
Did I my soul and fortunes consecrate—
So that, dear lords, if I be left behind
A moth of peace, and he go to the war,
The rites° for why I love him are bereft me,   *(of love or war); rights*
255 And I a heavy interim shall support°   *have to bear*
By his dear absence. Let me go with him.
OTHELLO   Let her have your voice.°   *agreement*
Vouch with me, heaven, I therefore beg it not
To please the palate of my appetite,
260 Nor to comply with heat° the young affects   *satisfy*
In my defunct and proper satisfaction,[7]
But to be free° and bounteous to her mind.   *liberal*
And heaven defend your good souls that you think
I will your serious and great business scant
265 When she is with me. No, when light-winged toys°   *diversions*
Of feathered Cupid seal° with wanton dullness   *blind*
My speculative and officed instrument[8]
That° my disports° corrupt and taint my business,   *So that / sexual pleasures*
Let housewives make a skillet of my helm,°   *helmet*
270 And all indign° and base adversities   *undignified*
Make head against my estimation.[9]
DUKE   Be it as you shall privately determine,
Either for her stay or going. Th'affair cries haste,
And speed must answer it.
FIRST SENATOR   You must away tonight.
275 OTHELLO   With all my heart.
DUKE   At nine i'th' morning here we'll meet again.
Othello, leave some officer behind,
And he shall our commission bring to you,
And such things else of quality and respect°   *weight and importance*
As doth import° you.   *concern*
280 OTHELLO   So please your grace, my ensign:
A man he is of honesty[1] and trust.

---

4. My strong feelings and assault on the constraints I was fated to endure.
5. *My heart's . . . lord:* I love him for what he is (military, adventurous). Q reads "utmost pleasure" for "very quality"—a formulation that makes Desdemona's response one of subordination rather than of identification, sexual and otherwise.
6. I saw Othello as he sees himself; or: Othello's face expresses his character; or, perhaps: I looked past his outward appearance (age, skin color) to his inner essence.
7. *Nor . . . satisfaction:* Nor to fulfill with passion youthful desires in the performed (though possibly suggesting defectiveness: "defunct") and fitting satisfaction (of marital relations).
8. My duty-bound faculties of sense.
9. Raise an army against my good reputation.
1. The first of many references to Iago's "honesty," all of them deeply ironic, some unwittingly so.

To his conveyance I assign my wife
With what else needful your good grace shall think
To be sent after me.

DUKE   Let it be so.

285   —Good night to everyone. [*to* BRABANZIO] And, noble signor,
If virtue no delighted° beauty lack,   *delightful*
Your son-in-law is far more fair than black.°   *(ethically); (racially)*

FIRST SENATOR   Adieu, brave Moor;[2] use Desdemona well.

BRABANZIO   Look to her,° Moor, if thou hast eyes to see: *Watch her carefully*
290   She has deceived her father, and may thee.

OTHELLO   My life upon her faith.

                  Exeunt [*all except* OTHELLO, DESDEMONA, IAGO,
                                 and RODERIGO].

                      Honest Iago,
My Desdemona must I leave to thee.
I prithee let thy wife attend on her,
And bring them after in the best advantage.[3]

295   —Come, Desdemona, I have but an hour
Of love, of wordly matter, and direction°   *directives*
To spend with thee. We must obey the time.

                   Exeunt [OTHELLO *and* DESDEMONA].

RODERIGO   Iago?

IAGO   What say'st thou, noble heart?

RODERIGO   What will I do, think'st thou?

IAGO   Why, go to bed and sleep.

300   RODERIGO   I will incontinently° drown myself!   *immediately*

IAGO   If thou dost, I shall never love thee after. Why, thou silly
    gentleman!

RODERIGO   It is silliness to live when to live is torment; and then
    have we a prescription° to die when death is our physician.   *right; doctor's order*

305   IAGO   Oh, villainous!° I have looked upon the world for four   *absurd; immoral(?)*
    times seven years and, since I could distinguish betwixt a bene-
    fit and an injury, I never found man that knew how to love
    himself. Ere I would say I would drown myself for the love of a
    guinea hen, I would change my humanity with a baboon.[4]

310   RODERIGO   What should I do? I confess it is my shame to be so
    fond, but it is not in my virtue° to amend it.   *native ability*

IAGO   Virtue? A fig!° 'Tis in ourselves that we are thus, or thus.   *(obscenity)*
    Our bodies are our gardens, to the which our wills are garden-
    ers, so that if we will plant nettles or sow lettuce, set hyssop°   *mint herb*
315   and weed up thyme, supply it with one gender° of herbs or   *type*
    distract it with many, either to have it sterile with idleness° or   *noncultivation*
    manured with industry, why the power and corrigible authority°   *ability to improve*
    of this lies in our wills. If the brain of our lives had not one
    scale of reason to poise° another of sensuality, the blood and   *counterweigh*
320   baseness of our natures would conduct us to most prepos-
    terous conclusions.° But we have reason to cool our raging   *outcomes*
    motions,° our carnal stings, or unbitted° lusts—whereof I take   *impulses / unrestrained*

---

2. **TEXTUAL COMMENT** *Moor* (line 288): an elastic term referring to any or all Muslims, heretics, North Africans, or, by way of general association with blackness, sub-Saharan Africans. Both F and Q foreground Othello's blackness through abusive terms such as "black ram," "sooty bosom," and the like (1.1.86, 1.2.70). While F exclusively refers to Othello by name in stage directions (though calling him "*Moor*" in its list of roles), the Q stage directions sometimes substitute "*Moor*" for Othello's name, thus perhaps emphasizing the ways in which early modern English actors created the appearance of black skin. See Digital Edition TC 1 (Folio edited text).

3. And bring them along at the most favorable moment.

4. *guinea hen:* prostitute; perhaps a disparaging reference to Guinea in West Africa, picked up by "baboon."

this that you call "love" to be a sect or scion.°   *offshoot*
RODERIGO It cannot be.
325 IAGO It is merely a lust of the blood and a permission of the
will. Come, be a man! Drown thyself? Drown cats and blind
puppies! I have professed me thy friend, and I confess me knit
to thy deserving with cables of perdurable° toughness. I could   *durable*
never better stead° thee than now. Put money in thy purse!   *help*
330 Follow thou the wars; defeat thy favor with an usurped beard.[5]
I say, put money in thy purse! It cannot be long that Desdemona should continue her love to the Moor—put money in
thy purse!—nor he his to her. It was a violent commencement° *an abruptly begun affair*
in her, and thou shalt see an answerable sequestration[6]—put
335 but money in thy purse! These Moors are changeable in their
wills—fill thy purse with money! The food that to him now is
as luscious as locusts[7] shall be to him shortly as bitter as *colo-*
quintida.[8] She must change for youth:° when she is sated with   *a youth*
his body, she will find the errors of her choice. Therefore put
340 money in thy purse! If thou wilt needs° damn thyself, do it a   *If you must*
more delicate way than drowning. Make all the money thou
canst. If sanctimony° and a frail vow betwixt an erring barbar-   *holy rite*
ian[9] and super-subtle° Venetian be not too hard for my wits   *deceptive*
and all the tribe of hell, thou shalt enjoy her. Therefore, make
345 money. A pox of drowning thyself! It is clean out of the way!°   *unacceptable*
Seek thou rather to be hanged in compassing° thy joy than to   *obtaining*
be drowned and go without her.
RODERIGO Wilt thou be fast° to my hopes if I depend on the   *duty bound*
issue?°   *outcome*
350 IAGO Thou art sure of me. Go, make money. I have told thee
often and I re-tell thee again and again: I hate the Moor. My
cause is hearted,° thine hath no less reason: let us be conjunc- *heartfelt*
tive° in our revenge against him. If thou canst cuckold him,   *joined*
thou dost thyself a pleasure, me a sport. There are many events
355 in the womb of Time which will be delivered. Traverse,° go,   *Go (to arms)*
provide thy money: we will have more of this tomorrow. Adieu.
RODERIGO Where shall we meet i'th' morning?
IAGO At my lodging.
RODERIGO   I'll be with thee betimes.°   *early*
IAGO Go to. Farewell. Do you hear, Roderigo?
360 RODERIGO I'll sell all my land!   *Exit.*
IAGO Thus do I ever make my fool my purse:
For I mine own gained knowledge should profane
If I would time expend with such snipe°   *fools*
But for my sport and profit. I hate the Moor,
365 And it is thought abroad° that twixt my sheets   *rumored*
He's done my office.° I know not if't be true,   *(sexual)*
But I, for mere suspicion in that kind,°   *regard*
Will do° as if for surety.° He holds° me well;   *act / it were true / likes*
The better shall my purpose work on him.
370 Cassio's a proper° man—let me see now: *handsome*
To get his place° and to plume up° my will   *position / gratify*
In double knavery? How? How? Let's see.

---

5. Disguise yourself to look more like a soldier with a
fake beard.
6. A correspondingly abrupt separation.
7. A sweet, exotic fruit, perhaps carob or honeysuckle.

8. Colocynth, a purgative—one of Iago's many references to the digestive tract.
9. Wandering (also mistaken) foreigner (savage; native
of Barbary in North Africa).

After some time, to abuse Othello's ears
That he is too familiar with his wife.[1]
375 He hath a person and a smooth dispose°   *manner*
To be° suspected, framed to make women false.   *That are to be*
The Moor is of a free° and open nature   *liberal*
That thinks men honest that but seem to be so,
And will as tenderly° be led by th' nose   *easily*
380 As asses are.
I have't! It is engendered. Hell and night
Must bring this monstrous birth to the world's light.[2]   [*Exit.*]

2.1 (Q 2.1)

Enter MONTANO, *and* [FIRST *and* SECOND]
    GENTLEMEN.

MONTANO   What from the cape can you discern at sea?
FIRST GENTLEMAN   Nothing at all. It is a high-wrought flood:°   *very rough sea*
  I cannot twixt the heaven and the main°   *sea*
  Descry° a sail.   *Discern*
5 MONTANO   Methinks the wind hath spoke aloud at land;
  A fuller blast ne'er shook our battlements.
  If it hath ruffianed° so upon the sea,   *raged*
  What ribs of oak, when mountains melt on them,
  Can hold the mortise?[1] What shall we hear of this?
10 SECOND GENTLEMAN   A segregation° of the Turkish fleet: *separation*
  For do but stand upon the foaming shore,
  The chidden billow[2] seems to pelt the clouds,
  The wind-shaked surge° with high and monstrous main°   *fountain / open sea*
  Seems to cast water on the burning Bear
15   And quench the guards of th'ever-fixèd pole.[3]
  I never did like molestation view°   *see such a tumult*
  On the enchafèd° flood.   *heated; tumultuous*
MONTANO   If that the Turkish fleet
  Be not ensheltered and embayed, they are drowned.
  It is impossible to bear it out.
        Enter [THIRD] GENTLEMAN.
20 THIRD GENTLEMAN   News, lads! Our wars are done.
  The desperate tempest hath so banged the Turks
  That their designment° halts. A noble ship of Venice   *plan*
  Hath seen a grievous wreck and sufferance
  On most part of their fleet.
MONTANO   How? Is this true?
25 THIRD GENTLEMAN   The ship is here put in,
  A Veronese.[4] Michael Cassio,
  Lieutenant to the warlike Moor, Othello,
  Is come on shore; the Moor himself at sea,
  And is in full commission here for Cyprus.
30 MONTANO   I am glad on't; 'tis a worthy governor.

---

1. "He" is Cassio (as in line 371), but "his" refers to Othello—a potential confusion of pronouns.
2. PERFORMANCE COMMENT. For some of the many ways of performing Iago's soliloquies, see Digital Edition PC 2.
2.1 Location: A seaport in Cyprus; outdoors near the harbor.
1. *What . . . mortise:* What ship (with "ribs of oak") can hold its joints ("mortise") together when "moun-

tains" of water pour on it?
2. The rising ocean, rebuked ("chidden") by the wind or repulsed by the land.
3. *burning Bear:* the constellation Ursa Minor. *guards:* probably two stars in the constellation that point in a line to the polestar, also in Ursa Minor.
4. Meaning unclear: originally from Verona, though now used by the Venetians; a cutter.

THIRD GENTLEMAN   But this same Cassio, though he speak of
    comfort
Touching° the Turkish loss, yet he looks sadly°   *About / somberly*
And prays the Moor be safe, for they were parted
With foul and violent tempest.
MONTANO   Pray heavens he be!
35   For I have served him, and the man commands
Like a full° soldier. Let's to the sea-side, ho,   *true*
As well to see the vessel that's come in
As to throw out our eyes for brave Othello,
Even till we make the main and th'aerial blue
An indistinct regard.[5]
40   THIRD GENTLEMAN   Come, let's do so,
For every minute is expectancy
Of more arrivancy.
        Enter CASSIO.
CASSIO   Thanks, you, the valiant of the warlike isle
That so approve the Moor! Oh, let the heavens
45   Give him defense against the elements,
For I have lost him on a dangerous sea.
MONTANO   Is he well shipped?
CASSIO   His bark is stoutly timbered, and his pilot
Of very expert and approved allowance:°   *known ability*
50   Therefore my hopes, not surfeited to death,°   *not excessive*
Stand in bold cure.°   *Are likely to be rewarded*
VOICES (*within*)   A sail! A sail! A sail!
CASSIO   What noise?
SECOND GENTLEMAN   The town is empty: on the brow° o'th' sea   *cliff at the edge*
Stand ranks of people and they cry, "A sail!"
55   CASSIO   My hopes do shape him for° the governor.   *make it out to be*
        [*A shot is heard.*]
SECOND GENTLEMAN   They do discharge their shot of courtesy.
Our friends, at least.
CASSIO [*to* SECOND GENTLEMAN]   I pray you, sir, go forth,
And give us truth who 'tis that is arrived.
SECOND GENTLEMAN   I shall.   *Exit.*
60   MONTANO   But, good lieutenant, is your general wived?
CASSIO   Most fortunately! He hath achieved° a maid   *won*
That paragons° description and wild fame,[6]   *stands above*
One that excels the quirks of blazoning° pens   *praise-giving*
And in th'essential vesture of creation
Does tire the engineer.[7]
        Enter [SECOND] GENTLEMAN.
65   —How now? Who has put in?
SECOND GENTLEMAN   'Tis one Iago, ensign to the general.
CASSIO   He's had most favorable and happy speed.
Tempests themselves, high seas, and howling winds,
The guttered° rocks and congregated° sands—   *jagged / accumulated*
70   Traitors ensteeped° to enclog the guiltless keel—   *underwater*
As having sense of beauty do omit°   *forgo*
Their mortal° natures, letting go safely by   *deadly*
The divine Desdemona.

5. *Even . . . regard:* Until we can't distinguish sea from
sky.
6. Unrestrained rumors.

7. *in . . . engineer:* whose natural beauty exhausts the
poet's capacity to invent praise.

MONTANO   What is she?

CASSIO   She that I spake of: our great captain's captain,
75   Left in the conduct of the bold Iago,
      Whose footing here anticipates our thoughts
      A sennight's speed.[8] Great Jove, Othello guard,°   *guard Othello*
      And swell his sail with thine own powerful breath,
      That he may bless this bay with his tall ship,
80   Make love's quick pants in Desdemona's arms,
      Give renewed fire to our extincted spirits—

              Enter DESDEMONA, IAGO, RODERIGO, *and* EMILIA.
                                          Oh, behold!
      The riches of the ship is come on shore.
      You men of Cyprus, let her have your knees.
              [*He kneels.*]
      Hail to thee, lady, and the grace of heaven
85   Before, behind thee, and on every hand
      Enwheel thee round.

DESDEMONA   I thank you, valiant Cassio.
              [CASSIO *rises.*]
      What tidings can you tell of my lord?

CASSIO   He is not yet arrived, nor know I aught
      But that he's well and will be shortly here.

90 DESDEMONA   Oh, but I fear! How lost you company?

CASSIO   The great contention of sea and skies
      Parted our fellowship—

VOICES (*within*)   A sail! A sail!

CASSIO   But hark, a sail!
              [*A shot is heard.*]

SECOND GENTLEMAN   They give this greeting to the citadel;
      This likewise is a friend.

CASSIO [*to* SECOND GENTLEMAN]   See for the news.
                          [*Exit* SECOND GENTLEMAN.]
95   —Good ensign, you are welcome. [*He kisses* EMILIA.] Wel-
          come, mistress.
      —Let it not gall your patience, good Iago,
      That I extend my manners: 'tis my breeding
      That gives me this bold show of courtesy.

IAGO   Sir, would she give you so much of her lips
100   As of her tongue° she oft bestows on me,   *(scolding); (kissing)*
      You would have enough.

DESDEMONA   Alas, she has no speech![9]

IAGO   In faith, too much:
      I find it still when I have leave to sleep.
      Marry, before your ladyship I grant
105   She puts her tongue a little in her heart,[1]
      And chides with thinking.

EMILIA   You have little cause to say so.

IAGO   Come on! Come on! You are pictures out of door,
      Bells in your parlors, wildcats in your kitchens,
110   Saints in your injuries, devils being offended,

---

8. *Whose . . . speed:* Whose arrival predates our expectations by a week.
9. Perhaps: Alas, the accused scolding chatterbox is

not even rising to her own defense (both a defense of
Emilia and a prod for her to speak).
1. She keeps her (critical) thoughts to herself.

Players in your housewifery, and housewives in your beds.[2]

DESDEMONA   Oh, fie upon thee, slanderer![3]

IAGO   Nay, it is true, or else I am a Turk:
You rise to play, and go to bed to work.

EMILIA   You shall not write my praise.

115   IAGO   No, let me not.

DESDEMONA   What wouldst write of me, if thou shouldst
   praise me?

IAGO   O gentle lady, do not put me to't,
For I am nothing if not critical.

DESDEMONA   Come on: assay.° There's one gone to the harbor?   *try*

120   IAGO   Ay, madam.

DESDEMONA   I am not merry, but I do beguile°   *disguise*
The thing I am° by seeming otherwise.   *(worried for Othello)*
Come, how wouldst thou praise me?[4]

IAGO   I am about it,
But, indeed, my invention comes from my pate

125   As birdlime[5] does from frieze:° it plucks out brains and all.   *coarse wool cloth*
But my muse labors° and thus she is delivered: *(in childbirth)*
"If she be fair and wise, fairness and wit,
The one's for use, the other useth it."[6]

DESDEMONA   Well praised. How if she be black and witty?

130   IAGO   "If she be black and thereto have a wit,
She'll find a white that shall her blackness fit."[7]

DESDEMONA   Worse and worse!

EMILIA   How if fair and foolish?

IAGO   "She never yet was foolish that was fair,
For even her folly° helped her to an heir."   *foolishness; lechery*

135   DESDEMONA   These are old fond° paradoxes to make fools laugh   *foolish*
i'th' alehouse. What miserable praise hast thou for her that's
foul° and foolish?   *ugly*

IAGO   "There's none so foul and foolish thereunto°   *to boot*
But does foul° pranks which fair and wise ones do."   *lascivious*

140   DESDEMONA   Oh, heavy ignorance: thou praisest the worst
best! But what praise couldst thou bestow on a deserving
woman indeed? One that in the authority of her merit did
justly put on the vouch° of very malice itself?   *compel the approval*

IAGO   "She that was ever fair and never proud,

145   Had tongue at will and yet was never loud,
Never lacked gold and yet went never gay,°[8]   *lavishly clothed*
Fled from her wish and yet said, 'Now I may';[8]
She that being angered, her revenge being nigh,
Bade her wrong stay° and her displeasure fly;   *sense of injury end*

150   She that in wisdom never was so frail

---

2. *You are . . . beds:* Iago shifts from Emilia to women
generally in this speech. *pictures:* models of silent propriety. *Bells:* Noisy. *kitchens:* perhaps domestic affairs
generally, rather than a specific room. *Saints:* Martyrs.
Players in your housewifery: Deceptive in managing
household expenses. *housewives:* wanton (perhaps
businesslike, or sparing of sexual favors).
3. TEXTUAL COMMENT This line is part of Iago's
speech in Q, where it may have been meant to be spoken by Emilia. For the different consequences of having Desdemona or Emilia utter this line, see Digital
Edition TC 2 (Folio edited text).

4. PERFORMANCE COMMENT For the various issues
raised by this scene in Cyprus's harbor—what appears
onstage, relations between Venetians and Cypriots,
possible sexual tension among the characters—see
Digital Edition PC 3.
5. Sticky substance used to trap small birds.
6. *The one's . . . it:* Intelligence makes use of beauty.
7. *black:* dark-haired or dark-complexioned. *white:*
fair-skinned person ("wight" means "person"). *blackness* (referring to hair or skin; also sexual). *fit:* (sexual).
8. Voluntarily withstood temptation even when given
the choice.

To change the cod's head for the salmon's tail;⁹
She that could think and never disclose her mind,
See suitors following and not look behind;
She was a wight,° if ever such wights were"—   *(play on "white," line 131)*

155   DESDEMONA   To do what?
IAGO   "To suckle fools and chronicle small beer."¹
DESDEMONA   Oh, most lame and impotent conclusion! —Do not
learn of him, Emilia, though he be thy husband. —How say
you, Cassio? Is he not a most profane and liberal° counselor?   *outspoken*

160   CASSIO   He speaks home,° madam: you may relish him   *forcefully*
More in° the soldier than in the scholar.   *as*
IAGO [*aside*]   He takes her by the palm. Ay, well said:° whisper!   *well done*
With as little a web as this will I ensnare as great a fly as
Cassio. Ay, smile upon her, do! I will give° thee in thine own   *shackle*

165   courtship.° [*to* CASSIO] You say true; 'tis so indeed. [*aside*] If   *courtliness*
such tricks as these strip you out of your lieutenantry, it had
been better you had not kissed your three fingers² so oft,
which now, again, you are most apt to play the sir° in. Very   *gentleman*
good: well kissed and excellent curtsy! [*to* CASSIO] 'Tis so

170   indeed. [*aside*] Yet again your fingers to your lips? Would they
were clyster-pipes° for your sake.   *enema tubes*
            [*Trumpets within.*]
—The Moor! I know his trumpet.
CASSIO   'Tis truly so.
DESDEMONA   Let's meet him and receive him.
            Enter OTHELLO *and Attendants.*
CASSIO   Lo, where he comes!
OTHELLO   O my fair warrior!
DESDEMONA   My dear Othello!

175   OTHELLO   It gives me wonder great as my content
To see you here before me. O my soul's joy!
If after every tempest come such calms,
May the winds blow till they have wakened death,
And let the laboring bark° climb hills of seas   *small ship*

180   Olympus-high,³ and duck again as low
As hell's from heaven. If it were now to die,
'Twere now to be most happy—for I fear
My soul hath her content so absolute
That not another comfort like to this
Succeeds° in unknown fate.°   *Will follow / future*

185   DESDEMONA   The heavens forbid
But that our loves and comforts should increase
Even as our days do grow.
OTHELLO   Amen to that, sweet powers!
I cannot speak enough of this content;
It° stops me here.° It is too much of joy.   *(Emotion) / now; in my heart*
            [*They kiss.*]

190   And this, and this, the greatest discords be
That e'er our hearts shall make.
IAGO [*aside*]   Oh, you are well tuned now,

---

9. To make an unworthy exchange. Probably also suggesting sexual infidelity: "cod" means "penis," and "tail"
equals "vulva."
1. To breast-feed babies and keep track of trivial
domestic goods. That is, such perfect virtue suits only

a dull, complacent, decidedly ungenteel housewife.
2. Kissing one's own hand was a common courtly
gesture from a gentleman to a lady.
3. Mount Olympus, home of the Greek gods and
hence too high for mortals.

But I'll set down the pegs that make this music,[4]
As honest as I am.

OTHELLO   Come, let us to the castle.
—News, friends! Our wars are done. The Turks are drowned.

195 How does my old acquaintance of this isle?
[to DESDEMONA] Honey, you shall be well desired° in Cyprus: *welcomed*
I have found great love amongst them. O my sweet,
I prattle out of fashion, and I dote
In mine own comforts. —I prithee, good Iago,

200 Go to the bay and disembark my coffers.
Bring thou the master° to the citadel: *captain*
He is a good one, and his worthiness
Does challenge° much respect. —Come, Desdemona.   *deserve*
—Once more, well met at Cyprus.

                     Exeunt [all but IAGO *and* RODERIGO].

205 IAGO   Do thou meet me presently at the harbor. Come thither.
If thou beest valiant—as they say base° men being in love   *lowly born*
have then a nobility in their natures more than is native to
them—list° me. The lieutenant tonight watches on the court   *listen to*
of guard.[5] First, I must tell thee this: Desdemona is directly

210 in love with him.

RODERIGO   With him? Why, 'tis not possible!

IAGO [*putting a finger to his lips*]   Lay thy finger thus, and let
thy soul be instructed. Mark me with what violence she first
loved the Moor but for bragging and telling her fantastical

215 lies. To love him still for prating? Let not thy discreet heart
think it. Her eye must be fed, and what delight shall she have
to look on the devil? When the blood is made dull with the act
of sport, there should° be a game° to inflame it and to give   *needs to / (sexual)*
satiety a fresh appetite: loveliness in favor,° sympathy in years,   *look; appearance*

220 manners, and beauties—all which the Moor is defective in.
Now, for want of these required conveniences,° her delicate   *agreements; advantages*
tenderness will find itself abused,[6] begin to heave the gorge,°   *feel nausea*
disrelish, and abhor the Moor: very nature will instruct her in
it, and compel her to some second choice. Now, sir, this

225 granted—as it is a most pregnant° and unforced position—   *obvious; (sexual)*
who stands so eminent in the degree of[7] this fortune as Cas-
sio does? A knave very voluble,° no further conscionable° than   *facile / no more ethical*
in putting on the mere form of civil and humane° seeming for   *courteous*
the better compass° of his salt° and most hidden loose affec-   *achievement / lewd*

230 tion. Why, none! Why, none! A slipper° and subtle knave, a   *slippery*
finder of occasion that has an eye can stamp and counterfeit
advantages, though true advantage[8] never present itself. A
devilish knave! Besides, the knave is handsome, young, and
hath all those requisites in him that folly° and green minds   *wantonness*

235 look after. A pestilent° complete knave, and the woman hath   *damnably*
found him already.

RODERIGO   I cannot believe that in her: she's full of most blessed
condition.

IAGO   Blessed fig's end!° The wine she drinks is made of   *(obscene)*

240 grapes. If she had been blessed, she would never have loved

---

4. I'll untune (by loosening the "pegs") that hold the
strings of a musical instrument taut.
5. Cassio is in charge of the watch at the guardhouse.
6. Mistreated; deceived.

7. *in the degree of*: as next in line for.
8. Who can (like a counterfeiter) mint his own opportunities.

the Moor. Blessed pudding!° Didst thou not see her paddle   *sausage*
with the palm of his hand? Didst not mark that?

RODERIGO   Yes, that I did; but that was but courtesy.

IAGO   Lechery, by this hand. An index and obscure prologue to
245   the history of lust and foul thoughts.[9] They met so near
with their lips that their breaths embraced together. Villainous thoughts, Roderigo! When these mutabilities so marshal
the way, hard at hand comes the master and main exercise:[1]
th'incorporate° conclusion. Pish! But, sir, be you ruled by me.   *fleshly; physical*
250   I have brought you from Venice. Watch you tonight for the
command; I'll lay't upon you.[2] Cassio knows you not. I'll not
be far from you. Do you find some occasion to anger Cassio,
either by speaking too loud, or tainting° his discipline, or   *insulting*
from what other course you please, which the time shall more
255   favorably minister.°   *provide*

RODERIGO   Well?

IAGO   Sir, he's rash and very sudden in choler,° and happily°   *anger / to our benefit*
may strike at you. Provoke him that he may, for even out of
that will I cause these of Cyprus to mutiny, whose qualifica-
260   tion shall come into no true taste again[3] but by the displanting
of Cassio. So shall you have a shorter journey to your desires
by the means I shall then have to prefer° them, and the impedi-   *promote*
ment most profitably removed, without the which there were
no expectation of our prosperity.

265 RODERIGO   I will do this, if you can bring it to any opportunity.

IAGO   I warrant thee. Meet me by and by at the citadel. I must
fetch his necessaries° ashore. Farewell.   *Othello's possessions*

RODERIGO   Adieu.   ***Exit.***

IAGO   That Cassio loves her, I do well believe't;
270   That she loves him, 'tis apt and of great credit.°   *likely and believable*
The Moor, howbeit that I endure him not,
Is of a constant, loving, noble nature,
And I dare think he'll prove to Desdemona
A most dear° husband. Now I do love her, too,   *affectionate; costly*
275   Not out of absolute lust—though, peradventure,°   *perhaps*
I stand accountant° for as great a sin—   *accountable*
But partly led to diet° my revenge,   *feed*
For that I do suspect the lusty Moor
Hath leaped into my seat,° the thought whereof   *slept with my wife*
280   Doth like a poisonous mineral gnaw my inwards,°   *innards*
And nothing can, or shall, content my soul
Till I am evened with him, wife for wife.
Or, failing so, yet that I put the Moor,
At least, into a jealousy so strong
285   That judgment cannot cure. Which thing to do,
If this poor trash of Venice, whom I trace
For his quick hunting, stand the putting-on,[4]
I'll have our Michael Cassio on the hip;°   *at my mercy*

---

9. *An . . . thoughts:* The analysis is to a dirty book.
index: table of contents. *obscure:* encoded. *history:*
story.
1. When these intimacies have cleared the way, the
main event follows close behind. Here, the analogy is
to an official procession.
2. Stand watch tonight. I'll see that you receive

orders.
3. *whose . . . again:* who will not be adequately
appeased.
4. *If . . . on:* If Roderigo, whom I follow (?), train (?),
puts weights on to slow him down (?), is successfully
set on the hunt when incited.

	Abuse° him to the Moor in the right garb°—	*Slander / manner*
290	For I fear Cassio with my night-cape,° too—	*wife (sexual)*
	Make the Moor thank me, love me, and reward me	
	For making him egregiously an ass	
	And practicing upon° his peace and quiet	*undermining*
	Even to madness. 'Tis here,° but yet confused:	*My plan is here*
295	Knavery's plain face is never seen till used. *Exit.*	

2.2 (Q 2.2)

Enter Othello's HERALD *with a proclamation.*

HERALD [*reads*] "It is Othello's pleasure, our noble and valiant
general, that upon certain tidings now arrived, importing the
mere perdition° of the Turkish fleet, every man put himself   *entire loss*
into triumph: some to dance, some to make bonfires, each
5   man to what sport and revels his addition° leads him. For,   *rank*
besides these beneficial news, it is the celebration of his nuptial." So much was his pleasure should be proclaimed. All
offices° are open, and there is full liberty of feasting from this   *storehouses*
present hour of five till the bell have told eleven. Bless the
10   isle of Cyprus and our noble general Othello!   *Exit.*

2.3 (Q 2.3)

Enter OTHELLO, DESDEMONA, CASSIO, *and Attendants.*

OTHELLO	Good Michael, look you to the guard tonight.	
	Let's teach ourselves that honorable stop°	*self-restraint*
	Not to out-sport° discretion.	*pass the limits of*
CASSIO	Iago hath direction what to do,	
5	But notwithstanding with my personal eye	
	Will I look to't.	
OTHELLO	Iago is most honest.	
	Michael, good night: tomorrow with your earliest	
	Let me have speech with you. —Come, my dear love.	
	The purchase made, the fruits are to ensue:	
10	That profit's yet to come tween me and you.¹	
	—Good night. *Exeunt* [OTHELLO *and* DESDEMONA].	
	Enter IAGO.	
CASSIO	Welcome, Iago. We must to the watch.	
IAGO	Not this hour, lieutenant: 'tis not yet ten o'th' clock.	
	Our general cast° us thus early for the love of his Desde-	*dismissed*
15	mona, who let us not therefore blame: he hath not yet made	
	wanton the night with her, and she is sport for Jove.	
CASSIO	She's a most exquisite lady.	
IAGO	And, I'll warrant her, full of game.°	*spirit; (sexual?)*
CASSIO	Indeed, she's a most fresh and delicate creature.	
20 IAGO	What an eye she has! Methinks it sounds a parley° to	*(military) call*
	provocation.	
CASSIO	An inviting eye, and yet methinks right modest.	
IAGO	And when she speaks, is it not an alarum° to love?	*a call (to arms)*
CASSIO	She is indeed perfection.	
25 IAGO	Well, happiness to their sheets. Come, lieutenant, I	
	have a stoup° of wine, and here without° are a brace of°	*bottle / outside / two*

2.2 Location: A street in Cyprus.   1. We haven't yet consummated our marriage.
2.3 Location: The citadel at Cyprus.

Cyprus gallants that would fain have a measure° to the health   *would like to drink*
of black Othello.

CASSIO   Not tonight, good Iago. I have very poor and unhappy
30   brains for drinking: I could well wish courtesy would invent
some other custom of entertainment.

IAGO   Oh, they are our friends! But one cup: I'll drink for you.

CASSIO   I have drunk but one cup tonight—and that was craft-
ily qualified,° too—and behold what innovation° it makes   *well diluted / disorder*
35   here. I am infortunate in the infirmity, and dare not task my
weakness with any more.

IAGO   What, man? 'Tis a night of revels. The gallants desire it.

CASSIO   Where are they?

IAGO   Here, at the door. I pray you call them in.

40 CASSIO   I'll do't, but it dislikes me.°   *Exit.*   *I don't like doing it*

IAGO   If I can fasten but one cup upon him
With that which he hath drunk tonight already,
He'll be as full of quarrel and offense
As my young mistress' dog. Now, my sick fool Roderigo,
45   Whom love hath turned almost the wrong side out,
To Desdemona hath tonight caroused
Potations pottle-deep, and he's to watch.[2]
Three else of Cyprus—noble swelling° spirits   *proud*
That hold their honors in a wary distance,[3]
50   The very elements° of this warlike isle—   *character(istic)s*
Have I tonight flustered with flowing cups,
And they watch, too. Now 'mongst this flock of drunkards
Am I put to° our Cassio in some action°   *to put / fight*
That may offend the isle.

       Enter CASSIO, MONTANO, *and [three]* GENTLEMEN
       [*with wine*].

          But here they come.

55   If consequence do but approve my dream,[4]
My boat sails freely both with wind and stream.°   *current*

CASSIO   Fore heaven, they have given me a rouse° already!   *full draft*

MONTANO   Good faith, a little one: not past a pint, as I am a
soldier!

60 IAGO   —Some wine, ho!

[*sings*]   And let me the cannikin° clink, clink,   *drinking vessel*
           And let me the cannikin clink.
           A soldier's a man, oh, man's life's but a span,
           Why, then, let a soldier drink!
65   Some wine, boys!

CASSIO   Fore heaven, an excellent song!

IAGO   I learned it in England, where indeed they are most
potent in potting.[5] Your Dane, your German, and your swag°-   *hanging*
bellied Hollander—drink, ho!—are nothing to your English.

70 CASSIO   Is your Englishman so exquisite in his drinking?

IAGO   Why, he drinks you with facility° your Dane dead drunk;   *easily drinks*
he sweats not to overthrow your Almain;° he gives your Hol-   *German*
lander a vomit ere the next pottle° can be filled.   *tankard*

CASSIO   To the health of our general!

---

2. *caroused . . . watch*: consumed drink to the bottom of the tankard, and he's set to watch Cassio.
3. Who are touchy about their honor.

4. If events turn out as I hope.
5. Most adept at drinking (self-referential joke).

75 MONTANO I am for it, lieutenant, and I'll do you justice.°   *match your drinking*
  IAGO   O sweet England!
    [*sings*]   King Stephen was and a worthy peer,
               His breeches cost him but a crown;
               He held them sixpence all too dear,
80   With that he called the tailor "loon."°   *lout*
               He was a wight of high renown
               And thou art but of low degree:
               'Tis pride° that pulls the country down,   *ostentatious clothing*
               And take thy old cloak about thee.
85   —Some wine, ho!
  CASSIO   Why, this is a more exquisite song than the other!
  IAGO   Will you hear't again?
  CASSIO   No, for I hold him to be unworthy of his place that does
    those things. Well, heaven's above all, and there be souls must
90   be saved, and there be souls must not be saved.[6]
  IAGO   It's true, good lieutenant.
  CASSIO   For mine own part, no offense to the general nor any
    man of quality,° I hope to be saved.   *rank*
  IAGO   And so do I, too, lieutenant.
95 CASSIO   Ay, but by your leave, not before me! The lieutenant is
    to be saved before the ensign. Let's have no more of this. Let's
    to our affairs. Forgive us our sins. —Gentlemen, let's look to
    our business. Do not think, gentlemen, I am drunk: this is my
    ensign, this is my right hand, and this is my left. I am not
100   drunk now: I can stand well enough and I speak well enough.
  GENTLEMEN   Excellent well.
  CASSIO   Why, very well, then: you must not think, then, that
    I am drunk.   *Exit.*
  MONTANO   To th' platform, masters. Come, let's set the watch.
                       [*Exeunt* GENTLEMEN.]
105 IAGO   You see this fellow that is gone before?
    He's a soldier fit to stand by Caesar
    And give direction; and do but see his vice:
    'Tis to his virtue a just equinox,°   *of equal size*
    The one as long as th'other. 'Tis pity of him.°   *It's a shame*
110   I fear the trust Othello puts him in
    On some odd time of his infirmity
    Will shake this island.
  MONTANO   But is he often thus?
  IAGO   'Tis evermore his prologue to his sleep:
    He'll watch the horologe a double set[7]
    If drink rock not his cradle.
115 MONTANO   It were well
    The general were put in mind of it.
    Perhaps he sees it not, or his good nature
    Prizes the virtue that appears in Cassio
    And looks not on his evils. Is not this true?—
        Enter RODERIGO.
120 IAGO [*aside*]   How now, Roderigo?
    I pray you, after the lieutenant: go!   [*Exit* RODERIGO.]
  MONTANO   —And 'tis great pity that the noble Moor

---

6. Referring to the idea of predestination, the belief held by Calvinist Protestants that some souls are des- tined from the outset to be saved and others damned.
7. He'll stay up twice around the clock.

Should hazard such a place as his own second
With one of an engraft° infirmity.   *ingrained*
125 It were an honest action to say so
To the Moor.
IAGO   Not I, for this fair island!
I do love Cassio well, and would do much
To cure him of this evil. But hark, what noise?
            Enter CASSIO *pursuing* RODERIGO.
CASSIO   You rogue! You rascal!
MONTANO   What's the matter, lieutenant?
130 CASSIO   A knave teach me my duty?
I'll beat the knave into a twiggen bottle.[8]
RODERIGO   Beat me?
CASSIO   Dost thou prate, rogue?
MONTANO   Nay, good lieutenant!
I pray you, sir, hold your hand.
CASSIO   Let me go, sir,
Or I'll knock you o'er the mazard.°   *head*
MONTANO   Come, come! You're drunk.
135 CASSIO   Drunk?
            [*They fight.*]
IAGO [*aside to* RODERIGO]   Away, I say! Go out and cry a mutiny.
                                    [*Exit* RODERIGO.]
—Nay, good lieutenant. Alas, gentlemen!
—Help, ho! —Lieutenant! Sir! —Montano!
—Help, masters! —Here's a goodly watch indeed.
            [*A bell rings.*]
140 Who's that which rings the bell? *Diablo*!° Ho!   *Devil!*
The town will rise. —Fie, fie, lieutenant,
You'll be ashamed for ever.
            Enter OTHELLO *and Attendants.*
OTHELLO   What is the matter here?
MONTANO   I bleed still. I am hurt to th' death. He dies!
OTHELLO   Hold, for your lives!
145 IAGO   Hold, ho! Lieutenant! Sir! Montano! Gentlemen!
Have you forgot all place of sense and duty?
Hold! The general speaks to you. Hold, for shame!
OTHELLO   Why, how now? Ho! From whence ariseth this?
Are we turned Turks, and to ourselves do that
150 Which heaven hath forbid the Ottomites?°   *(by raising a storm)*
For Christian shame, put by this barbarous brawl.
He that stirs next to carve for his own rage°   *draw a sword in anger*
Holds his soul light: he dies upon his motion.
[*to Attendants*] Silence that dreadful bell: it frights the isle
From her propriety.   [*Exit Attendant.*]
155   —What is the matter, masters?
—Honest Iago, that looks dead with grieving,
Speak. Who began this? On thy love I charge thee.
IAGO   I do not know. Friends all but now; even now
In quarter° and in terms like bride and groom   *Under control*
160 Devesting them° for bed; and then but now,   *Getting undressed*

---

8. *twiggen:* wicker-cased. Hence, smash to pieces or, perhaps, produce wicker-like lashes on Roderigo's back.

As if some planet° had unwitted men, *astrological influence*
Swords out, and tilting one at other's breasts
In opposition bloody. I cannot speak
Any beginning to this peevish odds,° *capricious quarrel*
165 And would in action glorious I had lost
Those legs that brought me to a part of it.
OTHELLO   How comes it, Michael, you are thus forgot?° *you thus forgot yourself*
CASSIO   I pray you, pardon me: I cannot speak.
OTHELLO   Worthy Montano, you were wont to be° civil: *you used to be*
170 The gravity and stillness of your youth
The world hath noted, and your name is great
In mouths of wisest censure.° What's the matter *judgment*
That you unlace your reputation thus,
And spend your rich opinion° for the name *reputation*
175 Of a night-brawler? Give me answer to it!
MONTANO   Worthy Othello, I am hurt to danger.
Your officer, Iago, can inform you
While I spare speech, which something now offends me,° *somewhat now pains me*
Of all that I do know. Nor know I aught° *anything*
180 By me that's said or done amiss this night,
Unless self-charity° be sometimes a vice, *care of oneself*
And to defend ourselves it be a sin
When violence assails us.
OTHELLO   Now, by heaven,
My blood begins my safer guides to rule
185 And passion, having my best judgment collied,[9]
Assays to lead the way! If I once stir
Or do but lift this arm, the best of you
Shall sink in my rebuke. Give me to know
How this foul rout began, who set it on,
190 And he that is approved in° this offense, *shown culpable of*
Though he had twinned with me, both at a birth,
Shall lose me. What, in a town of war
Yet° wild, the peoples' hearts brimful of fear, *Still*
To manage° private and domestic quarrel *carry on*
195 In night, and on the court and guard of safety?[1]
'Tis monstrous! Iago, who began't?
MONTANO [*to* IAGO]   If partially affined or league in office,[2]
Thou dost deliver more or less than truth,
Thou art no soldier.
IAGO   Touch me not so near.
200 I had rather have this tongue cut from my mouth
Than it should do offense to Michael Cassio.
Yet, I persuade myself, to speak the truth
Shall nothing wrong him. This it is, general:
Montano and myself being in speech,
205 There comes a fellow crying out for help
And Cassio following him with determined sword
To execute upon° him. Sir, this gentleman *attack*
          [*indicating* MONTANO]
Steps in to Cassio and entreats his pause.

9. Obscured by anger (choler); darkened racially.
1. And at the place where safety and security are at
stake (on the night watch).
2. *If . . . office:* If biased (in favor of Cassio) by your
ties to him or (by) your holding office together.

Myself the crying fellow did pursue
210 Lest by his clamor, as it so fell out,
The town might fall in fright. He, swift of foot,
Outran my purpose, and I returned then rather
For that° I heard the clink and fall of swords   *especially since*
And Cassio high in oath, which till tonight
215 I ne'er might say before. When I came back—
For this was brief—I found them close together
At blow and thrust, even as again they were
When you yourself did part them.
More of this matter cannot I report.
220 But men are men: the best sometimes forget.
Though Cassio did some little wrong to him,
As men in rage strike those that wish them best,
Yet surely Cassio, I believe, received
From him that fled some strange indignity
Which patience could not pass.°   *let pass*
225 OTHELLO   I know, Iago,
Thy honesty and love doth mince° this matter,   *minimize*
Making it light to Cassio. —Cassio, I love thee,
But never more be officer of mine.

Enter DESDEMONA [*and Attendants*].

Look if my gentle love be not raised up—
230 [*to* CASSIO] I'll make thee an example.
DESDEMONA   What is the matter, dear?
OTHELLO   All's well, sweeting.
Come away to bed. [*to* MONTANO] Sir, for your hurts
Myself will be your surgeon. [*to Attendants*] Lead him off.
—Iago, look with care about the town,
235 And silence those whom this vile brawl distracted.
—Come, Desdemona. 'Tis the soldier's life
To have their balmy slumbers waked with strife.

Exeunt [all but IAGO *and* CASSIO].

IAGO   What, are you hurt, lieutenant?
CASSIO   Ay, past all surgery.
240 IAGO   Marry, heaven forbid!
CASSIO   Reputation, reputation, reputation! Oh, I have lost my
reputation! I have lost the immortal part of myself, and what
remains is bestial. My reputation, Iago, my reputation!
IAGO   As I am an honest man, I had thought you had received
245 some bodily wound; there is more sense in that than in reputa-
tion. Reputation is an idle and most false imposition,° oft got   *artificial notion*
without merit and lost without deserving. You have lost no
reputation at all, unless you repute yourself such a loser.
What, man, there are more ways to recover the general again!
250 You are but now cast in his mood; a punishment more in policy[3] than in malice, even so as one would beat his offenseless
dog to affright an imperious lion. Sue to° him again, and he's   *Petition*
yours.
CASSIO   I will rather sue to be despised than to deceive so good a
255 commander with so slight, so drunken, and so indiscreet an
officer. Drunk? And speak parrot?° And squabble, swagger,   *rant on*
swear? And discourse fustian° with one's own shadow? O thou   *nonsense*

---

3. *cast . . . policy*: dismissed in anger—a matter of policy (of public example).

invisible spirit of wine, if thou hast no name to be known by, let
us call thee "devil."

260 IAGO What was he that you followed with your sword? What
had he done to you?

CASSIO I know not.

IAGO Is't possible?

CASSIO I remember a mass of things, but nothing distinctly; a
265 quarrel, but nothing wherefore.° Oh, that men should put   *but not why*
an enemy in their mouths° to steal away their brains! That   *should drink*
we should with joy, pleasance, revel, and applause transform
ourselves into beasts!

IAGO Why, but you are now well enough. How came you thus
270 recovered?

CASSIO It hath pleased the devil drunkenness to give place to
the devil wrath: one unperfectness shows me another to
make me frankly despise myself.

IAGO Come, you are too severe a moraler. As the time, the
275 place, and the condition of this country stands, I could heartily wish this had not befallen; but since it is as it is, mend it,
for your own good.

CASSIO I will ask him for my place again; he shall tell me I am
a drunkard. Had I as many mouths as Hydra,[4] such an
280 answer would stop them all. To be now a sensible man, by
and by a fool, and presently a beast! Oh, strange! Every inor-
dinate cup is unblessed, and the ingredient is a devil.

IAGO Come, come: good wine is a good familiar creature, if it
be well used. Exclaim no more against it. And, good lieuten-
285 ant, I think you think I love you?

CASSIO I have well approved° it, sir.—I, drunk?   *tested*

IAGO You, or any man living, may be drunk at a time, man. I
tell you what you shall do. Our general's wife is now the
general—I may say so, in this respect, for that he hath
290 devoted and given up himself to the contemplation, mark,   *devotion to / qualities*
and devotement of° her parts° and graces. Confess yourself
freely to her; importune her help to put you in your place°   *office*
again. She is of so free, so kind, so apt, so blessed a disposition, she holds it a vice in her goodness not to do more than
295 she is requested.[5] This broken joint[6] between you and her
husband entreat her to splinter° and, my fortunes against   *heal with a splint*
any lay° worth naming, this crack of your love shall grow   *wager*
stronger than it was before.

CASSIO You advise me well.

300 IAGO I protest,° in the sincerity of love and honest kindness.   *insist*

CASSIO I think it freely, and betimes° in the morning I will   *early*
beseech the virtuous Desdemona to undertake for me. I am
desperate of my fortunes if they check° me!   *stop*

IAGO You are in the right. Good night, lieutenant. I must to
305 the watch.

---

4. A mythical serpent with many heads who grew
two more when one was cut off.
5. In these lines, Iago may covertly defame Desdemona, unbeknownst to Cassio; line 289: "general" (generally accessible sexually); line 292: "put you in your
place" (penetration in intercourse); line 293: "free"
(generous, erotically open), "kind" (good-humored
about agreeing to make love), "apt" (inclined to help, to
engage in amorous behavior). Similar undertones mark
his ensuing soliloquy, lines 307–33.
6. (Of a bone).

CASSIO   Good night, honest Iago.   *Exit* CASSIO.

IAGO   And what's he, then, that says I play the villain
    When this advice is free I give, and honest,
    Probal° to thinking, and indeed the course   *Wise*
310   To win the Moor again? For 'tis most easy
    Th'inclining° Desdemona to subdue   *The well-disposed*
    In any honest suit: she's framed as fruitful°   *generous*
    As the free elements.° And then for her   *unconstrained nature*
    To win the Moor—were° to renounce his baptism,   *even if it were*
315   All seals and symbols of redeemed sin—
    His soul is so enfettered to her love
    That she may make, unmake, do what she list,
    Even as her appetite[7] shall play the god
    With his weak function.° How am I then a villain   *(intellectual?); (sexual)*
320   To counsel Cassio to this parallel° course   *suitable*
    Directly to his good? Divinity° of hell: *Theology*
    When devils will the blackest sins put on,
    They do suggest at first with heavenly shows,
    As I do now. For whiles this honest fool
325   Plies Desdemona to repair his fortune,
    And she for him pleads strongly to the Moor,
    I'll pour this pestilence into his° ear: *(Othello's)*
    That she repeals him° for her body's lust   *appeals for him*
    And, by how much she strives to do him good,
330   She shall undo her credit with the Moor.
    So will I turn her virtue into pitch[8]
    And out of her own goodness make the net
    That shall enmesh them all—
        Enter RODERIGO.

              —How now, Roderigo?
RODERIGO   I do follow here in the chase, not like a hound that
335   hunts but one that fills up the cry.° My money is almost   *a pack follower*
    spent; I have been tonight exceedingly well cudgeled; and I
    think the issue will be I shall have so much° experience for   *only this*
    my pains. And so, with no money at all and a little more wit,
    return again to Venice.
340 IAGO   How poor are they that have not patience!
    What wound did ever heal but by degrees?
    Thou know'st we work by wit and not by witchcraft,
    And wit depends on dilatory° time.   *drawn-out*
    Does't not go well? Cassio hath beaten thee,
345   And thou by that small hurt hath cashiered° Cassio.   *dismissed*
    Though other things grow fair against the sun,
    Yet fruits that blossom first will first be ripe.[9]
    Content thyself awhile. In troth, 'tis morning!
    Pleasure and action make the hours seem short.
350   Retire thee; go where thou art billeted.
    Away, I say! Thou shalt know more hereafter.
    Nay, get thee gone!   *Exit* RODERIGO.
           Two things are to be done:

---

7. *her appetite*: Despdemona's wishes or desire for Othello; perhaps, his appetite for her.
8. Black, sticky substance used as a snare. The more the thing caught in it tries to escape, the more stuck it becomes.

9. *Though . . . ripe*: Although others prosper only when fully in the sun, your plan will be successful even earlier in the day (metaphorically) because started first and allowed to develop slowly.

My wife must move for Cassio to her mistress—
I'll set her on;
355 Myself a while to draw the Moor apart
And bring him jump° when he may Cassio find   *exactly*
Soliciting his wife. Ay, that's the way.
Dull not device by coldness and delay.[1]   *Exit.*

3.1 (Q 3.1)
Enter CASSIO [*with*] MUSICIANS.

CASSIO   Masters, play here—I will content° your pains—   *reward*
Something that's brief, and bid "Good morrow, general."
[MUSICIANS *play.*]
[*Enter* CLOWN.]

CLOWN   Why, masters, have your instruments been in Naples,
that they speak i'th' nose thus?[1]

5 MUSICIAN   How, sir? How?

CLOWN   Are these, I pray you, wind instruments?[2]

MUSICIAN   Ay, marry are they, sir.

CLOWN   Oh, thereby hangs a tail!

MUSICIAN   Whereby hangs a tale, sir?

10 CLOWN   Marry, sir, by many a wind instrument that I know.
But, masters, here's money for you, and the general so likes
your music that he desires you, for love's sake,[3] to make no
more noise with it.

MUSICIAN   Well, sir, we will not!

15 CLOWN   If you have any music that may not° be heard, to't   *cannot*
again. But, as they say, to hear music the general does not
greatly care.

MUSICIAN   We have none such, sir.

CLOWN   Then put up your pipes in your bag, for I'll away. Go,
20 vanish into air. Away!   *Exeunt* MUSICIANS.

CASSIO   Dost thou hear, mine honest friend?

CLOWN   No, I hear not your honest friend: I hear you.

CASSIO   Prithee, keep up thy quillets.° There's a poor piece of   *pack up your puns*
gold for thee. If the gentlewoman that attends the general
25 be stirring, tell her there's one Cassio entreats her a little
favor of speech. Wilt thou do this?

CLOWN   She is stirring, sir. If she will stir hither, I shall seem°   *arrange*
to notify unto her.   *Exit* CLOWN.[4]
Enter IAGO.

CASSIO   In happy time,° Iago.   *I'm glad to see you*

IAGO   You have not been a-bed, then?

30 CASSIO   Why, no: the day had broke before we parted.
I have made bold, Iago, to send in to your wife:
My suit to her is that she will to virtuous
Desdemona procure me some access.

IAGO   I'll send her to you presently,°   *immediately*
35 And I'll devise a mean to draw the Moor

---

1. Don't let sluggishness and slowness to act weaken the plot.
3.1 Location: Outside Othello and Desdemona's room.
1. That they sound so nasal; perhaps a reference to venereal disease, often associated with Naples, or a phallic or anal joke.
2. The exchange that follows depends on the con-nections between wind instruments, flatulence, and "tale/tail."
3. Out of affection for him; so that his lovemaking won't be disturbed.
4. PERFORMANCE COMMENT For the consequences of cutting (or preserving) both the Clown's part (here and in 3.4) and the very brief 3.2, See Digital Edition PC 4.

Out of the way, that your converse and business
May be more free.

CASSIO I humbly thank you for't. *Exit* [IAGO].
I never knew
A Florentine° more kind and honest.   *Even a fellow Florentine*
Enter EMILIA.

40 EMILIA Good morrow, good lieutenant. I am sorry
For your displeasure,° but all will sure be well: *troubles*
The general and his wife are talking of it,
And she speaks for you stoutly. The Moor replies
That he you hurt is of great fame in Cyprus
45 And great affinity,° and that, in wholesome wisdom,   *well connected*
He might not but refuse you. But he protests he loves you,
And needs no other suitor but his likings
To bring you in again.

CASSIO   Yet, I beseech you,
If you think fit, or that it may be done,
50 Give me advantage of some brief discourse
With Desdemon alone.

EMILIA   Pray you, come in.
I will bestow you where you shall have time
To speak your bosom° freely.   *heart*

CASSIO   I am much bound to you.
[*Exeunt.*]

3.2 (Q 3.2)

Enter OTHELLO, IAGO, *and* GENTLEMEN.

OTHELLO These letters give, Iago, to the pilot,
And by him do my duties° to the Senate.   *send my respects*
That done, I will be walking on the works.°   *fortifications*
Repair there to me.

IAGO   Well, my good lord, I'll do't.
5 OTHELLO —This fortification, gentlemen, shall we see't?
GENTLEMEN We'll wait upon your lordship.   *Exeunt.*

3.3 (Q 3.3)

Enter DESDEMONA, CASSIO, *and* EMILIA.

DESDEMONA Be thou assured, good Cassio, I will do
All my abilities in thy behalf.

EMILIA Good madam, do. I warrant it grieves my husband
As if the cause were his.

5 DESDEMONA Oh, that's an honest fellow. —Do not doubt,
Cassio,
But I will have my lord and you again
As friendly as you were.

CASSIO   Bounteous madam,
Whatever shall become of Michael Cassio,
He's never anything but your true servant.

10 DESDEMONA I know't. I thank you. You do love my lord;
You have known him long and, be you well assured,
He shall in strangeness stand no farther off

3.2 Location: The citadel.   3.3 Location: The citadel's garden.

Than in a politic distance.[1]

CASSIO   Ay, but, lady,
That policy may either last so long,
15   Or feed upon such nice and waterish diet,
Or breed itself so out of circumstances[2]
That, I being absent, and my place supplied,°   *filled*
My general will forget my love and service.

DESDEMONA   Do not doubt° that. Before Emilia here   *fear*
20   I give thee warrant° of thy place. Assure thee: *assurance*
If I do vow a friendship, I'll perform it
To the last article. My lord shall never rest:
I'll watch him tame, and talk him out of patience;[3]
His bed shall seem a school, his board a shrift;°   *confessional*
25   I'll intermingle everything he does
With Cassio's suit. Therefore be merry, Cassio,
For thy solicitor° shall rather die   *advocate*
Than give thy cause away.°   *up*

      Enter OTHELLO *and* IAGO.[4]

EMILIA   Madam, here comes my lord.

CASSIO   Madam, I'll take my leave.

DESDEMONA   Why, stay and hear me speak.

30 CASSIO   Madam, not now: I am very ill at ease,
Unfit for mine own purposes.

DESDEMONA   Well, do your discretion.   *Exit* CASSIO.

IAGO   Ha! I like not that.

OTHELLO   What dost thou say?

IAGO   Nothing, my lord, or if—I know not what.

35 OTHELLO   Was not that Cassio parted from my wife?

IAGO   Cassio, my lord? No, sure. I cannot think it
That he would steal away so guilty-like,
Seeing your coming.

OTHELLO   I do believe 'twas he.

DESDEMONA   How now, my lord?

40   I have been talking with a suitor here,
A man that languishes in your displeasure.

OTHELLO   Who is't you mean?

DESDEMONA   Why, your lieutenant, Cassio. Good my lord,
If I have any grace or power to move you,
45   His present reconciliation take:°   *Accept him now*
For if he be not one that truly loves you,
That errs in ignorance and not in cunning,°   *not knowingly*
I have no judgment in an honest face.
I prithee call him back.

OTHELLO   Went he hence now?

50 DESDEMONA   I'sooth,° so humbled   *Truly*
That he hath left part of his grief with me
To suffer with him. Good love, call him back.

OTHELLO   Not now, sweet Desdemon. Some other time.

DESDEMONA   But shall't be shortly?

---

1. *He . . . distance:* He will distance himself from you only as much as good diplomacy requires.
2. *Or feed . . . circumstances:* Or persist based on such unimportant and poor justifications (perhaps: such pampered and juicy fare), or continue by chance.
3. I'll keep him awake until he obeys me, and talk to

him beyond his endurance.
4. TEXTUAL COMMENT For the difference between F's and Q's stage directions here, and the implications for understanding events as public or private, see Digital Edition TC 3 (Folio edited text).

OTHELLO   The sooner, sweet, for you.
DESDEMONA   Shall't be tonight at supper?
55 OTHELLO   No, not tonight.
DESDEMONA   Tomorrow dinner,° then?   *midday meal*
OTHELLO   I shall not dine at home:
      I meet the captains at the citadel.
DESDEMONA   Why, then, tomorrow night? On Tuesday morn?
      On Tuesday noon, or night? On Wednesday morn?
60 I prithee, name the time, but let it not
      Exceed three days. In faith, he's penitent,
      And yet his trespass, in our common reason°—   *normal judgment*
      Save that, they say, the wars must make example
      Out of her° best—is not almost a fault   *(war's)*
65 T'incur a private check.[5] When shall he come?
      Tell me, Othello. I wonder in my soul
      What you would ask me that I should deny,
      Or stand so mammering° on? What, Michael Cassio   *hesitating*
      That came a-wooing with you, and so many a time
70 When I have spoke of you dispraisingly
      Hath ta'en your part? To have so much to do
      To bring him in?° Trust me, I could do much.[6]   *into favor*
OTHELLO   Prithee, no more. Let him come when he will:
      I will deny thee nothing.
DESDEMONA   Why, this is not a boon.
75 'Tis as I should entreat you wear your gloves,
      Or feed on nourishing dishes, or keep you warm,
      Or sue to you to do a peculiar° profit   *particular*
      To your own person. Nay, when I have a suit
      Wherein I mean to touch your love indeed,
80 It shall be full of poise° and difficult weight,   *balanced judgment*
      And fearful to be granted.[7]
OTHELLO   I will deny thee nothing.
      Whereon, I do beseech thee, grant me this:
      To leave me but a little to myself.
85 DESDEMONA   Shall I deny you? No. Farewell, my lord.
OTHELLO   Farewell, my Desdemona. I'll come to thee straight.°   *immediately*
DESDEMONA   Emilia, come. [*to* OTHELLO] Be as your fancies
      teach° you: *as your whims lead*
      Whate'er you be, I am obedient.
                    Exeunt [DESDEMONA *and* EMILIA].
OTHELLO   Excellent wretch!° Perdition catch my soul   *(affectionate)*
90 But I do love thee; and when I love thee not,
      Chaos is come again.
IAGO   My noble lord?
OTHELLO   What dost thou say, Iago?
IAGO   Did Michael Cassio,
      When you wooed my lady, know of your love?
OTHELLO   He did, from first to last. Why dost thou ask?
95 IAGO   But for a satisfaction of my thought,
      No further harm.
OTHELLO   Why of thy thought, Iago?

---

5. *is . . . check:* is barely worth even private criticism.
6. Do much to make you regret your reluctance (?).
7. Desdemona argues that her request is trivial, that

only a far more serious "suit" (line 78) would be a real
test of his devotion.

IAGO I did not think he had been acquainted with her.

OTHELLO Oh, yes, and went between us very oft.

IAGO Indeed?

100 OTHELLO Indeed? Ay, indeed! Discern'st thou aught in that?
  Is he not honest?

IAGO Honest, my lord?

OTHELLO   Honest? Ay, honest.

IAGO My lord, for aught I know.

OTHELLO   What dost thou think?

IAGO Think, my lord?

105 OTHELLO "Think, my lord?" Alas, thou echo'st me
  As if there were some monster in thy thought
  Too hideous to be shown. Thou dost mean something.
  I heard thee say even now thou "lik'st not that"
  When Cassio left my wife. What didst not like?

110 And when I told thee he was of my counsel,°   *in my confidence*
  Of my whole course of wooing, thou cried'st "Indeed?"
  And didst contract and purse thy brow together
  As if thou then hadst shut up in thy brain
  Some horrible conceit.° If thou dost love me,   *conception*

115 Show me thy thought.

IAGO My lord, you know I love you.

OTHELLO   I think thou dost.
  And, for° I know thou'rt full of love and honesty   *since*
  And weigh'st thy words before thou giv'st them breath,
  Therefore these stops° of thine fright me the more: *disruptive pauses*

120 For such things in a false, disloyal knave
  Are tricks of custom,° but in a man that's just   *habitual*
  They're close dilations[8] working from the heart
  That passion cannot rule.°   *control*

IAGO   For Michael Cassio,
  I dare be sworn, I think that he is honest.

OTHELLO I think so too.

125 IAGO   Men should be what they seem,
  Or those that be not, would they might seem none.[9]

OTHELLO Certain, men should be what they seem.

IAGO Why, then, I think Cassio's an honest man.

OTHELLO Nay, yet there's more in this.

130 I prithee, speak to me as to thy thinkings
  As thou dost ruminate, and give thy worst of thoughts
  The worst of words.

IAGO   Good my lord, pardon me.
  Though I am bound to every act of duty,
  I am not bound to that: all slaves are free.°   *(to hide their thoughts)*

135 Utter my thoughts? Why, say they are vile and false—
  As where's that palace whereinto foul things
  Sometimes intrude not?—who has that breast so pure?—
  Wherein uncleanly apprehensions
  Keep leets and law-days, and in sessions sit

140 With meditations lawful?[1]

---

8. Involuntary hesitations (expansions, censures) of interior, close-kept secrets.
9. *Or . . . none:* If only those who are not what they seem didn't seem to be what they are not.

1. *Wherein . . . lawful:* (Even in pure breasts) illegitimate thoughts meet in court ("leets") from time to time (on "law-days") and debate (in court "session") with legitimate ones.

OTHELLO   Thou dost conspire against thy friend,° Iago,   (Othello)
  If thou but think'st him wronged and mak'st his ear
  A stranger to thy thoughts.
IAGO   I do beseech you,
  Though I perchance am vicious° in my guess—   culpably mistaken
145 As, I confess, it is my nature's plague
  To spy into abuses and of my jealousy°   suspicion; envy
  Shape faults that are not—that your wisdom
  From one that so imperfectly conceits°   imagines
  Would take no notice, nor build yourself a trouble
150 Out of his scattering° and unsure observance.   incoherent
  It were not° for your quiet, nor your good,   It would not be good
  Nor for my manhood, honesty, and wisdom
  To let you know my thoughts.
OTHELLO   What dost thou mean?
IAGO   Good name in man and woman, dear my lord,
155 Is the immediate jewel of their souls.
  Who steals my purse, steals trash: 'tis something, nothing;
  'Twas mine, 'tis his, and has been slave to thousands.
  But he that filches from me my good name
  Robs me of that which not enriches him
160 And makes me poor indeed.
OTHELLO   I'll know thy thoughts.
IAGO   You cannot, if my heart were in your hand,
  Nor shall not, whilst 'tis in my custody.
OTHELLO   Ha!
IAGO   Oh, beware, my lord, of jealousy!
  It is the green-eyed monster which doth mock
165 The meat it feeds on.[2] That cuckold lives in bliss
  Who, certain of his fate, loves not his wronger;[3]
  But, oh, what damnèd minutes tells he o'er°   does he note pass by
  Who dotes, yet doubts; suspects, yet soundly loves.
OTHELLO   Oh, misery![4]
170 IAGO   Poor and content is rich, and rich enough;
  But riches fineless° is as poor as winter   boundless
  To him that ever fears he shall be poor.
  Good heaven, the souls of all my tribe defend
  From jealousy!
OTHELLO   Why? Why is this?
175 Think'st thou I'd make a life of jealousy,
  To follow still the changes of the moon°   Always madly to waver
  With fresh suspicions? No, to be once in doubt
  Is to be resolved.° Exchange me for a goat   to be finally settled
  When I shall turn the business of my soul
180 To such exufflicate and blowed° surmises,   inflated and blown-up
  Matching thy inference.° 'Tis not to make me jealous   implication
  To say my wife is fair, feeds well, loves company,
  Is free of speech, sings, plays, and dances:
  Where virtue is, these are more virtuous.
185 Nor from mine own weak merits will I draw
  The smallest fear or doubt of her revolt,°   or worry of her betrayal

2. *which . . . on:* that tortures, as it consumes, the body and soul of the jealous person.
3. Who, knowing it is his fate to be cuckolded, doesn't love his wife.

4. PERFORMANCE COMMENT For different ways of playing Othello's psychological and physical response to Iago's temptation of him, see Digital Edition PC 5.

For she had eyes and chose me. No, Iago,
I'll see before I doubt; when I doubt, prove;
And, on the proof, there is no more but this:
190   Away at once with love or jealousy.
IAGO   I am glad of this, for now I shall have reason
To show the love and duty that I bear you
With franker spirit. Therefore, as I am bound,
Receive it from me, I speak not yet of proof:
195   Look to your wife; observe her well with Cassio.
Wear your eyes thus: not jealous, nor secure.
I would not have your free and noble nature
Out of self-bounty be abused.[5] Look to't.
I know our country° disposition well: *(obscene wordplay)*
200   In Venice they do let heaven see the pranks
They dare not show their husbands; their best conscience
Is not to leave't undone but kept unknown.
OTHELLO   Dost thou say so?
IAGO   She did deceive her father, marrying you;
205   And when she seemed to shake and fear your looks,
She loved them most.
OTHELLO   And so she did.
IAGO   Why, go to,° then!   *that's it*
She that so young could give out such a seeming
To seal her father's eyes up, close as oak[6]—
He thought 'twas witchcraft. But I am much to blame.
210   I humbly do beseech you of your pardon
For too much loving you.
OTHELLO   I am bound to thee for ever.
IAGO   I see this hath a little dashed your spirits.
OTHELLO   Not a jot, not a jot.
IAGO   Trust me, I fear it has.
215   I hope you will consider what is spoke
Comes from your love. But I do see you're moved.
I am to pray you not to strain my speech
To grosser issues,° nor to larger reach   *greater conclusions*
Than to suspicion.
OTHELLO   I will not.
220 IAGO   Should you do so, my lord,
My speech should fall into such vile success
Which my thoughts aimed not at. Cassio's my worthy friend.
My lord, I see you're moved.
OTHELLO   No, not much moved.
I do not think but Desdemona's honest.
225 IAGO   Long live she so, and long live you to think so.
OTHELLO   And yet, how nature erring from itself—
IAGO   Ay, there's the point! As, to be bold with you,
Not to affect° many proposed matches   *desire*
Of her own clime, complexion,° and degree,°   *nature, skin color / rank*
230   Whereto we see in all things nature tends.
Faugh!° One may smell in such a will most rank,   *(expressing disgust)*
Foul disproportions,° thoughts unnatural.   *abnormalities*
But pardon me, I do not in position°   *argument*

---

5. Be deceived on account of your own goodness.
6. Perhaps: To cover (the homonym "seel" means "to blind") her father's eyes as tightly as oak (a fine-grained wood).

Distinctly speak of her, though I may fear
235 Her will, recoiling to° her better judgment,   *resuming*
May fall to match you with her country forms,[7]
And happily° repent.   *perhaps*
OTHELLO   Farewell, farewell.
If more thou dost perceive, let me know more.
Set on thy wife to observe. Leave me, Iago.
240 IAGO My lord, I take my leave.
OTHELLO   Why did I marry? This honest creature doubtless
Sees and knows more, much more, than he unfolds.
IAGO My lord, I would I might entreat your honor
To scan this thing no farther: leave it to time.
245 Although 'tis fit that Cassio have his place—
For, sure, he fills it up with great ability—
Yet if you please to hold him off awhile,
You shall by that perceive him and his means.°   *(of regaining his job)*
Note if your lady strain his entertainment°   *urge his reception*
250 With any strong or vehement importunity:
Much will be seen in that. In the meantime,
Let me be thought too busy° in my fears—   *meddlesome*
As worthy cause I have to fear I am—
And hold her free,° I do beseech your honor.   *believe her innocent*
OTHELLO   Fear not my government.°   *self-conduct*
255 IAGO   I once more take my leave.
                           Exit.
OTHELLO   This fellow's of exceeding honesty,
And knows all quantities with a learned spirit
Of human dealings.[8] If I do prove her haggard,°   *wild (falconry)*
Though that her jesses were my dear heartstrings,
260 I'd whistle her off, and let her down the wind
To prey at fortune.[9] Haply, for° I am black   *Perhaps, because*
And have not those soft parts of° conversation°   *easy / manner; intercourse*
That chamberers° have, or for I am declined   *gallants; valets*
Into the vale of years—yet that's not much—
265 She's gone, I am abused,° and my relief   *deceived*
Must be to loathe her. O curse of marriage,
That we can call these delicate creatures ours
And not their appetites! I had rather be a toad
And live upon the vapor of a dungeon
270 Than keep a corner in the thing I love
For others' uses. Yet 'tis the plague to great ones:
Prerogatived° are they less than the base.°   *Privileged / lowborn*
'Tis destiny unshunnable, like death:
Even then, this forked plague is fated to us
When we do quicken.[1]
        Enter DESDEMONA *and* EMILIA.
275   Look where she comes!
If she be false, heaven mocked itself.
I'll not believe't.

---

7. May happen to compare you with Venetian (with obscene pun on "country") standards.
8. *quantities . . . of human dealings:* amounts of a commodity in civil commercial transactions (literal); characteristics of human behavior (metaphorical).
9. *Though . . . fortune:* Even if what tied her ("jesses"

were leg straps put on a hawk) were my own heartstrings, I'd set her loose downwind forever to hunt on her own.
1. *Even . . . quicken:* The "plague" of horns (imagined to grow from the forehead of a cuckold) is our fate as soon as we live.

DESDEMONA How now, my dear Othello?
  Your dinner, and the generous° islanders *noble*
  By you invited, do attend° your presence. *wait for*
OTHELLO I am to blame.
280 DESDEMONA Why do you speak so faintly?
  Are you not well?
OTHELLO I have a pain upon my forehead here.° *(from cuckold's horns)*
DESDEMONA Why, that's with watching;° 'twill away again. *from lack of sleep*
  Let me but bind it hard, within this hour
  It will be well.
285 OTHELLO Your napkin° is too little. *handkerchief*
  Let it alone.
    [*They drop the handkerchief.*]
    Come, I'll go in with you.
DESDEMONA I am very sorry that you are not well.
    Exeunt [OTHELLO *and* DESDEMONA].
EMILIA I am glad I have found this napkin:
  [*She picks up the handkerchief.*]
  This was her first remembrance from the Moor.
290 My wayward husband hath a hundred times
  Wooed me to steal it, but she so loves the token—
  For he conjured her[2] she should ever keep it—
  That she reserves it evermore about her
  To kiss and talk to. I'll have the work ta'en out,° *embroidery copied*
295 And giv't Iago. What he will do with it
  Heaven knows, not I.
  I nothing,° but to please his fantasy. *do (know; intend) nothing*
    Enter IAGO.
IAGO How now? What do you here alone?
EMILIA Do not you chide: I have a thing for you.
300 IAGO You have a thing for me? It is a common thing[3]—
EMILIA Ha!
IAGO —To have a foolish wife.
EMILIA Oh, is that all? What will you give me now
  For that same handkerchief?[4]
IAGO What handkerchief?
305 EMILIA What handkerchief?
  Why, that the Moor first gave to Desdemona;
  That which so often you did bid me steal.
IAGO Hast stolen it from her?
EMILIA No, but she let it drop by negligence,
310 And to th'advantage° I, being here, took't up. *taking the opportunity*
  Look, here 'tis.
IAGO A good wench. Give it me.
EMILIA What will you do with't, that you have been so earnest
  To have me filch it?
IAGO Why, what is that to you?
EMILIA If it be not for some purpose of import,
315 Give't me again. Poor lady, she'll run mad
  When she shall lack it.
IAGO Be not acknown on't.° *Conceal your role in it*

---

2. Made her swear; perhaps also an unwitting backward glance at Brabanzio's charge in 1.3 that Othello employed witchcraft to win Desdemona.
3. It is a vagina ("thing") available to all.

4. PERFORMANCE COMMENT For Emilia's behavior and various possible motives for taking the handkerchief and giving it to Iago, see Digital Edition PC 6.

I have use for it. Go, leave me.   *Exit* EMILIA.
I will in Cassio's lodging lose° this napkin,   *misplace; let loose*
And let him find it. Trifles light as air
320   Are to the jealous confirmations strong
As proofs of holy writ. This may do something.
The Moor already changes with my poison:
Dangerous conceits° are in their natures poisons   *ideas*
Which, at the first, are scarce found to distaste
325   But, with a little,° act upon the blood,   *(time)*
Burn like the mines of sulfur.[5]
     Enter OTHELLO.
                I did say so!
Look where he comes! Not poppy, nor mandragora,[6]
Nor all the drowsy syrups of the world
Shall ever medicine thee to that sweet sleep
Which thou owed'st° yesterday.   *owned*
330 OTHELLO   Ha! Ha! False to me?
IAGO   Why, how now, general? No more of that.
OTHELLO   Avaunt!° Be gone! Thou hast set me on the rack.   *Leave me!*
I swear 'tis better to be much abused°   *mistreated; deceived*
Than but to know't a little.
IAGO   How now, my lord?
335 OTHELLO   What sense had I in her stolen hours of lust?
I saw't not, thought it not, it harmed not me;
I slept the next night well, fed well, was free and merry;
I found not Cassio's kisses on her lips.
He that is robbed, not wanting° what is stolen,   *missing*
340   Let him not know't, and he's not robbed at all.
IAGO   I am sorry to hear this.
OTHELLO   I had been happy if the general camp,
Pioneers° and all, had tasted her sweet body,   *Manual laborers*
So° I had nothing known. Oh, now forever   *If*
345   Farewell the tranquil mind; farewell content;
Farewell the plumèd troops and the big wars
That makes ambition virtue! Oh, farewell,
Farewell the neighing steed and the shrill trump,
The spirit-stirring drum, th'ear-piercing fife,
350   The royal banner, and all quality,°   *merit*
Pride,° pomp, and circumstance° of glorious war.   *Magnificence / ceremony*
And O you mortal engines,° whose rude throats   *deadly cannons*
Th'immortal Jove's dread clamors° counterfeit,   *thunderclaps*
Farewell. Othello's occupation's gone.
355 IAGO   Is't possible, my lord?
OTHELLO   Villain, be sure thou prove my love a whore;
Be sure of it! Give me the ocular proof
Or, by the worth of mine eternal soul,
Thou hadst been better have been born a dog
360   Than answer my waked wrath.
IAGO   Is't come to this?
OTHELLO   Make me to see't, or at the least so prove it
That the probation° bear no hinge nor loop   *proof*

---

5. Pliny the Elder describes two islands of sulfur between mainland Italy and Sicily that were rumored to be always on fire.

6. A sleep-inducing substance made from the mandrake root.

To hang a doubt on, or woe upon thy life!
IAGO   My noble lord—
365 OTHELLO   If thou dost slander her and torture me,
Never pray more; abandon all remorse;
On horror's head horrors accumulate;
Do deeds to make heaven weep, all earth amazed;
For nothing canst thou to damnation add
Greater than that.
370 IAGO   O grace! O heaven forgive me!
Are you a man? Have you a soul, or sense?
God b'wi'you; take mine office.[7] O wretched fool°   *(to himself)*
That lov'st to make thine honesty a vice!°   *fault*
O monstrous world! Take note, take note, O world:
375 To be direct and honest is not safe.
I thank you for this profit° and, from hence,   *profitable lesson*
I'll love no friend, sith° love breeds such offense.   *since*
OTHELLO   Nay, stay: thou shouldst be honest.
IAGO   I should be wise, for honesty's a fool,
And loses that° it works for.   *what*
380 OTHELLO   By the world,[8]
I think my wife be honest, and think she is not;
I think that thou art just, and think thou art not.
I'll have some proof. My name, that was as fresh
As Dian's[9] visage, is now begrimed and black
385 As mine own face. If there be cords or knives,
Poison or fire, or suffocating streams,[1]
I'll not endure it. Would I were satisfied!
IAGO   I see you are eaten up with passion;
I do repent me that I put it to you.
You would be satisfied?
390 OTHELLO   Would? Nay, and I will!
IAGO   And may. But how? How satisfied, my lord?
Would you the supervision grossly gape on?[2]
Behold her topped?°   *sexually mounted*
OTHELLO   Death and damnation! Oh!
IAGO   It were a tedious° difficulty, I think,   *disagreeable*
395 To bring them to that prospect.° Damn them, then,   *viewable position*
If ever mortal eyes do see them bolster°   *use a pillow*
More° than their own. What, then? How, then?   *Other*
What shall I say? Where's satisfaction?
It is impossible you should see this,
400 Were they as prime° as goats, as hot as monkeys,   *lustful*
As salt as wolves in pride,[3] and fools as gross
As ignorance made drunk. But yet, I say,
If imputation and strong circumstances[4]—
Which lead directly to the door of truth—
405 Will give you satisfaction, you might have't.
OTHELLO   Give me a living° reason she's disloyal.   *legitimate*

---

7. Good-bye, I resign my official position (ensign).
8. Othello's speech (lines 380–87) does not appear in Q.
9. Diana, goddess of chastity and of the (pale) moon.
1. *cords . . . streams:* methods of suicide or murder.
2. *Would you the supervision . . . gape on?:* Would

you look ("gape") at the sight ("vision") from above ("super")? Would you, the person in the observer's position ("the supervision"), look ("gape") on?
3. As lecherous as wolves in heat.
4. If attribution of fault and strong circumstantial evidence.

IAGO   I do not like the office.
    But, sith I am entered in this cause so far—
    Pricked to't° by foolish honesty and love—   *Prodded on*
410   I will go on. I lay with Cassio lately
    And, being troubled with a raging tooth,
    I could not sleep. There are a kind of men
    So loose of soul that in their sleeps will mutter
    Their affairs: one of this kind is Cassio.
415   In sleep I heard him say, "Sweet Desdemona,
    Let us be wary. Let us hide our loves."
    And then, sir, would he grip and wring my hand,
    Cry, "O sweet creature!" then kiss me hard
    As if he plucked up kisses by the roots
420   That grew upon my lips; laid his leg o'er my thigh,
    And sighed, and kissed, and then cried, "Cursèd fate,
    That gave thee to the Moor!"
OTHELLO   Oh, monstrous! Monstrous!
IAGO   Nay, this was but his dream.
OTHELLO   But this denoted a foregone conclusion.°   *an earlier event*
425   'Tis a shrewd doubt,° though it be but a dream.   *reasonable fear*
IAGO   And this may help to thicken other proofs
    That do demonstrate thinly.
OTHELLO   I'll tear her all to pieces!
IAGO   Nay, yet be wise; yet we see nothing done.
    She may be honest yet. Tell me but this:
430   Have you not sometimes seen a handkerchief
    Spotted with strawberries in your wife's hand?
OTHELLO   I gave her such a one. 'Twas my first gift.
IAGO   I know not that, but such a handkerchief—
    I am sure it was your wife's—did I today
    See Cassio wipe his beard with.
435 OTHELLO   If it be that—
IAGO   If it be that, or any, it was hers.
    It speaks against her with the other proofs.
OTHELLO   Oh, that the slave° had forty thousand lives!   *(Cassio)*
    One is too poor, too weak for my revenge.
440   Now do I see 'tis true. Look here, Iago:
    All my fond love thus do I blow to heaven. 'Tis gone.
       [OTHELLO *kneels.*]
    Arise, black vengeance, from the hollow hell;
    Yield up, O love, thy crown and hearted throne°   *rule of the heart*
    To tyrannous hate. Swell, bosom, with thy fraught,°   *burden*
    For 'tis of aspics'° tongues.   *poisonous snakes'*
445 IAGO   Yet be content.
OTHELLO   Oh, blood! Blood! Blood!
IAGO   Patience, I say: your mind may change.
OTHELLO   Never, Iago! Like to the Pontic Sea,°   *Black Sea*
    Whose icy current and compulsive course
    Ne'er keeps retiring ebb, but keeps due on
450   To the Propontic and the Hellespont,[5]
    Even so my bloody thoughts, with violent pace,

5. The Pontic, or Black, Sea was said by the ancient Roman writer Pliny to flow in only one direction— into the Propontic, the body of water bounded by the straits of Bosphorus and the Dardanelles (Hellespont), the latter strait leading to the Aegean.

Shall ne'er look back, ne'er ebb to humble love
Till that a capable° and wide revenge   *capacious*
Swallow them up. Now, by yond marble heaven,
455 In the due reverence of a sacred vow
I here engage my words.

IAGO   Do not rise yet.

      [IAGO *kneels.*[6]]
Witness, you ever-burning lights above,
You elements that clip° us round about,   *embrace (sexual?)*
Witness that here Iago doth give up
460 The execution° of his wit, hands, heart,   *command*
To wronged Othello's service. Let him command,
And to obey shall be in me remorse,°   *pity (for Othello)*
What bloody business ever.

OTHELLO   I greet thy love
Not with vain thanks but with acceptance bounteous,
465 And will upon the instant put thee to't.°   *immediately test it*
Within these three days let me hear thee say
That Cassio's not alive.

IAGO   My friend is dead.
'Tis done at your request. But let her live.

OTHELLO   Damn her, lewd minx!° Oh, damn her! Damn her!   *wanton*
470 Come, go with me apart. I will withdraw
To furnish me with some swift means of death
For the fair devil. Now art thou my lieutenant.

IAGO   I am your own forever.   *Exeunt.*

3.4 (Q 3.4)

Enter DESDEMONA, EMILIA, *and* CLOWN.

DESDEMONA   Do you know, sirrah,[1] where lieutenant Cassio
lies?

CLOWN   I dare not say he lies anywhere.

DESDEMONA   Why, man?

5 CLOWN   He's a soldier, and for me to say a soldier lies, 'tis
stabbing.

DESDEMONA   Go to! Where lodges he?

CLOWN   To tell you where he lodges is to tell you where I lie.

DESDEMONA   Can anything be made of this?

10 CLOWN   I know not where he lodges, and for me to devise a
lodging and say, "He lies here," or "He lies there," were to lie
in mine own throat.°   *lie outrageously*

DESDEMONA   Can you inquire him out, and be edified by report?

CLOWN   I will catechize the world for him: that is, make ques-
15 tions and by them answer.°   *find the answer*

DESDEMONA   Seek him. Bid him come hither. Tell him I have
moved° my lord on his behalf, and hope all will be well.   *petitioned*

CLOWN   To do this is within the compass° of man's wit and,   *scope*
therefore, I will attempt the doing it.   *Exit* CLOWN.

20 DESDEMONA   Where should° I lose the handkerchief, Emilia?   *did*

EMILIA   I know not, madam.

DESDEMONA   Believe me, I had rather have lost my purse

---

6. Parody of the marriage ceremony.   1. A form of address to an inferior.
3.4 Location: Before the citadel.

Full of *crusados.*° And but° my noble Moor   *gold coins / but that*
Is true of mind and made of no such baseness
25 As jealous creatures are, it were enough
To put him to ill thinking.

EMILIA   Is he not jealous?

DESDEMONA   Who, he? I think the sun where he was born
Drew all such humors from him.[2]

          Enter OTHELLO.

EMILIA   Look where he comes.

DESDEMONA   I will not leave him now till Cassio be
30 Called to him. —How is't with you, my lord?

OTHELLO   Well, my good lady. [*aside*] Oh, hardness to dissemble!
—How do you, Desdemona?

DESDEMONA   Well, my good lord.

OTHELLO   Give me your hand. This hand is moist,° my lady.   *(sign of carnal desire)*

DESDEMONA   It hath felt no age, nor known no sorrow.

35 OTHELLO   This argues fruitfulness and liberal heart.[3]
Hot, hot, and moist: this hand of yours requires
A sequester from liberty, fasting, and prayer,
Much castigation, exercise devout,
For here's a young and sweating devil here
40 That commonly rebels. 'Tis a good hand,
A frank° one.   *(sexually) open*

DESDEMONA   You may indeed say so,
For 'twas that hand that gave away my heart.

OTHELLO   A liberal hand. The hearts of old gave hands,
But our new heraldry is hands, not hearts.[4]

45 DESDEMONA   I cannot speak of this. Come now, your
    promise.

OTHELLO   What promise, chuck?°   *woodchuck (affectionate)*

DESDEMONA   I have sent to bid Cassio come speak with you.

OTHELLO   I have a salt and sorry rheum° offends me.   *badly watering eyes*
Lend me thy handkerchief.

DESDEMONA   Here, my lord.

OTHELLO   That which I gave you.

50 DESDEMONA   I have it not about me.

OTHELLO   Not?

DESDEMONA   No, indeed, my lord.

OTHELLO   That's a fault. That handkerchief
Did an Egyptian to my mother give:
She was a charmer,° and could almost read   *sorceress*
55 The thoughts of people. She told her, while she kept it,
'Twould make her amiable,° and subdue my father   *desirable*
Entirely to her love; but if she lost it,
Or made a gift of it, my father's eye
Should hold her loathed, and his spirits should hunt
60 After new fancies. She, dying, gave it me,
And bid me, when my fate would have me wived,
To give it her.° I did so, and take heed on't;   *to my wife*
Make it a darling like° your precious eye;   *as dear to you as*

2. The four humors were bodily fluids, the mix of which was believed by classical and Renaissance thinkers to determine one's temperament. Desdemona here repeats a standard position—that the climate of Africa, in its effect on the bodily humors, prevented its inhabitants from easily succumbing to jealousy.
3. This demonstrates fertility (perhaps, by implication, lust) and a generous (loose) heart.
4. These days the joining of hands doesn't signify the joining of hearts.

To lose't or give't away were such perdition° *loss; damnation*
As nothing else could match.

65 DESDEMONA   Is't possible?

OTHELLO   'Tis true. There's magic in the web of it.
A sibyl,° that had numbered in the world *female prophet*
The sun to course two hundred compasses,⁵
In her prophetic fury sewed the work;

70 The worms were hallowed that did breed the silk;
And it was dyed in mummy,⁶ which the skillful
Conserved of° maidens' hearts. *Preserved out of*

DESDEMONA   Indeed? Is't true?

OTHELLO   Most veritable. Therefore look to't well.

DESDEMONA   Then would to heaven that I had never seen't!

75 OTHELLO   Ha! Wherefore?

DESDEMONA   Why do you speak so startingly° and rash? *impetuously*

OTHELLO   Is't lost? Is't gone? Speak, is't out o'th' way?

DESDEMONA   Bless us!

OTHELLO   Say you?

80 DESDEMONA   It is not lost—but what an if° it were? *an if = if*

OTHELLO   How?

DESDEMONA   I say it is not lost.

OTHELLO   Fetch't. Let me see't.

DESDEMONA   Why, so I can, but I will not now:
This is a trick to put me from my suit.

85 Pray you, let Cassio be received again.

OTHELLO   Fetch me the handkerchief! [*aside*] My mind misgives.

DESDEMONA   Come, come. You'll never meet a more sufficient° *complete*
man.

OTHELLO   The handkerchief!

DESDEMONA   A man that all his time
Hath founded his good fortunes on your love,
Shared dangers with you—

90 OTHELLO   The handkerchief!

DESDEMONA   In sooth, you are to blame.

OTHELLO   Away!
Exit OTHELLO.

EMILIA   Is not this man jealous?

DESDEMONA   I ne'er saw this before.
Sure, there's some wonder in this handkerchief;
I am most unhappy in the loss of it.

95 EMILIA   'Tis not a year or two shows us a man:⁷
They are all but° stomachs, and we all but food; *nothing but*
They eat us hungrily, and when they are full
They belch us.

Enter IAGO *and* CASSIO.

Look you, Cassio and my husband.

IAGO [*to* CASSIO]   There is no other way; 'tis she must do't.

100 [*He indicates* DESDEMONA.] And, lo, the happiness!⁸ Go and
importune her.

DESDEMONA   How now, good Cassio? What's the news with you?

CASSIO   Madam, my former suit. I do beseech you

---

5. *that . . . compasses:* who was two hundred years old.
6. Fluid drained from mummified bodies, supposedly magical.

7. Probably: It doesn't take long to see what men are made of.
8. What a happy coincidence (seeing Desdemona).

That by your virtuous means I may again
Exist, and be a member of his love
105 Whom I, with all the office of my heart,
Entirely honor. I would not be delayed.
If my offense be of such mortal° kind   *deadly*
That nor° my service past, nor present sorrows,   *neither*
Nor purposed° merit in futurity,°   *intended / the future*
110 Can ransom me into his love again,
But to know so° must be my benefit.   *Even to know this*
So° shall I clothe me in a forced content,   *If so*
And shut myself up in° some other course   *limit myself to*
To° Fortune's alms.   *To win*
DESDEMONA   Alas, thrice-gentle Cassio,
115 My advocation is not now in tune.⁹
My lord is not my lord, nor should I know him
Were he in favor° as in humor altered.   *appearance*
So help me every spirit sanctified,
As I have spoken for you all my best,
120 And stood within the blank of° his displeasure   *in the aim of*
For my free speech. You must awhile be patient:
What I can do, I will, and more I will
Than for myself I dare. Let that suffice you.
IAGO   Is my lord angry?
EMILIA   He went hence but now,
125 And certainly in strange unquietness.
IAGO   Can he be angry? I have seen the cannon
When it hath blown his ranks into the air
And, like the devil, from his very arm
Puffed his own brother¹—and is he angry?
130 Something of moment, then. I will go meet him.
There's matter in't indeed, if he be angry.
DESDEMONA   I prithee, do so.   *Exit* [IAGO].
                         Something, sure, of state,°   *state business*
Either from Venice or some unhatched practice°   *unfinished plot*
Made demonstrable° here in Cyprus to him,   *Revealed*
135 Hath puddled° his clear spirit; and in such cases   *fouled; dirtied*
Men's natures wrangle with inferior things,
Though great ones are their object. 'Tis even so:
For let our finger ache, and it endues°   *induces*
Our other healthful members even to a sense
140 Of pain. Nay, we must think men are not gods,
Nor of them look for such observancy°   *careful attention*
As fits the bridal.° Beshrew me° much, Emilia,   *wedding / (mild curse)*
I was—unhandsome° warrior as I am—   *unskilled*
Arraigning his unkindness with my soul,
145 But now I find I had suborned the witness,
And he's indicted falsely.²
EMILIA   Pray heaven it be
State matters, as you think, and no conception
Nor no jealous toy° concerning you.   *whim*
DESDEMONA   Alas the day! I never gave him cause.

---

9. My advocacy isn't working properly.
1. Blew up his own brother (and Othello wasn't angry
even then).

2. *suborned . . . falsely*: made the witness lie and so
accused Othello falsely.

150 EMILIA   But jealous souls will not be answered so.
      They are not ever jealous for the cause,
      But jealous for they're jealous: it is a monster
      Begot upon itself, born on itself.
DESDEMONA   Heaven keep the monster from Othello's mind!
155 EMILIA   Lady, amen.
DESDEMONA   I will go seek him. —Cassio, walk here about.
      If I do find him fit, I'll move your suit,
      And seek to effect it to my uttermost.
CASSIO   I humbly thank your ladyship.
                                    Exeunt [DESDEMONA *and* EMILIA].
      Enter BIANCA.[3]
BIANCA   Save you,° friend Cassio.   *God save you*
160 CASSIO   What make° you from home?   *brings*
      How is't with you, my most fair Bianca?
      Indeed, sweet love, I was coming to your house.
BIANCA   And I was going to your lodging, Cassio.
      What, keep a week away? Seven days and nights,
165   Eight score eight hours—and lovers' absent hours
      More tedious than the dial eight score times![4]
      Oh, weary reck'ning!°   *calculating*
CASSIO   Pardon me, Bianca.
      I have this while with leaden thoughts been pressed,
      But I shall in a more continuate° time   *opportune*
170   Strike off° this score of absence. Sweet Bianca,   *Make up*
            [*He gives her the handkerchief.*]
      Take me this work out.°   *Copy this embroidery*
BIANCA   O Cassio, whence came this?
      This is some token from a newer friend.
      To the felt absence now I feel a cause.
      Is't come to this? Well, well!
CASSIO   Go to,° woman!   *Stop it*
175   Throw your vile guesses in the devil's teeth
      From whence you have them. You are jealous now
      That this is from some mistress some remembrance.
      No, in good troth, Bianca.
BIANCA   Why, whose is it?
CASSIO   I know not, neither. I found it in my chamber.
180   I like the work well: ere it be demanded,°   *sought out*
      As like° enough it will, I would have it copied.   *likely*
      Take it, and do't, and leave me for this time.
BIANCA   Leave you? Wherefore?
CASSIO   I do attend here on the general,
185   And think it no addition,° nor my wish,   *(to my cause)*
      To have him see me womaned.°   *with a woman*
BIANCA   Why, I pray you?
CASSIO   Not that I love you not.
BIANCA   But that you do not love me.
      I pray you, bring me on the way a little,
      And say if I shall see you soon at night.
190 CASSIO   'Tis but a little way that I can bring you,

---

3. "Bianca" means "white" in Italian—perhaps part of the play's ironic reversal of conventional color imagery, given that Bianca is a "customer" (courte-san, 4.1.115).
4. *lovers'* . . . *times:* each hour lovers are parted is eight score (160) times more tedious than normal clock time.

For I attend here; but I'll see you soon.
BIANCA 'Tis very good. I must be circumstanced.[5]

Exeunt all.

4.1 (Q 4.1)

Enter OTHELLO *and* IAGO.

IAGO Will you think so?
OTHELLO   Think so, Iago?
IAGO   What,
   To kiss in private?
OTHELLO   An unauthorized kiss!
IAGO Or to be naked with her friend in bed
   An hour or more, not meaning any harm?
5 OTHELLO Naked in bed, Iago, and not mean harm?
   It is hypocrisy against the devil.[1]
   They that mean virtuously, and yet do so,
   The devil their virtue tempts, and they tempt heaven.[2]
IAGO If they do nothing, 'tis a venial slip;°   *an excusable sin*
   But if I give my wife a handkerchief—
10 OTHELLO   What then?
IAGO Why, then 'tis hers, my lord, and, being hers,
   She may, I think, bestow't on any man.
OTHELLO She is protectress of her honor, too.
   May she give that?
15 IAGO Her honor is an essence that's not seen:
   They° have it very oft that have it not.   *They are reputed to*
   But for the handkerchief—
OTHELLO By heaven, I would most gladly have forgot it!
   Thou said'st—oh, it comes o'er my memory
20 As doth the raven o'er the infectious house,[3]
   Boding to all—he had my handkerchief.
IAGO Ay, what of that?
OTHELLO   That's not so good now.
IAGO What if I had said I had seen him do you wrong?
   Or heard him say—as knaves be such abroad,[4]
25 Who, having by their own importunate suit,
   Or voluntary dotage of some mistress,
   Convinced or supplied° them, cannot choose   *Seduced or satisfied*
   But they must blab—
OTHELLO   Hath he said anything?
IAGO He hath, my lord, but be you well assured,
   No more than he'll unswear.
30 OTHELLO   What hath he said?
IAGO Why, that he did—I know not what he did.
OTHELLO What? What?
IAGO   Lie.
OTHELLO   With her?

---

5. Content with what circumstances offer.
4.1 Location: Before the citadel.
1. *Naked . . . devil:* By showing every sign of committing adultery but then stopping just in time, they
deliberately mislead the devil, who wrongly takes their
apparent intention to sin at face value (just as an
ordinary hypocrite deceives by professing virtue).

2. *they . . . heaven:* Those who mean well ("virtuously") but act in this lascivious fashion ("so") make it
easy for the devil successfully to tempt them, and they
violate the biblical prohibition against tempting God.
3. The raven was thought to be an ill omen and a
carrier of plague. *infectious:* plague-infested.
4. As such knaves do exist in the world.

IAGO   With her, on her, what you will.

OTHELLO   Lie with her? Lie on her? We say "lie on her"° when   *lie about her; (sexual)*
they belie° her. Lie with her? That's fulsome!° Handker-   *slander / nauseating*
35   chief! Confessions! Handkerchief! To⁵ confess and be
hanged for his labor. First to be hanged and then to confess.
I tremble at it. Nature would not invest herself in such shadowing passion without some instruction.⁶ It is not words
that shakes me thus—pish! Noses, ears, and lips! Is't possi-
40   ble? Confess? Handkerchief? Oh, devil!
          [*He*] *falls in a trance.*

IAGO   Work on,
My medicine works! Thus credulous fools are caught,
And many worthy and chaste dames, even thus
All guiltless, meet reproach. —What ho, my lord?
My lord, I say! Othello!
          Enter CASSIO.
45   —How now, Cassio?

CASSIO   What's the matter?

IAGO   My lord is fallen into an epilepsy.
This is his second fit; he had one yesterday.

CASSIO   Rub him about the temples.

50   IAGO   The lethargy° must have his° quiet course: *trance / its*
If not, he foams at mouth and, by and by,
Breaks out to savage madness. Look, he stirs.
Do you withdraw yourself a little while.
He will recover straight.° When he is gone,   *immediately*
55   I would on great occasion° speak with you.   [*Exit* CASSIO.]   *important matters*
—How is it, general? Have you not hurt your head?⁷

OTHELLO   Dost thou mock me?

IAGO   I mock you not, by heaven.
Would you would bear your fortune like a man.

OTHELLO   A hornèd man's a monster and a beast.

60   IAGO   There's many a beast, then, in a populous city,
And many a civil° monster.   *city-dwelling*

OTHELLO   Did he confess it?

IAGO   Good sir, be a man.
Think every bearded fellow that's but yoked
May draw with you?⁸ There's millions now alive
65   That nightly lie in those unproper beds
Which they dare swear peculiar.⁹ Your case is better.
Oh, 'tis the spite of hell, the fiend's arch-mock,°   *devil's greatest mock*
To lip° a wanton in a secure° couch   *kiss / an unsuspected*
And to suppose her chaste. No, let me know
70   And, knowing what I am,° I know what she shall be.   *(a cuckold)*

OTHELLO   Oh, thou art wise, 'tis certain.

IAGO   Stand you awhile apart.

---

5. Lines 35–40 do not appear in Q. Arguably, these
lines provide more time for Othello to drive himself
to distraction and hence make his collapse more
plausible.
6. *Nature . . . instruction*: It isn't natural that I would
feel such foreboding ("shadowing") emotion (jealousy) unless there were some cause for it.
7. Othello takes this as suggesting that he has grown

cuckold's horns.
8. *every . . . you*: every married man ("yoked," like an
ox, to his wife and hence to cuckoldry) labors ("draws")
under the same fate.
9. *That . . . peculiar*: Who lie in beds that don't belong
entirely to them but that they would swear are exclusively their own.

Confine yourself but in a patient list.°   *boundary; bearing; desire*
Whilst you were here, o'erwhelmed with your grief—
A passion most resulting° such a man—   *recoiling upon (?)*
75 Cassio came hither. I shifted him away,
And laid good 'scuses upon your ecstasy,°   *for your fit*
Bade him anon° return and here speak with me,   *soon*
The which he promised. Do but encave° yourself,   *Only hide*
And mark the fleers,° the jibes, and notable scorns   *sneers*
80 That dwell in every region of his face:
For I will make him tell the tale anew,
Where, how, how oft, how long ago, and when
He hath and is again to cope° your wife.   *copulate with*
I say but mark his gesture. Marry, patience!
85 Or I shall say you're all-in-all in spleen,°   *completely impulsive*
And nothing of a man.
OTHELLO   Dost thou hear, Iago?
I will be found most cunning in my patience,
But—dost thou hear?—most bloody.
IAGO   That's not amiss.
But yet keep time° in all. Will you withdraw?   *maintain control*
    [OTHELLO *withdraws.*]
90 Now will I question Cassio of Bianca,
A housewife that by selling her desires[1]
Buys herself bread and cloth. It is a creature
That dotes on Cassio, as 'tis the strumpet's plague
To beguile many and be beguiled by one.
95 He, when he hears of her, cannot restrain
From the excess of laughter.
            Enter CASSIO.
                    Here he comes.
As he shall smile, Othello shall go mad,
And his unbookish jealousy[2] must construe
Poor Cassio's smiles, gestures, and light behaviors
100 Quite in the wrong. [*to* CASSIO] How do you, lieutenant?
CASSIO The worser that you give me the addition°   *title*
Whose want even° kills me.   *lack just*
IAGO Ply Desdemona well, and you are sure on't.
Now, if this suit lay in Bianca's dower°   *dowry*
How quickly should you speed?
105 CASSIO   Alas, poor caitiff!°   *wretch*
OTHELLO [*apart*] Look how he laughs already.
IAGO I never knew woman love man so.
CASSIO Alas, poor rogue. I think indeed she loves me.
OTHELLO [*apart*] Now he denies it faintly, and laughs it out.
IAGO Do you hear, Cassio?—
110 OTHELLO [*apart*]   Now he importunes him
To tell it o'er. Go to: well said, well said.
IAGO   —She gives it out that you shall marry her.
Do you intend it?
CASSIO   Ha, ha, ha!

---

1. *housewife . . . selling her desires:* housewife (or hussy = prostitute) selling her desired body.
2. Naïve; ignorant of the high level of suspiciousness appropriate to an educated Venetian man—given

Othello's refusal to be jealous of Desdemona merely because she "loves company, / Is free of speech, . . . and dances" (3.3.182–83); not conforming to the bookish notion of the unjealous African.

OTHELLO [*apart*]   Do ye triumph, Roman?[3] Do you triumph?

115   CASSIO   I marry! What, a customer!° Prithee bear some char-   *courtesan*
      ity to my wit.° Do not think it so unwholesome. Ha, ha, ha!   *sense*

OTHELLO [*apart*]   So, so, so, so. They laugh that wins.

IAGO   Why, the cry goes that you marry her.

CASSIO   Prithee say true.

IAGO   I am a very villain else.°   *if it's not true (ironic)*

120   OTHELLO [*apart*]   Have you scored me?[4] Well.

CASSIO   This is the monkey's own giving out.° She is per-   *Bianca's own story*
      suaded I will marry her out of her own love and flattery, not
      out of my promise.

OTHELLO [*apart*]   Iago beckons me. Now he begins the story.
      [OTHELLO *moves closer.*]

125   CASSIO   She was here even now; she haunts me in every place.
      I was the other day talking on the sea-bank with certain
      Venetians, and thither comes the bauble° and falls me thus   *toy*
      about my neck.

OTHELLO [*apart*]   Crying, "O dear Cassio!", as it were: his ges-

130   ture imports° it.   *indicates*

CASSIO   So hangs, and lolls, and weeps upon me; so shakes
      and pulls me. Ha, ha, ha!

OTHELLO [*apart*]   Now he tells how she plucked him to my
      chamber. Oh, I see that nose of yours, but not that dog I shall

135   throw it to.[5]

CASSIO   Well, I must leave her company.
      Enter BIANCA.

IAGO   Before me, look where she comes!

CASSIO   'Tis such another fitchew.[6] Marry, a perfumed one!
      [*to* BIANCA] What do you mean by this haunting of me?

140   BIANCA   Let the devil and his dam° haunt you! What did you   *mother*
      mean by that same handkerchief you gave me even now? I
      was a fine fool to take it. I must take out° the work? A likely   *copy*
      piece of work,° that you should find it in your chamber and   *An implausible story*
      know not who left it there. This is some minx's token—and

145   I must take out the work? There, give it° your hobby-horse!°   *it to / loose woman*
      Wheresoever you had it, I'll take out no work on't.

CASSIO   How now, my sweet Bianca? How now? How now?

OTHELLO [*apart*]   By heaven, that should° be my handkerchief!   *must*

BIANCA   If you'll come to supper tonight, you may: if you will

150   not, come when you are next prepared for.[7]   *Exit.*

IAGO   After her! After her!

CASSIO   I must: she'll rail in the streets else.

IAGO   Will you sup there?

CASSIO   Yes, I intend so.

155   IAGO   Well, I may chance to see you, for I would very fain°   *be very well pleased to*
      speak with you.

CASSIO   Prithee, come. Will you?

IAGO   Go to. Say no more.   [*Exit* CASSIO.]

---

3. Perhaps Othello draws on associations either with
Rome's imperial successes (and subsequent collapse)
or with the Roman practice of holding celebratory
processions.
4. Wounded me; sexually conquered at my expense.
5. *I see . . . to:* I'm envisioning my revenge, but the

time is not yet quite right. Cutting off the enemy's
nose was understood as a form of retribution.
6. Polecat, associated with prostitutes because of its
bad smell and presumed lecherousness.
7. Come next time I prepare for you (never).

OTHELLO How shall I murder him, Iago?

160 IAGO Did you perceive how he laughed at his vice?

OTHELLO O Iago!

IAGO And did you see the handkerchief?

OTHELLO Was that mine?

IAGO Yours, by this hand. And to see how he prizes the foolish
165 woman, your wife: she gave it him, and he hath given it his
whore.

OTHELLO I would have him nine years a-killing.[8] A fine woman!
A fair woman! A sweet woman!

IAGO Nay, you must forget that.

170 OTHELLO Ay, let her rot and perish, and be damned tonight,
for she shall not live. No, my heart is turned to stone: I strike
it, and it hurts my hand. Oh, the world hath not a sweeter
creature: she might lie by an emperor's side, and command
him tasks.

175 IAGO Nay, that's not your way.°   (the way to think)

OTHELLO Hang her! I do but say what she is: so delicate with
her needle; an admirable musician—oh, she will sing the
savageness out of a bear!—of so high and plenteous wit and
invention°—   imagination

180 IAGO She's the worse for all this.

OTHELLO Oh, a thousand, a thousand times! And, then, of so
gentle° a condition!   highly born

IAGO Ay, too gentle.°   generous (sexually)

OTHELLO Nay, that's certain.

185 But yet the pity of it, Iago. O Iago, the pity of it, Iago!

IAGO If you are so fond° over her iniquity, give her patent° to foolish / license
offend; for if it touch not you, it comes near nobody.

OTHELLO I will chop her into messes!° Cuckold me!   pieces of food

IAGO Oh, 'tis foul in her.

190 OTHELLO With mine officer!

IAGO That's fouler.

OTHELLO Get me some poison, Iago, this night. I'll not expostulate with her, lest her body and beauty unprovide my mind° weaken my resolve
again. This night, Iago.

195 IAGO Do it not with poison. Strangle her in her bed, even the
bed she hath contaminated.

OTHELLO Good, good. The justice of it pleases. Very good.

IAGO And for Cassio, let me be his undertaker.° You shall hear murderer
more by midnight.

OTHELLO Excellent good.
[A trumpet sounds.]

200   What trumpet is that same?

IAGO I warrant, something from Venice.
Enter LODOVICO, DESDEMONA, and Attendants.
'Tis Lodovico: this comes from the Duke.
See, your wife's with him.

LODOVICO Save you, worthy general.

OTHELLO   With all my heart,° sir.   Thank you

205 LODOVICO The Duke and the senators of Venice greet you.
[He gives OTHELLO a letter.]

---

8. I would spend nine years killing him.

OTHELLO   I kiss the instrument° of their pleasures.°   *bearer / commands*
DESDEMONA   And what's the news, good cousin Lodovico?
IAGO   I am very glad to see you, signor.
   Welcome to Cyprus.
210 LODOVICO   I thank you. How does Lieutenant Cassio?
IAGO   Lives, sir.
DESDEMONA   Cousin, there's fallen between him and my lord
   An unkind° breach, but you shall make all well.   *unnatural; painful*
OTHELLO   Are you sure of that?
215 DESDEMONA   My lord?
OTHELLO [*reads*]   "This fail you not to do, as you will—"
LODOVICO [*to* DESDEMONA]   He did not call: he's busy in° the   *with*
   paper.
   Is there division twixt my lord and Cassio?
DESDEMONA   A most unhappy one. I would do much
220   T'atone° them, for the love I bear to Cassio.   *To reconcile*
OTHELLO   Fire and brimstone!
DESDEMONA   My lord?
OTHELLO   Are you wise?
DESDEMONA [*to* LODOVICO]   What, is he angry?
LODOVICO   Maybe the letter moved him,
   For, as I think, they do command him home,
   Deputing Cassio in his government.°   *official position*
DESDEMONA   Trust me, I am glad on't.
OTHELLO   Indeed?
225 DESDEMONA   My lord?
OTHELLO   I am glad to see you mad.[9]
DESDEMONA   Why, sweet Othello?
OTHELLO   Devil!
     [*He strikes her.*]
DESDEMONA   I have not deserved this!
LODOVICO   My lord! This would not be believed in Venice,
230   Though I should swear I saw't. 'Tis very much.°   *serious*
   Make her amends: she weeps.
OTHELLO   O devil! Devil!
   If that the earth could teem with° woman's tears,   *become pregnant by*
   Each drop she falls would prove a crocodile.[1]
   —Out of my sight!
DESDEMONA   I will not stay to offend you.
     [*She starts to leave.*]
235 LODOVICO   Truly obedient, lady.
   —I do beseech your lordship, call her back.
OTHELLO   Mistress.
DESDEMONA   My lord?
OTHELLO [*to* LODOVICO]   What would you° with her, sir?   *do you wish*
LODOVICO   Who? I, my lord?
OTHELLO   Ay, you did wish that I would make her turn.°   *return*
240   Sir, she can turn and turn,° and yet go on   *(sexually)*
   And turn again. And she can weep, sir, weep!

---

9. Perhaps Othello is pleased that she's rejoicing in Cassio's promotion and hence revealing their adulterous affair, which she would be "mad" to do in public and in front of him.

1. Each drop would cause the earth to conceive a crocodile (crocodiles proverbially wept false tears for their victims).

And she's obedient, as you say, obedient,
Very obedient. [*to* DESDEMONA] Proceed you in your tears.
[*to* LODOVICO] Concerning this, sir— [*to* DESDEMONA] Oh,
    well-painted passion!
245 —I am commanded home. [*to* DESDEMONA] Get you away.
I'll send for you anon. —Sir, I obey the mandate
And will return to Venice. [*to* DESDEMONA] Hence! Avaunt!°   *Begone*
                                    [*Exit* DESDEMONA.]
[*to* LODOVICO] Cassio shall have my place, and, sir, tonight
I do entreat that we may sup together.
250 You are welcome, sir, to Cyprus. —Goats and monkeys!²
                                        Exit.

LODOVICO   Is this the noble Moor whom our full Senate
Call all-in-all sufficient? Is this the nature
Whom passion could not shake? Whose solid virtue
The shot of accident nor dart of chance
Could neither graze nor pierce?
255 IAGO   He is much changed.
LODOVICO   Are his wits safe? Is he not light of brain?
IAGO   He's that he is: I may not breathe my censure.
What he might be—if what he might, he is not—
I would to heaven he were.³
LODOVICO   What, strike his wife?
260 IAGO   Faith, that was not so well. Yet would I knew
That stroke would prove the worst.
LODOVICO   Is it his use?°   *custom*
Or did the letters work upon his blood,°   *passions*
And new create his fault?
IAGO   Alas, alas!
It is not honesty in me to speak
265 What I have seen and known. You shall observe him,
And his own courses° will denote him so   *actions*
That I may save my speech. Do but go after,
And mark how he continues.
LODOVICO   I am sorry that I am deceived in him.   *Exeunt.*

4.2 (Q 4.2)
Enter OTHELLO *and* EMILIA.
OTHELLO   You have seen nothing, then?
EMILIA   Nor ever heard, nor ever did suspect.
OTHELLO   Yes? You have seen Cassio and she together?
EMILIA   But then I saw no harm; and then I heard
5 Each syllable that breath made up between them.
OTHELLO   What, did they never whisper?
EMILIA   Never, my lord.
OTHELLO   Nor send you out o'th' way?
EMILIA   Never.
OTHELLO   To fetch her fan, her gloves, her mask, nor nothing?
EMILIA   Never, my lord.

---

2. Symbols of lust (borrowing Iago's language, 3.3.400).
3. *He's that . . . were:* He is what he is (as Iago says of himself, "I am not what I am," 1.1.63). I won't express my judgment on whether he is sane. What he might be

(sane)—if, though he might be (sane), he is not—I wish he were (sane). That is: if he is not sane, I wish he were. Alternatively: if he is sane, I wish he were insane (because only that would excuse his bad behavior).
4.2 Location: The citadel.

10 OTHELLO   That's strange.
EMILIA   I durst, my lord, to wager she is honest:
     Lay down my soul at stake. If you think other,
     Remove your thought: it doth abuse your bosom.
     If any wretch have put this in your head,
15   Let heaven requit° it with the serpent's curse,[1]   *requite*
     For if she be not honest, chaste, and true,
     There's no man happy: the purest of their wives
     Is foul as slander.
OTHELLO   Bid her come hither. Go.   *Exit* EMILIA.
     She says enough. Yet she's a simple bawd
20   That cannot say as much.[2] This is a subtle whore,
     A closet, lock, and key° of villainous secrets;   *A hider*
     And yet she'll kneel and pray—I have seen her do't.
          Enter DESDEMONA *and* EMILIA.
DESDEMONA   My lord, what is your will?
OTHELLO   Pray you, chuck, come hither.
DESDEMONA   What is your pleasure?
OTHELLO   Let me see your eyes.
     Look in my face.
25 DESDEMONA   What horrible fancy's this?
OTHELLO [*to* EMILIA]   Some of your function,[3] mistress.
     Leave procreants° alone, and shut the door.   *copulators*
     Cough or cry "hem!" if anybody come.
     Your mystery, your mystery° may dispatch![4]   *Exit* EMILIA.   *profession*
30 DESDEMONA [*kneeling*]   Upon my knee, what doth your speech
          import?
     I understand a fury in your words.
OTHELLO   Why, what art thou?
DESDEMONA   Your wife, my lord: your true and loyal wife.
OTHELLO   Come, swear it! Damn thyself, lest, being°   *appearing*
35   Like one of heaven, the devils themselves
     Should fear to seize thee. Therefore be double damned:
     Swear thou art honest.
DESDEMONA   Heaven doth truly know it.
OTHELLO   Heaven truly knows that thou art false as hell.
DESDEMONA   To whom, my lord? With whom? How am I false?
40 OTHELLO   Ah, Desdemon! Away! Away! Away!
DESDEMONA   Alas the heavy day, why do you weep?
     Am I the motive of these tears, my lord?
     If haply° you my father do suspect   *perhaps*
     An instrument of this your calling back,
45   Lay not your blame on me. If you have lost him,
     I have lost him too.
OTHELLO   Had it pleased heaven
     To try me with affliction; had they° rained   *the heavens*
     All kind of sores and shames on my bare head;
     Steeped me in poverty to the very lips;
50   Given to captivity me and my utmost hopes,
     I should have found in some place of my soul
     A drop of patience. But, alas, to make me

---

1. In Genesis, the curse that God laid on the serpent
who deceived Eve.
2. *Yet . . . much:* Yet it would be a simpleminded go-
between who can't say as much as she did.
3. Fulfill your bawd's function by guarding the door.
4. May send you to your destination.

The fixèd figure for the time of scorn
To point his slow and moving finger at!⁵
55   Yet could I bear that too, well, very well.
But there, where I have garnered° up my heart,   *stored*
Where either I must live, or bear no life,
The fountain⁶ from the which my current runs,
Or else dries up—to be discarded thence,
60   Or keep it as a cistern for foul toads
To knot and gender° in! Turn thy complexion there,   *To couple and engender*
Patience, thou young and rose-lipped cherubin:
I here look grim as hell.⁷

DESDEMONA   I hope my noble lord esteems me honest.
65   OTHELLO   Oh, ay. As summer flies are in the shambles,°   *slaughter-house*
That quicken even with blowing.⁸ O thou weed,
Who art so lovely fair and smell'st so sweet
That the sense aches at thee! Would thou hadst never been
born!

DESDEMONA   Alas, what ignorant° sin have I committed?   *unwitting*
70   OTHELLO   Was this fair paper, this most goodly book,
Made to write "whore" upon? "What committed?"
"Committed?"⁹ O thou public commoner!°   *prostitute*
I should make very forges of my cheeks
That would to cinders burn up modesty,
75   Did I but speak thy deeds. "What committed?"
Heaven stops the nose at it, and the moon winks;°   *closes its eyes*
The bawdy° wind, that kisses all it meets,   *promiscuous*
Is hushed within the hollow mine of earth,°   *cave of the winds*
And will not hear't. "What committed?"

80   DESDEMONA   By heaven, you do me wrong!
OTHELLO   Are not you a strumpet?
DESDEMONA   No, as I am a Christian!
If to preserve this vessel for my lord
From any other foul, unlawful touch
Be not to be a strumpet, I am none.
OTHELLO   What, not a whore?
85   DESDEMONA   No, as I shall be saved!
OTHELLO   Is't possible?
DESDEMONA   O heaven, forgive us!
OTHELLO   I cry you mercy,° then;   *I beg your pardon*
I took you for that cunning whore of Venice
That married with Othello. [*He calls* EMILIA.] You, mistress,
Enter EMILIA.
90   That have the office opposite to Saint Peter,
And keeps the gate of hell. You, you! Ay, you!
We have done our course.° There's money for your pains.   *business*
[*He gives* EMILIA *money.*]
I pray you, turn the key, and keep our counsel.   *Exit.*
EMILIA   Alas, what does this gentleman conceive?°   *believe*

---

5. *The fixèd . . . at:* The designated object of scorn
for this scornful time to point (as on a clock face) its
slowly moving hand at.
6. Spring. The language here imagines Desdemona
as the source of Othello's emotional vitality.
7. *Turn . . . / hell:* Look there (or change your look for
the worse) at the thought of that, Patience, and you

"cherubin": I (or: Ay) here look infernally forbidding.
8. Who come to life (or bring their offspring to life
and hence make the meat foul) as soon as the eggs are
deposited. The point seems to be the speed of breeding, inferred from Desdemona's supposed infidelity.
9. Lines 72–75 do not appear in Q.

95 —How do you, madam? How do you, my good lady?

DESDEMONA Faith, half asleep.

EMILIA Good madam, what's the matter with my lord?

DESDEMONA With who?

EMILIA   Why, with my lord, madam.

DESDEMONA Who is thy lord?

EMILIA   He that is yours, sweet lady.

100 DESDEMONA I have none. Do not talk to me, Emilia.

I cannot weep, nor answers have I none

But what should go by water.° Prithee tonight   *appear in tears*

Lay on my bed my wedding sheets. Remember,

And call thy husband hither.

EMILIA   Here's a change indeed.   *Exit.*

105 DESDEMONA 'Tis meet° I should be used so, very meet.   *fitting*

How have I been behaved, that he might stick

The small'st opinion on my least misuse?[1]

       Enter IAGO *and* EMILIA.

IAGO What is your pleasure, madam?

How is't with you?

110 DESDEMONA I cannot tell. Those that do teach young babes

Do it with gentle means and easy tasks;

He might have chid me so, for, in good faith,

I am a child to chiding.°   *new to being reproached*

IAGO   What is the matter, lady?

EMILIA Alas, Iago, my lord hath so bewhored her,°   *called her whore*

115 Thrown such despite° and heavy terms upon her,   *spite*

That true hearts cannot bear it.

DESDEMONA Am I that name, Iago?

IAGO   What name, fair lady?

DESDEMONA Such as she said my lord did say I was.

EMILIA He called her "whore." A beggar in his drink

120 Could not have laid such terms upon his callet.°   *whore*

IAGO Why did he so?

DESDEMONA I do not know; I am sure I am none such.

IAGO Do not weep, do not weep. Alas the day!

EMILIA Hath she forsook so many noble matches,

125 Her father, and her country, and her friends,

To be called "whore"? Would it not make one weep?

DESDEMONA It is my wretched fortune.

IAGO   Beshrew° him for't.   *Curse*

How comes this trick° upon him?   *behavior*

DESDEMONA   Nay, heaven doth know.

EMILIA I will be hanged if some eternal villain,

130 Some busy° and insinuating rogue,   *meddling*

Some cogging,° cozening° slave, to get some office   *deceiving / cheating*

Have not devised this slander—I will be hanged else.

IAGO Fie, there is no such man: it is impossible.

DESDEMONA If any such there be, heaven pardon him.

135 EMILIA A halter° pardon him, and hell gnaw his bones!   *hangman's noose*

Why should he call her "whore"? Who keeps her company?

What place, what time, what form, what likelihood?

---

1. *that . . . misuse:* which would cause him to suspect even slightly my smallest fault. TEXTUAL COMMENT For the differences between F and Q in this, Desdemona's only soliloquy, see Digital Edition TC 4 (Folio edited text).

The Moor's abused by some most villainous knave,
Some base, notorious knave, some scurvy fellow.
140   O heavens, that° such companions thou'dst unfold,°   *would that / reveal*
And put in every honest hand a whip
To lash the rascals naked through the world,
Even from the East to th' West!
IAGO [*aside to* EMILIA]   Speak within door.°   *more softly*
EMILIA [*aside to* IAGO]   Oh, fie upon them! Some such squire°   *fellow*
    he was
145   That turned your wit the seamy-side·without,°   *wrong side out*
And made you to suspect me with the Moor.
IAGO [*aside to* EMILIA]   You are a fool. Go to!
DESDEMONA   Alas, Iago,
What shall I do to win my lord again?
Good friend, go to him—for, by this light of heaven,
150   I know not how I lost him. Here I kneel:[2]
If e'er my will did trespass 'gainst his love,
Either in discourse of thought or actual deed;
Or that mine eyes, mine ears, or any sense
Delighted them, or any other form;[3]
155   Or that I do not yet° and ever did   *still*
And ever will—though he do shake me off
To beggarly divorcement—love him dearly,
Comfort forswear me.° Unkindness may do much,   *Deny me (divine) solace*
And his unkindness may defeat my life
160   But never taint my love. I cannot say "whore":
It doth abhor me[4] now I speak the word—
To do the act that might the addition° earn,   *label*
Not the world's mass of vanity° could make me.   *all worldly splendor*
IAGO   I pray you, be content: 'tis but his humor.°   *mood*
165   The business of the state does him offense.
DESDEMONA   If 'twere no other—
IAGO   It is but so, I warrant.
    [*Trumpets sound.*]
Hark how these instruments summon to supper:
The messengers of Venice stay the meat.°   *are waiting to eat*
Go in, and weep not: all things shall be well.
              Exeunt DESDEMONA *and* EMILIA.
    Enter RODERIGO.
170   How now, Roderigo?
RODERIGO   I do not find that thou deal'st justly with me.
IAGO   What in the contrary?
RODERIGO   Every day thou dafts me with some device,[5] Iago,
    and rather, as it seems to me now, keep'st from me all conve-
175   niency° than suppliest me with the least advantage of hope.   *opportunity*
I will indeed no longer endure it, nor am I yet persuaded to
put up in peace what already I have foolishly suffered.
IAGO   Will you hear me, Roderigo?
RODERIGO   I have heard too much, and your words and per-
180   formances are no kin together.

---

2. Lines 150–63 (beginning with "Here") do not   4. Fill me with abhorrence; make me abhorrent, with
appear in Q.   a pun on "ab-whore."
3. Took pleasure in anyone but him.   5. You make a fool of me with some trick.

IAGO You charge me most unjustly.

RODERIGO With naught but truth. I have wasted myself out of
my means: the jewels you have had from me to deliver Desdemona would half have corrupted a votarist.° You have told me
she hath received them, and returned me expectations and
comforts of sudden respect and acquaintance, but I find none.

IAGO Well, go to.° Very well.

RODERIGO "Very well"? "Go to"? I cannot go to,° man, nor 'tis
not very well! Nay, I think it is scurvy,° and begin to find myself
fopped° in it.

IAGO Very well.

RODERIGO I tell you, 'tis not very well! I will make myself
known to Desdemona: if she will return me my jewels, I will
give over my suit, and repent my unlawful solicitation. If not,
assure yourself I will seek satisfaction of you.

IAGO You have said° now.

RODERIGO Ay, and said nothing but what I protest intend-
ment of doing.

IAGO Why, now I see there's mettle in thee, and even from this
instant do build on thee a better opinion than ever before.
Give me thy hand, Roderigo. Thou hast taken against me a
most just exception, but yet, I protest, I have dealt most
directly in thy affair.

RODERIGO It hath not appeared.

IAGO I grant indeed it hath not appeared, and your suspicion
is not without wit and judgment. But, Roderigo, if thou hast
that in thee indeed which I have greater reason to believe
now than ever—I mean purpose, courage, and valor—this
night show it. If thou, the next night following, enjoy not
Desdemona, take me from this world with treachery, and
devise engines for° my life.

RODERIGO Well, what is it? Is it within reason and compass?°

IAGO Sir, there is especial commission come from Venice to
depute Cassio in Othello's place.

RODERIGO Is that true? Why, then Othello and Desdemona
return again to Venice.

IAGO Oh, no. He goes into Mauretania[6] and taketh away with
him the fair Desdemona, unless his abode be lingered here
by some accident, wherein none can be so determinate° as
the removing of Cassio.

RODERIGO How do you mean, removing him?

IAGO Why, by making him uncapable of Othello's place:
knocking out his brains!

RODERIGO And that you would have me to do?

IAGO Ay, if you dare do yourself a profit and a right. He sups
tonight with a harlotry,° and thither will I go to him. He
knows not yet of his honorable fortune.° If you will watch
his going thence, which I will fashion° to fall out between
twelve and one, you may take him at your pleasure. I will be
near to second your attempt, and he shall fall between us.
Come: stand not amazed at it, but go along with me; I will
show you such a necessity in his death that you shall think

nun

(expresses remonstrance)
succeed sexually
shabby
made a fool

finished

plots against
possibility

effectual

prostitute
promotion
arrange

6. Country in the western Sahara.

yourself bound to put it on him. It is now high supper-time,
and the night grows to waste: about it!

235 RODERIGO I will hear further reason for this.

IAGO And you shall be satisfied.   *Exeunt.*

4.3 (Q 4.3)

Enter OTHELLO, LODOVICO, DESDEMONA, EMILIA,
and Attendants.

LODOVICO I do beseech you, sir, trouble yourself no further.

OTHELLO Oh, pardon me. 'Twill do me good to walk.

LODOVICO —Madam, good night. I humbly thank your ladyship.

DESDEMONA Your honor is most welcome.

5 OTHELLO Will you walk, sir? —O Desdemona—

DESDEMONA My lord?

OTHELLO Get you to bed on th'instant: I will be returned
forthwith. Dismiss your attendant there. Look't be done.

DESDEMONA I will, my lord.

                    Exeunt [OTHELLO, LODOVICO, *and Attendants*].

10 EMILIA How goes it now? He looks gentler than he did.

DESDEMONA He says he will return incontinent,°   *immediately*
And hath commanded me to go to bed,
And bid me to dismiss you.

EMILIA   Dismiss me?

DESDEMONA It was his bidding: therefore, good Emilia,

15 Give me my nightly wearing, and adieu.
We must not now displease him.

EMILIA I would you had never seen him!

DESDEMONA So would not I: my love doth so approve him
That even his stubbornness, his checks, his frowns

20 —Prithee, unpin me—have grace and favor.

EMILIA I have laid those sheets you bade me on the bed.

DESDEMONA All's one.° —Good Father, how foolish are our   *It doesn't matter*
minds!
—If I do die before, prithee shroud me
In one of these same sheets.

EMILIA   Come, come: you talk!

25 DESDEMONA My mother had a maid called Barbary:[1]
She was in love, and he she loved proved mad
And did forsake her. She had a song of "willow":
An old thing 'twas, but it expressed her fortune,
And she died singing it. That song tonight

30 Will not go from my mind.[2] I have much to do
But to[3] go hang my head all at one side
And sing it like poor Barbary. Prithee dispatch.

EMILIA Shall I go fetch your nightgown?

DESDEMONA   No, unpin me here.
This Lodovico is a proper man.

EMILIA A very handsome man.

35 DESDEMONA   He speaks well.

4.3 Location: Scene continues.
1. Iago compares Othello to a "Barbary horse"
(1.1.109).
2. Textual Comment Lines 30–49 ("I . . . next") do
not appear in Q. For the significance of sexuality in

this passage, the only one in the play where women
are alone together, see Digital Edition TC 5 (Folio
edited text).
3. I can barely bring myself not to.

EMILIA I know a lady in Venice would have walked barefoot
    to Palestine for a touch of his nether lip.
DESDEMONA [*sings*] The poor soul sat singing[4] by a sycamore
            tree:
    Sing all a green willow.[5]
40   Her hand on her bosom, her head on her knee:
    Sing willow, willow, willow.
    The fresh streams ran by her and murmured her
            moans:
    Sing willow, willow, willow.
    Her salt tears fell from her and softened the stones:
    Sing willow, willow, willow—
45 [*to* EMILIA]   Lay by these—
  [*sings*]   Willow, willow—
  [*to* EMILIA]   Prithee, hie thee:° he'll come anon.   *hurry*
  [*sings*]   "Sing all a green willow" must be my garland:
    Let nobody blame him, his scorn I approve—
  Nay, that's not next. —Hark, who is't that knocks?
50 EMILIA It's the wind.
DESDEMONA [*sings*] I called my love "false love" but what said he
            then?[6]
    Sing willow, willow, willow.
    "If I court more women, you'll couch with more men."
  [*to* EMILIA] So, get thee gone: good night. Mine eyes do itch.
  Doth that bode weeping?
55 EMILIA   'Tis neither here nor there.
DESDEMONA I have heard it said so. Oh, these men, these men![7]
  Dost thou in conscience think—tell me, Emilia—
  That there be women do abuse their husbands
  In such gross kind?°   *fashion*
  EMILIA   There be some such, no question.
60 DESDEMONA Wouldst thou do such a deed for all the world?
  EMILIA Why, would not you?
  DESDEMONA   No, by this heavenly light.
  EMILIA Nor I neither by this heavenly light:
  I might do't as well i'the dark.
  DESDEMONA Wouldst thou do such a deed for all the world?
65 EMILIA The world's a huge thing; it is a great price
  For a small vice.
  DESDEMONA   In troth, I think thou wouldst not.
  EMILIA In troth, I think I should, and undo't when I had
  done. Marry, I would not do such a thing for a joint ring,[8]
  nor for measures of lawn,° nor for gowns, petticoats, nor   *linen*
70 caps, nor any petty exhibition.° But for all the whole world?   *gift*
  Why, who would not make her husband a cuckold to make
  him a monarch? I should venture purgatory for't.
  DESDEMONA Beshrew me if I would do such a wrong
  For the whole world!

---

4. TEXTUAL COMMENT For the gendered significance
of "singing" here, which replaces "sighing" in the popular version of this song, as well as its relationship to
printing house processes, see Digital Edition TC 6
(Folio edited text).

5. A conventional symbol of disappointed love.
6. Lines 51–53 do not appear in Q.
7. Lines 56–59 do not appear in Q.
8. A cheap ring in separable halves.

75 EMILIA Why, the wrong is but a wrong i'the world and, hav-
ing the world for your labor, 'tis a wrong in your own world,
and you might quickly make it right!
DESDEMONA I do not think there is any such woman.
EMILIA Yes, a dozen! And as many to th' vantage as would
80 store the world they played for.[9]
But I do think it is their husbands' faults[1]
If wives do fall. Say that they slack their duties,°   marital duties
And pour our treasures into foreign laps;[2]
Or else break out in peevish jealousies,
85 Throwing restraint upon us; or say they strike us,
Or scant our former having in despite:[3]
Why, we have galls,° and, though we have some grace,   tempers
Yet have we some revenge. Let husbands know
Their wives have sense like them: they see and smell,
90 And have their palates both for sweet and sour,
As husbands have. What is it that they do
When they change us for others? Is it sport?
I think it is. And doth affection° breed it?   lust
I think it doth. Is't frailty that thus errs?
95 It is so, too. And have not we affections,
Desires for sport, and frailty, as men have?
Then let them use us well. Else let them know
The ills we do, their ills instruct us so.
DESDEMONA Good night, good night. Heaven me such uses°   habits
send
100 Not to pick bad from bad, but by bad, mend.[4]   *Exeunt.*

5.1 (Q 5.1)

Enter IAGO *and* RODERIGO.

IAGO Here, stand behind this balk:° straight° will he come.   timber beam / right away
Wear thy good rapier bare, and put it home.°   drive it into him
Quick, quick! Fear nothing; I'll be at thy elbow.
It makes us or it mars us. Think on that,
5 And fix most firm thy resolution.
RODERIGO Be near at hand; I may miscarry in't.
IAGO Here, at thy hand. Be bold, and take thy stand.
RODERIGO [*aside*] I have no great devotion to the deed;
And yet he hath given me satisfying reasons.
10 'Tis but a man gone. —Forth my sword: he dies!
[*He draws.*]
[IAGO *withdraws.*]
IAGO [*aside*] I have rubbed this young quat° almost to the   pimple
sense,°   to the quick
And he grows angry. Now, whether he kill Cassio,
Or Cassio him, or each do kill the other,
Every way makes my gain. Live Roderigo,°   If Roderigo lives
15 He calls me to a restitution large
Of gold and jewels that I bobbed from him°   defrauded him of
As gifts to Desdemona—

9. *And . . . for:* and as many more as it would take to
populate the world they gained by doing it.
1. Lines 81–98 do not appear in Q.
2. And give the semen that belongs to us to other
women.

3. Or reduce our allowances out of spite.
4. Not to take bad behavior as an example, but to
know what to avoid.
5.1 Location: A street in Cyprus.

It must not be. If Cassio do remain,
He hath a daily beauty in his life

20 That makes me ugly; and, besides, the Moor
May unfold° me to him: there stand I in much peril.   *reveal*
No, he must die. But so:° I heard him coming.   *so be it*
[*He draws.*]
Enter CASSIO.

RODERIGO   I know his gait, 'tis he. —Villain, thou diest!
[*He thrusts at* CASSIO.]

CASSIO   That thrust had been mine enemy indeed,

25 But that my coat is better° than thou know'st.   *thicker; more armored*
I will make proof of° thine.   *test*
[*He stabs* RODERIGO.]

RODERIGO   Oh, I am slain!
[IAGO *stabs* CASSIO.]

CASSIO   I am maimed forever! Help, ho! Murder! Murder!
[*Exit* IAGO.]
Enter OTHELLO [*apart*].

OTHELLO   The voice of Cassio. Iago keeps his word!

RODERIGO   Oh, villain that I am!

OTHELLO   It is even so.

30 CASSIO   Oh, help, ho! Light! A surgeon!

OTHELLO   'Tis he. O brave Iago, honest and just,
That hast such noble sense of thy friend's wrong;
Thou teachest me. —Minion,° your dear lies dead,   *Hussy*
And your unblest fate hies.° Strumpet, I come: *damnation hurries on*

35 For of° my heart those charms, thine eyes, are blotted;   *out of*
Thy bed, lust-stained, shall with lust's blood be spotted.
Exit OTHELLO.
Enter LODOVICO *and* GRAZIANO [*apart*].

CASSIO   What, ho? No watch? No passage?° Murder! Murder!   *passersby*

GRAZIANO [*to* LODOVICO]   'Tis some mischance. The voice is
very direful.

CASSIO   Oh, help!

40 LODOVICO [*to* GRAZIANO]   Hark!

RODERIGO   O wretched villain!

LODOVICO [*to* GRAZIANO]   Two or three groan! 'Tis heavy° night;   *dark*
These may be counterfeits. Let's think't unsafe
To come into° the cry without more help.   *go near*

45 RODERIGO   Nobody come? Then shall I bleed to death!
Enter IAGO [*with a light*].

LODOVICO [*to* GRAZIANO]   Hark!

GRAZIANO [*to* LODOVICO]   Here's one comes in his shirt, with
light and weapons.

IAGO   Who's there? Whose noise is this that cries on murder?

LODOVICO   We do not know.

IAGO   Do not you hear a cry?

CASSIO   Here! Here! For heaven sake, help me!

50 IAGO [*to* CASSIO]   What's the matter?

GRAZIANO [*to* LODOVICO]   This is Othello's ensign, as I take it.

LODOVICO [*to* GRAZIANO]   The same indeed: a very valiant fellow.

IAGO [*to* CASSIO]   What are you here, that cry so grievously?

CASSIO   Iago? Oh, I am spoiled, undone by villains!
Give me some help.

55 IAGO   O me, lieutenant!

What villains have done this?

CASSIO I think that one of them is hereabout
And cannot make° away.   get

IAGO   O treacherous villains!
[*to* LODOVICO *and* GRAZIANO] What are you there? Come in
and give some help.

RODERIGO Oh, help me there!

60 CASSIO   That's one of them!

IAGO [*to* RODERIGO] O murd'rous slave! O villain!
        [*He stabs* RODERIGO.]

RODERIGO O damned Iago! O inhuman dog!

IAGO Kill men i'th' dark? Where be these bloody thieves?
How silent is this town! Ho! Murder! Murder!

65 [*to* LODOVICO *and* GRAZIANO] What may you be? Are you of
good or evil?

LODOVICO As you shall prove us, praise us.

IAGO   Signor Lodovico?

LODOVICO He, sir.

IAGO I cry you mercy: here's Cassio hurt by villains.

GRAZIANO Cassio?

IAGO [*to* CASSIO] How is't, brother?

70 CASSIO   My leg is cut in two.

IAGO Marry, heaven forbid.
    —Light, gentlemen! I'll bind it with my shirt.
            Enter BIANCA.

BIANCA What is the matter, ho? Who is't that cried?

IAGO Who is't that cried?

BIANCA   O my dear Cassio!

75 My sweet Cassio! O Cassio! Cassio! Cassio!

IAGO O notable strumpet. —Cassio, may you suspect
Who they should be that have thus mangled you?

CASSIO No.

GRAZIANO I am sorry to find you thus; I have been to seek you.

IAGO [*to* LODOVICO *and* GRAZIANO] Lend me a garter. So.

80 [*He binds Cassio's leg.*]   Oh, for a chair°   litter
To bear him easily hence.

BIANCA Alas, he faints! O Cassio! Cassio! Cassio!

IAGO Gentlemen all, I do suspect this trash°   (Bianca)
To be a party in this injury.

85 —Patience awhile, good Cassio. [*to* LODOVICO *and* GRAZIANO]
Come, come,
Lend me a light. [*He goes to* RODERIGO.] Know we this face
or no?
Alas, my friend and my dear countryman,
Roderigo! No? Yes, sure. Yes, 'tis Roderigo!

GRAZIANO What, of Venice?

IAGO Even he, sir. Did you know him?

90 GRAZIANO   Know him? Ay.

IAGO Signor Graziano? I cry your gentle pardon;
These bloody accidents must excuse my manners
That so neglected you.

GRAZIANO   I am glad to see you.

IAGO —How do you, Cassio? —Oh, a chair! A chair!

95 GRAZIANO Roderigo?

IAGO He, he. 'Tis he.

[Enter Attendants with a chair.]
                              Oh, that's well said:° the chair.   *carried out*
Some good man bear him carefully from hence.
I'll fetch the general's surgeon. [*to* BIANCA] For you, mistress,
Save you your labor. —He that lies slain here, Cassio,
100   Was my dear friend. What malice was between you?
CASSIO   None in the world, nor do I know the man.
IAGO   What, look you pale? [*to Attendants*] Oh, bear him o'th'
       air.[1]   [*Exeunt Attendants with* CASSIO *and* RODERIGO.]
       [*to* LODOVICO *and* GRAZIANO] Stay you, good gentlemen. [*to*
       BIANCA] Look you pale, mistress?
       [*to* LODOVICO *and* GRAZIANO] Do you perceive the gastness°   *terror*
       of her eye?
105   [*to* BIANCA] Nay, if you stare we shall hear more anon.
       [*to* LODOVICO *and* GRAZIANO] Behold her well. I pray you,
       look upon her:
Do you see, gentlemen? Nay, guiltiness will speak,
Though tongues were out of use.
              [Enter EMILIA.]
EMILIA   Alas, what is the matter?
What is the matter, husband?
110   IAGO   Cassio hath here been set on in the dark
By Roderigo and fellows that are scaped:
He's almost slain, and Roderigo quite dead.
EMILIA   Alas, good gentleman! Alas, good Cassio!
IAGO   This is the fruits of whoring. Prithee, Emilia,
115   Go know of Cassio where he supped tonight.
       [*to* BIANCA] What, do you shake at that?
BIANCA   He supped at my house, but I therefore shake not.
IAGO   Oh, did he so? I charge you go with me.
EMILIA   Oh, fie upon thee, strumpet!
120   BIANCA   I am no strumpet, but of life as honest
As you that thus abuse me.
EMILIA   As I? Fie upon thee!
IAGO   Kind gentlemen, let's go see poor Cassio dressed.°   *bandaged*
       [*to* BIANCA]   Come, mistress, you must tell's another tale.
       —Emilia, run you to the citadel
125   And tell my lord and lady what hath happed.
       [*to* LODOVICO *and* GRAZIANO] Will you go on afore?
       [*aside*] This is the night
That either makes me or fordoes° me quite.   *Exeunt.*   *undoes*

5.2 (Q 5.2)
Enter OTHELLO [*with a light*,] *and* DESDEMONA *in
her bed.*[1]
OTHELLO   It is the cause,[2] it is the cause, my soul.
Let me not name it to you, you chaste stars:
It is the cause. Yet I'll not shed her blood,
Nor scar that whiter skin of hers than snow
5   And smooth as monumental alabaster;°   *stone used in tombs*

---

1. Out of the open air (thought to be bad for wounds).
5.2 Location: Desdemona and Othello's bedroom.
1. PERFORMANCE COMMENT For the problem of where on stage to place Desdemona's bed, as well as how Desdemona, Othello, and Iago are to be played

in this scene, see Digital Edition PC 7.
2. What matters is Desdemona's infidelity; the "cause" of justice, which Othello sees himself defending, as in the subsequent lines.

Yet she must die, else she'll betray more men.
Put out the light, and then put out the light.[3]
If I quench thee, thou flaming minister,°   *light that serves me*
I can again thy former light restore,
10   Should I repent me—but once put out thy light,
Thou cunning'st pattern of excelling nature,[4]
I know not where is that Promethean heat[5]
That can thy light relume.° When I have plucked thy rose,   *relight*
I cannot give it vital growth again:
15   It needs must wither. I'll smell thee on the tree.
        [*He kisses her.*]
Oh, balmy breath, that dost almost persuade
Justice to break her sword! One more, one more.
Be thus when thou art dead, and I will kill thee
And love thee after. One more, and that's the last.
        [*He kisses her.*]
20   So sweet was ne'er so fatal. I must weep,
But they are cruel tears. This sorrow's heavenly:
It strikes where it doth love.[6] She wakes!
DESDEMONA   Who's there? Othello?
OTHELLO   Ay, Desdemona.
DESDEMONA   Will you come to bed, my lord?
OTHELLO   Have you prayed tonight, Desdemon?
25 DESDEMONA   Ay, my lord.
OTHELLO   If you bethink yourself of any crime
Unreconciled as yet to heaven and grace,
Solicit° for it straight.   *Ask forgiveness*
DESDEMONA   Alack, my lord,
What may you mean by that?
30 OTHELLO   Well, do it, and be brief. I will walk by.
I would not kill thy unprepared spirit;
No, heavens forfend, I would not kill thy soul.
DESDEMONA   Talk you of killing?
OTHELLO   Ay, I do.
DESDEMONA   Then heaven have mercy on me!
OTHELLO   Amen, with all my heart.
35 DESDEMONA   If you say,° I hope you will not kill me.   *Since you say "amen"*
OTHELLO   Hum!
DESDEMONA   And yet I fear you, for you're fatal then
When your eyes roll so. Why I should fear I know not,
Since guiltiness I know not, but yet I feel I fear.
OTHELLO   Think on thy sins.
40 DESDEMONA   They are loves I bear to you.
OTHELLO   Ay, and for that thou diest.
DESDEMONA   That death's unnatural that kills for loving.
Alas, why gnaw you so your nether lip?
Some bloody passion shakes your very frame.
45   These are portents, but yet I hope, I hope,
They do not point on me.
OTHELLO   Peace, and be still.

---

3. This and the following lines compare the light of
Othello's lamp or torch to Desdemona's "light" of life.
4. You most cleverly wrought example of nature's work.
5. Life-giving fire. In Greek mythology, Prometheus
stole fire from heaven to give it to humankind; in a

different tradition, he is credited with animating
humankind from clay.
6. See Hebrews 12:6: "For whom the Lord loveth, he
chasteneth."

DESDEMONA   I will so. What's the matter?

OTHELLO   That handkerchief,
Which I so loved and gave thee, thou gav'st to Cassio.

DESDEMONA   No, by my life and soul! Send for the man,
50   And ask him.

OTHELLO   Sweet soul, take heed, take heed of perjury.
Thou art on thy death-bed.

DESDEMONA   I? But not yet to die?

OTHELLO   Presently.°   *Immediately*
Therefore confess thee freely of thy sin,
55   For to deny each article with oath
Cannot remove nor choke the strong conception
That I do groan withal:[7] thou art to die.

DESDEMONA   O heaven, have mercy on me!

OTHELLO   I say amen.

DESDEMONA   And have you mercy, too. I never did
60   Offend you in my life, never loved Cassio
But with such general warranty of heaven
As I might love. I never gave him token.

OTHELLO   By heaven, I saw my handkerchief in 's hand!
O perjured woman, thou dost stone° my heart,   *harden*
65   And makest me call what I intend to do
A murder, which I thought a sacrifice.
I saw the handkerchief.

DESDEMONA   He found it, then.
I never gave it him. Send for him hither:
Let him confess a truth.

OTHELLO   He hath confessed.

DESDEMONA   What, my lord?

OTHELLO   That he hath used thee.

70   DESDEMONA   How, unlawfully?

OTHELLO   Ay.

DESDEMONA   He will not say so.

OTHELLO   No, his mouth is stopped.
Honest Iago hath ta'en order for't.

DESDEMONA   Oh, my fear interprets. What, is he dead?

OTHELLO   Had all his hairs been lives, my great revenge
75   Had stomach for them all.

DESDEMONA   Alas, he is betrayed, and I undone.

OTHELLO   Out, strumpet! Weep'st thou for him to my face?

DESDEMONA   Oh, banish me, my lord, but kill me not.

OTHELLO   Down, strumpet!
    [*He attacks her.*]

80   DESDEMONA [*struggling*]   Kill me tomorrow; let me live tonight!

OTHELLO   Nay, if you strive—

DESDEMONA   But half an hour!

OTHELLO   Being done, there is no pause.[8]

DESDEMONA   But while I say one prayer!

OTHELLO   It is too late.
    [*He*] smothers her.

EMILIA (*at the door*)   My lord! My lord! What ho, my lord! My
    lord!

7. *Cannot . . . withal:* Cannot stop the strong conviction I have in your guilt (or the firm plan to kill you),
which makes me groan so. The metaphor is from

childbirth.
8. Now that I've started, there's no stopping.

85 OTHELLO   What noise is this? —Not dead? Not yet quite dead?
      I, that am cruel, am yet merciful:
      I would not have thee linger in thy pain.
      So. So.
          [*He smothers* DESDEMONA *again.*]
   EMILIA (*within*)   What ho, my lord! My lord!
   OTHELLO   Who's there?
   EMILIA [*within*]   O good my lord, I would speak a word with you.
90 OTHELLO   Yes. —'Tis Emilia. —By and by! —She's dead.
      'Tis like° she comes to speak of Cassio's death: likely
      The noise was high.° —Ha, no more moving?   commotion was loud
      Still as the grave. Shall she come in? Were't good?
      I think she stirs again! No. What's best to do?
95   If she come in, she'll sure speak to my wife.
      My wife! My wife! What wife? I have no wife.
      Oh, insupportable! Oh, heavy hour!
      Methinks it should be now a huge eclipse
      Of sun and moon, and that th'affrighted globe
      Did yawn at alteration.⁹
100 EMILIA [*within*]   I do beseech you
      That I may speak with you, O good my lord!
   OTHELLO   I had forgot thee. —Oh, come in, Emilia.
      —Soft!° —By and by. —Let me the curtains draw.   Quiet
      —Where art thou? What's the matter with thee now?
          Enter EMILIA.
105 EMILIA   O my good lord, yonder's foul murders done.
   OTHELLO   What? Now?
   EMILIA   But° now, my lord.   Just
   OTHELLO   It is the very error° of the moon: deviation
      She comes more nearer earth than she was wont,
      And makes men mad.
110 EMILIA   Cassio, my lord, hath killed
      A young Venetian called Roderigo.
   OTHELLO   Roderigo killed? And Cassio killed?
   EMILIA   No, Cassio is not killed.
   OTHELLO [*aside*]   Not Cassio killed? Then murder's out of tune,
      And sweet revenge grows harsh.
115 DESDEMONA   Oh, falsely, falsely murdered!
   EMILIA   Alas, what cry is that?
   OTHELLO   That? What?
   EMILIA   Out and alas, that was my lady's voice!
          [*She opens the bed curtains.*]
      Help! Help, ho! Help! —O lady, speak again!
      Sweet Desdemona! O sweet mistress, speak!
   DESDEMONA   A guiltless death I die.
120 EMILIA   Oh, who hath done this deed?
   DESDEMONA   Nobody. I myself. Farewell.
      Commend me to my kind lord. Oh, farewell!
          [*She dies.*]
   OTHELLO   Why, how should she be murdered?
   EMILIA   Alas, who knows?

---

9. Should gape at the change. Earthquakes were associated with eclipses.

OTHELLO   You hear her say herself it was not I.

125   EMILIA   She said so. I must needs report the truth.

OTHELLO   She's like a liar gone to burning hell:
'Twas I that killed her.

EMILIA   Oh, the more angel she, and you the blacker devil.

OTHELLO   She turned to folly,° and she was a whore.   *wantonness*

130   EMILIA   Thou dost belie her, and thou art a devil.

OTHELLO   She was false as water.

EMILIA   Thou art rash as fire to say
That she was false. Oh, she was heavenly true!

OTHELLO   Cassio did top her—ask thy husband else.°   *if you doubt it*
Oh, I were damned beneath all depth in hell

135   But that I did proceed upon just grounds
To this extremity. Thy husband knew it all.

EMILIA   My husband?

OTHELLO   Thy husband.

EMILIA   That she was false to wedlock?

OTHELLO   Ay, with Cassio. Had she been true,
If heaven would make me such another world

140   Of one entire and perfect chrysolite,°   *topaz*
I'd not have sold her for it.

EMILIA   My husband?

OTHELLO   Ay, 'twas he that told me on her first.
An honest man he is, and hates the slime
That sticks on filthy deeds—

EMILIA   My husband?

145   OTHELLO   What needs this iterance,° woman? I say, thy   *repetition*
husband.

EMILIA   O mistress! Villainy hath made mocks with° love.[1]   *at*
—My husband say she was false?

OTHELLO   He, woman.
I say, thy husband. Dost understand the word?
My friend, thy husband, honest, honest Iago.

150   EMILIA   If he say so, may his pernicious soul
Rot half a grain a day: he lies to th' heart.
She was too fond of her most filthy bargain.

OTHELLO   Ha!

EMILIA   Do thy worst!

155   This deed of thine is no more worthy heaven
Than thou wast worthy her.

OTHELLO   Peace, you were best.[2]

EMILIA   Thou hast not half that power to do me harm
As I have to be hurt. O gull!° O dolt,   *fool*
As ignorant as dirt. Thou hast done a deed—

160   I care not for thy sword: I'll make thee known,
Though I lost twenty lives. —Help! Help, ho! Help!
The Moor hath killed my mistress. Murder! Murder!

                    Enter MONTANO, GRAZIANO, *and* IAGO.

MONTANO   What is the matter? How now, general?

EMILIA   Oh, are you come, Iago? You have done well

165   That men must lay their murders on your neck.

---

1. Lines 146–49 do not appear in Q.
2. It would be best for you (to remain silent).

GRAZIANO What is the matter?
EMILIA [*to* IAGO] Disprove this villain, if thou beest a man.
  He says thou told'st him that his wife was false.
  I know thou didst not: thou'rt not such a villain.
170 Speak, for my heart is full.
IAGO I told him what I thought, and told no more
  Than what he found himself was apt and true.
EMILIA But did you ever tell him she was false?
IAGO I did.
175 EMILIA You told a lie, an odious, damned lie!
  Upon my soul, a lie, a wicked lie!
  She false with Cassio? Did you say with Cassio?
IAGO With Cassio, mistress. Go to, charm° your tongue.   silence
EMILIA I will not charm my tongue: I am bound to speak:
180 My mistress here lies murdered in her bed.[3]
MONTANO *and* GRAZIANO O heavens forfend!
EMILIA And your reports have set the murder on.
OTHELLO Nay, stare not, masters: it is true indeed.
GRAZIANO 'Tis a strange truth.
MONTANO   Oh, monstrous act!
185 EMILIA Villainy! Villainy! Villainy!
  I think upon't; I think I smell't. Oh, villainy!
  I thought so, then. I'll kill myself for grief.
  Oh, villainy! Villainy!
IAGO   What, are you mad?
  I charge you, get you home.
190 EMILIA Good gentlemen, let me have leave to speak.
  'Tis proper I obey him, but not now.
  —Perchance, Iago, I will ne'er go home.
OTHELLO Oh! Oh! Oh!
        [OTHELLO *falls on the bed.*]
EMILIA   Nay, lay thee down and roar,
  For thou hast killed the sweetest innocent
  That e'er did lift up eye.°   (to heaven)
195 OTHELLO   Oh, she was foul!
  [*to* GRAZIANO] I scarce did know you, uncle. There lies your
      niece,
  Whose breath, indeed, these hands have newly stopped.
  I know this act shows° horrible and grim.   appears
GRAZIANO Poor Desdemon. I am glad thy father's dead:
200 Thy match was mortal to him, and pure grief
  Shore his old thread in twain.[4] Did he live now,
  This sight would make him do a desperate turn,°   act
  Yea, curse his better angel from his side,
  And fall to reprobance.[5]
205 OTHELLO 'Tis pitiful, but yet Iago knows
  That she with Cassio hath the act of shame
  A thousand times committed. Cassio confessed it,
  And she did gratify his amorous works
  With that recognizance° and pledge of love   token

---

3. Lines 180–88 do not appear in Q.
4. Cut the thread of his life.
5. Reprobation, rejection by God—here for suicide, the unforgivably sinful act of despair, leading to eternal damnation.

210   Which I first gave her. I saw it in his hand:
It was a handkerchief, an antique token
My father gave my mother.[6]

EMILIA   O heaven! O heavenly powers!

IAGO   Come, hold your peace!

EMILIA   'Twill out, 'twill out. I, peace?
No, I will speak as liberal as the north.[7]

215   Let heaven, and men, and devils, let them all,
All, all cry shame against me, yet I'll speak.

IAGO   Be wise, and get you home.

        [*He draws.*]

EMILIA   I will not.

GRAZIANO   Fie! Your sword upon a woman?

EMILIA   O thou dull Moor, that handkerchief thou speak'st of
220   I found by fortune, and did give my husband:
For often, with a solemn earnestness—
More than indeed belonged to such a trifle—
He begged of me to steal't.

IAGO   Villainous whore!

EMILIA   She give it Cassio? No, alas, I found it,
And I did give't my husband.

225 IAGO   Filth! Thou liest.

EMILIA   By heaven, I do not. I do not, gentlemen.
    [*to* OTHELLO] O murd'rous coxcomb!° What should such a   *fool*
    fool
Do with so good a wife?

OTHELLO   Are there no stones° in heaven   *thunderbolts*
But what serves for the thunder? [*to* IAGO] Precious° villain!   *Absolute*
      [OTHELLO *runs at* IAGO; MONTANO *disarms him.*
      IAGO *stabs* EMILIA.][8]

230 GRAZIANO   The woman falls! Sure, he hath killed his wife.
                        [*Exit* IAGO.]

EMILIA   Ay! Ay! Oh, lay me by my mistress' side.
    [GRAZIANO *puts her on the bed.*][9]

GRAZIANO   He's gone, but his wife's killed.

MONTANO   'Tis a notorious villain. [*to* GRAZIANO] Take you
    this weapon,
Which I have recovered from the Moor.
235   Come, guard the door without; let him not pass,
But kill him rather. I'll after that same villain,
For 'tis a damned slave.   *Exeunt* [MONTANO *and* GRAZIANO].

OTHELLO   I am not valiant, neither,
But every puny whipster° gets my sword.   *insignificant person*
But why should honor outlive honesty?[1]
Let it go all.

240 EMILIA [*to* DESDEMONA]   What did thy song bode, lady?[2]
Hark, canst thou hear me? I will play the swan

---

6. Earlier, however, Othello says that his mother got the handkerchief not from his father but from "an Egyptian . . . charmer" (3.4.53–54).
7. As freely as the north wind.
8. TEXTUAL COMMENT For the significance of Othello's use of swords, and the difference between F's and Q's treatment of the matter, see Digital Edition TC 7 (Folio edited text).

9. TEXTUAL COMMENT For the different consequences of having Graziano honor, or ignore, Emilia's dying request, "Lay me by my mistress' side," see Digital Edition TC 8 (Folio edited text).
1. Why should military reputation outlive integrity?
2. Lines 240–42 ("What . . . willow.'") do not appear in Q.

And die in music. [*She sings.*] "Willow, willow, willow."
—Moor, she was chaste. She loved thee, cruel Moor.
So come my soul to bliss as I speak true;

245 So, speaking as I think, alas, I die.
　　　[*She dies.*]
OTHELLO　I have another weapon in this chamber:
It was a sword of Spain, the ice-brook's temper.°　　　　　*tempered in icy water*
Oh, here it is. —Uncle, I must come forth.
GRAZIANO [*within*]　If thou attempt it, it will cost thee dear:

250 Thou hast no weapon, and perforce must suffer.
OTHELLO　Look in upon me, then, and speak with me
Or, naked° as I am, I will assault thee.　　　　　　　　　*unarmed*
　　　[*Enter* GRAZIANO.]
GRAZIANO　What is the matter?
OTHELLO　　　　　　　　　　　Behold, I have a weapon:
A better never did itself sustain

255 Upon a soldier's thigh. I have seen the day
That, with this little arm and this good sword,
I have made my way through more impediments
Than twenty times your stop.° But, oh, vain boast!　　　*power to stop*
Who can control his fate? 'Tis not so now.

260 Be not afraid, though you do see me weaponed:[3]
Here is my journey's end; here is my butt°　　　　　　　*goal*
And very sea-mark° of my utmost sail.°　　　　　*beacon / voyage's limit*
Do you go back dismayed? 'Tis a lost° fear:　　　　　　*an unnecessary*
Man but a rush° against Othello's breast,　　　　　*Aim even a reed*

265 And he retires. Where should Othello go?
[*to* DESDEMONA] Now, how dost thou look now? O ill-starred
　　　wench,
Pale as thy smock. When we shall meet at count,°　　　*Judgment Day*
This look of thine will hurl my soul from heaven,
And fiends will snatch at it. Cold, cold, my girl?

270 Even like thy chastity. O cursèd, cursèd slave!
Whip me, ye devils,
From the possession of this heavenly sight;
Blow me about in winds, roast me in sulfur,
Wash me in steep-down gulfs of liquid fire.

275 O Desdemon! Dead, Desdemon, dead! Oh! Oh![4]
　　　Enter LODOVICO, CASSIO [*in a chair*], MONTANO, *and*
　　　IAGO [*as a prisoner*], *with* OFFICERS.
LODOVICO　Where is this rash and most unfortunate man?
OTHELLO　That's he that was Othello: here I am.
LODOVICO　Where is that viper? [*to* OFFICERS] Bring the
　　　villain forth.
OTHELLO　I look down towards his feet,[5] but that's a fable.

280 [*to* IAGO] If that thou beest a devil, I cannot kill thee.
　　　[*He stabs* IAGO.]
LODOVICO [*to* OFFICERS]　Wrench his sword from him!
IAGO　　　　　　　　　　　I bleed, sir, but not killed.
OTHELLO　I am not sorry, neither: I'd have thee live,
For, in my sense,° 'tis happiness to die.　　　　　　　*state of feeling*

---

3. Lines 260–66 do not appear in Q.
4. TEXTUAL COMMENT For the consequences of the metrical differences between F and Q in rendering Othello's grief in this line, see Digital Edition TC 9 (Folio edited text).
5. I look for the devil's cloven feet.

LODOVICO   O thou, Othello, that was once so good,
285   Fallen in the practice° of a cursèd slave,   *plot*
      What shall be said to thee?
OTHELLO   Why, anything.
      An honorable murderer, if you will,
      For naught I did in hate, but all in honor.
LODOVICO   This wretch hath part confessed his villainy.
290   Did you and he consent in Cassio's death?
OTHELLO   Ay.
CASSIO   Dear general, I never gave you cause!
OTHELLO   I do believe it, and I ask your pardon.
      Will you, I pray, demand that demi-devil
295   Why he hath thus ensnared my soul and body?
IAGO   Demand me nothing. What you know, you know:[6]
      From this time forth I never will speak word.
LODOVICO   What, not to pray?
GRAZIANO   Torments° will ope your lips.   *Tortures*
OTHELLO   Well, thou dost best.[7]
300   LODOVICO   Sir,
      You shall understand what hath befallen,
      Which, as I think, you know not. Here is a letter
      Found in the pocket of the slain Roderigo,
      And here another: the one of them imports
305   The death of Cassio, to be undertook
      By Roderigo.
OTHELLO   O villain!
CASSIO   Most heathenish and most gross!°   *monstrous*
LODOVICO   Now, here's another discontented paper°   *paper listing complaints*
      Found in his pocket, too, and this it seems
      Roderigo meant t' have sent this damnèd villain
310   But that, belike,° Iago in the interim   *most likely*
      Came in and satisfied him.
OTHELLO   O thou pernicious caitiff!°   *wretch*
      —How came you, Cassio, by that handkerchief
      That was my wife's?
CASSIO   I found it in my chamber,
      And he himself confessed it but even now
315   That there he dropped it for a special purpose
      Which wrought to his desire.
OTHELLO   O fool! Fool! Fool!
CASSIO   There is, besides, in Roderigo's letter
      How he upbraids Iago that he made him
      Brave° me upon the watch, whereon it came   *Defy*
320   That I was cast;° and even but now he spake,   *dismissed*
      After long seeming dead: Iago hurt him;
      Iago set him on.
LODOVICO [*to* OTHELLO]   You must forsake this room and go
          with us:
      Your power and your command is taken off,
325   And Cassio rules in Cyprus. For this slave,
      If there be any cunning cruelty

---

6. Iago's final pithy statement of identity or noniden-
tity. See 1.1.63, 4.1.257–59, and notes.

7. Addressed to Lodovico and Graziano or, ironically, to Iago.

That can torment him much and hold him° long,   *(alive)*
It shall be his. —You shall close° prisoner rest   *tightly confined*
Till that the nature of your fault be known
330   To the Venetian state. [*to* OFFICERS] Come, bring away.
OTHELLO   Soft you,° a word or two before you go.   *Wait*
I have done the state some service, and they know't—
No more of that. I pray you, in your letters,
When you shall these unlucky deeds relate,
335   Speak of me as I am; nothing extenuate,
Nor set down aught in malice. Then must you speak
Of one that loved not wisely, but too well;
Of one not easily jealous but, being wrought,
Perplexed in the extreme;⁸ of one whose hand,
340   Like the base Judean,⁹ threw a pearl away
Richer than all his tribe; of one whose subdued° eyes,   *(by grief)*
Albeit unusèd to the melting mood,
Drop tears as fast as the Arabian trees
Their medicinable gum.° Set you down this,   *myrrh*
345   And say, besides, that in Aleppo¹ once,
Where a malignant and a turbaned Turk
Beat a Venetian and traduced° the state,   *defamed*
I took by th' throat the circumcisèd dog
And smote him thus.
           [*He stabs himself.*]
LODOVICO   Oh, bloody period!°   *conclusion; sentence*
350   GRAZIANO   All that is spoke is marred.
OTHELLO [*to* DESDEMONA]   I kissed thee ere I killed thee. No
     way but this:
Killing myself, to die upon a kiss.
           [*He*] *dies*[.]
CASSIO   This did I fear—but thought he had no weapon—
For he was great of heart.
LODOVICO [*to* IAGO]   O Spartan dog,°   *(notoriously savage)*
355   More fell° than anguish, hunger, or the sea,   *cruel*
Look on the tragic loading of this bed:
This is thy work. The object poisons sight.
Let it be hid. —Graziano, keep° the house,   *guard*
And seize upon the fortunes of the Moor,
360   For they succeed on you. [*to* CASSIO] To you, Lord Governor,
Remains the censure° of this hellish villain: *sentence*
The time, the place, the torture—oh, enforce it.
Myself will straight aboard, and to the state
This heavy act with heavy heart relate.   *Exeunt.*

---

8. *not easily jealous . . . perplexed in the extreme:* The
first of these two statements echoes Desdemona's
earlier comment about Othello's disinclination to be
jealous (3.4.27–28); the second, an accompanying
geocultural belief of the time—that southern tem-
peraments, when once that disinclination was overcome, became extremely jealous.

9. TEXTUAL COMMENT For the differences between
F's anti-Semitic reading, "Judean," and Q's colonial-
ist reading, "Indian," see Digital Edition TC 10 (Folio
text).
1. Ottoman city in what later became Syria through
which Venice traded with the East.

King Lear

You have, King James told his eldest son a few years before Shakespeare wrote *King Lear,* a double obligation to love God: first because He made you a man, and second because He made you "a little God to sit on his Throne, and rule over other men." Whatever the realities of Renaissance kingship—realities that included the stern necessity of compromise, reciprocity, and restraint—the idea of sovereignty was closely linked to fantasies of divine omnipotence. From his exalted height, the sovereign looked down upon the tiny figures of the ordinary mortals below him. Their hopes, the material conditions of their miserable existence, their names, were of little interest, and yet the King knew that they too were looking back up at him. "For kings being public persons," James uneasily acknowledged, are set "upon a public stage, in the sight of all the people; where all the beholders' eyes are attentively bent to look and pry in the least circumstance of their secretest drifts." Under such circumstances, the sovereign's dream was to command, like God, not only unquestioning obedience but unqualified love.

In *King Lear,* Shakespeare explores the dark consequences of this dream not only in the state but also in the family, where the Renaissance father increasingly styled himself "a little God." If, as the play opens, the aged Lear, exercising his imperious will and demanding professions of devotion, is every inch a king, he is also by the same token every inch a father, the absolute ruler of a family that conspicuously lacks the alternative authority of a mother. Shakespeare's play invokes this royal and paternal sovereignty only to chronicle its destruction in scenes of astonishing cruelty and power. The very words "every inch a king" are spoken not by the confident figure of supreme authority whom we glimpse in the first moments but by the ruined old man who perceives in his feverish rage and madness that the fantasy of omnipotence is a fraud: "When the rain came to wet me once, and the wind to make me chatter, when the thunder would not peace at my bidding, there I found 'em, there I smelt 'em out. Go to, they are not men o'their words. They told me I was everything. 'Tis a lie. I am not ague-proof" (*The Tragedy of King Lear* [Folio text] 4.5.100–105; cf. *The History of King Lear* [Quarto text] 4.6.100–105).

"They told me I was everything": Shakespeare's culture continually staged public rituals of deference to authority. These rituals—kneeling, bowing, uncovering the head, and so forth—enacted respect for wealth, caste, power, and, at virtually every level of society, age. Jacobean England had a strong official regard for the rights and privileges of age. It told itself that, by the will of God and the natural order of things, authority gravitated to the old, particularly to old men, and it contrived to ensure that this proper, sanctified arrangement of society be everywhere respected.

"'Tis a lie": Shakespeare's culture continually told itself at the same time that without the control of property and the threat of punishment, any claim to authority was chillingly vulnerable to the ruthless ambitions of the young, the restless, and the discontented. The incessant, ritualized spectacles of sovereignty have a nervous air, as if no one quite believed all the grand claims to divine sanction for the rule of kings and fathers, as if those who ruled both states and families harbored a half-conscious fear that the elaborate hierarchical structure could vanish like a mirage, exposing their shivering, defenseless bodies.

In ordinary circumstances, the tension between the extravagant claim to divinely sanctioned authority and the queasy sense that this claim was baseless lay far below the surface. Men and women went about their lives making the quiet compromises people usually make: rulers understood that they were not in fact God omnipotent; wives and children found ways to make their wishes felt without rising in open rebellion; social rituals were observed with the blend of deference, light irony, and flexibility that enables the social order to maintain its equilibrium.

But *King Lear* is emphatically not about ordinary circumstances, quiet compromises, and equilibrium. It is about a crisis in which latent contradictions become all too manifest, polite fictions give way to unbearable truths, and all veils are stripped away. *King Lear* relentlessly stages a horrifying descent toward what the ruined King, contemplating the filthy, naked body of a mad beggar, calls "the thing itself": "Unaccommodated man is no more but such a poor, bare, forked animal as thou art" (F 3.4.98–100; cf. Q 3.4.93–95). Lear and the Earl of Gloucester, another old man whose terrible fate closely parallels Lear's, repeatedly look up at the heavens and call upon the gods for help, but the gods are silent. The despairing Gloucester concludes that the universe is actively malevolent—"As flies to wanton boys are we to th' gods: / They kill us for their sport" (F 4.1.38–39; cf. Q 4.1.37–38)—but the awful silence of the gods may equally be a sign of their indifference or their nonexistence.

The story of King Lear and his three daughters had been often told when Shakespeare undertook to make it the subject of a tragedy. The play, performed at court in December 1606, was probably written and first performed somewhat earlier, though not before 1603, since it contains allusions to a florid piece of anti-Catholic propaganda published in that year: Samuel Harsnett's *Declaration of Egregious Popish Imposture* (the source of the colorful names of the "foul fiends" by whom Shakespeare's mad beggar claims to be possessed). Thus, scholars generally assign Shakespeare's composition of *King Lear* to 1604–05, shortly after *Othello* (ca. 1601–03) and before *Macbeth* (ca. 1606): an astounding succession of tragic masterpieces.

King Lear first appeared in print in a Quarto published in 1608 entitled the *True Chronicle Historie of the life and death of King Lear*; a substantially different text, entitled *The Tragedie of King Lear* and grouped with the other tragedies, was printed in the 1623 First Folio. From the eighteenth century, when the difference between the two texts was first noted, editors, assuming that the texts were imperfect versions of the identical play, customarily conflated them, blending together the approximately one hundred Folio lines not printed in the Quarto with the approximately three hundred Quarto lines not printed in the Folio and selecting as best they could among the hundreds of particular alternative readings.

There is, however, a growing scholarly consensus that the 1608 text of *Lear* represents the play as Shakespeare first wrote it and that the 1623 text represents a substantial revision. The changes include what appears to be a serious rethinking of the armed struggle—whether it is to be imagined principally as a foreign invasion or a civil war—that brings about the denouement, as well as a reconsideration of the play's final moments. (See the Textual Introduction for further discussion.) Since this revision includes significant structural changes as well as many local details, the two texts provide a precious opportunity to glimpse Shakespeare's creative process as an artist and the collaborative work of his theater company. Accordingly, *The Norton Shakespeare* prints *The History of King Lear* (Q) and *The Tragedy of King Lear* (F) on facing pages, and the plays can be read independently of one another in the Digital Edition. In addition, we include a modern combined version of the play, so that readers will be able to judge for themselves the effects of the familiar editorial practice of stitching together the two texts. The combined text also provides readers with access to the version that has for centuries formed the basis for innumerable stage and, more recently, film productions.

When *King Lear* was first performed, it may have struck contemporaries as strangely timely in the wake of a lawsuit that had occurred in late 1603. The two elder daughters of a doddering gentleman named Sir Brian Annesley had attempted to get their father legally certified as insane, thereby enabling themselves to take over his estate, while his youngest daughter vehemently protested on her father's behalf. The youngest daughter's name happened to be Cordell, a name uncannily close to that of Lear's youngest daughter, Cordelia, who tries to save her father from the malevolent designs of her older sisters.

The Annesley case is worth invoking not only because the weird coincidence may have caught Shakespeare's attention but also because it directs our own attention to the ordinary family tensions and fears around which *King Lear,* for all of its wildness, violence, and strangeness, is constructed. Though the Lear story has the mythic

Cordeilla Queene. From Raphael Holinshed, *Chronicles of England, Scotland, and Ireland* (1577).

quality of a folktale (specifically, it resembles both the tale of Cinderella and the tale told in many cultures of a daughter who falls into disfavor for telling her father she loves him as much as salt), it was rehearsed in Shakespeare's time as a piece of authentic British history from the very ancient past (ca. 800 B.C.E.) and as an admonition to contemporary fathers not to put too much trust in the flattery of their children: "Remember what happened to old King Lear. . . ." In some versions of the story, including Shakespeare's, the warning centers on a decision to retire.

Retirement has come to seem a routine event, but in the patriarchal, gerontocratic culture of Tudor and Stuart England, it was generally shunned. When through illness or extreme old age it became unavoidable, retirement put a severe strain on the politics and psychology of deference by driving a wedge between status—what Lear at society's pinnacle calls "[t]he name and all th'addition to a king" (F 1.1.133; cf. Q 1.1.121)—and power. In both the state and the family, the strain could be somewhat eased by transferring power to the eldest legitimate male successor, but as the families of both the legendary Lear and the real Brian Annesley showed, such a successor did not always exist.

In the absence of a male heir, the aged Lear, determined to "shake all cares and business" from himself and confer them on "younger strengths," attempts to divide his kingdom equally among his daughters so that, as he puts it, "future strife / May be prevented now" (F 1.1.37–38, 42–43; cf. Q 1.1.37–38). This attempt is a disastrous failure. Critics have often argued that the roots of the failure lie in the division of the kingdom, that any parceling out of the land on a map would itself have provoked in the audience an ominous shudder, as it is clearly meant to do when the rebels spread out a map in anticipation of a comparable division in *1 Henry IV.* But perhaps to some observers at least, Lear's intended plan, under the circumstances, might have seemed to make strategic sense. After all, the play opens with the Earl of Gloucester and the Earl of Kent commenting without apparent disapproval on the King's scrupulous distribution of the shares. The plan is not, in any case, put to the test, and the principal focus of the tragedy lies elsewhere. Lear's folly is not (or not only) that he retires or even that he divides his kingdom, but rather that he rashly disinherits the only child who truly loves him—his youngest daughter.

Shakespeare contrives moreover to show that the problem of generational transition—and the related tensions in the family and the state—with which his characters are grappling does not simply result from the absence of a son and heir. In his most brilliant and complex use of a double plot, he intertwines the story of Lear and his three daughters with the story of Gloucester and his two sons, a tale he adapted from an episode in Philip Sidney's prose romance *Arcadia*. The fact that this second story is given unusually full and intense treatment, almost equal to the main plot, has the effect of suggesting that what is at stake extends beyond the royal family alone, that the roots of the tragedy lie deep in the nature of things. Gloucester has a legitimate heir, his elder son, Edgar, as well as an illegitimate son, Edmund, and in this family the tragic conflict originates not in an unusual manner of transferring property from one generation to another but rather in the reverse: Edmund seethes with murderous resentment at the disadvantage entirely customary for someone in his position, both as a younger son and as what was called a "base" or "natural" child. "Thou, Nature, art my goddess," he declares:

> Wherefore should I
> Stand in the plague of custom and permit
> The curiosity of nations to deprive me,
> For that I am some twelve or fourteen moonshines
> Lag of a brother? Why "bastard"? Wherefore "base" . . . ?
> (F 1.2.1–6; cf. Q 1.2.1–6)

For the seductive and ruthlessly ambitious Edmund, the social order and the language used to articulate it are merely arbitrary constraints, obstacles to the triumph of his will. He schemes to tear down the obstacles by playing on his father's fears, cleverly planting a forged letter in which his older brother appears to be plotting against his father's life. The letter's chilling sentences express Edmund's own impatience, his hatred of the confining power of custom, his disgusted observation of "the oppression of aged tyranny, who sways not as it hath power but as it is suffered" (F 1.2.48–49; cf. Q 1.2.47–48). Gloucester is predictably horrified and incensed; these are, as Edmund cunningly knows, the cold sentiments that the aged fear lie just beneath the surface of deference and flattery. The forged letter reflects back as well on the scene that has just concluded and on whose outcome Gloucester is brooding: a scene in which everyone, with the exception of the Earl of Kent, has tamely suffered a tyrannical old man to banish his youngest daughter for her failure to flatter him.

Stargazing. From John Cypriano, *A Most Strange and Wonderful Prophesy* (1595). "I should have been that I am had the maidenliest star in the firmament twinkled on my bastardizing" (F 1.2.118–20).

Why does Lear, who has already drawn up the map dividing the kingdom, stage the love test? In Shakespeare's principal source, an anonymous play called *The True Chronicle History of King Leir* (published in 1605 but dating from 1594 or earlier), there is a gratifyingly clear answer. Leir's strong-willed daughter Cordella has vowed that she will only marry a man whom she herself loves; Leir wishes her to marry the man he chooses for his own dynastic purposes. He stages the love test, anticipating that in competing with her sisters Cordella will declare that she loves her father best, at which point Leir will demand that she prove her love by marrying the suitor of his choice. The stratagem backfires, but its purpose is clear.

By stripping his character of a comparable motive, Shakespeare makes

Lear's act seem stranger, at once more arbitrary and more rooted in deep psychological needs. His Lear is a man who has determined to retire from power but who cannot endure dependence. Unwilling to lose his identity as an absolute authority both in the state and in the family, he arranges a public ritual—"Which of you shall we say doth love us most . . . ?" (F 1.1.49; cf. Q 1.1.43)—whose aim seems to be to allay his own anxiety by arousing it in his children. Since the shares have already been apportioned, Lear evidently wants his daughters to engage in a symbolic competition for his bounty without having to endure any of the actual consequences of such a competition; he wants, that is, to produce in them something like the effect of theater, where emotions run high and their practical effects are negligible. But in this absolutist theater—whose formal, ceremonial character Goneril and Regan perfectly understand—Cordelia refuses to perform: "What shall Cordelia speak? Love, and be silent" (F 1.1.60; cf. Q 1.1.54). When she says "Nothing," a word that echoes darkly throughout the play, Lear hears what he most dreads: emptiness, loss of respect, the extinction of identity. And when, under further interrogation, she declares that she loves her father "[a]ccording to my bond" (F 1.1.91; cf. Q 1.1.79), Lear understands these words too to be the equivalent of "nothing."

As Cordelia's subsequent actions demonstrate, his youngest daughter's bond is in reality something substantial and deep. It is linked to the primary sense of obligation that keeps the Fool from abandoning the fallen King, leads Gloucester to commit what is regarded as treason, and drives Kent to put his life at risk to serve his royal master. In the case of Cordelia, this bond extends beyond duty and service to include a sustaining, generous love, but it is a love that ultimately leads to her death. Here Shakespeare makes an even more startling departure not only from *The True Chronicle History of King Leir* but from all his known sources. The earliest of these, the account in Geoffrey of Monmouth's twelfth-century *Historia Regum Britanniae,* sets the pattern repeated in John Higgins's *Mirror for Magistrates* (1574 edition), William Warner's *Albions England* (1586), Raphael Holinshed's *Chronicles of England, Scotland, and Ireland* (2nd ed., 1587), and Edmund Spenser's *Faerie Queene* (1590, 2.10.27–32): the aged Lear is overthrown by his wicked daughters and their husbands, but he is restored to the throne by the army of his good daughter's husband, the King of France. The story then is one of loss and restoration: Lear resumes his reign, and when, "made ripe for death" by old age, as Spenser puts it, he dies, he is succeeded by Cordelia. The conclusion is not unequivocally happy; in all of the known chronicles, Cordelia rules worthily for several years and then, after being deposed and imprisoned by her nephews, in despair commits suicide. But Shakespeare's ending is unprecedented in its tragic devastation. When in act 5 Lear suddenly enters with the lifeless body of Cordelia in his arms, the original audience, secure in the expectation of a very different resolution, must have been doubly shocked, a shock cruelly reinforced when the signs that she might be reviving—"This feather stirs. She lives!" (F 5.3.239; cf. Q 5.3.261)—all prove false. In the Folio *Tragedy of King Lear,* the father apparently dies in the grip of the illusion that he detects some breath on his daughter's lips, but we know that Cordelia will, as he says a moment earlier, "come no more, / Never, never, never, never, never!" (F 5.3.283–84; cf. Q 5.3.303–04).

Those five reiterated words, the bleakest pentameter line Shakespeare ever wrote, are the climax of an extraordinary poetics of despair that is set in motion when Lear disinherits Cordelia and when Gloucester credits Edmund's lies about Edgar. *King Lear* has seemed to many modern readers and audiences the greatest of Shakespeare's tragedies precisely because of its anguished look into the heart of darkness, but its vision of suffering and evil has not always commanded unequivocal admiration. In the eighteenth century, Samuel Johnson wrote, "I was many years ago so shocked by Cordelia's death that I know not whether I ever endured to read again the last scenes of the play till I undertook to revise them as an editor." Johnson's contemporaries preferred a revision of Shakespeare's tragedy undertaken in 1681 by Nahum Tate. Finding the play "a Heap of Jewels, unstrung, and unpolisht," Tate proceeded to restring them in order to save Cordelia's life and to produce the unambiguous and happy triumph of the forces of good.

Only in the nineteenth century was Shakespeare's deeply pessimistic ending—the old generation dead or dying, the survivors shaken to the core, the ruling families all broken with no impending marriage to promise renewal—generally restored to theatrical performance and the tragedy's immense power fully acknowledged. Even passionate admirers of King Lear, however, continued to express deep uneasiness, repeatedly noting not only its unbearably painful close but also what Johnson first called the "improbability of Lear's conduct" and what Samuel Taylor Coleridge termed the plot's "glaring absurdity." Above all, critics questioned whether the tragedy was suitable for the stage. Coleridge compared the suffering Lear to one of Michelangelo's titanic figures, but the grandeur invoked by the comparison led his contemporary Charles Lamb to conclude flatly that "Lear is essentially impossible to be represented on stage." "To see Lear acted," Lamb wrote, "to see an old man tottering about the stage with a walking stick, turned out of doors by his daughters in a rainy night, has nothing in it but what is painful and disgusting." In such a view, King Lear could only be staged successfully in the imagination; there alone would Lear's passion be perceived not like ordinary human suffering but rather, in the marvelous characterization of another Romantic critic, William Hazlitt, "like a sea, swelling, chafing, raging, without bound, without hope, without beacon, or anchor." In the theater of the mind, Shakespeare's play could assume its true, stupendous proportions, enabling the reader to grasp its ultimate meaning. That meaning, the great early twentieth-century critic A. C. Bradley wrote, is that we must "renounce the world, hate it, and lose it gladly. The only real thing in it is the soul, with its courage, patience, devotion. And nothing outward can touch that." These are stirring words, but what about the body?

Brilliant modern stage performances and, more recently, films belying the view that King Lear is unactable have underscored not only the play's acute theatrical sophistication and self-awareness but also its emphasis on the body's inescapable centrality. If Shakespeare explores the extremes of the mind's anguish and the soul's devotion, he never forgets that his characters have bodies as well, bodies that have needs, cravings, and vulnerabilities.

Then as now, those vulnerabilities are at their most terrible in the poor, and King Lear insists with singular urgency on the crucial importance of noticing what those who are wrapped in their "[r]obes and furred gowns" (F 4.5.159; cf. Q 4.6.158) rarely if ever register. The world is full of people who have almost nothing to shield them from the harshness of the elements and the grotesque inequities of the state. When those in power see the bodies of what the play calls "unaccommodated man," they look away or merely pretend to see what in reality they ignore. "Get thee glass eyes," Lear says bitterly, "And, like a scurvy politician, / Seem to see the things thou dost not" (F 4.5.164–66; cf. Q 4.6.158–60).

Lear himself was blind in precisely this way, but he has been forced, as he puts it, "to feel what wretches feel" (F 3.4.35; cf. Q 3.4.31). When in this tragedy characters fall from high station, they plunge unprotected into a world of violent storms, murderous cruelty, and physical horror. The old King wanders raging on the heath, through a wild night of thunder and rain. Disguised as Poor Tom, a mad beggar possessed by demons, Gloucester's son Edgar enacts a life of utmost degradation: "Poor Tom, that eats the swimming frog, the toad, the tadpole, the wall-newt, and the water, that in the fury of his heart, when the foul fiend rages, eats cow dung for salads, swallows the old rat and the ditch dog, drinks the green mantle of the standing pool" (F 3.4.118–22; cf. Q 3.4.114–18). Gloucester's fate is even more terrible: betrayed by his son Edmund, he is seized in his own house by Lear's sadistic daughter Regan and her husband, Cornwall, tied to a chair, brutally interrogated, blinded, and then thrust bleeding out of doors.

Mental anguish in *King Lear*, then, is closely intertwined with physical anguish; the terrifying forces that are released by Lear's folly crash down upon both body and soul, just as the storm that rages on the heath seems at once an objective event and a symbolic representation of Lear's innermost being. The greatest expression of this intertwining in the play is Lear's madness, which brings together a devastating loss of identity; a relentless, radical assault on the hypocrisies of authority; and a demented, nauseated loathing of female sexuality. The loathing culminates in a fit of retching— "Fie, fie, fie! Pah, pah!"—followed by Lear's delusional attempt to find a physical remedy for his psychic pain: "Give me an ounce of civet, good apothecary; / Sweeten my imagination" (F 4.5.127–29; cf. Q 4.6.126–28). In fact, relief from the chaotic rage of madness comes in the wake of a deep, restorative sleep and a change of garments.

The body in *King Lear* is a site not only of abject misery, nausea, and pain but of care and a nascent moral and political awareness. In the midst of his mad ravings, Lear turns to the shivering Fool and asks, "Art cold?" (F 3.2.68; cf. Q 3.2.71). The simple question anticipates his recognition a few moments later that there is more suffering in the world than his own:

> Poor naked wretches, wheresoe'er you are,
> That bide the pelting of this pitiless storm,
> How shall your houseless heads and unfed sides,
> Your looped and windowed raggedness defend you
> From seasons such as these? Oh, I have ta'en
> Too little care of this!
> (F 3.4.29–34; cf. Q 3.4.25–30)

And if the world seems largely unjust and indifferent to human suffering, there are nonetheless throughout the play constant manifestations of generosity of body as well as soul. "Help me, help me!" cries the frightened Fool, to which Kent (disguised in order to serve the King, who has banished him) says simply, "Give me thy hand" (F 3.4.39–41; cf. Q 3.4.34–36). "What are you?" says the blind Gloucester to the son he has unjustly disinherited, to which the son, also in disguise, replies similarly, "Give me your hand" (F 4.5.213, 216; cf. Q 4.6.66). (In a moving moment from the Quarto, absent from the Folio version, two of Glouces-ter's servants not only react with horror to their master's blinding but also resolve to assist him: "Go thou. I'll fetch some flax and whites of eggs to apply to his bleeding face. Now, heaven help him!" [Q 3.7.105–06].) Such signs of goodness and empathy do not outweigh the harshness of the physical world of the play, let alone cancel out the vicious cru-elty of certain of its inhabitants, but they do qualify its moral bleakness.

It is possible to detect in *King Lear* one of the great structural

Tom Durie (1614). By Marcus Gheeraerts the Younger. Durie was the jester of Anne of Denmark, who was married to James I.

rhythms of Christianity: a passage through suffering, humiliation, and pain to a transcendent wisdom and love. Lear's initial actions were blind and selfish, but he comes to acknowledge his folly and, in an immensely poignant scene, to kneel down before the daughter he has wronged. Gloucester too learns that he was blind, even when his eyes could see, and he passes, by means of Edgar's strange deception at the imaginary cliff, from suicidal despair to patient resignation. "Men must endure / Their going hence even as their coming hither," Edgar wisely counsels his father. "Ripeness is all" (F 5.2.9–11; cf. Q 5.2.9–11).

But "ripeness," as the play shows, may entail resistance as well as resignation. For a time, evil seems to flourish in the world, but the forces of decency regroup themselves, and the wicked do not ultimately triumph. Edmund is killed by the brother he had tried to destroy; the loathsome Oswald is clubbed to death trying to murder Gloucester; one wicked sister poisons the other and then kills herself. And in an astonishing moment, radical in its political implications, the sadistic Duke of Cornwall is wounded by an upright servant. The anonymous servant—a nobody in the social world of the play—is Cornwall's own, but there are moments in which deference to authority is not enough, in which it is not acceptable merely to stand by and watch, in which the will to serve paradoxically requires violent disobedience. The servant is stabbed to death by the shocked and outraged Regan—"A peasant stand up thus?" (F 3.7.80; cf. Q 3.7.79)—but the Duke does not survive his wound, and the balance of power at that point in the play begins to shift.

Against self-interest and in the face of intolerable pressure, goodness and moral courage repeatedly shine forth. The Earl of Kent, banished by the rash Lear, dons a disguise in order to serve his king and master, and there are comparable acts of devoted service, political resolve, and self-sacrificing love from Edgar, Gloucester, Cordelia, and that remarkable figure the Fool. In one of the comic masterpieces of the sixteenth century, *The Praise of Folly,* the great Dutch humanist Erasmus used the fool as an emblem of the deepest Christian wisdom, revealed only when the pride, cruelty, and ambition of the world are shattered by a cleansing laughter. The shattering in *King Lear* is tragically violent and deadly, but the presence of the truth-telling Fool seems to point toward a comparable revelation.

Yet *King Lear,* set in a pagan world, resists the redemptive optimism that underlies the Christian vision (an optimism that led Dante to call his poem of damnation and salvation *The Divine Comedy*). The Fool's unnervingly perceptive observations sound far more corrosive than loving—he is, in Lear's words, "A bitter fool" (F 1.4.124; cf. Q 1.4.125)—and he disappears altogether in the third act. His moments of insight and those of all the other characters in the play are radically unstable, like brilliant flashes of lightning in a vast, dark landscape. Hence, for example, Lear's recognition of his folly in banishing Cordelia for her "most small fault" (F 1.4.232; cf. Q 1.4.250) is immediately followed by his hideous cursing of Goneril. His moving acknowledgment of the suffering of the poor, naked wretches is immediately followed by his inability to see the poor, naked wretch before him in any terms but his own: "Didst thou give all to thy daughters, and art thou come to this?" (F 3.4.48–49; cf. Q 3.4.43–44). And his appeal to patient resignation—"When we are born, we cry that we are come / To this great stage of fools" (F 4.5.176–77; cf. Q 4.6.170–71)—is immediately followed by a mad fantasy of revenge: "Then kill, kill, kill, kill, kill, kill!" (F 4.5.181; cf. Q 4.6.174). Every time we seem to have reached firm moral ground, the ground shifts, and we are kept, as Johnson observed, in "a perpetual tumult of indignation, pity, and hope." There are moments of apparent resolution: "Come, let's away to prison," says Lear to the weeping Cordelia, when they are captured by the enemy. "We two alone will sing like birds i'th' cage" (F 5.3.8–9; cf. Q 5.3.8–9). But a more terrible fate lies before them. "Some good I mean to do," says the dying Edmund, "Despite of mine own nature" (F 5.3.218–19; cf. Q 5.3.239–40). But his attempt to send a reprieve and therefore in some measure to redeem himself comes too late.

The play's nightmarish events continually lurch ahead of intentions, and even efforts to say "I have seen the worst" are frustrated.

The tragedy is not only that the intervals of moral resolution, mental lucidity, and spiritual calm are so brief, continually giving way to feverish grief and rage, but also that the modest human understandings, moving in their simplicity, cost such an enormous amount of pain. Edgar saves his father from despair but also in some sense breaks his father's heart. Cordelia's steadfast honesty, her refusal to flatter the father she loves, may be admirable but has disastrous consequences, and her attempt to save Lear only leads to her own death. For a sublime moment, Lear actually *sees* his daughter, understands her separateness, acknowledges her existence—"Do not laugh at me, / For as I am a man, I think this lady / To be my child Cordelia"—but it has taken the destruction of virtually his whole world for him to reach this recognition (F 4.6.65–67; cf. Q 4.7.69–71).

An apocalyptic dream of last judgment and redemption hovers over the entire tragedy, but it is a dream forever deferred. At the sight of the howling Lear with the dead Cordelia in his arms, the bystanders can only ask a succession of stunned questions:

> KENT   Is this the promised end?
> EDGAR   Or image of that horror.
>   (F 5.3.237–38; cf. Q 5.3.259–60)

Lear's own question a moment later seems the most terrible and the most important: "Why should a dog, a horse, a rat have life, / And thou no breath at all?" (F 5.3.282–83; cf. Q 5.3.302–03). It is a sign of *King Lear*'s astonishing freedom from orthodoxy that it refuses to offer any of the conventional answers to this question, answers that largely serve to conceal or deflect the mourner's anguish. Shakespeare's tragedy asks us not to turn away from evil, folly, and unbearable human pain but, seeing them face-to-face, to strengthen our capacity to speak the truth, to seek justice, and to love.

STEPHEN GREENBLATT

SELECTED BIBLIOGRAPHY

Cavell, Stanley. "The Avoidance of Love: A Reading of *King Lear.*" *Disowning Knowledge in Six Plays of Shakespeare.* Cambridge: Cambridge UP, 1987. 39–124. To face the frightening isolation of all humans, to grasp the difference between the knowledge of love and the acknowledgment of love, to understand that in order to see one must also allow oneself to be seen, to endure the shame of exposure—these are among *King Lear*'s radical insights.

de Grazia, Margreta. "The Ideology of Superfluous Things: *King Lear* as Period Piece." *Subject and Object in Renaissance Culture.* Ed. Margreta de Grazia, Maureen Quilligan, and Peter Stallybrass. Cambridge: Cambridge UP, 1996. 17–42. Asserts that far from being protomodern, the play depicts a world in which persons and things cannot be separated and superfluity is a sign of apocalypse.

Greenblatt, Stephen. "Shakespeare and the Exorcists." *Shakespearean Negotiations: The Circulation of Social Energy in Renaissance England.* Berkeley: U of California P, 1988. 94–128. Argues that Shakespeare draws theatrical energy from the contemporary practice of exorcism, a ritualized encounter with evil attacked by Protestant officials as a vicious, histrionic fraud.

Holland, Peter, ed. *"King Lear" and Its Afterlife. Shakespeare Survey* 55 (2002). Treating four centuries of adaptations, appropriations, performances, and interpretations, this essay collection focuses on plays, songs, and novels that draw on *King Lear.*

Jones, John. *Shakespeare at Work*. Oxford: Oxford UP, 1995. Points out that close attention to the Folio revisions of the Quarto text discloses a cunning symbolic design that links Lear's craziness to his obsession with quantity.

Kronenfeld, Judy. *"King Lear" and the Naked Truth: Rethinking the Language of Religion and Resistance*. Durham, NC: Duke UP, 1998. Claims that the play should be understood not through deconstruction or new historicism but through the common Christian culture that gave its terms meaning outside a polemical context.

Leggatt, Alexander. *King Lear*. 2nd ed. Manchester: Manchester UP, 2004. Explores interpretive problems through the history of twentieth-century stage and film productions.

Nuttall, A. D. *"King Lear." Why Does Tragedy Give Pleasure?* Oxford: Clarendon, 1996. 81–105. Argues that the play gives pleasure not by sealing off suffering in poetic form but by destroying the expected recognition and closure of tragedy.

Strier, Richard. *Resistant Structures: Particularity, Radicalism, and Renaissance Texts*. Berkeley: U of California P, 1995. 165–202. Asserts that in *King Lear* Shakespeare endorses a radical political position that, in extreme circumstances, counseled resistance to authority as the highest form of "good service."

Taylor, Gary, and Michael Warren, eds. *The Division of the Kingdoms: Shakespeare's Two Versions of "King Lear."* Oxford: Clarendon, 1983. This essay collection presents the case for the Quarto and Folio texts as distinct works and explores the consequences for interpreting *King Lear*.

FILMS

King Lear. 1953. Dir. Andrew McCullough, with Peter Brook. US. 73 min. Heavily cut—entirely without the Edgar–Edmund subplot—this version, filmed for live television, features the powerful presence of Orson Welles, along with a fine performance of the Fool by the Irish actor Michael MacLiammoir.

Korol Lir. 1969. Dir. Grigori Kozintsev and Iosif Shapiro. USSR. 139 min. This black-and-white film presents a wizened but childlike Lear in a peasant-filled wasteland; a romantic fable set in the Christian Middle Ages.

King Lear. 1971. Dir. Peter Brook. UK. 137 min. Men in pelts wander in a primitive tundra. Breaks in cinematic realism signal Lear's decline. With Paul Scofield and Jack MacGowran.

King Lear. 1982. Dir. Jonathan Miller. UK. 180 min. Michael Hordern's Lear draws upon director Miller's background in neurology to depict his character's mental deterioration.

King Lear. 1983. Dir. Michael Elliott. UK. 158 min. Laurence Olivier, nearly eighty years old, in his final *Lear*. A television production that opens at Stonehenge.

Ran. 1985. Dir. Akira Kurosawa. Japan. 160 min. Set in sixteenth-century feudal Japan, the story, loosely adapted from Shakespeare, is noted for its elegiac battle sequences and orgies of red. With Tatsuya Nakadai and Akira Terao.

King Lear. 1998. Dir. Richard Eyre. UK. 150 min. Garish hues and torch-lit interiors for an especially cruel Lear, with equally vicious Regan and Goneril. With Ian Holm and Victoria Hamilton.

King Lear. 2008. Dir. Trevor Nunn. UK. 172 min. Set in a vaguely Hapsburg-era Central European court, this production features a commanding Ian McKellen tormented by the discovery that he cannot compel love from his daughters.

TEXTUAL INTRODUCTION

King Lear presents the most fascinating, important, and contentious textual issues of the entire Shakespeare canon. The play exists in two early authoritative texts, the Quarto (Q1) of 1608 and the Folio (F) of 1623. For many years, it was presumed that each text was an imperfect and incomplete version of a lost, longer original. Consequently, *King Lear* was usually printed in a "conflated" text: that is, in an attempt to give readers and audiences as many as possible of Shakespeare's words, editors combined the two texts into a version of the play that was longer than either of the early texts. However, by the end of the twentieth century there was a general consensus that the two texts were sequential—that is, that the Quarto represents a first complete stage of the play and the Folio represents a later stage, which may be Shakespeare's revision of his own play. This consensus informs the decision of *The Norton Shakespeare* to print both texts, so as to enable readers to compare them, and in addition to print a text that merges material from both (discussed below).

The Quarto, as Peter Blayney argued in *The Texts of "King Lear" and Their Origins* (1982), was most probably printed from Shakespeare's "foul papers," or draft. Such drafts typically fail to provide necessary directions, use inconsistent speech prefixes, and include "false starts"—i.e., inconsistencies in the development of plot, structure, or characters. An instance of Shakespeare's characteristic patterns of composition in the Quarto text includes his use of generic speech prefixes (e.g., Edmund is *"Bastard"* in the speech prefixes). There are also signs of rapid revision. Such revisions may be signaled in verse by a hypermetric line (one with too many syllables for a pentameter) and in a prose line by a crowded right margin. Shakespeare may also have made further refinements and alterations as the play moved from the draft to the version used for performance. Q1, then, based as it appears to be on foul papers, most likely reflects the play as originally written and corrected; it may have been further revised before a "fair copy" was made that could serve as the basis for the "promptbook," or script from which the play was performed.

The Q1 text has acquired a second layer of alteration through correction during the printing process, as revealed by variant copies of Q1: for example, at 4.6.253, some copies read "my gayle" and others have been corrected to "my iayle." Occasionally, "corrections" of one word during printing have created errors in other words, as when Gonorill warns her husband, Albany, of the impending threat of attack by Cordelia's army: *"France . . . With plumed helme, thy slayer begins threats"* is corrected to *"France . . . With plumed helm, thy state begins thereat"* (4.2.58ff). Since the lines do not appear in the Folio text, we cannot know which parts of these first and second versions in Q1 are Shakespeare's own. While we have no proof that Shakespeare or his acting company authorized the printing of Q1, the use of his foul papers in its printing may suggest that the King's Men participated to some degree in this text's transmission.

The second significant version of the play is the text printed in the 1623 First Folio. The printer's copy for this text seems to have been the Second Quarto, one of the so-called Pavier Quartos, which were printed by the publisher Thomas Pavier without the authority of the King's Men in what seems to have been a first stab at a collection of Shakespeare's plays. The title page bears the false date of 1608, but in fact Q2 was printed eleven years later. This 1619 Q2 is largely identical to Q1, and printers of the First Folio evidently collated it against a King's Men theatrical manuscript.

The Folio contains about one hundred lines that do not appear in the Q1 text of the play, while the Q1 text contains about three hundred lines that do not appear in the F text. F intensifies the action in the last two acts through heavy cutting, particularly to focus on Lear himself. F deletes Q1's entire scene 4.3, in which Kent and a Gentleman discuss Cordelia's return, and, even more remarkably, cuts the "mock-trial" scene of Q1, in which Lear puts his daughters Gonorill and Regan on trial in absentia. It is above all the coherence of the changes from Q that has persuaded scholars that the Folio was a deliberate revision by Shakespeare of his own play.

Some of the streamlining of characters and action was probably done for stage economy. For example, the three Gentlemen in Q1 who chase the mad Lear in 4.6 are reduced to one Gentleman in the parallel scene (4.5) in F, and such Q1 characters as the Doctor are reduced to a generic Gentleman in F. But other economies notably alter the action, as in the blinding of Gloucester in 3.7, which concludes in Q1 with the decision of the two servants to follow and comfort him—lines not in F. In addition, the consolatory (if generic) final lines of the play, spoken by Albany in Q1, are given to Edgar here. This reassignment of lines, along with the omission of the mock-trial and all of 4.3, seems to suggest a carefully planned attempt by Shakespeare to alter the play's theatrical impact.

In addition to its reassigned speeches and omitted or cut scenes, the Folio text offers dozens of small, and seemingly minor, corrections and revisions. A striking example occurs in Cordelia's aside at F 1.1.60 (cf. Q1 1.1.54):

> F: What shall *Cordelia* speake? Loue, and be silent.
> Q1: What shall *Cordelia* doe, loue and be silent.

Throughout the play, Cordelia places an emphasis on action in Q1 and on language in F, and this type of consistent revision in characterization is also apparent in the presentations of Edmund, Kent, Edgar, and Gloucester.

Some editors attribute F's alterations to external censorship, noting, for example, the cuts of numerous references to France. However, enough references to France remain in F to suggest that censorship cannot have been the primary factor. The substantive variants between Q1 and F suggest the kinds of clear, coherent patterns of revision typical of an author. Whether this revision was done to suit a new venue, such as the Blackfriars indoor playhouse, or a changing group of personnel is not certain, and it is possible that Shakespeare may simply have wished to revise his tragedy.

Audiences and editors have traditionally been reluctant to entertain the idea that Shakespeare revised, particularly in the case of so great a play as *King Lear*. The Quarto, which has a substantial number of incoherent or misprinted lines, was thus labeled "bad" by a generation of editors, and the Folio, regarded as the sole authoritative text of the play, served as base text for their editions. Nonetheless, in an attempt to save passages that appeared only in Q1, editors produced texts that interpolated words, lines, passages, scenes, and characters from Q1 into F, even when these variants appeared contradictory, as in Kent's main speech in 3.1, in which, in Q1, he discusses the foreign war with France, whereas in F his subject is the civil war between Albany and Cornwall. Despite the conflict, such conflated editions included both sets of lines.

The Norton Shakespeare offers separate editions of Q1 and F *King Lear*. These editions attempt to present both Q1 and F in a form that makes them accessible to readers, ensuring that the differences between the texts are maintained but emending where necessary to address error. Whenever possible, Q1 has been emended on the basis of either Q2 or F. F's very occasional errors are corrected through emendation (from Q1 or Q2 when possible). Lineation has occasionally been silently corrected. Because printers did not discard sheets that had been printed before the proofreader corrected them and the press was stopped for corrections, all early modern books, including the First Folio, contain a mixture of uncorrected and corrected pages. These variants have been recorded unless they involve only changes in punctuation.

Because conflations of *King Lear* have been for three centuries the basis of performance, criticism, and interpretation, we also provide a "scars-and-stitches" edition of the play, based on the Folio. Unless they cannot structurally coexist with the material in F, lines, passages, and scenes (but not single words or phrases) that appear only in the Quarto have been interpolated into this base text. To signal their insertion, these interpolations are indented, printed in a slightly different typeface, and given different line numbers. Indifferent or disputable variants follow F; F's character names have been regularized to the spelling that has become standard in modern editions; and stage directions that appear in Q but not in F have been interpolated. In addition, as has been conventional practice, the long scene of 2.2, which continues in F until the end of the act, is divided into two further scenes, 2.3 and 2.4.

GRACE IOPPOLO

TEXTUAL BIBLIOGRAPHY

Blayney, Peter W. M. *The Texts of "King Lear" and Their Origins.* Cambridge: Cambridge UP, 1982.
Ioppolo, Grace. *Revising Shakespeare.* Cambridge: Harvard UP, 1991.
Taylor, Gary, and Michael Warren, eds. *The Division of the Kingdoms: Shakespeare's Two Versions of "King Lear."* Oxford: Clarendon, 1983.

PERFORMANCE NOTE

Though Shakespeare wrote longer plays than *King Lear* (*Hamlet, Cymbeline*), no other work so taxes the playgoer's emotional reserves, or so thoroughly implicates his or her sense of personal endurance in the experience of tragedy. Consequently, directors face unusual risks when cutting *Lear* for performance, a task already complicated by significant variants between the Quarto and Folio texts (see the Textual Introduction). Each production's handling of the play's length and textual cruxes can vary its balance between domestic and political concerns, and can determine whether audiences see a man journeying toward moral redemption or foundering, tormented, in a world void of morals or meaning.

Historically, Lear has most often been portrayed as a man "more sinned against than sinning," a rash yet loving father victimized by ungrateful daughters (F 3.2.60; cf. Q 3.2.61). Productions featuring sympathetic treatments sometimes give religious significance to Lear's atonement and death, or present a fractured fairy tale pitting Lear and Cordelia against a pair of matching harpies. Such choices clarify the audience's moral sympathies and can deepen the impact of a tragic outcome so contrary to its sense of justice. Increasingly, however, directors take more neutral positions, showing Lear's peremptory dismissals of Kent and Cordelia as more characteristic than anomalous, and letting Goneril and Regan act upon legitimate grievances. Such productions may show Cordelia as more prig than princess, and moderate her sisters' cruelty by giving them distinct personalities, affections, and insecurities. Whatever the approach, each production must strike balances between Lear's majesty and dotage, suffering and tyranny, reason and lunacy.

Gloucester, meanwhile, can charm or alienate audiences when discussing Edmund's bastardy, and Edgar can be an entitled favorite or a devoted brother and son. Such choices may condemn or almost justify Edmund, whose birth story can seem a source of anguish or a transparent excuse for villainy. Meanwhile, Kent can be a trusty servant or a bully; Lear's knights can be decorous guests or hooligans; the Fool can be a light-hearted jester or a bitter cynic. Other considerations for directors include staging the storm; accounting for the Fool's disappearance; extracting Gloucester's eyes; determining Edmund's familiarity with Goneril; representing Dover and explaining Edgar's reluctance to confide in his father; and devising a setting for a play that seems to demand cosmic grandeur and familial intimacy, timelessness, and specificity.

BRETT GAMBOA

The History of King Lear[1]

QUARTO

LEAR, King of Britain
GONORILL, eldest daughter to Lear
Duke of ALBANY, husband to Gonorill
REGAN, second daughter to Lear
Duke of CORNWALL, husband to Regan
CORDELIA, youngest daughter to Lear
King of FRANCE, suitor to Cordelia
Duke of BURGUNDY, suitor to Cordelia
FOOL, Lear's jester
Earl of GLOUCESTER
EDGAR, legitimate son to Gloucester, later disguised as Poor Tom
Edmund the BASTARD, illegitimate son to Gloucester
Earl of KENT, later disguised as Caius
Oswald, STEWARD to Gonorill
OLD MAN, a tenant of Gloucester
CURAN, a servant of Gloucester
SERVANTS to Cornwall
DOCTOR
CAPTAIN OF THE GUARD
CAPTAIN
HERALD
MESSENGER
KNIGHTS
GENTLEMEN
SERVANTS
Soldiers]

1.1[2] (F 1.1)

Enter KENT, GLOUCESTER,[3] *and [Edmund the]* BASTARD.

KENT I thought the King had more affected° the Duke of   *favored*
Albany° than Cornwall.   *Scotland*

GLOUCESTER It did always seem so to us. But now, in the division of the kingdoms, it appears not° which of the Dukes he   *is not clear*

5   values most, for equalities° are so weighed° that curiosity in   *shares / equal*
neither can make choice of either's moiety.[4]

KENT Is not this your son, my lord?

1. TEXTUAL COMMENT The first readers of the Quarto and Folio versions of *King Lear* would have confronted not only very different material books but also two different plays, as suggested by the titles of the earliest printed copies of the play. *King Lear* is either a "history" or a "tragedy," depending on which book one is reading. See Digital Edition TC 1 (Quarto edited text).
1.1 Location: King Lear's court.
2. TEXTUAL COMMENT One major difference between the Quarto and Folio texts is that the latter provides act and scene divisions while the former marks no such breaks. These notations suggest that Q1 of *King Lear* was printed from Shakespeare's "foul papers" (or first draft) and that the Folio text was printed from a later "fair copy" (or theatrical manuscript) written out by a scribe and checked against Q2. See Digital Edition TC 2 (Quarto edited text).
3. Pronounced "Gloster."
4. *that . . . moiety:* that careful scrutiny ("curiosity") of both parts cannot determine which portion ("moiety") is preferable.

The Tragedy of King Lear[1]

FOLIO

[THE PERSONS OF THE PLAY

LEAR, King of Britain
GONERILL, eldest daughter to Lear
Duke of ALBANY, husband to Gonerill
REGAN, second daughter to Lear
Duke of CORNWALL, husband to Regan
CORDELIA, youngest daughter to Lear
King of FRANCE, suitor to Cordelia
Duke of BURGUNDY, suitor to Cordelia
FOOL, Lear's jester
Earl of GLOUCESTER
EDGAR, legitimate son to Gloucester, later disguised as Poor Tom
EDMOND, illegitimate son to Gloucester
Earl of KENT, later disguised as Caius
Oswald, STEWARD to Gonerill
OLD MAN, a tenant of Gloucester
CURAN, a servant of Gloucester
SERVANTS to Cornwall
CAPTAIN
HERALD
MESSENGER
GENTLEMEN
KNIGHTS
Attendants, Servants, Soldiers]

1.1[2] (Q 1.1)

Enter KENT, GLOUCESTER,[3] *and* EDMOND.

KENT I thought the King had more affected° the Duke of   *favored*
    Albany° than Cornwall.   *Scotland*

GLOUCESTER It did always seem so to us. But now, in the divi-
    sion of the kingdom, it appears not° which of the Dukes he   *is not clear*
5   values most, for qualities° are so weighed° that curiosity in   *shares / equal*
    neither can make choice of either's moiety.[4]

KENT Is not this your son, my lord?

---

1. TEXTUAL COMMENT The first readers of the Quarto and Folio versions of *King Lear* would have confronted not only very different material books but also two different plays, as suggested by the titles of the earliest printed copies of the play. *King Lear* is either a "history" or a "tragedy," depending on which book one is reading. See Digital Edition TC 1 (Folio edited text).

1.1 Location: King Lear's court.

2. TEXTUAL COMMENT One major difference between the Quarto and Folio texts is that the latter provides act and scene divisions while the former marks no

such breaks. These notations suggest that Q1 of *King Lear* was printed from Shakespeare's "foul papers" (or first draft) and that the Folio text was printed from a later "fair copy" (or theatrical manuscript) written out by a scribe and checked against Q2. See Digital Edition TC 2 (Folio edited text).

3. Pronounced "Gloster."

4. *for . . . moiety:* because their qualities are so evenly weighted that careful scrutiny ("curiosity") of both parts cannot determine which portion ("moiety") is preferable.

GLOUCESTER   His breeding,° sir, hath been at my charge.⁵ I have   *upbringing*
so often blushed to acknowledge him that now I am brazed°   *hardened*
10   to it.
KENT   I cannot conceive° you.   *comprehend*
GLOUCESTER   Sir, this young fellow's mother could,⁶ whereupon she grew round-wombed and had indeed, sir, a son for
her cradle ere she had a husband for her bed. Do you smell
15   a fault?⁷
KENT   I cannot wish the fault undone, the issue° of it being so   *offspring; result*
proper.°   *handsome; right*
GLOUCESTER   But I have, sir, a son by order of law,° some year   *a legitimate son*
elder than this, who yet is no dearer in my account.° Though   *estimation*
20   this knave° came something saucily⁸ into the world before   *scamp; fellow*
he was sent for, yet was his mother fair, there was good sport
at his making, and the whoreson° must be acknowledged. —Do   *rogue; bastard*
you know this noble gentleman, Edmund?
BASTARD   No, my lord.
25   GLOUCESTER   My lord of Kent. Remember him hereafter as
my honorable friend.
BASTARD   My services to your lordship.
KENT   I must love you and sue° to know you better.   *seek*
BASTARD   Sir, I shall study deserving.°   *shall learn to deserve*
30   GLOUCESTER   He hath been out° nine years, and away he shall   *away; abroad*
again. The King is coming.

> *Sound a sennet.° Enter one bearing a coronet, then*   *fanfare of trumpets*
> LEAR, *then the Dukes of* ALBANY *and* CORNWALL,
> *next* GONORILL, REGAN, CORDELIA, *with followers*
> [*and* SERVANTS].

LEAR   Attend° my lords of France and Burgundy, Gloucester.   *Attend upon; escort*
GLOUCESTER   I shall, my liege.°   [*Exit.*]   *feudal superior*
LEAR   Meantime we° will express our darker° purposes.   *(royal "we") / more secret*
35   [*He points to map.*°]   The map there. Know we have divided
In three our kingdom, and 'tis our first intent
To shake all cares and business of our state,°   *position (as King)*
Confirming them on younger years.
The two great princes, France and Burgundy,
40   Great rivals in our youngest daughter's love,
Long in our court have made their amorous sojourn
And here are to be answered. Tell me, my daughters,

Which of you shall we say doth love us most,
That° we our largest bounty° may extend   *So that / generosity*
45   Where merit doth most challenge it?°   *best claim it*
Gonorill, our eldest born, speak first.

---

5. My responsibility; at my cost.   7. Sin, wrongdoing; female genitals.
6. Could conceive; punning on biological conception.   8. Somewhat rudely; somewhat shamefully.

GLOUCESTER His breeding,° sir, hath been at my charge.[5] I   *upbringing*
  have so often blushed to acknowledge him that now I am
10 brazed° to't.   *hardened*
KENT I cannot conceive° you.   *comprehend*
GLOUCESTER Sir, this young fellow's mother could,[6] where-
  upon she grew round-wombed, and had indeed, sir, a son for
  her cradle ere she had a husband for her bed. Do you smell
15 a fault?[7]
KENT I cannot wish the fault undone, the issue° of it being so   *offspring; result*
  proper.°   *handsome; right*
GLOUCESTER But I have a son, sir, by order of law,° some year   *a legitimate son*
  elder than this, who yet is no dearer in my account.° Though   *estimation*
20 this knave° came something saucily[8] to the world before he   *scamp; fellow*
  was sent for, yet was his mother fair, there was good sport at
  his making, and the whoreson° must be acknowledged.   *rogue; bastard*
  —Do you know this noble gentleman, Edmond?
EDMOND No, my lord.
25 GLOUCESTER My lord of Kent. Remember him hereafter as
  my honorable friend.
EDMOND My services to your lordship.
KENT I must love you and sue° to know you better.   *seek*
EDMOND Sir, I shall study deserving.°   *shall learn to deserve*
30 GLOUCESTER He hath been out° nine years, and away he shall   *away; abroad*
  again. The King is coming.
  Sennet.° Enter [one bearing a coronet,] King LEAR,   *Fanfare of trumpets*
  CORNWALL, ALBANY, GONERILL, REGAN, CORDELIA,
  and Attendants.
LEAR Attend° the lords of France and Burgundy, Gloucester.   *Attend upon; escort*
GLOUCESTER I shall, my lord.   *Exit.*
LEAR Meantime we° shall express our darker° purpose.   *(royal "we") / more secret*
35 Give me the map there. Know that we have divided
  In three our kingdom, and 'tis our fast° intent   *fixed*
  To shake all cares and business from our age,
  Conferring them on younger strengths, while we
  Unburdened crawl toward death. Our son° of Cornwall,   *son-in-law*
40 And you, our no-less-loving son of Albany,
  We have this hour a constant will to publish[9]
  Our daughters' several dowers,° that future strife   *individual dowries*
  May be prevented now. The princes, France and Burgundy,
  Great rivals in our youngest daughter's love,
45 Long in our court have made their amorous sojourn
  And here are to be answered. Tell me, my daughters,
  Since now we will divest us both of rule,
  Interest° of territory, cares of state,   *Legal title*
  Which of you shall we say doth love us most,
50 That° we our largest bounty° may extend   *So that / generosity*
  Where nature doth with merit challenge?[1] Gonerill,
  Our eldest born, speak first.

---

5. My responsibility; at my cost.
6. Could conceive; punning on biological conception.
7. Sin, wrongdoing; female genitals.
8. Somewhat rudely; somewhat shamefully.

9. A fixed determination to announce publicly.
1. *Where . . . challenge:* To the one whose natural love and deserving lay claim (to our generosity).

GONORILL   Sir, I do love you more than words can wield° the   *convey*
　　matter:
　Dearer than eyesight, space,° or liberty,   *freedom of movement*
　Beyond what can be valued rich or rare,
50　No less than life, with grace, health, beauty, honor,
　As much a child e'er loved, or father friend,
　A love that makes breath° poor and speech unable.   *language*
　Beyond all manner of so much° I love you.   *Beyond all comparison*
CORDELIA [*aside*]   What shall Cordelia do? Love and be
　　silent.
55　LEAR [*pointing to map*]   Of all these bounds,° even from this   *regions*
　　line to this,
　With shady forests and wide-skirted meads,°   *broad meadows*
　We make thee lady. To thine and Albany's issue°   *children; heirs*
　Be this perpetual. [*to* REGAN] What says our second
　　daughter,
　Our dearest Regan, wife to Cornwall? Speak.
60　REGAN   Sir, I am made of the selfsame metal° that my sister is   *spirit; substance*
　And prize me at her worth.° In my true heart   *believe myself her equal*
　I find she names my very deed of love, only she came short,
　That° I profess myself an enemy to all other joys   *In that*
　Which the most precious square of sense possesses,[9]
65　And find I am alone felicitate° in your dear highness' love.   *am only made happy*

CORDELIA [*aside*]   Then poor Cordelia, and yet not so, since I
　　am sure
　My love's more richer than my tongue.
LEAR [*pointing to map*]   To thee and thine hereditary ever
　Remain this ample third of our fair kingdom,
70　No less in space, validity,° and pleasure   *value*
　Than that confirmed° on Gonorill. [*to* CORDELIA] But now,   *fixed*
　　our joy,
　Although the last, not least in our dear love,

　What can you say to win a third more opulent
　Than your sisters'?
75　CORDELIA   Nothing, my lord.
LEAR   How? Nothing can come of nothing.[1] Speak again.

9. Which . . . possesses: That the body can enjoy. *precious square of sense*: measure of sensibility; or, perhaps, balanced and sensitive perception. The square may represent the even mixture of the body's four fluids, or humors.

1. *Ex nihilo nihil fit*, a maxim derived from Aristotle, was accepted by the Christian Middle Ages with the single exception of God having created the world out of nothing.

GONERILL   Sir, I love you more than word can wield° the   *convey*
    matter:
    Dearer than eyesight, space,° and liberty,   *freedom of movement*
55 Beyond what can be valued rich or rare,
    No less than life, with grace, health, beauty, honor,
    As much as child e'er loved or father found,
    A love that makes breath° poor and speech unable.   *language*
    Beyond all manner of so much° I love you.   *Beyond all comparison*
60 CORDELIA [*aside*]   What shall Cordelia speak? Love, and be
    silent.
    LEAR [*pointing to map*]   Of all these bounds,° even from this   *regions*
    line to this,
    With shadowy forests and with champaigns riched,°   *enriched plains*
    With plenteous rivers and wide-skirted meads,°   *broad meadows*
    We make thee lady. To thine and Albany's issues°   *children; heirs*
65 Be this perpetual. [*to* REGAN] What says our second
    daughter,
    Our dearest Regan, wife of Cornwall?
    REGAN   I am made of that self-mettle° as my sister   *same spirit; substance*
    And prize me at her worth.° In my true heart   *believe myself her equal*
    I find she names my very deed of love,
70 Only she comes too short, that° I profess   *in that*
    Myself an enemy to all other joys
    Which the most precious square of sense professes,[2]
    And find I am alone felicitate°   *am only made happy*
    In your dear highness' love.
    CORDELIA [*aside*]   Then, poor Cordelia,
75 And yet not so, since I am sure my love's
    More ponderous° than my tongue.   *weighty*
    LEAR [*pointing to map*]   To thee and thine hereditary ever,
    Remain this ample third of our fair kingdom,
    No less in space, validity,° and pleasure   *value*
80 Than that conferred on Gonerill. [*to* CORDELIA] Now, our
    joy,
    Although our last and least,° to whose young love   *youngest; smallest*
    The vines of France and milk of Burgundy
    Strive to be interest,° what can you say to draw   *admitted*
    A third more opulent than your sisters'? Speak.
85 CORDELIA   Nothing, my lord.
    LEAR   Nothing?
    CORDELIA   Nothing.
    LEAR   Nothing will come of nothing.[3] Speak again.

---

2. *Which . . . professes:* That the body can enjoy. *precious square of sense:* measure of sensibility; or, perhaps, balanced and sensitive perception. The square may represent the even mixture of the body's four fluids, or humors.

3. *Ex nihilo nihil fit,* a maxim derived from Aristotle, was accepted by the Christian Middle Ages with the single exception of God having created the world out of nothing.

CORDELIA   Unhappy that I am, I cannot heave
My heart into my mouth.[2] I love your majesty
According to my bond,° nor more nor less.   *filial duty*

80 LEAR   Go to, go to. Mend your speech a little,
Lest it may mar your fortunes.
CORDELIA   Good my lord,
You have begot me, bred me, loved me.
I return those duties back as are right fit:
Obey you, love you, and most honor you.

85 Why have my sisters husbands if they say they love you all?°   *exclusively*
Happily,° when I shall wed, that lord whose hand   *Perhaps; if lucky*
Must take my plight° shall carry half my love with him,   *marriage vow; condition*
Half my care and duty. Sure, I shall never
Marry like my sisters, to love my father all.
LEAR   But goes this with thy heart?

90 CORDELIA   Ay, good my lord.
LEAR   So young and so untender?
CORDELIA   So young, my lord, and true.°   *honest; faithful*
LEAR   Well, let it be so! Thy truth then be thy dower,[3]
For by the sacred radiance of the sun,

95 The mistress of Hecate,[4] and the might;
By all the operation of the orbs,
From whom we do exist and cease to be;[5]
Here I disclaim all my paternal care,
Propinquity,° and property of blood,°   *Closeness / kinship*

100 And as a stranger to my heart and me
Hold thee from this° forever. The barbarous Scythian,[6]   *this time*
Or he that makes his generation
Messes[7] to gorge his appetite,
Shall be as well neighbored, pitied, and relieved

105 As thou my sometime° daughter.   *former*

---

2. *I cannot heave . . . mouth:* Cf. "The heart of fools is in their mouth: but the mouth of the wise is in their heart" (Ecclesiastes 1:26).
3. PERFORMANCE COMMENT The opening sequence of *King Lear,* from Lear's entrance to his banishment of Cordelia, involves crucial interpretive choices for directors and performers, choices that center on the motivations of the central characters. See Digital Edition PC 1.
4. A classical goddess of the moon and the patron of

witchcraft, she was associated with the underworld, Hades.
5. *By all . . . be:* referring to the belief that the movements of stars and planets ("orbs") corresponded to physical and spiritual motions in a person and thus controlled his or her fate.
6. Notoriously savage Crimean nomads of classical antiquity.
7. *he . . . Messes:* he who makes meals of his children.

CORDELIA   Unhappy that I am, I cannot heave
90   My heart into my mouth.[4] I love your majesty
        According to my bond,° no more nor less.   *filial duty*
    LEAR   How, how, Cordelia? Mend your speech a little,
        Lest you may mar your fortunes.
    CORDELIA   Good my lord,
        You have begot me, bred me, loved me.
95   I return those duties back as are right fit:
        Obey you, love you, and most honor you.
        Why have my sisters husbands if they say
        They love you all?° Happily,° when I shall wed,   *completely / Perhaps; if lucky*
        That lord whose hand must take my plight° shall carry   *marriage vow; condition*
100   Half my love with him, half my care and duty.
        Sure, I shall never marry like my sisters.
    LEAR   But goes thy heart with this?
    CORDELIA   Ay, my good lord.
    LEAR   So young and so untender?
    CORDELIA   So young, my lord, and true.°   *honest; faithful*
105 LEAR   Let it be so: thy truth, then, be thy dower![5]
        For by the sacred radiance of the sun,
        The mysteries of Hecate[6] and the night,
        By all the operation of the orbs
        From whom we do exist and cease to be,[7]
110   Here I disclaim all my paternal care,
        Propinquity° and property of blood,°   *Closeness / kinship*
        And as a stranger to my heart and me
        Hold thee from this° forever. The barbarous Scythian,[8]   *this time*
        Or he that makes his generation messes[9]
115   To gorge his appetite, shall to my bosom
        Be as well neighbored, pitied, and relieved
        As thou my sometime° daughter.   *former*

---

4. *I cannot heave . . . mouth:* Cf. "The heart of fools is in their mouth: but the mouth of the wise is in their heart" (Ecclesiastes 1:26).
5. PERFORMANCE COMMENT The opening sequence of *King Lear*, from the Lear's entrance to his banishment of Cordelia, involves crucial interpretive choices for directors and performers, choices that center on the motivations of the central characters. See Digital Edition PC 1.
6. A classical goddess of the moon and the patron of witchcraft, she was associated with the underworld, Hades.
7. *By all . . . be:* referring to the belief that the movements of stars and planets ("orbs") corresponded to physical and spiritual motions in a person and thus controlled his or her fate.
8. Notoriously savage Crimean nomads of classical antiquity.
9. *he . . . messes:* he who makes meals of his children.

KENT   Good my liege—
LEAR   Peace, Kent! Come not between the dragon and his
              wrath!
         I loved her most and thought to set my rest[8]
         On her kind nursery.° Hence and avoid my sight.   care
110   So be my grave my peace,[9] as here I give
         Her father's heart from her. Call France! Who stirs?[1]
         Call Burgundy!   [Exeunt some SERVANTS.]
                          Cornwall and Albany,
         With my two daughters' dower digest° this third.   incorporate
         Let pride, which she calls "plainness,"° marry her.   directness
115   I do invest you jointly in my power,
         Preeminence, and all the large effects°   outward shows; trappings
         That troop with° majesty. Ourself by monthly course,   accompany
         With reservation of° an hundred knights,   legal right to retain
         By you to be sustained, shall our abode
120   Make with you by due turns. Only we still retain
         The name and all the additions° to a king.   prerogatives
         The sway,° revenue, execution of the rest,   power
         Beloved sons, be yours, which to confirm,
         This coronet[2] part betwixt you. [He hands them a coronet.]
KENT   Royal Lear,
125   Whom I have ever honored as my king,
         Loved as my father, as my master followed,
         As my great patron thought on in my prayers—
LEAR   The bow is bent and drawn; make from° the shaft.   get clear of
KENT   Let it fall° rather, though the fork° invade   strike here / arrowhead
130   The region of my heart. Be Kent unmannerly
         When Lear is mad. What wilt thou do, old man?
         Think'st thou that duty shall have dread to speak
         When power to flattery bows? To plainness° honor's bound   plain speaking
         When majesty stoops to folly. Reverse thy doom,°   Revoke your sentence
135   And in thy best consideration check°   halt
         This hideous rashness. Answer my life my judgment:[3]
         Thy youngest daughter does not love thee least,
         Nor are those empty-hearted whose low sound
         Reverbs no hollowness.°   Echoes no insincerity

8. To secure my repose; to stake my all, as in the
card game known as primero.
9. So may I rest in peace (probably an oath).
1. Does nobody stir? An order, with the force of "Get
moving."

2. Cordelia's crown, symbol of the endowment she
has forsworn.
3. Answer . . . judgment: I'll stake my life on my
opinion.

KENT   Good my liege—
LEAR   Peace, Kent!
         Come not between the dragon and his wrath!
120   I loved her most and thought to set my rest[1]
         On her kind nursery.° Hence and avoid my sight.   care
         So be my grave my peace,[2] as here I give
         Her father's heart from her. Call France! Who stirs?[3]
         Call Burgundy!   [*Exeunt some Attendants.*]
         Cornwall and Albany,
125   With my two daughters' dowers digest° the third.   incorporate
         Let pride, which she calls plainness,° marry her.   directness
         I do invest you jointly with my power,
         Preeminence, and all the large effects°   outward shows; trappings
         That troop with° majesty. Ourself by monthly course,   accompany
130   With reservation of° an hundred knights,   legal right to retain
         By you to be sustained, shall our abode
         Make with you by due turn. Only we shall retain
         The name and all th'addition° to a king. The sway,°   the prerogatives / power
         Revenue, execution of the rest,
135   Beloved sons, be yours, which to confirm,
         This coronet[4] part between you. [*He hands them a coronet.*]
KENT   Royal Lear,
         Whom I have ever honored as my king,
         Loved as my father, as my master followed,
         As my great patron thought on in my prayers—
140   LEAR   The bow is bent and drawn; make from° the shaft.   get clear of
         KENT   Let it fall° rather, though the fork° invade   strike here / arrowhead
         The region of my heart. Be Kent unmannerly
         When Lear is mad. What wouldst thou do, old man?
         Think'st thou that duty shall have dread to speak
145   When power to flattery bows?
         To plainness° honor's bound   plain speaking
         When majesty falls to folly. Reserve° thy state,°   Retain / rule; position
         And in thy best consideration check°   halt
         This hideous rashness. Answer my life my judgment:[5]
150   Thy youngest daughter does not love thee least,
         Nor are those empty-hearted whose low sounds
         Reverb no hollowness.°   Echo no insincerity

---

1. To secure my repose; to stake my all, as in the card
game known as primero.
2. So may I rest in peace (probably an oath).
3. Does nobody stir? An order, with the force of "Get
moving."

4. Cordelia's crown, symbol of the endowment she
has forsworn.
5. *Answer . . . judgment:* I'll stake my life on my opinion.

140	LEAR	Kent, on thy life, no more!	
	KENT	My life I never held but as a pawn°	*chess piece; stake*
		To wage° against thy enemies, nor fear to lose it	*wager*
		Thy safety being the motive.	
	LEAR	Out of my sight!	
145	KENT	See better, Lear, and let me still° remain	*always*
		The true blank° of thine eye.	*precise bull's-eye*
	LEAR	Now, by Apollo—	
	KENT	Now, by Apollo, King, thou swearest thy gods in vain.[4]	
	LEAR	Vassal, recreant!°	*traitor*
150	KENT	Do, kill thy physician,	
		And the fee bestow upon the foul disease.[5]	
		Revoke thy doom, or whilst I can vent clamor	
		From my throat I'll tell thee thou dost evil.	
	LEAR	Hear me! On thy allegiance, hear me!	
155		Since thou hast sought to make us break our vow,	
		Which we durst never yet; and with strayed° pride	*wayward; erring*
		To come between our sentence and our power,	
		Which nor our nature nor our place[6] can bear,	
		Our potency made good,° take thy reward.	*demonstrated*
160		Four days we do allot thee for provision,	
		To shield thee from diseases° of the world,	*discomforts*
		And on the fifth to turn thy hated back	
		Upon our kingdom. If, on the tenth day following,	
		Thy banished trunk° be found in our dominions,	*body*
165		The moment is thy death. Away! By Jupiter,	
		This shall not be revoked.	
	KENT	Why, fare thee well, King. Since thus thou wilt appear,	
		Friendship lives hence, and banishment is here.	
		[*to* CORDELIA] The gods to their protection take thee,	
		maid,	
170		That rightly thinks and hast most justly said.	
		[*to* GONORILL *and* REGAN] And your large speeches may	
		your deeds approve,[7]	
		That good effects may spring from words of love.	
		Thus, Kent, O princes, bids you all adieu;	
		He'll shape his old course in a country new.	
		Enter FRANCE *and* BURGUNDY *with* GLOUCESTER.	
175	GLOUCESTER	Here's France and Burgundy, my noble lord.	
	LEAR	My lord of Burgundy, we first address towards you,	
		Who with a king hath rivaled for our daughter.	
		What in the least will you require in present	
		Dower with her or cease your quest of love?	

---

4. You invoke your gods falsely and without effect.
5. *kill . . . disease:* you would not only kill the doctor but also hand his fee over to the disease.

6. Which neither my temperament nor my royal position.
7. And let your actions live up to your fine words.

LEAR   Kent, on thy life, no more!
KENT   My life I never held but as pawn°   *chess piece; stake*
　　To wage° against thine enemies; ne'er fear to lose it,   *wager*
　　Thy safety being motive.°   *(my) motivation*
155　LEAR   Out of my sight!
KENT   See better, Lear, and let me still° remain   *always*
　　The true blank° of thine eye.   *precise bull's-eye*
LEAR   Now, by Apollo—
KENT   Now, by Apollo, King,
　　Thou swear'st thy gods in vain.[6]
LEAR   O vassal! Miscreant!°   *Villain; unbeliever*
160　ALBANY *and* CORNWALL   Dear sir, forbear.
KENT   Kill thy physician and thy fee bestow
　　Upon the foul disease.[7] Revoke thy gift,
　　Or whilst I can vent clamor from my throat
　　I'll tell thee thou dost evil.
165　LEAR   Hear me, recreant!° On thine allegiance, hear me!   *traitor*
　　That thou hast sought to make us break our vows,
　　Which we durst never yet; and with strained° pride   *overblown*
　　To come betwixt our sentences and our power,
　　Which nor our nature nor our place[8] can bear,
170　Our potency made good,° take thy reward.   *demonstrated*
　　Five days we do allot thee for provision,
　　To shield thee from disasters of the world,
　　And on the sixth to turn thy hated back
　　Upon our kingdom. If, on the tenth day following,
175　Thy banished trunk° be found in our dominions,   *body*
　　The moment is thy death. Away! By Jupiter,
　　This shall not be revoked.
KENT   Fare thee well, King. Sith° thus thou wilt appear,   *Since*
　　Freedom lives hence, and banishment is here.
180　[*to* CORDELIA] The gods to their dear shelter take thee,
　　　maid,
　　That justly think'st and hast most rightly said.
　　[*to* GONERILL *and* REGAN] And your large speeches may
　　　your deeds approve.[9]
　　That good effects may spring from words of love.
　　Thus Kent, O princes, bids you all adieu.
185　He'll shape his old course in a country new.   *Exit.*
　　　　Flourish.° *Enter* GLOUCESTER *with* FRANCE *and*   *Fanfare of trumpets*
　　　　BURGUNDY [*and*] *Attendants.*
CORNWALL   Here's France and Burgundy, my noble lord.
LEAR   My lord of Burgundy,
　　We first address toward you, who with this king
　　Hath rivaled for our daughter. What in the least
190　Will you require in present dower with her
　　Or cease your quest of love?

---

6. You invoke your gods falsely and without effect.
7. *Kill . . . disease:* You would not only kill the doctor
but also hand his fee over to the disease.
8. Which neither my temperament nor my royal
position.
9. And let your actions live up to your fine words.

180 BURGUNDY   Royal majesty, I crave no more than what
    Your highness offered, nor will you tender° less.   *offer*
   LEAR   Right noble Burgundy, when she was dear to us
    We did hold her so, but now her price is fallen.
    Sir, there she stands. If aught within that little
185   Seeming substance,[8] or all of it with our displeasure
        pieced°   *joined*
    And nothing else, may fitly like° your grace,   *please*
    She's there, and she is yours.
   BURGUNDY   I know no answer.
   LEAR   Sir, will you with those infirmities she owes,°   *owns*
    Unfriended, new-adopted to our hate,
190   Covered with our curse and strangered° with our oath,   *estranged*
    Take her or leave her?
   BURGUNDY   Pardon me, royal sir, election makes not up
    On such conditions.[9]
   LEAR   Then leave her, sir, for, by the power that made me,
195   I tell you° all her wealth. [*to* FRANCE] For° you, great King, *inform you of / As for*
    I would not from your love make such a stray°   *stray so far*
    To° match you where I hate. Therefore, beseech you   *As to*
    To avert your liking° a more worthier way   *To turn your affections*
    Than on a wretch whom Nature is ashamed
200   Almost to acknowledge hers.
   FRANCE   This is most strange, that she, that even but now
    Was your best object, the argument° of your praise,   *theme*
    Balm of your age, most best, most dearest,
    Should in this trice° of time commit a thing   *moment*
205   So monstrous to dismantle° so many folds of favor. *as to strip off; disrobe*
    Sure, her offense must be of such unnatural degree
    That monsters it,° or you, for vouched affections,   *makes it monstrous*
    Fallen into taint,[1] which to believe of her
    Must be a faith that reason without miracle
210   Could never plant in me.
   CORDELIA   I yet beseech your majesty—
    If for I want° that glib and oily art   *because I lack*
    To speak and purpose not,° since what I well intend *and not intend*
    I'll do't before I speak—that you may know°   *acknowledge*
215   It is no vicious blot, murder, or foulness,
    No unclean action or dishonored step
    That hath deprived me of your grace and favor,
    But even for want of that for which I am rich:
    A still soliciting° eye and such a tongue   *An always-begging*
220   As I am glad I have not, though not to have it
    Hath lost me in your liking.
   LEAR   Go to, go to. Better thou hadst not been born
    Than not to have pleased me better.

---

8. *little / Seeming substance:* one who appears insubstantial; one who will not pretend.
9. A choice cannot be made under those terms.
1. *or . . . taint:* or else the love you earlier swore for

Cordelia must be regarded with suspicion. "Or" may also mean "before," in which case the phrase would mean "before the love you once proclaimed could have decayed."

BURGUNDY   Most royal majesty,
I crave no more than hath your highness offered,
Nor will you tender° less.   *offer*

LEAR   Right noble Burgundy,
When she was dear to us we did hold her so,
195   But now her price is fallen. Sir, there she stands.
If aught within that little-seeming substance,[1]
Or all of it with our displeasure pieced°   *joined*
And nothing more, may fitly like° your grace,   *please*
She's there, and she is yours.

BURGUNDY   I know no answer.

200   LEAR   Will you with those infirmities she owes,°   *owns*
Unfriended, new-adopted to our hate,
Dow'red with our curse and strangered° with our oath,   *estranged*
Take her or leave her?

BURGUNDY   Pardon me, royal sir,
Election makes not up in such conditions.[2]

205   LEAR   Then leave her, sir, for, by the power that made me,
I tell you° all her wealth. [*to* FRANCE] For° you, great King,   *inform you of / As for*
I would not from your love make such a stray°   *stray so far*
To° match you where I hate. Therefore, beseech you   *As to*
T'avert your liking° a more worthier way   *To turn your affections*
210   Than on a wretch whom Nature is ashamed
Almost t'acknowledge hers.

FRANCE   This is most strange,
That she, whom even but now was your object,
The argument° of your praise, balm of your age,   *theme*
The best, the dearest, should in this trice° of time   *moment*
215   Commit a thing so monstrous to dismantle°   *as to strip off; disrobe*
So many folds of favor. Sure, her offense
Must be of such unnatural degree
That monsters it,° or your fore-vouched affection   *makes it monstrous*
Fall into taint,[3] which to believe of her
220   Must be a faith that reason without miracle
Should never plant in me.

CORDELIA   I yet beseech your majesty—
If for I want° that glib and oily art   *because I lack*
To speak and purpose not,° since what I will intend,   *and not intend*
I'll do't before I speak—that you make known
225   It is no vicious blot, murder, or foulness,
No unchaste action or dishonored step
That hath deprived me of your grace and favor,
But even for want of that for which I am richer:
A still soliciting° eye and such a tongue   *An always begging*
230   That I am glad I have not, though not to have it
Hath lost me in your liking.

LEAR   Better thou hadst
Not been born than not t'have pleased me better.

---

1. *little-seeming substance:* one who appears insubstantial; one who will not pretend.
2. A choice cannot be made under those terms.
3. *or . . . taint:* or else the love you earlier swore for

Cordelia must be regarded with suspicion. "Or" may
also mean "before," in which case the phrase would
mean "before the love you once proclaimed could
have decayed."

FRANCE   Is it no more but this, a tardiness in nature,
225   That often leaves the history unspoke that it intends to do?[2]
       My lord of Burgundy, what say you to the lady?
       Love is not love when it is mingled with
       Respects° that stands aloof from the entire point.   *Considerations*
       Will you have her? She is herself and dower.
230 BURGUNDY   Royal Lear, give but that portion
       Which yourself proposed, and here I take Cordelia
       By the hand, Duchess of Burgundy,
     LEAR   Nothing, I have sworn.
     BURGUNDY [*to* CORDELIA]   I am sorry, then, you have so lost a
         father
235   That you must lose a husband.
     CORDELIA   Peace be with Burgundy. Since that respects
       Of fortune are his love, I shall not be his wife.
     FRANCE   Fairest Cordelia, that art most rich being poor,
       Most choice forsaken, and most loved despised,
240   Thee and thy virtues here I seize upon.
       Be it lawful I take up what's cast away.
       Gods, gods! 'Tis strange, that from their cold'st neglect
       My love should kindle to inflamed respect.°   *ardent regard*
       Thy dowerless daughter, King, thrown to my chance,
245   Is queen of us, of ours, and our fair France.
       Not all the dukes in wat'rish° Burgundy   *irrigated; watery; weak*
       Shall buy this unprized° precious maid of me.   *unappreciated*
       Bid them farewell, Cordelia; though unkind,°   *though they are unkind*
       Thou losest here° a better where° to find.   *this place / place*
250 LEAR   Thou hast her, France. Let her be thine,
       For we have no such daughter, nor shall ever see
       That face of hers again. Therefore be gone
       Without our grace, our love, our benison.°   *blessing*
       Come, noble Burgundy.
                 Exeunt LEAR *and* BURGUNDY[, *Dukes of* ALBANY
                      and CORNWALL, GLOUCESTER, *Edmund the*
                          BASTARD, *and* SERVANTS].
255 FRANCE   Bid farewell to your sisters.
     CORDELIA   The jewels of our father,
       With washèd eyes Cordelia leaves you.
       I know you what you are
       And like a sister am most loath to call your faults
260   As they are named.° Use well our father;   *are properly called*
       To your professed bosoms° I commit him.   *publicly proclaimed love*
       But yet, alas, stood I within his grace,
       I would prefer° him to a better place.   *promote; recommend*
       So farewell to you both.

---

2. *a tardiness . . . do:* a natural reserve that inhibits voicing one's intentions.

FRANCE   Is it but this, a tardiness in nature,
 Which often leaves the history unspoke
235 That it intends to do?[4] My lord of Burgundy,
 What say you to the lady? Love's not love
 When it is mingled with regards° that stands   *considerations*
 Aloof from th'entire point. Will you have her?
 She is herself a dowry.
BURGUNDY   Royal King,
240 Give but that portion which yourself proposed,
 And here I take Cordelia by the hand,
 Duchess of Burgundy.
LEAR Nothing, I have sworn; I am firm.
BURGUNDY [*to* CORDELIA] I am sorry, then, you have so lost
  a father
 That you must lose a husband.
245 CORDELIA   Peace be with Burgundy.
 Since that respect and fortunes are his love,
 I shall not be his wife.
FRANCE Fairest Cordelia, that art most rich being poor,
 Most choice forsaken, and most loved despised,
250 Thee and thy virtues here I seize upon.
 Be it lawful I take up what's cast away.
 Gods, gods! 'Tis strange, that from their cold'st neglect
 My love should kindle to enflamed respect.°   *ardent regard*
 Thy dowerless daughter, King, thrown to my chance,
255 Is Queen of us, of ours, and our fair France.
 Not all the dukes of wat'rish° Burgundy   *irrigated; watery; weak*
 Can buy this unprized,° precious maid of me.   *unappreciated*
 Bid them farewell, Cordelia; though unkind,° *though they are unkind*
 Thou losest here° a better where° to find.   *this place / place*
260 LEAR Thou hast her, France. Let her be thine, for we
 Have no such daughter, nor shall ever see
 That face of hers again. Therefore be gone
 Without our grace, our love, our benison.°   *blessing*
 —Come, noble Burgundy.
     Flourish. Exeunt [*all but* FRANCE, CORDELIA,
        GONERILL, *and* REGAN].
265 FRANCE Bid farewell to your sisters.
 CORDELIA The jewels of our father, with washed eyes
 Cordelia leaves you. I know you what you are
 And like a sister am most loath to call
 Your faults as they are named.° Love well our father; *are properly called*
270 To your professed bosoms° I commit him. *publicly proclaimed love*
 But yet, alas, stood I within his grace,
 I would prefer° him to a better place.   *promote; recommend*
 So farewell to you both.

4. *a tardiness . . . do:* a natural reserve that inhibits voicing one's intentions.

265 GONORILL   Prescribe not us our duties.
    REGAN   Let your study be to content your lord,
      Who hath received you at fortune's alms.[3]
      You have obedience scanted°   *neglected*
      And well are worth the worth that you have wanted.[4]
270 CORDELIA   Time shall unfold what pleated cunning hides;
      Who covers faults, at last shame them derides.[5]
      Well may you prosper.
    FRANCE   Come, fair Cordelia.
                      Exeunt FRANCE *and* CORDELIA.
    GONORILL   Sister, it is not a little I have to say of what most
      nearly appertains to us both. I think our father will hence to-
275   night.
    REGAN   That's most certain, and with you; next month with us.
    GONORILL   You see how full of changes° his age is; the obser-   *fickleness*
      vation we have made of it hath not been little.[6] He always
      loved our sister most, and with what poor judgment he hath
280   now cast her off appears too gross.°   *blatant*
    REGAN   'Tis the infirmity of his age, yet he hath ever but slen-
      derly known himself.
    GONORILL   The best and soundest of his time hath been but
      rash.[7] Then° must we look to receive from his age not alone   *Therefore*
285   the imperfection of long engrafted condition,° but there-   *deep-rooted habit*
      withal unruly waywardness that infirm and choleric years
      bring with them.
    REGAN   Such unconstant starts[8] are we like° to have from him   *likely*
      as this of Kent's banishment.
290 GONORILL   There is further compliment° of leave-taking between   *ceremony*
      France and him. Pray, let's hit° together. If our father carry   *join; strike*
      authority with such dispositions[9] as he bears, this last surren-
      der° of his will but offend° us.   *abdication / harm*
    REGAN   We shall further think on't.
295 GONORILL   We must do something, and i'th' heat.°   *Exeunt.*   *quickly*

---

3. As a charitable gift from fortune.
4. And you deserve to get no more love (from your husband) than you have given (to your father). "Want" plays on its alternative meanings of "lack" and "desire."
5. *Who . . . derides:* Those who hide their faults will in the end be put to shame.

6. We have observed it more than a little.
7. *The . . . rash:* Even in the prime of his life he was impetuous.
8. Such impulsive outbursts.
9. Frame of mind.

REGAN   Prescribe not us our duty.

GONERILL   Let your study
275   Be to content your lord, who hath received you
      At fortune's alms.⁵ You have obedience scanted°   *neglected*
      And well are worth the want that you have wanted.⁶

CORDELIA   Time shall unfold what plighted cunning hides;
      Who covers faults, at last with shame derides.⁷
      Well may you prosper.

280   FRANCE   Come, my fair Cordelia.
                                Exeunt FRANCE *and* CORDELIA.

GONERILL   Sister, it is not little I have to say of what most
      nearly appertains to us both. I think our father will hence
      tonight.

REGAN   That's most certain, and with you; next month with us.

285   GONERILL   You see how full of changes° his age is; the obser-   *fickleness*
      vation we have made of it hath been little.°   *in the smallest detail*
      our sister most, and with what poor judgment he hath now
      cast her off appears too grossly.°   *blatantly*

REGAN   'Tis the infirmity of his age, yet he hath ever but slen-
290   derly known himself.

GONERILL   The best and soundest of his time hath been but
      rash.⁸ Then° must we look from his age to receive not alone   *Therefore*
      the imperfections of long engraffed condition,° but there-   *deep-rooted habit*
      withal the unruly waywardness that infirm and choleric
295   years bring with them.

REGAN   Such unconstant starts⁹ are we like° to have from   *likely*
      him as this of Kent's banishment.

GONERILL   There is further compliment° of leave-taking   *ceremony*
      between France and him. Pray you let us sit together. If our
300   father carry authority with such disposition¹ as he bears,
      this last surrender° of his will but offend° us.   *abdication / harm*

REGAN   We shall further think of it.

GONERILL   We must do something, and i'th' heat.°   *Exeunt.*   *quickly*

---

5. As a charitable gift from fortune.
6. And you deserve to get no more love (from your
husband) than you have given (to your father). "Want"
plays on its alternative meanings of "lack" and "desire."
7. *Time . . . derides:* Time eventually exposes and

shames all hidden faults.
8. *The . . . rash:* Even in the prime of his life he was
impetuous.
9. Such impulsive outbursts.
1. Frame of mind.

1.2 (F 1.2)

Enter [Edmund the] BASTARD *alone.*

BASTARD Thou, Nature, art my goddess; to thy law
My services are bound.[1] Wherefore° should I   *Why*
Stand in the plague of custom[2] and permit
The curiosity° of nations to deprive me,   *legal niceties*
5   For that° I am some twelve or fourteen moonshines°   *Because / months*
Lag of° a brother? Why "bastard"? Wherefore "base,"   *Younger than*
When my dimensions are as well compact,°   *composed*
My mind as generous,° and my shape as true   *noble*
As honest° madam's issue?   *married; chaste*
10   Why brand they us with "base," "base bastardy"?
Who, in the lusty stealth of nature, take
More composition and fierce quality[3]
Than doth within a stale, dull-eyed bed go
To the creating of a whole tribe of fops°   *fools*
15   Got° 'tween a sleep and wake? Well, the   *Begotten*
"Legitimate" Edgar, I must have your land.
Our father's love is to° the bastard Edmund   *as much to*
As to the legitimate. Well, my legitimate, if
This letter speed° and my invention° thrive,   *succeed / plot*
20   Edmund the base shall to° th' legitimate.   *match up to; usurp*
I grow, I prosper. Now, gods, stand up for bastards!

Enter GLOUCESTER.

GLOUCESTER Kent banished thus? And France in choler
   parted?°   *in anger departed*
And the King gone tonight,° subscribed° his power,   *last night / limited*
Confined to exhibition?[4] All this done
25   Upon the gad?° —Edmund, how now, what news?   *spur of the moment*
BASTARD [*putting up a letter*] So please your lordship, none.
GLOUCESTER Why so earnestly seek you to put up that letter?
BASTARD I know no news, my lord.
GLOUCESTER What paper were you reading?

1.2 Location: The Earl of Gloucester's house.
1. Edmund declares the raw force of unsocialized and unregulated existence, as opposed to human law, to be his ruler; ironically, "nature" also means "natural filial affection." A "natural" was another word for a "bastard" (illegitimate child).
2. Submit to the imposition of inheritance law.
3. *Who . . . quality:* Whose begetting, by reason of its furtiveness and heightened excitement, requires bet-

ter execution and more vigor. Alternatively (with "take" meaning "give"), whose begetting produces (a person of) more mixture and vigor. "Composition," or mixture, may refer to the belief that the perfect offspring was conceived from an equal quantity of male and female essence and that physical and mental abnormalities were caused by a predominance of one or the other.
4. Pension; mere show without force.

1.2 (Q 1.2)

Enter EDMOND.

EDMOND Thou, Nature, art my goddess; to thy law	
My services are bound.¹ Wherefore° should I	*Why*
Stand in the plague of custom² and permit	
The curiosity° of nations to deprive me,	*legal niceties*
5	For that° I am some twelve or fourteen moonshines°	*Because / months*
Lag of° a brother? Why "bastard"? Wherefore "base,"	*Younger than*
When my dimensions are as well compact,°	*composed*
My mind as generous,° and my shape as true	*noble*
As honest° madam's issue? Why brand they us	*married; chaste*
10	With "base"? With "baseness," "bastardy"? Base? Base?	
Who, in the lusty stealth of nature, take	
More composition and fierce quality³	
Than doth within a dull, stale, tired bed	
Go to th' creating a whole tribe of fops°	*fools*
15	Got° 'tween a sleep and wake? Well, then,	*Begotten*
Legitimate Edgar, I must have your land.	
Our father's love is to° the bastard Edmond	*as much to*
As to th' legitimate. Fine word: "legitimate"!	
Well, my legitimate, if this letter speed°	*succeed*
20	And my invention° thrive, Edmond the base	*plot*
Shall to° th' legitimate. I grow. I prosper.	*match up to; usurp*
Now, gods, stand up for bastards!	

Enter GLOUCESTER.

GLOUCESTER Kent banished thus? And France in choler	
parted?°	*in anger departed*
And the King gone tonight,° prescribed° his power,	*last night / limited*
25	Confined to exhibition?⁴ All this done	
Upon the gad?° —Edmond, how now? What news?	*spur of the moment*
EDMOND [*putting up a letter*] So please your lordship, none.	
GLOUCESTER Why so earnestly seek you to put up that letter?	
EDMOND I know no news, my lord.	
30 | GLOUCESTER   What paper were you reading? | |

1.2 Location: The Earl of Gloucester's house.
1. Edmond declares the raw force of unsocialized and unregulated existence, as opposed to human law, to be his ruler; ironically, "nature" also means "natural filial affection." A "natural" was another word for a "bastard" (illegitimate child).
2. Submit to the imposition of inheritance law.
3. *Who . . . quality:* Whose begetting, by reason of its furtiveness and heightened excitement, requires bet-

ter execution and more vigor. Alternatively (with "take" meaning "give"), whose begetting produces (a person of) more mixture and vigor. "Composition," or mixture, may refer to the belief that the perfect off-spring was conceived from an equal quantity of male and female essence and that physical and mental abnormalities were caused by a predominance of one or the other.
4. Pension; mere show without force.

30 BASTARD Nothing, my lord,
   GLOUCESTER No? What needs then that terrible dispatch° of   *frightened haste*
   it into your pocket? The quality of nothing hath not such
   need to hide itself. Let's see. Come, if it be nothing, I shall
   not need spectacles.
35 BASTARD I beseech you, sir, pardon me. It is a letter from my
   brother that I have not all o'er-read. For so much as I have
   perused, I find it not fit for your liking.°   *pleasure*
   GLOUCESTER Give me the letter, sir.
   BASTARD I shall offend either to detain or give it. The con-
40   tents, as in part I understand them, are to blame.
   GLOUCESTER Let's see, let's see.
   BASTARD [*giving him a letter*] I hope, for my brother's justification, he wrote this but as an essay or taste⁵ of my virtue.
   GLOUCESTER ([*reading*] *a letter*) "This policy of age makes the
45   world bitter to the best of our times,⁶ keeps our fortunes
   from us till our oldness cannot relish them. I begin to find an
   idle and fond° bondage in the oppression of aged tyranny,   *a useless and foolish*
   who sways not as it hath power but as it is suffered.⁷ Come to
   me, that of this I may speak more. If our father would sleep
50   till I waked him, you should enjoy half his revenue forever
   and live the beloved of your brother. Edgar." Hum, conspiracy! "Slept till I waked him, you should enjoy half his revenue"! My son Edgar, had he a hand to write this, a heart and
   brain to breed it in? When came this to you? Who brought it?
55 BASTARD It was not brought me, my lord. There's the cunning
   of it. I found it thrown in at the casement° of my closet.°   *window / private room*
   GLOUCESTER You know the character° to be your brother's?   *handwriting*
   BASTARD If the matter° were good, my lord, I durst swear it   *content*
   were his, but in respect of that, I would fain° think it were not.   *gladly*
60 GLOUCESTER It is his?
   BASTARD It is his hand, my lord, but I hope his heart is not in
   the contents.
   GLOUCESTER Hath he never heretofore sounded you° in this   *sounded you out*
   business?
65 BASTARD Never, my lord. But I have often heard him maintain
   it to be fit that, sons at perfect age° and fathers declining, his   *at maturity*
   father should be as ward⁸ to the son, and the son manage the
   revenue.
   GLOUCESTER Oh, villain, villain! His very opinion in the let-
70   ter! Abhorred villain! Unnatural, detested, brutish villain;
   worse than brutish! Go, sir, seek him. Ay, apprehend him.
   Abominable villain! Where is he?

---

5. *but . . . taste:* simply as a proof or test. Both terms
derive from metallurgy.
6. The established primacy of the elderly embitters
us at the prime of our lives. *policy:* statecraft; crafti-
ness; established order.

7. *who . . . suffered:* which rules not because it is
powerful but because it is permitted to ("suffered").
8. A child under eighteen years of age who was
legally dependent, often orphaned.

EDMOND Nothing, my lord.

GLOUCESTER No? What needed then that terrible dispatch°   *frightened haste*
of it into your pocket? The quality of nothing hath not such
need to hide itself. Let's see. Come, if it be nothing, I shall
35   not need spectacles.

EDMOND I beseech you, sir, pardon me. It is a letter from my
brother that I have not all o'er-read, and, for so much as I
have perused, I find it not fit for your o'erlooking.

GLOUCESTER Give me the letter, sir.

40 EDMOND I shall offend either to detain or give it. The contents,
as in part I understand them, are to blame.

GLOUCESTER Let's see, let's see.

EDMOND [*giving him a letter*] I hope, for my brother's justification, he wrote this but as an essay or taste⁵ of my virtue.

45 GLOUCESTER (*reads*) "This policy and reverence of age makes
the world bitter to the best of our times,⁶ keeps our fortunes
from us till our oldness cannot relish them. I begin to find an
idle and fond° bondage in the oppression of aged tyranny,   *a useless and foolish*
who sways not as it hath power but as it is suffered.⁷ Come to
50   me, that of this I may speak more. If our father would sleep
till I waked him, you should enjoy half his revenue forever
and live the beloved of your brother. Edgar." Hum, conspiracy! "Sleep till I wake him, you should enjoy half his revenue"! My son Edgar, had he a hand to write this, a heart and
55   brain to breed it in? When came you to this? Who brought it?

EDMOND It was not brought me, my lord; there's the cunning
of it. I found it thrown in at the casement° of my closet.°   *window / private room*

GLOUCESTER You know the character° to be your brother's?   *handwriting*

EDMOND If the matter° were good, my lord, I durst swear it   *content*
60   were his, but in respect of that, I would fain° think it were not.   *gladly*

GLOUCESTER It is his?

EDMOND It is his hand, my lord, but I hope his heart is not in
the contents.

GLOUCESTER Has he never before sounded you° in this busi-   *sounded you out*
65   ness?

EDMOND Never, my lord. But I have heard him oft maintain it
to be fit that, sons at perfect age° and fathers declined, the   *at maturity*
father should be as ward⁸ to the son, and the son manage his
revenue.

70 GLOUCESTER Oh, villain, villain! His very opinion in the
letter! Abhorred villain! Unnatural, detested, brutish villain;
worse than brutish. Go, sirrah,⁹ seek him. I'll apprehend
him. Abominable villain! Where is he?

---

5. *but . . . taste:* simply as a proof or test. Both terms
derive from metallurgy.
6. The established primacy of the elderly embitters
us at the prime of our lives. *policy:* statecraft; crafti-
ness; established order.
7. *who . . . suffered:* which rules not because it is

powerful but because it is permitted to ("suffered").
8. A child under eighteen years of age who was legally
dependent, often orphaned.
9. A form of address used with children or social
inferiors.

BASTARD   I do not well know, my lord. If it shall please you to
suspend your indignation against my brother till you can
75   derive from him better testimony of this intent, you should
run a certain° course; where,° if you violently proceed against   *safe; reliable / whereas*
him, mistaking his purpose, it would make a great gap in
your own honor and shake in pieces the heart of his obedi-
ence. I dare pawn down° my life for him, he hath wrote this   *I dare stake*
80   to feel° my affection to your honor and to no further pretense   *feel out*
of danger.⁹

GLOUCESTER   Think you so?

BASTARD   If your honor judge it meet,° I will place you where   *appropriate*
you shall hear us confer of this and by an auricular° assur-   *audible*
85   ance have your satisfaction, and that without any further delay
than this very evening.

GLOUCESTER   He cannot be such a monster—

BASTARD   Nor is not, sure.

GLOUCESTER   —To his father, that so tenderly and entirely loves
90   him. Heaven and earth! Edmund, seek him out; wind me
into him.¹ I pray you, frame° your business after your own   *arrange*
wisdom. I would unstate myself to be in a due resolution.²

BASTARD   I shall seek him, sir, presently,° convey° the busi-   *immediately / carry out*
ness as I shall see means, and acquaint you withal.°   *therewith*
95   GLOUCESTER   These late° eclipses in the sun and moon por-   *recent*
tend no good to us.³ Though the wisdom of Nature can rea-
son thus and thus, yet Nature finds itself scourged by the
sequent effects.⁴ Love cools, friendship falls off, brothers
divide; in cities, mutinies; in countries, discords; palaces,
100   treason; the bond cracked between son and father. Find out
this villain, Edmund. It shall lose thee nothing. Do it carefully. And the noble and true-hearted Kent banished, his
offense honest. Strange, strange!   [*Exit.*]

BASTARD   This is the excellent foppery° of the world, that when   *foolishness*
105   we are sick in fortune, often the surfeit° of our own behavior,   *excesses*
we make guilty of° our disasters the sun, the moon, and the   *we hold responsible for*
stars, as if we were villains by necessity, fools by heavenly
compulsion, knaves, thieves, and treacherers° by spiritual   *traitors*
predominance,⁵ drunkards, liars, and adulterers by an
110   enforced obedience of planetary influence, and all that we
are evil in by a divine thrusting-on.° An admirable° evasion   *imposition / amazing*
of whoremaster man, to lay his goatish disposition to the

9. No further intention to do harm.
1. Worm your way into his confidence (with "me" as
an intensifier); worm your way into his confidence for
me ("me" as a dative of respect).
2. I would give up my rank and property to have my
doubts resolved.
3. The lunar and solar eclipses that were seen in London between September and October 1605, about a
year before the play's first recorded performance,

would have added spice to this superstitious belief in
the role of heavenly bodies as augurs of misfortune.
4. *Though . . . effects:* Though natural science may
explain the eclipses this way or that, Nature (and
family bonds) suffers in the effects that follow.
5. By the ascendancy of a particular planet. In the
universe as conceived by the second-century astrono-
mer Ptolemy, the planets revolved about the earth on
crystalline spheres.

EDMOND I do not well know, my lord. If it shall please you to
75 suspend your indignation against my brother till you can
derive from him better testimony of his intent, you should
run a certain° course; where,° if you violently proceed against   *safe; reliable / whereas*
him, mistaking his purpose, it would make a great gap in your
own honor and shake in pieces the heart of his obedience. I
80 dare pawn down° my life for him that he hath writ this to   *I dare stake*
feel° my affection to your honor and to no other pretense of   *feel out*
danger.[1]

GLOUCESTER Think you so?

EDMOND If your honor judge it meet,° I will place you where   *appropriate*
85 you shall hear us confer of this and by an auricular° assur-   *audible*
ance have your satisfaction, and that without any further
delay than this very evening.

GLOUCESTER He cannot be such a monster. Edmond, seek
him out; wind me into him,[2] I pray you. Frame° the business   *Arrange*
90 after your own wisdom. I would unstate myself to be in a
due resolution.[3]

EDMOND I will seek him, sir, presently,° convey° the business   *immediately / carry out*
as I shall find means, and acquaint you withal.°   *therewith*

GLOUCESTER These late° eclipses in the sun and moon por-   *recent*
95 tend no good to us.[4] Though the wisdom of Nature can
reason it thus and thus, yet Nature finds itself scourged by
the sequent effects.[5] Love cools, friendship falls off,
brothers divide; in cities, mutinies; in countries, discord;
in palaces, treason; and the bond cracked twixt son and
100 father. This villain of mine comes under the prediction:
there's son against father. The King falls from bias of
nature:[6] there's father against child. We have seen the best
of our time. Machinations, hollowness,° treachery, and all   *insincerity*
ruinous disorders follow us disquietly to our graves. Find
105 out this villain, Edmond. It shall lose thee nothing. Do it
carefully. And the noble and true-hearted Kent banished,
his offense: honesty! 'Tis strange!   *Exit.*

EDMOND This is the excellent foppery° of the world, that when   *foolishness*
we are sick in fortune, often the surfeits° of our own behav-   *excesses*
110 ior, we make guilty of° our disasters the sun, the moon, and   *we hold responsible for*
stars, as if we were villains on necessity, fools by heavenly
compulsion, knaves, thieves, and treacherers° by spherical pre-   *traitors*
dominance,[7] drunkards, liars, and adulterers by an enforced
obedience of planetary influence, and all that we are evil in
115 by a divine thrusting-on.° An admirable° evasion of whore-   *imposition / amazing*
master man, to lay his goatish disposition on the charge of a

---

1. No other intention to do harm.
2. Worm your way into his confidence (with "me" as
an intensifier); worm your way into his confidence for
me ("me" as a dative of respect).
3. I would give up my rank and property to have my
doubts resolved.
4. The lunar and solar eclipses that were seen in London between September and October 1605, about a
year before the play's first recorded performance,
would have added spice to this superstitious belief in
the role of heavenly bodies as augurs of misfortune.

5. *Though . . . effects:* Though natural science may
explain the eclipses this way or that, nature (and family bonds) suffers in the effects that follow.
6. The King deviates from his natural inclination. In
the game of bowls, the "bias" ("course") is the eccentric path taken by the weighted ball when thrown.
7. By the ascendancy of a particular planet. In the
universe as conceived by the second-century astrono-
mer Ptolemy, the planets revolved about the earth on
crystalline spheres.

charge of stars!⁶ My father compounded° with my mother   *coupled*
under the dragon's tail, and my nativity was under Ursa
115 Major,⁷ so that it follows I am rough and lecherous. Fut!° I   *By Christ's foot*
should have been that° I am had the maidenliest star of the   *what*
firmament twinkled on my bastardy.
    Enter EDGAR.
[*aside*] Edgar! And out he comes like the catastrophe° of the old   *resolution*
comedy. Mine° is villainous melancholy, with a sigh like them   *My cue; my role*
120 of Bedlam.⁸ —Oh, these eclipses do portend these divisions.
  EDGAR How now, brother Edmund, what serious contemplation are you in?
  BASTARD I am thinking, brother, of a prediction I read this
other day what should follow these eclipses.
125   EDGAR Do you busy yourself about that?
  BASTARD I promise you, the effects he writ of succeed° unhap-   *follow*
pily, as of unnaturalness between the child and the parent,
death, dearth, dissolutions of ancient amities, divisions in
state, menaces and maledictions against king and nobles,
130 needless diffidences,° banishment of friends, dissipation of   *baseless suspicions*
cohorts,⁹ nuptial breaches, and I know not what.
  EDGAR How long have you been a sectary astronomical?°   *a devotee of astrology*
  BASTARD Come, come, when saw you my father last?
  EDGAR Why, the night gone by.
135   BASTARD Spake you with him?
  EDGAR Two hours together.
  BASTARD Parted you in good terms? Found you no displeasure in him by word or countenance?°   *appearance; demeanor*
  EDGAR None at all.
140   BASTARD Bethink yourself wherein you may have offended
him and at my entreaty forbear° his presence till some little   *avoid*
time hath qualified° the heat of his displeasure, which at   *moderated*
this instant so rageth in him that with the mischief of your
person it would scarce allay.¹
145   EDGAR Some villain hath done me wrong.
  BASTARD That's my fear, brother. I advise you to the best: go
armed. I am no honest man if there be any good meaning
towards you. I have told you what I have seen and heard but
faintly, nothing like the image and horror of it. Pray you,
150 away!

---

6. *to lay . . . stars:* to hold the stars responsible for his
lustful desires. In Greek mythology, the satyr, a creature with goat-like characteristics, was notoriously
lecherous.
7. Constellations: "dragon's tail" = Draco and "Ursa
Major" = Great Bear.
8. Like the inmates of Bedlam. "Bethlehem," short-

ened to "Bedlam," was the name of the oldest and
best-known London madhouse.
9. Scattering of forces.
1. *with . . . allay:* even harming you bodily would
hardly relieve his anger; alternatively, with the irritant of your presence, it (Gloucester's anger) would
not be abated.

star!⁸ My father compounded° with my mother under the | *coupled*

dragon's tail, and my nativity was under Ursa Major,⁹ so that

it follows I am rough and lecherous. I should have been

120 that° I am had the maidenliest star in the firmament twin- | *what*

kled on my bastardizing.

    Enter EDGAR.

[*aside*] Pat,° he comes like the catastrophe° of the old com- | *On cue / resolution*

edy. My cue is villainous melancholy, with a sigh like Tom

o'Bedlam.¹ —Oh, these eclipses do portend these divisions.

125 [*Sings.*] Fa, sol, la, mi.²

EDGAR How now, brother Edmond, what serious contempla-

tion are you in?

EDMOND I am thinking, brother, of a prediction I read this

other day what should follow these eclipses.

130 EDGAR Do you busy yourself with that?

EDMOND I promise you, the effects he writes of succeed° | *follow*

unhappily. When saw you my father last?

EDGAR The night gone by.

EDMOND Spake you with him?

135 EDGAR Ay, two hours together.

EDMOND Parted you in good terms? Found you no displea-

sure in him by word nor countenance?° | *appearance; demeanor*

EDGAR None at all.

EDMOND Bethink yourself wherein you may have offended

140 him, and at my entreaty forbear° his presence until some | *avoid*

little time hath qualified° the heat of his displeasure, which | *moderated*

at this instant so rageth in him that with the mischief of

your person it would scarcely allay.³

EDGAR Some villain hath done me wrong.

145 EDMOND That's my fear. I pray you, have a continent forbear-

ance° till the speed of his rage goes slower, and, as I say, retire | *restrained absence*

with me to my lodging, from whence I will fitly° bring you to | *when suitable*

hear my lord speak. Pray ye go; there's my key. If you do stir

abroad, go armed.

150 EDGAR Armed, brother?

EDMOND Brother, I advise you to the best. I am no honest

man if there be any good meaning toward you. I have told

you what I have seen and heard but faintly, nothing like the

image and horror of it. Pray you, away!

---

8. *to lay . . . star:* to hold a star responsible for his lustful desires. In Greek mythology, the satyr, a creature with goat-like characteristics, was notoriously lecherous.

9. Constellations: "dragon's tail" = Draco and "Ursa Major" = Great Bear.

1. The usual name for lunatic beggars; "Bethlehem," shortened to "Bedlam," was the name of the oldest and best-known London madhouse.

2. The portion of the scale that Edmond sings is an augmented fourth, an interval considered at this time very discordant; it was sometimes referred to as *diabolus in musica* ("the devil in music"). *divisions:* social fractures; melodic embellishments.

3. *with . . . allay:* even harming you bodily ("mischief") would hardly relieve his anger; alternatively, with the irritant of your presence, it (Gloucester's anger) would not be abated.

EDGAR   Shall I hear from you anon?

BASTARD   I do serve you in this business.   *Exit* EDGAR.

A credulous father and a brother noble,
Whose nature is so far from doing harms
155   That he suspects none; on whose foolish honesty
My practices° ride easy. I see the business.[2]   *plots*
Let me, if not by birth, have lands by wit.°   *intelligence*
All with me's meet that I can fashion fit.[3]   *Exit.*

1.3 (F 1.3)

Enter GONORILL *and* GENTLEMAN.

GONORILL   Did my father strike my gentleman
For chiding of his fool?

GENTLEMAN   Yes, madam.

GONORILL   By day and night he wrongs me;
5   Every hour he flashes into one gross crime° or other   *offense*
That sets us all at odds. I'll not endure it.
His knights grow riotous, and himself upbraids us
On every trifle. When he returns from hunting
I will not speak with him. Say I am sick.
10   If you come slack of former services,[1]
You shall do well; the fault of it I'll answer.°   *answer for*

GENTLEMAN   He's coming, madam, I hear him.

GONORILL   Put on what weary negligence you please,
You and your fellow servants. I'd have it come
15   In° question. If he dislike it, let him   *Into*
To our sister, whose mind and mine I know
In that are one, not to be overruled.
Idle° old man, that still would manage those   *Foolish*
Authorities that he hath given away!
20   Now, by my life, old fools are babes again
And must be used with checks as flatteries when
They are seen abused.[2] Remember what I tell you.

GENTLEMAN   Very well, madam.

GONORILL   And let his knights have colder looks among you.
25   What grows of it no matter; advise your fellows so.
I would breed from hence occasions, and I shall.
That I may speak,[3] I'll write straight° to my sister   *straightaway*
To hold my very° course. Go prepare for dinner.   *exact*

Exeunt [*severally*].°   *separately*

---

2. It is now clear to me what needs to be done.
3. Anything is fine by me as long as I can make it serve my purpose. *meet*: justifiable; appropriate.
1.3 Location: The Duke of Albany's castle.
1. If you offer him less service (and respect) than before.

2. *old . . . abused:* When foolish old men act like children, rebukes are the kindest treatment when kind treatment is abused.
3. *I would . . . speak:* I wish to foster situations, and I shall, in which to speak my mind.

155 EDGAR Shall I hear from you anon?

EDMOND I do serve you in this business.   *Exit* EDGAR.

    A credulous father and a brother noble,

    Whose nature is so far from doing harms

    That he suspects none; on whose foolish honesty

160   My practices° ride easy. I see the business.[4]   *plots*

    Let me, if not by birth, have lands by wit.°   *intelligence*

    All with me's meet that I can fashion fit.[5]   *Exit.*

1.3 (Q 1.3)

Enter GONERILL, *and* [Oswald the] STEWARD.

GONERILL Did my father strike my gentleman

    For chiding of his fool?

STEWARD   Ay, madam.

GONERILL By day and night he wrongs me; every hour

    He flashes into one gross crime° or other   *offense*

5   That sets us all at odds. I'll not endure it.

    His knights grow riotous, and himself upbraids us

    On every trifle. When he returns from hunting,

    I will not speak with him. Say I am sick.

    If you come slack of former services,[1]

10   You shall do well; the fault of it I'll answer.°   *answer for*

STEWARD He's coming, madam, I hear him.

GONERILL Put on what weary negligence you please,

    You and your fellows.° I'd have it come to question.   *other servants*

    If he distaste° it, let him to my sister,   *dislike*

15   Whose mind and mine I know in that are one.

    Remember what I have said.

STEWARD   Well, madam.

GONERILL And let his knights have colder looks among you.

    What grows of it no matter; advise your fellows so.

    I'll write straight° to my sister to hold my course.   *straightaway*

20   Prepare for dinner.   *Exeunt* [severally].°   *separately*

4. It is now clear to me what needs to be done.

5. Anything is fine by me as long as I can make it serve my purpose. *meet*: justifiable; appropriate.

1.3 Location: The Duke of Albany's castle.

1. If you offer him less service (and respect) than before.

1.4 (F 1.4)

Enter KENT *[disguised as Caius].*

KENT   If but as well[1] I other accents borrow,
    That can my speech diffuse,° my good intent   *disguise*
    May carry through itself to that full issue°   *result*
    For which I razed my likeness.[2] Now, banished Kent,
5   If thou canst serve where thou dost stand condemned,
    Thy master, whom thou lovest, shall find thee full of labor.°   *ready for work*

Enter LEAR *[and* SERVANTS*].*

LEAR   Let me not stay° a jot for dinner; go get it ready.   *wait*

[Exit a SERVANT.*]*

    [to KENT*]* How now, what° art thou?   *who*

KENT   A man, sir.

10   LEAR   What dost thou profess?[3] What wouldst thou with us?

KENT   I do profess to be no less than I seem, to serve him
    truly that will put me in trust, to love him that is honest, to
    converse° with him that is wise and says little, to fear judg-   *associate*
    ment, to fight when I cannot choose,° and to eat no fish.[4]   *when I must*

15   LEAR   What art thou?

KENT   A very honest-hearted fellow and as poor as the King.

LEAR   If thou be as poor for a subject as he is for a king, thou'rt
    poor enough. What wouldst thou?

KENT   Service.

20   LEAR   Who wouldst thou serve?

KENT   You.

LEAR   Dost thou know me, fellow?

KENT   No, sir, but you have that in your countenance which I
    would fain° call master.   *gladly*

25   LEAR   What's that?

KENT   Authority.

LEAR   What services canst do?

KENT   I can keep honest counsel,° ride, run, mar a curious   *keep secrets*
    tale in telling it[5] and deliver a plain message bluntly. That
30   which ordinary men are fit for, I am qualified in, and the
    best of me is diligence.

LEAR   How old art thou?

KENT   Not so young to love a woman for singing, nor so old to
    dote on her for anything. I have years on my back forty-eight.

35   LEAR   Follow me. Thou shalt serve me if I like thee no worse
    after dinner. I will not part from thee yet. —Dinner, ho, din-
    ner! Where's my knave, my fool? *[to a* SERVANT*]* Go you and
    call my fool hither.   *[Exit a* SERVANT.*]*

Enter [Oswald the] STEWARD.

    You, sirrah, where's my daughter?

40   STEWARD   So please you—   *[Exit.]*

1.4 (Q 1.4)

Enter KENT [*disguised as Caius*].

KENT If but as well[1] I other accents borrow
    That can my speech diffuse,° my good intent — *disguise*
    May carry through itself to that full issue° — *result*
    For which I razed my likeness.[2] Now, banished Kent,
5   If thou canst serve where thou dost stand condemned,
    So may it come° thy master, whom thou lov'st, — *come to pass*
    Shall find thee full of labors.° — *helpful; keen*

        Horns within.° *Enter* LEAR *and* [KNIGHTS *as* — *Hunting horns offstage*
        Attendants.

LEAR Let me not stay° a jot for dinner; go get it ready. [*to* KENT] — *wait*
    How now, what° art thou? — *who*
10 KENT A man, sir.
LEAR What dost thou profess?[3] What wouldst thou with us?
KENT I do profess to be no less than I seem, to serve him
    truly that will put me in trust, to love him that is honest,
    to converse° with him that is wise and says little, to fear — *associate*
15   judgment, to fight when I cannot choose,° and to eat no — *when I must*
    fish.[4]
LEAR What art thou?
KENT A very honest-hearted fellow and as poor as the King.
LEAR If thou be'st as poor for a subject as he's for a king, thou
20   art poor enough. What wouldst thou?
KENT Service.
LEAR Who wouldst thou serve?
KENT You.
LEAR Dost thou know me, fellow?
25 KENT No, sir, but you have that in your countenance which I
    would fain° call master. — *gladly*
LEAR What's that?
KENT Authority.
LEAR What services canst thou do?
30 KENT I can keep honest counsel,° ride, run, mar a curious tale — *keep secrets*
    in telling it,[5] and deliver a plain message bluntly. That which
    ordinary men are fit for I am qualified in, and the best of me
    is diligence.
LEAR How old art thou?
35 KENT Not so young, sir, to love a woman for singing, nor
    so old to dote on her for anything. I have years on my back
    forty-eight.
LEAR Follow me. Thou shalt serve me if I like thee no worse
    after dinner. I will not part from thee yet. —Dinner, ho, din-
40   ner! Where's my knave? My fool? Go you and call my fool
    hither.   [*Exit a* KNIGHT.]

        Enter [*Oswald the*] STEWARD.

    You, you, sirrah, where's my daughter?
STEWARD So please you—   *Exit.*

1.4 Location: As before.
1. As well as disguising my appearance.
2. Disguised my appearance; shaved off my beard.
3. What is your job (profession)? Kent, in reply, uses "profess" punningly to mean "claim."
4. And not to be a Catholic or penitent (Catholics

were obliged to eat fish on specified occasions and as penance); alternatively, to be a manly man, a meat eater.
5. That is, Kent's plain, blunt speech would make him ill suited to tell a convoluted ("curious") tale.

LEAR   What says the fellow there? Call the clotpoll° back.   *blockhead*
                      [*Exeunt* KENT *and a* SERVANT.]
          Where's my fool, ho? I think the world's asleep.
                      [*Enter* KENT *and a* SERVANT.]
          How now, where's that mongrel?
KENT   He says, my lord, your daughter is not well.
45 LEAR   Why came not the slave back to me when I called him?
    SERVANT   Sir, he answered me in the roundest° manner, he   *bluntest; rudest*
          "would not."
    LEAR   'A° would not?   *He*
    SERVANT   My lord, I know not what the matter is, but to my
50   judgment, your highness is not entertained with that cere-
          monious affection as you were wont.° There's a great abate-   *accustomed to*
          ment appears as well in the general dependents° as in the   *servants*
          Duke himself also and your daughter.
    LEAR   Ha? Say'st thou so?
55 SERVANT   I beseech you pardon me, my lord, if I be mistaken,
          for my duty cannot be silent when I think your highness
          wronged.
    LEAR   Thou but remember'st° me of mine own conception.° I   *remind / perception*
          have perceived a most faint neglect of late, which I have
60   rather blamed as mine own jealous curiosity[6] than as a very
          pretense° and purport of unkindness. I will look further   *a true intention*
          into't. But where's this fool? I have not seen him this two
          days.
    SERVANT   Since my young lady's going into France, sir, the
65   fool hath much pined away.
    LEAR   No more of that, I have noted it. [*to* SERVANT] Go you
          and tell my daughter I would speak with her. [*to another*
          SERVANT] Go you, call hither my fool.
                      [*Exeunt two* SERVANTS.]
                      [*Enter Oswald the* STEWARD.]
          Oh, you, sir, you, sir, come you hither. Who am I, sir?
70 STEWARD   My lady's father.
    LEAR   "My lady's father"? My lord's knave! You whoreson dog,
          you slave, you cur!
    STEWARD   I am none of this, my lord. I beseech you pardon me.
    LEAR   [*striking the* STEWARD]   Do you bandy looks with me,
75   you rascal?
    STEWARD   I'll not be struck, my lord,
    KENT   [*tripping the* STEWARD]   Nor tripped neither, you base
          football player.[7]
    LEAR   I thank thee, fellow! Thou serv'st me, and I'll love thee.
80 KENT   [*to* STEWARD]   Come, sir, I'll teach you differences.°   *(of rank)*
          Away, away. If you will measure your lubber's length again,[8]
          tarry. But away, you have wisdom.   [*Exit* STEWARD.]

---

6. *jealous curiosity:* paranoid concern with niceties.   8. If you will be stretched out by me again. *lubber:*
7. Football was a rough street game played by the poor.   clumsy oaf.

LEAR   What says the fellow there? Call the clotpoll° back.   *blockhead*
                              [*Exit* SECOND KNIGHT.]
45   Where's my fool? Ho, I think the world's asleep.
                 [*Enter* SECOND KNIGHT.]
       How now? Where's that mongrel?
SECOND KNIGHT   He says, my lord, your daughter is not well.
LEAR   Why came not the slave back to me when I called him?
SECOND KNIGHT   Sir, he answered me in the roundest° manner,   *bluntest; rudest*
50   he would not.
LEAR   He would not?
SECOND KNIGHT   My lord, I know not what the matter is, but
       to my judgment your highness is not entertained with that
       ceremonious affection as you were wont.° There's a great   *accustomed to*
55   abatement of kindness appears as well in the general depen-
       dents° as in the Duke himself also and your daughter.   *servants*
LEAR   Ha? Say'st thou so?
SECOND KNIGHT   I beseech you pardon me, my lord, if I be
       mistaken, for my duty cannot be silent when I think your
60   highness wronged.
LEAR   Thou but rememberest° me of mine own conception.° I   *remind / perception*
       have perceived a most faint neglect of late, which I have
       rather blamed as mine own jealous curiosity[6] than as a very
       pretense° and purpose of unkindness. I will look further   *a true intention*
65   into't. But where's my fool? I have not seen him this two days.
SECOND KNIGHT   Since my young lady's going into France, sir,
       the fool hath much pined away.
LEAR   No more of that, I have noted it well. [*to* SECOND KNIGHT]
       Go you and tell my daughter I would speak with her. [*to*
70   *another* KNIGHT] Go you, call hither my fool.
                              [*Exeunt two* KNIGHTS.]
            Enter [*Oswald the*] STEWARD.
       Oh, you, sir, you, come you hither, sir. Who am I, sir?
STEWARD   My lady's father.
LEAR   "My lady's father"? My lord's knave! You whoreson dog,
       you slave, you cur!
75 STEWARD   I am none of these, my lord. I beseech your pardon.
LEAR [*striking him*]   Do you bandy looks with me, you rascal?
STEWARD   I'll not be strucken, my lord.
KENT [*tripping him*]   Nor tripped, neither, you base football
       player.[7]
80 LEAR   I thank thee, fellow. Thou serv'st me, and I'll love thee.
KENT [*to* STEWARD]   Come, sir, arise, away. I'll teach you
       differences.° Away, away. If you will measure your lubber's   *(of rank)*
       length again,[8] tarry. But away, go to; have you wisdom, so.
                              [*Exit* STEWARD.]

---

6. *jealous curiosity*: paranoid concern with niceties.   8. If you will be stretched out by me again. *lubber*:
7. Football was a rough street game played by the poor.   clumsy oaf.

LEAR [*to* KENT]   Now, friendly knave, I thank thee. [*He gives
him money.*] There's earnest of° thy service.   downpayment for
          Enter FOOL.[9]

85   FOOL   Let me hire him too. [*He hands* KENT *his cap.*] Here's my
          coxcomb.°   fool's cap
     LEAR   How now, my pretty knave, how dost thou?
     FOOL [*to* KENT]   Sirrah, you were best take my coxcomb.
     KENT   Why, Fool?
90   FOOL   Why, for taking one's part that's out of favor. Nay, an°   if
          thou canst not smile as the wind sits, thou'lt catch cold
          shortly.[1] There, take my coxcomb. Why, this fellow hath ban-
          ished two on 's daughters[2] and done the third a blessing
          against his will. If thou follow him, thou must needs wear
95   my coxcomb. How now, nuncle?° Would I had two coxcombs   (mine) uncle
          and two daughters.
     LEAR   Why, my boy?
     FOOL   If I gave them any living,° I'd keep my coxcombs myself.[3]   goods
          [*He hands him his cap.*] There's mine; beg another of thy
100   daughters.
     LEAR   Take heed, sirrah, the whip.
     FOOL   Truth is a dog that must to° kennel; he must be whipped   go to
          out, when the Lady Brach[4] may stand by the fire and stink.
     LEAR   A pestilent gull° to me.   annoyance; bitterness
105 FOOL   Sirrah, I'll teach thee a speech.
     LEAR   Do.
     FOOL   Mark it, uncle:
          Have more than thou showest,
          Speak less than thou knowest,
110   Lend less than thou owest,°   own
          Ride more than thou goest,°   walk
          Learn° more than thou trowest,°   Hear / believe
          Set less than thou throwest;[5]
          Leave thy drink and thy whore,
115   And keep in a-door,
          And thou shalt have more
          Than two tens to a score.[6]
     LEAR   This is nothing, Fool.
     FOOL   Then like the breath° of an unfeed° lawyer, you gave   speech / unpaid
120   me nothing for't. Can you make no use of nothing, uncle?
     LEAR   Why, no, boy, nothing can be made out of nothing.

9. PERFORMANCE COMMENT The Fool and Cordelia
never meet onstage, making it possible in some productions for one actor to play both roles. Some other
productions cast an older actor as the Fool, thus providing a third aging figure alongside Lear and Gloucester. See Digital Edition PC 2.
1. *an . . . shortly:* if you can't keep in favor with those in
power, you will soon find yourself left out in the cold.
2. By abdicating, Lear has in effect prevented his
eldest daughters from any longer being his subjects,

just as if he had "banished" them.
3. I'd be twice as much a fool.
4. *Lady Brach:* Lady Bitch. Pet dogs were often called
"Lady" such and such. The allusion is to Regan and
Gonorill, who are now being preferred to truthful
Cordelia.
5. Don't gamble everything on a single cast of the dice.
6. *And thou . . . score:* And there will be more than
two tens in your twenty—that is, you will become
richer.

LEAR Now, my friendly knave, I thank thee. [*He gives him*
85   *money.*] There's earnest of° thy service.   *downpayment for*
            Enter FOOL.[9]
FOOL Let me hire him too. [*He hands* KENT *his cap.*] Here's my
         coxcomb.°   *fool's cap*
LEAR How now, my pretty knave, how dost thou?
FOOL [*to* KENT] Sirrah, you were best take my coxcomb.
90 LEAR Why, my boy?
FOOL Why, for taking one's part that's out of favor. Nay, an thou
         canst not smile as the wind sits, thou'lt catch cold shortly.[1]
         There, take my coxcomb. Why, this fellow has banished two
         on 's daughters[2] and did the third a blessing against his will. If
95   thou follow him, thou must needs wear my coxcomb. How
         now, nuncle?° Would I had two coxcombs and two daughters.   *(mine) uncle*
LEAR Why, my boy?
FOOL If I gave them all my living,° I'd keep my coxcombs   *goods*
         myself.[3] [*He hands him his cap.*] There's mine; beg another of
100   thy daughters.
LEAR Take heed, sirrah, the whip.
FOOL Truth's a dog must to° kennel; he must be whipped out,   *go to*
         when the lady brach[4] may stand by th' fire and stink.
LEAR A pestilent gall° to me.   *annoyance; bitterness*
105 FOOL Sirrah, I'll teach thee a speech.
LEAR Do.
FOOL Mark it, nuncle:
         Have more than thou showest,
         Speak less than thou knowest,
110   Lend less than thou owest,°   *own*
         Ride more than thou goest,°   *walk*
         Learn° more than thou trowest,°   *Hear / believe*
         Set less than thou throwest;[5]
         Leave thy drink and thy whore,
115   And keep in a-door,
         And thou shalt have more
         Than two tens to a score.[6]
KENT This is nothing, Fool.
FOOL Then 'tis like the breath° of an unfeed° lawyer: you gave   *speech / unpaid*
120   me nothing for't. Can you make no use of nothing, nuncle?
LEAR Why, no, boy, nothing can be made out of nothing.

9. PERFORMANCE COMMENT The Fool and Cordelia never meet onstage, making it possible in some productions for one actor to play both roles. Some other productions cast an older actor as the Fool, thus providing a third aging figure alongside Lear and Gloucester. See Digital Edition PC 2.
1. *an . . . shortly:* if you can't keep in favor with those in power, you will soon find yourself left out in the cold.
2. By abdicating, Lear has in effect prevented his eldest daughters from any longer being his subjects, just as if he had "banished" them.
3. I'd be twice as much a fool.
4. Lady bitch. Pet dogs were often called "Lady" such and such. The allusion is to Regan and Gonerill, who are now being preferred to truthful Cordelia.
5. Don't gamble everything on a single cast of the dice.
6. *And thou . . . score:* And there will be more than two tens in your twenty—that is, you will become richer.

FOOL   Prithee, tell him so much the rent of his land comes
to.[7] He will not believe a fool.

LEAR   A bitter fool.

125 FOOL   Dost know the difference, my boy, between a bitter fool
and a sweet fool?

LEAR   No, lad, teach me.

FOOL   That lord that counseled thee
          To give away thy land,

130   Come place him here by me;
          Do thou for him stand.°   represent him
          The sweet and bitter fool
          Will presently appear,
          The one in motley[8] here,

135   [pointing to LEAR] The other found out there.

LEAR   Dost thou call me fool, boy?

FOOL   All thy other titles thou hast given away; that thou wast
born with.

KENT   This is not altogether fool,[9] my lord.

140 FOOL   No, faith, lords and great men will not let me. If I had a
monopoly out, they would have part in't, and ladies too. They
will not let me have all the fool to myself; they'll be snatch-
ing. Give me an egg, nuncle, and I'll give thee two crowns.

LEAR   What two crowns shall they be?

145 FOOL   Why, after I have cut the egg in the middle and ate up
the meat,° the two crowns of the egg. When thou clovest°   edible part / cleaved
thy crown i'th' middle and gavest away both parts, thou bor-
est[1] thy ass a'th'° back o'er the dirt. Thou hadst little wit° in   on your / sense
thy bald crown when thou gavest thy golden one away. If I

150   speak like myself° in this, let him be whipped that first finds   (like a fool)
it so.[2]

          [Sings.]   Fools had ne'er less wit in a year,
                         For wise men are grown foppish;[3]
                         They know not how their wits do wear,

155   Their manners are so apish.°   stupid; imitative

LEAR   When were you wont° to be so full of songs, sirrah?   accustomed

FOOL   I have used° it, nuncle, ever since thou mad'st thy daugh-   practiced
ters thy mother. For when thou gavest them the rod and putt'st
down thine own breeches,

160   [Sings.]   Then they for sudden joy did weep,
                         And I for sorrow sung,
                         That such a king should play bo-peep,°   (a child's game)
                         And go the fools among.

          Prithee, nuncle, keep a schoolmaster that can teach thy

165   Fool to lie. I would fain learn to lie.

---

7. Remind him that no land means no rent; with a
pun on "rent" meaning "torn," "divided."
8. Multicolored dress of a court jester.
9. Foolish, folly. In the next line, the Fool takes
"altogether fool" to mean "one who has cornered the
market on folly."

1. thou borest: you carried.
2. that . . . so: who first discovers for himself that
this is true; who first considers this to be foolish.
3. Fools . . . foppish: Professional fools have never
been as witless since wise men have lately outdone
them in idiocy.

FOOL   Prithee, tell him so much the rent of his land comes
    to.[7] He will not believe a fool.

LEAR   A bitter fool.

125   FOOL   Dost thou know the difference, my boy, between a bit-
    ter fool and a sweet one?

LEAR   No, lad, teach me.

FOOL   Nuncle, give me an egg, and I'll give thee two crowns.

LEAR   What two crowns shall they be?

130   FOOL   Why, after I have cut the egg i'th' middle and ate up the
    meat,° the two crowns of the egg. When thou clovest° thy   *edible part / cleaved*
    crown i'th' middle and gav'st away both parts, thou bor'st°   *you carried*
    thine ass on thy back o'er the dirt. Thou hadst little wit° in thy   *sense*
    bald crown when thou gav'st thy golden one away. If I speak

135   like myself° in this, let him be whipped that first finds it so.[8]   *(like a fool)*
    [*Sings.*]   Fools had ne'er less grace in a year,
               For wise men are grown foppish;[9]
               And know not how their wits to wear,
               Their manners are so apish.°   *stupid; imitative*

140   LEAR   When were you wont° to be so full of songs, sirrah?   *accustomed*

FOOL   I have used° it, nuncle, e'er since thou mad'st thy daugh-   *practiced*
    ters thy mothers. For when thou gav'st them the rod and putt'st
    down thine own breeches,
    [*Sings.*]   Then they for sudden joy did weep,

145   And I for sorrow sung,
               That such a king should play bo-peep,°   *(a child's game)*
               And go the fool among.
    Prithee, nuncle, keep a schoolmaster that can teach thy fool
    to lie. I would fain learn to lie.

---

7. Remind him that no land means no rent; with a
pun on "rent" meaning "torn," "divided."
8. *that . . . so:* who first discovers for himself that
this is true; who first considers this to be foolish.

9. *Fools . . . foppish:* Professional fools have never
been as witless since wise men have lately outdone
them in idiocy.

LEAR   An° you lie, we'll have you whipped.   *If*

FOOL   I marvel what kin° thou and thy daughters are! They'll   *how alike*
         have me whipped for speaking true, thou wilt have me
         whipped for lying, and sometime I am whipped for holding
170   my peace. I had rather be any kind of thing than a fool, and
         yet I would not be thee, nuncle. Thou hast pared thy wit
         o'both sides and left nothing in the middle. Here comes one
         of the parings.
              Enter GONORILL.

LEAR   How now, daughter, what makes that frontlet⁴ on?
175   Methinks you are too much o'late i'th' frown.

FOOL   Thou wast a pretty fellow when thou hadst no need to
         care for her frown. Now thou art an O without a figure.⁵ I
         am better than thou art now: I am a fool, thou art nothing.
         —Yes, forsooth, I will hold my tongue. So your face bids me,
180   though you say nothing.
         [*Sings.*]   Mum, mum,
                      He that keeps neither crust nor crumb,
                      Weary of all, shall want° some.   *lack; be in need of*
         [*He points to* GONORILL.] That's a shelled peascod.°   *empty pea pod; nothing*

185 GONORILL   Not only, sir, this, your all-licensed° Fool,   *unrestrained*
         But other of your insolent retinue
         Do hourly carp and quarrel, breaking forth
         In rank° and not-to-be-endurèd riots.   *foul; spreading*
         Sir, I had thought by making this well known unto you
190   To have found a safe° redress, but now grow fearful   *sure*
         By what yourself too late° have spoke and done,   *recently*
         That you protect this course and put it on°   *encourage it*
         By your allowance; which if you should, the fault
         Would not scape censure, nor the redress sleep;
195   Which in the tender of a wholesome weal⁶
         Might in their working do you that offense
         That else were shame, that then necessity
         Must call discreet proceedings.⁷

FOOL   For you trow, nuncle,
200   [*Sings.*]   The hedge-sparrow fed the cuckoo⁸ so long
                      That it had it head bit off by't young,°   *(the young cuckoo)*
                      So out went the candle,
                      And we were left darkling.°   *in the dark*

---

4. A headband; here, a metaphor for "frown."
5. A zero without a preceding digit to give it value;
nothing.
6. *tender of a wholesome weal*: maintenance of a
well-ordered commonwealth.
7. *which if you . . . proceedings*: if you do approve (of
your attendants' behavior), you will not escape criti-

cism, nor will it be without retribution, which for the
common good will cause you pain. While this would
otherwise be improper, it will be seen as a prudent
("discreet") action under the circumstances.
8. The cuckoo lays its eggs in the nests of other
birds, which then hatch and feed their offspring.

150 LEAR   An° you lie, sirrah, we'll have you whipped.   *If*

FOOL   I marvel what kin° thou and thy daughters are. They'll   *how alike*
have me whipped for speaking true, thou'lt have me whipped
for lying, and sometimes I am whipped for holding my peace.
I had rather be any kind o'thing than a fool, and yet I would
155 not be thee, nuncle. Thou hast pared thy wit o'both sides and
left nothing i'th' middle. Here comes one o'th' parings.

　　　　　Enter GONERILL.

LEAR   How now, daughter? What makes that frontlet[1] on? You
are too much of late i'th' frown.

FOOL   Thou wast a pretty fellow when thou hadst no need to
160 care for her frowning. Now thou art an O without a figure.[2]
I am better than thou art now: I am a fool, thou art nothing.
—Yes, forsooth, I will hold my tongue, so your face bids me,
though you say nothing.

[*Sings.*]　　　Mum, mum,
165 　　　　　He that keeps nor crust, nor crumb,
　　　　　Weary of all, shall want° some.   *lack; be in need of*

[*He points to* GONERILL.] That's a shelled peascod.°   *empty pea pod; nothing*

GONERILL   Not only, sir, this, your all-licensed° fool,   *unrestrained*
But other of your insolent retinue
170 Do hourly carp and quarrel, breaking forth
In rank° and not-to-be-endured riots. Sir,   *foul; spreading*
I had thought by making this well known unto you
To have found a safe° redress, but now grow fearful,   *sure*
By what yourself too late° have spoke and done,   *recently*
175 That you protect this course and put it on°   *encourage it*
By your allowance; which if you should, the fault
Would not scape censure, nor the redresses sleep;
Which in the tender of a wholesome weal[3]
Might in their working do you that offense
180 Which else were shame, that then necessity
Will call discreet proceeding.[4]

FOOL   For you know, nuncle,

[*Sings.*]　　　The hedge-sparrow fed the cuckoo[5] so long
　　　　　That its had its head bit off by its young;°   *(the young cuckoo)*
185 　　　　　So out went the candle,
　　　　　And we were left darkling.°   *in the dark*

---

1. A headband; here, a metaphor for "frown."
2. A zero without a preceding digit to give it value; nothing.
3. *tender of a wholesome weal:* maintenance of a well-ordered society.
4. *which if you . . . proceeding:* if you do approve (of your attendants' behavior), you will not escape criticism, nor will it be without retribution, which for the common good will cause you pain. While this would otherwise be improper, it will be seen as a prudent ("discreet") action under the circumstances.
5. The cuckoo lays its eggs in the nests of other birds, which then hatch and feed their offspring.

LEAR   Are you our daughter?

205   GONORILL   Come, sir, I would° you would make use of that   *wish*
Good wisdom whereof I know you are fraught°   *full*
And put away these dispositions,° that   *moods; attitudes*
Of late transform you from what you rightly are.

FOOL   May not an ass know when the cart draws the horse?

210   [*Sings.*] Whoop-jug,⁹ I love thee.

LEAR   Doth any here know me? Why, this is not Lear.
Doth Lear walk thus? Speak thus? Where are his eyes?
Either his notion,° weakness, or his discernings   *intellect*
Are lethargied. Sleeping or waking, ha!

215   Sure, 'tis not so. Who is it that can tell me who I am?
Lear's shadow? I would° learn that, for by the marks°   *wish to / evidence*
Of sovereignty, knowledge, and reason,
I should be false persuaded I had daughters.

FOOL   Which° they will make an obedient father.   *Whom*

220   LEAR [*to* GONORILL]   Your name, fair gentlewoman?

GONORILL   Come, sir, this admiration° is much of the savor   *excessive amazement*
Of other your new pranks. I do beseech you,
Understand my purposes aright:
As you are old and reverend, should° be wise.   *you should*

225   Here do you keep a hundred knights and squires,
Men so disordered,° so deboist° and bold,   *disorderly / debauched*
That this our court, infected with their manners,
Shows° like a riotous inn; epicurism° and lust   *Appears / gluttony*
Make more like a tavern or brothel

230   Than a great palace.¹ The shame itself doth speak
For instant remedy. Be thou desired
By her, that else will take the thing she begs,
A little to disquantity your train,°   *to reduce your retinue*
And the remainder that shall still depend°   *be retained*

235   To be such men as may besort° your age,   *befit*
That know themselves° and you.   *Who know their place*

LEAR   Darkness and devils! [*to his* SERVANTS] Saddle my
horses;
Call my train together. [*to* GONORILL] Degenerate bastard,
I'll not trouble thee. Yet° have I left a daughter.   *Still*

240   GONORILL   You strike my people, and your disordered rabble
Make servants of their betters!

---

9. Nickname for "Joan"; sobriquet for a whore.
1. PERFORMANCE COMMENT Productions must decide whether the king's followers are well-behaved "men of choicest parts," as Lear puts it, or a "disordered rabble," as Gonorill describes them. See Digital Edition PC 3.

LEAR   Are you our daughter?

GONERILL   I would° you would make use of your good   *wish*
         wisdom,
         Whereof I know you are fraught,° and put away   *full*
190   These dispositions,° which of late transport you   *moods; attitudes*
         From what you rightly are.

FOOL   May not an ass know when the cart draws the horse?
         [*Sings.*]   Whoop, jug,[6] I love thee.

LEAR   Does any here know me? This is not Lear.
195   Does Lear walk thus? Speak thus? Where are his eyes?
         Either his notion° weakens, his discernings   *intellect*
         Are lethargied. Ha! Waking?° 'Tis not so.   *Am I awake*
         Who is it that can tell me who I am?

FOOL   Lear's shadow.

200 LEAR [*to* GONERILL]   Your name, fair gentlewoman?

GONERILL   This admiration,° sir, is much o'th' savor   *excessive amazement*
         Of other your new pranks. I do beseech you
         To understand my purposes aright:
         As you are old and reverend, should° be wise.   *you should*
205   Here do you keep a hundred knights and squires,
         Men so disordered,° so debauched and bold,   *disorderly*
         That this our court, infected with their manners,
         Shows° like a riotous inn. Epicurism° and lust   *Appears / Gluttony*
         Makes it more like a tavern or a brothel
210   Than a graced° palace.[7] The shame itself doth speak   *an honored*
         For instant remedy. Be then desired
         By her, that else will take the thing she begs,
         A little to disquantity your train,°   *to reduce your retinue*
         And the remainders that shall still depend°   *be retained*
215   To be such men as may besort° your age,   *befit*
         Which know themselves° and you.   *Who know their place*

LEAR   Darkness and devils!
         Saddle my horses; call my train together.
         Degenerate bastard, I'll not trouble thee.
220   Yet° have I left a daughter.   *Still*

GONERILL   You strike my people, and your disordered rabble
         Make servants of their betters.

---

6. Nickname for "Joan"; sobriquet for a whore.
7. PERFORMANCE COMMENT Productions must decide whether the king's followers are well-behaved "men of choicest parts," as Lear puts it, or a "disordered rabble," as Gonerill describes them. See Digital Edition PC 3.

Enter [Duke of] ALBANY.

LEAR   We that too late repent 's! [*to* ALBANY] O sir, are you
    come?
    Is it your will that we prepare any horses?
    [*to* GONORILL] Ingratitude! Thou marble-hearted fiend,
245   More hideous when thou showest thee in a child
    Than the sea-monster! Detested kite,° thou liest!   *carrion-eating hawk*
    My train and men of choice and rarest parts°   *qualities*
    That all particulars of duty know,
    And in the most exact regard support
250   The worships of° their name. —O most small fault,   *honor accorded*
    How ugly didst thou in Cordelia show,
    That like an engine wrenched my frame of nature
    From the fixed place,² drew from my heart all love
    And added to the gall. O Lear, Lear!
255   Beat at this gate° that let thy folly in   *(his head)*
    And thy dear° judgment out. [*to his* SERVANTS] Go, go, my   *precious*
    people.   [*Exeunt* SERVANTS.]
ALBANY   My lord, I am guiltless as I am ignorant.
LEAR   It may be so, my lord. Hark, Nature, hear,
    Dear goddess! Suspend thy purpose if thou
260   Didst intend to make this creature fruitful.
    Into her womb convey sterility,
    Dry up in her the organs of increase,
    And from her derogate° body never spring   *debased*
    A babe to honor her. If she must teem,°   *breed*
265   Create her child of spleen,° that it may live   *malice*
    And be a thwart dis-utered° torment to her.   *a perverse unnatural*
    Let it stamp wrinkles in her brow of youth;
    With cadent° tears, fret° channels in her cheeks;   *flowing / carve*
    Turn all her mother's pains and benefits°   *cares and kind actions*
270   To laughter and contempt, that she may feel—
    That she may feel
    How sharper than a serpent's tooth it is
    To have a thankless child. —Go, go, my people!
ALBANY   Now, gods that we adore, whereof comes this?
275 GONORILL   Never afflict yourself to know the cause,
    But let his disposition have that scope
    That dotage gives it.
LEAR   What, fifty of my followers at a clap,
    Within a fortnight?
ALBANY   What is the matter, sir?
280 LEAR   I'll tell thee: life and death! [*to* GONORILL] I am
    ashamed
    That thou hast power to shake my manhood thus;
    That these hot tears that break from me perforce°   *against my will*
    Should make the worst blasts and fogs upon thee.

---

2. *like . . . place:* as a machine (or lever) dislocated my natural affections from their proper foundations.

Enter [Duke of] ALBANY.

LEAR Woe that° too late repents!   *Woe to him who*
    [*to* ALBANY] Is it your will? Speak, sir. Prepare my horses.
225   [*to* GONERILL] Ingratitude! Thou marble-hearted fiend,
    More hideous when thou show'st thee in a child
    Than the sea-monster.
ALBANY   Pray, sir, be patient.
LEAR [*to* GONERILL]   Detested kite,° thou liest!   *carrion-eating hawk*
    My train are men of choice and rarest parts°   *qualities*
230   That all particulars of duty know,
    And in the most exact regard support
    The worships of° their name. —O most small fault,   *honors accorded*
    How ugly didst thou in Cordelia show,
    Which, like an engine, wrenched my frame of nature
235   From the fixed place,[8] drew from my heart all love,
    And added to the gall. O Lear, Lear, Lear!
    Beat at this gate° that let thy folly in   *(his head)*
    And thy dear° judgment out. [*to his* KNIGHTS] Go, go, my   *precious*
       people.   [*Exeunt* KNIGHTS.]
ALBANY   My lord, I am guiltless as I am ignorant
    Of what hath moved you.
240 LEAR   It may be so, my lord.
    Hear, Nature, hear, dear goddess, hear:
    Suspend thy purpose if thou didst intend
    To make this creature fruitful.
    Into her womb convey sterility,
245   Dry up in her the organs of increase,
    And from her derogate° body never spring   *debased*
    A babe to honor her. If she must teem,°   *breed*
    Create her child of spleen,° that it may live   *malice*
    And be a thwart disnatured° torment to her.   *a perverse unnatural*
250   Let it stamp wrinkles in her brow of youth;
    With cadent° tears fret° channels in her cheeks;   *flowing / carve*
    Turn all her mother's pains and benefits°   *cares and kind actions*
    To laughter and contempt, that she may feel
    How sharper than a serpent's tooth it is
255   To have a thankless child. Away, away.
              Exeunt [LEAR *and* KENT].
ALBANY   Now gods that we adore,
    Whereof comes this?
GONERILL   Never afflict yourself to know more of it,
    But let his disposition have that scope
260   As° dotage gives it.   *Which*
       Enter LEAR.
LEAR   What, fifty of my followers at a clap?
    Within a fortnight?
ALBANY   What's the matter, sir?
LEAR   I'll tell thee:
    Life and death! [*to* GONERILL] I am ashamed
265   That thou hast power to shake my manhood thus,
    That these hot tears, which break from me perforce,°   *against my will*
    Should make thee worth them.
    Blasts and fogs upon thee!

8. *like . . . place*: as a machine (or lever), dislocated my natural affections from their proper foundations.

Untented woundings° of a father's curse,   *Undressed wounds*
285 Pierce every sense about thee! Old fond° eyes,   *foolish*
Beweep° this cause again, I'll pluck you out   *If you weep over*
And cast you with the waters that you make
To temper° clay. Yea, is't come to this? Yet   *soften*
Have I left a daughter, whom I am sure
290 Is kind and comfortable.°   *comforting*
When she shall hear this of thee, with her nails
She'll flay thy wolvish visage. Thou shalt find
That I'll resume the shape which thou dost think
I have cast off forever. Thou shalt, I warrant thee.
                                    [*Exeunt* LEAR *and* KENT.]
295 GONORILL   Do you mark that, my lord?
ALBANY   I cannot be so partial,° Gonorill,   *biased*
To° the great love I bear you—   *Because of*
GONORILL   Come, sir, no more.—
[*to* FOOL] You, more knave than fool, after your master.
300 FOOL   Nuncle Lear, nuncle Lear, tarry and take the Fool
          with.
A fox when one has caught her,
And such a daughter
Should sure° to the slaughter,   *surely be sent*
If my cap would buy a halter,°   *collar; noose*
305 So the Fool follows after.   [*Exit.*]

GONORILL   What, Oswald, ho!
          [*Enter Oswald the* STEWARD.]
STEWARD   Here, madam,
GONORILL   What, have you writ this letter to my sister?
STEWARD   Yes, madam.
GONORILL   Take you some company and away to horse.
310 Inform her full of my particular fears,
And thereto add such reasons of your own
As may compact° it more. Get you gone   *compound*
And hasten your return.   [*Exit* STEWARD.]
                    Now, my lord,
This milky gentleness and course of yours,
315 Though I dislike not, yet under pardon,°   *begging your pardon*
You're much more attasked° for want of wisdom   *taken to task; censured*
Than praise for harmful mildness.
ALBANY   How far your eyes may pierce,° I cannot tell;   *foresee*
Striving to better aught,° we mar what's well.   *anything*
GONORILL   Nay, then—
320 ALBANY   Well, well, the event.°   *Exeunt.*   *let's see the outcome*

	Th'untented woundings° of a father's curse	*The undressed wounds*
270	Pierce every sense about thee. Old fond° eyes,	*foolish*
	Beweep° this cause again, I'll pluck ye out	*If you weep over*
	And cast you with the waters that you lose°	*let loose*
	To temper° clay. Ha? Let it be so.	*soften*
	I have another daughter	
275	Who I am sure is kind and comfortable.°	*comforting*
	When she shall hear this of thee, with her nails	
	She'll flay thy wolvish visage. Thou shalt find	
	That I'll resume the shape which thou dost think	
	I have cast off forever. *Exit.*	

GONERILL Do you mark that?

280 ALBANY I cannot be so partial,° Gonerill, *biased*
To° the great love I bear you— *Because of*
GONERILL Pray you, content.° What, Oswald, ho? *be quiet*
[*to* FOOL] You, sir, more knave than fool, after your master.
FOOL Nuncle Lear, nuncle Lear,
285 Tarry, take the fool with thee.
A fox when one has caught her,
And such a daughter
Should sure° to the slaughter *surely be sent*
If my cap would buy a halter.° *collar; noose*
290 So the fool follows after. *Exit.*
GONERILL This man hath had good counsel. A hundred
knights?
'Tis politic° and safe to let him keep *prudent*
At point° a hundred knights; yes, that on every dream *Armed*
Each buzz,° each fancy, each complaint, dislike. *rumor*
295 He may enguard° his dotage with their powers *protect*
And hold our lives in mercy. Oswald, I say!
ALBANY Well, you may fear too far.
GONERILL Safer than trust too far.
Let me still° take away the harms I fear, *always*
300 Not° fear still to be taken. I know his heart; *Rather than*
What he hath uttered I have writ my sister.
If she sustain him and his hundred knights
When I have showed th'unfitness—
Enter [*Oswald the*] STEWARD.
How now, Oswald?
305 What, have you writ that letter to my sister?
STEWARD Ay, madam.
GONERILL Take you some company and away to horse.
Inform her full of my particular fear
And thereto add such reasons of your own
310 As may compact° it more. Get you gone *compound*
And hasten your return. [*Exit* STEWARD.]
[*to* ALBANY] No, no, my lord,
This milky gentleness and course of yours,
Though I condemn not, yet under pardon,° *begging your pardon*
You are much more at task° for want of wisdom *taken to task; censured*
315 Than praised for harmful mildness.
ALBANY How far your eyes may pierce,° I cannot tell; *foresee*
Striving to better, oft we mar what's well.
GONERILL Nay, then—
ALBANY Well, well, th'event.° *Exeunt.* *let's see the outcome*

1.5 (F 1.5)

Enter LEAR[, KENT, FOOL, *and a* SERVANT].

LEAR Go you before° to Gloucester¹ with these letters; acquaint   *on ahead*
my daughter no further with anything you know than comes
from her demand out of the letter.² If your diligence be not
speedy, I shall be there before you.

5 KENT I will not sleep, my lord, till I have delivered your
letter.   *Exit.*

FOOL If a man's brains were in his heels, were't not in danger
of kibes?°   *chilblains*

LEAR Ay, boy.

10 FOOL Then I prithee, be merry; thy wit shall ne'er go slipshod.³

LEAR Ha, ha, ha.

FOOL Shalt° see thy other daughter will use thee kindly, for   *Thou shalt*
though she's as like this as a crab⁴ is like an apple, yet I con°   *know*
what I can tell.

15 LEAR Why, what canst thou tell, my boy?

FOOL She'll taste as like this as a crab doth to a crab. Thou
canst not tell why one's nose stand in the middle of his face?

LEAR No.

FOOL Why, to keep his eyes on either side 's nose, that what a
20 man cannot smell out 'a° may spy into.   *he*

LEAR I did her wrong.

FOOL Canst tell how an oyster makes his shell?

LEAR No.

FOOL Nor I, neither, but I can tell why a snail has a house.

25 LEAR Why?

FOOL Why, to put his head in, not to give it away to his
daughter and leave his horns without a case.⁵

LEAR I will forget my nature.⁶ So kind a father! Be my horses
ready?

30 FOOL Thy asses° are gone about them. The reason why the   *(servants)*
seven stars° are no more than seven is a pretty reason.   *the Pleiades*

LEAR Because they are not eight.

FOOL Yes, thou wouldst make a good fool.

LEAR To take't again, perforce.⁷ Monster ingratitude!

35 FOOL If thou wert my fool, nuncle, I'd have thee beaten for
being old before thy time.

LEAR How's that?

FOOL Thou shouldst not have been old before thou hadst
been wise.

40 LEAR Oh, let me not be mad, sweet heaven! I would not be
mad! Keep me in temper.° I would not be mad! —Are the   *sane*
horses ready?

1.5 Location: Before Albany's castle.
1. To Gloucestershire, where Cornwall and Regan
reside.
2. *than . . . letter:* other than such questions as are
prompted by the letter.
3. Literally, your brains will not wear slippers (to
warm feet that are afflicted with chilblains); feet of
any intelligence would not walk toward Regan.
4. *crab:* crab apple; sour apple.

5. Protective covering for his head, or concealment
for his horns (horns were the conventional sign of a
cuckold). The Fool may be slyly implying that Lear's
wife cheated on him.
6. Lose my fatherly feelings. *nature:* character.
7. To take it back by force. Lear may refer to Gonorill's treachery, or he may be contemplating resuming
his authority.

1.5 (Q 1.5)

Enter LEAR, KENT [*disguised as Caius*], GENTLEMAN,
and FOOL.

LEAR [*to* KENT]   Go you before° to Gloucester[1] with these let-   *on ahead*
ters; acquaint my daughter no further with anything you
know than comes from her demand out of the letter.[2] If your
diligence be not speedy, I shall be there afore you.

5   KENT   I will not sleep, my lord, till I have delivered your letter.
                                                                Exit.

FOOL   If a man's brains were in 's heels, were't not in danger
of kibes?°   *chilblains*

LEAR   Ay, boy.

FOOL   Then, I prithee, be merry; thy wit shall not go slipshod.[3]

10   LEAR   Ha, ha, ha.

FOOL   Shalt° see thy other daughter will use thee kindly, for   *Thou shalt*
though she's as like this as a crab's° like an apple, yet I can   *crab apple; sour apple*
tell what I can tell.

LEAR   What canst tell, boy?

15   FOOL   She will taste as like this as a crab does to a crab. Thou
canst tell why one's nose stands i'th' middle on 's° face?   *of one's*

LEAR   No.

FOOL   Why, to keep one's eyes of either side 's nose, that what
a man cannot smell out he may spy into.

20   LEAR   I did her wrong.

FOOL   Canst tell how an oyster makes his shell?

LEAR   No.

FOOL   Nor I, neither, but I can tell why a snail has a house.

LEAR   Why?

25   FOOL   Why, to put 's head in, not to give it away to his daughters and leave his horns without a case.[4]

LEAR   I will forget my nature.[5] So kind a father! Be my horses
ready?

FOOL   Thy asses° are gone about 'em; the reason why the   *(servants)*
30   seven stars° are no more than seven is a pretty reason.   *the Pleiades*

LEAR   Because they are not eight.

FOOL   Yes, indeed; thou wouldst make a good fool.

LEAR   To take't again perforce.[6] Monster ingratitude!

FOOL   If thou wert my fool, nuncle, I'd have thee beaten for
35   being old before thy time.

LEAR   How's that?

FOOL   Thou shouldst not have been old till thou hadst been
wise.

LEAR   Oh, let me not be mad, not mad. Sweet heaven, keep me
40   in temper;° I would not be mad. —How now, are the horses   *sane*
ready?

1.5 Location: Before Albany's castle.
1. To Gloucestershire, where Cornwall and Regan
reside.
2. *than . . . letter:* other than such questions as are
prompted by the letter.
3. Literally, your brains will not wear slippers (to
warm feet that are afflicted with chilblains); feet of
any intelligence would not walk toward Regan.

4. Protective covering for his head, or concealment
for his horns (horns were the conventional sign of a
cuckold). The Fool may be slyly implying that Lear's
wife cheated on him.
5. Lose my fatherly feelings. *nature:* character.
6. To take it back by force. Lear may refer to Gonerill's treachery, or he may be contemplating resuming
his authority.

SERVANT   Ready, my lord.

LEAR [*to* FOOL]   Come, boy.   [*Exeunt* LEAR *and* SERVANT.]

45 FOOL   She that is maid now and laughs at my departure,
     Shall not be a maid long, except things be cut shorter.[8]

                                            Exit.

2.1 (F 2.1)

Enter [Edmund the] BASTARD *and* CURAN, *meeting.*

BASTARD   Save° thee, Curan.   *God save*

CURAN   And you, sir. I have been with your father and given
     him notice that the Duke of Cornwall and his duchess will
     be here with him tonight.

5 BASTARD   How comes that?

CURAN   Nay, I know not. You have heard of the news abroad.
     I mean the whispered ones, for there are yet but ear-bussing[1]
     arguments.

BASTARD   Not I. Pray you, what are they?

10 CURAN   Have you heard of no likely wars towards° twixt the   *impending*
     two Dukes of Cornwall and Albany?

BASTARD   Not a word.

CURAN   You may, then, in time. Fare you well, sir.   [*Exit.*]

BASTARD   The Duke be here tonight! The better best!

15   This weaves itself perforce° into my business.   *necessarily*
     My father hath set guard to take my brother,
     And I have one thing of a queasy question,[2]
     Which must ask briefness and Fortune help.

        Enter EDGAR [*above*].

     Brother, a word! Descend, brother, I say!

        [EDGAR *descends.*]

20   My father watches. Oh, fly this place!
     Intelligence is given where you are hid.
     You have now the good advantage of the night.
     Have you not spoken 'gainst the Duke of Cornwall aught?°   *anything*
     He's coming hither now in the night, i'th' haste,

25   And Regan with him. Have you nothing said
     Upon his party° against the Duke of Albany?   *On his (Cornwall's) side*
     Advise your—°   *Consider carefully*

EDGAR   I am sure on't,° not a word.   *of it*

BASTARD   I hear my father coming. Pardon me:
     [*He draws his sword.*] In cunning I must draw my sword
       upon you.

30   Seem to defend yourself; now quit you° well.   *acquit yourself*
     [*He shouts.*] Yield, come before my father. —Light here,
       here!
     [*to* EDGAR] Fly, brother, fly! —Torches, torches! [*to* EDGAR]
     So farewell!   [*Exit* EDGAR.]

---

8. *She . . . shorter:* A girl who would laugh at my leaving would be so foolish that she could not remain a virgin for long; "things" refers both to the unfolding event and to penises.

2.1 Location: Gloucester's castle.

1. *ear-bussing:* ear-kissing, from "buss" meaning "to kiss." Perhaps also a pun on "buzz" (rumor). Compare to Lear's use of the term in 1.4.294 in F.

2. And I have a hazardous and delicate problem.

GENTLEMAN   Ready, my lord.

LEAR   Come, boy.

FOOL   She that's a maid now and laughs at my departure,

45   Shall not be a maid long, unless things be cut shorter.[7]

Exeunt.

2.1 (Q 2.1)

Enter [EDMOND *the*] *bastard, and* CURAN, *severally.*°   separately

EDMOND   Save° thee, Curan.   God save

CURAN   And you, sir. I have been with your father and given
  him notice that the Duke of Cornwall and Regan, his duchess, will be here with him this night.

5 EDMOND   How comes that?

CURAN   Nay, I know not. You have heard of the news abroad,
  I mean the whispered ones, for they are yet but ear-kissing
  arguments.[1]

EDMOND   Not I. Pray you, what are they?

10 CURAN   Have you heard of no likely wars toward° twixt the   impending
  Dukes of Cornwall and Albany?

EDMOND   Not a word.

CURAN   You may do, then, in time. Fare you well, sir.   *Exit.*

EDMOND   The Duke be here tonight? The better best!

15 This weaves itself perforce° into my business.   necessarily
  My father hath set guard to take my brother,
  And I have one thing of a queasy question[2]
  Which I must act. Briefness and fortune work.°   be with me
      Enter EDGAR [*above*].
  Brother, a word! Descend, brother, I say.
      [EDGAR *descends.*]

20 My father watches. O sir, fly this place!
  Intelligence is given where you are hid.
  You have now the good advantage of the night.
  Have you not spoken 'gainst the Duke of Cornwall?
  He's coming hither now, i'th' night, i'th' haste,

25 And Regan with him. Have you nothing said
  Upon his party° 'gainst the Duke of Albany?   On his (Cornwall's) side
  Advise yourself.°   Consider carefully

EDGAR   I am sure on't,° not a word.   of it

EDMOND   I hear my father coming. Pardon me:
  [*He draws his sword.*] In cunning, I must draw my sword
      upon you.

30 Draw, seem to defend yourself. Now quit you° well.   acquit yourself
  [*He shouts.*] Yield, come before my father. —Light, ho, here!
  [*to* EDGAR] Fly, brother! —Torches, torches! [*to* EDGAR] So
      farewell!   [*Exit* EDGAR.]

---

7. *She . . . shorter*: A girl who would laugh at my leaving would be so foolish that she could not remain a
virgin for long; "things" refers both to the unfolding
event and to penises.

2.1 Location: Gloucester's castle.
1. Barely whispered affairs.
2. And I have a hazardous and delicate problem.

[*He wounds his arm.*] Some blood drawn on me would
  beget opinion°   *produce the impression*
Of my more fierce endeavor. I have seen
35 Drunkards do more than this in sport. [*He shouts.*] Father,
  father!
Stop, stop! No help?
        Enter GLOUCESTER [*and* SERVANTS].
GLOUCESTER   Now, Edmund, where is the villain?
BASTARD   Here stood he in the dark, his sharp sword out,
  Warbling of wicked charms, conjuring the moon
  To stand 's° auspicious mistress.   *To act as his*
40 GLOUCESTER   But where is he?
BASTARD   Look, sir, I bleed.
GLOUCESTER   Where is the villain, Edmund?
BASTARD   Fled this way, sir, when by no means he could—
GLOUCESTER   Pursue him, go after!   [*Exeunt* SERVANTS.]
                        By no means—what?
BASTARD   —Persuade me to the murder of your lordship,
45 But that° I told him the revengive° gods   *In response to that / revenging*
  'Gainst parricides did all their thunders bend;
  Spoke with how manifold and strong a bond
  The child was bound to the father. Sir,
  In a fine,° seeing how loathly opposite° I stood   *Finally / opposed*
50 To his unnatural purpose, with fell° motion   *deadly*
  With his preparèd sword he charges home°   *strikes to the heart of*
  My unprovided° body, lanced° mine arm,   *unprotected / struck*
  But when he saw my best alarumed spirits,
  Bold in the quarrel's rights,[3] roused to the encounter,
55 Or° whether gasted° by the noise I made,[4]   *Either / frightened*
  But suddenly he fled.
GLOUCESTER   Let him fly far.
  Not in this land shall he remain uncaught,
  And found, dispatch.° The noble Duke, my master,   *And once found, killed*
  My worthy arch° and patron, comes tonight.   *lord*
60 By his authority I will proclaim it
  That he which finds him shall deserve our thanks,
  Bringing the murderous caitiff° to the stake.[5]   *wretch*
  He that conceals him, death.
BASTARD   When I dissuaded him from his intent
65 And found him pight° to do it, with cursed° speech   *resolved / bitter*
  I threatened to discover° him. He replied,   *expose*
  "Thou unpossessing bastard, dost thou think,
  If I would stand against thee, could the reposure°   *placing*
  Of any trust, virtue, or worth in thee
70 Make thy words faithed?° No. What I should deny—   *credible*
  As this I would, ay, though thou didst produce
  My very character[6]—I'd turn it all
  To[7] thy suggestion, plot, and damned pretence,°   *intent*
  And thou must make a dullard of the world
75 If they not thought the profits of my death

---

3. *my best . . . rights:* that I was fully roused to action,   one could be burned.
made brave by righteousness.   6. Handwriting; but also, a true summary of my
4. From the jumbled syntax, it appears likely that Q   character.
has accidentally omitted a verse line.   7. *I'd . . . To:* I'd blame it all on.
5. Treachery and rebellion were crimes for which

[*He wounds his arm.*] Some blood drawn on me would beget
    opinion°   *produce the impression*
    Of my more fierce endeavor. I have seen drunkards
35   Do more than this in sport. [*He shouts.*] Father, father!
    Stop, stop! No help?
            Enter GLOUCESTER *and* SERVANTS, *with torches.*
GLOUCESTER   Now, Edmond, where's the villain?
EDMOND   Here stood he in the dark, his sharp sword out,
    Mumbling of wicked charms, conjuring the moon
40   To stand° auspicious mistress.   *To act as his*
GLOUCESTER   But where is he?
EDMOND   Look, sir, I bleed.
GLOUCESTER   Where is the villain, Edmond?
EDMOND   Fled this way, sir, when by no means he could—
GLOUCESTER   Pursue him, ho, go after.   [*Exeunt* SERVANTS.]
45   —By no means—what?
EDMOND   —Persuade me to the murder of your lordship,
    But that° I told him the revenging gods   *In response to that*
    'Gainst parricides did all the thunder bend;
    Spoke with how manifold and strong a bond
50   The child was bound to th' father. Sir, in fine,°   *finally.*
    Seeing how loathly opposite° I stood   *opposed*
    To his unnatural purpose, in fell° motion   *deadly*
    With his preparèd sword he charges home°   *strikes to the heart of*
    My unprovided° body, latched° mine arm,   *unprotected / struck*
55   And when he saw my best alarumed spirits
    Bold in the quarrel's right,[3] roused to th'encounter,
    Or whether gasted° by the noise I made,   *frightened*
    Full suddenly he fled.
GLOUCESTER   Let him fly far.
    Not in this land shall he remain uncaught,
60   And found, dispatch.° The noble Duke, my master,   *And once found, killed*
    My worthy arch° and patron, comes tonight.   *lord*
    By his authority I will proclaim it,
    That he which finds him shall deserve our thanks,
    Bringing the murderous coward to the stake.[4]
65   He that conceals him, death.
EDMOND   When I dissuaded him from his intent,
    And found him pight° to do it, with curst° speech   *resolved / bitter*
    I threatened to discover° him. He replied,   *expose*
    "Thou unpossessing bastard, dost thou think,
70   If I would stand against thee, would the reposal°   *placing*
    Of any trust, virtue, or worth in thee
    Make thy words faithed?° No, what should I deny—   *credible*
    As this I would, though thou didst produce
    My very character[5]—I'd turn it all
75   To[6] thy suggestion, plot, and damnèd practice,°   *scheming*
    And thou must make a dullard of the world,
    If they not thought the profits of my death

---

3. *my best . . . right:* that I was fully roused to action, made brave by righteousness.
4. Treachery and rebellion were crimes for which one could be burned.
5. Handwriting; but also, a true summary of my character.
6. *I'd . . . To:* I'd blame it all on.

Were very pregnant and potential spurs
To make thee seek it."[8]

GLOUCESTER   Strong° and fastened° villain,   *Flagrant / incorrigible*
Would he deny his letter? I never got° him!   *begot*
[*A sennet sounds.*]
Hark, the Duke's trumpets! I know not why he comes.

80   All ports° I'll bar. The villain shall not scape;   *seaports; exits*
The Duke must grant me that. Besides, his picture
I will send far and near, that all the kingdom
May have note of him[9] and of my land.
Loyal and natural° boy, I'll work the means   *loving; illegitimate*

85   To make thee capable.°   *legally able to inherit*
    Enter the Duke of CORNWALL [*and* REGAN].
CORNWALL   How now, my noble friend? Since I came hither,
Which I can call but now, I have heard strange news.
REGAN   If it be true, all vengeance comes too short
Which can pursue the offender. How dost my lord?

90   GLOUCESTER   Madam, my old heart is cracked, is cracked.
REGAN   What, did my father's godson seek your life?
He whom my father named, your Edgar?
GLOUCESTER   Ay, lady, lady; shame would have it hid.
REGAN   Was he not companion with the riotous knights

95   That tends° upon my father?   *attend*
GLOUCESTER   I know not, madam. 'Tis too bad, too bad.
BASTARD   Yes, madam, he was.
REGAN   No marvel, then, though° he were ill affected.°   *that / ill disposed*
'Tis they have put him on° the old man's death   *have urged him to seek*

100   To have the waste and spoil of his revenues.
I have this present evening from my sister
Been well informed of them, and with such cautions
That if they come to sojourn at my house,
I'll not be there.

CORNWALL   Nor I, assure thee, Regan.

105   Edmund, I heard that you have shown your father
A childlike office.°   *filial service*
BASTARD   'Twas my duty, sir.
GLOUCESTER   He did betray his practice° and received   *uncover his (Edgar's) plot*
This hurt you see, striving to apprehend him.
CORNWALL   Is he pursued?
GLOUCESTER   Ay, my good lord.

110   CORNWALL   If he be taken, he shall never more
Be feared of doing harm. Make your own purpose
How in my strength you please.[1] For you, Edmund,
Whose virtue and obedience doth this instant
So much commend itself, you shall be ours.

115   Natures of such deep trust we shall much need;
You we first seize on.
BASTARD   I shall serve you truly, however else.°   *if nothing else*
GLOUCESTER   For him, I thank your grace.

---

8. *And thou . . . it:* And do you think the world so stupid that it could not see the benefit you would get from
my death (and thus a motive for plotting to kill me)?
pregnant: full. *potential spurs:* powerful temptations.
9. Likenesses of outlaws were drawn up, printed,

and publicly displayed, sometimes with an offer of
reward as in "Wanted" posters.
1. *Make . . . please:* Devise your plots making use of
my forces and authority as you see fit.

Were very pregnant and potential spirits
To make thee seek it."[7]
GLOUCESTER   Oh, strange° and fastened° villain,   *unnatural / incorrigible*
80   Would he deny his letter, said he?
                    Tucket° within.   *Flourish of trumpets*
Hark, the Duke's trumpets. I know not where he comes.
All ports° I'll bar. The villain shall not scape;   *seaports; exits*
The Duke must grant me that. Besides, his picture
I will send far and near, that all the kingdom
85   May have due note of him,[8] and of my land,
Loyal and natural° boy, I'll work the means   *loving; illegitimate*
To make thee capable.°   *legally able to inherit*
          Enter CORNWALL, REGAN, *and Attendants.*
CORNWALL   How now, my noble friend? Since I came hither,
Which I can call but now, I have heard strangeness.
90   REGAN   If it be true, all vengeance comes too short
Which can pursue th'offender. How dost my lord?
GLOUCESTER   O madam, my old heart is cracked; it's cracked.
REGAN   What, did my father's godson seek your life?
He whom my father named, your Edgar?
95   GLOUCESTER   O lady, lady, shame would have it hid.
REGAN   Was he not companion with the riotous knights
That tended° upon my father?   *attend*
GLOUCESTER   I know not, madam. 'Tis too bad, too bad.
EDMOND   Yes, madam, he was of that consort.°   *company*
100 REGAN   No marvel, then, though° he were ill affected.°   *that / ill disposed*
'Tis they have put him on° the old man's death   *have urged him to seek*
To have th'expense° and waste of his revenues.   *use*
I have this present evening from my sister
Been well informed of them, and with such cautions
105 That if they come to sojourn at my house,
I'll not be there.
CORNWALL   Nor I, assure thee, Regan.
Edmond, I hear that you have shown your father
A childlike office.°   *filial service*
EDMOND   It was my duty, sir.
GLOUCESTER   He did bewray his practice° and received   *uncover his (Edgar's) plot*
110 This hurt you see, striving to apprehend him.
CORNWALL   Is he pursued?
GLOUCESTER   Ay, my good lord.
CORNWALL   If he be taken, he shall never more
Be feared of doing harm. Make your own purpose
How in my strength you please.[9] For you, Edmond,
115 Whose virtue and obedience doth this instant
So much commend itself, you shall be ours.
Natures of such deep trust we shall much need;
You we first seize on.
EDMOND   I shall serve you, sir, truly, however else.°   *if nothing else*
120 GLOUCESTER   For him, I thank your grace.

---

7. *And thou . . . it:* And do you think the world so stupid that it could not see the benefit you would get from
my death (and thus a motive for plotting to kill me)?
pregnant: full. *potential spirits:* powerful temptations.
8. Likenesses of outlaws were drawn up, printed,
and publicly displayed, sometimes with an offer of
reward as in "Wanted" posters.
9. *Make . . . please:* Devise your plots making use of
my forces and authority as you see fit.

CORNWALL   You know not why we came to visit you?

120   REGAN   Thus out of season—threat'ning dark-eyed night—
Occasions, noble Gloucester, of some poise,°   *weight*
Wherein we must have use of your advice.
Our father he hath writ—so hath our sister—
Of differences,° which I best thought it fit   *quarrels*
125   To answer from° our home. The several° messengers   *away from / various*
From hence attend° dispatch. Our good old friend,   *await*
Lay comforts to your bosom and bestow your needful°   *badly needed*
counsel
To our business, which craves the instant use.[2]

GLOUCESTER   I serve you, madam. Your graces are right
welcome.   *Exeunt.*

2.2 (F 2.2)

Enter KENT *[disguised as Caius] and [Oswald the]*
STEWARD.

STEWARD   Good even° to thee, friend. Art° of the house?   *evening / Are you a servant*
KENT   Ay.
STEWARD   Where may we set our horses?
KENT   I'th' mire.
5   STEWARD   Prithee, if thou love me,° tell me.   *if you will be so kind*
KENT   I love thee not.
STEWARD   Why, then, I care not for thee.
KENT   If I had thee in Lipsbury pinfold,[1] I would make thee
care for me.
10   STEWARD   Why dost thou use° me thus? I know thee not.   *treat*
KENT   Fellow, I know thee.
STEWARD   What dost thou know me for?
KENT   A knave, a rascal, an eater of broken meats,° a base,   *scraps*
proud, shallow, beggarly, three-suited, hundred pound, filthy,
15   worsted-stocking knave,[2] a lily-livered, action-taking knave,
a whoreson, glass-gazing, superfinical rogue, one-trunk-
inheriting slave,[3] one that wouldst be a bawd in way of good
service[4] and art nothing but the composition° of a knave,   *combination*
beggar, coward, pander, and the son and heir of a mongrel
20   bitch, whom I will beat into clamorous whining if thou deny
the least syllable of the addition.[5]
STEWARD   What a monstrous fellow art thou thus to rail on
one that's neither known of° thee nor knows thee.   *by*
KENT   What a brazen-faced varlet° art thou to deny thou   *rascal*
25   knowest me! Is it two days ago since I beat thee and tripped
up thy heels before the King? *[He draws his sword.]* Draw,

---

2. Which requires immediate attention.
2.2 Location: Before Gloucester's house.
1. If I had you in the enclosure of my mouth (gripped in my teeth). Lipsbury is probably an invented place-name. *pinfold:* pen, animal enclosure.
2. *three-suited . . . knave:* Oswald is being called a poor imitation of a gentleman. Servants were permitted three suits a year; one hundred pounds was the minimum qualification for the purchase of one of King James's knighthoods; a gentleman would wear stock-

ings of silk, not "worsted" (thick woolen material).
3. *lily-livered:* cowardly. *action-taking:* litigious, one who would rather use the law than his fists. *glass-gazing:* mirror-gazing. *superfinical:* overly finicky, fastidious. *one-trunk-inheriting:* owning only what would fill one trunk.
4. *one that . . . service:* one who would even be a pimp if called upon.
5. Of the descriptions Kent has just applied to him. *addition:* title (used ironically).

CORNWALL You know not why we came to visit you?

REGAN Thus out of season, threading dark-eyed night?
Occasions, noble Gloucester, of some prize,°   *weight*
Wherein we must have use of your advice.

125 Our father, he hath writ—so hath our sister—
Of differences,° which I best thought it fit   *quarrels*
To answer from° our home. The several° messengers   *away from / various*
From hence attend° dispatch. Our good old friend,   *await*
Lay comforts to your bosom and bestow

130 Your needful° counsel to our businesses,   *badly needed*
Which craves the instant use.[1]

GLOUCESTER   I serve you, madam.
Your graces are right welcome.   *Exeunt. Flourish.*

2.2 (Q 2.2)

Enter KENT [*disguised as Caius*] *and* [*Oswald the*]
STEWARD *severally.*°   *separately*

STEWARD Good dawning to thee, friend. Art° of this house? *Are you a servant*

KENT Ay.

STEWARD Where may we set our horses?

KENT I'th' mire.

5 STEWARD Prithee, if thou lov'st me,° tell me.   *if you will be so kind*

KENT I love thee not.

STEWARD Why, then, I care not for thee.

KENT If I had thee in Lipsbury pinfold,[1] I would make thee
care for me.

10 STEWARD Why dost thou use° me thus? I know thee not.   *treat*

KENT Fellow, I know thee.

STEWARD What dost thou know me for?

KENT A knave, a rascal, an eater of broken meats,° a base,   *scraps*
proud, shallow, beggarly, three-suited, hundred pound, filthy,

15 worsted-stocking knave,[2] a lily-livered, action-taking, whoreson, glass-gazing, super-serviceable finical rogue, one-trunk-
inheriting slave,[3] one that wouldst be a bawd in way of good
service[4] and art nothing but the composition° of a knave,   *combination*
beggar, coward, pander, and the son and heir of a mongrel

20 bitch. One whom I will beat into clamors whining if thou
deny'st the least syllable of thy addition.[5]

STEWARD Why, what a monstrous fellow art thou thus to rail
on one that is neither known of° thee nor knows thee!   *by*

KENT What a brazen-faced varlet° art thou to deny thou know- *rascal*

25 est me! Is it two days since I tripped up thy heels and beat
thee before the King? [*He draws his sword.*] Draw, you rogue, for

1. Which requires immediate attention.
2.2 Location: Before Gloucester's house.
1. If I had you in the enclosure of my mouth (gripped
in my teeth). Lipsbury is probably an invented place-
name. *pinfold:* pen, animal enclosure.
2. *three-suited . . . knave:* Oswald is being called a poor
imitation of a gentleman. Servants were permitted
three suits a year; one hundred pounds was the minimum qualification for the purchase of one of King
James's knighthoods; a gentleman would wear stockings of silk, not "worsted" (thick woolen material).

3. *lily-livered:* cowardly. *action-taking:* litigious; one
who would rather use the law than his fists. *glass-
gazing:* mirror-gazing. *super-serviceable:* overly officious, or too ready to serve. *finical:* finicky, fastidious.
one-trunk-inheriting: owning only what would fill one
trunk.
4. *one that . . . service:* one who would even be a
pimp if called upon.
5. Of the descriptions Kent has just applied to him.
addition: title (used ironically).

you rogue, for though it be night, the moon shines. I'll make
a sop of the moonshine[6] o'you. Draw, you whoreson, cullionly barber-monger![7] Draw!

STEWARD   Away, I have nothing to do with thee.

KENT   Draw, you rascal! You bring letters against the King,
and take Vanity the puppet's part against the royalty of her
father.[8] Draw, you rogue, or I'll so carbonado[9] your shanks—   *Come forward*
Draw, you rascal! Come your ways!°
[*He beats him.*]

STEWARD   Help, ho, murder, help!

KENT   Strike, you slave! Stand, rogue! Stand, you neat° slave.   *elegant; foppish*
Strike!

STEWARD   Help, ho, murder, help!

    Enter Edmund [*the* BASTARD] *with his rapier drawn,*
    GLOUCESTER, *the Duke and Duchess* [CORNWALL
    and REGAN].

BASTARD   How now, what's the matter?

KENT   With you, goodman boy, an't° you please. Come, I'll   *if*
flesh you.[1] Come on, young master!

GLOUCESTER   Weapons? Arms? What's the matter here?

CORNWALL   Keep peace, upon your lives. He dies that strikes
again! What's the matter?

REGAN   The messengers from our sister and the King?

CORNWALL   What's your difference?° Speak.   *quarrel*

STEWARD   I am scarce in breath, my lord.

KENT   No marvel; you have so bestirred your valor, you
cowardly rascal. Nature disclaims° in thee. A tailor made   *disowns her part*
thee![2]

CORNWALL   Thou art a strange fellow! A tailor make a man?

KENT   Ay, a tailor, sir. A stonecutter or a painter could not
have made him so ill,° though he had been but two hours at   *so badly*
the trade.

GLOUCESTER   Speak yet: how grew your quarrel?

STEWARD   This ancient ruffian, sir, whose life I have spared at
suit of° his gray beard—   *on account of*

KENT [*to* STEWARD] Thou whoreson zed,[3] thou unnecessary
letter! —My lord, if you'll give me leave, I will tread this
unbolted° villain into mortar and daub the walls of a jakes°   *unsifted; coarse /*
with him. [*to* STEWARD] "Spare my gray beard," you wag-tail![4]   *privy; toilet*

CORNWALL   Peace, sir! You beastly knave, you have no
reverence.°   *respect*

KENT   Yes, sir, but anger has a privilege.

CORNWALL   Why art thou angry?

Line numbers: 30, 35, 40, 45, 50, 55, 60, 65

---

6. Kent proposes to skewer and pierce Oswald so that
his body might be made into something insubstantial
(like moonshine). Alternatively, perhaps Kent is proposing to scramble Oswald's body into a substance
resembling the popular sixteenth- and seventeenth-
century pudding called "eggs in moonshine." *sop:*
piece of bread to be steeped or dunked in soup.
7. *cullionly barber-monger:* despicable frequenter of
hairdressers. *cullion:* testicle.
8. *and take . . . father:* and support Gonorill, here
depicted as a dressed-up doll whose pride is contrasted with Lear's kingliness.
9. Slash or score as one would the surface of meat in
preparation for broiling.

1. I'll initiate you into fighting, as a hunting dog is
given the taste of blood to rouse it for the chase.
2. Tailors, considered effeminate, were stock objects
of mockery. Kent has suggested that Oswald is
worthless apart from the value he derives from his
external garments.
3. The letter Z (zed) was considered superfluous
because it could be replaced by S; consequently, it
was omitted from many dictionaries.
4. A common English bird that takes its name from
the up-and-down flicking of its tail; this, and its
characteristic hopping from foot to foot, causes it to
appear nervous. Alternatively, a contemptuous term
for a harlot.

though it be night, yet the moon shines. I'll make a sop o'th'
moonshine of you,[6] you whoreson, cullionly barber-monger.[7]
Draw!

30 STEWARD   Away, I have nothing to do with thee.

KENT   Draw, you rascal! You come with letters against the
King and take Vanity the puppet's part against the royalty
of her father?[8] Draw, you rogue, or I'll so carbonado[9] your
shanks—Draw, you rascal! Come your ways!°   *Come forward*
[*He beats him.*]

35 STEWARD   Help, ho, murder, help!

KENT   Strike, you slave! Stand, rogue! Stand, you neat° slave!   *elegant; foppish*
Strike!

STEWARD   Help, ho, murder, murder!

Enter [EDMOND *the*] *bastard,* CORNWALL, REGAN,
GLOUCESTER, SERVANTS.

EDMOND   How now, what's the matter? Part!

40 KENT [*to* STEWARD]   With you, goodman boy, if you please.
Come, I'll flesh ye.[1] Come on, young master.

GLOUCESTER   Weapons? Arms? What's the matter here?

CORNWALL   Keep peace, upon your lives! He dies that strikes
again! What is the matter?

45 REGAN   The messengers from our sister and the King?

CORNWALL   What is your difference?° Speak.   *quarrel*

STEWARD   I am scarce in breath, my lord.

KENT   No marvel; you have so bestirred your valor, you
cowardly rascal. Nature disclaims° in thee. A tailor[2] made   *disowns her part*
50 thee!

CORNWALL   Thou art a strange fellow. A tailor make a man?

KENT   A tailor, sir. A stonecutter or a painter could not have
made him so ill,° though they had been but two years o'th'°   *so badly / at the*
trade.

55 CORNWALL   Speak yet: how grew your quarrel?

STEWARD   This ancient ruffian, sir, whose life I have spared at
suit of° his gray beard—   *on account of*

KENT [*to* STEWARD]   Thou whoreson zed,[3] thou unnecessary
letter! —My lord, if you will give me leave, I will tread
60 this unbolted° villain into mortar and daub the wall of a   *unsifted; coarse*
jakes° with him. [*to* STEWARD] "Spare my gray beard," you   *privy; toilet*
wagtail![4]

CORNWALL   Peace, sirrah!
You beastly knave, know you no reverence?°   *respect*

65 KENT   Yes, sir, but anger hath a privilege.

CORNWALL   Why art thou angry?

---

6. Kent proposes to skewer and pierce Oswald so that
his body might be made into something insubstantial
(like moonshine). Alternatively, perhaps Kent is proposing to scramble Oswald's body into a substance
resembling the popular sixteenth- and seventeenth-
century pudding called "eggs in moonshine." *sop:*
piece of bread to be steeped or dunked in soup.
7. *cullionly barber-monger: cullion:* testicle.
8. *and take . . . father:* and support Gonerill, here
depicted as a dressed-up doll whose pride is contrasted with Lear's kingliness.
9. Slash or score, as one would the surface of meat in
preparation for broiling.

1. I'll initiate you into fighting, as a hunting dog is
given the taste of blood to rouse it for the chase.
2. Tailors, considered effeminate, were stock objects
of mockery. Kent has suggested that Oswald is worthless apart from the value he derives from his external
garments.
3. The letter Z (zed) was considered superfluous
because it could be replaced by S; consequently, it was
omitted from many dictionaries.
4. A common English bird that takes its name from
the up-and-down flicking of its tail; this, and its
characteristic hopping from foot to foot, causes it to
appear nervous. Alternatively, a contemptuous term
for a harlot.

KENT　That such a slave as this should wear a sword
　　That° wears no honesty. Such smiling rogues　　　　　　　　　　*Who*
　　As these like rats oft bite those cords⁵ in twain
　　Which are too entrench° to unloose; smooth° every passion　　*intricate / flatter*
70　That in the natures of their lords rebel,
　　Being oil to fire, snow to their colder moods,
　　Renege,° affirm, and turn their halcyon beaks⁶　　　　　　　　*Deny*
　　With every gale and vary° of their masters,　　　　　　　　　*mood*
　　Knowing naught like days but following.
75　A plague upon your epileptic° visage!　　　　　　　*distorted; grimacing*
　　Smoile you° my speeches as° I were a fool?　　　*Do you smile at / as if*
　　Goose, an I had you upon Sarum plain,
　　I'd send you cackling home to Camelot.⁷
CORNWALL　What, art thou mad, old fellow?
80　GLOUCESTER　How fell you out? Say that.
KENT　No contraries° hold more antipathy　　　　　　　　　　*opposites*
　　Than I and such a knave.
CORNWALL　Why dost thou call him knave? What's his
　　offense?
KENT　His countenance likes° me not.　　　　　　　　　　　　*pleases*
85　CORNWALL　No more perchance does mine, or his, or hers.
KENT　Sir, 'tis my occupation to be plain.
　　I have seen better faces in my time
　　Than stands on any shoulder that I see
　　Before me at this instant.
90　CORNWALL　This is a fellow who, having been praised
　　For bluntness, doth affect a saucy roughness
　　And constrains the garb quite from his nature.⁸
　　He cannot flatter, he; he must be plain;
　　He must speak truth, an they will take't so;
95　If not, he's plain.⁹ These kind of knaves I know,
　　Which in this plainness harbor more craft
　　And more corrupter ends than twenty silly ducking
　　Observants that stretch their duties nicely.¹
KENT　Sir, in good sooth, or in sincere verity,
100　Under the allowance of your grand aspect,²
　　Whose influence like the wreath of radiant fire
　　In flickering Phoebus' front°—　　　　　　　　*the sun god's forehead*
CORNWALL　What mean'st thou by this?
KENT　To go out of my dialogue,° which you discommend so　*normal mode of speech*
105　　much. I know, sir, I am no flatterer. He that beguiled you in
　　a plain accent was a plain knave, which for my part I will not

5. Bonds of kinship, affection, marriage, or rank.
6. It was believed that the kingfisher (in Greek, *hal-cyon*) could be used as a weather vane when dead: suspended by a fine thread, its beak would turn whatever way the wind blew.
7. *Goose . . . Camelot:* Comparing him to a cackling goose, Kent tells Oswald that if he had him on Salisbury Plain, he would drive him all the way to Camelot, the legendary home of King Arthur.
8. *And constrains . . . nature:* and assumes the appearance although it is untrue to his real self. Alternatively (with "his" meaning "its"): and distorts the true shape

of plainness from what it naturally is (by turning it into disrespect).
9. If they will accept (Kent's attitude), well and good; if not, he is a plainspoken man (and does not care).
1. *than . . . nicely:* than twenty obsequious attendants who constantly bow idiotically and who perform their functions with excessive diligence ("nicely").
2. With the permission of your great countenance. "Aspect" also refers to the astrological position of a planet; Kent's bombastic language here raises Cornwall to the mock-heroic proportions of a heavenly body.

KENT   That such a slave as this should wear a sword
      Who wears no honesty. Such smiling rogues as these
      Like rats oft bite the holy cords[5] a-twain,
70   Which are t'intrince° t'unloose; smooth° every passion   *too intricate / flatter*
      That in the natures of their lords rebel,
      Being oil to fire, snow to the colder moods,
      Revenge affirm, and turn their halcyon beaks[6]
      With every gall and vary° of their masters,   *irritation and mood*
75   Knowing naught, like dogs, but following.
      A plague upon your epileptic° visage!   *distorted; grimacing*
      Smoile you° my speeches as° I were a fool?   *Do you smile at / as if*
      Goose, if I had you upon Sarum Plain,
      I'd drive ye cackling home to Camelot.[7]
80 CORNWALL   What, art thou mad, old fellow?
GLOUCESTER   How fell you out? Say that.
KENT   No contraries° hold more antipathy   *opposites*
      Than I and such a knave.
CORNWALL   Why dost thou call him knave? What is his
      fault?°   *offense*
85 KENT   His countenance likes° me not.   *pleases*
CORNWALL   No more, perchance, does mine, nor his, nor
      hers.
KENT   Sir, 'tis my occupation to be plain.
      I have seen better faces in my time
      Than stands on any shoulder that I see
      Before me at this instant.
90 CORNWALL   This is some fellow
      Who, having been praised for bluntness, doth affect
      A saucy roughness and constrains the garb
      Quite from his nature.[8] He cannot flatter, he.
      An honest mind and plain, he must speak truth
95   An they will take it so; if not, he's plain.[9]
      These kind of knaves I know, which in this plainness
      Harbor more craft and more corrupter ends
      Than twenty silly-ducking observants
      That stretch their duties nicely.[1]
100 KENT   Sir, in good faith, in sincere verity,
      Under th'allowance of your great aspect,[2]
      Whose influence like the wreath of radiant fire
      On flick'ring Phoebus' front°—   *the sun god's forehead*
CORNWALL   What mean'st by this?
KENT   To go out of my dialect,° which you discommend so   *normal mode of speech*
105   much. I know, sir, I am no flatterer. He that beguiled you in
      a plain accent was a plain knave, which for my part I will not

---

5. Bonds of kinship, affection, marriage, or rank.
6. It was believed that the kingfisher (in Greek, *halcyon*) could be used as a weather vane when dead: suspended by a fine thread, its beak would turn whatever way the wind blew.
7. *Goose . . . Camelot:* Comparing him to a cackling goose, Kent tells Oswald that if he had him on Salisbury Plain, he would drive him all the way to Camelot, the legendary home of King Arthur.
8. *and constrains . . . nature:* and assumes the appearance although it is untrue to his real self. Alternatively (with "his" meaning "its"): and distorts the true

shape of plainness from what it naturally is (by turning it into disrespect).
9. If they will accept (Kent's attitude), well and good; if not, he is a plainspoken man (and does not care).
1. *Than . . . nicely:* Than twenty obsequious attendants who constantly bow idiotically and who perform their functions with excessive diligence ("nicely").
2. With the permission of your great countenance. "Aspect" also refers to the astrological position of a planet; Kent's bombastic language here raises Cornwall to the mock-heroic proportions of a heavenly body.

be, though I should win your displeasure to entreat me to't.[3]
CORNWALL [to STEWARD]   What's the offense you gave him?
STEWARD   I never gave him any.

110   It pleased the King his master very late°   lately
To strike at me upon his misconstruction,°   misunderstanding (me)
When he, conjunct° and flattering his displeasure,   in league with
Tripped me behind; being down, insulted,° railed,   I being down, he insulted
And put upon him such a deal of man that,

115   That worthied him,[4] got praises of the King;
For him attempting who was self-subdued,[5]
And in the fleshment° of this dread exploit   excitement; flush
Drew on me here again.
KENT   None of these rogues and cowards, but Ajax is their

120   fool.[6]
CORNWALL   Bring forth the stocks, ho!
You stubborn miscreant knave, you reverend° braggart,   old; revered
We'll teach you.
KENT   I am too old to learn.
Call not your stocks for me. I serve the King,

125   On whose employments I was sent to you.
You should do small respect, show too bold malice,
Against the grace° and person° of my master,   majesty / personal honor
Stopping° his messenger.   By stocking
CORNWALL   Fetch forth the stocks! As I have life and honor,

130   There shall he sit till noon.
REGAN   Till noon? Till night, my lord, and all night too.
KENT   Why, madam, if I were your father's dog,
You could not use me so.
REGAN   Sir, being° his knave, I will.   since you are

135   CORNWALL   This is a fellow of the selfsame nature
Our sister° speak of. —Come, bring away the stocks.   sister-in-law
[Enter a SERVANT with the stocks.]
GLOUCESTER   Let me beseech your grace not to do so;
His fault is much, and the good King his master
Will check° him for't. Your purposed° low correction   reprimand / intended

140   Is such as basest and 'temnest° wretches   condemnest; most condemned
For pilf'rings and most common trespasses
Are punished with. The King must take it ill
That he's so slightly valued in his messenger,
Should have him thus restrained.
CORNWALL   I'll answer° that.   be responsible for

145   REGAN   My sister may receive it much more worse
To have her gentlemen abused, assaulted,
For following° her affairs. —Put in his legs.   carrying out
[KENT is put in the stocks.]
Come, my good lord, away.
[Exeunt all but GLOUCESTER and KENT.]
GLOUCESTER [to KENT]   I am sorry for thee, friend. 'Tis the
Duke's pleasure,

150   Whose disposition all the world well knows
Will not be rubbed° nor stopped. I'll entreat for thee.   obstructed

---

3. *He that . . . to't:* The person who tried to hood-
wink you with plain speaking was, indeed, a pure
knave—something I won't be, even if you were to beg
me to be one (a plain knave, or flatterer).
4. *And put . . . worthied him:* And put on such a show
of manliness that he was thought a worthy fellow.

5. For attacking a man who had already surrendered
(Kent attacking Oswald).
6. *None . . . fool:* Such rogues and cowards as these
talk as if they were greater warriors (and blusterers)
than Ajax; such rogues always make even mighty
Ajax out to be a fool.

be, though I should win your displeasure to entreat me to't.[3]

CORNWALL [*to* STEWARD]　What was th'offense you gave him?

STEWARD　I never gave him any.

110 It pleased the King his master very late°　　　　　　　　　　*lately*
To strike at me upon his misconstruction,°　　　*misunderstanding (me)*
When he, compact° and flattering his displeasure,　　　*in league with*
Tripped me behind; being down, insulted,° railed,　*I being down, he insulted*
And put upon him such a deal of man
115 That worthied him,[4] got praises of the King,
For him attempting who was self-subdued,[5]
And in the fleshment° of this dread exploit,　　　　*excitement; flush*
Drew on me here again.

KENT　None of these rogues and cowards
But Ajax is their fool.[6]

120 CORNWALL　　　　　　　　Fetch forth the stocks!

[*Exit a* SERVANT.]

You stubborn, ancient knave, you reverend° braggart,　　　*old; revered*
We'll teach you.

KENT　　　　　　Sir, I am too old to learn.
Call not your stocks for me. I serve the King,
On whose employment I was sent to you.
125 You shall do small respects, show too bold malice
Against the grace° and person° of my master,　　　*majesty / personal honor*
Stocking° his messenger.　　　　　　　　　　　　　　*By stocking*

CORNWALL　　　　　　　Fetch forth the stocks.
As I have life and honor, there shall he sit till noon.

REGAN　Till noon? Till night, my lord, and all night too.

130 KENT　Why, madam, if I were your father's dog,
You should not use me so.

REGAN　Sir, being° his knave, I will.　　　　　　　　*since you are*

Stocks brought out [*by a* SERVANT].

CORNWALL　This is a fellow of the selfsame color°　　　　*character*
Our sister° speaks of. —Come, bring away the stocks.　*sister-in-law*

135 GLOUCESTER　Let me beseech your grace not to do so;
The King his master needs must take it ill
That he, so slightly valued in his messenger,
Should have him thus restrained.

CORNWALL　　　　　　　　I'll answer° that.　　　*be responsible for*

REGAN　My sister may receive it much more worse
140 To have her gentleman abused, assaulted.

CORNWALL　Come, my lord, away.

Exeunt [CORNWALL *and* REGAN].

GLOUCESTER　I am sorry for thee, friend. 'Tis the Duke's
　　pleasure,
Whose disposition, all the world well knows,
Will not be rubbed° nor stopped. I'll entreat for thee.　　*obstructed*

---

3. *He that . . . to't:* The person who tried to hood-wink you with plain speaking was, indeed, a pure knave—something I won't be, even if you were to beg me to be one (a plain knave, or flatterer).
4. *And put . . . worthied him:* And put on such a show of manliness that he was thought a worthy fellow.

5. For attacking a man who had already surrendered (Kent attacking Oswald).
6. *None . . . fool:* Such rogues and cowards as these talk as if they were greater warriors (and blusterers) than Ajax; such rogues always make even mighty Ajax out to be a fool.

KENT   Pray you, do not, sir. I have watched° and traveled   *gone without sleep*
    hard;
    Sometime I shall sleep on't, the rest I'll whistle.
    A good man's fortune may grow out at heels.[7]
155   Give° you good morrow.   *God give*
GLOUCESTER   The Duke's to blame in this; 'twill be ill
    took.   *[Exit.]*
KENT   Good King, that must approve° the common saw,°   *prove / saying*
    Thou out of heaven's benediction comest
    To the warm sun.[8]
160   *[He takes out a letter.]* Approach, thou beacon[9] to this
      underglobe,
    That by thy comfortable beams I may
    Peruse this letter. Nothing almost sees my wrack
    But misery.[1] I know 'tis from Cordelia,
    Who hath most fortunately been informed
165   Of my obscurèd° course and shall find time   *hidden; disguised*
    From this enormous state,° seeking to give   *awful state of affairs*
    Losses their remedies. All weary and overwatch,°   *too long awake*
    Take vantage,° heavy eyes, not to behold   *the opportunity*
    This shameful lodging. Fortune, good night;
170   Smile; once more turn thy wheel.[2]
          [He] sleeps [and remains onstage].
          Enter EDGAR.
EDGAR   I hear myself proclaimed°   *declared an outlaw*
    And by the happy° hollow of a tree   *opportune*
    Escaped the hunt. No port° is free; no place   *seaport; exit*
    That guard and most unusual vigilance
175   Dost not attend my taking.° While° I may scape   *await my capture / Until*
    I will preserve myself and am bethought°   *resolved*
    To take the basest and most poorest shape
    That ever penury in contempt of° man   *for*
    Brought near to beast. My face I'll grime with filth,
180   Blanket my loins, elf all my hair with knots,[3]
    And with presented° nakedness outface   *exposed*
    The wind and persecution of the sky.
    The country gives me proof and precedent
    Of Bedlam beggars, who, with roaring voices,
185   Strike° in their numbed and mortified° bare arms   *Stick / deadened*
    Pins, wooden pricks, nails, sprigs of rosemary,
    And with this horrible object° from low service,   *spectacle*
    Poor pelting° villages, sheepcotes, and mills,   *paltry; contemptible*
    Sometime with lunatic bans,° sometime with prayers,   *curses*
190   Enforce their charity. Poor Turlygod,[4] poor Tom!
    That's something yet. Edgar I nothing am.[5]   *Exit.*
        Enter King [LEAR, FOOL, *and a* KNIGHT].
LEAR   'Tis strange that they should so depart from hence
    And not send back my messenger.

---

7. The fortunes of even good men sometimes wear thin.

8. *Thou ... sun:* You come from the blessing of heaven into the heat of the sun (go from good to bad).

9. That is, the sun.

1. *Nothing ... misery:* Only those suffering misery are granted miracles; any comfort seems miraculous to those who are miserable.

2. The goddess Fortune was traditionally depicted with a wheel to signify her mutability and caprice. She was believed to take pleasure in arbitrarily lowering those at the top of her wheel and raising those at the bottom.

3. Tangle the hair into "elf locks," supposed to be a favorite trick of malicious elves.

4. A word of unknown origin.

5. Edgar, I am nothing; I am no longer Edgar.

145 KENT Pray, do not, sir. I have watched° and traveled hard; *gone without sleep*
  Some time I shall sleep out, the rest I'll whistle.
  A good man's fortune may grow out at heels.[7]
  Give° you good morrow. *God give*
  GLOUCESTER The Duke's to blame in this; 'twill be ill
  taken. *Exit.*
150 KENT Good King, that must approve° the common saw,° *prove / saying*
  Thou out of heaven's benediction com'st
  To the warm sun.[8]
  Approach, thou beacon[9] to this under-globe,
  That by thy comfortable beams I may
155 Peruse this letter. Nothing almost sees miracles
  But misery.[1] I know 'tis from Cordelia,
  Who hath most fortunately been informed
  Of my obscurèd° course and shall find time *hidden; disguised*
  From this enormous state,° seeking to give *awful state of affairs*
160 Losses their remedies. All weary and o'er-watched,° *too long awake*
  Take vantage,° heavy eyes, not to behold *the opportunity*
  This shameful lodging. Fortune, goodnight,
  Smile once more; turn thy wheel.[2]
    [*Sleeps and remains onstage.*]
    Enter EDGAR.
  EDGAR I heard myself proclaimed° *declared an outlaw*
165 And by the happy° hollow of a tree *opportune*
  Escaped the hunt. No port° is free; no place *seaport; exit*
  That guard and most unusual vigilance
  Does not attend my taking.° Whiles° I may scape, *await my capture / Until*
  I will preserve myself and am bethought° *resolved*
170 To take the basest and most poorest shape
  That ever penury in contempt of° man *for*
  Brought near to beast. My face I'll grime with filth,
  Blanket my loins, elf all my hairs in knots,[3]
  And with presented° nakedness outface *exposed*
175 The winds and persecutions of the sky.
  The country gives me proof and precedent
  Of Bedlam beggars who, with roaring voices,
  Strike° in their numbed and mortified° arms *Stick / deadened*
  Pins, wooden pricks, nails, sprigs of rosemary,
180 And with this horrible object° from low farms, *spectacle*
  Poor pelting° villages, sheepcotes, and mills, *paltry; contemptible*
  Sometimes with lunatic bans,° sometime with prayers, *curses*
  Enforce their charity. Poor Turlygod,[4] poor Tom.
  That's something yet. Edgar I nothing am.[5] *Exit.*
    Enter LEAR, FOOL, *and* GENTLEMAN.[6]
185 LEAR 'Tis strange that they should so depart from home
  And not send back my messengers.

---

7. The fortunes of even good men sometimes wear thin.
8. *Thou . . . sun:* You come from the blessing of heaven into the heat of the sun (go from good to bad).
9. That is, the sun.
1. *Nothing . . . misery:* Only those suffering misery are granted miracles; any comfort seems miraculous to those who are miserable.
2. The goddess Fortune was traditionally depicted with a wheel to signify her mutability and caprice.

She was believed to take pleasure in arbitrarily lowering those at the top of her wheel and raising those at the bottom.
3. Tangle the hair into "elf locks," supposed to be a favorite trick of malicious elves.
4. A word of unknown origin.
5. Edgar, I am nothing; I am no longer Edgar.
6. F seems to reserve "Gentleman" for this particular character, who returns in 5.3.

KNIGHT   As I learned, the night before there was
195   No purpose° of his remove.°   *intention / change of*
KENT   Hail to thee, noble master.   *residence*
LEAR   How, mak'st thou this shame thy pastime?
FOOL   Ha, ha, look, he wears crewel garters.[6]
    Horses are tied by the heels, dogs and bears
200   By th' neck, monkeys by th' loins, and men
    By th' legs. When a man's overlusty at legs,[7]
    Then he wears wooden netherstocks.°   *knee socks*
LEAR   What's° he that hath so much thy place° mistook   *Who's / position*
    To set thee here?
205   KENT   It is both he and she: your son° and daughter.   *son-in-law*
LEAR   No.
KENT   Yes.
LEAR   No, I say.
KENT   I say yea.
LEAR   No, no, they would not.
KENT   Yes, they have.
LEAR   By Jupiter, I swear no. They durst not do't;
210   They would not, could not do't. 'Tis worse than murder
    To do upon respect[8] such violent outrage.
    Resolve° me with all modest° haste which way   *Inform / reasonable*
    Thou mayst deserve or they purpose this usage
    Coming from us.
KENT   My lord, when at their home
215   I did commend° your highness' letters to them,   *deliver*
    Ere I was risen from the place that showed
    My duty kneeling, came there a reeking° post,°   *sweating / messenger*
    Stewed in his haste, half breathless, panting forth,
    From Gonorill his mistress, salutations,
220   Delivered letters 'spite of intermission,[9]
    Which presently° they read. On whose contents   *immediately*
    They summoned up their men,° straight° took horse,   *retinue / straightaway*
    Commanded me to follow and attend the leisure
    Of their answer, gave me cold looks,
225   And meeting here the other messenger,
    Whose welcome I perceived had poisoned mine—
    Being the very° fellow that of late   *same*
    Displayed so saucily° against your highness—   *Acted so insolently*
    Having more man° than wit° about me, drew.   *courage / sense*
230   He raised the house with loud and coward cries.
    Your son and daughter found this trespass worth°   *deserving of*
    This shame which here it suffers.

---

6. Worsted garters, punning on "cruel." Crewel is a thin yarn made of twisted fibers. The Fool is actually referring to the stocks in which Kent's feet are held.
7. When a man's liable to run away.

8. To do to one who deserves respect.
9. Regardless of interrupting me; despite the interruptions in his account (as he gasped for breath).

GENTLEMAN As I learned,
The night before there was no purpose in them°   *they had no intention*
Of this remove.°   *change of residence*

KENT Hail to thee, noble master.

LEAR Ha? Mak'st thou this shame thy pastime?

KENT No, my lord.

190 FOOL Ha, ha, he wears cruel garters![7] Horses are tied by the
heads, dogs and bears by th' neck, monkeys by th' loins, and
men by th' legs. When a man's overlusty at legs,[8] then he
wears wooden nether-stocks.°   *knee socks*

LEAR What's° he that hath so much thy place° mistook   *Who's / position*
To set thee here?

195 KENT It is both he and she:
Your son° and daughter.   *son-in-law*

LEAR No.

KENT Yes.

LEAR No, I say.

200 KENT I say yea.

LEAR By Jupiter, I swear no.

KENT By Juno,[9] I swear ay.

LEAR They durst not do't;
They could not, would not do't. 'Tis worse than murder
205 To do upon respect[1] such violent outrage.
Resolve° me with all modest° haste which way   *Inform / reasonable*
Thou mightst deserve, or they impose, this usage,
Coming from us.

KENT My lord, when at their home
I did commend° your highness' letters to them,   *deliver*
210 Ere I was risen from the place that showed
My duty kneeling, came there a reeking° post,°   *sweating / messenger*
Stewed in his haste, half breathless, painting° forth   *panting*
From Gonerill, his mistress, salutations,
Delivered letters 'spite of intermission,[2]
215 Which presently° they read. On those contents   *immediately*
They summoned up their meiny,° straight° took horse,   *retinue / straightaway*
Commanded me to follow and attend
The leisure of their answer, gave me cold looks,
And meeting here the other messenger,
220 Whose welcome I perceived had poisoned mine—
Being the very° fellow which of late   *same*
Displayed so saucily° against your highness—   *Acted so insolently*
Having more man° than wit° about me, drew.   *courage / sense*
He raised the house with loud and coward cries.
225 Your son and daughter found this trespass worth°   *deserving of*
The shame which here it suffers.

---

7. Worsted garters, punning on "crewel," a thin yarn. The Fool is actually referring to the stocks in which Kent's feet are held.
8. When a man's liable to run away.
9. Queen of the Roman gods and wife of Jupiter, with whom she constantly quarreled.
1. To do to one who deserves respect.
2. Regardless of interrupting me; despite the interruptions in his account (as he gasped for breath).

LEAR   Oh, how this mother° swells up toward my heart!   *hysteria*
    Hysterica passio, down, thou climbing sorrow,[1]
235   Thy element's° below! Where is this daughter?   *natural place is*
KENT   With the Earl, sir: within.
LEAR   Follow me not; stay there.   [*Exit.*]
KNIGHT   Made you no more offense than what you speak of?
KENT   No. How chance the King comes with so small a train?
240 FOOL   An° thou hadst been set in the stocks for that question,   *If*
    thou hadst well deserved it.
KENT   Why, Fool?
FOOL   We'll set thee to school to an ant, to teach thee there's
    no laboring in the winter.[2] All that follow their noses are led
245   by their eyes but blind men, and there's not a nose among a
    hundred but can smell him that's stinking.° Let go thy hold   *(as his fortunes decay)*
    when a great wheel runs down a hill, lest it break thy neck
    with following it. But the great one that goes up the hill,[3] let
    him draw thee after. When a wise man gives thee better
250   counsel, give me mine again. I would have none but knaves
    follow it, since a fool gives it.
    [*Sings.*]   That sir that serves for gain,
        And follows but for form,
        Will pack° when it begin to rain,   *pack up and go*
255   And leave thee in the storm.
        But I will tarry; the Fool will stay,
        And let the wise man fly.
        The knave turns fool that runs away,[4]
        The fool no knave, pardie.°   *by God (pardieu)*
260 KENT   Where learned you this, Fool?
FOOL   Not in the stocks.
    Enter LEAR *and* GLOUCESTER.
LEAR   Deny to speak with me? They're sick, they're weary?
    They traveled hard tonight? Mere justice.
    Ay, the images of revolt and flying off![5]
    Fetch me a better answer.

---

1. Hysterica . . . *sorrow*: *Hysterica passio* (a Latin expression originating in the Greek *steiros*, "suffering in the womb") was an inflammation of the senses. In Renaissance medicine, vapors from the abdomen were thought to rise up through the body, and in women, the uterus itself was thought to wander around.
2. Ants, proverbially prudent, store food in the summer and thus do not work in the winter. Implicitly, a wise person should know better than to look for sustenance to an old man who has fallen on wintry times.
3. A great wheel is a figure for Lear and of Fortune's wheel itself, which has swung downward.
4. The scoundrel who runs away is the real fool.
5. *images of*: signs of. *flying off*: desertion; insurrection.

FOOL   Winter's not gone yet, if the wild geese fly that way.[3]
Fathers that wear rags
Do make their children blind.[4]
230   But fathers that bear bags
Shall see their children kind.
Fortune, that arrant whore,
Ne'er turns the key° to th' poor.   *opens the door*
But for all this, thou shalt have as many dolors[5] for thy
235   daughters as thou canst tell° in a year.   *count*
LEAR   Oh, how this mother° swells up toward my heart!   *hysteria*
Hysterica passio, down, thou climbing sorrow,[6]
Thy element's° below! Where is this daughter?   *natural place is*
KENT   With the Earl, sir, here within.
240   LEAR   Follow me not. Stay here.   *Exit.*
GENTLEMAN   Made you no more offense but what you
speak of?
KENT   None. How chance the King comes with so small a
number?
245   FOOL   An thou hadst been set i'th' stocks for that question,
thou'dst well deserved it.
KENT   Why, Fool?
FOOL   We'll set thee to school to an ant, to teach thee there's
no laboring i'th' winter.[7] All that follow their noses are led
250   by their eyes but blind men, and there's not a nose among
twenty but can smell him that's stinking.° Let go thy hold   *(as his fortunes decay)*
when a great wheel runs down a hill,[8] lest it break thy neck
with following. But the great one that goes upward, let him
draw thee after. When a wise man gives thee better counsel,
255   give me mine again. I would have none but knaves follow it
since a fool gives it.
[*Sings.*]   That sir which serves and seeks for gain,
And follows but for form,
Will pack° when it begins to rain,   *pack up and go*
260   And leave thee in the storm,
But I will tarry; the Fool will stay,
And let the wise man fly.
The knave turns fool that runs away,[9]
The Fool no knave, pardie.°   *by God (pardieu)*
Enter LEAR *and* GLOUCESTER.
265   KENT   Where learned you this, Fool?
FOOL   Not i'th' stocks, Fool.
LEAR   Deny to speak with me?
They are sick? They are weary?
They have traveled all the night? Mere fetches,°   *ruses; pretexts*
270   The images of revolt and flying off.[1]
Fetch me a better answer.

---

3. Things will get worse according to such omens.
4. Blind to their father's needs.
5. Pains, sorrows; punning on "dollar," the English term for the German "thaler," a large silver coin.
6. Hysterica . . . *sorrow: Hysterica passio* (a Latin expression originating in the Greek *steiros,* "suffering in the womb") was an inflammation of the senses. In Renaissance medicine, vapors from the abdomen were thought to rise up through the body, and in women, the uterus itself was thought to wander around.

7. Ants, proverbially prudent, store food in the summer and thus do not work in the winter. Implicitly, a wise person should know better than to look for sustenance to an old man who has fallen on wintry times.
8. A great wheel is a figure for Lear and of Fortune's wheel itself, which has swung downward.
9. The scoundrel who runs away is the real fool.
1. *images of:* signs of. *flying off:* desertion; insurrection.

265 GLOUCESTER   My dear lord,
     You know the fiery quality° of the Duke,   *disposition*
     How unremoveable and fixed he is
     In his own course.
     LEAR   Vengeance, death, plague, confusion!°   *destruction*
270 What "fiery quality"? Why, Gloucester, Gloucester,
     I'd speak with the Duke of Cornwall and his wife.

     GLOUCESTER   Ay, my good lord.
     LEAR   The King would speak with Cornwall, the dear father
     Would with his daughter speak, commands her service.
275 "Fiery Duke"? Tell the hot Duke that Lear—
     No, but not yet, maybe he is not well.
     Infirmity doth still° neglect all office°   *always / obligation*
     Whereto our health is bound. We are not ourselves
     When nature, being oppressed, command the mind
280 To suffer with the body. I'll forbear,
     And am fallen out with my more headier will⁶
     To take° the indisposed and sickly fit   *mistake*
     For the sound man. Death on my state!⁷ Wherefore°   *Why*
     Should he sit here? This act persuades me
285 That this remotion° of the Duke and her   *remoteness; aloofness*
     Is practice° only. Give me my servant forth.   *trickery*
     Tell the Duke and 's wife I'll speak with them
     Now, presently.° Bid them come forth and hear me,   *at once*
     Or at their chamber door I'll beat the drum
290 Till it cry sleep to death.⁸
     GLOUCESTER   I would have all well betwixt you.
     LEAR   Oh, my heart, my heart!
     FOOL   Cry to it, nuncle, as the Cockney° did to the eels when   *Londoner (city woman)*
     she put 'em i'th' paste° alive. She rapped 'em o'th' coxcombs°   *pie; pastry / heads*
295 with a stick and cried, "Down, wantons,° down!" 'Twas her   *rogues*
     brother that, in pure kindness to his horse, buttered his hay.⁹
                    Enter Duke [of CORNWALL] *and* REGAN.
     LEAR   Good morrow to you both.
     CORNWALL   Hail to your grace.
                    [KENT *here set at liberty*.]
     REGAN   I am glad to see your highness.
     LEAR   Regan, I think you are. I know what reason
300 I have to think so. If thou shouldst not be glad,
     I would divorce me from thy mother's tomb,
     Sepulch'ring° an adultress. [*to* KENT] Yea, are you free?   *Because it entombed*
     Some other time for that. —Beloved Regan,
     Thy sister is naught.° O Regan, she hath tied   *wicked; nothing*
305 Sharp-toothed unkindness, like a vulture, here.¹
     I can scarce speak to thee. Thou'lt not believe

6. And disagree with my (earlier) more rash intention.
7. May my royal authority end (an oath). Ironically, this has already happened.
8. Till the noise kills sleep.
9. Like that of his sister (who wanted to make eel pie without killing the eels), his kindness was misplaced:

horses will not eat buttered hay. The anecdote about the eels is reminiscent of Lear's attempt earlier in the scene to quell his grieving heart: "*Hysterica passio*, down, thou climbing sorrow."
1. Lear probably gestures to his heart.

GLOUCESTER My dear lord,
You know the fiery quality° of the Duke,   *disposition*
How unremoveable and fixed he is
In his own course.

LEAR   Vengeance, plague, death, confusion!°   *destruction*
275   "Fiery"? What "quality"? Why, Gloucester, Gloucester,
I'll speak with the Duke of Cornwall and his wife.

GLOUCESTER   Well, my good lord, I have informed them so.

LEAR   Informed them? Dost thou understand me, man?

GLOUCESTER   Ay, my good lord.

280   LEAR   The King would speak with Cornwall. The dear father
Would with his daughter speak, commands, tends° service.   *awaits*
Are they informed of this? My breath and blood!
Fiery? The fiery Duke? Tell the hot Duke that—
No, but not yet; maybe he is not well.

285   Infirmity doth still° neglect all office°   *always / obligation*
Whereto our health is bound. We are not ourselves
When nature, being oppressed, commands the mind
To suffer with the body. I'll forbear
And am fallen out with my more headier will,[2]

290   To take° the indisposed and sickly fit   *mistake*
For the sound man. Death on my state![3] Wherefore°   *Why*
Should he sit here? This act persuades me
That this remotion° of the Duke and her   *remoteness; aloofness*
Is practice° only. Give me my servant forth.   *trickery*

295   Go tell the Duke and 's wife I'd speak with them
Now, presently.° Bid them come forth and hear me,   *at once*
Or at their chamber door I'll beat the drum
Till it cry sleep to death.[4]

GLOUCESTER   I would have all well betwixt you.   *Exit.*

300   LEAR   Oh, me, my heart! My rising heart! But down.

FOOL   Cry to it, nuncle, as the Cockney° did to the eels when   *Londoner (city woman)*
she put 'em i'th' paste° alive. She knapped 'em o'th' cox-   *pie; pastry*
combs° with a stick and cried, "Down, wantons,° down!"   *heads / rogues*
'Twas her brother that, in pure kindness to his horse, but-

305   tered his hay.[5]

                Enter CORNWALL, REGAN, GLOUCESTER, [*and*]
                SERVANTS.

LEAR   Good morrow to you both.

CORNWALL   Hail to your grace.

                KENT *here set at liberty.*

REGAN   I am glad to see your highness.

LEAR   Regan, I think you are. I know what reason
I have to think so. If thou shouldst not be glad,

310   I would divorce me from thy mother's tomb,
Sepulch'ring° an adultress. [*to* KENT] Oh, are you free?   *Because it entombed*
Some other time for that. —Beloved Regan,
Thy sister's naught!° O Regan, she hath tied   *wicked; nothing*
Sharp-toothed unkindness, like a vulture, here.[6]

315   I can scarce speak to thee. Thou'lt not believe

---

2. And disagree with my (earlier) more rash intention.
3. May my royal authority end (an oath). Ironically, this has already happened.
4. Till the noise kills sleep.
5. Like that of his sister (who wanted to make eel pie without killing the eels), his kindness was misplaced:

horses will not eat buttered hay. The anecdote about the eels is reminiscent of Lear's attempt earlier in the scene to quell his grieving heart: "Hysterica passio, down, thou climbing sorrow."
6. Lear probably gestures to his heart.

Of how deprived a quality—O Regan!

REGAN   I pray, sir, take patience. I have hope
You less know how to value her desert
310 Than she to slack her duty.[2]

LEAR   My curses on her!
REGAN   O sir, you are old;
Nature° on you stands on the very verge   Life
Of her confine.° You should be ruled and led   Of its limit
By some discretion° that discerns your state   discreet person
315 Better than you yourself. Therefore, I pray
That to our sister you do make return.
Say you have wronged her, sir.
LEAR   Ask her forgiveness?
Do you mark how this becomes the house?[3]
Dear daughter, I confess that I am old;
320 Age° is unnecessary. [*He kneels.*] On my knees, I beg   An old man
That you'll vouchsafe me raiment,° bed, and food.   promise me clothing
REGAN   Good sir, no more; these are unsightly tricks.
Return you to my sister.
LEAR [*rising*]   No, Regan,
She hath abated° me of half my train,   deprived
325 Looked black upon me, struck me with her tongue
Most serpent-like upon the very heart.
All° the stored vengeances of heaven fall   Let all
On her ungrateful top.° Strike her young bones,   head
You taking° airs, with lameness.   infectious; malignant
CORNWALL   Fie, fie, sir.
330 LEAR   You nimble lightnings, dart your blinding flames
Into her scornful eyes. Infect her beauty,
You fen-sucked fogs, drawn by the powerful sun[4]
To fall and blast her pride.
REGAN   Oh, the blest gods! So will you wish on me
335 When the rash mood—
LEAR   No, Regan, thou shalt never have my curse;
The tender-hested° nature shall not give thee o'er   pledged to tenderness
To harshness. Her eyes are fierce, but thine
Do comfort and not burn. 'Tis not in thee
340 To grudge my pleasures, to cut off my train,
To bandy hasty words, to scant my sizes,°   reduce my allowances
And, in conclusion, to oppose the bolt°   lock the door
Against my coming in. Thou better knowest
The offices° of nature, bond of childhood,   duties
345 Effects° of courtesy, dues of gratitude.   Actions
Thy half of the kingdom hast thou not forgot,
Wherein I thee endowed.

---

2. *I have . . . duty*: I expect that you are worse at
valuing her merit than she is at neglecting her duty.
The double negative here ("less," "slack") is acceptable Jacobean usage.

3. Do you see how appropriate this is among members of a family (spoken ironically)?
4. The sun was thought to suck poisonous vapors
from marshy ground.

With how depraved a quality—O Regan!
REGAN   I pray you, sir, take patience. I have hope
    You less know how to value her desert
    Than she to scant her duty.[7]
    LEAR   Say? How is that?
320   REGAN   I cannot think my sister in the least
    Would fail her obligation. If, sir, perchance
    She have restrained the riots of your followers,
    'Tis on such ground and to such wholesome end
    As clears her from all blame.
    LEAR   My curses on her!
325   REGAN   O sir, you are old;
    Nature° in you stands on the very verge   *Life*
    Of his confine.° You should be ruled and led   *Of its limit*
    By some discretion° that discerns your state   *discreet person*
    Better than you yourself. Therefore, I pray you
330   That to our sister you do make return.
    Say you have wronged her.
    LEAR   Ask her forgiveness?
    Do you but mark how this becomes the house?[8]
    Dear daughter, I confess that I am old;
    Age° is unnecessary. [*He kneels.*] On my knees I beg   *An old man*
335   That you'll vouchsafe me raiment,° bed, and food.   *promise me clothing*
    REGAN   Good sir, no more; these are unsightly tricks.
    Return you to my sister.
    LEAR [*rising*]   Never, Regan.
    She hath abated° me of half my train,   *deprived*
    Looked black upon me, struck me with her tongue
340   Most serpent-like upon the very heart.
    All° the stored vengeances of heaven fall   *Let all*
    On her ingrateful top.° Strike her young bones,   *head*
    You taking° airs, with lameness.   *infectious; malignant*
    CORNWALL   Fie, sir, fie!
    LEAR   You nimble lightnings, dart your blinding flames
345   Into her scornful eyes. Infect her beauty,
    You fen-sucked fogs, drawn by the pow'rful sun[9]
    To fall and blister.
    REGAN   Oh, the blest gods!
    So will you wish on me when the rash mood is on.
    LEAR   No, Regan, thou shalt never have my curse.
350   Thy tender-hafted[1] nature shall not give
    Thee o'er to harshness. Her eyes are fierce, but thine
    Do comfort and not burn. 'Tis not in thee
    To grudge my pleasures, to cut off my train,
    To bandy hasty words, to scant my sizes,°   *reduce my allowances*
355   And, in conclusion, to oppose the bolt°   *lock the door*
    Against my coming in. Thou better know'st
    The offices° of nature, bond of childhood,   *duties*
    Effects° of courtesy, dues of gratitude.   *Actions*
    Thy half o'th' kingdom hast thou not forgot,
    Wherein I thee endowed.

7. *I have . . . duty:* I expect that you are worse at valuing her merit than she is at neglecting her duty. The
double negative here ("less," "scant") is acceptable
Jacobean usage.
8. Do you see how appropriate this is among members of a family (spoken ironically)?
9. The sun was thought to suck poisonous vapors
from marshy ground.
1. Tenderly placed; firmly set in a tender disposition
(as a knife blade into its haft).

REGAN   Good sir, to th' purpose.°   *get to the point*
LEAR   Who put my man i'th' stocks?
    [*A sennet sounds.*]
CORNWALL   What trumpet's that?
    Enter [*Oswald the*] STEWARD.
350   REGAN   I know't my sister's; this approves° her letters   *confirms*
    That she would soon be here. [*to* STEWARD] Is your lady
      come?
LEAR   This is a slave whose easy-borrowed pride[5]
    Dwells in the fickle grace of her 'a° follows.   *he*
    [*He strikes* STEWARD.] Out, varlet,° from my sight!   *wretch*
                  [*Exit* STEWARD.]
CORNWALL   What means your grace?
    Enter GONORILL.
355   GONORILL   Who struck my servant? Regan, I have good hope
    Thou didst not know on't.°   *of it*
LEAR   Who comes here? O heavens,
    If you do love old men, if your sweet sway allow
    Obedience, if yourselves are old, make it your cause;
    Send down and take my part.
360   [*to* GONORILL] Art not ashamed to look upon this beard?
    O Regan, wilt thou take her by the hand?
GONORILL   Why not by the hand, sir? How have I offended?
    All's not offense that indiscretion finds
    And dotage terms so.
LEAR   O sides,[6] you are too tough!
365   Will you yet hold? How came my man i'th' stocks?
CORNWALL   I set him there, sir, but his own disorders°   *disorderly behavior*
    Deserved much less advancement.[7]
LEAR   You, did you?
REGAN   I pray you, father, being weak, seem so.°   *behave so*
    If till the expiration of your month
370   You will return and sojourn with my sister,
    Dismissing half your train, come then to me.
    I am now from home and out of that provision
    Which shall be needful for your entertainment.
LEAR   Return to her, and fifty men dismissed?
375   No, rather I abjure all roofs and choose
    To wage against the enmity of the air,
    To be a comrade with the wolf and owl,
    Necessity's sharp pinch.[8] Return with her?
    Why, the hot blood in France that dowerless
380   Took our youngest born, I could as well be brought
    To knee° his throne and squire-like pension beg,   *kneel to*
    To keep base life afoot. Return with her?
    Persuade me rather to be slave and sumpter°   *packhorse*
    To this detested groom.°   *(the Steward)*
GONORILL   At your choice, sir.
385   LEAR   Now, I prithee, daughter, do not make me mad.
    I will not trouble thee, my child; farewell.
    We'll no more meet, no more see one another.
    But yet thou art my flesh, my blood, my daughter,

---

5. Unmerited and unpaid-for arrogance; "pride" may also refer to Oswald's fine clothing received for his services to Gonorill.
6. Chest, where Lear's heart is swelling with emotion.

7. Deserved far worse treatment.
8. *To wage . . . pinch:* To counter the harshness of the elements with the hardness brought on by necessity. *pinch:* stress, pressure.

360 REGAN   Good sir, to th' purpose.°   *get to the point*

LEAR   Who put my man i'th' stocks?

         Enter [Oswald the] STEWARD. *Tucket within.*

CORNWALL   What trumpet's that?

REGAN   I know't my sister's; this approves° her letter   *confirms*

   That she would soon be here. [*to* STEWARD] Is your lady

     come?

LEAR   This is a slave whose easy borrowed pride[2]

365   Dwells in the sickly grace of her he follows.

   [*to* STEWARD] Out, varlet,° from my sight.   *wretch*

CORNWALL   What means your grace?

LEAR   Who stocked my servant? Regan, I have good hope

   Thou didst not know on't.°   *of it*

      Enter GONERILL.

                     Who comes here? O heavens,

   If you do love old men, if your sweet sway

370   Allow obedience, if you yourselves are old,

   Make it your cause: send down and take my part.

   [*to* GONERILL] Art not ashamed to look upon this beard?

   O Regan, will you take her by the hand?

GONERILL   Why not by th' hand, sir? How have I offended?

375   All's not offense that indiscretion finds

   And dotage terms so.

LEAR   O sides,[3] you are too tough! Will you yet hold?

   How came my man i'th' stocks?

CORNWALL   I set him there, sir, but his own disorders°   *disorderly behavior*

   Deserved much less advancement.[4]

380 LEAR   You, did you?

REGAN   I pray you, father, being weak, seem so.°   *behave so*

   If till the expiration of your month

   You will return and sojourn with my sister,

   Dismissing half your train, come then to me.

385   I am now from home and out of that provision

   Which shall be needful for your entertainment.

LEAR   Return to her, and fifty men dismissed?

   No, rather I abjure all roofs and choose

   To wage against the enmity o'th' air,

390   To be a comrade with the wolf and owl,

   Necessity's sharp pinch.[5] Return with her?

   Why, the hot-blooded France, that dowerless took

   Our youngest born, I could as well be brought

   To knee° his throne and squire-like pension beg,   *kneel to*

395   To keep base life afoot. Return with her?

   Persuade me rather to be slave and sumpter°   *packhorse*

   To this detested groom.°   *(Oswald)*

GONERILL   At your choice, sir.

LEAR   I prithee, daughter, do not make me mad.

   I will not trouble thee, my child; farewell.

400   We'll no more meet, no more see one another.

   But yet thou art my flesh, my blood, my daughter,

---

2. Unmerited and unpaid-for arrogance; "pride" may also refer to Oswald's fine clothing received for his services to Gonerill.

3. Chest, where Lear's heart is swelled with emotion.

4. Deserved far worse treatment.

5. *To wage . . . pinch:* To counter the harshness of the elements with the hardness brought on by necessity. *pinch:* stress, pressure.

Or rather a disease that lies within my flesh,
390 Which I must needs call mine. Thou art a boil,
A plague sore, an embossed° carbuncle in my   *a swollen*
Corrupted blood. But I'll not chide thee.
Let shame come when it will; I do not call° it.   *call upon*
I do not bid the thunder-bearer° shoot,   *(Jove)*
395 Nor tell tales of thee to high-judging Jove.
Mend° when thou canst; be better at thy leisure.   *Make amends*
I can be patient; I can stay with Regan,
I and my hundred knights.
REGAN   Not altogether so, sir. I look not for° you yet,   *I did not expect*
400 Nor am provided for your fit welcome.
Give ear, sir, to my sister, for those
That mingle reason with your passion[9]
Must be content to think you are old, and so.
But she knows what she does.
405 LEAR   Is this well° spoken now?   *earnestly*
REGAN   I dare avouch° it, sir. What, fifty followers?   *vouch for*
Is it not well? What should you need of more?
Yea, or so many, sith° that both charge° and danger   *since / expense*
Speaks 'gainst so great a number? How in a house
410 Should many people under two commands
Hold amity? 'Tis hard, almost impossible.
GONORILL   Why might not you, my lord, receive attendance
From those that she calls servants or from mine?
REGAN   Why not, my lord? If then they chanced to slack°   *neglect*
you,
415 We could control them. If you will come to me—
For now I spy a danger—I entreat you
To bring but five-and-twenty; to no more
Will I give place or notice.°   *acknowledgment*
LEAR   I gave you all—
REGAN   And in good time° you gave it.   *it was about time*
420 LEAR   —Made you my guardians, my depositaries,°   *trustees*
But kept a reservation° to be followed   *reserved a right*
With such a number. What, must I come to you
With five-and-twenty, Regan? Said you so?
REGAN   And speak't again, my lord: no more with me.
425 LEAR   Those wicked creatures yet do seem well-favored°   *attractive*
When others are more wicked; not being the worst
Stands in some rank of praise.[1] [to GONORILL] I'll go with
thee:
Thy fifty yet doth double five-and-twenty,
And thou art twice her love.
GONORILL   Hear me, my lord.
430 What need you five-and-twenty, ten, or five
To follow in a house where twice so many
Have a command to tend you?
REGAN   What needs one?
LEAR   Oh, reason not the need! Our basest beggars
Are in the poorest thing superfluous.[2]
435 Allow not° nature more than nature needs,   *If you don't allow*
Man's life is cheap as beast's. Thou art a lady:

---

9. For those who temper your passionate argument
with their own calm reasoning.
1. Deserves some degree ("rank") of praise.

2. *Our . . . superfluous:* Even the lowliest beggars
have something more than the barest minimum.

    Or rather a disease that's in my flesh
    Which I must needs call mine. Thou art a boil,
    A plague sore, or embossèd° carbuncle   *swollen*
405   In my corrupted blood. But I'll not chide thee.
    Let shame come when it will; I do not call° it.   *call upon*
    I do not bid the thunder-bearer° shoot,   *(Jove)*
    Nor tell tales of thee to high-judging Jove.
    Mend° when thou canst; be better at thy leisure.   *Make amends*
410   I can be patient: I can stay with Regan,
    I and my hundred knights.
REGAN   Not altogether so.
    I looked not for° you yet, nor am provided   *I did not expect*
    For your fit welcome. Give ear, sir, to my sister,
    For those that mingle reason with your passion[6]
415   Must be content to think you old and so.
    But she knows what she does.
LEAR   Is this well° spoken?   *earnestly*
REGAN   I dare avouch° it, sir. What, fifty followers?   *vouch for*
    Is it not well? What should you need of more?
    Yea, or so many, sith° that both charge° and danger *since / expense*
420   Speak 'gainst so great a number? How in one house
    Should many people under two commands
    Hold amity? 'Tis hard, almost impossible.
GONERILL   Why might not you, my lord, receive attendance
    From those that she calls servants, or from mine?
425 REGAN   Why not, my lord?
    If then they chanced to slack° ye,   *neglect*
    We could control them. If you will come to me—
    For now I spy a danger—I entreat you
    To bring but five-and-twenty; to no more
430   Will I give place or notice.°   *acknowledgment*
LEAR   I gave you all—
REGAN   And in good time° you gave it.   *it was about time*
LEAR   —Made you my guardians, my depositaries,°   *trustees*
    But kept a reservation° to be followed   *reserved a right*
    With such a number. What, must I come to you
435   With five-and-twenty, Regan? Said you so?
REGAN   And speak't again, my lord; no more with me.
LEAR   Those wicked creatures yet do look well-favored° *attractive*
    When others are more wicked; not being the worst
    Stands in some rank of praise.[7] [*to* GONERILL] I'll go with thee:
440   Thy fifty yet doth double five-and-twenty,
    And thou art twice her love.
GONERILL   Hear me, my lord.
    What need you five-and-twenty? Ten? Or five?
    To follow in a house where twice so many
    Have a command to tend you?
REGAN   What need one?
445 LEAR   Oh, reason not the need! Our basest beggars
    Are in the poorest thing superfluous.[8]
    Allow not° nature more than nature needs,   *If you don't allow*
    Man's life is cheap as beast's. Thou art a lady:

---

6. For those who temper your passionate argument with their own calm reasoning.
7. Deserves some degree ("rank") of praise.

8. *Our . . . superfluous:* Even the lowliest beggars have something more than the barest minimum.

If only to go warm were gorgeous,
Why, nature needs not what thou gorgeous wearest,
Which scarcely keeps thee warm.³ But for true need,
440   You heavens, give me that patience,° patience I need.   endurance
You see me here, you gods, a poor old fellow,
As full of grief as age, wretched in both.
If it be you that stirs these daughters' hearts
Against their father, fool me not too much
445   To bear it lamely.⁴ Touch me with noble anger.
Oh, let not women's weapons, water drops,
Stain my man's cheeks. No, you unnatural hags,
I will have such revenges on you both
That all the world shall—I will do such things—
450   What they are, yet I know not, but they shall be
The terrors of the earth! You think I'll weep.
No, I'll not weep. I have full cause of weeping,
But this heart shall break in a hundred thousand flows,°   fragments
Or e'er° I'll weep. O Fool, I shall go mad.   Before
                    Exeunt LEAR, [GLOUCESTER,] KENT, *and* FOOL.
455   CORNWALL   Let us withdraw, 'twill be a storm.
REGAN   This house is little; the old man and his people
Cannot be well bestowed.°   lodged
GONORILL   'Tis his own blame hath put himself from° rest   deprived himself of
And must needs taste his folly.
460   REGAN   For his particular,° I'll receive him gladly,   single self
But not one follower.
CORNWALL   So am I purposed. Where is my lord of Gloucester?
REGAN   Followed the old man forth.
                    Enter GLOUCESTER.
                                      He is returned.
GLOUCESTER   The King is in high rage and will° I know not   will go
whither.
465   REGAN   'Tis good to give him way; he leads himself.
GONORILL   My lord, entreat him by no means to stay.
GLOUCESTER   Alack, the night comes on, and the bleak winds
Do sorely rustle. For many miles about there's not a bush.
REGAN   O sir, to willful men
470   The injuries that they themselves procure
Must be their schoolmasters. Shut up your doors.
He is attended with a desperate° train,   violent
And what they may incense° him to, being apt   incite
To have his ear abused,° wisdom bids fear.   deceived
475   CORNWALL   Shut up your doors, my lord. 'Tis a wild night.
My Regan counsels well. Come out o'th' storm.   *Exeunt.*

---

3. *If . . . thee warm:* If gorgeousness in clothes is
measured by the warmth they provide, your elaborate
clothes are superfluous, for they barely cover your
body.
4. *fool . . . lamely:* do not make me so foolish as to
accept it meekly.

If only to go warm were gorgeous,
450 Why, nature needs not what thou gorgeous wear'st,
Which scarcely keeps thee warm.⁹ But for true need,
You heavens, give me that patience,° patience I need!   *endurance*
You see me here, you gods, a poor old man,
As full of grief as age, wretched in both.
455 If it be you that stirs these daughters' hearts
Against their father, fool me not so much
To bear it tamely.¹ Touch me with noble anger,
And let not women's weapons, water drops,
Stain my man's cheeks. No, you unnatural hags,
460 I will have such revenges on you both
That all the world shall—I will do such things—
What they are, yet I know not, but they shall be
The terrors of the earth! You think I'll weep.
No, I'll not weep. I have full cause of weeping.
          Storm and tempest.
465 But this heart shall break into a hundred thousand flaws°   *fragments*
Or e'er° I'll weep. O Fool, I shall go mad.   *Before*
          Exeunt [with GLOUCESTER, KENT, FOOL,
                    and Attendants].
CORNWALL   Let us withdraw; 'twill be a storm.
REGAN   This house is little; the old man and 's people
Cannot be well bestowed.°   *lodged*
470 GONERILL   'Tis his own blame hath put himself from° rest   *deprived himself of*
And must needs taste his folly.
REGAN   For his particular,° I'll receive him gladly,   *single self*
But not one follower.
GONERILL   So am I purposed.
Where is my lord of Gloucester?
          Enter GLOUCESTER.
475 CORNWALL   Followed the old man forth; he is returned.
GLOUCESTER   The King is in high rage.
CORNWALL   Whither is he going?
GLOUCESTER   He calls to horse, but will° I know not whither.   *will go*
CORNWALL   'Tis best to give him way; he leads himself.
480 GONERILL   My lord, entreat him by no means to stay.
GLOUCESTER   Alack, the night comes on, and the high winds
Do sorely ruffle.° For many miles about   *bluster*
There's scarce a bush.
REGAN   O sir, to willful men
The injuries that they themselves procure
485 Must be their schoolmasters. Shut up your doors:
He is attended with a desperate° train,   *violent*
And what they may incense° him to, being apt   *incite*
To have his ear abused,° wisdom bids fear.   *deceived*
CORNWALL   Shut up your doors, my lord; 'tis a wild night.
490 My Regan counsels well: come out o'th' storm.   *Exeunt.*

---

9. *If . . . thee warm:* If gorgeousness in clothes is measured by the warmth they provide, your elaborate clothes are superfluous, for they barely cover your body.
1. *fool . . . tamely:* do not make me so foolish as to accept it meekly.

3.1 (F 3.1)

Enter KENT *[disguised as Caius] and a* GENTLEMAN *at several°* doors.   separate

KENT What's here beside foul weather?

GENTLEMAN One minded like the weather, most unquietly.

KENT I know you. Where's the King?

GENTLEMAN Contending with the fretful element;

5   Bids the wind blow the earth into the sea,

Or swell the curlèd waters 'bove the main,°   mainland

That things might change or cease; tears his white hair,

Which the impetuous blasts, with eyeless rage,

Catch in their fury and make nothing of;

10   Strives in his little world of man to outscorn

The to-and-fro conflicting wind and rain

This night, wherein the cub-drawn bear would couch,[1]

The lion and the belly-pinchèd wolf

Keep their fur dry. Unbonneted° he runs   Hatless; uncrowned

And bids what will take all.

15 KENT   But who is with him?

GENTLEMAN None but the Fool, who labors to out-jest

His heart-struck injuries.[2]

KENT   Sir, I do know you

And dare upon the warrant of my art[3]

Commend a dear° thing to you. There is division,   Entrust a crucial

20   Although as yet the face of it be covered

With mutual cunning, twixt Albany and Cornwall.

But true it is, from France[4] there comes a power

Into this scattered kingdom, who, already wise in° our   aware of

negligence,

Have secret feet in some of our best ports,

25   And are at point° to show their open banner.   ready

Now to you: if on my credit you dare build° so far   if you trust me

To make your speed to Dover, you shall find

Some that will thank you, making just° report   accurate

Of how unnatural and bemadding° sorrow   maddening

30   The King hath cause to plain.°   complain

I am a gentleman of blood and breeding

And from some knowledge and assurance

Offer this office° to you.   role; duty

GENTLEMAN I will talk farther with you.

KENT   No, do not.

35   For confirmation that I am much more

Than my out-wall,° open this purse and take   outward appearance

What it contains. If you shall see Cordelia—

As fear not but you shall—show her this ring,

And she will tell you who your fellow° is   (Kent himself)

3.1 Location: Bare, open country.
1. In which even the bear, though starving, having been sucked dry ("drawn") by its cub, would not go out to forage.
2. *to out-jest*: to relieve with laughter; to exorcise through ridicule. *heart-struck injuries*: injuries (from the betrayal of his paternal love) that penetrated to the heart.
3. On the basis of my skill (at judging people).

4. TEXTUAL COMMENT There is substantial variation between the Quarto and Folio texts in Kent's speech in 3.1 about the sources of political unrest. While Kent points to French foreign invasion in the Quarto, the Folio text presents a vision of civil unrest between Cornwall and Albany. Some scholars have proposed political censorship as a possible explanation for the stark difference between Kent's speeches. See Digital Edition TC 3 (Quarto edited text).

3.1 (Q 3.1)

Storm still. Enter KENT [*disguised as Caius*] *and a*
GENTLEMAN, *severally.*°   separately

KENT Who's there besides foul weather?

GENTLEMAN One minded like the weather, most unquietly.

KENT I know you. Where's the King?

GENTLEMAN Contending with the fretful elements;

5   Bids the wind blow the earth into the sea,
       Or swell the curlèd waters 'bove the main,°   mainland
       That things might change or cease.

KENT But who is with him?

GENTLEMAN None but the Fool, who labors to out-jest
       His heart-struck injuries.[1]

10   KENT   Sir, I do know you
       And dare upon the warrant of my note[2]
       Commend a dear° thing to you. There is division,   Entrust a crucial
       Although as yet the face of it is covered
       With mutual cunning, twixt Albany and Cornwall,[3]

15   Who have—as who have not that their great stars
       Throned and set high[4]—servants, who seem no less,°   who appear as such
       Which are to France the spies and speculations°   observers
       Intelligent of[5] our state. What hath been seen,
       Either in snuffs and packings° of the Dukes,   quarrels and plots

20   Or the hard rein° which both of them hath borne   treatment
       Against the old kind King, or something deeper,
       Whereof, perchance, these are but furnishings.°   pretexts

GENTLEMAN I will talk further with you.

KENT   No, do not.
       For confirmation that I am much more

25   Than my out-wall,° open this purse and take   outward appearance
       What it contains. If you shall see Cordelia—
       As fear not but you shall—show her this ring,
       And she will tell you who that fellow° is   (Kent himself)

3.1 Location: Bare, open country.
1. *to out-jest:* to relieve with laughter; to exorcise
through ridicule. *heart-struck injuries:* injuries (from
the betrayal of his paternal love) that penetrated to
the heart.
2. On the basis of my skill (at judging people).
3. TEXTUAL COMMENT There is substantial variation
between the Quarto and Folio texts in Kent's speech
in 3.1 about the sources of political unrest. While

Kent points to French foreign invasion in the Quarto,
the Folio text presents a vision of civil unrest between
Cornwall and Albany. Some scholars have proposed
political censorship as a possible explanation for the
stark difference between Kent's speeches. See Digital Edition TC 3 (Folio edited text).
4. *as . . . high:* as has everybody who has been favored
by destiny.
5. Supplying intelligence about; too well informed of.

40 That yet you do not know. Fie on this storm!
    I will go seek the King.
GENTLEMAN Give me your hand. Have you no more to say?
KENT Few words, but to effect° more than all yet: *but in importance*
    That when we have found the King—
45 I'll° this way, you that—he that first lights *I'll go*
    On him holla the other. *Exeunt [severally].*° *separately*

3.2 (F 3.2)

Enter LEAR and FOOL.

LEAR Blow wind and crack your cheeks! Rage, blow,
    You cataracts° and hurricanos, spout *waterspouts*
    Till you have drenched the steeples, drowned the cocks!° *weather vanes*
    You sulphurous and thought-executing fires,[1]
5   Vaunt-couriers° to oak-cleaving thunderbolts, *Forerunners*
    Singe my white head. And thou, all-shaking thunder,
    Smite flat the thick rotundity of the world,
    Crack Nature's mold, all germens° spill at once *seeds*
    That make ingrateful man.
10 FOOL O nuncle, court holy water[2] in a dry house is better
    than this rainwater out a-door. Good nuncle, in, and ask thy
    daughter's blessing. Here's a night pities neither wise man
    nor fool.
LEAR Rumble thy bellyful! Spit fire, spout rain!
15 Nor rain, wind, thunder, fire are my daughters.
    I task° not you, you elements, with unkindness; *blame*
    I never gave you kingdom, called you children.
    You owe me no subscription.° Why, then, let fall *obedience; allegiance*
    Your horrible pleasure. Here I stand your slave,
20 A poor, infirm, weak, and despised old man.
    But yet I call you servile ministers,° *agents*
    That have with two pernicious daughters joined
    Your high-engendered battle° 'gainst a head *heaven-bred force*
    So old and white as this. Oh, 'tis foul!
25 FOOL He that has a house to put his head in has a good
    headpiece.° *hat; brain*
    The codpiece that will house
    Before the head has any,
    The head and he shall louse;
30 So beggars marry many.[3]
    The man that makes his toe
    What he his heart should make,
    Shall have a corn, cry "Woe,"
    And turn his sleep to wake.[4]
35 For there was never yet fair woman but she made mouths in
    a glass.[5]

3.2 Location: As before.
1. *thought-executing fires:* Either meaning lightning that strikes as swiftly as thought or lightning that puts an end to thought.
2. Sprinkled blessings of a courtier, flattery.
3. *The codpiece . . . many:* Whoever finds his penis a lodging before providing shelter for his head will end up in lice-infested poverty and live in married beggary. *codpiece:* a pouchlike covering for the male genitals, often conspicuous, particularly in the costume of a

fool.
4. *The man . . . wake:* The man who values an inferior part of his body over the part that is truly valuable will suffer from and lose sleep over that inferior part.
5. She practiced making pretty faces in a mirror. The Fool probably refers to Regan's and Gonorill's vanity, or the line may be thrown in to soften the harshness of his satire.

That yet you do not know. Fie on this storm!
I will go seek the King.

30 GENTLEMAN   Give me your hand.
 Have you no more to say?

 KENT Few words, but to effect° more than all yet: *but in importance*
 That when we have found the King—in which your pain
 That way, I'll this[6]—he that first lights on him
35 Holla the other.   *Exeunt [severally].°*   *separately*

3.2 (Q 3.2)
Storm still. Enter LEAR *and* FOOL.

 LEAR Blow winds and crack your cheeks! Rage, blow,
 You cataracts° and hurricanos, spout   *waterspouts*
 Till you have drenched our steeples, drowned the cocks.° *weather vanes*
 You sulph'rous and thought-executing fires,[1]
5 Vaunt-couriers° of oak-cleaving thunderbolts,   *Forerunners*
 Singe my white head. And thou, all-shaking thunder,
 Strike flat the thick rotundity o'th' world,
 Crack Nature's molds, all germens° spill at once   *seeds*
 That makes ingrateful man.

10 FOOL O nuncle, court holy water[2] in a dry house is better
 than this rainwater out o'door. Good nuncle, in! Ask thy
 daughters' blessing. Here's a night pities neither wise men
 nor fools.

 LEAR Rumble thy bellyful! Spit fire, spout rain!
15 Nor rain, wind, thunder, fire are my daughters.
 I tax° not you, you elements, with unkindness: *blame*
 I never gave you kingdom, called you children.
 You owe me no subscription.° Then let fall   *obedience; allegiance*
 Your horrible pleasure. Here I stand your slave,
20 A poor, infirm, weak, and despised old man.
 But yet I call you servile ministers,°   *agents*
 That will with two pernicious daughters join
 Your high-engendered battles° 'gainst a head   *heaven-bred forces*
 So old and white as this. Oh, ho! 'Tis foul.

25 FOOL He that has a house to put 's head in has a good
 headpiece.°   *hat; brain*
 The codpiece that will house
 Before the head has any,
 The head and he shall louse;
30 So beggars marry many.[3]
 The man that makes his toe
 What he his heart should make,
 Shall of a corn cry woe
 And turn his sleep to wake.[4]
35 For there was never yet fair woman but she made mouths in
 a glass.[5]

---

6. *in which . . . this:* in which effort you will go that
way and I this way.
3.2 Location: As before.
1. *thought-executing fires:* meaning either lightning
that strikes as swiftly as thought or lightning that
puts an end to thought.
2. Sprinkled blessings of a courtier; flattery.
3. *The codpiece . . . many:* Whoever finds his penis a
lodging before providing shelter for his head will end
up in lice-infested poverty and live in married beggary.

codpiece: a pouchlike covering for the male genitals,
often conspicuous, particularly in the costume of a
fool.
4. *The man . . . wake:* The man who values an inferior part of his body over the part that is truly valuable
will suffer from and lose sleep over that inferior part.
5. She practiced making pretty faces in a mirror. The
Fool probably refers to Regan's and Gonerill's vanity,
or the line may be thrown in to soften the harshness
of his satire.

LEAR [*sitting down*]   No, I will be the pattern of all patience.
          Enter KENT [*disguised as Caius*].
  I will say nothing.
KENT   Who's there?

40 FOOL   Marry, here's grace and a codpiece: that's a wise man
    and a fool.[6]
KENT   Alas, sir, sit you here?
  Things that love night love not such nights as these.
  The wrathful skies gallow° the very wanderer   *frighten*
45 Of the dark and makes them keep° their caves.   *keep inside*
  Since I was man, such sheets of fire,
  Such bursts of horrid thunder, such groans of
  Roaring wind and rain I ne'er remember
  To have heard. Man's nature cannot carry°   *bear*
  The affliction, nor the force.
50 • LEAR   Let the great gods
  That keep this dreadful pother° o'er our heads   *commotion*
  Find out their enemies now. Tremble, thou wretch,
  That hast within thee undivulgèd crimes
  Unwhipped of° justice. Hide thee, thou bloody hand,   *Unpunished by*
55 Thou perjured and thou simular° man of virtue   *simulating; pretending*
  That art incestuous. Caitiff,° in pieces shake,   *Wretch*
  That under covert and convenient seeming°   *fitting hypocrisy*
  Hast practiced on° man's life.   *against*
  Close° pent-up guilts, rive° your concealed centers   *Secret / split open*
60 And cry these dreadful summoners grace.[7]
  I am a man more sinned against than sinning.
KENT   Alack, bareheaded?
  Gracious my lord, hard by here is a hovel.
  Some friendship will it lend you 'gainst the tempest.
65 Repose you there whilst I to this hard house°—   *household*
  More hard than is the stone whereof 'tis raised,
  Which° even but now demanding after me,   *Who*
  Denied me to come in—return and force
  Their scanted° courtesy.   *grudging*
70 LEAR   My wit begins to turn.
  [*to* FOOL] Come on, my boy. How dost, my boy? Art cold?
  I am cold myself. Where is this straw, my fellow?
  The art° of our necessities is strange   *skill; alchemy*
  That can make vile things precious. Come, your hovel.
75 Poor fool and knave, I have one part of my heart
  That sorrows yet for thee.
FOOL [*sings*][8]   He that has a little tiny wit,°   *sense*
             With heigh-ho, the wind and the rain,
             Must make content with his fortunes fit,
80   For the rain it raineth every day.
LEAR   True, my good boy. Come, bring us to this hovel.
                         [*Exeunt.*]

---

6. The supposedly wise King is symbolized by royal grace, the Fool by his codpiece (here, slang for "penis"). The Fool speaks ironically: the King, as he has pointed out, is now the foolish one. *Marry:* By the Virgin Mary (a mild oath).

7. *And cry . . . grace:* And pray for mercy from these elements that bring you to justice.
8. The following song is an adaptation of one sung by the Clown at the end of *Twelfth Night*.

Enter KENT [*disguised as Caius*].

LEAR [*sitting down*]   No, I will be the pattern of all
   patience.
I will say nothing.

KENT   Who's there?

40 FOOL   Marry, here's grace and a codpiece: that's a wise man
and a fool.[6]

KENT   Alas, sir, are you here? Things that love night
Love not such nights as these. The wrathful skies
Gallow° the very wanderers of the dark   *Frighten*

45 And make them keep° their caves. Since I was man,   *keep inside*
Such sheets of fire, such bursts of horrid thunder,
Such groans of roaring wind and rain I never
Remember to have heard. Man's nature cannot carry°   *bear*
Th'affliction nor the fear.

LEAR   Let the great gods

50 That keep this dreadful pudder° o'er our heads   *commotion*
Find out their enemies now. Tremble, thou wretch,
That hast within thee undivulgèd crimes
Unwhipped of° justice. Hide thee, thou bloody hand,   *Unpunished by*
Thou perjured and thou simular° of virtue   *simulator; pretender*

55 That art incestuous. Caitiff,° to pieces shake,   *Wretch*
That under covert and convenient seeming°   *fitting hypocrisy*
Has practiced on° man's life. Close° pent-up guilts,   *against / Secret*
Rive° your concealing continents° and cry   *Split open / coverings*
These dreadful summoners grace.[7] I am a man
More sinned against than sinning.

60 KENT   Alack, bareheaded?
Gracious my lord, hard by here is a hovel;
Some friendship will it lend you 'gainst the tempest.
Repose you there, while I to this hard house°—   *household*
More harder than the stones whereof 'tis raised,

65 Which° even but now, demanding° after you,   *Who / I demanding*
Denied me to come in—return and force
Their scanted° courtesy.   *grudging*

LEAR   My wits begin to turn.
Come on, my boy. How dost, my boy? Art cold?
I am cold myself. Where is this straw, my fellow?

70 The art° of our necessities is strange   *skill; alchemy*
And can make vile things precious. Come, your hovel.
Poor fool and knave, I have one part in my heart
That's sorry yet for thee.

FOOL [*sings*][8] He that has and° a little tiny wit,°   *even / sense*

75   With heigh-ho, the wind and the rain,
          Must make content with his fortunes fit,
          Though the rain it raineth every day.

LEAR   True, boy. Come, bring us to this hovel.

                    Exeunt [LEAR *and* KENT].

---

6. The supposedly wise King is symbolized by royal grace, the Fool by his codpiece (here, slang for "penis"). The Fool speaks ironically: the King, as he has pointed out, is now the foolish one. *Marry:* By the Virgin Mary (a mild oath).

7. *and cry . . . grace:* and pray for mercy from these elements that bring you to justice.
8. The following song is an adaptation of one sung by the Clown at the end of *Twelfth Night.*

3.3 (F 3.3)

Enter GLOUCESTER *and [Edmund] the* BASTARD *with lights.*

GLOUCESTER Alack, alack, Edmund, I like not this unnatural
dealing. When I desired their leave that I might pity° him,   *relieve*
they took from me the use of mine own house, charged me
on pain of their displeasure neither to speak of him, entreat
5   for him, nor any way sustain him.

BASTARD Most savage and unnatural!

GLOUCESTER Go to,° say you nothing. There's a division betwixt   *(an expletive)*
the Dukes and a worse matter than that. I have received a
letter this night—'tis dangerous to be spoken. I have locked
10   the letter in my closet.° These injuries the King now bears will   *private chamber*
be revenged home:° there's part of a power° already landed.   *to the hilt / an army*
We must incline to¹ the King. I will seek him and privily°   *secretly; privately*
relieve him. Go you and maintain talk with the Duke, that
my charity be not of him perceived. If he ask for me, I am ill
15   and gone to bed. Though I die for't, as no less is threatened
me, the King my old master must be relieved. There is some
strange thing toward.° Edmund, pray you be careful. *Exit.*   *coming*

BASTARD This courtesy,° forbid° thee, shall the Duke   *act of kindness / forbidden*
Instantly know, and of that letter too.
20   This seems a fair deserving² and must draw me
That which my father loses: no less than all.
Then younger rises when the old do fall.   *Exit.*

3.3 Location: At Gloucester's castle.   2. This seems an action that deserves to be rewarded.
1. We must take the side of.

FOOL This is a brave night to cool a courtesan.[9] I'll speak a
80 prophecy ere I go:[1]
    When priests are more in word than matter,°   *real virtue*
    When brewers mar their malt with water,
    When nobles are their tailors' tutors,[2]
    No heretics burned but wenches' suitors,[3]
85 When every case in law is right,°   *just*
    No squire in debt, nor no poor knight,
    When slanders do not live in tongues,
    Nor cutpurses° come not to throngs,   *pickpockets*
    When usurers tell their gold i'th' field,[4]
90 And bawds and whores do churches build,
    Then shall the realm of Albion° come to great confusion.°   *Britain / decay*
    Then comes the time, who lives to see't,
    That going° shall be used° with feet.   *walking / practiced*
    This prophecy Merlin shall make, for I live before his time.[5]
                                                            Exit.

3.3 (Q 3.3)

Enter GLOUCESTER *and* EDMOND.

GLOUCESTER Alack, alack, Edmond, I like not this unnatural
    dealing. When I desired their leave that I might pity° him,   *relieve*
    they took from me the use of mine own house, charged me
    on pain of perpetual displeasure neither to speak of him,
5   entreat for him, or any way sustain him.
EDMOND Most savage and unnatural!
GLOUCESTER Go to,° say you nothing. There is division between   *(an expletive)*
    the Dukes and a worse matter than that. I have received a
    letter this night—'tis dangerous to be spoken. I have locked
10 the letter in my closet.° These injuries the King now bears will   *private chamber*
    be revenged home.° There is part of a power already footed.[1]   *to the hilt*
    We must incline to[2] the King; I will look him and privily°   *secretly; privately*
    relieve him. Go you and maintain talk with the Duke, that my
    charity be not of him perceived. If he ask for me, I am ill and
15 gone to bed. If I die for it, as no less is threatened me, the King
    my old master must be relieved. There is strange things
    toward,° Edmond. Pray you be careful.   *Exit.*   *coming*
EDMOND This courtesy,° forbid° thee, shall the Duke   *act of kindness / forbidden*
    Instantly know and of that letter too.
20 This seems a fair deserving[3] and must draw me
    That which my father loses: no less than all.
    The younger rises when the old doth fall.   *Exit.*

---

9. To cool even the hot lusts of a prostitute.
1. What follows is a parody of the pseudo-Chaucerian "Merlin's Prophecy" from *The Art of English Poesy.*
2. When noblemen follow fashion more closely than their tailors do.
3. When the only heretics burned are faithless lovers, who burn from venereal disease.
4. When usurers can count their profits openly

(because they have no shady dealings to hide).
5. Merlin was the great wizard at the legendary court of King Arthur. Lear's Britain is set in an even more distant past.
3.3 Location: At Gloucester's castle.
1. Part of an army already on the move.
2. We must take the side of.
3. This seems an action that deserves to be rewarded.

3.4 (F 3.4)

Enter LEAR, KENT [*disguised as Caius*], *and* FOOL.

KENT   Here is the place, my lord. Good my lord, enter.
  The tyranny of the open night's too rough
  For nature° to endure.   *human weakness*
LEAR   Let me alone.
KENT   Good my lord, enter.
LEAR   Wilt break my heart?
5   KENT   I had rather break mine own. Good my lord, enter.
LEAR   Thou think'st 'tis much that this tempestuous storm
  Invades us to the skin; so 'tis to thee.
  But where the greater malady is fixed,°   *rooted*
  The lesser is scarce felt. Thou'dst shun a bear,
10   But if thy flight lay toward the roaring sea,
  Thou'dst meet the bear i'th' mouth. When the mind's free,°   *unburdened*
  The body's delicate.° This tempest in my mind   *sensitive*
  Doth from my senses take all feeling else,
  Save° what beats: their filial ingratitude.   *Except*
15   Is it not as° this mouth should tear this hand   *as if*
  For lifting food to't? But I will punish sure.
  No, I will weep no more— In such a night as this!
  O Regan, Gonorill, your old kind father
  Whose frank heart gave you all! Oh, that way madness lies.
20   Let me shun that; no more of that.
KENT   Good my lord, enter.
LEAR   Prithee, go in thyself; seek thy own ease.   [*Exit* FOOL.]
  This tempest will not give me leave to° ponder   *allow me to*
  On things would hurt me more. But I'll go in.

25   Poor naked wretches, wheresoe'er you are,
  That bide° the pelting of this pitiless night,   *endure; dwell in*
  How shall your houseless heads and unfed sides,°   *starved ribs*
  Your looped and windowed[1] raggedness defend you
  From seasons such as these? Oh, I have ta'en
30   Too little care of this! Take physic, pomp;[2]
  Expose thyself to feel what wretches feel,
  That thou mayst shake the superflux[3] to them
  And show the heavens more just.
          [*Enter* FOOL.]
FOOL   Come not in here, nuncle. Here's a spirit! Help me,
35   help me!
KENT   Give me thy hand. Who's there?
FOOL   A spirit. He says his name's Poor Tom.
KENT   What art thou that dost grumble there in the straw?
  Come forth.

3.4 Location: Open country, before a cattle shed.   2. Cure yourself, pompous person.
1. *looped and windowed*: full of holes and vents;   3. Superfluity; bodily discharge, suggested by
"windowed" could also refer to cloth worn through to   "physic" (which also has the meaning of "purgative")
semitransparency, like the oilcloth window "panes"   in line 30. Excess here is also excess of wealth.
of the poor.

3.4 (Q 3.4)

Enter LEAR, KENT [disguised as Caius], and FOOL.

KENT   Here is the place, my lord. Good my lord, enter.
    The tyranny of the open night's too rough
    For nature° to endure.   *human weakness*
            Storm still.

LEAR   Let me alone.

KENT   Good my lord, enter here.

LEAR   Wilt break my heart?

5   KENT   I had rather break mine own.
    Good my lord, enter.

LEAR   Thou think'st 'tis much that this contentious storm
    Invades us to the skin; so 'tis to thee.
    But where the greater malady is fixed,°   *rooted*
10   The lesser is scarce felt. Thou'dst shun a bear,
    But if thy flight lay toward the roaring sea,
    Thou'dst meet the bear i'th' mouth. When the mind's free,°   *unburdened*
    The body's delicate.° The tempest in my mind   *sensitive*
    Doth from my senses take all feeling else,
15   Save° what beats there: filial ingratitude.   *Except*
    Is it not as° this mouth should tear this hand   *as if*
    For lifting food to't? But I will punish home.°   *thoroughly*
    No, I will weep no more. In such a night
    To shut me out? Pour on, I will endure.
20   In such a night as this? O Regan, Gonerill,
    Your old kind father, whose frank heart gave all!
    Oh, that way madness lies. Let me shun that;
    No more of that.

KENT   Good my lord, enter here.

LEAR   Prithee, go in thyself; seek thine own ease.
25   This tempest will not give me leave to° ponder   *allow me to*
    On things would hurt me more, but I'll go in.
    [to FOOL] In, boy, go first. You houseless poverty,°   *poor*
    Nay, get thee in; I'll pray, and then I'll sleep.   *Exit [FOOL].*
    Poor naked wretches, wheresoe'er you are,
30   That bide° the pelting of this pitiless storm,   *endure; dwell in*
    How shall your houseless heads and unfed sides,°   *starved ribs*
    Your looped and windowed[1] raggedness defend you
    From seasons such as these? Oh, I have ta'en
    Too little care of this! Take physic, pomp;[2]
35   Expose thyself to feel what wretches feel,
    That thou mayst shake the superflux[3] to them
    And show the heavens more just.

EDGAR *[within]*   Fathom and half,[4] fathom and half. Poor Tom!
         Enter FOOL.

FOOL   Come not in here, nuncle. Here's a spirit! Help me,
40   help me!

KENT   Give me thy hand. Who's there?

FOOL   A spirit, a spirit! He says his name's Poor Tom.

KENT   What art thou that dost grumble there i'th' straw?
    Come forth.

3.4 Location: Open country, before a cattle shed.
1. *looped and windowed:* full of holes and vents; "windowed" could also refer to cloth worn through to semitransparency, like the oilcloth window "panes" of the poor.
2. Cure yourself, pompous person.

3. Superfluity; bodily discharge, suggested by "physic" (which also has the meaning of "purgative") in line 34. Excess here is also excess of wealth.
4. "Nine feet," a sailor's cry when taking soundings to gauge the depth of water.

[Enter EDGAR *disguised as Poor Tom.]*

40   EDGAR   Away, the foul fiend follows me! Through the sharp
hawthorn blows the cold wind.[4] Go to thy cold bed and
warm thee.[5]

    LEAR   Hast thou given all to thy two daughters, and art thou
come to this?

45   EDGAR   Who gives anything to Poor Tom, whom the foul fiend
hath led through fire, and through ford and whirlpool, o'er
bog and quagmire, that has laid knives under his pillow and
halters in his pew, set ratsbane by his pottage,[6] made him
proud of heart to ride on a bay trotting horse over four-
50   inched bridges,[7] to course° his own shadow for° a traitor.   *hunt / as*
Bless thy five wits![8] Tom's a-cold. Bless thee from whirl-
winds, star-blasting, and taking.[9] Do Poor Tom some charity, whom the foul fiend vexes. There could I have him now,
and there, and there again.[1]

55   LEAR   What, his daughters brought him to this pass?
    —Couldst thou save nothing? Didst thou give them all?

    FOOL   Nay, he reserved a blanket, else we had been all
shamed.

    LEAR   Now all the plagues that in the pendulous° air   *overhanging; portentous*
60   Hang fated o'er men's faults fall on thy daughters.

    KENT   He hath no daughters, sir.

    LEAR   Death, traitor! Nothing could have subdued nature
To such a lowness but his unkind daughters.
Is it the fashion that discarded fathers
65   Should have thus little mercy on their flesh?
Judicious punishment! 'Twas this flesh
Begot those pelican[2] daughters.

  EDGAR *[sings]*   Pilicock sat on pilicock's hill, a lo, lo, lo.[3]

    FOOL   This cold night will turn us all to fools and madmen.

70   EDGAR   Take heed o'th' foul fiend, obey thy parents, keep thy
words justly, swear not, commit not with man's sworn spouse,
set not thy sweetheart on proud array.[4] Tom's a-cold.

    LEAR   What hast thou been?

  EDGAR   A servingman, proud in heart and mind, that curled
75   my hair, wore gloves in my cap,[5] served the lust of my mistress' heart, and did the act of darkness with her. Swore as
many oaths as I spake words and broke them in the sweet
face of heaven. One that slept in the contriving of lust and
waked to do it. Wine loved I deeply, dice dearly, and in
80   woman out-paramoured the Turk.[6] False of heart, light of

---

4. *Through . . . wind:* Perhaps a fragment from a ballad.

5. *Go . . . thee:* This expression is also used by the drunken beggar Christopher Sly in *The Taming of the Shrew,* Induction 1.

6. *laid knives . . . potage:* these are all means by which the foul fiend tempts Tom to commit suicide. *halters:* nooses. *ratsbane:* rat poison. *pottage:* soup.

7. Impossibly narrow, and probably suicidal to attempt without diabolical help.

8. The five wits were common wit, imagination, fantasy, estimation, and memory (from medieval and Renaissance cognitive theory).

9. *whirlwinds, star-blasting:* malign astrological influences capable of causing sickness or death. *tak-*

ing: infection; bewitchment.

1. As Edgar speaks this sentence, he might kill vermin on his body as if they were devils.

2. Greedy. Young pelicans were reputed to feed on blood from the wounds they made in their mother's breast; in some versions, they first killed their father.

3. A fragment of an old rhyme, followed by hunting cries or a ballad refrain; "Pilicock" was both a term of endearment and a euphemism for "penis."

4. *obey . . . array:* these are fragments from the Ten Commandments.

5. Favors from his mistress. In Petrarchan poetry, wooers are "servants" to their ladies.

6. And had more women than the Turkish sultan had in his royal harem.

Enter EDGAR *[disguised as Poor Tom].*

45 EDGAR Away, the foul fiend follows me! Through the sharp
hawthorn blow the winds.[5] Hum, go to thy bed and warm
thee.[6]

LEAR Didst thou give all to thy daughters, and art thou come
to this?

50 EDGAR Who gives anything to Poor Tom, whom the foul fiend
hath led through fire and through flame, through sword and
whirlpool, o'er bog and quagmire, that hath laid knives under
his pillow and halters in his pew, set ratsbane by his porridge,[7]
made him proud of heart to ride on a bay trotting horse over
55 four-inched[8] bridges, to course° his own shadow for° a traitor.   hunt / as
Bless thy five wits![9] Tom's a-cold. Oh, do, de, do, de, do, de,
bless thee from whirlwinds, star-blasting, and taking![1] Do
Poor Tom some charity, whom the foul fiend vexes. There
could I have him now, and there, and there again, and there![2]

Storm still.

60 LEAR Has his daughters brought him to this pass?
—Couldst thou save nothing? Wouldst thou give 'em all?

FOOL Nay, he reserved a blanket, else we had been all
shamed.

LEAR Now all the plagues that in the pendulous° air   overhanging; portentous
65 Hang fated o'er men's faults light on thy daughters.

KENT He hath no daughters, sir.

LEAR Death, traitor! Nothing could have subdued nature
To such a lowness but his unkind daughters.
Is it the fashion that discarded fathers
70 Should have thus little mercy on their flesh?
Judicious punishment! 'Twas this flesh begot
Those pelican[3] daughters.

EDGAR *[sings]* Pillicock sat on Pillicock hill, alow, alow,
loo, loo.[4]

FOOL This cold night will turn us all to fools and madmen.

75 EDGAR Take heed o'th' foul fiend, obey thy parents, keep thy
word's justice, swear not, commit not with man's sworn
spouse, set not thy sweetheart on proud array.[5] Tom's a-cold.

LEAR What hast thou been?

EDGAR A servingman, proud in heart and mind, that curled
80 my hair, wore gloves in my cap,[6] served the lust of my mistress' heart and did the act of darkness with her. Swore as
many oaths as I spake words and broke them in the sweet
face of heaven. One that slept in the contriving of lust and
waked to do it. Wine loved I dearly, dice dearly, and in
85 woman out-paramoured the Turk.[7] False of heart, light of

5. *Through . . . winds:* Perhaps a fragment from a
ballad.
6. *go . . . thee:* This expression is also used by the
drunken beggar Christopher Sly in *The Taming of the
Shrew,* Induction 1.
7. *laid knives . . . porridge:* these are all means by
which the foul fiend tempts Tom to commit suicide.
halters: nooses. *ratsbane:* rat poison.
8. Impossibly narrow, and probably suicidal to attempt
without diabolical help.
9. The five wits were common wit, imagination, fantasy, estimation, and memory (from medieval and
Renaissance cognitive theory).
1. *whirlwinds, star-blasting:* malign astrological
influences capable of causing sickness or death. *tak-*

ing: infection; bewitchment.
2. As Edgar speaks this sentence, he might kill vermin on his body as if they were devils.
3. Greedy. Young pelicans were reputed to feed on
blood from the wounds they made in their mother's
breast; in some versions, they first killed their father.
4. A fragment of an old rhyme, followed by hunting
cries or a ballad refrain; "Pillicock" was both a term
of endearment and a euphemism for "penis."
5. *obey . . . array:* these are fragments from the Ten
Commandments.
6. Favors from his mistress. In Petrarchan poetry,
wooers are "servants" to their ladies.
7. And had more women than the Turkish sultan had
in his royal harem.

ear,° bloody of hand. Hog in sloth, fox in stealth, wolf in   *rumor-hungry*
greediness, dog in madness, lion in prey. Let not the creaking of shoes[7] nor the rustlings of silks betray thy poor heart
to women. Keep thy foot[8] out of brothel, thy hand out of
85   placket,[9] thy pen from lender's book, and defy the foul fiend.
Still through the hawthorn blows the cold wind.
[*Sings.*]   Heigh, no, nonny.
Dolphin, my boy, my boy! Cease! Let him trot by.[1]

LEAR   Why, thou wert better in thy grave than to answer°   *encounter*
90   with thy uncovered body this extremity of the skies.° Is man   *violent weather*
no more but this? Consider him well. Thou owest the worm
no silk, the beast no hide, the sheep no wool, the cat[2] no
perfume. Here's three on 's° are sophisticated. Thou art the   *of us*
thing itself. Unaccommodated[3] man is no more but such a
95   poor, bare, forked° animal as thou art. [*He begins to undress.*]   *two-legged*
Off, off, you lendings!° Come on.   *borrowed clothes*

FOOL   Prithee, nuncle, be content. This is a naughty° night to   *foul*
swim in. Now a little fire in a wild° field were like an old   *barren; lustful*
lecher's heart: a small spark, all the rest in° body cold. Look,   *of his*
100   here comes a walking fire.
              Enter GLOUCESTER [*with a torch*].

EDGAR   This is the foul fiend Fliberdegibek.[4] He begins at
curfew° and walks till the first cock.° He gives the web and   *9:00 P.M. / midnight*
the pin,[5] squeans° the eye and makes the harelip, mildews   *causes squints in*
the white° wheat, and hurts the poor creature of earth.   *nearly ripe*
105   Swithold footed thrice the old,[6]
He met the night mare and her nine-fold[7]
Bid her "Oh, light,"
And her troth plight°   *And gave her word*
And aroint thee,° witch, aroint thee!   *begone*
110   KENT   How fares your grace?
LEAR   What's° he?   *Who's*
KENT   Who's there? What is't you seek?
GLOUCESTER   What are you there? Your names?
EDGAR   Poor Tom, that eats the swimming frog, the toad, the
115   tadpole, the wall-newt, and the water,° that in the fury of his   *water newt*
heart, when the foul fiend rages, eats cow dung for salads,
swallows the old rat and the ditch dog,[8] drinks the green
mantle° of the standing pool, who is whipped from tithing°   *scum / parish*
to tithing and stock-punished° and imprisoned, who hath   *put in stocks*
120   had three suits to his back, six shirts to his body.
Horse to ride, and weapon to wear.
But mice and rats and such small deer[9]
Hath been Tom's food for seven long year.
Beware my follower! Peace, snulbug!° Peace, thou fiend!   *(a Harsnett devil)*

7. Creaking shoes were a fashionable affectation.
8. Punning on the French *foutre* ("fuck").
9. Slits in skirts or petticoats.
1. These phrases are probably from songs and proverbs. *Dolphin:* dauphin; the heir to the French throne,
sometimes identified with the devil by the English.
2. Civet, in Shakespeare's time the major source of
musk for perfume.
3. Naked; without the trappings of civilization.
4. A devil drawn from folk beliefs but famous for his
prominent place in Samuel Harsnett's *Declaration of
Egregious Popish Impostures* (1603); the frequent borrowings from Harsnett in *King Lear* set the earliest

possible composition date for the play.
5. *web and the pin:* cataract.
6. Swithald (or St. Withold), an early English saint
famous for healing, traversed the hilly countryside
three times.
7. *night mare:* a demon, not necessarily in the shape
of a horse; *nine-fold* might suggest an entourage of
demons and familiars, or the many folds (coils) of a
snake.
8. A dog found dead in a ditch.
9. *deer:* animals. These verses are adapted from a
romance popular in Shakespeare's time, *Bevis of
Hampton.*

ear,° bloody of hand. Hog in sloth, fox in stealth, wolf in | *rumor-hungry*
greediness, dog in madness, lion in prey. Let not the creaking of shoes[8] nor the rustling of silks betray thy poor heart
to woman. Keep thy foot[9] out of brothels, thy hand out of
90 plackets,[1] thy pen from lenders' books, and defy the foul
fiend. Still through the hawthorn blows the cold wind, says
suum, mun, nonny. Dolphin, my boy, boy, cease. Let him
trot by.[2]

    Storm still.

LEAR Thou wert better in a grave than to answer° with thy | *encounter*
95 uncovered body this extremity of the skies.° Is man no more | *violent weather*
than this? Consider him well. Thou ow'st the worm no silk,
the beast no hide, the sheep no wool, the cat[3] no perfume.
Ha? Here's three on 's° are sophisticated. Thou art the thing | *of us*
itself. Unaccommodated[4] man is no more but such a poor,
100 bare, forked° animal as thou art. [*He begins to undress.*] Off, | *two-legged*
off, you lendings.° Come, unbutton here. | *borrowed clothes*

    Enter GLOUCESTER, *with a torch.*

FOOL Prithee, nuncle, be contented. 'Tis a naughty° night to | *foul*
swim in. Now a little fire in a wild° field were like an old | *barren; lustful*
lecher's heart: a small spark, all the rest on 's° body cold. | *of his*
105 Look, here comes a walking fire.

EDGAR This is the foul Flibbertigibbet![5] He begins at curfew° | *9:00 p.m.*
and walks at first cock.° He gives the web and the pin,[6] | *midnight*
squints the eye and makes the harelip, mildews the white° | *near-ripe*
wheat, and hurts the poor creature of earth.
110 Swithold footed thrice the old,[7]
He met the night mare and her nine-fold;[8]
Bid her alight and her troth plight,° | *and gave her word*
And aroint thee,° witch, aroint thee. | *begone*

KENT How fares your grace?

115 LEAR What's° he? | *Who's*

KENT Who's there? What is't you seek?

GLOUCESTER What are you there? Your names?

EDGAR Poor Tom, that eats the swimming frog, the toad, the
tadpole, the wall-newt, and the water,° that in the fury of his | *water newt*
120 heart, when the foul fiend rages, eats cow dung for salads,
swallows the old rat and the ditch dog,[9] drinks the green
mantle° of the standing pool, who is whipped from tithing° | *scum / parish*
to tithing and stocked,° punished, and imprisoned, who | *put in stocks*
hath three suits to his back, six shirts to his body.
125 Horse to ride, and weapon to wear.
But mice and rats and such small deer[1]
Have been Tom's food for seven long year.
Beware my follower! Peace, Smulkin!° Peace, thou fiend. | *(a Harsnett devil)*

---

8. Creaking shoes were a fashionable affectation.
9. Punning on the French *foutre* ("fuck").
1. Slits in skirts or petticoats.
2. These phrases are probably from songs and proverbs. *Dolphin:* dauphin; the heir to the French
throne, sometimes identified with the devil by the
English.
3. Civet, in Shakespeare's time the major source of
musk for perfume.
4. Naked; without the trappings of civilization.
5. A devil drawn from folk beliefs but famous for his
prominent place in Samuel Harsnett's *Declaration of
Egregious Popish Impostures* (1603); the frequent borrowings from Harsnett in *King Lear* set the earliest

possible composition date for the play.
6. *web and the pin:* cataract.
7. Swithin (or St. Withold), an early English saint
famous for healing, traversed the hilly countryside
three times. *old:* wold; uplands.
8. *night mare:* a demon, not necessarily in the shape
of a horse; *nine-fold* might suggest an entourage of
demons and familiars, or the many folds (coils) of a
snake.
9. A dog found dead in a ditch.
1. *deer:* animals. These verses are adapted from a
romance popular in Shakespeare's time, *Bevis of
Hampton.*

125 GLOUCESTER [*to* LEAR]   What, hath your grace no better
    company?
  EDGAR   The prince of darkness is a gentleman, Modo he's
    called and Mahu.[1]
  GLOUCESTER   Our flesh and blood is grown so vile, my lord,
130   That it doth hate what gets° it.   *begets*
  EDGAR   Poor Tom's a-cold.
  GLOUCESTER   Go in with me. My duty cannot suffer°   *permit me*
    To obey in all your daughters' hard commands.
    Though their injunction be to bar my doors
135   And let this tyrannous night take hold upon you,
    Yet have I ventured to come seek you out
    And bring you where both food and fire is ready.
  LEAR   First let me talk with this philosopher,
    [*to* EDGAR] What is the cause of thunder?
140 KENT   My good lord, take his offer; go into the house.
  LEAR   I'll talk a word with this most learned Theban.°   *(Greek sage)*
    What is your study?°   *field of expertise*
  EDGAR   How to prevent the fiend and to kill vermin.
  LEAR   Let me ask you one word in private.
145 KENT [*to* GLOUCESTER]   Importune him to go, my lord; his wits
    Begin to unsettle.
  GLOUCESTER   Canst thou blame him?
    His daughters seek his death. O that good Kent,
    He said it would be thus, poor banished man!
    Thou sayest the King grows mad. I'll tell thee, friend,
150   I am almost mad myself. I had a son
    Now outlawed° from my blood, 'a° sought my life   *disowned / he*
    But lately, very late.° I loved him, friend,   *recently*
    No father his son dearer. True to tell thee,
    The grief hath crazed my wits.
155   What a night's this! I do beseech your grace—
  LEAR   Oh, cry you mercy.° —Noble philosopher, your   *beg your pardon*
    company.
  EDGAR   Tom's a-cold.
  GLOUCESTER [*to* EDGAR]   In, fellow, there, in th' hovel. Keep
    thee warm.
  LEAR   Come, let's in all.
  KENT   This way, my lord.
160 LEAR   With him I will keep still, with my philosopher.
  KENT   Good my lord, soothe° him. Let him take the fellow.   *humor*
  GLOUCESTER   Take him you on.°   *on ahead*
  KENT [*to* EDGAR]   Sirrah, come on, go along with us.
  LEAR   Come, good Athenian.°   *Greek philosopher*
165 GLOUCESTER   No words, no words, hush.
  EDGAR   Child Rowland[2] to the dark town come,
    His word° was still° "Fie, fo, and fum,   *motto / always*
    I smell the blood of a British[3] man."   [*Exeunt.*]

---

1. Modo and Mahu, more Harsnett devils, were
commanding generals of the hellish troops.
2. *Child:* an aspirant to knighthood. Rowland is the
famous hero of the Charlemagne legends.

3. "An Englishman" usually appears in this rhyme
from the cycle of tales of which "Jack and the
Beanstalk" is the best known. The alteration befits
Lear's ancient Britain.

GLOUCESTER   What, hath your grace no better company?

130 EDGAR   The Prince of Darkness is a gentleman. Modo he's
called and Mahu.[2]

GLOUCESTER   Our flesh and blood, my lord, is grown so vile
That it doth hate what gets° it.   *begets*

EDGAR   Poor Tom's a-cold.

135 GLOUCESTER   Go in with me. My duty cannot suffer°   *permit me*
T'obey in all your daughters' hard commands.
Though their injunction be to bar my doors
And let this tyrannous night take hold upon you,
Yet have I ventured to come seek you out

140 And bring you where both fire and food is ready.

LEAR   First let me talk with this philosopher.
[*to* EDGAR] What is the cause of thunder?

KENT   Good my lord, take his offer;
Go into th' house.

145 LEAR   I'll talk a word with this same learned Theban.°   *(Greek sage)*
What is your study?°   *field of expertise*

EDGAR   How to prevent the fiend and to kill vermin.

LEAR   Let me ask you one word in private.

KENT [*to* GLOUCESTER]   Importune him once more to go, my
lord,
His wits begin t'unsettle.

150 GLOUCESTER   Canst thou blame him?
Storm still.
His daughters seek his death. Ah, that good Kent,
He said it would be thus, poor banished man!
Thou sayest the King grows mad. I'll tell thee, friend,
I am almost mad myself. I had a son,

155 Now outlawed° from my blood. He sought my life   *disowned*
But lately, very late.° I loved him, friend,   *recently*
No father his son dearer. True to tell thee,
The grief hath crazed my wits. What a night's this?
I do beseech your grace—

LEAR   Oh, cry you mercy,° sir.   *beg your pardon*

160 —Noble philosopher, your company.

EDGAR   Tom's a-cold.

GLOUCESTER [*to* EDGAR]   In, fellow, there: into th' hovel.
Keep thee warm.

LEAR   Come, let's in all.

KENT   This way, my lord.

LEAR   With him
I will keep still, with my philosopher.

165 KENT [*to* GLOUCESTER]   Good my lord, soothe° him.   *humor*
Let him take the fellow.

GLOUCESTER   Take him you on.°   *on ahead*

KENT   Sirrah, come on. Go along with us.

LEAR   Come, good Athenian.°   *Greek philosopher*

GLOUCESTER   No words, no words, hush.

170 EDGAR   Child Rowland[3] to the dark tower came,
His word° was still° "Fie, fo, and fum;   *motto / always*
I smell the blood of a British[4] man."   *Exeunt.*

---

2. Modo and Mahu, more Harsnett devils, were
commanding generals of the hellish troops.
3. *Child:* an aspirant to knighthood. Roland is the
famous hero of the Charlemagne legends.

4. "An Englishman" usually appears in this rhyme
from the cycle of tales of which "Jack and the
Beanstalk" is the best known. The alteration befits
Lear's ancient Britain.

3.5 (F 3.5)

Enter CORNWALL *and* [*Edmund the*] BASTARD.

CORNWALL   I will have my revenge ere I depart the house.

BASTARD   How, my lord, I may be censured,° that nature° thus   *judged / kinship*
gives way to loyalty, something fears me° to think of.   *I am somewhat afraid*

CORNWALL   I now perceive it was not altogether your brother's
5   evil disposition made him seek his° death, but a provoking   *(Gloucester's)*
merit set a-work by a reprovable badness in himself.[1]

BASTARD   How malicious is my fortune that I must repent to
be just! This is the letter he spoke of, which approves him an
intelligent party to the advantages of France.[2] O heavens,
10   that his treason were not, or not I the detector.

CORNWALL   Go with me to the Duchess.

BASTARD   If the matter of this paper be certain, you have
mighty business in hand.

CORNWALL   True or false, it hath made thee Earl of Gloucester.
15   Seek out where thy father is, that he may be ready for our
apprehension.°   *arrest*

BASTARD [*aside*]   If I find him comforting the King, it will
stuff his° suspicion more fully. [*to* CORNWALL] I will per-   *(Cornwall's)*
severe in my course of loyalty, though the conflict be sore
20   between that and my blood.°   *filial duty*

CORNWALL   I will lay trust upon thee, and thou shalt find a
dearer father in my love.   *Exeunt.*

3.6 (F 3.6)

Enter GLOUCESTER *and* LEAR, KENT [*disguised as
Caius*], FOOL, *and* [EDGAR *disguised as Poor*] Tom.

GLOUCESTER   Here is better than the open air; take it thankfully. I will piece out° the comfort with what addition I can.   *augment*
I will not be long from you.

KENT   All the power of his wits have given way to impatience.[1]
5   The gods° deserve your kindness.   [*Exit* GLOUCESTER.]   *May the gods*

EDGAR   Fratereto° calls me and tells me Nero is an angler in   *(a Harsnett devil)*
the lake of darkness.[2] Pray, innocent, beware the foul fiend.

FOOL   Prithee, nuncle, tell me whether a madman be a
gentleman or a yeoman.[3]
10   LEAR   A king, a king! To have a thousand with red burning
spits come hissing in upon them.

3.5 Location: At Gloucester's castle.
1. *a provoking . . . himself:* Gloucester's own wickedness deservedly triggered the blameworthy evil in
Edgar.
2. *which . . . France:* which proves him a spy and an
informer in the aid of France; "party," or faction, was
usually a term of opprobrium in the Renaissance.
3.6 Location: Within an outbuilding of Gloucester's.

1. Rage; inability to bear more suffering.
2. In Chaucer's *Monk's Tale*, the infamously cruel
Roman emperor Nero is found fishing in hell (lines
485–86).
3. A free landowner but not a member of the gentry,
lacking official family arms and the distinctions they
confer. Shakespeare seems to have procured a coat of
arms for his father in 1596.

3.5 (Q 3.5)

Enter CORNWALL *and* EDMOND.

CORNWALL   I will have my revenge ere I depart his house.

EDMOND   How, my lord, I may be censured,° that nature° thus *judged / kinship*
gives way to loyalty, something fears me° to think of. *I am somewhat afraid*

CORNWALL   I now perceive it was not altogether your brother's
5   evil disposition made him seek his° death, but a provoking *(Gloucester's)*
merit set a-work by a reprovable badness in himself.[1]

EDMOND   How malicious is my fortune that I must repent to
be just! This is the letter which he spoke of, which approves
him an intelligent party to the advantages of France.[2] O
10   heavens, that this treason were not, or not I the detector.

CORNWALL   Go with me to the Duchess.

EDMOND   If the matter of this paper be certain, you have mighty
business in hand.

CORNWALL   True or false, it hath made thee Earl of Glouces-
15   ter. Seek out where thy father is, that he may be ready for our
apprehension.° *arrest*

EDMOND [*aside*]   If I find him comforting the King, it will stuff
his° suspicion more fully. [*to* CORNWALL] I will persevere in *(Cornwall's)*
my course of loyalty, though the conflict be sore between
20   that and my blood.° *filial duty*

CORNWALL   I will lay trust upon thee, and thou shalt find a
dear father in my love. *Exeunt.*

3.6 (Q 3.6)

Enter KENT [*disguised as Caius*] *and* GLOUCESTER.

GLOUCESTER   Here is better than the open air; take it thankfully. I will piece out° the comfort with what addition I can. *augment*
I will not be long from you.

KENT   All the power of his wits have given way to his impa-
5   tience.[1] The gods° reward your kindness. *May the gods*

Exit [GLOUCESTER].

Enter LEAR, EDGAR [*disguised as Poor Tom*],
and FOOL.

EDGAR   Fraretto° calls me and tells me Nero is an angler in *(a Harsnett devil)*
the lake of darkness.[2] Pray, innocent, and beware the foul
fiend.

FOOL   Prithee, nuncle, tell me whether a madman be a gentle-
10   man or a yeoman.[3]

LEAR   A king, a king.

FOOL   No, he's a yeoman that has a gentleman to° his son, for *for*
he's a mad yeoman that sees his son a gentleman before
him.

15   LEAR   To have a thousand with red burning spits
Come hizzing in upon 'em.

3.5 Location: At Gloucester's castle.
1. *a provoking . . . himself*: Gloucester's own wickedness deservedly triggered the blameworthy evil in
Edgar.
2. *which . . . France*: which proves him a spy and an
informer in the aid of France; "party," or faction, was
usually a term of opprobrium in the Renaissance.
3.6 Location: Within an outbuilding of Gloucester's.

1. Rage; inability to bear more suffering.
2. In Chaucer's *Monk's Tale*, the infamously cruel
Roman emperor Nero is found fishing in hell (lines
485–86).
3. A free landowner but not a member of the gentry,
lacking official family arms and the distinctions they
confer. Shakespeare seems to have procured a coat of
arms for his father in 1596.

EDGAR   The foul fiend bites my back.

FOOL   He's mad that trusts in the tameness of a wolf, a horse's
health, a boy's love, or a whore's oath.

15   LEAR   It shall be done;[4] I will arraign° them straight.°   *prosecute / immediately*

[*to* EDGAR] Come, sit thou here, most learned Justice.

[*to the* FOOL] Thou, sapient sir, sit here —No, you she-foxes—

EDGAR   Look where he stands and glares. Want'st thou eyes[5]
at trial, madam?

20   [*Sings.*]   Come o'er the broom, Bessy, to me.[6]

FOOL [*sings*]   Her boat hath a leak,
And she must not speak,
Why she dares not come over to thee.

EDGAR   The foul fiend haunts poor Tom in the voice of a

25   nightingale. Hoppedance° cries in Tom's belly for two white°   *(a demon) / fresh*
herring. Croak° not, black angel. I have no food for thee.   *Growl*

KENT [*to* LEAR   How do you, sir? Stand you not so amazed.
Will you lie down and rest upon the cushions?

LEAR   I'll see their trial first: bring in their evidence.

30   [*to* EDGAR] Thou robèd man of justice, take thy place,

[*to the* FOOL] And thou, his yokefellow of equity,°   *partner of law*
Bench° by his side. You are o'th' commission:° sit you too.   *Sit / judiciary*

EDGAR   Let us deal justly.

[*Sings.*]   Sleepest or wakest, thou jolly shepherd?

35   Thy sheep be in the corn,°   *grain*
And for one blast of thy minikin° mouth,   *dainty*
Thy sheep shall take no harm.

Purr, the cat is gray.[7]

LEAR   Arraign her first: 'tis Gonorill, I here take my oath

40   before this honorable assembly, kicked the poor King her
father.

FOOL   Come hither, mistress. Is your name Gonorill?

LEAR   She cannot deny it.

FOOL   Cry you mercy, I took you for a joint-stool.[8]

45   LEAR   And here's another whose warped looks proclaim
What store° her heart is made on.° Stop her there.   *material / of*
Arms, arms, sword, fire, corruption in the place!
False Justicer, why hast thou let her scape?

---

4. TEXTUAL COMMENT Lear's "mock-trial" of Gonorill and Regan, in absentia, appears only in Q1
(3.6.15–48). The trial does not appear in F and was
probably cut by Shakespeare rather than omitted
due to a printer's error. See Digital Edition TC 4
(Quarto edited text).
5. *eyes:* eyeballs (?).

6. From an old song.
7. Purr the cat is another devil; such devils in the
shape of cats were the familiars of witches.
8. I beg your pardon, I mistook you for a stool. An
idiom of the day expressing annoyance at being
slighted. Here, the part of Gonorill is actually being
played by a stool.

EDGAR Bless thy five wits.

50 KENT Oh, pity. Sir, where is the patience now
     That you so oft have boasted to retain?

EDGAR [aside] My tears begin to take his part so much
     They'll mar my counterfeiting.

LEAR The little dogs and all,°   *Even the little dogs*
55   Trey, Blanche, and Sweetheart, see, they bark at me.

EDGAR Tom will throw his head at° them; avaunt,° you curs! *will threaten (?) / begone*
     Be thy mouth or° black or white,   *either*
     Tooth that poisons° if it bite,   *gives rabies*
     Mastiff, greyhound, mongrel grim,
60   Hound or spaniel, brach° or him,   *bitch*
     Bobtail tyke, or trundle-tail,[9]
     Tom will make them weep and wail;
     For with throwing thus my head,
     Dogs leap the hatch[1] and all are fled.
65   Loudla, doodla, come march to wakes,° and fairs,   *parish festivals*
     And market towns. Poor Tom, thy horn is dry.[2]

LEAR Then let them anatomize° Regan, see what breeds about   *dissect*
     her heart. Is there any cause in nature that makes this hard-
     ness? [to EDGAR] You, sir, I entertain° you for one of my hun- *retain*
70   dred, only I do not like the fashion of your garments. You'll
     say they are Persian° attire, but let them be changed.   *oriental; splendid*

KENT Now, good my lord, lie here awhile.

LEAR Make no noise, make no noise. Draw the curtains,° so,   *bed curtains*
     so, so. We'll go to supper i'th' morning, so, so, so.
          [He falls asleep.]
          Enter GLOUCESTER.

75 GLOUCESTER Come hither, friend. Where is the King my
     master?

KENT Here, sir, but trouble him not. His wits are gone.

GLOUCESTER Good friend, I prithee, take him in thy arms.
     I have o'erheard a plot of death upon° him,   *against*
     There is a litter ready; lay him in't
80   And drive towards Dover, friend, where thou shalt meet
     Both welcome and protection. Take up thy master;
     If thou shouldst dally half an hour, his life
     With thine and all that offer to defend him
     Stand in assurèd loss.° Take up the King   *Are certainly doomed*
85   And follow me, that will to some provision
     Give thee quick conduct.[3]

---

9. Short-tailed mongrel, or long-tailed.
1. Dogs leap over the lower half of a divided door.
2. A begging formula that refers to the horn vessel
that vagabonds carried for drink; the covert sense is

that Edgar has run out of Bedlamite inspiration.
3. *that . . . conduct:* who will quickly guide you to
some supplies.

EDGAR   Bless thy five wits.[4]

KENT   Oh, pity. Sir, where is the patience now
That you so oft have boasted to retain?

20 EDGAR   [aside]   My tears begin to take his part so much
They mar my counterfeiting.

LEAR   The little dogs and all,°   *Even the little dogs*
Trey, Blanche, and Sweetheart, see, they bark at me.

EDGAR   Tom will throw his head at° them. Avaunt,° you curs!   *will threaten (?) / Begone*

25 Be thy mouth or° black or white,   *either*
Tooth that poisons° if it bite,   *gives rabies*
Mastiff, greyhound, mongrel grim,
Hound or spaniel, brach° or him,   *bitch*
Or bobtail tyke, or trundle tail,[5]

30 Tom will make him weep and wail;
For with throwing thus my head,
Dogs leapt the hatch[6] and all are fled.
Do, de, de, de. Sessa.[7] Come, march to wakes,° and fairs,   *parish festivals*
and market towns. Poor Tom, thy horn is dry.[8]

35 LEAR   Then let them anatomize° Regan, see what breeds   *dissect*
about her heart. Is there any cause in nature that makes
these hard hearts? [to EDGAR] You, sir, I entertain° for one of   *retain*
my hundred, only I do not like the fashion of your garments.
You will say they are Persian,° but let them be changed.   *oriental; splendid*

40 KENT   Now, good my lord, lie here and rest awhile.

LEAR   Make no noise, make no noise. Draw the curtains,° so,   *bed curtains*
so. We'll go to supper i'th' morning.

FOOL   And I'll go to bed at noon.

Enter GLOUCESTER.

GLOUCESTER   Come hither, friend. Where is the King my
master?

45 KENT   Here, sir, but trouble him not. His wits are gone.

GLOUCESTER   Good friend, I prithee, take him in thy arms.
I have o'erheard a plot of death upon° him.   *against*
There is a litter ready: lay him in't
And drive toward Dover, friend, where thou shalt meet

50 Both welcome and protection. Take up thy master;
If thou shouldst dally half an hour, his life
With thine and all that offer to defend him
Stand in assurèd loss.° Take up, take up,   *Are certainly doomed*
And follow me, that will to some provision

55 Give thee quick conduct.[9] Come, come, away.   *Exeunt.*

---

4. TEXTUAL COMMENT Lear's "mock-trial" of Gonerill and Regan, in absentia, appears only in Q1
(3.6.12–49). The trial does not appear in F and was
probably cut by Shakespeare rather than omitted due
to a printer's error. See Digital Edition TC 4 (Folio
edited text).
5. Short-tailed mongrel, or long-tailed.
6. Dogs leaped over the lower half of a divided door.

7. Apparently nonsense, although "Sessa" may be a
version of the French *cessez* ("stop" or "hush").
8. A begging formula that refers to the horn vessel
that vagabonds carried for drink; the covert sense is
that Edgar has run out of Bedlamite inspiration.
9. *that . . . conduct:* who will quickly guide you to
some supplies.

KENT   Oppressed nature sleeps.
        This rest might yet have balmed° thy broken sinews,°   soothed / nerves
        Which, if convenience° will not allow,   circumstances
        Stand in hard cure.° [to the FOOL] Come, help to bear thy   Will be hard to cure
        master.
90   Thou must not stay behind.
        GLOUCESTER   Come, come away.   Exeunt [all but EDGAR].
        EDGAR   When we our betters see bearing our° woes,   our same
        We scarcely think our miseries our foes.
        Who alone suffers, suffers most i'th' mind,
95   Leaving free° things and happy shows° behind.   carefree / scenes
        But then the mind much sufferance doth o'erskip,
        When grief hath mates and bearing° fellowship.   pain; suffering
        How light and portable my pain seems now,
        When that which makes me bend makes the King bow:
100   He° childed as I fathered. Tom, away.   He is
        Mark the high noises° and thyself bewray°   important rumors / reveal
        When false opinion, whose wrong thoughts defile thee,
        In thy just proof repeals and reconciles thee.[4]
        What° will hap° more tonight, safe scape the King,   Whatever / chance
105   Lurk, lurk.   [Exit.]

---

4. *In . . . thee:* When true evidence pardons you and reconciles you (with your father).

3.7 (F 3.7)

Enter CORNWALL, REGAN, GONORILL, *[Edmund the]*
BASTARD[, *and three* SERVANTS].

CORNWALL [*to* GONORILL] Post° speedily to my lord your hus-   Ride
band; show him this letter. The army of France is landed. [*to*
SERVANTS] Seek out the villain Gloucester!

[*Exeunt two or three* SERVANTS.]

REGAN Hang him instantly.

5 GONORILL Pluck out his eyes.

CORNWALL Leave him to my displeasure. Edmund, keep you
our sister° company. The revenge we are bound¹ to take upon   sister-in-law
your traitorous father are not fit for your beholding. Advise
the Duke where you are going to a most festinate prepara-
10 tion.² We are bound° to the like. Our post° shall be swift and   committed / messengers
intelligence° betwixt us. Farewell, dear sister. Farewell, my   convey information
lord of Gloucester.

Enter STEWARD.

How now, where's the King?

STEWARD My lord of Gloucester hath conveyed him hence.

15 Some five- or six-and-thirty of his° knights,   (Lear's)
Hot questrists° after him, met him at gate,   searchers
Who, with some other of the lord's° dependents,   (Gloucester's)
Are gone with him towards Dover, where they boast
To have well-armed friends.

20 CORNWALL Get horses for your mistress.   [*Exit* STEWARD.]

GONORILL Farewell, sweet lord and sister.

CORNWALL Edmund, farewell.

Exeunt GONORILL *and* [*Edmund the*] BASTARD.

Go seek the traitor Gloucester.

Pinion him° like a thief; bring him before us.   Tie his arms
Though we may not pass° upon his life   pass sentence
25 Without the form° of justice, yet our power   official proceedings
Shall do a courtesy³ to our wrath, which men may blame
But not control. Who's there, the traitor?

Enter GLOUCESTER *brought in by two or three*
[SERVANTS].

REGAN Ingrateful fox, 'tis he.

CORNWALL Bind fast his corky° arms.   withered

[SERVANTS *bind* GLOUCESTER.]

GLOUCESTER What means your graces? Good my friends,
consider

30 You are my guests. Do me no foul play, friends.

CORNWALL Bind him, I say.

REGAN Hard, hard! O filthy traitor!

GLOUCESTER Unmerciful lady, as you are, I am true.

CORNWALL To this chair bind him. —Villain, thou shalt find—

GLOUCESTER By the kind gods, 'tis most ignobly done

35 To pluck me by the beard.°   (an extreme insult)

REGAN So white° and such a traitor?   white-haired; venerable

---

3.7 Location: At Gloucester's castle.
1. Bound by duty; expected by destiny.
2. *Advise . . . preparation:* When you reach Albany,
tell the Duke to prepare quickly.
3. Shall allow a courtesy or an indulgence; shall
bow to.

3.7 (Q 3.7)

Enter CORNWALL, REGAN, GONERILL, [EDMOND *the*]
bastard, and SERVANTS.

CORNWALL [*to* GONERILL] Post° speedily to my lord, your hus-   *Ride*
band; show him this letter. The army of France is landed. [*to*
SERVANTS] Seek out the traitor Gloucester.

        [*Exeunt* SERVANTS.]

REGAN Hang him instantly.

5 GONERILL Pluck out his eyes.

CORNWALL Leave him to my displeasure. Edmond, keep you
our sister° company. The revenges we are bound[1] to take   *sister-in-law*
upon your traitorous father are not fit for your beholding.
Advise the Duke where you are going to a most festinate
10 preparation.[2] We are bound° to the like. Our posts° shall be *committed / messengers*
swift and intelligent° betwixt us. Farewell, dear sister. Fare- *well informed*
well, my lord of Gloucester.

    Enter [*Oswald the*] STEWARD.

How now? Where's the King?

STEWARD My lord of Gloucester hath conveyed him hence.
15 Some five- or six-and-thirty of his° knights,   *(Lear's)*
Hot questrists° after him, met him at gate,   *searchers*
Who, with some other of the lord's° dependents,   *(Gloucester's)*
Are gone with him toward Dover, where they boast
To have well-armed friends.

20 CORNWALL Get horses for your mistress.

GONERILL Farewell, sweet lord and sister.

CORNWALL Edmond, farewell.

    Exeunt GONERILL [*and* EDMOND].

    Go seek the traitor Gloucester;

Pinion him° like a thief; bring him before us.   *Tie his arms*
Though well we may not pass° upon his life   *pass sentence*
25 Without the form° of justice, yet our power   *official proceedings*
Shall do a court'sy[3] to our wrath, which men
May blame but not control.

    Enter GLOUCESTER *and* SERVANTS.

    Who's there? The traitor?

REGAN Ingrateful fox, 'tis he.

CORNWALL   Bind fast his corky° arms.   *withered*

GLOUCESTER What means your graces? Good my friends,
consider
30 You are my guests. Do me no foul play, friends.

CORNWALL Bind him, I say.

    [SERVANTS *bind* GLOUCESTER.]

REGAN   Hard, hard! O filthy traitor!

GLOUCESTER Unmerciful lady, as you are, I'm none.

CORNWALL To this chair bind him. —Villain, thou shalt find—

GLOUCESTER By the kind gods, 'tis most ignobly done
35 To pluck me by the beard.°   *(an extreme insult)*

REGAN So white° and such a traitor?   *white-haired; venerable*

3.7 Location: At Gloucester's castle.
1. Bound by duty; expected by destiny.
2. *Advise . . . preparation*: When you reach Albany,

tell the Duke to prepare quickly.
3. Shall allow a courtesy or an indulgence; shall
bow to.

GLOUCESTER   Naughty° lady,   *Wicked*
  These hairs which thou dost ravish from my chin
  Will quicken° and accuse thee. I am your host;   *come alive*
  With robbers' hands my hospitable favors°   *features*
40 You should not ruffle° thus. What will you do?   *snatch at*
CORNWALL   Come, sir, what letters had you late° from   *lately*
  France?
REGAN   Be simple,° answerer, for we know the truth.   *direct*
CORNWALL   And what confederacy have you with the traitors
  Late-footed° in the kingdom?   *Recently on the move*
45 REGAN   To whose hands you have sent the lunatic King?
  Speak.
GLOUCESTER   I have a letter guessingly set down,[4]
  Which came from one that's of a neutral heart
  And not from one opposed.
CORNWALL   Cunning.
REGAN   And false.
CORNWALL   Where hast thou sent the King?
GLOUCESTER   To Dover.
50 REGAN   Wherefore° to Dover? Wast thou not charged° at   *Why / commanded*
  peril—
CORNWALL   Wherefore to Dover? Let him first answer that!
GLOUCESTER   I am tied to th' stake, and I must stand the
  course.[5]
REGAN   Wherefore to Dover, sir?
GLOUCESTER   Because I would not see thy cruel nails
55 Pluck out his poor old eyes, nor thy fierce sister
  In his anointed[6] flesh, rash° boarish fangs.   *slash; cut*
  The sea, with such a storm on his loved head
  In hell-black night endured, would have laid° up   *risen*
  And quenched the stellèd° fires. Yet, poor old heart,   *stars'*
60 He holped° the heavens to rage.   *helped*
  If wolves had at thy gate heard that dern° time   *dreary; dreadful*
  Thou shouldst have said, "Good Porter, turn the key."°   *(to open the door)*
  All cruels else subscribed,[7] but I shall see
  The wingèd vengeance[8] overtake such children.
65 CORNWALL   See't shalt thou never. Fellows,° hold the chair.   *Servants*
  —Upon those eyes of thine, I'll set my foot.
GLOUCESTER   He that will think° to live till he be old,   *Whoever hopes*
  Give me some help! —Oh, cruel! O ye gods!
  [CORNWALL *plucks out Gloucester's eye.*]
REGAN   One side will mock another: t'other too.
70 CORNWALL   If you see vengeance—
FIRST SERVANT   Hold your hand, my lord.
  I have served ever since I was a child,
  But better service have I never done you
  Than now to bid you hold.
REGAN   How now, you dog?

---

4. Written without confirmation; speculative.
5. An image from bearbaiting, in which a bear on a short tether had to fight off an assault by dogs.
6. Consecrated with holy oils (as part of a king's coronation).

7. All other cruel beasts would have pity, but not you; I can accept the cruelty of all creatures, but not yours.
8. Swift or heaven-sent revenge; either an angel of God or the Furies, who were flying executors of divine vengeance in classical mythology.

GLOUCESTER   Naughty° lady,   *Wicked*
  These hairs which thou dost ravish from my chin
  Will quicken° and accuse thee. I am your host;   *come alive*
  With robbers' hands my hospitable favors°   *features*
40   You should not ruffle° thus. What will you do?   *snatch at*
CORNWALL   Come, sir, what letters had you late° from   *lately*
  France?
REGAN   Be simple-answered,° for we know the truth.   *straightforward*
CORNWALL   And what confederacy have you with the traitors
  Late footed° in the kingdom?   *Recently on the move*
REGAN   To whose hands
45   You have sent the lunatic King? Speak.
GLOUCESTER   I have a letter guessingly set down[4]
  Which came from one that's of a neutral heart
  And not from one opposed.
CORNWALL   Cunning.
REGAN   And false.
CORNWALL   Where hast thou sent the King?
50 GLOUCESTER   To Dover.
REGAN   Wherefore° to Dover?   *Why*
  Wast thou not charged° at peril—   *commanded*
CORNWALL   Wherefore to Dover? Let him answer that.
GLOUCESTER   I am tied to th' stake, and I must stand the
  course.[5]
55 REGAN   Wherefore to Dover?
GLOUCESTER   Because I would not see thy cruel nails
  Pluck out his poor old eyes, nor thy fierce sister
  In his anointed[6] flesh stick boarish fangs.
  The sea, with such a storm as his bare head
60   In hell-black night endured, would have buoyed° up   *risen*
  And quenched the stellèd° fires,   *stars'*
  Yet poor old heart, he holp° the heavens to rain.   *helped*
  If wolves had at thy gate howled that stern° time,   *dreary; dreadful*
  Thou shouldst have said, "Good porter, turn the key,°   *(to open the door)*
65   All cruels else subscribe."[7] But I shall see
  The wingèd vengeance[8] overtake such children.
CORNWALL   See't shalt thou never. Fellows,° hold the chair.   *Servants*
  —Upon these eyes of thine, I'll set my foot.
    [*He plucks out Gloucester's eye.*]
GLOUCESTER   He that will think° to live till he be old,   *Whoever hopes*
70   Give me some help! —Oh, cruel! O you gods!
REGAN   One side will mock another: th'other too.
CORNWALL   If you see vengeance—
FIRST SERVANT   Hold your hand, my lord.
  I have served you ever since I was a child,
  But better service have I never done you
  Than now to bid you hold.
75 REGAN   How now, you dog?

---

4. Written without confirmation; speculative.
5. An image from bearbaiting, in which a bear on a short tether had to fight off an assault by dogs.
6. Consecrated with holy oils (as part of a king's coronation).

7. All other cruel beasts would have pity, but not you; I can accept the cruelly of all creatures, but not yours.
8. Swift or heaven-sent revenge; either an angel of God or the Furies, who were flying executors of divine vengeance in classical mythology.

75 FIRST SERVANT If you did wear a beard upon your chin,
   I'd shake it on this quarrel.[9] What do you mean?°   *intend*
   CORNWALL My villein?°   *servant; villain*
   FIRST SERVANT Why, then, come on and take the chance of
      anger![1]
         [*They*] *draw and fight.*
   REGAN Give me thy sword. A peasant stand up thus?
         She takes a sword and runs at him behind.
80 FIRST SERVANT Oh, I am slain! [*to* GLOUCESTER] My lord, yet
      have you one eye left
      To see some mischief° on him. Oh!   *injury*
         [*He dies.*]
   CORNWALL Lest it see more, prevent it. Out, vile jelly![2]
         [*He plucks out Gloucester's other eye.*]
      Where is thy luster now?
   GLOUCESTER All dark and comfortless? Where's my son
      Edmund?
85 Edmund, unbridle all the sparks of Nature[3]
   To quit° this horrid act.   *requite; avenge*
   REGAN   Out, villain!
      Thou call'st on him that hates thee. It was he
      That made the overture of° thy treasons to us,   *revealed*
      Who is too good to pity thee.
90 GLOUCESTER Oh, my follies! Then Edgar was abused.°   *slandered*
      Kind gods, forgive me that and prosper him.
   REGAN Go thrust him out at gates, and let him smell
      His way to Dover. How is't my lord? How look you?°   *How do you feel*
   CORNWALL I have received a hurt. Follow me, lady.
95   [*to* SERVANTS] Turn out that eyeless villain; throw this
         slave
      Upon the dunghill.
                 [*Exeunt* SERVANTS *with* GLOUCESTER *and*
                           First Servant's body.]
         Regan, I bleed apace;
      Untimely comes this hurt. Give me your arm.
                     Exeunt [CORNWALL *and* REGAN].[4]
   SECOND SERVANT I'll never care what wickedness I do if this
      man come to good.[5]
100 THIRD SERVANT If she live long, and in the end meet the old°   *usual*
      course of death, women will all turn monsters.
   SECOND SERVANT Let's follow the old Earl and get the Bed-
      lam° to lead him where he would. His madness allows itself   *madman*
      to anything.
105 THIRD SERVANT Go thou. I'll fetch some flax and whites of
      eggs to apply to his bleeding face. Now, heaven help him!
                     Exeunt [*severally*].°   *separately*

---

9. I'd pluck it over this point; I'd issue a challenge.
1. Take the risk of fighting when angry; take the fortune of one who is governed by his anger.
2. PERFORMANCE COMMENT Should a production
minimize gore in this shocking scene, or emphasize
it? For the implications of the staging, see Digital
Edition PC 4.
3. All the warmth of filial love; all the anger that
your father has received such treatment.
4. TEXTUAL COMMENT Some critics have called the

play's blinding scene the "cruelest" in all of English
literature. Yet the two texts differ in their portrayals
of this cruelty. Notably, the Quarto version culminates
with Cornwall's two servants pledging to avenge
Gloucester's blinding. Their absence in the Folio version denies the audience even this brief expression of
sympathy. See Digital Edition TC 5 (Quarto edited
text).
5. *I'll . . . good:* Because this may be a sign that evil
goes unpunished. *this man:* Cornwall.

FIRST SERVANT If you did wear a beard upon your chin,
I'd shake it on this quarrel.[9] What do you mean?°   *intend*
CORNWALL [*drawing his sword*] My villein?°   *servant; villain*
FIRST SERVANT Nay, then, come on, and take the chance of
anger.[1]
[*They fight, and* CORNWALL *is wounded.*]
80   REGAN Give me thy sword. A peasant stand up thus?
[*She*] *kills him.*
FIRST SERVANT Oh, I am slain! [*to* GLOUCESTER] My lord, you
have one eye left
To see some mischief° on him. Oh!   *injury*
[*He dies.*]
CORNWALL Lest it see more, prevent it. Out, vile jelly![2]
[*He plucks out Gloucester's other eye.*]
Where is thy luster now?
85   GLOUCESTER All dark and comfortless?
Where's my son Edmond?
Edmond, enkindle all the sparks of nature[3]
To quit° this horrid act.   *requite; avenge*
REGAN   Out, treacherous villain!
Thou call'st on him that hates thee. It was he
90   That made the overture of° thy treasons to us,   *revealed*
Who is too good to pity thee.
GLOUCESTER Oh, my follies! Then Edgar was abused!°   *slandered*
Kind gods, forgive me that, and prosper him.
REGAN Go, thrust him out at gates, and let him smell
95   His way to Dover. How is't, my lord? How look you?°   *How do you feel*
CORNWALL I have received a hurt. Follow me, lady.
[*to* SERVANTS] Turn out that eyeless villain. Throw this slave
Upon the dunghill.
                    Exeunt [SERVANTS] *with* GLOUCESTER [*and First
                                              Servant's body*].
Regan, I bleed apace;
Untimely comes this hurt. Give me your arm.
                    Exeunt [CORNWALL *and* REGAN].[4]

---

9. I'd pluck it over this point; I'd issue a challenge.
1. Take the risk of fighting when angry; take the fortune of one who is governed by his anger.
2. PERFORMANCE COMMENT Should a production minimize gore in this shocking scene, or emphasize it? For the implications of the staging, see Digital Edition PC 4.
3. All the warmth of filial love; all the anger that your father has received such treatment.

4. TEXTUAL COMMENT Some critics have called the play's blinding scene the "cruelest" in all of English literature. Yet the two texts differ in their portrayals of this cruelty. Notably, the Quarto version culminates with Cornwall's two servants pledging to avenge Gloucester's blinding. Their absence in the Folio version denies the audience even this brief expression of sympathy. See Digital Edition TC 5 (Folio edited text).

4.1 (F 4.1)

Enter EDGAR *[disguised as Poor Tom].*

EDGAR   Yet better thus and known to be contemned,°   despised
    Than still° contemned and flattered to be worst.   always
    The lowest and most dejected thing of Fortune
    Stands still in experience, lives not in fear.[1]
5   The lamentable change is from the best,
    The worst returns to laughter.[2]

Enter GLOUCESTER, *led by an* OLD MAN.

    Who's here? My father, parti-eyed![3] World, world, O world!
    But that thy strange mutations make us hate thee,
    Life would not yield to age.[4]
OLD MAN   O my good lord,
10   I have been your tenant and your father's
    Tenant this fourscore—
GLOUCESTER   Away, get thee away! Good friend, be gone.
    Thy comforts° can do me no good at all;   assistance
    Thee they may hurt.
15 OLD MAN   Alack, sir, you cannot see your way.
GLOUCESTER   I have no way and therefore want no eyes.
    I stumbled when I saw. Full oft 'tis seen
    Our means secure us, and our mere defects
    Prove our commodities.[5] Ah, dear son Edgar,
20   The food° of thy abusèd° father's wrath,   fuel; prey / deceived
    Might I but live to see thee in° my touch,   through
    I'd say I had eyes again.
OLD MAN   How now, who's there?
EDGAR *[aside]*   O gods! Who is't can say, "I am at the worst"?
25   I am worse than e'er I was.
OLD MAN   'Tis poor mad Tom.
EDGAR *[aside]*   And worse I may be yet. The worst is not
    As long as we can say, "This is the worst."
OLD MAN   Fellow, where goest?
30 GLOUCESTER   Is it a beggar man?
OLD MAN   Madman and beggar too.
GLOUCESTER   'A° has some reason, else he could not beg.   He
    In the last night's storm, I such a fellow saw,
    Which made me think a man a worm. My son
35   Came then into my mind, and yet my mind
    Was then scarce friends with him. I have heard more since.
    As flies are to th' wanton° boys are we to th' gods: playful; careless
    They bit us for their sport.

4.1 Location: Open country.
1. *Stands . . . fear:* Remains calmly upright because there is no fear of falling further.
2. *The lamentable . . . laughter:* The change to be lamented is one that alters the best of circumstances; the worst luck can only improve.
3. Multicolored like a fool's costume (red with blood under white dressings).
4. *But . . . age:* If there were no strange reversals of fortune to make the world hateful, we would not consent to aging and death.
5. *Our means . . . commodities:* Our wealth makes us overconfident, and our utter deprivation proves to be beneficial.

4.1 (Q 4.1)

Enter EDGAR [*disguised as Poor Tom*].

EDGAR Yet better thus and known to be contemned°   despised
　　　Than still° contemned and flattered. To be worst,   always
　　　The lowest and most dejected thing of fortune
　　　Stands still in esperance, lives not in fear.[1]
5　　The lamentable change is from the best,
　　　The worst returns to laughter.[2] Welcome, then,
　　　Thou unsubstantial air that I embrace.
　　　The wretch that thou hast blown unto the worst
　　　Owes nothing° to thy blasts.   (*because he can't pay*)

Enter GLOUCESTER *and an* OLD MAN.

10　　But who comes here? My father, poorly led?
　　　World, world, O world!
　　　But that thy strange mutations make us hate thee,
　　　Life would not yield to age.[3]

OLD MAN O my good lord, I have been your tenant
15　　And your father's tenant these fourscore years.

GLOUCESTER Away, get thee away! Good friend, be gone.
　　　Thy comforts° can do me no good at all;   assistance
　　　Thee, they may hurt.

OLD MAN　　　　　　You cannot see your way.

GLOUCESTER I have no way and therefore want no eyes.
20　　I stumbled when I saw. Full oft 'tis seen
　　　Our means secure us, and our mere defects
　　　Prove our commodities.[4] O dear son Edgar,
　　　The food° of thy abusèd° father's wrath,   fuel; prey / deceived
　　　Might I but live to see thee in° my touch,   through
　　　I'd say I had eyes again.

25　OLD MAN　　　　　　How now? Who's there?

EDGAR [*aside*] O gods! Who is't can say, "I am at the worst"?
　　　I am worse than e'er I was.

OLD MAN　　　　　　'Tis poor mad Tom.

EDGAR [*aside*] And worse I may be yet; the worst is not
　　　So long as we can say, "This is the worst."

OLD MAN Fellow, where goest?

30　GLOUCESTER　　　　　Is it a beggar man?

OLD MAN Madman and beggar too.

GLOUCESTER He has some reason, else he could not beg.
　　　I'th' last night's storm, I such a fellow saw
　　　Which made me think a man a worm. My son
35　　Came then into my mind, and yet my mind
　　　Was then scarce friends with him.
　　　I have heard more since.
　　　As flies to wanton° boys are we to th' gods: playful; careless
　　　They kill us for their sport.

4.1 Location: Open country.
1. *Stands . . . fear:* Remains in hope ("esperance")
because there is no fear of falling further.
2. *The lamentable . . . laughter:* The change to be
lamented is one that alters the best of circumstances;
the worst luck can only improve.

3. *But . . . age:* If there were no strange reversals of
fortune to make the world hateful, we would not
consent to aging and death.
4. *Our means . . . commodities:* Our wealth makes us
overconfident, and our utter deprivation proves to be
beneficial.

EDGAR [*aside*]   How should this be?
  Bad is the trade that must play the fool to sorrow,[6]
40 Ang'ring itself and others. [*to* GLOUCESTER] Bless thee,
    master.
GLOUCESTER Is that the naked fellow?
OLD MAN   Ay, my lord.
GLOUCESTER Then prithee, get thee gone. If for my sake
  Thou wilt o'ertake us here a mile or twain
  I'th' way toward Dover, do it for ancient love,[7]
45 And bring some covering for this naked soul,
  Who I'll entreat to lead me.
OLD MAN Alack, sir, he is mad.
GLOUCESTER 'Tis the time's plague when[8] madmen lead the
    blind.
  Do as I bid thee, or rather do thy pleasure.
50 Above the rest, be gone.
OLD MAN I'll bring him the best 'parrel° that I have,   *apparel; clothing*
  Come on't what will.   [*Exit.*]
GLOUCESTER   Sirrah, naked fellow.
EDGAR Poor Tom's a-cold. [*aside*] I cannot dance it farther.[9]
GLOUCESTER Come hither, fellow.
55 EDGAR Bless thy sweet eyes, they bleed.
GLOUCESTER Know'st thou the way to Dover?
EDGAR Both stile and gate, horse-way, and footpath. Poor Tom
  hath been scared out of his good wits. Bless the good man
  from the foul fiend. Five fiends have been in poor Tom at
60 once: of lust, as Obidicut; Hobbididence, prince of dumb-
  ness; Mahu of stealing; Modo of murder; Stiberdigebit of
  mopping and mowing,[1] who since possesses chambermaids
  and waiting women. So bless thee, master.
GLOUCESTER Here, take this purse, thou whom the heavens'
    plagues
65 Have humbled to all strokes.° That I am wretched   *to accept all blows*
  Makes thee the happier. Heavens deal so still.°   *always*
  Let the superfluous and lust-dieted man[2]
  That stands° your ordinance,° that will not see   *resists / authority*
  Because he does not feel, feel your power quickly.
70 So distribution should undo excess,
  And each man have enough. Dost thou know Dover?
EDGAR Ay, master.
GLOUCESTER There is a cliff whose high and bending° head   *overhanging*
  Looks firmly in the confinèd deep.[3]
75 Bring me but to the very brim of it,
  And I'll repair the misery thou dost bear
  With something rich about me.
  From that place I shall no leading need.
EDGAR Give me thy arm. Poor Tom shall lead thee.
           [*Exit* GLOUCESTER *led by* EDGAR.]

---

6. It is a bad business to have to play the fool in the face of sorrow.
7. For the sake of our long and loyal relationship (as master and servant).
8. The time is truly sick when.

9. I cannot continue the charade.
1. Grimacing and making faces.
2. Let the overprosperous man who indulges his appetite.
3. Looks fearsomely into the straits below.

EDGAR [*aside*]   How should this be?
40   Bad is the trade that must play fool to sorrow,[5]
        Ang'ring itself and others. [*to* GLOUCESTER] Bless thee,
            master.
GLOUCESTER   Is that the naked fellow?
OLD MAN   Ay, my lord.
GLOUCESTER   Get thee away. If for my sake
        Thou wilt o'ertake us hence a mile or twain
45   I'th' way toward Dover, do it for ancient love,[6]
        And bring some covering for this naked soul,
        Which I'll entreat to lead me.
OLD MAN   Alack, sir, he is mad.
GLOUCESTER   'Tis the time's plague when[7] madmen lead the
            blind.
        Do as I bid thee, or rather do thy pleasure.
50   Above the rest, be gone.
OLD MAN   I'll bring him the best 'parrel° that I have,   *apparel; clothing*
        Come on't what will.   *Exit.*
GLOUCESTER   Sirrah, naked fellow—
EDGAR   Poor Tom's a-cold. [*aside*] I cannot daub it further.[8]
55   GLOUCESTER   Come hither, fellow.
EDGAR [*aside*]   And yet I must. —Bless thy sweet eyes, they
            bleed.
GLOUCESTER   Know'st thou the way to Dover?
EDGAR   Both stile and gate, horse-way and footpath. Poor
60   Tom hath been scared out of his good wits. Bless thee, good-
        man's° son, from the foul fiend.   *householder's*
GLOUCESTER   Here, take this purse, thou whom the heav'ns'
            plagues
        Have humbled to all strokes.° That I am wretched   *to accept all blows*
        Makes thee the happier. Heavens deal so still.°   *always*
65   Let the superfluous and lust-dieted man,[9]
        That slaves° your ordinance,° that will not see   *defers to / authority*
        Because he does not feel, feel your power quickly.
        So distribution should undo excess,
        And each man have enough. Dost thou know Dover?
70   EDGAR   Ay, master.
GLOUCESTER   There is a cliff whose high and bending° head   *overhanging*
        Looks fearfully in the confinèd deep.[1]
        Bring me but to the very brim of it,
        And I'll repair the misery thou dost bear
75   With something rich about me. From that place
        I shall no leading need.
EDGAR   Give me thy arm;
        Poor Tom shall lead thee.   *Exeunt.*

---

5. It is a bad business to have to play the fool in the face of sorrow.
6. For the sake of our long and loyal relationship (as master and servant).
7. The time is truly sick when.
8. I cannot continue the charade. *daub*: mask, plaster.
9. Let the overprosperous man who indulges his appetite.
1. Looks fearsomely into the straits below.

4.2 (F 4.2)

Enter GONORILL *and [Edmund the]* BASTARD.

GONORILL   Welcome, my lord. I marvel our mild husband
  Not° met us on the way.   Has not

Enter [Oswald the] STEWARD.

  Now, where's your master?

STEWARD   Madam, within, but never man so changed.
  I told him of the army that was landed;
5 He smiled at it. I told him you were coming;
  His answer was, "The worse." Of Gloucester's treachery,
  And of the loyal service of his son,
  When I informed him, then he called me "sot"°   fool
  And told me I had turned the wrong side out.[1]
10 What he should most dislike seems pleasant to him;
  What like, offensive.

GONORILL [*to* BASTARD]   Then shall you go no further.
  It is the cowish° terror of his spirit   cowardly
  That dares not undertake. He'll not feel wrongs
  Which tie him to an answer.[2] Our wishes on the way
15 May prove effects.[3] Back, Edmund, to my brother;°   brother-in-law
  Hasten his musters° and conduct his powers.°   call-up of troops / armies
  I must change arms at home and give the distaff[4]
  Into my husband's hands. This trusty servant
  Shall pass between us. Ere long, you are like° to hear—   likely
20 If you dare venture in your own behalf—
  A mistress's° command. Wear this; spare speech;[5]   (playing on "lover's")
  Decline your head. This kiss, if it durst speak,
  Would stretch thy spirits up into the air.
  Conceive,° and fare you well.   Understand (my meaning)

25 BASTARD   Yours in° the ranks of death.   even in

GONORILL   My most dear Gloucester, to thee woman's
  services are due.   [*Exit* BASTARD.]
  A fool usurps my bed.[6]

STEWARD   Madam, here comes my lord.   Exit.

[*Enter* ALBANY.]

GONORILL   I have been worth the whistling.[7]

30 ALBANY   O Gonorill,
  You are not worth the dust which the rude wind
  Blows in your face. I fear your disposition.
  That nature which contemns i'th'° origin   despises its
  Cannot be bordered certain° in itself.   defended securely
35 She that herself will sliver and disbranch°   split
  From her material sap, perforce must wither
  And come to deadly use.[8]

Scene 4.2 Location: Before Albany's castle.
1. I had reversed things (by mistaking loyalty for treachery).
2. He'll . . . answer: He'll ignore insults that would provoke him to retaliate.
3. May be put into action.
4. A device used in spinning and thus emblematic of the female role. To "change arms," therefore, is to swap the male and female identities.
5. TEXTUAL COMMENT The printing of 4.2 in Q1 shows an unusual amount of stop-press correction in the lines of Gonorill and Albany from 21 to 61. While such correction should improve the text, here the "corrections" often confuse the lines further. Editors have proposed various reasons for the scene's

textual problems (what editors would call a "textual crux"), ranging from printer errors to Shakespeare's own emendation of the text. See Digital Edition TC 6 (Quarto edited text).
6. Continuing the inversion of roles, Albany, who should be the head of the family, is seen by Gonorill as a subservient member with no right to control her.
7. At one time, you would have come to welcome me home; referring to the proverb "It is a poor dog that is not worth the whistling."
8. She . . . use: The allusion is probably biblical: "But that which beareth thorns and briers is reproved, and is near unto cursing; whose end is to be burned" (Hebrews 6:8). come to deadly use: be destroyed; be used for burning.

4.2 (Q 4.2)

Enter GONERILL, [EDMOND *the*] *bastard, and* [Oswald *the*] STEWARD.

GONERILL Welcome, my lord. I marvel our mild husband
  Not° met us on the way. [*to* STEWARD] Now, where's your   *Has not*
    master?
STEWARD Madam, within, but never man so changed.
  I told him of the army that was landed;
5 He smiled at it. I told him you were coming;
  His answer was, "The worse." Of Gloucester's treachery,
  And of the loyal service of his son,
  When I informed him, then he called me "sot"°   *fool*
  And told me I had turned the wrong side out.[1]
10 What most he should dislike seems pleasant to him;
  What like, offensive.
GONERILL [*to* EDMOND]   Then shall you go no further.
  It is the cowish° terror of his spirit   *cowardly*
  That dares not undertake. He'll not feel wrongs
  Which tie him to an answer.[2] Our wishes on the way
15 May prove effects.[3] Back, Edmond, to my brother;°   *brother-in-law*
  Hasten his musters° and conduct his powers.°   *call-up of troops / armies*
  I must change names° at home and give the distaff[4]   *exchange roles*
  Into my husband's hands. This trusty servant
  Shall pass between us. Ere long you are like° to hear—   *likely*
20 If you dare venture in your own behalf—
  A mistress's° command. Wear this; spare speech;   *(playing on "lover's")*
  Decline your head. This kiss, if it durst speak,
  Would stretch thy spirits up into the air.
  Conceive,° and fare thee well.   *Understand (my meaning)*
EDMOND Yours in° the ranks of death.   *Exit.*   *even in*
25 GONERILL   My most dear Gloucester!
  Oh, the difference of man and man!
  To thee a woman's services are due;
  My fool usurps my body.[5]
STEWARD Madam, here comes my lord.   [*Exit.*]
    Enter ALBANY.
GONERILL I have been worth the whistle.[6]
30 ALBANY   O Gonerill,
  You are not worth the dust which the rude wind
  Blows in your face.

4.2 Location: Before Albany's castle.
1. I had reversed things (by mistaking loyalty for treachery).
2. *He'll . . . answer:* He'll ignore insults that would provoke him to retaliate.
3. May be put into action.
4. A device used in spinning and thus emblematic of the female role. To "change names," therefore, is to swap the marking of male and female identities.
5. My idiot husband presumes to possess me.
6. At one time, you would have come to welcome me home; referring to the proverb "It is a poor dog that is not worth the whistling."

GONORILL　No more, the text is foolish.

ALBANY　Wisdom and goodness to the vile seem vile;
40　Filths savor but themselves. What have you done?
Tigers, not daughters, what have you performed?
A father and a gracious agèd man,
Whose reverence even the head-lugged° bear would lick,   *dragged by the head*
Most barbarous, most degenerate, have you madded.°   *driven mad*
45　Could my good brother° suffer you to do it?   *brother-in-law*
A man, a prince, by him so benefited!
If that the heavens do not their visible spirits
Send quickly down to tame the vile offenses,
It will come.
50　Humanity must perforce° prey on itself   *inevitably*
Like monsters of the deep.

GONORILL　 Milk-livered° man,   *Cowardly*
That bearest a cheek for blows, a head for wrongs,[9]
Who hast not in thy brows an eye discerning
Thine honor from thy suffering,[1] that not know'st
55　Fools do those villains pity who are punished
Ere they have done their mischief. Where's thy drum?°   *(to muster troops)*
France spreads his banners in our noiseless° land   *peaceful*
With plumèd helm. Thy state begins thereat
Whilst thou, a moral° fool, sits still and cries,   *moralizing*
"Alack, why does he so?"
60　ALBANY　 See thyself, devil!
Proper deformity seems not in the fiend
So horrid as in woman.[2]

GONORILL　 O vain° fool!   *useless*

ALBANY　Thou changèd and self-covered[3] thing, for shame!
Bemonster not thy feature. Were't my fitness°   *If it were appropriate*
65　To let these hands obey my blood,
They are apt enough to dislocate and tear
Thy flesh and bones. Howe'er° thou art a fiend,   *Although*
A woman's shape doth shield thee.

GONORILL　Marry, your manhood, mew[4]—

Enter a GENTLEMAN.

70　ALBANY　What news?

GENTLEMAN　O my good lord, the Duke of Cornwall's dead,
Slain by his servant, going to put out
The other eye of Gloucester.

ALBANY　 Gloucester's eyes?

GENTLEMAN　A servant that he bred, 'thralled with remorse,°   *shaken with pity*
75　Opposed against the act, bending° his sword   *directing*
To° his great master, who, thereat enraged,   *Against*

9. *for wrongs:* fit for abuse; ready for cuckold's horns.
1. *discerning . . . suffering:* that can distinguish
between an insult to your honor and something you
should patiently endure.
2. *Proper . . . woman:* Deformity (of morals) is appropriate in the devil and so less horrid than in woman,
from whom virtue is expected. Albany may hold a
mirror in front of Gonorill, since Jacobean women
sometimes wore small mirrors attached to their
dresses.
3. Altered and with your true (womanly) self concealed.
4. Assert your feeble masculinity (with a derisive catcall, "mew"). Alternatively: get control of your manhood; restrain ("mew") it. *Marry:* By the Virgin Mary.

GONERILL   Milk-livered° man,   *Cowardly*

That bear'st a cheek for blows, a head for wrongs,[7]

Who hast not in thy brows an eye discerning

35   Thine honor from thy suffering.[8]

ALBANY   See thyself, devil!

Proper deformity seems not in the fiend

So horrid as in woman.[9]

GONERILL   O vain° fool!   *useless*

     Enter a MESSENGER.

MESSENGER   O my good lord, the Duke of Cornwall's dead,

40   Slain by his servant, going to put out

The other eye of Gloucester.

ALBANY   Gloucester's eyes?

MESSENGER   A servant that he bred, thrilled with remorse,°   *shaken with pity*

Opposed against the act, bending° his sword   *directing*

To° his great master, who, threat-enragèd,   *Against*

---

7. *for wrongs:* fit for abuse; ready for cuckold's horns.
8. *discerning . . . suffering:* that can distinguish between an insult to your honor and something you should patiently endure.
9. *Proper . . . woman:* Deformity (of morals) is appropriate in the devil and so less horrid than in woman, from whom virtue is expected. Albany may hold a mirror in front of Gonerill, since Jacobean women sometimes wore small mirrors attached to their dresses.

Flew on him and amongst them felled him dead,
But not without that harmful stroke which since
Hath plucked him after.[5]

80 ALBANY   This shows you are above, you Justices,°   *Judges*
That these our nether crimes[6] so speedily can venge.
But, oh, poor Gloucester! Lost he his other eye?
GENTLEMAN   Both, both, my lord.
This letter, madam, craves a speedy answer.
'Tis from your sister.

85 GONORILL [*aside*]   One way I like this well:[7]
But being° widow, and my Gloucester with her,   *her being*
May all the building on my fancy pluck
Upon my hateful life.[8] Another way the news is not so took.[9]
[*to* GENTLEMAN] I'll read and answer.   *Exit.*

90 ALBANY   Where was his son when they did take his eyes?
GENTLEMAN   Come with my lady hither.
ALBANY   He is not here.
GENTLEMAN   No, my good lord, I met him back° again.   *returning*
ALBANY   Knows he the wickedness?
GENTLEMAN   Ay, my good lord. 'Twas he informed against
him

95 And quit the house on purpose that their punishment
Might have the freer course.
ALBANY   Gloucester, I live
To thank thee for the love thou showed'st the King
And to revenge thy eyes. Come hither, friend;
Tell me what more thou knowest.   *Exeunt.*

4.3

Enter KENT [*disguised as Caius*] *and a* GENTLEMAN.

KENT   Why the King of France is so suddenly gone back,
know you no reason?
GENTLEMAN   Something he left imperfect° in the state, which   *unsettled*
since his coming forth is thought of,° which imports° to the   *remembered / portends*
5   kingdom so much fear and danger that his personal return
was most required and necessary.
KENT   Who hath he left behind him general?
GENTLEMAN   The Marshal of France, Monsieur la Far.
KENT   Did your letters pierce the Queen to any demonstration
10   of grief?
GENTLEMAN   I say she took them, read them in my presence,
And now and then an ample tear trilled down
Her delicate cheek. It seemed she was a queen
Over her passion, who,° most rebel-like,   *which*
Sought to be king o'er her.

---

5. Has sent him to follow his servant into death.
6. Lower crimes, and so committed on earth, but also suggesting that the deeds smack of the nether-world of hell.
7. Because a political rival has been eliminated.
8. *May . . . life:* May pull down all of my built-up fantasies and thus make my life hateful.
9. The news may be taken otherwise.

45 Flew on him and amongst them felled him dead,
But not without that harmful stroke which since
Hath plucked him after.[1]

ALBANY   This shows you are above,
You Justices,° that these our nether crimes[2]   *Judges*
So speedily can venge. But oh, poor Gloucester!
Lost he his other eye?

50 MESSENGER   Both, both, my lord.
This letter, madam, craves a speedy answer:
'Tis from your sister.

GONERILL [*aside*]   One way I like this well;[3]
But being° widow, and my Gloucester with her,   *her being*
May all the building in my fancy pluck
55 Upon my hateful life.[4] Another way
The news is not so tart.° I'll read and answer.   *bitter*

ALBANY   Where was his son when they did take his eyes?

MESSENGER   Come with my lady hither.

ALBANY   He is not here.

MESSENGER   No, my good lord, I met him back° again.   *returning*
60 ALBANY   Knows he the wickedness?

MESSENGER   Ay, my good lord. 'Twas he informed against
    him
And quit the house on purpose, that their punishment
Might have the freer course.

ALBANY   Gloucester, I live
To thank thee for the love thou showed'st the King
65 And to revenge thine eyes. Come hither, friend;
Tell me what more thou know'st.   *Exeunt.*

---

1. Has sent him to follow his servant into death.
2. Lower crimes, and so committed on earth, but also suggesting that the deeds smack of the nether-world of hell.
3. Because a political rival has been eliminated.
4. *May . . . life:* May pull down all of my built-up fantasies and thus make my life hateful.

15 KENT   Oh, then, it moved her.
    GENTLEMAN   Not to a rage. Patience and sorrow stream
        Who should express her goodliest.¹ You have seen
        Sunshine and rain at once; her smiles and tears
        Were like a better way. Those happy smilets
20   That played on her ripe lip seem not to know
        What guests were in her eyes, which parted thence
        As pearls from diamonds dropped. In brief,
        Sorrow would be a rarity° most beloved,   gem
        If all could so become it.²
25 KENT   Made she no verbal question?
    GENTLEMAN   Faith, once or twice she heaved the name of
            father
        Pantingly forth, as if it pressed her heart,
        Cried, "Sisters, sisters, shame of ladies, sisters!
        Kent, father, sisters! What, i'th' storm, i'th' night?
30   Let pity not be believed."³ There she shook
        The holy water from her heavenly eyes,
        And clamor° moistened her. Then away she started,°   crying / sprang
        To deal with grief alone.
    KENT   It is the stars,
        The stars above us, govern our conditions.
35   Else one self mate and make⁴ could not beget
        Such different issues.° You spoke not with her since?   offspring
    GENTLEMAN   No.
    KENT   Was this before the King returned?
    GENTLEMAN   No, since.
    KENT   Well, sir, the poor distressèd Lear's i'th' town,
40   Who sometime in his better tune° remembers   state of mind
        What we are come about, and by no means
        Will yield° to see his daughter.   consent
    GENTLEMAN   Why, good sir?
    KENT   A sovereign shame so elbows° him: his own   prods; nudges
            unkindness,
        That stripped her from his benediction, turned her
45   To foreign casualties,° gave her dear rights   risks
        To his dog-hearted daughters. These things sting his mind
        So venomously that burning shame
        Detains him from Cordelia.
    GENTLEMAN   Alack, poor gentleman!
50 KENT   Of Albany's and Cornwall's powers you heard not?
    GENTLEMAN   'Tis so, they are afoot.
    KENT   Well, sir, I'll bring you to our master Lear
        And leave you to attend him. Some dear cause°   Some important reason
        Will in concealment wrap me up awhile.
55   When I am known aright, you shall not grieve°   regret
        Lending me this acquaintance.° I pray you   news
        Go along with me.   *Exeunt.*

4.3 Location: Near the French camp at Dover.   3. Never believe in pity; compassion cannot exist.
1. Which should best express her feelings.   4. Or else the same pair of spouses; "mate" and "make"
2. If everyone wore it so beautifully.   may describe either partner.

4.4 (F 4.3)

Enter CORDELIA, DOCTOR, *and others* [*including*
GENTLEMEN].

CORDELIA   Alack, 'tis he! Why, he was met even now,
As mad as the vent sea, singing aloud,
Crowned with rank fumitor and furrow weeds,[1]
With burdocks, hemlock, nettles, cuckoo flowers,
Darnell, and all the idle° weeds that grow   *useless*
In our sustaining corn. A century° is sent forth.   *battalion*
Search every acre in the high-grown field
And bring him to our eye.   [*Exeunt three* GENTLEMEN.]
                        What can man's wisdom
In the restoring° his bereaved sense? He that can help him   *Do to restore*
Take all my outward° worth.   *material*
DOCTOR   There is means, madam.
Our foster nurse of nature[2] is repose,
The which he lacks. That to provoke in him
Are many simples operative,[3] whose power
Will close the eye of anguish.
CORDELIA   All blest secrets,
All you unpublished virtues° of the earth,   *obscure healing plants*
Spring with my tears; be aidant and remediate°   *healing and remedial*
In the good man's distress. Seek, seek for him,
Lest his ungoverned rage dissolve the life
That wants° the means to lead it.   *lacks*
Enter MESSENGER.
MESSENGER   News, madam:
The British powers° are marching hitherward.   *armies*
CORDELIA   'Tis known before; our preparation stands
In expectation of them. O dear father,
It is thy business that I go about![4]
Therefore great France
My mourning and important° tears hath pitied.   *urgent; solicitous*
No blown° ambition doth our arms incite,   *inflated*
But love, dear love, and our aged father's right.[5]
Soon may I hear and see him!   *Exeunt.*

Line numbers: 5, 10, 15, 20, 25

4.4 Location: The French camp at Dover.
1. Fumitor was used against brain sickness. Furrow weeds, like the other weeds in the following lines, grow in the furrows of plowed fields.
2. *Our . . . nature:* That which comforts and nourishes human nature.
3. *That . . . operative:* To induce that ("repose") in

him, there are many effective medicinal herbs.
4. The line echoes Christ's explanation of his mission in Luke 2:49: "I must go about my father's business."
5. *No . . . right:* 1 Corinthians 13:4–5 in the Bishops' Bible (1568) says that love "swelleth not, dealeth not dishonestly, seeketh not her own."

4.3 (Q 4.4)

Enter with drum and colors, CORDELIA, GENTLEMEN,
and Soldiers.

CORDELIA   Alack, 'tis he. Why, he was met even now,
As mad as the vexèd sea, singing aloud.
Crowned with rank fumitor and furrow weeds,[1]
With burdocks, hemlock, nettles, cuckoo flowers,
5   Darnel, and all the idle° weeds that grow   *useless*
In our sustaining corn. A century° send forth;   *battalion (100 men)*
Search every acre in the high-grown field
And bring him to our eye.   [*Exit a* GENTLEMAN.]
                              What can man's wisdom
In the restoring° his bereavèd sense? He that helps him,   *Do to restore*
Take all my outward° worth.   *material*
10   GENTLEMAN   There is means, madam.
Our foster nurse of nature[2] is repose,
The which he lacks. That to provoke in him
Are many simples operative,[3] whose power
Will close the eye of anguish.
CORDELIA   All blest secrets,
15   All you unpublished virtues° of the earth,   *obscure healing plants*
Spring with my tears; be aidant and remediate°   *healing and remedial*
In the good man's desires. Seek, seek for him,
Lest his ungoverned rage dissolve the life
That wants° the means to lead it.   *lacks*
                     Enter MESSENGER.
MESSENGER   News, madam:
20   The British powers° are marching hitherward.   *armies*
CORDELIA   'Tis known before. Our preparation stands
In expectation of them. O dear father,
It is thy business that I go about![4] Therefore great France
My mourning and importuned° tears hath pitied.   *importunate; solicitous*
25   No blown° ambition doth our arms incite,   *inflated*
But love, dear love, and our agèd father's right.[5]
Soon may I hear and see him!   *Exeunt.*

4.3 Location: The French camp at Dover.
1. Fumitor was used against brain sickness. Furrow
weeds, like the other weeds in the following lines,
grow in the furrows of plowed fields.
2. *Our . . . nature:* That which comforts and nourishes human nature.
3. *That . . . operative:* To induce that ("repose") in

him, there are many effective medicinal herbs.
4. The line echoes Christ's explanation of his mission
in Luke 2:49: "I must go about my father's business."
5. *No . . . right:* 1 Corinthians 13:4–5 in the Bishops'
Bible (1568) says that love "swelleth not, dealeth not
dishonestly, seeketh not her own."

4.5 (F 4.4)

Enter REGAN *and* [*Oswald the*] STEWARD.

REGAN But are my brother's powers° set forth?   *(Albany's forces)*

STEWARD   Ay, madam.

REGAN Himself in person?

STEWARD   Madam, with much ado;°   *trouble*

   Your sister is the better soldier.

REGAN Lord Edmund spake not with your lady at home?

5 STEWARD No, madam.

REGAN What might import° my sister's letters to him?   *mean*

STEWARD I know not, lady.

REGAN Faith, he is posted° hence on serious matter—   *sent*

   It was great ignorance, Gloucester's eyes being out,

10   To let him live. Where he arrives, he moves

   All hearts against us—and now, I think, is gone

   In pity of his misery° to dispatch his nighted° life,   *(ironic) / darkened*

   Moreover to descry° the strength o'th' army.   *investigate*

STEWARD I must needs after° him with my letters.   *go after*

15 REGAN Our troop sets forth tomorrow; stay with us.

   The ways are dangerous.

STEWARD   I may not, madam;

   My lady charged° my duty in this business.   *commanded*

REGAN Why should she write to Edmund? Might not you

   Transport her purposes by word? Belike°   *Perhaps*

20   Something—I know not what. I'll love° thee much: *reward*

   Let me unseal the letter.

STEWARD   Madam, I'd rather—

REGAN I know your lady does not love her husband.

   I am sure of that, and at her late° being here   *recently*

   She gave strange oeillades° and most speaking looks   *amorous glances*

25   To noble Edmund. I know you are of her bosom.°   *in her confidence*

STEWARD Ay, madam.

REGAN I speak in understanding,° for I know't.   *with certainty*

   Therefore, I do advise you take this note.°   *take note of this*

   My lord is dead. Edmund and I have talked,

30   And more convenient° is he for my hand   *appropriate*

   Than for your lady's. You may gather° more.   *infer*

   If you do find him, pray you give him this,[1]

   And, when your mistress hears thus much from you,

   I pray, desire her call her wisdom to her.[2] So, farewell.

35   If you do chance to hear of that blind traitor,

   Preferment falls on him that cuts him off.°   *cuts his life short*

STEWARD Would I could meet him, madam, I would show

   What lady I do follow.

REGAN   Fare thee well.   *Exeunt* [*severally*].°   *separately*

4.5 Location: At Gloucester's castle.

1. This information, but possibly another letter or token.

2. *desire . . . to her:* tell her to come to her senses.

4.4 (Q 4.5)

Enter REGAN *and* [*Oswald the*] STEWARD.

REGAN   But are my brother's powers° set forth?   (*Albany's forces*)
STEWARD   Ay, madam.
REGAN   Himself in person there?
STEWARD   Madam, with much ado;°   *trouble*
    Your sister is the better soldier.
REGAN   Lord Edmond spake not with your lord at home?
5 STEWARD   No, madam.
REGAN   What might import° my sister's letter to him?   *mean*
STEWARD   I know not, lady.
REGAN   Faith, he is posted° hence on serious matter—   *sent*
    It was great ignorance, Gloucester's eyes being out,
10   To let him live. Where he arrives, he moves
    All hearts against us. Edmond, I think, is gone,
    In pity of his misery,° to dispatch   (*ironic*)
    His nighted° life; moreover to descry°   *darkened / investigate*
    The strength o'th' enemy.
15 STEWARD   I must needs after° him, madam, with my letter.   *go after*
REGAN   Our troops set forth tomorrow; stay with us.
    The ways are dangerous.
STEWARD   I may not, madam:
    My lady charged° my duty in this business.   *commanded*
REGAN   Why should she write to Edmond?
20   Might not you transport her purposes by word? Belike°   *Perhaps*
    Some things—I know not what. I'll love° thee much: *reward*
    Let me unseal the letter.
STEWARD   Madam, I had rather—
REGAN   I know your lady does not love her husband.
    I am sure of that, and at her late° being here,   *recently*
25   She gave strange oeillades° and most speaking looks   *amorous glances*
    To noble Edmond. I know you are of her bosom.°   *in her confidence*
STEWARD   I, madam?
REGAN   I speak in understanding.° Y'are; I know't.   *with certainty*
    Therefore I do advise you take this note.°   *take note of this*
30   My lord is dead. Edmond and I have talked,
    And more convenient° is he for my hand   *appropriate*
    Than for your lady's. You may gather° more.   *infer*
    If you do find him, pray you give him this,[1]
    And when your mistress hears thus much from you,
35   I pray, desire her call her wisdom to her.[2]
    So, fare you well.
    If you do chance to hear of that blind traitor,
    Preferment falls on him that cuts him off.°   *cuts his life short*
STEWARD   Would I could meet, madam; I should show
    What party I do follow.
40 REGAN   Fare thee well.   *Exeunt* [*severally*].°   *separately*

4.4 Location: At Gloucester's castle.
1. This information, but possibly another letter or

token.
2. *desire . . . to her:* tell her to come to her senses.

4.6 (F 4.5)

Enter GLOUCESTER *and* [EDGAR *disguised as a peasant*].

GLOUCESTER   When shall we come to th' top of that same°   *agreed-upon*
hill?

EDGAR   You do climb it up now. Look how we labor.

GLOUCESTER   Methinks the ground is even.

EDGAR   Horrible steep; hark, do you hear the sea?

5 GLOUCESTER   No, truly.

EDGAR   Why, then, your other senses grow imperfect
By your eyes' anguish.

GLOUCESTER   So may it be indeed.
Methinks thy voice is altered, and thou speakest
With better phrase and matter° than thou didst.   *sense*

10 EDGAR   You're much deceived. In nothing am I changed
But in my garments.

GLOUCESTER   Methinks you're better spoken.

EDGAR   Come on, sir. Here's the place. Stand still. How
fearful
And dizzy 'tis to cast one's eyes so low!

15 The crows and choughs° that wing the midway air¹   *jackdaws*
Show° scarce so gross° as beetles. Halfway down   *Appear / big*
Hangs one that gathers samphire;° dreadful trade!   *seaweed*
Methinks he seems no bigger than his head.
The fishermen that walk upon the beach

20 Appear like mice, and yon tall anchoring bark°   *ship*
Diminished to her cock;° her cock a buoy   *dinghy*
Almost too small for sight. The murmuring surge,
That on the unnumbered° idle pebble chafes,   *innumerable*
Cannot be heard. It's so high, I'll look no more,

25 Lest my brain turn and the° deficient sight   *my*
Topple° down headlong.   *Topple me*

GLOUCESTER   Set me where you stand.

EDGAR   Give me your hand; you are now within a foot
Of th'extreme verge. For all beneath the moon
Would I not leap upright.²

GLOUCESTER   Let go my hand.

30 Here, friend, 's another purse, in it a jewel
Well worth a poor man's taking. Fairies and gods
Prosper it³ with thee. Go thou farther off.
Bid me farewell, and let me hear thee going.

EDGAR   Now, fare you well, good sir.

GLOUCESTER   With all my heart.

35 EDGAR [*aside*]   Why I do trifle thus with his despair
Is done to cure it.

GLOUCESTER (*kneels*)   O you mighty gods,
This world I do renounce, and in your sights
Shake patiently my great affliction off.

4.6 Location: Near Dover.
1. The air between cliff and sea.
2. I would not jump up and down (for fear of losing

my balance).
3. Make it increase. Fairies were sometimes believed
to hoard and multiply treasure.

4.5 (Q 4.6)

Enter GLOUCESTER *and* EDGAR [*disguised as a peasant*].

GLOUCESTER   When shall I come to th' top of that same° hill?   *agreed-upon*
EDGAR   You do climb up it now. Look how we labor.
GLOUCESTER   Methinks the ground is even.
EDGAR   Horrible steep.
   Hark, do you hear the sea?
GLOUCESTER   No, truly.
5 EDGAR   Why, then your other senses grow imperfect
   By your eyes' anguish.
GLOUCESTER   So may it be indeed.
   Methinks thy voice is altered, and thou speak'st
   In better phrase and matter° than thou didst.   *sense*
EDGAR   You're much deceived. In nothing am I changed
10   But in my garments.
GLOUCESTER   Methinks you're better spoken.
EDGAR   Come on, sir,
   Here's the place. Stand still. How fearful
   And dizzy 'tis to cast one's eyes so low!
   The crows and choughs° that wing the midway air[1]   *jackdaws*
15 Show° scarce so gross° as beetles. Halfway down   *Appear / big*
   Hangs one that gathers samphire:° dreadful trade!   *seaweed*
   Methinks he seems no bigger than his head.
   The fishermen that walked upon the beach
   Appear like mice, and yond tall anchoring bark°   *ship*
20 Diminished to her cock;° her cock, a buoy   *dinghy*
   Almost too small for sight. The murmuring surge,
   That on th'unnumbered° idle pebble chafes,   *innumerable*
   Cannot be heard so high. I'll look no more,
   Lest my brain turn and the° deficient sight   *my*
25 Topple° down headlong.   *Topple me*
GLOUCESTER   Set me where you stand.
EDGAR   Give me your hand.
   You are now within a foot of th'extreme verge.
   For all beneath the moon would I not leap upright.[2]
GLOUCESTER   Let go my hand.
30   Here, friend, 's another purse. In it, a jewel
   Well worth a poor man's taking. Fairies and gods
   Prosper it[3] with thee. Go thou further off.
   Bid me farewell, and let me hear thee going.
EDGAR   Now, fare ye well, good sir.
GLOUCESTER   With all my heart.
35 EDGAR [*aside*]   Why I do trifle thus with his despair
   Is done to cure it.
GLOUCESTER   O you mighty gods!
      [*He kneels.*]
   This world I do renounce, and in your sights
   Shake patiently my great affliction off.

4.5 Location: Near Dover.
1. The air between cliff and sea.
2. I would not jump up and down (for fear of losing

my balance).
3. Make it increase. Fairies were sometimes believed
to hoard and multiply treasure.

If I could bear it longer and not fall

40 To quarrel° with your great opposeless wills,   *Into conflict*
My snuff and loathèd part of nature[4] should
Burn itself out. If Edgar live, oh, bless!
Now fellow, fare thee well.
   He falls.
EDGAR   Gone, sir; farewell,
And yet I know not how conceit may rob

45 The treasury of life, when life itself
Yields to the theft.[5] Had he been where he thought,
By this° had thought been past. Alive or dead?[6]   *now*
[*to* GLOUCESTER] Ho, you, sir! Hear you, sir? Speak.
Thus might he pass° indeed, yet he revives.   *pass away*
—What are you, sir?

50 GLOUCESTER   Away and let me die.
EDGAR Hadst thou been aught° but goss'mer, feathers, air, *anything*
So many fathom down precipitating,°   *plunging*
Thou hadst shivered° like an egg. But thou dost breathe, *shattered*
Hast heavy substance, bleed'st not, speakest, art sound.

55 Ten masts at each° make not the altitude   *end to end*
Which thou hast perpendicularly fell.
Thy life's a miracle. Speak yet again.
GLOUCESTER But have I fallen or no?
EDGAR From the dread summons of this chalky bourn.[7]

60 Look up a-height, the shrill gorged° lark so far   *shrill-voiced*
Cannot be seen or heard. Do but look up.
GLOUCESTER Alack, I have no eyes.
Is wretchedness deprived° that benefit   *deprived of*
To end itself by death? 'Twas yet some comfort

65 When misery could beguile° the tyrant's rage   *cheat*
And frustrate his proud will.
EDGAR   Give me your arm.
Up, so; how feel you your legs? You stand.
GLOUCESTER Too well, too well.
EDGAR   This is above all strangeness.
Upon the crown of the cliff, what thing was that
Which parted from you?

70 GLOUCESTER   A poor unfortunate beggar.
EDGAR As I stood here below, methoughts his eyes
Were two full moons, 'a had a thousand noses,
Horns whelked° and waved like the enridgèd sea.   *twisted*
It was some fiend. Therefore, thou happy father,°   *lucky old man*

75 Think that the clearest° gods, who made their honors *purest; most illustrious*
Of men's impossibilities,[8] have preserved thee.
GLOUCESTER I do remember now. Henceforth I'll bear
Affliction till it do cry out itself,
"Enough, enough," and die. That thing you speak of,

80 I took it for a man. Often would it say,

---

4. The scorched and hateful remnant of my lifetime. *snuff:* end of a candlewick.
5. *And yet . . . theft:* Edgar worries that the imagined scenario ("conceit") he has invented may be enough to kill his father, particularly as Gloucester wishes for ("yields to") his own death.
6. PERFORMANCE COMMENT Like readers, audiences cannot initially be certain whether the cliff is "real"

(within the play's fictive world) or imaginary, and the resulting tension makes for one of Shakespeare's most fascinating scenes. See Digital Edition PC 5.
7. The white chalk cliffs of Dover, which make a boundary ("bourn") between land and sea.
8. *who . . . impossibilities:* who attained honor for themselves by performing deeds impossible to men.

	If I could bear it longer and not fall	
40	To quarrel° with your great opposeless wills,	*Into conflict*
	My snuff and loathèd part of nature[4] should	
	Burn itself out. If Edgar live, oh, bless him!	
	Now, fellow, fare thee well.	

EDGAR   Gone, sir. Farewell.

         [GLOUCESTER *falls down.*]

	And yet I know not how conceit may rob	
45	The treasury of life, when life itself	
	Yields to the theft.[5] Had he been where he thought,	
	By this° had thought been past. Alive or dead?[6]	*now*
	[*to* GLOUCESTER] Ho, you, sir! Friend, hear you, sir? Speak.	
	Thus might he pass° indeed. Yet he revives.	*pass away*
	—What are you, sir?	
50	GLOUCESTER Away and let me die.	
	EDGAR Hadst thou been aught° but goss'mer, feathers, air,	*anything*
	So many fathom down precipitating,°	*plunging*
	Thou'dst shivered° like an egg. But thou dost breathe,	*shattered*
	Hast heavy substance, bleed'st not, speak'st, art sound.	
55	Ten masts at each° make not the altitude	*end to end*
	Which thou hast perpendicularly fell.	
	Thy life's a miracle. Speak yet again.	
	GLOUCESTER But have I fall'n or no?	
	EDGAR From the dread summit of this chalky bourn.[7]	
60	Look up a-height, the shrill-gorged° lark so far	*shrill-voiced*
	Cannot be seen or heard. Do but look up.	
	GLOUCESTER Alack, I have no eyes.	
	Is wretchedness deprived° that benefit	*deprived of*
	To end itself by death? 'Twas yet some comfort	
65	When misery could beguile° the tyrant's rage	*cheat*
	And frustrate his proud will.	
	EDGAR Give me your arm.	
	Up, so. How is't? Feel you your legs? You stand.	
	GLOUCESTER Too well, too well.	
	EDGAR This is above all strangeness.	
	Upon the crown o'th' cliff, what thing was that	
	Which parted from you?	
70	GLOUCESTER A poor unfortunate beggar.	
	EDGAR As I stood here below, methought his eyes	
	Were two full moons. He had a thousand noses,	
	Horns whelked° and waved like the enragèd sea.	*twisted*
	It was some fiend. Therefore, thou happy father,°	*lucky old man*
75	Think that the clearest° gods, who make them honors	*purest; most illustrious*
	Of men's impossibilities,[8] have preserved thee.	
	GLOUCESTER I do remember now. Henceforth I'll bear	
	Affliction till it do cry out itself,	
	"Enough, enough," and die. That thing you speak of,	
80	I took it for a man. Often 'twould say,	

---

4. The scorched and hateful remnant of my lifetime. *snuff:* end of a candlewick.
5. *And yet . . . theft:* Edgar worries that the imagined scenario ("conceit") he has invented may be enough to kill his father, particularly as Gloucester wishes for ("yields to") his own death.
6. PERFORMANCE COMMENT Like readers, audiences cannot initially be certain whether the cliff is "real"

(within the play's fictive world) or imaginary, and the resulting tension makes for one of Shakespeare's most fascinating scenes. See Digital Edition PC 5.
7. The white chalk cliffs of Dover, which make a boundary ("bourn") between land and sea.
8. *who . . . impossibilities:* who attain honor for themselves by performing deeds impossible to men.

"The fiend, the fiend." He led me to that place.

EDGAR   Bear free and patient thoughts.

Enter LEAR *mad.*

                                 But who comes here?

The safer sense will ne'er accommodate

His master thus.[9]

85   LEAR   No, they cannot touch me for coining,[1] I am the King
himself.

EDGAR *[aside]*   O thou side-piercing sight!

LEAR   Nature is above art in that respect.[2] There's your press
money.[3] That fellow handles his bow like a crow-keeper.[4]

90   Draw me a clothier's yard.[5] Look, look, a mouse. Peace, peace,
this toasted cheese will do it.° There's my gauntlet; I'll prove it   *(lure the mouse)*
on a giant.[6] Bring up the brown-bills.[7] Oh, well flown, bird,°   *arrow*
in the air. Ha, give the word.°   *password*

EDGAR   Sweet marjoram.[8]

95   LEAR   Pass.

GLOUCESTER   I know that voice.

LEAR   Ha, Gonorill, ha, Regan! They flattered me like a dog°   *fawningly*
and told me I had white hairs in my beard ere the black ones
were there.[9] To say "Ay" and "No" to everything I said "Ay"

100   and "No" to was no good divinity.[1] When the rain came to
wet me once, and the wind to make me chatter, when the
thunder would not peace at my bidding, there I found°   *understood*
them, there I smelt them out. Go to, they are not men of
their words. They told me I was everything. 'Tis a lie. I am

105   not ague-proof.°   *immune to illness*

GLOUCESTER   The trick° of that voice I do well remember,   *peculiarity*
Is't not the King?

LEAR   Ay, every inch a king!

When I do stare, see how the subject quakes.

I pardon that man's life. —What was thy cause,°   *crime*

110   Adultery? Thou shalt not die for adultery.

No, the wren goes to't, and the small gilded fly

Do lecher in my sight.

Let copulation thrive, for Gloucester's bastard son

Was kinder to his father than my daughters

115   Got 'tween the lawful sheets. To't, luxury,° pell-mell,   *lechery*

For I lack soldiers. Behold yon simp'ring dame,

Whose face between her forks presageth snow,[2]

That minces° virtue, and do shake the head   *affects*

To hear of° pleasure's name.   *even of*

120   The fitchew nor the soiled horse[3] goes to't

With a more riotous appetite. Down from the waist

---

9. *The . . . thus:* A sane mind would never allow its
possessor to dress up in this way.
1. Because minting money was the prerogative of the
King, nobody could overtake or equal ("touch") him.
2. My true feelings will always outvalue others' hypocrisy; my natural supremacy surpasses any attempt to
create a false new reign. This image may also be based
on coining (see note 1, above).
3. Fee paid to a soldier impressed, or forced, into the
army.
4. A person hired as a scarecrow and thus unfit for
anything else.
5. Draw the bowstring the full length of the arrow (a
standard English arrow was a cloth yard [37 inches]

long).
6. I'll defend my stand even against a giant. To throw
down an armored glove ("gauntlet") was to issue a
challenge.
7. Brown painted pikes; the soldiers carrying them.
8. Used medicinally against madness.
9. Told me I had wisdom before age.
1. *no good divinity*: poor theology (because insincere);
from James 5:12: "Let your yea be yea; nay, nay."
2. Whose expression implies cold chastity. "Face"
refers to the area between her legs ("forks"), as well as
to her literal facial expression as framed by the aristocratic lady's starched headpiece, also called a "fork."
3. Neither the polecat nor a horse full of fresh grass.

"The fiend, the fiend." He led me to that place.

EDGAR   Bear free and patient thoughts.

    Enter LEAR.

                                   But who comes here?

The safer sense will ne'er accommodate

His master thus.[9]

85   LEAR   No, they cannot touch me° for crying. I am the King   *lay hands on me*
himself.

EDGAR [*aside*]   O thou side-piercing sight!

LEAR   Nature's above art in that respect.[1] There's your press
money.[2] That fellow handles his bow like a crow-keeper.[3]

90   Draw me a clothier's yard.[4] Look, look, a mouse! Peace, peace,
this piece of toasted cheese will do't.° There's my gauntlet; I'll   *(lure the mouse)*
prove it on a giant.[5] Bring up the brown bills.[6] Oh, well flown,
bird!° I'th' clout, i'th' clout! Whew. Give the word.°   *arrow / password*

EDGAR   Sweet marjoram.[7]

95   LEAR   Pass.

GLOUCESTER   I know that voice.

LEAR   Ha! Gonerill with a white beard? They flattered me like
a dog° and told me I had the white hairs in my beard ere the   *fawningly*
black ones were there.[8] To say "Ay" and "No" to everything

100   that I said "Ay" and "No" to was no good divinity.[9] When the
rain came to wet me once, and the wind to make me chatter,
when the thunder would not peace at my bidding, there I
found° 'em, there I smelt 'em out. Go to, they are not men   *understood*
o'their words. They told me I was everything. 'Tis a lie. I am

105   not ague-proof.°   *immune to illness*

GLOUCESTER   The trick° of that voice, I do well remember.   *peculiarity*
Is't not the King?

LEAR   Ay, every inch a king!
When I do stare, see how the subject quakes.
I pardon that man's life. —What was thy cause?°   *crime*

110   Adultery? Thou shalt not die. Die for adultery?
No, the wren goes to't, and the small gilded fly
Does lecher in my sight. Let copulation thrive,
For Gloucester's bastard son was kinder to his father
Than my daughters got 'tween the lawful sheets.

115   To't, luxury,° pell-mell, for I lack soldiers.   *lechery*
Behold yond simp'ring dame,
Whose face between her forks presages snow,[1]
That minces° virtue and does shake the head   *affects*
To hear of° pleasure's name.   *even of*

120   The fitchew nor the soiled horse[2] goes to't
With a more riotous appetite.
Down from the waist they are centaurs,[3]

---

9. *The . . . thus:* A sane mind would never allow its
possessor to dress up in this way.
1. My true feelings will always outvalue others' hypocrisy; my natural supremacy surpasses any attempt to
create a false new reign.
2. Fee paid to a soldier impressed, or forced, into the
army.
3. A person hired as a scarecrow and thus unfit for
anything else.
4. Draw the bowstring the full length of the arrow (a
standard English arrow was a cloth yard [37 inches]
long).
5. I'll defend my stand even against a giant. To throw
down an armored glove ("gauntlet") was to issue a

challenge.
6. Brown painted pikes; the soldiers carrying them.
7. Used medicinally against madness.
8. Told me I had wisdom before age.
9. *no good divinity:* poor theology (because insincere);
from James 5:12: "Let your yea be yea; nay, nay."
1. Whose expression implies cold chastity. "Face"
refers to the area between her legs ("forks") as well as
to her literal facial expression as framed by the aristocratic lady's starched headpiece, also called a "fork."
2. Neither the polecat nor a horse full of fresh grass.
3. Lecherous mythological creatures that have a
human body above the waist and the legs and torso of
a horse below.

They're centaurs,[4] though women all above.
But° to the girdle° do the gods inherit;°   *Only / waist / own*
Beneath is all the fiend's. There's hell,[5] there's darkness,
125   There's the sulphury pit: burning, scalding,
Stench, consummation. Fie, fie, fie, pah, pah!
—Give me an ounce of civet,[6] good apothecary,
To sweeten my imagination. There's money for thee.
GLOUCESTER   Oh, let me kiss that hand.
130   LEAR   Here, wipe it first. It smells of mortality.
GLOUCESTER   O ruined piece° of nature, this great world   *masterpiece*
Should so wear out to naught.[7] Do you know me?
LEAR   I remember thy eyes well enough. Dost thou squiny° on   *squint*
me? No, do thy worst, blind Cupid, I'll not love. Read thou
135   that challenge; mark the penning of't.
GLOUCESTER   Were all the letters suns, I could not see one.
EDGAR [*aside*]   I would not take° this from report; it is,   *believe*
And my heart breaks at it.
LEAR   Read.
140   GLOUCESTER   What, with the case° of eyes?   *sockets*
LEAR   Oh, ho, are you there with me?[8] No eyes in your head,
nor no money in your purse? Your eyes are in a heavy case,[9]
your purse in a light, yet you see how this world goes.
GLOUCESTER   I see it feelingly.°   *by touch; painfully*
145   LEAR   What, art mad? A man may see how the world goes with
no eyes. Look with thy ears. See how yon justice rails upon
yon simple° thief. Hark in thy ear. Handy, dandy,[1] which is   *lowly; innocent*
the thief, which is the justice? Thou hast seen a farmer's dog
bark at a beggar?
150   GLOUCESTER   Ay, sir.
LEAR   And the creature run from the cur. There thou mightst
behold the great image of authority; a dog's obeyed in office.
—Thou rascal beadle,[2] hold° thy bloody hand.   *restrain*
Why dost thou lash that whore? Strip thine own back;
155   Thy blood hotly lusts to use her in that kind°   *way*
For which thou whipp'st her. The usurer hangs the cozener.[3]
Through tattered rags small vices do appear;
Robes and furred gowns hides all. Get thee glass eyes,
And, like a scurvy politician,[4]
160   Seem to see the things thou dost not. No, now,
Pull off my boots, harder, harder, so.
EDGAR [*aside*]   Oh, matter and impertinency° mixed!   *sense and nonsense*
Reason in madness.

---

4. Lecherous mythological creatures that have a human body above the waist and the legs and torso of a horse below.
5. Shakespeare's frequent term for female genitals. Cf. Sonnets 129 and 144.
6. Perfume derived from the anal gland of the civet.
7. Shall decay to nothing in the same way. In Renaissance philosophy, humans were analogous to the cosmos, standing for the whole in miniature and as its

masterpiece.
8. Is that what you are telling me?
9. In a sad condition; playing on "case" as "sockets."
1. Pick a hand, as in a child's guessing game.
2. The parish officer responsible for whippings.
3. The ruinous moneylender, prosperous enough to be made a judge, convicts the ordinary cheat.
4. A vile schemer. In early modern England, "politician" meant an ambitious, even Machiavellian, upstart.

Though women all above.
But° to the girdle° do the gods inherit;°   *Only / waist / own*
125 Beneath is all the fiend's. There's hell,[4] there's darkness,
There is the sulphurous pit: burning, scalding,
Stench, consumption. Fie, fie, fie! Pah, pah!
—Give me an ounce of civet,[5] good apothecary;
Sweeten my imagination. There's money for thee.
GLOUCESTER Oh, let me kiss that hand.
130 LEAR   Let me wipe it first.
It smells of mortality.
GLOUCESTER O ruined piece° of nature, this great world   *masterpiece*
Shall so wear out to naught.[6] Dost thou know me?
LEAR I remember thine eyes well enough. Dost thou squiny°   *squint*
135 at me? No, do thy worst, blind Cupid. I'll not love. Read
thou this challenge; mark but the penning of it.
GLOUCESTER Were all thy letters suns, I could not see.
EDGAR [*aside*] I would not take° this from report;   *believe*
It is, and my heart breaks at it.
140 LEAR Read.
GLOUCESTER What, with the case° of eyes?   *socket*
LEAR Oh, ho, are you there with me?[7] No eyes in your head,
nor no money in your purse? Your eyes are in a heavy case,[8]
your purse in a light, yet you see how this world goes.
145 GLOUCESTER I see it feelingly.°   *by touch; painfully*
LEAR What, art mad? A man may see how this world goes with
no eyes. Look with thine ears. See how yond justice rails
upon yond simple° thief. Hark in thine ear. Change places,   *lowly; innocent*
and handy-dandy,[9] which is the justice, which is the thief?
150 Thou hast seen a farmer's dog bark at a beggar?
GLOUCESTER Ay, sir.
LEAR And the creature° run from the cur. There thou mightst   *wretch*
behold the great image of authority; a dog's obeyed in office.
—Thou rascal beadle,[1] hold° thy bloody hand.   *restrain*
155 Why dost thou lash that whore? Strip thy own back;
Thou hotly lusts to use her in that kind°   *way*
For which thou whipp'st her. The usurer hangs the
        cozener.[2]
Through tattered clothes great vices do appear;
Robes and furred gowns hide all. Plate° sins with gold,   *Armor; gild*
160 And the strong lance of justice hurtless° breaks.   *harmlessly*
Arm it in rags, a pigmy's straw does pierce it.
None does offend; none, I say, none. I'll able° 'em.   *authorize*
Take that of me, my friend, who have the power
To seal th'accuser's lips. Get thee glass eyes,
165 And, like a scurvy politician,[3]
Seem to see the things thou dost not. Now, now, now, now.
Pull off my boots, harder, harder, so.
EDGAR [*aside*] Oh, matter and impertinency° mixed!   *sense and nonsense*
Reason in madness.

---

4. Shakespeare's frequent term for female genitals. Cf. Sonnets 129 and 144.
5. Perfume derived from the anal gland of the civet.
6. Shall decay to nothing in the same way. In Renaissance philosophy, humans were analogous to the cosmos, standing for the whole in miniature and as its masterpiece.
7. Is that what you are telling me?

8. In a sad condition; playing on "case" as "sockets."
9. Pick a hand, as in a child's guessing game.
1. The parish officer responsible for whippings.
2. The ruinous moneylender, prosperous enough to be made a judge, convicts the ordinary cheat.
3. A vile schemer. In early modern England, "politician" meant an ambitious, even Machiavellian, upstart.

LEAR   If thou wilt weep my fortune, take my eyes.
165   I know thee well enough: thy name is Gloucester.
    Thou must be patient. We came crying hither.
    Thou knowest the first time that we smell the air
    We wail and cry. I will preach to thee, mark me.
GLOUCESTER   Alack, alack the day!
170   LEAR   When we are born, we cry that we are come
    To this great stage of fools. This° a good block.[5]   This is
    It were a delicate° stratagem to shoe   subtle
    A troop of horse with fell,[6] and when I have stole upon
    These son-in-laws, then kill, kill, kill, kill, kill, kill!
        Enter three GENTLEMEN.
175   FIRST GENTLEMAN   Oh, here he is. Lay hands upon him, sirs.
    [*to* LEAR] Your most dear—
    LEAR   No rescue? What, a prisoner? I am e'en
    The natural fool[7] of fortune. Use° me well;   Treat
    You shall have ransom. Let me have a surgeon:
180   I am cut to the brains.
    FIRST GENTLEMAN   You shall have anything.
    LEAR   No seconds?° All myself?   supporters
    Why, this would make a man of salt[8] to use
    His eyes for garden water-pots, ay, and
    Laying° autumn's dust.   Settling
    FIRST GENTLEMAN   Good sir—
185   LEAR   I will die bravely,[9] like a bridegroom.
    What? I will be jovial. Come, come,
    I am a king, my masters. Know you that?
    FIRST GENTLEMAN   You are a royal one, and we obey you.
    LEAR   Then there's life° in't, nay, an° you get it,   hope / if
190   You shall get it with running.
            Exit King [LEAR] *running*[*, pursued by
                two* GENTLEMEN].
    FIRST GENTLEMAN   A sight most pitiful in the meanest wretch,
    Past speaking of in a king. Thou hast one daughter
    Who redeems nature from the general curse
    Which twain hath brought her to.[1]
    EDGAR   Hail, gentle° sir.   noble
195   FIRST GENTLEMAN   Sir, speed you.° What's your will?   God speed you
    EDGAR   Do you hear aught of a battle toward?°   coming
    FIRST GENTLEMAN   Most sure and vulgar,° everyone hears   commonly known
        that
    That can distinguish sense.°   Who can understand
    EDGAR   But by your favor, how near's the other army?
200   FIRST GENTLEMAN   Near and on speed for't; the main°   main army
        descries°   scouts
    Stand'st on the hourly thoughts.°   Are expected forthwith
    EDGAR   I thank you, sir. That's all.

5. Stage (often called "scaffold" and hence linked to
an executioner's block); block used to shape a felt hat
(such as the hat removed by a preacher before a sermon); mounting block (such as the stump or stock
Lear may have sat on to remove his boots).
6. The skin or hide of an animal, to muffle the sound
of the approaching cavalry.
7. Born plaything; playing on "natural" as "mentally
deficient."
8. A man reduced to nothing but the salt his tears

deposit.
9. "Die" plays on the Renaissance sense of "have an
orgasm."
1. *Who . . . to:* Who restores proper meaning and
order to a universe plagued by the crimes of the other
two daughters; alluding to the fall of humankind and
the natural world caused by the sin of Adam and Eve
and to the universal redemption brought about by
Christ's sacrifice.

170 LEAR If thou wilt weep my fortunes, take my eyes.
I know thee well enough: thy name is Gloucester.
Thou must be patient. We came crying hither.
Thou know'st the first time that we smell the air
We wail and cry. I will preach to thee. Mark.
175 GLOUCESTER Alack, alack the day.
LEAR When we are born, we cry that we are come
To this great stage of fools. This° a good block.[4]   *This is*
It were a delicate° stratagem to shoe   *subtle*
A troop of horse with felt.[5] I'll put't in proof,°   *to the test*
180 And when I have stol'n upon these son-in-laws,
Then kill, kill, kill, kill, kill, kill!

      Enter a GENTLEMAN.

GENTLEMAN Oh, here he is. Lay hand upon him. [*to* LEAR] Sir,
Your most dear daughter—
LEAR No rescue? What, a prisoner? I am even
185 The natural fool[6] of fortune. Use° me well;   *Treat*
You shall have ransom. Let me have surgeons:
I am cut to th' brains.
GENTLEMAN   You shall have anything.
LEAR No seconds?° All myself?   *supporters*
Why, this would make a man a man of salt,[7]
190 To use his eyes for garden water-pots. I will die bravely,[8]
Like a smug° bridegroom. What? I will be jovial.   *an elegant*
Come, come, I am a king, masters. Know you that?
GENTLEMAN You are a royal one, and we obey you.
LEAR Then there's life° in't. Come; an° you get it,   *hope / if*
195 You shall get it by running. Sa, sa, sa, sa.[9]   *Exit.*

GENTLEMAN A sight most pitiful in the meanest wretch,
Past speaking of in a king. Thou hast a daughter
Who redeems nature from the general curse,
Which twain have brought her to.[1]
EDGAR Hail, gentle° sir.   *noble*
200 GENTLEMAN   Sir, speed you.° What's your will?   *God speed you*
EDGAR Do you hear aught, sir, of a battle toward?°   *coming*
GENTLEMAN Most sure and vulgar:°   *commonly known*
Everyone hears that which can distinguish sound.
EDGAR But, by your favor, how near's the other army?
205 GENTLEMAN Near and on speedy foot; the main descry°   *appearance*
Stands on the hourly thought.°   *Is expected forthwith*
EDGAR I thank you, sir, that's all.

4. Stage (often called "scaffold" and hence linked to an executioner's block); block used to shape a felt hat (such as the hat removed by a preacher before a sermon); mounting block (such as the stump or stock Lear may have sat on to remove his boots).
5. Hat material, to muffle the sound of the approaching cavalry.
6. Born plaything; playing on "natural" as "mentally deficient."
7. A man reduced to nothing but the salt his tears deposit.
8. With courage; showily. "Die" plays on the Renaissance sense of "have an orgasm."
9. A cry to encourage dogs in the hunt.
1. *Who . . . to:* Who restores proper meaning and order to a universe plagued by the crimes of the other two daughters; alluding to the fall of humankind and the natural world caused by the sin of Adam and Eve and to the universal redemption brought about by Christ's sacrifice.

FIRST GENTLEMAN   Though that the Queen on° special   *for*
cause° is here,   *reason*
Her army is moved on.
EDGAR   I thank you, sir.
                                          Exit [FIRST GENTLEMAN].
205   GLOUCESTER   You ever gentle gods, take my breath from me.
Let not my worser spirit[2] tempt me again
To die before you please.
EDGAR   Well pray you, father.[3]
GLOUCESTER   Now, good sir, what are you?
EDGAR   A most poor man, made lame by fortune's blows,
210   Who by the art of known and feeling° sorrows   *profound*
Am pregnant to° good pity. Give me your hand;   *disposed to feel*
I'll lead you to some biding.°   *resting place*
GLOUCESTER   Hearty thanks,
The bounty and benison of heaven to boot, to boot.[4]
                                    Enter [*Oswald the*] STEWARD.
STEWARD   A proclaimed prize![5] Most happy!°   *lucky*
215   That eyeless head of thine was first framed° flesh   *made of*
To raise my fortunes. Thou most unhappy traitor,
Briefly thyself remember.[6] [*He draws his sword.*] The sword
is out
That must destroy thee.
GLOUCESTER   Now let thy friendly hand
Put strength enough to't.
STEWARD [*to* EDGAR]   Wherefore, bold peasant,
220   Durst thou support a published° traitor? Hence,   *proclaimed*
Lest the infection° of his fortune take   *(deathly) sickness*
Like° hold on thee. Let go his arm.   *The same*
EDGAR [*drawing his sword and speaking in a country accent*]
Chill[7] not let go, sir, without 'cagion.°   *occasion*
STEWARD   Let go, slave, or thou diest!
225   EDGAR   Good gentleman, go your gait.° Let poor voke pass.   *be on your way*
An chud° have been swaggered out of my life, it would not   *If I could*
have been so long by a vortnight. Nay, come not near the old
man! Keep out, che vore ye, or I'll try whether your costard
or my bat be the harder.[8] I'll be plain with you.
230   STEWARD   Out, dunghill!
                          They fight.
EDGAR   Chill pick your teeth, sir; come, no matter for your
foins.°   *sword thrusts*
STEWARD   Slave, thou hast slain me! Villain, take my purse.
If ever thou wilt thrive, bury my body;
235   And give the letters which thou find'st about me
To Edmund, Earl of Gloucester. Seek him out upon°   *within*
The British party. Oh, untimely death! Death!
                          He dies.

2. Wicked inclination; bad angel.
3. A term of respect for an elderly man.
4. To send you reward in addition to my thanks.
5. A wanted man, with a bounty on his life.
6. Recollect and pray forgiveness for your sins.

7. I will; dialect from Somerset was a stage convention for peasant dialogue.
8. *che vor ye . . . harder:* I warrant you, or I'll test whether your head or my cudgel is harder. *costard:* a kind of apple.

GENTLEMAN   Though that the Queen on° special cause° is   *for / reason*
      here,
   Her army is moved on.
EDGAR   I thank you, sir.   *Exit* [GENTLEMAN].
210 GLOUCESTER   You ever gentle gods, take my breath from me.
   Let not my worser spirit[2] tempt me again
   To die before you please.
EDGAR   Well pray you, father.[3]
GLOUCESTER   Now, good sir, what are you?
EDGAR   A most poor man, made tame to fortune's blows,
215   Who by the art of known and feeling° sorrows,   *profound*
   Am pregnant to° good pity. Give me your hand;   *disposed to feel*
   I'll lead you to some biding.°   *resting place*
GLOUCESTER   Hearty thanks.
   The bounty and the benison of heaven
   To boot and boot.[4]
           Enter [*Oswald the*] STEWARD.
STEWARD   A proclaimed prize![5] Most happy!°   *lucky*
220   That eyeless head of thine was first framed° flesh   *made of*
   To raise my fortunes. Thou old unhappy traitor,
   Briefly thyself remember.[6] [*He draws his sword.*] The sword
      is out
   That must destroy thee.
GLOUCESTER   Now let thy friendly hand
   Put strength enough to't.
STEWARD [*to* EDGAR]   Wherefore, bold peasant,
225   Dar'st thou support a published° traitor? Hence,   *proclaimed*
   Lest that th'infection° of his fortune take   *(deathly) sickness*
   Like° hold on thee. Let go his arm.   *The same*
EDGAR [*drawing his sword and speaking in a country accent*]
   Chill[7] not let go, zir, without vurther 'casion.°   *further occasion*
STEWARD   Let go, slave, or thou diest.
230 EDGAR   Good gentleman, go your gait,° and let poor volk pass. *be on your way*
   An chud ha'° been zwaggered out of my life, 'twould not ha'   *If I could have*
   been zo long as 'tis by a vortnight. Nay, come not near th'old
   man! Keep out, che vor' ye, or I'll try whither your costard or
   my ballow be the harder.[8] Chill be plain with you.
235 STEWARD   Out, dunghill!
EDGAR   Chill pick your teeth, zir! Come, no matter vor your
   foins.°   *sword thrusts*
           [*They fight.*]
STEWARD   Slave, thou hast slain me! Villain, take my purse.
   If ever thou wilt thrive, bury my body,
240   And give the letters which thou find'st about me
   To Edmond, Earl of Gloucester. Seek him out
   Upon° the English party. Oh, untimely death, death!   *Within*
           [*He dies.*]

---

2. Wicked inclination; bad angel.
3. A term of respect for an elderly man.
4. In addition to my thanks, and may it bring you some worldly reward.
5. A wanted man, with a bounty on his life.
6. Recollect and pray forgiveness for your sins.

7. I will; dialect from Somerset was a stage convention for peasant dialogue.
8. *che vor' ye . . . harder:* I warrant you, or I shall test whether your head or my cudgel is harder. *costard:* a kind of apple.

EDGAR   I know thee well: a serviceable° villain,   *an officious*
　　　As duteous to the vices of thy mistress
　　　As badness would desire.
240 GLOUCESTER   What, is he dead?
EDGAR   Sit you down, father, rest you.
　　　Let's see his pockets. These letters that he speaks of
　　　May be my friends. He's dead; I am only sorry
　　　He had no other deathsman.° [*He opens the letter.*] Let us see.   *executioner*
245 Leave,° gentle wax,[9] and manners blame us not.   *By your leave*
　　　To know our enemy's minds, we'd rip their hearts.
　　　Their° papers is more lawful.   *To rip their*
　　　([*Reads*] *a letter.*) "Let your reciprocal vows be remembered.
　　　You have many opportunities to cut him off. If your will
250 want° not, time and place will be fruitfully offered. There is   *lacks*
　　　nothing done° if he return the conqueror; then am I the   *accomplished*
　　　prisoner and his bed my jail, from the loathed warmth
　　　whereof deliver me and supply° the place for your labor.[1]   *fill*
　　　Your wife (so I would say), your affectionate servant, and for
255 you her own for venture,[2] Gonorill."
　　　Oh, indistinguished space of woman's wit![3]
　　　A plot upon her virtuous husband's life,
　　　And the exchange° my brother. Here in the sands   *substitute*
　　　Thee I'll rake up,° the post unsanctified°   *cover up / unholy messenger*
260 Of murderers lechers, and in the mature time°   *when the time is ripe*
　　　With this ungracious° paper strike the sight   *ungodly*
　　　Of the death-practiced Duke.[4] For him, 'tis well
　　　That of thy death and business I can tell.
GLOUCESTER   The King is mad. How stiff is my vile sense[5]
265 That I stand up and have ingenious feeling[6]
　　　Of my huge sorrows? Better I were distract;°   *mad*
　　　So should my thoughts be fencèd from my griefs,
　　　And woes by wrong° imaginations lose   *false*
　　　The knowledge of themselves.
　　　　　　A drum afar off.
EDGAR   Give me your hand.
270 Far off methinks I hear the beaten drum.
　　　Come, father, I'll bestow° you with a friend.   *Exeunt.*   *lodge*

---

9. The wax seal on the letter.
1. *for your labor:* as a reward for your endeavors, and
for further sexual exertion.
2. *for you . . . venture:* one willing to risk all for you;
all yours, if you dare be so bold.

3. Limitless extent of woman's cunning.
4. Of the Duke whose death is plotted.
5. How obstinate is my unwanted power of reason.
6. That I remain upright and firm in my sanity and
have rational perceptions.

EDGAR   I know thee well: a serviceable° villain,   *an officious*
As duteous to the vices of thy mistress
As badness would desire.
245 GLOUCESTER   What, is he dead?
EDGAR   Sit you down, father; rest you.
Let's see these pockets. The letters that he speaks of
May be my friends. He's dead; I am only sorry
He had no other deathsman.° [*He opens the letter.*] Let   *executioner*
us see.
250 Leave,° gentle wax,[9] and manners blame us not.   *By your leave*
To know our enemies' minds, we rip their hearts;
Their° papers is more lawful.   *To rip their*
          [*He*] *reads the letter.*
"Let our reciprocal vows be remembered. You have many
opportunities to cut him off. If your will want° not, time and   *lacks*
255 place will be fruitfully offered. There is nothing done° if he   *accomplished*
return the conqueror; then am I the prisoner and his bed my
jail, from the loathed warmth whereof deliver me, and sup-
ply° the place for your labor.[1] Your (wife, so I would say)   *fill*
affectionate servant, Gonerill."
260 Oh, indistinguished space of woman's will![2]
A plot upon her virtuous husband's life,
And the exchange° my brother! Here in the sands   *substitute*
Thee I'll rake up,° the post unsanctified°   *cover up / unholy messenger*
Of murderous lechers, and in the mature time°   *when the time is ripe*
265 With this ungracious° paper strike the sight   *ungodly*
Of the death-practiced Duke.[3] For him, 'tis well
That of thy death and business I can tell.
GLOUCESTER   The King is mad. How stiff is my vile sense[4]
That I stand up and have ingenious feeling[5]
270 Of my huge sorrows? Better I were distract;°   *mad*
So should my thoughts be severed from my griefs,
          Drum afar off.
And woes by wrong° imaginations lose   *false*
The knowledge of themselves.
EDGAR   Give me your hand.
Far off methinks I hear the beaten drum.
275 Come, father, I'll bestow° you with a friend.   *Exeunt.*   *lodge*

9. The wax seal on the letter.
1. *for your labor:* as a reward for your endeavors, and
for further sexual exertion.
2. Limitless extent of woman's willfulness. As with
"hell" in line 125, "will" might also refer to a woman's
genitals.
3. Of the Duke whose death is plotted.
4. How obstinate is my unwanted power of reason.
5. That I remain upright and firm in my sanity and
have rational perceptions.

4.7 (F 4.6)

Enter CORDELIA, KENT [*dressed as Caius*], *and*
DOCTOR[, *and* GENTLEMAN].

CORDELIA   O thou good Kent, how shall I live and work
　　To match thy goodness? My life will be too short
　　And every measure° fail me.　　　　　　　　　　　　　　　　*attempt*
KENT　　To be acknowledged, madam, is o'erpaid.°　　　　*is more than enough*
5　　All my reports go[1] with the modest truth,
　　Nor more, nor clipped, but so.[2]
CORDELIA　　　　　　　　　　Be better suited;°　　　　　　*attired*
　　These weeds° are memories of those worser hours.　　　*clothes*
　　I prithee, put them off.
KENT　　Pardon me, dear madam.
10　　Yet to be known shortens my made intent.[3]
　　My boon I make it[4] that you know° me not　　　　　　　*acknowledge*
　　Till time and I think meet.°　　　　　　　　　　　　　　　*suitable*
CORDELIA   Then be't so. [*to* DOCTOR] My good lord, how does
　　the King?
DOCTOR　　Madam, sleeps still.
15　CORDELIA   O you kind gods,
　　Cure this great breach in his abusèd nature.
　　The untuned and hurrying senses, oh, wind up[5]
　　Of this child-changèd[6] father.
DOCTOR　　So please your majesty
20　That we may wake the King? He hath slept long.
CORDELIA   Be governed by your knowledge and proceed
　　I'th' sway° of your own will. Is he arrayed?°　　　　*By the authority / clothed*
DOCTOR   Ay, madam. In the heaviness of his sleep
　　We put fresh garments on him.
25　GENTLEMAN   Good madam, be by when we do awake him;
　　I doubt not of his temperance.°　　　　　　　　　　　　*calmness*
CORDELIA　　　　　　　　　　Very well.
　　　　[*Music plays.*]
DOCTOR   Please you draw near; louder the music there.
　　　　[*Enter* LEAR *in a chair carried by* SERVANTS.]
CORDELIA   O my dear father, restoration
　　Hang thy medicine on my lips, and let this kiss
30　Repair those violent harms that my two sisters
　　Have in thy reverence° made.　　　　　　　　　　　　　　*aged dignity*
KENT　　　　　　　　　　Kind and dear princess.
CORDELIA   Had you not[7] been their father, these white
　　flakes°　　　　　　　　　　　　　　　　　　　　　　　*locks of hair*
　　Had challenged° pity of them. Was this a face　　　　　*Would have provoked*
　　To be exposed against the warring winds,

4.7 Location: The French camp at Dover.　　　　5. *The . . . up:* Reorder his confused and delirious
1. May all accounts of me agree.　　　　　　　mind. The image is of tightening the strings of a lute.
2. Not greater or less, but exactly the modest amount　　6. Changed by his children; changed into a child;
I deserve.　　　　　　　　　　　　　　　　　playing on a musical key change.
3. Revealing myself now would abort my designs.　　7. Even if you had not.
4. The reward I beg is.

4.6 (Q 4.7)

Enter CORDELIA, KENT [*dressed as Caius*], *and*
GENTLEMAN.

CORDELIA   O thou good Kent, how shall I live and work
To match thy goodness? My life will be too short
And every measure° fail me.   *attempt*
KENT   To be acknowledged, madam, is o'erpaid.°   *is more than enough*
5   All my reports go¹ with the modest truth,
Nor more, nor clipped, but so.²
CORDELIA   Be better suited;°   *attired*
These weeds° are memories of those worser hours.   *clothes*
I prithee, put them off.
KENT   Pardon, dear madam,
Yet to be known shortens my made intent.³
10   My boon I make it⁴ that you know° me not   *acknowledge*
Till time and I think meet.°   *suitable*
CORDELIA   Then be't so, my good lord.
—How does the King?
GENTLEMAN   Madam, sleeps still.
CORDELIA   O you kind gods,
Cure this great breach in his abusèd nature.
15   Th'untuned and jarring senses, oh, wind up⁵
Of this child-changed⁶ father.
GENTLEMAN   So please your majesty
That we may wake the King? He hath slept long.
CORDELIA   Be governed by your knowledge and proceed
I'th' sway° of your own will. Is he arrayed?°   *By the authority / clothed*
Enter LEAR *in a chair carried by* SERVANTS.
20   GENTLEMAN   Ay, madam. In the heaviness of sleep,
We put fresh garments on him.
Be by, good madam, when we do awake him;
I doubt of his temperance.°   *calmness*
CORDELIA   O my dear father, restoration hang
25   Thy medicine on my lips, and let this kiss
Repair those violent harms that my two sisters
Have in thy reverence° made.   *aged dignity*
KENT   Kind and dear princess.
CORDELIA   Had you not⁷ been their father, these white
     flakes°   *locks of hair*
Did challenge° pity of them. Was this a face   *Would have provoked*
30   To be opposed against the jarring winds?

4.6 Location: The French camp at Dover.
1. May all accounts of me agree.
2. Not greater or less, but exactly the modest amount
I deserve.
3. Revealing myself now would abort my designs.
4. The reward I beg is.

5. *Th'untuned . . . up:* Reorder his confused and
delirious mind. The image is of tightening the strings
of a lute.
6. Changed by his children; changed into a child;
playing on a musical key change.
7. Even if you had not.

35 To stand against the deep dread-bolted thunder,
 In the most terrible and nimble stroke
 Of quick cross lightning to watch° —poor *perdu*![8]—   *to stand guard*
 With this thin helm?° Mine injurious dog,   *helmet (of hair)*
 Though he had bit me, should have stood that night
40 Against my fire. And wast thou fain,° poor father,   *obliged*
 To hovel thee with swine and rogues forlorn
 In short° and musty straw? Alack, alack,   *scant; broken*
 'Tis wonder that thy life and wits at once
 Had not concluded all!° —He wakes. Speak to him.   *altogether*
45 DOCTOR Madam, do you, 'tis fittest.
 CORDELIA How does my royal lord? How fares your majesty?
 LEAR You do me wrong to take me out o'th' grave.
 Thou art a soul in bliss, but I am bound
 Upon a wheel of fire, that mine own tears
 Do scald like molten lead.[9]
50 CORDELIA   Sir, know me.
 LEAR You're a spirit, I know. Where did you die?
 CORDELIA Still, still, far wide.°   *unbalanced*
 DOCTOR He's scarce awake. Let him alone a while.
 LEAR Where have I been? Where am I? Fair daylight?
55 I am mightily abused.° I should e'en die with pity   *wronged; deceived*
 To see another thus. I know not what to say.
 I will not swear these are my hands. Let's see,
 I feel this pin prick. Would I were assured
 Of my condition.
 CORDELIA [*kneeling*] Oh, look upon me, sir,
60 And hold your hands in benediction o'er me.
    [LEAR *kneels.*]
 No, sir, you must not kneel.
 LEAR [*rising*]   Pray do not mock.
 I am a very foolish fond° old man,   *silly*
 Fourscore and upward, and, to deal plainly,
 I fear I am not in my perfect mind.
65 Methinks I should know you and know this man.
 Yet I am doubtful, for I am mainly° ignorant   *entirely*
 What place this is, and all the skill I have
 Remembers not these garments, nor I know not
 Where I did lodge last night. Do not laugh at me,
70 For as I am a man, I think this lady
 To be my child Cordelia.
 CORDELIA   And so I am.
 LEAR Be your tears wet?[1] Yes, faith. I pray, weep not.
 If you have poison for me I will drink it.
 I know you do not love me, for your sisters
75 Have, as I do remember, done me wrong.
 You have some cause; they have not.
 CORDELIA   No cause, no cause.

8. Lost one; in military terms, a dangerously exposed
sentry.
9. *but I . . . lead:* Lear puts himself in either hell or
purgatory, both places of such punishment in medi-

eval accounts. Compare also to the classical myth of
Ixion, bound by Zeus to a spinning wheel of fire.
1. Are your tears real? Is this really happening?

Mine enemy's dog, though he had bit me,
Should have stood that night against my fire.
And wast thou fain,° poor father,   obliged
To hovel thee with swine and rogues forlorn
35   In short° and musty straw? Alack, alack,   scant; broken
'Tis wonder that thy life and wits at once
Had not concluded all.° —He wakes; speak to him.   altogether
GENTLEMAN   Madam, do you, 'tis fittest.
CORDELIA   How does my royal lord?
40   How fares your majesty?
LEAR   You do me wrong to take me out o'th' grave.
Thou art a soul in bliss, but I am bound
Upon a wheel of fire, that mine own tears
Do scald like molten lead.[8]
CORDELIA   Sir, do you know me?
45   LEAR   You are a spirit, I know. Where did you die?
CORDELIA   Still, still, far wide.°   unbalanced
GENTLEMAN   He's scarce scarce awake. Let him alone a while.
LEAR   Where have I been? Where am I? Fair daylight?
I am mightily abused.° I should e'en die with pity   wronged; deceived
50   To see another thus. I know not what to say.
I will not swear these are my hands. Let's see,
I feel this pin prick. Would I were assured
Of my condition.
CORDELIA [kneeling]   Oh, look upon me, sir,
And hold your hand in benediction o'er me.
[LEAR kneels.]
You must not kneel.
55   LEAR [rising]   Pray do not mock me.
I am a very foolish, fond° old man,   silly
Fourscore and upward,
Not an hour more nor less,
And to deal plainly,
60   I fear I am not in my perfect mind.
Methinks I should know you and know this man.
Yet I am doubtful, for I am mainly° ignorant   entirely
What place this is, and all the skill I have
Remembers not these garments, nor I know not
65   Where I did lodge last night. Do not laugh at me,
For as I am a man, I think this lady
To be my child Cordelia.
CORDELIA   And so I am. I am.
LEAR   Be your tears wet?[9] Yes, faith. I pray, weep not.
If you have poison for me, I will drink it.
70   I know you do not love me, for your sisters
Have, as I do remember, done me wrong.
You have some cause; they have not.
CORDELIA   No cause, no cause.

---

8. *but I . . . lead:* Lear puts himself in either hell or
purgatory, both places of such punishment in medieval accounts. Compare also to the classical myth of
Ixion, bound by Zeus to a spinning wheel of fire.
9. Are your tears real? Is this really happening?

LEAR Am I in France?
KENT   In your own kingdom, sir.
LEAR Do not abuse° me.   deceive; mock
DOCTOR Be comforted, good madam. The great rage
80   You see is cured in him, and yet it is
     Danger to make him even o'er° the time   go over
     He has lost. Desire him to go in;
     Trouble him no more till further settling.°   until his mind eases
CORDELIA Will't please your highness walk?
85   LEAR You must bear with me. Pray now, forget and forgive.
     I am old and foolish.
               Exeunt [LEAR *and* CORDELIA]; KENT *and*
                         GENTLEMAN *remain.*
GENTLEMAN Holds it true, sir, that the Duke of Cornwall was
     so slain?
KENT Most certain, sir.
90   GENTLEMAN Who is conductor° of his people?   commander
KENT As 'tis said, the bastard son of Gloucester.
GENTLEMAN They say Edgar, his banished son, is with the
     Earl of Kent in Germany.
KENT Report° is changeable. 'Tis time to look about.° The   Rumor / prepare defenses
95   powers of the kingdom approach apace.
GENTLEMAN The arbitrament° is like to be bloody. Fare you   encounter
     well, sir.   [*Exit.*]
KENT My point and period[2] will be thoroughly wrought,
     Or° well or ill as this day's battle's fought.   *Exit.*   For

5.1 (F 5.1)

               Enter Edmund [*the* BASTARD], REGAN, *and their*
                         powers.
BASTARD Know° of the Duke if his last purpose hold,[1]   Inquire
     Or whether since he is advised by aught[2]
     To change the course. He's full of alteration[3]
     And self reproving. Bring his constant pleasure.°   his settled intent
5   REGAN Our sister's man is certainly miscarried.[4]
BASTARD 'Tis to be doubted,° madam,   feared
REGAN   Now, sweet lord,
     You know the goodness I intend upon you.
     Tell me but truly, but then speak the truth:
     Do you not love my sister?
BASTARD   Ay, honored° love.   honorable
10   REGAN But have you never found my brother's way
     To the forfended[5] place?

2. The purpose and end of my life; literally, the full
stop.
5.1 Location: The British camp near Dover.
1. If his previous intention (to wage war) remains firm.
2. Since then anything has persuaded him.

3. A tendency to give up his intentions or put aside
his responsibilities.
4. Has surely come to grief by some accident.
5. Forbidden, by the prohibition against adultery.

LEAR   Am I in France?
KENT   In your own kingdom, sir.
LEAR   Do not abuse° me.   *deceive; mock*
75 GENTLEMAN   Be comforted, good madam; the great rage
       You see is killed in him. Desire him to go in;
       Trouble him no more till further settling.°   *until his mind eases*
    CORDELIA   Will't please your highness walk?
    LEAR   You must bear with me.
       Pray you now, forget and forgive.
80   I am old and foolish.   *Exeunt.*

5.1 (Q 5.1)

Enter with drum and colors,° EDMOND, REGAN,   *regimental flags*
       GENTLEMEN, *and Soldiers.*
    EDMOND   Know° of the Duke if his last purpose hold,[1]   *Inquire*
       Or whether since he is advised by aught[2]
       To change the course. He's full of alteration[3]
       And self-reproving. Bring his constant pleasure.°   *his settled intent*
5   REGAN   Our sister's man is certainly miscarried.[4]
    EDMOND   'Tis to be doubted,° madam.   *feared*
    REGAN   Now, sweet lord,
       You know the goodness I intend upon you.
       Tell me but truly, but then speak the truth:
       Do you not love my sister?
    EDMOND   In honored° love.   *honorable*
10 REGAN   But have you never found my brother's way
       To the forfended[5] place?

5.1 Location: The British camp near Dover.
1. If his previous intention (to wage war) remains firm.
2. Since then anything has persuaded him.

3. A tendency to give up his intentions or put aside his responsibilities.
4. Has surely come to grief by some accident.
5. Forbidden, by the prohibition against adultery.

BASTARD   That thought abuses° you.   *deceives*

REGAN   I am doubtful° that you have been conjunct°   *suspicious / complicit*

     And bosomed with° her—as far as we call hers.[6]   *enamored of*

BASTARD   No, by mine honor, madam.

15   REGAN   I never shall endure her. Dear my lord,

     Be not familiar° with her.   *intimate*

BASTARD   Fear° me not. She and the Duke, her husband—   *Doubt*

     Enter ALBANY *and* GONORILL *with troops.*

GONORILL [*aside*]   I had rather lose the battle than that sister

     Should loosen° him and me.   *disunite*

20   ALBANY   Our very loving sister, well be-met.°   *met*

     For this I hear: the King is come to his daughter,

     With others whom the rigor° of our state°   *harshness / government*

     Forced to cry out. Where I could not be honest°   *honorable*

     I never yet was valiant. For this business,

25   It touches° us as France invades our land,   *concerns*

     Not bolds° the King, with others whom I fear   *Does not embolden*

     Most just and heavy causes make oppose.[7]

BASTARD   Sir, you speak nobly.

REGAN   Why is this reasoned?[8]

GONORILL   Combine together 'gainst the enemy,

30   For these domestic poor particulars°   *minor details*

     Are not to° question here.   *the*

ALBANY   Let us, then, determine with the ancient° of war   *experienced officer(s)*

     On our proceedings.

BASTARD   I shall attend you presently° at your tent.   *in a moment*

35   REGAN   Sister, you'll go with us?

GONORILL   No.

REGAN   'Tis most convenient;° pray you go with us.[9]   *suitable*

GONORILL   Oh, ho, I know the riddle.° I will go.   *disguised meaning*

     Enter EDGAR [*disguised*].

EDGAR [*to* ALBANY]   If e'er your grace had speech with man

     so poor,

     Hear me one word.

ALBANY [*to the others*]   I'll overtake you.

     Exeunt [BASTARD, GONORILL, *and* REGAN

     with their troops and powers].

40   Speak.

EDGAR   Before you fight the battle, ope this letter.

     If you have victory, let the trumpet sound

     For him that brought it. Wretched though I seem,

     I can produce a champion that will prove°   *defend*

45   What is avouchèd° there. If you miscarry,°   *asserted / perish*

     Your business of the world hath so an end.

     Fortune love you.

ALBANY   Stay till I have read the letter.

---

6. In total intimacy; all the way.

7. *It . . . oppose:* The invasion concerns us only insofar as France has invaded Britain, not because it has
emboldened Lear, who has just cause to attack.

8. What is the point of this kind of speech?

9. Regan wants Gonorill to go with Albany and her,
rather than with Edmund.

EDMOND   No, by mine honor, madam.

REGAN   I never shall endure her. Dear my lord,
  Be not familiar° with her.   *intimate*
EDMOND   Fear° not. She and the Duke, her husband—   *Doubt*
      Enter with drum and colors, ALBANY, GONERILL,
      Soldiers.

15 ALBANY   Our very loving sister, well be-met.°   *met*
      —Sir, this I heard: the King is come to his daughter,
      With others whom the rigor° of our state°   *harshness / government*
      Forced to cry out.

REGAN   Why is this reasoned?[6]
GONERILL   Combine together 'gainst the enemy.
20   For these domestic and particular broils°   *minor details*
      Are not the question here.
ALBANY   Let's then determine with th'ancient° of war   *experienced officer(s)*
      On our proceeding.
REGAN   Sister, you'll go with us?[7]
25 GONERILL   No.
REGAN   'Tis most convenient;° pray go with us.   *suitable*
GONERILL   Oh, ho, I know the riddle!° I will go.   *disguised meaning*
                          Exeunt both the armies.
            Enter EDGAR [*disguised*].
EDGAR [*to* ALBANY]   If e'er your grace had speech with man
      so poor,
      Hear me one word.
ALBANY [*to the others*]   I'll overtake you.
                    [*Exeunt* EDMOND, GONERILL, *and* REGAN.]
                          Speak.
30 EDGAR   Before you fight the battle, ope this letter.
      If you have victory, let the trumpet sound
      For him that brought it. Wretched though I seem,
      I can produce a champion that will prove°   *defend*
      What is avouchèd° there. If you miscarry,°   *asserted / perish*
35   Your business of the world hath so an end,
      And machination° ceases. Fortune loves you.   *plotting*
ALBANY   Stay till I have read the letter.

6. What is the point of this kind of speech?
7. Regan wants Gonerill to go with Albany and her, rather than with Edmond.

EDGAR   I was forbid it.
　　When time shall serve, let but the herald cry
50　And I'll appear again.
ALBANY   Why, fare thee well. I will o'erlook the paper.
　　　　　　　　　　　　　　　　　　　　Exit [EDGAR].
　　　　Enter Edmund [the BASTARD].
BASTARD   The enemy's in view; draw up your powers.°　　　　　*troops*
　　Hard is the guess° of their great strength and forces　　*estimate*
　　By diligent discovery,° but your haste is now urged on you.　*spying*
55　ALBANY   We will greet the time.[1]　　　　　　　　　*Exit.*
BASTARD   To both these sisters have I sworn my love,
　　Each jealous° of the other, as the stung　　　　　　*suspicious*
　　Are of the adder. Which of them shall I take?
　　Both, one, or neither? Neither can be enjoyed
60　If both remain alive. To take the widow
　　Exasperates, makes mad, her sister Gonorill,
　　And hardly° shall I carry out my side,°　　*with difficulty / plan*
　　Her husband being alive. Now, then, we'll use
　　His countenance[2] for the battle, which being done,
65　Let her that would be rid of him devise
　　His speedy taking-off. As for his mercy
　　Which he intends to Lear and to Cordelia,
　　The battle done, and they within our power,
　　Shall° never see his pardon. For my state°　　*They shall / condition*
70　Stands on° me to defend, not to debate.　　*Exit.*　　*Obliges*

5.2 (F 5.2)

Alarum.[1] Enter the powers of France over the stage,
CORDELIA *with her father in her hand[, and exeunt].*
Enter EDGAR *[disguised as a peasant] and*
GLOUCESTER.

EDGAR   Here, father,[2] take the shadow of this bush
　　For your good host.° Pray that the right may thrive.　*shelter*
　　If ever I return to you again, I'll bring you comfort.　*Exit.*
GLOUCESTER   Grace go with you, sir.
　　　　Alarum° and retreat. [Enter EDGAR.]　　*Trumpet signal*
5　EDGAR   Away, old man! Give me thy hand, away!
　　King Lear hath lost: he and his daughter ta'en.
　　Give me thy hand, come on.
GLOUCESTER   No farther, sir, a man may rot even° here.　*right*
EDGAR   What, in ill thoughts again? Men must endure
10　Their going hence even as their coming hither.
　　Ripeness is all.[3] Come on.　　　　　　　*[Exeunt.]*

---

1. We will be ready to meet the occasion.
2. Authority or backing; also suggesting "face," to be used like a mask for Edmund's ambition.
5.2 Location: The rest of the play takes place near the battlefield.
1. Trumpet call to battle.

2. See note to 4.6.207.
3. To await the destined time is the most important thing, as fruit falls only when ripe (playing on Gloucester's "rot," line 8); readiness for death is our only duty (compare *Hamlet* 5.2.194, "The readiness is all").

EDGAR   I was forbid it.
When time shall serve, let but the herald cry,
And I'll appear again.   *Exit.*

40 ALBANY   Why, fare thee well. I will o'erlook thy paper.
      Enter EDMOND.
EDMOND   The enemy's in view; draw up your powers.°   *troops*
Here is the guess° of their true strength and forces   *estimate*
By diligent discovery,° but your haste   *spying*
Is now urged on you.
    ALBANY   We will greet the time.[8]   *Exit.*
45 EDMOND   To both these sisters have I sworn my love,
Each jealous° of the other, as the stung   *suspicious*
Are of the adder. Which of them shall I take?
Both? One? Or neither? Neither can be enjoyed
If both remain alive. To take the widow
50 Exasperates, makes mad, her sister Gonerill,
And hardly° shall I carry out my side,°   *with difficulty / plan*
Her husband being alive. Now, then, we'll use
His countenance[9] for the battle, which being done,
Let her who would be rid of him devise
55 His speedy taking-off. As for the mercy
Which he intends to Lear and to Cordelia,
The battle done, and they within our power,
Shall° never see his pardon. For my state°   *They shall / condition*
Stands on° me to defend, not to debate.   *Exit.*   *Obliges*

5.2 (Q 5.2)

Alarum within.[1] Enter with drum and colors, LEAR,
CORDELIA, *and Soldiers, over the stage, and exeunt.*
Enter EDGAR [*disguised as a peasant*] *and*
GLOUCESTER.
EDGAR   Here, father,[2] take the shadow of this tree
For your good host.° Pray that the right may thrive.   *shelter*
If ever I return to you again,
I'll bring you comfort.
GLOUCESTER   Grace go with you, sir.   *Exit* [EDGAR].
      Alarum° and retreat within.   *Trumpet signal*
      Enter EDGAR.
5 EDGAR   Away, old man, give me thy hand, away!
King Lear hath lost: he and his daughter ta'en.
Give me thy hand. Come on.
GLOUCESTER   No further, sir, a man may rot even° here.   *right*
EDGAR   What, in ill thoughts again? Men must endure
10 Their going hence even as their coming hither;
Ripeness is all.[3] Come on.
GLOUCESTER   And that's true too.   *Exeunt.*

---

8. We will be ready to meet the occasion.
9. Authority or backing; also suggesting "face," to be used like a mask for Edmond's ambition.
5.2 Location: The rest of the play takes place near the battlefield.
1. Trumpet call to battle (backstage).

2. See note to 4.5.212.
3. To await the destined time is the most important thing, as fruit falls only when ripe (playing on Gloucester's "rot," line 8); readiness for death is our only duty (compare *Hamlet* 5.2.199, "The readiness is all").

5.3 (F 5.3)

Enter Edmund [the BASTARD*, and* CAPTAIN OF THE
GUARD], *with* LEAR *and* CORDELIA *prisoners[,
guarded].*[1]

BASTARD   Some officers! Take them away. Good guard,
  Until their greater pleasures[2] best be known
  That are to censure° them.   *judge*
CORDELIA   We are not the first
  Who with best meaning° have incurred the worst.   *intention*
5 For thee, oppressèd King, am I cast down;°   *(into unhappiness)*
  Myself could else out-frown false fortune's frown.[3]
  Shall we not see these daughters and these sisters?
LEAR   No, no, come, let's away to prison.
  We two alone will sing like birds i'th' cage.
10 When thou dost ask me blessing, I'll kneel down
  And ask of thee forgiveness. So we'll live,
  And pray, and sing, and tell old tales and laugh
  At gilded butterflies,[4] and hear poor rogues
  Talk of court news, and we'll talk with them too—
15 Who loses, and who wins, who's in, who's out—
  And take upon 's the mystery of things
  As if we were God's spies. And we'll wear out°   *outlast*
  In a walled prison packs and sects of great ones
  That ebb and flow by th' moon.[5]
BASTARD   Take them away.
20 LEAR   Upon such sacrifices,[6] my Cordelia,
  The gods themselves throw incense. Have I caught thee?
  He that parts us shall bring a brand from heaven
  And fire us hence like foxes.[7] Wipe thine eyes.
  The good shall devour 'em, flesh and fell,[8]
25 Ere they shall make us weep. We'll see 'em starve first. Come.
    [Exit with CORDELIA*, guarded by* GENTLEMEN*.]*
BASTARD   Come hither, Captain. Hark.
  Take thou this note; go follow them to prison.
  One step I have advanced° thee; if thou dost   *promoted*
  As this instructs thee, thou dost make thy way
30 To noble fortunes. Know thou this: that men
  Are as the time is. To be tender-minded
  Does not become a sword;° thy great employment   *befit a swordsman*
  Will not bear question.° Either say thou'lt do't   *discussion*
  Or thrive by other means.
CAPTAIN OF THE GUARD   I'll do't, my lord.
35 BASTARD   About it, and write happy when thou hast done.[9]
  Mark, I say, instantly, and carry it° so   *carry it out*
  As I have set it down.

5.3
1. TEXTUAL COMMENT There are differences between
the entrance and exit directions in the Quarto and
Folio versions of 5.3. Q1's entrance of the "Captain"
late in the scene is replaced by the entrance of the
"Messenger" in F. The deletion of extraneous roles is
not unusual in the later revisions of plays, but this
scene's revision in F suggests that too many "Captains" are wandering the stage in Q1. See Digital Edition TC 7 (Quarto edited text).
2. *Good . . . pleasures:* Guard them well until the
desires of those greater persons.

3. Otherwise, I could be defiant in the face of bad
fortune.
4. Gaudy courtiers.
5. *packs . . . moon:* followers and factions of important people whose position at court varies as the tide.
6. Upon such sacrifices as we are or as you have made.
7. *shall . . . foxes:* must have divine aid to do so. The
image is of using a torch to smoke foxes out of their
holes—or, in the case of Lear and Cordelia, prison
cells.
8. *flesh and fell:* meat and skin; entirely.
9. Go to it, and call yourself happy when you are done.

5.3 (Q 5.3)

Enter in conquest with drum and colors, EDMOND;
LEAR *and* CORDELIA *as prisoners; Soldiers,* CAPTAIN.[1]

EDMOND Some officers! Take them away. Good guard
    Until their greater pleasures[2] first be known
    That are to censure° them.   *judge*
CORDELIA   We are not the first
    Who with best meaning° have incurred the worst.   *intention*
5   For thee, oppressèd King, I am cast down.°   *(into unhappiness)*
    Myself could else out-frown false fortune's frown.[3]
    Shall we not see these daughters and these sisters?
LEAR   No, no, no, no. Come, let's away to prison.
    We two alone will sing like birds i'th' cage.
10   When thou dost ask me blessing, I'll kneel down
    And ask of thee forgiveness. So we'll live,
    And pray, and sing, and tell old tales, and laugh
    At gilded butterflies,[4] and hear poor rogues
    Talk of court news, and we'll talk with them too—
15   Who loses, and who wins; who's in, who's out—
    And take upon 's the mystery of things,
    As if we were God's spies. And we'll wear out,°   *outlast*
    In a walled prison, packs and sects of great ones,
    That ebb and flow by th' moon.[5]
EDMOND   Take them away.
20 LEAR   Upon such sacrifices,[6] my Cordelia,
    The gods themselves throw incense. Have I caught thee?
    He that parts us shall bring a brand from heaven,
    And fire us hence like foxes.[7] Wipe thine eyes.
    The good years shall devour them, flesh and fell,[8]
25   Ere they shall make us weep.
    We'll see 'em starved first. Come.
          Exeunt [*Soldiers with* LEAR *and* CORDELIA].
EDMOND Come hither, Captain. Hark.
    Take thou this note; go follow them to prison.
    One step I have advanced° thee; if thou dost   *promoted*
30   As this instructs thee, thou dost make thy way
    To noble fortunes. Know thou this: that men
    Are as the time is. To be tender-minded
    Does not become a sword;° thy great employment   *befit a swordsman*
    Will not bear question.° Either say thou'lt do't   *discussion*
35   Or thrive by other means.
CAPTAIN   I'll do't, my lord.
EDMOND About it, and write happy when th' hast done.[9]
    Mark, I say instantly, and carry it so°   *carry it out*
    As I have set it down.   *Exit* CAPTAIN.

5.3
1. TEXTUAL COMMENT There are differences between
the entrance and exit directions in the Q1 and F versions of 5.3. Q1's entrance of the "Captain" late in the
scene is replaced by the entrance of the "Messenger"
in F. The deletion of extraneous roles is not unusual
in the later revisions of plays, but this scene's revision
in F suggests that too many "Captains" are wandering
the stage in Q1. See Digital Edition TC 6 (Folio
edited text).
2. *Good . . . pleasures:* Guard them well until the
desires of those greater persons.
3. Otherwise, I could be defiant in the face of bad
fortune.

4. Gaudy courtiers.
5. *packs . . . moon:* followers and factions of important people whose position at court varies as the tide.
6. Upon such sacrifices as we are or as you have
made.
7. *shall . . . foxes:* must have divine aid to do so. The
image is of using a torch to smoke foxes out of their
holes—or, in the case of Lear and Cordelia, prison
cells.
8. *flesh and fell:* meat and skin; entirely. The precise
meaning of "good years" has not been explained; it
may signify simply the passage of time or may suggest
some ominous, destructive power.
9. Go to it, and call yourself happy when you are done.

CAPTAIN OF THE GUARD   I cannot draw a cart, nor eat dried
    oats;°   *(like a horse)*
  If it be man's work, I'll do't.   [*Exit.*]
      Enter [*the*] *Duke* [*of* ALBANY], *the two Ladies*
      [GONORILL *and* REGAN, *another* CAPTAIN], *and others.*

40   ALBANY   Sir, you have showed today your valiant strain,°   *qualities; heritage*
    And Fortune led you well. You have the captives
    That were the opposites° of this day's strife.   *opponents*
    We do require them of you, so to use° them   *treat*
    As we shall find their merits and our safety
    May equally determine.
45   BASTARD   Sir, I thought it fit
    To send the old and miserable King
    To some retention° and appointed guard,   *confinement*
    Whose° age has charms in it, whose title more,   *(Lear's)*
    To pluck the common bosom[1] of his side
50   And turn our impressed lances° in our eyes   *conscripted lancers*
    Which[2] do command them. With him I sent the Queen.
    My reason all the same, and they are ready
    Tomorrow or at further space° to appear   *at a future point*
    Where you shall hold your session.° At this time,   *court of judgment*
55   We sweat and bleed. The friend hath lost his friend,
    And the best quarrels, in the heat, are cursed
    By those that feel their sharpness.[3]
    The question of Cordelia and her father
    Requires a fitter place.
    ALBANY   Sir, by your patience,
60   I hold you but a subject of° this war,   *in waging*
    Not as a brother.
    REGAN   That's as we list° to grace him.   *choose*
    Methinks our pleasure should have been demanded[4]
    Ere you had spoke so far. He led our powers,°   *armies*
    Bore the commission of my place and person,
65   The which immediate° may well stand up   *close connection*
    And call itself your brother.
    GONORILL   Not so hot.°   *Not so fast*
    In his own grace° he doth exalt himself   *merit*
    More than in your advancement.[5]
    REGAN   In my right,
    By me invested, he compeers° the best.   *equals*
70   GONORILL   That were the most[6] if he should husband you.
    REGAN   Jesters do oft prove prophets.
    GONORILL   Holla, holla!
    That eye that told you so looked but asquint.[7]
    REGAN   Lady, I am not well, else I should answer
    From a full-flowing stomach.° —General,   *anger*
75   Take thou my soldiers, prisoners, patrimony.
    Witness the world that I create thee here
    My lord and master.

---

1. To garner the affection of the populace.
2. *in our eyes / Which:* in the eyes of us who.
3. *And . . . sharpness:* And in the heat of battle, even the most just wars are cursed by those who must suffer the fighting.
4. I think you should have inquired into my wishes.

5. In the honors you confer upon him.
6. That investiture would be complete.
7. Squinting was a proverbial effect of jealousy, because of the tendency to look suspiciously at potential rivals.

Flourish. Enter ALBANY, GONERILL, REGAN, *Soldiers.*

ALBANY Sir, you have showed today your valiant strain,° *qualities; heritage*
40 And fortune led you well. You have the captives
 Who were the opposites° of this day's strife. *opponents*
 I do require them of you, so to use° them *treat*
 As we shall find their merits and our safety
 May equally determine.
EDMOND   Sir, I thought it fit
45 To send the old and miserable King to some retention,° *confinement*
 Whose° age had charms in it, whose title more, *(Lear's)*
 To pluck the common bosom[1] on his side
 And turn our impressed lances° in our eyes *conscripted lancers*
 Which[2] do command them. With him I sent the Queen,
50 My reason all the same, and they are ready
 Tomorrow or at further space° t'appear *at a future point*
 Where you shall hold your session.° *court of judgment*

ALBANY   Sir, by your patience,
 I hold you but a subject of° this war, *in waging*
 Not as a brother.
REGAN   That's as we list° to grace him. *choose*
55 Methinks our pleasure might have been demanded[3]
 Ere you had spoke so far. He led our powers,° *armies*
 Bore the commission of my place and person,
 The which immediacy° may well stand up *close connection*
 And call itself your brother.
GONERILL   Not so hot.° *Not so fast*
60 In his own grace° he doth exalt himself *merit*
 More than in your addition.[4]
REGAN   In my rights,
 By me invested, he compeers° the best. *equals*
ALBANY That were the most[5] if he should husband you.
REGAN Jesters do oft prove prophets.
GONERILL   Holla, holla!
65 That eye that told you so looked but asquint.[6]
REGAN Lady, I am not well, else I should answer
 From a full-flowing stomach.° —General, *anger*
 Take thou my soldiers, prisoners, patrimony;
 Dispose of them, of me. The walls° is thine. *fortress of my heart*
70 Witness the world that I create thee here
 My lord and master.

---

1. To garner the affection of the populace.
2. *in our eyes / Which:* in the eyes of us who.
3. I think you should have inquired into my wishes.
4. In the honors you confer upon him.

5. That investiture would be complete.
6. Squinting was a proverbial effect of jealousy, because of the tendency to look suspiciously at potential rivals.

GONORILL   Mean you to enjoy him, then?

ALBANY   The let-alone° lies not in your good will.   *veto*

BASTARD   Nor in thine, lord.

ALBANY   Half-blooded° fellow, yes.   *Bastard*

80   BASTARD   Let the drum strike,[8] and prove my title good.

ALBANY   Stay, yet; hear reason. Edmund, I arrest thee
     On capital treason, and in thine attaint[9]
     This gilded serpent. [*to* REGAN] For your claim, fair sister,°   *sister-in-law*
     I bar it in the interest of my wife.

85   'Tis she is subcontracted to this lord,
     And I her husband contradict the banns.°   *marriage announcement*
     If you will marry, make your love to me:
     My lady is bespoke. —Thou art armed, Gloucester;
     If none appear to prove upon thy head

90   Thy heinous, manifest, and many treasons,
     There is my pledge. [*He throws down his gauntlet.*] I'll prove
         it on thy heart
     Ere I taste bread, thou art in nothing less°   *in no way less guilty*
     Than I have here proclaimed thee.

REGAN   Sick, oh, sick!

GONORILL [*aside*]   If not, I'll ne'er trust poison.

95   BASTARD [*throwing down his gauntlet*]   There's my exchange.
     What° in the world he is   *Whoever*
     That names me traitor, villain-like he lies.
     Call by thy trumpet; he that dares approach
     On him, on you—who not—I will maintain
     My truth and honor firmly.

ALBANY   A herald, ho!

100   BASTARD   A herald, ho, a herald.

ALBANY   Trust to thy single virtue,° for thy soldiers,   *your unassisted power*
     All levied in my name, have in my name
     Took their discharge.

REGAN   This sickness grows upon me.

ALBANY   She is not well; convey her to my tent.
               [*Exit* REGAN *with* GENTLEMEN.]
       [*Enter a* HERALD.]

105   Come hither, Herald. Let the trumpet sound,
     And read out this. [*He hands him a letter.*]

---

8. Perhaps to announce the betrothal or a challenge.
9. And in order to accuse you; and as one who shares your corruption or crime.

GONERILL   Mean you to enjoy him?

ALBANY   The let-alone° lies not in your good will.   *veto*

EDMOND   Nor in thine, lord.

ALBANY   Half-blooded° fellow, yes.   *Bastard*

REGAN   Let the drum strike,[7] and prove my title thine.

75   ALBANY   Stay yet; hear reason. Edmond, I arrest thee
       On capital treason, and in thy arrest[8]
       This gilded serpent. [*to* REGAN] For your claim, fair sister,°   *sister-in-law*
       I bar it in the interest of my wife.
       'Tis she is subcontracted to this lord,
80   And I her husband contradict your banns.°   *marriage announcement*
       If you will marry, make your loves to me:
       My lady is bespoke.

GONERILL   An interlude!°   *A farce*

ALBANY   Thou art armed, Gloucester. Let the trumpet sound.
       If none appear to prove upon thy person
85   Thy heinous, manifest, and many treasons,
       There is my pledge. I'll make° [*throwing down his gauntlet*]   *prove*
          it on thy heart,
       Ere I taste bread, thou art in nothing less°   *in no way less guilty*
       Than I have here proclaimed thee.

REGAN   Sick, oh, sick!

GONERILL [*aside*]   If not, I'll ne'er trust medicine.°   *poison (euphemistic)*

90   EDMOND [*throwing down his gauntlet*]   There's my exchange.
       What° in the world he's   *Whoever*
       That names me traitor, villain-like he lies.
       Call by the trumpet. He that dares approach
       On him, on you—who not—I will maintain
       My truth and honor firmly.

ALBANY   A herald, ho!

       Enter a HERALD.

95   Trust to thy single virtue,° for thy soldiers,   *your unassisted power*
       All levied in my name, have in my name
       Took their discharge.

REGAN   My sickness grows upon me.

ALBANY   She is not well; convey her to my tent.

                                [*Exit* REGAN, *attended.*]

       Come hither, Herald; let the trumpet sound,
100   And read out this. [*He hands him a letter.*]

---

7. Perhaps to announce the betrothal or a challenge.
8. And in order to accuse you; and as one who shares your corruption or crime.

CAPTAIN   Sound trumpet!
      [*A trumpet sounds.*]
HERALD [*reads*]   "If any man of quality or degree, in the host
    of the army, will maintain upon Edmund, supposed Earl of
    Gloucester, that he's a manifold traitor, let him appear at
110   the third sound of the trumpet. He is bold in his defense."
BASTARD   Sound!
      [*A trumpet sounds.*]
    Again!
      [*A trumpet sounds.*]
      Enter EDGAR [*in armor*] *at the third sound, a trumpet*
      before him.
ALBANY   Ask him his purposes: why he appears
    Upon this call o'th' trumpet.
115   HERALD   What° are you? Your name and quality°   *Who / degree; rank*
    And why you answer this present summons?
EDGAR   Oh, know my name is lost, by treason's tooth
    Bare-gnawn and canker-bit.[1] Yet ere I move't,°   *make my declaration*
    Where is the adversary I come to cope withal?°   *to encounter with*
120   ALBANY   Which is that adversary?
EDGAR   What's he that speaks for Edmund, Earl of
    Gloucester?
BASTARD   Himself. What sayest thou to him?
EDGAR   Draw thy sword,
    That° if my speech offend a noble heart, thy arm   *So that*
    May do thee justice. [*He draws his sword.*] Here is mine.
125   Behold, it is the privilege of my tongue,
    My oath, and my profession. I protest,
    Maugre° thy strength, youth, place, and eminence,   *Despite*
    Despite thy victor-sword and fire-new° fortune,   *newly minted*
    Thy valor and thy heart,° thou art a traitor,   *courage*
130   False to thy gods, thy brother, and thy father,
    Conspirant 'gainst this high illustrious prince,
    And from th'extremest upward° of thy head,   *top*
    To the descent° and dust beneath thy feet,   *lowest part; sole*
    A most toad-spotted[2] traitor. Say thou no,
135   This sword, this arm, and my best spirits
    Are bent° to prove upon thy heart, whereto I speak,   *ready*
    Thou liest.
BASTARD   In wisdom I should ask thy name,
    But since thy outside looks so fair and warlike,
    And that° thy being some say[3] of breeding breathes,   *since*
140   By right of knighthood,° I disdain and spurn.   *(to ask your name)*
    Here do I toss those treasons to thy head.
    With the hell-hated° lie o'erturned thy heart,   *hated as much as hell*

---

1. *canker-bit:* worm-eaten.   3. Taste (from "assay"); utterance.
2. Venomous, like a toad; spotted with disgrace.

A trumpet sounds.

HERALD (*reads*) "If any man of quality or degree, within the
lists of the army, will maintain upon Edmond, supposed
Earl of Gloucester, that he is a manifold traitor, let him
appear by the third sound of the trumpet. He is bold in his
105 defense."

    First trumpet [sounds].

Again!

    Second trumpet [sounds].

Again!

    Third trumpet [sounds].
    Trumpet answers within.
    Enter EDGAR, *armed.*

ALBANY Ask him his purposes: why he appears
Upon this call o'th' trumpet.

HERALD What° are you?	*Who*

110 Your name, your quality,° and why you answer   *degree; rank*
This present summons?

EDGAR Know my name is lost,	

By treason's tooth bare-gnawn and canker-bit,°   *worm-eaten*
Yet am I noble as the adversary
I come to cope.°   *to encounter*

ALBANY   Which is that adversary?

115 EDGAR What's he that speaks for Edmond, Earl of
    Gloucester?

EDMOND Himself. What say'st thou to him?

EDGAR Draw thy sword,	

That° if my speech offend a noble heart,   *So that*
Thy arm may do thee justice. [*He draws his sword.*] Here is
    mine.
Behold, it is my privilege,
120 The privilege of mine honors,
My oath, and my profession. I protest,
Maugre° thy strength, place, youth, and eminence,   *Despite*
Despite thy victor-sword and fire-new° fortune,   *newly minted*
Thy valor and thy heart,° thou art a traitor,   *courage*
125 False to thy gods, thy brother, and thy father,
Conspirant 'gainst this high illustrious prince,
And from th'extremest upward° of thy head   *top*
To the descent° and dust below thy foot   *lowest part; sole*
A most toad-spotted⁹ traitor. Say thou no,
130 This sword, this arm, and my best spirits are bent°   *ready*
To prove upon thy heart, whereto I speak,
Thou liest.

EDMOND   In wisdom I should ask thy name,
But since thy outside looks so fair and warlike,
And that° thy tongue some say¹ of breeding breathes,   *since*
135 What safe and nicely I might well delay
By rule of knighthood, I disdain and spurn.²
Back do I toss these treasons to thy head,
With the hell-hated° lie o'erwhelm thy heart,   *hated as much as hell*

---

9. Venomous, like a toad; spotted with disgrace.
1. Taste (from "assay"); utterance.
2. *And . . . spurn:* And since your speech may suggest high birth, I will not stick safely and meticulously to the rules of knighthood (which do not require a knight to fight an unknown opponent) and refuse to fight you.

Which, for° they yet glance by and scarcely bruise,   *since*
This sword of mine shall give them instant way°   *access*
145 Where they shall rest forever. —Trumpets, speak.
      [*Alarums. They fight, and* EDGAR *vanquishes*
      BASTARD.]
ALBANY[4] Save° him, save him!   *Spare*
GONORILL   This is mere practice,° Gloucester!   *trickery*
By the law of arms thou art not bound to answer
An unknown opposite.° Thou art not vanquished,   *opponent*
But cozened and beguiled.°   *cheated and deceived*
ALBANY [*showing her a letter*]   Stop your mouth, dame,
150 Or with this paper shall I stopple° it.   *plug*
Thou worse than anything, read thine own evil!
Nay, no tearing, lady; I perceive you know't.
GONORILL   Say if I do, the laws are mine, not thine.
Who shall arraign° me for't?   *prosecute*
155 ALBANY   Most monstrous! Know'st thou this paper?
GONORILL   Ask me not what I know.   *Exit.*
ALBANY   Go after her, she's desperate; govern° her.   *restrain*
                            [*Exeunt some* SERVANTS.]
BASTARD   What you have charged me with, that have I done,
And more, much more; the time will bring it out.
160 'Tis past, and so am I. But what art thou
That hast this fortune on me?[5] If thou beest noble,
I do forgive thee.
EDGAR   Let's exchange charity.°   *forgiveness*
[*He removes his helmet.*] I am no less in blood than thou
          art, Edmund;
If more, the more thou hast wronged me.
165 My name is Edgar and thy father's son.
The gods are just, and of our pleasant virtues
Make instruments to scourge us:
The dark and vicious place where thee he got[6]
Cost him his eyes.
BASTARD   Thou hast spoken truth.
170 The wheel° is come full circled; I am here.[7]   *Fortune's wheel*
ALBANY [*to* EDGAR]   Methought thy very gait did prophesy
A royal nobleness. I must embrace thee.
Let sorrow split my heart if I did ever hate
Thee or thy father.
EDGAR   Worthy prince, I know't.
175 ALBANY   Where have you hid yourself?
How have you known the miseries of your father?
EDGAR   By nursing them, my lord. List° a brief tale,   *Listen to*
And, when 'tis told, oh, that my heart would burst!
The bloody proclamation to escape[8]
180 That followed me so near—oh, our lives' sweetness,

---

4. Both Q and F give this speech to "Alb." (for "Albany"), which may be a compositor's mistake for "All."
5. Who have this good fortune at my expense.
6. The adulterous bed in which you were conceived; or, possibly, the vagina. *got:* begot.
7. Back at the lowest point.
8. In order to escape the sentence of death.

140	Which, for° they yet glance by and scarcely bruise, This sword of mine shall give them instant way° Where they shall rest for ever. —Trumpets, speak. *Alarums. Fights.*	*since* *access*

ALBANY[3]   Save° him, save him!   *Spare*

GONERILL   This is practice,° Gloucester!   *trickery*

    By th' law of war thou wast not bound to answer

    An unknown opposite.° Thou art not vanquished,   *opponent*

    But cozened and beguiled.°   *cheated and deceived*

145   ALBANY [*showing her a letter*]   Shut your mouth, dame,

    Or with this paper shall I stop° it. Hold,° sir,   *plug / Behold*

    Thou worse than any name, read thine own evil.

    No tearing, lady; I perceive you know it.

GONERILL   Say if I do, the laws are mine, not thine.

150   Who can arraign° me for't?   *Exit.*   *prosecute*

ALBANY [*to* EDMOND]   Most monstrous! Oh, know'st thou this

      paper?

EDMOND   Ask me not what I know.

ALBANY   Go after her. She's desperate; govern° her.   *restrain*

                    [*Exeunt some Soldiers.*]

EDMOND   What you have charged me with, that have I done,

155   And more, much more; the time will bring it out.

    'Tis past, and so am I. But what art thou

    That hast this fortune on me?[4] If thou'rt noble,

    I do forgive thee.

EDGAR   Let's exchange charity.°   *forgiveness*

    [*He removes his helmet.*] I am no less in blood than thou

      art, Edmond;

160   If more, the more th' hast wronged me.

    My name is Edgar and thy father's son.

    The gods are just, and of our pleasant vices

    Make instruments to plague us:

    The dark and vicious place where thee he got[5]

    Cost him his eyes.

165   EDMOND   Th' hast spoken right, 'tis true:

    The wheel° is come full circle. I am here.[6]   *Fortune's wheel*

ALBANY [*to* EDGAR]   Methought thy very gait did prophesy

    A royal nobleness. I must embrace thee.

    Let sorrow split my heart if ever I

    Did hate thee or thy father.

170   EDGAR   Worthy prince, I know't.

ALBANY   Where have you hid yourself?

    How have you known the miseries of your father?

EDGAR   By nursing them, my lord. List° a brief tale,   *Listen to*

    And when 'tis told, oh, that my heart would burst!

175   The bloody proclamation to escape,[7]

    That followed me so near—oh, our lives' sweetness,

---

3. Both Q and F give this speech to "*Alb.*" (for "Albany"), which may be a compositor's mistake for "*All.*"
4. Who have this good fortune at my expense.
5. The adulterous bed in which you were conceived; or, possibly, the vagina. *got:* begot.
6. Back at the lowest point.
7. In order to escape the sentence of death.

That with the pain of death would hourly die,
Rather than die at once⁹—taught me to shift
Into a madman's rags, to assume a semblance
That very° dogs disdained, and in this habit   *even*
185   Met I my father with his bleeding rings° —   *sockets*
The precious stones° new lost—became his guide,   *eyes*
Led him, begged for him, saved him from despair.
Never—O father—revealed myself unto him
Until some half hour past, when I was armed.
190   Not sure, though hoping of this good success,°   *conclusion*
I asked his blessing and from first to last
Told him my pilgrimage. But his flawed° heart,   *cracked*
Alack, too weak the conflict to support,
Twixt two extremes of passion, joy and grief,
195   Burst smilingly.
BASTARD   This speech of yours hath moved me
And shall perchance do good. But speak you on;
You look as you had something more to say.
ALBANY   If there be more, more woeful, hold it in,
For I am almost ready to dissolve,°   *melt into tears*
200   Hearing of this.
EDGAR   This would have seemed a period° to such   *conclusion*
As love not sorrow, but another to amplify° too much   *enlarge; extend*
Would make much more and top extremity.
Whilst I was big in clamor,° came there in a man,   *lamenting loudly*
205   Who having seen me in my worst estate
Shunned my abhorred society, but then finding
Who 'twas that so endured, with his strong arms
He fastened on my neck and bellowed out
As he'd burst heaven, threw me on my father,
210   Told the most piteous tale of Lear and him°   *himself*
That ever ear received, which, in recounting,
His grief grew puissant,° and the strings of life   *powerful*
Began to crack twice. Then the trumpets sounded.
And there I left him tranced.
ALBANY   But who was this?
215   EDGAR   Kent, sir, the banished Kent, who in disguise
Followed his enemy king¹ and did him service
Improper° for a slave.   *Unfit even*
        Enter one [a GENTLEMAN] *with a bloody knife.*
GENTLEMAN   Help, help!
ALBANY   What kind of help? What means that bloody knife?
GENTLEMAN   It's hot! It smokes! It came even from the heart of—
220   ALBANY   Who, man? Speak!
GENTLEMAN   —Your lady, sir, your lady—and her sister
By her is poisoned; she hath confessed it.

That we the pain of death would hourly die
Rather than die at once[8]—taught me to shift
Into a madman's rags, t'assume a semblance
180 That very° dogs disdained, and in this habit   *even*
Met I my father with his bleeding rings°—   *sockets*
Their precious stones° new lost—became his guide,   *eyes*
Led him, begged for him, saved him from despair.
Never—oh, fault—revealed myself unto him
185 Until some half hour past, when I was armed.
Not sure, though hoping of this good success,°   *conclusion*
I asked his blessing and from first to last
Told him our pilgrimage. But his flawed° heart,   *cracked*
Alack, too weak the conflict to support,
190 Twixt two extremes of passion, joy and grief,
Burst smilingly.
EDMOND   This speech of yours hath moved me
And shall perchance do good. But speak you on;
You look as you had something more to say.
ALBANY   If there be more, more woeful, hold it in,
195 For I am almost ready to dissolve,°   *melt into tears*
Hearing of this.

    Enter a GENTLEMAN [*with a bloody knife*].
GENTLEMAN   Help, help! Oh, help!
EDGAR   What kind of help?
ALBANY   Speak, man.
EDGAR   What means this bloody knife?
GENTLEMAN   'Tis hot! It smokes! It came even from the
    heart of—
    Oh, she's dead.
200 ALBANY   Who dead? Speak, man.
GENTLEMAN   Your lady, sir, your lady—and her sister
    By her is poisoned; she confesses it.

---

8. *our . . . once:* how sweet must life be that we prefer the constant pain of dying to death itself.

BASTARD   I was contracted to them both; all three
      Now marry° in an instant.   *unite (in death)*
225 ALBANY   Produce their bodies, be they alive or dead.
      This justice of the heavens that makes us tremble
      Touches us not with pity.
                  Enter KENT.
EDGAR   Here comes Kent, sir.
ALBANY   Oh, 'tis he. The time will not allow
      The compliment that very manners urges.[2]
230 KENT   I am come to bid my king and master
      Aye° good night. Is he not here?   *Forever*
ALBANY   Great thing of° us forgot!   *by*
      Speak, Edmund, where's the King? And where's Cordelia?
            The bodies of Gonorill and Regan are brought in.
      See'st thou this object,° Kent?   *spectacle*
KENT   Alack, why thus?
235 BASTARD   Yet° Edmund was beloved: *Despite all*
      The one the other poisoned for my sake
      And after slew herself.
ALBANY   Even so; cover their faces.
BASTARD   I pant for life. Some good I mean to do
240 Despite of my own nature. Quickly send—
      Be brief° —into th' castle, for my writ[3]   *speedy*
      Is on the life of Lear and on Cordelia.
      Nay, send in time!
ALBANY   Run, run, oh, run!
EDGAR   To who, my lord? —Who hath the office?° Send   *commission*
245 Thy token of reprieve.
BASTARD   Well thought on! Take my sword. The Captain,
      Give it the° Captain!   *to the*
ALBANY [*to* EDGAR]   Haste thee for thy life.   [*Exit* EDGAR.]
BASTARD   He hath commission from thy wife and me
      To hang Cordelia in the prison and to lay
250 The blame upon her own despair,
      That she fordid herself.[4]
ALBANY   The gods defend her! Bear him hence awhile.
                  [*Edmund the* BASTARD *is carried out by*
                        CAPTAIN *and some* SERVANTS.]
            Enter LEAR *with* CORDELIA *in his arms*[, EDGAR, *and*
            CAPTAIN OF THE GUARD].
LEAR   Howl, howl, howl, howl! Oh, you are men of stones!
      Had I your tongues and eyes, I would use them so
255 That heaven's vault should crack! She's gone forever.
      I know when one is dead and when one lives;
      She's dead as earth. Lend me a looking glass.

---

2. *The compliment . . . urges:* the ceremony that barest custom demands.
3. Order of execution.

4. Destroyed herself. In most of Shakespeare's
source texts for the play, Cordelia does in fact kill
herself after reigning for some years.

EDMOND   I was contracted to them both; all three
   Now marry° in an instant.   *unite (in death)*
     Enter KENT.
EDGAR   Here comes Kent.
205 ALBANY   Produce the bodies, be they alive or dead.
     Gonerill and Regan's bodies brought out.
   This judgment of the heavens that makes us tremble
   Touches us not with pity. Oh, is this he?
   The time will not allow the compliment
   Which very manners urges.[9]
KENT   I am come
210 To bid my king and master aye° good night.   *forever*
   Is he not here?
ALBANY   Great thing of° us forgot!   *by*
   Speak, Edmond, where's the King? And where's Cordelia?
   Seest thou this object,° Kent?   *spectacle*
KENT   Alack, why thus?
EDMOND   Yet° Edmond was beloved: *Despite all*
215 The one the other poisoned for my sake
   And after slew herself.
ALBANY   Even so. Cover their faces.
EDMOND   I pant for life. Some good I mean to do
   Despite of mine own nature. Quickly send—
220 Be brief° in it—to th' castle, for my writ[1]   *speedy*
   Is on the life of Lear and on Cordelia.
   Nay, send in time.
ALBANY   Run, run, oh, run!
EDGAR   To who, my lord? —Who has the office?°   *commission*
   Send thy token of reprieve.
EDMOND   Well thought on. Take my sword,
   Give it the° Captain.   *to the*
225 EDGAR   Haste thee for thy life!
                [*Exit* GENTLEMAN.]
EDMOND   He hath commission from thy wife and me
   To hang Cordelia in the prison and
   To lay the blame upon her own despair,
   That she fordid herself.[2]
230 ALBANY   The gods defend her! Bear him hence awhile.
       [EDMOND *is carried out by Soldiers.*]
     Enter LEAR, *with* CORDELIA *in his arms[, and*
     GENTLEMAN].
LEAR   Howl, howl, howl! Oh, you are men of stones!
   Had I your tongues and eyes, I'd use them so
   That heaven's vault should crack. She's gone forever.
   I know when one is dead and when one lives;
235 She's dead as earth. Lend me a looking glass,

---

9. *the complement . . . urges:* the ceremony that barest custom demands.
1. Order of execution.

2. Destroyed herself. In most of Shakespeare's
source texts for the play, Cordelia does in fact kill
herself after reigning for some years.

If that her breath will mist or stain the stone,[5]
Why, then, she lives.

KENT   Is this the promised end?[6]

EDGAR   Or image of that horror?

260   ALBANY   Fall and cease.[7]

LEAR   This feather stirs. She lives![8] If it be so,
It is a chance which does redeem all sorrows
That ever I have felt.

KENT   Ay, my good master.

LEAR   Prithee, away.

EDGAR   'Tis noble Kent, your friend.

265   LEAR   A plague upon your murderous traitors all!
I might have saved her; now she's gone forever.
Cordelia, Cordelia, stay a little. Ha,
What is't thou sayest? Her voice was ever soft,
Gentle, and low, an excellent thing in women.

270   —I killed the slave that was a-hanging thee.

CAPTAIN OF THE GUARD   'Tis true, my lords, he did.

LEAR   Did I not, fellow? I have seen the day,
With my good biting falchion° I would   *light sword*
Have made them skip. I am old now,

275   And these same crosses spoil me.[9] Who are you?
Mine eyes are not o'the best, I'll tell you straight.°   *recognize you soon*

KENT   If Fortune bragged of two she loved or hated,
One of them we behold.[1]

LEAR   Are not you Kent?

KENT   The same: your servant Kent. Where is your servant
Caius?°   *(Kent's pseudonym)*

280   LEAR   He's a good fellow, I can tell that;
He'll strike, and quickly, too. He's dead and rotten.

KENT   No, my good lord, I am the very man—

LEAR   I'll see that straight.[2]

KENT   —That from your life of difference and decay[3]
Have followed your sad steps.

285   LEAR   You're welcome hither.

KENT   Nor no man else.[4] All's cheerless, dark and deadly.°   *deathly*
Your eldest daughters have fordone° themselves   *destroyed*
And desperately° are dead.   *in despair*

LEAR   So think I, too.

---

5. Mica, or stone polished to a mirror finish.
6. Doomsday; expected end of the play. In no version of the story previous to Shakespeare's does Cordelia die at this point.
7. Let the world collapse and end.
8. PERFORMANCE COMMENT Each production must determine whether to sustain suspense regarding the possibility that Cordelia is still alive or to make it clear that her father is raving over a corpse. See Digital Edition PC 6.
9. And these recent adversities have weakened me; and these parries I could once match would now destroy me.

1. *If . . . behold:* If there were only two supreme examples in the world of Fortune's ability to raise up and cast down, Lear would be one; alternatively, we are each of us one (Lear and Kent are here looking at each other).
2. I'll attend to that shortly; I'll comprehend that in a moment.
3. Who from the beginning of your alteration and deterioration.
4. No, neither I nor anyone else is welcome. Alternatively, I am that man, not disguised as anyone else.

If that her breath will mist or stain the stone,[3]
Why, then, she lives.

KENT   Is this the promised end?[4]

EDGAR   Or image of that horror.

ALBANY   Fall and cease.[5]

LEAR   This feather stirs. She lives![6] If it be so,
240 It is a chance which does redeem all sorrows
That ever I have felt.

KENT   O my good master.

LEAR   Prithee, away.

EDGAR   'Tis noble Kent, your friend.

LEAR   A plague upon you murderers, traitors all!
I might have saved her; now she's gone forever.
245 Cordelia, Cordelia, stay a little. Ha,
What is't thou say'st? Her voice was ever soft,
Gentle, and low, an excellent thing in woman.
—I killed the slave that was a-hanging thee.

GENTLEMAN   'Tis true, my lords, he did.

LEAR   Did I not, fellow?
250 I have seen the day, with my good biting falchion°   *light sword*
I would have made him skip. I am old now,
And these same crosses spoil me.[7] Who are you?
Mine eyes are not o'th' best, I'll tell you straight.°   *recognize you soon*

KENT   If Fortune brag of two she loved and hated,
255 One of them we behold.[8]

LEAR   This is a dull sight;[9] are you not Kent?

KENT   The same: your servant Kent.
Where is your servant Caius?°   *(Kent's pseudonym)*

LEAR   He's a good fellow, I can tell you that;
260 He'll strike, and quickly, too. He's dead and rotten.

KENT   No, my good lord, I am the very man—

LEAR   I'll see that straight.[1]

KENT   —That from your first of difference and decay[2]
Have followed your sad steps.

LEAR   You are welcome hither.
265 KENT   Nor no man else.[3]
All's cheerless, dark, and deadly.°   *deathly*
Your eldest daughters have fordone° themselves   *destroyed*
And desperately° are dead.   *in despair*

LEAR   Ay, so I think.

---

3. Mica, or stone polished to a mirror finish.

4. Doomsday; expected end of the play. In no version of the story previous to Shakespeare's does Cordelia die at this point.

5. Let the world collapse and end.

6. PERFORMANCE COMMENT Each production must determine whether to sustain suspense regarding the possibility that Cordelia is still alive or to make it clear that her father is raving over a corpse. See Digital Edition PC 6.

7. And these recent adversities have weakened me; and these parries I could once match would now destroy me.

8. *If . . . behold:* If there were only two supreme examples in the world of Fortune's ability to raise up and cast down, Lear would be one; alternatively, we are each of us one (Lear and Kent are here looking at each other).

9. This is a sad sight; my vision is failing.

1. I'll attend to that shortly; I'll comprehend that in a moment.

2. Who from the beginning of your alteration and deterioration.

3. No, neither I nor anyone else is welcome. Alternatively, I am that man, not disguised as anyone else.

ALBANY   He knows not what he sees, and vain° it is   *in vain*
That we present us to him.

290 EDGAR   Very bootless.°   *futile*

Enter CAPTAIN.

CAPTAIN   Edmund is dead, my lord.

ALBANY   That's but a trifle here.
You lords and noble friends, know our intent:
What comfort to this decay° may come   *ruin; destruction*
Shall be applied. For us, we will resign

295 During the life of this old majesty
To him our absolute power; [*to* EDGAR] you to your rights,
With boot° and such addition° as your honor   *reward / distinction*
Have more than merited. All friends shall taste
The wages of their virtue and all foes

300 The cup of their deservings. Oh, see, see!

LEAR   And my poor fool[5] is hanged. No, no life.
Why should a dog, a horse, a rat have life
And thou no breath at all? Oh, thou wilt come no more.
Never, never, never! —Pray you, undo

305 This button. Thank you, sir. Oh, oh, oh, oh![6]
                    [*He faints.*]

EDGAR   He faints. My lord, my lord?

LEAR   Break, heart, I prithee, break!
                    [*He dies.*]

EDGAR   Look up, my lord!

KENT   Vex not his ghost.[7] Oh, let him pass!
He hates him that would upon the rack[8]

310 Of this tough world stretch him out longer.

EDGAR   Oh, he is gone indeed.

KENT   The wonder is he hath endured so long.
He but usurped his life.[9]

ALBANY   Bear them from hence. Our present business

315 Is to general woe. [*to* KENT *and* EDGAR] Friends of my soul,
        you twain
Rule in this kingdom and the gored° state sustain.   *wounded; bloody*

KENT   I have a journey, sir, shortly to go.
My master calls, and I must not say no.

ALBANY[1]   The weight of this sad time we must obey;

320 Speak what we feel, not what we ought to say.
The oldest have borne most; we that are young
Shall never see so much, nor live so long.   [*Exeunt.*]

---

5. A term of endearment, here used for Cordelia, though it also recalls the disappearance of Lear's Fool after 3.6.
6. TEXTUAL COMMENT All the source plays for the King Lear story show Lear and Cordelia prevailing, with Cordelia surviving and accepting the role of Lear's successor as monarch. In the Folio text, unlike in the Quarto text, Lear apparently thinks that his attempts to revive her are successful. See Digital Edition TC 8 (Quarto edited text).
7. Do not disturb his departing soul.
8. Instrument of torture, used to stretch its victims.

9. From death, which already had a claim on it.
1. TEXTUAL COMMENT One of the apparently minor but nevertheless significant differences between the two early texts of *King Lear* is that in the Quarto I text the last lines of the play are given to Albany, whereas in the Folio they are given to Edgar. These powerful lines suggest that their speaker will inherit political leadership, and editors who conflate the two texts face the challenge of selecting which character should stand as the moral and political spokesperson at the end of the play. See Digital Edition TC 9 (Quarto edited text).

ALBANY He knows not what he says, and vain° is it   *in vain*
    That we present us to him.
        Enter a MESSENGER.
270 EDGAR   Very bootless.°   *futile*
MESSENGER   Edmond is dead, my lord.
ALBANY   That's but a trifle here.
    You lords and noble friends, know our intent:
    What comfort to this great decay° may come   *ruin; destruction*
    Shall be applied. For us, we will resign
275   During the life of this old majesty
    To him our absolute power; [*to* EDGAR] you to your rights,
    With boot° and such addition° as your honors   *reward / distinction*
    Have more than merited. All friends shall
    Taste the wages of their virtue and all foes
280   The cup of their deservings. Oh, see, see!
LEAR   And my poor fool[4] is hanged. No, no, no life?
    Why should a dog, a horse, a rat have life,
    And thou no breath at all? Thou'lt come no more,
    Never, never, never, never, never!
285   Pray you, undo this button. Thank you, sir.
    Do you see this? Look on her! Look, her lips,
    Look there. Look there![5]
        He dies.
EDGAR   He faints. My lord, my lord.
KENT   Break, heart, I prithee, break.
EDGAR   Look up, my lord.
KENT   Vex not his ghost.[6] Oh, let him pass! He hates him
290   That would upon the rack[7] of this tough world
    Stretch him out longer.
EDGAR   He is gone indeed.
KENT   The wonder is he hath endured so long.
    He but usurped his life.[8]
ALBANY   Bear them from hence. Our present business
295   Is general woe. [*to* KENT *and* EDGAR] Friends of my soul,
      you twain
    Rule in this realm and the gored° state sustain.   *wounded; bloody*
KENT   I have a journey, sir, shortly to go.
    My master calls me. I must not say no.
EDGAR[9]   The weight of this sad time we must obey;
300   Speak what we feel, not what we ought to say.
    The oldest hath borne most; we that are young
    Shall never see so much, nor live so long.
        Exeunt with a dead march.

---

4. A term of endearment, here used for Cordelia, though it also recalls the disappearance of Lear's Fool after 3.6.

5. TEXTUAL COMMENT All the source plays for the King Lear story show Lear and Cordelia prevailing, with Cordelia surviving and accepting the role of Lear's successor as monarch. In F, unlike in Q, Lear apparently thinks that his attempts to revive her are successful. See Digital Edition TC 7 (Folio edited text).

6. Do not disturb his departing soul.

7. Instrument of torture, used to stretch its victims.

8. From death, which already had a claim on it.

9. TEXTUAL COMMENT One of the apparently minor but nevertheless significant differences between the two early texts of *King Lear* is that in Q1 the last lines of the play are given to Albany, whereas in F they are given to Edgar. These powerful lines suggest that their speaker will inherit political leadership, and editors who conflate the two texts face the challenge of selecting which character should stand as the moral and political spokesperson at the end of the play. See Digital Edition TC 8 (Folio edited text).

King Lear[1]

COMBINED TEXT*

[THE PERSONS OF THE PLAY

LEAR, King of Britain
GONERIL, eldest daughter to Lear
Duke of ALBANY, husband to Goneril
REGAN, second daughter to Lear
Duke of CORNWALL, husband to Regan
CORDELIA, youngest daughter to Lear
King of FRANCE, suitor to Cordelia
Duke of BURGUNDY, suitor to Cordelia
FOOL, Lear's jester
Earl of GLOUCESTER
EDGAR, legitimate son to Gloucester, later disguised as Poor Tom
EDMUND, illegitimate son to Gloucester
Earl of KENT, later disguised as Caius
OSWALD, steward to Goneril
OLD MAN, a tenant of Gloucester
CURAN, a servant of Gloucester
SERVANTS to Cornwall
CAPTAIN
HERALD
MESSENGER
GENTLEMEN
KNIGHTS
SERVANTS
Attendants, Soldiers]

1.1[2]

Enter KENT, GLOUCESTER,[3] *and* EDMUND.

KENT I thought the King had more affected° the Duke of
 Albany° than Cornwall.
                favored
                Scotland

GLOUCESTER It did always seem so to us. But now, in the division of the kingdom, it appears not° which of the Dukes he
              is not clear
5 values most, for qualities° are so weighed° that curiosity in
            shares / equal
 neither can make choice of either's moiety.[4]

KENT Is not this your son, my lord?

GLOUCESTER His breeding,° sir, hath been at my charge.[5] I
               upbringing

---

1. TEXTUAL COMMENT The first readers of the Quarto and Folio versions of *King Lear* would have confronted not only very different material books but also two different plays, as suggested by the titles of the earliest printed copies of the play. *King Lear* is either a "history" or a "tragedy," depending on which book one is reading. See Digital Edition TC 1 (combined text).
*Text based on the Folio, with interpolated lines, passages, and scenes from Q1.
2. TEXTUAL COMMENT One major difference between the Quarto and Folio texts is that the latter provides act and scene divisions while the former marks no

such breaks. These notations suggest that Q1 of *King Lear* was printed from Shakespeare's "foul papers" (or first draft) and that F was printed from a later "fair copy" (or theatrical manuscript) written out by a scribe and checked against Q2. See Digital Edition TC 2 (combined text).
1.1 Location: King Lear's court.
3. Pronounced "Gloster."
4. for . . . *moiety*: their qualities are so evenly weighted that careful scrutiny ("curiosity") of both parts cannot determine which portion ("moiety") is preferable.
5. My responsibility; at my cost.

have so often blushed to acknowledge him that now I am
10 brazed° to't.   *hardened*

KENT   I cannot conceive° you.   *comprehend*

GLOUCESTER   Sir, this young fellow's mother could,[6] whereupon she grew round-wombed, and had, indeed, sir, a son for
her cradle ere she had a husband for her bed. Do you smell a
15 fault?[7]

KENT   I cannot wish the fault undone, the issue° of it being so   *offspring; result*
proper.°   *handsome; right*

GLOUCESTER   But I have a son, sir, by order of law,° some year   *a legitimate son*
elder than this, who yet is no dearer in my account.° Though   *estimation*
20 this knave° came something saucily[8] to the world before he   *scamp; fellow*
was sent for, yet was his mother fair, there was good sport at
his making, and the whoreson° must be acknowledged. —Do   *rogue; bastard*
you know this noble gentleman, Edmund?

EDMUND   No, my lord.

25 GLOUCESTER   My lord of Kent. Remember him hereafter as
my honorable friend.

EDMUND   My services to your lordship.

KENT   I must love you and sue° to know you better.   *seek*

EDMUND   Sir, I shall study deserving.°   *shall learn to deserve*

30 GLOUCESTER   He hath been out° nine years, and away he shall   *away; abroad*
again. The King is coming.

   Sennet.° Enter [one bearing a coronet,] King LEAR,   *Fanfare of trumpets*
   CORNWALL, ALBANY, GONERIL, REGAN, CORDELIA,
   and Attendants.

LEAR   Attend the lords of France and Burgundy, Gloucester.

GLOUCESTER   I shall, my lord.°   *Exit.*   *feudal superior*

LEAR   Meantime we° shall express our darker° purpose.   *(royal "we") / more secret*
35 Give me the map there. Know that we have divided
In three our kingdom, and 'tis our fast° intent   *fixed*
To shake all cares and business from our age,
Conferring them on younger strengths, while we
Unburdened crawl toward death. Our son° of Cornwall   *son-in-law*
40 And you, our no-less-loving son of Albany,
We have this hour a constant will to publish[9]
Our daughters' several dowers,° that future strife   *individual dowries*
May be prevented now. The princes, France and Burgundy,
Great rivals in our youngest daughter's love,
45 Long in our court have made their amorous sojourn
And here are to be answered. Tell me, my daughters,
Since now we will divest us both of rule,
Interest° of territory, cares of state,   *Legal title*
Which of you shall we say doth love us most,
50 That° we our largest bounty° may extend   *So that / generosity*
Where nature doth with merit challenge?[1] Goneril,
Our eldest born, speak first.

GONERIL   Sir, I love you more than word can wield° the   *convey*
matter;
Dearer than eyesight, space,° and liberty,   *freedom of movement*
55 Beyond what can be valued rich or rare,
No less than life, with grace, health, beauty, honor,

---

6. Could conceive; punning on biological conception.
7. Sin, wrongdoing; female genitals.
8. Somewhat rudely; somewhat shamefully.

9. A fixed determination to announce publicly.
1. *Where . . . challenge:* To the one whose natural
love and deserving lay claim (to our generosity).

As much as child e'er loved or father found,
A love that makes breath° poor and speech unable. *language*
Beyond all manner of so much° I love you. *Beyond all comparison*

60 CORDELIA [*aside*] What shall Cordelia speak? Love, and be
 silent.

LEAR [*pointing to map*] Of all these bounds,° even from this *regions*
 line to this,
With shadowy forests and with champaigns riched° *enriched plains*
With plenteous rivers and wide-skirted meads,° *broad meadows*
We make thee lady. To thine and Albany's issues° *children; heirs*

65 Be this perpetual. [*to* REGAN] What says our second daughter,
Our dearest Regan, wife of Cornwall?

REGAN I am made of that self-mettle° as my sister *same spirit; substance*
And prize me at her worth.° In my true heart *believe myself her equal*
I find she names my very deed of love,

70 Only she comes too short, that° I profess *in that*
Myself an enemy to all other joys
Which the most precious square of sense professes,[2]
And find I am alone felicitate° *am only made happy*
In your dear highness' love.

CORDELIA [*aside*]   Then, poor Cordelia,

75 And yet not so, since I am sure my love's
More ponderous° than my tongue. *weighty*

LEAR [*pointing to map*] To thee and thine hereditary ever,
Remain this ample third of our fair kingdom,
No less in space, validity,° and pleasure *value*

80 Than that conferred on Goneril. [*to* CORDELIA] Now, our joy,
Although our last and least,° to whose young love *youngest; smallest*
The vines of France and milk of Burgundy
Strive to be interest,° what can you say to draw *admitted*
A third more opulent than your sisters'? Speak.

85 CORDELIA Nothing, my lord.

LEAR Nothing?

CORDELIA Nothing.

LEAR Nothing will come of nothing.[3] Speak again.

CORDELIA Unhappy that I am, I cannot heave

90 My heart into my mouth.[4] I love your majesty
According to my bond,° no more nor less. *filial duty*

LEAR How, how, Cordelia? Mend your speech a little,
Lest you may mar your fortunes.

CORDELIA   Good my lord,
You have begot me, bred me, loved me.

95 I return those duties back as are right fit:
Obey you, love you, and most honor you.
Why have my sisters husbands if they say
They love you all?° Happily,° when I shall wed, *completely / Perhaps; if lucky*
That lord whose hand must take my plight° shall carry *marriage vow; condition*

100 Half my love with him, half my care and duty.
Sure, I shall never marry like my sisters,

101.1 *To love my father all.*

---

2. *Which . . . professes:* That the body can enjoy. *precious square of sense:* measure of sensibility; or, perhaps, balanced and sensitive perception. The square may represent the even mixture of the body's four fluids, or humors.
3. *Ex nihilo nihil fit,* a maxim derived from Aristotle,

was accepted by the Christian Middle Ages with the single exception of God having created the world out of nothing.
4. *I cannot heave . . . mouth:* Cf. "The heart of fools is in their mouth: but the mouth of the wise is in their heart" (Ecclesiastes 1:26).

LEAR   But goes thy heart with this?

CORDELIA   Ay, my good lord.

LEAR   So young and so untender?

CORDELIA   So young, my lord, and true.°   *honest; faithful*

105   LEAR   Let it be so: thy truth, then, be thy dower![5]
     For by the sacred radiance of the sun,
     The mysteries of Hecate[6] and the night;
     By all the operation of the orbs,
     From whom we do exist and cease to be;[7]
110   Here I disclaim all my paternal care,
     Propinquity° and property of blood,°   *Closeness / kinship*
     And as a stranger to my heart and me,
     Hold thee from this° forever. The barbarous Scythian,[8]   *this time*
     Or he that makes his generation messes[9]
115   To gorge his appetite, shall to my bosom
     Be as well neighbored, pitied, and relieved
     As thou my sometime° daughter.   *former*

KENT   Good my liege—

LEAR   Peace, Kent!
     Come not between the dragon and his wrath!
120   I loved her most and thought to set my rest[1]
     On her kind nursery.° Hence and avoid my sight.   *care*
     So be my grave my peace,[2] as here I give
     Her father's heart from her. Call France! Who stirs?[3]
     Call Burgundy!   [*Exeunt some Attendants.*]
     Cornwall and Albany,
125   With my two daughters' dowers digest° the third.   *incorporate*
     Let pride, which she calls plainness,° marry her.   *directness*
     I do invest you jointly with my power,
     Preeminence, and all the large effects°   *outward shows; trappings*
     That troop with° majesty. Ourself by monthly course,   *accompany*
130   With reservation of° an hundred knights,   *legal right to retain*
     By you to be sustained, shall our abode
     Make with you by due turn. Only we shall retain
     The name and all th'addition° to a king. The sway,°   *the prerogatives / power*
     Revenue, execution of the rest,
135   Beloved sons, be yours, which to confirm,
     This coronet[4] part between you. [*He hands them the
     coronet.*]

KENT   Royal Lear,
     Whom I have ever honored as my king,
     Loved as my father, as my master followed,
     As my great patron thought on in my prayers—
140   LEAR   The bow is bent and drawn; make from° the shaft.   *get clear of*

KENT   Let it fall° rather, though the fork° invade   *strike home / arrowhead*
     The region of my heart. Be Kent unmannerly

---

5. PERFORMANCE COMMENT The opening sequence
of *King Lear*, from the king's entrance to his banishment of Cordelia, involves crucial interpretive choices
for directors and performers, choices that center on
the motivations of the central characters. See Digital
Edition PC 1.
6. A classical goddess of the moon and the patron of
witchcraft, she was associated with the underworld,
Hades.
7. *By all . . . be:* Referring to the belief that the movements of stars and planets ("orbs") corresponded to
physical and spiritual motions in a person and thus

controlled his or her fate.
8. Notoriously savage nomads of classical antiquity.
9. *he . . . messes:* he who makes meals of his parents
or his children.
1. To secure my repose; to stake my all, as in the card
game known as primero.
2. So may I rest in peace (probably an oath).
3. Does nobody stir? An order, with the force of "Get
moving."
4. Cordelia's crown, symbol of the endowment she
has forsworn.

When Lear is mad. What wouldst thou do, old man?
Think'st thou that duty shall have dread to speak
145 When power to flattery bows?
To plainness° honor's bound   *plain speaking*
When majesty falls to folly. Reserve° thy state,°   *Retain / rule; position*
And in thy best consideration check°   *halt*
This hideous rashness. Answer my life my judgment:⁵
150 Thy youngest daughter does not love thee least,
Nor are those empty-hearted whose low sounds
Reverb no hollowness.°   *Echo no insincerity*

LEAR   Kent, on thy life, no more!

KENT   My life I never held but as pawn°   *chess piece; stake*
To wage° against thine enemies; ne'er fear to lose it,   *wager*
Thy safety being motive.°   *(my) motivation*

155 LEAR   Out of my sight!

KENT   See better, Lear, and let me still° remain   *always*
The true blank° of thine eye.   *precise bull's-eye*

LEAR   Now, by Apollo—

KENT   Now, by Apollo, King,
Thou swear'st thy gods in vain.⁶

LEAR   O vassal! Miscreant!°   *Villain; unbeliever*

160 ALBANY *and* CORNWALL   Dear sir, forbear.

KENT   Kill thy physician and thy fee bestow
Upon the foul disease.⁷ Revoke thy gift,
Or whilst I can vent clamor from my throat
I'll tell thee thou dost evil.

165 LEAR   Hear me, recreant!° On thine allegiance, hear me!   *traitor*
That thou hast sought to make us break our vows,
Which we durst never yet; and with strained° pride   *overblown*
To come betwixt our sentences and our power,
Which nor our nature nor our place⁸ can bear.
170 Our potency made good,° take thy reward.   *demonstrated*
Five days we do allot thee for provision,
To shield thee from disasters of the world,
And on the sixth to turn thy hated back
Upon our kingdom. If, on the tenth day following,
175 Thy banished trunk° be found in our dominions,   *body*
The moment is thy death. Away! By Jupiter,
This shall not be revoked.

KENT   Fare thee well, King. Sith° thus thou wilt appear,   *Since*
Freedom lives hence, and banishment is here.
180 [*to* CORDELIA] The gods to their dear shelter take thee, maid,
That justly think'st and hast most rightly said.
[*to* GONERIL *and* REGAN] And your large speeches may your
    deeds approve,⁹
That good effects may spring from words of love.
Thus Kent, O princes, bids you all adieu.
185 He'll shape his old course in a country new.   *Exit.*

            Flourish.° Enter GLOUCESTER *with* FRANCE *and*   *Fanfare of trumpets*
            BURGUNDY [*and*] *Attendants.*

---

5. *Answer . . . judgment:* I'll stake my life on my
opinion.
6. You invoke your gods falsely and without effect.
7. *Kill . . . disease:* You would not only kill the doctor

but also hand his fee over to the disease.
8. Which neither my temperament nor my royal
position.
9. And let your actions live up to your fine words.

CORNWALL   Here's France and Burgundy, my noble lord.
LEAR   My lord of Burgundy,
   We first address toward you, who with this king
   Hath rivaled for our daughter. What in the least
190   Will you require in present dower with her
   Or cease your quest of love?
BURGUNDY   Most royal majesty,
   I crave no more than hath your highness offered,
   Nor will you tender° less.   *offer*
LEAR   Right noble Burgundy,
   When she was dear to us we did hold her so,
195   But now her price is fallen. Sir, there she stands.
   If aught within that little-seeming substance,[1]
   Or all of it with our displeasure pieced°   *joined*
   And nothing more, may fitly like° your grace,   *please*
   She's there, and she is yours.
BURGUNDY   I know no answer.
200   LEAR   Will you with those infirmities she owes,°   *owns*
   Unfriended, new-adopted to our hate,
   Dow'red with our curse and strangered° with our oath,   *estranged*
   Take her or leave her?
BURGUNDY   Pardon me, royal sir,
   Election makes not up in such conditions.[2]
205   LEAR   Then leave her, sir, for, by the power that made me,
   I tell you° all her wealth. [*to* FRANCE] For° you, great King,   *inform you of / As for*
   I would not from your love make such a stray°   *stray so far*
   To° match you where I hate. Therefore, beseech you   *As to*
   T'avert your liking° a more worthier way   *To turn your affections*
210   Than on a wretch whom Nature is ashamed
   Almost t'acknowledge hers.
FRANCE   This is most strange,
   That she, whom even but now was your object,
   The argument° of your praise, balm of your age,   *theme*
   The best, the dearest, should in this trice° of time   *moment*
215   Commit a thing so monstrous to dismantle°   *as to strip off; disrobe*
   So many folds of favor. Sure, her offense
   Must be of such unnatural degree
   That monsters it,° or your fore-vouched affection   *makes it monstrous*
   Fall into taint,[3] which to believe of her
220   Must be a faith that reason without miracle
   Should never plant in me.
CORDELIA   I yet beseech your majesty—
   If for I want° that glib and oily art   *because I lack*
   To speak and purpose not,° since what I will intend,   *and not intend*
   I'll do't before I speak—that you make known
225   It is no vicious blot, murder, or foulness,
   No unchaste action or dishonored step
   That hath deprived me of your grace and favor,
   But even for want of that for which I am richer:

---

1. *little-seeming substance:* one who appears insubstantial; one who will not pretend.
2. A choice cannot be made under those terms.
3. *or . . . taint:* or else the love you earlier swore for

Cordelia must be regarded with suspicion. "Or" may
also mean "before," in which case the phrase would
mean "before the love you once proclaimed could have
decayed."

A still soliciting° eye and such a tongue　　　　　　　　*An always-begging*
230　That I am glad I have not, though not to have it
　　Hath lost me in your liking.

LEAR　　　　　　　　　　　　Better thou hadst
　　Not been born than not t'have pleased me better.

FRANCE　Is it but this, a tardiness in nature,
　　Which often leaves the history unspoke
235　That it intends to do?[4] My lord of Burgundy
　　What say you to the lady? Love's not love
　　When it is mingled with regards° that stands　　　　　*considerations*
　　Aloof from th'entire point. Will you have her?
　　She is herself a dowry.

BURGUNDY　　　　　　　　Royal King,
240　Give but that portion which yourself proposed
　　And here I take Cordelia by the hand,
　　Duchess of Burgundy.

LEAR　Nothing, I have sworn; I am firm.

BURGUNDY [*to* CORDELIA]　I am sorry, then, you have so lost a
　　　father
　　That you must lose a husband.

245　CORDELIA　　　　　　　　　Peace be with Burgundy.
　　Since that respect and fortunes are his love,
　　I shall not be his wife.

FRANCE　Fairest Cordelia, that art most rich being poor,
　　Most choice forsaken, and most loved despised,
250　Thee and thy virtues here I seize upon.
　　Be it lawful I take up what's cast away.
　　Gods, gods! 'Tis strange, that from their cold'st neglect
　　My love should kindle to enflamed respect.°　　　　　*ardent regard*
　　Thy dowerless daughter, King, thrown to my chance,
255　Is Queen of us, of ours, and our fair France.
　　Not all the dukes of wat'rish° Burgundy　　　　*irrigated; watery; weak*
　　Can buy this unprized,° precious maid of me.　　　　*unappreciated*
　　Bid them farewell, Cordelia; though unkind,°　　*though they are unkind*
　　Thou losest here° a better where° to find.　　　　*this place / place*
260　LEAR　Thou hast her, France. Let her be thine, for we
　　Have no such daughter, nor shall ever see
　　That face of hers again. Therefore be gone
　　Without our grace, our love, our benison.°　　　　　*blessing*
　　—Come, noble Burgundy.

　　　　　　　　　Flourish. Exeunt [*all but* FRANCE, CORDELIA,
　　　　　　　　　　　　　　　　　　GONERIL, *and* REGAN].

265　FRANCE　Bid farewell to your sisters.

CORDELIA　The jewels of our father, with washed eyes
　　Cordelia leaves you. I know you what you are
　　And like a sister am most loath to call
　　Your faults as they are named.° Love well our father;　　*are properly called*
270　To your professed bosoms° I commit him.　　*publicly proclaimed love*
　　But yet, alas, stood I within his grace,
　　I would prefer° him to a better place.　　　　　*promote; recommend*
　　So farewell to you both.

REGAN　Prescribe not us our duty.

---

4. *a tardiness . . . do*: a natural reserve that inhibits voicing one's intentions.

GONERIL   Let your study
275   Be to content your lord, who hath received you
       At fortune's alms.[5] You have obedience scanted°   *neglected*
       And well are worth the want that you have wanted.[6]
CORDELIA   Time shall unfold what plighted cunning hides;
       Who covers faults, at last with shame derides.[7]
       Well may you prosper.
280 FRANCE   Come, my fair Cordelia.
                         Exeunt FRANCE *and* CORDELIA.
GONERIL   Sister, it is not little I have to say of what most nearly
       appertains to us both. I think our father will hence tonight.
REGAN   That's most certain and with you; next month with us.
GONERIL   You see how full of changes° his age is; the observa-   *fickleness*
       tion we have made of it hath been little.° He always loved our   *in the smallest detail*
       sister most, and with what poor judgment he hath now cast
       her off appears too grossly.°   *blatantly*
REGAN   'Tis the infirmity of his age, yet he hath ever but slen-
       derly known himself.
290 GONERIL   The best and soundest of his time hath been but
       rash.[8] Then° must we look from his age to receive not alone   *Therefore*
       the imperfections of long engraffed condition,° but there-   *deep-rooted habit*
       withal the unruly waywardness that infirm and choleric
       years bring with them.
295 REGAN   Such unconstant starts[9] are we like° to have from   *likely*
       him as this of Kent's banishment.
GONERIL   There is further compliment° of leave-taking between   *ceremony*
       France and him. Pray you let us sit together. If our father
       carry authority with such disposition[1] as he bears, this last
300   surrender° of his will but offend° us.   *abdication / harm*
REGAN   We shall further think of it.
GONERIL   We must do something, and i'th' heat.°   *Exeunt.*   *quickly*

1.2

       Enter EDMUND.
EDMUND   Thou, Nature, art my goddess; to thy law
       My services are bound.[1] Wherefore° should I   *Why*
       Stand in the plague of custom[2] and permit
       The curiosity° of nations to deprive me,   *legal niceties*
5   For that° I am some twelve or fourteen moonshines°   *Because / months*
       Lag of° a brother? Why "bastard"? Wherefore "base,"   *Younger than*
       When my dimensions are as well compact,°   *composed*
       My mind as generous° and my shape as true   *noble*
       As honest° madam's issue? Why brand they us   *married; chaste*
10   With "base"? With "baseness," "bastardy"? Base? Base?
       Who, in the lusty stealth of nature, take

5. As a charitable gift from fortune.
6. And you deserve to get no more love (from your husband) than you have given (to your father). "Want" plays on its alternative meanings of "lack" and "desire."
7. *Time . . . derides:* Time eventually exposes and shames all hidden faults.
8. *The . . . rash:* Even in the prime of his life he was impetuous.

9. Such impulsive outbursts.
1. Frame of mind.
1.2 Location: The Earl of Gloucester's house.
1. Edmund declares the raw force of unsocialized and unregulated existence, as opposed to human law, to be his ruler; ironically, "nature" also means "natural filial affection." A "natural" was another word for "bastard" (illegitimate child).
2. Submit to the imposition of inheritance law.

More composition and fierce quality³
Than doth within a dull, stale, tired bed
Go to th' creating a whole tribe of fops°   *fools*
15 Got° 'tween a sleep, and wake? Well, then,   *Begotten*
Legitimate Edgar, I must have your land.
Our father's love is to° the bastard Edmund   *as much to*
As to th' legitimate. Fine word: "legitimate"!
Well, my legitimate, if this letter speed°   *succeed*
20 And my invention° thrive, Edmund the base   *plot*
Shall to° th' legitimate. I grow. I prosper.   *match up to; usurp*
Now, gods, stand up for bastards!
   Enter GLOUCESTER.
GLOUCESTER Kent banished thus? And France in choler
  parted?°   *in anger departed*
And the King gone tonight,° prescribed° his power, *last night / limited*
25 Confined to exhibition?⁴ All this done
Upon the gad?° —Edmund, how now? What news? *spur of the moment*
EDMUND [*putting up a letter*] So please your lordship, none.
GLOUCESTER Why so earnestly seek you to put up that letter?
EDMUND I know no news, my lord.
30 GLOUCESTER What paper were you reading?
EDMUND Nothing, my lord.
GLOUCESTER No? What needed then that terrible dispatch° *frightened haste*
of it into your pocket? The quality of nothing hath not such
need to hide itself. Let's see. Come, if it be nothing, I shall
35 not need spectacles.
EDMUND I beseech you, sir, pardon me. It is a letter from my
brother that I have not all o'er-read, and, for so much as I
have perused, I find it not fit for your o'erlooking.
GLOUCESTER Give me the letter, sir.
40 EDMUND I shall offend either to detain or give it. The contents, as in part I understand them, are to blame.
GLOUCESTER Let's see; let's see.
EDMUND [*giving him a letter*] I hope, for my brother's justification, he wrote this but as an essay or taste⁵ of my virtue.
45 GLOUCESTER (*reads*) "This policy and reverence of age makes
the world bitter to the best of our times,⁶ keeps our fortunes
from us till our oldness cannot relish them. I begin to find an
idle and fond° bondage in the oppression of aged tyranny, *a useless and foolish*
who sways not as it hath power but as it is suffered.⁷ Come to
50 me, that of this I may speak more. If our father would sleep
till I waked him, you should enjoy half his revenue forever
and live the beloved of your brother. Edgar." Hum, conspiracy! "Sleep till I wake him, you should enjoy half his revenue"! My son Edgar, had he a hand to write this, a heart and
55 brain to breed it in? When came you to this? Who brought it?

---

3. *Who . . . quality:* Whose begetting, by reason of its
furtiveness and heightened excitement, requires better execution and more vigor. Alternatively (with
"take" meaning "give"), whose begetting produces (a
person of) more mixture and vigor. "Composition," or
mixture, may refer to the belief that the perfect offspring was conceived from an equal quantity of male
and female essence and that physical and mental
abnormalities were caused by a predominance of one

or the other.
4. Pension; mere show without force.
5. *but . . . taste:* simply as a proof or test. Both terms
derive from metallurgy.
6. The established primacy of the elderly embitters
us at the prime of our lives. *policy:* statecraft; crafti-
ness; established order.
7. *who . . . suffered:* which rules not because it is
powerful but because it is permitted to ("suffered").

EDMUND   It was not brought me, my lord; there's the cunning of it. I found it thrown in at the casement° of my closet.°

GLOUCESTER   You know the character° to be your brother's?

EDMUND   If the matter° were good, my lord, I durst swear it
60   were his, but in respect of that, I would fain° think it were not.

GLOUCESTER   It is his?

EDMUND   It is his hand, my lord, but I hope his heart is not in the contents.

GLOUCESTER   Has he never before sounded you° in this
65   business?

EDMUND   Never, my lord. But I have heard him oft maintain it to be fit that, sons at perfect age° and fathers declined, the father should be as ward[8] to the son, and the son manage his revenue.

70   GLOUCESTER   Oh, villain, villain! His very opinion in the letter! Abhorred villain! Unnatural, detested, brutish villain; worse than brutish! Go, sirrah,[9] seek him. I'll apprehend him. Abominable villain! Where is he?

EDMUND   I do not well know, my lord. If it shall please you to
75   suspend your indignation against my brother till you can derive from him better testimony of his intent, you should run a certain° course; where,° if you violently proceed against him, mistaking his purpose, it would make a great gap in your own honor and shake in pieces the heart of his obedience. I dare
80   pawn down° my life for him that he hath writ this to feel° my affection to your honor and to no other pretense of danger.[1]

GLOUCESTER   Think you so?

EDMUND   If your honor judge it meet,° I will place you where you shall hear us confer of this and by an auricular° assur-
85   ance have your satisfaction, and that without any further delay than this very evening.

GLOUCESTER   He cannot be such a monster—

87.1   EDMUND   *Nor is not, sure.*

GLOUCESTER   *—To his father that so tenderly and entirely loves him. Heaven and earth!* Edmund, seek him out; wind me into him,[2] I pray you. Frame° the business after your own wisdom. I would unstate
90   myself to be in a due resolution.[3]

EDMUND   I will seek him, sir, presently,° convey° the business as I shall find means and acquaint you withal.°

GLOUCESTER   These late° eclipses in the sun and moon portend no good to us.[4] Though the wisdom of Nature can rea-
95   son it thus and thus, yet Nature finds itself scourged by the sequent effects.[5] Love cools, friendship falls off, brothers divide; in cities, mutinies; in countries, discord; in palaces, treason; and the bond cracked twixt son and father. This villain of mine comes under the prediction: there's son against

Right margin glosses:

window / private room
handwriting
content
gladly

sounded you out

at maturity

safe; reliable / whereas

I dare stake / feel out

appropriate
audible

Arrange

immediately / carry out
therewith
recent

8. A child under eighteen years of age who was legally dependent, often orphaned.
9. A form of address used with children or social inferiors.
1. No further intention to do harm.
2. Worm your way into his confidence (with "me" as an intensifier); worm your way into his confidence for me ("me" as a term of respect).
3. I would give up my rank and property to have my doubts resolved.
4. The lunar and solar eclipses that were seen in London between September and October 1605, about a year before the play's first recorded performance, would have added spice to this superstitious belief in the role of heavenly bodies as augurs of misfortune.
5. *Though . . . effects:* Though natural science may explain the eclipses this way or that, nature (and family bonds) suffers in the effects that follow.

100 father. The King falls from bias of nature:[6] there's father
against child. We have seen the best of our time. Machina-
tions, hollowness,° treachery and all ruinous disorders fol-   *insincerity*
low us disquietly to our graves. Find out this villain,
Edmund. It shall lose thee nothing. Do it carefully. And the
105 noble and true-hearted Kent banished, his offense: honesty!
'Tis strange!   *Exit.*

EDMUND   This is the excellent foppery° of the world, that when   *foolishness*
we are sick in fortune, often the surfeits° of our own behavior,   *excesses*
we make guilty of° our disasters the sun, the moon, and stars,   *we hold responsible for*
110 as if we were villains on necessity, fools by heavenly compul-
sion, knaves, thieves, and treacherers° by spherical predomi-   *traitors*
nance,[7] drunkards, liars, and adulterers by an enforced
obedience of planetary influence, and all that we are evil in
by a divine thrusting-on.° An admirable° evasion of whore-   *imposition / amazing*
115 master man to lay his goatish disposition on the charge of a
star![8] My father compounded° with my mother under the   *coupled*
dragon's tail, and my nativity was under Ursa Major,[9] so that
it follows I am rough and lecherous. I should have been that°   *what*
I am had the maidenliest star in the firmament twinkled on
120 my bastardizing.
          Enter EDGAR.
[*aside*] Pat,° he comes like the catastrophe° of the old com-   *On cue / resolution*
edy. My cue is villainous melancholy, with a sigh like Tom
o'Bedlam.[1] —Oh, these eclipses do portend these divisions.
[*Sings.*]   Fa, sol, la, mi.[2]
125 EDGAR   How now, brother Edmund, what serious contemplation are you in?
EDMUND   I am thinking, brother, of a prediction I read this
other day what should follow these eclipses.
EDGAR   Do you busy yourself with that?
130 EDMUND   I promise you, the effects he writes of succeed°   *follow*
unhappily,
131.1   *as of unnaturalness between the child and the parent,*
          death, dearth, dissolutions of ancient amities, divisions in
          state, menaces and maledictions against king and nobles,
          needless diffidences,° banishment of friends, dissipation   *baseless suspicions*
131.5   *of cohorts,[3] nuptial breaches, and I know not what.*
     EDGAR   *How long have you been a sectary astronomical?°*   *a devotee of astrology*
     BASTARD   *Come, come,*
EDMUND   when saw you my father last?
EDGAR   The night gone by.
EDMUND   Spake you with him?
135 EDGAR   Ay, two hours together.
EDMUND   Parted you in good terms? Found you no displea-
sure in him by word nor countenance?°   *appearance; demeanor*

---

6. The King deviates from his natural inclination. In
the game of bowls, the "bias" ("course") is the eccentric path taken by the weighted ball when thrown.
7. By the ascendancy of a particular planet. In the
universe as conceived by the second-century astrono-
mer, Ptolemy, the planets revolved about the earth on
crystalline spheres.
8. *to lay . . . star:* to hold a star responsible for his
lustful desires. In Greek mythology, the satyr, a creature with goat-like characteristics, was notoriously
lecherous.

9. Constellations: "dragon's tail" = Draco and "Ursa
Major" = Great Bear.
1. The usual name for lunatic beggars; "Bethlehem,"
shortened to "Bedlam," was the name of the oldest
and best-known London madhouse.
2. The portion of the scale Edmund sings is an augmented fourth, an interval considered at this time
very discordant; it was sometimes referred to as
diabolus in musica ("the devil in music"). *divisions:*
social fractures; melodic embellishments.
3. Scattering of forces.

EDGAR   None at all.

EDMUND   Bethink yourself wherein you may have offended
140   him, and at my entreaty forbear° his presence until some   *avoid*
        little time hath qualified° the heat of his displeasure, which   *moderated*
        at this instant so rageth in him that with the mischief of
        your person it would scarcely allay.[4]

EDGAR   Some villain hath done me wrong.

145 EDMUND   That's my fear. I pray you, have a continent forbear-
        ance° till the speed of his rage goes slower, and, as I say,   *restrained absence*
        retire with me to my lodging, from whence I will fitly° bring   *when suitable*
        you to hear my lord speak. Pray ye go; there's my key. If you
        do stir abroad, go armed.

150 EDGAR   Armed, brother?

EDMUND   Brother, I advise you to the best. I am no honest man
        if there be any good meaning toward you. I have told you
        what I have seen and heard but faintly, nothing like the image
        and horror of it. Pray you, away!

155 EDGAR   Shall I hear from you anon?

EDMUND   I do serve you in this business.   *Exit* EDGAR.
        A credulous father and a brother noble,
        Whose nature is so far from doing harms
        That he suspects none; on whose foolish honesty
160   My practices° ride easy. I see the business.[5]   *plots*
        Let me, if not by birth, have lands by wit.°   *intelligence*
        All with me's meet that I can fashion fit.[6]   *Exit.*

1.3

Enter GONERIL *and* [*Oswald the*] STEWARD.

GONERIL   Did my father strike my gentleman
        For chiding of his fool?

STEWARD   Ay, madam.

GONERIL   By day and night he wrongs me; every hour
        He flashes into one gross crime° or other   *offense*
5   That sets us all at odds. I'll not endure it.
        His knights grow riotous, and himself upbraids us
        On every trifle. When he returns from hunting,
        I will not speak with him. Say I am sick.
        If you come slack of former services,[1]
10   You shall do well; the fault of it I'll answer.°   *answer for*

STEWARD   He's coming, madam, I hear him.

GONERIL   Put on what weary negligence you please,
        You and your fellows.° I'd have it come to question.   *the other servants*
        If he distaste it, let him to my sister,
15   Whose mind and mine I know in that are one,
15.1   *Not to be overruled. Idle° old man,*   *Foolish*
            That still would manage those authorities
            That he hath given away! Now, by my life,
            Old fools are babes again and must be used
15.5   *With checks as flatteries when they are seen abused.[2]*

---

4. *with . . . allay:* even harming you bodily ("mis-chief") would hardly relieve his anger; alternatively, with the irritant of your presence, it (Gloucester's anger) would not be abated.
5. It is now clear to me what needs to be done.
6. Anything is fine by me as long as I can make it serve my purpose. *meet:* justifiable; appropriate.

1.3 Location: The Duke of Albany's castle.
1. If you offer him less service (and respect) than before.
2. *Old . . . abused:* When foolish old men act like children, rebukes are the kindest treatment when kind treatment is abused.

Remember what I have said.

STEWARD   Well, madam.

GONERIL   And let his knights have colder looks among you.
What grows of it no matter; advise your fellows so.
I'll write straight° to my sister to hold my course.   *straightaway*
20 Prepare for dinner.   *Exeunt [severally].*°   *separately*

1.4

Enter KENT *[disguised as Caius].*

KENT   If but as well[1] I other accents borrow
That can my speech diffuse,° my good intent   *disguise*
May carry through itself to that full issue°   *result*
For which I razed my likeness.[2] Now, banished Kent,
5 If thou canst serve where thou dost stand condemned,
So may it come° thy master, whom thou lov'st,   *come to pass*
Shall find thee full of labors.°   *helpful; keen*
        Horns within.° *Enter* LEAR *and [*KNIGHTS *as]*   *Hunting horns offstage*
        Attendants.

LEAR   Let me not stay° a jot for dinner; go get it ready.   *wait*
[*to* KENT] How now, what° art thou?   *who*
10 KENT   A man, sir.
LEAR   What dost thou profess?[3] What wouldst thou with us?
KENT   I do profess to be no less than I seem, to serve him
truly that will put me in trust, to love him that is honest, to
converse° with him that is wise and says little, to fear judg-   *associate*
15 ment, to fight when I cannot choose,° and to eat no fish.[4]   *when I must*
LEAR   What art thou?
KENT   A very honest-hearted fellow and as poor as the King.
LEAR   If thou be'st as poor for a subject as he's for a king, thou
art poor enough. What wouldst thou?
20 KENT   Service.
LEAR   Who wouldst thou serve?
KENT   You.
LEAR   Dost thou know me, fellow?
KENT   No, sir, but you have that in your countenance which I
25 would fain° call master.   *gladly*
LEAR   What's that?
KENT   Authority.
LEAR   What services canst thou do?
KENT   I can keep honest counsel,° ride, run, mar a curious tale   *keep secrets*
30 in telling it,[5] and deliver a plain message bluntly. That which
ordinary men are fit for I am qualified in, and the best of me
is diligence.
LEAR   How old art thou?
KENT   Not so young, sir, to love a woman for singing, nor so
35 old to dote on her for anything. I have years on my back
forty-eight.
LEAR   Follow me. Thou shalt serve me if I like thee no worse
after dinner. I will not part from thee yet. —Dinner, ho,

1.4 Location: As before.
1. As well as disguising my appearance.
2. Disguised my appearance; shaved off my beard.
3. What is your job (profession)? Kent, in reply, uses
"profess" punningly to mean "claim."
4. And not to be a Catholic or penitent (Catholics

were obliged to eat fish on specified occasions and as
penance); alternatively, to be a manly man, a meat
eater.
5. That is, Kent's plain, blunt speech would make
him ill suited to tell a convoluted ("curious") tale.

dinner! Where's my knave? My fool? Go you and call my fool
40   hither.   [*Exit a* KNIGHT.]
            Enter [Oswald the] STEWARD.
        You, you, sirrah, where's my daughter?
        STEWARD   So please you—   *Exit.*
        LEAR   What says the fellow there? Call the clotpoll° back.   blockhead
                                        [*Exit* SECOND KNIGHT.]
        Where's my fool? Ho, I think the world's asleep.
            [*Enter* SECOND KNIGHT.]
45   How now? Where's that mongrel?
        SECOND KNIGHT   He says, my lord, your daughter is not well.
        LEAR   Why came not the slave back to me when I called him?
        SECOND KNIGHT   Sir, he answered me in the roundest° man-   bluntest; rudest
            ner, he would not.
50   LEAR   He would not?
        SECOND KNIGHT   My lord, I know not what the matter is, but
            to my judgment your highness is not entertained with that
            ceremonious affection as you were wont.° There's a great   accustomed to
            abatement of kindness appears as well in the general depen-
55   dents° as in the Duke himself also and your daughter.   servants
        LEAR   Ha? Say'st thou so?
        SECOND KNIGHT   I beseech you pardon me, my lord, if I be mis-
            taken, for my duty cannot be silent when I think your high-
            ness wronged.
60   LEAR   Thou but rememberest° me of mine own conception.° I   remind / perception
            have perceived a most faint neglect of late, which I have
            rather blamed as mine own jealous curiosity[6] than as a very
            pretense° and purpose of unkindness. I will look further   a true intention
            into't. But where's my fool? I have not seen him this two days.
65   SECOND KNIGHT   Since my young lady's going into France, sir,
            the fool hath much pined away.
        LEAR   No more of that, I have noted it well. [*to* SECOND KNIGHT]
            Go you and tell my daughter I would speak with her. [*to
            another* KNIGHT] Go you, call hither my fool.
                                        [*Exeunt both* KNIGHTS.]
            Enter [Oswald the] STEWARD.
70   Oh, you, sir, you, come you hither, sir. Who am I, sir?
        STEWARD   My lady's father.
        LEAR   "My lady's father"? My lord's knave! You whoreson dog,
            you slave, you cur!
        STEWARD   I am none of these, my lord. I beseech your pardon.
75   LEAR [*striking him*]   Do you bandy looks with me, you rascal?
        STEWARD   I'll not be strucken, my lord.
        KENT [*tripping him*]   Nor tripped, neither, you base football
            player.[7]
        LEAR   I thank thee, fellow. Thou serv'st me, and I'll love thee.
80   KENT [*to* STEWARD]   Come, sir, arise, away. I'll teach you dif-
            ferences.° Away, away. If you will measure your lubber's   (of rank)
            length again,[8] tarry. But away, go to; have you wisdom, so.

6. *jealous curiosity*: paranoid concern with niceties.   8. If you will be stretched out by me again. *lubber:*
7. Football was a rough street game played by the   clumsy oaf.
poor.

LEAR   Now, my friendly knave, I thank thee. [*He gives him* *money.*] There's earnest of° thy service.   *downpayment for*
   Enter FOOL.[9]

85 FOOL   Let me hire him too. [*He hands* KENT *his cap.*] Here's my coxcomb.°   *fool's cap*

LEAR   How now, my pretty knave, how dost thou?

FOOL [*to* KENT]   Sirrah, you were best take my coxcomb.

LEAR   Why, my boy?

90 FOOL   Why, for taking one's part that's out of favor. Nay, an° *if* thou canst not smile as the wind sits, thou'lt catch cold shortly.[1] There, take my coxcomb. Why, this fellow has banished two on 's daughters[2] and did the third a blessing against his will. If thou follow him, thou must needs wear my coxcomb. How now, nuncle?°　Would I had two coxcombs and *(mine) uncle* two daughters.

LEAR   Why, my boy?

FOOL   If I gave them all my living,° I'd keep my coxcombs *goods* myself.[3] [*He hands him his cap.*] There's mine; beg another of
100 thy daughters.

LEAR   Take heed, sirrah, the whip.

FOOL   Truth's a dog that must to° kennel; he must be whipped *go to* out, when the lady brach[4] may stand by th' fire and stink.

LEAR   A pestilent gall° to me.   *annoyance; bitterness*

105 FOOL   Sirrah, I'll teach thee a speech.

LEAR   Do.

FOOL   Mark it, nuncle:
Have more than thou showest,
Speak less than thou knowest,
110 Lend less than thou owest,°   *own*
Ride more than thou goest,°   *walk*
Learn° more than thou trowest,°   *Hear / believe*
Set less than thou throwest;[5]
Leave thy drink and thy whore,
115 And keep in a-door,
And thou shalt have more
Than two tens to a score.[6]

KENT   This is nothing, Fool.

FOOL   Then 'tis like the breath° of an unfeed° lawyer: you gave *speech / unpaid*
120 me nothing for't. Can you make no use of nothing, nuncle?

LEAR   Why, no, boy, nothing can be made out of nothing.

FOOL   Prithee, tell him so much the rent of his land comes to.[7] He will not believe a fool.

LEAR   A bitter fool.

125 FOOL   Dost thou know the difference, my boy, between a bitter fool and a sweet one?

LEAR   No, lad, teach me.

---

9. Performance Comment The Fool and Cordelia never meet onstage, making it possible in some productions for one actor to play both roles. Some other productions cast an older actor as the Fool, thus providing a third aging figure alongside Lear and Gloucester. See Digital Edition PC 2.
1. *an . . . shortly:* if you can't keep in favor with those in power, you will soon find yourself left out in the cold.
2. By abdicating, Lear has in effect prevented his eldest daughters from any longer being his subjects, just as if he had "banished" them.

3. I'd be twice as much a fool.
4. Lady bitch. Pet dogs were often called "Lady" such and such. The allusion is to Regan and Goneril, who are now being preferred to truthful Cordelia.
5. Don't gamble everything on a single cast of the dice.
6. *And thou . . . score:* And there will be more than two tens in your twenty—that is, you will become richer.
7. Remind him that no land means no rent; with a pun on "rent" meaning "torn," "divided."

127.1	FOOL *That lord that counseled thee*	
	To give away thy land,	
	Come place him here by me;	
	Do thou for him stand.°	*represent him*
127.5	*The sweet and bitter fool*	
	Will presently appear,	
	The one in motley[8] *here,*	
	[*pointing to* LEAR] *The other found out there.*	
	LEAR *Dost thou call me fool, boy?*	
127.10	FOOL *All thy other titles thou hast given away; that thou*	
	was born with.	
	KENT *This is not altogether fool,*[9] *my lord.*	
	FOOL *No, faith, lords and great men will not let me. If I*	
	had a monopoly out, they would have part in't, and	
127.15	*ladies too. They will not let me have all the fool to*	
	myself, they'll be snatching.	

Nuncle, give me an egg, and I'll give thee two crowns.

LEAR What two crowns shall they be?

130 FOOL Why, after I have cut the egg i'th' middle and ate up the meat,° the two crowns of the egg. When thou clovest° thy crowns i'th' middle and gav'st away both parts, thou bor'st° thine ass on thy back o'er the dirt. Thou hadst little wit° in thy bald crown when thou gav'st thy golden one away. If I
135 speak like myself° in this, let him be whipped that first finds it so.[1]

     [*Sings.*]   Fools had ne'er less grace in a year,
                  For wise men are grown foppish;[2]
                  And know not how their wits to wear,
140   Their manners are so apish.°

LEAR When were you wont° to be so full of songs, sirrah?

FOOL I have used° it, nuncle, e'er since thou mad'st thy daughters thy mothers. For when thou gav'st them the rod and putt'st down thine own breeches,
145   [*Sings.*]   Then they for sudden joy did weep,
                  And I for sorrow sung,
                  That such a king should play bo-peep,°
                  And go the fool among.

Prithee, nuncle, keep a schoolmaster that can teach thy fool
150 to lie. I would fain learn to lie.

LEAR An° you lie, sirrah, we'll have you whipped.

FOOL I marvel what kin° thou and thy daughters are. They'll have me whipped for speaking true, thou'lt have me whipped for lying, and sometimes I am whipped for holding my peace.
155 I had rather be any kind o'thing than a fool, and yet I would not be thee, nuncle. Thou hast pared thy wit o'both sides and left nothing i'th' middle. Here comes one o'th' parings.

     Enter GONERIL.

LEAR How now, daughter? What makes that frontlet[3] on? You are too much of late i'th' frown.

Marginal glosses:
- *represent him* (127.4)
- *edible part / cleaved* (130)
- *you carried* (132)
- *sense* (132)
- *(like a fool)* (135)
- *stupid; imitative* (140)
- *accustomed* (141)
- *practiced* (142)
- *(a child's game)* (148)
- *If* (151)
- *how alike* (152)

---

8. Multicolored dress of a court jester.
9. Foolish, folly. In the next line, the Fool takes "altogether fool" to mean "one who has cornered the market on folly."
1. *that . . . so:* who first discovers for himself that this

is true; who first considers this to be foolish.
2. *Fools . . . foppish:* Professional fools have never been as witless since wise men have lately outdone them in idiocy.
3. A headband; here, a metaphor for "frown."

160 FOOL Thou wast a pretty fellow when thou hadst no need to
care for her frowning. Now thou art an O without a figure.[4]
I am better than thou art now: I am a fool, thou art nothing.
—Yes, forsooth, I will hold my tongue, so your face bids me,
though you say nothing.

165 [*Sings.*]　　　Mum, mum,
　　　　　　He that keeps nor crust, nor crumb,
　　　　　　Weary of all, shall want° some.　　　　　　*lack; be in need of*
[*He points to* GONERIL.] That's a shelled peascod.°　　*empty pea pod; nothing*
GONERIL Not only, sir, this, your all-licensed° fool,　　*unrestrained*
170 But other of your insolent retinue
Do hourly carp and quarrel, breaking forth
In rank° and not-to-be-endured riots. Sir,　　　　　　*foul; spreading*
I had thought by making this well known unto you
To have found a safe° redress, but now grow fearful　　*sure*
175 By what yourself too late° have spoke and done,　　　*recently*
That you protect this course and put it on°　　　　　　*encourage it*
By your allowance; which if you should, the fault
Would not scape censure, nor the redresses sleep;
Which in the tender of a wholesome weal[5]
180 Might in their working do you that offense
Which else were shame, that then necessity
Will call discreet proceeding.[6]
FOOL For you know, nuncle,
[*Sings.*] The hedge-sparrow fed the cuckoo[7] so long
185 　　　　That its had its head bit off by its young;°　　*(the young cuckoo)*
　　　　So out went the candle,
　　　　And we were left darkling.°　　　　　　　　*in the dark*
LEAR Are you our daughter?
GONERIL I would° you would make use of your good　　*wish*
　　wisdom,
190 Whereof I know you are fraught,° and put away　　　*full*
These dispositions,° which of late transport you　　*moods; attitudes*
From what you rightly are.
FOOL May not an ass know when the cart draws the horse?
[*Sings.*]　　　Whoop, jug,[8] I love thee.
195 LEAR Does any here know me? This is not Lear.
Does Lear walk thus? Speak thus? Where are his eyes?
Either his notion° weakens, his discernings　　　　　*intellect*
Are lethargied. Ha! Waking?° 'Tis not so.　　　　　*Am I awake*
Who is it that can tell me who I am?
200 FOOL Lear's shadow.
LEAR [*to* GONERIL] Your name, fair gentlewoman?
GONERIL This admiration,° sir, is much o'th' savor　　*excessive amazement*
Of other your new pranks. I do beseech you
To understand my purposes aright:
205 As you are old and reverend, should be wise.
Here do you keep a hundred knights and squires,

---

4. A zero without a preceding digit to give it value;
nothing.
5. *tender of a wholesome weal*: maintenance of a well-
ordered commonwealth.
6. *which if you . . . proceeding*: if you do approve (of
your attendants' behavior), you will not escape criticism, nor will it be without retribution, which for the
common good will cause you pain. While this would
otherwise be improper, it will be seen as a prudent
("discreet") action under the circumstances.
7. The cuckoo lays its eggs in the nests of other
birds, which then hatch and feed their offspring.
8. Nickname for "Joan"; sobriquet for a whore.

Men so disordered,° so debauched and bold,   *disorderly*
That this our court, infected with their manners,
Shows° like a riotous inn. Epicurism° and lust   *Appears / Gluttony*
210   Makes it more like a tavern or a brothel
Than a graced° palace.⁹ The shame itself doth speak   *an honored*
For instant remedy. Be then desired
By her, that else will take the thing she begs,
A little to disquantity your train,°   *to reduce your retinue*
215   And the remainders that shall still depend,°   *be retained*
To be such men as may besort° your age,   *befit*
Which know themselves° and you.   *Who know their place*
  LEAR   Darkness and devils!
Saddle my horses; call my train together.
220   Degenerate bastard, I'll not trouble thee.
Yet° have I left a daughter.   *Still*
  GONERIL   You strike my people, and your disordered rabble
Make servants of their betters.
        Enter [Duke of] ALBANY.
  LEAR   Woe that° too late repents!   *Woe to him who*
225   [*to* ALBANY] Is it your will? Speak, sir. Prepare my horses.
[*to* GONERIL] Ingratitude! Thou marble-hearted fiend,
More hideous when thou show'st thee in a child
Than the sea-monster!
  ALBANY   Pray, sir, be patient.
  LEAR [*to* GONERIL]   Detested kite,° thou liest!   *carrion-eating hawk*
230   My train are men of choice and rarest parts°   *qualities*
That all particulars of duty know,
And in the most exact regard support
The worships of° their name. —O most small fault,   *honors accorded*
How ugly didst thou in Cordelia show,
235   Which, like an engine, wrenched my frame of nature
From the fixed place,¹ drew from my heart all love,
And added to the gall. O Lear, Lear, Lear!
Beat at this gate° that let thy folly in   *(his head)*
And thy dear° judgment out. [*to his* KNIGHTS] Go, go, my   *precious*
    people.   [*Exeunt* KNIGHTS.]
240   ALBANY   My lord, I am guiltless as I am ignorant
Of what hath moved you.
  LEAR   It may be so, my lord.
Hear, Nature, hear, dear goddess, hear:
Suspend thy purpose, if thou didst intend
To make this creature fruitful.
245   Into her womb convey sterility,
Dry up in her the organs of increase,
And from her derogate° body never spring   *debased*
A babe to honor her. If she must teem,°   *breed*
Create her child of spleen,° that it may live   *malice*
250   And be a thwart disnatured° torment to her.   *a perverse unnatural*
Let it stamp wrinkles in her brow of youth;
With cadent° tears fret° channels in her cheeks;   *flowing / carve*
Turn all her mother's pains and benefits°   *cares and kind actions*

---

9. PERFORMANCE COMMENT Productions must decide
whether the king's followers are well-behaved "men
of choicest parts," as Lear puts it, or a "disordered
rabble," as Goneril describes them. See Digital Edi-

tion PC 3.
1. *like . . . place:* as a machine (or lever), dislocated
my natural affections from their proper foundations.

To laughter and contempt, that she may feel
255 How sharper than a serpent's tooth it is
To have a thankless child. Away, away.
Exeunt [LEAR *and* KENT].
ALBANY   Now gods that we adore,
Whereof comes this?
GONERIL   Never afflict yourself to know more of it,
260 But let his disposition have that scope
As° dotage gives it.   *Which*
Enter LEAR.
LEAR   What, fifty of my followers at a clap?
Within a fortnight?
ALBANY   What's the matter, sir?
LEAR   I'll tell thee:
265 Life and death! [*to* GONERIL] I am ashamed
That thou hast power to shake my manhood thus,
That these hot tears, which break from me perforce,°   *against my will*
Should make thee worth them.
Blasts and fogs upon thee!
270 Th'untented woundings° of a father's curse   *The undressed wounds*
Pierce every sense about thee. Old fond° eyes,   *foolish*
Beweep° this cause again, I'll pluck ye out   *If you weep over*
And cast you with the waters that you lose°   *let loose*
To temper° clay. Ha? Let it be so.   *soften*
275 I have another daughter
Who I am sure is kind and comfortable.°   *comforting*
When she shall hear this of thee, with her nails
She'll flay thy wolvish visage. Thou shalt find
That I'll resume the shape which thou dost think
I have cast off forever.   *Exit.*
280 GONERIL   Do you mark that?
ALBANY   I cannot be so partial,° Goneril,   *biased*
To° the great love I bear you—   *Because of*
GONERIL   Pray you, content.° What, Oswald, ho?   *be quiet*
[*to* FOOL] You, sir, more knave than fool, after your master.
285 FOOL   Nuncle Lear, nuncle Lear,
Tarry, take the fool with thee.
A fox when one has caught her,
And such a daughter
Should sure° to the slaughter   *surely be sent*
290 If my cap would buy a halter.°   *collar; noose*
So the fool follows after.   *Exit.*
GONERIL   This man hath had good counsel. A hundred
knights?
'Tis politic° and safe to let him keep   *prudent*
At point° a hundred knights; yes, that on every dream   *Armed*
295 Each buzz,° each fancy, each complaint, dislike.   *rumor*
He may enguard° his dotage with their powers   *protect*
And hold our lives in mercy. Oswald, I say!
ALBANY   Well, you may fear too far.
GONERIL   Safer than trust too far.
300 Let me still° take away the harms I fear,   *always*
Not° fear still to be taken. I know his heart;   *Rather than*
What he hath uttered I have writ my sister.

If she sustain him and his hundred knights
When I have showed th'unfitness.—
   Enter [Oswald the] STEWARD.
305 How now, Oswald?
What, have you writ that letter to my sister?
STEWARD Ay, madam.
GONERIL Take you some company and away to horse.
Inform her full of my particular fear
310 And thereto add such reasons of your own
As may compact° it more. Get you gone   *compound*
And hasten your return.   [*Exit* STEWARD.]
[*to* ALBANY]   No, no, my lord,
This milky gentleness and course of yours,
Though I condemn not, yet under pardon°   *begging your pardon*
315 You are much more at task° for want of wisdom *taken to task; censured*
Than praised for harmful mildness.
ALBANY How far your eyes may pierce,° I cannot tell;   *foresee*
Striving to better, oft we mar what's well.
GONERIL Nay, then—
ALBANY   Well, well, th'event.° *Exeunt.* *let's see the outcome*

1.5

Enter LEAR, KENT [*disguised as Caius*], GENTLEMAN,
and FOOL.

LEAR [*to* KENT] Go you before° to Gloucester¹ with these let- *on ahead*
ters; acquaint my daughter no further with anything you
know than comes from her demand out of the letter.² If your
diligence be not speedy, I shall be there afore you.
5 KENT I will not sleep, my lord, till I have delivered your letter.
                  Exit.
FOOL If a man's brains were in 's heels were't not in danger of
kibes?°   *chilblains*
LEAR Ay, boy.
FOOL Then, I prithee, be merry; thy wit shall not go slipshod.³
10 LEAR Ha, ha, ha.
FOOL Shalt° see thy other daughter will use thee kindly, for *Thou shalt*
though she's as like this as a crab's° like an apple, yet I can *crab apple; sour apple*
tell what I can tell.
LEAR What canst tell, boy?
15 FOOL She will taste as like this as a crab does to a crab. Thou
canst tell why one's nose stands i'th' middle on 's° face? *of one's*
LEAR No.
FOOL Why, to keep one's eyes of either side 's nose, that what
a man cannot smell out he may spy into.
20 LEAR I did her wrong.
FOOL Canst tell how an oyster makes his shell?
LEAR No.
FOOL Nor I, neither, but I can tell why a snail has a house.
LEAR Why?

1.5 Location: Before Albany's castle.
1. To Gloucestershire, where Cornwall and Regan
reside.
2. *than . . . letter:* other than such questions as are

prompted by the letter.
3. Literally, your brains will not wear slippers (to
warm feet that are afflicted with chilblains); feet of
any intelligence would not walk toward Regan.

25   FOOL   Why, to put 's head in, not to give it away to his daughters and leave his horns without a case.[4]

     LEAR   I will forget my nature.[5] So kind a father! Be my horses
ready?

     FOOL   Thy asses° are gone about 'em; the reason why the seven   *(servants)*
30 stars° are no more than seven is a pretty reason.   *the Pleiades*

     LEAR   Because they are not eight.

     FOOL   Yes, indeed, thou wouldst make a good fool.

     LEAR   To tak't again perforce.[6] Monster ingratitude!

     FOOL   If thou wert my fool, nuncle, I'd have thee beaten for
35 being old before thy time.

     LEAR   How's that?

     FOOL   Thou shouldst not have been old till thou hadst been
wise.

     LEAR   Oh, let me not be mad, not mad. Sweet heaven, keep me
40 in temper;° I would not be mad. —How now, are the horses   *sane*
ready?

     GENTLEMAN   Ready, my lord.

     LEAR   Come, boy.

     FOOL   She that's a maid now and laughs at my departure,
45 Shall not be a maid long, unless things be cut shorter.[7]

                                         Exeunt.

2.1

     *Enter [*EDMUND *the] Bastard, and* CURAN, *severally.*°   *separately*

     EDMUND   Save° thee, Curan.   *God save*

     CURAN   And you, sir. I have been with your father and given
him notice that the Duke of Cornwall and Regan, his duchess, will be here with him this night.

5   EDMUND   How comes that?

     CURAN   Nay, I know not. You have heard of the news abroad,
I mean the whispered ones, for they are yet but ear-kissing
arguments.[1]

     EDMUND   Not I. Pray you, what are they?

10 CURAN   Have you heard of no likely wars toward° twixt the   *impending*
Dukes of Cornwall and Albany?

     EDMUND   Not a word.

     CURAN   You may do, then, in time. Fare you well, sir.   *Exit.*

     EDMUND   The Duke be here tonight? The better best!
15 This weaves itself perforce° into my business.   *necessarily*
My father hath set guard to take my brother,
And I have one thing of a queasy question[2]
Which I must act. Briefness and fortune work.°   *be with me*

        Enter EDGAR [*above*].

Brother, a word! Descend, brother, I say.

---

4. Protective covering for his head or concealment for his horns (horns were the conventional sign of a cuckold). The Fool may be slyly implying that Lear's wife cheated on him.

5. Lose my fatherly feelings. *nature:* character.

6. To take it back by force. Lear may refer to Goneril's treachery, or he may be contemplating resuming his authority.

7. *She . . . shorter:* A girl who would laugh at my leaving would be so foolish that she could not remain a virgin for long; "things" refers both to the unfolding event and to penises.

2.1 Location: Gloucester's castle.

1. Barely whispered affairs.

2. And I have a hazardous and delicate problem.

[EDGAR *descends.*]

20 My father watches. O sir, fly this place!
Intelligence is given where you are hid.
You have now the good advantage of the night.
Have you not spoken 'gainst the Duke of Cornwall?
He's coming hither now, i'th' night, i'th' haste

25 And Regan with him. Have you nothing said
Upon his party° 'gainst the Duke of Albany?   *On his (Cornwall's) side*
Advise yourself.°   *Consider carefully*

EDGAR   I am sure on't,° not a word.   *of it*

EDMUND   I hear my father coming. Pardon me:
[*He draws his sword.*] In cunning, I must draw my sword
    upon you.

30 Draw, seem to defend yourself. Now quit you° well.   *acquit yourself*
[*He shouts.*] Yield, come before my father. —Light, ho, here!
[*to* EDGAR] Fly, brother! —Torches, torches! [*to* EDGAR] So
    farewell.   [*Exit* EDGAR.]
[*He wounds his arm.*] Some blood drawn on me would beget
    opinion°   *produce the impression*
Of my more fierce endeavor. I have seen drunkards

35 Do more than this in sport. [*He shouts.*] Father, father!
Stop, stop! No help?

Enter GLOUCESTER *and* SERVANTS, *with torches.*

GLOUCESTER   Now, Edmund, where's the villain?

EDMUND   Here stood he in the dark, his sharp sword out,
Mumbling of wicked charms, conjuring the moon

40 To stand° auspicious mistress.   *To act as his*

GLOUCESTER   But where is he?

EDMUND   Look, sir, I bleed.

GLOUCESTER   Where is the villain, Edmund?

EDMUND   Fled this way, sir, when by no means he could—

GLOUCESTER   Pursue him, ho, go after.   [*Exeunt* SERVANTS.]

45   —By no means—what?

EDMUND   —Persuade me to the murder of your lordship,
But that° I told him the revenging gods   *In response to that*
'Gainst parricides did all the thunder bend;
Spoke with how manifold and strong a bond

50 The child was bound to th' father. Sir, in fine,°   *finally*
Seeing how loathly opposite° I stood   *opposed*
To his unnatural purpose, in fell° motion   *deadly*
With his preparèd sword he charges home°   *strikes to the heart of*
My unprovided° body, latched° mine arm,   *unprotected / struck*

55 And when he saw my best alarumed spirits
Bold in the quarrel's right,[3] roused to th'encounter,
Or whether gasted° by the noise I made,   *frightened*
Full suddenly he fled.

GLOUCESTER   Let him fly far.
Not in this land shall he remain uncaught;

60 And found, dispatch.° The noble Duke, my master,   *And once found—killed*
My worthy arch° and patron, comes tonight.   *lord*
By his authority I will proclaim it,
That he which finds him shall deserve our thanks,

---

3. *my best . . . right:* that I was fully roused to action, made brave by righteousness.

Bringing the murderous coward to the stake.[4]
65 He that conceals him, death.
EDMUND   When I dissuaded him from his intent,
And found him pight° to do it, with curst° speech   *resolved / bitter*
I threatened to discover° him. He replied,   *expose*
"Thou unpossessing bastard, dost thou think,
70 If I would stand against thee, would the reposal°   *placing*
Of any trust, virtue, or worth in thee
Make thy words faithed?° No, what should I deny—   *credible*
As this I would, though thou didst produce
My very character[5]—I'd turn it all
75 To[6] thy suggestion, plot, and damnèd practice,°   *scheming*
And thou must make a dullard of the world,
If they not thought the profits of my death
Were very pregnant and potential spirits
To make thee seek it."[7]
GLOUCESTER   Oh, strange° and fastened° villain,   *unnatural / incorrigible*
80 Would he deny his letter, said he?
80.1   *I never got° him!*   *begot*
                Tucket° within.   *Flourish of trumpets*
Hark, the Duke's trumpets. I know not where he comes.
All ports° I'll bar. The villain shall not scape.   *seaports; exits*
The Duke must grant me that. Besides, his picture
I will send far and near that all the kingdom
85 May have due note of him,[8] and of my land,
Loyal and natural° boy, I'll work the means   *loving; illegitimate*
To make thee capable.°   *legally able to inherit*
        Enter CORNWALL, REGAN, *and Attendants.*
CORNWALL   How now, my noble friend? Since I came hither,
Which I can call but now, I have heard strangeness.
90 REGAN   If it be true, all vengeance comes too short
Which can pursue th'offender. How dost my lord?
GLOUCESTER   O madam, my old heart is cracked; it's cracked.
REGAN   What, did my father's godson seek your life?
He whom my father named, your Edgar?
95 GLOUCESTER   O lady, lady, shame would have it hid.
REGAN   Was he not companion with the riotous knights
That tended° upon my father?   *attend*
GLOUCESTER   I know not, madam. 'Tis too bad, too bad.
EDMUND   Yes, madam, he was of that consort.°   *company*
100 REGAN   No marvel, then, though° he were ill affected.°   *that / ill disposed*
'Tis they have put him on° the old man's death   *have urged him to seek*
To have th'expense° and waste of his revenues.   *the use*
I have this present evening from my sister
Been well informed of them and with such cautions
105 That if they come to sojourn at my house,
I'll not be there.
CORNWALL   Nor I, assure thee, Regan.
Edmund, I hear that you have shown your father

4. Treachery and rebellion were crimes for which
one could be burned.
5. Handwriting; but also, a true summary of my character.
6. *I'd . . . To:* I'd blame it all on.
7. *And thou . . . it:* And do you think the world so stupid that it could not see the benefit you would get from
my death (and thus a motive for plotting to kill me)?
pregnant: full. *potential spirits:* powerful temptations.
8. Likenesses of outlaws were drawn up, printed,
and publicly displayed, sometimes with an offer of
reward as in "Wanted" posters.

A childlike office.°   *filial service*
EDMUND   It was my duty, sir.
GLOUCESTER   He did bewray his practice° and received   *uncover his (Edgar's) plot*
110   This hurt you see, striving to apprehend him.
CORNWALL   Is he pursued?
GLOUCESTER   Ay, my good lord.
CORNWALL   If he be taken, he shall never more
      Be feared of doing harm. Make your own purpose
      How in my strength you please.⁹ For you, Edmund,
115   Whose virtue and obedience doth this instant
      So much commend itself, you shall be ours.
      Natures of such deep trust we shall much need;
      You we first seize on.
EDMUND   I shall serve you, sir, truly, however else.°   *if nothing else*
120   GLOUCESTER   For him, I thank your grace.
CORNWALL   You know not why we came to visit you?
REGAN   Thus out of season, threading dark-eyed night?
      Occasions, noble Gloucester, of some prize,°   *weight*
      Wherein we must have use of your advice.
125   Our father, he hath writ, so hath our sister,
      Of differences,° which I best thought it fit   *quarrels*
      To answer from° our home. The several° messengers   *away from / various*
      From hence attend° dispatch. Our good old friend,   *await*
      Lay comforts to your bosom and bestow
130   Your needful° counsel to our businesses,   *badly needed*
      Which craves the instant use.¹
GLOUCESTER   I serve you, madam.
      Your graces are right welcome.   ***Exeunt. Flourish.***

2.2

Enter KENT [*disguised as Caius*] *and* [*Oswald the*]
     STEWARD *severally.*°   *separately*
STEWARD   Good dawning to thee, friend. Art° of this house?   *Are you a servant*
KENT   Ay.
STEWARD   Where may we set our horses?
KENT   I'th' mire.
5   STEWARD   Prithee, if thou lov'st me,° tell me.   *if you will be so kind*
KENT   I love thee not.
STEWARD   Why, then, I care not for thee.
KENT   If I had thee in Lipsbury pinfold,¹ I would make thee
      care for me.
10   STEWARD   Why dost thou use° me thus? I know thee not.   *treat*
KENT   Fellow, I know thee.
STEWARD   What dost thou know me for?
KENT   A knave, a rascal, an eater of broken meats,° a base,   *scraps*
      proud, shallow, beggarly, three-suited, hundred pound, filthy,
15   worsted-stocking knave,² a lily-livered, action-taking, whore-
      son, glass-gazing, super-serviceable finical rogue, one-trunk-

---

9. *Make . . . please:* Devise your plots making use of
my forces and authority as you see fit.
1. Which requires immediate attention.
2.2 Location: Before Gloucester's house.
1. If I had you in the enclosure of my mouth (gripped
in my teeth). Lipsbury is probably an invented place-
name. *pinfold:* pen, animal enclosure.

2. *three-suited . . . knave:* Oswald is being called a poor
imitation of a gentleman. Servants were permitted
three suits a year; one hundred pounds was the minimum qualification for the purchase of one of King
James's knighthoods; a gentleman would wear stockings of silk, not "worsted" (thick woolen material).

inheriting slave,³ one that wouldst be a bawd in way of good
service⁴ and art nothing but the composition° of a knave, beg-   *combination*
gar, coward, pander, and the son and heir of a mongrel bitch.
20   One whom I will beat into clamors whining if thou deny'st
the least syllable of thy addition.⁵
STEWARD   Why, what a monstrous fellow art thou thus to rail
on one that is neither known of° thee nor knows thee!   *by*
KENT   What a brazen-faced varlet° art thou to deny thou know-   *rascal*
25   est me! Is it two days since I tripped up thy heels and beat
thee before the King? [*He draws his sword.*] Draw, you rogue,
for though it be night, yet the moon shines. I'll make a sop
o'th' moonshine⁶ of you, you whoreson, cullionly barber-
monger.⁷ Draw!
STEWARD   Away, I have nothing to do with thee.
30   KENT   Draw, you rascal! You come with letters against the
King and take Vanity the puppet's part against the royalty of
her father?⁸ Draw, you rogue, or I'll so carbonado⁹ your
shanks—Draw, you rascal! Come your ways!°   *Come forward*
[*He beats him.*]
STEWARD   Help, ho, murder, help!
35   KENT   Strike, you slave! Stand, rogue! Stand, you neat° slave!   *elegant; foppish*
Strike!
STEWARD   Help, ho, murder, murder!
   Enter [EDMUND *the*] *Bastard,* CORNWALL, REGAN,
    GLOUCESTER, SERVANTS.
EDMUND   How now, what's the matter? Part!
KENT [*to* STEWARD]   With you, goodman boy, if you please.
40   Come, I'll flesh ye.¹ Come on, young master.
GLOUCESTER   Weapons? Arms? What's the matter here?
CORNWALL   Keep peace, upon your lives! He dies that strikes
again! What is the matter?
REGAN   The messengers from our sister and the King?
45   CORNWALL   What is your difference?° Speak.   *quarrel*
STEWARD   I am scarce in breath, my lord.
KENT   No marvel; you have so bestirred your valor, you cow-
ardly rascal. Nature disclaims° in thee. A tailor² made thee!   *disowns her part*
CORNWALL   Thou art a strange fellow. A tailor make a man?
50   KENT   A tailor, sir. A stonecutter or a painter could not have
made him so ill,° though they had been but two years o'th'   *so badly*
trade.
CORNWALL   Speak yet: how grew your quarrel?

---

3. *lily-livered:* cowardly. *action-taking:* litigious, one
who would rather use the law than his fists. *glass-
gazing:* mirror-gazing. *super-serviceable:* overly officious, or too ready to serve. *finical:* finicky, fastidious.
one-trunk-inheriting: owning only what would fill
one trunk.
4. *one that . . . service:* one who would even be a pimp
if called upon.
5. Of the descriptions Kent has just applied to him.
addition: title (used ironically).
6. Kent proposes to skewer and pierce Oswald so that
his body might be made into something insubstantial
(like moonshine). Alternatively, perhaps Kent is proposing to scramble Oswald's body into a substance
resembling the popular sixteenth- and seventeenth-

century pudding called "eggs in moonshine." *sop:*
piece of bread to be steeped or dunked in soup.
7. *cullionly barber-monger:* despicable frequenter of
hairdressers. *cullion:* testicle.
8. *and take . . . father:* and support Goneril, here
depicted as a dressed-up doll whose pride is contrasted
with Lear's kingliness.
9. Slash or score as one would the surface of meat in
preparation for broiling.
1. I'll initiate you into fighting, as a hunting dog is
given the taste of blood to rouse it for the chase.
2. Tailors, considered effeminate, were stock objects
of mockery. Kent has suggested that Oswald is worthless apart from the value he derives from his external
garments.

STEWARD   This ancient ruffian, sir, whose life I have spared at
55   suit of° his gray beard—   *on account of*
KENT [*to* STEWARD]   Thou whoreson zed,[3] thou unnecess-
     ary letter! —My lord, if you will give me leave, I will tread
     this unbolted° villain into mortar and daub the wall of a   *unsifted; coarse*
     jakes° with him. [*to* STEWARD] "Spare my gray beard," you   *privy; toilet*
60   wagtail![4]
CORNWALL   Peace, sirrah!
     You beastly knave, know you no reverence?°   *respect*
KENT   Yes, sir, but anger hath a privilege.
CORNWALL   Why art thou angry?
65   KENT   That such a slave as this should wear a sword
     Who wears no honesty. Such smiling rogues as these
     Like rats oft bite the holy cords[5] a-twain,
     Which are t'intrince° t'unloose; smooth° every passion   *too intricate / flatter*
     That in the natures of their lords rebel,
70   Being oil to fire, snow to the colder moods,
     Revenge, affirm, and turn their halcyon beaks[6]
     With every gall and vary° of their masters,   *irritation and mood*
     Knowing naught, like dogs, but following.
     A plague upon your epileptic° visage!   *distorted; grimacing*
75   Smile you° my speeches as° I were a fool?   *Do you smile at / as if*
     Goose, if I had you upon Sarum Plain,
     I'd drive ye cackling home to Camelot.[7]
CORNWALL   What, art thou mad, old fellow?
GLOUCESTER   How fell you out? Say that.
80   KENT   No contraries° hold more antipathy   *opposites*
     Than I and such a knave.
CORNWALL   Why dost thou call him knave? What is his fault?°   *offense*
KENT   His countenance likes° me not.   *pleases*
CORNWALL   No more, perchance, does mine, nor his, nor hers.
85   KENT   Sir, 'tis my occupation to be plain.
     I have seen better faces in my time
     Than stands on any shoulder that I see
     Before me at this instant.
CORNWALL   This is some fellow
     Who, having been praised for bluntness, doth affect
90   A saucy roughness and constrains the garb
     Quite from his nature.[8] He cannot flatter, he.
     An honest mind and plain, he must speak truth
     An they will take it so; if not, he's plain.[9]
     These kind of knaves I know, which in this plainness
95   Harbor more craft and more corrupter ends
     Than twenty silly-ducking observants

3. The letter Z (zed) was considered superfluous because it could be replaced by S; consequently, it was omitted from many dictionaries.
4. A common English bird that takes its name from the up-and-down flicking of its tail; this, and its characteristic hopping from foot to foot, causes it to appear nervous. Alternatively, a contemptuous term for a harlot.
5. Bonds of kinship, affection, marriage, or rank.
6. It was believed that the kingfisher (in Greek, *halcyon*) could be used as a weather vane when dead: suspended by a fine thread, its beak would turn what-ever way the wind blew.
7. *Goose . . . Camelot:* Comparing him to a cackling goose, Kent tells Oswald that if he had him on Salisbury Plain, he would drive him all the way to Camelot, the legendary home of King Arthur.
8. *and constrains . . . nature:* and assumes the appearance although it is untrue to his real self. Alternatively (with "his" meaning "its"): and distorts the true shape of plainness from what it naturally is (by turning it into disrespect).
9. If they will accept (Kent's attitude), well and good; if not, he is a plainspoken man (and does not care).

That stretch their duties nicely.[1]

KENT   Sir, in good faith, in sincere verity,
      Under th'allowance of your great aspect,[2]

100   Whose influence like the wreath of radiant fire
      On flick'ring Phoebus' front°—   *the sun god's forehead*

CORNWALL   What mean'st by this?

KENT   To go out of my dialect,° which you discommend so   *normal mode of speech*
      much. I know, sir, I am no flatterer. He that beguiled you in
      a plain accent was a plain knave, which for my part I will not

105   be, though I should win your displeasure to entreat me to't.[3]

CORNWALL [*to* STEWARD]   What was th'offense you gave him?

STEWARD   I never gave him any.
      It pleased the King his master very late°   *lately*
      To strike at me upon his misconstruction,°   *misunderstanding (me)*

110   When he, compact° and flattering his displeasure,   *in league with*
      Tripped me behind; being down, insulted,° railed,   *I being down, he insulted*
      And put upon him such a deal of man
      That worthied him,[4] got praises of the King,
      For him attempting who was self-subdued,[5]

115   And in the fleshment° of this dread exploit,   *excitement; flush*
      Drew on me here again.

KENT   None of these rogues and cowards
      But Ajax is their fool.[6]

CORNWALL   Fetch forth the stocks!
                                             [*Exit a* SERVANT.]
      You stubborn, ancient knave, you reverend° braggart,   *old; revered*
      We'll teach you.

120   KENT   Sir, I am too old to learn.
      Call not your stocks for me. I serve the King,
      On whose employment I was sent to you.
      You shall do small respects, show too bold malice
      Against the grace° and person° of my master,   *majesty / personal honor*
      Stocking° his messenger.   *By stocking*

125   CORNWALL   Fetch forth the stocks.
      As I have life and honor, there shall he sit till noon.

REGAN   Till noon? Till night, my lord, and all night too.

KENT   Why, madam, if I were your father's dog,
      You should not use me so.

130   REGAN   Sir, being° his knave, I will.   *since you are*
                 Stocks brought out [*by a* SERVANT].

CORNWALL   This is a fellow of the selfsame color°   *character*
      Our sister° speaks of. —Come, bring away the stocks.   *sister-in-law*

GLOUCESTER   Let me beseech your grace not to do so;

133.1   *His fault is much, and the good King his master*
      Will check° him for't. Your purposed° low correction   *reprimand / intended*
      Is such as basest and 'temnest[7] wretches

---

1. *Than . . . nicely:* Than twenty obsequious attendants who constantly bow idiotically and who perform
their functions with excessive diligence ("nicely").
2. With the permission of your great countenance.
"Aspect" also refers to the astrological position of a
planet; Kent's bombastic language here raises Cornwall to the mock-heroic proportions of a heavenly body.
3. *He that . . . to't:* The person who tried to hoodwink
you with plain speaking was, indeed, a pure knave—
something I won't be, even if you were to beg me to be

one (a plain knave, or flatterer).
4. *And put . . . worthied him:* And put on such a show
of manliness that he was thought a worthy fellow.
5. For attacking a man who had already surrendered
(Kent attacking Oswald).
6. *None . . . fool:* Such rogues and cowards as these
talk as if they were greater warriors (and blusterers)
than Ajax; such rogues always make even mighty Ajax
out to be a fool.
7. Condemnest; most condemned.

> For pilf'rings and most common trespasses
133.5   Are punished with.
The King his master needs must take it ill
135   That he, so slightly valued in his messenger,
Should have him thus restrained.

CORNWALL   I'll answer° that.   *be responsible for*
REGAN   My sister may receive it much more worse
To have her gentleman abused, assaulted,
138.1   For following° her affairs. —Put in his legs.   *carrying out*
CORNWALL   Come, my lord, away.

Exeunt [CORNWALL *and* REGAN].

140   GLOUCESTER   I am sorry for thee, friend. 'Tis the Duke's
pleasure,
Whose disposition, all the world well knows,
Will not be rubbed° nor stopped. I'll entreat for thee.   *obstructed*
KENT   Pray, do not, sir. I have watched° and traveled hard;   *gone without sleep*
Some time I shall sleep out, the rest I'll whistle.
145   A good man's fortune may grow out at heels.[8]
Give° you good morrow.   *God give*
GLOUCESTER   The Duke's to blame in this; 'twill be ill taken.

Exit.

KENT   Good King, that must approve° the common saw,°   *prove / saying*
Thou out of heaven's benediction com'st
150   To the warm sun.[9]
Approach, thou beacon[1] to this under-globe,
That by thy comfortable beams I may
Peruse this letter. Nothing almost sees miracles
But misery.[2] I know 'tis from Cordelia,
155   Who hath most fortunately been informed
Of my obscurèd° course and shall find time   *hidden; disguised*
From this enormous state,° seeking to give   *awful state of affairs*
Losses their remedies. All weary and o'er-watched,°   *too long awake*
Take vantage,° heavy eyes, not to behold   *the opportunity*
160   This shameful lodging. Fortune, good night,
Smile once more; turn thy wheel.[3]

[*Sleeps and remains onstage.*]

2.3

Enter EDGAR.

EDGAR   I heard myself proclaimed°   *declared an outlaw*
And by the happy° hollow of a tree   *opportune*
Escaped the hunt. No port° is free; no place   *seaport; exit*
That guard and most unusual vigilance
5   Does not attend my taking.° Whiles° I may scape,   *await my capture / Until*
I will preserve myself and am bethought°   *resolved*
To take the basest and most poorest shape
That ever penury in contempt of° man   *for*
Brought near to beast. My face I'll grime with filth,

---

8. The fortunes of even good men sometimes wear thin.
9. *Thou . . . sun:* You come from the blessing of heaven into the heat of the sun (go from good to bad).
1. That is, the sun.
2. *Nothing . . . misery:* Only those suffering misery are granted miracles; any comfort seems miraculous to those who are miserable.
3. The goddess Fortune was traditionally depicted with a wheel to signify her mutability and caprice. She was believed to take pleasure in arbitrarily lowering those at the top of her wheel and raising those at the bottom.
2.3 Location: As before.

10   Blanket my loins, elf all my hairs in knots,[1]
   And with presented° nakedness outface   *exposed*
   The winds and persecutions of the sky.
   The country gives me proof and precedent
   Of Bedlam beggars who, with roaring voices,
15   Strike° in their numbed and mortified° arms   *Stick / deadened*
   Pins, wooden pricks, nails, sprigs of rosemary,
   And with this horrible object° from low farms,   *spectacle*
   Poor pelting° villages, sheepcotes, and mills,   *paltry; contemptible*
   Sometimes with lunatic bans,° sometime with prayers,   *curses*
20   Enforce their charity. Poor Turlygod,[2] poor Tom:
   That's something yet. Edgar I nothing am.[3]   *Exit.*

2.4

Enter LEAR, FOOL, *and* GENTLEMAN.

LEAR   'Tis strange that they should so depart from home
   And not send back my messengers.

GENTLEMAN   As I learned,
   The night before there was no purpose in them°   *they had no intention*
   Of this remove.°   *change of residence*

KENT   Hail to thee, noble master.

LEAR   Ha? Mak'st thou this shame thy pastime?

5 KENT   No, my lord.

FOOL   Ha, ha, he wears cruel garters![1] Horses are tied by the
   heads, dogs and bears by th' neck, monkeys by th' loins, and
   men by th' legs. When a man's overlusty at legs,[2] then he
   wears wooden nether-stocks.°   *knee socks*

10 LEAR   What's° he that hath so much thy place° mistook   *Who's / position*
   To set thee here?

KENT   It is both he and she:
   Your son° and daughter.   *son-in-law*

LEAR   No.

KENT   Yes.

15 LEAR   No, I say.

KENT   I say yea.

LEAR   By Jupiter, I swear no.

KENT   By Juno,[3] I swear ay.

LEAR   They durst not do't;
20   They could not, would not do't. 'Tis worse than murder
   To do upon respect[4] such violent outrage.
   Resolve° me with all modest° haste, which way   *Inform / reasonable*
   Thou mightst deserve, or they impose, this usage,
   Coming from us.

KENT   My lord, when at their home
25   I did commend° your highness' letters to them,   *deliver*
   Ere I was risen from the place, that showed
   My duty kneeling, came there a reeking° post,°   *sweating / messenger*
   Stewed in his haste, half breathless, painting° forth   *panting*

---

1. Tangle the hair into "elf locks," supposed to be a favorite trick of malicious elves.
2. A word of unknown origin.
3. Edgar, I am nothing; I am no longer Edgar.
2.4 Location: As before.
1. Worsted garters, punning on "crewel." Crewel is a thin yarn made of twisted fibers. The Fool is actually referring to the stocks in which Kent's feet are held.
2. When a man's liable to run away.
3. Queen of the Roman gods and wife of Jupiter, with whom she constantly quarreled.
4. To do to one who deserves respect.

From Goneril, his mistress, salutations,
30 Delivered letters 'spite of intermission,[5]
Which presently° they read. On those contents   *immediately*
They summoned up their meiny,° straight° took horse,   *retinue / straightaway*
Commanded me to follow and attend
The leisure of their answer, gave me cold looks,
35 And meeting here the other messenger,
Whose welcome I perceived had poisoned mine—
Being the very° fellow which of late   *same*
Displayed so saucily° against your highness—   *Acted so insolently*
Having more man° than wit° about me, drew.   *courage / sense*
40 He raised the house with loud and coward cries.
Your son and daughter found this trespass worth°   *deserving of*
The shame which here it suffers.
FOOL   Winter's not gone yet, if the wild geese fly that way.[6]
Fathers that wear rags
45 Do make their children blind.[7]
But fathers that bear bags
Shall see their children kind.
Fortune, that arrant whore,
Ne'er turns the key° to th' poor.   *opens the door*
50 But for all this, thou shalt have as many dolors[8] for thy daugh-
ters as thou canst tell° in a year.   *count*
LEAR   Oh, how this mother° swells up toward my heart!   *hysteria*
Hysterica passio, down, thou climbing sorrow,[9]
Thy element's° below! Where is this daughter?   *natural place is*
55 KENT   With the Earl, sir, here within.
LEAR   Follow me not. Stay here.   *Exit.*
GENTLEMAN   Made you no more offense but what you speak of?
KENT   None. How chance the King comes with so small a
number?
60 FOOL   An° thou hadst been set i'th' stocks for that question,   *If*
thou'dst well deserved it.
KENT   Why, Fool?
FOOL   We'll set thee to school to an ant, to teach thee there's
no laboring i'th' winter.[1] All that follow their noses are led by
65 their eyes but blind men, and there's not a nose among twenty
but can smell him that's stinking.° Let go thy hold when a   *(as his fortunes decay)*
great wheel runs down a hill,[2] lest it break thy neck with fol-
lowing. But the great one that goes upward, let him draw thee
after. When a wise man gives thee better counsel, give me
70 mine again. I would have none but knaves follow it since a
fool gives it.
[*Sings.*]   That sir which serves and seeks for gain,
And follows but for form,
Will pack° when it begins to rain,   *pack up and go*

---

5. Regardless of interrupting me; despite the interruptions in his account (as he gasped for breath).
6. Things will get worse according to such omens.
7. Blind to their father's needs.
8. Pains, sorrows; punning on "dollar," the English
term for the German "thaler," a large silver coin.
9. Hysterica . . . *sorrow: Hysterica passio* (a Latin
expression originating in the Greek *steiros*, "suffering
in the womb") was an inflammation of the senses. In
Renaissance medicine, vapors from the abdomen were
thought to rise up through the body, and in women,
the uterus itself was thought to wander around.
1. Ants, proverbially prudent, store food in the summer and thus do not work in the winter. Implicitly, a
wise person should know better than to look for sustenance to an old man who has fallen on wintry times.
2. A great wheel is a figure for Lear and of Fortune's
wheel itself, which has swung downward.

75   And leave thee in the storm,
        But I will tarry; the Fool will stay,
        And let the wise man fly.
        The knave turns fool that runs away,[3]
        The Fool no knave, pardie.°   *by God (pardieu)*
     Enter LEAR *and* GLOUCESTER.

80 KENT   Where learned you this, Fool?
    FOOL   Not i'th' stocks, Fool.
    LEAR   Deny to speak with me?
    They are sick? They are weary?
    They have traveled all the night? Mere fetches,°   *ruses; pretexts*
85 The images of revolt and flying off.[4]
    Fetch me a better answer.
    GLOUCESTER   My dear lord,
    You know the fiery quality° of the Duke,   *disposition*
    How unremoveable and fixed he is
    In his own course.
    LEAR   Vengeance, plague, death, confusion!°   *destruction*
90 "Fiery"? What "quality"? Why, Gloucester, Gloucester,
    I'll speak with the Duke of Cornwall and his wife.
    GLOUCESTER   Well, my good lord, I have informed them so.
    LEAR   Informed them? Dost thou understand me, man?
    GLOUCESTER   Ay, my good lord.
95 LEAR   The King would speak with Cornwall. The dear father
    Would with his daughter speak, commands, tends° service.   *awaits*
    Are they informed of this? My breath and blood!
    Fiery? The fiery Duke? Tell the hot Duke that—
    No, but not yet; maybe he is not well.
100 Infirmity doth still° neglect all office°   *always / obligation*
    Whereto our health is bound. We are not ourselves
    When nature, being oppressed, commands the mind
    To suffer with the body. I'll forbear
    And am fallen out with my more headier will,[5]
105 To take° the indisposed and sickly fit   *mistake*
    For the sound man. Death on my state![6] Wherefore°   *Why*
    Should he sit here? This act persuades me
    That this remotion° of the Duke and her   *remoteness; aloofness*
    Is practice° only. Give me my servant forth.   *trickery*
110 Go tell the Duke and 's wife I'd speak with them
    Now, presently.° Bid them come forth and hear me,   *at once*
    Or at their chamber door I'll beat the drum
    Till it cry sleep to death.[7]
    GLOUCESTER   I would have all well betwixt you.   *Exit.*
115 LEAR   Oh, me, my heart! My rising heart! But down.
    FOOL   Cry to it, nuncle, as the Cockney° did to the eels when   *Londoner (city woman)*
    she put 'em i'th' paste° alive. She knapped 'em o'th' coxcombs°   *pie; pastry / heads*
    with a stick and cried, "Down, wantons,° down!" 'Twas her   *rogues*
    brother that, in pure kindness to his horse, buttered his hay.[8]

---

3. The scoundrel who runs away is the real fool.
4. *images of*: signs of. *flying off*: desertion; insurrection.
5. And disagree with my (earlier) more rash intention.
6. May my royal authority end (an oath). Ironically, this has already happened.

7. Till the noise kills sleep.
8. Like that of his sister (who wanted to make eel pie without killing the eels), his kindness was misplaced: horses will not eat buttered hay. The anecdote about the eels is reminiscent of Lear's attempt earlier in the scene to quell his grieving heart: "*Hysterica passio*, down, thou climbing sorrow."

Enter CORNWALL, REGAN, GLOUCESTER, [*and*]
SERVANTS.

LEAR   Good morrow to you both.

120 CORNWALL   Hail to your grace.

   KENT *here set at liberty.*

REGAN   I am glad to see your highness.

LEAR   Regan, I think you are. I know what reason
   I have to think so. If thou shouldst not be glad,
   I would divorce me from thy mother's tomb,
125   Sepulch'ring° an adulteress. [*to* KENT] Oh, are you free?   Because it entombed
   Some other time for that. —Beloved Regan,
   Thy sister's naught!° O Regan, she hath tied   wicked; nothing
   Sharp-toothed unkindness, like a vulture, here.[9]
   I can scarce speak to thee. Thou'lt not believe
130   With how depraved a quality—O Regan!

REGAN   I pray you, sir, take patience. I have hope
   You less know how to value her desert
   Than she to scant her duty.[1]

LEAR   Say? How is that?

REGAN   I cannot think my sister in the least
135   Would fail her obligation. If, sir, perchance
   She have restrained the riots of your followers,
   'Tis on such ground and to such wholesome end
   As clears her from all blame.

LEAR   My curses on her!

REGAN   O sir, you are old;
140   Nature° in you stands on the very verge   Life
   Of his confine.° You should be ruled and led   Of its limit
   By some discretion° that discerns your state   discreet person
   Better than you yourself. Therefore I pray you
   That to our sister you do make return.
   Say you have wronged her.

145 LEAR   Ask her forgiveness?
   Do you but mark how this becomes the house?[2]
   Dear daughter, I confess that I am old;
   Age° is unnecessary. [*He kneels.*] On my knees I beg   An old man
   That you'll vouchsafe me raiment,° bed, and food.   promise me clothing

150 REGAN   Good sir, no more; these are unsightly tricks.
   Return you to my sister.

LEAR [*rising*]   Never, Regan.
   She hath abated° me of half my train,   deprived
   Looked black upon me, struck me with her tongue
   Most serpent-like upon the very heart.
155   All° the stored vengeances of heaven fall   Let all
   On her ingrateful top.° Strike her young bones,   head
   You taking° airs, with lameness.   infectious; malignant

CORNWALL   Fie, sir, fie!

LEAR   You nimble lightnings, dart your blinding flames
   Into her scornful eyes. Infect her beauty,
160   You fen-sucked fogs, drawn by the pow'rful sun[3]

---

9. Lear probably gestures to his heart.
1. *I have . . . duty:* I expect that you are worse at
valuing her merit than she is at neglecting her duty.
The double negative here ("less," "scant") is acceptable Jacobean usage.

2. Do you see how appropriate this is among members of a family (spoken ironically)?
3. The sun was thought to suck poisonous vapors
from marshy ground.

To fall and blister.
REGAN   O the blest gods!
So will you wish on me when the rash mood is on.
LEAR   No, Regan, thou shalt never have my curse.
Thy tender-hafted[4] nature shall not give
165   Thee o'er to harshness. Her eyes are fierce, but thine
Do comfort and not burn. 'Tis not in thee
To grudge my pleasures, to cut off my train,
To bandy hasty words, to scant my sizes,°   *reduce my allowances*
And, in conclusion, to oppose the bolt°   *lock the door*
170   Against my coming in. Thou better know'st
The offices° of nature, bond of childhood,   *duties*
Effects° of courtesy, dues of gratitude.   *Actions*
Thy half o'th' kingdom hast thou not forgot,
Wherein I thee endowed.
REGAN   Good sir, to th' purpose.°   *get to the point*
LEAR   Who put my man i'th' stocks?
        Enter [Oswald the] STEWARD. Tucket within.
175 CORNWALL   What trumpet's that?
REGAN   I know't my sister's; this approves° her letter   *confirms*
That she would soon be here. [*to* STEWARD] Is your lady come?
LEAR   This is a slave whose easy borrowed pride[5]
Dwells in the sickly grace of her he follows.
[*to* STEWARD] Out, varlet,° from my sight.   *wretch*
180 CORNWALL   What means your grace?
LEAR   Who stocked my servant? Regan, I have good hope
Thou didst not know on't.°   *of it*
       Enter GONERIL.
                  Who comes here? O heavens,
If you do love old men, if your sweet sway
Allow obedience, if you yourselves are old,
185   Make it your cause: send down and take my part.
[*to* GONERIL] Art not ashamed to look upon this beard?
O Regan, will you take her by the hand?
GONERIL   Why not by th' hand, sir? How have I offended?
All's not offense that indiscretion finds
190   And dotage terms so.
LEAR   O sides,[6] you are too tough! Will you yet hold?
How came my man i'th' stocks?
CORNWALL   I set him there, sir, but his own disorders°   *disorderly behavior*
Deserved much less advancement.[7]
LEAR   You, did you?
195 REGAN   I pray you, father, being weak, seem so.°   *behave so*
If till the expiration of your month
You will return and sojourn with my sister,
Dismissing half your train, come then to me.
I am now from home and out of that provision
200   Which shall be needful for your entertainment.
LEAR   Return to her, and fifty men dismissed?
No, rather, I abjure all roofs and choose

---

4. Tenderly placed; firmly set in a tender disposition (as a knife blade into its haft).
5. Unmerited and unpaid-for arrogance; "pride" may also refer to Oswald's fine clothing received for his services to Goneril.
6. Chest, where Lear's heart is swelling with emotion.
7. Deserved far worse treatment.

To wage against the enmity o'th' air,
To be a comrade with the wolf and owl,
205 Necessity's sharp pinch.⁸ Return with her?
Why, the hot-blooded France, that dowerless took
Our youngest born, I could as well be brought
To knee° his throne and squire-like pension beg,   *kneel to*
To keep base life afoot. Return with her?
210 Persuade me rather to be slave and sumpter°   *packhorse*
To this detested groom.°   *the Steward*
GONERIL   At your choice, sir.
LEAR   I prithee, daughter, do not make me mad.
I will not trouble thee, my child; farewell.
We'll no more meet, no more see one another.
215 But yet thou art my flesh, my blood, my daughter,
Or rather a disease that's in my flesh
Which I must needs call mine. Thou art a boil,
A plague sore, or embossèd° carbuncle   *a swollen*
In my corrupted blood. But I'll not chide thee.
220 Let shame come when it will; I do not call° it.   *call upon*
I do not bid the thunder-bearer° shoot,   *(Jove)*
Nor tell tales of thee to high-judging Jove.
Mend° when thou canst; be better at thy leisure.   *Make amends*
I can be patient: I can stay with Regan,
I and my hundred knights.
225 REGAN   Not altogether so.
I looked not for° you yet, nor am provided   *I did not expect*
For your fit welcome. Give ear, sir, to my sister,
For those that mingle reason with your passion⁹
Must be content to think you old and so.
But she knows what she does.
230 LEAR   Is this well° spoken?   *earnestly*
REGAN   I dare avouch° it, sir. What, fifty followers? *vouch for*
Is it not well? What should you need of more?
Yea, or so many, sith° that both charge° and danger   *since / expense*
Speak 'gainst so great a number? How in one house
235 Should many people under two commands
Hold amity? 'Tis hard, almost impossible.
GONERIL   Why might not you, my lord, receive attendance
From those that she calls servants, or from mine?
REGAN   Why not, my lord?
240 If then they chanced to slack° ye,   *neglect*
We could control them. If you will come to me—
For now I spy a danger—I entreat you
To bring but five-and-twenty; to no more
Will I give place or notice.°   *acknowledgment*
LEAR   I gave you all—
245 REGAN   And in good time° you gave it.   *it was about time*
LEAR   —Made you my guardians, my depositaries,°   *trustees*
But kept a reservation° to be followed   *reserved a right*
With such a number. What, must I come to you
With five-and-twenty, Regan? Said you so?

---

8. *To wage . . . pinch:* To counter, like predators, the
harshness of the elements with the hardness brought
on by necessity. *pinch:* stress, pressure.

9. For those who temper your passionate argument
with their own calm reasoning.

250 REGAN   And speak't again, my lord; no more with me.
  LEAR   Those wicked creatures yet do look well-favored°   *attractive*
      When others are more wicked; not being the worst
      Stands in some rank of praise.¹ I'll go with thee:
      Thy fifty yet doth double five-and-twenty,
      And thou art twice her love.
255 GONERIL   Hear me, my lord.
      What need you five-and-twenty? Ten? Or five?
      To follow in a house where twice so many
      Have a command to tend you?
  REGAN   What need one?
  LEAR   Oh, reason not the need! Our basest beggars
260   Are in the poorest thing superfluous.²
      Allow not° nature more than nature needs,   *If you don't allow*
      Man's life is cheap as beast's. Thou art a lady:
      If only to go warm were gorgeous,
      Why, nature needs not what thou gorgeous wear'st,
265   Which scarcely keeps thee warm.³ But for true need,
      You heavens, give me that patience,° patience I need!   *endurance*
      You see me here, you gods, a poor old man,
      As full of grief as age, wretched in both.
      If it be you that stirs these daughters' hearts
270   Against their father, fool me not so much
      To bear it tamely.⁴ Touch me with noble anger,
      And let not women's weapons, water drops,
      Stain my man's cheeks. No, you unnatural hags,
      I will have such revenges on you both
275   That all the world shall—I will do such things—
      What they are, yet I know not, but they shall be
      The terrors of the earth! You think I'll weep.
      No, I'll not weep. I have full cause of weeping.
          Storm and tempest.
      But this heart shall break into a hundred thousand flaws°   *fragments*
280   Or e'er° I'll weep. O Fool, I shall go mad.   *Before*
          Exit [with GLOUCESTER, KENT, FOOL,
                    and Attendants].
  CORNWALL   Let us withdraw; 'twill be a storm.
  REGAN   This house is little; the old man and 's people
      Cannot be well bestowed.°   *lodged*
  GONERIL   'Tis his own blame hath put himself from° rest   *deprived himself of*
285   And must needs taste his folly.
  REGAN   For his particular,° I'll receive him gladly,   *single self*
      But not one follower.
  GONERIL   So am I purposed.
      Where is my lord of Gloucester?
          Enter GLOUCESTER.
  CORNWALL   Followed the old man forth; he is returned.
290 GLOUCESTER   The King is in high rage.
  CORNWALL   Whither is he going?
  GLOUCESTER   He calls to horse, but will° I know not whither.   *will go*
  CORNWALL   'Tis best to give him way; he leads himself.

---

1. Deserves some degree ("rank") of praise.
2. *Our . . . superfluous:* Even the lowliest beggars
have something more than the barest minimum.
3. *If . . . thee warm:* If gorgeousness in clothes is
measured by the warmth they provide, your elaborate clothes are superfluous, for they barely cover
your body.
4. *fool . . . tamely:* do not make me so foolish as to
accept it meekly.

GONERIL My lord, entreat him by no means to stay.

295 GLOUCESTER Alack, the night comes on, and the high winds

Do sorely ruffle.° For many miles about   *bluster*

There's scarce a bush.

REGAN   O sir, to willful men,

The injuries that they themselves procure

Must be their schoolmasters. Shut up your doors:

300 He is attended with a desperate° train,   *violent*

And what they may incense° him to, being apt   *incite*

To have his ear abused,° wisdom bids fear.   *deceived*

CORNWALL Shut up your doors, my lord; 'tis a wild night.

My Regan counsels well: come out o'th' storm.   *Exeunt.*

3.1

Storm still. Enter KENT *[disguised as Caius] and a*
GENTLEMAN, *severally.*°   *separately*

KENT Who's there besides foul weather?

GENTLEMAN One minded like the weather, most unquietly.

KENT I know you. Where's the King?

GENTLEMAN Contending with the fretful elements:

5 Bids the wind blow the earth into the sea,

Or swell the curlèd waters 'bove the main,°   *mainland*

That things might change or cease;

7.1   *tears his white hair,*

Which the impetuous blasts, with eyeless rage,

Catch in their fury and make nothing of;

Strives in his little world of man to outscorn

7.5 *The to-and-fro conflicting wind and rain*

This night, wherein the cub-drawn bear would couch,[1]

The lion and the belly-pinchèd wolf

Keep their fur dry. Unbonneted° *he runs*   *Hatless; uncrowned*

And bids what will take all.

KENT But who is with him?

GENTLEMAN None but the Fool, who labors to out-jest

His heart-struck injuries.[2]

10 KENT   Sir, I do know you

And dare upon the warrant of my note[3]

Commend a dear° thing to you. There is division, *Entrust a crucial*

Although as yet the face of it is covered

With mutual cunning, twixt Albany and Cornwall,[4]

15 Who have—as who have not that their great stars

Throned and set high[5]—servants, who seem no less,° *who appear as such*

Which are to France the spies and speculations°   *observers*

Intelligent[6] of our state. What hath been seen,

Either in snuffs and packings° of the Dukes,   *quarrels and plots*

20 Or the hard rein° which both of them hath borne   *treatment*

3.1 Location: Bare, open country.
1. In which even the bear, though starving, having
been sucked dry ("drawn") by its cub, would not go
out to forage.
2. *to out-jest:* to relieve with laughter; to exorcise
through ridicule. *heart-struck injuries:* injuries (from
the betrayal of his paternal love) that penetrated to
the heart.
3. On the basis of my skill (at judging people).
4. TEXTUAL COMMENT There is substantial variation
between the Quarto and Folio texts in Kent's speech

in 3.1 about the sources of political unrest. While
Kent points to French foreign invasion in the Quarto,
the Folio text presents a vision of civil unrest between
Cornwall and Albany. Some scholars have proposed
political censorship as a possible explanation for the
stark difference between Kent's speeches. See Digital Edition TC 3 (combined text).
5. *as . . . high:* as has everybody who has been favored
by destiny.
6. Supplying intelligence about; too well informed of.

Against the old kind King, or something deeper,
Whereof, perchance, these are but furnishings.°   *pretexts*
22.1   *But true it is, from France there comes a power*
Into this scattered kingdom, who, already wise in° our   *aware of*
negligence,
Have secret feet in some of our best ports,
And are at point° to show their open banner.   *ready*
22.5   *Now to you: if on my credit you dare build° so far*   *if you trust me*
To make your speed to Dover, you shall find
Some that will thank you, making just° report   *accurate*
Of how unnatural and bemadding° sorrow   *maddening*
The King hath cause to plain.°   *complain*
22.10 *I am a gentleman of blood and breeding*
And from some knowledge and assurance
Offer this office° to you.   *role; duty*
GENTLEMAN   I will talk further with you.
KENT   No, do not.
For confirmation that I am much more
25   Than my out-wall,° open this purse and take   *outward appearance*
What it contains. If you shall see Cordelia—
As fear not but you shall—show her this ring,
And she will tell you who that fellow° is   *(Kent himself)*
That yet you do not know. Fie on this storm!
I will go seek the King.
30   GENTLEMAN   Give me your hand.
Have you no more to say?
KENT   Few words, but to effect° more than all yet: *but in importance*
That when we have found the King—in which your pain
That way, I'll this[7]—he that first lights on him
35   Holla the other.   *Exeunt [severally].*

3.2

Storm still. Enter LEAR *and* FOOL.
LEAR   Blow winds and crack your cheeks! Rage, blow,
You cataracts° and hurricanos, spout   *waterspouts*
Till you have drenched our steeples, drowned the cocks.°   *weather vanes*
You sulph'rous and thought-executing fires,[1]
5   Vaunt-couriers° of oak-cleaving thunderbolts,   *Forerunners*
Singe my white head. And thou, all-shaking thunder,
Strike flat the thick rotundity o'th' world,
Crack Nature's molds, all germens° spill at once   *seeds*
That makes ingrateful man.
10   FOOL   O nuncle, court holy water[2] in a dry house is better
than this rainwater out o' door. Good nuncle, in! Ask thy
daughters' blessing. Here's a night pities neither wise men
nor fools.
LEAR   Rumble thy bellyful! Spit fire, spout rain!
15   Nor rain, wind, thunder, fire are my daughters.
I tax° not you, you elements, with unkindness;   *blame*
I never gave you kingdom, called you children.

---

7. *in which . . . this:* in which effort you will go that
way and I this way.
3.2 Location: As before.
1. *thought-executing fires:* either meaning lightning

that strikes as swiftly as thought or lightning that
puts an end to thought.
2. Sprinkled blessings of a courtier; flattery.

You owe me no subscription.° Then let fall   *obedience; allegiance*
Your horrible pleasure. Here I stand your slave,
20 A poor, infirm, weak, and despised old man.
But yet I call you servile ministers,°   *agents*
That will with two pernicious daughters join
Your high-engendered battles° 'gainst a head   *heaven-bred forces*
So old and white as this. Oh, ho! 'Tis foul.
25 FOOL He that has a house to put 's head in has a good
  headpiece.°   *hat; brain*
  The codpiece that will house
  Before the head has any,
  The head and he shall louse;
30 So beggars marry many.³
  The man that makes his toe
  What he his heart should make,
  Shall of a corn cry woe
  And turn his sleep to wake.⁴
35 For there was never yet fair woman but she made mouths in
  a glass.⁵
    Enter KENT *[disguised as Caius].*
LEAR *[sitting down]* No, I will be the pattern of all patience.
  I will say nothing.
KENT Who's there?
40 FOOL Marry, here's grace and a codpiece: that's a wise man
  and a fool.⁶
KENT Alas, sir, are you here? Things that love night
  Love not such nights as these. The wrathful skies
  Gallow° the very wanderers of the dark   *Frighten*
45 And make them keep° their caves. Since I was man, *keep inside*
  Such sheets of fire, such bursts of horrid thunder,
  Such groans of roaring wind and rain I never
  Remember to have heard. Man's nature cannot carry° *bear*
  Th'affliction, nor the fear.
  LEAR   Let the great gods
50 That keep this dreadful pudder° o'er our heads, *commotion*
  Find out their enemies now. Tremble, thou wretch,
  That hast within thee undivulgèd crimes
  Unwhipped of° justice. Hide thee, thou bloody hand, *Unpunished by*
  Thou perjured and thou simular° of virtue   *simulator; pretender*
55 That art incestuous. Caitiff,° to pieces shake,   *Wretch*
  That under covert and convenient seeming° *fitting hypocrisy*
  Has practiced on° man's life. Close° pent-up guilts, *against / Secret*
  Rive° your concealing continents° and cry *Split open / coverings*
  These dreadful summoners grace.⁷ I am a man
  More sinned against than sinning.

---

3. *The codpiece . . . many:* Whoever finds his penis a
lodging before providing shelter for his head will end
up in lice-infested poverty and live in married beggary. *codpiece:* a pouchlike covering for the male
genitals, often conspicuous, particularly in the costume of a fool.
4. *The man . . . wake:* The man who values an inferior part of his body over the part that is truly valuable will suffer from and lose sleep over that inferior
part.
5. She practiced making pretty faces in a mirror. The

Fool probably refers to Regan's and Goneril's vanity,
or the line may be thrown in to soften the harshness
of his satire.
6. The supposedly wise King is symbolized by royal
grace, the Fool by his codpiece (here, slang for "penis").
The Fool speaks ironically: the King, as he has pointed
out, is now the foolish one. *Marry:* By the Virgin Mary
(a mild oath).
7. *and cry . . . grace:* and pray for mercy from these
elements that bring you to justice.

60 KENT   Alack, bareheaded?
    Gracious my lord, hard by here is a hovel;
    Some friendship will it lend you 'gainst the tempest.
    Repose you there, while I to this hard house°—   *household*
    More harder than the stones whereof 'tis raised,
65 Which° even but now, demanding° after you,   *Who / I demanding*
    Denied me to come in—return and force
    Their scanted° courtesy.   *grudging*
    LEAR   My wits begin to turn.
    Come on, my boy. How dost, my boy? Art cold?
    I am cold myself. Where is this straw, my fellow?
70 The art° of our necessities is strange   *skill; alchemy*
    And can make vile things precious. Come, your hovel.
    Poor fool and knave, I have one part in my heart
    That's sorry yet for thee.
    FOOL [*sings*]⁸ He that has and° a little tiny wit,°   *even / sense*
75   With heigh-ho, the wind and the rain,
            Must make content with his fortunes fit,
            Though the rain it raineth every day.
    LEAR   True, boy. Come, bring us to this hovel.
                                    Exeunt [LEAR *and* KENT].
    FOOL   This is a brave night to cool a courtesan.⁹ I'll speak a
80 prophecy ere I go:¹
    When priests are more in word than matter,°   *real virtue*
    When brewers mar their malt with water,
    When nobles are their tailors' tutors,²
    No heretics burned, but wenches' suitors,³
85 When every case in law is right,°   *just*
    No squire in debt, nor no poor knight,
    When slanders do not live in tongues,
    Nor cutpurses° come not to throngs,   *pickpockets*
    When usurers tell their gold i'th' field,⁴
90 And bawds and whores do churches build,
    Then shall the realm of Albion° come to great confusion.°   *Britain / decay*
    Then comes the time, who lives to see't,
    That going° shall be used° with feet.   *walking / practiced*
    This prophecy Merlin shall make, for I live before his time.⁵
                                                    Exit.

3.3
Enter GLOUCESTER *and* EDMUND.
GLOUCESTER Alack, alack, Edmund, I like not this unnatural
    dealing. When I desired their leave that I might pity° him,   *relieve*
    they took from me the use of mine own house, charged me
    on pain of perpetual displeasure neither to speak of him,
5   entreat for him, or any way sustain him.
EDMUND Most savage and unnatural!

---

8. The following song is an adaptation of one sung by
the Clown at the end of *Twelfth Night.*
9. To cool even the hot lusts of a prostitute.
1. What follows is a parody of the pseudo-Chaucerian
"Merlin's Prophecy" from *The Art of English Poesy.*
2. When noblemen follow fashion more closely than
their tailors do.
3. When the only heretics burned are faithless lov-

ers, who burn from venereal disease.
4. When usurers can count their profits openly
(because they have no shady dealings to hide).
5. Merlin was the great wizard at the legendary
court of King Arthur. Lear's Britain is set in an even
more distant past.
3.3 Location: At Gloucester's castle.

GLOUCESTER Go to,° say you nothing. There is division between   *(an expletive)*
the Dukes and a worse matter than that. I have received a let-
ter this night—'tis dangerous to be spoken. I have locked the
10   letter in my closet.° These injuries the King now bears will be   *private chamber*
revenged home.° There is part of a power already footed.[1]   *to the hilt*
We must incline to[2] the King; I will look him and privily°   *secretly; privately*
relieve him. Go you and maintain talk with the Duke, that
my charity be not of him perceived. If he ask for me, I am ill
15   and gone to bed. If I die for it, as no less is threatened me,
the King my old master must be relieved. There is strange
things toward,° Edmund. Pray you, be careful.   *Exit.*   *coming*
EDMUND This courtesy,° forbid° thee, shall the Duke   *act of kindness / forbidden*
Instantly know, and of that letter too.
20   This seems a fair deserving[3] and must draw me
That which my father loses: no less than all.
The younger rises when the old doth fall.   *Exit.*

3.4

Enter LEAR, KENT *[disguised as Caius,] and* FOOL.

KENT Here is the place, my lord. Good my lord, enter.
The tyranny of the open night's too rough
For nature° to endure.   *human weakness*
          Storm still.
LEAR   Let me alone.
KENT Good my lord, enter here.
LEAR   Wilt break my heart?
5   KENT I had rather break mine own.
Good my lord, enter.
LEAR Thou think'st 'tis much that this contentious storm
Invades us to the skin; so 'tis to thee.
But where the greater malady is fixed,°   *rooted*
10   The lesser is scarce felt. Thou'dst shun a bear,
But if thy flight lay toward the roaring sea,
Thou'dst meet the bear i'th' mouth. When the mind's free,°   *unburdened*
The body's delicate.° The tempest in my mind   *sensitive*
Doth from my senses take all feeling else,
15   Save° what beats there: filial ingratitude.   *Except*
Is it not as° this mouth should tear this hand   *as if*
For lifting food to't? But I will punish home.°   *thoroughly*
No, I will weep no more. In such a night
To shut me out? Pour on, I will endure.
20   In such a night as this? O Regan, Goneril,
Your old kind father, whose frank heart gave all!
Oh, that way madness lies. Let me shun that,
No more of that.
KENT   Good my lord, enter here.
LEAR Prithee, go in thyself; seek thine own ease.
25   This tempest will not give me leave to° ponder   *allow me to*
On things would hurt me more, but I'll go in.
[*to* FOOL] In, boy, go first. You houseless poverty,°   *poor*
Nay, get thee in; I'll pray, and then I'll sleep.   *Exit* [FOOL].

---

1. Part of an army already on the move.   3. This seems an action that deserves to be rewarded.
2. We must take the side of.   3.4 Location: Open country, before a cattle shed.

Poor naked wretches, wheresoe'er you are,
30 That bide° the pelting of this pitiless storm,   *endure; dwell in*
How shall your houseless heads and unfed sides,°   *starved ribs*
Your looped and windowed[1] raggedness defend you
From seasons such as these? Oh, I have ta'en
Too little care of this! Take physic, pomp;[2]
35 Expose thyself to feel what wretches feel,
That thou mayst shake the superflux[3] to them
And show the heavens more just.

EDGAR [*within*]   Fathom and half,[4] fathom and half. Poor Tom!
       Enter FOOL.

FOOL   Come not in here, nuncle. Here's a spirit! Help me, help
40 me!

KENT   Give me thy hand. Who's there?

FOOL   A spirit, a spirit! He says his name's Poor Tom.

KENT   What art thou that dost grumble there i'th' straw? Come
forth.
       Enter EDGAR [*disguised as Poor Tom*].

45 EDGAR   Away, the foul fiend follows me! Through the sharp hawthorn blow the winds.[5] Hum, go to thy bed and warm thee.[6]

LEAR   Didst thou give all to thy daughters, and art thou come
to this?

EDGAR   Who gives anything to Poor Tom, whom the foul fiend
50 hath led through fire and through flame, through sword and
whirlpool, o'er bog and quagmire, that hath laid knives under
his pillow and halters in his pew, set ratsbane by his porridge,[7]
made him proud of heart to ride on a bay trotting horse over
four-inched bridges,[8] to course° his own shadow for° a traitor.   *hunt / as*
55 Bless thy five wits![9] Tom's-a-cold. Oh, do, de, do, de, do, de,
bless thee from whirlwinds, star-blasting, and taking![1] Do
Poor Tom some charity, whom the foul fiend vexes. There
could I have him now, and there, and there again, and there.[2]
       Storm still.

LEAR   Has his daughters brought him to this pass?
60 —Couldst thou save nothing? Wouldst thou give 'em all?

FOOL   Nay, he reserved a blanket, else we had been all
shamed.

LEAR   Now all the plagues that in the pendulous° air   *overhanging; portentous*
Hang fated o'er men's faults light on thy daughters.

65 KENT   He hath no daughters, sir.

LEAR   Death, traitor! Nothing could have subdued nature
To such a lowness but his unkind daughters.
Is it the fashion that discarded fathers

---

1. *looped and windowed:* full of holes and vents; "windowed" could also refer to cloth worn through to semitransparency, like the oilcloth window "panes" of the
poor.
2. Cure yourself, pompous person.
3. Superfluity; bodily discharge, suggested by "physic"
(which also has the meaning of "purgative") in line
34. Excess here is also excess of wealth.
4. "Nine feet," a sailor's cry when taking soundings
to gauge the depth of water.
5. *Through . . . winds:* Perhaps a fragment from a
ballad.
6. *go . . . thee:* this expression is also used by the
drunken beggar Christopher Sly in *The Taming of*

the Shrew, Induction 1.
7. *laid knives . . . porridge:* these are all means by
which the foul fiend tempts Tom to commit suicide.
halters: nooses. *ratsbane:* rat poison.
8. Impossibly narrow, and probably suicidal to attempt
without diabolical help.
9. The five wits were common wit, imagination, fantasy, estimation, and memory (from medieval and
Renaissance cognitive theory).
1. *whirlwinds, star-blasting:* malign astrological influences capable of causing sickness or death. *taking:*
infection; bewitchment.
2. As Edgar speaks this sentence, he might kill vermin on his body as if they were devils.

Should have thus little mercy on their flesh?
70 Judicious punishment! 'Twas this flesh begot
Those pelican[3] daughters.
EDGAR [sings]   Pillicock sat on Pillicock hill, alow,
        alow, loo, loo.[4]
FOOL   This cold night will turn us all to fools and madmen.
EDGAR   Take heed o'th' foul fiend, obey thy parents, keep thy
75 word's justice, swear not, commit not with man's sworn
    spouse, set not thy sweetheart on proud array.[5] Tom's a-cold.
LEAR   What hast thou been?
EDGAR   A serving man, proud in heart and mind, that curled
    my hair, wore gloves in my cap,[6] served the lust of my mis-
80 tress' heart and did the act of darkness with her. Swore as
    many oaths as I spake words and broke them in the sweet
    face of heaven. One that slept in the contriving of lust and
    waked to do it. Wine loved I dearly, dice dearly, and in woman
    out-paramoured the Turk.[7] False of heart, light of ear,° bloody   *rumor-hungry*
85 of hand. Hog in sloth, fox in stealth, wolf in greediness, dog
    in madness, lion in prey. Let not the creaking of shoes[8] nor
    the rustling of silks betray thy poor heart to woman. Keep thy
    foot[9] out of brothels, thy hand out of plackets,[1] thy pen from
    lender's books, and defy the foul fiend. Still through the haw-
90 thorn blows the cold wind, says suum, mun, nonny. Dolphin,
    my boy, boy, cease. Let him trot by.[2]

        Storm still.

LEAR   Thou wert better in a grave than to answer° with thy   *encounter*
    uncovered body this extremity of the skies.° Is man no more   *violent weather*
    than this? Consider him well. Thou ow'st the worm no silk,
95 the beast no hide, the sheep no wool, the cat[3] no perfume.
    Ha? Here's three on 's° are sophisticated. Thou art the thing   *of us*
    itself. Unaccommodated[4] man is no more but such a poor,
    bare, forked° animal as thou art. [*He begins to undress.*] Off,   *two-legged*
    off, you lendings.° Come, unbutton here.   *borrowed clothes*

        Enter GLOUCESTER, *with a torch.*

100 FOOL   Prithee, nuncle, be contented. 'Tis a naughty° night to   *foul*
    swim in. Now a little fire in a wild° field were like an old   *barren; lustful*
    lecher's heart: a small spark, all the rest on 's° body cold.   *of his*
    Look, here comes a walking fire.
EDGAR   This is the foul Flibbertigibbet![5] He begins at curfew°   *9:00 p.m.*
105 and walks at first cock.° He gives the web and the pin,[6]   *midnight*
    squints the eye and makes the harelip, mildews the white°   *near-ripe*
    wheat, and hurts the poor creature of earth.

3. Greedy. Young pelicans were reputed to feed on blood from the wounds they made in their mother's breast; in some versions, they first killed their father.
4. A fragment of an old rhyme, followed by hunting cries or a ballad refrain; "Pillicock" was both a term of endearment and a euphemism for "penis."
5. *obey . . . array:* these are fragments from the Ten Commandments.
6. Favors from his mistress. In Petrarchan poetry, wooers are "servants" to their ladies.
7. And had more women than the Turkish sultan had in his royal harem.
8. Creaking shoes were a fashionable affectation.
9. Punning on the French *foutre* ("fuck").

1. Slits in skirts or petticoats.
2. These phrases are probably snatches from songs and proverbs. *Dolphin:* dauphin; the heir to the French throne, sometimes identified with the devil by the English.
3. Civet, in Shakespeare's time the major source of musk for perfume.
4. Naked; without the trappings of civilization.
5. A devil drawn from folk beliefs but famous for his prominent place in Samuel Harsnett's *Declaration of Egregious Popish Impostures* (1603); the frequent borrowings from Harsnett in *King Lear* set the earliest possible composition date for the play.
6. *web and the pin:* cataract.

Swithold footed thrice the old,[7]
He met the night mare and her nine-fold;[8]
110 Bid her alight and her troth plight,°   *and gave her word*
And aroint thee,° witch, aroint thee.   *begone*
KENT   How fares your grace?
LEAR   What's° he?   *Who's*
KENT   Who's there? What is't you seek?
115 GLOUCESTER   What are you there? Your names?
EDGAR   Poor Tom, that eats the swimming frog, the toad, the
tadpole, the wall-newt, and the water,° that in the fury of his   *water newt*
heart, when the foul fiend rages, eats cow dung for salads,
swallows the old rat and the ditch dog,[9] drinks the green
120 mantle° of the standing pool, who is whipped from tithing°   *scum / parish*
to tithing and stocked,° punished, and imprisoned, who hath   *put in stocks*
three suits to his back, six shirts to his body.
Horse to ride, and weapon to wear.
But mice and rats and such small deer[1]
125 Have been Tom's food for seven long year.
Beware my follower! Peace, Smulkin!° Peace, thou fiend.   *(a Harsnett devil)*
GLOUCESTER   What, hath your grace no better company?
EDGAR   The Prince of Darkness is a gentleman. Modo he's
called and Mahu.[2]
130 GLOUCESTER   Our flesh and blood, my lord, is grown so vile
That it doth hate what gets° it.   *begets*
EDGAR   Poor Tom's a-cold.
GLOUCESTER   Go in with me. My duty cannot suffer°   *permit me*
T'obey in all your daughters' hard commands.
135 Though their injunction be to bar my doors
And let this tyrannous night take hold upon you,
Yet have I ventured to come seek you out
And bring you where both fire and food is ready.
LEAR   First let me talk with this philosopher.
140 [*to* EDGAR] What is the cause of thunder?
KENT   Good my lord, take his offer;
Go into th' house.
LEAR   I'll talk a word with this same learned Theban.°   *(Greek sage)*
What is your study?°   *field of expertise*
145 EDGAR   How to prevent the fiend and to kill vermin.
LEAR   Let me ask you one word in private.
KENT [*to* GLOUCESTER]   Importune him once more to go, my lord,
His wits begin t'unsettle.
GLOUCESTER   Canst thou blame him?
      Storm still.
His daughters seek his death. Ah, that good Kent,
150 He said it would be thus, poor banished man!
Thou sayest the King grows mad. I'll tell thee, friend,
I am almost mad myself. I had a son,
Now outlawed° from my blood. He sought my life   *disowned*

---

7. St. Swithin (or Withold), an early English saint famous for healing, traversed the hilly countryside three times. *old:* wold; uplands.
8. *night mare:* a demon, not necessarily in the shape of a horse; *nine-fold* might suggest an entourage of demons and familiars, or the many folds (coils) of a snake.

9. A dog found dead in a ditch.
1. *deer:* animals. These verses are adapted from a romance popular in Shakespeare's time, *Bevis of Hampton.*
2. Modo and Mahu, more Harsnett devils, were commanding generals of the hellish troops.

But lately, very late.° I loved him, friend,   *recently*
155 No father his son dearer. True to tell thee,
The grief hath crazed my wits. What a night's this?
I do beseech your grace—
LEAR   Oh, cry you mercy,° sir.   *beg your pardon*
—Noble philosopher, your company.
EDGAR   Tom's a-cold.
GLOUCESTER [*to* EDGAR]   In, fellow, there: into th' hovel.
160   Keep thee warm.
LEAR   Come, let's in all.
KENT   This way, my lord.
LEAR   With him
I will keep still, with my philosopher.
KENT [*to* GLOUCESTER]   Good my lord, soothe° him.   *humor*
Let him take the fellow.
GLOUCESTER   Take him you on.°   *on ahead*
165 KENT   Sirrah, come on. Go along with us.
LEAR   Come, good Athenian.°   *Greek philosopher*
GLOUCESTER   No words, no words, hush.
EDGAR   Child Rowland³ to the dark tower came,
His word° was still° "Fie, fo, and fum;   *motto / always*
170 I smell the blood of a British⁴ man."   *Exeunt.*

3.5

Enter CORNWALL *and* EDMUND.
CORNWALL   I will have my revenge ere I depart his house.
EDMUND   How, my lord I may be censured,° that nature° thus   *judged / kinship*
gives way to loyalty, something fears me° to think of.   *I am somewhat afraid*
5 CORNWALL   I now perceive it was not altogether your brother's
evil disposition made him seek his° death, but a provoking   *(Gloucester's)*
merit set a-work by a reproveable badness in himself.¹
EDMUND   How malicious is my fortune that I must repent to
be just! This is the letter which he spoke of, which approves
him an intelligent party to the advantages of France.²
10 O heavens, that this treason were not, or not I the detector.
CORNWALL   Go with me to the Duchess.
EDMUND   If the matter of this paper be certain, you have mighty
business in hand.
CORNWALL   True or false, it hath made thee Earl of Glouces-
15 ter. Seek out where thy father is that he may be ready for our
apprehension.°   *arrest*
EDMUND [*aside*]   If I find him comforting the King, it will
stuff his° suspicion more fully. [*to* CORNWALL] I will per-   *(Cornwall's)*
severe in my course of loyalty, though the conflict be sore
20 between that and my blood.°   *filial duty*
CORNWALL   I will lay trust upon thee, and thou shalt find a
dear father in my love.   *Exeunt.*

---

3. *Child*: an aspirant to knighthood. Roland is the
famous hero of the Charlemagne legends.
4. "An Englishman" usually appears in this rhyme
from the cycle of tales of which "Jack and the
Beanstalk" is the best known. The alteration befits
Lear's ancient Britain.
3.5 Location: At Gloucester's castle.

1. *a provoking . . . himself*: Gloucester's own wickedness deservedly triggered the blameworthy evil in
Edgar.
2. *which . . . France*: which proves him a spy and an
informer in the aid of France; "party," or faction, was
usually a term of opprobrium in the Renaissance.

3.6

Enter KENT *[disguised as Caius] and* GLOUCESTER.

GLOUCESTER Here is better than the open air; take it thank-
fully. I will piece out° the comfort with what addition I can.   *augment*
I will not be long from you.

KENT All the power of his wits have given way to his impa-
5   tience.[1] The gods° reward your kindness.   *May the gods*

Exit [GLOUCESTER].

Enter LEAR, EDGAR *[disguised as Poor Tom,]*
and FOOL.

EDGAR Fraterretto° calls me and tells me Nero is an angler in   *(a Harsnett devil)*
the lake of darkness.[2] Pray, innocent, and beware the foul
fiend.

FOOL Prithee, nuncle, tell me whether a madman be a gentle-
10   man or a yeoman.[3]

LEAR A king, a king.

FOOL No, he's a yeoman that has a gentleman to° his son, for   *for*
he's a mad yeoman that sees his son a gentleman before him.

LEAR To have a thousand with red burning spits
15   Come hizzing in upon 'em.

15.1   EDGAR *The foul fiend bites my back.*[4]

FOOL *He's mad that trusts in the tameness of a wolf, a*
horse's health, a boy's love, or a whore's oath.

LEAR *It shall be done; I will arraign° them straight.°*   *prosecute / immediately*
15.5   *[to* EDGAR*] Come, sit thou here, most learned Justice.*
[to the FOOL*] Thou, sapient sir, sit here —No, you she-foxes—*

EDGAR *Look where he stands and glares. Want'st thou*
eyes° at trial, madam?   *observers*
[Sings.]   Come o'er the broom, Bessy, to me.[5]

15.10 FOOL *[sings]   Her boat hath a leak,*[6]
And she must not speak,
Why she dares not come over to thee.

EDGAR *The foul fiend haunts poor Tom in the voice of a*
nightingale. Hoppedance° cries in Tom's belly for two   *(a demon)*
15.15 *white° herring. Croak° not, black angel. I have no food*   *fresh / Growl*
for thee.

KENT *[to* LEAR*] How do you, sir? Stand you not so amazed.*
Will you lie down and rest upon the cushions?

LEAR *I'll see their trial first: bring in their evidence.*
15.20 *[to* EDGAR*] Thou robèd man of justice, take thy place,*
[to the FOOL*] And thou, his yokefellow of equity,°*   *partner of law*
Bench° by his side. You are o'th' commission:° sit you too.   *Sit / judiciary*

EDGAR *Let us deal justly.*
[Sings.]   Sleepest or wakest, thou jolly shepherd?
15.25 *Thy sheep be in the corn,°*   *grain*
And for one blast of thy minikin° mouth,   *dainty*
Thy sheep shall take no harm.

3.6 Location: Within an outbuilding of Gloucester's.
1. Rage; inability to bear more suffering.
2. In Chaucer's *Monk's Tale*, the infamously cruel
Roman emperor Nero is found fishing in hell (lines
485–86).
3. A free landowner but not a member of the gentry,
lacking official family arms and the distinctions they
confer. Shakespeare seems to have procured a coat of
arms for his father in 1596.

4. TEXTUAL COMMENT Lear's "mock-trial" of Goneril
and Regan, in absentia, appears only in Q1 (3.6.12
–48). The trial does not appear in F and was probably
cut by Shakespeare rather than omitted due to a
printer's error. See Digital Edition TC 4 (combined
text).
5. From an old song. *broom:* a small stream.
6. She has venereal disease.

Purr, the cat is gray.[7]

LEAR *Arraign her first: 'tis Goneril, I here take my oath*
15.30 *before this honorable assembly, kicked the poor King*
her father.

FOOL *Come hither, mistress. Is your name Goneril?*

LEAR *She cannot deny it.*

FOOL *Cry you mercy, I took you for a joint-stool.*[8]

15.35 LEAR *And here's another whose warped looks proclaim*
What store° *her heart is made on.°* *Stop her there.*　　　　　material / of
Arms, arms, sword, fire, corruption in the place!
False Justicer, why hast thou let her scape?

EDGAR Bless thy five wits.

KENT Oh, pity. Sir, where is the patience now
That you so oft have boasted to retain?

EDGAR [*aside*] My tears begin to take his part so much
20 They mar my counterfeiting.

LEAR The little dogs and all,°　　　　　Even the little dogs
Trey, Blanche, and Sweetheart, see, they bark at me.

EDGAR Tom will throw his head at° them. Avaunt,° you curs!　will threaten (?) / Begone
Be thy mouth or° black or white,　　　　　either
25 Tooth that poisons° if it bite,　　　　　gives rabies
Mastiff, greyhound, mongrel grim,
Hound or spaniel, brach,° or him,　　　　　bitch
Or bobtail tyke, or trundle tail,[9]
Tom will make him weep and wail;
30 For with throwing thus my head,
Dogs leapt the hatch[1] and all are fled.
Do, de, de, de. Sessa.[2] Come, march to wakes,° and fairs, and　parish festivals
market towns. Poor Tom, thy horn is dry.[3]

LEAR Then let them anatomize° Regan, see what breeds about　dissect
35 her heart. Is there any cause in nature that makes these
hard hearts? [*to* EDGAR] You, sir, I entertain° for one of my　retain
hundred, only I do not like the fashion of your garments.
You will say they are Persian,° but let them be changed.　oriental; splendid

KENT Now, good my lord, lie here and rest awhile.

40 LEAR Make no noise, make no noise. Draw the curtains,° so,　bed curtains
so. We'll go to supper i'th' morning.

FOOL And I'll go to bed at noon.

Enter GLOUCESTER.

GLOUCESTER Come hither, friend. Where is the King my master?

KENT Here, sir, but trouble him not. His wits are gone.

45 GLOUCESTER Good friend, I prithee, take him in thy arms.
I have o'erheard a plot of death upon° him.　　　　　against
There is a litter ready: lay him in't
And drive toward Dover, friend, where thou shalt meet
Both welcome and protection. Take up thy master;
50 If thou shouldst dally half an hour, his life
With thine and all that offer to defend him

---

7. Purr the cat is another devil; such devils in the
shape of cats were the familiars of witches.
8. I beg your pardon, I mistook you for a stool. An
idiom of the day expressing annoyance at being
slighted. Here the part of Goneril is actually being
played by a stool.
9. Short-tailed mongrel, or long-tailed.

1. Dogs leap over the lower half of a divided door.
2. Apparently nonsense, although "Sessa" may be a
version of the French *cessez* ("stop" or "hush").
3. A begging formula that refers to the horn vessel
that vagabonds carried for drink; the covert sense is
that Edgar has run out of Bedlamite inspiration.

Stand in assurèd loss.° Take up, take up,　　　　　　　　　　*Are certainly doomed*
And follow me, that will to some provision
Give thee quick conduct.[4]

54.1　　KENT　*Oppressed nature sleeps.*
　　　　This rest might yet have balmed° thy broken sinews,°　　　*soothed / nerves*
　　　　Which, if convenience will not allow,
　　　　Stand in hard cure.° [to the FOOL] *Come, help to bear*　　　*Will be hard to cure*
　　　　　　thy master.
54.5　　　*Thou must not stay behind.*

55　　GLOUCESTER　*Come, come away.*　　　*Exeunt [all but* EDGAR].

55.1　　EDGAR　*When we our betters see bearing our° woes,*　　　　*our same*
　　　　We scarcely think our miseries our foes.
　　　　Who alone suffers, suffers most i'th' mind,
　　　　Leaving free° things and happy shows° behind.　　　*carefree / scenes*
55.5　　*But then the mind much sufferance doth o'er-skip,*
　　　　When grief hath mates and bearing° fellowship.　　　*pain; suffering*
　　　　How light and portable my pain seems now,
　　　　When that which makes me bend makes the King bow:
　　　　He° childed as I fathered. Tom, away.　　　　　　　*He is*
55.10　　*Mark the high noises° and thyself bewray°*　　　*important rumors / reveal*
　　　　When false opinion, whose wrong thoughts defile thee,
　　　　In thy just proof repeals and reconciles thee.[5]
　　　　What° will hap° more tonight, safe scape the King.　　　*Whatever / chance*
　　　　Lurk, lurk.　　　　　　　　　　　　[Exit.]

3.7

Enter CORNWALL, REGAN, GONERIL, [EDMUND *the*]
bastard, and SERVANTS.

CORNWALL [*to* GONERIL]　Post° speedily to my lord, your hus-　　*Ride*
band; show him this letter. The army of France is landed.
[*to* SERVANTS] Seek out the traitor Gloucester.
　　　　　　　　　　　　　[*Exeunt* SERVANTS.]

REGAN　Hang him instantly.
5　GONERIL　Pluck out his eyes.

CORNWALL　Leave him to my displeasure. Edmund, keep you
our sister° company. The revenges we are bound[1] to take　　*sister-in-law*
upon your traitorous father are not fit for your beholding.
Advise the Duke where you are going to a most festinate
10　preparation.[2] We are bound° to the like. Our posts° shall be　*committed / messengers*
swift and intelligent° betwixt us. Farewell, dear sister. Fare-　*well informed*
well, my lord of Gloucester.
　　　　Enter [Oswald the] STEWARD.
How now? Where's the King?

STEWARD　My lord of Gloucester hath conveyed him hence.
15　Some five- or six-and-thirty of his° knights,　　　　　　*(Lear's)*
Hot questrists° after him, met him at gate,　　　　　　*searchers*
Who, with some other of the lord's° dependents,　　　　*(Gloucester's)*
Are gone with him toward Dover, where they boast
To have well-armed friends.

20　CORNWALL　Get horses for your mistress.

---

4. *that . . . conduct:* who will quickly guide you to
some supplies.
5. *In . . . thee:* When true evidence pardons you and
reconciles you (with your father).

3.7 Location: At Gloucester's castle.
1. Bound by duty; expected by destiny.
2. *Advise . . . preparation:* When you reach Albany,
tell the Duke to prepare quickly.

GONERIL Farewell, sweet lord and sister.
CORNWALL Edmund, farewell.

Exeunt GONERIL [*and* EDMUND].

Go seek the traitor Gloucester;
Pinion him° like a thief, bring him before us.   *Tie his arms*
Though well we may not pass° upon his life   *pass sentence*
25 Without the form° of justice, yet our power   *official proceedings*
Shall do a court'sy³ to our wrath, which men
May blame but not control.

Enter GLOUCESTER *and* SERVANTS.

Who's there? The traitor?
REGAN Ingrateful fox, 'tis he.
CORNWALL   Bind fast his corky° arms.   *withered*
GLOUCESTER What means your graces? Good my friends,
    consider
30 You are my guests. Do me no foul play, friends.
CORNWALL Bind him, I say.

[SERVANTS *bind* GLOUCESTER.]

REGAN   Hard, hard! O filthy traitor!
GLOUCESTER Unmerciful lady, as you are, I'm none.
CORNWALL To this chair bind him. —Villain, thou shalt find—
GLOUCESTER By the kind gods, 'tis most ignobly done
35 To pluck me by the beard.°   *(an extreme insult)*
REGAN So white° and such a traitor?   *white-haired; venerable*
GLOUCESTER   Naughty° lady,   *Wicked*
These hairs which thou dost ravish from my chin
Will quicken° and accuse thee. I am your host;   *come alive*
With robbers' hands my hospitable favors°   *features*
40 You should not ruffle° thus. What will you do?   *snatch at*
CORNWALL Come, sir, what letters had you late° from France?   *lately*
REGAN Be simple-answered,° for we know the truth.   *straightforward*
CORNWALL And what confederacy have you with the traitors
Late footed° in the kingdom?   *Recently on the move*
REGAN   To whose hands
45 You have sent the lunatic King? Speak.
GLOUCESTER I have a letter guessingly set down⁴
Which came from one that's of a neutral heart
And not from one opposed.
CORNWALL   Cunning.
REGAN   And false.
CORNWALL Where hast thou sent the King?
50 GLOUCESTER To Dover.
REGAN Wherefore° to Dover?   *Why*
Wast thou not charged° at peril—   *commanded*
CORNWALL Wherefore to Dover? Let him answer that.
GLOUCESTER I am tied to th' stake, and I must stand the
    course.⁵
55 REGAN Wherefore to Dover?
GLOUCESTER Because I would not see thy cruel nails
Pluck out his poor old eyes, nor thy fierce sister

3. Shall allow a courtesy or an indulgence; shall bow to.
4. Written without confirmation; speculative.
5. An image from bearbaiting, in which a bear on a
short tether had to fight off an assault by dogs.

In his anointed[6] flesh stick boarish fangs.
The sea, with such a storm as his bare head
60 In hell-black night endured, would have buoyed° up   *risen*
And quenched the stellèd° fires.   *stars'*
Yet poor old heart, he holp° the heavens to rain.   *helped*
If wolves had at thy gate howled that stern° time,   *dreary; dreadful*
Thou shouldst have said, "Good porter, turn the key,°   *(to open the door)*
65 All cruels else subscribe."[7] But I shall see
The wingèd vengeance[8] overtake such children.
CORNWALL   See't shalt thou never. Fellows,° hold the chair.   *Servants*
    —Upon these eyes of thine, I'll set my foot.
        [*He plucks out Gloucester's eye.*]
GLOUCESTER   He that will think° to live till he be old,   *Whoever hopes*
70 Give me some help! —Oh, cruel! O you gods!
REGAN   One side will mock another: th'other too.
CORNWALL   If you see vengeance—
FIRST SERVANT   Hold your hand, my lord.
I have served you ever since I was a child,
But better service have I never done you
Than now to bid you hold.
75 REGAN   How now, you dog?
FIRST SERVANT   If you did wear a beard upon your chin,
I'd shake it on this quarrel.[9] What do you mean?°   *intend*
CORNWALL [*drawing his sword*]   My villein?°   *servant; villain*
FIRST SERVANT   Nay, then, come on and take the chance of
    anger.[1]
        [*They fight, and* CORNWALL *is wounded.*]
80 REGAN   Give me thy sword. A peasant stand up thus?
        [*She*] *kills him.*
FIRST SERVANT   Oh, I am slain! [*to* GLOUCESTER] My lord, you
    have one eye left
To see some mischief° on him. Oh!   *injury*
    [*He dies.*]
CORNWALL   Lest it see more, prevent it. Out, vile jelly![2]
        [*He plucks out Gloucester's other eye.*]
Where is thy luster now?
85 GLOUCESTER   All dark and comfortless?
Where's my son Edmund?
Edmund, enkindle all the sparks of nature[3]
To quit° this horrid act.   *requite; avenge*
REGAN   Out, treacherous villain!
Thou call'st on him that hates thee. It was he
90 That made the overture of° thy treasons to us,   *revealed*
Who is too good to pity thee.
GLOUCESTER   Oh, my follies! Then Edgar was abused!°   *slandered*
Kind gods, forgive me that, and prosper him.
REGAN   Go, thrust him out at gates, and let him smell
95 His way to Dover. How is't, my lord? How look you?°   *How do you feel*

---

6. Consecrated with holy oils (as part of a king's coronation).
7. All other beasts would have pity, but not you; I can accept the cruelty of all creatures, but not yours.
8. Swift or heaven-sent revenge; either an angel of God or the Furies, who were flying executors of divine vengeance in classical mythology.
9. I'd pluck it over this point; I'd issue a challenge.

1. Take the risk of fighting when angry; take the fortune of one who is governed by his anger.
2. PERFORMANCE COMMENT Should a production minimize gore in this shocking scene, or emphasize it? For the implications of the staging, see Digital Edition PC 4.
3. All the warmth of filial love; all the anger that your father has received such treatment.

CORNWALL   I have received a hurt. Follow me, lady.
[*to* SERVANTS] Turn out that eyeless villain. Throw this slave
Upon the dunghill.
                    Exeunt [Servants] with GLOUCESTER
                              [*and First Servant's body*].
Regan, I bleed apace;
Untimely comes this hurt. Give me your arm.
                    *Exeunt [*CORNWALL *with* REGAN].[4]

99.1   SECOND SERVANT   *I'll never care what wickedness I do if*
       this man come to good.[5]
       THIRD SERVANT   *If she live long, and in the end meet the*   usual
       old° *course of death, women will all turn monsters.*
99.5   SECOND SERVANT   *Let's follow the old Earl and get the*
       Bedlam° *to lead him where he would. His madness*   madman
       allows itself to anything.
       THIRD SERVANT   *Go thou. I'll fetch some flax and whites of*
       eggs to apply to his bleeding face. Now, heaven help him!
                              Exeunt [severally].°   separately

4.1

Enter EDGAR [*disguised as Poor Tom*].
EDGAR   Yet better thus and known to be contemned°   despised
Than still° contemned and flattered. To be worst,   always
The lowest and most dejected thing of fortune
Stands still in esperance, lives not in fear.[1]
5   The lamentable change is from the best,
The worst returns to laughter.[2] Welcome, then,
Thou unsubstantial air that I embrace.
The wretch that thou hast blown unto the worst
Owes nothing° to thy blasts.   (*because he can't pay*)
                    Enter GLOUCESTER *and an* OLD MAN.
10   But who comes here? My father, poorly led?
World, world, O world!
But that thy strange mutations make us hate thee,
Life would not yield to age.[3]
OLD MAN   O my good lord, I have been your tenant
15   And your father's tenant these fourscore years.
GLOUCESTER   Away, get thee away! Good friend, be gone.
Thy comforts° can do me no good at all;   assistance
Thee, they may hurt.
OLD MAN   You cannot see your way.
GLOUCESTER   I have no way and therefore want no eyes.
20   I stumbled when I saw. Full oft 'tis seen
Our means secure us, and our mere defects
Prove our commodities.[4] O dear son Edgar,
The food° of thy abusèd° father's wrath,   *fuel; prey / despised*

---

4. TEXTUAL COMMENT Some critics have called the play's blinding scene the "cruelest" in all of English literature. Yet the two texts differ in their portrayals of this cruelty. Notably, the Quarto version culminates with Cornwall's two servants pledging to avenge Gloucester's blinding. Their absence in the Folio version denies the audience even this brief expression of sympathy. See Digital Edition TC 5 (combined text).
5. *I'll . . . good:* because this may be a sign that evil goes unpunished. *this man:* Cornwall.
4.1 Location: Open country.

1. *Stands . . . fear:* Remains in hope ("esperance") because there is no fear of falling further.
2. *The lamentable . . . laughter:* The change to be lamented is one that alters the best of circumstances; the worst luck can only improve.
3. *But . . . age:* If there were no strange reversals of fortune to make the world hateful, we would not consent to aging and death.
4. *Our means . . . commodities:* Our wealth makes us overconfident, and our utter deprivation proves to be beneficial.

Might I but live to see thee in° my touch,   *through*
I'd say I had eyes again.
25   OLD MAN   How now? Who's there?
EDGAR [*aside*]   O gods! Who is't can say, "I am at the worst"?
I am worse than e'er I was.
OLD MAN   'Tis poor mad Tom.
EDGAR [*aside*]   And worse I may be yet; the worst is not
So long as we can say, "This is the worst."
OLD MAN   Fellow, where goest?
30   GLOUCESTER   Is it a beggar man?
OLD MAN   Madman and beggar too.
GLOUCESTER   He has some reason, else he could not beg.
I'th' last night's storm, I such a fellow saw
Which made me think a man a worm. My son
35   Came then into my mind, and yet my mind
Was then scarce friends with him.
I have heard more since.
As flies to wanton° boys are we to th' gods: *playful; careless*
They kill us for their sport.
EDGAR [*aside*]   How should this be?
40   Bad is the trade that must play fool to sorrow,[5]
Ang'ring itself and others. [*to* GLOUCESTER] Bless thee,
master.
GLOUCESTER   Is that the naked fellow?
OLD MAN   Ay, my lord.
GLOUCESTER   Get thee away. If for my sake
Thou wilt o'ertake us hence a mile or twain
45   I'th' way toward Dover, do it for ancient love,[6]
And bring some covering for this naked soul,
Which I'll entreat to lead me.
OLD MAN   Alack, sir, he is mad.
GLOUCESTER   'Tis the time's plague when[7] madmen lead the
blind.
Do as I bid thee, or rather do thy pleasure.
50   Above the rest, be gone.
OLD MAN   I'll bring him the best 'parrel° that I have,   *apparel; clothing*
Come on't what will.   *Exit.*
GLOUCESTER   Sirrah, naked fellow—
EDGAR   Poor Tom's a-cold. [*aside*] I cannot daub it further.[8]
55   GLOUCESTER   Come hither, fellow.
EDGAR [*aside*]   And yet I must. —Bless thy sweet eyes, they
bleed.
GLOUCESTER   Know'st thou the way to Dover?
EDGAR   Both stile and gate, horse-way and footpath. Poor
60   Tom hath been scared out of his good wits. Bless thee, goodman's° son, from the foul fiend.   *householder's*
61.1   *Five fiends have been in*
poor Tom at once: of lust, as Obidicut; Hobbididence,
prince of dumbness; Mahu of stealing; Modo of mur-
der; Stiberdigebit of mopping and mowing,[9] *who since*
61.5   *possesses chambermaids and waiting women. So bless*
thee, master.

---

5. It is a bad business to have to play the fool in the
face of sorrow.
6. For the sake of our long and loyal relationship (as
master and servant).

7. The time is truly sick when.
8. I cannot continue the charade. *daub:* mask, plaster.
9. Grimacing and making faces.

GLOUCESTER   Here, take this purse, thou whom the heav'ns'
    plagues
    Have humbled to all strokes.° That I am wretched   *to accept all blows*
    Makes thee the happier. Heavens deal so still.°   *always*
65   Let the superfluous and lust-dieted man,[1]
    That slaves° your ordinance,° that will not see   *defers to / authority*
    Because he does not feel, feel your power quickly.
    So distribution should undo excess,
    And each man have enough. Dost thou know Dover?
70 EDGAR   Ay, master.
    GLOUCESTER   There is a cliff whose high and bending° head   *overhanging*
    Looks fearfully in the confinèd deep.[2]
    Bring me but to the very brim of it,
    And I'll repair the misery thou dost bear
75   With something rich about me. From that place
    I shall no leading need.
    EDGAR   Give me thy arm;
    Poor Tom shall lead thee.   *Exeunt.*

4.2

Enter GONERIL, [EDMUND *the*] *bastard, and* [Oswald
the] STEWARD.

GONERIL   Welcome, my lord. I marvel our mild husband
    Not° met us on the way. [*to* STEWARD] Now, where's your   *Has not*
    master?
    STEWARD   Madam, within, but never man so changed.
    I told him of the army that was landed:
5   He smiled at it. I told him you were coming.
    His answer was, "The worse." Of Gloucester's treachery,
    And of the loyal service of his son,
    When I informed him, then he called me "sot"°   *fool*
    And told me I had turned the wrong side out.[1]
10   What most he should dislike seems pleasant to him;
    What like, offensive.
    GONERIL [*to* EDMUND]   Then shall you go no further.
    It is the cowish° terror of his spirit   *cowardly*
    That dares not undertake. He'll not feel wrongs
    Which tie him to an answer.[2] Our wishes on the way
15   May prove effects.[3] Back, Edmund, to my brother;°   *brother-in-law*
    Hasten his musters° and conduct his powers.°   *call-up of troops / armies*
    I must change names° at home and give the distaff[4]   *exchange roles*
    Into my husband's hands. This trusty servant
    Shall pass between us. Ere long you are like° to hear—   *likely*
20   If you dare venture in your own behalf—
    A mistress's° command. Wear this; spare speech;   *(playing on "lover's")*
    Decline your head. This kiss, if it durst speak,
    Would stretch thy spirits up into the air.
    Conceive,° and fare thee well.   *Understand my meaning*
    EDMUND   Yours in° the ranks of death.   *Exit.*   *even in*

---

1. Let the overprosperous man who indulges his
appetite.
2. Looks fearsomely into the straits below.
4.2 Location: Before Albany's castle.
1. I had reversed things (by mistaking loyalty for
treachery).

2. *He'll . . . answer:* He'll ignore insults that would
provoke him to retaliate.
3. May be put into action.
4. A device used in spinning and thus emblematic of
the female role. To "change names," therefore, is to
swap the marking of male and female identities.

25   GONERIL   My most dear Gloucester!
      Oh, the difference of man and man!
      To thee a woman's services are due;
      My fool usurps my body.[5]

      STEWARD   Madam, here comes my lord.   [*Exit.*]
            Enter ALBANY.

      GONERIL   I have been worth the whistle.[6]

30   ALBANY   O Goneril,
      You are not worth the dust which the rude wind
      Blows in your face.

32.1   *I fear your disposition.*
            That nature which contemns i'th' origin°   despises its origin
            Cannot be bordered certain° in itself.   be defended securely
            She that herself will sliver and disbranch°   split
32.5   *From her material sap, perforce must wither*
            And come to deadly use.[7]

      GONERIL   *No more, the text is foolish.*

      ALBANY   *Wisdom and goodness to the vile seem vile;*
            Filths savor but themselves. What have you done?
32.10   *Tigers, not daughters, what have you performed?*
            A father and a gracious agèd man,
            Whose reverence even the head-lugged° bear would lick,   dragged by the head
            Most barbarous, most degenerate, have you madded.°   driven mad
            Could my good brother° suffer you to do it?   brother-in-law
32.15   *A man, a prince, by him so benefited!*
            If that the heavens do not their visible spirits
            Send quickly down to tame the vile offenses,
            It will come.
            Humanity must perforce° prey on itself   inevitably
32.20   *Like monsters of the deep.*

      GONERIL   Milk-livered° man,   Cowardly
      That bear'st a cheek for blows, a head for wrongs,[8]
35   Who hast not in thy brows an eye discerning
      Thine honor from thy suffering,[9]

36.1   *that not know'st*
            Fools do those villains pity who are punished
            Ere they have done their mischief. Where's thy drum?°   (to muster troops)
            France spreads his banners in our noiseless° land   peaceful
36.5   *With plumèd helm. Thy state begins thereat*
            Whilst thou, a moral° fool, sits still and cries,   moralizing
            "Alack, why does he so?"

      ALBANY   See thyself, devil!
      Proper deformity seems not in the fiend
      So horrid as in woman.[1]

      GONERIL   O vain° fool!   useless

39.1   ALBANY   *Thou changèd, and self-covered[2] thing, for shame!*
            Bemonster not thy feature. Were't my fitness°   If it were appropriate

5. My idiot husband presumes to possess me.
6. At one time, you would have come to welcome me home; referring to the proverb "It is a poor dog that is not worth the whistling."
7. *She . . . use:* The allusion is probably biblical: "But that which beareth thorns and briers is reproved, and is near unto cursing; whose end is to be burned" (Hebrews 6:8). *come to deadly use:* be destroyed; be used for burning.
8. *for wrongs:* fit for abuse; ready for cuckold's horns.

9. *discerning . . . suffering:* that can distinguish between an insult to your honor and something you should patiently endure.
1. *Proper . . . woman:* Deformity (of morals) is appropriate in the devil and so less horrid than in woman, from whom virtue is expected. Albany may hold a mirror in front of Goneril, since Jacobean women sometimes wore small mirrors attached to their dresses.
2. Altered and with your true (womanly) self concealed.

To let these hands obey my blood,
They are apt enough to dislocate and tear
39.5 *Thy flesh and bones. Howe'er° thou art a fiend,* Although
A woman's shape doth shield thee.
GONERIL   *Marry, your manhood, mew*[3]—
Enter a GENTLEMAN.[4]
ALBANY   *What news?*
40 MESSENGER   O my good lord, the Duke of Cornwall's dead,
Slain by his servant, going to put out
The other eye of Gloucester.
ALBANY   Gloucester's eyes?
MESSENGER   A servant that he bred, thrilled with remorse,°   shaken with pity
Opposed against the act, bending° his sword   directing
45 To° his great master, who, threat-enragèd,   Against
Flew on him and amongst them felled him dead,
But not without that harmful stroke which since
Hath plucked him after.[5]
ALBANY   This shows you are above,
You justices,° that these our nether crimes[6]   Judges
50 So speedily can venge. But oh, poor Gloucester!
Lost he his other eye?
MESSENGER   Both, both, my lord.
This letter, madam, craves a speedy answer:
'Tis from your sister.
GONERIL [*aside*]   One way I like this well:[7]
But being° widow, and my Gloucester with her,   her being
55 May all the building in my fancy pluck
Upon my hateful life.[8] Another way
The news is not so tart.° I'll read and answer.   bitter
ALBANY   Where was his son when they did take his eyes?
MESSENGER   Come with my lady hither.
ALBANY   He is not here.
60 MESSENGER   No, my good lord, I met him back° again.   returning
ALBANY   Knows he the wickedness?
MESSENGER   Ay, my good lord. 'Twas he informed against him
And quit the house on purpose, that their punishment
Might have the freer course.
ALBANY   Gloucester, I live
65 To thank thee for the love thou showed'st the King
And to revenge thine eyes. Come hither, friend;
Tell me what more thou know'st.   *Exeunt.*

4.3

Enter KENT [*disguised as Caius*] *and a* GENTLEMAN.
KENT   *Why the King of France is so suddenly gone back,*
know you no reason?
GENTLEMAN   *Something he left imperfect° in the state,*   unsettled
which since his coming forth is thought of,° which   remembered

3. Assert your feeble masculinity (with a derisive catcall, "mew"). Alternatively, get control of your manhood; restrain ("mew") it. *Marry:* By the Virgin Mary.
4. Q's Gentleman becomes a Messenger in F.
5. Has sent him to follow his servant into death.
6. Lower crimes, and so committed on earth, but

also suggesting that the deeds smack of the netherworld of hell.
7. Because a political rival has been eliminated.
8. *May . . . life:* May pull down all of my built-up fantasies and thus make my life hateful.
4.3 Location: Near the French camp at Dover.

5 imports° to the kingdom so much fear and danger that   *portends*
    his personal return was most required and necessary.
KENT   Who hath he left behind him general?
GENTLEMAN   The Marshal of France, Monsieur la Far.
KENT   Did your letters pierce the Queen to any demon-
10   stration of grief?
GENTLEMAN   I say she took them, read them in my presence,
    And now and then an ample tear trilled down
    Her delicate cheek. It seemed she was a queen
    Over her passion, who,° most rebel-like,   *which*
    Sought to be king o'er her.
15 KENT   Oh, then, it moved her.
GENTLEMAN   Not to a rage. Patience and sorrow stream
    Who should express her goodliest.[1] You have seen
    Sunshine and rain at once; her smiles and tears
    Were like a° better way. Those happy smilets   *Were similar in a*
20   That played on her ripe lip seem not to know
    What guests were in her eyes, which parted thence
    As pearls from diamonds dropped. In brief,
    Sorrow would be a rarity° most beloved,   *gem*
    If all could so become it.[2]
25 KENT   Made she no verbal question?
GENTLEMAN   Faith, once or twice she heaved the name
      of father
    Pantingly forth, as if it pressed her heart,
    Cried, "Sisters, sisters, shame of ladies, sisters!
    Kent, father, sisters! What, i'th' storm, i'th' night?
30   Let pity not be believed."[3] There she shook
    The holy water from her heavenly eyes,
    And clamor° moistened her. Then away she started,°   *crying / sprang*
    To deal with grief alone.
KENT   It is the stars,
    The stars above us, govern our conditions.
35   Else one self mate and make[4] could not beget
    Such different issues.° You spoke not with her since?   *offspring*
GENTLEMAN   No.
KENT   Was this before the King returned?
GENTLEMAN   No, since.
KENT   Well, sir, the poor distressèd Lear's i'th' town,
40   Who sometime in his better tune° remembers   *state of mind*
    What we are come about, and by no means
    Will yield° to see his daughter.   *consent*
GENTLEMAN   Why, good sir?
KENT   A sovereign shame so elbows° him: his own   *prods; nudges*
      unkindness,
    That stripped her from his benediction, turned her
45   To foreign casualties,° gave her dear rights   *risks*
    To his dog-hearted daughters. These things sting his mind
    So venomously that burning shame
    Detains him from Cordelia.
GENTLEMAN   Alack, poor gentleman!

---

1. Which should best express her feelings.
2. If everyone wore it so beautifully.
3. Never believe in pity; compassion cannot exist.

4. Or else the same pair of spouses; "mate" and "make"
may describe either partner.

50   KENT   *Of Albany's and Cornwall's powers you heard not?*
    GENTLEMAN   *'Tis so, they are afoot.*
    KENT   *Well, sir, I'll bring you to our master Lear*
      And leave you to attend him. Some dear cause°   Some important reason
      Will in concealment wrap me up awhile.
55   *When I am known aright, you shall not grieve°*   regret
      Lending me this acquaintance.° I pray you   news
      Go along with me.   *Exeunt.*

4.4

Enter with drum and colors, CORDELIA, GENTLEMEN,
and Soldiers.

  CORDELIA   Alack, 'tis he. Why, he was met even now
  As mad as the vexèd sea, singing aloud.
  Crowned with rank fumitor and furrow weeds,[1]
  With burdocks, hemlock, nettles, cuckoo flowers,
5   Darnel, and all the idle° weeds that grow   useless
  In our sustaining corn. A century° send forth;   battalion (100 men)
  Search every acre in the high-grown field
  And bring him to our eye.   [*Exit a* GENTLEMAN.]
                      What can man's wisdom
  In the restoring° his bereavèd sense? He that helps him,   Do to restore
  Take all my outward° worth.   material
10   GENTLEMAN   There is means, madam.
  Our foster nurse of nature[2] is repose,
  The which he lacks. That to provoke in him
  Are many simples operative,[3] whose power
  Will close the eye of anguish.
  CORDELIA   All blest secrets,
15   All you unpublished virtues° of the earth,   obscure healing plants
  Spring with my tears; be aidant and remediate°   healing and remedial
  In the good man's desires. Seek, seek for him,
  Lest his ungoverned rage dissolve the life
  That wants° the means to lead it.   lacks
        Enter MESSENGER.
  MESSENGER   News, madam:
20   The British powers° are marching hitherward.   armies
  CORDELIA   'Tis known before. Our preparation stands
  In expectation of them. O dear father,
  It is thy business that I go about![4] Therefore great France
  My mourning and importuned° tears hath pitied.   importunate; solicitous
25   No blown° ambition doth our arms incite,   inflated
  But love, dear love, and our agèd father's right.[5]
  Soon may I hear and see him!   *Exeunt.*

4.5

Enter REGAN *and* [*Oswald the*] STEWARD.
  REGAN   But are my brother's powers° set forth?   (Albany's forces)

4.4 Location: The French camp at Dover.
1. Fumitor was used against brain sickness. Furrow weeds, like the other weeds in the following lines, grow in the furrows of plowed fields.
2. *Our . . . nature:* That which comforts and nourishes human nature.
3. *That . . . operative:* To induce that ("repose") in

him, there are many effective medicinal herbs.
4. The line echoes Christ's explanation of his mission in Luke 2:49: "I must go about my father's business."
5. *No . . . right:* 1 Corinthians 13:4–5 in the Bishops' Bible (1568) says that love "swelleth not, dealeth not dishonestly, seeketh not her own."
4.5 Location: At Gloucester's castle.

STEWARD   Ay, madam.
REGAN   Himself in person there?
STEWARD   Madam, with much ado;°   *trouble*
   Your sister is the better soldier.
REGAN   Lord Edmund spake not with your lord at home?
5 STEWARD   No, madam.
REGAN   What might import° my sister's letter to him?   *mean*
STEWARD   I know not, lady.
REGAN   Faith, he is posted° hence on serious matter—   *sent*
   It was great ignorance, Gloucester's eyes being out,
10   To let him live. Where he arrives, he moves
   All hearts against us. Edmund, I think, is gone,
   In pity of his misery,° to dispatch   *(ironic)*
   His nighted° life, moreover to descry°   *darkened / investigate*
   The strength o'th' enemy.
15 STEWARD   I must needs after° him, madam, with my letter.   *go after*
REGAN   Our troops set forth tomorrow; stay with us.
   The ways are dangerous.
STEWARD   I may not, madam:
   My lady charged° my duty in this business.   *commanded*
REGAN   Why should she write to Edmund?
20   Might not you transport her purposes by word? Belike°   *Perhaps*
   Some things—I know not what. I'll love° thee much: *reward*
   Let me unseal the letter.
STEWARD   Madam, I had rather—
REGAN   I know your lady does not love her husband.
   I am sure of that, and at her late° being here,   *recently*
25   She gave strange oeillades° and most speaking looks   *amorous glances*
   To noble Edmund. I know you are of her bosom.°   *in her confidence*
STEWARD   I, madam?
REGAN   I speak in understanding.° Y'are; I know't.   *with certainty*
   Therefore I do advise you take this note.°   *take note of this*
30   My lord is dead. Edmund and I have talked,
   And more convenient° is he for my hand   *appropriate*
   Than for your lady's. You may gather° more.   *infer*
   If you do find him, pray you give him this,[1]
   And when your mistress hears thus much from you,
35   I pray, desire her call her wisdom to her.[2]
   So, fare you well.
   If you do chance to hear of that blind traitor,
   Preferment falls on him that cuts him off.°   *cuts his life short*
STEWARD   Would I could meet, madam; I should show
   What party I do follow.
40 REGAN   Fare thee well.   *Exeunt [severally].*°   *separately*

4.6

Enter GLOUCESTER *and* EDGAR [*disguised as
a peasant*].
GLOUCESTER   When shall I come to th' top of that same° hill?   *agreed-upon*
EDGAR   You do climb up it now. Look how we labor.
GLOUCESTER   Methinks the ground is even.

---

1. This information, but possibly another letter or   2. *desire . . . to her:* tell her to come to her senses.
token.   **4.6** Location: Near Dover.

EDGAR   Horrible steep.
   Hark, do you hear the sea?
GLOUCESTER   No, truly.
5   EDGAR Why, then, your other senses grow imperfect
   By your eyes' anguish.
GLOUCESTER   So may it be indeed.
   Methinks thy voice is altered, and thou speak'st
   In better phrase and matter° than thou didst.   *sense*
EDGAR You're much deceived. In nothing am I changed
10   But in my garments.
GLOUCESTER Methinks you're better spoken.
EDGAR   Come on, sir,
   Here's the place. Stand still. How fearful
   And dizzy 'tis to cast one's eyes so low!
   The crows and choughs° that wing the midway air[1]   *jackdaws*
15   Show° scarce so gross° as beetles. Halfway down   *Appear / big*
   Hangs one that gathers samphire:° dreadful trade!   *seaweed*
   Methinks he seems no bigger than his head.
   The fishermen that walked upon the beach
   Appear like mice, and yond tall anchoring bark°   *ship*
20   Diminished to her cock;° her cock a buoy   *dinghy*
   Almost too small for sight. The murmuring surge,
   That on th'unnumbered° idle pebble chafes,   *innumerable*
   Cannot be heard so high. I'll look no more,
   Lest my brain turn and the° deficient sight   *my*
25   Topple° down headlong.   *Topple me*
GLOUCESTER Set me where you stand.
EDGAR   Give me your hand.
   You are now within a foot of th'extreme verge.
   For all beneath the moon would I not leap upright.[2]
GLOUCESTER Let go my hand.
30   Here, friend, 's another purse. In it, a jewel
   Well worth a poor man's taking. Fairies and gods
   Prosper it[3] with thee. Go thou further off.
   Bid me farewell, and let me hear thee going.
EDGAR Now, fare ye well, good sir.
GLOUCESTER   With all my heart.
35   EDGAR [*aside*] Why I do trifle thus with his despair
   Is done to cure it.
GLOUCESTER   O you mighty gods!
       [*He kneels.*]
   This world I do renounce, and in your sights
   Shake patiently my great affliction off.
   If I could bear it longer and not fall
40   To quarrel° with your great opposeless wills,   *Into conflict*
   My snuff and loathèd part of nature[4] should
   Burn itself out. If Edgar live, oh, bless him!
   Now, fellow, fare thee well.
EDGAR   Gone, sir. Farewell.
      [GLOUCESTER *falls down.*]

---

1. The air between cliff and sea.
2. I would not jump up and down (for fear of losing my balance).
3. Make it increase. Fairies were sometimes believed to hoard and multiply treasure.
4. The scorched and hateful remnant of my lifetime. *snuff*: end of a candlewick.

And yet I know not how conceit may rob
45 The treasury of life, when life itself
Yields to the theft.[5] Had he been where he thought,
By this° had thought been past. Alive or dead?[6]   *now*
[*to* GLOUCESTER] Ho, you, sir! Friend, hear you, sir? Speak.
Thus might he pass° indeed. Yet he revives.   *pass away*
—What are you, sir?
50 GLOUCESTER   Away and let me die.
EDGAR   Hadst thou been aught° but goss'mer, feathers, air,   *anything*
So many fathom down precipitating,°   *plunging*
Thou'dst shivered° like an egg. But thou dost breathe,   *shattered*
Hast heavy substance, bleed'st not, speak'st, art sound.
55 Ten masts at each° make not the altitude   *end to end*
Which thou hast perpendicularly fell.
Thy life's a miracle. Speak yet again.
GLOUCESTER   But have I fall'n or no?
EDGAR   From the dread summit of this chalky bourn.[7]
60 Look up a-height, the shrill-gorged° lark so far   *shrill-voiced*
Cannot be seen or heard. Do but look up.
GLOUCESTER   Alack, I have no eyes.
Is wretchedness deprived° that benefit   *deprived of*
To end itself by death? 'Twas yet some comfort
65 When misery could beguile° the tyrant's rage   *cheat*
And frustrate his proud will.
EDGAR   Give me your arm.
Up, so. How is't? Feel you your legs? You stand.
GLOUCESTER   Too well, too well.
EDGAR   This is above all strangeness.
Upon the crown o'th' cliff, what thing was that
Which parted from you?
70 GLOUCESTER   A poor unfortunate beggar.
EDGAR   As I stood here below, methought his eyes
Were two full moons. He had a thousand noses,
Horns whelked° and waved like the enragèd sea.   *twisted*
It was some fiend. Therefore, thou happy father,°   *lucky old man*
75 Think that the clearest° gods, who make them honors   *purest; most illustrious*
Of men's impossibilities,[8] have preserved thee.
GLOUCESTER   I do remember now. Henceforth I'll bear
Affliction till it do cry out itself,
"Enough, enough," and die. That thing you speak of,
80 I took it for a man. Often 'twould say
"The fiend, the fiend." He led me to that place.
EDGAR   Bear free and patient thoughts.
            Enter LEAR.
                                    But who comes here?
The safer sense will ne'er accommodate
His master thus.[9]

---

5. *And yet . . . theft:* Edgar worries that the imagined scenario ("conceit") he has invented may be enough to kill his father, particularly as Gloucester wishes for ("yields to") his own death.
6. PERFORMANCE COMMENT Like readers, audiences cannot initially be certain whether the cliff is "real" (within the play's fictive world) or imaginary, and the resulting tension makes for one of Shakespeare's

most fascinating scenes. See Digital Edition PC 5.
7. The white chalk cliffs of Dover, which make a boundary ("bourn") between land and sea.
8. *who . . . impossibilities:* who attain honor for themselves by performing deeds impossible to men.
9. *The . . . thus:* A sane mind would never allow its possessor to dress up in this way.

85 LEAR No, they cannot touch me° for crying. I am the King   *lay hands on me*
himself.

EDGAR [*aside*] O thou side-piercing sight!

LEAR Nature's above art in that respect.[1] There's your press
money.[2] That fellow handles his bow like a crow-keeper.[3] Draw
90 me a clothier's yard.[4] Look, look, a mouse! Peace, peace, this
piece of toasted cheese will do't.° There's my gauntlet; I'll prove   *(lure the mouse)*
it on a giant.[5] Bring up the brown bills.[6] Oh, well-flown, bird!°   *arrow*
I'th' clout,° i'th' clout! Whew. Give the word.°   *bull's-eye / password*

EDGAR Sweet marjoram.[7]

95 LEAR Pass.

GLOUCESTER I know that voice.

LEAR Ha! Goneril with a white beard? They flattered me like
a dog° and told me I had the white hairs in my beard ere the   *fawningly*
black ones were there.[8] To say "Ay" and "No" to everything
100 that I said "Ay" and "No" to was no good divinity.[9] When the
rain came to wet me once, and the wind to make me chatter,
when the thunder would not peace at my bidding, there I
found° 'em, there I smelt 'em out. Go to, they are not men   *understood*
o'their words. They told me I was everything. 'Tis a lie. I am
105 not ague-proof.°   *immune to illness*

GLOUCESTER The trick° of that voice, I do well remember.   *peculiarity*
Is't not the King?

LEAR   Ay, every inch a king!
When I do stare, see how the subject quakes.
I pardon that man's life. —What was thy cause?°   *crime*
110 Adultery? Thou shalt not die. Die for adultery?
No, the wren goes to't, and the small gilded fly
Does lecher in my sight. Let copulation thrive,
For Gloucester's bastard son was kinder to his father
Than my daughters got 'tween the lawful sheets.
115 To't, luxury,° pell-mell, for I lack soldiers.   *lechery*
Behold yond simp'ring dame,
Whose face between her forks presages snow,[1]
That minces° virtue and does shake the head   *affects*
To hear of° pleasure's name.   *even of*
120 The fitchew nor the soiled horse[2] goes to't
With a more riotous appetite.
Down from the waist they are centaurs,[3]
Though women all above.
But° to the girdle° do the gods inherit;°   *Only / waist / own*

---

1. My true feelings will always outweigh others'
hypocrisy; my natural supremacy surpasses any
attempt to create a false new reign.
2. Fee paid to a soldier impressed, or forced, into the
army.
3. A person hired as a scarecrow and thus unfit for
anything else.
4. Draw the bowstring the full length of the arrow (a
standard English arrow was a cloth yard [37 inches]
long).
5. I'll defend my stand even against a giant. To throw
down an armored glove ("gauntlet") was to issue a
challenge.

6. Brown painted pikes; the soldiers carrying them.
7. Used medicinally against madness.
8. Told me I had wisdom before age.
9. *no good divinity:* poor theology (because insincere);
from James 5:12: "Let your yea be yea; nay, nay."
1. Whose expression implies cold chastity. "Face"
refers to the area between her legs ("forks"), as well as
to her literal facial expression as framed by the aristocratic lady's starched headpiece, also called a "fork."
2. Neither the polecat nor a horse full of fresh grass.
3. Lecherous mythological creatures that have a
human body above the waist and the legs and torso of
a horse below.

125   Beneath is all the fiend's. There's hell,[4] there's darkness,
    There is the sulphurous pit: burning, scalding,
    Stench, consumption. Fie, fie, fie! Pah, pah!
    —Give me an ounce of civet,[5] good apothecary;
    Sweeten my imagination. There's money for thee.
    GLOUCESTER   Oh, let me kiss that hand.

130   LEAR   Let me wipe it first.
    It smells of mortality.
    GLOUCESTER   O ruined piece° of nature, this great world   *masterpiece*
    Shall so wear out to naught.[6] Dost thou know me?
    LEAR   I remember thine eyes well enough. Dost thou squiny°   *squint*

135   at me? No, do thy worst, blind Cupid. I'll not love. Read
    thou this challenge; mark but the penning of it.
    GLOUCESTER   Were all thy letters suns, I could not see.
    EDGAR [*aside*]   I would not take° this from report;   *believe*
    It is, and my heart breaks at it.

140   LEAR   Read.
    GLOUCESTER   What, with the case° of eyes?   *socket*
    LEAR   Oh, ho, are you there with me?[7] No eyes in your head,
    nor no money in your purse? Your eyes are in a heavy case,[8]
    your purse in a light, yet you see how this world goes.

145   GLOUCESTER   I see it feelingly.°   *by touch; painfully*
    LEAR   What, art mad? A man may see how this world goes
    with no eyes. Look with thine ears. See how yond justice
    rails upon yond simple° thief. Hark in thine ear. Change   *lowly; innocent*
    places, and handy-dandy,[9] which is the justice, which is the

150   thief? Thou hast seen a farmer's dog bark at a beggar?
    GLOUCESTER   Ay, sir.
    LEAR   And the creature° run from the cur. There thou mightst   *wretch*
    behold the great image of authority; a dog's obeyed in office.
    —Thou rascal beadle,[1] hold° thy bloody hand.   *restrain*

155   Why dost thou lash that whore? Strip thy own back;
    Thou hotly lusts to use her in that kind°   *way*
    For which thou whipp'st her. The usurer hangs the
        cozener.[2]
    Through tattered clothes great vices do appear.
    Robes and furred gowns hide all. Plate° sins with gold,   *Armor; gild*

160   And the strong lance of justice hurtless° breaks.   *harmlessly*
    Arm it in rags; a pigmy's straw does pierce it.
    None does offend; none, I say, none. I'll able° 'em.   *authorize*
    Take that of me, my friend, who have the power
    To seal th'accuser's lips. Get thee glass eyes,

165   And, like a scurvy politician,[3]
    Seem to see the things thou dost not. Now, now, now, now.
    Pull off my boots, harder, harder, so.
    EDGAR [*aside*]   Oh, matter and impertinency° mixed!   *sense and nonsense*
    Reason in madness.

---

4. Shakespeare's frequent term for female genitals. Cf. Sonnets 129 and 144.
5. Perfume derived from the anal gland of the civet.
6. Shall decay to nothing in the same way. In Renaissance philosophy, humans were perfectly analogous to the cosmos, standing for the whole in miniature and as its masterpiece.
7. Is that what you are telling me?

8. In a sad condition; playing on "case" as "sockets."
9. Pick a hand, as in a child's guessing game.
1. The parish officer responsible for whippings.
2. The ruinous moneylender, prosperous enough to be made a judge, convicts the ordinary cheat.
3. A vile schemer. In early modern England, "politician" meant an ambitious, even Machiavellian, upstart.

170 LEAR If thou wilt weep my fortunes, take my eyes.
I know thee well enough: thy name is Gloucester.
Thou must be patient. We came crying hither.
Thou know'st, the first time that we smell the air
We wail and cry. I will preach to thee. Mark.

175 GLOUCESTER Alack, alack the day.

LEAR When we are born, we cry that we are come
To this great stage of fools. This° a good block.[4]   *This is*
It were a delicate° stratagem to shoe   *subtle*
A troop of horse with felt.[5] I'll put't in proof,°   *to the test*
180 And when I have stol'n upon these son-in-laws,
Then kill, kill, kill, kill, kill, kill!

        Enter a GENTLEMAN.

GENTLEMAN Oh, here he is. Lay hand upon him. [*to* LEAR] Sir,
Your most dear daughter—

LEAR No rescue? What, a prisoner? I am even
185 The natural fool[6] of fortune. Use° me well;   *Treat*
You shall have ransom. Let me have surgeons:
I am cut to th' brains.

GENTLEMAN   You shall have anything.

LEAR No seconds?° All myself?   *supporters*
Why, this would make a man a man of salt,[7]
190 To use his eyes for garden water-pots. I will die[8] bravely,
Like a smug° bridegroom. What? I will be jovial.   *an elegant*
Come, come, I am a king, masters. Know you that?

GENTLEMAN You are a royal one, and we obey you.

LEAR Then there's life° in't. Come; an° you get it,   *hope / if*
195 You shall get it by running. Sa, sa, sa, sa.[9]   *Exit.*

GENTLEMAN A sight most pitiful in the meanest wretch,
Past speaking of in a king. Thou hast a daughter
Who redeems nature from the general curse,
Which twain have brought her to.[1]

EDGAR Hail, gentle° sir.   *noble*
200 GENTLEMAN   Sir, speed you.° What's your will?   *God speed you*

EDGAR Do you hear aught, sir, of a battle toward?°   *coming*

GENTLEMAN Most sure and vulgar:°   *commonly known*
Everyone hears that which° can distinguish sound.   *who*

EDGAR But, by your favor, how near's the other army?

205 GENTLEMAN Near and on speedy foot; the main descry°   *appearance*
Stands on the hourly thought.°   *Is expected forthwith*

EDGAR I thank you, sir, that's all.

GENTLEMAN Though that the Queen on° special cause° is here, *for / reason*
Her army is moved on.

EDGAR   I thank you, sir. *Exit* [GENTLEMAN].

210 GLOUCESTER You ever gentle gods, take my breath from me.

---

4. Stage (often called "scaffold" and hence linked to an executioner's block); block used to shape a felt hat (such as the hat removed by a preacher before a sermon); mounting block (such as the stump or stock Lear may have sat on to remove his boots).
5. Hat material, to muffle the sound of the approaching cavalry.
6. Born plaything; playing on "natural" as "mentally deficient."
7. A man reduced to nothing but the salt his tears

deposit.
8. "Die" plays on the Renaissance sense of "have an orgasm."
9. A cry to encourage dogs in the hunt.
1. *Who . . . to:* Who restores proper meaning and order to a universe plagued by the crimes of the other two daughters; alluding to the fall of humankind and the natural world caused by the sin of Adam and Eve and to the universal redemption brought about by Christ's sacrifice.

Let not my worser spirit[2] tempt me again
To die before you please.
EDGAR   Well pray you, father.[3]
GLOUCESTER   Now, good sir, what are you?
EDGAR   A most poor man, made tame to fortune's blows,
215   Who, by the art of known and feeling° sorrows,   *profound*
Am pregnant to° good pity. Give me your hand,   *disposed to feel*
I'll lead you to some biding.°   *resting place*
GLOUCESTER   Hearty thanks.
The bounty and the benison of heaven
To boot and boot.[4]
            Enter [Oswald the] STEWARD.
STEWARD   A proclaimed prize![5] Most happy!°   *lucky*
220   That eyeless head of thine was first framed° flesh   *made of*
To raise my fortunes. Thou old unhappy traitor,
Briefly thyself remember.[6] [*He draws his sword.*] The sword
    is out
That must destroy thee.
GLOUCESTER   Now let thy friendly hand
Put strength enough to't.
STEWARD [*to* EDGAR]   Wherefore, bold peasant,
225   Dar'st thou support a published° traitor? Hence,   *proclaimed*
Lest that th'infection° of his fortune take   *(deathly) sickness*
Like° hold on thee. Let go his arm.   *The same*
EDGAR [*drawing his sword and speaking in a country accent*]
Chill[7] not let go, zir, without vurther 'casion.°   *further occasion*
STEWARD   Let go, slave, or thou diest.
230   EDGAR   Good gentleman, go your gait,° and let poor volk pass.   *be on your way*
An chud ha'° been zwaggered out of my life, 'twould not ha'   *If I could have*
been zo long as 'tis by a vortnight. Nay, come not near th'old
man! Keep out, che vor' ye, or I'll try whither your costard or
my ballow be the harder.[8] Chill be plain with you.
235   STEWARD   Out, dunghill.
EDGAR   Chill pick your teeth, zir! Come, no matter vor your
foins.°   *sword thrusts*
            [*They fight.*]
STEWARD   Slave, thou hast slain me! Villain, take my purse.
If ever thou wilt thrive, bury my body,
240   And give the letters which thou find'st about me
To Edmund, Earl of Gloucester. Seek him out
Upon° the English party. Oh, untimely death, death!   *Within*
            [*He dies.*]
EDGAR   I know thee well: a serviceable° villain,   *an officious*
As duteous to the vices of thy mistress
As badness would desire.
245   GLOUCESTER   What, is he dead?
EDGAR   Sit you down, father; rest you.
Let's see these pockets. The letters that he speaks of
May be my friends. He's dead; I am only sorry

2. Wicked inclination; bad angel.
3. A term of respect for an elderly man.
4. In addition to my thanks, and may it bring you
some worldly reward.
5. A wanted man, with a bounty on his life.
6. Recollect and pray forgiveness for your sins.

7. I will; dialect from Somerset was a stage convention for peasant dialogue.
8. *che vor' ye . . . harder:* I warrant you, or I shall test
whether your head or my cudgel is harder. *costard:* a
kind of apple.

He had no other deathsman.° [*He opens the letter.*] Let   *executioner*
us see;
250   Leave,° gentle wax,[9] and manners blame us not.   *By your leave*
To know our enemies' minds, we rip their hearts;
Their° papers is more lawful.   *To rip their*
        [*He*] *reads the letter.*
"Let our reciprocal vows be remembered. You have many
opportunities to cut him off. If your will want° not, time and   *lacks*
255   place will be fruitfully offered. There is nothing done° if he   *accomplished*
return the conqueror; then am I the prisoner and his bed my
jail, from the loathed warmth whereof deliver me, and supply°   *fill*
the place for your labor.[1] Your (wife, so I would say), affectionate servant,
259.1   *and for you her own for venture,*
260   Goneril."
Oh, indistinguished space of woman's will![2]
A plot upon her virtuous husband's life,
And the exchange° my brother! Here in the sands   *substitute*
Thee I'll rake up,° the post unsanctified°   *cover up / unholy messenger*
265   Of murderous lechers, and in the mature time°   *when the time is ripe*
With this ungracious° paper strike the sight   *ungodly*
Of the death-practiced Duke.[3] For him, 'tis well
That of thy death and business I can tell.
GLOUCESTER   The King is mad. How stiff is my vile sense[4]
270   That I stand up and have ingenious feeling[5]
Of my huge sorrows? Better I were distract;°   *mad*
So should my thoughts be severed from my griefs,
        Drum afar off.
And woes by wrong° imaginations lose   *false*
The knowledge of themselves.
EDGAR   Give me your hand.
275   Far off methinks I hear the beaten drum.
Come, father, I'll bestow° you with a friend.   *Exeunt.*   *lodge*

4.7

Enter CORDELIA, KENT [*dressed as Caius*], *and*
GENTLEMAN.
CORDELIA   O thou good Kent, how shall I live and work
To match thy goodness? My life will be too short
And every measure° fail me.   *attempt*
KENT   To be acknowledged, madam, is o'erpaid.°   *is more than enough*
5   All my reports go[1] with the modest truth,
Nor more, nor clipped, but so.[2]
CORDELIA   Be better suited;°   *attired*
These weeds° are memories of those worser hours.   *clothes*
I prithee, put them off.
KENT   Pardon, dear madam,
Yet to be known shortens my made intent.[3]

9. The wax seal on the letter.
1. *for your labor:* as a reward for your endeavors, and
for further sexual exertion.
2. Limitless extent of woman's willfulness. As with
"hell" in line 125, "will" might also refer to a woman's
genitals.
3. Of the Duke whose death is plotted.
4. How obstinate is my unwanted power of reason.

5. That I remain upright and firm in my sanity and
have rational perceptions.
4.7 Location: The French camp at Dover.
1. May all accounts of me agree.
2. Not greater or less, but exactly the modest amount
I deserve.
3. Revealing myself now would abort my designs.

10　My boon I make it[4] that you know° me not　　　　　　　　　　　*acknowledge*
　　Till time and I think meet.°　　　　　　　　　　　　　　　　　　*suitable*
CORDELIA　　　　　　　　　Then be't so, my good lord.
　—How does the King?
GENTLEMAN　　　　　　　Madam, sleeps still.
CORDELIA　O you kind gods,
　Cure this great breach in his abusèd nature.
15　Th'untuned and jarring senses, oh, wind up[5]
　Of this child-changed[6] father.
GENTLEMAN　　　　　　　　So please your majesty,
　That we may wake the King? He hath slept long.
CORDELIA　Be governed by your knowledge and proceed
　I'th' sway° of your own will. Is he arrayed?°　　　　*By the authority / clothed*
　　　　Enter LEAR *in a chair carried by* SERVANTS.
20　GENTLEMAN　Ay, madam. In the heaviness of sleep,
　We put fresh garments on him.
　Be by, good madam, when we do awake him;
　I doubt of his temperance.°　　　　　　　　　　　　　　　　　　*calmness*
CORDELIA　O my dear father, restoration hang
25　Thy medicine on my lips, and let this kiss
　Repair those violent harms that my two sisters
　Have in thy reverence° made.　　　　　　　　　　　　　　　*aged dignity*
KENT　　　　　　　　　　　Kind and dear princess.
CORDELIA　Had you not[7] been their father, these white flakes°　　*locks of hair*
　Did challenge° pity of them. Was this a face　　　　　　　　*Would provoke*
30　To be opposed against the jarring winds,
30.1　　*To stand against the deep dread-bolted thunder,*
　　　In the most terrible and nimble stroke
　　　Of quick cross lightning to watch°—poor perdu![8]—　　*to stand guard*
　　　With this thin helm?°　　　　　　　　　　　　　　　*helmet (of hair)*
　Mine enemy's dog, though he had bit me,
　Should have stood that night against my fire.
　And wast thou fain,° poor father,　　　　　　　　　　　　　　*obliged*
　To hovel thee with swine and rogues forlorn
35　In short° and musty straw? Alack, alack,　　　　　　　　*scant; broken*
　'Tis wonder that thy life and wits at once
　Had not concluded all.° —He wakes; speak to him.　　　　　*altogether*
GENTLEMAN　Madam, do you, 'tis fittest.
CORDELIA　How does my royal lord?
40　How fares your majesty?
LEAR　You do me wrong to take me out o'th' grave.
　Thou art a soul in bliss, but I am bound
　Upon a wheel of fire, that mine own tears
　Do scald like molten lead.[9]
CORDELIA　　　　　　　　Sir, do you know me?
45　LEAR　You are a spirit, I know. Where did you die?
CORDELIA　Still, still, far wide.°　　　　　　　　　　　　　*unbalanced*
GENTLEMAN　He's scarce awake. Let him alone a while.

---

4. The reward I beg is.
5. *Th'untuned . . . up:* Reorder his confused and
delirious mind. The image is of tightening the strings
of a lute.
6. Changed by his children; changed into a child;
playing on a musical key change.
7. Even if you had not.

8. Lost one; in military terms, a dangerously exposed
sentry.
9. *but I . . . lead:* Lear puts himself in either hell or
purgatory, both places of such punishment in medieval accounts. Compare also the classical myth of
Ixion, bound by Zeus to a spinning wheel of fire.

LEAR   Where have I been? Where am I? Fair daylight?
   I am mightily abused.° I should e'en die with pity   *wronged; deceived*
50   To see another thus. I know not what to say.
   I will not swear these are my hands. Let's see,
   I feel this pin prick. Would I were assured
   Of my condition.
CORDELIA [*kneeling*]   Oh, look upon me, sir,
   And hold your hand in benediction o'er me.
         [LEAR *kneels.*]
   You must not kneel.
55   LEAR [*rising*]   Pray, do not mock me.
   I am a very foolish, fond° old man,   *silly*
   Fourscore and upward,
   Not an hour more nor less,
   And to deal plainly,
60   I fear I am not in my perfect mind.
   Methinks I should know you and know this man,
   Yet I am doubtful, for I am mainly° ignorant   *entirely*
   What place this is, and all the skill I have
   Remembers not these garments, nor I know not
65   Where I did lodge last night. Do not laugh at me,
   For, as I am a man, I think this lady
   To be my child Cordelia.
CORDELIA   And so I am. I am.
LEAR   Be your tears wet?[1] Yes, faith. I pray, weep not.
   If you have poison for me, I will drink it.
70   I know you do not love me, for your sisters
   Have, as I do remember, done me wrong.
   You have some cause; they have not.
CORDELIA   No cause, no cause.
LEAR   Am I in France?
KENT   In your own kingdom, sir.
LEAR   Do not abuse° me.   *deceive; mock*
75   GENTLEMAN   Be comforted, good madam; the great rage
   You see is killed in him. Desire him to go in;
   Trouble him no more till further settling.°   *until his mind eases*
CORDELIA   Will't please your highness walk?
LEAR   You must bear with me.
   Pray you now, forget and forgive,
80   I am old and foolish.
               Exeunt [LEAR *and* CORDELIA;
               KENT *and* GENTLEMAN *remain*].
80.1   GENTLEMAN   *Holds it true, sir, that the Duke of Corn-*
   wall was so slain?
   KENT   *Most certain, sir.*
   GENTLEMAN   *Who is conductor° of his people?*   *commander*
80.5   KENT   *As 'tis said, the bastard son of Gloucester.*
   GENTLEMAN   *They say Edgar, his banished son, is with*
   the Earl of Kent in Germany.
   KENT   *Report° is changeable. 'Tis time to look about.°*   *Rumor / prepare defenses*
   The powers of the kingdom approach apace.

---

1. Are your tears real? Is this really happening?

80.10   GENTLEMEN   *The arbitrament° is like to be bloody. Fare*   *encounter*
       you well, sir.   *[Exit.]*
       KENT   *My point and period² will be thoroughly wrought,*
       Or° well or ill as this day's battle's fought.   *Exit.*   *For*

5.1

Enter with drum and colors,° EDMUND, REGAN,   *regimental flags*
GENTLEMEN, and Soldiers.

    EDMUND   Know° of the Duke if his last purpose hold,[1]   *Inquire*
    Or whether since he is advised by aught²
    To change the course. He's full of alteration³
    And self-reproving. Bring his constant pleasure.°   *his settled intent*
5   REGAN   Our sister's man is certainly miscarried.⁴
    EDMUND   'Tis to be doubted,° madam.   *feared*
    REGAN   Now, sweet lord,
    You know the goodness I intend upon you.
    Tell me but truly, but then speak the truth:
    Do you not love my sister?
    EDMUND   In honored° love.   *honorable*
10   REGAN   But have you never found my brother's way
    To the forfended⁵ place?
11.1   EDMUND   *That thought abuses° you.*   *deceives*
    REGAN   *I am doubtful° that you have been conjunct°*   *suspicious / complicit*
    And bosomed with° her—as far as we call hers.⁶   *enamored of*
    EDMUND   No, by mine honor, madam.
    REGAN   I never shall endure her. Dear my lord,
    Be not familiar° with her.   *intimate*
15   EDMUND   Fear° not. She and the Duke her husband—   *Doubt*
    Enter with drum and colors, ALBANY, GONERIL,
    Soldiers.
15.1   GONERIL *[aside]*   *I had rather lose the battle than that sister*
    Should loosen° him and me.   *disunite*
    ALBANY   Our very loving sister, well be-met.
    —Sir, this I heard: the King is come to his daughter
    With others, whom the rigor° of our state°   *harshness / government*
    Forced to cry out.
19.1   *Where I could not be honest°*   *honorable*
    I never yet was valiant. For this business,
    It touches° us as France invades our land,   *concerns*
    Not bolds° the King, with others whom I fear   *Does not embolden*
19.5   *Most just and heavy causes make oppose.⁷*
    EDMUND   *Sir, you speak nobly.*
20   REGAN   Why is this reasoned?⁸
    GONERIL   Combine together 'gainst the enemy.
    For these domestic and particular broils°   *minor details*
    Are not the question here.
    ALBANY   Let's then determine with th'ancient° of war   *experienced officer(s)*
25   On our proceeding.

---

2. The purpose and end of my life; literally, the full stop.
5.1 Location: The British camp near Dover.
1. If his previous intention (to wage war) remains firm.
2. Since then anything has persuaded him.
3. A tendency to give up his intentions or put aside his responsibilities.

4. Has surely come to grief by some accident.
5. Forbidden, by the prohibition against adultery.
6. In total intimacy; all the way.
7. *It . . . oppose:* The invasion concerns us only insofar that France has invaded Britain, not because it has emboldened Lear, who has just cause to attack.
8. What is the point of this kind of speech?

REGAN   Sister, you'll go with us?[9]

GONERIL   No.

REGAN   'Tis most convenient;° pray go with us.   *suitable*

GONERIL   Oh, ho, I know the riddle!° I will go.   *disguised meaning*

Exeunt both the armies.

Enter EDGAR [*disguised*].

30   EDGAR [*to* ALBANY]   If e'er your grace had speech with man
                so poor,
        Hear me one word.

ALBANY [*to the others*]   I'll overtake you.

[*Exeunt* EDMUND, GONERIL, *and* REGAN.]
                                        Speak.

EDGAR   Before you fight the battle, ope this letter.
        If you have victory, let the trumpet sound
        For him that brought it. Wretched though I seem,
35   I can produce a champion that will prove°   *defend*
        What is avouchèd° there. If you miscarry,°   *asserted / perish*
        Your business of the world hath so an end,
        And machination° ceases. Fortune loves you.   *plotting*

ALBANY   Stay till I have read the letter.

EDGAR   I was forbid it.

40   When time shall serve, let but the herald cry,
        And I'll appear again.   *Exit.*

ALBANY   Why, fare thee well. I will o'erlook thy paper.

Enter EDMUND.

EDMUND   The enemy's in view; draw up your powers.°   *troops*
        Here is the guess° of their true strength and forces   *estimate*
45   By diligent discovery,° but your haste   *spying*
        Is now urged on you.

ALBANY   We will greet the time.[1]   *Exit.*

EDMUND   To both these sisters have I sworn my love,
        Each jealous° of the other, as the stung   *suspicious*
        Are of the adder. Which of them shall I take?
50   Both? One? Or neither? Neither can be enjoyed
        If both remain alive. To take the widow
        Exasperates, makes mad, her sister Goneril,
        And hardly° shall I carry out my side,°   *with difficulty / plan*
        Her husband being alive. Now, then, we'll use
55   His countenance[2] for the battle, which being done,
        Let her who would be rid of him devise
        His speedy taking-off. As for the mercy
        Which he intends to Lear and to Cordelia,
        The battle done, and they within our power,
60   Shall° never see his pardon. For my state°   *They shall / condition*
        Stands on° me to defend, not to debate.   *Exit.*   *Obliges*

---

9. Regan wants Goneril to go with Albany and her,   2. Authority or backing; also suggesting "face," to be
rather than with Edmund.   used like a mask for Edmund's ambition.
1. We will be ready to meet the occasion.

5.2

Alarum within.[1] *Enter with drum and colors,* LEAR,
CORDELIA, *and Soldiers, over the stage, and exeunt.*
Enter EDGAR [*disguised as a peasant*] *and*
GLOUCESTER.

EDGAR   Here, father,[2] take the shadow of this tree
For your good host.° Pray that the right may thrive.   *shelter*
If ever I return to you again,
I'll bring you comfort.

GLOUCESTER   Grace go with you, sir. *Exit* [EDGAR].
Alarum and retreat° within.   *trumpet signal*
Enter EDGAR.

5   EDGAR   Away, old man, give me thy hand, away!
King Lear hath lost; he and his daughter ta'en.
Give me thy hand. Come on.

GLOUCESTER   No further, sir, a man may rot even° here.   *right*

EDGAR   What, in ill thoughts again? Men must endure
10   Their going hence even as their coming hither;
Ripeness is all.[3] Come on.

GLOUCESTER   And that's true too.   *Exeunt.*

5.3

Enter in conquest with drum and colors, EDMUND;
LEAR *and* CORDELIA, *as prisoners; Soldiers,* CAPTAIN.[1]

EDMUND   Some officers! Take them away. Good guard,
Until their greater pleasures[2] first be known
That are to censure° them.   *judge*

CORDELIA   We are not the first
Who with best meaning° have incurred the worst.   *intention*
5   For thee, oppressèd King, I am cast down.°   *(into unhappiness)*
Myself could else out-frown false fortune's frown.[3]
Shall we not see these daughters and these sisters?

LEAR   No, no, no, no. Come, let's away to prison.
We two alone will sing like birds i'th' cage.
10   When thou dost ask me blessing, I'll kneel down
And ask of thee forgiveness. So we'll live,
And pray, and sing, and tell old tales, and laugh
At gilded butterflies,[4] and hear poor rogues
Talk of court news, and we'll talk with them too—
15   Who loses, and who wins; who's in, who's out—
And take upon 's the mystery of things,
As if we were God's spies. And we'll wear out,°   *outlast*
In a walled prison, packs and sects of great ones,
That ebb and flow by th' moon.[5]

EDMUND   Take them away.

20   LEAR   Upon such sacrifices,[6] my Cordelia,

5.2 Location: The rest of the play takes place near
the battlefield.
1. Trumpet call to battle (backstage).
2. See note to 4.6.212.
3. To await the destined time is the most important
thing, as fruit falls only when ripe (playing on Gloucester's "rot," line 8); readiness for death is our only duty
(compare *Hamlet* 5.2.194, "the readiness is all").
5.3
1. TEXTUAL COMMENT There are differences between
the entrance and exit directions in the First Quarto
and the Folio versions of 5.3. Q1's entrance of the
"Captain" late in the scene is replaced by the entrance

of the "Messenger" in F. The deletion of extraneous
roles is not unusual in the later revisions of plays, but
this scene's revision in F suggests that too many
"Captains" are wandering the stage in Q1. See Digital
Edition TC 6 (combined text).
2. *Good . . . pleasures:* Guard them well until the
desires of those greater persons.
3. Otherwise, I could be defiant in the face of bad
fortune.
4. Gaudy courtiers.
5. *packs . . . moon:* followers and factions of important people whose positions at court vary as the tide.
6. Upon such sacrifices as we are or as you have made.

The gods themselves throw incense. Have I caught thee?
He that parts us shall bring a brand from heaven
And fire us hence like foxes.[7] Wipe thine eyes.
The good years shall devour them, flesh and fell,[8]
25   Ere they shall make us weep.
We'll see 'em starved first. Come.
        Exeunt [Soldiers with LEAR *and* CORDELIA].
EDMUND   Come hither, Captain. Hark.
Take thou this note; go follow them to prison.
One step I have advanced° thee; if thou dost   *promoted*
30   As this instructs thee, thou dost make thy way
To noble fortunes. Know thou this: that men
Are as the time is. To be tender-minded
Does not become a sword;° thy great employment   *befit a swordsman*
Will not bear question.° Either say thou'lt do't   *discussion*
Or thrive by other means.
35 CAPTAIN   I'll do't, my lord.
EDMUND   About it, and write happy when th' hast done.[9]
Mark, I say, instantly, and carry it° so   *carry it out*
As I have set it down.
38.1   CAPTAIN   *I cannot draw a cart, nor eat dried oats;*°   *(like a horse)*
     If it be man's work, I'll do't.   *Exit* CAPTAIN.
      Flourish. Enter ALBANY, GONERIL, REGAN, *Soldiers.*
ALBANY   Sir, you have showed today your valiant strain,°   *qualities; heritage*
40   And fortune led you well. You have the captives
Who were the opposites° of this day's strife.   *opponents*
I do require them of you, so to use° them   *treat*
As we shall find their merits and our safety
May equally determine.
EDMUND   Sir, I thought it fit
45   To send the old and miserable King to some retention,°   *confinement*
Whose° age had charms in it, whose title more,   *(Lear's)*
To pluck the common bosom[1] on his side
And turn our impressed lances° in our eyes   *conscripted lancers*
Which[2] do command them. With him I sent the Queen,
50   My reason all the same, and they are ready
Tomorrow or at further space° t'appear   *at a future point*
Where you shall hold your session.°   *court of judgment*
52.1   *At this time*
    We sweat and bleed. The friend hath lost his friend,
    And the best quarrels, in the heat, are cursed
    By those that feel their sharpness.[3]
52.5   *The question of Cordelia and her father*
    Requires a fitter place.
ALBANY   Sir, by your patience,
I hold you but a subject of° this war,   *in waging*
Not as a brother.
55 REGAN   That's as we list° to grace him.   *choose*

---

7. **shall . . . foxes:** must have divine aid to do so. The image is of using a torch to smoke foxes out of their holes—or, in the case of Lear and Cordelia, prison cells.
8. **flesh and fell:** meat and skin; entirely. The precise meaning of "good years" has not been explained; it may signify simply the passage of time or may suggest some ominous, destructive power.
9. Go to it, and call yourself happy when you are done.
1. To garner the affection of the populace.
2. **in our eyes / Which:** in the eyes of us who.
3. **And . . . sharpness:** And in the heat of battle, even the most just wars are cursed by those who must suffer the fighting.

Methinks our pleasure might have been demanded[4]
Ere you had spoke so far. He led our powers,°   *armies*
Bore the commission of my place and person,
The which immediacy° may well stand up   *close connection*
And call itself your brother.

60   GONERIL   Not so hot.°   *Not so fast*
In his own grace° he doth exalt himself   *merit*
More than in your addition.[5]

REGAN   In my rights,
By me invested, he compeers° the best.   *equals*

ALBANY   That were the most[6] if he should husband you.

REGAN   Jesters do oft prove prophets.

65   GONERIL   Holla, holla!
That eye that told you so looked but asquint.[7]

REGAN   Lady, I am not well, else I should answer
From a full-flowing stomach.° —General,   *anger*
Take thou my soldiers, prisoners, patrimony;

70   Dispose of them, of me. The walls° is thine.   *fortress of my heart*
Witness the world that I create thee here
My lord and master.

GONERIL   Mean you to enjoy him?

ALBANY   The let-alone° lies not in your good will.   *veto*

EDMUND   Nor in thine, lord.

ALBANY   Half-blooded° fellow, yes.   *Bastard*

75   REGAN   Let the drum strike,[8] and prove my title thine.

ALBANY   Stay yet; hear reason. Edmund, I arrest thee
On capital treason, and in thy arrest[9]
This gilded serpent. [*to* REGAN] For your claim, fair sister,°   *sister-in-law*
I bar it in the interest of my wife.

80   'Tis she is subcontracted to this lord,
And I her husband contradict your banns.°   *marriage announcement*
If you will marry, make your loves to me:
My lady is bespoke.

GONERIL   An interlude!°   *A farce*

ALBANY   Thou art armed, Gloucester. Let the trumpet sound.

85   If none appear to prove upon thy person
Thy heinous, manifest, and many treasons,
There is my pledge. [*He throws down his gauntlet.*] I'll make
     it on thy heart,
Ere I taste bread, thou art in nothing less°   *in no way less guilty*
Than I have here proclaimed thee.

REGAN   Sick, oh, sick!

90   GONERIL [*aside*]   If not, I'll ne'er trust medicine.°   *poison (euphemistic)*

EDMUND [*throwing down his gauntlet*]   There's my exchange.
What° in the world he's   *Whoever*
That names me traitor, villain-like he lies.
Call by the trumpet. He that dares approach
On him, on you—who not—I will maintain
My truth and honor firmly.

95   ALBANY   A herald, ho!

---

4. I think you should have inquired into my wishes.
5. In the honors you confer upon him.
6. That investiture would be complete.
7. Squinting was a proverbial effect of jealousy, because of the tendency to look suspiciously at poten-

tial rivals.
8. Perhaps to announce the betrothal or a challenge.
9. And in order to accuse you; and as one who shares your corruption or crime.

Enter a HERALD.

Trust to thy single virtue,° for thy soldiers,   *your unassisted power*
All levied in my name, have in my name
Took their discharge.
REGAN   My sickness grows upon me.
ALBANY   She is not well; convey her to my tent.

                          [*Exit* REGAN, *attended.*]

100   Come hither, Herald; let the trumpet sound,
And read out this. [*He hands him a letter.*]
      A trumpet sounds.
HERALD (*reads*)   "If any man of quality or degree, within the
lists of the army, will maintain upon Edmund, supposed Earl
of Gloucester, that he is a manifold traitor, let him appear by
105   the third sound of the trumpet. He is bold in his defense."
      First trumpet [*sounds*].
Again!
      Second trumpet [*sounds*].
Again!
      Third trumpet [*sounds*].
      Trumpet answers within.
      Enter EDGAR, *armed.*
ALBANY   Ask him his purposes; why he appears
Upon this call o'th' trumpet.
HERALD   What° are you?   *Who*
110   Your name, your quality,° and why you answer   *degree; rank*
This present summons?
EDGAR   Know my name is lost,
By treason's tooth bare-gnawn and canker-bit,°   *worm-eaten*
Yet am I noble as the adversary
I come to cope.°   *to encounter*
ALBANY   Which is that adversary?
115   EDGAR   What's he that speaks for Edmund, Earl of
    Gloucester?
EDMUND   Himself. What say'st thou to him?
EDGAR   Draw thy sword,
That° if my speech offend a noble heart,   *So that*
Thy arm may do thee justice. [*He draws his sword.*] Here is
   mine.
Behold, it is my privilege,
120   The privilege of mine honors,
My oath, and my profession. I protest,
Maugre° thy strength, place, youth, and eminence,   *Despite*
Despite thy victor-sword, and fire-new° fortune,   *newly minted*
Thy valor and thy heart,° thou art a traitor,   *courage*
125   False to thy gods, thy brother, and thy father,
Conspirant 'gainst this high illustrious prince,
And from th'extremest upward° of thy head   *top*
To the descent° and dust below thy foot   *lowest part; sole*
A most toad-spotted[1] traitor. Say thou no,
130   This sword, this arm, and my best spirits are bent°   *ready*
To prove upon thy heart, whereto I speak,
Thou liest.

---

1. Venomous, like a toad; spotted with disgrace.

EDMUND   In wisdom I should ask thy name,
But since thy outside looks so fair and warlike,
And that thy tongue some say[2] of breeding breathes,
135 What safe and nicely I might well delay
By rule of knighthood, I disdain and spurn.[3]
Back do I toss these treasons to thy head,
With the hell-hated° lie o'erwhelm thy heart,   hated as much as hell
Which for° they yet glance by and scarcely bruise,   since
140 This sword of mine shall give them instant way°   access
Where they shall rest for ever. —Trumpets, speak.
          Alarums. Fights.
ALBANY[4]   Save° him, save him!   Spare
GONERIL   This is practice,° Gloucester!   trickery
By th' law of war thou wast not bound to answer
An unknown opposite.° Thou art not vanquished   opponent
But cozened and beguiled.°   cheated and deceived
145 ALBANY [*showing her a letter*]   Shut your mouth, dame,
Or with this paper shall I stop° it. Hold,° sir,   plug / Behold
Thou worse than any name, read thine own evil.
No tearing, lady; I perceive you know it.
GONERIL   Say if I do, the laws are mine, not thine.
150 Who can arraign° me for't?   *Exit.*   prosecute
ALBANY [*to* EDMUND]   Most monstrous! Oh, know'st thou this
     paper?
EDMUND   Ask me not what I know.
ALBANY   Go after her. She's desperate; govern° her.   restrain
          [*Exeunt some Soldiers.*]
EDMUND   What you have charged me with, that have I done,
155 And more, much more; the time will bring it out.
'Tis past, and so am I. But what art thou
That hast this fortune on me?[5] If thou'rt noble,
I do forgive thee.
EDGAR   Let's exchange charity.°   forgiveness
[*He removes his helmet.*] I am no less in blood than thou
     art, Edmund;
160 If more, the more th' hast wronged me.
My name is Edgar and thy father's son.
The gods are just and of our pleasant vices
Make instruments to plague us:
The dark and vicious place where thee he got[6]
Cost him his eyes.
165 EDMUND   Th' hast spoken right, 'tis true:
The wheel° is come full circle. I am here.[7]   Fortune's wheel
ALBANY [*to* EDGAR]   Methought thy very gait did prophesy
A royal nobleness. I must embrace thee.
Let sorrow split my heart if ever I
Did hate thee or thy father.
170 EDGAR   Worthy prince, I know't.

---

2. Taste (from "assay"); utterance.
3. *And . . . spurn:* And since your speech may suggest high birth, I will not stick safely and meticulously to the rules of knighthood (which do not require a knight to fight an unknown opponent) and refuse to fight you.

4. Both F and Q give this speech to "*Alb.*" (for Albany), which may be a compositor's error for "*All.*"
5. Who have this good fortune at my expense.
6. The adulterous bed in which you were conceived; or, possibly, the vagina. *got:* begot.
7. Back at the lowest point.

ALBANY Where have you hid yourself?
    How have you known the miseries of your father?
  EDGAR By nursing them, my lord. List° a brief tale,   *Listen to*
    And when 'tis told, oh, that my heart would burst!
175   The bloody proclamation to escape,[8]
    That followed me so near—oh, our lives' sweetness,
    That we the pain of death would hourly die
    Rather than die at once[9]—taught me to shift
    Into a madman's rags, t'assume a semblance
180   That very° dogs disdained, and in this habit   *even*
    Met I my father with his bleeding rings°—   *sockets*
    Their precious stones° new lost—became his guide,   *eyes*
    Led him, begged for him, saved him from despair.
    Never—oh, fault—revealed myself unto him
185   Until some half hour past, when I was armed.
    Not sure, though hoping of this good success,°   *conclusion*
    I asked his blessing and from first to last
    Told him our pilgrimage. But his flawed° heart,   *cracked*
    Alack, too weak the conflict to support,
190   Twixt two extremes of passion, joy and grief,
    Burst smilingly.
  EDMUND   This speech of yours hath moved me
    And shall perchance do good. But speak you on;
    You look as you had something more to say.
  ALBANY If there be more, more woeful, hold it in,
195   For I am almost ready to dissolve,°   *melt into tears*
    Hearing of this.
196.1   EDGAR *This would have seemed a period° to such*   *conclusion*
      As love not sorrow, but another to amplify° too much   *enlarge; extend*
      Would make much more and top extremity.
      Whilst I was big in clamor,° came there in a man,   *lamenting loudly*
196.5   *Who having seen me in my worst estate*
      Shunned my abhorred society, but then finding
      Who 'twas that so endured, with his strong arms
      He fastened on my neck and bellowed out
      As he'd burst heaven, threw me on my father,
196.10   *Told the most piteous tale of Lear and him°*   *himself*
      That ever ear received, which, in recounting,
      His grief grew puissant,° and the strings of life   *powerful*
      Began to crack twice. Then the trumpets sounded.
      And there I left him tranced.
    ALBANY   *But who was this?*
196.15   EDGAR *Kent, sir, the banished Kent, who in disguise*
      Followed his enemy king[1] and did him service
      Improper° for a slave.   *Unfit even*
      Enter a GENTLEMAN [*with a bloody knife*].
  GENTLEMAN Help, help! Oh, help!
  EDGAR   What kind of help?
  ALBANY   Speak, man.
  EDGAR What means this bloody knife?
  GENTLEMAN 'Tis hot! It smokes! It came even from the heart of—

---

8. In order to escape the sentence of death.
9. *our . . . once:* how sweet must life be that we prefer the constant pain of dying to death itself.

1. Because Lear had previously banished him. *enemy:*
hostile.

Oh, she's dead.

200 ALBANY   Who dead? Speak, man.

GENTLEMAN   Your lady, sir, your lady—and her sister
By her is poisoned; she confesses it.

EDMUND   I was contracted to them both; all three
Now marry° in an instant.   *unite (in death)*
Enter KENT.

EDGAR   Here comes Kent.

205 ALBANY   Produce the bodies, be they alive or dead.
Goneril and Regan's bodies brought out.
This judgment of the heavens that makes us tremble
Touches us not with pity. Oh, is this he?
The time will not allow the compliment
Which very manners urges.²

KENT   I am come

210 To bid my king and master aye° good night.   *forever*
Is he not here?

ALBANY   Great thing of° us forgot!   *by*
Speak, Edmund, where's the King? And where's Cordelia?
Seest thou this object,° Kent?   *spectacle*

KENT   Alack, why thus?

EDMUND   Yet° Edmund was beloved: *Despite all*

215 The one the other poisoned for my sake
And after slew herself.

ALBANY   Even so. Cover their faces.

EDMUND   I pant for life. Some good I mean to do
Despite of mine own nature. Quickly send—

220 Be brief° in it—to th' castle, for my writ³   *speedy*
Is on the life of Lear and on Cordelia.
Nay, send in time.

ALBANY   Run, run, oh, run!

EDGAR   To who, my lord? —Who has the office?°   *commission*
Send thy token of reprieve.

EDMUND   Well thought on. Take my sword,
Give it the° Captain.   *to the*

225 EDGAR   Haste thee for thy life!
                                      [*Exit* GENTLEMAN.]

EDMUND   He hath commission from thy wife and me
To hang Cordelia in the prison and
To lay the blame upon her own despair,
That she fordid herself.⁴

230 ALBANY   The gods defend her! Bear him hence awhile.
                    [EDMUND *is carried out by Soldiers.*]
Enter LEAR, *with* CORDELIA *in his arms[, and*
GENTLEMAN].

LEAR   Howl, howl, howl! Oh, you are men of stones!
Had I your tongues and eyes, I'd use them so
That heaven's vault should crack. She's gone forever.
I know when one is dead and when one lives;

235 She's dead as earth. Lend me a looking glass,

---

2. *the compliment . . . urges:* the ceremony that barest custom demands.
3. Order of execution.

4. Destroyed herself. In most of Shakespeare's
source texts for the play, Cordelia does in fact kill
herself after reigning for some years.

If that her breath will mist or stain the stone,[5]
Why, then, she lives.[6]
KENT   Is this the promised end?[7]
EDGAR   Or image of that horror.
ALBANY   Fall and cease.[8]
LEAR   This feather stirs. She lives! If it be so,
240   It is a chance which does redeem all sorrows
        That ever I have felt.
KENT   O my good master.
LEAR   Prithee, away.
EDGAR   'Tis noble Kent, your friend.
LEAR   A plague upon you murderers, traitors all!
        I might have saved her; now she's gone forever.
245   Cordelia, Cordelia, stay a little. Ha,
        What is't thou say'st? Her voice was ever soft,
        Gentle, and low, an excellent thing in woman.
        —I killed the slave that was a-hanging thee.
GENTLEMAN   'Tis true, my lords, he did.
LEAR   Did I not, fellow?
250   I have seen the day, with my good biting falchion°   light sword
        I would have made him skip. I am old now,
        And these same crosses spoil me.[9] Who are you?
        Mine eyes are not o'th' best, I'll tell you straight.°   recognize you soon
KENT   If Fortune brag of two she loved and hated,
255   One of them we behold.[1]
LEAR   This is a dull sight;[2] are you not Kent?
KENT   The same: your servant Kent.
        Where is your servant Caius?°   (Kent's pseudonym)
LEAR   He's a good fellow, I can tell you that;
260   He'll strike, and quickly, too. He's dead and rotten.
KENT   No, my good lord, I am the very man—
LEAR   I'll see that straight.[3]
KENT   —That from your first of difference and decay[4]
        Have followed your sad steps.
LEAR   You are welcome hither.
265 KENT   Nor no man else.[5]
        All's cheerless, dark, and deadly.°   deathly
        Your eldest daughters have fordone° themselves   destroyed
        And desperately° are dead.   in despair
LEAR   Ay, so I think.
ALBANY   He knows not what he says, and vain° is it   in vain
        That we present us to him.
            Enter a MESSENGER.
270 EDGAR   Very bootless.°   futile
MESSENGER   Edmund is dead, my lord.

---

5. Mica, or stone polished to a mirror finish.
6. PERFORMANCE COMMENT Each production must determine whether to sustain suspense regarding the possibility that Cordelia is still alive or to make it clear that her father is raving over a corpse. See Digital Edition PC 6.
7. Doomsday; expected end of the play. In no version of the story previous to Shakespeare's does Cordelia die at this point.
8. Let the world collapse and end.
9. And these recent adversities have weakened me; and these parries I could once match would now destroy me.

1. *If . . . behold:* If there were only two supreme examples in the world of Fortune's ability to raise up and cast down, Lear would be one; alternatively, we are each of us one (Lear and Kent are here looking at each other).
2. This is a sad sight; my vision is failing.
3. I'll attend to that shortly; I'll comprehend that in a moment.
4. Who from the beginning of your alteration and deterioration.
5. No, neither I nor anyone else is welcome. Alternatively, I am that man, not disguised as anyone else.

ALBANY   That's but a trifle here.
    You lords and noble friends, know our intent:
    What comfort to this great decay° may come   *ruin; destruction*
    Shall be applied. For us, we will resign
275 During the life of this old majesty
    To him our absolute power; [*to* EDGAR] you to your rights,
    With boot° and such addition° as your honors   *reward / distinction*
    Have more than merited. All friends shall
    Taste the wages of their virtue and all foes
280 The cup of their deservings. Oh, see, see!
LEAR   And my poor fool⁶ is hanged. No, no, no life?
    Why should a dog, a horse, a rat have life,
    And thou no breath at all? Thou'lt come no more,
    Never, never, never, never, never!
285 Pray you, undo this button. Thank you, sir.
    Do you see this? Look on her! Look, her lips,
    Look there. Look there!⁷
        He dies.
EDGAR   He faints. My lord, my lord.
KENT   Break, heart, I prithee, break.
EDGAR   Look up, my lord.
KENT   Vex not his ghost.⁸ Oh, let him pass! He hates him
290 That would upon the rack⁹ of this tough world
    Stretch him out longer.
EDGAR   He is gone indeed.
KENT   The wonder is he hath endured so long.
    He but usurped his life.¹
ALBANY   Bear them from hence. Our present business
295 Is general woe. [*to* KENT *and* EDGAR] Friends of my soul,
        you twain
    Rule in this realm and the gored° state sustain.   *wounded; bloody*
KENT   I have a journey, sir, shortly to go.
    My master calls me. I must not say no.
EDGAR²   The weight of this sad time we must obey;
300 Speak what we feel, not what we ought to say.
    The oldest hath borne most; we that are young
    Shall never see so much, nor live so long.
                    Exeunt with a dead march.

6. A term of endearment, here used for Cordelia, though it also recalls the disappearance of Lear's Fool after 3.6.
7. TEXTUAL COMMENT All the source plays for the King Lear story show Lear and Cordelia prevailing, with Cordelia surviving and accepting the role of Lear's successor as monarch. In the Folio text, unlike in the Quarto text, Lear apparently thinks that his attempts to revive her are successful. See Digital Edition TC 7 (combined text).
8. Do not disturb his departing soul.
9. Instrument of torture, used to stretch its victims.

1. From death, which already had a claim on it.
2. TEXTUAL COMMENT One of the apparently minor but nevertheless significant differences between the two early texts of *King Lear* is that in the First Quarto text the last lines of the play are given to Albany, whereas in the Folio they are given to Edgar. These powerful lines suggest that their speaker will inherit political leadership, and conflating editors face the challenge of selecting which character should stand as the moral and political spokesperson at the end of the play. See Digital Edition TC 8 (combined text).

Timon of Athens

In a jewelry advertisement, a handsome man and a beautiful woman share a rapturous embrace. A large diamond sparkles on the woman's finger; apparently, the impressive ring symbolizes a love equally magnificent. Although the deliberate confusion of emotional and financial investments seems crass once it is explicitly recognized, the ad can only be effective at selling jewelry if it captures something people know, or wish, to be true. What does love have to do with money? How closely entwined are friendship and material self-interest? Are persons esteemed for intrinsic personal characteristics or for the glamor of their possessions? Are affluent communities or prosperous individuals especially likely to confuse sheer wealth with other forms of value? *Timon of Athens* asks such questions with a fierce relentlessness unusual for Shakespeare. In the past four decades its tale of debt-fueled extravagance followed by ruin has inspired a series of memorable productions that have drawn connections between the world of the play and our own society, with its rampant consumerism and its precarious reliance upon borrowed funds.

It is probably no coincidence that *Timon*'s schematic plot and static characters seem closer to the satiric drama of Shakespeare's contemporaries than to the other tragedies that Shakespeare was writing around 1605–08, the probable date of its composition. Recent scholarship strongly suggests that *Timon* is a collaborative work, about a third of which was written by Shakespeare's fellow dramatist Thomas Middleton. (Middleton seems to have been responsible for act 1, scene 2, the long party scene, and for most of the third act, when Timon's fortunes turn; he may have contributed to other parts of the play as well.) In many of his comedies, Middleton addresses the selfishness and hypocrisy of the commercial London of his day. He frequently portrays young spendthrifts struggling, as Timon does, in the clutches of predatory lenders. At the same time, the connections between *Timon* and Shakespeare's other plays are clear enough. The plot derives from that Shakespearean favorite, Plutarch's *Lives*, which also provided the sources for *Julius Caesar, Antony and Cleopatra,* and *Coriolanus. Timon* has strong affinities to *The Merchant of Venice* in its concern with the connections between material and intangible goods, and between friendship and moneylending. The play's jaundiced view of ancient Greece recalls *Troilus and Cressida*, as does its evasion of ordinary generic categories: although its protagonist dies at the end, its title does not promise a tragedy but merely a "life." The hero's sensational degradation from preeminence to utter penury, and his ferociously misanthropic reaction to that humiliation, has often prompted comparison with *King Lear.*

Timon opens on a panorama of glittering abundance. Purveyors of luxury goods—art, poems, jewels, textiles—flock to Timon's palace in hope of reward. Like advertisers today, they claim that their goods have a symbolic significance that goes beyond their obvious beauty or utility: these items give concrete expression to the ineffable virtues of their possessor. "Things of like value differing in the owners / Are prizèd by their masters," fawns the Jeweler. "You mend the jewel by the wearing it" (1.1.172–73, 174). The guests at Timon's sumptuous banquet are likewise loud in their admiration for their host. Their conversation turns almost obsessively upon Timon's apparently inexhaustible fortune.

And no wonder—for Timon seems not merely rich but unique. His generosity is characterized by what the Poet calls "magic of bounty," an outflow uncannily unbalanced by any apparent countereffort at acquisition. While ordinary owners have the power merely to transfer, not actually to generate, new goods, Timon seems freed from such basic material laws. He dispenses his "bounty" as if he were a god empowered to create wealth from nothing. But Timon's "magic" relies on a trick that he himself resolutely ignores. Using his lands as collateral, he borrows the money he needs to buy expensive presents and keep a lavish table. The recipients of his hospitality are often the same men to whom he is indebted.

To Timon's surprise, but hardly to the audience's, his elaborate charade collapses in the play's second act. Why has he behaved so self-destructively? We are given clues to his motives when, in the course of his banquet, he and his guests explicitly and implicitly offer several theories about the relationship of his "bounty" both to the social weal and to his own self-conception. Timon desires love and admiration, and in Athenian society, as in many others, money proves a potent way of getting both. The adjectives "good," "worthy," "free," "kind," "gentle," and "noble" echo through the first act—their simultaneously economic and moral significance tending to break down any difference between the two domains. When Ventidius offers to return the large sum that Timon has spent releasing him from prison, Timon refuses:

> You mistake my love.
> I gave it freely ever, and there's none
> Can truly say he gives if he receives.
> (1.2.9–11)

Typically, love and money are here almost inextricable. Is the "it" that Timon freely gives the love to which he refers in the previous line or the money he has bestowed upon Ventidius? Moreover, Timon's generosity is entangled with a desire for mastery. By always giving, never receiving, Timon attempts to force his beneficiaries into an endlessly grateful and therefore subordinate role. His conduct recalls that of the chiefs of the Native American tribes of the Pacific Northwest, who consolidated their status by "potlatches," great parties at which they would give away virtually all their possessions, thus compelling their guests to serve them in the future. In such a system, divesting oneself of wealth, not accumulating it, is the primary mode of acquiring status.

In the socioeconomic world of the potlatch, in which the recipient of a gift is profoundly obliged to the donor, Timon might well escape serious financial danger. His "courtiers" would have to repay him somehow, in kind or in service. Timon briefly imagines such a system when he rhapsodizes at his dinner party: "We are born to do benefits, and what better or properer can we call our own than the riches of our friends? Oh, what a precious comfort 'tis to have so many like brothers commanding one another's fortunes!" (1.2.97–100). Unfortunately, not only is this communitarian vision at odds with Timon's insistence on entirely unilateral gift-giving, but it is grossly out of kilter with the covetous society in which he actually lives. When Timon pays Ventidius's debt, Ventidius's messenger declares that "Your lordship ever binds him" (1.1.106); likewise the First Lord claims to be "virtuously bound" by Timon's generosity (1.2.223). Yet by the middle of act 2, they have already lost any sense of commitment to their erstwhile benefactor. Timon's "bonds," the legal instruments that enable his lenders to seize his lands when he forfeits cash repayment, turn out to be more "binding" than the unwritten ties of gratitude. In Athens, tangible goods are considered more real than intangible ones, legal commitments more real than obligations informally imposed.

Apemantus, hovering on the margins of Timon's dinner party, introduces an alternative economic language early in the play: the audience's perception of the entire banquet extravaganza is filtered through his commentary. Apemantus is a Cynic, that is, a follower of a Greek philosophical school that repudiated conventional desires for wealth and social prominence and regarded many forms of human interaction as hypocritical and self-serving. For Timon, magnanimity apparently comes naturally and gifts express sociability. For Apemantus, by contrast, people are naturally greedy and antisocial: protestations of friendship and gratitude conceal an impulse to accumulate wealth at the expense of another, just as lavishness conceals a desire for adulation. In such circumstances, the Cynic philosopher preserves his safety and integrity by repudiating his need both for property and for other people:

> Immortal gods, I crave no pelf.
> I pray for no man but myself.
> Grant I may never prove so fond
> To trust a man on his oath or bond,
> Or a harlot for her weeping,
> Or a dog that seems a-sleeping,
> Or a keeper with my freedom,
> Or my friends if I should need 'em.
> (1.2.62–69)

To Timon's generous trustfulness, Apemantus counterpoises a self-protective suspicion. The difference in the way the two men conceive of human nature correlates with a difference in the way they imagine the material world. Timon believes that wealth is endlessly renewable and thus endlessly sharable without decrease. Apemantus believes that resources are strictly limited and that one person's gain must entail another person's loss. Thus what Timon sees as banquet pleasantries amount, in Apemantus's view, to a form of cannibalism. "O you gods! What a number of men eats Timon, and he sees 'em not? It grieves me to see so many dip their meat in one man's blood" (1.2.40–42). Both of these apparently opposite attitudes, however—Timon's romanticism and Apemantus's reductiveness—are actually rooted in a conviction that one's possessions, or the lack of them, centrally determine the way one thinks of oneself and interacts with other people. Arguably, Apemantus's cannibal imagery makes the shared materialism of the two men's attitudes especially obvious to a Christian audience; for that vision of Timon's banquet parodies, in grotesquely literal terms, the dispersal of Christ's spiritual body in the Communion ceremony.

Most scholars believe that *Timon of Athens* was written between 1606 and 1608, several years after the accession of James I to the English throne. There are good reasons why Timon's particular economic dilemma would interest dramatists observing the contemporary scene in these years. If the play was, as many argue, left unfinished and unproduced, perhaps it was too incendiary to be safely performed in Jacobean England: although most of Shakespeare's plays reflect to some extent the time in which they were written, *Timon* is unusual in its brutally direct topical relevance. In the first decade of the seventeenth century, the traditional aristocratic virtues of openhanded generosity and carelessness of expense were coming into increasingly acute conflict with the limited means upon which the great nobles could actually draw. As England became an international trading power, luxuries once unheard of became available to people with the money to buy them. As tastes grew more sophisticated, noblemen who wished to impress peers and subordinates with the splendor of their "bounty" were forced into ever greater expenditures. The result was an extraordinary expansion in the credit markets. The worst offender in this respect was King James, who—like Timon—showered his favorites with expensive gifts, a habit that created staggering deficits in the Royal Exchequer. By 1608, royal indebtedness had reached crisis proportions, and other members of the upper aristocracy were likewise floating on a sea of debt and credit.

Shakespeare, or Shakespeare and Middleton, thus bears witness to a society in the process of a crucial economic transition—a transition that affects more than financial matters narrowly defined. In the first act, Timon assumes that his money transactions are accompanied by affection on the part of the giver and gratitude on the part of the recipient. In an informal, small-scale credit system, the difference between love and money, and between loans and gifts, may indeed become blurred, for friends may help one another financially on occasion. In Jacobean England, however, the inability of the upper classes to live within their means overstrained the limits of "friendly understanding": for few people then or now lend really substantial sums of money out of sheer amiability. Borrowing and lending thus increasingly became business matters transacted between relative strangers, divorced from rather than continuous with friendship and patronage relationships. Usury, a practice traditionally deplored and even illegal, was nonetheless widespread and increasingly accepted as a necessary fact of life.

A fiscally prudent, hardworking businessman, Shakespeare may well have been shocked on occasion at the profligacy of the patrons upon whose expansiveness he and his theater company partly depended. Certainly he recognized acutely that the motives of the Poet and the Painter do not differ from the motives of the other courtiers: "artists" in Athens are as venal as everybody else. What seems to have intrigued him most, however, is the way in which an apparently rather limited social phenomenon—aristocratic reliance on credit—necessarily affects social and even biological relations that seem far removed from moneylending. Uniquely among Shakespeare's plays, *Timon* is nearly bereft of women. The few who do briefly appear—the Amazons of act 1, Alcibiades' whores in act 4—are pointedly excluded from the "normal" marital relationships in which most socially useful reproductive activity traditionally takes place. In this nearly all-male world, the language of erotic intimacy is reserved for interactions among men. Exchanges of money and commodities take over some of the functions of procreative sexual intimacy, an appropriation that can easily be construed as perverse or depraved. Lending money at interest seems especially corrupt: *Timon of Athens* draws upon an ancient tradition of imagining usury to be a form of unnatural "breeding." After his disillusionment, Timon continually and deliberately conflates lust with greed, the venereal with the venal. Syphilis and its symptoms are not merely analogies for, but are perhaps even the consequences of, economic iniquity.

Despite the virtual absence of

Penthesilea, Queen of the Amazons. Drawing by Inigo Jones. From *The Masque of Queens* (1609), by Ben Jonson.

Dame Fortune, blind, standing on a ball with wings (to show how quickly her favors may fly away). From George Wither, *A Collection of Emblems* (1635).

actual women, allegorical representations of female power play an important rhetorical role in *Timon of Athens*. The first half of the play is dominated by the allegorical figure of Fortune. The Poet describes her as a "sovereign lady" enthroned "upon a high and pleasant hill" (1.1.69, 64), huge, omnipotent, and whimsical, raising and crushing her struggling male subjects for no apparent reason. In the second half of the play, "Mother Earth" has some of the same threatening demeanor. The ruined Timon forsakes Athens for the wilderness outside it, rather as Shakespeare's lovers had done in that drastically different play *A Midsummer Night's Dream*. In *Dream*, the woods outside Athens are a lushly sexual place, but in *Timon*, roughly the same geographical locale is unusually harsh and minimalist. Like the whores to whom Timon compares her, Mother Earth is barren, refusing to surrender the roots for which Timon digs and instead yielding only the gold he had hoped to flee. Thus, for all the energy spent exposing the "unnaturalness" of Athenians' economic relations, a potentially restorative "natural" alternative is wholly lacking.

In many respects, Timon's disillusioned ferocity simply inverts, recoils from, the generous courtesy he had manifested throughout act 1. Yet not everything changes: there is a clear continuity to Timon's personality in the first and second halves of the play. Initially, as a wealthy patron and benefactor, Timon isolates himself from others by making himself a god of generosity. Later, as an indigent, he similarly sets himself apart, cursing mankind with all the immoderation with which he once blessed it. Shakespeare was fascinated throughout his career by self-absorbed, almost solipsistic characters: Adonis in *Venus and Adonis*, the young man of the sonnets, Malvolio in *Twelfth Night* "sick of self-love." Timon exemplifies an extreme version of this egocentrism, his sense of his own separateness untouched even after his conception of human nature has been poisoned at its source. He not only dies alone, but—in the possibly corrupt text that has come down to us—mysteriously manages to bury himself and engrave his own epitaph: an epitaph that typically, and perversely, both demands that passersby remember him and orders them to "Seek not my name" (5.5.71).

The necessarily social medium of the drama finds true hermits impossible to accommodate. For most of acts 4 and 5, various acquaintances crowd to Timon's cave as they once crowded to his palace, some to commiserate or to offer advice, some to investigate rumors that Timon had discovered gold while digging for roots to eat. The disillusioned Timon no longer wants gold, because it has value only insofar as it can be exchanged, and thus requires that its users form relationships with other human beings. So, ironically, the man who once blessed his "friends" with treasure once again gives it away to them, this time with his curses. The sense of separateness Timon has always possessed makes satiric alienation congenial to him; but, like many satirists, he is an ambiguous figure. The satirist can tell truths about society because his disengagement gives him the standing to criticize practices he regards as corrupt. At the same time, his observational acuteness—his refusal to accept the complacencies of the majority—bespeaks a certain imbalance. The satirist's misanthropy coexists curiously with an inability to mind his own business. The tone of the play's latter acts thus becomes profoundly equivocal. Are we supposed to agree with Timon that virtually all human values and activities can be plausibly reduced to money and the greed for it? Certainly the action of the play gives us ample reason to share his disgust at his erstwhile friends. Or is his rage disproportionate to the adversities he endures? Just as the Timon of the early acts can be variously characterized as noble and foolish, the later Timon has seemed to some critics a sublimely disappointed idealist, to others a petulant whiner.

A few characters suggest that Timon's unmitigated misanthropy is too simple and incomplete. The steward Flavius's loyalty to his former master defies the terms of Timon's blanket condemnation of all humankind, as Timon reluctantly acknowledges. Throughout *Timon,* low-ranking characters—having less to gain from greed—display an acute sense of gratitude and obligation sadly lacking in their "betters." All Timon's servants, not merely Flavius, seem dismayed by their master's ruin; and in 3.4, the usurers' servants, talking among themselves, freely condemn the commands they are forced to carry out. But Timon prefers to believe that rapacity is a universal human trait, not a more limited, class-linked phenomenon. Reduced to rags and roots though he is, Timon cannot help being a snob. And to some extent, his status consciousness seems justified: for if the servants are kindhearted, they are also ineffectual. Their lack of resources prevents them from remedying the social problems they witness.

Alcibiades provides a more formidable alternative to the Athenian usurers, although the connection between this subplot and the main action is sketchy. Certainly he does not escape, or seek to disentangle, the interconnections between love and money that eventually seem so poisonous to Timon: when he visits Timon in the cave, he comes with a prostitute on each arm. Nonetheless, in his brief appearances, Alcibiades testifies to the existence of a less restricted, more complex sociopolitical world than the one we witness for most of the play. Whereas, for instance, Timon's function in Athens seems mainly to give expensive dinner parties, Alcibiades insists that Timon has performed important military services for the state: that his "bounty" has had a political and executive, as well as a sheerly economic, aspect. Unfortunately, the relationship between Timon and Alcibiades, as well as the relationship between the city's politics and its social organization, is left largely undeveloped in the text of the play as it has come down to us. The soldier, pursuing his vocation in the bleak world beyond the city walls, is imagined as partly outside the economic system in which other characters are enmeshed. Like the hermit-satirist, he has the special credibility that comes with distance. But whereas Timon's detachment is the product of a merely negative disgust, Alcibiades' involves allegiance to a different set of positive values. In 3.6, not only does he risk himself to defend a friend, but the terms of his defense hint at a code of behavior divorced from cash rewards and penalties.

At the end of the play, after Timon's death, the Athenian senators invite Alcibiades and his army back into the city. He will, they hope, "Approach the fold and cull th'infected forth" (5.5.43), as a shepherd kills the sick animals of his flock in order to keep disease from spreading to the remainder. The senators argue that greed is merely the failing of a degenerate few, not the universal human trait Timon had believed it to be. Alcibiades seems to accept this claim, agreeing to renounce the indiscriminate violence of a war against all Athens in favor of the more targeted punishment of particular offenders. But the play entertains this alternative view of Timon's plight too late and too hastily to carry much conviction, and the apparent optimism of the conclusion thus seems unearned. How Alcibiades' invasion will reform Athens is hard to imagine.

KATHARINE EISAMAN MAUS

SELECTED BIBLIOGRAPHY

Bailey, Amanda. "*Timon of Athens*, Forms of Payback, and the Genre of Debt." *English Literary Renaissance* 41 (2011): 375–400. Examines *Timon's* connection to the system of credit and debt in early modern England.

Chorost, Michael. "Biological Finance in Shakespeare's *Timon of Athens*." *English Literary Renaissance* 21 (1991): 349–70. Looks at gift and money economies in *Timon* and the language of biological reproduction in which they are described.

Jowett, John. "Middleton and Debt in *Timon of Athens*." *Money and the Age of Shakespeare: Essays in New Economic Criticism*. Ed. Linda Woodbridge. New York: Palgrave Macmillan, 2003. Argues that the play reflects the economic attitudes of Thomas Middleton, Shakespeare's probable collaborator.

Kahn, Coppélia. "'Magic of Bounty': *Timon of Athens*, Jacobean Patronage, and Maternal Power." *Shakespeare Quarterly* 38 (1987): 34–57. Analyzes *Timon's* links to the contradictory practices of Jacobean court patronage.

Lupton, Julia. "Job of Athens, Timon of Uz." *Thinking with Shakespeare: Essays on Politics and Life*. Chicago: U of Chicago P, 2011. 131–61. Compares reversals of fortune in the stories of Timon and the biblical Job.

Nuttall, A. D. *Timon of Athens*. Harvester New Critical Introductions to Shakespeare. Hemel Hempstead: Harvester Wheatsheaf, 1989. Offers chapters on stage history and critical reception, followed by a detailed commentary on the play.

Paster, Gail Kern. *The Idea of the City in the Age of Shakespeare*. Athens: U of Georgia P, 1985. 99–108. Looks at *Timon's* bleak vision of urban life, as enacted in the hero's transformation from philanthropist to misanthrope.

Scott, Alison V. *Selfish Gifts: The Politics of Exchange and English Courtly Literature, 1580–1628*. Madison, NJ: Fairleigh Dickinson UP, 2005. Describes the culture of patronage and self-seeking upon which *Timon* comments.

FILM

Timon of Athens. 1981. Dir. Jonathan Miller. UK. 128 min. Sepia-toned BBC-TV production featuring Athenians in Jacobean dress. Jonathan Pryce stars as an initially clueless and eventually very battered Timon. Effectively slimy performances in the subsidiary roles.

TEXTUAL INTRODUCTION

The survival of *Timon of Athens* is largely a matter of chance, as evidence suggests that it was not originally to be included in the 1623 Folio. The Folio marks the play's first appearance in print, together with seventeen other Shakespeare plays that had not been published in an earlier quarto edition.

The play's initial textual history is tied to a dispute over the rights to Shakespeare's *Troilus and Cressida*. The printing syndicate that united to publish the First Folio had planned to include the latter play, but came into difficulties over ownership of the text. As a stopgap, *Timon of Athens* was brought in to fill up the pages left available by the missing *Troilus and Cressida*. This sequence of events is suggested by the fact that *Timon* occupies less space in the Folio than was allotted to it. The run of signatures, or pages, is too short, and the play was printed with an unusual degree of "white space," suggesting that the printers were trying to stretch it to cover more pages. Further, the initial "Catalogue" or list of plays does not include *Troilus*, which is located between the tragedies and histories in a run of signatures that is out of place. But the strongest evidence that *Timon* replaced *Troilus* occurs in a canceled sheet, which prints the first two pages of *Troilus*, that survives in a handful of copies following *Romeo and Juliet*. *Timon* is placed after *Romeo and Juliet* in most copies of the Folio. The canceled sheet indicates that early plans had gone awry.

So we are lucky that *Timon* survives at all, which raises a question as to why those collecting the Folio's plays—Shakespeare's fellow actors John Hemminges and Henry Condell—would initially seek to exclude the text. The answer probably lies in the likelihood that *Timon of Athens* was a collaborative effort, almost certainly written in part by Thomas Middleton. Similarly coauthored plays, *Pericles* and *The Two Noble Kinsmen*, were also left out of the Folio. That being said, other coauthored Shakespeare plays were included, so the exact reasons for excluding *Timon* from the initial conception of the volume cannot be fully determined.

Another possible reason for not including the play is the unsatisfactory nature of the text itself. *Timon* as it stands seems to lack the tidiness required to bring a play onto the stage, and as such it might reflect an early authorial draft, rather than a working theatrical copy. It is full of false starts and repetitions. Famously, Timon's epitaph at the end of the play includes two mutually contradictory rhyming couplets (see Digital Edition TC 9). The names of characters are frequently altered, as when Ventidius becomes Ventigius in 1.2, or when Apemantus is described as Apermantus in 1.1 and 1.2. The play also has several confusing moments in which servants are called by their masters' names. While the characters cause confusion in places, the dialogue can be said to be even more difficult to follow. The text contains patchy verse and errant lineation, with prose set as verse and verse set as prose. Characters switch between the two in a way that is uncharacteristic of Shakespeare, but does happen in Middleton's works. The dialogue also can be very opaque, and editors make frequent emendations to try to bring sense to seemingly corrupt passages. The text therefore poses challenges to readers attempting to make sense of its language and constant stream of thinly developed characters. Yet the text is not so corrupt as to disguise the obvious rhetorical and emotive power of the protagonist, and its inconsistencies make for a surprisingly contemporary play, one whose sometimes jarring scenic cadences have been well received on the stage.

Eugene Giddens

PERFORMANCE NOTE

In general, directors of *Timon of Athens* view the protagonist predominantly as either a reckless prodigal bringing misery on himself or a magnanimous benefactor driven to desperation by parasitic Athenians. While productions can incorporate elements of both characterizations, they must decide how responsible Timon is for his downfall, a decision that impacts the second half's representation of his misanthropy. Some productions present Timon's generosity as transparently egocentric, his subsequent degradation then seeming a just punishment for vanity. Others make clear that Timon's vice is not self-love but excessive, guileless love for others, his fall the more tragic for proceeding from overabundant faith in his friends. In either case, Timon can deliver his invectives as a disconsolate wretch, a raging madman, or a visionary, depending on whether directors and actors see sadness, regret, or spiritual abnegation mingled with his cynicism. Timon's apparent lack of familial ties has also inspired productions to explain his wild generosity as founded on a desperate need for emotional intimacy, thus helping to excuse the fault and ennoble the character.

Though *Timon* is rarely produced, its preoccupations with wealth and greed give it urgent contemporary relevance, and productions commonly use modern dress and present-day substitutes for Athens. Nicholas Hytner's 2012 production, for example, began with Timon dedicating a room in a London art gallery while an Occupy-style protest took place nearby, the second half reducing him to a homeless figure pushing a cart under a bridge. Productions can use such contemporary parallels to dignify Timon—for example, by indicating that a market crash, rather than personal extravagance, is responsible for Timon's ruin. Like Timon, the secondary characters are often treated analogically or allegorized, but all productions must decide whether Apemantus is a well-meaning sage or a surly cynic, and whether Alcibiades is Athens' great hope or a new form of devourer. Both characters can seem pained by or indifferent to Timon's afflictions, while Flavius can remain a loyal steward or grasp after gold as eagerly as the rest. Other considerations in performance include staging the masque, the physical prominence of the gold and other gifts, and settling the text's contradictory versions of Timon's epitaph.

BRETT GAMBOA

The Life of Timon of Athens

THE PERSONS OF THE PLAY

TIMON of Athens
POET
PAINTER
JEWELER
MERCHANT
OLD ATHENIAN
LUCIUS
LUCULLUS } flattering lords and senators
SEMPRONIUS
VENTIDIUS, false friend to Timon
APEMANTUS, a churlish philosopher
ALCIBIADES, an Athenian captain
CUPID, a character in the masque
Masquers, LADIES as Amazons
FLAMINIUS
SERVILIUS } servants to Timon
LUCILIUS
Flavius, Timon's STEWARD
CAPHIS, a servant
Two of VARRO'S SERVANTS
TITUS, a servant
HORTENSIUS, a servant
PHILOTUS, a servant
LUCIUS' SERVANT
ISIDORE'S SERVANT
Other SERVANTS and Attendants
Four of Timon's FRIENDS
LORDS
SENATORS
BANDITTI, or thieves
MESSENGERS
FOOL
PAGE
Three STRANGERS
PHRYNIA
TIMANDRA
SOLDIERS

1.1

Enter POET, PAINTER, JEWELER, *[and]* MERCHANT *at several doors.*[1]

POET Good day, sir.
PAINTER   I am glad you're well.
POET I have not seen you long. How goes the world?

1.1 Location: Timon's house, Athens.
1. TEXTUAL COMMENT The stage direction in the Folio

text leaves it unclear how many people enter at this juncture; see Digital Edition TC 1 for clarification.

PAINTER	It wears,° sir, as it grows.°	*wears out / ages*
POET	Ay, that's well known.	

But what particular rarity, what strange,
5   Which manifold record° not matches? See,   *all recorded history*
    Magic of bounty,° all these spirits thy power   *generosity*
    Hath conjured to attend—I know the merchant.

PAINTER   I know them both: th'other's a jeweler.
MERCHANT [*to* JEWELER]   Oh, 'tis a worthy lord.°   *(Timon)*
JEWELER   Nay, that's most fixed.°   *definite*
10 MERCHANT   A most incomparable man, breathed° as it were,   *trained; inspired*
    To an untirable and continuate° goodness: *habitual*
    He passes.°   *excels*

JEWELER [*showing the jewel*]   I have a jewel here.
MERCHANT   Oh, pray let's see it. For the Lord Timon, sir?
15 JEWELER   If he will touch the estimate.° But for that—   *meet the price*
POET [*to himself*]   When we for recompense have praised the vile,
    It stains the glory in that happy° verse,   *appropriate*
    Which aptly sings the good.
MERCHANT   'Tis a good form.°   *shape*
JEWELER   And rich. Here is a water,° look ye.   *luster*
20 PAINTER [*to* POET]   You are rapt, sir, in some work, some dedication
    To the great lord.[2]
POET   A thing slipped idly from me.
    Our poesy is as a gum° which oozes   *sap*
    From whence 'tis nourished. The fire i'th' flint
    Shows not till it be struck. Our gentle flame
25   Provokes° itself, and like the current flies   *Generates*
    Each bound it chases.[3] What have you there?
PAINTER   A picture, sir. When comes your book forth?
POET   Upon the heels of my presentment,[4] sir.
    Let's see your piece.
PAINTER [*showing the painting*]   'Tis a good piece.
30 POET   So 'tis. This comes off well and excellent.
PAINTER   Indifferent.°   *So-so*
POET   Admirable! How this grace
    Speaks his own standing;[5] what a mental power
    This eye shoots forth! How big imagination
    Moves in this lip! To th' dumbness° of the gesture   *muteness*
35   One might interpret.°   *supply words*
PAINTER   It is a pretty mocking° of the life.   *imitation*
    Here is a touch: is't good?
POET   I will say of it,
    It tutors nature. Artificial strife°   *The striving of art*
    Lives in these touches livelier than life.
       Enter certain SENATORS.
40 PAINTER   How this lord is followed.
POET   The senators of Athens, happy men.
PAINTER   Look, more.
              [*More* SENATORS *pass over the stage,*
               and all the SENATORS *exeunt.*]

---

2. Poets dedicated their volumes to wealthy patrons in hopes of financial reward.
3. *like . . . chases:* like the river overflows its banks.
4. As soon as I have presented it formally (to Timon).
5. Imparts the dignity of his estate.

POET   You see this confluence, this great flood of visitors.
 I have in this rough work shaped out a man
45 Whom this beneath[6] world doth embrace and hug
 With amplest entertainment.° My free drift°   *hospitality / meaning*
 Halts not particularly[7] but moves itself
 In a wide sea of wax.[8] No leveled malice
 Infects one comma in the course I hold
50 But flies an eagle flight, bold, and forth° on,   *straight*
 Leaving no tract° behind.   *trace*
PAINTER   How shall I
 Understand you?
POET   I will unbolt° to you.   *disclose*
 You see how all conditions, how all minds,
 As well of glib and slipp'ry creatures as
55 Of grave and austere quality, tender° down   *give*
 Their services to Lord Timon. His large fortune,
 Upon his good and gracious nature hanging,
 Subdues and properties° to his love and tendance° *appropriates / attendance*
 All sorts of hearts. Yea, from the glass-faced[9] flatterer
60 To Apemantus, that few things loves better
 Than to abhor himself, even he drops down
 The knee before him and returns° in peace   *leaves*
 Most rich in Timon's nod.
PAINTER   I saw them speak together.
POET   Sir, I have upon a high and pleasant hill
65 Feigned° Fortune to be throned. The base o'th' mount *Imagined*
 Is ranked with all deserts,[1] all kind of natures
 That labor on the bosom of this sphere
 To propagate their states.° Amongst them all   *improve their fortunes*
 Whose eyes are on this sovereign lady fixed,
70 One do I personate° of Lord Timon's frame,   *depict*
 Whom Fortune with her ivory hand wafts° to her,   *beckons*
 Whose present grace° to present slaves and servants *graciousness*
 Translates his rivals.[2]
PAINTER   'Tis conceived to scope.°   *correctly*
 This throne, this Fortune, and this hill, methinks,
75 With one man beckoned from the rest below,
 Bowing his head against the sleepy mount
 To climb his happiness,° would be well expressed   *good fortune*
 In our condition.[3]
POET   Nay, sir, but hear me on:
 All those which were his fellows° but of late,   *equals*
80 Some better than his value, on the moment
 Follow his strides, his lobbies fill with tendance,[4]
 Rain sacrificial° whisperings in his ear,   *respectful*

6. Sublunar (in Ptolemaic astronomy, the earth was the center of the universe and the moon its closest satellite; things beyond the moon were eternally fixed, but things in the sublunar "sphere" died or changed).
7. Does not criticize individuals.
8. "Wide sea of wax" is perhaps a misprint in the Folio text, but possibly the Poet is contrasting the breadth of his inspiration with the small size of the wax tablets on which poems were written in classical times.

leveled: aimed (at a particular person).
9. Reflecting his patron's moods.
1. Is lined with people of all degrees of virtue.
2. *to present . . . rivals:* instantly converts Timon's rivals to his slaves and servants.
3. *would . . . condition:* would be a good expression of the human condition; would make a good design for a painter.
4. *his . . . tendance:* crowd his rooms to visit him.

Make sacred even his stirrup,⁵ and through him
Drink the free air.
PAINTER   Ay, marry, what of these?
85 POET   When Fortune in her shift and change of mood
Spurns° down her late belovèd, all his dependents   *Kicks*
Which labored after him to the mountain's top,
Even on their knees and hands, let him set down,
Not one accompanying his declining foot.
90 PAINTER   'Tis common:
A thousand moral paintings I can show
That shall demonstrate these quick blows of Fortune's
More pregnantly° than words. Yet you do well   *forcibly*
To show Lord Timon that mean° eyes have seen   *base people's*
95 The foot above the head.
            Trumpets sound.
            Enter Lord TIMON, *addressing himself courteously*
            to every suitor[, with MESSENGER *from* VENTIDIUS,
            LUCILIUS, *and* SERVANTS].
TIMON [*to* MESSENGER]   Imprisoned is he, say you?
MESSENGER   Ay, my good lord, five talents⁶ is his debt,
His means most short, his creditors most strait.°   *severe*
Your honorable letter he desires
100 To those° have shut him up, which failing,   *those who*
Periods° his comfort.   *Ends*
TIMON   Noble Ventidius, well!
I am not of that feather° to shake off   *sort*
My friend when he must need me. I do know him
A gentleman that well deserves a help,
105 Which he shall have. I'll pay the debt and free him.
MESSENGER   Your lordship ever binds° him.   *obligates*
TIMON   Commend me to him. I will send his ransom,
And, being enfranchised,° bid him come to me.   *set free*
'Tis not enough to help the feeble up
110 But to support him after. Fare you well.
MESSENGER   All happiness to your honor.   *Exit.*
            Enter an OLD ATHENIAN.
OLD ATHENIAN   Lord Timon, hear me speak.
TIMON   Freely, good father.
OLD ATHENIAN   Thou hast a servant named Lucilius.
TIMON   I have so. What of him?
115 OLD ATHENIAN   Most noble Timon, call the man before thee.
TIMON   Attends he here or no? Lucilius!
LUCILIUS   Here, at your lordship's service.
OLD ATHENIAN   This fellow here, Lord Timon, this thy creature,
By night frequents my house. I am a man
120 That from my first have been inclined to thrift,
And my estate deserves an heir more raised°   *exalted*
Than one which holds a trencher.⁷

---

5. By holding it reverently as he mounts.
6. A large unit of money, usually taken as equivalent to several thousand dollars. The value of a "talent" is inconsistent from scene to scene in *Timon*; these dis-

crepancies are often cited as evidence for incomplete revision of the text.
7. Platter (one who waits on table).

TIMON   Well, what further?

OLD ATHENIAN   One only daughter have I, no kin else,
On whom I may confer what I have got.
125 The maid is fair, o'th' youngest for a bride,
And I have bred her° at my dearest cost   *brought her up*
In qualities of the best. This man of thine
Attempts her love. I prithee, noble lord,
Join with me to forbid him her resort.°   *company*
Myself have spoke in vain.
130 TIMON   The man is honest.
OLD ATHENIAN   Therefore he will be,[8] Timon.
His honesty rewards him in itself;
It must not bear° my daughter.   *carry off*
TIMON   Does she love him?
OLD ATHENIAN   She is young and apt.°   *impressionable*
135 Our own precedent° passions do instruct us   *former*
What levity's in youth.
TIMON [*to* LUCILIUS]   Love you the maid?
LUCILIUS   Ay, my good lord, and she accepts of it.
OLD ATHENIAN   If in her marriage my consent be missing,
I call the gods to witness, I will choose
140 Mine heir from forth the beggars of the world
And dispossess her all.
TIMON   How shall she be endowed°   *What dowry will she have*
If she be mated with an equal husband?
OLD ATHENIAN   Three talents on the present; in future, all.
TIMON   This gentleman of mine hath served me long.
145 To build his fortune I will strain a little,
For 'tis a bond° in men. Give him thy daughter.   *duty of friendship*
What you bestow, in him I'll counterpoise
And make him weigh with her.
OLD ATHENIAN   Most noble lord,
Pawn me to this your honor,[9] she is his.
150 TIMON   My hand to thee, mine honor on my promise.
LUCILIUS   Humbly I thank your lordship. Never may
That state or fortune fall into my keeping
Which is not owed to you.   *Exit* [*with* OLD ATHENIAN].
POET [*to* TIMON]   Vouchsafe° my labor   *Accept*
And long live your lordship!
155 TIMON   I thank you. You shall hear from me anon.°   *soon*
Go not away. —What have you there, my friend?
PAINTER   A piece of painting which I do beseech
Your lordship to accept.
TIMON   Painting is welcome.
The painting is almost the natural° man.   *actual*
160 For since dishonor traffics° with man's nature,   *has dealings*
He is but outside.° These penciled figures are   *only superficial*
Even such as they give out.[1] I like your work,
And you shall find I like it. Wait attendance

---

8. He will behave honorably (and chastely).   1. Just what they profess to be.
9. If you pledge your honor to do this.

Till you hear further from me.

PAINTER   The gods preserve ye.

165 TIMON   Well fare you, gentleman. [*to* JEWELER] Give me your
      hand.
      We must needs dine together. Sir, your jewel
      Hath suffered under² praise.

JEWELER   What, my lord, dispraise?

TIMON   A mere° satiety of commendations.   *An utter*
      If I should pay you for't as 'tis extolled,
      It would unclew° me quite.   *ruin*

170 JEWELER   My lord, 'tis rated
      As those which sell would give.³ But you well know
      Things of like value differing in the owners
      Are prizèd by their masters.⁴ Believe't, dear lord,
      You mend° the jewel by the wearing it.   *improve*

TIMON   Well mocked.°   *You're kidding*

      Enter APEMANTUS.

175 MERCHANT   No, my good lord, he speaks the common tongue,°   *general opinion*
      Which all men speak with him.

TIMON   Look who comes here. Will you be chid?°   *scolded*

JEWELER   We'll bear° with your lordship.   *suffer*

MERCHANT   He'll spare none.

TIMON   Good morrow to thee, gentle Apemantus.

180 APEMANTUS   Till I be gentle, stay thou for thy good morrow—
      When thou art Timon's dog and these knaves honest.⁵

TIMON   Why dost thou call them knaves? Thou know'st them not.

APEMANTUS   Are they not Athenians?

TIMON   Yes.

185 APEMANTUS   Then I repent not.

JEWELER   You know me, Apemantus?

APEMANTUS   Thou know'st I do. I called thee by thy name.

TIMON   Thou art proud, Apemantus!

APEMANTUS   Of nothing so much as that I am not like Timon.

190 TIMON   Whither art going?

APEMANTUS   To knock out an honest Athenian's brains.

TIMON   That's a deed thou'lt die for.

APEMANTUS   Right, if doing nothing⁶ be death by th' law.

TIMON   How lik'st thou this picture, Apemantus?

195 APEMANTUS   The best for the innocence.⁷

TIMON   Wrought he not well that painted it?

APEMANTUS   He wrought better that made the painter, and
      yet he's but a filthy piece of work.

PAINTER   You're a dog.⁸

200 APEMANTUS   Thy mother's of my generation. What's she, if I
      be a dog?

TIMON   Wilt dine with me, Apemantus?

---

2. Has been inundated by (but the Jeweler misunderstands).
3. At what a merchant would pay (the wholesale price).
4. Are valued as their owners are valued.
5. *stay . . . honest:* wait for a polite greeting until you are changed into your own dog or (an equally unlikely prospect) until these crooks become honest.
6. Since there are no honest Athenians.
7. For its inability to harm anyone.
8. "Dog" is not merely a term of contempt; Apemantus is a Cynic philosopher, a school whose name derived from the Greek *kynē*, "dog."

APEMANTUS   No, I eat not[9] lords.

TIMON   An° thou shouldst, thou'dst anger ladies.   *If*

205 APEMANTUS   Oh, they eat lords. So they come by great bellies.

TIMON   That's a lascivious apprehension.[1]

APEMANTUS   So thou apprehend'st it, take it for thy labor.

TIMON   How dost thou like this jewel, Apemantus?

APEMANTUS   Not so well as plain-dealing, which will not cost

210 a man a doit.°   *tiny coin*

TIMON   What dost thou think 'tis worth?

APEMANTUS   Not worth my thinking.

     How now, poet?

POET   How now, philosopher?

APEMANTUS   Thou liest.

POET   Art not one?

APEMANTUS   Yes.

POET   Then I lie not.

APEMANTUS   Art not a poet?

POET   Yes.

APEMANTUS   Then thou liest.

215 Look in thy last work, where thou hast feigned him° a worthy   *(Timon)*
     fellow.

POET   That's not feigned. He is so.

APEMANTUS   Yes, he is worthy of thee and to pay thee for thy
     labor. He that loves to be flattered is worthy o'th' flatterer.

220 Heavens, that I were a lord!

TIMON   What wouldst do then, Apemantus?

APEMANTUS   E'en as Apemantus does now: hate a lord with
     my heart.

TIMON   What, thyself?

225 APEMANTUS   Ay.

TIMON   Wherefore?

APEMANTUS   That I had no angry wit[2] to be a lord. —Art not
     thou a merchant?

MERCHANT   Ay, Apemantus.

230 APEMANTUS   Traffic confound° thee, if the gods will not.   *May business ruin*

MERCHANT   If traffic do it, the gods do it.

APEMANTUS   Traffic's thy god, and thy god confound thee.
          Trumpet sounds. Enter a MESSENGER.

TIMON   What trumpet's that?

MESSENGER   'Tis Alcibiades and some twenty horse,°   *horsemen*

235 All of companionship.°   *in one group*

TIMON [*to* SERVANT]   Pray, entertain them; give them guide to us.
                                   [*Exit* SERVANT.]
     You must needs dine with me. Go not you hence
     Till I have thanked you. [*to* PAINTER] When dinner's done
     Show me this piece. I am joyful of your sights.°   *to see you*
          Enter ALCIBIADES *with* [SOLDIERS *on horseback*].

240 —Most welcome, sir!

APEMANTUS [*aside*]   So, so, there! Aches contract and starve°   *ruin*
     your supple joints. That there should be small love amongst

---

9. I do not devour the substance of.   2. Foresight (so I could avoid it).
1. Interpretation; grasping.

these sweet knaves and all this courtesy! The strain of man's
bred out° into baboon and monkey.   *degenerated*
245 ALCIBIADES [*to* TIMON]   Sir, you have saved my longing,° and I   *anticipated my desire*
feed
Most hungerly on your sight.
TIMON   Right welcome, sir!
Ere we depart we'll share a bounteous time
In different pleasures. Pray you, let us in.
                                          Exeunt [*all but* APEMANTUS].
             Enter two LORDS.
FIRST LORD   What time o'day is't, Apemantus?
APEMANTUS   Time to be honest.
250 FIRST LORD   That time serves still.°   *always*
APEMANTUS   The most accursèd thou that still omitt'st° it.   *do not take advantage of*
SECOND LORD   Thou art going to Lord Timon's feast?
APEMANTUS   Ay, to see meat fill knaves and wine heat fools.
SECOND LORD   Fare thee well, fare thee well.
255 APEMANTUS   Thou art a fool to bid me farewell twice.
SECOND LORD   Why, Apemantus?
APEMANTUS   Shouldst have kept one to thyself, for I mean to
give thee none.
FIRST LORD   Hang thyself!
260 APEMANTUS   No, I will do nothing at thy bidding. Make thy
requests to thy friend.
SECOND LORD   Away, unpeaceable dog, or I'll spurn° thee hence.   *kick*
APEMANTUS   I will fly like a dog the heels o'th' ass.
FIRST LORD   He's opposite° to humanity.   *antagonistic*
265 Come, shall we in and taste Lord Timon's bounty?
He outgoes° the very heart° of kindness.   *surpasses / essence*
SECOND LORD   He pours it out. Plutus, the god of gold,
Is but his steward. No meed° but he repays   *gift*
Sevenfold above itself; no gift to him
270 But breeds the giver a return exceeding
All use of quittance.°   *customary interest rates*
FIRST LORD   The noblest mind he carries
That ever governed man.
SECOND LORD   Long may he live in fortunes. Shall we in?
FIRST LORD   I'll keep you company.   *Exeunt.*

1.2

Oboes playing loud music.
A great banquet served in [*by Flavius the* STEWARD
and SERVANTS], *and then enter Lord* TIMON, *the*
[SENATORS], *the Athenian* LORDS, [ALCIBIADES, *and*]
VENTIDIUS *which Timon redeemed from prison. Then*
comes dropping° after all APEMANTUS *discontentedly*   *entering casually*
like himself.°   *in everyday clothes*
VENTIDIUS   Most honored Timon,
It hath pleased the gods to remember
My father's age and call him to long peace.°   *eternal rest*
He is gone happy and has left me rich.

1.2 Location: Timon's banqueting room.

5   Then, as in grateful virtue I am bound
       To your free° heart, I do return those talents,   generous
       Doubled with thanks and service, from whose help
       I derived liberty.
TIMON   Oh, by no means,
       Honest Ventidius. You mistake my love.
10   I gave it freely ever, and there's none
       Can truly say he gives if he receives.
       If our betters play at that game,° we must not dare   pretend generosity
       To imitate them. Faults that are rich° are fair.   of rich people
VENTIDIUS   A noble spirit!
       [The LORDS stand.]
15 TIMON   Nay, my lords,
       Ceremony was but devised at first
       To set a gloss on¹ faint deeds, hollow welcomes,
       Recanting goodness,² sorry ere 'tis shown.
       But where there is true friendship, there needs none.°   no ceremony
20   Pray, sit. More welcome are ye to my fortunes
       Than my fortunes to me.
       [They sit.]
FIRST LORD   My lord, we always have confessed it.
APEMANTUS   Ho, ho, confessed it? Hanged it, have you not?
TIMON   O Apemantus, you are welcome!
25 APEMANTUS   No. You shall not make me welcome:
       I come to have thee° thrust me out of doors.   provoke you to
TIMON   Fie, thou'rt a churl.° Ye've got a humor there   rude one
       Does not become a man. 'Tis much to blame.
       They say, my lords, *Ira furor brevis est,*³
30   But yond man is ever angry.
       Go, let him have a table by himself,
       For he does neither affect° company,   like
       Nor is he fit for't, indeed.
APEMANTUS   Let me stay at thine apperil,° Timon.   risk
35   I come to observe; I give thee warning on't.
TIMON   I take no heed of thee. Thou'rt an Athenian,
       Therefore welcome. I myself would have no power;⁴
       Prithee, let my meat make thee silent.
APEMANTUS   I scorn thy meat. 'Twould choke me, for I should
40   ne'er flatter thee. O you gods! What a number of men eats
       Timon, and he sees 'em not! It grieves me to see so many dip
       their meat in one man's blood, and all° the madness is, he   the height of
       cheers them up,° too.   encourages them
       I wonder men dare trust themselves with men.
45   Methinks they should invite them without knives:⁵
       Good for their meat, and safer for their lives.
       There's much example for't. The fellow that sits next him,
       now parts° bread with him, pledges the breath of him in a   shares
       divided draft,⁶ is the readiest man to kill him. 'T has been
50   proved. If I were a huge° man, I should fear to drink at meals,   great

---

1. To give a fine appearance to.
2. Generosity that demands repayment or that is immediately revoked.
3. Anger is brief insanity (Latin).

4. Wish no power to silence you.
5. Renaissance dinner guests brought their own silverware.
6. *pledges . . . draft*: toasts his health in a shared cup.

Lest they should spy my windpipe's dangerous notes.[7]
Great men should drink with harness° on their throats.   *armor*
TIMON [*drinking to a* LORD]   My lord, in heart. And let the
      health° go round.   *shared cup*
SECOND LORD   Let it flow° this way, my good lord.   *circulate*
55   APEMANTUS   "Flow this way"? A brave° fellow. He keeps his   *fine (ironic)*
      tides[8] well. Those healths will make thee and thy state look ill,
      Timon.
      Here's that which is too weak to be a sinner:
      Honest water, which ne'er left man i'th' mire.
60   This and my food are equals; there's no odds.
      Feasts are too proud to give thanks to the gods.
                    Apemantus' grace.
            Immortal gods, I crave no pelf.°   *property (contemptuous)*
            I pray for no man but myself.
            Grant I may never prove so fond°   *foolish*
65   To trust man on his oath or bond,
            Or a harlot for her weeping,
            Or a dog that seems a-sleeping,
            Or a keeper° with my freedom,   *jailer*
            Or my friends if I should need 'em.
70   Amen. So fall to't.
            Rich men sin, and I eat root.
      Much good dich° thy good heart, Apemantus.   *may it do*
TIMON   Captain Alcibiades, your heart's in the field° now.   *battlefield*
ALCIBIADES   My heart is ever at your service, my lord.
75   TIMON   You had rather be at a breakfast of enemies° than a *(at a battle)*
      dinner of friends.
ALCIBIADES   So they were bleeding new, my lord, there's no
      meat like 'em. I could wish my best friend at such a feast.
APEMANTUS   Would all those flatterers were thine enemies
      then,
80   That then thou mightst kill 'em and bid me to 'em.
FIRST LORD   Might we but have that happiness, my lord, that
      you would once use our hearts,[9] whereby we might express
      some part of our zeals,° we should think ourselves forever   *love*
      perfect.°   *happy*
85   TIMON   Oh, no doubt, my good friends, but the gods them-
      selves have provided that I shall have much help from you.
      How had you been my friends else? Why have you that
      charitable title° from thousands?[1] Did not you chiefly belong *loving name*
      to my heart? I have told more of you to myself than you can
90   with modesty speak in your own behalf, and thus far I con-
      firm you.[2] O you gods, think I, what need we have any
      friends, if we should ne'er have need of 'em? They were the
      most needless creatures living, should we ne'er have use for
      'em, and would most resemble sweet instruments hung up in
95   cases that keeps their sounds to themselves. Why, I have
      often wished myself poorer that I might come nearer to you.

---

7. *my . . . notes:* the indications, when I drink, of
where my windpipe is (so they can cut my throat).
8. He observes his opportunity (joking, with wordplay on "flow," that the Second Lord is ensuring that
he gets plenty to drink).
9. Would test of our affection.

1. Timon seems to mean, "Why are you, of all the
thousands of Athenians, called my friends?" but also
possibly, "Why do so many thousands of people call
you their friends?"
2. In your claim to be my friends.

We are born to do benefits, and what better or properer° can   *more suitably*
we call our own than the riches of our friends? Oh, what a
precious comfort 'tis to have so many like brothers
100   commanding³ one another's fortunes! Oh, joy's e'en made
away° ere't can be born. Mine eyes cannot hold out water,   *destroyed (by tears)*
methinks. To forget their° faults, I drink to you.   *(my eyes')*

APEMANTUS   Thou weep'st to make them drink, Timon.

SECOND LORD   Joy had the like° conception in our eyes   *same kind of*
105   And, at that instant, like a babe sprung up.

APEMANTUS   Ho, ho! I laugh to think that babe a bastard.⁴

THIRD LORD [*to* TIMON]   I promise you, my lord, you moved me
    much.

APEMANTUS   Much.
     Sound tucket.°   *trumpet flourish*

TIMON   What means that trump? How now?
     Enter SERVANT.

110   SERVANT   Please you, my lord, there are certain ladies most
    desirous of admittance.

TIMON   Ladies? What are their wills?

SERVANT   There comes with them a forerunner, my lord,
    which bears that office,° to signify their pleasures.°   *function / desires*

115   TIMON   I pray let them be admitted.
     Enter CUPID.

CUPID   Hail to thee, worthy Timon, and to all
    That of his bounties taste. The five best senses
    Acknowledge thee their patron and come freely
    To gratulate° thy plenteous bosom.°   *greet / generous heart*
120   There taste, touch, all, pleased from thy table rise.
    They° only now come but to feast thine eyes.   *(the masquers)*

TIMON   They're welcome all! Let 'em have kind admittance.
    Music make their welcome.

FIRST LORD   You see, my lord, how ample you're beloved.
     Enter the masque of LADIES [*as*] *Amazons with lutes in*
     *their hands, dancing and playing.*⁵

125   APEMANTUS   Hoy-day, what a sweep of vanity comes this way!
    They dance? They are madwomen.
    Like madness is the glory° of this life   *vain display*
    As this pomp shows to a little oil and root.⁶
    We make ourselves fools to disport° ourselves   *amuse*
130   And spend our flatteries to drink° those men   *toast; drink up*
    Upon whose age we void° it up again   *old age we spit*
    With poisonous spite and envy.
    Who lives that's not depraved or depraves?
    Who dies that bears not one spurn° to their graves   *insult*
135   Of their friends' gift?°   *giving*
    I should fear those that dance before me now
    Would one day stamp upon me. 'T has been done.
    Men shut their doors against a setting sun.
     The LORDS *rise from table with much adoring of*
     TIMON, *and to show their loves each single out an*
     Amazon, and all dance, men with women, a lofty
     strain or two to the oboes and cease.

---

3. *commanding*: having at their command.
4. That is, the guests' tears are illegitimate.
5. TEXTUAL COMMENT The masque is a courtly entertainment. For information on the masque genre in the
early seventeenth century, see Digital Edition TC 2.
6. As this feast compares to a meager meal.

TIMON You have done our pleasures much grace, fair ladies,
140   Set a fair fashion on° our entertainment,   *Made elegant*
  Which was not half so beautiful and kind.
  You have added worth unto't and luster,
  And entertained me with mine own device.[7]
  I am to thank you for't.
145 FIRST LADY My lord, you take us even at the best.[8]
APEMANTUS Faith, for the worst is filthy and would not hold
  taking,[9] I doubt me.
TIMON Ladies, there is an idle° banquet attends you.   *a trifling*
  Please you to dispose° yourselves.   *seat*
150 ALL LADIES Most thankfully, my lord.
                Exeunt [LADIES *and* CUPID].
TIMON Flavius.
STEWARD My lord.
TIMON The little casket bring me hither.
STEWARD Yes, my lord. [*aside*] More jewels yet?
155   There is no crossing him in 's humor,°   *whim*
  Else I should tell him well, i'faith I should,
  When all's spent, he'd be crossed[1] then, an° he could.   *if*
  'Tis pity bounty had not eyes behind,[2]
  That man might ne'er be wretched for his mind.[3]   *Exit.*
160 FIRST LORD Where be our men?
SERVANT Here, my lord, in readiness.
SECOND LORD Our horses.   [*Exit* SERVANT.]
TIMON O my friends, I have one word to say to you—
  Look you, my good lord,
165   I must entreat you honor me so much
  As to advance° this jewel. Accept it and wear it,   *improve (by your worth)*
  Kind my lord.
      [TIMON *gives the jewel.*]
FIRST LORD I am so far already in your gifts.
ALL LORDS So are we all.
         Enter [FIRST] SERVANT.
170 FIRST SERVANT My lord, there are certain nobles of the Sen-
  ate newly alighted and come to visit you.
TIMON They are fairly° welcome.   [*Exit* FIRST SERVANT.]   *graciously*
         Enter Flavius [*the* STEWARD].
STEWARD I beseech your honor, vouchsafe me a word; it does
  concern you near.
175 TIMON Near? Why, then, another time I'll hear thee. I prithee,
  let's be provided to show them entertainment.
STEWARD I scarce know how.
         Enter [*a* SECOND] SERVANT.
SECOND SERVANT May it please your honor, Lord Lucius
  Out of his free love hath presented to you
180   Four milk-white horses trapped° in silver.   *bedecked*
TIMON I shall accept them fairly. Let the presents

---

7. Plan. Timon may be implying that he himself
arranged the entertainment, or merely that it was
designed for him by his admirers.
8. You consider our efforts in the best possible light.
9. Would not be worth noting; would not endure sex-

ual penetration (because of venereal disease).
1. He'd want to have his debts canceled.
2. 'Tis a pity generosity is not more careful.
3. *for his mind:* because of his (generous) intentions.

Be worthily entertained.°   [*Exit* SECOND SERVANT.]   *accepted*
    Enter a THIRD SERVANT.
                How now, what news?
THIRD SERVANT   Please you, my lord, that honorable gentle-
    man Lord Lucullus entreats your company tomorrow to
185   hunt with him, and he's sent your honor two brace° of   *pairs*
    greyhounds.
TIMON   I'll hunt with him, and let them be received
    Not without fair reward.   [*Exit* THIRD SERVANT.]
STEWARD [*aside*]   What will this come to?
    He commands us to provide and give great gifts,
190   And all out of an empty coffer;
    Nor will he know his purse, or yield° me this: *allow*
    To show him what a beggar his heart is,
    Being of no power to make his wishes good.
    His promises fly so beyond his state°   *estate*
195   That what he speaks is all in debt. He owes
    For every word. He is so kind that he now
    Pays interest for't. His land's put to their books.°   *mortgaged*
    Well, would I were gently put out of office
    Before I were forced out.
200   Happier is he that has no friend to feed
    Than such that do e'en enemies exceed.[4]
    I bleed inwardly for my lord.   *Exit.*
TIMON [*to* LORDS]   You do yourselves
    Much wrong; you bate° too much of your own merits.   *undervalue*
    [*to* SECOND LORD] Here, my lord, a trifle of our love.
205 SECOND LORD   With more than common thanks I will receive it.
    THIRD LORD   Oh, he's the very soul of bounty.
TIMON [*to* FIRST LORD]   And now I remember, my lord, you gave
    Good words the other day of a bay courser°   *horse*
    I rode on. 'Tis yours because you liked it.
210 FIRST LORD   Oh, I beseech you, pardon me, my lord, in that.[5]
TIMON   You may take my word, my lord; I know no man
    Can justly praise but what he does affect.°   *desire*
    I weigh my friends' affection with mine own.
    I'll tell you true, I'll call to° you.   *on*
ALL LORDS   Oh, none so welcome.
215 TIMON   I take all and your several visitations
    So kind to heart. 'Tis not enough to give.
    Methinks I could deal kingdoms to my friends
    And ne'er be weary. Alcibiades,
    Thou art a soldier, therefore seldom rich.
220   It comes in charity to thee, for all thy living
    Is 'mongst the dead, and all the lands thou hast
    Lie in a pitched field.
ALCIBIADES   Ay, defiled[6] land, my lord.
FIRST LORD   We are so virtuously bound.
TIMON   And so am I to you.

---

4. Who ruin themselves faster than enemies could.
5. That is, I wasn't hinting for the horse.
6. Lined with ranks of soldiers; punning on Ecclesias-

ticus 13:1, "He that toucheth pitch, shall be defiled
with it."

225 SECOND LORD So infinitely endeared.°   *obliged*
   TIMON All to you. —Lights, more lights!
   FIRST LORD The best of happiness, honor, and fortunes
     Keep with you, Lord Timon.
   TIMON Ready for his friends.

          Exeunt [all but TIMON *and* APEMANTUS].

   APEMANTUS   What a coil's° here,   *commotion is*
230 Serving of becks° and jutting out of bums.   *bowing*
   I doubt whether their legs° be worth the sums   *curtsies*
   That are given for 'em. Friendship's full of dregs.
   Methinks false hearts should never have sound legs.
   Thus honest fools lay out their wealth on curtsies.
235 TIMON Now, Apemantus, if thou wert not sullen,
   I would be good to thee.
   APEMANTUS No, I'll nothing. For if I should be bribed too,
     there would be none left to rail upon thee, and then thou
     wouldst sin the faster. Thou giv'st so long, Timon, I fear me
240 thou wilt give away thyself in paper° shortly. What needs   *promissory notes*
     these feasts, pomps, and vainglories?
   TIMON Nay, an you begin to rail on society once, I am sworn
     not to give regard° to you.   *pay attention*
     Farewell, and come with better music.   *Exit.*
   APEMANTUS   So.
245 Thou wilt not hear me now; thou shalt not then.
   I'll lock thy heaven° from thee. Oh, that men's ears   *(my redemptive guidance)*
     should be
   To counsel deaf, but not to flattery.   *Exit.*

2.1

          Enter a SENATOR.

   SENATOR And late five thousand. To Varro and to Isidore
   He owes nine thousand, besides my former sum,
   Which makes it five-and-twenty. Still in motion
   Of raging waste?[1] It cannot hold,° it will not.   *last*
5 If I want gold, steal but a beggar's dog
   And give it Timon, why, the dog coins gold!
   If I would sell my horse and buy twenty more
   Better than he, why, give my horse to Timon.
   Ask nothing, give it him; it foals me straight
10 And able horses.[2] No porter[3] at his gate,
   But rather one that smiles and still invites
   All that pass by. It cannot hold. No reason
   Can sound his state in safety.[4] —Caphis, ho!
   Caphis, I say!

          Enter CAPHIS.

   CAPHIS   Here, sir, what is your pleasure?
15 SENATOR Get on your cloak, and haste you to Lord Timon.
   Importune him for my moneys. Be not ceased°   *put off*
   With slight denial, nor then silenced when

2.1 Location: A Senator's house.
1. *Still . . . waste*: Still keeping up unending
extravagance.
2. *it . . . horses*: it immediately "gives birth to" full-

grown horses (not "foals," baby horses).
3. Gatekeeper (who restricts entrance).
4. *No reason . . . safety*: No rational person can investigate his financial situation and believe it safe.

"Commend me to your master," and the cap
Plays in the right hand[5] thus, but tell him
20   My uses cry to me. I must serve my turn
Out of mine own.[6] His days and times are past,
And my reliances on his fracted° dates   broken
Have smit° my credit. I love and honor him   hurt
But must not break my back to heal his finger.
25   Immediate are my needs, and my relief
Must not be tossed and turned[7] to me in words
But find supply immediate. Get you gone.
Put on a most importunate aspect,
A visage of demand, for I do fear
30   When every feather sticks in his own wing[8]
Lord Timon will be left a naked gull,°   an unfledged bird; dupe
Which flashes now a phoenix. Get you gone!
CAPHIS   I go, sir.
SENATOR   "I go, sir"? [He gives him bonds.] Take the bonds
        along with you,
And have the dates in. Come.
CAPHIS   I will, sir.
35   SENATOR   Go.   Exeunt.

2.2

Enter STEWARD with many bills in his hand.
STEWARD   No care, no stop—so senseless of expense
That he will neither know how to maintain it
Nor cease his flow of riot,° takes no account   his wastefulness
How things go from him, nor resume° no care   takes
5   Of what is to continue. Never mind
Was to be so unwise to be so kind.[1]
What shall be done? He will not hear till feel.°   he suffers
I must be round° with him, now he comes from hunting.   frank
Fie, fie, fie, fie!
        Enter CAPHIS, ISIDORE['S SERVANT], and VARRO['S
        SERVANT].
10   CAPHIS   Good even, Varro. What, you come for money?
VARRO'S SERVANT   Is't not your business too?
CAPHIS   It is—and yours too, Isidore?
ISIDORE'S SERVANT   It is so.
CAPHIS   Would we were all dischargèd.
VARRO'S SERVANT   I fear it.
CAPHIS   Here comes the lord.
        Enter TIMON and his train [of LORDS, with ALCIBIADES].
15   TIMON   So soon as dinner's done we'll forth again,
My Alcibiades—
        [CAPHIS approaches TIMON.]
                —With me? What is your will?
CAPHIS   My lord, here is a note of certain dues.°   debts

---

5. when . . . hand: that is, with friendly speech and
gestures.
6. serve . . . own: pay for my needs with my own money.
7. Returned (like a tennis ball).

8. When everything is returned to its proper owner.
2.2 Location: Before Timon's house.
1. Never . . . kind: Never was anyone so idiotically
generous.

TIMON Dues? Whence are you?

CAPHIS   Of Athens here, my lord.

TIMON Go to my steward.

20 CAPHIS Please it your lordship, he hath put me off

To the succession of new days this month.°   *Every day for a month*

My master is awaked° by great occasion°   *driven / need*

To call upon his own° and humbly prays you   *own money*

That, with your other noble parts, you'll suit[2]

In giving him his right.

25 TIMON   Mine honest friend,

I prithee but repair° to me next morning.   *come back*

CAPHIS Nay, good my lord.

TIMON   Contain thyself, good friend.

VARRO'S SERVANT [*giving bond to* TIMON] One Varro's servant,

my good lord.

ISIDORE'S SERVANT [*giving bond to* TIMON] From Isidore. He

humbly prays your speedy payment.

30 CAPHIS If you did know, my lord, my master's wants.

VARRO'S SERVANT 'Twas due on forfeiture,[3] my lord, six weeks

and past.

ISIDORE'S SERVANT Your steward puts me off, my lord, and I

Am sent expressly to your lordship.

TIMON   Give me breath.

—I do beseech you, good my lords, keep on.°   *go ahead*

I'll wait upon you instantly.

       [*Exeunt* LORDS *with* ALCIBIADES.]

35 [*to* STEWARD]   Come hither, pray you.

How goes the world that I am thus encountered

With clamorous demands of debt, broken bonds,

And the detention of° long-since-due debts   *failure to pay*

Against my honor?

STEWARD [*to* SERVANTS] Please you, gentlemen,

40 The time is unagreeable to this business.

Your importunacy cease till after dinner,

That I may make his lordship understand

Wherefore you are not paid.

TIMON [*to* SERVANTS] Do so, my friends. [*to* STEWARD] See them

well entertained.   [*Exit.*]

45 STEWARD Pray, draw near.   *Exit.*

    Enter APEMANTUS *and* FOOL.

CAPHIS Stay, stay, here comes the Fool with Apemantus.

Let's ha' some sport with 'em.

VARRO'S SERVANT Hang him, he'll abuse us.

ISIDORE'S SERVANT A plague upon him, dog.

50 VARRO'S SERVANT How dost, Fool?

APEMANTUS Dost dialogue with thy shadow?[4]

VARRO'S SERVANT I speak not to thee.

APEMANTUS No, 'tis to thyself. [*to* FOOL] Come away.

ISIDORE'S SERVANT There's the Fool[5] hangs on your back

55 already.

---

2. That you'll act in accordance with your noble
qualities.
3. On penalty of forfeiting the security.
4. With your reflection (implying that Varro's Ser-

vant is also a fool).
5. The name "fool." In Renaissance England, wrong-
doers were punished by being made to wear signs
declaring their offenses.

APEMANTUS   No, thou stand'st single.° Thou'rt not on him yet.   alone (in being a fool)

CAPHIS   Where's the Fool now?

APEMANTUS   He last asked the question. Poor rogues and usurers' men, bawds between gold and want.[6]

60   ALL SERVANTS   What are we, Apemantus?

APEMANTUS   Asses.

ALL SERVANTS   Why?

APEMANTUS   That you ask me what you are and do not know
yourselves. —Speak to 'em, Fool.

65   FOOL   How do you, gentlemen?

ALL SERVANTS   Gramercies,° good Fool. How does your mistress?   Many thanks

FOOL   She's e'en° setting on water to scald such chickens[7] as   just now
you are. Would we could see you at Corinth.[8]

APEMANTUS   Good, gramercy.

Enter PAGE.

70   FOOL   Look you, here comes my master's page.

PAGE [*to* FOOL]   Why, how now, captain? What do you in this
wise company? —How dost thou, Apemantus?

APEMANTUS   Would I had a rod[9] in my mouth that I might
answer thee profitably.

75   PAGE   Prithee, Apemantus, read me the superscription° of   address
these letters. I know not which is which.

APEMANTUS   Canst not read?

PAGE   No.

APEMANTUS   There will little learning die, then, that day thou
80   art hanged. This is to Lord Timon, this to Alcibiades. Go,
thou wast born a bastard, and thou'lt die a bawd.

PAGE   Thou wast whelped a dog, and thou shalt famish° a   die
dog's death. Answer not; I am gone.   *Exit.*

APEMANTUS   E'en so thou outrunn'st grace.[1] —Fool, I will go
85   with you to Lord Timon's.

FOOL   Will you leave me there?

APEMANTUS   If Timon stay at home.[2] —You three serve three
usurers?

ALL SERVANTS   Ay, would they served us.°   treated us well

90   APEMANTUS   So would I: as good a trick as ever hangman
served thief.

FOOL   Are you three usurers' men?

ALL SERVANTS   Ay, Fool.

FOOL   I think no usurer but has a fool to his servant. My mis-
95   tress is one,[3] and I am her fool. When men come to borrow
of your masters, they approach sadly and go away merry, but
they enter my master's house merrily and go away sadly.[4]
The reason of this?

VARRO'S SERVANT   I could render one.

---

6. *bawds . . . want:* go-betweens making deals
between moneylenders and those who need loans.
7. In order to remove the feathers (a "plucked bird"
was a hoodwinked fool; compare 2.1.31); also, syphi-
litics were "sweated" in tubs of very hot water.
8. Greek city famous for prostitution.
9. From Proverbs 26:3–4: "Unto the horse belongeth
a whip, to the ass a bridle, and a rod to the fool's
back. Answer not a fool according to his foolishness,

lest thou also be like him."
1. You run away from profitable instruction.
2. There will be a fool at Timon's house as long as he
is at home.
3. She is a "usurer" in the sense that she lends her
body for financial gain; the connection between usury
and prostitution was traditional.
4. According to Aristotle, all creatures are sad after
sexual intercourse.

APEMANTUS Do it then, that we may account thee a whoremaster and a knave, which notwithstanding thou shalt be
 no less esteemed.
VARRO'S SERVANT What is a whoremaster, Fool?
FOOL A fool in good clothes, and something like thee. 'Tis a
 spirit. Sometime't appears like a lord, sometime like a lawyer, sometime like a philosopher, with two stones[5] more
 than 's° artificial one. He is very often like a knight, and   *than his*
 generally in all shapes that man goes up and down in from
 fourscore to thirteen, this spirit walks in.
VARRO'S SERVANT Thou art not altogether a fool.
FOOL Nor thou altogether a wise man. As much foolery as I
 have, so much wit thou lack'st.
APEMANTUS That answer might have become° Apemantus.   *suited*
ALL SERVANTS Aside, aside! Here comes Lord Timon.
   Enter TIMON *and* STEWARD.
APEMANTUS Come with me, Fool, come.
FOOL I do not always follow lover, elder brother, and woman:[6]
 sometime the philosopher. [*Exeunt* APEMANTUS *and* FOOL.]
STEWARD [*to* SERVANTS] Pray you, walk near. I'll speak with
  you anon.   *Exeunt* [SERVANTS].
TIMON You make me marvel wherefore ere this time
 Had you not fully laid my state before me,[7]
 That I might so have rated° my expense   *regulated*
 As I had leave of means.°   *As means permitted*
STEWARD   You would not hear me.
 At many leisures I proposed.
TIMON   Go to.°   *(impatient exclamation)*
 Perchance some single vantages° you took   *isolated opportunities*
 When my indisposition° put you back,   *disinclination*
 And that unaptness made your minister°   *allowed you*
 Thus to excuse yourself.
STEWARD   O my good lord,
 At many times I brought in my accounts,
 Laid them before you. You would throw them off
 And say you found them in mine honesty.[8]
 When for some trifling present you have bid me
 Return so much,° I have shook my head and wept,   *a large sum*
 Yea, 'gainst th'authority of manners,° prayed you   *with rude bluntness*
 To hold your hand more close. I did endure
 Not seldom nor no slight checks° when I have   *rebukes*
 Prompted you in° the ebb of your estate   *Urged you to note*
 And your great flow of debts. My lovèd lord,
 Though you hear now too late, yet now's a time°   *by now*
 The greatest of your having[9] lacks a half
 To pay your present debts.
TIMON   Let all my land be sold.
STEWARD 'Tis all engaged,° some forfeited and gone,   *mortgaged*
 And what remains will hardly stop the mouth

---

5. Testicles. In alchemy, the "philosopher's stone"
was thought to turn base metals into gold.
6. All figures associated with folly.

7. Described my financial status.
8. You gauged their accuracy by my honesty.
9. The most generous estimate of your wealth.

Of present dues.° The future comes apace.   *debts*
What shall defend the interim, and at length°   *in the long term*
145 How goes our reckoning?
    TIMON   To Lacedaemon° did my land extend.   *Sparta*
    STEWARD   O my good lord, the world is but a word.
    Were it all yours to give it in a breath,
    How quickly were it gone.
    TIMON   You tell me true.
150 STEWARD   If you suspect my husbandry° or falsehood,   *household management*
    Call me before th'exactest auditors
    And set me on the proof. So the gods bless me,
    When all our offices° have been oppressed   *kitchens and workrooms*
    With riotous feeders, when our vaults have wept
155 With drunken spilth° of wine, when every room   *spilling*
    Hath blazed with lights and brayed with minstrelsy,
    I have retired me to a wasteful cock[1]
    And set mine eyes at flow.
    TIMON   Prithee, no more.
    STEWARD   "Heavens," have I said, "the bounty of this lord!
160 How many prodigal bits° have slaves and peasants   *extravagant morsels*
    This night englutted? Who is not Timon's?°   *devoted to Timon*
    What heart, head, sword, force, means, but is Lord Timon's?
    Great Timon, noble, worthy, royal Timon!"
    Ah, when the means are gone that buy this praise,
165 The breath is gone whereof this praise is made.
    Feast won, fast° lost. One cloud of winter showers: *quickly; while fasting*
    These flies are couched.°   *lying unseen*
    TIMON   Come, sermon me no further.
    No villainous° bounty yet hath passed my heart.   *shameful*
    Unwisely, not ignobly, have I given.
170 Why dost thou weep? Canst thou the conscience° lack   *conviction*
    To think I shall lack friends? Secure thy heart.
    If I would broach° the vessels of my love   *tap (like a wine barrel)*
    And try the argument° of hearts by borrowing,   *test the contents*
    Men and men's fortunes could I frankly° use   *as freely*
    As I can bid thee speak.
175 STEWARD   Assurance bless your thoughts.[2]
    TIMON   And in some sort° these wants of mine are crowned°   *respect / exalted*
    That I account them blessings. For by these
    Shall I try friends. You shall perceive how you
    Mistake my fortunes: I am wealthy in my friends.
180 —Within there, Flaminius, Servilius?
              Enter three SERVANTS *[including* FLAMINIUS *and*
              SERVILIUS*].*
    ALL SERVANTS   My lord, my lord.
    TIMON   I will dispatch you severally:° [*to* SERVILIUS] you to   *separately*
    Lord Lucius, [*to* FLAMINIUS] to Lord Lucullus you—I hunted
    with his honor today— [*to third* SERVANT] you to Sempro-
185 nius. Commend me to their loves, and I am proud, say, that
    my occasions° have found time° to use 'em toward a supply   *needs / occasion*
    of money. Let the request be fifty talents.°   *(a huge sum)*

---

1. I have sat down beside a wine spout, left waste-   2. May your hopes be well founded.
fully flowing.

FLAMINIUS As you have said, my lord.   [*Exeunt* SERVANTS.]
STEWARD Lord Lucius and Lucullus? Humph!
190 TIMON Go you, sir, to the senators,
    Of whom, even to the state's best health,[3] I have
    Deserved this hearing. Bid 'em send o'th' instant
    A thousand talents to me.
STEWARD   I have been bold,
    For that I knew it the most general° way,   *usual*
195   To them to use your signet[4] and your name,
    But they do shake their heads, and I am here
    No richer in return.
TIMON   Is't true? Can 't be?
STEWARD They answer in a joint and corporate voice
    That now they are at fall,° want° treasure, cannot   *low ebb / lack*
200 Do what they would, are sorry. You are honorable,
    But yet they could have wished—they know not—
    Something hath been amiss; a noble nature
    May catch a wrench;° would all were well; 'tis pity.   *suffer a misfortune*
    And so intending° other serious matters,   *pretending; attending to*
205 After distasteful looks and these hard fractions,°   *phrases*
    With certain half-caps° and cold-moving nods,   *reluctant salutations*
    They froze me into silence.
TIMON   You gods, reward them!
    Prithee, man, look cheerily.° These old fellows   *cheerful*
    Have their ingratitude in them hereditary.
210 Their blood is caked, 'tis cold, it seldom flows.
    'Tis lack of kindly[5] warmth they are not kind.
    And nature, as it grows again toward earth,°   *the grave*
    Is fashioned for the journey dull and heavy.
    Go to Ventidius. Prithee, be not sad;
215 Thou art true and honest. Ingeniously I speak;
    No blame belongs to thee. Ventidius lately
    Buried his father, by whose death he's stepped
    Into a great estate. When he was poor,
    Imprisoned, and in scarcity of friends
220 I cleared him with five talents. Greet him from me.
    Bid him suppose some good° necessity   *urgent*
    Touches his friend, which craves to be remembered
    With° those five talents. That had, give't these fellows *By return of*
    To whom 'tis instant due. Never speak or think
225 That Timon's fortunes 'mong his friends can sink.
STEWARD I would I could not think it. That thought is bounty's
    foe;
    Being free° itself, it thinks all others so.   *Exeunt.*   *generous*

3.1

[*Enter*] FLAMINIUS *waiting to speak with a lord*[,
LUCULLUS]. *From his master enters a* SERVANT *to him.*
SERVANT I have told my lord of you. He is coming down to you.
FLAMINIUS I thank you, sir.
    Enter LUCULLUS.
SERVANT Here's my lord.

---

3. Greatest welfare (see 4.3.92–95).   5. Natural, caring.
4. Signet ring (token of authorization).   3.1 Location: Lucullus's house.

LUCULLUS [*aside*] One of Lord Timon's men? A gift, I war-
5   rant. Why, this hits right: I dreamt of a silver basin and ewer°   *pitcher*
  tonight. —Flaminius, honest Flaminius, you are very respec-
  tively° welcome, sir! [*to* SERVANT] Fill me some wine.   *respectfully*
                                     [*Exit* SERVANT.]
  And how does that honorable, complete, freehearted gentleman of Athens, thy very bountiful good lord and master?
10 FLAMINIUS His health is well, sir.
  LUCULLUS I am right glad that his health is well, sir. And what
  hast thou there under thy cloak, pretty Flaminius?
  FLAMINIUS Faith, nothing but an empty box, sir, which in my
  lord's behalf I come to entreat your honor to supply, who,
15   having great and instant° occasion to use fifty talents, hath   *urgent*
  sent to your lordship to furnish him, nothing doubting your
  present° assistance therein.   *immediate*
  LUCULLUS La, la, la, la, "nothing doubting," says he? Alas,
  good lord! A noble gentleman 'tis, if he would not keep so
20   good a house.° Many a time and often I ha' dined with him   *such lavish hospitality*
  and told him on't, and come again to supper to him of pur-
  pose to have him[1] spend less, and yet he would embrace no
  counsel, take no warning by my coming. Every man has his
  fault, and honesty° is his. I ha' told him on't, but I could   *generosity*
25   ne'er get him from't.
        Enter SERVANT *with wine.*
  SERVANT Please your lordship, here is the wine.
  LUCULLUS Flaminius, I have noted thee always wise. Here's
  to thee!
        [*He drinks.*]
  FLAMINIUS Your lordship speaks your pleasure.°   *It pleases you to say so*
30 LUCULLUS I have observed thee always for a towardly° prompt   *promising*
  spirit, give thee thy due, and one that knows what belongs
  to reason° and canst use the time well, if the time use thee   *is reasonable*
  well[2]—good parts in thee![3] [*to* SERVANT] Get you gone,
  sirrah.   [*Exit* SERVANT.]
35   Draw nearer, honest Flaminius. Thy lord's a bountiful gentleman, but thou art wise, and thou know'st well enough,
  although thou com'st to me, that this is no time to lend
  money, especially upon bare° friendship without security.   *mere*
  [*He gives coins.*] Here's three solidares° for thee. Good boy,   *shillings*
40   wink at me,[4] and say thou saw'st me not. Fare thee well.
  FLAMINIUS Is't possible the world should so much differ,°   *alter*
  And we alive that lived? [*He throws back the coins.*] Fly,
    damned baseness,
  To him that worships thee.
  LUCULLUS Ha! Now I see thou art a fool and fit for thy master.
                                       Exit.
45 FLAMINIUS May these add to the number that may scald thee.°   *(in hell)*
  Let molten coin be thy damnation,
  Thou disease of a friend, and not himself.°   *not a true friend*
  Has friendship such a faint and milky heart
  It turns° in less than two nights? O you gods!   *curdles*

---

1. *of . . . him:* in order to persuade him to.
2. *canst . . . thee well:* know how to use an
opportunity.
3. To your good qualities (a toast).
4. Close your eyes to me.

50	I feel my master's passion.° This slave	*suffering*
	Unto this hour has my lord's meat in him.	
	Why should it thrive and turn to nutriment,	
	When he is turned to poison?	
	Oh, may diseases only work upon't,	
55	And when he's sick to death, let not that part of nature	
	Which my lord paid for be of any power	
	To expel sickness, but prolong his hour.° *Exit.*	*(of suffering)*

3.2
Enter LUCIUS *with three* STRANGERS.

LUCIUS   Who, the Lord Timon? He is my very good friend and
an honorable gentleman.

FIRST STRANGER   We know him for no less, though we are but
strangers to him. But I can tell you one thing, my lord, and
5   which I hear from common rumors: now Lord Timon's happy
hours are done and past, and his estate shrinks from him.

LUCIUS   Fie, no, do not believe it! He cannot want for money.

SECOND STRANGER   But believe you this, my lord, that not
long ago one of his men was with the Lord Lucullus to bor-
10   row so many talents, nay urged extremely for't, and showed
what necessity belonged to't, and yet was denied.

LUCIUS   How?

SECOND STRANGER   I tell you, denied, my lord.

LUCIUS   What a strange case was that! Now before the gods,
15   I am ashamed on't. Denied that honorable man? There was
very little honor showed in't. For my own part, I must needs
confess I have received some small kindnesses from him, as
money, plate, jewels, and such like trifles—nothing comparing to his. Yet had he mistook him[1] and sent to me, I should
20   ne'er have denied his occasion so many talents.
      Enter SERVILIUS.

SERVILIUS [*aside*] See, by good hap yonder's my lord. I have	
sweat° to see his honor. [*to* LUCIUS] My honored lord.	*hurried*

LUCIUS   Servilius? You are kindly met, sir. [*He starts to leave.*]

Fare thee well. Commend me to thy honorable virtuous	
25 lord, my very exquisite° friend.	*extraordinary*

SERVILIUS May it please your honor, my lord hath sent—	
LUCIUS Ha? What has he sent? I am so much endeared° to	*obliged*

that lord; he's ever sending. How shall I thank him, think'st
thou? And what has he sent now?

30   SERVILIUS   He's only sent his present occasion now, my lord,
requesting your lordship to supply his instant use with so
many talents.

LUCIUS   I know his lordship is but merry with me.
He cannot want fifty, five hundred[2] talents.

35   SERVILIUS   But in the meantime he wants less, my lord.
If his occasion were not virtuous,
I should not urge it half so faithfully.

LUCULLUS   Dost thou speak seriously, Servilius?

SERVILIUS   Upon my soul 'tis true, sir.

3.2 Location: A public place.
1. Not overestimated Lucullus's generosity.

2. This number possibly retains Shakespeare's revision from "five hundred" to "fifty" or vice versa.

40 LUCIUS   What a wicked beast was I to disfurnish myself against
such a good time³ when I might ha' shown myself honorable!
How unluckily it happened that I should purchase the day
before for a little part° and undo a great deal of honor! Ser-   *small investment*
vilius, now before the gods, I am not able to do, the more
45 beast, I say! I was sending to use° Lord Timon myself—   *make use of*
these gentlemen can witness—but I would not for the
wealth of Athens I had done't now. Commend me bounti-
fully to his good lordship, and I hope his honor will conceive
the fairest° of me, because I have no power to be kind. And   *think the best*
50 tell him this from me: I count it one of my greatest afflic-
tions, say, that I cannot pleasure° such an honorable gentle-   *gratify*
man. Good Servilius, will you befriend me so far as to use
mine own words to him?
SERVILIUS   Yes, sir, I shall.
55 LUCIUS   I'll look you out° a good turn, Servilius.   *seek to do you*

           Exit SERVILIUS.⁴

—True as you said: Timon is shrunk indeed,
And he that's once denied will hardly speed.°   *Exit.*   *prosper*
FIRST STRANGER   Do you observe this, Hostilius?
SECOND STRANGER   Ay, too well.
FIRST STRANGER   Why, this is the world's soul,° and just of the   *essence*
same piece°   *(of cloth)*
60 Is every flatterer's spirit. Who can call him his friend
That dips in the same dish?⁵ For in my knowing
Timon has been this lord's father,°   *patron*
And kept his° credit with his purse,   *sustained (Lucius's)*
Supported his estate, nay, Timon's money
65 Has paid his men their wages. He ne'er drinks
But Timon's silver treads upon his lip,
And yet (oh, see the monstrousness of man
When he looks out° in an ungrateful shape!)   *shows himself*
He does deny him, in respect of his,⁶
70 What charitable men afford to beggars.
THIRD STRANGER   Religion groans at it.
FIRST STRANGER   For mine own part,
I never tasted° Timon in my life,   *had experience of*
Nor came any of his bounties over me
To mark me for his friend. Yet, I protest,
75 For his right noble mind, illustrious virtue,
And honorable carriage,°   *conduct*
Had his necessity made use of me,
I would have put my wealth into donation,°   *given my wealth*
And the best half should have returned to him,
80 So much I love his heart. But I perceive
Men must learn now with pity to dispense,
For policy° sits above conscience.   *Exeunt.*   *calculation*

---

3. *disfurnish . . . time:* be unprepared for such a fine
occasion.
4. TEXTUAL COMMENT In the Folio this stage direction is placed one line earlier, suggesting that Lucius
speaks to Servilius as he is going out. See Digital

Edition TC 3 for a discussion of this change.
5. Alluding to Judas's betrayal of Christ after the
Last Supper.
6. In proportion to what he owns.

3.3

Enter [Timon's] third SERVANT *with* SEMPRONIUS,
another of Timon's friends.

SEMPRONIUS   Must he needs trouble me in't? Humph! 'Bove
  all others?
He might have tried Lord Lucius, or Lucullus,
And now Ventidius is wealthy too,
Whom he redeemed from prison. All these
Owes their estates unto him.
5   SERVANT   My lord,
They have all been touched° and found base metal,   *tested for purity*
For they have all denied him.
  SEMPRONIUS   How![1] Have they denied him?
Has Ventidius and Lucullus denied him,
And does he send to me? Three? Humph!
10   It shows but little love or judgment in him.
Must I be his last refuge? His friends like physicians
Thrive, give him over.[2] Must I take th' cure upon me?
He's much disgraced me in't. I'm angry at him,
That might have known my place.[3] I see no sense for't,
15   But his occasions might have wooed me first.
For in my conscience,° I was the first man   *on my word*
That ere received gift from him,
And does he think so backwardly of me now
That I'll requite it last? No!
20   So it may prove an argument° of laughter   *a subject*
To th' rest, and 'mongst lords be thought a fool.
I'd rather than the worth of thrice the sum
He'd sent to me first, but for my mind's sake;[4]
I'd such a courage to do him good. But now return,
25   And with their faint reply this answer join:
Who bates° mine honor shall not know my coin.   *Exit.*   *undervalues*
  SERVANT   Excellent. Your lordship's a goodly villain. The devil
knew not what he did when he made man politic.° He   *calculating*
crossed[5] himself by't, and I cannot think but in the end the
30   villainies of man will set him clear.[6] How fairly° this lord   *fully; speciously*
strives to appear foul, takes virtuous copies° to be wicked.   *precepts*
Like those[7] that under hot ardent zeal would set whole
realms on fire, of such a nature is his politic love.
This was my lord's best hope. Now all are fled
35   Save only the gods. Now his friends are dead.
Doors that were ne'er acquainted with their wards°   *locks*
Many a bounteous year must be employed
Now to guard sure° their master.   *safely*
And this is all a liberal° course allows: *generous*
40   Who cannot keep his wealth must keep his house.[8]   *Exit.*

3.3 Location: Sempronius's house.
1. TEXTUAL COMMENT The exclamation point is a question mark in the Folio. The two forms of punctuation were not always distinguished in the early modern period, so a modernized edition must often choose between them. See Digital Edition TC 4.
2. Thrive, while abandoning him to death.
3. That is, his place in Timon's list of friends.
4. If only on account of my disposition to him.

5. Thwarted (by making men his equal); canceled from the list of debtors.
6. Will make him look innocent; will free him from debt.
7. Religious fanatics; perhaps alludes to the Catholic Gunpowder Plot to blow up King James I and Parliament in 1605.
8. Must stay indoors (for fear of arrest).

3.4

Enter [two of] VARRO'S *[*SERVANTS*] meeting others, all*
[servants of] Timon's creditors, to wait for his coming
out. Then enter LUCIUS' *[*SERVANT,*]* HORTENSIUS, *and*
*[*TITUS*].*

VARRO'S FIRST SERVANT Well met. Good morrow, Titus and
    Hortensius.
TITUS The like to you, kind Varro.
HORTENSIUS Lucius, what, do we meet together?
LUCIUS' SERVANT Ay, and I think one business does command
    us all.
    For mine is money.
5 TITUS   So is theirs and ours.
        Enter PHILOTUS.
LUCIUS' SERVANT And Sir Philotus, too!
PHILOTUS   Good day, at once.
LUCIUS' SERVANT Welcome, good brother!
    What do you think the hour?
PHILOTUS   Laboring for° nine.   *Approaching*
LUCIUS' SERVANT So much?
PHILOTUS   Is not my lord° seen yet?   *(Timon)*
LUCIUS' SERVANT   Not yet.
10 PHILOTUS I wonder on't. He was wont to shine° at seven.   *used to rise*
LUCIUS' SERVANT Ay, but the days are waxed shorter with him.
    You must consider that a prodigal course
    Is like the sun's,[1]
    But not like his° recoverable, I fear.   *(the sun's)*
15 'Tis deepest winter in Lord Timon's purse. That is:
    One may reach deep enough and yet find little.
PHILOTUS I am of° your fear for that.   *I share*
TITUS I'll show you how t'observe a strange event:
    [*to* HORTENSIUS] Your lord sends now for money?
HORTENSIUS   Most true, he does.
20 TITUS And he wears jewels now of Timon's gift,
    For° which I wait for money.   *For the purchase of*
HORTENSIUS   It is against my heart.°   *desire*
LUCIUS' SERVANT Mark how strange it shows:
    Timon in this should pay more than he owes;
    And e'en° as if your lord should wear rich jewels   *just*
25 And send for money for 'em.[2]
HORTENSIUS I'm weary of this charge,° the gods can witness.   *task*
    I know my lord hath spent of Timon's wealth,
    And now ingratitude makes it worse than stealth.°   *stealing*
VARRO'S FIRST SERVANT Yes, mine's three thousand crowns.
    What's yours?
30 LUCIUS' SERVANT Five thousand, mine.
VARRO'S FIRST SERVANT 'Tis much° deep, and it should seem   *very*
    by th' sum
    Your master's confidence was above mine.°   *(my master's)*
    Else surely his° had equaled.   *(my master's loan)*
      Enter FLAMINIUS.
TITUS One of Lord Timon's men.

3.4 Location: Timon's house.   2. And demand payment from Timon for supplying
1. That is, waning after the summer solstice.   them.

35 LUCIUS' SERVANT   Flaminius! Sir, a word. Pray, is my lord
   Ready to come forth?
FLAMINIUS   No, indeed he is not.
TITUS   We attend his lordship. Pray, signify so much.
FLAMINIUS   I need not tell him that; he knows you are
   Too diligent.   [*Exit.*]
   Enter STEWARD *in a cloak, muffled.*
40 LUCIUS' SERVANT   Ha! Is not that his steward muffled so?
   He goes away in a cloud.° Call him, call him!   *concealed; in trouble*
TITUS [*to* STEWARD]   Do you hear, sir?
VARRO'S SECOND SERVANT [*to* STEWARD]   By your leave, sir.
STEWARD   What do ye ask of me, my friend?
TITUS   We wait for certain money here, sir.
45 STEWARD   Ay,
   If money were as certain as your waiting,
   'Twere sure enough.
   Why then preferred° you not your sums and bills   *brought forward*
   When your false masters ate of my lord's meat?
50   Then they could smile and fawn upon his debts
   And take down th'interest into their gluttonous maws.
   You do yourselves but wrong to stir me up.
   Let me pass quietly.
   Believe't, my lord and I have made an end;°   *finished with each other*
55   I have no more to reckon, he to spend.
LUCIUS' SERVANT   Ay, but this answer will not serve.
STEWARD   If 'twill not serve,[3] 'tis not so base as you,
   For you serve knaves.   [*Exit.*]
VARRO'S FIRST SERVANT   How? What does his cashiered° wor-   *dismissed*
60 ship mutter?[4]
VARRO'S SECOND SERVANT   No matter what. He's poor, and
   that's revenge enough. Who can speak broader[5] than he that
   has no house to put his head in? Such may rail against great
   buildings.
   Enter SERVILIUS.
65 TITUS   Oh, here's Servilius. Now we shall know some answer.
SERVILIUS   If I might beseech you, gentlemen, to repair° some   *return*
   other hour, I should derive° much from't. For take't of my   *gain*
   soul, my lord leans wondrously to discontent. His comfort-
   able° temper has forsook him; he's much out of health and   *cheerful*
70 keeps his chamber.
LUCIUS' SERVANT   Many do keep their chambers are not sick,[6]
   And, if it be so far beyond his health,
   Methinks he should the sooner pay his debts
   And make a clear way to the gods.
SERVILIUS   Good gods!
75 TITUS   We cannot take this for answer, sir.
FLAMINIUS (*within*)   Servilius, help! My lord, my lord!
   Enter TIMON *in a rage.*
TIMON   What, are my doors opposed against my passage?
   Have I been ever free,° and must my house   *at liberty; generous*

---

3. Suffice (but in line 58, "wait on").
4. TEXTUAL COMMENT This line, like many in *Timon*, is set as prose but has a pattern of stresses suggestive of blank verse. For a discussion of the way the lan-guage of the play often hovers between verse and prose, see Digital Edition TC 5.
5. More freely; more out of doors.
6. That is, they are avoiding arrest for debt.

Be my retentive° enemy? My jail?   *confining; niggardly*
80 The place which I have feasted, does it now
    Like all mankind show me an iron heart?
LUCIUS' SERVANT Put in° now, Titus.   *Make your claim*
TITUS   My lord, here is my bill.
LUCIUS' SERVANT Here's mine.
VARRO'S FIRST SERVANT   And mine, my lord.
VARRO'S SECOND SERVANT   And ours, my lord.
PHILOTUS All our bills.
85 TIMON Knock me down with 'em; cleave me to the girdle.[7]
LUCIUS' SERVANT Alas, my lord.
TIMON Cut my heart in° sums.   *into*
TITUS Mine, fifty talents.
TIMON Tell° out my blood.   *Count*
LUCIUS' SERVANT   Five thousand crowns, my lord.
90 TIMON Five thousand drops pays that. [to VARRO'S SERVANTS]
    What yours? And yours?
VARRO'S FIRST SERVANT My lord—
VARRO'S SECOND SERVANT My lord—
TIMON Tear me, take me, and the gods fall upon you.
                               Exit TIMON.
HORTENSIUS Faith, I perceive our masters may throw their
95   caps at° their money. These debts may well be called desper-   *cease pursuing*
    ate° ones, for a madman owes 'em.   *Exeunt.*   *hopeless; insane*

3.5

Enter TIMON [*and* STEWARD].
TIMON They have e'en put[1] my breath from me, the slaves.
    Creditors? Devils!
STEWARD My dear lord—
TIMON What if it should be so?[2]
5 STEWARD My lord—
TIMON I'll have it so. —My steward!
STEWARD   Here, my lord.
TIMON So fitly?° Go, bid all my friends again,   *conveniently*
    Lucius, Lucullus, and Sempronius, usurers all.[3]
    I'll once more feast the rascals.
STEWARD   O my lord,
10 You only speak from your distracted soul.
    There's not so much left to furnish out
    A moderate table.
TIMON   Be it not in thy care.°   *your responsibility*
    Go, I charge thee, invite them all. Let in the tide
    Of knaves once more. My cook and I'll provide.   *Exeunt.*

---

7. Timon puns on "bills" (line 84) as weapons (halberds).
3.5 Location: Scene continues.
1. Have taken (referring to Timon's breathlessness and to the proverb "Air is free").

2. Timon is referring to a plan he has just thought of.
3. TEXTUAL COMMENT The Folio reads "*Vllorxa,*" probably a compositor's error, emended here to "usurers." For the rationale behind the emendation, see Digital Edition TC 6.

3.6

Enter three SENATORS *at one door,* ALCIBIADES
meeting them, with Attendants.

FIRST SENATOR My lord, you have my voice to't.° The fault's°   *vote for it / crime is*
   bloody;
   'Tis necessary he should die.
   Nothing emboldens sin so much as mercy.
SECOND SENATOR Most true. The law shall bruise 'em.
5 ALCIBIADES Honor, health, and compassion to the Senate.
FIRST SENATOR Now, captain—
ALCIBIADES I am an humble suitor to your virtues.
   For pity is the virtue° of the law,   *essence*
   And none but tyrants use it cruelly.
10 It pleases time and fortune to lie heavy
   Upon a friend of mine, who in hot blood
   Hath stepped into° the law, which is past depth   *(as into quicksand)*
   To those that without heed do plunge into't.
   He is a man, setting his fate° aside, of comely virtues,   *deed*
15 Nor did he soil the fact with cowardice—
   An honor in him which buys out his fault°—   *redeems his crime*
   But with a noble fury and fair spirit.
   Seeing his reputation touched to death,°   *fatally besmirched*
   He did oppose his foe:
20 And with such sober and unnoted[1] passion
   He did behoove° his anger, ere 'twas spent,   *control*
   As if he had but proved an argument.
FIRST SENATOR You undergo° too strict a paradox,   *undertake*
   Striving to make an ugly deed look fair.
25 Your words have took such pains as if they labored
   To bring manslaughter into form[2] and set quarreling
   Upon the head° of valor, which indeed   *In the category of*
   Is valor misbegot and came into the world
   When sects and factions were newly born.
30 He's truly valiant that can wisely suffer
   The worst that man can breathe,° and make his wrongs his   *utter*
     outsides,°   *merely external things*
   To wear them like his raiment, carelessly,
   And ne'er prefer° his injuries to his heart,   *promote*
   To bring it into danger.
35 If wrong be evils and enforce us kill,
   What folly 'tis to hazard life for ill.
ALCIBIADES My lord—
FIRST SENATOR You cannot make gross sins look clear;
   To revenge is no valor, but to bear.°   *endure (is valor)*
ALCIBIADES My lords, then, under favor,° pardon me   *by your leave*
40 If I speak like a captain.
   Why do fond° men expose themselves to battle   *foolish*
   And not endure all threats, sleep upon't,
   And let the foes quietly cut their throats
   Without repugnancy?° If there be   *resistance*

3.6 Location: The Senate house.   2. To make manslaughter legal.
1. Unnoticed (because moderate).

45   Such valor in the bearing,° what make we   *enduring*
       Abroad?³ Why, then, women are more valiant
       That stay at home, if bearing carry it,°   *wins the day*
       And the ass more captain than the lion,
       The fellow loaden with irons° wiser than the judge,   *shackles*
50   If wisdom be in suffering. O my lords,
       As you are great, be pitifully good.°   *good in showing pity*
       Who cannot condemn rashness in cold blood?
       To kill, I grant, is sin's extremest gust,°   *outburst*
       But in defense, by mercy,⁴ 'tis most just.
55   To be in anger is impiety,
       But who is man that is not angry?
       Weigh but the crime with this.
    SECOND SENATOR   You breathe in vain.
    ALCIBIADES   In vain?
       His service done at Lacedaemon and Byzantium
60   Were a sufficient briber for his life.
    FIRST SENATOR   What's that?
    ALCIBIADES   Why, I say, my lords, he's done fair° service   *fine*
       And slain in fight many of your enemies.
       How full of valor did he bear himself
65   In the last conflict and made plenteous wounds!
    SECOND SENATOR   He has made too much plenty with him.
       He's a sworn rioter;° he has a sin   *committed reveler*
       That often drowns him and takes his valor prisoner.⁵
       If there were no foes, that were enough
70   To overcome him. In that beastly fury
       He has been known to commit outrages
       And cherish factions.° 'Tis inferred° to us   *foster dissension / alleged*
       His days are foul and his drink dangerous.
    FIRST SENATOR   He dies.
    ALCIBIADES   Hard fate! He might have died in war.
75   My lords, if not for any parts° in him—   *good qualities*
       Though his right arm might purchase his own time⁶
       And be in debt to none—yet, more to move you,
       Take° my deserts to his and join 'em both.   *Combine*
       And for I know your reverend ages love security,⁷
80   I'll pawn my victories, all my honor, to you
       Upon his good returns.°   *repayment (of your trust)*
       If by this crime he owes the law his life,
       Why, let the war receive't in valiant gore;
       For law is strict, and war is nothing more.
85   FIRST SENATOR   We are for law. He dies. Urge it no more
       On height of our° displeasure. Friend or brother,   *At risk of our highest*
       He forfeits his own blood that spills another.
    ALCIBIADES   Must it be so? It must not be.
       My lords, I do beseech you know me.
    SECOND SENATOR   How?
    ALCIBIADES   Call me to your remembrances.
90   THIRD SENATOR   What?

---

3. *what make we / Abroad*: why do we (men) go
outdoors?
4. But self-defense, considered mercifully.
5. *sin . . . prisoner*: that is, drunkenness.

6. Though performance in battle might redeem him
for the duration of his life.
7. Collateral (as on a loan); safety.

ALCIBIADES   I cannot think but your age has forgot me.
It could not else° be I should prove so base   *otherwise*
To sue and be denied such common grace.
My wounds ache at you.
FIRST SENATOR   Do you dare our anger?
95   'Tis in few words but spacious° in effect: *great*
We banish thee forever.
ALCIBIADES   Banish me?
Banish your dotage, banish usury
That makes the Senate ugly.
FIRST SENATOR   If after two-days' shine Athens contain thee,
100   Attend our weightier judgment, and, not to swell our spirit,°   *anger*
He shall be executed presently.°   *Exeunt* [SENATORS].   *immediately*
ALCIBIADES   Now the gods keep you old enough that you may
           live
Only in bone,° that none may look on you!   *as skeletons*
I'm worse than mad; I have kept back their foes
105   While they have told° their money and let out   *counted*
Their coin upon large interest, I myself
Rich only in large hurts. All those, for this?
Is this the balsam° that the usuring Senate   *ointment*
Pours into captains' wounds? Banishment!
110   It comes not ill; I hate not to be banished.
It is a cause worthy my spleen and fury
That I may strike at Athens. I'll cheer up
My discontented troops and lay for hearts.°   *win their support*
'Tis honor with most lands° to be at odds;   *the richest*
115   Soldiers should brook° as little wrongs as gods.   *Exit.*   *endure*

3.7

Enter diverse [of Timon's] FRIENDS, [SENATORS
including LUCIUS, LUCULLUS, *and* SEMPRONIUS,]
at several doors.[1]

FIRST FRIEND   The good time of day to you, sir.
SECOND FRIEND   I also wish it to you. I think this honorable
   lord did but try° us this other day.   *test*
FIRST FRIEND   Upon that were my thoughts tiring[2] when we
5   encountered.° I hope it is not so low with him as he made it   *met*
   seem in the trial of his several friends.
SECOND FRIEND   It should not be, by the persuasion° of his   *evidence*
   new feasting.
FIRST FRIEND   I should think so. He hath sent me an earnest
10   inviting, which many my near occasions° did urge me to put   *my many urgent affairs*
   off, but he hath conjured me beyond them, and I must needs
   appear.
SECOND FRIEND   In like manner was I in debt° to my importu-   *I needed to attend*
   nate business, but he would not hear my excuse. I am sorry
15   when he sent to borrow of me that my provision was out.

3.7 Location: Timon's house.
1. TEXTUAL COMMENT The individual friends are not
named in the stage directions to this scene, nor in
the speech prefixes, although Lucius, Sempronius,

and Lucullus were invited to Timon's party in 3.5.
See Digital Edition TC 7 for a discussion of their
anonymity in this scene.
2. Feeding (as a hawk tears flesh).

FIRST FRIEND I am sick of that grief, too, as I understand how
all things go.³

SECOND FRIEND Every man hears so. What would he have
borrowed of you?

20 FIRST FRIEND A thousand pieces.

SECOND FRIEND A thousand pieces?

FIRST FRIEND What of you?

SECOND FRIEND He sent to me, sir—here he comes.

    Enter TIMON *and Attendants.*

TIMON With all my heart, gentlemen both, and how fare you?

25 FIRST FRIEND Ever at the best, hearing well of your lordship.

SECOND FRIEND The swallow follows not summer more willing than we your lordship.

TIMON [*aside*] Nor more willingly leaves winter; such summer
birds are men. —Gentlemen, our dinner will not recom-

30 pense this long stay. Feast your ears with the music a while,
if they will fare° so harshly o'th' trumpet's sound. We shall   *sustain themselves*
to't presently.

FIRST FRIEND I hope it remains not unkindly with your lordship that I returned you an empty messenger.

35 TIMON O sir, let it not trouble you.

SECOND FRIEND My noble lord—

TIMON Ah, my good friend, what cheer?

    The banquet brought in.

SECOND FRIEND My most honorable lord, I am e'en° sick of   *utterly*
shame that when your lordship this other day sent to me I

40 was so unfortunate a beggar.

TIMON Think not on't, sir.

SECOND FRIEND If you had sent but two hours before—

TIMON Let it not cumber° your better remembrance. [*He*   *burden*
calls.] Come, bring in all together.

    [*Enter* SERVANTS *with dishes.*]

45 SECOND FRIEND All covered dishes.

FIRST FRIEND Royal cheer,° I warrant you.   *dining*

THIRD FRIEND Doubt not that, if money and the season can
yield it.

FIRST FRIEND How do you? What's the news?

50 THIRD FRIEND Alcibiades is banished. Hear you of it?

BOTH Alcibiades banished?

THIRD FRIEND 'Tis so, be sure of it.

FIRST FRIEND How? How?

SECOND FRIEND I pray you upon what?°   *what grounds*

55 TIMON My worthy friends, will you draw near?

THIRD FRIEND I'll tell you more anon. Here's a noble feast
toward.°   *coming up*

SECOND FRIEND This is the old⁴ man still.

THIRD FRIEND Wilt hold? Wilt hold?°   *last*

60 SECOND FRIEND It does, but time will,° and so—   *"time will tell"*

THIRD FRIEND I do conceive.°   *understand*

TIMON Each man to his stool with that spur° as he would to   *speed*
the lip of his mistress. Your diet shall be in all places alike.

---

3. *as . . . go:* now that I understand the real situation.   4. Familiar (in his generosity).

Make not a city feast[5] of it, to let the meat cool ere we can
65   agree upon the first place.° Sit, sit.   *place of honor*
        [*They sit.*]
    The gods require our thanks:
    You great benefactors, sprinkle our society with thankful-
    ness. For your own gifts make yourselves praised. But reserve
    still[6] to give, lest your deities be despised. Lend to each man
70   enough that one need not lend to another. For were your
    godheads to borrow of men, men would forsake the gods.
    Make the meat be beloved more than the man that gives it.
    Let no assembly of twenty be without a score of villains. If
    there sit twelve women at the table, let a dozen of them be as
75   they are.° The rest of your foes, O gods, the senators of Ath-   *(that is, unchaste)*
    ens, together with the common leg° of people, what is amiss   *mob*
    in them, you gods, make suitable for destruction. For these
    my present friends, as they are to me nothing, so in nothing
    bless them, and to nothing are they welcome. —Uncover,
80   dogs, and lap!
        [*The dishes, containing only hot water, are uncovered.*]
SOME FRIEND   What does his lordship mean?
SOME OTHER   I know not.
TIMON   May you a better feast never behold,
    You knot of mouth-friends.[7] Smoke and lukewarm water
85   Is your perfection. This is Timon's last,
    Who stuck and spangled you with flatteries,
    Washes it off and sprinkles in your faces
    Your reeking° villainy. [*He throws water at them.*] Live loathed   *steaming; stinking*
        and long,
    Most smiling, smooth, detested parasites,
90   Courteous destroyers, affable wolves, meek bears,
    You fools of fortune, trencher-friends,° time's flies,[8]   *mealtime friends*
    Cap-and-knee° slaves, vapors, and minute-jacks.[9]   *Sycophantic*
    Of man and beast, the infinite malady[1]
    Crust you quite o'er. What, dost thou go?
        [*He beats them.*]
95   Soft,° take thy physic° first—thou, too, and thou: *Wait / medicine*
    Stay, I will lend thee money, borrow none.
    What, all in motion?   [*Exeunt* FRIENDS *and* SENATORS.]
                  Henceforth be no feast
    Whereat a villain's not a welcome guest.
    Burn, house! Sink, Athens! Henceforth hated be
100   Of Timon, man, and all humanity.   *Exit* [*with* SERVANTS].
        Enter the SENATORS, [*Timon's* FRIENDS,] *with other*
        LORDS.
FIRST FRIEND   How now, my lords?
SECOND FRIEND   Know you the quality° of Lord Timon's fury?   *nature*
THIRD FRIEND   Push,° did you see my cap?   *(impatient expression)*
FOURTH FRIEND   I have lost my gown.

---

5. Feast as given by London dignitaries, in which seating arrangements were thought socially significant.
6. But always hold back something.
7. You group of insincere (or gluttonous) friends.

8. That is, vanishing in cold weather.
9. Mannequins that strike bells on medieval clocks;
hence, timeservers.
1. May every disease of man and beast.

FIRST FRIEND   He's but a mad lord, and naught but humors°   *unstable moods*
105   sways him. He gave me a jewel th'other day, and now he has
       beat it out of my hat.
       Did you see my jewel?
SECOND FRIEND   Did you see my cap?
THIRD FRIEND   Here 'tis.
FOURTH FRIEND   Here lies my gown.
FIRST FRIEND   Let's make no stay.
SECOND FRIEND   Lord Timon's mad.
THIRD FRIEND   I feel't upon my bones.
110   FOURTH FRIEND   One day he gives us diamonds, next day stones.
                   Exeunt the SENATORS, [*other* LORDS, *and*
                                   Timon's FRIENDS].

4.1

       Enter TIMON.
TIMON   Let me look back upon thee. O thou wall
        That girdles in those wolves, dive in the earth
        And fence not Athens. Matrons, turn incontinent.°   *unchaste*
        Obedience, fail in children. Slaves and fools,
5   Pluck the grave-wrinkled Senate from the bench
        And minister in their steads. To general filths°   *common whores*
        Convert o'th' instant green[1] virginity.
        Do't in your parents' eyes! Bankrupts, hold fast:°   *refuse to pay*
        Rather than render back, out with your knives
10   And cut your trusters'° throats. Bound° servants, steal;   *creditors' / Indentured*
        Large-handed robbers your grave masters are
        And pill° by law. Maid, to thy master's bed;   *plunder*
        Thy mistress is o'th' brothel. Son of sixteen,
        Pluck the lined° crutch from thy old limping sire;   *padded*
15   With it, beat out his brains. Piety and fear,
        Religion to the gods, peace, justice, truth,
        Domestic awe,[2] night-rest and neighborhood,°   *neighborliness*
        Instruction, manners, mysteries,° and trades,   *crafts*
        Degrees,° observances,[3] customs, and laws,   *Social ranks*
20   Decline to your confounding° contraries,   *destroying*
        And yet confusion live. Plagues incident to men,
        Your potent and infectious fevers heap
        On Athens ripe for stroke.° Thou cold sciatica,°   *to be struck / nerve pain*
        Cripple our senators that their limbs may halt°   *limp*
25   As lamely as their manners. Lust and liberty,°   *licentiousness*
        Creep in the minds and marrows[4] of our youth,
        That 'gainst the stream of virtue they may strive
        And drown themselves in riot.° Itches, blains,°   *debauchery / sores*
        Sow all th'Athenian bosoms, and their crop
30   Be general leprosy. Breath infect breath,
        That their society,° as their friendship, may   *company*
        Be merely° poison. Nothing I'll bear from thee   *wholly*
        But nakedness, thou detestable town.
        Take thou that too, with multiplying bans.°   *curses*

4.1 Location: Outside the walls of Athens.   2. Household government.
1. Young, newly menstruating girls often suffered   3. Respectful customs.
anemia, then called "greensickness" and thought to   4. Thought to be the site of vigor; proverbially melted
be curable by sexual satisfaction.   by lust.

35   Timon will to the woods, where he shall find
      Th'unkindest beast more kinder[5] than mankind.
      The gods confound—hear me, you good gods all!—
      Th'Athenians both within and out that wall,
      And grant as Timon grows his hate may grow
40   To the whole race of mankind, high and low.
      Amen.   *Exit.*

4.2

Enter STEWARD *with two or three* SERVANTS.

FIRST SERVANT   Hear you, Master Steward, where's our master?
      Are we undone, cast off, nothing remaining?
STEWARD   Alack, my fellows, what should I say to you?
      Let me be recorded by the righteous gods,
      I am as poor as you.
5   FIRST SERVANT   Such a house broke?
      So noble a master fallen? All gone, and not
      One friend to take his° fortune by the arm   *(Timon's)*
      And go along with him?
SECOND SERVANT   As we do turn our backs
      From our companion thrown into his grave,
10 So his familiars to[1] his buried fortunes
      Slink all away, leave their false vows with him
      Like empty purses picked. And his poor self,
      A dedicated° beggar to the air,   *Abandoned as a*
      With his disease of all-shunned poverty,
15 Walks like contempt alone.—More of our fellows.

Enter other SERVANTS.

STEWARD   All broken implements of a ruined house.
THIRD SERVANT   Yet do our hearts wear Timon's livery,°   *servants' uniforms*
      That see I by our faces we are fellows still,
      Serving alike in sorrow. Leaked is our bark,°   *sailboat*
20 And we poor mates stand on the dying° deck,   *sinking*
      Hearing the surges threat.° We must all part   *waves threaten*
      Into this sea of air.
STEWARD   Good fellows all,
      The latest° of my wealth I'll share amongst you.   *last bit*
      Wherever we shall meet, for Timon's sake
25 Let's yet be fellows. Let's shake our heads and say,
      As 'twere a knell unto our master's fortunes,
      "We have seen better days." [*He gives them money.*] Let each
         take some.
      Nay, put out all your hands. Not one word more.
      Thus part we rich in sorrow, parting poor.

            Embrace and [SERVANTS] *part several ways.*

30 Oh, the fierce° wretchedness that glory brings us!   *excessive*
      Who would not wish to be from wealth exempt,
      Since riches point to misery and contempt?
      Who would be so mocked with glory, or to live
      But in a dream of friendship,

---

5. Gentler; more nearly akin.   1. So his intimate friends from (a "familiar" could
4.2 Location: Timon's house.   also be a flattering devil).

35   To have his pomp and all what state compounds[2]
    But only painted like his varnished friends?
    Poor honest lord, brought low by his own heart,
    Undone by goodness. Strange unusual blood,°   *disposition*
    When man's worst sin is he does too much good.
40   Who then dares to be half so kind again?
    For bounty that makes° gods do still mar men.   *characterizes*
    My dearest lord, blest to be most accursed,
    Rich only to be wretched. Thy great fortunes
    Are made thy chief afflictions. Alas, kind lord,
45   He's flung in rage from this ingrateful seat°   *residence*
    Of monstrous friends.
    Nor has he with him to supply° his life,   *resources to maintain*
    Or that° which can command it.   *(money)*
    I'll follow and inquire him out.
50   I'll ever serve his mind with my best will;
    Whilst I have gold, I'll be his steward still.   *Exit.*

4.3

Enter TIMON *in the woods.*

TIMON   O blessèd breeding sun,[1] draw from the earth
    Rotten° humidity. Below thy sister's[2] orb   *Putrid*
    Infect the air. Twinned brothers of one womb,
    Whose procreation, residence,° and birth   *time in the womb*
5   Scarce is dividant,° touch them with several° fortunes: *separable / different*
    The greater scorns the lesser. Not nature,
    To whom all sores° lay siege, can bear great fortune,   *afflictions*
    But by contempt of nature.[3]
    Raise me[4] this beggar, and deny't that lord,
10   The senators shall bear contempt hereditary,° *as if he had inherited it*
    The beggar native° honor.   *inborn*
    It is the pasture lards[5] the brother's sides,
    The want that makes him lean. Who dares, who dares
    In purity of manhood stand upright
15   And say, "This man's a flatterer"? If one be,
    So are they all, for every grece° of fortune   *step on the staircase*
    Is smoothed by that below.[6] The learnèd pate°   *head*
    Ducks° to the golden fool. All's obliquy.°   *Bows / deviousness*
    There's nothing level° in our cursèd natures   *straight; consistent*
20   But direct villainy. Therefore be abhorred,
    All feasts, societies, and throngs of men.
    His semblable,° yea himself, Timon disdains.   *His own image*
    Destruction, fang° mankind. [*He digs.*] Earth, yield me roots. *seize*
    Who seeks for better of thee, sauce his palate
25   With thy most operant° poison. [*He discovers gold.*] What is *potent*
      here?
    Gold? Yellow, glittering, precious gold?

---

2. And all that splendor is made of.
4.3 Location: Outside Athens.
1. The sun was supposed to be able to generate vermin spontaneously and to foment infection.
2. The moon's; see note to 1.1.45.
3. Without scorning those of like nature.

4. This "me" is an example of the so-called ethic dative
("for me"), used to emphasize the verb. See also line
113.
5. Fattens ("pasture" suggests both owning and eating from the land).
6. By the people standing on the step below.

No, gods, I am no idle° votarist—   *frivolous*
Roots, you clear heavens! Thus much of this will make
Black white, foul fair, wrong right,
30   Base noble, old young, coward valiant.
Ha, you gods! Why this? What, this, you gods? Why, this
Will lug your priests and servants from your sides,
Pluck stout men's pillows from below their heads.°   *(to kill them)*
This yellow slave
35   Will knit and break religions, bless th'accursed,
Make the hoar° leprosy adored, place° thieves   *gray / appoint to office*
And give them title, knee,° and approbation   *reverence*
With senators on the bench. This is it
That makes the wappered° widow wed again.   *worn out*
40   She whom the spittle-house° and ulcerous sores   *hospital*
Would cast the gorge° at, this embalms and spices   *vomit*
To th'April day⁷ again. Come, damnèd earth,°   *gold*
Thou common whore of mankind that puts odds°   *quarrels*
Among the rout° of nations, I will make thee   *rabble*
Do⁸ thy right nature.
                    March afar off.
45   Ha, a drum? Thou'rt quick.⁹
But yet I'll bury thee. [*He buries gold.*] Thou'lt go, strong
    thief,
When gouty keepers of thee cannot stand—
Nay, stay thou out for earnest.°   *as a pledge*
                    Enter ALCIBIADES *with* [SOLDIERS *marching to*]
                    drum and fife in warlike manner, and PHRYNIA
                    and TIMANDRA.
ALCIBIADES   What art thou there? Speak.
TIMON   A beast as thou art. The canker¹ gnaw thy heart
50   For showing me again the eyes of man.
ALCIBIADES   What is thy name? Is man so hateful to thee,
That art thyself a man?
TIMON   I am *Misanthropos*° and hate mankind.   *man-hater (Greek)*
For thy part, I do wish thou wert a dog,
That I might love thee something.°   *somewhat*
55   ALCIBIADES   I know thee well,
But in thy fortunes am unlearned and strange.²
TIMON   I know thee, too, and more than that I know thee
I not desire° to know. Follow thy drum.   *do not desire*
With man's blood paint the ground gules,° gules.   *red (heraldic term)*
60   Religious canons, civil laws are cruel.
Then what should war be? This fell° whore of thine   *dreadful*
Hath in her more destruction than thy sword,
For all her cherubin look.
PHRYNIA   Thy lips rot off!°   *(as in syphilis)*
TIMON   I will not kiss thee; then the rot returns
65   To thine own lips again.
ALCIBIADES   How came the noble Timon to this change?

---

7. To youthful freshness.   9. Swift to bring strife; alive.
8. Act according to (by concealing gold and yielding   1. Spreading ulcer; cankerworm.
roots).   2. Am ignorant and unacquainted.

TIMON   As the moon does, by wanting° light to give.   *lacking*
But then renew I could not like the moon;
There were no suns to borrow of.

70   ALCIBIADES   Noble Timon, what friendship may I do thee?

TIMON   None, but to maintain my opinion.

ALCIBIADES   What is it, Timon?

TIMON   Promise me friendship, but perform none. If thou wilt
not promise, the gods plague thee, for thou art a man. If

75   thou dost perform, confound° thee, for thou art a man.   *damn*

ALCIBIADES   I have heard in some sort° of thy miseries.   *to some extent*

TIMON   Thou saw'st them when I had prosperity.

ALCIBIADES   I see them now. Then was a blessèd time.

TIMON   As thine is now, held with a brace° of harlots.   *pair*

80   TIMANDRA   Is this th'Athenian minion° whom the world   *favorite*
Voiced° so regardfully?   *Spoke of*

TIMON   Art thou Timandra?

TIMANDRA   Yes.

TIMON   Be a whore still. They love thee not that use thee.
Give them diseases, leaving with thee their lust.

85   Make use of thy salt° hours. Season° the slaves   *lecherous / Prepare*
For tubs and baths;³ bring down rose-cheeked youth
To the tub-fast and the diet.

TIMANDRA   Hang thee, monster!

ALCIBIADES   Pardon him, sweet Timandra, for his wits
Are drowned and lost in his calamities.

90   I have but little gold of late, brave Timon,
The want whereof doth daily make° revolt   *cause*
In my penurious band. I have heard and grieved
How cursèd Athens, mindless of thy worth,
Forgetting thy great deeds, when neighbor states

95   But for thy sword and fortune trod upon them⁴—

TIMON   I prithee, beat thy drum, and get thee gone.

ALCIBIADES   I am thy friend and pity thee, dear Timon.

TIMON   How dost thou pity him whom thou dost trouble?
I had rather be alone.

ALCIBIADES   Why, fare thee well.
[*He offers* TIMON *gold.*] Here is some gold for thee.

100 TIMON   Keep it; I cannot eat it.

ALCIBIADES   When I have laid proud Athens on a heap—

TIMON   Warr'st thou 'gainst Athens?

ALCIBIADES   Ay, Timon, and have cause.

TIMON   The gods confound them all in thy conquest,
And thee after when thou hast conquerèd.

105 ALCIBIADES   Why me, Timon?

TIMON   That by killing of villains thou wast born to conquer
my country.
Put up thy gold.
[*He offers* ALCIBIADES *gold.*]
                       Go on, here's gold, go on!

---

3. Used, with "diet" (line 87), to treat venereal   4. Alcibiades suggests that Timon's money and mili-
disease.   tary expertise saved Athens in the past.

	Be as a planetary plague,[5] when Jove	
110	Will o'er some high-viced city hang his poison	
	In the sick air. Let not thy sword skip one.	
	Pity not honored age for his white beard;	
	He is an usurer. Strike me° the counterfeit matron:	*Strike for me*
	It is her habit° only that is honest;	*attire*
115	Herself's a bawd. Let not the virgin's cheek	
	Make soft thy trenchant° sword, for those milk paps°	*cutting / breasts*
	That through the window-bars° bore at men's eyes	*openwork bodice*
	Are not within the leaf° of pity writ,	*page*
	But set them down horrible traitors. Spare not the babe	
120	Whose dimpled smiles from fools exhaust° their mercy.	*draw out*
	Think it a bastard, whom the oracle	
	Hath doubtfully° pronounced the throat shall cut,	*ambiguously*
	And mince it sans° remorse. Swear against objects;[6]	*without*
	Put armor on thine ears and on thine eyes,	
125	Whose proof° nor yells of mothers, maids, nor babes,	*strength*
	Nor sight of priests in holy vestments bleeding	
	Shall pierce a jot. There's gold to pay thy soldiers.	
	Make large confusion and, thy fury spent,	
	Confounded be thyself. Speak not, be gone.	
130	ALCIBIADES [*taking gold*] Hast thou gold yet? I'll take the gold thou givest me,	
	Not all thy counsel.	
	TIMON Dost thou or dost thou not, heaven's curse upon thee.	
	PHRYNIA *and* TIMANDRA Give us some gold, good Timon; hast thou more?	
	TIMON Enough to make a whore forswear her trade	
135	And to make whores a bawd. Hold up, you sluts,	
	Your aprons mountant.[7] [*He gives them gold.*] You are not oathable,[8]	
	Although I know you'll swear, terribly swear	
	Into strong shudders and to heavenly agues°	*fevers*
	Th'immortal gods that hear you. Spare your oaths;	
140	I'll trust to your conditions.° Be whores still,	*occupations; characters*
	And he whose pious breath seeks to convert you,	
	Be strong in whore, allure him, burn him up.°	*inflame him; infect him*
	Let your close° fire predominate his smoke,[9]	*secret*
	And be no turncoats. Yet may your pains six months	
145	Be quite contrary,° and thatch your poor thin roofs	*Make you suffer intensely*
	With burdens of the dead[1]—some that were hanged—	
	No matter. Wear them, betray with them, whore still.	
	Paint° till a horse may mire° upon your face.	*Use cosmetics / get stuck*
	A pox of wrinkles!	
	PHRYNIA *and* TIMANDRA Well, more gold, what then?	
150	Believe't that we'll do anything for gold.	
	TIMON Consumptions° sow	*Diseases*
	In hollow bones of man, strike their sharp shins,[2]	

---

5. Plagues were thought to be caused by the influence of the other planets.
6. Vow not to listen to protests.
7. Your skirts lifted ("mountant," a heraldic term, puns on "sexual mounting").

8. Capable of being bound on oath.
9. Overcome his "pious breath" (line 141).
1. *thatch . . . dead:* wear wigs made of corpses' hair to cover your syphilitic baldness.
2. Syphilis causes bone degeneration.

And mar men's spurring![3] Crack the lawyer's voice
That he may never more false title plead,
155 Nor sound his quillets° shrilly. Hoar the flamen[4]   *quibbles*
That scold'st against the quality° of flesh   *nature*
And not believes himself. Down with the nose,
Down with it flat,[5] take the bridge quite away
Of him that his particular° to foresee   *self-interest*
160 Smells from the general weal.[6] Make curled-pate ruffians
    bald,
And let the unscarred braggarts of the war
Derive some pain from you. Plague all,
That your activity may defeat and quell
The source of all erection.[7] There's more gold.
165 Do you damn others, and let this damn you,
And ditches grave you all.[8]

PHRYNIA *and* TIMANDRA   More counsel with more money,
    bounteous Timon!

TIMON   More whore, more mischief first. I have given you
    earnest.°   *a down payment*

ALCIBIADES   Strike up the drum towards Athens. Farewell,
    Timon.
170 If I thrive well, I'll visit thee again.

TIMON   If I hope well, I'll never see thee more.

ALCIBIADES   I never did thee harm.

TIMON   Yes, thou spok'st well of me.

ALCIBIADES   Call'st thou that harm?

TIMON   Men daily find it.° Get thee away,   *discover it to be so*
    And take thy beagles° with thee.   *fawning curs (the whores)*

175 ALCIBIADES   We but offend him.
    [*to drummers*] Strike!   *Exeunt* [*all but* TIMON].

TIMON [*digging*]   That nature being sick of° man's unkindness   *through excess of*
    Should yet be hungry! Common° mother, thou   *Universal*
    Whose womb unmeasurable and infinite breast
180 Teems° and feeds all, whose selfsame mettle°   *Breeds / substance*
    Whereof thy proud child, arrogant man, is puffed,
    Engenders the black toad and adder blue,
    The gilded newt and eyeless venomed worm,
    With all th'abhorrèd births below crisp° heaven,   *clear*
185 Whereon Hyperion's quick'ning° fire doth shine,   *the sun's life-giving*
    Yield him who all the human sons do hate
    From forth thy plenteous bosom one poor root.
    Ensear° thy fertile and conceptious womb;   *Dry up*
    Let it no more bring out ingrateful man.
190 Go great° with tigers, dragons, wolves, and bears;   *pregnant*
    Teem with new monsters, whom thy upward° face   *upturned*
    Hath to the marbled mansion° all above   *heavens*
    Never presented.—Oh, a root! Dear thanks.
    Dry up thy marrows,° vines, and plough-torn leas,°   *pulpy fruits / fields*
195 Whereof ingrateful man with liquorish drafts[9]

---

3. Horseback riding; sexual intercourse. *Crack:* Ruin
(an ulcerous larynx is an effect of syphilis).
4. Whiten the priest (with syphilis or leprosy).
5. Syphilis sometimes causes the bridge of the nose
to collapse.

6. The image suggests a dog leaving the pack to pursue its own quarry.
7. Sexual erection; social advancement.
8. May you all suffer squalid deaths.
9. Sweet, lust-inducing drinks.

And morsels unctuous° greases his pure mind,   *oily*
That from it all consideration° slips.   *rationality*
    Enter APEMANTUS.
More man? Plague, plague!
APEMANTUS   I was directed hither. Men report
200   Thou dost affect° my manners and dost use them.   *like; imitate*
TIMON   'Tis, then, because thou dost not keep a dog
Whom I would imitate. Consumption catch thee!
APEMANTUS   This is in thee a nature but infected,[1]
A poor unmanly melancholy sprung
205   From change of future. Why this spade, this place,
This slave-like habit,° and these looks of care?   *costume*
Thy flatterers yet wear silk, drink wine, lie soft,
Hug their diseased perfumes,° and have forgot   *perfumed women*
That ever Timon was. Shame not these woods
210   By putting on the cunning of a carper.[2]
Be thou a flatterer now, and seek to thrive
By that which has undone thee. Hinge thy knee,
And let his very breath whom thou'lt observe°   *pay court to*
Blow off thy cap. Praise his most vicious strain,°   *trait*
215   And call it excellent. Thou wast told thus.
Thou gav'st thine ears like tapsters° that bade welcome   *bartenders*
To knaves and all approachers. 'Tis most just
That thou turn rascal.° Hadst thou wealth again,   *knave; solitary deer*
Rascals should have't. Do not assume my likeness.
220 TIMON   Were I like thee, I'd throw away myself.
APEMANTUS   Thou hast cast away thyself being like thyself,
A madman so long, now a fool. What think'st—
That the bleak air, thy boisterous chamberlain,°   *personal servant*
Will put thy shirt on warm? Will these moist trees,
225   That have outlived the eagle, page° thy heels   *follow at*
And skip when thou point'st out?[3] Will the cold brook,
Candied° with ice, caudle thy morning taste[4]   *Encrusted*
To cure thy o'ernight's surfeit? Call the creatures
Whose naked natures live in° all the spite   *exposed to*
230   Of wreakful° heaven, whose bare unhousèd trunks°   *vengeful / bodies*
To the conflicting elements exposed
Answer° mere nature. Bid them flatter thee.   *Obey*
Oh, thou shalt find—
TIMON   A fool of thee. Depart!
APEMANTUS   I love thee better now than ere I did.
TIMON   I hate thee worse.
APEMANTUS   Why?
235 TIMON   Thou flatter'st misery.
APEMANTUS   I flatter not but say thou art a caitiff.°   *wretch*
TIMON   Why dost thou seek me out?
APEMANTUS   To vex thee.
TIMON   Always a villain's office, or a fool's.
Dost please thyself in't?
APEMANTUS   Ay.
TIMON   What, a knave, too?

---

1. That is, not innately misanthropic or converted by philosophical argument.
2. The knowledge of a faultfinder.
3. And jump to get whatever you indicate.
4. Give you a hot drink in the morning.

240 APEMANTUS   If thou didst put this sour cold habit° on   *dress; disposition*
        To castigate thy pride, 'twere well. But thou
        Dost it enforcèdly.° Thou'dst courtier be again   *by compulsion*
        Wert thou not beggar. Willing misery
        Outlives incertain° pomp, is crowned⁵ before.   *insecure*
245   The one° is filling still,° never complete;   *("incertain pomp") / always*
        The other at high wish.⁶ Best state, contentless,⁷
        Hath a distracted and most wretched being,
        Worse than the worst, content.⁸
        Thou shouldst desire to die, being miserable.
250 TIMON   Not by his breath that is more miserable.⁹
        Thou art a slave, whom Fortune's tender arm
        With favor never clasped, but bred a dog.
        Hadst thou like us from our first swathe proceeded¹
        The sweet degrees² that this brief world affords
255   To such as° may the passive drudges of it   *To those who*
        Freely command, thou wouldst have plunged thyself
        In general riot,° melted down thy youth   *debauchery*
        In different beds of lust, and never learned
        The icy precepts of respect,° but followed   *restraint; judgment*
260   The sugared game° before thee. But myself,   *sweet quarry*
        Who had the world as my confectionary,
        The mouths, the tongues, the eyes, and hearts of men
        At duty° more than I could frame° employment—   *my service / provide*
        That numberless upon me stuck as leaves
265   Do on the oak—have with one winter's brush
        Fell from their boughs and left me open, bare,
        For every storm that blows. I to bear this,
        That never knew but better,° is some burden.   *anything but good fortune*
        Thy nature did commence in sufferance;° time   *suffering*
270   Hath made thee hard° in't. Why shouldst thou hate men?   *hardened*
        They never flattered thee. What hast thou given?
        If thou wilt curse, thy father, that poor rag,°   *wretch*
        Must be thy subject, who in spite put stuff
        To³ some she-beggar and compounded° thee   *constituted*
275   Poor rogue hereditary.° Hence, be gone!   *by birth*
        If thou hadst not been born the worst of men,
        Thou hadst been a knave and flatterer.
    APEMANTUS   Art thou proud yet?
    TIMON   Ay, that I am not thee.
    APEMANTUS   I that I was no prodigal.
280 TIMON   I that I am one now.
        Were all the wealth I have shut up° in thee,   *contained*
        I'd give thee leave to hang it. Get thee gone.
        That° the whole life of Athens were in this,   *Would that*
        Thus would I eat it.
            [*He bites the root.*]
    APEMANTUS [*offering food*]   Here, I will mend° thy feast.   *improve*
285 TIMON   First mend thy company. Take away thyself.

---

5. Finds fulfillment.   than I.
6. (Misery) at the height of its wish.   1. From our swaddling clothes mounted.
7. The greatest prosperity, if not contented.   2. Social ranks; steps on Fortune's ladder.
8. The least prosperity, living contented.   3. *put stuff / To:* ejaculated into.
9. Not at the command of someone even unhappier

APEMANTUS   So I shall mend mine own, by th' lack of thine.

TIMON   'Tis not well mended so; it is but botched.[4]
If not, I would it were.

APEMANTUS   What wouldst thou have to[5] Athens?

TIMON   Thee thither in a whirlwind. If thou wilt,

290   Tell them there I have gold. Look, so I have.

APEMANTUS   Here is no use for gold.

TIMON   The best and truest.
For here it sleeps and does no hired harm.

APEMANTUS   Where liest a-nights, Timon?

TIMON   Under that's above me.° Where feed'st thou a-days,   (the sky)

295   Apemantus?

APEMANTUS   Where my stomach finds meat,° or rather where   food
I eat it.

TIMON   Would poison were obedient and knew my mind.

APEMANTUS   Where wouldst thou send it?

300   TIMON   To sauce thy dishes.

APEMANTUS   The middle of humanity thou never knewest,
but the extremity of both ends. When thou wast in thy gilt
and thy perfume, they mocked thee for too much curiosity;°   delicacy
in thy rags thou know'st none, but art despised for the con-

305   trary. There's a medlar[6] for thee. Eat it.

TIMON   On what I hate I feed not.

APEMANTUS   Dost hate a medlar?

TIMON   Ay, though it look like thee.

APEMANTUS   An° thou'dst hated meddlers sooner, thou shouldst   If

310   have loved thyself better now. What man didst thou ever
know unthrift° that was beloved after[7] his means?   prodigal

TIMON   Who, without those means thou talk'st of, didst thou
ever know beloved?

APEMANTUS   Myself.

315   TIMON   I understand thee. Thou hadst some means to keep a
dog.[8]

APEMANTUS   What things in the world canst thou nearest
compare to thy flatterers?

TIMON   Women nearest, but men, men are the things them-

320   selves. What wouldst thou do with the world, Apemantus, if
it lay in thy power?

APEMANTUS   Give it° the beasts to be rid of the men.   Give it to

TIMON   Wouldst thou have thyself fall in the confusion° of   overthrow
men and remain a beast with the beasts?

325   APEMANTUS   Ay, Timon.

TIMON   A beastly ambition, which the gods grant thee t'attain
to. If thou wert the lion, the fox would beguile thee. If thou
wert the lamb, the fox would eat thee. If thou wert the fox,
the lion would suspect thee when peradventure° thou wert   perchance

330   accused by the ass. If thou wert the ass, thy dullness would
torment thee, and still° thou lived'st but as a breakfast to   always
the wolf. If thou wert the wolf, thy greediness would afflict

---

4. It is fixed badly (because Apemantus will still have to endure himself).
5. Have conveyed to (but Timon changes the meaning).
6. A pear eaten when rotten; with puns in the fol-

lowing lines on "lecher," "whore," and "interfering person."
7. In proportion to; after losing. *means:* money.
8. Which flattered its master for meager reward (or perhaps "dog" refers to Apemantus himself).

thee and oft thou shouldst hazard thy life for thy dinner.
Wert thou the unicorn, pride and wrath would confound
335   thee and make thine own self the conquest of thy fury.[9]
Wert thou a bear, thou wouldst be killed by the horse.[1] Wert
thou a horse, thou wouldst be seized by the leopard. Wert
thou a leopard, thou wert german° to the lion, and the spots   *related*
of thy kindred[2] were jurors on thy life. All thy safety were
340   remotion,° and thy defense absence. What beast couldst   *remaining away*
thou be that were not subject to a beast, and what a beast
art thou already, that seest not thy loss in transformation?[3]
APEMANTUS   If thou couldst please me with speaking to me,
thou mightst have hit upon it here.[4] The commonwealth of
345   Athens is become a forest of beasts.
TIMON   How, has the ass broke the wall, that thou art out of
the city?
APEMANTUS   Yonder comes a poet and a painter.[5] The plague
of company light upon thee! I will fear to catch it and give
350   way.° When I know not what else to do, I'll see thee again.   *go away*
TIMON   When there is nothing living but thee, thou shalt be
welcome. I had rather be a beggar's dog than Apemantus.
APEMANTUS   Thou art the cap[6] of all the fools alive.
TIMON   Would thou wert clean enough to spit upon.
355   APEMANTUS   A plague on thee. Thou art too bad to curse.
TIMON   All villains that do stand by thee are pure.°   *(by comparison)*
APEMANTUS   There is no leprosy but what thou speak'st.
TIMON   If I name thee, I'll beat thee, but I should
Infect my hands.
APEMANTUS   I would my tongue could rot them off.
360   TIMON   Away, thou issue° of a mangy dog!   *offspring; discharge*
Choler does kill me that thou art alive.
I swoon to see thee.
APEMANTUS   Would thou wouldst burst.
TIMON   Away, thou tedious rogue!
       [*He throws a stone at* APEMANTUS.]
I am sorry I shall lose a stone by thee.
365   APEMANTUS   Beast!
TIMON   Slave!
APEMANTUS   Toad!
TIMON   Rogue, rogue, rogue!
I am sick of this false world and will love naught
370   But even° the mere necessities upon't.   *Except*
Then, Timon, presently° prepare thy grave.   *at once*
Lie where the light foam of the sea may beat
Thy gravestone daily; make thine epitaph,
That death in° me at others' lives may laugh.   *through*
       [*He looks at his gold.*]
375   O thou sweet king-killer and dear divorce
Twixt natural sun and fire, thou bright defiler

---

9. The legendary unicorn could be trapped by a
hunter who stood in front of a tree; when the unicorn
charged, the hunter stepped aside and the unicorn's
horn stuck fast in the tree.
1. Bears were supposedly hated by horses.
2. Lion's crimes; leopard's spots.

3. Being transformed to a beast.
4. *thou . . . here:* what you've just said would please
me.
5. They do not appear until 5.1 (perhaps a sign of
revision).
6. Supreme instance (with wordplay on "fool's cap").

Of Hymen's° purest bed, thou valiant Mars,[7]   *god of marriage*
Thou ever-young, fresh, loved, and delicate wooer,
Whose blush° doth thaw the consecrated snow[8]   *glow*
380   That lies on Dian's lap, thou visible god,
That sold'rest close impossibilities[9]
And mak'st them kiss, that speak'st with every tongue
To every purpose, O thou touch° of hearts,   *touchstone*
Think thy slave, man, rebels, and by thy virtue°   *power*
385   Set them into confounding odds,° that beasts   *men at ruinous strife*
May have the world in empire.

APEMANTUS   Would 'twere so,
But not till I am dead. I'll say thou'st gold:
Thou wilt be thronged to shortly.

TIMON   Thronged to?

APEMANTUS   Ay.

TIMON   Thy back,[1] I prithee.

APEMANTUS   Live, and love thy misery.

390   TIMON   Long live so, and so die. I am quit.°   *rid of you*

        Enter the BANDITTI.

APEMANTUS   More things like men. Eat, Timon, and abhor
    them.   *Exit.*

FIRST BANDIT   Where should he have° this gold? It is some   *have obtained; have put*
    poor fragment, some slender ort° of his remainder. The   *scrap*
    mere want of gold and the falling from of his friends drove
395   him into this melancholy.

SECOND BANDIT   It is noised° he hath a mass of treasure.   *rumored*

THIRD BANDIT   Let us make the assay° upon him. If he care   *test; assault*
    not for't, he will supply us easily; if he covetously reserve it,
    how shall's get it?

400   SECOND BANDIT   True, for he bears it not about him. 'Tis hid.

FIRST BANDIT   Is not this he?

SECOND *and* THIRD BANDITS   Where?

SECOND BANDIT   'Tis his description.

THIRD BANDIT   He! I know him.

405   ALL   Save° thee, Timon.   *God save*

TIMON   Now, thieves—

ALL   Soldiers, not thieves.

TIMON   Both, too, and women's sons.

ALL   We are not thieves, but men that much do want.°   *are very needy*

TIMON   Your greatest want is you want much of meat.°   *food*
410   Why should you want? Behold, the earth hath roots.
Within this mile break forth a hundred springs.
The oaks bear mast,° the briars scarlet hips.[2]   *acorns (fed to swine)*
The bounteous housewife Nature on each bush
Lays her full mess° before you. Want? Why want?   *serving*
415   FIRST BANDIT   We cannot live on grass, on berries, water,
    As beasts and birds and fishes.

TIMON   Nor on the beasts themselves, the birds, and fishes:
You must eat men. Yet thanks I must you con°   *render*

---

7. Adulterous lover of Venus and the god of war.
8. The snow of chastity, of which the goddess Diana was patroness.

9. That tightly solders together incompatible things.
1. Show me your back (go away).
2. Rose hips (sour fruit).

That you are thieves professed, that you work not
420 In holier shapes, for there is boundless theft
In limited° professions. [*He gives them gold.*] Rascal thieves,   *legitimate*
Here's gold. Go, suck the subtle° blood o'th' grape   *delicate; deceptive*
Till the high fever seethe° your blood to froth,   *boil (by drunkenness)*
And so scape hanging.° Trust not the physician.   *(by dying of a fever)*
425 His antidotes are poison, and he slays
More than you rob. Take wealth and lives together—
Do, villain, do. Since you protest° to do't   *openly profess*
Like workmen,° I'll example you with³ thievery: *skilled artisans*
The sun's a thief and with his great attraction°   *power to draw up*
430 Robs the vast sea. The moon's an arrant⁴ thief,
And her pale fire she snatches from the sun.
The sea's a thief, whose liquid surge resolves°   *melts*
The moon into salt tears.⁵ The earth's a thief,
That feeds and breeds by a composture° stolen   *manure*
435 From general° excrement. Each thing's a thief.   *universal*
The laws, your curb and whip,° in their rough power   *restraint and punishment*
Has unchecked theft.⁶ Love not yourselves. Away!
Rob one another. There's more gold; cut throats.
All that you meet are thieves. To Athens go;
440 Break open shops. Nothing can you steal
But thieves do lose it. Steal less for° this I give you,   *because of*
And gold confound you howsoe'er.° Amen.   *whatever you do*
THIRD BANDIT   He's almost charmed me from my profession
by persuading me to it.
445 FIRST BANDIT   'Tis in the malice° of mankind that he thus   *out of hatred*
advises us, not to have us thrive in our mystery.°   *profession*
SECOND BANDIT   I'll believe him as an enemy⁷ and give over
my trade.
FIRST BANDIT   Let us first see peace in Athens.° There is no   *(an unlikely prospect)*
450 time so miserable but a man may be true.°   *may repent*

Exeunt [BANDITTI].

Enter the STEWARD *to* TIMON.

STEWARD   O you gods!
Is yond despised and ruinous° man my lord?   *ruined*
Full of decay and failing? Oh, monument
And wonder of good deeds evilly bestowed!⁸
455 What an alteration of honor has desperate want made.
What viler thing upon the earth than friends,
Who can bring noblest minds to basest ends.
How rarely does it meet with this time's guise,
When man was wished to love his enemies.⁹
460 Grant I may ever love, and rather woo,
Those that would mischief me than those that do.¹
He's caught me in his eye. I will present
My honest grief unto him, and as my lord
Still serve him with my life. —My dearest master.

---

3. I'll give you precedents for.
4. Unmitigated; wandering (errant). The moon was considered auspicious to thieves.
5. Tides supposedly resulted from the sea drawing moisture from the moon.
6. Have unlimited power to steal.
7. As I would an enemy (that is, not at all).

8. Bestowed on ungrateful people.
9. *How . . . enemies:* How perfectly it accords with the customary exhortation to love one's enemies (since friends are one's undoing).
1. Those who would like to injure me, rather than those who really do so.

TIMON   Away, what art thou?

STEWARD   Have you forgot me, sir?

TIMON   Why dost ask that? I have forgot all men.
   Then, if thou grunt'st, thou'rt a man. I have forgot thee.

STEWARD   An honest poor servant of yours.

TIMON   Then I know thee not.
   I never had honest man about me. Ay, all
470   I kept were knaves to serve in meat° to villains.   *serve food*

STEWARD   The gods are witness,
   Ne'er did poor steward wear a truer grief
   For his undone lord than mine eyes for you.

TIMON   What, dost thou weep? Come nearer. Then I love thee
475   Because thou art a woman° and disclaim'st   *(in weeping)*
   Flinty mankind, whose eyes do never give°   *succumb*
   But through lust and laughter. Pity's sleeping.
   Strange times that weep with laughing, not with weeping.

STEWARD   I beg of you to know me, good my lord,
480   T'accept my grief, [*showing* TIMON *money*] and whilst this
      poor wealth lasts
   To entertain° me as your steward still.   *employ*

TIMON   Had I a steward
   So true, so just, and now so comfortable?°   *comforting*
   It almost turns my dangerous° nature wild.   *savage*
485   Let me behold thy face. Surely, this man
   Was born of woman.
   Forgive my general and exceptless° rashness,   *indiscriminate*
   You perpetual sober gods. I do proclaim
   One honest man. Mistake me not, but one—
490   No more, I pray—and he's a steward.
   How fain° would I have hated all mankind,   *willingly*
   And thou redeem'st thyself. But all save thee,
   I fell° with curses.   *cut down*
   Methinks thou art more honest now than wise,
495   For, by oppressing and betraying me,
   Thou mightst have sooner got another service.
   For many so arrive at second masters
   Upon° their first lord's neck. But tell me true—   *By stepping on*
   For I must ever doubt though ne'er so sure—
500   Is not thy kindness subtle,° covetous,   *treacherous*
   If not a usuring kindness, and, as rich men deal gifts,
   Expecting in return twenty for one?

STEWARD   No, my most worthy master, in whose breast
   Doubt and suspect,° alas, are placed too late.   *suspicion*
505   You should have feared false times when you did feast.
   Suspect still° comes where an estate is least.   *always*
   That which I show, heaven knows, is merely love,
   Duty, and zeal to your unmatched mind,
   Care of your food and living, and believe it,
510   My most honored lord,
   For° any benefit that points to me,   *As for*
   Either in hope,° or present, I'd exchange   *the future*
   For this one wish: that you had power and wealth
   To requite° me by making rich yourself.   *repay*
515   TIMON [*offering gold*]   Look thee, 'tis so, thou singly honest
      man.

Here, take. The gods out of my misery
Has sent thee treasure. Go, live rich and happy,
But thus conditioned:[2] thou shalt build from° men,   *away from*
Hate all, curse all, show charity to none,
520 But let the famished flesh slide from the bone
Ere thou relieve the beggar. Give to dogs
What thou deniest to men. Let prisons swallow 'em,
Debts wither 'em to nothing; be men° like blasted woods, *let men be*
And may diseases lick up their false bloods.
525 And so farewell and thrive.
STEWARD Oh, let me stay and comfort you, my master.
TIMON If thou hat'st curses,
Stay not. Fly, whilst thou art blest and free;
Ne'er see thou man, and let me ne'er see thee.
   Exeunt [TIMON *to his cave and* STEWARD *separately*].

5.1

  Enter POET *and* PAINTER.
PAINTER As I took note of the place, it cannot be far where he
 abides.
POET What's to be thought of him? Does the rumor hold for
 true that he's so full of gold?
5 PAINTER Certain. Alcibiades reports it. Phrynia and Timandra had gold of him. He likewise enriched poor straggling
 soldiers with great quantity. 'Tis said he gave unto his steward a mighty sum.
POET Then this breaking° of his has been but a try° for his *bankruptcy / test*
10 friends?
PAINTER Nothing else. You shall see him a palm[1] in Athens
 again and flourish with the highest. Therefore, 'tis not amiss
 we tender our loves to him in this supposed distress of his. It
 will show honestly in us and is very likely to load our purposes° *to reward our efforts*
15 with what they travail° for, if it be a just and true report that *labor; travel*
 goes° of his having.° *circulates / property*
POET What have you now to present unto him?
PAINTER Nothing at this time but my visitation. Only I will
 promise him an excellent piece.
20 POET I must serve him so too, tell him of an intent that's
 coming toward him.
PAINTER Good as the best.° Promising is the very air° o'th' *That's excellent / fashion*
 time. It opens the eyes of expectation. Performance is ever
 the duller for his° act, and, but in the plainer and simpler *its*
25 kind of people, the deed of saying° is quite out of use. To *doing what one says*
 promise is most courtly and fashionable; performance is a
 kind of will or testament which argues a great sickness in
 his judgment that makes it.[2]
   Enter TIMON *from his cave.*[3]
TIMON [*aside*] Excellent workman! Thou canst not paint a
30 man so bad as is thyself.

---

2. But on this condition.
5.1 Location: Outside Athens.
1. The highest tree: alluding to Psalm 92:12, "The
righteous shall flourish like a palm tree."
2. That is, only those close to death worry about ful-

filling their vows.
3. TEXTUAL COMMENT This stage direction suggests
that Timon's cave is either a stage door or a curtained
alcove at the back of the stage; see Digital Edition
TC 8 for a discussion of the theatrical possibilities.

POET   I am thinking what I shall say I have provided for him.
It must be a personating° of himself—a satire against the   *representation*
softness of prosperity, with a discovery° of the infinite flat-   *revelation*
teries that follow youth and opulency.

35 TIMON [*aside*]   Must thou needs stand° for a villain in thine   *model*
own work? Wilt thou whip thine own faults in other men?
Do so; I have gold for thee.
POET   Nay, let's seek him.
Then do we sin against our own estate,°   *condition in life*
40 When we may profit meet° and come too late.   *make a profit*
PAINTER   True.
When the day serves° before black-cornered night,   *allows*
Find what thou want'st by free and offered light.
Come.
45 TIMON [*aside*]   I'll meet you at the turn.[4]
What a god's gold that he is worshippèd
In a baser temple than where swine feed?
'Tis thou that rigg'st the bark° and plow'st the foam,   *puts sails on the boat*
Settlest admired reverence in a slave.[5]
50 To thee be worship and thy saints for aye;°   *ever*
Be crowned with plagues that thee alone obey.
Fit° I meet them.   *It is fit*
          [*He comes forward.*]
POET   Hail, worthy Timon!
PAINTER   Our late noble master!
TIMON   Have I once° lived to see two honest men?   *really*
55 POET   Sir,
Having often of your open bounty tasted,
Hearing you were retired,° your friends fall'n off,   *had gone away*
Whose thankless natures—oh, abhorrèd spirits!—
Not all the whips of heaven are large enough—
60 What, to you,
Whose star-like nobleness gave life and influence[6]
To their whole being!—I am rapt° and cannot cover   *overwhelmed*
The monstrous bulk of this ingratitude
With any size[7] of words.
65 TIMON   Let it go naked. Men may see't the better.
You that are honest, by being what you are,
Make them° best seen and known.   *(the "abhorrèd spirits")*
PAINTER   He and myself
Have travailed° in the great shower of your gifts   *worked*
And sweetly felt it.
TIMON   Ay, you are honest men.
70 PAINTER   We are hither come to offer you our service.
TIMON   Most honest men, why, how shall I requite you?
Can you eat roots and drink cold water? No?
BOTH   What we can do, we'll do to do you service.
TIMON   You're honest men. You've heard that I have gold.
75 I am sure you have. Speak truth; you're honest men.

---

4. I'll meet you when you come around the corner;
I'll trick you in return.
5. Makes an unworthy person be revered.
6. Explained astrologically, "influence" was a sub-

stance thought to stream forth from stars and affect
events on earth.
7. Amount; sizing, a layer applied to walls prior to
painting.

PAINTER So it is said, my noble lord, but therefore
   Came not my friend, nor I.
TIMON Good honest men. [to PAINTER] Thou draw'st a
   counterfeit°   *picture; fake*
   Best in all Athens. Thou'rt indeed the best;
   Thou counterfeit'st most lively.
80 PAINTER   So, so, my lord.
TIMON E'en so, sir, as I say. [to POET] And for thy fiction,°   *poetry; lying*
   Why, thy verse swells with stuff so fine and smooth
   That thou art even natural° in thine art.   *lifelike; idiotic*
   But for all this, my honest-natured friends,
85 I must needs say you have a little fault—
   Marry, 'tis not monstrous in you, neither wish I
   You take much pains to mend.
BOTH   Beseech your honor
   To make it known to us.
TIMON   You'll take it ill.
BOTH Most thankfully, my lord.
TIMON   Will you indeed?
90 BOTH Doubt it not, worthy lord.
TIMON There's never a one of you but trusts a knave
   That mightily deceives you.
BOTH   Do we, my lord?
TIMON Ay, and you hear him cog,° see him dissemble,   *cheat*
   Know his gross patchery,° love him, feed him,   *roguery*
95 Keep° in your bosom, yet remain assured   *Keep him*
   That he's a made-up° villain.   *complete*
PAINTER I know none such, my lord.
POET Nor I.
TIMON Look you, I love you well. I'll give you gold.
100 Rid me these villains from your companies.
   Hang them or stab them, drown them in a draft,°   *stream; cesspool*
   Confound° them by some course, and come to me,   *Destroy*
   I'll give you gold enough.
BOTH Name them, my lord. Let's know them.
105 TIMON You that way and you this, but two in company.
   Each man apart, all single and alone,
   Yet an archvillain keeps him company.[8]
   [to one] If where thou art two villains shall not be,
   Come not near him. [to the other] If thou wouldst not reside
110 But where one villain is, then him abandon.
      [TIMON attacks them.]
   Hence, pack,° there's gold. You came for gold, ye slaves.   *go away*
   You have work for me; there's payment, hence!
   You are an alchemist;[9] make gold of that!
   Out, rascal dogs!
        Exeunt [POET *and* PAINTER. *Exit* TIMON *to his cave*].

---

8. That is, both of you are archvillains.
9. That is, one who can translate base metal (the beating) into gold.

5.2

Enter STEWARD *and two* SENATORS.

STEWARD   It is vain that you would speak with Timon,
    For he is set so only to himself°   *so self-isolated*
    That nothing but himself which looks like man
    Is friendly with° him.   *congenial to*
FIRST SENATOR   Bring us to his cave.
5   It is our part and promise to th'Athenians
    To speak with Timon.
SECOND SENATOR   At all times alike
    Men are not still° the same. 'Twas time and griefs   *always*
    That framed him thus. Time with his fairer hand
    Offering the fortunes of his former days,
10   The former man may make him. Bring us to him
    And chance it as it may.
STEWARD   Here is his cave.
    [*He calls.*] Peace and content be here! Lord Timon, Timon,
    Look out and speak to friends. Th'Athenians
    By two of their most reverend Senate greet thee.
15   Speak to them, noble Timon.
            Enter TIMON *out of his cave.*
TIMON   Thou sun that comforts, burn! —Speak, and be hanged.
    For each true word, a blister, and each false°   *let each false word*
    Be as a cantherizing° to the root o'th' tongue,   *cauterizing*
    Consuming it with speaking.
FIRST SENATOR   Worthy Timon—
20 TIMON   Of none but such as you, and you of Timon.[1]
FIRST SENATOR   The senators of Athens greet thee, Timon.
TIMON   I thank them and would send them back the plague,
    Could I but catch it for them.
FIRST SENATOR   Oh, forget
    What we are sorry for ourselves in thee![2]
25   The senators with one consent of° love   *unanimous*
    Entreat thee back to Athens, who have thought
    On special dignities,° which vacant lie   *titles; offices*
    For thy best use and wearing.
FIRST SENATOR   They confess
    Toward thee forgetfulness too general gross,°   *obvious and extreme*
30   Which now the public body,° which doth seldom   *republic*
    Play the recanter,° feeling in itself   *Change its mind*
    A lack of Timon's aid, hath sense withal
    Of its own fall,° restraining° aid to Timon,   *failure / withholding*
    And send forth us to make their sorrowed render,° *to apologize sadly*
35   Together with a recompense more fruitful
    Than their offense can weigh down by the dram,[3]
    Ay, even such heaps and sums of love and wealth
    As shall to thee blot out what wrongs were theirs
    And write in thee the figures[4] of their love,
    Ever to read them thine.
40 TIMON   You witch° me in it,   *bewitch*

5.2 Location: Scene continues.
1. That is, we deserve each other.
2. In the injuries we did you.

3. Can outweigh even by painstaking calculation.
4. Distinctive marks; numbers in an account book.

Surprise me to the very brink of tears.
Lend me a fool's heart and a woman's eyes,
And I'll beweep these comforts, worthy senators.
FIRST SENATOR   Therefore so please thee to return with us,
45 And of our Athens, thine and ours, to take
The captainship. Thou shalt be met with thanks,
Allowed° with absolute power, and thy good name   *Vested*
Live with authority. So soon we shall drive back
Of Alcibiades th'approaches wild,
50 Who like a boar too savage doth root up
His country's peace.
SECOND SENATOR   And shakes his threat'ning sword
Against the walls of Athens.
FIRST SENATOR   Therefore, Timon—
TIMON   Well, sir, I will. Therefore I will, sir, thus:
If Alcibiades kill my countrymen,
55 Let Alcibiades know this of Timon:
That Timon cares not. But if he sack fair Athens
And take our goodly agèd men by th' beards,
Giving our holy virgins to the stain°   *(by rape)*
Of contumelious,° beastly, mad-brained war,   *insolent*
60 Then let him know, and tell him Timon speaks it,
In pity of our agèd and our youth,
I cannot choose but tell him that I care not,
And let him take't at worst.[5] For their knives care not,
While you have throats to answer.° For myself,   *suitable for cutting*
65 There's not a whittle° in th'unruly camp   *pocketknife*
But I do prize it at my love before
The reverend'st throat in Athens. So I leave you
To the protection of the prosperous gods,
As thieves to keepers.
STEWARD   Stay not. All's in vain.
70 TIMON   Why, I was writing of my epitaph.
It will be seen tomorrow. My long sickness
Of health and living now begins to mend,
And nothing° brings me all things. Go, live still.   *oblivion*
Be Alcibiades your plague, you his,
And last so long enough.
75 FIRST SENATOR   We speak in vain.
TIMON   But yet I love my country and am not
One that rejoices in the common wrack,°   *ruin*
As common bruit° doth put it.   *rumor*
FIRST SENATOR   That's well spoke.
TIMON   Commend me to my loving countrymen.
80 FIRST SENATOR   These words become your lips as they pass
    through them.
SECOND SENATOR   And enter in our ears like great triumphers[6]
In their applauding gates.[7]
TIMON   Commend me to them,
And tell them that to ease them of their griefs,
Their fears of hostile strokes, their aches, losses,

---

5. Interpret what I say in the worst possible way.
6. Like conquerors returning home.
7. Gates full of applauding fellow citizens.

85   Their pangs of love, with other incident throes°   *natural torments*
        That nature's fragile vessel doth sustain
        In life's uncertain voyage, I will some kindness do them.
        I'll teach them to prevent° wild Alcibiades' wrath.   *forestall*
        FIRST SENATOR   I like this well. He will return again.
90   TIMON   I have a tree which grows here in my close,°   *enclosure*
        That mine own use° invites me to cut down,   *purpose*
        And shortly must I fell it. Tell my friends,
        Tell Athens, in the sequence of degree°   *in order of rank*
        From high to low throughout, that, whoso please
95   To stop affliction, let him take his haste,
        Come hither ere my tree hath felt the ax,
        And hang himself. I pray you, do my greeting.
        STEWARD   Trouble him no further. Thus you still shall find him.
        TIMON   Come not to me again, but say to Athens
100   Timon hath made his everlasting mansion°   *(his grave)*
        Upon the beachèd verge° of the salt flood,°   *edge / sea*
        Who once a day with his embossèd° froth   *foaming*
        The turbulent surge shall cover. Thither come,
        And let my gravestone be your oracle.°   *source of revelation*
105   Lips, let four° words go by and language end;   *(that is, few)*
        What is amiss, plague and infection mend.
        Graves only be men's works and death their gain.
        Sun, hide thy beams. Timon hath done his reign.   *Exit.*
        FIRST SENATOR   His discontents are unremovably
110   Coupled to nature.°   *Intrinsic to his nature*
        SECOND SENATOR   Our hope in him is dead. Let us return
        And strain what other means is left unto us
        In our dear peril.
        FIRST SENATOR   It requires swift foot.   *Exeunt.*

5.3

Enter two other SENATORS *with a* MESSENGER.

THIRD SENATOR   Thou hast painfully discovered.[1] Are his files°   *troops*
        As full as thy report?
MESSENGER   I have spoke the least.°   *estimated low*
        Besides, his expedition° promises present° approach.   *speed / immediate*
FOURTH SENATOR   We stand much hazard if they bring not
        Timon.
5   MESSENGER   I met a courier, one mine ancient friend,
        Whom though in general part° we were opposed,   *public matters*
        Yet our old love made° a particular force   *exerted*
        And made us speak like friends. This man was riding
        From Alcibiades to Timon's cave
10   With letters of entreaty, which imported°   *urged*
        His fellowship i'th' cause against your city,
        In part for his sake moved.
                Enter the other SENATORS.
THIRD SENATOR   Here come our brothers.
FIRST SENATOR   No talk of Timon. Nothing of him expect.
        The enemy's drum is heard, and fearful scouring°   *hostile action*

5.3 Location: Outside the walls of Athens.   1. Carefully reconnoitered; told us painful news.

15   Doth choke the air with dust. In and prepare.
       Ours is the fall, I fear, our foes the snare.   *Exeunt.*

5.4

Enter a SOLDIER *in the woods, seeking* TIMON.

SOLDIER   By all description this should be the place.
      Who's here? Speak, ho! No answer? What is this?
          "Timon is dead, who hath outstretched his span.
          Some beast read this; there does not live a man."

5   Dead, sure, and this his grave. What's on this tomb
      I cannot read. The character I'll take with wax.[1]

Our captain hath in every figure° skill,	*kind of writing*
An aged° interpreter, though young in days.	*experienced*
Before proud Athens he's set down by this,°	*laid siege by this time*
10 Whose fall the mark° of his ambition is. *Exit.*	*goal*

5.5

Trumpets sound. Enter ALCIBIADES *with his powers°*   *army*
before Athens.

ALCIBIADES Sound° to this coward and lascivious town	*Proclaim*

      Our terrible approach.
          Sounds a parley.[1]
          The SENATORS *appear upon the walls.*[2]
      Till now you have gone on and filled the time
      With all licentious measure,[3] making your wills
5   The scope of justice.[4] Till now myself and such

As slept° within the shadow of your power	*dwelled*

      Have wandered with our traversed[5] arms and breathed
      Our sufferance[6] vainly. Now the time is flush,

When crouching marrow° in the bearer strong	*latent vigor*
10 Cries of itself, "No more." Now breathless° wrong	*exhausted*

      Shall sit and pant in your great chairs of ease,

And pursy° insolence shall break his wind°	*short-winded / pant; fart*
With fear and horrid° flight.	*terrified*

FIRST SENATOR   Noble and young,

When thy first griefs were but a mere conceit,°	*merely imagined*

15   Ere thou hadst power or we had cause of fear,
      We sent to thee to give thy rages balm,
      To wipe out our ingratitude, with loves
      Above their quantity.[7]

SECOND SENATOR   So did we woo
      Transformèd Timon to our city's love

20 By humble message and by promised means.°	*wealth*

      We were not all unkind, nor all deserve

The common° stroke of war.	*indiscriminate*

FIRST SENATOR   These walls of ours
      Were not erected by their hands from whom

5.4 Location: Outside Athens.
1. By making an impression of the letters. The soldier is evidently reading a notice of some kind in lines 3–4, yet in lines 5–6 he claims to be unable to read the writing on the tombstone, perhaps because the script is unfamiliar, or because the epitaph is in a foreign language (later translated by Alcibiades).
5.5 Location: Outside the walls of Athens.
1. Trumpet call to negotiate.

2. Probably on the upper gallery at stage rear.
3. All kinds of licentious conduct.
4. *making . . . justice:* making justice conform to your whims.
5. Crossed (as part of military training).
6. *breathed / Our sufferance:* voiced our grievances.
7. *loves . . . quantity:* friendly gestures greater than your grievances.

You have received your grief. Nor are they such
25 That these great towers, trophies,° and schools[8] should fall   *monuments*
For private faults in them.°   *(the offenders)*
SECOND SENATOR   Nor are they living
Who were the motives that you first went out.[9]
Shame, that they wanted° cunning, in excess   *lacked*
Hath broke their hearts. March, noble lord,
30 Into our city with thy banners spread.
By decimation and a tithèd death,[1]
If thy revenges hunger for that food
Which nature loathes, take thou the destined tenth,
And by the hazard of the spotted die
Let die the spotted.[2]
35 FIRST SENATOR   All have not offended.
For those that were,° it is not square° to take   *(living) / fair*
On those that are, revenge. Crimes like lands
Are not inherited. Then, dear countryman,
Bring in thy ranks, but leave without° thy rage.   *outside*
40 Spare thy Athenian cradle° and those kin   *birthplace*
Which in the bluster of thy wrath must fall
With those that have offended. Like a shepherd
Approach the fold and cull th'infected forth,°   *pick out the corrupt*
But kill not altogether.
SECOND SENATOR   What thou wilt,
45 Thou rather shalt enforce it with thy smile
Than hew to't with thy sword.
FIRST SENATOR   Set but thy foot
Against our rampired° gates, and they shall ope,   *barricaded*
So° thou wilt send thy gentle heart before   *If*
To say thou'lt enter friendly.
SECOND SENATOR   Throw thy glove
50 Or any token° of thine honor else   *pledge*
That thou wilt use the wars as thy redress
And not as our confusion.° All thy powers°   *ruin / army*
Shall make their harbor° in our town till we   *lodging*
Have sealed° thy full desire.   *satisfied*
ALCIBIADES [*throwing his glove*]   Then there's my glove.
55 Descend and open your unchargèd ports.°   *unattacked gates*
Those enemies of Timon's and mine own,
Whom you yourselves shall set out for reproof,°   *select for punishment*
Fall, and no more. And to atone° your fears   *allay*
With my more noble meaning, not a man°   *soldier*
60 Shall pass his quarter° or offend the stream   *leave his assigned place*
Of regular justice[3] in your city's bounds
But shall be remedied to° your public laws   *punished according to*
At heaviest answer.°   *penalty*
BOTH SENATORS   'Tis most nobly spoken.
ALCIBIADES Descend, and keep your words.
    Enter a [SOLDIER].

---

8. Public buildings.
9. Who were those who prompted your banishment.
1. Killing one of every ten persons, chosen by lot.

2. Corrupt (punning on the spots of dice).
3. *offend . . . justice:* violate the ordinary laws.

65 SOLDIER My noble general, Timon is dead,
　　　Entombed upon the very hem° o'th' sea,　　　　　　　　　　　　　*edge*
　　　And on his gravestone this insculpture,° which　　　　　　　*inscription*
　　　With wax I brought away, whose soft impression
　　　Interprets for my poor ignorance.
　　　　　　ALCIBIADES *reads the epitaph.*[4]
70　　　　　"Here lies a wretchèd corpse of wretchèd soul bereft.
　　　　　Seek not my name. A plague consume you wicked
　　　　　　caitiffs° left.　　　　　　　　　　　　　　　　　*wretches*
　　　　　Here lie I, Timon, who alive all living men did hate.
　　　　　Pass by and curse thy fill, but pass and stay not here
　　　　　　thy gait."
　　　These well express in thee thy latter spirits.°　　　　　　　*sentiments*
75　　　Though thou abhorred'st in us our humane griefs,
　　　Scorned'st our brain's flow,[5] and those our droplets which
　　　From niggard[6] nature fall, yet rich conceit°　　　　　　　*imagination*
　　　Taught thee to make vast Neptune weep for aye°　　　　　　*ever*
　　　On thy low grave, on faults forgiven. Dead
80　　Is noble Timon, of whose memory
　　　Hereafter more. Bring me into your city,
　　　And I will use the olive° with my sword,　　　　　　*(symbol of peace)*
　　　Make war breed peace, make peace stint° war, make each　　*stop*
　　　Prescribe to other as each other's leech.[7]
85　　Let our drums strike.　　　　　　　　　　　　*Exeunt.*

---

4. TEXTUAL COMMENT The epitaph seems to consist of two mutually contradictory couplets, perhaps suggesting incomplete revision or collaboration, or perhaps indicating Timon's profoundly conflicted state of mind. See Digital Edition TC 9 for a fuller discussion.

5. Tears were thought to exude from the brain.
6. "Niggard" because teardrops are tiny compared with the sea, Neptune (line 78).
7. Physician (because war purges peace of its decadence, and peace purges war of its violence).

Macbeth

On May 19, 1603, a scant two months after the death of Queen Elizabeth and the accession to the English throne of the Scottish King James, Shakespeare's company, the Chamberlain's Men, was formally declared to be the King's Men. The players had every reason to be grateful to their royal master for this lucrative distinction and to be attentive to his pleasure and interest. It has long been argued that one of the most striking signs of their gratitude is *Macbeth,* based on a story from Scottish history particularly apt for a monarch who traced his line back to Banquo, the noble thane whose murder Macbeth orders after he has killed King Duncan. Shakespeare's Scottish play is far too complex about the nature of power—and far too frightening—to have served as a simple piece of flattery. But the King's Men must have calculated that the Jacobean court, where the play was frequently performed, would find the tragedy's vision gripping.

As so often with Shakespeare, we do not have a secure date for either the composition or the first performance of *Macbeth.* The first printed text is in the 1623 First Folio, but the play, usually dated 1606, has always seemed the most topical of Shakespeare's great tragedies, cannily alert at once to King James's personal obsessions and to contemporary events. The most unnerving of those events was the 1605 Gunpowder Plot, an assassination attempt that riveted the attention of the entire kingdom and had long-term political and psychological consequences. A small group of conspirators, embittered by what they perceived as James's unwillingness to extend toleration to Roman Catholics, smuggled barrels of gunpowder into the basement beneath the House of Lords and allegedly planned to set off a massive explosion that would blow up the King and his family, along with most of the government, at the ceremonial opening of England's Parliament. According to the official account, the King himself saved the day by brilliantly interpreting a subtle hint in an intercepted letter. On the night before the intended attempt, officers arrested one of the principal conspirators, Guy Fawkes, who revealed under torture the names of his collaborators.

How is it possible to confront and triumph over terror? What are the dark roots of treason? Whom can you trust? Surface appearances may deceive; apparently straightforward statements may conceal dangerous ambiguities; it is important to read between the lines. Among those hunted down and brought to trial was Father Henry Garnet, head of the clandestine Jesuit mission in England. Swearing that he was innocent, Garnet pointed out that there was no evidence against him, but the government prosecutors made much of the fact that he was the author of *A Treatise of Equivocation,* a book showing how to give misleading answers under oath. Convicted of treason, he was hanged, drawn, and quartered, and his head was set on a pole on London Bridge.

Written in the wake of this national trauma, Shakespeare's whole play is haunted by equivocation. At a harrowing moment in *Macbeth,* in the immediate wake of the murder of the sleeping King Duncan, an insistent knocking is heard at the castle gate. (The knocking is a simple device, but in performance it almost always has a thrilling effect, famously characterized by the Romantic critic Thomas de Quiney as the first reflux of the ordinary human world upon the fiendish.) A porter, roused by the hammering on the door but still half drunk from the evening's revelry, appears, and the play lurches suddenly toward macabre comedy. As he grumblingly goes to unlock the gate, the porter imagines that he is the gatekeeper in hell, opening the door to new arrivals. "Here's an equivocator," he says of one of these imaginary sinners, "that could swear in both the scales against either scale, who committed treason enough for God's sake, yet could not equivocate to heaven. Oh, come in, equivocator" (2.3.7–10). This treasonous equivocator knocking on hell's gate is almost certainly an allusion to the recently executed Henry Garnet.

The Gunpowder Plot was only one of the King's sources of anxiety. Not surprising for someone whose mother and father had both been killed, James had a horror of assassination and was convinced that there were many plots against his life. He also held a powerful conviction that a king was a sacred figure, God's own representative on earth. Regicide, in this view, was close to the ultimate crime, a demonic assault not simply on an individual and a community but on the fundamental order of the universe. James, who had written a learned book on witchcraft, suspected the hand of the devil in any plot against an anointed king, believed that witches had at various points in his own life conspired to harm him or render him impotent, and feared the existence of occult, invisible forces bent on bringing all things to ruin.

In several of his earlier plays, most notably *Richard II*, Shakespeare's characters give voice to the theory that the king is God's deputy on earth and consequently that attacks upon him are evil. The theory is by no means simply endorsed in any of these plays, and it jostles up against a thoroughly secular analysis of power politics and the manipulation of ideology. But kingship's claim to sacred authority is voiced exceptionally powerfully in *Macbeth* (not in Scotland alone, but also in neighboring England, where, as Malcolm tells Macduff, the touch of the pious King Edward cures disease). Exceptionally powerful too in this play is the metaphysical horror of regicide. The murder of Duncan is marked in the natural world with dreadful signs and portents, and in the human world with an overpowering sense of devastation ironically given its most eloquent expression by the murderer Macbeth:

> Renown and grace is dead.
> The wine of life is drawn, and the mere lees
> Is left this vault to brag of.
> (2.3.91–93)

Macbeth is speaking hypocritically—"Look like th'innocent flower," his wife had counseled him, "But be the serpent under't" (1.5.63–64)—and yet, at least in one interpretation of the part, he is saying what he himself knows to be the grim truth. Far more than any other of Shakespeare's villains, more than the homicidal Richard III, the treacherous Claudius in *Hamlet*, and the cold-hearted Iago in *Othello*, Macbeth is tormented by an awareness of the wickedness of what he is doing. Endowed with a clear-eyed grasp of the difference between good and evil, he chooses evil, even though the choice mystifies and sickens him.

Before he has taken the irrevocable step, Macbeth tries to recover his moral bearings. The deed he is contemplating, he begins by telling himself, would work only if he could control all consequences, so that his blow "Might be the be-all and the end-all" (1.7.5). But he grasps that there is no possibility of such complete control and therefore no hope of practical success. His thoughts then turn to the overwhelming ethical arguments against the murder: he is not only the King's kinsman and subject but also his host, "Who should against his murderer shut the door, / Not bear the knife myself" (1.7.15–16). And from these considerations, practical and ethical, Macbeth's restless, brooding mind rises higher, imagining that the murdered Duncan's virtues will plead like angels against the "deep damnation of his taking-off":

> And Pity, like a naked newborn babe
> Striding the blast, or heaven's cherubim horsed
> Upon the sightless couriers of the air,
> Shall blow the horrid deed in every eye,
> That tears shall drown the wind.
> (1.7.20–25)

Henry IV of France (1553–1610) administers the royal touch, thought to cure scrofula. An etching by Pierre Firens, in André Du Laurens' *De mirabili strumas sanandi vi solis Galliae regibus . . .* (Paris, 1609). See *Macbeth* 4.3.141–59.

No one else in the play has a moral sensibility so intense or so visionary, no one else imagines so vividly the forces that lie beyond the ordinary and familiar horizon of human experience. Macbeth understands exactly what is at stake and what he must do: "We will," he tells his wife decisively, "proceed no further in this business" (1.7.31).

Why, then, does he change his mind and commit a crime he cannot even contemplate without horror? A significant part of the answer lies in the instigation of his formidable wife. When we first glimpse Lady Macbeth, she is reading a letter. (Reading was by no means a universal achievement for women of the early seventeenth century, let alone the eleventh, when the play's events are set, but Shakespeare frequently represents it in his plays in a variety of contexts.) The letter makes her burn with visions of the "golden round" that "fate and metaphysical aid" (1.5.26–27) seem to have conferred upon her husband. But though she speaks of the crown as if it were already on Macbeth's head, she fears that he is too full of the "milk of human kindness" (1.5.15) to seize what has been promised him. She resolves then to "chastise" her husband, to urge him, in a phrase taken from archery that has a strong sexual undercurrent, to screw his courage to the sticking place. Lady Macbeth manipulates him in two principal ways. The first is through sexual taunting:

> Art thou afeard
> To be the same in thine own act and valor
> As thou art in desire?
> . . . .
> When you durst do it, then you were a man.
>   (1.7.39–41, 49)

And the second is through the terrible force of her determination:

> I have given suck and know
> How tender 'tis to love the babe that milks me;
> I would, while it was smiling in my face,
> Have plucked my nipple from his boneless gums
> And dashed the brains out, had I so sworn as you
> Have done to this.
>
> (1.7.54–59)

These words, and the gestures that viscerally intensify them onstage, cannot by them-selves account for Macbeth's decision. He counters his wife's sexual taunting with a clear sense of the proper boundaries of his identity as a male and as a human being: "I dare do all that may become a man; / Who dares do more is none" (1.7.46–47). As for Lady Macbeth's fantasy of murdering her infant, its horror might have served rather to deter Macbeth from his unnatural crime than to spur him toward it.

Virtually everyone is subject to terrible dreams and lawless fantasies—"Merciful powers," Banquo prays, "Restrain in me the cursèd thoughts that nature / Gives way to in repose" (2.1.7–9)—but not everyone crosses the fatal line from criminal desire to criminal act. That in crossing this line Macbeth murders a man toward whom he should be grateful, loyal, and protective deepens the mystery of his crime, linking it to a long current of theological and philosophical brooding on the nature of evil. For St. Augustine, the great fourth-century Church Father, evil in its most radical form is gratuitous—that is, without an explicable rationale or motivation—and this notion of gratuitousness haunts subsequent thinkers, including those far from Christian ortho-doxy. Thus the Florentine Niccolò Machiavelli, notorious in the sixteenth century for free-thinking, writes in chapter 37 of his *Discourses* that "when men are no longer obliged to fight from necessity, they fight from ambition, which passion is so powerful in the hearts of men that it never leaves them, no matter to what height they may rise." The reason for this, Machiavelli proposes, is that "nature has created men so that they desire everything, but are unable to attain it; desire being thus always greater than the faculty of acquiring, discontent with what they have and dissatisfaction with them-selves result from it."

Macbeth and Lady Macbeth act on ambition, restless desire, and a will to power normally kept in check by the pragmatic, ethical, and religious considerations to which the wavering Macbeth initially gives voice. Lady Macbeth in effect works to liberate that will to power in her husband, freeing him from his "sickly" fears of damna-tion so that he can act with a ruthless blend of murderous violence and cunning. In her radically disenchanted, coolly skeptical view, the murder of the King can be undertaken without fear of guilty conscience, vengeful ghosts, or divine judgment: "The sleeping and the dead," she tells her shaken husband, "Are but as pictures; 'tis the eye of child-hood / That fears a painted devil" (2.2.56–58).

This reassurance, Shakespeare's tragedy shows, is hopelessly shallow. As the spec-tral dagger, the ghost sitting in Macbeth's chair, and the indelible bloodstains on Lady Macbeth's hands all chillingly demonstrate, the secure distinction between represen-tation and reality, the dead and the living, repeatedly breaks down, not simply for the characters but for the spectators as well. In most productions, the dagger and the blood are visible only to the diseased minds of the murderers, but Banquo's ghost is almost always palpably present onstage, visible to the audience as well as to the unhinged Macbeth, though invisible to everyone around him. Moreover, the dream of a "clean" regicide proves psychologically untenable. Lady Macbeth, who had vaunted that she would readily kill her own infant in the pursuit of her ambition, finds that a family resemblance prevents her from sticking a dagger in the sleeping King: "Had he not resembled / My father as he slept, I had done't" (2.2.12–13).

The seizure of the crown brings with it feverish sleeplessness, brooding anxiety about security, and an overwhelming sense of defilement. Macbeth and Lady Macbeth are equally devastated, but the psychological trajectory in the wake of the crime is not the same for the two conspirators. Initially frozen in moral numbness, Lady Macbeth experiences a gradual decomposition, a growing horror that breaks forth unforgettably in the sleepwalking scene with her compulsive attempts to free herself of the smell and stain of blood: "All the perfumes of Arabia will not sweeten this little hand" (5.1.44–45). Initially gripped by a heightened sensitivity to fear, a dread that threatens inward decomposition, Macbeth experiences a gradual hardening and deadening of the self:

> Tomorrow and tomorrow and tomorrow
> Creeps in this petty pace from day to day
> To the last syllable of recorded time. . . .
> (5.5.19–21)

Macbeth's murderous attempt to make himself "perfect" (3.4.22), as he puts it, leads by a grim irony to a state of absolute numbness, so that his life story, indeed any life story, seems to him in the end "a tale / Told by an idiot, full of sound and fury, / Signifying nothing" (5.5.26–28).

The assassination also proves, as Macbeth had foreseen, politically untenable. There is always someone who escapes the murderer's net, someone who poses a threat or seeks to redress an injury or simply remembers what it felt like to be free and unafraid. It is impossible to tie up all the loose ends, to break the chain of action and reaction, to reach a stable resting place. There are no clean murders. One crime leads to another and then to another, without bringing the criminal any closer to the security or contentment that each desperate act is meant to achieve. Macbeth cannot stop the bloody acts; instead he must multiply and extend them. Where Lady Macbeth had only fantasized the murder of children, Macbeth actually undertakes that and other crimes until he dreams, in his half-crazed words to the "secret, black, and midnight hags" (4.1.47), of universal destruction.

It is Macbeth's first encounter with these hags—the weird (or, in the original spelling, "weyward" or "weyard") sisters—that seems to initiate his descent toward murder and tyranny. But what kind of power do these malevolent bearded women have over Macbeth? Are they responsible, by magical influence or by planting the idea in his mind, for his decision to kill Duncan? Are they somehow privy to a predestined fate, as if they have seen the script of the tragedy before it is performed? Or, alternatively, are they uncanny emblems of Macbeth's psychological condition, a kind of screen onto which he projects his "horrible imaginings" (1.3.140)? The word "weird," in one of its etymologies, derives from the Old English word for "fate," but do the women Shakespeare depicts, trafficking in ambiguous prophecies, fretting over village squabbles, mumbling charms, actually control destiny (or, what amounts to the same thing, the tragedy's plot)? What is the nature of these strange creatures that "look not like th'inhabitants o'th' earth," as Banquo observes, "And yet are on't" (1.3.42–43)?

Actors' responses to these questions have ranged wildly, though virtually all productions have recognized that the witches' scenes are among the most theatrically powerful and compelling in the play and that it matters a great deal whether they are made up to look grotesque or stately, perversely comical or terrifying. Scholarly responses have been complicated by the high probability that not all of the witchcraft scenes are by Shakespeare himself: it appears that 3.5 and part of 4.1, the scenes featuring the goddess Hecate, were added to the play sometime after its first performance and incorporate songs derived from Thomas Middleton's play *The Witch*. (The Folio text of Macbeth, and hence *The Norton Shakespeare*, cites only the first words of these songs, but they were probably sung in full onstage: recordings of these songs can be found in the Digital Edition.) But even if we set aside the problems raised by these interpolated scenes, the status of the witches in Shakespeare's play remains uncertain and seems to be so by design. "What are you?" asks Macbeth when he first encounters the eerie, sexually ambiguous figures, and he receives in reply his

Macbeth and Banquo encounter the weird sisters (1.3). From Raphael Holinshed, *The First Volume of the Chronicles of England, Scotland, and Ireland* (1577).

own name: "All hail, Macbeth!" (1.3.48–49). Banquo urgently renews the inquiry, asking the creatures before his eyes if they truly exist or are only figments of his imagination; but his question, too, remains unanswered. When Macbeth and Banquo demand to know more, the witches vanish: "what seemed corporal / Melted as breath into the wind" (1.3.82–83). "As breath into the wind"—*Macbeth* is a tragedy of meltings, vanishing boundaries, and liminal states.

Much of the play transpires on the border between fantasy and reality, a sickening betwixt-and-between where a "horrid image" in the mind has the uncanny power to produce bodily effects "Against the use of nature" (1.3.137, 139), where one mind is present to the innermost fantasies of another, where manhood threatens to vanish and murdered men walk and blood cannot be washed off. If these effects could be unequivocally attributed to the agency of the witches, the audience would at least have the security of a defined and focused fear. Alternatively, if the witches could be definitively dismissed as fantasy or fraud, the audience would at least have the clear-eyed certainty of witnessing human causes in an altogether secular world. But instead, it remains fascinatingly difficult to determine how much agency either Macbeth or his wife actually possesses, how much their choices are governed by political calculations in a radically unstable kingdom, how much they are in the grip of forces they barely understand.

Shakespeare achieves the remarkable effect of a nebulous infection, a bleeding of the demonic into the secular and the secular into the demonic. The most famous instance of this effect is Lady Macbeth's great invocation of the "spirits / That tend on mortal thoughts" (1.5.38–39) to unsex her, fill her with cruelty, make thick her blood, and exchange her milk for gall. The speech appears to be a conjuration of demonic powers, an act of witchcraft in which the "murdering ministers" are directed to bring about a set of changes in her body. She calls these ministers "sightless substances" (1.5.47): though invisible, they are—as she conceives them—not figures of speech or projections of her mind, but objective, substantial beings or forces. (Macbeth similarly seems to imagine invisible but objective forces when he speaks of "the sightless couriers of the air," 1.7.23.) But the fact that the spirits she invokes are "sightless" already moves this passage away from the literal existence of the weird sisters and toward the metaphorical use of "spirits" in her speech of a few moments earlier: "Hie thee hither, / That I may pour my spirits in thine ear" (1.5.23–24). The spirits she

Witchcraft in Scotland. From *News from Scotland* (1591).

speaks of here are manifestly figurative—they refer to the bold words, the undaunted mettle, and the sexual taunts with which she intends to incite Macbeth to murder Duncan—but, like all of her expressions of will and passion, they strain toward bodily realization, even as they convey a psychic and hence invisible inwardness. That is, there is something uncannily literal about Lady Macbeth's influence on her husband, as if marital intimacy were akin to demonic possession, as if she had contrived to inhabit his mind, as if, in other words, she had literally poured her spirits in his ear. Conversely, there is something uncannily figurative about the "sightless substances" she invokes, as if the spirit world, the realm of "fate and metaphysical aid," were only a metaphor for her blind and murderous desires, as if the weird sisters were condensations of her own breath.

In Shakespeare's plays, as in those of his contemporaries, evildoers may wreak havoc for a time, but in the final restoration of order and justice, they and their principal accomplices are almost inevitably punished. Thus, at the close of *Macbeth*, not only are Macbeth and Lady Macbeth dead, but the victorious Malcolm also speaks of settling scores with "the cruel ministers / Of this dead butcher and his fiend-like Queen" (5.7.98–99). Yet though the play has deeply implicated the witches in Macbeth's monstrous assault on the fabric of civilized life, there is no gesture toward punishing them, no sign that the victors are even aware of their existence. This omission is the more striking if we recall that at the time Shakespeare wrote his play, the authorities in England and Scotland were bringing women to trial on charges of witchcraft and executing them. The theatrical power of *Macbeth* seems bound up with its refusal to resolve the questions raised by the witches. At once marginal and central to the play, they are only briefly and intermittently onstage, but they are still suggestively present when we cannot see them, when the threats they embody are absorbed in the ordinary relations of everyday life.

"There's no art / To find the mind's construction in the face" (1.4.11–12), says the baffled Duncan about a man who had betrayed his trust, but Macbeth confronts a deeper perplexity, an appalling mystery within himself:

> My thought, whose murder yet is but fantastical,
> Shakes so my single state of man
> That function is smothered in surmise,
> And nothing is but what is not.
>
> (1.3.141–44)

The witches have something to do with this inner torment, but what that something is remains as elusive as the dagger that Macbeth sees before him, handle toward his hand. Scotland is sick, "Almost afraid to know itself" (4.3.165). But the sickness cannot be isolated in a conspiracy of witches. If violence stirs in the hinterlands, where marauding armies struggle, it breeds more murderously still in the inmost circles of the realm, where the ruler feels most secure: "This castle hath a pleasant seat," says Duncan, going unwittingly to his death. "The air nimbly and sweetly recommends itself / Unto our gentle senses" (1.6.1–3).

If there is sexual disturbance out on the heath, where the bearded hags stir the ingredients of their hideous cauldron, there is deeper sexual disturbance at home, in the murderous intimacy of the marriage bond: "When you durst do it, then you were a man" (1.7.49). If the mind is subject to "supernatural soliciting" (1.3.132) from some bizarre place, it is gripped still more terribly and irresistibly by "horrible imaginings" (1.3.140) from within. If you are anxious about your future, scrutinize your best friends. If you are worried about losing your manhood, it is not enough to hunt for witches; look to your wife. If you are worried about demonic temptation, fear your own dreams. And if you fear spiritual desolation, turn your eyes on the contents not only of the cauldron but of your skull: "Oh, full of scorpions is my mind, dear wife!" (3.2.35).

The men who persecuted witches in Shakespeare's age were determined to compel full confessions, to pass judgment, and to escape from the terror of the inexplicable, the unforeseen, the aimlessly malignant. In *Macbeth*, the audience is given something better than confession, for it has visible proof of the demonic in action, but this visibility turns out to be as maddeningly equivocal or frustrating as the witches' riddling words. The "wayward" witches appear and disappear, their promises and prophecies all tricks, like practical jokes with appalling consequences. The ambiguous language of the play subverts the illusory certainties of sight, and the forces of renewed order, Malcolm and Macduff, are themselves strangely unstable. Malcolm, who spins an elaborate fantasy of his own viciousness, and Macduff, who abandons his wife and children to their slaughter, are peculiar emblems of a renewed, divinely sanctioned order. Shakespeare may have set out to please the king, but it is difficult to see how the king, if he paid any attention to the tragedy that the King's Men offered him, could be reassured. The ambiguities of demonic agency are never resolved, and its horror spreads like a mist through a murky landscape. "What is't you do?" Macbeth asks the weird sisters, who answer, "A deed without a name" (4.1.48).

By the play's close, Macbeth has begun "To doubt th'equivocation of the fiend / That lies like truth" (5.5.43–44). Equivocations are lies with mental reservations, words with double meanings, puns, twists of emphasis, and plays on false interpretations (such as the meaning of the phrase "not of woman born"). Like the witches— and, for that matter, like concepts of gender and authority and social order—language in *Macbeth* is a boundary-stalker, neither a trustworthy guide nor a manifest illusion. Words sit dangerously in a middle ground; they must be brought under control, but they always threaten to slide into lies or magic charms or riddles or sheer emptiness. It is this emptiness with which Macbeth seems haunted at the end, with his vision of life as "a tale told by an idiot." If the closing moments of the play invite us to recoil from this black hole—after all, the tyrant is killed and his severed head held up for all to see—they also invite us to recoil from too confident and simple a celebration of the triumph of grace. For somewhere beyond the immediate circle of order restored, the witches are dancing around the cauldron, and, the play seems to imply, the cauldron is in every one of us.

STEPHEN GREENBLATT

SELECTED BIBLIOGRAPHY

Adelman, Janet. "'Born of Woman': Fantasies of Maternal Power in *Macbeth*." *Cannibals, Witches, and Divorce: Estranging the Renaissance*. Ed. Marjorie Garber. Baltimore, MD: Johns Hopkins UP, 1987. 90–121. Argues that *Macbeth* represents dueling fantasies of absolute, destructive female power and of escape from that power; masculine authority is consolidated in the end by eliminating the feminine.

Bradley, A. C. *Shakespearean Tragedy: Lectures on "Hamlet," "Othello," "King Lear," "Macbeth."* London: Macmillan, 1905. Presents *Macbeth* as the most concentrated, classical, and fast-paced of Shakespeare's great tragedies, producing unequaled dread with its dark atmosphere and sublime central characters.

Calderwood, James L. *If It Were Done: "Macbeth" and Tragic Action*. Amherst: U of Massachusetts P, 1986. Looks at how *Macbeth* subverts the models of *Hamlet* and Aristotelian poetics, interrogating the nature of tragedy and the role of violence as both a threat to and a source of social order.

Greenblatt, Stephen. "Shakespeare Bewitched." *New Historical Literary Study: Essays on Reproducing Texts, Representing History*. Ed. Jeffrey N. Cox and Larry J. Reynolds. Princeton, NJ: Princeton UP, 1993. 108–35. Examines how in writing *Macbeth* Shakespeare drew upon both the king's belief in witchcraft and a skeptical critique of such belief by Reginald Scot.

Harris, Jonathan Gil. "The Smell of *Macbeth*." *Shakespeare Quarterly* 58 (2007): 465–86. Reflects on the smell of gunpowder used for stage effects in the early performances of *Macbeth* and the associations that smell would have had for the audience.

Howard, Jean E. "Shakespeare, Geography, and the Work of Genre on the Early Modern Stage." *Modern Language Quarterly* 64.3 (2003): 299–322. Analyzes how Scotland's mingled contemporary reputation for nobility and savagery allowed Shakespeare to desacralize kingship.

Kastan, David Scott. "*Macbeth* and the 'Name of the King.'" *Shakespeare After Theory*. New York: Routledge, 1999. 165–82. Explores how insistent doubling, blending the figures of the king and tyrant, undermines the attempt in *Macbeth* to contain violence by restoring moral order.

Mullaney, Steven. "Lying Like Truth: Riddle, Representation, and Treason." *The Place of the Stage: License, Play, and Power in Renaissance England*. Chicago: U of Chicago P, 1988. 116–34. Argues that, like the Jacobean spectacle of a traitor on the scaffold, *Macbeth* reveals the generative power of equivocation, challenging the absolutes of royal authority.

Norbrook, David. "*Macbeth* and the Politics of Historiography." *Politics of Discourse: The Literature and History of Seventeenth-Century England*. Ed. Kevin Sharpe and Steven Zwicker. Berkeley: U of California P, 1987. 78–116. Argues that, embroiled in seventeenth-century debates over writing Scottish history, Shakespeare raised the specter of justified regicide even as he drew on King James's monarchist views.

Orgel, Stephen. "Macbeth and the Antic Round." *The Authentic Shakespeare and Other Problems of the Early Modern Stage*. New York: Routledge, 2002. 159–72. Analyzes how revisions to the witches' scenes link theatrical spectacle to psychological inwardness and heighten the paradoxical role of women.

FILMS

Macbeth. 1948. Dir. Orson Welles. USA. 107 mins. Expressionist, low-budget production, starring Welles and Jeanette Nolan.

Throne of Blood. 1957. Dir. Akira Kurosawa. Japan. 105 mins. Kabuki-influenced production set in feudal Japan stars Toshiro Mifune and Isuzu Yamada.

Macbeth. 1971. Dir. Roman Polanski. UK. 140 mins. Bleak, misty, bloody vision, with strikingly young leads, Jon Finch and Francesca Annis.

Macbeth. 1979. Dir. Philip Casson. UK. 146 mins. Minimalist production for television with doubling actors and simple sets. Ian McKellen and Judi Dench star.

Men of Respect. 1989. Dir. William Reilly. USA. 113 mins. John Turturro stars as a mafia hitman who murders his boss (Rod Steiger). With Stanley Tucci as Malcolm and Peter Boyle as Macduff.

Maqbool. 2003. Dir. Vishal Bhardwaj. India. 132 mins. Set in the Mumbai underworld, with the witches as two corrupt, fortune-telling policemen.

Macbeth. 2010. Dir. Rupert Goold. UK. 160 mins. Patrick Stewart and Kate Fleetwood star in a production that evokes the Soviet Union in the time of Stalin and his henchmen. The witches are murderous hospital nurses.

TEXTUAL INTRODUCTION

The sole early modern text for *The Tragedy of Macbeth* appears in Shakespeare's First Folio (1623, sigs. ll6–nn4) between *Julius Caesar* and *Hamlet*. At 2,084 lines, *Macbeth* is one of Shakespeare's shortest plays (longer only than *The Comedy of Errors* and *The Tempest*) and by far the shortest of Shakespeare's tragedies, which average 3,030 lines, excluding the collaborative and possibly incomplete *Timon of Athens* at 2,299 lines. The text is about 95 percent verse and 5 percent prose and shows minimal proof correction. The Second Folio (1632) has no independent textual authority, but it presents some suggested alternative readings.

The brevity of *Macbeth* suggests that the play may be an abridgment. Many have noted inconsistencies in the action, which suggest revision or at least complicated transmission: Ross, for example, reports that Cawdor's betrayal began the conflict (1.2.55) but Macbeth knows nothing of his treachery (1.3.73–74). Lennox tells of Macduff's flight to England and Macbeth's rebuffed messenger to him in 3.6, but Macbeth is shocked and angry in 4.1 to discover that Macduff is gone, "Fled to England?" (line 141).

The copy text for the Folio may have been a promptbook or a transcription of one. The relatively complete record of entrances and exits and the relatively clear designation of characters may signal origins in the theater, though many scholars now regard such signals as inconclusive. A. R. Braunmuller (263) notes some additional evidence of theatrical provenance: in his view the Folio erroneously incorporates a theatrical instruction—"Ring the bell!" (2.3.75)—and contains numerous "professionally terse" stage directions for sound and lighting ("*Hautboys. Torches*," 1.7.0 SD) and for supernumeraries ("*Drum and colors*," 5.2.0 SD, 5.4.0 SD, 5.5.0 SD, 5.6.0 SD, 5.7.64 SD4). The printed text divides the play into acts and scenes, though modern editors have questioned the division between 2.2 and 2.3 because the location remains the same, Macbeth's castle, and the action is continuous; some have also argued for more scenic divisions in act 5 (see Digital Edition TC 10 at 5.7.64 SD). Two workmen, dubbed Compositor A and Compositor B, competently set the type to convert the manuscript to print, but A sometimes arranged blank verse into irregular lines and B sometimes set prose as verse (see Digital Edition TC 5 at 3.1.75).

As Braunmuller explains (275–79), scholars generally agree that Folio *Macbeth* shows signs of theatrical interpolation. The text includes instances of "repetition brackets," identical lines in close proximity that may mark an addition between them.

The repeated command, "Look to the lady" (2.3.116, 122; see Digital Edition TC 4 at 2.3.115 SD) brackets Malcolm and Donaldbain's worried conversation about their future, a possible addition. Gary Taylor argues that the repeated phrase "How wilt thou do for a father?" (4.2.38, 56–57) brackets a conversation inserted to reflect the Overbury trials and hangings of 1615–16 (Taylor and Lavagnino, pp. 394–97). Malcolm's dialogue with the English Doctor (4.3, a curiously otiose anticipation of the Scottish Doctor of Physic, 5.1), including the discussion on the "king's evil" (140–59), occurs between lines that may be linked to make up a pentameter ("'Tis hard to reconcile" and "See who comes here"). Many have thought the dialogue a digressive addition by Shakespeare or another for a court performance; others have defended the passage as developing the contrast between the good King Edward, a miraculous healer, and the evil tyrant Macbeth. Others have questioned Malcolm and Macduff's previous dialogue in this scene because it raises doubts about the character of the heir apparent and does not advance the action. (Actors who play Macbeth are grateful for the break before the closing action, however.) Most also believe the Hecate speeches (3.5 and 4.1.39ff), so different in style from the other witches' verse, are additions by another playwright for later performance; others believe them to be Shakespearean.

The leading candidate for that other playwright, a collaborator or adaptor of Shakespeare's *Macbeth*, is Thomas Middleton. Evidence for the identification consists mainly in the cues for two songs, "Come away, come away" (3.5.35 SD) and "Black spirits" (4.1.43 SD), which appear in full in Middleton's *The Witch* (1616?) (see Digital Edition TC 8 at 3.5.35 SD). Gary Taylor has argued that Middleton revised Shakespeare's play in 1616 and wrote an additional 151 lines, as well as 72 lines with Shakespeare, for a total of about 11 percent of the Folio text (Taylor and Lavagnino, pp. 383–97). For this reason he and John Lavagnino include *Macbeth* in the Oxford edition of Thomas Middleton's *Collected Works* (2007). In a *TLS* article (2010) and in a study with Marcus Dahl and Marina Tarlinskaya (2010), Brian Vickers has argued against Middleton's presence in *Macbeth*. Using software programs to detect three-word collocations in the canons of Shakespeare and Middleton, and examining diction and syntax, Vickers argues that the lines attributed to Middleton are demonstrably Shakespearean. Responding that the Vickers–Dahl–Tarlinskaya databases are incomplete and their methods flawed, Taylor and others have defended the Middleton attributions. The debate is ongoing.

ROBERT S. MIOLA

TEXTUAL BIBLIOGRAPHY

Braunmuller, A. R., ed. *Macbeth*. Cambridge: Cambridge UP, 1997, rev. 2008.
Taylor, Gary. "*Macbeth* and Middleton." *Macbeth*. Ed. Robert S. Miola. 2nd ed. New York: Norton, 2014. 296–305.
Taylor, Gary, and John Lavagnino, eds. *Thomas Middleton and Early Modern Textual Culture: A Companion to the Collected Works*. Oxford: Oxford UP, 2007.
Vickers, Brian. "Disintegrated: Did Thomas Middleton Really Adapt *Macbeth*?" *Times Literary Supplement*, 28 May 2010, 13–14.
Vickers, Brian, Marcus Dahl, and Marina Tarlinskaya. "An Enquiry into Middleton's Supposed 'Adaptation' of *Macbeth*." *London Forum for Authorship Studies* (2010), seminar paper: http://ies.sas.ac.uk/events/seminars/LFAS/index.htm.

PERFORMANCE NOTE

Macbeth generates considerable theatrical energy by exploiting tensions and intersections between fate and human agency. While directors typically strive to maintain the sense of moral uncertainty that makes tragedy possible, they cannot sidestep questions regarding Macbeth's responsibility for Duncan's murder. Do the witches plant the seed of ambition or invite Macbeth to act on existing desires? Do they foretell fate or set the sequence of gruesome events in motion? Is Lady Macbeth an accessory to murder or its chief architect? Do the dagger, Banquo's ghost, and the divining apparitions portend supernatural intrusion or a tormented conscience? Each production's answers determine the level of sympathy or dread the audience feels for the protagonist, and can decide whether the witches appear as earthly hags, ghostly temptresses, or disembodied voices; Lady Macbeth as an ambitious partner, controlling mother, or fourth witch; Macbeth as a man tortured from within or without.

The title role requires actors to oscillate convincingly between hero and tyrant, portraying a man whose savagery and coldness are as genuine as his hesitancy and remorse. The challenge intensifies in the play's second half, when the protagonist diminishes considerably in dramatic opportunity, influence, and psychological depth, even as the play slackens its invigorating pace, compression, and conflict. Productions can attempt to maintain interest and stave off anticlimax by underplaying the early acts; spectacularly staging the supernatural phenomena; cutting Siward, trimming Malcolm, and focusing on Macduff's revenge plot; assigning political topicality to Macbeth's fall; or emphasizing the inverse developmental arcs of the Macbeths, or their parallel descents into madness. However addressed, the challenges help explain why no other play has seen so many celebrated actors disappoint in—or simply avoid—the title role.

The portrayals of the supporting cast further influence audiences' reception of the Macbeths. Duncan can be a martyr or an imperious warlord; Malcolm, a worthy successor or naïve underling; the Porter, a comic or an ominous figure; and Macduff, like Banquo, can personify loyalty and valor, or compromise his virtues with jealousy or self-loathing. Other dramaturgical considerations include clarifying the muddled events discussed in 3.6; motivating Ross's reticence and sudden disclosure (see Digital Edition PC 6); deciding whether Macbeth dies onstage or off, and representing his severed head; and determining whether notes of optimism, despair, or tragic irony dominate the play's final moments.

Brett Gamboa

The Tragedy of Macbeth

[THE PERSONS OF THE PLAY

KING Duncan of Scotland
MALCOLM, later Prince of Cumberland, eldest son to King Duncan
DONALDBAIN, son to King Duncan
CAPTAIN in King Duncan's army

MACBETH, Thane of Glamis, later Thane of Cawdor, later King of Scotland
LADY MACBETH
Three MURDERERS
PORTER at Macbeth's castle
SEYTON, servant to Macbeth
GENTLEWOMAN, servant to Lady Macbeth
DOCTOR OF PHYSIC, attending Lady Macbeth

Six WITCHES, including the three weird sisters
HECATE, queen of the witches

BANQUO, a thane
FLEANCE, son to Banquo

MACDUFF, Thane of Fife
WIFE to Macduff
SON to Macduff and Wife

LENNOX
ROSS
MENTEITH } thanes
ANGUS
CAITHNESS

English DOCTOR
OLD MAN
SIWARD, Earl of Northumberland
YOUNG SIWARD
Three APPARITIONS: an armed head, a bloody child, a child crowned
MESSENGER
LORDS
SERVANTS
SOLDIERS

Lords, Attendants, Drummers, a Sewer, a show of eight kings]

1.1
Thunder and lightning. Enter three WITCHES.[1]
FIRST WITCH   When shall we three meet again?

1.1 Location: An open place.
1. PERFORMANCE COMMENT Stage productions often include novel or spectacular approaches to representing the witches, but the most urgent decisions concern their ontological status—supernatural visionaries or earthly psychics?—and the extent of their power to influence the action. See Digital Edition PC 1.

In thunder, lightning, or in rain?[2]
SECOND WITCH   When the hurly-burly's° done,   *tumult is*
  When the battle's lost and won.
5   THIRD WITCH   That will be ere the set of sun.
FIRST WITCH   Where the place?
SECOND WITCH   Upon the heath.
THIRD WITCH   There to meet with Macbeth.
FIRST WITCH   I come, Grimalkin!
10   ALL   Paddock[3] calls anon!°   *at once*
  Fair is foul, and foul is fair,
  Hover through the fog and filthy air.   *Exeunt.*

1.2

Alarum within. Enter KING [*Duncan*], MALCOLM,
DONALDBAIN, LENNOX, *with Attendants, meeting a*
bleeding CAPTAIN.°   *staff officer*
KING   What bloody man is that? He can report,
  As seemeth by his plight, of the revolt
  The newest state.
MALCOLM   This is the sergeant
  Who like a good and hardy soldier fought
5   'Gainst my captivity. —Hail, brave friend!
  Say to the King the knowledge of the broil°   *battle*
  As thou didst leave it.
CAPTAIN   Doubtful it stood,
  As two spent° swimmers that do cling together   *exhausted*
  And choke their art.[1] The merciless Macdonald—
10   Worthy to be a rebel, for to that°   *that end*
  The multiplying villainies of nature[2]
  Do swarm upon him—from the Western Isles°   *Hebrides and Ireland*
  Of kerns and galloglasses[3] is supplied;
  And Fortune, on his damnèd quarrel[4] smiling,
15   Showed° like a rebel's whore. But all's too weak,   *Appeared*
  For brave Macbeth—well he deserves that name°—   *epithet*
  Disdaining Fortune with his brandished steel,
  Which smoked with bloody execution,
  Like valor's minion° carved out his passage   *favorite*
20   Till he faced the slave,°   *(Macdonald)*
  Which° ne'er shook hands nor bade farewell to him,   *Who*
  Till he unseamed him from the nave to th' chops,[5]
  And fixed his head upon our battlements.
KING   O valiant cousin,° worthy gentleman!   *kinsman*
25   CAPTAIN   As whence the sun 'gins his reflection,[6]
  Shipwrecking storms and direful thunders,
  So from that spring° whence comfort seemed to come,   *source; (season)*
  Discomfort swells.° Mark, King of Scotland, mark: *wells up*
  No sooner justice had, with valor armed,
30   Compelled these skipping° kerns to trust their heels,   *mobile; fleeing*
  But the Norwegian lord, surveying vantage,°   *seeing his chance*

---

2. Witches were thought to be able to cause bad
weather.
3. Paddock, a toad, and Grimalkin, a gray cat, are
the witches' familiars, or attendant evil spirits.
1.2 Location: A camp near the battlefield.
1. And confound their skill in swimming.
2. The evil aspects of his own nature; the villainous
progeny of nature (the mercenaries).

3. *kerns:* lightly armed Irish foot soldiers. *galloglasses:*
ax-wielding horsemen.
4. Macdonald's cursed rebellion.
5. Ripped him open from the navel to the jaw, as one
would rip open the seam of a garment.
6. Begins its return after the spring equinox, thought
to cause turbulent weather. F2 adds "breaking" to
the end of line 26.

With furbished° arms and new supplies of men   *polished*
    Began a fresh assault.
KING Dismayed not this our captains, Macbeth and Banquo?
35 CAPTAIN Yes, as sparrows eagles or the hare the lion.
    If I say sooth, I must report they were
    As cannons overcharged with double cracks;[7]
    So they doubly redoubled strokes upon the foe.
    Except° they meant to bathe in reeking wounds,   *Unless*
40   Or memorize another Golgotha,[8]
    I cannot tell—
    But I am faint. My gashes cry for help.
KING So well thy words become thee as thy wounds;
    They smack of honor both. —Go, get him surgeons.
                              [*Exit* CAPTAIN, *attended.*]
    Enter ROSS *and* ANGUS.
    Who comes here?
45 MALCOLM   The worthy Thane[9] of Ross.
    LENNOX What a haste looks through his eyes!
    So should he look that seems to° speak things strange.   *seems about to*
ROSS God save the King!
KING Whence cam'st thou, worthy thane?
50 ROSS From Fife, great King,
    Where the Norwegian banners flout° the sky   *mock*
    And fan our people cold.°   *cold with fear*
    Norway° himself, with terrible numbers,   *The King of Norway*
    Assisted by that most disloyal traitor,
55   The Thane of Cawdor, began a dismal° conflict,   *an ominous*
    Till that° Bellona's bridegroom,[1] lapped in proof,[2]   *Until*
    Confronted him with self-comparisons,°   *comparable deeds*
    Point° against point, rebellious arm 'gainst arm,   *Swordpoint*
    Curbing his lavish° spirit. And to conclude,   *wild*
    The victory fell on us—
KING   Great happiness!—
60 ROSS   —That now Sweno,
    The Norways'° king, craves composition.°   *Norwegians' / a truce*
    Nor would we deign him burial of his men
    Till he disbursèd at Saint Colme's Inch[3]
    Ten thousand dollars[4] to our general use.
65 KING No more that Thane of Cawdor shall deceive
    Our bosom interest.[5] Go pronounce his present° death,   *immediate*
    And with his former title greet Macbeth.
ROSS I'll see it done.
KING What he hath lost noble Macbeth hath won.   *Exeunt.*

1.3

Thunder. Enter the three WITCHES.
FIRST WITCH Where hast thou been, sister?
SECOND WITCH Killing swine.
THIRD WITCH Sister, where thou?

---

7. Overloaded with double charges of gunpowder.
8. Or make the battlefield as memorable as Golgotha, the "place of skulls" where Jesus was crucified.
9. Title of Scottish nobility.
1. Macbeth, imagined as husband to Bellona, the Roman goddess of war.
2. Clad in tested armor.

3. Incholm, the island of St. Columba in the Firth of Forth.
4. German and Spanish coins (first minted in the sixteenth century, 500 years after the events of the play).
5. Our closest concerns.
1.3 Location: An open place.

FIRST WITCH   A sailor's wife had chestnuts in her lap,
5   And munched, and munched, and munched.
"Give me," quoth I.
"Aroint thee,° witch!" the rump-fed runnion[1] cries.   Begone
Her husband's to Aleppo gone, master o'the *Tiger*,
But in a sieve I'll thither sail,
10   And like a rat without a tail,
I'll do, I'll do, and I'll do.
SECOND WITCH   I'll give thee a wind.
FIRST WITCH   Thou'rt kind.
THIRD WITCH   And I another.
15   FIRST WITCH   I myself have all the other,°   others
And the very ports they blow,°   blow from
All the quarters° that they know   directions
I'th' shipman's card.°   compass card
I'll drain him dry as hay.
20   Sleep shall neither night nor day
Hang upon his penthouse lid;[2]
He shall live a man forbid.°   cursed
Weary sennights° nine times nine   weeks
Shall he dwindle, peak,° and pine.   waste away
25   Though his bark cannot be lost,
Yet it shall be tempest-tossed.
Look what I have.
SECOND WITCH   Show me, show me.
FIRST WITCH   Here I have a pilot's thumb,
30   Wrecked as homeward he did come.
        Drum within.
THIRD WITCH   A drum, a drum!
Macbeth doth come!
ALL [*dancing in a circle*]   The weird[3] sisters, hand in hand,
Posters° of the sea and land,   Swift travelers
35   Thus do go, about, about,
Thrice to thine, and thrice to mine,
And thrice again to make up nine.
Peace, the charm's wound up.
        Enter MACBETH *and* BANQUO.
MACBETH   So foul and fair a day I have not seen.
40   BANQUO   How far is't called° to Forres? What are these,   said to be
So withered and so wild in their attire,
That look not like th'inhabitants o'th' earth,
And yet are on't? —Live you? Or are you aught
That man may question?° You seem to understand me   interrogate
45   By each at once her choppy° finger laying   chapped
Upon her skinny lips. You should be women,
And yet your beards forbid me to interpret
That you are so.
MACBETH   Speak, if you can. What are you?
FIRST WITCH   All hail, Macbeth! Hail to thee, Thane of Glamis!
50   SECOND WITCH   All hail, Macbeth! Hail to thee, Thane of Cawdor!
THIRD WITCH   All hail, Macbeth, that shalt be king hereafter!

---

1. The fat-rumped, mangy slut.
2. Eyelid, which projects out over the eye like the sloping roof of a penthouse.
3. TEXTUAL COMMENT This crucial word appears throughout F as both "weyard" and "weyward." For further details on the issue of its ambiguous spelling and meaning, see Digital Edition TC 1.

BANQUO   Good sir, why do you start and seem to fear
    Things that do sound so fair? —I'th' name of truth,
    Are ye fantastical° or that indeed   *imaginary*
55   Which outwardly ye show? My noble partner
    You greet with present grace° and great prediction   *title*
    Of noble having° and of royal hope   *estate*
    That he seems rapt withal.[4] To me you speak not.
    If you can look into the seeds of time
60   And say which grain will grow and which will not,
    Speak then to me, who neither beg nor fear
    Your favors nor your hate.
FIRST WITCH   Hail!
SECOND WITCH   Hail!
65   THIRD WITCH   Hail!
FIRST WITCH   Lesser than Macbeth, and greater.
SECOND WITCH   Not so happy,° yet much happier.   *fortunate*
THIRD WITCH   Thou shalt get° kings, though thou be none.   *beget*
    So all hail, Macbeth and Banquo!
70   FIRST WITCH   Banquo and Macbeth, all hail!
MACBETH   Stay, you imperfect° speakers, tell me more.   *incomplete*
    By Finel's° death I know I am Thane of Glamis,   *Macbeth's father's*
    But how of Cawdor? The Thane of Cawdor lives,
    A prosperous gentleman, and to be king
75   Stands not within the prospect of belief,
    No more than to be Cawdor. Say from whence
    You owe° this strange intelligence,° or why   *possess / information*
    Upon this blasted° heath you stop our way   *blighted*
    With such prophetic greeting. Speak, I charge you.
                                               WITCHES *vanish.*
80   BANQUO   The earth hath bubbles as the water has,
    And these are of them. Whither are they vanished?
MACBETH   Into the air. And what seemed corporal°   *corporeal*
    Melted as breath into the wind. Would they had stayed.
BANQUO   Were such things here as we do speak about?
85   Or have we eaten on the insane root[5]
    That takes the reason prisoner?
MACBETH   Your children shall be kings.
BANQUO   You shall be king.
MACBETH   And Thane of Cawdor too. Went it not so?
BANQUO   To th' selfsame tune and words. —Who's here?
                    Enter ROSS *and* ANGUS.
90   ROSS   The King hath happily received, Macbeth,
    The news of thy success; and when he reads°   *considers*
    Thy personal venture° in the rebels' fight,   *exploits*
    His wonders and his praises do contend
    Which should be thine or his. Silenced with that,[6]
95   In viewing o'er the rest o'th' selfsame day,
    He finds thee in the stout Norwegian ranks,
    Nothing° afeard of what thyself didst make,   *Not at all*
    Strange images° of death. As thick as hail   *forms*
    Came post° with post, and every one did bear   *messenger*
100   Thy praises in his kingdom's great defense

---

4. He seems entranced by these predictions.
5. Of the root causing insanity, possibly hemlock.
6. *His wonders . . . that:* Duncan does not know

whether to speak of his astonishment or his admiration, and so is silent.

And poured them down before him.

ANGUS   We are sent
To give thee from our royal master thanks,
Only to herald thee into his sight,
Not pay thee.

105   ROSS   And for an earnest° of a greater honor,   *a pledge*
He bade me, from him, call thee Thane of Cawdor;
In which addition,° hail, most worthy thane,   *title*
For it is thine.

BANQUO   What, can the devil speak true?

MACBETH   The Thane of Cawdor lives. Why do you dress me
In borrowed robes?

110   ANGUS   Who was the thane lives yet,
But under heavy judgment bears that life
Which he deserves to lose.
Whether he was combined° with those of Norway,   *allied*
Or did line the rebel° with hidden help   *support Macdonald*

115   And vantage,° or that with both he labored   *benefit*
In his country's wrack,[7] I know not.
But treasons capital, confessed and proved,
Have overthrown him.

MACBETH [*aside*]   Glamis, and Thane of Cawdor!
The greatest is behind.° —Thanks for your pains.   *to come*

120   [*aside to* BANQUO] Do you not hope your children shall be kings,
When those that gave the Thane of Cawdor to me
Promised no less to them?

BANQUO [*aside to* MACBETH] That trusted home°   *completely*
Might yet enkindle° you unto the crown,   *encourage*
Besides the Thane of Cawdor. But 'tis strange,

125   And oftentimes to win us to our harm,
The instruments of darkness tell us truths,
Win us with honest trifles, to betray's°   *betray us*
In deepest consequence.
—Cousins, a word, I pray you.

[*He converses apart with* ROSS *and* ANGUS.]

MACBETH [*aside*]   Two truths are told,

130   As happy prologues to the swelling act[8]
Of th'imperial theme. —I thank you, gentlemen.
[*aside*] This supernatural soliciting°   *temptation*
Cannot be ill, cannot be good. If ill,
Why hath it given me earnest of success

135   Commencing in a truth? I am Thane of Cawdor.
If good, why do I yield to that suggestion
Whose horrid image doth unfix my hair
And make my seated heart knock at my ribs
Against the use° of nature? Present fears   *custom*

140   Are less than horrible imaginings.
My thought, whose murder yet is but fantastical,[9]
Shakes so my single state of man[1]
That function° is smothered in surmise,° *capacity to act / speculation*
And nothing is but what is not.

145   BANQUO   Look how our partner's rapt.

---

7. He worked to bring about his country's ruin.
8. To the developing action, or climactic dramatic action.
9. In which murder is so far only a fantasy.

1. My undivided self. Macbeth feels that his wholeness is coming apart under the pressure of his criminal thought.

MACBETH [*aside*]   If chance will have me king, why, chance
    may crown me
    Without my stir.°   *effort*
BANQUO   New honors come upon him,
    Like our strange° garments, cleave not to their mold°   *new / wearer's form*
    But with the aid of use.
MACBETH [*aside*]   Come what come may,
150   Time and the hour runs through the roughest day.[2]
BANQUO   Worthy Macbeth, we stay° upon your leisure.   *wait; attend*
MACBETH   Give me your favor.° My dull brain was wrought°   *pardon / agitated*
    With things forgotten. Kind gentlemen, your pains
    Are registered° where every day I turn   *recorded (in my memory)*
155   The leaf to read them. Let us toward the King.
    [*aside to* BANQUO] Think upon what hath chanced, and at
    more time,
    The interim having weighed it, let us speak
    Our free hearts° each to other.   *unconcealed thoughts*
BANQUO [*aside to* MACBETH]   Very gladly.
MACBETH [*aside to* BANQUO]   Till then, enough. —Come, friends.
                                  Exeunt.

1.4

Flourish. Enter KING, LENNOX, MALCOLM,
    DONALDBAIN, *and Attendants.*
KING   Is execution done on Cawdor? Or° not   *Or are*
    Those in commission[1] yet returned?
MALCOLM   My liege,
    They are not yet come back. But I have spoke
    With one that saw him die, who did report
5   That very frankly he confessed his treasons,
    Implored your highness' pardon, and set forth
    A deep repentance. Nothing in his life
    Became him like the leaving it. He died
    As one that had been studied° in his death   *practiced*
10   To throw away the dearest thing he owed°   *owned*
    As 'twere a careless° trifle.   *an uncared-for*
KING   There's no art
    To find the mind's construction in the face.
    He was a gentleman on whom I built
    An absolute trust.
          Enter MACBETH, BANQUO, ROSS, *and* ANGUS.
                 O worthiest cousin!
15   The sin of my ingratitude even now
    Was heavy on me. Thou art so far before°   *ahead*
    That swiftest wing of recompense is slow
    To overtake thee. Would thou hadst less deserved,
    That the proportion both of thanks and payment
20   Might have been mine.[2] Only I have left to say,
    More is thy due than more than all can pay.
MACBETH   The service and the loyalty I owe
    In doing it pays itself. Your highness' part
    Is to receive our duties, and our duties

---

2. *Come . . . day:* What must happen will happen one
way or another.
1.4 Location: A camp near the battlefield.

1. Those charged to execute Cawdor.
2. *That . . . mine:* That the King's rewards would be
generously proportional to Macbeth's desert.

25   Are to your throne and state, children and servants,
     Which do but what they should by doing everything
     Safe toward° your love and honor.   *To safeguard*

KING   Welcome hither.
     I have begun to plant thee and will labor
     To make thee full of growing. —Noble Banquo,
30   That hast no less deserved nor must be known
     No less to have done so, let me enfold thee
     And hold thee to my heart.

BANQUO   There if I grow,
     The harvest is your own.

KING   My plenteous joys,
     Wanton° in fullness, seek to hide themselves   *Unrestrained*
35   In drops of sorrow. —Sons, kinsmen, thanes,
     And you whose places are the nearest,° know   *nearest to the throne*
     We will establish our estate³ upon
     Our eldest, Malcolm, whom we name hereafter
     The Prince of Cumberland;⁴ which honor must
40   Not unaccompanied invest him only,⁵
     But signs of nobleness, like stars, shall shine
     On all deservers. [*to* MACBETH] From hence to Inverness,° *Macbeth's castle*
     And bind us further to you.⁶

MACBETH   The rest is labor which is not used for you.⁷
45   I'll be myself the harbinger⁸ and make joyful
     The hearing of my wife with your approach.
     So humbly take my leave.

KING   My worthy Cawdor!

MACBETH [*aside*]   The Prince of Cumberland! That is a step
     On which I must fall down or else o'erleap,
50   For in my way it lies. Stars, hide your fires,
     Let not light see my black and deep desires;
     The eye wink at the hand;⁹ yet let that be°   *be done*
     Which the eye fears, when it is done, to see.   *Exit.*

KING   True, worthy Banquo, he is full so valiant,¹
55   And in his commendations I am fed;
     It is a banquet to me. Let's after him,
     Whose care is gone before to bid us welcome.
     It is a peerless kinsman.   *Flourish. Exeunt.*

1.5

Enter Macbeth's Wife [LADY MACBETH]¹ *alone with
a letter.*

LADY MACBETH [*reading*] "They met me in the day of success,
    and I have learned by the perfect'st° report they have more *most accurate*
    in them than mortal knowledge. When I burnt in desire to
    question them further, they made themselves air, into which
5   they vanished. Whiles I stood rapt in the wonder of it came

---

3. We will settle the succession of the kingdom. At the time, the Scottish crown was not hereditary.
4. Title of the Scottish heir apparent.
5. *which . . . only:* honors will not be bestowed on Malcolm alone.
6. And make me further indebted to you by your hospitality.
7. Even repose seems wearisome when it is not dedicated to your purposes.

8. Forerunner; messenger sent ahead to arrange royal lodgings.
9. Let the eye deliberately ignore what the hand does.
1. As valiant as you say.
1.5 Location: Inverness, Macbeth's castle.
1. TEXTUAL COMMENT Surprisingly to modern readers, this character is never named "Lady Macbeth" throughout F. For more on the issue of naming and character, see Digital Edition TC 2.

missives° from the King, who all-hailed me 'Thane of Caw-   *messengers*
dor,' by which title before these weird sisters saluted me and
referred me to the coming on of time with 'Hail, king that
shalt be!' This have I thought good to deliver° thee, my dear-   *inform*
10   est partner of greatness, that thou mightst not lose the dues
of rejoicing by being ignorant of what greatness is promised
thee. Lay it to thy heart, and farewell."
Glamis thou art, and Cawdor, and shalt be
What thou art promised. Yet do I fear° thy nature;   *doubt*
15   It is too full o'th' milk of human kindness
To catch the nearest° way. Thou wouldst be great,   *most expedient*
Art not without ambition, but without
The illness° should attend it. What thou wouldst highly,   *wickedness (that)*
That wouldst thou holily; wouldst not play false,
20   And yet wouldst wrongly win. Thou'dst have, great Glamis,
That which cries, "Thus thou must do" if thou have it,
And that which rather thou dost fear to do
Than wishest should be undone. Hie° thee hither,   *Hasten*
That I may pour my spirits in thine ear
25   And chastise with the valor of my tongue
All that impedes thee from the golden round,°   *crown*
Which fate and metaphysical° aid doth seem   *supernatural*
To have thee crowned withal.°   *with*

      Enter MESSENGER.

                                  What is your tidings?
MESSENGER   The King comes here tonight.
LADY MACBETH   Thou'rt mad to say it!
30   Is not thy master with him, who, were't so,
Would have informed for preparation?
MESSENGER   So please you, it is true. Our thane is coming.
One of my fellows had the speed of° him,   *outdistanced*
Who, almost dead for breath, had scarcely more
Than would make up his message.
35   LADY MACBETH   Give him tending;
He brings great news.   *Exit* MESSENGER.
                   The raven[2] himself is hoarse
That croaks the fatal entrance of Duncan
Under my battlements. Come, you spirits
That tend on mortal° thoughts, unsex me here,   *attend deadly*
40   And fill me from the crown to the toe top-full
Of direst cruelty! Make thick my blood,
Stop up th'access and passage to remorse,°   *pity*
That no compunctious visitings of nature
Shake my fell° purpose nor keep peace° between   *cruel / intervene*
45   Th'effect and it.[3] Come to my woman's breasts
And take my milk for° gall, you murd'ring ministers,°   *in exchange for / agents*
Wherever in your sightless° substances   *invisible*
You wait on° nature's mischief. Come, thick night,   *assist*
And pall° thee in the dunnest° smoke of hell,   *envelop / darkest*
50   That my keen knife see not the wound it makes,
Nor heaven peep through the blanket of the dark
To cry, "Hold, hold!"[4]

---

2. The raven was considered a bird of ill omen.
3. My purpose and its accomplishment.
4. PERFORMANCE COMMENT Actors playing Lady

Macbeth can choose to emphasize or downplay the
witchlike implication of her summoning of spirits.
See Digital Edition PC 2.

Enter MACBETH.

                                Great Glamis, worthy Cawdor,
Greater than both by the all-hail hereafter!
Thy letters have transported me beyond

55   This ignorant present, and I feel now
The future in the instant.

MACBETH   My dearest love,
Duncan comes here tonight.

LADY MACBETH   And when goes hence?

MACBETH   Tomorrow, as he purposes.

LADY MACBETH   Oh, never

Shall sun that morrow see!

60   Your face, my thane, is as a book where men
May read strange matters. To beguile the time,
Look like the time;[5] bear welcome in your eye,
Your hand, your tongue. Look like th'innocent flower,
But be the serpent under't. He that's coming

65   Must be provided for. And you shall put
This night's great business into my dispatch,°   *management*
Which shall to all our nights and days to come
Give solely sovereign sway and masterdom.

MACBETH   We will speak further.

LADY MACBETH   Only look up clear.°   *appear innocent*

70   To alter favor[6] ever is to fear.
Leave all the rest to me.   *Exeunt.*

1.6

Hautboys° *and torches. Enter* KING, MALCOLM,   *Oboes*
    DONALDBAIN, BANQUO, LENNOX, MACDUFF, ROSS,
    ANGUS, *and Attendants.*

KING   This castle hath a pleasant seat.°   *location*
The air nimbly and sweetly recommends itself
Unto our gentle senses.

BANQUO   This guest of summer,
The temple-haunting martlet,[1] does approve°   *prove*

5   By his loved mansionry° that the heavens' breath   *nest building*
Smells wooingly here. No jutty,° frieze,   *projection*
Buttress, nor coign of vantage,° but this bird   *convenient corner*
Hath made his pendent bed and procreant° cradle.   *for breeding*
Where they must breed and haunt, I have observed,
The air is delicate.

Enter LADY MACBETH.

10   KING   See, see, our honored hostess!
—The love that follows us sometime is our trouble,
Which still we thank as love.[2] Herein I teach you
How you shall bid God 'ield us for your pains,
And thank us for your trouble.[3]

LADY MACBETH   All our service,

15   In every point twice done and then done double,

---

5. *To . . . like the time:* To deceive the world, match your expression to the occasion.
6. To alter your facial expression and thereby arouse suspicion.
1.6 Location: Outside Macbeth's castle.
1. A bird, the martin, that often built its nest in churches.

2. *The . . . love:* Love bestowed upon us sometimes causes us inconvenience, but we are still grateful for it.
3. *bid . . . trouble:* ask God to reward ("yield") me for the trouble I cause you.

Were° poor and single° business to contend   *Would be / small*
Against those honors deep and broad wherewith
Your majesty loads our house. For those of old,
And the late dignities heaped up to them,
We rest your hermits.[4]

20 KING   Where's the Thane of Cawdor?
We coursed him at the heels° and had a purpose   *followed him closely*
To be his purveyor;[5] but he rides well,
And his great love, sharp as his spur, hath holp° him   *helped*
To his home before us. Fair and noble hostess,
We are your guest tonight.

25 LADY MACBETH   Your servants ever
Have theirs, themselves, and what is theirs in count°   *account*
To make their audit at your highness' pleasure,
Still to return your own.[6]

KING   Give me your hand;
Conduct me to mine host. We love him highly
30 And shall continue our graces towards him.
By your leave,[7] hostess.   *Exeunt.*

1.7

Hautboys. Torches. Enter a Sewer,° and divers   *Butler*
SERVANTS *with dishes and service over the stage.*
Then enter MACBETH.

MACBETH   If it were done when 'tis done, then 'twere well
It were done quickly. If th'assassination
Could trammel up the consequence and catch
With his surcease success[1]—that but this blow
5   Might be the be-all and the end-all!—here,°   *in this world*
But here, upon this bank and shoal[2] of time,
We'd jump° the life to come. But in these cases   *risk*
We still have judgment[3] here, that° we but teach   *in that*
Bloody instructions which, being taught, return
10   To plague th'inventor. This even-handed° justice   *impartial*
Commends th'ingredients° of our poisoned chalice   *the contents*
To our own lips. He's here in double trust:
First, as I am his kinsman and his subject,
Strong both against the deed; then, as his host,
15   Who should against his murderer shut the door,
Not bear the knife myself. Besides, this Duncan
Hath borne his faculties° so meek, hath been   *authority*
So clear° in his great office, that his virtues   *blameless*
Will plead like angels, trumpet-tongued, against
20   The deep damnation of his taking-off;°   *murder*
And Pity, like a naked newborn babe

---

4. We remain your beadsmen (monks hired to pray for their employers).
5. Attendant who preceded the King when he traveled and procured foodstuffs for the royal party.
6. *Your servants . . . own:* Your servants hold all that they have in trust from you, and they are always ready to settle accounts and return to you what is yours.
7. By your permission. A request for permission to enter, or perhaps for a formal kiss.
1.7 Location: A courtyard or an anteroom in Macbeth's castle.

1. *If th'assassination . . . success:* If only I could gain success with Duncan's death (his "surcease"); if only the assassination were the end of the matter. *trammel up the consequence:* restrain the subsequent sequence of events, as in a trammel, or net.
2. Sandbar. The mortal span is seen as a narrow piece of land in the river of time. F has "Schoole," and "bank" may also mean "bench," suggesting that life is a time of instruction and probation.
3. We are invariably punished.

Striding the blast,[4] or heaven's cherubim horsed
Upon the sightless couriers[5] of the air,
Shall blow the horrid deed in every eye,
25 That tears shall drown the wind.[6] I have no spur
To prick the sides of my intent, but only
Vaulting ambition, which o'erleaps itself
And falls on th'other[7]—

        Enter LADY MACBETH.

                How now? What news?
LADY MACBETH   He has almost supped. Why have you left the
   chamber?
MACBETH   Hath he asked for me?
30 LADY MACBETH   Know you not he has?
MACBETH   We will proceed no further in this business.
He hath honored me of late, and I have bought°   *won*
Golden opinions from all sorts of people,
Which would be worn now in their newest gloss,
Not cast aside so soon.
35 LADY MACBETH   Was the hope drunk
Wherein you dressed yourself? Hath it slept since?
And wakes it now to look so green° and pale   *sickly*
At what it did so freely? From this time
Such I account thy love. Art thou afeard
40 To be the same in thine own act and valor
As thou art in desire? Wouldst thou have that°   *(the crown)*
Which thou esteem'st the ornament of life,
And live a coward in thine own esteem,
Letting "I dare not" wait upon "I would,"
Like the poor cat i'th' adage?[8]
45 MACBETH   Prithee, peace!
I dare do all that may become a man;
Who dares do more is none.
LADY MACBETH   What beast was't, then,
That made you break° this enterprise to me?   *broach*
When you durst do it, then you were a man;
50 And to be more than what you were, you would
Be so much more the man. Nor time nor place
Did then adhere,° and yet you would make both.   *agree*
They have made themselves, and that their fitness now
Does unmake you. I have given suck and know
55 How tender 'tis to love the babe that milks me;
I would, while it was smiling in my face,
Have plucked my nipple from his boneless gums
And dashed the brains out, had I so sworn as you
Have done to this.
MACBETH   If we should fail?
LADY MACBETH   We fail?[9]
60 But° screw your courage to the sticking-place,[1]   *Just*

---

4. Astride the storm provoked by Duncan's death.
5. The invisible runners, the winds.
6. Tears will fall like heavy rain, which was believed
to still the wind.
7. That is, the other side. The image is of a rider
vaulting over his horse instead of into his saddle, or
of a horseman who clears a high obstacle but falls on
the other side.
8. Proverbial: "The cat would eat fish but does not

dare to wet her feet."
9. Textual Comment F's version of this speech may
be understood either as a question ("We fail?") or as a
declaration ("We fail!"). For more on the issue of
early modern typography and its interpretative flexibility, see Digital Edition TC 3.
1. The notch on a crossbow that holds the string,
which is cranked or screwed taut.

And we'll not fail. When Duncan is asleep—
Whereto the rather shall his day's hard journey
Soundly invite him—his two chamberlains°   *bedroom attendants*
Will I with wine and wassail° so convince°   *carousing / overpower*
65   That memory, the warder° of the brain,   *guard*
Shall be a fume, and the receipt° of reason   *receptacle*
A limbeck[2] only. When in swinish sleep
Their drenchèd natures lies as in a death,
What cannot you and I perform upon
70   Th'unguarded Duncan? What not put upon
His spongy officers, who shall bear the guilt
Of our great quell?°   *murder*
MACBETH   Bring forth men-children only,
For thy undaunted mettle° should compose   *substance*
Nothing but males. Will it not be received,°   *believed*
75   When we have marked with blood those sleepy two
Of his own chamber and used their very daggers,
That they have done't?
LADY MACBETH   Who dares receive it other,
As we shall make our griefs and clamor roar
Upon his death?
MACBETH   I am settled, and bend up
80   Each corporal° agent to this terrible feat.[3]   *bodily*
Away, and mock° the time with fairest show;   *deceive*
False face must hide what the false heart doth know.   *Exeunt.*

2.1

Enter BANQUO *and* FLEANCE, *with a torch before him.*
BANQUO   How goes the night, boy?[1]
FLEANCE   The moon is down; I have not heard the clock.
BANQUO   And she goes down at twelve.
FLEANCE   I take't 'tis later, sir.
BANQUO   Hold, take my sword. There's husbandry° in heaven;   *thrift*
5   Their candles are all out. Take thee that,[2] too.
A heavy summons° lies like lead upon me,   *summons to sleep*
And yet I would not sleep. Merciful powers,[3]
Restrain in me the cursèd thoughts that nature
Gives way to in repose.
Enter MACBETH *and a* SERVANT *with a torch.*
Give me my sword!
10   —Who's there?
MACBETH   A friend.
BANQUO   What, sir, not yet at rest? The King's abed.
He hath been in unusual pleasure
And sent forth great largesse° to your offices.[4]   *gifts*
15   This diamond he greets your wife withal,
By the name of most kind hostess, and shut up°   *concluded*
In measureless content.
    [*He gives a diamond.*]
MACBETH   Being unprepared,

2. Alembic, the upper part of a still to which fumes
rise. The wine will make the memory a fume that
will fill and cloud the brain, the "receptacle of
reason."
3. PERFORMANCE COMMENT Productions must consider why Macbeth agrees to undertake Duncan's
murder so soon after resolving against it and how

Lady Macbeth manages to instigate him to do so. See
Digital Edition PC 3.
2.1 Location: The courtyard of Macbeth's castle.
1. How much of the night has passed?
2. Some article of clothing or armor.
3. Angels invoked as protection against demons.
4. Household departments.

Our will became the servant to defect,
Which else should free have wrought.[5]

BANQUO   All's well.
20 I dreamt last night of the three weird sisters.
To you they have showed some truth.

MACBETH   I think not of them.
Yet, when we can entreat an hour to serve,
We would spend it in some words upon that business,
If you would grant the time.

BANQUO   At your kind'st leisure.
25 MACBETH If you shall cleave to my consent, when 'tis,[6]
It shall make honor for you.

BANQUO   So° I lose none   Provided
In seeking to augment it, but still keep
My bosom franchised° and allegiance clear,°   guiltless / unstained
I shall be counseled.°   receptive

MACBETH   Good repose the while.
30 BANQUO Thanks, sir; the like to you.

                          Exit BANQUO [*with* FLEANCE].

MACBETH Go bid thy mistress, when my drink is ready,
She strike upon the bell. Get thee to bed.   *Exit* [SERVANT].
Is this a dagger which I see before me,
The handle toward my hand? Come, let me clutch thee.[7]
35 I have thee not, and yet I see thee still.
Art thou not, fatal vision, sensible°   perceptible
To feeling as to sight? Or art thou but
A dagger of the mind, a false creation,
Proceeding from the heat-oppressèd° brain?   fevered
40 I see thee yet in form as palpable
As this which now I draw.

                          [*He draws a dagger.*]

Thou marshall'st° me the way that I was going,   guide
And such an instrument I was to use.
Mine eyes are made the fools o'th' other senses,
45 Or else worth all the rest. I see thee still,
And on thy blade and dudgeon° gouts° of blood,   handle / drops
Which was not so before. There's no such thing.
It is the bloody business which informs°   creates shapes
Thus to mine eyes. Now o'er the one half world
50 Nature seems dead, and wicked dreams abuse°   deceive
The curtained sleep. Witchcraft celebrates
Pale Hecate's off'rings,[8] and withered Murder,
Alarumed° by his sentinel the wolf,   Roused
Whose howl's his watch,° thus with his stealthy pace,   watchword
55 With Tarquin's[9] ravishing strides, towards his design°   prey
Moves like a ghost. Thou sure and firm-set earth,
Hear not my steps, which way they walk, for fear
Thy very stones prate of my whereabout
And take the present horror° from the time,   *i.e.,* terrible stillness
60 Which now suits with it. Whiles I threat, he lives;

5. *Being . . . wrought:* Our desire to entertain the King liberally was constrained by the fact that we were unprepared. *defect:* deficiency. *free:* freely.
6. If you will support my opinion or my cause when the time comes.
7. PERFORMANCE COMMENT Whether or not the dagger that Macbeth attempts to clutch appears to the audience is a decision that every director of the play needs to make. See Digital Edition PC 4.
8. Sacrificial rites offered to Hecate, Greek goddess of witchcraft and of the moon.
9. A Roman prince who ravished the chaste matron Lucrece. Shakespeare tells the story in *The Rape of Lucrece.*

Words to the heat of deeds too cold breath gives.
    A bell rings.
I go, and it is done. The bell invites me.
Hear it not, Duncan, for it is a knell
That summons thee to heaven or to hell.   *Exit.*

2.2

Enter LADY MACBETH.

LADY MACBETH   That which hath made them drunk hath
    made me bold;
What hath quenched them hath given me fire.
    [*An owl shrieks.*]
                              Hark! Peace!
It was the owl that shrieked, the fatal bellman°   *night watchman*
Which gives the stern'st good-night.[1] He is about it.
5   The doors are open, and the surfeited grooms°   *attendants*
Do mock their charge° with snores. I have drugged their   *duty*
    possets,°   *mulled milk and wine*
That death and nature do contend about them
Whether they live or die.
    Enter MACBETH [*with bloody daggers*].[2]
MACBETH   Who's there? What ho!
LADY MACBETH [*to herself*]   Alack, I am afraid they have awaked,
10   And 'tis not done. Th'attempt and not the deed
Confounds° us. Hark! I laid their daggers ready;   *Ruins*
He could not miss 'em. Had he not resembled
My father as he slept, I had done't. —My husband?
MACBETH   I have done the deed. Didst thou not hear a noise?
15 LADY MACBETH   I heard the owl scream and the crickets cry.
    Did not you speak?
MACBETH   When?
LADY MACBETH   Now.
MACBETH   As I descended?
20 LADY MACBETH   Ay.
MACBETH   Hark, who lies i'th' second chamber?
LADY MACBETH   Donaldbain.
MACBETH   This is a sorry sight.
LADY MACBETH   A foolish thought to say a sorry sight.
25 MACBETH   There's one did laugh in 's sleep, and one cried
    "Murder!"
That they did wake each other. I stood and heard them.
But they did say their prayers and addressed them°   *settled themselves*
Again to sleep.
LADY MACBETH   There are two lodged together.
MACBETH   One cried, "God bless us!" and "Amen" the other,
30   As° they had seen me with these hangman's[3] hands.   *As if*
List'ning their fear, I could not say "Amen"
When they did say, "God bless us!"
LADY MACBETH   Consider it not so deeply.
MACBETH   But wherefore could not I pronounce "Amen"?
35   I had most need of blessing, and "Amen"

2.2 Location: Scene continues with only a brief pause.
1. A bell was rung outside the cells of condemned
prisoners the night before they were to be executed.
2. Some editors have Macbeth first enter onto the
upper stage space (line 8), then exit to descend the inner

stairs during Lady Macbeth's speech before entering
again onto the main stage at line 13.
3. Bloodstained. The hangman had to disembowel
and quarter his victims.

Stuck in my throat.

LADY MACBETH   These deeds must not be thought°   *thought on*
After these ways; so, it will make us mad.

MACBETH   Methought I heard a voice cry, "Sleep no more!
Macbeth does murder sleep"—the innocent sleep,

40   Sleep that knits up the raveled° sleeve of care,   *unraveled*
The death of each day's life, sore labor's bath,
Balm of hurt minds, great nature's second course,[4]
Chief nourisher in life's feast—

LADY MACBETH   What do you mean?

MACBETH   Still it cried, "Sleep no more!" to all the house;

45   "Glamis hath murdered sleep, and therefore Cawdor
Shall sleep no more! Macbeth shall sleep no more!"

LADY MACBETH   Who was it that thus cried? Why, worthy thane,
You do unbend° your noble strength to think   *slacken*
So brainsickly of things. Go get some water,

50   And wash this filthy witness° from your hand.   *evidence*
Why did you bring these daggers from the place?
They must lie there. Go, carry them and smear
The sleepy grooms with blood.

MACBETH   I'll go no more.
I am afraid to think what I have done.
Look on't again I dare not.

55   LADY MACBETH   Infirm of purpose!
Give me the daggers. The sleeping and the dead
Are but as pictures; 'tis the eye of childhood
That fears a painted devil. If he do bleed,
I'll gild[5] the faces of the grooms withal,
For it must seem their guilt.   *Exit [with the daggers].*
        Knock within.

60   MACBETH   Whence is that knocking?
How is't with me, when every noise appalls me?
What hands are here? Ha, they pluck out mine eyes!
Will all great Neptune's ocean wash this blood
Clean from my hand? No, this my hand will rather

65   The multitudinous seas incarnadine,°   *turn red*
Making the green one red.[6]
       Enter LADY MACBETH.

LADY MACBETH   My hands are of your color, but I shame
To wear a heart so white. (*Knock.*) I hear a knocking
At the south entry. Retire we to our chamber.

70   A little water clears us of this deed.
How easy is it then. Your constancy
Hath left you unattended.[7] (*Knock.*) Hark, more knocking.
Get on your nightgown, lest occasion call us
And show us to be watchers.[8] Be not lost

75   So poorly in your thoughts.

MACBETH   To know my deed 'twere best not know myself.[9]
      (*Knock.*)
Wake Duncan with thy knocking. I would thou couldst!
                Exeunt.

---

4. Second, and most nourishing, course of a meal; second, or alternative, habit or practice.
5. Coat as if with gold leaf. Gold was often called red; compare 2.3.109.
6. *one red:* entirely red.

7. *Your . . . unattended:* Your resolve has deserted you.
8. Those who have stayed awake.
9. It is better that I lose consciousness altogether than face my deed.

2.3

Enter a PORTER. *Knocking within.*

PORTER   Here's a knocking indeed! If a man were porter of hell
gate, he should have old° turning the key. (*Knock.*) Knock, *plenty of*
knock, knock. Who's there, i'th' name of Beelzebub?° Here's a *(a devil)*
farmer that hanged himself on th'expectation of plenty.[1] Come
in time![2] Have napkins° enough about you; here you'll sweat *handkerchiefs*
5   for't. (*Knock.*) Knock, knock. Who's there, in th'other devil's
name? Faith, here's an equivocator[3] that could swear in both
the scales against either scale, who committed treason enough
for God's sake, yet could not equivocate to heaven. Oh, come
in, equivocator. (*Knock.*) Knock, knock, knock. Who's there?
10   Faith, here's an English tailor come hither for stealing out of a
French hose.[4] Come in, tailor. Here you may roast your goose.[5]
(*Knock.*) Knock, knock. Never at quiet? What are you? But
this place is too cold for hell. I'll devil-porter it no further. I
had thought to have let in some of all professions that go the
15   primrose way to th'everlasting bonfire. (*Knock.*) Anon, anon.
[*He opens the gate.*] —I pray you, remember° the porter. *tip*

Enter MACDUFF *and* LENNOX.

MACDUFF   Was it so late, friend, ere you went to bed,
That you do lie so late?
20   PORTER   Faith, sir, we were carousing till the second cock,° *3:00 A.M.*
and drink, sir, is a great provoker of three things.
MACDUFF   What three things does drink especially provoke?
PORTER   Marry,° sir, nose-painting,[6] sleep, and urine. Lech- *Indeed*
ery, sir, it provokes and unprovokes: it provokes the desire
25   but it takes away the performance. Therefore, much drink
may be said to be an equivocator with lechery: it makes him
and it mars him; it sets him on and it takes him off; it persuades him and disheartens him, makes him stand to° and *maintain an erection*
not stand to; in conclusion, equivocates him in a sleep[7] and,
30   giving him the lie,[8] leaves him.
MACDUFF   I believe drink gave thee the lie last night.
PORTER   That it did, sir, i'the very throat on me.[9] But I requited
him for his lie and, I think, being too strong for him, though
he took up my legs sometime, yet I made a shift to cast him.[1]
35   MACDUFF   Is thy master stirring?

Enter MACBETH.

Our knocking has awaked him. Here he comes.

[Exit PORTER.]

LENNOX   Good morrow, noble sir.

2.3 Location: Scene continues, perhaps after a short
pause.
1. *Here's . . . plenty:* A farmer had hoarded grain to
sell at high prices but was ruined by a crop surplus
that forced prices down.
2. Good timing.
3. One who speaks ambiguously. An allusion to the
Jesuit doctrine that a seemingly false statement was
not a lie (and therefore not repugnant to God) if the
speaker had in mind a different meaning in which
the utterance was true. Possibly an allusion to the
1606 trial of the Jesuit Henry Garnet for involvement
in the Gunpowder Plot to blow up the Houses of Parliament; Father Garnet had written a treatise defending equivocation for Catholics being persecuted for
their beliefs.

4. Tight-fitting breeches, which would easily reveal
the tailor's attempt to skimp on the cloth supplied
him for their manufacture. He had apparently been
able to do so undetected when loose-fitting breeches
were in fashion.
5. Heat your smoothing iron.
6. Reddening of the nose through drink.
7. Gives him an erotic experience in dreams only.
8. An elaborate pun: calling him a liar; laying him
out flat; making him urinate ("lye," or urine).
9. *i'the . . . me:* provoking a duel by insulting me with
a deliberate lie.
1. *being . . . cast him:* the effects of drunkenness are
described in the language of a wrestling match. *cast:*
throw off; vomit.

MACBETH   Good morrow, both.

MACDUFF   Is the King stirring, worthy thane?

MACBETH   Not yet.

MACDUFF   He did command me to call timely° on him.   *early*
    I have almost slipped the hour.

40   MACBETH   I'll bring you to him.

MACDUFF   I know this is a joyful trouble to you,
    But yet 'tis one.

MACBETH   The labor we delight in physics pain.[2]
    This is the door.

MACDUFF   I'll make so bold to call,

45   For 'tis my limited° service.   *Exit* MACDUFF.   *appointed*

LENNOX   Goes the King hence today?

MACBETH   He does; he did appoint so.

LENNOX   The night has been unruly. Where we lay,
    Our chimneys were blown down and, as they say,

50   Lamentings heard i'th' air, strange screams of death,
    And prophesying with accents terrible
    Of dire combustion° and confused events,   *tumult*
    New hatched to th' woeful time. The obscure bird[3]
    Clamored the livelong night. Some say the earth
    Was feverous and did shake.

55   MACBETH   'Twas a rough night.

LENNOX   My young remembrance cannot parallel
    A fellow to it.
            Enter MACDUFF.

MACDUFF   Oh, horror, horror, horror!
    Tongue nor heart cannot conceive nor name thee!

60   MACBETH *and* LENNOX   What's the matter?

MACDUFF   Confusion° now hath made his masterpiece!   *Ruin*
    Most sacrilegious murder hath broke ope
    The Lord's anointed temple° and stole thence   *(the King's body)*
    The life o'th' building!

MACBETH   What is't you say? The life?

65   LENNOX   Mean you his majesty?

MACDUFF   Approach the chamber and destroy your sight
    With a new Gorgon.[4] Do not bid me speak.
    See, and then speak yourselves.
              Exeunt MACBETH *and* LENNOX.
    —Awake, awake!
    Ring the alarum bell! Murder and treason!

70   Banquo and Donaldbain, Malcolm, awake!
    Shake off this downy sleep, death's counterfeit,
    And look on death itself! Up, up, and see
    The great doom's image!° Malcolm, Banquo,   *replica of Doomsday*
    As from your graves rise up and walk like sprites

75   To countenance° this horror! —Ring the bell![5]   *suit; behold*
        Bell rings. Enter LADY MACBETH.

LADY MACBETH   What's the business
    That such a hideous trumpet calls to parley
    The sleepers of the house? Speak, speak!

---

2. Pleasure in labor mitigates its laboriousness.
3. The owl, bird of darkness.
4. A mythical monster with a woman's figure and snakes for hair, the sight of whose face turned behold-ers to stone. Medusa was one of the three Gorgons.
5. Macduff's imperative to ring the bell may have been a stage direction mistakenly incorporated into his speech. For more, see the Textual Introduction.

MACDUFF O gentle lady,
80 'Tis not for you to hear what I can speak.
The repetition° in a woman's ear   *report*
Would murder as it fell.
      Enter BANQUO.
—O Banquo, Banquo! Our royal master's murdered!
LADY MACBETH Woe, alas! What, in our house?
85 BANQUO Too cruel anywhere.
Dear Duff, I prithee, contradict thyself,
And say it is not so.
      Enter MACBETH, LENNOX, *and* ROSS.
MACBETH Had I but died an hour before this chance,°   *occurrence*
I had lived a blessèd time, for from this instant
90 There's nothing serious in mortality.°   *worth living for*
All is but toys.° Renown and grace is dead.   *trifles*
The wine of life is drawn, and the mere lees
Is left this vault° to brag of.   *wine vault; world*
      Enter MALCOLM *and* DONALDBAIN.
DONALDBAIN What is amiss?
MACBETH   You are and do not know't.
95 The spring, the head, the fountain of your blood
Is stopped, the very source of it is stopped.
MACDUFF Your royal father's murdered.
MALCOLM   Oh! By whom?
LENNOX Those of his chamber, as it seemed, had done't.
Their hands and faces were all badged° with blood;   *marked*
100 So were their daggers, which unwiped we found
Upon their pillows. They stared and were distracted;
No man's life was to be trusted with them.
MACBETH Oh, yet I do repent me of my fury
That I did kill them.
MACDUFF   Wherefore did you so?
105 MACBETH Who can be wise, amazed, temp'rate and furious,
Loyal and neutral in a moment? No man.
Th'expedition° of my violent love   *haste*
Outran the pauser,° reason. Here lay Duncan,   *delayer*
His silver skin laced with his golden blood,
110 And his gashed stabs looked like a breach in nature
For ruin's wasteful° entrance; there the murderers,   *destructive*
Steeped in the colors of their trade, their daggers
Unmannerly breeched with gore.⁶ Who could refrain
That had a heart to love, and in that heart
Courage to make's love known?
115 LADY MACBETH [*fainting*]⁷   Help me hence, ho!
MACDUFF Look to the lady!
MALCOLM [*aside to* DONALDBAIN] Why do we hold our tongues,
That most may claim this argument° for ours?   *subject*
DONALDBAIN [*aside to* MALCOLM] What should be spoken here,
      where our fate,
Hid in an auger-hole,° may rush and seize us?   *in a cranny (in ambush)*
120 Let's away. Our tears are not yet brewed.

---

6. Covered—as if with breeches—with blood.
7. TEXTUAL COMMENT Since the seventeenth century, performers and editors have had Lady Macbeth
faint at this moment; however, F lacks an explicit
stage direction to indicate what exactly happens. For
more on this issue, see Digital Edition TC 4.

MALCOLM [*aside to* DONALDBAIN]   Nor our strong sorrow upon
    the foot of motion.[8]
BANQUO   Look to the lady.   [*Exit* LADY MACBETH, *attended.*]
    And when we have our naked frailties hid,°   *clothed*
    That suffer in exposure, let us meet
125   And question° this most bloody piece of work   *discuss*
    To know it further. Fears and scruples° shake us.   *doubts*
    In the great hand of God I stand, and thence
    Against the undivulged pretense I fight
    Of treasonous malice.[9]
MACDUFF   And so do I.
ALL   So, all!
130 MACBETH   Let's briefly° put on manly readiness,°   *quickly / clothes; resolve*
    And meet i'th' hall together.
ALL   Well contented.
            Exeunt [*all but* MALCOLM *and* DONALDBAIN].
MALCOLM   What will you do? Let's not consort with them.
    To show an unfelt sorrow is an office
    Which the false man does easy. I'll to England.
135 DONALDBAIN   To Ireland, I. Our separated fortune
    Shall keep us both the safer. Where we are,
    There's daggers in men's smiles. The nearer in blood,
    The nearer bloody.[1]
MALCOLM   This murderous shaft that's shot
    Hath not yet lighted,° and our safest way   *fallen*
140   Is to avoid the aim. Therefore, to horse,
    And let us not be dainty of° leave-taking,   *polite about*
    But shift° away. There's warrant° in that theft   *slip / justification*
    Which steals itself[2] when there's no mercy left.   *Exeunt.*

2.4

Enter ROSS *with an* OLD MAN.
OLD MAN   Threescore and ten I can remember well,
    Within the volume of which time I have seen
    Hours dreadful and things strange, but this sore night
    Hath trifled former knowings.[1]
ROSS   Ha, good father,
5   Thou seest the heavens, as troubled with man's act,
    Threatens his bloody stage. By th' clock 'tis day,
    And yet dark night strangles the traveling lamp.°   *sun*
    Is't night's predominance° or the day's shame   *ascendancy*
    That darkness does the face of earth entomb
    When living light should kiss it?
10 OLD MAN   'Tis unnatural,
    Even like the deed that's done. On Tuesday last
    A falcon, tow'ring in her pride of place,[2]
    Was by a mousing owl[3] hawked at and killed.
ROSS   And Duncan's horses—a thing most strange and certain—

---

8. *Nor . . . motion:* Nor has our strong sorrow yet
begun to express itself.
9. *Against . . . malice:* I will fight against the hidden
purpose behind this treasonous act.
1. *The nearer . . . bloody:* The closer the kinship, the
nearer the danger of murder.
2. *Which steals itself:* Malcolm alludes to the fact that

he and Donaldbain intend to "steal" away from the
castle.
2.4 Location: Not far from Macbeth's castle.
1. Has made previous experiences seem trifling.
2. Mounting to her highest point in the sky before
swooping down.
3. An owl that usually feeds on mice.

15 Beauteous and swift, the minions° of their race,   *darlings*
 Turned wild in nature, broke their stalls, flung out,
 Contending 'gainst obedience, as° they would   *as if*
 Make war with mankind.
OLD MAN   'Tis said they ate each other.
ROSS They did so, to th'amazement of mine eyes
 That looked upon't.
    Enter MACDUFF.
20   Here comes the good Macduff.
 How goes the world, sir, now?
MACDUFF   Why, see you not?
ROSS Is't known who did this more than bloody deed?
MACDUFF Those that Macbeth hath slain.
ROSS   Alas, the day!
 What good could they pretend?[4]
MACDUFF   They were suborned.°   *bribed*
25 Malcolm and Donaldbain, the King's two sons,
 Are stol'n away and fled, which puts upon them
 Suspicion of the deed.
ROSS   'Gainst nature still!
 Thriftless ambition that will ravin up°   *devour*
 Thine own life's means! Then 'tis most like
30 The sovereignty will fall upon Macbeth.
MACDUFF He is already named and gone to Scone[5]
 To be invested.
ROSS   Where is Duncan's body?
MACDUFF Carried to Colmekill,[6]
 The sacred storehouse of his predecessors
 And guardian of their bones.
35 ROSS   Will you to Scone?
MACDUFF No, cousin, I'll to Fife.[7]
ROSS   Well, I will thither.
MACDUFF Well may you see things well done there. Adieu,
 Lest our old robes sit easier than our new.
ROSS Farewell, father.
40 OLD MAN God's benison° go with you and with those *blessing*
 That would make good of bad and friends of foes.
             Exeunt all.

3.1

 Enter BANQUO.
BANQUO Thou hast it now—King, Cawdor, Glamis, all
 As the weird women promised, and I fear
 Thou play'dst most foully for't. Yet it was said
 It should not stand in thy posterity[1]
5 But that myself should be the root and father
 Of many kings. If there come truth from them—
 As upon thee, Macbeth, their speeches shine°— *smile favorably*
 Why by the verities on thee made good
 May they not be my oracles as well
10 And set me up in hope? But hush, no more.

---

4. What good could they expect to gain from the murder?
5. Ancient royal city where Scottish kings were invested with the ceremonial symbols of authority.
6. Iona, the burial place of Scottish kings.
7. Macduff is the Thane of Fife.
3.1 Location: The royal palace at Forres.
1. It should not pass to your descendants.

Sennet° sounded. Enter MACBETH *as King,* LADY
[MACBETH *as Queen,*] LENNOX, ROSS, LORDS, *and*
Attendants.

  Trumpet call

MACBETH Here's our chief guest.

LADY MACBETH   If he had been forgotten,
 It had been as a gap in our great feast,
 And all-thing° unbecoming.   *entirely*

MACBETH Tonight we hold a solemn° supper, sir, *formal*
 And I'll request your presence.

15 BANQUO   Let your highness
 Command upon me, to the which my duties
 Are with a most indissoluble tie
 Forever knit.

MACBETH   Ride you this afternoon?

BANQUO Ay, my good lord.

20 MACBETH We should have else desired your good advice,
 Which still° hath been both grave° and prosperous, *always / weighty*
 In this day's council; but we'll take[2] tomorrow.
 Is't far you ride?

BANQUO As far, my lord, as will fill up the time
25 Twixt this and supper. Go not my horse the better,[3]
 I must become a borrower of the night
 For a dark hour or twain.

MACBETH   Fail not our feast.

BANQUO My lord, I will not.

MACBETH We hear our bloody cousins are bestowed° *lodged*
30 In England and in Ireland, not confessing
 Their cruel parricide, filling their hearers
 With strange invention.° But of that tomorrow, *falsehood*
 When therewithal we shall have cause of state
 Craving us jointly.[4] Hie you to horse. Adieu,
35 Till you return at night. Goes Fleance with you?

BANQUO Ay, my good lord. Our time does call upon's.

MACBETH I wish your horses swift and sure of foot,
 And so I do commend° you to their backs. *entrust*
 Farewell.   *Exit* BANQUO.
40 —Let every man be master of his time
 Till seven at night. To make society
 The sweeter welcome, we will keep ourself
 Till supper-time alone. While° then, God be with you. *Till*
   Exeunt LORDS [*and all but* MACBETH *and a* SERVANT].
 —Sirrah, a word with you: attend those men
45 Our pleasure?

SERVANT They are, my lord, without° the palace gate. *outside*

MACBETH Bring them before us.   *Exit* SERVANT.
 To be thus is nothing, but to be safely thus.[5]
 Our fears in° Banquo stick° deep,   *of / prick*
50 And in his royalty of nature° reigns   *natural nobility*
 That which would be feared. 'Tis much he dares;
 And to° that dauntless temper of his mind *added to*
 He hath a wisdom that doth guide his valor
 To act in safety. There is none but he
55 Whose being I do fear, and under him

---

2. Take it (Banquo's advice).
3. If my horse does not go faster than I expect.
4. *cause . . . jointly:* state business demanding our joint

attention.
5. *To be thus . . . thus:* To be a king is no good unless
one can reign in safety ("thus" refers to "king").

My genius° is rebuked, as it is said[6]   *tutelary spirit*
Mark Antony's was by Caesar.° He chid the sisters   *Octavius Caesar*
When first they put the name of king upon me,
And bade them speak to him; then, prophet-like,
60 They hailed him father to a line of kings.
Upon my head they placed a fruitless crown
And put a barren scepter in my grip,
Thence to be wrenched with° an unlineal hand,   *by*
No son of mine succeeding. If't be so,
65 For Banquo's issue have I filed° my mind,   *defiled*
For them the gracious° Duncan have I murdered,   *full of grace*
Put rancors° in the vessel of my peace   *bitterness*
Only for them, and mine eternal jewel°   *soul*
Given to the common enemy of man°   *(the devil)*
70 To make them kings—the seeds of Banquo kings!
Rather than so, come fate into the list,°   *arena*
And champion me to th'utterance![7] —Who's there!

    Enter SERVANT *and two* MURDERERS.

[*to* SERVANT] Now go to the door, and stay there till we call.
                       Exit SERVANT.

—Was it not yesterday we spoke together?
MURDERERS It was, so please your highness.
75 MACBETH   Well, then; now,[8]
Have you considered of my speeches? Know
That it was he in the times past which held you
So under° fortune, which you thought had been   *out of favor with*
Our innocent self. This I made good to you
80 In our last conference, passed in probation° with you *reviewed the proof*
How you were borne in hand,° how crossed,° the instruments,[9] *deceived / thwarted*
Who wrought with them, and all things else that might
To half a soul and to a notion crazed[1]
Say, "Thus did Banquo."
FIRST MURDERER   You made it known to us.
85 MACBETH I did so, and went further, which is now
Our point of second meeting. Do you find
Your patience so predominant in your nature
That you can let this go? Are you so gospeled[2]
To pray for this good man and for his issue,
90 Whose heavy hand hath bowed you to the grave
And beggared yours° for ever?   *your family*
FIRST MURDERER   We are men, my liege.
MACBETH Ay, in the catalogue ye go for men,
As hounds and greyhounds, mongrels, spaniels, curs,
Shoughs, water-rugs, and demi-wolves[3] are clept°   *called*
95 All by the name of dogs. The valued file[4]
Distinguishes the swift, the slow, the subtle,
The housekeeper,° the hunter—every one   *watchdog*

---

6. Said by Plutarch. Shakespeare paraphrases him in *Antony and Cleopatra* (2.3).
7. And fight with me in single combat to the death (i.e., the uttermost).
8. TEXTUAL COMMENT In F, lines 75–79 appear highly metrically irregular, which this edition has attempted to rearrange. For more on the issue of F's erratic lineation and the work of textual editing, see Digital

Edition TC 5.
9. Agents.
1. Even to a half-wit or to a crazed mind.
2. Imbued with the gospel spirit.
3. Shaggy lapdogs, water dogs (for fowling), and crossbreeds between wolf and dog.
4. List specifying the value of the catalogued items.

According to the gift which bounteous nature
Hath in him closed,° whereby he does receive   *enclosed*
100 Particular addition from the bill
That writes them all alike;[5] and so of men.
Now, if you have a station° in the file,   *position*
Not i'th' worst rank of manhood, say't,
And I will put that business in your bosoms
105 Whose execution takes your enemy off,
Grapples you to the heart and love of us,
Who wear our health but sickly in his life,
Which in his death were perfect.
SECOND MURDERER   I am one, my liege,
Whom the vile blows and buffets of the world
110 Have so incensed that I am reckless what
I do to spite the world.
FIRST MURDERER   And I another,
So weary with disasters, tugged with° fortune,   *mauled by*
That I would set° my life on any chance   *risk*
To mend it or be rid on't.°   *of it*
MACBETH   Both of you
Know Banquo was your enemy.
115 MURDERERS   True, my lord.
MACBETH   So is he mine, and in such bloody distance°   *enmity*
That every minute of his being thrusts
Against my near'st of life.[6] And though I could
With barefaced power sweep him from my sight
120 And bid my will avouch° it, yet I must not,   *warrant*
For° certain friends that are both his and mine,   *Because of*
Whose loves I may not drop, but wail° his fall   *must bewail*
Who I myself struck down. And thence it is
That I to your assistance do make love,°   *I crave your aid*
125 Masking the business from the common eye
For sundry weighty reasons.
SECOND MURDERER   We shall, my lord,
Perform what you command us.
FIRST MURDERER   Though our lives—
MACBETH   Your spirits shine through you. Within this hour, at most,
I will advise you where to plant yourselves,
130 Acquaint you with the perfect spy o'th' time,[7]
The moment on't, for't must be done tonight,
And something° from the palace, always thought°   *at some distance / remember*
That I require a clearness.[8] And with him—
To leave no rubs° nor botches in the work—   *flaws*
135 Fleance, his son that keeps him company,
Whose absence is no less material to me
Than is his father's, must embrace the fate
Of that dark hour. Resolve yourselves apart.[9]
I'll come to you anon.
MURDERERS   We are resolved, my lord.
140 MACBETH   I'll call upon you straight; abide within.

Exeunt [MURDERERS].

---

5. *Particular . . . alike:* Distinction apart from a catalogue that lists them indiscriminately.
6. My most vital part, the heart.
7. *Acquaint . . . on't:* I will give you full and precise

instructions as to when it is to be done.
8. A clearance (from suspicion).
9. Make up your minds privately.

It is concluded. Banquo, thy soul's flight,
If it find heaven, must find it out tonight.   [*Exit.*]

3.2

Enter LADY MACBETH *and a* SERVANT.

LADY MACBETH   Is Banquo gone from court?
SERVANT   Ay, madam, but returns again tonight.
LADY MACBETH   Say to the King I would attend his leisure
  For a few words.
SERVANT   Madam, I will.   *Exit.*
LADY MACBETH   Naught's had, all's spent,
5 Where our desire is got without content.°   *happiness*
  'Tis safer to be that which we destroy
  Than by destruction dwell in doubtful joy.

Enter MACBETH.

  How now, my lord? Why do you keep alone,
  Of sorriest° fancies your companions making,   *most wretched*
10 Using° those thoughts which should indeed have died *Entertaining*
  With them they think on? Things without all remedy
  Should be without regard.° What's done is done.   *not considered*
MACBETH   We have scorched° the snake, not killed it.   *slashed*
  She'll close° and be herself, whilst our poor malice *heal*
15 Remains in danger of her former tooth.[1]
  But let the frame of things disjoint, both the worlds suffer,[2]
  Ere we will eat our meal in fear, and sleep
  In the affliction of these terrible dreams
  That shake us nightly. Better be with the dead,
20 Whom we, to gain our peace, have sent to peace,
  Than on the torture° of the mind to lie   *rack*
  In restless ecstasy.° Duncan is in his grave.   *frenzy*
  After life's fitful fever he sleeps well.
  Treason has done his worst; nor steel, nor poison,
25 Malice domestic, foreign levy,[3] nothing
  Can touch him further.
LADY MACBETH   Come on, gentle my lord,
  Sleek o'er your rugged looks. Be bright and jovial
  Among your guests tonight.
MACBETH   So shall I, love,
  And so, I pray, be you. Let your remembrance
30 Apply° to Banquo; present him eminence°   *Be given / favor*
  Both with eye and tongue—unsafe the while, that we
  Must lave our honors in these flattering streams[4]
  And make our faces vizards° to our hearts,   *masks*
  Disguising what they are.
LADY MACBETH   You must leave this.
35 MACBETH   Oh, full of scorpions is my mind, dear wife!
  Thou know'st that Banquo and his Fleance lives.
LADY MACBETH   But in them nature's copy's[5] not eterne.°   *everlasting*
MACBETH   There's comfort yet; they are assailable.

3.2 Location: The palace.
1. *our . . . tooth:* we remain in danger of her fangs,
which are as dangerous as they were before she was
slashed. *poor malice:* weak enmity.
2. Let the universe fall apart, and heaven and earth
suffer destruction.
3. An army levied abroad against Scotland.

4. *unsafe . . . streams:* we are unsafe at present, so we
must make our reputations look clean by flattering
others; we are unsafe as long as we must flatter.
5. Lease on life (a copyhold lease was subject to cancellation and therefore "not eterne"); the individual
human cast from nature's mold.

Then be thou jocund. Ere the bat hath flown
40   His cloistered° flight, ere to black Hecate's summons   *restricted*
  The shard-born[6] beetle with his drowsy hums
  Hath rung night's yawning peal,[7] there shall be done
  A deed of dreadful note.
LADY MACBETH   What's to be done?
MACBETH   Be innocent of the knowledge, dearest chuck,[8]
45   Till thou applaud the deed. —Come, seeling[9] night,
  Scarf up° the tender eye of pitiful day,   *Blindfold*
  And with thy bloody and invisible hand
  Cancel and tear to pieces that great bond°   *(Banquo's lease on life)*
  Which keeps me pale! Light thickens,
50   And the crow makes wing to th' rooky° wood;   *full of rooks*
  Good things of day begin to droop and drowse,
  Whiles night's black agents to their preys do rouse.
  —Thou marvel'st at my words, but hold thee still.
  Things bad begun make strong themselves by ill.
55   So, prithee, go with me.   *Exeunt.*

3.3

Enter three MURDERERS.
FIRST MURDERER   But who did bid thee join with us?
THIRD MURDERER   Macbeth.
SECOND MURDERER [*to* FIRST MURDERER]   He needs not our
  mistrust, since he delivers
  Our offices and what we have to do
  To the direction just.[1]
FIRST MURDERER [*to* THIRD MURDERER]   Then stand with us.
5   The West yet glimmers with some streaks of day.
  Now spurs the lated° traveler apace   *belated*
  To gain the timely inn, and near approaches
  The subject of our watch.
THIRD MURDERER   Hark, I hear horses.
BANQUO (*within*)   Give us a light there, ho!
SECOND MURDERER   Then 'tis he. The rest
10   That are within the note of expectation°   *list of expected guests*
  Already are i'th' court.
FIRST MURDERER   His horses go about.[2]
THIRD MURDERER   Almost a mile, but he does usually.
  So all men do from hence to th' palace gate
  Make it their walk.
        Enter BANQUO *and* FLEANCE, *with a torch.*
15 SECOND MURDERER   A light, a light!
THIRD MURDERER   'Tis he.
FIRST MURDERER   Stand to't.
BANQUO   It will be rain tonight.
FIRST MURDERER   Let it come down![3]
    [*They attack.* FIRST MURDERER *puts out the light.*]
BANQUO   Oh, treachery!

---

6. Born in dung ("shards"); carried on scaly wings ("shard-borne").
7. Macbeth likens the beetle's humming to a bell, signaling the time for sleep.
8. Chick (term of endearment).
9. Eye-closing. Falcons' eyelids were sewn shut ("seeled") as part of their training.

3.3 Location: Near the palace.
1. *He . . . just:* We need not mistrust this man, since he knows perfectly Macbeth's instructions to us.
2. Are led (by servants) to the stables.
3. TEXTUAL COMMENT For the variety of ways that Shakespeare's short lines can be read or performed, see Digital Edition TC 6.

20   Fly, good Fleance, fly, fly, fly!
    Thou mayst revenge. —O slave!
        [BANQUO *dies.* FLEANCE *escapes.*]
THIRD MURDERER   Who did strike out the light?
FIRST MURDERER   Was't not the way?°   *proper thing*
THIRD MURDERER   There's but one down. The son is fled.
SECOND MURDERER   We have lost best half of our affair.
25 FIRST MURDERER   Well, let's away and say how much is done.
                 Exeunt [*with Banquo's body*].

3.4

Banquet prepared. Enter MACBETH, LADY MACBETH,
  ROSS, LENNOX, LORDS, *and Attendants.*
MACBETH   You know your own degrees;° sit down.   *ranks; places*
    At first and last,[1] the hearty welcome.
LORDS   Thanks to your majesty.
MACBETH   Ourself will mingle with society
5   And play the humble host.
    Our hostess keeps her state,° but in best time   *chair of state*
    We will require° her welcome.   *request*
LADY MACBETH   Pronounce it for me, sir, to all our friends,
    For my heart speaks they are welcome.
      Enter FIRST MURDERER [*and stands aside*].
10 MACBETH   See, they encounter° thee with their hearts' thanks.   *answer*
    Both sides are even. Here I'll sit, i'th' midst.
    Be large° in mirth; anon we'll drink a measure   *unrestrained*
    The table round.
      [*He converses apart with the* FIRST MURDERER.]
             There's blood upon thy face.
FIRST MURDERER   'Tis Banquo's, then.
15 MACBETH   'Tis better thee without than he within.[2]
    Is he dispatched?
FIRST MURDERER   My lord, his throat is cut. That I did for him.
MACBETH   Thou art the best o'th' cutthroats.
    Yet he's good that did the like for Fleance;
20   If thou didst it, thou art the nonpareil.°   *paragon (without equal)*
FIRST MURDERER   Most royal sir, Fleance is scaped.
MACBETH   Then comes my fit again. I had else been perfect,
    Whole as the marble, founded° as the rock,   *immovable*
    As broad and general° as the casing° air,   *unconstrained / surrounding*
25   But now I am cabined, cribbed,° confined, bound in   *penned up*
    To saucy° doubts and fears. But Banquo's safe?   *importunate*
FIRST MURDERER   Ay, my good lord, safe in a ditch he bides,
    With twenty trenchèd gashes on his head,
    The least a death to nature.
MACBETH   Thanks for that.
30   There the grown serpent lies; the worm° that's fled   *young serpent*
    Hath nature that in time will venom breed,
    No teeth for th' present. Get thee gone. Tomorrow
    We'll hear ourselves° again.   *Exit* FIRST MURDERER.   *confer*
LADY MACBETH   My royal lord,
    You do not give the cheer.° The feast is sold   *entertain*

3.4 Location: The palace.   2. Better on you than inside him.
1. To one and all.

35   That is not often vouched, while 'tis a-making,
      'Tis given with welcome.³ To feed° were best at home;   *Mere eating*
      From thence° the sauce to meat is ceremony: *Away from home*
      Meeting were° bare without it.   *Company would be*

          Enter the Ghost of BANQUO *and sits in Macbeth's place.*⁴

      MACBETH   Sweet remembrancer.°   *reminder*
      —Now, good digestion wait on appetite,
      And health on both.

40   LENNOX   May't please your highness, sit.

      MACBETH   Here had we now our country's honor roofed,⁵
      Were the graced person of our Banquo present,
      Who may I rather challenge for° unkindness   *accuse of*
      Than pity for mischance.

      ROSS   His absence, sir,
45   Lays blame upon his promise. Please't your highness
      To grace us with your royal company?

      MACBETH [*seeing his place occupied*]   The table's full.

      LENNOX   Here is a place reserved, sir.

      MACBETH   Where?

      LENNOX   Here, my good lord. What is't that moves your highness?

      MACBETH   Which of you have done this?

50   LORDS   What, my good lord?

      MACBETH [*to Ghost of* BANQUO]   Thou canst not say I did it.
          Never shake
      Thy gory locks at me!

      ROSS   Gentlemen, rise. His highness is not well.

      LADY MACBETH   Sit, worthy friends. My lord is often thus
55   And hath been from his youth. Pray you, keep seat.
      The fit is momentary; upon a thought°   *in a moment*
      He will again be well. If much you note him,
      You shall offend him and extend his passion.°   *prolong his suffering*
      Feed, and regard him not.

          [*She converses apart with* MACBETH.]
                               Are you a man?

60   MACBETH   Ay, and a bold one that dare look on that
      Which might appall the devil!

      LADY MACBETH   Oh, proper stuff!°   *mere nonsense*
      This is the very painting of your fear;
      This is the air-drawn dagger⁶ which you said
      Led you to Duncan. Oh, these flaws° and starts,   *outbursts*
65   Impostors to° true fear, would well become   *compared with*
      A woman's story at a winter's fire,
      Authorized by her grandam. Shame itself!
      Why do you make such faces? When all's done,
      You look but on a stool.

      MACBETH   Prithee, see there!
70   Behold, look, lo! How say you?
      Why, what care I? [*to Ghost of* BANQUO] If thou canst nod,
          speak too.
      If charnel houses and our graves must send

---

3. *The . . . welcome:* A feast is like a purchased ("sold")
meal if it is not often affirmed ("vouched") to the
guests, while the feast is taking place, that they are
welcome.
4. TEXTUAL COMMENT F's stage direction for the
Ghost of Banquo's entrance leaves some uncertainty
about when precisely he appears on the stage, with

implications for the scene's theatrical effect. For further details on the issue of early modern stage directions, see Digital Edition TC 7.
5. All the Scottish nobility under one roof.
6. The dagger drawn on, or carried on, the air
(2.1.33ff).

Those that we bury back, our monuments
Shall be the maws of kites.[7]   [*Exit Ghost of* BANQUO.][8]
75   LADY MACBETH   What, quite unmanned in folly?
MACBETH   If I stand here, I saw him.
LADY MACBETH   Fie, for shame!
MACBETH   Blood hath been shed ere now, i'th' olden time,
Ere humane statute purged the gentle weal;[9]
Ay, and since, too, murders have been performed,
80   Too terrible for the ear. The times has been
That, when the brains were out, the man would die,
And there an end. But now they rise again,
With twenty mortal murders° on their crowns,°   *deadly wounds / heads*
And push us from our stools. This is more strange
Than such a murder is.
85   LADY MACBETH   My worthy lord,
Your noble friends do lack you.
MACBETH   I do forget.
—Do not muse° at me, my most worthy friends.   *wonder*
I have a strange infirmity, which is nothing
To those that know me. Come, love and health to all;
90   Then I'll sit down. Give me some wine; fill full.
          Enter Ghost [of BANQUO].
I drink to th' general joy o'th' whole table
And to our dear friend Banquo, whom we miss.
Would he were here! To all and him we thirst,°   *drink*
And all to all.[1]
LORDS   Our duties and the pledge.°   *toast*
          [*They drink.*]
95   MACBETH [*to Ghost of* BANQUO]   Avaunt, and quit my sight!
Let the earth hide thee!
Thy bones are marrowless, thy blood is cold;
Thou hast no speculation° in those eyes   *sight*
Which thou dost glare with.
LADY MACBETH   Think of this, good peers,
But as a thing of custom; 'tis no other,
100   Only it spoils the pleasure of the time.
MACBETH   What man dare, I dare.
Approach thou like the rugged Russian bear,
The armed° rhinoceros, or th' Hyrcan[2] tiger!   *armored*
Take any shape but that,° and my firm nerves°   *(Banquo's) / sinews*
105   Shall never tremble. Or be alive again,
And dare me to the desert° with thy sword.   *deserted place*
If trembling I inhabit then,[3] protest me
The baby of a girl.[4] Hence, horrible shadow,
Unreal mock'ry, hence!   [*Exit Ghost of* BANQUO.]
                        Why, so. Being gone,
110   I am a man again. —Pray you, sit still.
LADY MACBETH   You have displaced the mirth, broke the good
          meeting
With most admired° disorder.   *wondered at*

---

7. *If . . . kites:* If the dead return from their graves, nothing will prevent them from being consumed by birds of prey, making graves of their stomachs.
8. PERFORMANCE COMMENT Productions have to decide how to stage the appearance of Banquo's ghost at the banquet, or indeed whether to bring the figure of Banquo on stage at all. See Digital Edition PC 5.

9. Before human or humane (Elizabethans did not spell the two words differently) law cleansed the commonwealth and made it peaceable.
1. All good wishes to everyone.
2. From Hyrcania, a region near the Caspian Sea.
3. If then I tremble; if, trembling, I stay indoors.
4. A baby girl; a girl's doll.

MACBETH   Can such things be,
  And overcome° us like a summer's cloud,   *pass over*
  Without our special wonder? You make me strange
115 Even to the disposition that I owe,[5]
  When now I think you can behold such sights
  And keep the natural ruby of your cheeks
  When mine is blanched with fear.
    ROSS   What sights, my lord?
  LADY MACBETH   I pray you, speak not; he grows worse and worse.
120 Question enrages° him. At once, good night.   *Talk aggravates*
  Stand not upon the order of your going,
  But go at once.[6]
    LENNOX   Good night, and better health
  Attend his majesty.
  LADY MACBETH   A kind good night to all.
                              Exeunt LORDS [*and Attendants*].
  MACBETH   It will have blood, they say; blood will have blood.
125 Stones have been known to move and trees to speak;
  Augurs° and understood relations[7] have   *Auguries*
  By maggot-pies and choughs and rooks[8] brought forth°   *revealed*
  The secret'st man of blood.° What is the night?[9]   *murderer*
  LADY MACBETH   Almost at odds with morning, which is which.
130 MACBETH   How say'st thou[1] that Macduff denies his person
  At our great bidding?
  LADY MACBETH   Did you send to him, sir?
  MACBETH   I hear it by the way,° but I will send.   *indirectly*
  There's not a one of them but in his house
  I keep a servant fee'd.° I will° tomorrow—   *paid to spy / will go*
135 And betimes° I will—to the weird sisters.   *early*
  More shall they speak, for now I am bent° to know   *determined*
  By the worst means the worst. For mine own good
  All causes° shall give way. I am in blood   *other concerns*
  Stepped in so far that, should I° wade no more,°   *were I to / no farther*
140 Returning were° as tedious as go° o'er.   *would be / going*
  Strange things I have in head that will to hand,
  Which must be acted ere they may be scanned.[2]
  LADY MACBETH   You lack the season° of all natures, sleep.   *preservative*
  MACBETH   Come, we'll to sleep. My strange and self-abuse°   *self-delusion*
145 Is the initiate fear that wants hard use.[3]
  We are yet but young in deed.°   *Exeunt.*   *crime*

3.5

Thunder. Enter the three WITCHES, *meeting* HECATE.

FIRST WITCH   Why, how now, Hecate? You look angerly.
  HECATE   Have I not reason, beldams,° as you are   *hags*
  Saucy and overbold? How did you dare
  To trade and traffic with Macbeth
5 In riddles and affairs of death,
  And I, the mistress of your charms,

---

5. *You . . . owe:* You make me a stranger to my own
nature, which I had supposed brave.
6. *Stand . . . once:* Do not follow the order of precedence in departing, but all go at once.
7. Formerly hidden, now revealed relationships
between causes and effects.
8. Magpies, traditionally sacrificed by augurers, and
birds (choughs and rooks) of the crow family.

9. What time of night is it?
1. What do you think of the fact.
2. *ere . . . scanned:* at once, before they can be
considered.
3. Is the fear of a novice who lacks toughening
experience.
3.5 Location: An open place.

The close° contriver of all harms,   *secret*
Was never called to bear my part,
Or show the glory of our art?
10 And, which is worse, all you have done
Hath been but for a wayward son,
Spiteful and wrathful, who, as others do,
Loves for his own ends, not for you.
But make amends now. Get you gone,
15 And at the pit of Acheron°   *a river in hell*
Meet me i'th' morning. Thither he
Will come to know his destiny.
Your vessels and your spells provide,
Your charms and everything beside.
20 I am for th'air. This night I'll spend
Unto a dismal and a fatal end.¹
Great business must be wrought ere noon.
Upon the corner of the moon
There hangs a vap'rous drop profound;²
25 I'll catch it ere it come to ground.
And that, distilled by magic sleights,
Shall raise such artificial sprites³
As by the strength of their illusion
Shall draw him on to his confusion.
30 He shall spurn fate, scorn death, and bear
His hopes 'bove wisdom, grace, and fear.
And you all know security°   *overconfidence*
Is mortals' chiefest enemy.
              Music and a song.
Hark, I am called. My little spirit, see,
35 Sits in a foggy cloud and stays for me.   [*Exit.*]
        Sing within:° "*Come away, come away,*" *etc.*⁴   *offstage*
FIRST WITCH Come, let's make haste. She'll soon be back again.
                                                       Exeunt.

3.6

Enter LENNOX *and another* LORD.

LENNOX My former speeches have but hit your thoughts,
Which can interpret farther.¹ Only I say
Things have been strangely borne.° The gracious Duncan   *carried on*
Was pitied of Macbeth; marry, he was dead.²
5 And the right valiant Banquo walked too late,
Whom you may say, if't please you, Fleance killed,
For Fleance fled; men must not walk too late.
Who cannot want the thought° how monstrous   *can help thinking*
It was for Malcolm and for Donaldbain
10 To kill their gracious father? Damnèd fact,°   *deed*
How it did grieve Macbeth! Did he not straight
In pious° rage the two delinquents tear,   *loyal*
That were the slaves of drink and thralls° of sleep?   *slaves*

---

1. Working toward a disastrous and fateful end.
2. Of deep or hidden significance; ready to fall.
3. Spirits produced by magic art.
4. TEXTUAL COMMENT F's directions for the witches' song might indicate that *Macbeth* was revised, perhaps by Thomas Middleton, whose play *The Witch* includes an elaborately staged performance of a song with the same first line. For more on the issue, along with musical recordings, see Digital Edition TC 8.
3.6 Location: Somewhere in Scotland.
1. *My . . . farther:* What I have said has coincided with your thoughts. I need not say more; you can draw your own further conclusions.
2. *The . . . dead:* Macbeth pitied Duncan after he was dead, but not before. *of:* by.

Was not that nobly done? Ay, and wisely, too,
15 For 'twould have angered any heart alive
To hear the men deny't. So that I say
He has borne all things well. And I do think
That had he Duncan's sons under his key—
As, an't° please heaven, he shall not—they should find   *if it*
20 What 'twere to kill a father. So should Fleance.
But peace. For from broad words[3] and 'cause he failed
His presence at the tyrant's feast, I hear
Macduff lives in disgrace. Sir, can you tell
Where he bestows himself?°   *lodges*

LORD   The son of Duncan,
25 From whom this tyrant holds° the due of birth,°   *withholds / birthright*
Lives in the English court and is received
Of the most pious Edward[4] with such grace
That the malevolence of fortune nothing
Takes from his high respect.[5] Thither Macduff
30 Is gone to pray the holy King, upon his aid,°   *in aid of Malcolm*
To wake Northumberland and warlike Siward,
That by the help of these, with Him above
To ratify the work, we may again
Give to our tables meat,° sleep to our nights,   *food*
35 Free from our feasts and banquets bloody knives,[6]
Do faithful homage, and receive free[7] honors—
All which we pine for now. And this report
Hath so exasperate the King[8] that he
Prepares for some attempt of war.

40 LENNOX   Sent he to Macduff?

LORD   He did, and with° an absolute "Sir, not I,"   *on receiving*
The cloudy messenger turns me his back
And hums, as who should say, "You'll rue the time
That clogs me with this answer."[9]

LENNOX   And that well might
45 Advise him to a caution, t'hold what distance
His wisdom can provide.[1] Some holy angel
Fly to the court of England and unfold
His message ere he come, that a swift blessing
May soon return to this our suffering country
Under a hand accursed.[2]

50 LORD   I'll send my prayers with him. *Exeunt.*

4.1

Thunder. Enter the three WITCHES.

FIRST WITCH   Thrice the brinded° cat hath mewed.   *brindled; streaked*

SECOND WITCH   Thrice, and once the hedge-pig° whined.   *hedgehog*

---

3. As a result of his plain speaking.
4. *received . . . Edward:* received by the saintly King Edward (Edward the Confessor, reigned 1042–1066).
5. *nothing . . . takes:* does not deprive Malcolm of respect.
6. Free our feasts from bloody knives.
7. Freely given; enjoyed in freedom.
8. TEXTUAL COMMENT "Has so exasperated Macbeth." F, however, reads "their King." For more on the issue of textual confusions and how editors propose solutions, see Digital Edition TC 9.

9. *He did . . . answer:* Macduff says, "Sir, not I." The scowling ("cloudy") messenger from Macbeth turns his back and hums. His rudeness seems to say ominously, "You'll rue the time that burdens ('clogs') me with this answer."
1. *Advise . . . provide:* Warn Macduff to keep as far from Macbeth as he can.
2. *suffering . . . accursed:* country suffering under an accursed hand.
4.1 Location: A cave with a boiling cauldron.

THIRD WITCH   Harpier° cries, "'Tis time, 'tis time!"   *(her familiar)*
FIRST WITCH   Round about the cauldron go;
5   In the poisoned entrails throw.
Toad, that under cold stone
Days and nights has thirty-one
Sweltered venom sleeping got,[1]
Boil thou first i'th' charmèd pot.
10   ALL   Double, double, toil and trouble;
Fire burn, and cauldron bubble.
SECOND WITCH   Fillet° of a fenny° snake   *Slice / from the swamps*
In the cauldron boil and bake;
Eye of newt and toe of frog,
15   Wool of bat and tongue of dog,
Adder's fork° and blind-worm's sting,   *forked tongue*
Lizard's leg and owlet's wing,
For a charm of powerful trouble,
Like a hell-broth boil and bubble.
20   ALL   Double, double, toil and trouble;
Fire burn, and cauldron bubble.
THIRD WITCH   Scale of dragon, tooth of wolf,
Witches' mummy,° maw and gulf[2]   *mummified flesh*
Of the ravined° salt-sea shark,   *ravenous; glutted*
25   Root of hemlock digged i'th' dark,
Liver of blaspheming Jew,
Gall of goat, and slips of yew
Slivered° in the moon's eclipse,   *Cut off*
Nose of Turk and Tartar's[3] lips,
30   Finger of birth-strangled babe
Ditch-delivered by a drab,°   *whore*
Make the gruel thick and slab.°   *viscous*
Add thereto a tiger's chawdron,°   *entrails*
For th'ingredients of our cauldron.
35   ALL   Double, double, toil and trouble;
Fire burn, and cauldron bubble.
SECOND WITCH   Cool it with a baboon's blood;
Then the charm is firm and good.
   Enter HECATE *and the other three* WITCHES.
HECATE   Oh, well done. I commend your pains,
40   And every one shall share i'th' gains.
And now about the cauldron sing,
Live elves and fairies in a ring,
Enchanting all that you put in.
   Music and a song, "Black spirits," etc.
SECOND WITCH   By the pricking of my thumbs,
45   Something wicked this way comes.
Open, locks, whoever knocks!
   Enter MACBETH.
MACBETH   How now, you secret, black, and midnight hags?
What is't you do?
ALL WITCHES   A deed without a name.
MACBETH   I conjure you by that which you profess,°   *(the black arts)*
50   Howe'er you come to know it, answer me.

---

1. *has . . . got:* has for thirty-one days and nights exuded poison formed during sleep.

2. Stomach and gullet.
3. Both thought of as cruel pagans.

Though you untie the winds and let them fight
Against the churches, though the yeasty° waves   *foamy*
Confound° and swallow navigation up,   *Defeat*
Though bladed corn° be lodged° and trees blown down,   *ripe wheat / beaten down*
55   Though castles topple on their warders' heads,
Though palaces and pyramids do slope°   *bend*
Their heads to their foundations, though the treasure
Of nature's germens[4] tumble all together
Even till destruction sicken,° answer me   *be surfeited*
To what I ask you.
FIRST WITCH   Speak.
SECOND WITCH   Demand.
60   THIRD WITCH   We'll answer.
FIRST WITCH   Say if thou'dst rather hear it from our mouths,
Or from our masters.
MACBETH   Call 'em; let me see 'em.
FIRST WITCH   Pour in sow's blood that hath eaten
Her nine farrow;° grease that's sweaten°   *litter of nine / sweated*
65   From the murderer's gibbet° throw   *gallows*
Into the flame.
ALL WITCHES   Come high or low,
Thyself and office° deftly show![5]   *function*
          Thunder. FIRST APPARITION, *an armed° head.*   *armored*
MACBETH   Tell me, thou unknown power—
FIRST WITCH   He knows thy thought.
Hear his speech, but say thou naught.
70   FIRST APPARITION   Macbeth, Macbeth, Macbeth. Beware
          Macduff,
Beware the Thane of Fife. Dismiss me. Enough.
                              He descends.
MACBETH   Whate'er thou art, for thy good caution, thanks;
Thou hast harped° my fear aright. But one word more—   *guessed*
FIRST WITCH   He will not be commanded. Here's another,
75   More potent than the first.
          Thunder. SECOND APPARITION, *a bloody child.*
SECOND APPARITION   Macbeth, Macbeth, Macbeth.
MACBETH   Had I three ears, I'd hear thee.
SECOND APPARITION   Be bloody, bold, and resolute; laugh to
          scorn
The power of man, for none of woman born
80   Shall harm Macbeth.
                              [He] descends.
MACBETH   Then live, Macduff. What need I fear of thee?
But yet I'll make assurance double sure
And take a bond of fate.[6] Thou shalt not live,
That I may tell pale-hearted fear it lies,
And sleep in spite of thunder.
          Thunder. THIRD APPARITION, *a child crowned, with a*
          tree in his hand.[7]
85   What is this

---

4. Seeds from which all nature grows. According to
Renaissance theories of biology, if they were tumbled
together, they would become barren or produce only
monsters.
5. PERFORMANCE COMMENT No scene in *Macbeth*
raises more dramaturgical questions and challenges

than 4.1, which features Hecate, a trio of apparitions,
the return of Banquo's ghost, and at least eight spectral
kings. See Digital Edition PC 6.
6. Make a contract with fate.
7. Signifying Malcolm. The tree anticipates 5.5.33ff.

That rises like the issue of a king,
And wears upon his baby brow the round
And top of sovereignty?°   (crown)

ALL WITCHES   Listen, but speak not to't.

THIRD APPARITION   Be lion-mettled, proud, and take no care
90   Who chafes, who frets, or where conspirers are.
Macbeth shall never vanquished be until
Great Birnam Wood to high Dunsinane Hill
Shall come against him.

                                          [He] descends.

MACBETH   That will never be.
Who can impress° the forest, bid the tree   *force into service*
95   Unfix his earth-bound root? Sweet bodements,° good.   *omens*
Rebellious dead,[8] rise never till the Wood
Of Birnam rise, and our high-placed Macbeth
Shall live the lease of nature,° pay his breath   *natural life span*
To time and mortal custom.[9] Yet my heart
100 Throbs to know one thing: tell me, if your art
Can tell so much, shall Banquo's issue ever
Reign in this kingdom?

ALL WITCHES   Seek to know no more.

MACBETH   I will be satisfied. Deny me this,
And an eternal curse fall on you! Let me know.
           [The cauldron descends.] Hautboys.
105 Why sinks that cauldron? And what noise° is this?   *music*

FIRST WITCH   Show!

SECOND WITCH   Show!

THIRD WITCH   Show!

ALL WITCHES   Show his eyes, and grieve his heart;
110 Come like shadows, so depart.
     A show of eight kings, and BANQUO *last; [the eighth*
     king] with a glass° in his hand.   *mirror*

MACBETH   Thou art too like the spirit of Banquo. Down!
Thy crown does sear mine eyeballs! And thy heir,
Thou other gold-bound brow, is like the first.
A third is like the former. —Filthy hags,
115 Why do you show me this? —A fourth! Start,° eyes!   *Bulge out*
What, will the line stretch out to th' crack of doom?
Another yet? A seventh! I'll see no more.
And yet the eighth appears, who bears a glass
Which shows me many more; and some I see
120 That two-fold balls and treble scepters[1] carry.
Horrible sight! Now, I see 'tis true,
For the blood-boltered[2] Banquo smiles upon me,
And points at them for his.[3]
           [The show of kings and BANQUO *vanish.]*
               What, is this so?

FIRST WITCH   Ay, sir, all this is so. But why
125 Stands Macbeth thus amazedly?°   *entranced*
Come, sisters, cheer we up his sprites,°   *spirits*

8. Perhaps Banquo. Some editors emend to "Rebellious head" or "Rebellion's head," where "head" means
"army."
9. The custom of mortality; natural death.
1. James I was crowned twice, once as King of Scotland and later as King of England. He carried one orb
at each coronation. "Treble scepters" refers to the fact
that he held two scepters in the English coronation
and one in the Scottish, or perhaps to his claim to be
King of Britain, France, and Ireland.
2. Having hair matted with blood.
3. Banquo was the legendary founder of the Stuart
dynasty.

And show the best of our delights.
I'll charm the air to give a sound,
While you perform your antic round,°   *fantastic dance*
130   That this great king may kindly say
Our duties did his welcome pay.⁴

          Music. The WITCHES *dance and vanish.*

MACBETH   Where are they? Gone? Let this pernicious hour
Stand aye° accursèd in the calendar!   *ever*
Come in, without there.

         Enter LENNOX.

LENNOX   What's your grace's will?
MACBETH   Saw you the weird sisters?
135   LENNOX   No, my lord.
MACBETH   Came they not by you?
LENNOX   No, indeed, my lord.
MACBETH   Infected be the air whereon they ride,
And damned all those that trust them! I did hear
The galloping of horse. Who was't came by?
140   LENNOX   'Tis two or three, my lord, that bring you word
Macduff is fled to England.
MACBETH   Fled to England?
LENNOX   Ay, my good lord.
MACBETH *[aside]*   Time, thou anticipat'st° my dread exploits.   *forestall*
The flighty purpose never is o'ertook
145   Unless the deed go with it.⁵ From this moment
The very firstlings° of my heart shall be   *first notions*
The firstlings° of my hand. And even now,   *first acts*
To crown my thoughts with acts, be it thought and done.
The castle of Macduff I will surprise,
150   Seize upon Fife, give to th'edge o'th' sword
His wife, his babes, and all unfortunate souls
That trace him in his line. No boasting like a fool;
This deed I'll do before this purpose cool.
But no more sights. —Where are these gentlemen?
155   Come, bring me where they are.   *Exeunt.*

4.2

     Enter Macduff's WIFE, *her* SON, *and* ROSS.

WIFE   What had he done to make him fly the land?
ROSS   You must have patience, madam.
WIFE   He had none;
His flight was madness. When our actions do not,
Our fears do make us traitors.¹
ROSS   You know not
5   Whether it was his wisdom or his fear.
WIFE   Wisdom? To leave his wife, to leave his babes,
His mansion, and his titles° in a place   *estates*
From whence himself does fly? He loves us not;
He wants° the natural touch.° For the poor wren,   *lacks / affection*
10   The most diminutive of birds, will fight,
Her young ones in her nest, against the owl.

---

4. Our service repaid the welcome he gave us.
5. *The flighty . . . it:* The fleeting intention is never realized unless the deed is done immediately.
4.2 Location: Macduff's castle in Fife.

1. *When . . . traitors:* Even when we have committed no treason, our fear of suspicion makes us behave as though we are guilty.

All is the fear and nothing is the love,
As little is the wisdom, where the flight
So runs against all reason.

ROSS   My dearest coz,°   *kinswoman*

15   I pray you, school° yourself. But, for your husband,   *control*
He is noble, wise, judicious, and best knows
The fits o'th' season.[2] I dare not speak much further,
But cruel are the times when we are traitors
And do not know ourselves;[3] when we hold rumor

20   From what we fear, yet know not what we fear,[4]
But float upon a wild and violent sea,
Each way and none.[5] I take my leave of you;
Shall° not be long but° I'll be here again.   *It shall / before*
Things at the worst will cease or else climb upward

25   To what they were before. [*to the* SON] My pretty cousin,
Blessing upon you.

WIFE   Fathered he is, and yet he's fatherless.

ROSS   I am so much a fool, should I stay longer
It would be my disgrace and your discomfort.[6]
I take my leave at once.   *Exit* ROSS.

30 WIFE   Sirrah, your father's dead.
And what will you do now? How will you live?

SON   As birds do, mother.

WIFE   What, with worms and flies?

SON   With what I get, I mean, and so do they.

WIFE   Poor° bird, thou'dst never fear the net nor lime,[7]   *Pitiful*

35   The pitfall nor the gin.°   *snare*

SON   Why should I, mother? Poor° birds they are not set for.   *Worthless*
My father is not dead, for all your saying.

WIFE   Yes, he is dead. How wilt thou do for a father?

SON   Nay, how will you do for a husband?

40 WIFE   Why, I can buy me twenty at any market.

SON   Then you'll buy 'em to sell again.

WIFE   Thou speak'st with all thy wit, and yet, i'faith, with wit
enough for thee.

SON   Was my father a traitor, mother?

45 WIFE   Ay, that he was.

SON   What is a traitor?

WIFE   Why, one that swears and lies.[8]

SON   And be all traitors that do so?

WIFE   Every one that does so is a traitor and must be hanged.

50 SON   And must they all be hanged that swear° and lie?   *speak profanely*

WIFE   Every one.

SON   Who must hang them?

WIFE   Why, the honest men.

SON   Then the liars and swearers are fools, for there are liars and

55   swearers enough to beat the honest men and hang up them.

WIFE   Now, God help thee, poor monkey! But how wilt thou
do for a father?

---

2. The violent convulsions of the present time; what befits the time.
3. *we . . . ourselves:* we are denounced as traitors but do not know why; we have no self-knowledge.
4. *when . . . fear:* when we believe rumors inspired by our fears, but those fears are themselves vague.

5. In every direction, and so finally in none.
6. I would disgrace myself and embarrass you by weeping (or perhaps by lingering).
7. Birdlime, a sticky substance smeared on twigs to catch small birds.
8. Takes an oath and breaks it.

SON If he were dead, you'd weep for him; if you would not, it
were a good sign that I should quickly have a new father.

60 WIFE Poor prattler, how thou talk'st!

Enter a MESSENGER.

MESSENGER Bless you, fair dame. I am not to you known,
Though in your state of honor I am perfect.⁹
I doubt° some danger does approach you nearly.   fear
If you will take a homely° man's advice,   plain
65 Be not found here; hence with your little ones.
To fright you thus, methinks, I am too savage;
To do worse to you were fell cruelty,¹
Which is too nigh your person.² Heaven preserve you.
I dare abide no longer.   *Exit* MESSENGER.

WIFE   Whither should I fly?
70 I have done no harm. But I remember now
I am in this earthly world, where to do harm
Is often laudable, to do good sometime
Accounted dangerous folly. Why, then, alas,
Do I put up that womanly defense,
To say I have done no harm?

Enter MURDERERS.

75   What are these faces?
MURDERER Where is your husband?
WIFE I hope in no place so unsanctified
Where such as thou mayst find him.
MURDERER   He's a traitor.
SON Thou liest, thou shag-haired villain!
MURDERER [*stabbing him*]   What, you egg!
Young fry° of treachery.   spawn
80 SON   He has killed me, mother.
Run away, I pray you!

[*He dies.*]

Exit [WIFE] *crying* "Murder!" [*followed by*
MURDERERS *with Son's body*].

4.3

Enter MALCOLM *and* MACDUFF.

MALCOLM Let us seek out some desolate shade and there
Weep our sad bosoms empty.
MACDUFF   Let us rather
Hold fast the mortal° sword and like good men   deadly
Bestride our downfall birthdom.¹ Each new morn
5 New widows howl, new orphans cry, new sorrows
Strike heaven on the face, that° it resounds   so that
As if it felt with Scotland and yelled out
Like syllable of dolor.°   A similar cry of pain
MALCOLM   What I believe, I'll wail;
What know, believe; and what I can, redress;
10 As I shall find the time to friend,° I will.   favorable
What you have spoke, it may be so, perchance.
This tyrant, whose sole° name blisters our tongues,   mere

---

9. Though I know perfectly well your high rank (an
apology for bursting in).
1. *To fright . . . cruelty:* Even to frighten you by speaking of such danger is savage; actually to harm you

would be brutal ("fell") cruelty.
2. Such cruelty is already too near you.
4.3 Location: England, before King Edward's palace.
1. Stand in defense over our downfallen native land.

Was once thought honest. You have loved him well;
He hath not touched° you yet. I am young, but something   *injured*
15 You may deserve of him through me,[2] and wisdom°   *it's prudent*
To offer up a weak, poor, innocent lamb
T'appease an angry god.

MACDUFF   I am not treacherous.

MALCOLM   But Macbeth is.
A good and virtuous nature may recoil
20 In an imperial charge.[3] But I shall crave your pardon.
That which you are my thoughts cannot transpose;°   *transform*
Angels are bright still though the brightest° fell.   *(Lucifer)*
Though all things foul would wear the brows of grace,
Yet grace must still look so.[4]

MACDUFF   I have lost my hopes.[5]

25 MALCOLM   Perchance even there where I did find my doubts.[6]
Why in that rawness° left you wife and child,   *unprotected condition*
Those precious motives,° those strong knots of love,   *inducements to devotion*
Without leave-taking? I pray you,
Let not my jealousies° be your dishonors   *suspicions*
30 But mine own safeties.° You may be rightly just,   *safeguards*
Whatever I shall think.

MACDUFF   Bleed, bleed, poor country!
Great tyranny, lay thou thy basis° sure,   *foundation*
For goodness dare not check thee; wear thou thy wrongs,°   *wrongful gains*
The title is affeered.° —Fare thee well, lord.   *confirmed*
35 I would not be the villain that thou think'st
For the whole space that's in the tyrant's grasp
And the rich East to boot.°   *as well*

MALCOLM   Be not offended.
I speak not as in absolute fear° of you.   *complete distrust*
I think our country sinks beneath the yoke;
40 It weeps, it bleeds, and each new day a gash
Is added to her wounds. I think withal°   *nonetheless*
There would be hands uplifted in my right,
And here from gracious England° have I offer   *the King of England*
Of goodly thousands. But, for all this,
45 When I shall tread upon the tyrant's head
Or wear it on my sword, yet my poor country
Shall have more vices than it had before,
More suffer and more sundry° ways than ever,   *in more various*
By him that shall succeed.

MACDUFF   What° should he be?   *Who*

50 MALCOLM   It is myself I mean, in whom I know
All the particulars° of vice so grafted   *varieties*
That, when they shall be opened,° black Macbeth   *disclosed*
Will seem as pure as snow, and the poor state
Esteem him as a lamb, being compared
With my confineless° harms.   *infinite*

55 MACDUFF   Not in the legions
Of horrid hell can come a devil more damned

---

2. *I . . . me:* I am inexperienced, but you might gain favor with Macbeth by betraying me. *deserve:* F reads "discerne."
3. *recoil . . . charge:* give way to a royal command.
4. *Though . . . so:* Though everything evil disguises itself as virtue, virtue still looks like itself.
5. Hopes of Malcolm's help in a campaign against Macbeth.
6. Doubts of Macduff's loyalty, because he has left his wife and children.

In evils to top Macbeth.

MALCOLM   I grant him bloody,
Luxurious,° avaricious, false, deceitful,   *Lecherous*
Sudden,° malicious, smacking of every sin   *Violent*
60   That has a name. But there's no bottom, none,
In my voluptuousness: your wives, your daughters,
Your matrons, and your maids could not fill up
The cistern of my lust, and my desire
All continent° impediments would o'erbear   *restraining; chaste*
65   That did oppose my will. Better Macbeth
Than such an one to reign.

MACDUFF   Boundless intemperance
In nature° is a tyranny. It hath been   *human nature*
Th'untimely emptying of the happy throne
And fall of many kings. But fear not yet°   *nevertheless*
70   To take upon you what is yours. You may
Convey° your pleasures in a spacious plenty   *Manage secretly*
And yet seem cold;° the time° you may so hoodwink.°   *chaste / age / deceive*
We have willing dames enough. There cannot be
That vulture in you to devour so many
75   As will to greatness dedicate themselves,
Finding it so inclined.

MALCOLM   With this there grows
In my most ill-composed affection° such   *character*
A stanchless° avarice that, were I king,   *An insatiable*
I should cut off the nobles for their lands,
80   Desire his jewels and this other's house,
And my more-having would be as a sauce
To make me hunger more, that I should forge
Quarrels unjust against the good and loyal,
Destroying them for wealth.

MACDUFF   This avarice
85   Sticks deeper, grows with more pernicious root
Than summer-seeming[7] lust, and it hath been
The sword° of our slain kings. Yet do not fear;   *undoing*
Scotland hath foisons° to fill up your will   *plenty*
Of your mere own.[8] All these are portable,
90   With other graces weighed.[9]

MALCOLM   But I have none. The king-becoming graces—
As justice, verity, temp'rance, stableness,
Bounty, perseverance, mercy, lowliness,°   *humility*
Devotion, patience, courage, fortitude—
95   I have no relish° of them, but abound   *trace*
In the division° of each several° crime,   *variations / separate*
Acting it many ways. Nay, had I power, I should
Pour the sweet milk of concord into hell,
Uproar the universal peace, confound
All unity on earth.
100 MACDUFF   O Scotland, Scotland!

MALCOLM   If such a one be fit to govern, speak.
I am as I have spoken.

---

7. Appropriate to youth ("summer") but passing with age, unlike avarice; summerlike.
8. *Scotland . . . own:* Scotland is bountiful enough to satisfy your greed with your own royal property alone.
9. *All . . . weighed:* All the vices you have described are bearable, when counterbalanced with your other graces.

MACDUFF   Fit to govern?
No, not to live. O nation miserable,
With an untitled° tyrant, bloody-sceptered!   *a usurping*
105   When shalt thou see thy wholesome days again,
Since that the truest issue of thy throne
By his own interdiction° stands accused   *declaration of unfitness*
And does blaspheme his breed?° —Thy royal father   *disgrace his heritage*
Was a most sainted king; the queen that bore thee,
110   Oft'ner upon her knees than on her feet,
Died[1] every day she lived. Fare thee well.
These evils thou repeat'st upon thyself
Hath banished me from Scotland. —O my breast,
Thy hope ends here.
MALCOLM   Macduff, this noble passion,
115   Child of integrity, hath from my soul
Wiped the black scruples,° reconciled my thoughts   *dark suspicions*
To thy good truth and honor. Devilish Macbeth
By many of these trains° hath sought to win me   *stratagems*
Into his power, and modest wisdom° plucks me   *prudent moderation*
120   From over-credulous haste. But God above
Deal between thee and me. For even now
I put myself to thy direction and
Unspeak° mine own detraction, here abjure   *Retract*
The taints and blames I laid upon myself
125   For° strangers to my nature. I am yet   *As*
Unknown to woman, never was forsworn,
Scarcely have coveted what was mine own,
At no time broke my faith, would not betray
The devil to his fellow, and delight
130   No less in truth than life. My first false speaking
Was this upon myself. What I am truly
Is thine and my poor country's to command,
Whither, indeed, before thy here-approach,
Old Siward with ten thousand warlike men
135   Already at a point° was setting forth.   *prepared*
Now we'll together, and the chance of goodness
Be like our warranted quarrel.[2] Why are you silent?
MACDUFF   Such welcome and unwelcome things at once
'Tis hard to reconcile.
          Enter a[n English] DOCTOR.
140   MALCOLM   Well, more anon. [*to the* DOCTOR] Comes the King
forth, I pray you?
DOCTOR   Ay, sir. There are a crew of wretched souls
That stay° his cure. Their malady convinces   *await*
The great assay of art,[3] but at his touch—
Such sanctity hath heaven given his hand—
They presently amend.°   *heal*
145   MALCOLM   I thank you, Doctor. *Exit* [DOCTOR].
MACDUFF   What's the disease he means?
MALCOLM   'Tis called the Evil.[4]

---

1. Was dead to the world. ("By your rejoicing which I have in Christ Jesus our Lord, I die daily," 1 Corinthians 15:31.)
2. *the . . . quarrel:* may the chance of success be equal to the justice of our cause.
3. *convinces . . . art:* defeats the best efforts of medical skill.
4. "The king's evil," scrofula, thought to be cured by the royal touch.

A most miraculous work in this good King,
Which often since my here-remain in England
I have seen him do. How he solicits° heaven — moves by entreaty
150 Himself best knows; but strangely visited° people, — afflicted
All swoll'n and ulcerous, pitiful to the eye,
The mere° despair of surgery, he cures, — utter
Hanging a golden stamp° about their necks, — coin
Put on with holy prayers; and, 'tis spoken,
155 To the succeeding royalty he leaves
The healing benediction. With this strange virtue,° — power
He hath a heavenly gift of prophecy,
And sundry blessings hang about his throne
That speak him full of grace.° — divine grace

        Enter ROSS.

MACDUFF   See who comes here.
160 MALCOLM   My countryman, but yet I know° him not. — recognize
MACDUFF   My ever gentle cousin, welcome hither.
MALCOLM   I know him now. Good God, betimes° remove — quickly
     The means that makes us strangers.
ROSS   Sir, amen.
MACDUFF   Stands Scotland where it did?
ROSS   Alas, poor country,
165 Almost afraid to know itself. It cannot
Be called our mother, but our grave, where nothing
But who knows nothing is once seen to smile;[5]
Where sighs and groans and shrieks that rend the air
Are made, not marked;° where violent sorrow seems — noticed
170 A modern ecstasy.° The dead man's knell — commonplace emotion
Is there scarce asked for who,[6] and good men's lives
Expire before the flowers in their caps,
Dying or ere° they sicken. — before
MACDUFF   Oh, relation° — report
     Too nice° and yet too true! — detailed
MALCOLM   What's the newest grief?
175 ROSS   That of an hour's age doth hiss the speaker;[7]
     Each minute teems° a new one. — yields
MACDUFF   How does my wife?
ROSS   Why, well.
MACDUFF   And all my children?
ROSS   Well too.
MACDUFF   The tyrant has not battered at their peace?
ROSS   No, they were well at peace when I did leave 'em.
180 MACDUFF   Be not a niggard of your speech. How goes't?
ROSS   When I came hither to transport the tidings
Which I have heavily° borne, there ran a rumor — gravely
Of many worthy fellows that were out,[8]
Which was to my belief witnessed the rather° — made more credible
185 For that I saw the tyrant's power° afoot. — army
Now is the time of° help. [*to* MALCOLM] Your eye in Scotland — moment for
Would create soldiers, make our women fight
To doff° their dire distresses. — remove
MALCOLM   Be't their comfort

---

5. No one smiles except he who knows nothing.
6. Scarcely anyone asks for whom it is rung.
7. Cause the speaker to be hissed for telling old news.
8. Out in the field, in arms to rebel.

We are coming thither. Gracious England hath
190 Lent us good Siward and ten thousand men—
An older and a better soldier none°   *there is none*
That Christendom gives out.°   *proclaims; provides*

ROSS   Would I could answer
This comfort with the like. But I have words
That would be howled out in the desert air,
Where hearing should not latch° them.   *catch*

195 MACDUFF   What concern they?
The general cause, or is it a fee-grief°   *private woe*
Due to° some single breast?   *Owned by*

ROSS   No mind that's honest
But in it shares some woe, though the main part
Pertains to you alone.

MACDUFF   If it be mine,
200 Keep it not from me; quickly let me have it.

ROSS   Let not your ears despise my tongue forever,
Which shall possess them with the heaviest sound
That ever yet they heard.

MACDUFF   Hum—I guess at it.

ROSS   Your castle is surprised, your wife and babes
205 Savagely slaughtered. To relate the manner
Were, on the quarry of these murdered deer,
To add the death of you.[9]

MALCOLM   Merciful heaven!
What, man, ne'er pull your hat upon your brows.°   *conceal your grief*
Give sorrow words. The grief that does not speak
210 Whispers the o'er-fraught° heart and bids it break.   *overburdened*

MACDUFF   My children too?

ROSS   Wife, children, servants—
All that could be found.

MACDUFF   And I must be° from thence?   *had to be*
My wife killed too?

ROSS   I have said.

MALCOLM   Be comforted.
Let's make us med'cines of our great revenge
215 To cure this deadly grief.

MACDUFF   He has no children. All my pretty ones?
Did you say all? Oh, hell-kite! All?
What, all my pretty chickens and their dam
At one fell swoop?

MALCOLM   Dispute° it like a man.   *Fight*

220 MACDUFF   I shall do so.
But I must also feel it as a man.
I cannot but remember such things were
That were most precious to me. Did heaven look on
And would not take their part? Sinful Macduff,
225 They were all struck for° thee. Naught° that I am,   *on account of / Wicked*
Not for their own demerits but for mine
Fell slaughter on their souls. Heaven rest them now.

MALCOLM   Be this the whetstone of your sword. Let grief
Convert° to anger; blunt not the heart, enrage it.   *Be changed*

---

9. To tell how they were murdered would be to add
your death to the heap of slaughtered game ("quarry").
PERFORMANCE COMMENT In performance Ross's
reluctant delivery of the news about Macduff's wife
and children involves several interpretive questions
for directors, beginning with why Ross initially lies
when asked about the family. See Digital Edition
PC 7.

230 MACDUFF   Oh, I could play the woman with mine eyes
     And braggart with my tongue. But, gentle heavens,
     Cut short all intermission.° Front to front°   *delay / Face-to-face*
     Bring thou this fiend of Scotland and myself.
     Within my sword's length set him. If he scape,
     Heaven forgive him too.
235 MALCOLM   This tune goes manly.
     Come, go we to the King. Our power° is ready;   *army*
     Our lack is nothing but our leave.[1] Macbeth
     Is ripe for shaking, and the powers above
     Put on their instruments.[2] Receive what cheer you may;
240 The night is long that never finds the day.   *Exeunt.*

5.1

Enter a DOCTOR OF PHYSIC° *and a waiting*   *Physician*
GENTLEWOMAN.

DOCTOR OF PHYSIC   I have two nights watched with you but can
     perceive no truth in your report. When was it she last walked?
GENTLEWOMAN   Since his majesty went into the field,° I have   *battlefield*
     seen her rise from her bed, throw her nightgown upon her,
5   unlock her closet,° take forth paper, fold it, write upon't, read   *chest*
     it, afterwards seal it, and again return to bed, yet all this
     while in a most fast sleep.
DOCTOR OF PHYSIC   A great perturbation in nature, to receive at
     once the benefit of sleep and do the effects of watching.° In   *act as if awake*
10   this slumbery agitation,° besides her walking and other actual°   *movement / active*
     performances, what at any time have you heard her say?
GENTLEWOMAN   That, sir, which I will not report after her.
DOCTOR OF PHYSIC   You may to me, and 'tis most meet° you should.   *proper*
GENTLEWOMAN   Neither to you nor anyone, having no witness
15   to confirm my speech.
        Enter LADY MACBETH *with a taper.*
     Lo, you, here she comes. This is her very guise° and, upon   *exact habit*
     my life, fast asleep. Observe her; stand close.°   *concealed*
DOCTOR OF PHYSIC   How came she by that light?
GENTLEWOMAN   Why, it stood by her. She has light by her
20   continually; 'tis her command.
DOCTOR OF PHYSIC   You see her eyes are open.
GENTLEWOMAN   Ay, but their sense are shut.
DOCTOR OF PHYSIC   What is it she does now? Look how she
     rubs her hands.
25 GENTLEWOMAN   It is an accustomed action with her to seem
     thus washing her hands. I have known her continue in this
     a quarter of an hour.
LADY MACBETH   Yet here's a spot.
DOCTOR OF PHYSIC   Hark, she speaks. I will set down what
30   comes from her to satisfy° my remembrance the more strongly.   *support*
LADY MACBETH   Out, damned spot! Out, I say! One, two, why,
     then, 'tis time to do't. Hell is murky. Fie, my lord, fie, a sol-
     dier and afeard? What need we fear? Who knows it when
     none can call our power to account? Yet who would have
35   thought the old man to have had so much blood in him?

---

1. We have only to take leave of the King.
2. Arm themselves; set us to work as their agents.

5.1 Location: Macbeth's castle in Dunsinane.

DOCTOR OF PHYSIC   Do you mark that?

LADY MACBETH   The Thane of Fife had a wife. Where is she
   now? What, will these hands ne'er be clean? No more o'that,
   my lord, no more o'that. You mar all with this starting.°   *startled movement*
40 DOCTOR OF PHYSIC   Go to, go to.° You have known what you   *(expression of reproof)*
   should not.

GENTLEWOMAN   She has spoke what she should not, I am sure
   of that. Heaven knows what she has known.

LADY MACBETH   Here's the smell of the blood still. All the per-
45   fumes of Arabia will not sweeten this little hand. Oh, oh, oh!

DOCTOR OF PHYSIC   What a sigh is there! The heart is sorely
   charged.°   *burdened*

GENTLEWOMAN   I would not have such a heart in my bosom
   for the dignity° of the whole body.   *high rank (as Queen)*

50 DOCTOR OF PHYSIC   Well, well, well.

GENTLEWOMAN   Pray God it be, sir.

DOCTOR OF PHYSIC   This disease is beyond my practice.° Yet I   *skill*
   have known those which have walked in their sleep who
   have died holily in their beds.

55 LADY MACBETH   Wash your hands, put on your nightgown,
   look not so pale. I tell you yet again, Banquo's buried; he
   cannot come out on 's° grave.   *of his*

DOCTOR OF PHYSIC   Even so?

LADY MACBETH   To bed, to bed. There's knocking at the gate.
60   Come, come, come, come, give me your hand. What's done
   cannot be undone. To bed, to bed, to bed.   *Exit.*

DOCTOR OF PHYSIC   Will she go now to bed?

GENTLEWOMAN   Directly.

DOCTOR OF PHYSIC   Foul whisp'rings are abroad. Unnatural
   deeds
65 Do breed unnatural troubles. Infected minds
To their deaf pillows will discharge their secrets.
More needs she the divine° than the physician.   *priest*
God, God, forgive us all. Look after her;
Remove from her the means of all annoyance,°   *self-injury*
70 And still keep eyes upon her. So, good night.
My mind she has mated,° and amazed my sight.   *bewildered*
I think but dare not speak.

GENTLEWOMAN   Good night, good Doctor. *Exeunt.*

5.2

Drum and colors.° Enter MENTEITH, CAITHNESS,   *flag-bearers*
   ANGUS, LENNOX, *Soldiers.*

MENTEITH   The English power is near, led on by Malcolm,
   His uncle Siward, and the good Macduff.
   Revenges burn in them, for their dear causes
   Would to the bleeding° and the grim alarm°   *bloody / call to battle*
   Excite° the mortified° man.   *Rouse / insensible; dead*

5 ANGUS   Near Birnam Wood
   Shall we well° meet them; that way are they coming.   *doubtless*

CAITHNESS   Who knows if Donaldbain be with his brother?

LENNOX   For certain, sir, he is not. I have a file°   *roster*
   Of all the gentry. There is Siward's son

5.2 Location: The country near Dunsinane.

10 And many unrough° youths that even now   *beardless*
    Protest their first of manhood.[1]

MENTEITH   What does the tyrant?

CAITHNESS   Great Dunsinane he strongly fortifies.
    Some say he's mad; others that lesser hate him
    Do call it valiant fury, but for certain

15   He cannot buckle his distempered° cause   *disease-swollen*
    Within the belt° of rule.   *restraint*

ANGUS   Now does he feel
    His secret murders sticking on his hands;
    Now minutely° revolts upbraid his faith-breach.   *every minute*
    Those he commands move only in command,°   *under constraint*

20   Nothing in love. Now does he feel his title
    Hang loose about him, like a giant's robe
    Upon a dwarfish thief.

MENTEITH   Who then shall blame
    His pestered° senses to recoil and start,   *tormented*
    When all that is within him does condemn
    Itself for being there?

25 CAITHNESS   Well, march we on
    To give obedience where 'tis truly owed.
    Meet we the med'cine° of the sickly weal,°   *(Malcolm) / state*
    And with him pour we in our country's purge
    Each drop of us.

LENNOX   Or so much as it needs
30   To dew° the sovereign° flower and drown the weeds.   *bedew / royal; curative*
    Make we our march towards Birnam.   *Exeunt, marching.*

5.3

Enter MACBETH, DOCTOR [OF PHYSIC], *and Attendants.*

MACBETH   Bring me no more reports. Let them fly all.°   *Let all thanes desert*
    Till Birnam Wood remove to Dunsinane
    I cannot taint° with fear. What's the boy Malcolm?   *be infected*
    Was he not born of woman? The spirits that know
5   All mortal consequences° have pronounced me thus: *human destinies*
    "Fear not, Macbeth. No man that's born of woman
    Shall e'er have power upon thee." Then fly, false thanes,
    And mingle with the English epicures![1]
    The mind I sway° by and the heart I bear   *rule myself*
10   Shall never sag with doubt nor shake with fear.

    Enter SERVANT.

    The devil damn thee black, thou cream-faced loon!°   *rogue*
    Where gott'st thou that goose look?

SERVANT   There is ten thousand—

MACBETH   Geese, villain?

SERVANT   Soldiers, sir.

MACBETH   Go prick thy face and over-red thy fear,[2]
15   Thou lily-livered[3] boy. What soldiers, patch?°   *fool*
    Death of° thy soul! Those linen cheeks of thine   *on*
    Are counselors to fear.° What soldiers, whey-face?   *Teach others to fear*

SERVANT   The English force, so please you.

---

1. Declare for the first time that they are men.
5.3 Location: Macbeth's castle in Dunsinane.
1. Lovers of easy, luxurious living.

2. Redden your fearful pallor.
3. Lacking blood in your liver (thought to be the seat of courage); cowardly.

MACBETH   Take thy face hence.   [*Exit* SERVANT.]
                                  —Seyton! —I am sick at heart,
20 When I behold —Seyton, I say! —This push°   crisis
    Will cheer⁴ me ever or disseat° me now.   dethrone
    I have lived long enough. My way of life
    Is fall'n into the sere,° the yellow leaf,   withered
    And that which should accompany old age,
25 As° honor, love, obedience, troops of friends,   Such as
    I must not look to have, but in their stead
    Curses, not loud but deep, mouth-honor,° breath,   lip service
    Which the poor heart would fain deny and dare not.
    —Seyton!
          Enter SEYTON.
SEYTON   What's your gracious pleasure?
30 MACBETH   What news more?
SEYTON   All is confirmed, my lord, which was reported.
MACBETH   I'll fight till from my bones my flesh be hacked.
    Give me my armor.
SEYTON   'Tis not needed yet.
MACBETH   I'll put it on.
35 Send out more horses, skirr° the country round,   scour
    Hang those that talk of fear. Give me mine armor.
    —How does your patient, Doctor?
DOCTOR OF PHYSIC   Not so sick, my lord,
    As she is troubled with thick-coming fancies
    That keep her from her rest.
MACBETH   Cure her of that.
40 Canst thou not minister to a mind diseased,
    Pluck from the memory a rooted sorrow,
    Raze out the written troubles of⁵ the brain,
    And with some sweet oblivious° antidote   causing forgetfulness
    Cleanse the stuffed bosom of that perilous stuff
    Which weighs upon the heart?
45 DOCTOR OF PHYSIC   Therein the patient
    Must minister to himself.
MACBETH   Throw physic° to the dogs! I'll none of it.   medicine
    —Come, put mine armor on; give me my staff.°   lance
    —Seyton, send out. —Doctor, the thanes fly from me.
50 —Come, sir, dispatch.° —If thou couldst, Doctor, cast   hurry
    The water⁶ of my land, find her disease,
    And purge it to a sound and pristine health,
    I would applaud thee to the very echo
    That should applaud again. —Pull't off, I say.⁷
55 —What rhubarb, senna,° or what purgative drug   (medicinal plant)
    Would scour° these English hence? Hear'st thou of them?   purge
DOCTOR OF PHYSIC   Ay, my good lord. Your royal preparation
    Makes us hear something.
MACBETH   —Bring it⁸ after me.
    I will not be afraid of death and bane°   destruction

---

4. Comfort; enthrone or establish (punning on "cheer/ chair").
5. Erase the troubles engraved in.
6. *cast / The water*: analyze the urine as a method of diagnosis.
7. A piece of armor is not properly fitted; Macbeth orders the attendant to take it off.
8. The armor not yet on Macbeth.

60   Till Birnam forest come to Dunsinane.
                    Exeunt [all but the DOCTOR OF PHYSIC].
DOCTOR OF PHYSIC   Were I from Dunsinane away and clear,
    Profit again should hardly draw me here.⁹   [*Exit.*]

5.4

Drum and colors. Enter MALCOLM, SIWARD, MACDUFF,
YOUNG SIWARD, MENTEITH, CAITHNESS, ANGUS, *and*
SOLDIERS, *marching.*

MALCOLM   Cousins, I hope the days are near at hand
    That chambers° will be safe.   bedrooms
MENTEITH   We doubt it nothing.°   not at all
SIWARD   What wood is this before us?
MENTEITH   The Wood of Birnam.
MALCOLM   Let every soldier hew him down a bough
5   And bear't before him. Thereby shall we shadow°   conceal
    The numbers of our host and make discovery°   reconnaissance
    Err in report of us.
SOLDIER   It shall be done.
SIWARD   We learn no other but the confident tyrant
    Keeps still in Dunsinane and will endure
    Our setting down before't.°   laying siege to it
10   MALCOLM   'Tis his main hope.
    For where there is advantage to be given,¹
    Both more and less° have given him the revolt,   great and lowly
    And none serve with him but constrainèd things
    Whose hearts are absent too.
MACDUFF   Let our just censures
15   Attend the true event,² and put we on
    Industrious soldiership.
SIWARD   The time approaches
    That will with due decision make us know
    What we shall say we have and what we owe.
    Thoughts speculative their unsure hopes relate,
20   But certain issue strokes must arbitrate³—
    Towards which, advance the war.   *Exeunt, marching.*

5.5

Enter MACBETH, SEYTON, *and* SOLDIERS, *with drum
and colors.*

MACBETH   Hang out our banners on the outward walls.
    The cry is still, "They come!" Our castle's strength
    Will laugh a siege to scorn. Here let them lie
    Till famine and the ague° eat them up.   fever
5   Were they not forced° with those that should be ours,   reinforced
    We might have met them dareful,° beard to beard,   boldly
    And beat them backward home.
        A cry within of women.
                    What is that noise?

---

9. No large fees could lure me back.
5.4 Location: The country near Birnam Wood.
1. Where the opportunity presents itself.
2. *Let . . . event:* Let our judgments await the actual
outcome.

3. *Thoughts . . . arbitrate:* Speculation produces hopes
and unconfirmed optimism, but the issue will only be
decided by action.
5.5 Location: Macbeth's castle.

SEYTON   It is the cry of women, my good lord.   [*Exit.*]

MACBETH   I have almost forgot the taste of fears.

10 The time has been my senses would have cooled°   *been chilled with terror*
To hear a night-shriek, and my fell of hair°   *hair on my skin*
Would at a dismal treatise° rouse and stir   *story*
As life were in't. I have supped full with horrors.
Direness, familiar to my slaughterous thoughts,
Cannot once start° me.   *startle*
              [*Re-enter* SEYTON.]

15   Wherefore was that cry?

SEYTON   The Queen, my lord, is dead.

MACBETH   She should have died hereafter;[1]
There would have been a time for such a word.
Tomorrow and tomorrow and tomorrow

20 Creeps in this petty pace from day to day
To the last syllable of recorded time,
And all our yesterdays have lighted fools
The way to dusty death. Out, out, brief candle.
Life's but a walking shadow, a poor player

25 That struts and frets his hour upon the stage
And then is heard no more. It is a tale
Told by an idiot, full of sound and fury,
Signifying nothing.
              Enter a MESSENGER.
Thou com'st to use thy tongue; thy story quickly.

30 MESSENGER   Gracious my lord,
I should report that which I say I saw,
But know not how to do't.

MACBETH   Well, say, sir.

MESSENGER   As I did stand my watch upon the hill,
I looked toward Birnam, and anon methought
The wood began to move.

35 MACBETH   Liar and slave!

MESSENGER   Let me endure your wrath if't be not so.
Within this three mile may you see it coming,
I say, a moving grove.

MACBETH   If thou speak'st false,
Upon the next tree shalt thou hang alive

40 Till famine cling° thee; if thy speech be sooth,°   *wither / truth*
I care not if thou dost for me as much.
I pull in° resolution and begin   *rein in*
To doubt th'equivocation of the fiend
That lies like truth. "Fear not, till Birnam Wood

45 Do come to Dunsinane"—and now a wood
Comes toward Dunsinane. Arm, arm, and out!
If this which he avouches does appear,
There is nor flying hence nor tarrying here.
I 'gin to be aweary of the sun,

50 And wish th'estate° o'th' world were now undone.   *ordered structure*
Ring the alarum bell! Blow, wind, come, wrack!°   *ruin*
At least we'll die with harness° on our back.   *Exeunt.* *armor*

---

1. She would certainly have died someday; she should have died at another, more peaceful time.

5.6

Drum and colors. Enter MALCOLM, SIWARD, MACDUFF,
and their army, with boughs.

MALCOLM   Now near enough. Your leafy screens throw down
And show° like those you are. You, worthy uncle,   appear
Shall with my cousin, your right noble son,
Lead our first battle.° Worthy Macduff and we   battalion
5   Shall take upon's what else remains to do,
According to our order.°   battle plan
SIWARD   Fare you well.
Do we but find the tyrant's power° tonight,   army
Let us be beaten if we cannot fight.
MACDUFF   Make all our trumpets speak. Give them all breath,
10   Those clamorous harbingers of blood and death!

> *Exeunt. Alarums continued.*

5.7

Enter MACBETH.

MACBETH   They have tied me to a stake. I cannot fly,
But bearlike I must fight the course.[1] What's he
That was not born of woman? Such a one
Am I to fear, or none.

> *Enter* YOUNG SIWARD.

YOUNG SIWARD   What is thy name?
5   MACBETH   Thou'lt be afraid to hear it.
YOUNG SIWARD   No, though thou call'st thyself a hotter name
Than any is in hell.
MACBETH   My name's Macbeth.
YOUNG SIWARD   The devil himself could not pronounce a title
More hateful to mine ear.
MACBETH   No, nor more fearful.
10   YOUNG SIWARD   Thou liest, abhorrèd tyrant! With my sword
I'll prove the lie thou speak'st.

> *Fight, and* YOUNG SIWARD *slain.*

MACBETH   Thou wast born of woman.
But swords I smile at, weapons laugh to scorn,
Brandished by man that's of a woman born.

> *Exit [with the body].*

> *Alarums. Enter* MACDUFF.

15   MACDUFF   That way the noise is. Tyrant, show thy face!
If thou beest slain and with° no stroke of mine,   by
My wife and children's ghosts will haunt me still.°   always
I cannot strike at wretched kerns,° whose arms   Irish foot soldiers
Are hired to bear their staves.° Either thou, Macbeth,   spears
20   Or else my sword with an unbattered edge
I sheathe again, undeeded.[2] There thou shouldst be;
By this great clatter one of greatest note
Seems bruited.° Let me find him, Fortune,   announced
And more I beg not.
> *Exit. Alarums.*

> *Enter* MALCOLM *and* SIWARD.

25   SIWARD   This way, my lord. The castle's gently rendered.°   surrendered

---

5.6 Location: Scene continues.
5.7 Location: Scene continues.
1. Referring to the practice of bearbaiting, in which a

bear was tied to a stake and set upon by dogs. *course:*
round of bearbaiting.
2. Having accomplished no deeds.

The tyrant's people on both sides do fight;
The noble thanes do bravely in the war;
The day almost itself professes yours,
And little is to do.

MALCOLM We have met with foes
That strike beside us.[3]

30 SIWARD Enter, sir, the castle. *Exeunt. Alarums.*

Enter MACBETH.

MACBETH Why should I play the Roman fool° and die   *the suicide*
On mine own sword? Whiles I see lives, the gashes
Do better upon them.

Enter MACDUFF.

MACDUFF Turn, hellhound, turn!

MACBETH Of all men else I have avoided thee.
35 But get thee back. My soul is too much charged
With blood of thine already.

MACDUFF I have no words.
My voice is in my sword, thou bloodier villain
Than terms can give thee out!°   *words can describe*

Fight. Alarums.

MACBETH Thou losest labor.°   *waste effort*
As easy mayst thou the intrenchant° air   *incapable of being cut*
40 With thy keen sword impress° as make me bleed.   *mark*
Let fall thy blade on vulnerable crests.
I bear a charmèd life which must not yield
To one of woman born.

MACDUFF Despair° thy charm,   *Despair of*
And let the angel° whom thou still hast served   *(evil) spirit*
45 Tell thee, Macduff was from his mother's womb
Untimely° ripped.   *Prematurely*

MACBETH Accursèd be that tongue that tells me so,
For it hath cowed° my better part of man.   *intimidated*
And be these juggling fiends no more believed,
50 That palter° with us in a double sense,   *equivocate*
That keep the word of promise to our ear
And break it to our hope. I'll not fight with thee.

MACDUFF Then yield thee, coward,
And live to be the show and gaze° o'th' time.   *spectacle*
55 We'll have thee, as our rarer monsters° are,   *prodigies*
Painted upon a pole[4] and underwrit,
"Here may you see the tyrant."

MACBETH I will not yield,
To kiss the ground before young Malcolm's feet,
And to be baited° with the rabble's curse.   *harassed*
60 Though Birnam Wood be come to Dunsinane,
And thou opposed, being of no woman born,
Yet I will try the last.° Before my body   *last resort*
I throw my warlike shield. Lay on, Macduff,
And damned be him that first cries, "Hold, enough!"

Exeunt fighting. Alarums.

---

3. Fight on our side; deliberately miss us.
4. Painted on a cloth or board supported by a pole as a form of advertisement.

Enter [MACBETH *and* MACDUFF] *fighting, and*
MACBETH *slain.*[5]

[*Exit* MACDUFF *with Macbeth's body.*]
Retreat[6] *and flourish. Enter, with drum and colors,*
MALCOLM, SIWARD, ROSS, *Thanes, and* SOLDIERS.

65 MALCOLM   I would° the friends we miss were safe arrived.   wish
SIWARD   Some must go off;° and yet, by these[7] I see   die
So great a day as this is cheaply bought.
MALCOLM   Macduff is missing, and your noble son.
ROSS   Your son, my lord, has paid a soldier's debt.
70 He only lived but till he was a man,
The which no sooner had his prowess confirmed
In the unshrinking station[8] where he fought,
But like a man he died.
SIWARD   Then he is dead?
ROSS   Ay, and brought off the field. Your cause of sorrow
75 Must not be measured by his worth, for then
It hath no end.
SIWARD   Had he his hurts before?°   on his front
ROSS   Ay, on the front.
SIWARD   Why, then, God's soldier be he.
Had I as many sons as I have hairs,
I would not wish them to a fairer death.
And so, his knell is knolled.
80 MALCOLM   He's worth more sorrow,
And that I'll spend for him.
SIWARD   He's worth no more.
They say he parted° well and paid his score,   departed
And so, God be with him. Here comes newer comfort.
Enter MACDUFF *with Macbeth's head.*
MACDUFF   Hail, King, for so thou art. Behold where stands[9]
85 Th'usurper's cursèd head. The time is free.°   free from tyranny
I see thee compassed with thy kingdom's pearl,[1]
That speak my salutation in their minds,
Whose voices I desire aloud with mine:
Hail, King of Scotland!
ALL   Hail, King of Scotland!
Flourish.
90 MALCOLM   We shall not spend a large expense of time
Before we reckon with° your several loves   make an accounting of
And make us even with you.° My thanes and kinsmen,   reward your loyalty
Henceforth be earls, the first that ever Scotland
In such an honor named. What's more to do,
95 Which would be planted newly with the time,[2]
As calling home our exiled friends abroad
That fled the snares of watchful tyranny,
Producing forth[3] the cruel ministers°   agents
Of this dead butcher and his fiend-like queen—
100 Who, as 'tis thought, by self and violent hands°   her own violent hands

---

5. TEXTUAL COMMENT F's stage directions for the fight between Macbeth and Macduff can be interpreted in different ways, with implications for the play's dramatic structure. For more on this issue, see Digital Edition TC 10.
6. A trumpet call signaling the end of the battle.
7. To judge from those who are present.
8. Post from which he did not shrink.
9. Presumably upon a pole or lance.
1. I see you surrounded by your nobles, here called the "pearl" of the kingdom.
2. Which should be performed at the beginning of this new era.
3. Bringing forward for trial.

Took off her life—this, and what needful else
That calls upon us, by the grace of grace,
We will perform in measure, time, and place.[4]
So, thanks to all at once and to each one
105 Whom we invite to see us crowned at Scone.

Flourish. Exeunt all.

4. In due order, at the proper time and place.

Antony and Cleopatra

What if Shakespeare had had second thoughts about *Romeo and Juliet*? He might have tried something different. In this version, the lovers, neither youthful nor married to each other, conduct a long-standing, adulterous relationship. Romeo, thinking Juliet dead because she has sent a messenger with that lie, kills himself—though with a sword rather than poison. He partly bungles the job, however, and hence takes a while to expire. Juliet resolves to follow suit but delays for the entire fifth act before killing herself—though with poison rather than a sword. And when they are both finally dead, the audience may be less likely to lament the loss of "star-crossed lovers" than celebrate the fulfillment of heroic passion.

Shakespeare did have second thoughts about *Romeo and Juliet;* he called these second thoughts *Antony and Cleopatra* (1606–early 1607). The last of Shakespeare's three love tragedies, the play also rewrites *Othello,* the middle work of this group, converting its threat from the East, there represented by Turks, into both threat and opportunity from the East, here represented by Egyptians. All three tragedies set their domestic concerns thematically against the backdrop of bloody political conflict, but formally against the expectations of romantic comedy. All three seem like derailed comedies. But *Antony and Cleopatra* replaces the emphasis on youth of romantic comedy, of *Romeo and Juliet,* and even of Desdemona in *Othello,* with the most complex portrayal of mature love in Shakespeare's dramatic career.

In the romantic comedies, problem plays, and romances, the female protagonist often dominates the scene. But in the tragedies that Shakespeare composed from roughly 1599 to 1608, *Antony and Cleopatra* is the only such candidate. Moreover, following a series of tragedies—*Hamlet, Othello, King Lear,* and *Macbeth*—in which the protagonist's psychology is consistently probed, *Antony and Cleopatra* almost completely avoids soliloquy. Antony's and Cleopatra's motives often remain opaque—arguably, even to themselves. We never learn why Antony thinks marriage to Octavia will solve his political problems, why Cleopatra flees at Actium, why she negotiates with Caesar in the last act. Instead of self-revelation, the play offers contradictory framing commentary by minor figures, who try to rein in their masters with a mix of praise and ridicule, usually without success, and who are accordingly victims of Antony's and Cleopatra's tragic extravagance. These external perspectives help impart an epic feel, as do the geographical and scenic shifts, which also produce a loose, fragmentary, and capacious structure alien to classically inspired notions of dramatic form. *Antony and Cleopatra* is thus a new kind of tragedy. Its restlessness is of a piece with that of *Pericles,* perhaps the next play Shakespeare wrote and the first of his late romances. And the intimations of transcendence with which *Antony and Cleopatra* ends point toward the magical or supernatural resolutions of the romances more generally.

The play may also be compared to Shakespeare's other Roman tragedies, *Julius Caesar* and *Coriolanus.* All are based on Thomas North's translation of *Plutarch's Lives of the Noble Grecians and Romans* (1579)—Shakespeare's favorite source, with the exception of Raphael Holinshed's *Chronicles of England, Scotland, and Ireland,* and one that he follows closely here. All three plays rely heavily on blank verse while almost entirely avoiding rhyme, though in *Antony and Cleopatra* (and *Coriolanus*) the heavy use of enjambment imparts a naturalistic, sometimes even colloquial, feel to poetic dialogue. Still, the use of blank verse for serious subjects is introduced into English by the Earl of Surrey's sixteenth-century translation of part of the *Aeneid* (19 B.C.E.), Virgil's epic of

Octavius Caesar, later known as Augustus, as on this medal. From Guillaume Du Choul, *Discours de la Religion des Anciens Romains* (1567 ed.).

the legendary founding of Rome, itself understood in the poet's own day as an allegory of the city-state's bloody transition from republic (rule by senatorial aristocracy) to empire (monarchical power).

It is this transition that Shakespeare dramatizes in *Julius Caesar* and *Antony and Cleopatra*. Chronologically, *Antony* picks up where *Julius Caesar* leaves off. That earlier play focuses on Caesar's assassination by republicans, led by Brutus and Cassius, and the assassins' subsequent defeat at the hands of Mark Antony (Caesar's lieutenant) and Octavius Caesar (Caesar's young grandnephew and adoptive son). *Antony and Cleopatra*, which covers the period from 40 to 30 B.C.E., completes the narrative of Roman civil war and the final destruction of the Republic. The Mediterranean's dominant military power, Rome is ruled by the triumvirate of Lepidus, Octavius Caesar, and Mark Antony, who govern, respectively, the Mediterranean portions of Africa, Europe, and Asia. Accordingly, *Antony and Cleopatra* turns away from *Julius Caesar*'s emphasis on Rome's internal political system, looking instead to its imperial domains. The stylistic restraint befitting Brutus's republican austerity yields to hyperbolic verse corresponding to the Empire's grandeur. This would seem the theater for legendary, even mythic, performance: Antony is associated with Hercules, and Antony and Cleopatra with Mars and Venus.

Yet *Antony and Cleopatra* investigates the possibility of such performance in a postheroic world. It offers an epic view of the political arena but deprives that arena of heroic significance. Mark Antony and Octavius Caesar contend for political supremacy, but the love between Antony and Cleopatra occupies center stage. The work then asks whether heroism can be transplanted to the private terrain of love. Much of the play's fascination arises from this intertwining of empire and sexuality. Plutarch and other classical writers were preoccupied with what for them was the opposition between the virtue of the conquering West and the luxury of the subjugated East. This understanding of empire re-emerged in the Renaissance during a new era of Western expansion, marked by an increasingly racialized and still-sexualized view of non-European peoples. Just months before the probable first performance of the play, King James authorized the establishment of an English colony in North America—an undertaking that resulted in the founding of Jamestown the following year. As in other Western European countries at the time, Rome was the central model of empire. The view of Egypt was more mixed: preeminent source of ancient wisdom, it threatened to transmit its decadence to the victors, even though Rome had defeated it.

Accordingly, *Antony and Cleopatra* elicits complicated judgments. Rendering this complexity has often proven difficult in performance. Long supplanted on the stage by John Dryden's *All for Love* (1678), which recasts Shakespeare's story as a tragedy of private life, the play came into its own only after 1800 in the heyday of the British Empire, with Cleopatra embodying Oriental sexual vice. The text seems to justify this interpretation: Rome is contrasted to Egypt, West to East, the conquerors to the conquered. Rapid shifts of scene across enormous distances accentuate this division. A sober, masculine military ethos opposes a frivolous, feminized, sexualized court. Opportunism drives Antony's marriage to Octavia, while love and sexual desire drive his relationship with Cleopatra; he chooses between fidelity to a chaste, white wife and adultery with a promiscuous, "tawny," "black" seductress (1.1.6, 1.5.28). That seductress has a smaller political role than in Plutarch. Though Cleopatra's political maneuvering remains considerable, this change accentuates the basic conflict. Where Caesar follows rational self-interest (he is the "universal landlord," 3.13.72), Antony revels in extravagant generosity and challenges Caesar to one-on-one combat. Young Caesar is a bureaucrat of the future, old Antony a warrior of the past. Caesar's concerns are public, Antony's private. Antony is guilty by association with his brother and his previous wife, Fulvia, who attack Caesar. By contrast, Caesar promises that "The time of universal peace is near" (4.6.5), an assertion that anticipates the Pax Romana (Roman Peace) he instituted throughout the Empire and the birth of Christ in a Roman province during his rule.

Yet the play seems to create such dichotomies only to undermine them. Antony boasts of his valor at Philippi, while Caesar "alone / Dealt on lieutenantry" (battled exclusively through his officers; 3.11.38–39). Earlier, however, Antony's "officer" Ventidius remarks, "Caesar and Antony have ever won / More in their officer than person" (3.1.16–17). Caesar's promise of "universal peace" is anticipated in a version of Christ's Last Supper that Antony shares with his followers:

> Tend me tonight.
> May be it is the period of your duty.
> Haply you shall not see me more, or if,
> A mangled shadow. Perchance tomorrow
> You'll serve another master.
> (4.2.24–28)

Enobarbus, who functions like a skeptical chorus, criticizes Antony for moving his friends to tears. But that skepticism is itself challenged. It leads Enobarbus to become a Judas figure who betrays his master by defecting to Caesar and who dies shortly thereafter, his heart broken by Antony's generosity.

Even the geographical contrast of the play partly dissolves into parallelisms: Roman war is eroticized, Egyptian love militarized. The external representation of the lovers' relationship, the absence of scenes of them alone, and their pride in exhibiting their affair intensify the feeling that love and war influence each other, that there is no distinction between public and private. Furthermore, love is on both sides of the divide, albeit with a difference. When the work opens, Antony's neglect of military command is criticized as "this dotage of our general's" (1.1.1) by Philo (a name that means "love in friendship"), a figure invented by Shakespeare. Late in the play, Antony, focused exclusively on Cleopatra, is heroically preceded in suicide by his aptly named servant Eros (romantic love), a figure from Plutarch.

The eroticization of Rome also takes the form of powerful feelings directed toward Antony. Octavius Caesar at times acts almost as if he were the son—rather than grandnephew and adopted son—of Cleopatra's former lover, Julius Caesar, whose paternal role Antony has usurped. Caesar is disgusted by Antony and Cleopatra's theatrical coronation:

> At the feet sat
> Caesarion, whom they call my father's son,
> And all the unlawful issue that their lust
> Since then hath made between them.
> (3.6.5–8)

Note the possible confusion between Antony and the older Caesar and the definite one between Caesarion and the younger Caesar, both of whom are "my father's son." At Antony's death, Caesar movingly recalls his foe:

> thou, my brother, my competitor
> In top of all design, my mate in empire,

> Friend and companion in the front of war,
> The arm of mine own body, and the heart
> Where mine his thoughts did kindle. . . .
>
> (5.1.42–46)

By calling Antony his "brother" and "mate," and by invoking a meeting of "heart" and mind, Caesar suggests an intimacy between the two men that recalls Renaissance celebrations of male friendship but that also borders on the erotic. But he neutralizes any filial anxiety he may feel by describing Antony first as "my brother" and then as a subordinate, "The arm of mine own body."

Most important, this strategy of undermining distinctions drains the political world of meaning. *Julius Caesar*'s struggle between republic and empire arises only peripherally in *Antony and Cleopatra,* where it is voiced by Pompey (2.6.10–19), who is bought off, attacked, and finally murdered by the triumvirs. The Republic is thus virtually dead when *Antony and Cleopatra* opens. Egypt's independence is at stake, although this occurs only to Cleopatra. That leaves just the conflict between Antony and Caesar, two ambitious men. The end of the Roman civil war is important, but it is hard either to celebrate Caesar's victory or to lament Antony's defeat. The consequent disabused view of political power might be an implicit critique of the centralizing monarchs of Shakespeare's own time.

Still, the political symbolism of the two men is antithetical. Caesar astutely adopts republican style, whereas Antony offends Roman sensibilities with his monarchical trappings (3.6.1–19). Antony's antagonist does not emulate the older Caesar, whose sexual and military conquests were intertwined (3.13.83–86). Hence, the younger Caesar represents not the preservation but the diminution of Roman values, a constriction of a heroic culture of which Antony is the last survivor. The play insists that politics and sex (or any kind of grandeur) are sundered, that one can no longer have it both ways.

Certainly, Antony and Cleopatra cannot. The play characterizes them through a language of greatness, shared by protagonists and minor figures alike, only to subvert that rhetoric through other commentary and especially the behavior of Antony and Cleopatra themselves. Although Shakespeare makes them more sympathetic than does Plutarch, they remain self-absorbed and self-destructive—lying, ignoring urgent business, acting impulsively, bullying underlings, reveling in vulgarity, betraying each other. They are also militarily peripheral, as the fighting scenes, except for the first Battle of Alexandria, testify. Shakespeare's uncharacteristic decision to follow classical theater and keep all combat offstage leaves a feeling of being let down, as observers report on the debacle. Enobarbus laments at Actium:

> Naught, naught, all naught! I can behold no longer:
> Th'Antoniad, the Egyptian admiral,
> With all their sixty fly and turn the rudder.
>
> (3.10.1–3)

At the play's last battle, it is Antony's turn:

> All is lost!
> This foul Egyptian hath betrayed me!
> My fleet hath yielded to the foe, and yonder
> They cast their caps up and carouse together
> Like friends long lost.
>
> (4.12.9–13)

But this is not the whole story. Antony and Cleopatra are great not despite their failings but because of them. Inability to fit into Caesar's narrowed world of self-discipline sets them apart. Their grandeur can be described only through paradoxical hyperbole. Antony's heart "is become the bellows and the fan / To cool a gypsy's lust": his heart is a fan that cools Cleopatra's lust by satisfying it, but in so doing he rekindles her passion, as if his heart were also a bellows (1.1.9–10). Similarly, when Cleopatra meets Antony, "pretty dimpled boys" (2.2.214) attend her

> With divers colored fans whose wind did seem
> To glow the delicate cheeks which they did cool,
> And what they undid did.
>
> (2.2.215–17)

When told that marriage to Octavia will force Antony to abandon Cleopatra, Enobarbus demurs in the play's most famous lines:

> Never, he will not.
> Age cannot wither her, nor custom stale
> Her infinite variety. Other women cloy
> The appetites they feed, but she makes hungry
> Where most she satisfies.
>
> (2.2.246–50)

These passages might be considered accounts of middle-aged lust. The trick of the play is to convince the audience that they are about love. Antony's feelings are easier to believe than Cleopatra's: he is the one who gives up an empire. By contrast, Cleopatra's teasing frivolity, comic jealousy, and cold calculation render her motives suspect. Yet Shakespeare gives her passages of extraordinary dignity early in the play, when Antony decides to leave her upon hearing of his wife Fulvia's death:

> Courteous lord, one word.
> Sir, you and I must part, but that's not it.
> Sir, you and I have loved, but there's not it—
> That you know well. Something it is I would—
> Oh, my oblivion is a very Antony,
> And I am all forgotten.
>
> (1.3.87–92)

Cleopatra experiences something more than she can express. Its articulation thus takes the form of a failure to articulate. There is an echo of this when Enobarbus describes her to his fellow Romans: "her own person . . . beggared all description" (2.2.209–10). Here, however, Cleopatra tries to convey her meaning through a witticism: her forgetfulness makes her like Antony, who is forgetful of her. She forgets and is forgotten. But when Antony misses the point, thinking he has merely witnessed idle wordplay, she corrects him:

> 'Tis sweating labor
> To bear such idleness so near the heart
> As Cleopatra this. But, sir, forgive me,
>
> . . . .
> . . . be deaf to my unpitied folly,
> And all the gods go with you.
>
> (1.3.94–100)

In short, Cleopatra's playfulness is the surface of her essential depth, her "sweating labor" like that of childbirth.

The last two acts test that depth, ultimately making Cleopatra the play's central character. The protagonists' sphere of activity is reduced to Alexandria. Cleopatra sends Antony a manipulative report of her death, he botches his suicide in response, and she then refuses to leave her monument to attend him as he lies dying. Instead, she hoists him up to her with the comment, "Here's sport indeed. How heavy weighs my lord!" (4.15.33), where "sport" is both playful and bitter, where "weighs" carries both physical and psychological meaning, and, hence, where the scene combines comedy with pathos. Antony's politically climactic death proves a false ending that shifts central significance to the final act. Egypt and Cleopatra are what matter.

Egypt is associated throughout with the overflowing that Antony is faulted for at the outset. Antony declares his love for Cleopatra by rejecting the state he rules: "Let Rome in Tiber melt and the wide arch / Of the ranged empire fall!" (1.1.34–35). Upon hearing of Antony's marriage to Octavia, Cleopatra prays, "Melt Egypt into Nile, and kindly creatures / Turn all to serpents!" (2.5.79–80). This apocalyptic imagery dissolves all distinction. It is tied to the play's account of spontaneous generation: "Your serpent of Egypt is bred now of your mud by the operation of your sun. So is your crocodile" (2.7.26–27). More generally, it contributes to the play's insistence on the inseparability of the human and natural worlds, perhaps with a gesture toward the new notion of an infinite universe, clothed in the language of the Christian Bible: "Then must thou needs find out new heaven, new earth" (1.1.17).

Psychologically, this language anticipates Antony's loss of self when he thinks Cleopatra has betrayed him. His body seems to him as "indistinct / As water is in water" (4.14.10–11). The language of liquefaction is also connected to the confusion of gender identity. Antony "is not more manlike / Than Cleopatra, nor the queen of Ptolemy / More womanly than he" (1.4.5–7). And Cleopatra reports, "I . . . put my tires and mantles on him, whilst / I wore his sword Philippan" (2.5.21–23). This behavior either confuses gender roles, thereby leading to Antony's flight at Actium, or overcomes a destructive opposition.

Cleopatra, who metaphorically overflows boundaries, is literally linked to Egypt and specifically to the Egyptian goddess Isis (3.6.17), who is invoked several times, probably owing to Plutarch's *On Isis and Osiris*. Isis is the sister-wife of Osiris, whom she restores after he is pursued to his death by his brother-rival, Typhon. The conclusion thus seeks the regenerative powers of the Nile in Cleopatra. It asks whether she is the equivalent of Isis, whether she is the wife of Antony (Osiris), whether she restores him after he is pursued to his death by his brother (Caesar).

This is the work of Cleopatra's suicide, which justifies these imagistic patterns and Antony's decision to die for her. In Shakespeare's earlier tragedies, we may desire the protagonists' deaths because life has lost its meaning for them. But *Antony and Cleopatra* goes further, convincing us that the two lovers' suicides are a heroic achievement, that anything less would constitute failure. The ending also evokes the synthesis precluded by the play's dichotomies but implied by its subtler patterns. Cleopatra dies the death of a Roman man:

> My resolution's placed, and I have nothing
> Of woman in me. Now from head to foot
> I am marble constant. Now the fleeting moon
> No planet is of mine.
>
> (5.2.237–40)

She also dies the death of a faithful Roman wife:

> Methinks I hear
> Antony call. I see him rouse himself
> To praise my noble act. . . .
> . . . .
> . . . Husband, I come.
> Now to that name, my courage prove my title.
>
> (5.2.279–84)

By taking the poisonous asp to her breast, she becomes a Roman mother as well, in a passage that recalls her earlier intense feeling in the language of childbirth:

> Peace, peace.
> Dost thou not see my baby at my breast,

That sucks the nurse asleep.

. . . .

As sweet as balm, as soft as air, as gentle.
O Antony! Nay, I will take thee too.
    [*She applies another asp.*]
                    (5.2.304–08)

Since the Folio lacks the stage direction included here, the final line can mean that
she takes Antony to her breast, like a mother comforting her infant son.

The Nile delta, showing the northern end of the river as it flows into the Mediterranean Sea. Alexandria is visible near the upper left-hand corner. From a map in
Sebastian Münster's *Cosmographia universalis* (1550).

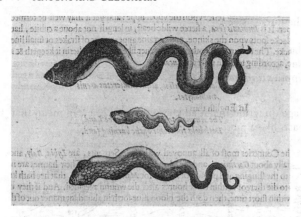

The Clown wishes Cleopatra "joy o'th' worm" (5.2.275) as she prepares to commit suicide. From Edward Topsell's *History of Serpents* (1608).

But "O Antony" is also a cry of orgasm that recalls Cleopatra's earlier sexual assertions, "I am again for Cydnus / To meet Mark Antony" (5.2.227–28) and "Husband, I come" (5.2.283), and looks ahead to Charmian's sexually ecstatic dying words, which Shakespeare added to his source: "Ah, soldier!" (5.2.324). Furthermore, Cleopatra's manner of death is clearly Egyptian. The asp recalls Antony's description of her as "my serpent of old Nile" (1.5.25). Thus, Rome and Egypt, Antony and Cleopatra, martial valor and sexual ecstasy are united in death as they cannot be in life. "Dido and her Aeneas" (4.14.53), in Antony's vision soon to be eclipsed by himself and Cleopatra, wander together through the afterlife of the play. But Dido and Aeneas remain unreconciled in the *Aeneid*, Shakespeare's source for the characters. There, Aeneas abandons Dido, whom Virgil modeled on the historical Cleopatra and thus associated with Eastern sensuality. The abandonment is justified in the name of a higher cause—Rome. Thus, Aeneas, despite his extramarital affair, functions as fictional forerunner not of Antony but of Octavius Caesar. Insofar as *Antony and Cleopatra* leads the audience to believe that its protagonists will end up together, then, it answers the *Aeneid*, distancing itself from Roman and, by extension, Renaissance imperialism. You *can* have it both ways. East and West, conquered and conqueror, are affirmed in a final synthesis.

Yet countercurrents trouble Cleopatra's "Immortal longings" (5.2.277). She resolves on suicide not when she learns that Antony killed himself for her but when she becomes certain that Caesar plans to lead her in humiliating triumph in Rome. Recognizing that her suicide will ruin Caesar's plans, she takes pleasure in imagining that Antony will "mock / The luck of Caesar," that the asp will "call great Caesar ass / Unpolicied" (5.2.281–82, 303–04). This rhetoric cleans up earlier dubious behavior and puts the best face on defeat. Heroic aristocratic individualism can act in the world only by leaving it. Moreover, the concluding, domestic Cleopatra reduces to a conventional gender role a woman who challenged sexual hierarchy. At her death, Cleopatra "lies / A lass unparalleled" (5.2.311–12). This eulogy juxtaposes the extravagant Latinate "unparalleled" with the homespun "lass," a word that matches Cleopatra's own rhetoric—"Husband," "baby," and "nurse." Moreover, in echoing her contempt for "Caesar [the] ass / Unpolicied," the phrase praises her at his expense. Alternatively, however, has *Antony and Cleopatra* presented "lies alas unparalleled"?

The answer depends on the relationship between the ending and the partly incompatible preceding material. Most critics have found the conclusion affirmative. But the work registers ambivalence to the last, in Cleopatra's account of the response she expects at Rome:

> The quick comedians
> Extemporally will stage us and present
> Our Alexandrian revels. Antony
> Shall be brought drunken forth, and I shall see

Some squeaking Cleopatra boy my greatness
I'th' posture of a whore.

(5.2.215–20)

Cleopatra shudders at the absurdity of a boy actor badly impersonating her, yet the part of Cleopatra in *Antony and Cleopatra* was originally performed by a boy. This reminder punctures the dramatic illusion just when it seems most essential. It looks back to Cleopatra's blurring of gender division. It emphasizes Cleopatra's own artifice—a veteran actress in her final performance. Shakespeare here flaunts his medium. But if it is impossible to "boy" Cleopatra's "greatness," to represent her adequately, perhaps that is an invitation, as she has earlier suggested, to look beyond what can be shown, to take seriously her "immortal longings."

WALTER COHEN

SELECTED BIBLIOGRAPHY

Archer, John Michael. "Antiquity and Degeneration in *Antony and Cleopatra.*" *Race, Ethnicity, and Power in the Renaissance.* Ed. Joyce Green MacDonald. Madison, NJ: Fairleigh Dickinson UP, 1997. 145–64. Explores the ambivalent image of Egypt in the Renaissance, combining reverence for its antique wisdom with anxiety about contagious decadence.

Deats, Sara Munson, ed. *Antony and Cleopatra: New Critical Essays.* New York: Routledge, 2005. Presents fourteen new essays, including Munson's own opening survey of criticism and performance.

Egan, Gabriel. *Green Shakespeare: From Ecopolitics to Ecocriticism.* London: Routledge, 2006. 108–19. Examines Antony and Cleopatra's sex without generation versus the Nile's generation without sex (spontaneous generation), the latter seen as an exceeding of bounds that levels humans with the rest of the natural world.

Geisweidt, Edward. "'The Nobleness of Life': Spontaneous Generation and Excremental Life in *Antony and Cleopatra.*" *Ecocritical Shakespeare.* Ed. Lynne Bruckner and Dan Brayton. Farnham, Surrey: Ashgate, 2011. 89–103. Discusses erosion of the hierarchy between human and animal through the Nile's ability to produce life from its fertile dung and comparison of Antony and Caesar to excrement.

Loomba, Ania. *Shakespeare, Race, and Colonialism.* Oxford: Oxford UP, 2002. 112–34. Explores links of empire, gender ambiguity, skin color, gypsies, and role playing.

Madeleine, Richard, ed. *Antony and Cleopatra.* Cambridge: Cambridge UP, 1998. Offers a book-length history of productions of *Antony and Cleopatra,* combined with an edition of the play annotated with accounts of various performance decisions.

Oates, Joyce Carol. "The Tragedy of Imagination in *Antony and Cleopatra.*" *Living with Shakespeare: Essays by Writers, Actors, and Directors.* Ed. Susannah Carson. New York: Vintage, 2013. 418–32. Sees the play as an atypical tragedy in which the protagonists' illusions, sustained by comic and hyperbolic language, are never demystified by reality.

Singh, Jyotsna G. "The Politics of Empathy in *Antony and Cleopatra*: A View from Below." *A Companion to Shakespeare's Works.* Ed. Richard Dutton and Jean E. Howard. Vol. 1: *The Tragedies.* Oxford: Blackwell, 2003. 411–29. Presents a critique of character-based scholarship and performances focusing on Cleopatra, in favor of a broader view of tragedy centered on the sufferings of the minor characters and drawing on Brecht's theory of alienation, or distancing, effects.

Weil, Judith. *Service and Dependency in Shakespeare's Plays.* Cambridge: Cambridge UP, 2005. 91–104. Examines Enobarbus and Charmian's flattery, combined with mockery, aimed at Antony and Cleopatra, and Cleopatra's similar strategy with Antony.

Wofford, Susanne L., ed. *Shakespeare's Late Tragedies: A Collection of Critical Essays.* Upper Saddle River, NJ: Prentice-Hall, 1996. Presents five essays on *Antony and Cleopatra* from the 1980s and 1990s, plus substantial discussion of the play in three other more general pieces; primarily issues of subjectivity, race, gender, empire, and performance.

FILM

Antony and Cleopatra. 1974. Dir. Jon Scoffield. UK. 161 min. Based on the 1972 Royal Shakespeare Company production starring Janet Suzman as an intelligent, "tawny," feminist Cleopatra. Focuses on love at the expense of politics.

TEXTUAL INTRODUCTION

The Tragedy of Anthonie, and Cleopatra was entered in the Stationers' Register on May 20, 1608, by the book publisher Edward Blount as if it were soon to be published, but for some reason the play was not printed until its inclusion in the First Folio of Shakespeare's plays in 1623. The comparatively clean Folio text requires very little emendation and serves as the base text for this edition. The text is likely drawn from a transcript of Shakespeare's original draft. The initial stage direction for 1.2 announces the entrance of Lamprius, Rannius, and Lucilius, but they have no speaking lines. Such "ghost characters" suggest an authorial manuscript rather than the kind of copy marked by a prompter who would normally note the specific entrances and exits required of the actors. This may explain why in the Folio Dolabella is mistakenly directed to enter at 5.2.315 and then again, properly, at 5.2.325. Some of the stage directions are descriptive, indicating the playwright's conception of what the action should look like. The initial stage direction for 3.1, "*Enter Ventidius as it were in triumph, the dead body of Pacorus borne before him*," for example, gives an impression of the scene but no details about the actual staging. Other stage directions permissively direct three or four characters to enter, leaving the exact number of soldiers, attendants, or servants to be decided by the actors. At other places, the Folio has no stage directions where modern editors supply them, as in 5.2.35–36, where the dialogue indicates that Caesar's soldiers suddenly seize Cleopatra but no stage direction is provided. Because many of the Folio spellings are uncharacteristic of Shakespeare's usual practice, editors believe the copy used was not his own manuscript but a transcript very close to the original.

The central challenge in editing *Antony and Cleopatra* is to determine how lines in the Folio should be organized in a modernized version. The compositors who set the original manuscript copy into print worked from a handwritten draft that economized on paper by running lines of poetry together. As dialogue moved from one speaker to another, the compositors set each speech without indentation, regardless of whether the iambic pentameter line was to be shared between two speakers. In some places they were careless, and in other spots, finding a line too long to fit tidily in their half-page column, they cut it in two. But problems with lineation cannot all be laid at the compositors' feet. In the latter part of Shakespeare's career when *Antony and Cleopatra* was written, the dramatist used a high proportion of short and shared lines, often eschewing metrical regularity for a more realistic representation of the way people speak. Sometimes Shakespeare uses a series of short lines to heighten a scene's emotional effect, as in 2.2.169–75 when Antony, Caesar, and Lepidus discuss the military threat posed by Pompey. At other times it is difficult to distinguish prose from verse. In 1.2, for example, Charmian, Alexas, and Iras conduct their bawdy repartee in prose, but the Soothsayer's lines are metrically regular. The alternation of verse lines with prose in this scene sets up the characters' opposing perspectives until the mood shifts again with Cleopatra's entrance and a return to consistent blank verse.

With so many variables, it is not surprising that the arrangement of *Antony and Cleopatra*'s lines of text often varies from edition to edition. *The Norton Shakespeare* takes a conservative approach, adopting many traditional changes to the Folio lineation. When the dialogue moves rapidly back and forth between characters, as in Cleopatra's confrontation with the Messenger in 2.5, it employs split lines to indicate the dialogue's rhythm. In other passages, especially when short lines are metrically irregular, they are printed as single lines of text.

Ever since the eighteenth century, it has been customary to regularize Shakespeare's character names in accordance with his source, Thomas North's English translation of *Plutarch's Lives of the Noble Greeks and Romans*. While a few recent editions have returned to the Folio's spellings—"Anthony" instead of "Antony," for example—*The Norton Shakespeare* adheres to the speech prefixes most commonly associated with the play.

The Folio provides a heading for act 1, scene 1, but offers no act and scene divisions after that. As performed by the King's Company in the Globe, *Antony and Cleopatra* would have been staged continuously, with action flowing rapidly from Rome to Egypt, from battlefield to palace—all without interruption. Shakespeare's eighteenth-century editors imposed a five-act structure on the text and divided each act into separate scenes. Although *The Norton Shakespeare* follows that tradition in its assignment of act and scene numbers, the action should be conceived of as continuous.

VIRGINIA MASON VAUGHAN

PERFORMANCE NOTE

Theater companies frequently avoid *Antony and Cleopatra*, a widely admired but tremendously challenging play with a history of disappointing the audience. Its sixty speaking roles and ever-shifting locations can tax the resources of any company; its abundance of short scenes, some little more than fragments, frustrates efforts at abridgment or adaptation. Furthermore, as the plot concerns legendary tragic figures and world-shaping events, yet progresses mostly through scenes appropriate to satire (comic exchanges, domestic situations), directors must strike difficult balances between epic and intimate aspects and between competing genres. The more successful productions in recent years emphasize the lovers' fading glories and ultimate transcendence over the political events and favor designs that facilitate fluid transitions between scenes—complemented often by actors cast in multiple roles—over attempts to evoke the grandeur of ancient cities. But there are no easy solutions.

All of the foregoing challenges seem trivial, though, when compared to those presented by the title roles. In commending Cleopatra for "her infinite variety," Enobarbus efficiently summarizes the role's challenges: it seems to want an actor both calculating and rash, coquettish and queenly, aging and yet irresistible, one who can perform passions both feigned and sincere and who can ensure that spectators are able to tell the difference. The actor playing Antony has the even more unreasonable task of justifying his reputation as a brave soldier, brilliant tactician, and constant lover, despite a glaring lack of scenes or soliloquies centered on love or war. In addition, he must appear a mythic figure and a fallen one, at once, and must earn attention while continually being overshadowed by his scene partners (especially Cleopatra, but also Caesar, Enobarbus, and Eros). Both roles, then, require extreme versatility while providing limitless possibilities for emphasis. Versatility benefits lesser roles, too—Caesar combines callous efficiency with moments of tenderness for Lepidus and Octavia; Enobarbus is a center of lyricism, cynicism, and pathos, both character and choric figure. Other considerations in production include Antony's motives for marrying and hastily abandoning Octavia; Cleopatra's purpose in negotiating with Thidias in 3.13; hoisting Antony at the monument (see Digital Edition PC 3); and Cleopatra's spectacular suicide.

BRETT GAMBOA

The Tragedy of
Antony and Cleopatra

[THE PERSONS OF THE PLAY

MARK ANTONY (Marcus Antonius), triumvir of Rome

Antony's friends and followers:
PHILO
DEMETRIUS
Domitius ENOBARBUS
VENTIDIUS
SILIUS
EROS
CANIDIUS
SCARUS
DERCETUS
Lamprius
Rannius
Lucilius

OCTAVIUS CAESAR, triumvir of Rome

Caesar's friends and followers:
MAECENAS
AGRIPPA
TAURUS
DOLABELLA
THIDIAS
PROCULEIUS
Gallus

LEPIDUS, triumvir of Rome

CLEOPATRA, Queen of Egypt

Attendants to Cleopatra:
CHARMIAN
IRAS
ALEXAS
MARDIAN, a eunuch
EGYPTIAN
DIOMEDES
SELEUCUS, treasurer to Cleopatra

POMPEY (Sextus Pompeius)

Pompey's supporters:
MENAS
VARRIUS
Menecrates

OCTAVIA, sister to Caesar, wife to Antony
SOOTHSAYER
AMBASSADOR from Antony

SENTRY
WATCHMEN
MESSENGERS
CAPTAINS
SOLDIERS
BOY
GUARDSMEN
ATTENDANTS
CLOWN
SERVITORS *or* SERVANTS]

1.1

Enter DEMETRIUS *and* PHILO.

PHILO	Nay, but this dotage° of our general's	*absurd infatuation*
	O'erflows the measure.[1] Those his goodly eyes,	
	That o'er the files and musters° of the war	*lines of troops*
	Have glowed like plated° Mars, now bend, now turn	*armored*
5	The office° and devotion of their view	*duty*
	Upon a tawny front.[2] His captain's heart,	
	Which in the scuffles of great fights hath burst	
	The buckles on his breast, reneges all temper[3]	
	And is become the bellows and the fan	
	To cool a gypsy's° lust.	*Egyptian's; hussy's*

Flourish.° Enter ANTONY, CLEOPATRA, *her ladies*   *Trumpet fanfare*
[CHARMIAN *and* IRAS, *and*] *the train° with eunuchs*   *retinue*
fanning her.

10	Look where they come!	
	Take but good note, and you shall see in him	
	The triple pillar of the world[4] transformed	
	Into a strumpet's fool. Behold and see.	
CLEOPATRA	If it be love indeed, tell me how much.	
15 ANTONY	There's beggary° in the love that can be reckoned.	*little value*
CLEOPATRA	I'll set a bourn° how far to be beloved.	*boundary*
ANTONY	Then must thou needs find out new heaven, new earth.[5]	

Enter a MESSENGER.

MESSENGER	News, my good lord, from Rome.	
ANTONY	Grates° me! The sum.°	*Irks / summary*
20 CLEOPATRA	Nay, hear them, Antony.	
	Fulvia° perchance is angry. Or, who knows	*(Antony's wife)*
	If the scarce-bearded Caesar[6] have not sent	
	His powerful mandate to you: "Do this, or this;	

1.1 Location: Cleopatra's palace, Alexandria.
1. Goes beyond suitable bounds.
2. A face or forehead of dark complexion (referring to Cleopatra; see the Introduction); military "front," or battle line.
3. Abandons all temperance ("temper" is also the hardness of tempered steel).
4. Antony, Octavius Caesar, and Lepidus were the three triumvirs ruling the Roman Empire (most of the known world, for Romans).

5. Alluding anachronistically to Revelation 21:1 ("I saw a new heaven, and a new earth"), and perhaps both to the cosmological revolution initiated by Copernicus and to the discovery of the New World. This second meaning may connect to the imperial theme of the play—its sense of geographical expansiveness and European geographical expansion.
6. The opening of the play is set in 40 B.C.E., when Octavius Caesar was twenty-three years old; Antony was almost twenty years his senior.

	Take in° that kingdom, and enfranchise° that!	*Annex / liberate*
	Perform't, or else we damn thee."	
25	ANTONY How,° my love?	*What*

ANTONY   How,° my love?   *What*
CLEOPATRA   Perchance? Nay, and most like!⁷

You must not stay here longer. Your dismission°   *marching orders*
Is come from Caesar; therefore hear it, Antony.
Where's Fulvia's process?°—Caesar's, I would say—both?   *summons*
Call in the messengers. As I am Egypt's queen,
Thou blushest, Antony, and that blood of thine
Is Caesar's homager°—else so° thy cheek pays shame   *Pays Caesar homage / or else*
When shrill-tongued Fulvia scolds. The messengers!

ANTONY   Let Rome in Tiber melt and the wide arch
Of the ranged° empire fall! Here is my space.   *orderly; extensive*
Kingdoms are clay. Our dungy° earth alike   *made of manure*
Feeds beast as man. The nobleness of life
Is to do thus,° when such a mutual⁸ pair   *act as we do*
And such a twain can do't, in which I bind—
On pain of punishment—the world to weet°   *recognize*
We stand up peerless.

CLEOPATRA   Excellent falsehood!
Why did he marry Fulvia and not love her?
I'll seem the fool I am not. Antony
Will be himself.⁹

ANTONY   But stirred¹ by Cleopatra.
Now for the love of love and her soft hours,
Let's not confound° the time with conference° harsh.   *ruin / conversation*
There's not a minute of our lives should stretch
Without some pleasure now. What sport° tonight?   *entertainment*

CLEOPATRA   Hear the ambassadors!

ANTONY   Fie, wrangling Queen!
Whom every thing becomes—to chide, to laugh,
To weep; whose every passion fully strives
To make itself in thee fair and admired.
No messenger but thine,² and all alone
Tonight we'll wander through the streets and note
The qualities of people. Come, my queen,
Last night you did desire it. [*to the* MESSENGER] Speak not
to us.   *Exeunt* [*the* MESSENGER, ANTONY,
                              and CLEOPATRA] *with the train.*

DEMETRIUS   Is Caesar with° Antonius prized° so slight?   *by / esteemed*
PHILO   Sir, sometimes when he is not Antony,
He comes too short of that great property°   *unique characteristic*
Which still° should go with Antony.   *always*

DEMETRIUS   I am full sorry
That he approves° the common liar who   *proves correct*
Thus speaks of him at Rome, but I will hope
Of better deeds tomorrow. Rest you happy.   *Exeunt.*

---

7. It is most likely, rather than merely possible, that Fulvia is angry or Caesar has sent orders.
8. Having the same feelings for each other; well-matched.
9. *I'll . . . himself:* I'll appear to believe Antony's falsehood, although I am really not so credulous; he will continue in his folly. (But Antony construes the words he hears as a compliment. It is also possible that Antony hears Cleopatra's entire speech.)
1. Aroused; motivated; disturbed.
2. I will hear only what you have to say.

1.2[1]

Enter ENOBARBUS, *Lamprius, a* SOOTHSAYER, *Rannius,*
Lucilius, CHARMIAN, IRAS, MARDIAN *the eunuch,*
and ALEXAS.[2]

CHARMIAN   Lord Alexas, sweet Alexas, most anything Alexas,
almost most absolute° Alexas, where's the Soothsayer that   *perfect*
you praised so to th' Queen? Oh, that I knew this husband,
which you say must change his horns[3] with garlands.

5 ALEXAS   Soothsayer!

SOOTHSAYER   Your will?

CHARMIAN   Is this the man? —Is't you, sir, that know things?

SOOTHSAYER   In nature's infinite book of secrecy
A little I can read.

10 ALEXAS   Show him your hand.

ENOBARBUS   Bring in the banquet° quickly; wine enough   *light meal; dessert*
Cleopatra's health to drink.

CHARMIAN   [*giving her hand to the* SOOTHSAYER]   Good sir,
give me good fortune.

15 SOOTHSAYER   I make not, but foresee.

CHARMIAN   Pray then, foresee me one.

SOOTHAYER   You shall be yet far fairer than you are.

CHARMIAN   He means in flesh.°   *(by getting fatter)*

IRAS   No, you shall paint° when you are old.   *use cosmetics*

20 CHARMIAN   Wrinkles forbid.

ALEXAS   Vex not his prescience; be attentive.

CHARMIAN   Hush.

SOOTHSAYER   You shall be more beloving than beloved.

CHARMIAN   I had rather heat my liver with drinking.[4]

25 ALEXAS   Nay, hear him.

CHARMIAN   Good now,° some excellent fortune! Let me be   *Please; fine; begin*
married to three kings in a forenoon and widow them all; let
me have a child at fifty, to whom Herod of Jewry[5] may do
homage. Find me° to marry me with Octavius Caesar, and   *Find in my palm*

30 companion me° with my mistress.   *make me equal*

SOOTHSAYER   You shall outlive the lady whom you serve.

CHARMIAN   Oh, excellent! I love long life better than figs.[6]

SOOTHSAYER   You have seen and proved° a fairer former fortune   *undergone*
Than that which is to approach.

35 CHARMIAN   Then belike° my children shall have no names.°   *likely / be bastards*
Prithee, how many boys and wenches must I have?

SOOTHSAYER   If every of your wishes had a womb
And fertile every wish, a million.

CHARMIAN   Out, fool! I forgive thee for a witch.[7]

40 ALEXAS   You think none but your sheets are privy to your wishes?

CHARMIAN   [*to* SOOTHSAYER]   Nay, come, tell Iras hers.

1.2 Location: Scene continues.
1. TEXTUAL COMMENT For the rationale behind the
division of the play into scenes, despite the likelihood
that the play presents continuous action, see Digital
Edition TC 1.
2. TEXTUAL COMMENT The presence of "ghost
characters"—those with no speaking part—suggests
that the play was printed from a manuscript not yet
revised for performance. See Digital Edition TC 2.
3. Must adorn his (proverbial) cuckold's horns.
4. Both falling in love and excessive drinking were
thought to inflame the liver, the seat of the passions.

5. Anachronistic: Charmian wants homage to her
child even from Herod, Cleopatra's enemy, who was
to become proverbial for his brutality to children for
his Massacre of the Innocents in an effort to kill the
infant Jesus.
6. Genitalia (possibly proverbial); lines 31–32 also
foreshadow 5.2.232–324.
7. Since you are a soothsayer, I will let you speak
freely and will not persecute you as a witch; I will
forgive your outlandish prognostications because
they are unlikely to come true.

ALEXAS We'll know all our fortunes.

ENOBARBUS Mine, and most of our fortunes tonight, shall be
drunk to bed.

45 IRAS [giving her hand to SOOTHSAYER] There's a palm pre-
sages chastity,° if nothing else.   (a dry palm)

CHARMIAN E'en as the o'erflowing Nilus presageth famine.[8]

IRAS Go, you wild° bedfellow, you cannot soothsay.   licentious

CHARMIAN Nay, if an oily palm° be not a fruitful prognostica-   (sign of sensuality)
50 tion,° I cannot scratch mine ear. [to SOOTHSAYER] Prithee,   sign of fertility
tell her but a workaday° fortune.   an everyday

SOOTHSAYER Your fortunes are alike.

IRAS But how, but how? Give me particulars!

SOOTHSAYER I have said.

55 IRAS Am I not an inch of fortune better than she?

CHARMIAN Well, if you were but an inch of fortune better than
I, where would you choose it?

IRAS Not in my husband's nose!°   (sexual innuendo)

CHARMIAN Our worser° thoughts heavens mend. Alexas—   lascivious
60 come, his fortune, his fortune. Oh, let him marry a woman
that cannot go, sweet Isis,[9] I beseech thee, and let her die,
too, and give him a worse, and let worse follow worse, till
the worst of all follow him laughing to his grave, fiftyfold a
cuckold. Good Isis, hear me this prayer, though thou deny
65 me a matter of more weight, good Isis, I beseech thee.

IRAS Amen, dear goddess, hear that prayer of the people!
For, as it is a heartbreaking to see a handsome man loose-
wived,° so it is a deadly sorrow to behold a foul knave uncuck-   wedded to an adulteress
olded. Therefore, dear Isis, keep decorum° and fortune him   do the right thing
70 accordingly.

CHARMIAN Amen.

ALEXAS Lo now, if it lay in their hands to make me a cuckold,
they would make themselves whores, but they'd do't.°   in order to do so

Enter CLEOPATRA.

ENOBARBUS Hush, here comes Antony.

75 CHARMIAN Not he, the Queen.

CLEOPATRA Saw you my lord?

ENOBARBUS No, lady.

CLEOPATRA Was he not here?

CHARMIAN No, madam.

80 CLEOPATRA He was disposed to mirth, but on the sudden
A Roman° thought hath struck him. Enobarbus!   of Rome; serious

ENOBARBUS Madam.

CLEOPATRA Seek him, and bring him hither. Where's Alexas?

ALEXAS Here, at your service. My lord approaches.

Enter ANTONY *with a* MESSENGER.

85 CLEOPATRA We will not look upon him: Go with us.

Exeunt [all but ANTONY and the MESSENGER].

MESSENGER Fulvia, thy wife, first came into the field.°   battlefield

ANTONY Against my brother Lucius?[1]

MESSENGER Ay,
But soon that war had end, and the time's state°   situation at the time

---

8. Ironic: the silt brought down by the flooding Nile
each year gave Egypt its fertile soil.
9. Egyptian goddess of fertility, as well as of the earth

and moon. For the comparison of Cleopatra to Isis, see
the Introduction. *go:* come (sexual); bear children.
1. Lucius Antonius, Roman consul.

90   Made friends of them, jointing their force 'gainst Caesar,
     Whose better issue° in the war from Italy   *greater success*
     Upon the first encounter drave them.°   *drove them out*
ANTONY   Well, what worst?
MESSENGER   The nature of bad news infects the teller.[2]
95   ANTONY   When it concerns the fool or coward. On.
     Things that are past are done with me. 'Tis thus:
     Who tells me true, though in his tale lie death,
     I hear him as° he flattered.   *as if*
MESSENGER   Labienus[3]—
     This is stiff news—hath with his Parthian force
100 Extended° Asia. From Euphrates   *Seized*
     His conquering banner shook, from Syria
     To Lydia, and to Ionia,
     Whilst—
ANTONY   Antony, thou wouldst say.
MESSENGER   O my lord!
ANTONY   Speak to me home,° mince not the general tongue.[4]   *plainly*
105 Name Cleopatra as she is called in Rome;
     Rail thou in Fulvia's phrase,° and taunt my faults   *words*
     With such full license as both truth and malice
     Have power to utter. Oh, then we bring forth weeds
     When our quick winds lie still, and our ills told us
110 Is as our earing.[5] Fare thee well awhile.
MESSENGER   At your noble pleasure.   *Exit* MESSENGER.
          Enter SECOND MESSENGER.
ANTONY   From Sicyon,[6] ho, the news! Speak there.
SECOND MESSENGER   The man from Sicyon—
ANTONY   Is there such a one?
SECOND MESSENGER   He stays upon° your will.   *He attends*
ANTONY   Let him appear.
          [*Exit* SECOND MESSENGER.]
115 These strong Egyptian fetters I must break,
     Or lose myself in dotage.
          Enter THIRD MESSENGER *with a letter.*
                    What are you?
THIRD MESSENGER   Fulvia, thy wife, is dead.
ANTONY   Where died she?
MESSENGER   In Sicyon.
     Her length of sickness, with what else more serious
     Importeth thee° to know, this bears.   *Is important for you*
          [*He gives* ANTONY *the letter.*]
120 ANTONY   Forbear° me.   *Leave*
          [*Exit* THIRD MESSENGER.]

---

2. Makes the teller hated by the hearer. For examples, see 2.5 and 3.13.
3. Quintus Labienus, who was sent by Brutus and Cassius following their killing of Julius Caesar (see *Julius Caesar*) to garner support from the Parthians, an Asian people whose empire came to include much of Mesopotamia (Iraq) and Persia (Iran) and who regularly warred with Rome. After Brutus's and Cassius's defeat at Philippi by Antony, Octavius Caesar, and Lepidus, Labienus defected to take command of the Parthian army and began a war against the Romans, conquering some of their provinces in what is now the Middle East (lines 100–102)—provinces Antony was supposed to protect.
4. Do not play down common opinion.
5. *Oh . . . earing*: Antony compares his recent behavior to an unplowed field: just as the field sprouts weeds when it remains untilled (by hand or) by a "quick" (fertile) wind, he falls into "ill" habits when he is not forced to face criticism (to undergo "earing," plowing).
6. City in Greece where Antony left Fulvia.

There's a great spirit gone. Thus did I desire it.
What our contempts doth often hurl from us,
We wish it ours again. The present pleasure,
By revolution low'ring,[7] does become
125   The opposite of itself. She's° good, being gone.   *Fulvia is*
The hand could° pluck her back that shoved her on.   *would wish to*
I must from this enchanting° queen break off.   *spellbinding*
Ten thousand harms, more than the ills I know,
My idleness doth hatch. How now, Enobarbus!

    Enter ENOBARBUS.

ENOBARBUS   What's your pleasure, sir?
130   ANTONY   I must with haste from hence.
ENOBARBUS   Why, then we kill[8] all our women. We see how
mortal an unkindness is to them; if they suffer our departure, death's the word.
ANTONY   I must be gone.
135   ENOBARBUS   Under a compelling occasion, let women die. It
were pity to cast them away for nothing, though between
them and a great cause, they should be esteemed nothing.
Cleopatra, catching but the least noise of this, dies instantly.
I have seen her die twenty times upon far poorer moment.°   *for far less reason*
140   I do think there is mettle° in death, which commits some   *(sexual) potency; courage*
loving act upon her, she hath such a celerity° in dying.   *speed*
ANTONY   She is cunning past man's thought.
ENOBARBUS   Alack, sir, no! Her passions are made of nothing
but the finest part of pure love. We cannot call her winds
145   and waters, sighs and tears—they are greater storms and
tempests than almanacs can report. This cannot be cunning
in her; if it be, she makes a shower of rain as well as Jove.[9]
ANTONY   Would I had never seen her!
ENOBARBUS   O sir, you had then left unseen a wonderful piece
150   of work,° which not to have been blest withal° would have   *masterpiece / with*
discredited your travel.[1]
ANTONY   Fulvia is dead.
ENOBARBUS   Sir.
ANTONY   Fulvia is dead.
155   ENOBARBUS   Fulvia?
ANTONY   Dead.
ENOBARBUS   Why, sir, give the gods a thankful sacrifice.
When it pleaseth their deities to take the wife of a man from
him, it shows to man the tailors of the earth, comforting
160   therein, that when old robes° are worn out, there are mem-   *clothes; women*
bers[2] to make new. If there were no more women but Fulvia,
then had you indeed a cut, and the case to be lamented.
This grief is crowned with consolation; your old smock brings
forth a new petticoat, and indeed, the tears live in an onion
165   that should water this sorrow.°   *don't shed any real tears*

7. Growing lower by turning (as of a wheel, such as Fortune's).
8. Alluding to achieving an orgasm. Throughout the scene, the words "kill," "death," and "dying" all carry this bawdy resonance. "Nothing," which Enobarbus repeats, may refer to the female genitals.
9. Jupiter; ruler of the gods: one of his duties was to govern rain.

1. Would have cast doubt on your success as a traveler. "Travel" also suggests "travail," or work, as in "piece of work" (lines 149–50).
2. Limbs; sexual organs. The sexual innuendo is continued in "cut" (line 162: severe blow; slash in a garment; vagina), "case" (line 162: situation; set of clothes; vagina), and "broachèd" (lines 166, 168: opened or pricked).

ANTONY The business she hath brochèd in the state,
Cannot endure my absence.
ENOBARBUS And the business you have broached here cannot
be without you, especially that of Cleopatra's, which wholly
170 depends on your abode.°   *staying on here*
ANTONY No more light answers. Let our officers
Have notice what we purpose. I shall break
The cause of our expedience° to the Queen   *haste*
And get her leave to part. For not alone
175 The death of Fulvia, with more urgent touches°   *concerns*
Do strongly speak to us, but the letters, too,
Of many our contriving friends[3] in Rome
Petition us at home.° Sextus Pompeius   *to go home*
Hath given the dare to Caesar and commands
180 The empire of the sea.[4] Our slippery° people,   *inconstant*
Whose love is never linked to the deserver
Till his deserts are past, begin to throw°   *ascribe (the title of)*
Pompey the Great and all his dignities
Upon his son, who, high in name and power—
185 Higher than both in blood and life°—stands up   *vitality and energy*
For the main soldier;° whose quality going on,   *acts like the top soldier*
The sides o'th' world may danger.[5] Much is breeding,
Which like the courser's hair hath yet but life,
And not a serpent's poison.[6] Say our pleasure,
190 To such whose place° is under us, requires   *rank*
Our quick remove from hence.
ENOBARBUS   I shall do't.

1.3

Enter CLEOPATRA, CHARMIAN, ALEXAS, *and* IRAS.

CLEOPATRA Where is he?
CHARMIAN   I did not see him since.°   *recently*
CLEOPATRA See where he is, who's with him, what he does.
I did not send you.[1] If you find him sad,°   *serious*
Say I am dancing; if in mirth, report
5 That I am sudden sick. Quick and return.   [*Exit* ALEXAS.]
CHARMIAN Madam, methinks if you did love him dearly,
You do not hold the method° to enforce   *act appropriately*
The like from him.
CLEOPATRA   What should I do, I do not?°   *What else should I do?*
CHARMIAN In each thing give him way. Cross him in nothing.
10 CLEOPATRA Thou teachest like a fool the way to lose him.
CHARMIAN Tempt° him not so too far. I wish—forbear°—   *Test / that you'd forbear*
In time we hate that which we often fear.

      Enter ANTONY.

But here comes Antony.
CLEOPATRA   I am sick and sullen.°   *dispirited*
ANTONY I am sorry to give breathing° to my purpose.   *voice*

---

3. Of many friends acting on our behalf.
4. Sextus Pompey was the younger son of Pompey the Great, who was a foe of Julius Caesar (see *Julius Caesar* 1.1). Previously an outlaw, the Pompey of the play had gained control of the shipping routes around Sicily.
5. *whose . . . danger:* whose accomplishments and char-
acter, should they continue to succeed, might endanger the entire arrangement of the world.
6. A horse's ("courser's," line 188) hair was believed to become a live snake if put in water.
1.3 Location: Scene continues.
1. Do not say I sent you.

15 CLEOPATRA   Help me away, dear Charmian, I shall fall.
       It cannot be thus long; the sides of nature²
       Will not sustain it.
    ANTONY   Now, my dearest queen—
    CLEOPATRA   Pray you, stand farther from me.
    ANTONY   What's the matter?
    CLEOPATRA   I know by that same eye there's some good news.
20   What? Says the married woman° you may go?   (Fulvia)
       Would she had never given you leave to come!
       Let her not say 'tis I that keep you here.
       I have no power upon you. Hers you are.
    ANTONY   The gods best know—
    CLEOPATRA   Oh, never was there queen
25   So mightily betrayed! Yet at the first
       I saw the treasons planted.
    ANTONY   Cleopatra—
    CLEOPATRA   Why should I think you can be mine and true—
       Though you in swearing shake the thronèd gods³—
       Who have been false to Fulvia? Riotous madness,
30   To be entangled with those mouth-made° vows,   hypocritical
       Which break themselves in swearing.°   as they are made
    ANTONY   Most sweet queen—
    CLEOPATRA   Nay, pray you seek no color° for your going,   excuse
       But bid farewell, and go. When you sued staying,°   entreated to remain
       Then was the time for words. No going then;
35   Eternity was in our° lips and eyes,   (royal plural)
       Bliss in our brows' bent,° none our parts° so poor   curve / of our parts was
       But was a race of heaven. They are so still,
       Or thou, the greatest soldier of the world,
       Art turned the greatest liar.
    ANTONY   How now, lady?
40 CLEOPATRA   I would I had thy inches;° thou shouldst know   size (phallic)
       There were a heart in Egypt.⁴
    ANTONY   Hear me, Queen.
       The strong necessity of time commands
       Our services awhile, but my full heart
       Remains in use° with you. Our Italy   in trust
45   Shines o'er with civil swords.° Sextus Pompeius   swords of civil war
       Makes his approaches to the port of Rome;°   Ostia (sixteen miles away)
       Equality of two domestic powers
       Breed scrupulous faction.° The hated, grown to strength,   distrustful dissent
       Are newly grown to love.° The condemnèd° Pompey,   popularity / banished
50   Rich in his father's honor, creeps° apace   insinuates himself
       Into the hearts of such as have not thrived
       Upon the present state,° whose numbers threaten,   government
       And quietness grown sick of rest would purge
       By any desperate change.⁵ My more particular,°   personal motivation
55   And that which most with you should safe° my going,   sanction
       Is Fulvia's death.
    CLEOPATRA   Though age from folly could not give me freedom

---

2. This cannot go on much longer; the bodily frame.   the country (Queen) of Egypt.
3. When Jupiter swore an oath, Mount Olympus, home   5. *And . . . change:* And peace, made ill by inactivity,
of the gods, was supposed to shake.   wishes to purge itself of impurities by a violently act-
4. There were courage (to respond to such insults) in   ing remedy.

It does from childishness. Can Fulvia die?

ANTONY   She's dead, my queen.

[*He shows the letters.*]

60   Look here, and at thy sovereign leisure read
The garboils° she awaked; at the last, best[6]—   upheavals
See when and where she died.

CLEOPATRA   Oh, most false love!
Where be the sacred vials[7] thou shouldst fill
With sorrowful water? Now I see, I see,

65   In Fulvia's death how mine received shall be.

ANTONY   Quarrel no more, but be prepared to know
The purposes I bear, which are, or cease°   continue, or not
As you shall give th'advice. By the fire°   sun
That quickens Nilus' slime,[8] I go from hence

70   Thy soldier-servant, making peace or war
As thou affects.°   choose

CLEOPATRA   Cut my lace,[9] Charmian, come—
But let it be. I am quickly ill and well,
So[1] Antony loves.

ANTONY   My precious queen, forbear
And give true evidence° to his love which stands   be an honest witness
An honorable trial.

75   CLEOPATRA   So Fulvia told me.
I prithee, turn aside and weep for her,
Then bid adieu to me and say the tears
Belong to Egypt.° Good now, play one scene   Cleopatra
Of excellent dissembling, and let it look
Like perfect honor.

80   ANTONY   You'll heat my blood° no more!   make me angry

CLEOPATRA   You can do better yet: but this is meetly.°   fairly good (acting)

ANTONY   Now, by my sword!

CLEOPATRA   And target.[2] Still he mends.°   improves
But this is not the best. Look, prithee, Charmian,
How this Herculean Roman does become

85   The carriage of his chafe.°   His posture of rage

ANTONY   I'll leave you, lady.

CLEOPATRA   Courteous lord, one word.
Sir, you and I must part, but that's not it.
Sir, you and I have loved, but there's not it—

90   That you know well. Something it is I would—
Oh, my oblivion is a very Antony,
And I am all forgotten.[3]

ANTONY   But that your royalty
Holds idleness your subject, I should take you
For idleness itself.[4]

CLEOPATRA   'Tis sweating labor°   work; birth pains

6. The best news last; Fulvia was at her best at the end of her life.
7. Renaissance writers thought that the Romans filled small bottles with tears to place in graves; also, where are your sad and watery eyes ("vials")?
8. That causes plants to grow in the silt that the Nile deposits.
9. Cutting the strings would be quicker than untying the lace on her bodice to relieve her from her feigned fainting spell.

1. As long as; thus (falsely).
2. Shield. Cleopatra parodies the blustering oaths of heroic drama.
3. *my . . . forgotten:* my memory has deserted me as you are doing, and I have forgotten everything (am totally forgotten—by Antony).
4. *But . . . itself:* If you were not queen over your flippancy and hence in full control of it, I would think that you were flippancy itself.

95   To bear such idleness° so near the heart   *flippancy; laziness*
      As Cleopatra this. But, sir, forgive me,
      Since my becomings° kill me when they do not   *transformations; graces*
      Eye° well to you. Your honor calls you hence;   *Look*
      Therefore be deaf to my unpitied folly,
100   And all the gods go with you. Upon your sword
      Sit laurel victory,° and smooth success   *the laurels of victory*
      Be strewed before your feet.
      ANTONY   Let us go. Come.
      Our separation so abides and flies,⁵
      That thou residing here goes yet with me,
105   And I hence fleeting here remain with thee.
      Away.   *Exeunt.*

1.4

Enter Octavius [CAESAR] reading a letter, LEPIDUS,
and their train.

CAESAR   You may see, Lepidus, and henceforth know,
      It is not Caesar's natural vice to hate
      Our great competitor.° From Alexandria   *ally; rival*
      This is the news: he fishes, drinks, and wastes
5   The lamps of night in revel; is not more manlike
      Than Cleopatra, nor the queen of Ptolemy¹
      More womanly than he; hardly gave audience² or
      Vouchsafed to think he had partners. You shall find there°   *(in the letter); (in Egypt)*
      A man who is th'abstract° of all faults   *the paradigm*
      That all men follow.
10   LEPIDUS   I must not think there are
      Evils enough to darken all his goodness.
      His faults in him seem as the spots of heaven,°   *stars*
      More fiery by night's blackness—hereditary,
      Rather than purchased,° what he cannot change,   *acquired*
15   Than° what he chooses.   *Rather than*
      CAESAR   You are too indulgent. Let's grant it is not
      Amiss to tumble on the bed of Ptolemy,
      To give a kingdom for a mirth,° to sit   *joke*
      And keep the turn of° tippling with a slave,   *take turns at*
20   To reel the streets at noon, and stand the buffet°   *come to blows*
      With knaves that smell of sweat. Say° this becomes him—   *Even if*
      As his composure° must be rare indeed   *And his character*
      Whom these things cannot blemish—yet must Antony
      No way excuse his foils° when we do bear   *faults*
25   So great weight in° his lightness. If he filled   *as a result of*
      His vacancy° with his voluptuousness,   *leisure*
      Full surfeits and the dryness of his bones³
      Call on° him for't. But to confound° such time   *Afflict / waste*
      That drums° him from his sport and speaks as loud   *summons*
30   As his own state° and ours, 'tis to be chid   *public responsibility*

5. Consists so much of both remaining together and
being separated (in that we are united by the shared
experience of it).
1.4 Location: Rome.
1. Julius Caesar had commanded Cleopatra to marry
her half brother Ptolemy XIV (acceptable within the
Egyptian royal family); she was said to have had Ptolemy poisoned.
2. Hardly listened (to Octavius's messenger, in 1.1).
3. *Full . . . bones:* Ill health caused by overeating and
venereal disease.

As we rate° boys who, being mature in knowledge,   *upbraid*
Pawn their experience to their present pleasure
And so rebel to judgment.⁴
    Enter a MESSENGER.
LEPIDUS   Here's more news.
MESSENGER   Thy biddings have been done, and every hour,
35   Most noble Caesar, shalt thou have report
How 'tis abroad. Pompey is strong at sea,
And it appears he is beloved of those
That only have feared Caesar.⁵ To the ports
The discontents° repair, and men's reports   *discontented people*
Give him° much wronged.   *Say he is*
40 CAESAR   I should have known no less.
It hath been taught us from the primal state⁶
That he which is was wished until he were,⁷
And the ebbed° man, ne'er loved till ne'er worth love,   *fallen*
Comes feared° by being lacked. This common body,°   *Is revered / The people*
45 Like to a vagabond flag° upon the stream,   *drifting reed*
Goes to and back, lackeying° the varying tide   *following slavishly*
To rot itself with motion.
    [*Enter a* SECOND MESSENGER.]
SECOND MESSENGER   Caesar, I bring thee word:
Menecrates and Menas, famous pirates,°   *(allied with Pompey)*
Makes the sea serve them, which they ear° and wound   *plow*
50 With keels of every kind. Many hot inroads
They make in Italy; the borders maritime°   *coastal territories*
Lack blood° to think on't, and flush° youth revolt.   *Go pallid / spirited*
No vessel can peep forth but 'tis as soon
Taken as seen—for Pompey's name strikes more
Than could his war resisted.⁸
55 CAESAR   Antony,
Leave thy lascivious wassails.° When thou once   *drunken revels*
Was beaten from Modena,⁹ where thou slew'st
Hirsius and Pansa, consuls, at thy heel
Did famine follow, whom thou fought'st against,
60 Though daintily brought up, with patience more
Than savages could suffer. Thou didst drink
The stale° of horses and the gilded° puddle   *urine / slime-covered*
Which beasts would cough at.° Thy palate then did deign°   *refuse (to drink) / accept*
The roughest berry on the rudest hedge.
65 Yea, like the stag when snow the pasture sheets,°   *covers*
The barks of trees thou browsèd.° On the Alps   *fed upon*
It is reported thou didst eat strange flesh
Which some did die to look on. And all this—
It wounds thine honor that I speak it now—
70 Was borne so like a soldier that thy cheek
So much as lanked° not.   *grew thin*

---

4. *being . . . judgment:* being old enough to know better, abandon their wisdom in favor of momentary pleasure and thus act against their better judgment.
5. That obeyed Caesar only out of fear.
6. Since the first society was organized.
7. That man who rules was supported until he began to rule.

8. *Pompey's . . . resisted:* Pompey's name alone is more powerful than his forces would be if confronted in battle.
9. Site of a battle in which Antony was defeated by the combined armies of Octavius Caesar and the Roman Senate, at the instigation of Cicero.

LEPIDUS 'Tis pity of him.
CAESAR   Let his shames quickly
    Drive him to Rome. 'Tis time we twain
    Did show ourselves i'th' field, and to that end
75 Assemble we immediate council. Pompey
    Thrives in our idleness.
LEPIDUS   Tomorrow, Caesar,
    I shall be furnished to inform you rightly
    Both what° by sea and land I can be able°   *what forces / assemble*
    To front° this present time.   *To confront the enemy at*
CAESAR   Till which encounter,
80 It is my business too. Farewell.
LEPIDUS   Farewell, my lord. What you shall know meantime
    Of stirs° abroad, I shall beseech you, sir,   *incidents*
    To let me be partaker.
CAESAR   Doubt not, sir.
    I knew it for my bond.°   *Exeunt.*   *responsibility*

1.5

Enter CLEOPATRA, CHARMIAN, IRAS, *and* MARDIAN.

CLEOPATRA   Charmian!
CHARMIAN   Madam?
CLEOPATRA   Ha, ha! Give me to drink mandragora.[1]
CHARMIAN   Why, madam?
5   CLEOPATRA   That I might sleep out this great gap of time
    My Antony is away.
CHARMIAN   You think of him too much.
CLEOPATRA   Oh, 'tis treason.
CHARMIAN   Madam, I trust not so.
CLEOPATRA   Thou, eunuch Mardian!
MARDIAN   What's your highness' pleasure?
CLEOPATRA   Not now to hear thee sing.[2] I take no pleasure
10 In aught[3] an eunuch has. 'Tis well for thee
    That, being unseminared,° thy freer thoughts   *castrated*
    May not fly forth of Egypt. Hast thou affections?°   *desires*
MARDIAN   Yes, gracious madam.
CLEOPATRA   Indeed?
15 MARDIAN   Not in deed, madam, for I can do° nothing   *(sexually)*
    But what indeed is honest° to be done.   *chaste; moral*
    Yet have I fierce affections and think
    What Venus did with Mars.[4]
CLEOPATRA   O Charmian,
    Where think'st thou he is now? Stands he, or sits he?
20 Or does he walk? Or is he on his horse?
    Oh, happy horse to bear the weight of Antony!
    Do bravely, horse, for wot'st° thou whom thou mov'st,   *know*
    The demi-Atlas[5] of this earth, the arm°   *champion*
    And burgonet° of men. He's speaking now   *helmet; guardian*

1.5 Location: Alexandria.
1. A narcotic, made from the mandrake plant.
2. Castrati were used in Italian music from the end of
the sixteenth century, and Shakespeare associates singing eunuchs with the eastern Mediterranean in *Twelfth
Night* and *A Midsummer Night's Dream*; they are not
thought to have been used as singers in ancient Rome.

3. In anything; in the nothing. The eunuch has nothing instead of testicles.
4. Venus, goddess of love (married to Vulcan), and
Mars, god of war, were lovers.
5. Octavius and Antony between them rule the
world—Lepidus having conveniently been forgotten—
as Atlas bore it on his shoulders.

25 Or murmuring, "Where's my serpent of old Nile?"[6]
(For so he calls me). Now I feed myself
With most delicious poison. Think on me
That am with Phoebus'° amorous pinches black   *the sun god's*
And wrinkled deep in time. Broad-fronted° Caesar,°   *Broad-browed / (Julius)*
30 When thou wast here above the ground, I was
A morsel for a monarch, and great Pompey[7]
Would stand and make his eyes grow in my brow;
There would he anchor his aspect° and die°   *gaze / (sexual)*
With looking on his life.
        Enter ALEXAS *from* [ANTONY].
35 ALEXAS   Sovereign of Egypt, hail!
CLEOPATRA   How much unlike art thou Mark Antony!
Yet coming from him, that great med'cine[8] hath
With his tinct° gilded thee.   *power; color*
How goes it with my brave° Mark Antony?   *magnificent*
40 ALEXAS   Last thing he did, dear queen,
He kissed—the last of many doubled kisses—
This orient[9] pearl. His speech sticks in my heart.
CLEOPATRA   Mine ear must pluck it thence.
ALEXAS   "Good friend," quoth he,
"Say the firm° Roman to great Egypt° sends   *loyal; resolute / Cleopatra*
45 This treasure of an oyster: at whose foot,
To mend° the petty present, I will piece°   *improve / add to*
Her opulent throne with kingdoms. All the East,"
Say thou, "shall call her mistress." So he nodded,
And soberly did mount an arm-gaunt steed,[1]
50 Who neighed so high that what I would have spoke
Was beastly dumbed° by him.   *drowned out*
CLEOPATRA   What was he, sad or merry?
ALEXAS   Like to the time o'th' year between th'extremes
Of hot and cold, he was nor° sad nor merry.   *neither*
55 CLEOPATRA   Oh, well-divided° disposition! Note him,   *balanced*
Note him, good Charmian, 'tis the man, but note him.
He was not sad, for he would shine on those
That make their looks by his;[2] he was not merry,
Which seemed to tell them his remembrance lay
60 In Egypt with his joy—but between both.
Oh, heavenly mingle! Be'st thou sad or merry,
The violence of either thee becomes,
So does it no man else. —Mett'st thou my posts?°   *messengers*
ALEXAS   Ay, madam, twenty several° messengers.   *separate*
Why do you send so thick?
65 CLEOPATRA   Who's° born that day   *Whoever is*
When I forget to send to Antony,
Shall die a beggar. Ink and paper, Charmian.
Welcome, my good Alexas! Did I, Charmian,
Ever love Caesar so?

---

6. See 2.7.26–27 for the superstition that snakes formed spontaneously in the Nile mud; the asp in particular was associated with Isis, with whom Cleopatra identifies herself.
7. Gneius Pompey, older brother of Sextus Pompey (the character in this play) and son of Pompey the Great. But Cleopatra's phrasing makes him sound like the father.

8. Elixir of life: sought by alchemists, it was thought to be able to turn base metals to gold and cure all disease.
9. From India (more lustrous than European pearls).
1. Thin but fiery war horse. TEXTUAL COMMENT For Shakespeare's invention of compound words like this one, see Digital Edition TC 3.
2. Who are dependent on his mood; who reflect his appearance in their own.

CHARMIAN   Oh, that brave Caesar!
70 CLEOPATRA   Be choked with such another emphasis,
    Say "the brave Antony."
CHARMIAN   The valiant Caesar.
CLEOPATRA   By Isis, I will give thee bloody teeth,
    If thou with Caesar paragon° again   compare
    My man of men.
CHARMIAN   By your most gracious pardon,
    I sing but after you.
75 CLEOPATRA   My salad days,
    When I was green° in judgment, cold in blood,°   immature / feeling
    To say as I said then. But come, away;
    Get me ink and paper.
    He shall have every day a several greeting
80 Or I'll unpeople Egypt.³   *Exeunt.*

2.1

Enter POMPEY, Menecrates, *and* MENAS,¹ *in*
warlike manner.

POMPEY   If the great gods be just, they shall assist
    The deeds of justest men.
MENAS   Know, worthy Pompey,
    That what they do delay they not deny.
POMPEY   Whiles we are suitors to their throne, decays
    The thing we sue for.²
5   MENAS   We, ignorant of ourselves,
    Beg often our own harms, which the wise powers
    Deny us for our° good. So find we profit   our own
    By losing of our prayers.
POMPEY   I shall do well.
    The people love me, and the sea is mine;
10 My powers are crescent,° and my auguring° hope   growing / prophesying
    Says it° will come to th' full.³ Mark Antony   (my military power)
    In Egypt sits at dinner and will make
    No wars without doors.⁴ Caesar gets money where
    He loses hearts. Lepidus flatters both,
15 Of° both is flattered; but he neither loves,°   By / loves neither
    Nor either cares for him.
MENAS   Caesar and Lepidus
    Are in the field. A mighty strength they carry.
POMPEY   Where have you this? 'Tis false.
MENAS   From Silvius, sir.
POMPEY   He dreams. I know they are in Rome together
20 Looking° for Antony. But all the charms° of love,   Waiting / incantations
    Salt° Cleopatra, soften thy waned⁵ lip!   Lecherous
    Let witchcraft join with beauty, lust with both;
    Tie up the libertine in a field of feasts;

---

3. If not, it will be only because I have run out of
Egyptians to act as messengers (or: because I have
killed all Egyptians).
2.1 Location: Pompey's headquarters (in Sicily).
1. TEXTUAL COMMENT For the assignment to Menas
of all dialogue with the speech prefix *Mene* in F, see
Digital Edition TC 4.
2. *Whiles . . . for:* While we are beseeching the gods,

what we request is losing its value.
3. Like the "crescent" moon.
4. Outside doors. Antony is concerned only with the
wars of love, conducted indoors.
5. Withered; decreased, like the moon, perhaps in
implicit contrast to the "crescent" and potentially
"full" moon of Pompey's "powers" (lines 10–11).

Keep his brain fuming.° Epicurean[6] cooks,   *drunk*
25 Sharpen with cloyless sauce[7] his appetite,
That sleep and feeding may prorogue° his honor   *postpone*
Even till a Lethe'd dullness[8]—
    Enter VARRIUS.
                     How now, Varrius?

VARRIUS   This is most certain that I shall deliver:
Mark Antony is every hour in Rome
30 Expected. Since he went from Egypt 'tis
A space for farther travel.[9]

POMPEY   I could have given less° matter   *less crucial*
A better ear. Menas, I did not think
This amorous surfeiter would have donned his helm°   *helmet*
35 For such a petty war. His soldiership
Is twice the other twain. But let us rear°   *elevate*
The higher our opinion,° that our stirring   *(of ourselves)*
Can from the lap of Egypt's widow° pluck   *(see note to 1.4.6)*
The ne'er-lust-wearied Antony.

MENAS   I cannot hope°   *suppose*
40 Caesar and Antony shall well greet together.
His wife that's dead did trespasses to° Caesar;   *offended against*
His brother warred upon him, although I think
Not moved° by Antony.   *prompted*

POMPEY   I know not, Menas,
How lesser enmities may give way to greater.
45 Were't not that we stand up against them all,
'Twere pregnant° they should square° between themselves,   *evident / argue*
For they have entertainèd° cause enough   *sustained*
To draw their swords. But how the fear of us
May cement their divisions° and bind up   *unite them*
50 The petty difference, we yet not know.
Be't as our gods will have't! It only stands
Our lives upon to use[1] our strongest hands.
Come, Menas.   *Exeunt.*

2.2
    Enter ENOBARBUS *and* LEPIDUS.
LEPIDUS   Good Enobarbus, 'tis a worthy deed,
And shall become you well, to entreat your captain
To soft and gentle speech.

ENOBARBUS   I shall entreat him
To answer like himself.[1] If Caesar move° him,   *angers*
5 Let Antony look over Caesar's head
And speak as loud as Mars. By Jupiter,
Were I the wearer of Antonio's beard,
I would not shave't today.[2]

LEPIDUS   'Tis not a time for private stomaching.°   *quarrels*
10 ENOBARBUS   Every time serves for the matter that is then born in't.

---

6. The philosopher Epicurus and his followers believed that the gods took no interest in humans' actions and that the only aim of life was to seek pleasure.
7. Sauce that never wearies or disgusts.
8. Drinking the water of Lethe, one of the rivers bounding Hades, was believed to cause total loss of memory.
9. Sufficient time to have traveled even farther (than between Egypt and Rome).
1. *It . . . use:* Our lives depend entirely on the use of.
2.2 Location: Rome.
1. To answer in a manner appropriate to his character.
2. Plucking a man's beard was an insult; Enobarbus wants Antony to give Octavius the chance to insult him. Possibly, Enobarbus is suggesting not that Antony act heroically but that he merely look the part.

LEPIDUS   But small to greater matters must give way.

ENOBARBUS   Not if the small come first.

LEPIDUS   Your speech is passion.° But pray you stir   *not reasoned*
   No embers° up. Here comes the noble Antony.   *old resentments*
    Enter ANTONY *and* VENTIDIUS.

15   ENOBARBUS   And yonder Caesar.
    Enter CAESAR, MAECENAS, *and* AGRIPPA.

ANTONY [*to* VENTIDIUS]   If we compose° well here, to Parthia.   *reach agreement*
   Hark, Ventidius.
    [*They confer apart.*]

CAESAR   I do not know, Maecenas, ask Agrippa.

LEPIDUS   Noble friends.

20   That which combined us was most great, and let not
   A leaner° action rend us. What's amiss,   *less important*
   May it be gently heard. When we debate
   Our trivial difference loud,° we do commit   *loudly; violently*
   Murder in° healing wounds. Then, noble partners,   *in the process of*
25   The rather for° I earnestly beseech,   *Especially because*
   Touch you the sourest points with sweetest terms,
   Nor curstness grow° to th' matter.   *Do not let ill temper add*

ANTONY   'Tis spoken well.
   Were we° before our armies, and to° fight,   *If we were / about to*
   I should do thus.[3]
    Flourish.

30   CAESAR   Welcome to Rome.

ANTONY   Thank you.

CAESAR   Sit.

ANTONY   Sit, sir.
    [*They sit.*]

CAESAR   Nay, then.

35   ANTONY   I learn you take things ill which are not so,
   Or being,° concern you not.   *being ill*

CAESAR   I must be laughed at,
   If or° for nothing, or a little, I   *either*
   Should say myself offended, and with you
   Chiefly i'th'° world; more laughed at, that I should   *Of all the*
40   Once name you derogately° when to sound   *censoriously*
   Your name it not concerned me.

ANTONY   My being in Egypt, Caesar, what was't to you?

CAESAR   No more than my residing here at Rome
   Might be to you in Egypt. Yet if you there
45   Did practice on° my state, your being in Egypt   *scheme against*
   Might be my question.°   *concern*

ANTONY   How intend you, practiced?

CAESAR   You may be pleased to catch at° mine intent   *grasp*
   By what did here befall me. Your wife and brother
   Made wars upon me, and their contestation
50   Was theme for you—you were the word of war.[4]

ANTONY   You do mistake your business. My brother never
   Did urge me in his act.[5] I did inquire° it,   *inquire into*
   And have my learning from some true reports°   *reliable sources*

---

3. Formally embrace you, as I do now; possibly, speak as you request.
4. *contestation . . . war:* war was meant as an exam-
ple for you to follow (had you as its theme)—your name was the war cry (war was waged in your name).
5. Claimed to be acting as my proxy.

That drew their swords with you. Did he not rather
55 Discredit my authority with yours
And make the wars alike against my stomach,°   *wish*
Having alike° your cause? Of this, my letters   *Since I shared*
Before did satisfy you. If you'll patch a quarrel,
As matter whole you have to make it with,[6]
It must not be with this.
60 CAESAR   You praise yourself
By laying defects of judgment to me, but
You patched up your excuses.
ANTONY   Not so, not so!
I know you could not lack—I am certain on't—
Very necessity of this thought,[7] that I,
65 Your partner in the cause 'gainst which he fought,
Could not with graceful eyes attend[8] those wars
Which fronted° mine own peace. As for my wife,   *opposed*
I would you had her spirit in such another.
The third o'th' world is yours, which with a snaffle[9]
70 You may pace° easy, but not such a wife.   *train to walk*
ENOBARARBUS   Would we had all such wives, that the men
    might go to wars with the women.
ANTONY   So much uncurbable,° her garboils,° Caesar,   *uncontrollable / tumults*
Made out of her impatience—which not wanted°   *did not lack*
75 Shrewdness of policy too—I grieving grant
Did you too much disquiet. For that you must
But° say I could not help it.   *Only*
CAESAR   I wrote to you,
When rioting in Alexandria you
Did pocket up my letters and with taunts
80 Did gibe my missive out of audience.[1]
ANTONY   Sir, he fell upon° me ere admitted then.   *broke in on*
Three kings I had newly feasted, and did want
Of what I was[2] i'th' morning. But next day
I told him of myself,° which was as much   *my situation*
85 As to have asked him pardon. Let this fellow
Be nothing° of our strife; if we contend   *Be no part*
Out of our question° wipe him.   *dispute*
CAESAR   You have broken
The article° of your oath, which you shall never   *terms*
Have tongue to charge me with.
90 LEPIDUS   Soft, Caesar!
ANTONY   No, Lepidus, let him speak.
The honor is sacred which he talks on now,
Supposing that I lacked it.[3] But on, Caesar—
The article of my oath?
95 CAESAR   To lend me arms and aid when I required them,
The which you both denied.
ANTONY   Neglected rather—

---

6. *If . . . with:* If you'll patch together an old quarrel
with trivia, when you have enough material to make a
new one (or, possibly, as if you had enough material to
make one).
7. *I know . . . thought:* I'm confident that you must
have been aware.
8. Could not look with approval on.
9. Bridle (one without a curb, for good-tempered

horses).
1. Scoffed my messenger out of your (public) hearing
(referring to 1.1).
2. *did . . . was:* was not myself.
3. *The honor . . . it:* What Caesar speaks of now is my
sacred honor, which he assumes I lack (even assuming
I lack it).

And then when poisoned hours had bound me up
From mine own knowledge.[4] As nearly as I may,
I'll play the penitent to you. But mine honesty
100   Shall not make poor my greatness, nor my power
Work without it.[5] Truth is that Fulvia,
To have me out of Egypt, made war here,
For which myself, the ignorant motive, do
So far ask pardon as befits mine honor°   *dignity*
To stoop in such a case.

105 LEPIDUS   'Tis noble spoken.

MAECENAS   If it might please you to enforce no further
The griefs° between ye; to forget them quite   *grievances*
Were to remember that the present need
Speaks to atone you.°   *Is to reconcile you*

LEPIDUS   Worthily spoken, Maecenas.

110 ENOBARBUS   Or if you borrow one another's love for the instant,
you may, when you hear no more words of Pompey, return it
again. You shall have time to wrangle in when you have nothing else to do.

ANTONY   Thou art a soldier only. Speak no more.

115 ENOBARBUS   That truth should be silent I had almost forgot.

ANTONY   You wrong this presence;° therefore speak no more! *(noble) company*

ENOBARBUS   Go to, then. Your considerate stone.[6]

CAESAR   I do not much dislike the matter° but   *content*
The manner of his speech, for't cannot be
120   We shall remain in friendship, our conditions°   *dispositions*
So diff'ring in their acts. Yet if I knew
What hoop should hold us staunch,° from edge to edge *watertight; bound*
O'th' world I would pursue it.

AGRIPPA   Give me leave, Caesar.

125 CAESAR   Speak, Agrippa.

AGRIPPA   Thou hast a sister by the mother's side,
Admired Octavia. Great Mark Antony
Is now a widower.

CAESAR   Say not so, Agrippa;
If Cleopatra heard you, your reproof
130   Were well deserved of rashness.[7]

ANTONY   I am not married, Caesar. Let me hear
Agrippa further speak.

AGRIPPA   To hold you in perpetual amity,
To make you brothers, and to knit your hearts
135   With an unslipping knot, take Antony°   *let Antony take*
Octavia to° his wife, whose beauty claims   *for*
No worse a husband than the best of men,
Whose virtue and whose general graces speak
That which none else can utter.[8] By this marriage
140   All little jealousies,° which now seem great,   *mistrusts*
And all great fears, which now import° their dangers, *bring along*
Would then be nothing. Truths would be tales,

---

4. *bound . . . knowledge:* prevented me from realiz-
ing what I was doing.
5. *mine . . . it:* my honorable behavior (in admitting a
fault) will not diminish my power, nor shall my power
operate without honor.
6. Very well, then; still and silent, but capable of
thought.
7. *your . . . rashness:* the reproof you would receive
would befit your rashness.
8. *speak . . . utter:* speak for themselves; speak more
powerfully than in any other woman.

Where now half-tales be truths.[9] Her love to both
Would each to other and all loves to both
145 Draw after her. Pardon what I have spoke,
For 'tis a studied, not a present° thought,   *sudden*
By duty ruminated.

ANTONY   Will Caesar speak?

CAESAR   Not till he hears how Antony is touched°   *reacts*
With° what is spoke already.   *To*

150 ANTONY   What power is in Agrippa,
If I would say, "Agrippa, be it so,"
To make this good?

CAESAR   The power of Caesar, and
His power unto Octavia.

ANTONY   May I never
To this good purpose, that so fairly shows,
155 Dream of impediment![1] Let me have thy hand.
Further this act of grace, and from this hour
The heart of brothers govern in our loves
And sway our great designs.

CAESAR   There's my hand.
A sister I bequeath° you, whom no brother   *hand over to*
160 Did ever love so dearly. Let her live
To join our kingdoms and our hearts, and never
Fly off our loves again.[2]

LEPIDUS   Happily, amen!

ANTONY   I did not think to draw my sword 'gainst Pompey,
For he hath laid strange° courtesies and great   *uncommon*
165 Of late upon me. I must thank him, only°   *at least*
Lest my remembrance° suffer ill report—   *gratitude*
At heel of° that, defy him.   *Right after*

LEPIDUS   Time calls upon's.
Of° us must Pompey presently° be sought,   *By / immediately*
Or else he seeks out us.

170 ANTONY   Where lies he?

CAESAR   About the Mount Misena.[3]

ANTONY   What is his strength by land?

CAESAR   Great, and increasing,
But by sea he is an absolute master.

175 ANTONY   So is the fame.°   *report*
Would we had spoke together!° Haste we for it,   *(earlier)*
Yet ere we put ourselves in arms, dispatch we
The business we have talked of.

CAESAR   With most gladness,
And do° invite you to my sister's view,   *I do*
180 Whither straight I'll lead you.

ANTONY   Let us, Lepidus, not lack your company.

LEPIDUS   Noble Antony, not sickness should detain me.

Flourish. Exeunt [CAESAR, ANTONY, LEPIDUS,
and VENTIDIUS]. ENOBARBUS, AGRIPPA,
and MAECENAS *remain.*

---

9. *Truths . . . truths:* True reports, even if they were
disturbing, could be passed over, regarded as hear-
say, where now incomplete rumors are accepted as
truth.
1. *May . . . impediment:* alluding to the Anglican
marriage service, as does Sonnet 116: "Let me not to

the marriage of true minds / Admit impediments." so
fairly shows: appears so attractive.
2. *never . . . again:* may our love for each other never
again desert us.
3. Misenum, a hilly outcropping at the northern end
of the Bay of Naples.

MAECENAS Welcome from Egypt, sir.

ENOBARBUS Half the heart° of Caesar, worthy Maecenas. —My   *Beloved friend*
185 honorable friend, Agrippa!

AGRIPPA Good Enobarbus!

MAECENAS We have cause to be glad that matters are so well
digested.° You stayed well by't⁴ in Egypt.   *settled*

ENOBARBUS Ay, sir, we did sleep day out of countenance⁵ and
190 made the night light° with drinking.   *bright; merry*

MAECENAS Eight wild boars roasted whole at a breakfast and
but twelve persons there. Is this true?

ENOBARBUS This was but as a fly by° an eagle. We had much   *compared with*
more monstrous matter of feast, which worthily deserved
195 noting.

MAECENAS She's a most triumphant° lady, if report be square°   *magnificent / fair*
to her.

ENOBARBUS When she first met Mark Antony, she pursed up
his heart upon the river of Cydnus.⁶

200 AGRIPPA There she appeared indeed, or my reporter devised°   *imagined*
well for her.

ENOBARBUS I will tell you.
The barge° she sat in, like a burnished throne   *oar-driven ship*
Burned on the water. The poop° was beaten gold,   *upper deck*
205 Purple° the sails, and so perfumèd that   *(royal dye)*
The winds were lovesick with them. The oars were silver,
Which to the tune of flutes kept stroke and made
The water which they beat to follow faster,
As° amorous of their strokes. For° her own person,   *As if / As for*
210 It beggared all description. She did lie
In her pavilion—cloth of gold, of tissue⁷—
O'er-picturing that Venus where we see
The fancy outwork nature.⁸ On each side her
Stood pretty dimpled boys, like smiling Cupids,
215 With divers colored fans whose wind did seem
To glow° the delicate cheeks which they did cool,   *make glow*
And what they undid did.

AGRIPPA   Oh, rare for Antony.

ENOBARBUS Her gentlewomen like the Nereides,°   *sea nymphs*
So many mermaids, tended her i'th' eyes°   *under her watchful eyes*
220 And made their bends adornings.⁹ At the helm
A seeming mermaid steers. The silken tackle°   *sails and ropes*
Swell with the touches of those flower-soft hands
That yarely frame° the office. From the barge   *artfully carry out*
A strange invisible perfume hits the sense
225 Of the adjacent wharfs.° The city cast   *banks*
Her people out upon° her, and Antony,   *toward*
Enthroned i'th' marketplace, did sit alone
Whistling to th'air, which, but for vacancy,¹
Had° gone to gaze on Cleopatra too,   *Would have*
And made a gap in nature.

---

4. You hung in there; you had a high old time.
5. We disconcerted day by sleeping through it and
did not see what it looked like.
6. She took possession of his heart on the Cydnus
River in Cilicia, Asia Minor (Turkey), on which the
city of Tarsus stood.
7. Fabric interwoven with gold thread.

8. *O'er-picturing . . . nature:* Outdoing even the picture of Venus in which the artist outdid nature.
9. Made their curtsies additions to the decoration.
1. Which, if not for the fact that its absence would
have left a vacuum (already in Shakespeare's time proverbially impossible in nature).

230 AGRIPPA   Rare Egyptian!

ENOBARBUS   Upon her landing, Antony sent to her,
   Invited her to supper. She replied,
   It should be better he became her guest,
   Which she entreated. Our courteous Antony,
235   Whom ne'er the word of "No" woman heard speak,
   Being barbered ten times o'er, goes to the feast,
   And for his ordinary° pays his heart   *public meal at an inn*
   For what his eyes eat only.

AGRIPPA   Royal wench!
   She made great Caesar° lay his sword to bed;   *(Julius)*
   He ploughed her, and she cropped.[2]

240 ENOBARBUS   I saw her once
   Hop forty paces through the public street
   And, having lost her breath, she spoke and panted
   That° she did make defect° perfection,   *So that / her panting*
   And breathless pour breath forth.

245 MAECENAS   Now Antony must leave her utterly.

ENOBARBUS   Never, he will not.
   Age cannot wither her, nor custom stale°   *familiarity diminish*
   Her infinite variety. Other women cloy
   The appetites they feed, but she makes hungry
250   Where most she satisfies. For vilest things
   Become themselves° in her, that° the holy priests   *Are becoming / so that*
   Bless her when she is riggish.°   *acts like a slut*

MAECENAS   If beauty, wisdom, modesty can settle
   The heart of Antony, Octavia is
   A blessèd lottery° to him.   *prize*

255 AGRIPPA   Let us go.
   Good Enobarbus, make yourself my guest
   Whilst you abide here.

ENOBARBUS   Humbly, sir, I thank you.   *Exeunt.*

2.3

Enter ANTONY, CAESAR, OCTAVIA *between them.*

ANTONY   The world and my great office will sometimes
   Divide me from your bosom.

OCTAVIA   All which time,
   Before the gods my knee shall bow my prayers
   To them for you.

ANTONY   Good night, sir. —My Octavia,
5   Read not my blemishes in the world's report.
   I have not kept my square,° but that° to come   *stayed in line / what's*
   Shall all be done by th' rule.[1] Good night, dear lady.
   —Good night, sir.

CAESAR   Good night.   *Exeunt* [CAESAR *and* OCTAVIA].

Enter SOOTHSAYER.

10 ANTONY   Now, sirrah,[2] you do wish yourself in Egypt?

2. She bore Caesarion. After the assassination of
Julius Caesar in 44 B.C.E., Cleopatra returned from
Rome, where she had accompanied him, to Egypt.
There she reigned with their son, who became Ptolemy XV, after she ordered the death of her half
brother. See 1.4.6 with note and 2.1.38. On Antony
and Cleopatra's plans for Ptolemy XV, see 3.6.1–16.

On Ptolemy XV's fate, see note to 5.2.358.
2.3 Location: Scene continues.
1. Regulation; ruler, as unit of measure (picking up
"square," line 6, a measuring tool).
2. Term by which a subordinate or social inferior is
addressed.

SOOTHSAYER Would I had never come from thence,
  Nor you thither!
ANTONY   If you can, your reason?
SOOTHSAYER I see it in my motion,° have it not in my tongue;   *intuition*
  But yet hie° you to Egypt again.   *hurry*
ANTONY   Say to me,
15 Whose fortunes shall rise higher: Caesar's or mine?
SOOTHSAYER Caesar's.
  Therefore, O Antony, stay not by his side.
  Thy demon—that thy spirit[3] which keeps thee—is
  Noble, courageous, high, unmatchable,
20 Where Caesar's is not. But near him thy angel
  Becomes afeard, as° being o'er-powered. Therefore   *as if*
  Make space enough between you.
ANTONY   Speak this no more.
SOOTHSAYER To none but thee—no more but when° to thee.   *not at all except*
  If thou dost play with him at any game,
25 Thou art sure to lose, and of° that natural luck   *by*
  He beats thee 'gainst the odds. Thy luster thickens°   *Your brightness dims*
  When he shines by. I say again, thy spirit
  Is all afraid to govern thee near him,
  But he away, 'tis noble.
ANTONY   Get thee gone.
30 Say to Ventidius I would speak with him.

                Exit [SOOTHSAYER].

  He shall to Parthia. Be it art or hap,°   *talent or luck*
  He° hath spoken true. The very dice obey him,°   *(the soothsayer) / (Caesar)*
  And in our sports my better cunning° faints   *capability*
  Under his chance.° If we draw lots, he speeds;°   *luck / succeeds*
35 His cocks do win the battle still of° mine   *always against*
  When it is all to naught, and his quails ever
  Beat mine, inhooped, at odds.[4] I will to Egypt.
  And though I make this marriage for my peace,
  I'th' East my pleasure lies.

      Enter VENTIDIUS.

             Oh, come, Ventidius.
40 You must to Parthia; your commission's ready.
  Follow me and receive't.   *Exeunt.*

2.4

Enter LEPIDUS, MAECENAS, *and* AGRIPPA.

LEPIDUS Trouble yourselves no further. Pray you hasten
  Your generals after.[1]
AGRIPPA   Sir, Mark Antony
  Will e'en but° kiss Octavia, and we'll follow.   *merely*
LEPIDUS Till I shall see you in your soldiers' dress,
  Which will become you both, farewell.
5 MAECENAS   We shall,
  As I conceive the journey, be at the Mount°   *Mount Misenum*
  Before you, Lepidus.
LEPIDUS   Your way is shorter.

---

3. *Thy demon . . . spirit:* Your guardian angel, which
is the spirit.
4. *When . . . odds:* When the odds completely favor
me, and when our quails are placed in a round enclosure to make them fight, his always beat mine, against
all odds.
2.4 Location: Scene continues.
1. *hasten . . . after:* follow your leaders.

My purposes do draw me° much about;   *force me to go*
You'll win two days upon me.
MAECENAS *and* AGRIPPA   Sir, good success.
10 LEPIDUS Farewell.   *Exeunt.*

2.5

Enter CLEOPATRA, CHARMIAN, IRAS, *and* ALEXAS.
CLEOPATRA Give me some music—music, moody° food   *melancholy*
Of us that trade in love.
CHARMIAN, IRAS, *and* ALEXAS The music, ho!
Enter MARDIAN *the eunuch.*
CLEOPATRA Let it alone. Let's to billiards. Come, Charmian.
CHARMIAN My arm is sore. Best play with Mardian.
5 CLEOPATRA As well a woman with an eunuch played
As with a woman. Come, you'll play with me, sir?
MARDIAN As well as I can, madam.
CLEOPATRA And when good will is showed, though't come too
short¹
The actor may plead pardon. I'll none now.°   *I won't play now*
10 Give me mine angle.° We'll to th' river. There,   *fishing rod*
My music playing far off, I will betray°   *catch*
Tawny-finned fishes. My bended hook shall pierce
Their slimy jaws, and as I draw them up,
I'll think them every one an Antony
And say, "Aha! You're caught!"
15 CHARMIAN   'Twas merry when
You wagered on your angling, when your diver
Did hang a salt° fish on his hook which he   *preserved*
With fervency drew up.
CLEOPATRA   That time? Oh, times!
.I laughed him out of patience, and that night
20 I laughed him into patience, and next morn,
Ere the ninth hour, I drunk him to his bed,
Then put my tires and mantles° on him, whilst   *headdresses and robes*
I wore his sword Philippan.²
Enter a MESSENGER.
Oh, from Italy!
Ram thou thy fruitful tidings in mine ears
That long time have been barren.
25 MESSENGER   Madam, madam!
CLEOPATRA Antonio's dead? If thou say so, villain,
Thou kill'st thy mistress; but well and free—
If thou so yield° him—there is gold, and here   *report*
My bluest veins to kiss, a hand that kings
30 Have lipped and trembled kissing.
MESSENGER First, madam, he is well.
CLEOPATRA Why, there's more gold. But, sirrah, mark, we use
To say the dead are well. Bring it to that,
The gold I give thee will I melt and pour
35 Down thy ill-uttering throat.
MESSENGER Good madam, hear me.
CLEOPATRA Well, go to, I will.

2.5 Location: Alexandria.
1. Referring to Mardian's sexual incapacity.

2. The sword with which Antony had beaten Brutus
and Cassius at Philippi.

But there's no goodness in thy face. If Antony
Be free and healthful, so tart a favor°   *so sour an expression*
40   To trumpet such good tidings! If not well,
Thou shouldst come like a fury[3] crowned with snakes,
Not like a formal° man.   *Not in the shape of a*

MESSENGER   Will't please you hear me?
CLEOPATRA   I have a mind to strike thee ere thou speak'st.
Yet if thou say Antony lives, 'tis well,
45   Or friends with Caesar, or not captive to him,
I'll set thee in a shower of gold and hail
Rich pearls upon thee.

MESSENGER   Madam, he's well.
CLEOPATRA   Well said.
MESSENGER   And friends with Caesar.
CLEOPATRA   Thou'rt an honest man.
MESSENGER   Caesar and he are greater friends than ever.
CLEOPATRA   Make thee a fortune from me.
50   MESSENGER   But yet, madam—
CLEOPATRA   I do not like "But yet." It does allay°   *dissipate*
The good precedence.° Fie upon "But yet"!   *preceding good news*
"But yet" is as a jailor to bring forth
Some monstrous malefactor. Prithee, friend,
55   Pour out the pack of matter to mine ear,°   *Give me all the news*
The good and bad together. He's friends with Caesar,
In state of health, thou say'st, and thou say'st, free.

MESSENGER   Free, madam, no! I made no such report.
He's bound unto Octavia.
CLEOPATRA   For what good turn?°   *good deed*
MESSENGER   For the best turn i'th' bed.
60   CLEOPATRA   I am pale, Charmian.
MESSENGER   Madam, he's married to Octavia.
CLEOPATRA   The most infectious pestilence upon thee!
          [*She*] *strikes him down.*
MESSENGER   Good madam, patience!
CLEOPATRA   What say you?
          [*She*] *strikes him.*
Hence, horrible villain, or I'll spurn° thine eyes   *kick*
65   Like balls before me! I'll unhair thy head;
          She hales° *him up and down.*   *drags*
Thou shalt be whipped with wire and stewed in brine,
Smarting in ling'ring pickle.°   *salt water*
MESSENGER   Gracious madam,
I that do bring the news made not the match!
CLEOPATRA   Say 'tis not so! A province I will give thee
70   And make thy fortunes proud. The blow thou hadst
Shall make thy peace for moving me to rage,
And I will boot° thee with what° gift beside   *compensate / whatever*
Thy modesty can beg.
MESSENGER   He's married, madam.
CLEOPATRA   Rogue, thou hast lived too long.
          [*She*] *draws a knife.*
MESSENGER   Nay, then I'll run.
75   What mean you, madam? I have made no fault.   *Exit.*

---

3. In Greek mythology, a female avenging spirit.

CHARMIAN   Good madam, keep yourself within yourself.°   *restrain yourself*
The man is innocent.
CLEOPATRA   Some innocents scape° not the thunderbolt.   *escape*
Melt Egypt into Nile, and kindly° creatures   *harmless*
80   Turn all to serpents! Call the slave again.
Though I am mad, I will not bite him. Call!
CHARMIAN   He is afeard to come.
CLEOPATRA   I will not hurt him.
These hands do lack nobility that they strike
A meaner° than myself, since I myself   *One of lower rank*
Have given myself the cause.°   *(by loving Antony)*
        Enter the MESSENGER *again.*
85   Come hither, sir.
Though it be honest, it is never good
To bring bad news. Give to a gracious message
An host° of tongues, but let ill tidings tell   *A multitude*
Themselves when they be felt.[4]
MESSENGER   I have done my duty.
90   CLEOPATRA   Is he married?
I cannot hate thee worser than I do
If thou again say "Yes."
MESSENGER   He's married, madam.
CLEOPATRA   The gods confound° thee. Dost thou hold there still?   *destroy*
MESSENGER   Should I lie, madam?
CLEOPATRA   Oh, I would thou didst,
95   So° half my Egypt were submerged and made   *Even if*
A cistern° for scaled snakes. Go, get thee hence!   *reservoir; chamber pot*
Hadst thou Narcissus[5] in thy face, to me
Thou wouldst appear most ugly. He is married?
MESSENGER   I crave your highness' pardon.
CLEOPATRA   He is married?
100 MESSENGER   Take no offense that I would not° offend you;   *since I don't want to*
To punish me for what you make me do
Seems much unequal.° He's married to Octavia.   *most unfair*
CLEOPATRA   Oh, that his fault should make a knave° of thee,   *villain*
That art not what thou'rt sure of![6] Get thee hence.
105 The merchandise which thou hast brought from Rome
Are all too dear for me. Lie they upon thy hand,[7]
And be undone° by 'em.   [*Exit* MESSENGER.]   *ruined (financially)*
CHARMIAN   Good your highness, patience!
CLEOPATRA   In praising Antony, I have dispraised Caesar.
CHARMIAN   Many times, madam.
110 CLEOPATRA   I am paid for't now. Lead me from hence.
I faint. O Iras, Charmian—'tis no matter.
Go to the fellow, good Alexas. Bid him
Report the feature° of Octavia, her years,   *appearance*
Her inclination.° Let him not leave out   *disposition*
115 The color of her hair. Bring me word quickly.
                                    [*Exit* ALEXAS.]
Let him forever go—let him not! Charmian,
Though he be painted one way like a Gorgon,

4. *let . . . felt:* bad news is best revealed by letting the   6. Who are not bad, unlike the offense you know
victim feel the effects.   about.
5. In Greek mythology, a surpassingly beautiful young   7. Leave with your goods unsold.
man.

The other way's a Mars.[8] [*to* MARDIAN] Bid you Alexas
Bring me word how tall she is. Pity me, Charmian,
120 But do not speak to me. Lead me to my chamber. *Exeunt.*

2.6

Flourish. Enter POMPEY *and* MENAS *at one door with
drum and trumpet. At another* [*door enter*] CAESAR,
LEPIDUS, ANTONY, ENOBARBUS, MAECENAS, *and*
AGRIPPA *with* SOLDIERS *marching.*

POMPEY   Your hostages I have, so have you mine,
And we shall talk before we fight.
CAESAR   Most meet°   *fitting*
That first we come to words, and therefore have we
Our written purposes° before us sent,   *offers*
5 Which if thou hast considered, let us know
If 'twill tie up° thy discontented sword   *lead you to put aside*
And carry back to Sicily much tall° youth   *courageous*
That else must perish here.
POMPEY   To you all three,
The senators alone° of this great world,   *sole governors*
10 Chief factors° for the gods: I do not know   *agents*
Wherefore° my father[1] should revengers want,°   *why / lack*
Having a son and friends, since Julius Caesar,
Who at Philippi the good Brutus ghosted,[2]
There saw you laboring for him.° What was't   *on his behalf*
15 That moved pale Cassius to conspire? And what
Made all-honored, honest,° Roman Brutus,   *honorable*
With the armed rest, courtiers° of beauteous freedom,   *seekers*
To drench° the Capitol, but that they would   *(in blood)*
Have one man but a man?° And that is it   *(and not a king)*
20 Hath made me rig° my navy. At whose burden   *equip*
The angered ocean foams, with which I meant
To scourge th'ingratitude that despiteful Rome
Cast on my noble father.
CAESAR   Take your time.
ANTONY   Thou canst not fear° us, Pompey, with thy sails.   *intimidate*
25 We'll speak with° thee at sea. At land thou know'st   *engage*
How much we do o'ercount° thee.   *outnumber*
POMPEY   At land indeed
Thou dost o'ercount me of my father's house.[3]
But, since the cuckoo builds not for himself,[4]
Remain in't as thou mayst.°   *as long as you can*
LEPIDUS   Be pleased to tell us,

---

8. Cleopatra imagines Antony as a figure in a perspective painting: popular in Shakespeare's time, they showed different images according to the angle from which they were viewed. In classical mythology, a Gorgon was one of three female monsters with snakes for hair whose horrific appearance could turn others to stone.
2.6 Location: Near Misenum, Italy.
1. Pompey the Great. After being defeated by Julius Caesar at Pharsalia, Pompey the Great fled to Egypt and was there assassinated by agents of Ptolemy, Cleopatra's half brother (prior to the events in *Julius Caesar*; see note to 1.4.6). In *Julius Caesar*, Julius

Caesar is then himself assassinated by the Roman republican conspirators, including Cassius and Brutus, who are in turn killed by the triumvirs (see note to 1.2.98). The younger Pompey thus believes that by making war on the triumvirate, he avenges his father's death and the deaths of Brutus and Cassius (and, therefore, fights for the Republic).
2. Caesar appeared as a ghost to Brutus at the Battle of Philippi.
3. Plutarch records that Antony agreed to buy the elder Pompey's house but ultimately refused to pay for it.
4. The cuckoo lays eggs in the nests of other birds, rather than building a nest of its own.

30   For this is from the present,° how you take   *beside the point*
         The offers we have sent you.
     CAESAR   There's the point.
     ANTONY   Which do not be entreated to,° but weigh   *convinced unfairly of*
         What it is worth embraced.°   *if you consent*
     CAESAR   And what may follow
         To try a larger fortune.[5]
     POMPEY   You have made me offer
35   Of Sicily, Sardinia, and I must
         Rid all the sea of pirates; then, to send
         Measures of wheat to Rome. This 'greed upon,
         To part with unhacked edges° and bear back   *unused swords*
         Our targes undinted.°   *shields untouched*
     CAESAR, ANTONY, *and* LEPIDUS   That's our offer.
     POMPEY   Know, then,
40   I came before you here a man prepared
         To take this offer. But Mark Antony
         Put me to some impatience. Though I lose
         The praise of it by telling, you must know,
         When Caesar and your brother were at blows,
45   Your mother came to Sicily and did find
         Her welcome friendly.
     ANTONY   I have heard it, Pompey,
         And am well studied for° a liberal thanks,   *intend to offer*
         Which I do owe you.
     POMPEY   Let me have your hand.
         [*They shake hands.*]
     I did not think, sir, to have met you here.
50   ANTONY   The beds i'th' East are soft, and thanks to you
         That called me timelier° than my purpose° hither,   *earlier / intention*
         For I have gained by't.
     CAESAR   Since I saw you last,
         There's a change upon you.
     POMPEY   Well, I know not
         What counts harsh fortune casts upon my face,[6]
55   But in my bosom shall she never come
         To make my heart her vassal.
     LEPIDUS   Well met here.
     POMPEY   I hope so, Lepidus. Thus we are agreed.
     I crave our composition° may be written   *pact*
         And sealed between us.
     CAESAR   That's the next to do.
60   POMPEY   We'll feast each other ere we part, and let's
         Draw lots who shall begin.°   *act as host*
     ANTONY   That will I, Pompey.
     POMPEY   No, Antony, take the lot, but first or last,
         Your fine Egyptian cookery shall have
         The fame. I have heard that Julius Caesar
         Grew fat with feasting there.
65   ANTONY   You have heard much.
     POMPEY   I have fair° meaning, sir.   *amicable*
     ANTONY   And fair° words to them.   *(ironic)*

---

5. If you try (by fighting us) for a still larger fortune than we have offered.

6. What accounts cruel fortune calculates (by marking notches, like wrinkles).

POMPEY   Then so much have I heard,
And I have heard Apollodorus carried[7]—

ENOBARBUS   No more that. He did so.

70 POMPEY   What, I pray you?

ENOBARBUS   A certain queen to Caesar in a mattress.

POMPEY   I know thee now. How far'st thou, soldier?

ENOBARBUS   Well, and well am like to do, for I perceive
Four feasts are toward.°   °to come

POMPEY   Let me shake thy hand,
75 I never hated thee. I have seen thee fight
When I have envied thy behavior.

ENOBARBUS   Sir,
I never loved you much, but I ha' praised ye,
When you have well deserved ten times as much
As I have said you did.

POMPEY   Enjoy thy plainness;°   °matter-of-fact speech
80 It nothing ill becomes thee.
Aboard my galley I invite you all.
Will you lead, lords?

CAESAR, ANTONY, and LEPIDUS   Show's the way, sir.

POMPEY   Come.

Exeunt all but ENOBARBUS *and* MENAS.

MENAS [*aside*]   Thy father, Pompey, would ne'er have made
this treaty. [*to* ENOBARBUS] You and I have known,° sir.   °met each other

85 ENOBARBUS   At sea, I think.

MENAS   We have, sir.

ENOBARBUS   You have done well by water.

MENAS   And you by land.

ENOBARBUS   I will praise any man that will praise me, though
90 it cannot be denied what I have done by land.

MENAS   Nor what I have done by water.

ENOBARBUS   Yes, something you can deny for your own safety.
You have been a great thief by sea.

MENAS   And you by land.

95 ENOBARBUS   There I deny my land service, but give me your
hand, Menas. If our eyes had authority,° here they might   °(to make an arrest)
take two thieves kissing.[8]

MENAS   All men's faces are true,° whatsoe'er their hands are.   °honest

ENOBARBUS   But there is never a fair woman has a true° face.   °(without makeup)

100 MENAS   No slander°—they steal hearts.   °That's true

ENOBARBUS   We came hither to fight with you.

MENAS   For my part, I am sorry it is turned to a drinking.
Pompey doth this day laugh away his fortune.

ENOBARBUS   If he do, sure he cannot weep't back again.

105 MENAS   You've said,° sir. We looked not for Mark Antony here.   °spoken truly
Pray you, is he married to Cleopatra?

ENOBARBUS   Caesar's sister is called Octavia.

MENAS   True, sir. She was the wife of Caius Marcellus.

ENOBARBUS   But she is now the wife of Marcus Antonius.

110 MENAS   Pray ye,° sir?   °Really

ENOBARBUS   'Tis true.

---

7. Alluding to the story that Cleopatra gained access to her lover, Julius Caesar, by having herself rolled up in a sleeping mat that Apollodorus carried into the palace (told in Plutarch).
8. Arrest two thieves embracing; catch two thieving hands in a handshake, plotting together.

MENAS   Then is Caesar and he forever knit together.

ENOBARBUS   If I were bound to divine° of this unity, I would   *make predictions*
not prophesy so.

115   MENAS   I think the policy of that purpose made more⁹ in the
marriage than the love of the parties.

ENOBARBUS   I think so too. But you shall find the band that
seems to tie their friendship together will be the very strangler
of their amity. Octavia is of a holy, cold, and still conversation.°   *disposition*

120   MENAS   Who would not have his wife so?

ENOBARBUS   Not he that himself is not so, which is Mark
Antony. He will to his Egyptian dish again. Then shall the
sighs of Octavia blow the fire up in Caesar, and—as I said
before—that which is the strength of their amity shall prove

125   the immediate author° of their variance.° Antony will use his   *cause / enmity*
affection where it is. He married but his occasion here.¹

MENAS   And thus it may be. Come, sir, will you aboard? I have
a health° for you.   *toast*

ENOBARBUS   I shall take it, sir; we have used our throats in Egypt.

130   MENAS   Come, let's away.   *Exeunt.*

2.7

Music plays.
Enter two or three SERVANTS *with a banquet.*¹

FIRST SERVANT   Here they'll be, man. Some o'their plants are
ill-rooted² already. The least wind i'th' world will blow them
down.

SECOND SERVANT   Lepidus is high-colored.

5   FIRST SERVANT   They have made him drink alms-drink.³

SECOND SERVANT   As they pinch one another by the disposition,⁴ he cries out, "No more," reconciles them to his
entreaty,° and himself to th' drink.   *(to stop arguing)*

FIRST SERVANT   But it raises the greater war between him and

10   his discretion.

SECOND SERVANT   Why, this it is to have a name° in great men's   *only a nominal place*
fellowship. I had as lief° have a reed that will do me no service   *just as soon*
as a partisan I could not heave.⁵

FIRST SERVANT   To be called into a huge sphere, and not to be

15   seen to move in't, are the holes where eyes should be, which
pitifully disaster the cheeks.⁶

A sennet° sounded.   *flourish of trumpets*

Enter CAESAR, ANTONY, POMPEY, LEPIDUS, AGRIPPA,
MAECENAS, ENOBARBUS, [*and*] MENAS, *with other*
CAPTAINS [*and a* BOY].

ANTONY   Thus do they, sir. They take the flow° o'th' Nile   *measure the depth*
By certain scales i'th'° pyramid. They know   *marks on the*

---

9. I think the politics of that "unity" weighed more
heavily.
1. *Antony . . . here:* Antony will act on his desire
where it really is located (Egypt). He married out of
self-interest here.
2.7 Location: Pompey's galley, off Misenum.
1. One of the courses of the feast, possibly dessert.
2. *their . . . rooted:* the soles of the feet of the (drunken)
leaders are unsteady; the alliance between Antony and
Caesar is shaky.
3. Drink given out of charity; in this case, extra
rounds given to reconcile the parties each time they

quarrel; one too many.
4. As they irritate one another according to their
natures.
5. As a spear I could not lift (position without power).
6. *To be . . . cheeks:* To be placed in high circles
where one is incapable of moving is like having,
instead of eyes, empty eye sockets that disfigure one's
face. (In Ptolemaic astronomy, a planet "moves"
within its "sphere," one of a series of concentric circles of which the universe is formed, with the earth at
the center. A planet's ill influence causes "disaster"—
literally, "bad star.")

	By th' height, the lowness, or the mean° if dearth	*middle position*
20	Or foison° follow. The higher Nilus swells,	*abundance*
	The more it promises; as it ebbs, the seedsman	
	Upon the slime and ooze scatters his grain,	
	And shortly comes to harvest.	

LEPIDUS You've strange serpents there?

25 ANTONY Ay, Lepidus.

LEPIDUS Your serpent of Egypt is bred now of your mud by the operation of your sun. So is your crocodile.

ANTONY They are so.

POMPEY Sit, and some wine. A health to Lepidus!

30 LEPIDUS I am not so well as I should be, but I'll ne'er out.°   *leave; miss a round*

ENOBARBUS [*aside*] Not till you have slept. I fear me you'll be in° till then.   *remain; be drunk*

LEPIDUS Nay, certainly, I have heard the Ptolemies' pyramises[7] are very goodly things. Without contradiction I have heard

35 that.

MENAS [*aside to* POMPEY] Pompey, a word.

POMPEY [*aside to* MENAS] Say in mine ear. What is't?

MENAS Forsake thy seat, I do beseech thee, captain, And hear me speak a word.

40 POMPEY (*whispering in* [*Menas'*] *ear*) Forbear° me till anon.   *Wait for*
—This wine for Lepidus.

LEPIDUS What manner o'thing is your crocodile?

ANTONY It is shaped, sir, like itself, and it is as broad as it hath breadth. It is just so high as it is, and moves with it° own   *its*

45 organs. It lives by that which nourisheth it, and the elements once out of it, it transmigrates.[8]

LEPIDUS What color is it of?

ANTONY Of it own color, too.

LEPIDUS 'Tis a strange serpent.

50 ANTONY 'Tis so, and the tears of it are wet.°   *deceitful crocodile tears*

CAESAR Will this description satisfy him?

ANTONY With the health that Pompey gives him, else he is a very epicure.°   *an insatiable glutton*

[MENAS *whispers to* POMPEY.]

POMPEY Go hang, sir, hang! Tell me of that? Away!

55 Do as I bid you. —Where's this cup I called for?

MENAS [*aside to* POMPEY] If for the sake of merit° thou wilt   *past deeds*
hear me, rise from thy stool.

POMPEY I think thou'rt mad. [*They step aside.*] The matter?

MENAS I have ever held my cap off to° thy fortunes.   *ever served*

60 POMPEY Thou hast served me with much faith. What's else to say? —Be jolly, lords.

ANTONY These quicksands, Lepidus, keep off them, for you sink.

MENAS Wilt thou be lord of all the world?

POMPEY   What say'st thou?

MENAS Wilt thou be lord of the whole world? That's twice.

POMPEY How should that be?

65 MENAS   But entertain° it,   *consider*
And though thou think me poor, I am the man
Will give thee all the world.

---

7. Pyramids (drunken speech).
8. Passes into other forms of life: referring to Pythagoras's theory, apparently of Egyptian origin,

that at death the soul moves into another newborn living thing.

POMPEY Hast thou drunk well?	
MENAS No, Pompey, I have kept me from the cup.	
Thou art, if thou dar'st be, the earthly Jove.	
70 Whate'er the ocean pales° or sky inclips°	encloses / embraces
Is thine, if thou wilt ha't.	
POMPEY Show me which way?	
MENAS These three world-sharers, these competitors°	allies
Are in thy vessel. Let me cut the cable,	
And when we are put off,° fall to their throats.	(from shore)
All there is thine.	
75 POMPEY Ah, this thou shouldst have done	
And not have spoke on't. In me 'tis villainy;	
In thee't had been good service. Thou must know,	
'Tis not my profit that does lead mine honor,	
Mine honor it.⁹ Repent that e'er thy tongue	
80 Hath so betrayed thine act.¹ Being done unknown,	
I should have found it afterwards well done,	
But must condemn it now. Desist, and drink.	
MENAS [aside] For this, I'll never follow thy palled° fortunes	diminished
more.	
Who seeks and will not take when once 'tis offered	
Shall never find it more.	
85 POMPEY This health to Lepidus.	
ANTONY Bear him ashore. I'll pledge it° for him, Pompey.	drink the toast
ENOBARBUS Here's to thee, Menas.	
MENAS Enobarbus, welcome.	
POMPEY Fill till the cup be hid.	
ENOBARBUS [pointing to the servant carrying LEPIDUS] There's	
a strong fellow, Menas.	
90 MENAS Why?	
ENOBARBUS 'A° bears the third part of the world, man. See'st not?	He
MENAS The third part then he is drunk—would it were all,	
That it might go on wheels!°	easily; out of control
ENOBARBUS Drink thou. Increase the reels.°	revels; spinning
95 MENAS Come.	
POMPEY This is not yet an Alexandrian feast.	
ANTONY It ripens towards it. Strike the vessels,° ho!	Open more casks
Here's to Caesar!	
CAESAR I could well forbear't.	
It's monstrous° labor when I wash my brain	unnatural
And° it grow fouler.	If as a result
100 ANTONY Be a child o'th' time.	
CAESAR Possess it. I'll make answer,²	
But I had rather fast from all° four days	for all of
Than drink so much in one.	
ENOBARBUS Ha, my brave emperor,	
Shall we dance now the Egyptian bacchanals³	
105 And celebrate our drink?	
POMPEY Let's ha't, good soldier.	
ANTONY Come, let's all take hands,	

9. 'Tis . . . it: It is my honor that precedes or is the basis of my profit.
1. Treacherously disclosed your intentions and so made it impossible to carry them out.

2. Take it, and I'll drink, too; be in command of the time, I say.
3. Wild, drunken revels in honor of Bacchus, god of wine and revelry.

Till that the conquering wine hath steeped our sense
In soft and delicate Lethe.°   *oblivion*
ENOBARBUS   All take hands.
110 Make battery to° our ears with the loud music,   *Besiege*
The while I'll place you; then the boy shall sing.
The holding° every man shall beat° as loud   *refrain / beat out*
As his strong sides can volley.°   *fire off*

Music plays. ENOBARBUS *places them hand in hand.*

The Song.

BOY [*sings*]   Come thou monarch of the vine,
115   Plumpy Bacchus with pink eyne!⁴
          In thy fats our cares be drowned,
          With thy grapes our hairs be crowned.
               Cup us till the world go round;
               Cup us till the world go round.

120 CAESAR   What would you more? Pompey, good night. —Good
brother,°   *Brother-in-law*
Let me request you off.° Our graver business   *to come ashore*
Frowns at this levity. Gentle lords, let's part.
You see we have burned° our cheeks. Strong Enobarb   *flushed*
Is weaker than the wine, and mine own tongue
125 Splits° what it speaks. The wild disguise° hath almost   *Deforms / drunkenness*
Anticked us all.° What needs more words? Good night.   *Made us all clowns*
Good Antony, your hand.
POMPEY   I'll try you° on the shore.   *test your drinking*
ANTONY   And shall, sir—give's your hand.
POMPEY   O Antony, you have my father's house.
130 But what? We are friends! Come down into the boat.
ENOBARBUS   Take heed you fall not.

        [*Exeunt all but* ENOBARBUS *and* MENAS.]
          Menas, I'll not° on shore.   *not go*
MENAS   No, to my cabin. These drums, these trumpets, flutes!
What!
Let Neptune hear we bid a loud farewell
To these great fellows. Sound and be hanged. Sound out!

Sound a flourish with drums.

135 ENOBARBUS   Hoo! Says 'a.° There's my cap!   *he*
[*He throws his cap in the air.*]
MENAS   Hoo! Noble captain, come.   *Exeunt.*

3.1

Enter VENTIDIUS *as it were in triumph, the dead body*
of Pacorus borne before him[, *with* SILIUS *and other*
SOLDIERS].

VENTIDIUS   Now, darting Parthia,¹ art thou struck, and now
Pleased fortune does of Marcus Crassus'² death
Make me revenger. Bear the King's son's body
Before our army. Thy° Pacorus, Orades,   *Your son*
Pays this for Marcus Crassus.
5 SILIUS   Noble Ventidius,

---

4. Half-closed and red from drinking.
3.1 Location: Syria.
1. Parthian cavalry advanced while flinging darts,
then retreated while shooting arrows. "Parthia" here

refers to both the nation and its king, Orodes.
2. A member, with Pompey the Great and Julius
Caesar, of the first triumvirate, treacherously and
cruelly killed in defeat by Orodes in 53 B.C.E.

Whilst yet with Parthian blood thy sword is warm,
The fugitive Parthians follow.[3] Spur through Media,[4]
Mesopotamia, and the shelters whither
The routed fly. So thy grand captain Antony
10 Shall set thee on triumphant° chariots and   *triumphal*
Put garlands on thy head.
VENTIDIUS   O Silius, Silius,
I have done enough. A lower place,° note well,   *man of low rank*
May make too great an act. For learn this, Silius;
Better to leave undone than by our deed
15 Acquire too high a fame when him we serve's away.
Caesar and Antony have ever won
More in their officer than person.[5] Sossius,
One of my place in Syria, his° lieutenant,   *(Antony's)*
For quick accumulation of renown,
20 Which he achieved by th' minute,° lost his favor.   *more of every minute*
Who does i'th' wars more than his captain can
Becomes his captain's captain, and ambition,
The soldier's virtue, rather makes choice of loss
Than gain which darkens him.°   *eclipses his renown*
25 I could do more to do Antonius good,
But 'twould offend him. And in his offense
Should my performance perish.°   *lose its value*
SILIUS   Thou hast, Ventidius, that°   *(discretion)*
Without the which a soldier and his sword
30 Grants scarce° distinction. Thou wilt write to Antony?   *Scarcely admits of*
VENTIDIUS   I'll humbly signify what in his name—
That magical word of war—we have effected;
How with his banners and his well-paid ranks
The ne'er-yet-beaten horse° of Parthia   *cavalry*
We have jaded° out o'th' field.   *chased like tired nags*
35 SILIUS   Where is he now?
VENTIDIUS   He purposeth to Athens, whither with what haste
The weight we must convey with 's will permit,
We shall appear before him. —On there! Pass along!
                            Exeunt.

3.2

Enter AGRIPPA *at one door,* ENOBARBUS *at another.*
AGRIPPA   What, are the brothers parted?°°   *brothers-in-law gone*
ENOBARBUS   They have dispatched° with Pompey. He is gone; *finished the business*
The other three are sealing.° Octavia weeps   *signing their pact*
To part from Rome. Caesar is sad, and Lepidus,
5 Since Pompey's feast—as Menas says—is troubled
With the greensickness.[1]
AGRIPPA   'Tis a noble Lepidus.
ENOBARBUS   A very fine one. Oh, how he loves Caesar!
AGRIPPA   Nay, but how dearly he adores Mark Antony!

---

3. Chase the fleeing Parthians.
4. The land between Persia and Armenia, east of Mesopotamia—part of the Parthian Empire.
5. Owing more to the skill of their officers than to their own skill.

3.2 Location: Rome.
1. Anemia in adolescent, lovesick girls (hence, a feminizing attribute): here, used humorously for Lepidus's hangover and its effect, as well as ironically for his overblown affection for Caesar and Antony.

ENOBARBUS   Caesar? Why, he's the Jupiter of men.

10   AGRIPPA   What's Antony? The god of Jupiter?

ENOBARBUS   Spake you of Caesar? How, the nonpareil?°   *incomparable*

AGRIPPA   O Antony! O thou Arabian bird![2]

ENOBARBUS   Would you praise Caesar? Say "Caesar." Go no
   further.

AGRIPPA   Indeed, he plied them both with excellent praises.

15   ENOBARBUS   But he loves Caesar best, yet he loves Antony.

Hoo! Hearts, tongues, figures,° scribes, bards, poets cannot   *(of speech); numbers*

Think, speak, cast,° write, sing, number!° Hoo!   *calculate / make verses*

His love to Antony. But as for Caesar—

Kneel down, kneel down, and wonder.

AGRIPPA   Both he loves.

ENOBARBUS   They are his shards[3] and he their beetle.
   [*Trumpets sound within.*]

20   So,

This is° to horse. Adieu, noble Agrippa.   *calls us*

AGRIPPA   Good fortune, worthy soldier, and farewell.
          Enter CAESAR, ANTONY, LEPIDUS, *and* OCTAVIA.

ANTONY   No further, sir.

CAESAR   You take from me a great part of myself.

25   Use me well in't. —Sister, prove such a wife

As my thoughts make thee, and as my farthest band

Shall pass on thy approof.[4] —Most noble Antony,

Let not the piece° of virtue which is set   *paragon*

Betwixt us as the cement of our love

30   To keep it builded, be the ram to batter

The fortress of it. For better might we

Have loved without this mean° if on both parts   *intermediary*

This be not cherished.

ANTONY   Make me not offended

In° your distrust.   *By*

CAESAR   I have said.

ANTONY   You shall not find,

35   Though you be therein curious,° the least cause   *overly probing*

For what you seem to fear. So the gods keep you

And make the hearts of Romans serve your ends.

We will here part.

CAESAR   Farewell, my dearest sister, fare thee well.

40   The elements be kind to thee and make

Thy spirits all of comfort. Fare thee well.

OCTAVIA   My noble brother.

ANTONY   The April's in her eyes;° it is love's spring,   *She weeps*

And these the showers to bring it on. Be cheerful.

45   OCTAVIA   Sir, look well to my husband's° house, and—   *(Antony's)*

CAESAR   What, Octavia?

OCTAVIA   I'll tell you in your ear.

ANTONY   Her tongue will not obey her heart, nor can

Her heart inform her tongue. The swansdown feather

---

2. The phoenix, a legendary, self-resurrecting bird,
only one of which existed at a time. It was believed to
live for several centuries, to die in flames, and to be
reborn from its own ashes.
3. Dung patches (between which the beetle crawls
to feed and breed); perhaps, wing cases (with which

the beetle flies).
4. *and as . . . approof*: and (such a wife) as to make
my largest contractual commitment (also, my closest
tie of affection: here, Caesar's to Octavia) approved
on the basis of what you will prove to be.

That stands upon the swell at the full of tide
And neither way inclines.[5]
50 ENOBARBUS [aside to AGRIPPA]   Will Caesar weep?
AGRIPPA   He has a cloud in 's face.
ENOBARBUS   He were the worse for that were he a horse;[6]
So is he being a man.
AGRIPPA   Why, Enobarbus,
When Antony found Julius Caesar dead,
55   He cried almost to roaring. And he wept
When at Philippi he found Brutus slain.
ENOBARBUS   That year, indeed, he was troubled with a rheum.°   *flu; watery eyes*
What willingly he did confound° he wailed,°   *destroy / mourned*
Believe't, till I weep too.
CAESAR   No, sweet Octavia,
60   You shall hear from me still.° The time shall not   *constantly*
Outgo[7] my thinking on° you.   *of*
ANTONY   Come, sir, come,
I'll wrestle with you in my strength of love.
Look, here I have you. [He embraces CAESAR.] Thus I let you go,
And give you to the gods.
CAESAR   Adieu. Be happy.
65 LEPIDUS   Let all the number of the stars give light
To thy fair way.
CAESAR   Farewell, farewell.
      ([He] kisses OCTAVIA.)
ANTONY   Farewell.
                                    Trumpets sound. Exeunt.

3.3

      Enter CLEOPATRA, CHARMIAN, IRAS, and ALEXAS.
CLEOPATRA   Where is the fellow?
ALEXAS   Half afeard to come.
CLEOPAPTRA   Go to, go to! Come hither, sir.
      Enter the MESSENGER as before.
ALEXAS   Good majesty,
Herod of Jewry[1] dare not look upon you
But when you are well pleased.
CLEOPATRA   That Herod's head
5   I'll have, but how, when Antony is gone
Through whom I might command it? —Come thou near.
MESSENGER   Most gracious majesty.
CLEOPATRA   Didst thou behold Octavia?
MESSENGER   Ay, dread queen.
CLEOPATRA   Where?
MESSENGER   Madam, in Rome.
I looked her in the face and saw her led
10   Between her brother and Mark Antony.
CLEOPATRA   Is she as tall as me?
MESSENGER   She is not, madam.
CLEOPATRA   Didst hear her speak? Is she shrill-tongued or low?

5. *the swansdown . . . inclines:* (she is like) the feather of a swan's down that floats in still water, unmoving (just as she can't speak) when the tide is about to turn. Octavia's emotions, balanced between brother and husband, are too strong to allow speech.
6. A horse with a cloud—a dark rather than a white star—on its face was supposedly ill tempered.
7. *The . . . / Outgo:* Even time will not endure beyond.
3.3 Location: Alexandria.
1. Renowned for his irrational cruelty. See note to 1.2.28.

MESSENGER   Madam, I heard her speak; she is low voiced.
CLEOPATRA   That's not so good.° He cannot like her long.   *favorable to Octavia*
15 CHARMIAN   Like her? O Isis, 'tis impossible!
CLEOPATRA   I think so, Charmian—dull of tongue and dwarfish!
    What majesty is in her gait? Remember,
    If ere thou look'st on majesty.
MESSENGER   She creeps.
    Her motion and her station° are as one.   *standing still*
20 She shows° a body rather than a life,   *seems to be*
    A statue than° a breather.   *rather than*
CLEOPAPTRA   Is this certain?
MESSENGER   Or I have no observance.°   *powers of observation*
CHARMIAN   Three in Egypt cannot make better note.[2]
CLEOPATRA   He's very knowing; I do perceive't.
25 There's nothing in her yet.
    The fellow has good judgment.
CHARMIAN   Excellent.
CLEOPATRA   Guess at her years, I prithee.
MESSENGER   Madam, she was a widow.
CLEOPATRA   Widow? Charmian, hark.
30 MESSENGER   And I do think she's thirty.°   *(Cleopatra was 38)*
CLEOPATRA   Bear'st thou her face in mind? Is't long or round?
MESSSENGER   Round, even to faultiness.
CLEOPATRA   For the most part, too, they are foolish that are so.
    Her hair, what color?
MESSENGER   Brown, madam, and her forehead
    As low as she would wish it.[3]
35 CLEOPATRA   There's gold for thee.
    Thou must not take my former sharpness ill.
    I will employ thee back° again. I find thee   *to go back to Rome*
    Most fit for business. Go, make thee ready.
    Our letters are prepared.   [*Exit* MESSENGER.]
CHARMIAN   A proper° man.   *An admirable*
40 CLEOPATRA   Indeed, he is so. I repent me much
    That so I harried him. Why, methinks by him°   *by his account*
    This creature's no such thing.°   *nothing special*
CHARMIAN   Nothing, madam.
CLEOPATRA   The man hath seen some majesty and should know.
CHARMIAN   Hath he seen majesty? Isis else defend,
45 And serving you so long.[4]
CLEOPATRA   I have one thing more to ask him yet, good Charmian.
    But 'tis no matter; thou shalt bring him to me
    Where I will write. All may be well enough.
CHARMIAN   I warrant you, madam.   *Exeunt.*

3.4

Enter ANTONY *and* OCTAVIA.
ANTONY   Nay, nay, Octavia, not only that—
    That were excusable, that and thousands more
    Of semblable° import—but he hath waged   *like*
    New wars 'gainst Pompey; made his will and read it

---

2. *Three . . . note:* There are not three better witnesses
in all Egypt.
3. So that she would wish it no lower: high foreheads
were admired.

4. *Isis . . . long:* He surely has, considering how long
he's served you. *else defend:* May Isis prevent it from
being otherwise.
3.4 Location: Athens.

5	To public ear;[1] spoke scantly° of me.	*meanly*
	When perforce he could not	
	But pay me terms of honor, cold and sickly	
	He vented them—most narrow measure° lent me.	*little credit*
	When the best hint° was given him, he not took't	*opportunity*
	Or did it from his teeth.°	*insincerely*

OCTAVIA   O my good lord,
10   Believe not all, or, if you must believe,
      Stomach° not all. A more unhappy lady,   *Resent*
      If this division chance, ne'er stood between
      Praying for both parts.
15   The good gods will mock me presently:°   *at once*
      When I shall pray, "Oh, bless my lord and husband,"
      Undo° that prayer by crying out as loud,   *I'll then undo*
      "Oh, bless my brother." Husband win, win brother,
      Prays and destroys the prayer[2]—no midway
      Twixt these extremes at all.
20 ANTONY   Gentle Octavia,
      Let your best love draw to that point which seeks
      Best to preserve it.[3] If I lose mine honor,
      I lose myself. Better I were not yours
      Than yours so branchless.° But as you requested,   *amputated*
25   Yourself shall go between 's. The meantime, lady,
      I'll raise the preparation of a war
      Shall stain your brother.° Make your soonest haste,   *dim his luster*
      So° your desires are yours.   *In this way; If*
  OCTAVIA   Thanks to my lord.
      The Jove of power make me, most weak, most weak,
30   Your reconciler. Wars twixt you twain would be
      As if the world should cleave and that slain men
      Should solder up the rift.[4]
  ANTONY   When it appears to you where this begins,°   *who started this*
      Turn your displeasure that way, for our faults
35   Can never be so equal that your love
      Can equally move with° them. Provide° your going,   *judge / Prepare for*
      Choose your own company, and command what cost
      Your heart has mind to.   *Exeunt.*

3.5

Enter ENOBARBUS *and* EROS.

ENOBARBUS   How now, friend Eros?

EROS   There's strange news come, sir.

ENOBARBUS   What, man?

EROS   Caesar and Lepidus have made wars upon Pompey.

5	ENOBARBUS This is old. What is the success?°	*outcome*

EROS   Caesar, having made use of him° in the wars 'gainst Pom-   *(Lepidus)*
      pey, presently denied him rivality,° would not let him partake   *equal partnership*
      in the glory of the action, and not resting° here, accuses him   *stopping*
      of letters he had formerly wrote to Pompey. Upon his° own   *(Caesar's)*
10   appeal° seizes him, so the poor third is up° till death enlarge *accusation / imprisoned*
      his confine.

---

1. Caesar's act implies promises to the public.
2. Wishing well for husband and then brother is to pray and then to undermine the prayer.
3. *Let . . . it*: Choose the one of us (Antony or Caesar)

who best strives to preserve your love.
4. *that . . . rift*: many deaths would be needed to repair the breach.
3.5 Location: Scene continues.

ENOBARBUS   Then, world, thou hast a pair of chaps,° no more,°   *jaws / (than two)*
    And throw° between them all the food thou hast,   *if you should throw*
    They'll grind the one the other. Where's Antony?
15 EROS   He's walking in the garden, thus, and spurns°   *kicks*
    The rush° that lies before him; cries, "Fool Lepidus!"   *rushes*
    And threats the throat of that his officer°   *of that officer of his*
    That murdered Pompey.[1]
ENOBARBUS   Our great navy's rigged.°   *prepared*
EROS   For Italy and Caesar. More,° Domitius: *There's more (to say)*
20   My lord desires you presently. My news
    I might have told hereafter.
ENOBARBUS   'Twill be naught[2]—
    But let it be. Bring me to Antony.
EROS   Come, sir.   *Exeunt.*

3.6

Enter AGRIPPA, MAECENAS, *and* CAESAR.

CAESAR   Contemning° Rome, he has done all this and more   *Despising*
    In Alexandria. Here's the manner of't:
    I'th' marketplace on a tribunal° silvered,   *platform*
    Cleopatra and himself in chairs of gold
5   Were publicly enthroned. At the feet sat
    Caesarion, whom they call my father's[1] son,
    And all the unlawful issue that their lust
    Since then hath made between them. Unto her
    He gave the stablishment° of Egypt, made her   *full possession*
10   Of lower Syria, Cyprus, Lydia,[2]
    Absolute queen.
MAECENAS   This in the public eye?
CAESAR   I'th' common showplace where they exercise,[3]
    His sons were there proclaimed the kings of kings;
    Great Media, Parthia, and Armenia
15   He gave to Alexander. To Ptolemy he assigned
    Syria, Cilicia, and Phoenicia. She
    In th' habiliments° of the goddess Isis   *costume*
    That day appeared, and oft before gave audience,
    As 'tis reported, so.°   *in this costume*
20 MAECENAS   Let Rome be thus informed.
AGRIPPA   Who, queasy with° his insolence already,   *sick of*
    Will their good thoughts call° from him.   *remove*
CAESAR   The people knows it and have now received
    His accusations.
AGRIPPA   Who does he accuse?
25 CAESAR   Caesar, and that having in Sicily
    Sextus Pompeius spoiled,° we had not rated° him   *ransacked / allotted*
    His part o'th' isle.° Then does he say he lent me   *(Sicily)*
    Some shipping unrestored.° Lastly, he frets   *not returned (by me)*
    That Lepidus of the triumvirate

---

1. Historically, though Shakespeare leaves Antony's responsibility for the killing unclear, Pompey was said to have been murdered at the command of Antony, who here regrets the death because Pompey might have been a useful ally against Caesar.
2. Of no consequence; extremely harmful.
3.6 Location: Rome.
1. Julius Caesar (who adopted his grandnephew Octavius as his son). See 2.2.239–40 with note and note to 5.2.358.
2. District on the western coast of Asia Minor. Shakespeare took the name from North's translation of Plutarch, but the original has "Libya."
3. In the arena (theater) where they engage in sports (perform).

30 Should be deposed, and being that,° we detain   *being deposed*
   All his revenue.
AGRIPPA   Sir, this should be answered.
CAESAR   'Tis done already and the messenger gone.
   I have told him Lepidus was grown too cruel,
   That he his high authority abused
35 And did deserve his change. For° what I have conquered,   *As for*
   I grant him part; but then in his Armenia
   And other of his conquered kingdoms, I
   Demand the like.
MAECENAS   He'll never yield to that.
CAESAR   Nor must not then be yielded to in this.

     Enter OCTAVIA *with her train.*

40 OCTAVIA   Hail, Caesar, and my lord. Hail, most dear Caesar!
CAESAR   That ever I should call thee castaway!
OCTAVIA   You have not called me so, nor have you cause.
CAESAR   Why have you stol'n upon us thus? You come not
   Like Caesar's sister. The wife of Antony
45 Should have an army for an usher and
   The neighs of horse to tell of her approach
   Long ere she did appear. The trees by th' way
   Should have borne men, and expectation fainted,
   Longing for what it had not. Nay, the dust
50 Should have ascended to the roof of heaven,
   Raised by your populous troops. But you are come
   A market maid to Rome, and have prevented°   *(by coming too early)*
   The ostentation° of our love, which, left unshown,   *public display*
   Is often left unloved.[4] We should have met you
55 By sea and land, supplying every stage°   *(of the voyage)*
   With an augmented greeting.
OCTAVIA   Good my lord,
   To come thus was I not constrained, but did it
   On my free will. My lord, Mark Antony,
   Hearing that you prepared for war, acquainted
60 My grievèd ear withal, whereon I begged
   His pardon for° return.   *permission to*
CAESAR   Which soon he granted,
   Being an abstract 'tween his lust and him.
OCTAVIA   Do not say so, my lord.
CAESAR   I have eyes upon him,
   And his affairs come to me on the wind.
   Where is he now?
65 OCTAVIA   My lord, in Athens.
CAESAR   No, my most wronged sister. Cleopatra
   Hath nodded him to her. He hath given his empire
   Up to a whore, who° now are levying   *both of them*
   The kings o'th' earth for war. He hath assembled
70 Bocchus, the King of Libya; Archelaus
   Of Cappadocia; Philadelphos, King
   Of Paphlagonia; the Thracian king, Adallas;
   King Manchus of Arabia; King of Pont;
   Herod of Jewry; Mithridates, King

---

4. Is often thought not to be love at all. Or, *which . . . unloved:* lack of opportunity to demonstrate love often leads to its actual decline.

75 Of Comagene; Polemon and Amintas,
The Kings of Mede and Lycaonia,[5]
With a more larger° list of scepters.   *yet longer*
OCTAVIA Ay me, most wretched,
That have my heart parted betwixt two friends
That does afflict each other.
80 CAESAR   Welcome hither.
Your letters did withhold our° breaking forth *restrain me from*
Till we perceived both how you were wrong° led *wrongly*
And we in negligent danger.° Cheer your heart. *danger from negligence*
Be you not troubled with the time,° which drives *present business*
85 O'er your content° these strong necessities, *contentment*
But let determined things to destiny
Hold unbewailed their way.[6] Welcome to Rome,
Nothing more dear to me. You are abused
Beyond the mark° of thought, and the high gods *limits*
90 To do you justice makes his ministers°   *agents*
Of us and those that love you. Best of comfort,
And ever welcome to us.
AGRIPPA   Welcome, lady.
MAECENAS Welcome, dear madam.
Each heart in Rome does love and pity you.
95 Only th'adulterous Antony, most large° *unlimited*
In his abominations, turns you off
And gives his potent regiment° to a trull° *powerful rule / whore*
That noises it° against us.   *cries out*
OCTAVIA   Is it so, sir?
CAESAR Most certain. Sister, welcome. Pray you,
100 Be ever known to patience. My dear'st sister! *Exeunt.*

3.7

Enter CLEOPATRA *and* ENOBARBUS.

CLEOPATRA I will be° even with thee, doubt it not. *get*
ENOBARBUS But why, why, why?
CLEOPATRA Thou hast forespoke° my being in these wars *opposed*
And say'st it is not fit.
ENOBARBUS   Well, is it, is it?
5 CLEOPATRA If not denounced° against us, why should not we *If war is declared*
Be there in person?
ENOBARBUS   Well, I could reply:
If we should serve with horse and mares together,
The horse were merely lost.[1] The mares would bear° *seduce; carry*
A soldier and his horse.
CLEOPATRA   What is't you say?
10 ENOBARBUS Your presence needs must puzzle° Antony, *distract*
Take from his heart, take from his brain, from 's time,
What should not then be spared. He is already
Traduced° for levity, and 'tis said in Rome *Slandered*
That Photinus, an eunuch, and your maids
Manage this war.
15 CLEOPATRA   Sink Rome,° and their tongues rot *To hell with Rome*

---

5. All kings from the East.
6. *let . . . way*: let predetermined events go to their
destined conclusions without complaint.
3.7 Location: Antony's camp, near Actium, Greece.

1. *If . . . lost*: If we take both male and female horses
(whores) to the wars, the males would have no hope
of triumphing, because of the females ("merely"
equals "mare-ly").

That speak against us! A charge° we bear i'th' war,   *An expense; duty*
And as the president of my kingdom will
Appear there for° a man. Speak not against it;   *as if I were*
I will not stay behind.
    Enter ANTONY *and* CANIDIUS.
20 ENOBARBUS Nay, I have done. Here comes the Emperor.
 ANTONY Is it not strange, Canidius,
  That from Tarentum and Brundusium[2]
  He could so quickly cut° the Ionian° Sea   *cut across / Adriatic*
  And take in° Toryne?° —You have heard on't, sweet? *overrun / (near Actium)*
25 CLEOPATRA Celerity is never more admired°   *wondered at*
  Than by the negligent.
 ANTONY   A good rebuke,
  Which might have well becomed the best of men
  To taunt at slackness. Canidius, we
  Will fight with him by sea.
 CLEOPATRA   By sea, what else?
 CANIDIUS Why will my lord do so?
30 ANTONY   For that he dares us to't.
 ENOBARBUS So hath my lord dared him to single fight.
 CANIDIUS Ay, and to wage this battle at Pharsalia,°   *(near Actium)*
  Where Caesar fought with Pompey. But these offers
  Which serve not for his vantage, he shakes off,
  And so should you.
35 ENOBARBUS   Your ships are not well manned,
  Your mariners are muleteers,° reapers, people   *mule drivers*
  Engrossed° by swift impress.° In Caesar's fleet *Amassed / conscription*
  Are those that often have 'gainst Pompey fought.
  Their ships are yare,° yours heavy. No disgrace   *smooth running*
40 Shall fall° you for refusing him at sea,   *befall*
  Being prepared for land.
 ANTONY   By sea, by sea.
 ENOBARBUS Most worthy sir, you therein throw away
  The absolute soldiership you have by land,
  Distract° your army, which doth most consist   *Divert*
45 Of war-marked footmen, leave unexecuted°   *untapped*
  Your own renownèd knowledge, quite forgo
  The way which promises assurance,° and   *victory*
  Give up yourself merely° to chance and hazard *completely*
  From firm security.
 ANTONY   I'll fight at sea.
50 CLEOPATRA I have sixty sails, Caesar none better.
 ANTONY Our overplus of shipping will we burn,[3]
  And with the rest full manned, from th' head° of Actium *promontory*
  Beat th'approaching Caesar. But if we fail,
  We then can do't at land.
    Enter a MESSENGER.
      Thy business?
55 MESSENGER The news is true, my lord. He is descried;° *He has been seen*
  Caesar has taken Toryne.   [*Exit* MESSENGER.]
 ANTONY Can he be there in person? 'Tis impossible!

2. Ports in southeastern Italy.
3. Antony seems to have burned his excess ("over-plus") ships because he did not have enough sailors

to man them adequately and feared that they could easily be taken by Octavius Caesar.

Strange, that his power° should be. Canidius,   *his entire army*
Our nineteen legions thou shalt hold by land,
60   And our twelve thousand horse. We'll to our ship.
—Away, my Thetis.[4]
        Enter a SOLDIER.[5]
               How now, worthy soldier?
SOLDIER   O noble emperor, do not fight by sea.
Trust not to rotten planks. Do you misdoubt
This sword and these my wounds? Let th'Egyptians
65   And the Phoenicians go a-ducking.° We   *to sea*
Have used to conquer standing on the earth
And fighting foot to foot.
ANTONY   Well, well, away!
      Exeunt ANTONY, CLEOPATRA, *and* ENOBARBUS.
SOLDIER   By Hercules, I think I am i'th' right.
CANIDIUS   Soldier, thou art, but his whole action grows
70   Not in the power on't.[6] So our leader's led,
And we are women's men.
SOLDIER   You keep by land
The legions and the horse whole, do you not?
CANIDIUS   Marcus Octavius, Marcus Justeius,
Publicola, and Caelius are for sea,
75   But we keep whole° by land. This speed of Caesar's   *stay undivided*
Carries beyond° belief.   *Exceeds*
SOLDIER   While he was yet in Rome,
His power went out in such distractions° as   *separate detachments*
Beguiled all spies.
CANIDIUS   Who's his lieutenant, hear you?
SOLDIER   They say one Taurus.
CANIDIUS   Well I know the man.
      Enter a MESSENGER.
80 MESSENGER   The Emperor calls, Canidius.
CANIDIUS   With news the time's with labor and throws forth
Each minute, some.[7]   *Exeunt.*

3.8

    Enter CAESAR *with his army, marching*[*, and* TAURUS].
CAESAR   Taurus?
TAURUS   My lord?
CAESAR   Strike not by land; keep whole.° Provoke not battle   *stay in reserve*
Till we have done at sea. Do not exceed
5   The prescript° of this scroll. Our fortune lies   *written orders*
Upon this jump.°   *Exeunt.*   *ploy*

3.9

    Enter ANTONY *and* ENOBARBUS.
ANTONY   Set we our squadrons on yond side o'th' hill
In eye° of Caesar's battle,° from which place   *view / battle line*
We may the number of the ships behold
And so proceed accordingly.   *Exeunt.*

---

4. Sea goddess, mother of the Greek hero Achilles.
5. TEXTUAL COMMENT For the significance of the possible identification of this unnamed soldier with the character Scarus in 3.10, see Digital Edition TC 5.
6. His entire plan is made without taking into account

his resources.
7. *throws . . . some:* each minute, more news is born.
3.8 Location: Near Actium.
3.9 Location: Scene continues.

3.10

CANIDIUS *marcheth with his land army one way over
the stage, and* TAURUS, *the lieutenant of Caesar, the
other way. After their going in is heard the noise of a
sea fight. Alarum. Enter* ENOBARBUS.

ENOBARBUS   Naught, naught, all naught!° I can behold no longer: *lost; ruined*
  Th'Antoniad, the Egyptian admiral,° *flagship*
  With all their sixty fly and turn the rudder.
  To see't mine eyes are blasted.° *(as if by lightning)*
   Enter SCARUS.

SCARUS   Gods and goddesses,
  All the whole synod° of them! *assembly*
5 ENOBARBUS   What's° thy passion? *What provokes*
SCARUS   The greater cantle° of the world is lost *corner; portion*
  With° very ignorance.° We have kissed away *Through / idiocy*
  Kingdoms and provinces.
ENOBARBUS   How appears the fight?
SCARUS   On our side, like the tokened pestilence,[1]
10   Where death is sure. Yon ribald nag of Egypt—
  Whom leprosy o'ertake—i'th' midst o'th' fight,
  When vantage like a pair of twins appeared
  Both as the same[2]—or rather, ours the elder°— *ours the stronger*
  The breeze upon her[3] like a cow in June,
  Hoists sails and flies.
15 ENOBARBUS   That I beheld.
  Mine eyes did sicken at the sight and could not
  Endure a further view.
SCARUS   She once being loofed,[4]
  The noble ruin° of her magic, Antony, *casualty*
  Claps on his sea-wing,° and—like a doting mallard°— *sails / male duck*
20   Leaving the fight in° height, flies after her! *at its*
  I never saw an action of such shame.
  Experience, manhood, honor ne'er before
  Did violate so itself.
ENOBARBUS   Alack, alack!
   Enter CANIDIUS.
CANIDIUS   Our fortune on the sea is out of breath
25   And sinks most lamentably. Had our general
  Been what he knew himself,° it had gone well. *(to be)*
  Oh, he has given example for our flight
  Most grossly by his own!
ENOBARBUS   Ay, are you thereabouts?° Why, then, good night *of the same mind*
  indeed.
30 CANIDIUS   Toward Peloponnesus are they fled.
SCARUS   'Tis easy to't,° and there I will attend *to reach that place*
  What further comes.
CANIDIUS   To Caesar will I render
  My legions and my horse. Six kings already
  Show me the way of yielding.
ENOBARBUS   I'll yet follow

3.10 Location: Scene continues.
1. Plague manifested in tokens (red spots presaging death).
2. When the fight could have gone either way.
3. Bitten by a gadfly; driven by a breeze.
4. Luffed—prepared to sail close to the wind (ready to leave); aloof.

35 The wounded chance° of Antony, though my reason   *fortune*
   Sits in the wind against me.°   [*Exeunt.*]   *Opposes*

3.11

Enter ANTONY *with* ATTENDANTS.

ANTONY   Hark, the land bids me tread no more upon't.
It is ashamed to bear me. Friends, come hither.
I am so lated° in the world that I   *lost in the dark*
Have lost my way forever. I have a ship
5 Laden with gold. Take that; divide it. Fly,
And make your peace with Caesar.
ATTENDANTS   Fly? Not we.
ANTONY   I have fled myself, and have instructed cowards
To run and show their shoulders.° Friends, begone!   *backs*
I have myself resolved upon a course
10 Which has no need of you. Begone!
My treasure's in the harbor. Take it. Oh,
I followed that° I blush to look upon.   *that which*
My very hairs do mutiny, for the white
Reprove the brown for rashness, and they them°   *they the others*
15 For fear and doting. Friends, begone! You shall
Have letters from me to some friends that will
Sweep° your way for you. Pray you, look not sad,   *Clear*
Nor make replies of loathness.° Take the hint°   *reluctance / chance*
Which my despair proclaims. Let that be left
20 Which leaves° itself. To the seaside straightway!   *ceases to be; flees*
I will possess you of that ship and treasure.
Leave me, I pray, a little°—pray you now,   *for a brief time*
Nay, do so, for indeed I have lost command;°   *the right to command you*
Therefore I pray you. I'll see you by and by.
                                   [*Exeunt* ATTENDANTS.]
          [ANTONY] *sits down.*
     Enter CLEOPATRA, *led by* CHARMIAN, [IRAS,] *and* EROS.
25 EROS   Nay, gentle madam, to him, comfort him.
IRAS   Do, most dear queen.
CHARMIAN   Do, why, what else?
CLEOPATRA   Let me sit down. O Juno!
ANTONY   No, no, no, no, no.
30 EROS   See you here, sir?
ANTONY   Oh, fie, fie, fie!
CHARMIAN   Madam.
IRAS   Madam, oh, good empress!
EROS   Sir, sir.
35 ANTONY   Yes, my lord, yes! He° at Philippi kept   *(Octavius)*
His sword e'en like a dancer,° while I struck   *(for decoration only)*
The lean and wrinkled Cassius, and 'twas I
That the mad Brutus ended.° He alone   *defeated*
Dealt on lieutenantry° and no practice had   *Fought through others*
40 In the brave squares° of war, yet now—no matter.   *fine formations*
CLEOPATRA   Ah, stand by.
EROS   The Queen, my lord! The Queen!
IRAS   Go to him, madam. Speak to him;
He's unqualitied° with very shame.   *lost his sense of self*

3.11 Location: Alexandria.

45 CLEOPATRA [*rising*] Well, then, sustain me. Oh!

EROS Most noble sir, arise. The Queen approaches;
Her head's declined, and death will seize her but°   *unless*
Your comfort makes the rescue.

ANTONY I have offended reputation,
A most unnoble swerving.°   *slippage*

50 EROS   Sir, the Queen.

ANTONY Oh, whither hast thou led me, Egypt? See
How I convey my shame out of° thine eyes,   *out of sight of; from*
By looking back° what I have left behind   *recalling*
'Stroyed° in dishonor.   *Destroyed*

CLEOPATRA   O my lord, my lord!

55 Forgive my fearful sails. I little thought
You would have followed.

ANTONY   Egypt, thou knew'st too well
My heart was to thy rudder tied by th' strings,
And thou shouldst tow me after. O'er my spirit
Thy full supremacy thou knew'st and that

60 Thy beck° might from the bidding of the gods   *call*
Command me.

CLEOPATRA   Oh, my pardon.

ANTONY   Now I must
To the young man[1] send humble treaties,° dodge   *appeals*
And palter in the shifts of lowness,[2] who
With half the bulk o'th' world played as I pleased,

65 Making and marring fortunes. You did know
How much you were my conqueror, and that
My sword, made weak by my affection,° would   *desire*
Obey it on all cause.°   *for any reason*

CLEOPATRA   Pardon, pardon!

ANTONY Fall° not a tear, I say. One of them rates°   *Weep / is worth*

70 All that is won and lost. Give me a kiss.
    [*They kiss.*]
Even this repays me.
We sent our schoolmaster.° Is 'a° come back?   *tutor to our children / he*
Love, I am full of lead. —Some wine
Within there, and our viands!° Fortune knows   *food*

75 We scorn her most when most she offers blows.   *Exeunt.*

3.12

Enter CAESAR, [THIDIAS,] AGRIPPA, *and* DOLABELLA,
    with others.

CAESAR Let him appear that's come from Antony.
Know you him?

DOLABELLA   Caesar, 'tis his schoolmaster—
An argument° that he is plucked, when hither   *A proof*
He sends so poor a pinion° of his wing,   *an outer feather*

5 Which° had superfluous kings for messengers   *He who*
Not many moons gone by.

    Enter AMBASSADOR *from Antony.*

CAESAR   Approach and speak.

---

1. Octavius Caesar at this time (31 B.C.E.) was thirty-
two years old, Antony fifty-one.
2. *dodge . . . lowness:* shuffle and play fast and loose
in the shifty ways of a man brought low.
3.12 Location: Caesar's camp, Egypt.

AMBASSADOR   Such as I am, I come from Antony.
I was of late as petty° to his ends   *inconsequential*
As is the morn dew on the myrtle leaf
To his grand sea.[1]

10   CAESAR   Be't so. Declare thine office.°   *business*

AMBASSADOR   Lord of his fortunes, he salutes thee and
Requires° to live in Egypt, which not granted,   *Asks*
He lessens his requests and to thee sues
To let him breathe between the heavens and earth

15   A private man in Athens. This for him.
Next, Cleopatra does confess thy greatness,
Submits her to thy might, and of thee craves
The circle° of the Ptolomies for her heirs,   *crown*
Now hazarded to thy grace.°   *placed at your mercy*

CAESAR   For Antony,
20   I have no ears to his request. The Queen
Of audience nor desire shall fail, so[2] she
From Egypt drive her all-disgracèd friend
Or take his life there. This if she perform
She shall not sue unheard. So to them both.

AMBASSADOR   Fortune pursue thee!

25   CAESAR   Bring° him through the bands.°   *Escort / ranks*

               [*Exit* AMBASSADOR, *attended.*]

[*to* THIDIAS] To try thy eloquence, now 'tis time. Dispatch;
From Antony win Cleopatra. Promise,
And in our name, what she requires; add more
(From thine invention°) offers. Women are not   *imagination*
30   In° their best fortunes strong, but want will perjure   *While in*
The ne'er-touched vestal.[3] Try thy cunning, Thidias;
Make thine own edict° for thy pains, which we   *Command your reward*
Will answer as a law.

THIDIAS   Caesar, I go.

CAESAR   Observe how Antony becomes his flaw,°   *reacts to his fall*
35   And what thou think'st his very action speaks
In every power that moves.[4]

THIDIAS   Caesar, I shall.   *Exeunt.*

3.13

Enter CLEOPATRA, ENOBARBUS, CHARMIAN, *and* IRAS.

CLEOPATRA   What shall we do, Enobarbus?

ENOBARBUS   Think,° and die.   *(about our misery)*

CLEOPATRA   Is Antony or we in fault for this?

ENOBARBUS   Antony only, that would make his will°   *lust*
Lord of his reason. What though° you fled   *What if*
5   From that great face of war, whose several ranges°   *battle lines*
Frighted each other? Why should he follow?
The itch of his affection should not then
Have nicked° his captainship at such a point,   *bettered (gambling term)*
When half to half the world opposed, he being
10   The merèd° question? 'Twas a shame no less   *disputed*

1. In relation to the great sea, ultimate source of dew, that is Antony.
2. Shall not fail to receive either a hearing or fulfillment of her wishes, as long as.
3. *want . . . vestal:* need will make the purest virgin break her vows.
4. *his very . . . moves:* his actions themselves reveal in every move he makes.
3.13 Location: Alexandria.

Than was his loss to course° your flying flags   *chase*
And leave his navy gazing.

CLEOPATRA   Prithee, peace.

Enter the AMBASSADOR *with* ANTONY.

ANTONY   Is that his answer?

AMBASSADOR   Ay, my lord.

15 ANTONY   The Queen shall then have courtesy, so° she   *as long as*
Will yield us up.

AMBASSADOR   He says so.

ANTONY   Let her know't.
—To the boy Caesar send this grizzled head,
And he will fill thy wishes to the brim
With principalities.

CLEOPATRA   That head, my lord?

20 ANTONY   To him again. Tell him he wears the rose
Of youth upon him, from which the world should note
Something particular.° His coin, ships, legions,   *anticipate the remarkable*
May be a coward's,[1] whose ministers° would prevail   *aides; underlings*
Under the service of a child as soon°   *as well*

25 As i'th' command of Caesar. I dare him therefore
To lay his gay caparisons° apart   *showy adornments*
And answer me declined,[2] sword against sword,
Ourselves alone. I'll write it. Follow me.

[*Exeunt* ANTONY *and* AMBASSADOR.]

ENOBARBUS [*aside*]   Yes, like enough. High-battled° Caesar will   *With many troops*

30 Unstate° his happiness and be staged to th' show[3]   *Overthrow*
Against a sworder! I see men's judgments are
A parcel of° their fortunes, and things outward   *Consistent with*
Do draw the inward quality after them
To suffer all alike.° That he should dream,   *To decay together*

35 Knowing all measures,[4] the full Caesar will
Answer° his emptiness. Caesar, thou hast subdued   *Fight; reply to*
His judgment too.[5]

Enter a SERVANT.

SERVANT   A messenger from Caesar.

CLEOPATRA   What, no more ceremony? See, my women,
Against the blown° rose may they stop their nose   *decaying*

40 That° kneeled unto the buds. —Admit him, sir.   *Who once*

ENOBARBUS [*aside*]   Mine honesty° and I begin to square.°   *honor / square off; argue*
The loyalty well held° to fools does make   *given*
Our faith mere° folly. Yet he that can endure   *complete*
To follow with allegiance a fall'n lord

45 Does conquer him that did his master conquer
And earns a place i'th' story.

Enter THIDIAS.

CLEOPATRA   Caesar's will?

THIDIAS   Hear it apart.

CLEOPATRA   None but friends. Say boldly.

---

1. Could just as well be a coward's (unless he does something special by himself).
2. And meet me past my prime, in my misfortune.
3. Be displayed to the public gaze (as in the London theater or Roman gladiatorial combat).
4. Having known the best and worst of times ("all measures" of fortune, both "full[ness]" and "empti-

ness," lines 35–36).
5. PERFORMANCE COMMENT For the consequences of treating Enobarbus's speech here as an aside (as the stage direction indicates), as a private address to Cleopatra, or as an aside overheard by Cleopatra, see Digital Edition PC 1.

THIDIAS   So haply° are they friends to Antony.   *possibly*
ENOBARBUS   He needs as many, sir, as Caesar has,
50   Or needs not us.[6] If Caesar please, our master
        Will leap to be his friend. For us, you know,
        Whose he is we are, and that is Caesar's.
THIDIAS   So,
        Thus then, thou most renowned: Caesar entreats,
        Not to consider° in what case thou stand'st   *be concerned*
        Further than he is Caesar.[7]
55 CLEOPATRA   Go on; right royal.°   *most generous*
THIDIAS   He knows that you embrace not Antony
        As you did love, but as you feared him.
CLEOPATRA   Oh.
THIDIAS   The scars upon your honor, therefore, he
        Does pity as constrainèd° blemishes,   *involuntary*
        Not as deserved.
60 CLEOPATRA   He is a god and knows
        What is most right. Mine honor was not yielded,
        But conquered merely.
ENOBARBUS [*aside*]   To be sure of that,
        I will ask Antony. Sir, sir, thou art so leaky
        That we must leave thee to thy sinking, for
        Thy dearest quit thee.   *Exit* ENOBARBUS.
65 THIDIAS   Shall I say to Caesar
        What you require° of him? For he partly begs   *request*
        To be desired to give. It much would please him,
        That of his fortunes you should make a staff
        To lean upon. But it would warm his spirits
70   To hear from me you had left Antony
        And put yourself under his shroud,°   *protection; burial sheet*
        The universal landlord.
CLEOPATRA   What's your name?
THIDIAS   My name is Thidias.
CLEOPATRA   Most kind messenger,
        Say to great Caesar this in deputation:°   *as my representative*
75   I kiss his conqu'ring hand. Tell him I am prompt
        To lay my crown at 's feet and there to kneel.
        Tell him from his all-obeying° breath I hear   *which all obey*
        The doom of Egypt.[8]
THIDIAS   'Tis your noblest course.
        Wisdom and fortune combating together,
80   If that the former dare but what it can,[9]
        No chance may shake it. Give me grace to lay
        My duty on your hand.
        [*He kisses her hand.*]
CLEOPATRA   Your Caesar's father oft,
        When he hath mused of taking kingdoms in,°   *subduing kingdoms*
85   Bestowed his lips on that unworthy place
        As° it rained kisses.   *As if*
        Enter ANTONY *and* ENOBARBUS.

6. *Or needs not us:* If the situation is truly hopeless,
he doesn't even need our friendship.
7. Beyond remembering that he is Caesar—and hence
nobly generous in forgiving insult and injury (but with

a more sinister undertone as well).
8. What he destines for Egypt and its queen.
9. If the wise man confines his daring to what is
possible.

ANTONY   Favors? By Jove that thunders![1]
   What art thou, fellow?
THIDIAS   One that but performs
   The bidding of the fullest° man and worthiest   *most successful*
   To have command obeyed.
ENOBARBUS   You will be whipped.
90 ANTONY Approach there! Ah, you kite!° Now gods and devils!   *bird of prey; whore*
   Authority melts from me. Of late, when I cried, "Ho!"
   Like boys unto a muss[2] kings would start forth
   And cry, "Your will?" Have you no ears? I am
   Antony yet.
        Enter SERVANT[S].
         Take hence this jack° and whip him.   *knave*
95 ENOBARBUS [*aside*] 'Tis better playing with a lion's whelp°   *cub*
   Than with an old one dying.
ANTONY   Moon and stars,
   Whip him! Were't twenty of the greatest tributaries
   That do acknowledge Caesar, should I find them
   So saucy with the hand of she here—what's her name
100 Since she was Cleopatra?[3] Whip him, fellows,
   Till like a boy you see him cringe° his face   *distort*
   And whine aloud for mercy. Take him hence.
THIDIAS Mark Antony!
ANTONY   Tug him away! Being whipped,
   Bring him again; the jack of Caesar's shall
105 Bear us an errand to him.
         Exeunt [SERVANTS] *with* THIDIAS.
   You were half blasted° ere I knew you! Ha?   *decayed*
   Have I my pillow left unpressed in Rome,
   Forborne the getting° of a lawful race,   *begetting*
   And by a gem of women, to be abused
   By one that looks on feeders?°   *parasites; servants*
110 CLEOPATRA   Good my lord.
ANTONY You have been a boggler° ever,   *fickle one*
   But when we in our viciousness grow hard
   (Oh, misery on't), the wise gods seal[4] our eyes
   In our own filth, drop our clear judgments, make us
115 Adore our errors, laugh at 's while we strut
   To our confusion.
CLEOPATRA   Oh, is't come to this?
ANTONY I found you as a morsel cold upon
   Dead Caesar's trencher.° Nay, you were a fragment°   *plate / leftover*
   Of Gneius Pompey's[5]—besides what hotter hours
120 Unregistered in vulgar fame° you have   *base gossip*
   Luxuriously° picked out. For I am sure,   *Wantonly*
   Though you can guess what temperance should be,
   You know not what it is.
CLEOPATRA   Wherefore is this?

---

1. PERFORMANCE COMMENT For the different views of both Cleopatra and Antony that follow from having Cleopatra's response to Thidias seem a betrayal of Antony or, at the other extreme, an effort to protect her defeated lover, see Digital Edition PC 2.
2. Game in which small items were tossed to the ground for children to snatch and grab.

3. Antony's question suggests that since Cleopatra's behavior has changed, her name must have changed as well.
4. Blind: hawks' eyes were sealed (sewn up) to tame them.
5. Older brother of the Pompey of the play and son of Pompey the Great. See note to 1.5.31.

ANTONY   To let a fellow that will take rewards
125   And say, "God quit° you" be familiar with   *repay*
    My playfellow, your hand, this kingly seal
    And plighter° of high hearts. Oh, that I were   *pledger*
    Upon the hill of Basan to outroar
    The hornèd herd,[6] for I have savage cause,
130   And to proclaim it civilly were like
    A haltered° neck which does the hangman thank   *in the noose*
    For being yare° about him.   *swift*

         Enter a SERVANT *with* THIDIAS.
                Is he whipped?

SERVANT   Soundly, my lord.
ANTONY   Cried he? and begged a pardon?
135 SERVANT   He did ask favor.
ANTONY   If that thy father live, let him repent
    Thou wast not made his daughter, and be thou sorry
    To follow Caesar in his triumph, since
    Thou hast been whipped for following him. Henceforth
140   The white hand of a lady fever thee;[7]
    Shake thou to look on't. Get thee back to Caesar.
    Tell him thy entertainment.° Look° thou say   *treatment / See that*
    He makes me angry with him, for he seems
    Proud and disdainful, harping on what I am,
145   Not what he knew I was. He makes me angry,
    And at this time most easy 'tis to do't,
    When my good stars that were my former guides
    Have empty left their orbs° and shot their fires   *spheres*
    Into th'abysm of hell. If he mislike
150   My speech and what is done, tell him he has
    Hipparchus, my enfranchèd° bondman, whom   *emancipated*
    He may at pleasure whip, or hang, or torture,
    As he shall like to quit° me. Urge it thou.   *requite*
    Hence with thy stripes.° Begone!   *wounds*

        Exeunt [SERVANT *and*] THIDIAS.

CLEOPATRA   Have you done yet?
155 ANTONY   Alack, our terrene moon[8] is now eclipsed,
    And it portends alone the fall of Antony.
CLEOPATRA   I must stay his time.[9]
ANTONY   To flatter Caesar, would you mingle eyes
    With one that ties his points.[1]
CLEOPATRA   Not know me yet?
ANTONY   Cold-hearted toward me?
160 CLEOPATRA   Ah, dear, if I be so,
    From my cold heart let heaven engender hail,
    And poison it in the source, and the first stone
    Drop in my neck.° As it determines,° so   *throat / turns to liquid*
    Dissolve my life; the next Caesarion smite;
165   Till by degrees the memory of my womb,°   *my children*
    Together with my brave Egyptians all,

---

6. Alluding to the bulls of the hill of Basan (Bashan) in Psalms 68:15 and 22:12; Antony sees himself as a cuckold (a man whose wife has committed adultery), conventionally imagined with horns.
7. May the white hand of a lady make you shiver with fear, as from a fever.

8. Terrestrial moon goddess—Cleopatra.
9. I must hold my tongue until he is over his rage.
1. *would . . . points*: would you flirt with one of his servants? *points*: laces (attaching stockings to other clothing).

By the discandying° of this pelleted storm   *dissolving*
Lie graveless till the flies and gnats of Nile
Have buried them for prey!
ANTONY   I am satisfied.
170 Caesar sets down in° Alexandria, where   *besieges*
I will oppose his fate.[2] Our force by land
Hath nobly held, our severed navy too
Have knit again, and fleet,° threat'ning most sealike.   *are afloat*
Where hast thou been, my heart?° Dost thou hear, lady?   *bravery*
175 If from the field I shall return once more
To kiss these lips, I will appear in blood.°   *bloody; vigorous*
I and my sword will earn our chronicle.°   *historical reputation*
There's hope in't yet.
CLEOPATRA   That's my brave lord.
ANTONY   I will be treble-sinewed, -hearted, -breathed,
180 And fight maliciously.° For when mine hours   *furiously*
Were nice[3] and lucky, men did ransom° lives   *buy their*
Of° me for jests.° But now I'll set my teeth   *From / trinkets*
And send to darkness all that stop me. Come,
Let's have one other gaudy° night. Call to me   *merry*
185 All my sad captains. Fill our bowls once more;
Let's mock the midnight bell.[4]
CLEOPATRA   It is my birthday.
I had thought t'have held it poor,° but since my lord   *modestly commemorated it*
Is Antony again, I will be Cleopatra.
ANTONY   We will yet do well.
190 CLEOPATRA   Call all his noble captains to my lord.
ANTONY   Do so. We'll speak to them, and tonight I'll force
The wine peep through their scars. Come on, my queen,
There's sap in't° yet. The next time I do fight   *vigor in (our cause)*
I'll make death love me, for I will contend°   *do battle*
195 Even with his pestilent° scythe.   *plague-dealing*
                 Exeunt [all but ENOBARBUS].
ENOBARBUS   Now he'll outstare° the lightning. To be furious°   *stare down / in a frenzy*
Is to be frighted out of fear, and in that mood
The dove will peck the estridge;° and I see still°   *a kind of hawk / always*
A diminution in our captain's brain
200 Restores his heart. When valor preys on reason,
It eats the sword it fights with. I will seek
Some way to leave him.   *Exit.*

4.1

Enter CAESAR, AGRIPPA, *and* MAECENAS, *with his*
army, CAESAR *reading a letter.*
CAESAR   He calls me "boy" and chides as° he had power   *as though*
To beat me out of Egypt. My messenger
He hath whipped with rods—dares me to personal combat,
Caesar to Antony! Let the old ruffian know
5 I have many other ways to die; meantime
Laugh at° his challenge.   *Mock*
MAECENAS   Caesar must think,

---

2. I will resist his apparently destined victory.
3. *Were nice:* Permitted me to pick and choose, to act with noble generosity; were lascivious; were pampered.
4. Let's make a mockery of the hour by revelry; let's mock the death knell that fate seems to ring for us.
4.1 Location: Caesar's camp, before Alexandria.

When one so great begins to rage, he's hunted
Even to falling. Give him no breath,° but now   *time to catch breath*
Make boot° of his distraction.° Never anger   *Take advantage / fury*
Made good guard for itself.
10 CAESAR   Let our best heads°   *officers*
Know that tomorrow the last of many battles
We mean to fight. Within our files° there are   *troops*
Of those that served Mark Antony but late,
Enough to fetch him in.° See it done,   *capture him*
15 And feast the army. We have store to do't,
And they have earned the waste.° Poor Antony! *Exeunt.*   *expense*

4.2

Enter ANTONY, CLEOPATRA, ENOBARBUS, CHARMIAN,
IRAS, ALEXAS, *with others.*
ANTONY He will not fight with me, Domitius?
ENOBARBUS   No.
ANTONY Why should he not?
ENOBARBUS He thinks, being twenty times of better fortune,
He is twenty men to one.
ANTONY   Tomorrow, soldier,
5 By sea and land I'll fight. Or° I will live,   *Either*
Or bathe my dying honor in the blood
Shall make it live again. Woo't thou° fight well?   *Will you*
ENOBARBUS I'll strike, and cry, "Take all!"°   *Winner take all*
ANTONY   Well said. Come on;
Call forth my household servants.
          Enter [some] SERVITORS.
                          Let's tonight
10 Be bounteous at our meal. Give me thy hand;
Thou hast been rightly honest. So hast thou,
Thou, and thou, and thou. You have served me well,
And kings have been your fellows.°   *companions*
CLEOPATRA *[aside to* ENOBARBUS]   What means this?
ENOBARBUS *[aside to* CLEOPATRA] 'Tis one of those odd tricks
    which sorrow shoots
Out of the mind.
15 ANTONY   And thou art honest, too.
I wish I could be made° so many men,   *split up into*
And all of you clapped up together in
An Antony, that I might do you service
So good as you have done.
SERVITORS   The gods forbid.
20 ANTONY Well, my good fellows, wait on me tonight.
Scant not my cups, and make as much of me
As when mine empire was your fellow° too   *fellow servant*
And suffered° my command.   *obeyed*
CLEOPATRA *[aside to* ENOBARBUS] What does he mean?
ENOBARBUS *[aside to* CLEOPATRA] To make his followers weep.
ANTONY   Tend me tonight.
25 May be it is the period° of your duty.   *end*
Haply° you shall not see me more, or if,°   *Maybe / if you do*

4.2 Location: Alexandria.

A mangled shadow.° Perchance tomorrow   *phantom*
You'll serve another master. I look on you
As one that takes his leave. Mine honest friends,
30   I turn you not away, but, like a master
Married to your good service, stay till death.¹
Tend me tonight two hours—I ask no more—
And the gods yield° you for't!   *reward*
ENOBARBUS   What mean you, sir,
To give them this discomfort? Look, they weep,
35   And I, an ass, am onion-eyed.° For shame!   *weepy*
Transform us not to women.
ANTONY   Ho, ho, ho!
Now the witch take° me if I meant it thus.   *bewitch*
Grace grow where those drops fall! My hearty friends,
You take me in too dolorous a sense,
40   For I spake to you for your comfort, did desire you
To burn this night with torches. Know, my hearts,
I hope well of tomorrow, and will lead you
Where rather I'll expect victorious life
Than death and honor. Let's to supper. Come,
45   And drown consideration.°   *Exeunt.*   *serious thoughts*

4.3

Enter a company of SOLDIERS.
FIRST SOLDIER   Brother, goodnight. Tomorrow is the day.
SECOND SOLDIER   It will determine one way. Fare you well.°   *Good luck*
Heard you of nothing strange about° the streets?   *in*
FIRST SOLDER   Nothing. What news?
5   SECOND SOLDIER   Belike° 'tis but a rumor. Good night to you.   *Most likely*
FIRST SOLDIER   Well, sir, good night.
      [*Enter*] *other* SOLDIERS [*to meet them*].
SECOND SOLDIER   Soldiers, have careful watch.
THIRD SOLDIER   And you. Good night, good night.
      They place themselves in every corner of the stage.
SECOND SOLDIER   Here we,¹ and if tomorrow
10   Our navy thrive, I have an absolute hope
Our landmen will stand up.°   *make a stand*
FIRST SOLDIER   'Tis a brave army and full of purpose.
      Music of the hautboys° is under the stage.   *oboes*
SECOND SOLDIER   Peace, what noise?
FIRST SOLDIER   List, list.
15   SECOND SOLDIER   Hark.
FIRST SOLDIER   Music i'th' air.
THIRD SOLDIER   Under the earth.
FOURTH SOLDIER   It signs° well, does it not?   *bodes*
THIRD SOLDIER   No.
20   FIRST SOLDIER   Peace, I say! What should this mean?
SECOND SOLDIER   'Tis the god Hercules whom Antony loved
Now leaves him.
FIRST SOLDIER   Walk. Let's see if other watchmen
Do hear what we do.

---

1. Antony considers himself a good "master" because he will remain loyal to ("stay" with) his followers until his (imminent) death.

4.3 Location: Outside Cleopatra's palace, Alexandria.
1. Here are our positions.

SECOND SOLDIER How now, masters?°   *good sirs*
  [*They*] *speak together.*[2]
25 ALL How now? How now? Do you hear this?
FIRST SOLDIER Ay, is't not strange?
THIRD SOLDIER Do you hear, masters? Do you hear?
FIRST SOLDIER Follow the noise so far as we have quarter.[3]
  Let's see how it will give off.°   *end*
ALL   Content. 'Tis strange. *Exeunt.*

4.4

Enter ANTONY *and* CLEOPATRA, *with* [CHARMIAN
  and] *others.*

ANTONY Eros, mine armor, Eros!
CLEOPATRA   Sleep a little.
ANTONY No, my chuck.° Eros, come, mine armor, Eros!   *my dear*
  Enter EROS.
  Come, good fellow, put thine iron on.[1]
  If fortune be not ours today, it is
  Because we brave° her. Come.   *dare*
5 CLEOPATRA   Nay, I'll help too.
  What's this for?
ANTONY   Ah, let be, let be. Thou art
  The armorer of my heart. False, false.° This, this.   *wrong*
CLEOPATRA Sooth,° la. I'll help. Thus it must be.   *Truly*
ANTONY   Well, well,
  We shall thrive now. —See'st thou, my good fellow?
  Go, put on thy defenses.°   *armor*
10 EROS   Briefly,° sir.   *Soon*
CLEOPATRA Is not this buckled well?
ANTONY   Rarely, rarely.°   *very well*
  He that unbuckles this, till we do please
  To daff't° for our repose, shall hear a storm.   *remove it*
  —Thou fumblest, Eros, and my queen's a squire°   *attendant to a knight*
15 More tight° at this than thou. Dispatch.° —O love,   *able / Finish*
  That thou couldst see my wars today, and knew'st
  The royal occupation, thou shouldst see
  A workman° in't.   *An expert*
          Enter an armed SOLDIER.
                    Good morrow to thee. Welcome.
  Thou look'st like him that knows a warlike charge.°   *purpose*
20 To business that we love we rise betime°   *early*
  And go to't with delight.
SOLDIER   A thousand, sir,
  Early though't be, have on their riveted trim°   *armor*
  And at the port expect you.
          Shout. Trumpets flourish.
          Enter CAPTAINS *and* SOLDIERS.
CAPTAIN The morn is fair. Good morrow, general.
SOLDIERS Good morrow, general.
25 ANTONY   'Tis well blown,[2] lads.

---

2. Individual soldiers probably address different questions and comments to one another rather than speaking in chorus.
3. As far as the limit of our watch.
4.4 Location: Cleopatra's palace.

1. Clothe me in that piece of armor of mine that
you have.
2. Well sounded (of the trumpet); well started (of the
morning).

This morning, like the spirit of a youth
That means to be of note, begins betimes.
[*to* CLEOPATRA] So, so. Come, give me that. This way. Well
   said.°   *Well done*
Fare thee well, dame. Whate'er becomes of me,
30 This is a soldier's kiss. Rebukable,
And worthy shameful check° it were to stand   *reprimand*
On more mechanic° compliment. I'll leave thee   *coarse*
Now like a man of steel. —You that will fight,
Follow me close. I'll bring you to't. —Adieu.
           Exeunt [ANTONY, EROS, CAPTAINS, *and* SOLDIERS].
CHARMIAN   Please you retire to your chamber?
35 CLEOPATRA   Lead me.
He goes forth gallantly. That he and Caesar might
Determine this great war in single fight,
Then Antony—but now —Well, on.   *Exeunt.*

4.5

Trumpets sound. Enter ANTONY, EROS[, *and a* SOLDIER].
SOLDIER   The gods make this a happy° day to Antony!   *fortunate*
ANTONY   Would thou and those thy scars had once° prevailed   *earlier*
To make me fight at land!
SOLDIER   Hadst thou done so,
The kings that have revolted° and the soldier   *deserted*
5   That has this morning left thee would have still
Followed thy heels.
ANTONY   Who's gone this morning?
SOLDIER   Who?
One ever near thee. Call for Enobarbus;
He shall not hear thee, or from Caesar's camp
Say, "I am none of thine."
ANTONY   What sayest thou?
SOLDIER   Sir,
He is with Caesar.
10 EROS   Sir, his chests and treasure
He has not with him.
ANTONY   Is he gone?
SOLDIER   Most certain.
ANTONY   Go, Eros; send his treasure after. Do it.
Detain no jot, I charge thee. Write to him—
I will subscribe°—gentle adieus and greetings.   *sign my name*
15 Say that I wish he never find more cause
To change a master. Oh, my fortunes have
Corrupted honest men. Dispatch. —Enobarbus!   *Exeunt.*

4.6

Flourish. Enter AGRIPPA, CAESAR, *with* ENOBARBUS
   and DOLABELLA.
CAESAR   Go forth, Agrippa, and begin the fight.
Our will is Antony be took alive.
Make it so known.
AGRIPPA   Caesar, I shall.   [*Exit* AGRIPPA.]

4.5 Location: Antony's camp, Alexandria.   4.6 Location: Caesar's camp, Alexandria.

5   CAESAR   The time of universal peace is near.¹
        Prove this° a prosp'rous day, the three-nooked world²   *If this proves*
        Shall bear the olive° freely.   *sign of peace*
           Enter a MESSENGER.
  MESSENGER   Antony
        Is come into the field.
  CAESAR   Go charge Agrippa
        Plant those that have revolted in the van,°   *front lines*
10   That Antony may seem to spend his fury
        Upon himself.°   *Exeunt [all but* ENOBARBUS].   *On his former troops*
  ENOBARBUS   Alexas did revolt and went to Jewry on
        Affairs of Antony; there did dissuade°   *persuade*
        Great Herod to incline himself to Caesar
15   And leave his master Antony. For this pains,
        Caesar hath hanged him. Canidius and the rest
        That fell away have entertainment° but   *employment*
        No honorable trust. I have done ill,
        Of which I do accuse myself so sorely
20   That I will joy no more.
          Enter a SOLDIER *of Caesar's.*
  SOLDIER   Enobarbus, Antony
        Hath after thee sent all thy treasure, with
        His bounty overplus. The messenger
        Came on my guard° and at thy tent is now   *on my watch*
        Unloading of his mules.
25   ENOBARBUS   I give it you.
  SOLDIER   Mock not, Enobarbus,
        I tell you true. Best you safed the bringer
        Out of the host.³ I must attend mine office,°   *look after my duties*
        Or would have done't myself. Your emperor
30   Continues still a Jove.   *Exit.*
  ENOBARBUS   I am alone the° villain of the earth   *the single greatest*
        And feel I am so most.⁴ O Antony,
        Thou mine of bounty, how wouldst thou have paid
        My better service when my turpitude
35   Thou dost so crown with gold! This blows° my heart.   *swells; bursts*
        If swift thought° break it not, a swifter mean°   *regret / means (suicide)*
        Shall outstrike thought; but thought will do't, I feel.
        I fight against thee? No, I will go seek
        Some ditch wherein to die. The foul'st best fits
40   My latter part of life.   *Exit.*

4.7

Alarum, drums, and trumpets.
Enter AGRIPPA *[and* SOLDIERS].
  AGRIPPA   Retire!° We have engaged ourselves too far.   *Sound the retreat*
        Caesar himself has work,° and our oppression°   *is beset / what we face*

---

1. Octavius Caesar, later the Emperor Augustus, was known for the Pax Romana—Roman peace—of his reign; the phrase also alludes to the birth of Christ, which occurred while Augustus was emperor. See the Introduction.
2. Three-cornered world. Referring (in descending order of probability) to Europe, Asia, Africa (the triumvirate's holdings); the three races descended from Noah's sons (Japhet, Shem, Ham); earth, sea, sky. The

three races of Noah can to an extent be superimposed on the three continents and may connect with the later religious connotations of the Roman Empire. See the previous note.
3. *Best . . . host:* It would be best if you ensured safe conduct through the lines for the messenger who brought the treasure.
4. I, more than anyone else, know this to be true of me.
4.7 Location: The battlefield, Alexandria.

Exceeds what we expected.   *Exeunt.*
     Alarums. Enter ANTONY *and* SCARUS, *wounded.*

SCARUS   O my brave emperor, this is fought indeed!
5   Had we done so at first, we had droven them home
   With clouts° about their heads.   *bandages; blows*
ANTONY   Thou bleed'st apace.
SCARUS   I had a wound here that was like a T,
   But now 'tis made an H.[1]
     [*Sound retreat*] *far off.*
ANTONY   They do retire.
SCARUS   We'll beat 'em into bench-holes.° I have yet   *latrine holes*
10   Room for six scotches° more.   *gashes*
     Enter EROS.
EROS   They are beaten, sir, and our advantage serves
   For a fair victory.
SCARUS   Let us score° their backs,   *slash*
   And snatch 'em up, as° we take hares—behind!   *in the same way as*
   'Tis sport to maul a runner.°   *coward*
ANTONY   I will reward thee
15   Once for thy sprightly° comfort, and tenfold   *cheerful*
   For thy good valor. Come thee on!
SCARUS   I'll halt° after.   *Exeunt.*   *limp*

4.8

     Alarum. Enter ANTONY *again in a march;* SCARUS,
     with others.
ANTONY   We have beat him to his camp. Run one before,
   And let the Queen know of our gests.°   [*Exit a* SOLDIER.]   *deeds*
                             Tomorrow
   Before the sun shall see's, we'll spill the blood
   That has today escaped. I thank you all,
5   For doughty-handed° are you, and have fought   *brave*
   Not as° you served the cause, but as't had been   *as though*
   Each man's like mine. You have shown all Hectors.[1]
   Enter the city, clip° your wives, your friends;   *embrace*
   Tell them your feats, whilst they with joyful tears
10   Wash the congealment from your wounds and kiss
   The honored gashes whole.
     Enter CLEOPATRA.
   [*to* SCARUS]   Give me thy hand;
   To this great fairy° I'll commend thy acts,   *enchantress*
   Make her thanks bless thee. [*to* CLEOPATRA] O thou day° o'th'   *light*
     world,
   Chain mine armed neck. Leap thou, attire and all,
15   Through proof of harness° to my heart, and there   *impenetrable armor*
   Ride on the pants° triumphing.   *heartbeats*
CLEOPATRA   Lord of lords!
   O infinite virtue,° com'st thou smiling from   *valor*
   The world's great snare uncaught?
ANTONY   My nightingale,
   We have beat them to their beds. What, girl, though gray

---

1. *wound . . . H:* The wound was originally shaped like a T, but another gash across its bottom has made it look like an H turned sideways (punning on "ache," pronounced "aitch").

4.8 Location: Scene continues.
1. You have all fought like Hector (the greatest of the Trojan warriors).

20 Do something° mingle with our younger brown, yet ha' we   *somewhat*
A brain that nourishes our nerves° and can   *muscles*
Get goal for goal of youth.² Behold this man.
Commend unto his lips thy favoring hand.
[*She offers* scarus *her hand.*]
—Kiss it, my warrior. —He hath fought today
25 As if a god in hate of mankind had
Destroyed in such a shape.

CLEOPATRA   I'll give thee, friend,
An armor all of gold. It was a king's.

ANTONY He has deserved it, were it carbuncled°   *bejeweled*
Like holy Phoebus' car.° Give me thy hand.   *the sun god's chariot*
30 Through Alexandria make a jolly march.
Bear our hacked targets like° the men that owe° them.   *shields as befits / own*
Had our great palace the capacity
To camp° this host, we all would sup together   *put up*
And drink carouses to the next day's fate,
35 Which promises royal° peril. —Trumpeters,   *great*
With brazen din blast you the city's ear.
Make mingle with our rattling taborins,°   *small drums*
That heaven and earth may strike their sounds together,
Applauding our approach.   [*Trumpets sound.*] *Exeunt.*

4.9

Enter a SENTRY *and his company* [*of* WATCH];
ENOBARBUS *follows.*

SENTRY If we be not relieved within this hour,
We must return to th' court of guard.° The night   *guardroom*
Is shiny,° and they say we shall embattle°   *bright / go to battle*
By th' second hour i'th' morn.
5 FIRST WATCH This last day was a shrewd° one to 's.   *bad*

ENOBARBUS Oh, bear me witness, night—

SECOND WATCH What man is this?

FIRST WATCH   Stand close,° and list° him.   *hidden / listen to*
[*They stand aside.*]

ENOBARBUS —Be witness to me, O thou blessèd moon,
When men revolted° shall upon record   *deserters*
10 Bear hateful memory, poor Enobarbus did
Before thy face repent.

SENTRY   Enobarbus?

SECOND WATCH Peace! Hark further.

ENOBARBUS O sovereign mistress of true melancholy,°   *(the moon)*
The poisonous damp of night disponge° upon me,   *pour down*
15 That life, a very rebel to my will,
May hang no longer on me. Throw my heart
Against the flint and hardness of my fault,
Which,° being dried with grief, will break to powder   *(his heart)*
And finish all foul thoughts. O Antony,
20 Nobler than my revolt is infamous,
Forgive me in thine own particular,¹
But let the world rank me in register°   *its records*

---

2. Compete with any youth. Antony is clearly referring here to the "boy" Caesar, but also, possibly, to his
own boyhood.

4.9 Location: Caesar's camp.
1. In whatever aspects of this business concern
only you.

A master-leaver and a fugitive.°   *deserter*
O Antony! O Antony!
          [*He dies.*]²
FIRST WATCH   Let's speak to him.
25 SENTRY   Let's hear him, for the things he speaks
     May concern Caesar.
SECOND WATCH   Let's do so. But he sleeps.
SENTRY   Swoons rather, for so bad a prayer as his
     Was never yet for° sleep.   *in preparation for*
FIRST WATCH   Go we to him.
SECOND WATCH   Awake, sir, awake! Speak to us.
FIRST WATCH   Hear you, sir?
30 SENTRY   The hand of death hath raught° him.   *taken*
          Drums afar off.
     Hark, the drums demurely° wake the sleepers.   *with subdued sound*
     Let us bear him to th' court of guard.
     He is of note. Our hour is fully out.°   *expired*
SECOND WATCH   Come on, then. He may recover yet.
                         Exeunt [with the body].

4.10

Enter ANTONY *and* SCARUS *with their army.*
ANTONY   Their preparation is today by sea;
     We please them not by land.
SCARUS   For both, my lord.
ANTONY   I would they'd fight i'th' fire, or i'th' air;
     We'd fight there too.¹ But this it is: our foot°   *foot soldiers*
5   Upon the hills adjoining to the city
     Shall stay with us—order for sea is given;
     They have put forth° the haven—   *departed from*
     Where their appointment° we may best discover   *purpose; battle plan*
     And look on their endeavor.   *Exeunt.*

4.11

Enter CAESAR *and his army.*
CAESAR   But being° charged, we will be still° by land—   *Unless we're / inactive*
     Which, as I take't, we shall, for his best force
     Is forth to man his galleys. To the vales,°   *valleys*
     And hold our best advantage.°   *Exeunt.*   *take the best position*

4.12

Alarum afar off, as at a sea fight.
Enter ANTONY *and* SCARUS.
ANTONY   Yet they are not joined.° Where yond pine does stand,   *(in battle)*
     I shall discover all. I'll bring thee word
     Straight° how 'tis like° to go.   *Exit.*   *Promptly / likely*
SCARUS   Swallows have built
     In Cleopatra's sails their nests. The augurs°   *soothsayers*
5   Say they know not, they cannot tell; look grimly
     And dare not speak their knowledge. Antony
     Is valiant and dejected, and by starts

---

2. Enobarbus's death is not yet obvious to those onstage   1. As well as in the other elements, earth and water.
and, depending on how the moment is played, may not   **4.11** Location: Scene continues.
be to the audience either.   **4.12** Location: Scene continues.
4.10 Location: The battlefield.

His fretted° fortunes give him hope and fear   *diminished*
Of what he has and has not.
     Enter ANTONY.
ANTONY   All is lost!

10 This foul Egyptian hath betrayed me!
My fleet hath yielded to the foe, and yonder
They cast their caps up and carouse together
Like friends long lost. Triple-turned whore![1] 'Tis thou
Hast sold me to this novice, and my heart

15 Makes only wars on thee. Bid them all fly,
For when I am revenged upon my charm,°   *sorceress*
I have done all. Bid them all fly! Be gone!   [*Exit* SCARUS.]
O sun, thy uprise shall I see no more.
Fortune and Antony part here; even here

20 Do we shake hands.° All come to this? The hearts   *(before parting)*
That spanieled° me at heels, to whom I gave   *fawned upon*
Their wishes, do discandy,° melt their sweets   *melt*
On blossoming Caesar, and this pine° is barked[2]   *(Antony)*
That overtopped them all. Betrayed I am.

25 Oh, this false soul of Egypt! This grave° charm,   *deadly*
Whose eye becked° forth my wars and called them home,   *beckoned*
Whose bosom was my crownet,° my chief end,°   *coronet / reward*
Like a right° gypsy, hath at fast and loose[3]   *true*
Beguiled° me to the very heart of loss.°   *Cheated / ruin*
What, Eros, Eros!
     Enter CLEOPATRA.

30   Ah, thou spell! Avaunt.°   *Leave me*
CLEOPATRA   Why is my lord enraged against his love?
ANTONY   Vanish, or I shall give thee thy deserving
And blemish Caesar's triumph.° Let him take thee   *triumphal procession*
And hoist thee up to the shouting plebeians!

35 Follow his chariot like the greatest spot°   *taint*
Of all thy sex. Most monster-like be shown
For poor'st diminutives,[4] for dolts, and let
Patient Octavia plough thy visage up
With her preparèd° nails!   *Exit* CLEOPATRA.   *specially sharpened*
                   'Tis well thou'rt gone,

40 If it be well to live. But better 'twere
Thou fell'st into° my fury, for one death   *a victim to*
Might have prevented many. Eros, ho!
The shirt of Nessus[5] is upon me. Teach me,
Alcides, thou mine ancestor, thy rage.

45 Let me lodge Lichas on the horns o'th' moon,
And with those hands that grasped the heaviest club
Subdue my worthiest self.° The witch shall die!   *commit suicide*
To the young Roman boy she hath sold me, and I fall
Under this plot. She dies for't. Eros, ho!   *Exit.*

1. Cleopatra is "triple-turned" because disloyal to three (Julius Caesar, Pompey, and Antony); alluding to her changing political allegiances.
2. Stripped of its bark (and so killed).
3. *fast and loose:* a cheating game played by gypsies.
4. For the benefit of (in place of) the lowest people (dwarfs).
5. Hercules, also known as Alcides (line 44), with whom Antony is repeatedly compared, fatally wounded the centaur Nessus with poisoned arrows for trying to rape his wife, Deianira. Nessus gave her some of his blood, falsely claiming that it would act as a love potion. Years later, she smeared some of the deadly blood on a shirt and sent it to Hercules, for whom it produced an agonizing death. Before succumbing and blaming Lichas (line 45), who had brought the shirt, Hercules cast him into the sea. When Deianira realized what she had done, she killed herself.

4.13

Enter CLEOPATRA, CHARMIAN, IRAS[, *and*] MARDIAN.

CLEOPATRA   Help me, my women! Oh, he's more mad
Than Telamon for his shield;[1] the boar of Thessaly[2]
Was never so embossed.[3]

CHARMIAN   To th' monument![4]
There lock yourself, and send him word you are dead.
5   The soul and body rive° not more in parting   *separate*
Than greatness going off.°   *leaving someone*

CLEOPATRA   To th' monument!
Mardian, go tell him I have slain myself.
Say that the last I spoke was "Antony,"
And word it, prithee, piteously. Hence, Mardian,
10   And bring me° how he takes my death. To th' monument!   *bring me word*
                                                          Exeunt.

4.14

Enter ANTONY *and* EROS.

ANTONY   Eros, thou yet behold'st me?

EROS   Ay, noble lord.

ANTONY   Sometime we see a cloud that's dragonish,°   *in a dragon's shape*
A vapor sometime like a bear or lion,
A towered citadel, a pendant° rock,   *hanging*
5   A forkèd mountain or blue promontory
With trees upon't that nod unto the world
And mock our eyes with air. Thou hast seen these signs.
They are black vesper's pageants.[1]

EROS   Ay, my lord.

ANTONY   That which is now a horse, even with a thought
10   The rack dislimns° and makes it indistinct   *cloud dims*
As water is in water.

EROS   It does, my lord.

ANTONY   My good knave° Eros, now thy captain is   *boy*
Even such a body. Here I am Antony,
Yet cannot hold this visible shape, my knave.
15   I made these wars for Egypt and the Queen,
Whose heart I thought I had, for she had mine,
Which, whilst it was mine, had annexed unto't
A million more, now lost. She, Eros, has
Packed cards° with Caesar and false played my glory   *Stacked the deck*
20   Unto an enemy's triumph.°   *victory; trump card*
Nay, weep not, gentle Eros, there is left us
Ourselves to end ourselves.

Enter MARDIAN.

                              Oh, thy vile lady,
She has robbed me of my sword.°   *valor; manhood*

MARDIAN   No, Antony,

4.13 Location: Alexandria.
1. Ajax, also known as Telamon, went mad and killed
himself after the capture of Troy when he was not
awarded Achilles' shield.
2. Sent by Diana to lay waste Calydon (killed by
Meleager).
3. Was never so exhaustedly foaming at the mouth—
that is, was never driven to such extremity (a hunt-

ing term).
4. The tomb that Cleopatra, forseeing her death, had
built.
4.14 Location: Scene continues.
1. Illusory spectacles heralding the approach of night—
with a probable allusion to funerals and death. (Pageants were originally moving stages on which miracle
plays were presented.)

My mistress loved thee, and her fortunes mingled
With thine entirely.
25 ANTONY   Hence, saucy° eunuch! Peace!   *disrespectful*
She hath betrayed me and shall die the death.
MARDIAN Death of one person can be paid but once,
And that she has discharged. What thou wouldst do
Is done unto thy hand.° The last she spake   *for you*
30 Was, "Antony, most noble Antony!"
Then in the midst a tearing groan did break
The name of Antony. It was divided
Between her heart and lips.² She rendered° life   *gave up*
Thy name so° buried in her.   *With thy name in this way*
ANTONY   Dead then?
MARDIAN   Dead.
35 ANTONY Unarm, Eros. The long day's task is done,
And we must sleep. [*to* MARDIAN] That thou depart'st hence safe
Does pay thy labor richly. Go.   *Exit* MARDIAN.
Off, pluck off!
[EROS *unarms him.*]
The sevenfold shield³ of Ajax cannot keep
The battery° from my heart. Oh, cleave my sides!   *onslaught*
40 Heart, once be stronger than thy continent°—   *container*
Crack thy frail case. Apace,° Eros, apace!   *Quickly*
No more a soldier. —Bruisèd pieces,° go!   *(of armor)*
You have been nobly borne. —From me awhile.   *Exit* EROS.
I will o'ertake thee, Cleopatra, and
45 Weep for my pardon. So it must be, for now
All length° is torture. Since the torch° is out,   *longer life / (Cleopatra)*
Lie down and stray no farther. Now all labor
Mars what it does. Yea, very force entangles
Itself with strength.⁴ Seal° then, and all is done.   *Finish the deed*
50 Eros! —I come, my queen. —Eros! —Stay for me,
Where souls do couch on flowers;⁵ we'll hand in hand,
And with our sprightly port° make the ghosts gaze.   *cheerful stance*
Dido and her Aeneas shall want troops,⁶
And all the haunt° be ours. —Come, Eros, Eros!   *place; ghosts*
Enter EROS.
EROS What would my lord?
55 ANTONY   Since Cleopatra died,
I have lived in such dishonor that the gods
Detest my baseness. I, that with my sword
Quartered the world and o'er green Neptune's back°   *on the sea*
With ships made cities,⁷ condemn myself to lack°   *for lacking*
60 The courage of a woman—less noble mind
Than she which by her death our Caesar tells,
"I am conqueror of myself." Thou art sworn, Eros,
That when the exigent° should come, which now   *urgent need*

---

2. *It . . . lips:* It was half-uttered.
3. A shield made of brass lined with six thicknesses of oxhide.
4. *very . . . strength:* strength defeats itself by its own exertions.
5. Lie ("couch") in the Elysian Fields of the blessed dead in the mythological underworld.
6. Shall lack followers. Dido, Queen of Carthage, commits suicide after being abandoned by her lover,

Aeneas, legendary Trojan founder of Rome, in Virgil's *Aeneid;* they are not reconciled in the underworld. Dido, who originally hailed from Phoenicia, is meant to recall Cleopatra. In leaving her, Aeneas places public responsibility above personal desire—unlike Antony but very much like Octavius Caesar, whom Virgil intended him to resemble.
7. Put so many ships to sea that the fleet resembled a city.

Is come indeed, when I should see behind me
65 Th'inevitable prosecution° of   *pursuit*
Disgrace and horror, that on my command
Thou then wouldst kill me. Do't. The time is come.
Thou strik'st not me—'tis Caesar thou defeat'st.
Put color in thy cheek.
EROS   The gods withhold me!°   *God forbid*
70 Shall I do that which all the Parthian darts,
Though enemy, lost aim and could not?
ANTONY   Eros,
Wouldst thou be windowed° in great Rome and see   *looking from a window*
Thy master thus with pleached° arms, bending down   *tied*
His corrigible° neck, his face subdued   *submissive*
75 To penetrative° shame; whilst the wheeled seat°   *piercing / chariot*
Of fortunate Caesar, drawn before him, branded
His baseness that ensued?[8]
EROS   I would not see't.
ANTONY   Come, then, for with a wound I must be cured.
Draw that thy honest° sword, which thou hast worn   *honorable*
Most useful for thy country.
80 EROS   O sir, pardon me.
ANTONY   When I did make thee free, swor'st thou not then
To do this when I bade thee? Do it at once,
Or thy precedent° services are all   *earlier*
But accidents unpurposed.° Draw, and come.   *But pointless events*
85 EROS   Turn from me then that noble countenance
Wherein the worship° of the whole world lies.   *esteem; worth*
ANTONY   Lo thee!
        [*He turns away.*]
EROS   My sword is drawn.
ANTONY   Then let it do at once
The thing why thou hast drawn it.
EROS   My dear master,
90 My captain and my emperor, let me say,
Before I strike this bloody stroke, farewell.
ANTONY   'Tis said, man, and farewell.
EROS   Farewell, great chief. Shall I strike now?
ANTONY   Now, Eros.
EROS   Why, there, then! ([*He*] *kills himself.*) Thus I do escape
    the sorrow
Of Antony's death.
95 ANTONY   Thrice-nobler than myself,
Thou teachest me, O valiant Eros, what
I should and thou couldst not. My queen and Eros
Have by their brave instruction got upon° me   *gained ahead of*
A nobleness in record.° But I will be   *history*
100 A bridegroom in my death and run into't
As to a lover's bed.[9] Come, then, and Eros,
Thy master dies thy scholar; to do thus
I learned of thee. [*He falls on his sword.*] How, not dead?
Not dead?

---

8. *branded . . . ensued:* indicated, as if by a criminal's brand, the humiliation of the man who followed.
9. *But . . . bed:* Death is here treated as a form of erotic union or climax, with Antony as the bridegroom and death (and Cleopatra) the bride.

The guard, ho! Oh, dispatch° me!   *finish*
    Enter a [company of the] GUARD[, *one of them*
    DERCETUS].
FIRST GUARD   What's the noise?
105 ANTONY   I have done my work ill, friends. Oh, make an end
    Of what I have begun.
SECOND GUARD   The star is fall'n.
FIRST GUARD   And time is at his period.°   *its end*
ALL THE GUARD   Alas, and woe.
ANTONY   Let him that loves me, strike me dead.
FIRST GUARD   Not I.
110 SECOND GUARD   Nor I.
THIRD GUARD   Nor anyone.
              Exeunt [all the GUARD *but* DERCETUS].
DERCETUS   Thy death and fortunes bid thy followers fly.
    [He takes Antony's sword.]
    This sword, but shown to Caesar with this tidings,
    Shall enter me° with him.   *gain me favor*
    Enter DIOMEDES.
115 DIOMEDES   Where's Antony?
DERCETUS   There, Diomed, there.
DIOMEDES   Lives he? Wilt thou not answer, man?
                      [Exit DERCETUS.]
ANTONY   Art thou there, Diomed? Draw thy sword and give me
    Sufficing° strokes for death.   *Enough*
DIOMEDES   Most absolute lord,
120   My mistress Cleopatra sent me to thee.
ANTONY   When did she send thee?
DIOMEDES   Now, my lord.
ANTONY   Where is she?
DIOMEDES   Locked in her monument. She had a prophesying
    fear
    Of what hath come to pass; for when she saw—
    Which never shall be found°—you did suspect   *(to be true)*
125   She had disposed° with Caesar, and that your rage   *made an alliance*
    Would not be purged, she sent you word she was dead.
    But fearing since how it might work, hath sent
    Me to proclaim the truth, and I am come,
    I dread, too late.
130 ANTONY   Too late, good Diomed. Call my guard, I prithee.
DIOMEDES   What ho! The Emperor's guard! The guard, what ho!
    Come, your lord calls.
        Enter [some] of the GUARD *of Antony.*
ANTONY   Bear me, good friends, where Cleopatra bides.°   *waits; dwells*
    'Tis the last service that I shall command you.
135 FIRST GUARD   Woe, woe are we, sir, you may not live to wear
    All your true followers out.°   *outlive your followers*
ALL THE GUARD   Most heavy day!
ANTONY   Nay, good my fellows, do not please sharp fate
    To grace° it with your sorrows. Bid that welcome   *By gracing*
    Which comes to punish us, and we punish it
140   Seeming to bear it lightly. Take me up.
    I have led you oft; carry me now, good friends,
    And have my thanks for all.
        Exeunt, bearing ANTONY [*and* EROS].

4.15

Enter CLEOPATRA *and her maids aloft, with* CHARMIAN *and* IRAS.

CLEOPATRA O Charmian, I will never go from hence.

CHARMIAN Be comforted, dear madam.

CLEOPATRA   No, I will not.
All strange and terrible events are welcome,
But comforts we despise. Our size of sorrow

5   Proportioned to our cause must be as great
As that which makes it.

Enter DIOMEDES [*below*].

                              How now? Is he dead?

DIOMEDES His death's upon him, but not dead.
Look out o'th' other side your monument;
His guard have brought him thither.

Enter ANTONY [*below*] *and the* GUARD [*bearing him*].

10 CLEOPATRA O sun,
Burn the great sphere thou mov'st in; darkling[1] stand
The varying shore o'th' world. O Antony,
Antony, Antony! Help, Charmian, help Iras, help!
Help friends below! Let's draw him hither.

ANTONY   Peace!

15 Not Caesar's valor hath o'erthrown Antony,
But Antony's hath triumphed on itself.

CLEOPATRA So it should be that none but Antony
Should conquer Antony, but woe 'tis so!

ANTONY I am dying, Egypt, dying. Only

20 I here importune death° awhile until   ask death to wait
Of many thousand kisses, the poor last
I lay upon thy lips.

CLEOPATRA   I dare not,° dear.   dare not come down
Dear my lord, pardon! I dare not
Lest I be taken. Not th'imperious show°   triumphal procession

25 Of the full-fortuned Caesar ever shall
Be brooched° with me; if knife, drugs, serpents have   decorated
Edge, sting, or operation,° I am safe.   power
Your wife Octavia, with her modest eyes
And still conclusion,° shall acquire no honor   silent judgment

30 Demuring° upon me. But come, come Antony.   Gazing solemnly
—Help me, my women! —We must draw thee up.
Assist, good friends!

[*They begin lifting* ANTONY.]

ANTONY   Oh, quick, or I am gone.

CLEOPATRA Here's sport indeed. How heavy weighs my lord!
Our strength is all gone into heaviness°—   sadness; weight

35 That makes the weight. Had I great Juno's power,
The strong-winged Mercury should fetch thee up
And set thee by Jove's side. Yet, come a little.
Wishers were ever fools. Oh, come, come, come!

They heave ANTONY *aloft to* CLEOPATRA.[2]

4.15 Location: Cleopatra's monument, Alexandria.
1. *O . . . darkling:* For the spheres in which the sun, like the planets and stars, was thought to move around the earth, see note to 2.7.16. If the sun burned its sphere, presumably it would move out of orbit, thus

leaving the earth in darkness ("darkling").
2. TEXTUAL COMMENT For the problem of visualizing this as stage action, see Digital Edition TC 6. PERFORMANCE COMMENT For how modern productions have dealt with this problem, see Digital Edition PC 3.

And welcome, welcome. Die when thou hast lived;°   *lived again*
40   Quicken° with kissing. Had my lips that power,   *Revive*
       Thus would I wear them out.
               [*She kisses him.*]
    ALL   A heavy sight.
    ANTONY   I am dying, Egypt, dying.
       Give me some wine and let me speak a little.
45   CLEOPATRA   No, let me speak, and let me rail so high
       That the false hussy Fortune break her wheel,
       Provoked by my offense.°   *insults*
    ANTONY   One word, sweet queen.
       Of Caesar seek your honor with your safety. Oh!
    CLEOPATRA   They do not go together.
    ANTONY   Gentle, hear me.
50   None about Caesar trust but Proculeius.
    CLEOPATRA   My resolution and my hands I'll trust,
       None about Caesar.
    ANTONY   The miserable change now at my end
       Lament° nor sorrow at, but please your thoughts   *Neither lament*
55   In feeding them with those my former fortunes,
       Wherein I lived the greatest prince o'th' world,
       The noblest, and do now not basely die,
       Not cowardly put off my helmet to
       My countryman—a Roman by a Roman
60   Valiantly vanquished. Now my spirit is going.
       I can no more.
    CLEOPATRA   Noblest of men, woo't° die?   *will you*
       Hast thou no care of me? Shall I abide
       In this dull world, which in thy absence is
       No better than a sty? —Oh, see, my women,
65   The crown o'th' earth doth melt. —My lord?
              [ANTONY *dies.*]
       Oh, withered is the garland° of the war;   *crowning glory*
       The soldier's pole[3] is fall'n. Young boys and girls
       Are level now with men. The odds° is gone,   *distinction among humans*
       And there is nothing left remarkable
       Beneath the visiting moon.
70   CHARMIAN   Oh, quietness, lady.
    IRAS   She's dead, too, our sovereign.
    CHARMIAN   Lady!
    IRAS   Madam!
    CHARMIAN   O madam, madam, madam!
75   IRAS   Royal Egypt! Empress!
    CHARMIAN   Peace, peace, Iras!
    CLEOPATRA   No more but e'en° a woman and commanded   *just (no longer Queen)*
       By such poor passion as the maid that milks
       And does the meanest chores. It were for° me   *would befit*
80   To throw my scepter at the injurious gods
       To tell them that this world did equal theirs
       Till they had stol'n our jewel. All's but naught.
       Patience is sottish,° and impatience does   *foolish*
       Become a dog that's mad. Then is it sin
85   To rush into the secret house of death
       Ere death dare come to us? How do you, women?

---

3. Polestar; military standard; phallus.

What, what, good cheer! Why, how now, Charmian?
My noble girls! Ah, women, women! Look!
Our lamp is spent; it's out. Good sirs,° take heart.   (*to the women*)
90 We'll bury him, and then, what's brave,° what's noble,   *fine*
Let's do't after the high Roman fashion
And make death proud to take us. Come, away!
This case of that huge spirit now is cold.
Ah, women, women! Come, we have no friend
95 But resolution and the briefest° end.   *fastest*

    Exeunt, bearing off Antony's body.

5.1

Enter CAESAR *with* AGRIPPA, DOLABELLA,
[MAECENAS, GALLUS, *and* PROCULEIUS,]
his council of war.

CAESAR Go to him, Dolabella, bid him yield.
Being so frustrate, tell him he mocks
The pauses that he makes.[1]
DOLABELLA   Caesar, I shall.

    [*Exit* DOLABELLA.]
Enter DERCETUS *with the sword of Antony.*

CAESAR Wherefore is that? And what art thou that dar'st
Appear thus° to us?   (*with a drawn weapon*)
5 DERCETUS   I am called Dercetus.
Mark Antony I served, who best was worthy
Best to be served. Whilst he stood up and spoke
He was my master, and I wore my life
To spend° upon his haters. If thou please   *expend*
10 To take me to thee, as I was to him
I'll be to Caesar; if thou pleasest not,
I yield thee up my life.
CAESAR   What is't thou say'st?
DERCETUS I say, O Caesar, Antony is dead.
CAESAR The breaking° of so great a thing should make   *end; telling*
15 A greater crack!° The round world   *noise; fracture*
Should have shook lions into civil° streets   *city*
And citizens to their° dens. The death of Antony   (*the lions'*)
Is not a single doom—in the name lay
A moiety° of the world.   *half*
DERCETUS   He is dead, Caesar,
20 Not by a public minister of justice,
Nor by a hired knife, but that self° hand   *same*
Which writ his honor in the acts it did
Hath, with the courage which the heart did lend it,
Splitted the heart. This is his sword.
25 I robbed his wound of it. Behold it stained
With his most noble blood.
CAESAR   Look you sad, friends?
The gods rebuke me,° but it is tidings   (*for my tears*)
To wash the eyes of kings.
DOLABELLA   And strange it is,
That nature must compel us to lament
Our most persisted deeds.°   *What we persevered in*

5.1 Location: Caesar's camp.   1. *he mocks . . . makes*: his delays are a mere mockery.

30 MAECENAS   His taints and honors
   Waged° equal with° him.   *Fought as if / in*
  DOLABELLA   A rarer spirit never
   Did steer humanity,° but you gods will give us   *govern (any) man*
   Some faults to make us men. Caesar is touched.
  MAECENAS   When such a spacious mirror's set before him,
   He needs must see himself.
35 CAESAR   O Antony,
   I have followed° thee to this, but we do lance°   *pursued / wound to cure*
   Diseases in our bodies. I must perforce
   Have shown to thee such a declining day[2]
   Or look on thine. We could not stall° together   *live in peace*
40 In the whole world. But yet let me lament
   With tears as sovereign° as the blood of hearts   *as efficacious*
   That thou, my brother, my competitor°   *comrade; foe*
   In top of all design,° my mate in empire,   *In the greatest ventures*
   Friend and companion in the front of war,
45 The arm of mine own body, and the heart
   Where mine his° thoughts did kindle—that our stars   *its*
   Unreconcilable should divide
   Our equalness° to this. Hear me, good friends—   *partnership*
         Enter an EGYPTIAN.
   But I will tell you at some meeter season.°   *fitter time*
50 The business of this man looks out of him.
   We'll hear him what he says. —Whence are you?
  EGYPTIAN   A poor Egyptian yet. The Queen, my mistress,
   Confined in all she has—her monument—
   Of thy intents desires instruction,
55 That she preparedly may frame herself
   To th' way she's forced to.
  CAESAR   Bid her have good heart.
   She soon shall know of us by some of ours
   How honorable and how kindly we
   Determine for her. For Caesar cannot live
   To be ungentle.
60 EGYPTIAN   So. The gods preserve thee.   *Exit.*
  CAESAR   Come hither, Proculeius. Go and say
   We purpose her no shame. Give her what comforts
   The quality° of her passion° shall require,   *strength / grief*
   Lest in her greatness by some mortal stroke
65 She do defeat us. For her life in Rome
   Would be eternal in our triumph.[3] Go,
   And with your speediest bring us what she says
   And how you find of her.
  PROCULEIUS   Caesar, I shall.   *Exit.*
  CAESAR   Gallus, go you along.   [*Exit* GALLUS.]
                    Where's Dolabella,
   To second Proculeius?
70 ALL BUT CAESAR   Dolabella!
  CAESAR   Let him alone, for I remember now
   How he's employed. He shall in time be ready.

---

2. *I must . . . day:* I would have had to exhibit my demise to you. *perforce:* necessarily.
3. *her life . . . triumph:* her presence alive in Rome

would bring eternal renown to my triumphal procession.

Go with me to my tent, where you shall see
How hardly° I was drawn into this war,   *unwillingly*
75   How calm and gentle I proceeded still
In all my writings.° Go with me and see   *(letters to Antony)*
What I can show in this.   *Exeunt.*

5.2

Enter CLEOPATRA, CHARMIAN, IRAS, *and* MARDIAN.

CLEOPATRA   My desolation does begin to make
A better life. 'Tis paltry to be Caesar;
Not being Fortune, he's but Fortune's knave,°   *servant*
A minister of her will. And it is great
5   To do that thing° that ends all other deeds,   *(suicide)*
Which shackles accidents and bolts up change,
Which sleeps and never palates more the dung,
The beggar's nurse and Caesar's.[1]
Enter PROCULEIUS.[2]

PROCULEIUS   Caesar sends greeting to the Queen of Egypt,
10   And bids thee study on° what fair demands   *give thought to*
Thou mean'st to have him grant thee.

CLEOPATRA   What's thy name?

PROCULEIUS   My name is Proculeius.

CLEOPATRA   Antony
Did tell me of you, bade me trust you, but
I do not greatly care to be deceived
15   That° have no use for trusting.[3] If your master   *(I) who*
Would have a queen his beggar, you must tell him
That majesty to keep decorum must
No less beg than a kingdom. If he please
To give me conquered Egypt for my son,
20   He gives me so much of mine own as° I   *that*
Will kneel to him with thanks.

PROCULEIUS   Be of good cheer.
You're fall'n into a princely hand. Fear nothing.
Make your full reference° freely to my lord,   *case*
Who is so full of grace that it flows over
25   On all that need. Let me report to him
Your sweet dependency,° and you shall find   *meek obeisance*
A conqueror that will pray in aid for kindness[4]
Where he for grace is kneeled to.

CLEOPATRA   Pray you, tell him
I am his fortune's vassal, and I send him
30   The greatness he has got.[5] I hourly learn
A doctrine of obedience and would gladly
Look him i'th' face.

PROCULEIUS   This I'll report, dear lady.
Have comfort, for I know your plight is pitied

5.2 Location: Cleopatra's monument.
1. *Which sleeps . . . Caesar's:* Which brings a sleep in which we no longer taste the produce of the earth ("dung"), nourisher of all from beggar to emperor.
2. Cleopatra and her women are inside the monument, the others outside it.
3. Cleopatra claims not to care whether she is deceived, in the hope that Proculeius will relax his guard and

reveal Caesar's intentions. But she may also mean that she doesn't like being deceived, knowing as she does the perils of misplaced trust.
4. Who will beg help in finding new ways to be kind.
5. *I am . . . got:* I do homage to his good fortune, and I acknowledge the great position he has won. "Send him" may suggest Cleopatra's sense of superiority in conferring greatness upon Caesar.

Of° him that caused it.   *By*

[*Enter Roman* SOLDIERS, *who seize* CLEOPATRA
from behind.]⁶

35 [*to* SOLDIERS] You see how easily she may be surprised.
Guard her till Caesar come.

IRAS   Royal Queen!

CHARMIAN   O Cleopatra, thou art taken, Queen!

CLEOPATRA [*drawing a dagger*]   Quick, quick, good hands.

PROCULEIUS [*seizing the dagger*]   Hold, worthy lady, hold!
Do not yourself such wrong, who are in this
Relieved° but not betrayed.   *Rescued*

40 CLEOPATRA   What, of° death, too,   *deprived of*
That rids our dogs of languish?⁷

PROCULEIUS   Cleopatra,
Do not abuse my master's bounty by
Th'undoing of yourself. Let the world see
His nobleness well acted, which your death
Will never let come forth.°   *allow to be displayed*

45 CLEOPATRA   Where art thou, death?
Come hither, come! Come, come, and take a queen
Worth many babes and beggars!⁸

PROCULEIUS   Oh, temperance, lady!

CLEOPATRA   Sir, I will eat no meat,° I'll not drink, sir;   *food*
If idle talk will once be necessary⁹

50 I'll not sleep, neither. This mortal house° I'll ruin,   *My body*
Do Caesar what he can. Know, sir, that I
Will not wait pinioned¹ at your master's court,
Nor once be chastised with the sober eye
Of dull Octavia. Shall they hoist me up

55 And show me to the shouting varletry°   *rabble*
Of censuring Rome? Rather a ditch in Egypt
Be gentle grave unto me; rather on Nilus' mud
Lay me stark naked and let the water-flies
Blow me into abhorring!² Rather make

60 My country's high pyramids my gibbet,°   *gallows*
And hang me up in chains!

PROCULEIUS   You do extend
These thoughts of horror further than you shall
Find cause in Caesar.

              Enter DOLABELLA.

DOLABELLA   Proculeius,
What thou hast done, thy master Caesar knows,

65 And he hath sent for thee. For the Queen,
I'll take her to my guard.

PROCULEIUS   So, Dolabella,
It shall content me best. Be gentle to her.
—To Caesar I will speak what° you shall please,   *whatever*
If you'll employ me to him.

---

6. TEXTUAL COMMENT For the difficulty of understanding what happens in lines 33–37, perhaps
because intervening material has been lost, see Digital Edition TC 7.
7. Which rids even our dogs of protracted demise.
8. *babes and beggars:* death's cheapest victims; those
most often "Relieved" (line 39) by the great.

9. (Even) if useless words are at times needed (to
keep me awake); if I am forced to engage in pointless
chatter.
1. Will not serve shackled (or: will not wait like a
bird with clipped wings).
2. Lay their eggs on me (thereby breeding maggots)
so that I become disgusting, abhorrent.

CLEOPATRA   Say, I would die.

                         Exit PROCULEIUS [*with* SOLDIERS].

70   DOLABELLA   Most noble empress, you have heard of me?

CLEOPATRA   I cannot tell.

DOLABELLA   Assuredly you know me.

CLEOPATRA   No matter, sir, what I have heard or known.

    You laugh when boys or women tell their dreams,

    Is't not your trick?°   *custom*

DOLABELLA   I understand not, madam.

75   CLEOPATRA   I dreamt there was an emperor Antony.

    Oh, such another sleep, that I might see

    But such another man.

DOLABELLA   If it might please ye—

CLEOPATRA   His face was as the heav'ns, and therein stuck°   *were stuck*

    A sun and moon, which kept their course and lighted

    The little O, th'earth.

80   DOLABELLA   Most sovereign creature!

CLEOPATRA   His legs bestrid° the ocean; his reared arm   *straddled*

    Crested[3] the world. His voice was propertied

    As all the tunèd spheres,[4] and that to friends.

    But when he meant to quail° and shake the orb,°   *awe / globe*

85   He was as rattling thunder. For his bounty,

    There was no winter in't. An Antony it was,

    That grew the more by reaping. His delights

    Were dolphin-like; they showed his back above°   *they rose above*

    The element they lived in.[5] In his livery°   *service*

90   Walked crowns and crownets.° Realms and islands were   *kings and princes*

    As plates° dropped from his pocket.   *silver coins*

DOLABELLA   Cleopatra—

CLEOPATRA   Think you there was or might be such a man

    As this I dreamt of?

DOLABELLA   Gentle madam, no.

CLEOPATRA   You lie up to the hearing of the gods!

95   But if there be, nor ever were one such,

    It's past the size of dreaming.[6] Nature wants stuff

    To vie strange forms with fancy, yet t'imagine

    An Antony were nature's piece 'gainst fancy,

    Condemning shadows quite.[7]

DOLABELLA   Hear me, good madam.

100   Your loss is as yourself, great, and you bear it

    As answering to the° weight. Would I might never   *Appropriately, given its*

    O'ertake° pursued success, but° I do feel   *Achieve / unless*

    By the rebound° of yours a grief that suits   *reflection*

    My very heart at root!

CLEOPATRA   I thank you, sir.

105   Know you what Caesar means to do with me?

DOLABELLA   I am loath to tell you what I would you knew.

CLEOPATRA   Nay, pray you, sir.

DOLABELLA   Though he be honorable—

---

3. Formed a crest over (as in heraldry).

4. *was . . . spheres:* sounded like the music of the spheres, supposedly produced by the harmonious structure of the universe. See note to 2.7.16.

5. Just as the dolphin's back appears above the water.

6. My vision of him surpasses what can be dreamed.

7. *Nature . . . quite:* Nature lacks material to compete with the remarkable visions of the imagination in creating fantastic forms; but by imagining and creating Antony, nature has produced a masterpiece that outstrips even fancy and thus discredits imaginary conceptions.

CLEOPATRA   He'll lead me then in triumph?

DOLABELLA   Madam, he will; I know't.

          Flourish.

          Enter PROCULEIUS, CAESAR, GALLUS, MAECENAS, *and*
          others of his train.

110 ALL°   Make way there! Caesar!   *(Caesar's train)*

CAESAR   Which is the Queen of Egypt?

DOLABELLA   It is the Emperor, madam.

          CLEOPATRA *kneels.*

CAESAR   Arise. You shall not kneel.
     I pray you rise. Rise, Egypt.

CLEOPATRA   Sir, the gods

115 Will have it thus.° My master and my lord,   *(that I obey you)*
     I must obey.

          [*She rises.*]

CAESAR   Take to you no hard thoughts.
     The record of what injuries you did us,
     Though written in our flesh, we shall remember
     As things but done by chance.

CLEOPATRA   Sole sir° o'th' world,   *lord*

120 I cannot project° mine own cause so well   *lay out*
     To make it clear,° but do confess I have   *innocent seeming*
     Been laden with like frailties, which before
     Have often shamed our sex.

CAESAR   Cleopatra, know,
     We will extenuate rather than enforce.°   *emphasize (faults)*

125 If you apply yourself° to our intents,   *conform*
     Which towards you are most gentle, you shall find
     A benefit in this change. But if you seek
     To lay on me a cruelty° by taking   *charge of cruelty*
     Antony's course, you shall bereave yourself

130 Of my good purposes and put your children
     To that destruction which I'll guard them from,
     If thereon you rely. I'll take my leave.

CLEOPATRA   And may through all the world.[8] 'Tis yours, and we
     Your scutcheons° and your signs of conquest shall   *captured shields*

135 Hang in what place you please. Here, my good lord.
          [*She holds out a paper.*]

CAESAR   You shall advise me in all for° Cleopatra.   *concerning*

CLEOPATRA   This is the brief° of money, plate, and jewels   *summary*
     I am possessed of. 'Tis exactly valued,
     Not petty things admitted.° Where's Seleucus?   *Except trivial things*
          [*Enter* SELEUCUS.]

140 SELEUCUS   Here, madam.

CLEOPATRA   This is my treasurer. Let him speak, my lord,
     Upon his peril that I have reserved
     To myself nothing. Speak the truth, Seleucus.

SELEUCUS   Madam, I had rather seal° my lips   *sew up*

145 Than to my peril speak that which is not.

CLEOPATRA   What have I kept back?

SELEUCUS   Enough to purchase what you have made known.

CAESAR   Nay, blush not, Cleopatra. I approve
     Your wisdom in the deed.

8. As you may (take your leave and go) anywhere (as ruler of the world).

CLEOPATRA   See, Caesar! Oh, behold,
150   How pomp is followed!⁹ Mine° will now be yours,   *My followers*
    And should we shift estates,° yours would be mine.   *change positions*
    The ingratitude of this Seleucus does
    Even make me wild. —O slave, of no more trust
    Than love that's hired! What, goest thou back? Thou shalt
155   Go back, I warrant thee, but I'll catch thine eyes,
    Though° they had wings. Slave! Soulless villain!   *Even if*
    Dog! Oh, rarely° base!   *exceptionally*
CAESAR   Good queen, let us entreat you—
CLEOPATRA   O Caesar, what a wounding shame is this,
    That thou vouchsafing° here to visit me,   *stooping to come*
160   Doing the honor of thy lordliness
    To one so meek, that mine own servant should
    Parcel° the sum of my disgraces by   *Particularize; add to*
    Addition of his envy!° Say, good Caesar,   *spite*
    That I some lady° trifles have reserved,   *ladylike*
165   Immoment toys,° things of such dignity   *Worthless trinkets*
    As we greet modern° friends withal,° and say   *everyday / with*
    Some nobler token I have kept apart
    For Livia° and Octavia to induce   *(Caesar's wife)*
    Their mediation, must I be unfolded
170   With° one that I have bred! The gods! It smites me   *turned in by*
    Beneath the fall I have. —Prithee, go hence,
    Or I shall show the cinders° of my spirits   *smoldering coals*
    Through th'ashes of my chance.° Wert thou a man,   *fortune*
    Thou wouldst have mercy on me.
CAESAR   Forbear, Seleucus.
                       [*Exit* SELEUCUS.]
175   CLEOPATRA   Be it known that we, the greatest, are misthought°   *misjudged*
    For things that others do; and when we fall,
    We answer others' merits in our name¹—
    Are therefore to be pitied.
CAESAR   Cleopatra,
    Not what you have reserved nor what acknowledged
180   Put we i'th' roll of conquest. Still be't yours.
    Bestow° it at your pleasure, and believe   *Dispense*
    Caesar's no merchant to make prize° with you   *haggle*
    Of things that merchants sold. Therefore be cheered;
    Make not your thoughts your prisons.² No, dear Queen,
185   For we intend so to dispose you as
    Yourself shall give us counsel. Feed and sleep.
    Our care and pity is so much upon you
    That we remain your friend. And so, adieu.
CLEOPATRA   My master and my lord!
CAESAR   Not so. Adieu.
           Flourish. Exeunt CAESAR *and his train*
                [*including* DOLABELLA].
190   CLEOPATRA   He words me, girls, he words me, that I should not
    Be noble to myself.³ But hark thee, Charmian.

---

9. How the great are served.
1. We are responsible for the deeds committed by others in our names (an effort to shift the blame to Seleucus).

2. Don't think yourself a prisoner; don't be imprisoned by (or in) your thoughts.
3. *He words . . . myself*: He puts me off from committing suicide with mere words.

IRAS   Finish, good lady. The bright day is done,
    And we are for the dark.
CLEOPATRA [*to* CHARMIAN]   Hie thee again.°   *Hurry back*
    I have spoke already, and it is provided.
    Go, put it to the haste.°   *Do it quickly*
195 CHARMIAN   Madam, I will.
              Enter DOLABELLA.
DOLABELLA   Where's the Queen?
CHARMIAN   Behold, sir.
                                        [*Exit* CHARMIAN.]
CLEOPATRA   Dolabella!
DOLABELLA   Madam, as thereto sworn by your command,
    Which my love makes religion° to obey,   *compels me*
    I tell you this: Caesar through Syria
200 Intends his journey, and within three days
    You with your children will he send before.
    Make your best use of this. I have performed
    Your pleasure and my promise.
CLEOPATRA   Dolabella,
    I shall remain your debtor.
DOLABELLA   I your servant.
205 Adieu, good Queen. I must attend on Caesar.
CLEOPATRA   Farewell, and thanks.   *Exit* [DOLABELLA].
                        Now, Iras, what think'st thou?
    Thou, an Egyptian puppet, shall be shown
    In Rome as well as I. Mechanic slaves°   *Laborers*
    With greasy aprons, rules,° and hammers shall   *measuring sticks*
210 Uplift us to the view. In their thick° breaths,   *foul*
    Rank° of gross diet,° shall we be enclouded   *Stinking / coarse food*
    And forced to drink° their vapor.   *inhale*
IRAS   The gods forbid!
CLEOPATRA   Nay, 'tis most certain, Iras. Saucy lictors°   *Insolent law officers*
    Will catch at us like strumpets, and scald° rhymers   *scurvy*
215 Ballad us out o'tune. The quick comedians
    Extemporally° will stage us and present   *In improvised manner*
    Our Alexandrian revels. Antony
    Shall be brought drunken forth, and I shall see
    Some squeaking Cleopatra boy[4] my greatness
    I'th' posture of a whore.
220 IRAS   O the good gods!
CLEOPATRA   Nay, that's certain.
IRAS   I'll never see't! For I am sure my nails
    Are stronger than mine eyes.
CLEOPATRA   Why, that's the way
    To fool their preparation and to conquer
    Their most absurd intents.
              Enter CHARMIAN.
225   Now, Charmian!
    Show° me, my women, like a queen. Go, fetch   *Display*
    My best attires. I am again for Cydnus
    To meet Mark Antony.[5] Sirrah Iras, go!
    Now, noble Charmian, we'll dispatch° indeed,   *hurry; finish*

---

4. Cleopatra's part will be played by a boy (as it was   5. See 2.2.198–238.
in Shakespeare's day).

230 And when thou hast done this chore, I'll give thee leave
To play till doomsday. Bring our crown and all.

[*Exit* IRAS.]

A noise within.
Wherefore's this noise?

Enter a GUARDSMAN.

GUARDSMAN   Here is a rural fellow
That will not be denied your highness' presence.
He brings you figs.

CLEOPATRA   Let him come in.   *Exit* GUARDSMAN.

235   What° poor an instrument   *How*
May do a noble deed! He brings me liberty.
My resolution's placed,° and I have nothing   *unwavering*
Of woman in me. Now from head to foot
I am marble constant. Now the fleeting° moon   *changeable*
No planet is of mine.

Enter GUARDSMAN *and* CLOWN° [*with basket*].   *a rustic*

240 GUARDSMAN   This is the man.

CLEOPATRA   Avoid,° and leave him.   *Exit* GUARDSMAN.   *Withdraw*
Hast thou the pretty worm[6] of Nilus there
That kills and pains not?

CLOWN   Truly I have him, but I would not be the party that
245   should desire you to touch him, for his biting is immortal.[7]
Those that do die of it do seldom or never recover.

CLEOPATRA   Remember'st thou any that have died on't?°   *of it*

CLOWN   Very many; men and women too! I heard of one of
them no longer than yesterday—a very honest° woman, but   *truthful; chaste*
250   something given to lie,° as a woman should not do but in the   *fib; lie with men*
way of honesty—how she died° of the biting of it, what pain   *perished; had an orgasm*
she felt. Truly, she makes a very good report o'th' worm. But
he that will believe all that they say shall never be saved by
half that they do.[8] But this is most falliable;° the worm's an   *(error for "infallible")*
255   odd worm.

CLEOPATRA   Get thee hence, farewell.

CLOWN   I wish you all joy of the worm.

CLEOPATRA   Farewell.

CLOWN   You must think this, look you, that the worm will do
260   his kind.°   *what's in its nature*

CLEOPATRA   Ay, ay, farewell.

CLOWN   Look you, the worm is not to be trusted but in the
keeping of wise people. For indeed, there is no goodness in
the worm.

265 CLEOPATRA   Take thou no care; it shall be heeded.

CLOWN   Very good. Give it nothing, I pray you, for it is not worth
the feeding.

CLEOPATRA   Will it eat me?

CLOWN   You must not think I am so simple but I know the
270   devil himself will not eat a woman. I know that a woman is
a dish for the gods, if the devil dress° her not. But truly,   *prepare (food); clothe*

---

6. Snake or serpent. In the Clown's description (lines 244–52), the "worm" also suggests the penis.
7. Comic error: the Clown means the opposite, but as so often occurs with such malapropisms in Shakespeare, the mistake reveals an unintended truth. See Cleopatra's "Immortal longings" (line 277).

8. Perhaps the point is that a woman "given to lie" (line 250) is not to be believed. If Cleopatra acts on this "good report o'th' worm," she will "never be saved" (lines 252–53): she will die and, in Christian terms, will lose hope of salvation by committing suicide.

these same whoreson° devils do the gods great harm in their   *accursed*
women. For in every ten that they make, the devils mar five.
CLEOPATRA   Well, get thee gone. Farewell.
275   CLOWN   Yes, forsooth. I wish you joy o'th' worm.   *Exit.*
        [*Enter* IRAS *with robe and crown.*]
      CLEOPATRA   Give me my robe; put on my crown. I have
        Immortal longings in me. Now no more
        The juice of Egypt's grape shall moist this lip.
        Yare,° yare, good Iras. Quick! Methinks I hear   *Briskly*
280   Antony call. I see him rouse himself
        To praise my noble act. I hear him mock
        The luck of Caesar, which the gods give men
        To excuse their° after wrath. Husband, I come.   *(the gods')*
        Now to that name, my courage prove my title.
285   I am fire and air. My other elements
        I give to baser life.[9] So, have you done?
        Come, then, and take the last warmth of my lips.
        Farewell, kind Charmian, Iras, long farewell.
         [*She kisses* CHARMIAN *and* IRAS, *who falls and dies.*]
        Have I the aspic° in my lips? Dost fall?   *asp*
290   If thou and nature can so gently part,
        The stroke of death is as a lover's pinch,
        Which hurts and is desired. Dost thou lie still?
        If thus thou vanishest, thou tell'st the world,
        It is not worth leave-taking.
295   CHARMIAN   Dissolve, thick cloud, and rain, that I may say
        The gods themselves do weep.
      CLEOPATRA   This proves me base.°   *ignoble*
        If she first meet the curlèd° Antony,   *curly-haired*
        He'll make demand of° her and spend that kiss   *question; (sexual)*
        Which is my heaven to have. Come, thou mortal wretch;°   *deadly creature*
         [*She applies an asp.*]
300   With thy sharp teeth this knot intrinsicate°   *intricate*
        Of life at once untie. Poor venomous fool,
        Be angry and dispatch. Oh, couldst thou speak
        That I might hear thee call great Caesar ass
        Unpolicied.°   *Outsmarted*
      CHARMIAN   O eastern star!°   *(Venus; Cleopatra)*
      CLEOPATRA   Peace, peace.
305   Dost thou not see my baby at my breast,
        That sucks the nurse asleep.
      CHARMIAN   Oh, break! Oh, break!
      CLEOPATRA   As sweet as balm, as soft as air, as gentle.
        O Antony! Nay, I will take thee too.
         [*She applies another asp.*]
        What° should I stay—   *Why*
         [*She*] *dies.*
310   CHARMIAN   In this wild world? So, fare thee well.
        Now boast thee, death, in thy possession lies
        A lass unparalleled. Downy windows° close,   *eyelids*

---

9. *I am . . . life:* The "other elements" (line 285) are earth and water, the lower and heavier elements traditionally linked to women and thought to explain their fickleness. Cleopatra is particularly associated with these elements through her equation with (the mud of) Egypt. By asserting that she is only "fire and air," she is claiming to be manly (as in lines 237–38) and is also referring to the separation of the soul from the body at death.

And golden Phoebus never be beheld
Of eyes again so royal. Your crown's awry.
315 I'll mend it,° and then play—   set it right
   Enter the GUARD *rustling*° *in.*   clattering
FIRST GUARD Where's the Queen?
CHARMIAN   Speak softly. Wake her not.
FIRST GUARD Caesar hath sent—
CHARMIAN   Too slow a messenger.
   [*She applies an asp.*]
Oh, come apace, dispatch. I partly feel thee.
FIRST GUARD Approach, ho! All's not well. Caesar's beguiled.°   deceived
320 SECOND GUARD There's Dolabella sent from Caesar. Call him.
          [*Exit a* GUARD.]
FIRST GUARD What work is here, Charmian? Is this well done?
CHARMIAN It is well done and fitting for a princess
Descended of so many royal kings.
Ah, soldier!
   CHARMIAN *dies.*
   Enter DOLABELLA.
DOLABELLA How goes it here?
SECOND GUARD   All dead.
325 DOLABELLA   Caesar, thy thoughts
Touch their effects° in this. Thyself art coming   Are realized
To see performed the dreaded act which thou
So sought'st to hinder.
   Enter CAESAR *and all his train, marching.*
ALL A way there, a way for Caesar!
330 DOLABELLA O sir, you are too sure an augurer.
That° you did fear is done.   What
CAESAR   Bravest at the last,
She leveled at° our purposes and, being royal,   discerned rightly
Took her own way. The manner of their deaths?
I do not see them bleed.
DOLABELLA   Who was last with them?
335 FIRST GUARD A simple countryman that brought her figs.
This was his basket.
CAESAR   Poisoned then.
FIRST GUARD   O Caesar,
This Charmian lived but now; she stood and spake.
I found her trimming up the diadem
On her dead mistress. Tremblingly she stood,
And on the sudden dropped.
340 CAESAR   Oh, noble weakness!
If they had swallowed poison, 'twould appear
By external swelling; but she looks like sleep,
As° she would catch another Antony   As if
In her strong toil° of grace.   snare
DOLABELLA   Here on her breast
345 There is a vent of blood and something blown;°   emitted; swollen
The like is on her arm.
FIRST GUARD This is an aspic's trail, and these fig leaves
Have slime upon them, such as th'aspic leaves
Upon the caves of Nile.
CAESAR   Most probable
350 That so she died, for her physician tells me

    She hath pursued conclusions° infinite   *trial outcomes*
    Of easy ways to die. Take up her bed,
    And bear her women from the monument.
    She shall be buried by her Antony.
355   No grave upon the earth shall clip° in it   *embrace*
    A pair so famous. High events as these
    Strike° those that make° them, and their story is   *Afflict / cause*
    No less in pity than his glory[1] which
    Brought them to be lamented. Our army shall
360   In solemn show attend this funeral,
    And then to Rome. Come, Dolabella, see
    High order in this great solemnity.
            Exeunt all[, the GUARDS *bearing the dead bodies].*

---

1. *their . . . glory:* there is no less pity in their story than there is glory in the exploits of Caesar. The immodesty of these lines, in the guise of praise, recalls Caesar's ambiguous grief, his combination of calculation and sentiment, at the news of Antony's death in 5.1. The historical Octavius Caesar went on to order the murder of Ptolemy XV (Caesarion), Cleopatra's son by Julius Caesar. Since Julius Caesar was Octavius's great-uncle and adoptive father, this act, which ended the Ptolemaic dynasty, might be seen as fratricide. See 2.2.239–40, with note, and 3.6.1–16, with note to line 6. By contrast, after Antony and Cleopatra's deaths, the historical Octavia, over her brother Octavius's objections, raised Antony's children by Fulvia and Cleopatra, as well as her own five children by Antony and a previous husband.

Coriolanus

Hērōs, the Greek word for "hero," originally meant "warrior." By Homer's time, eight centuries before the birth of Christ, the term was already beginning to be applied by extension to other kinds of praiseworthy people, but even today the military connotations of the word remain strong. The Latin word for "virtue" has a similar history, as the ancient historian Plutarch remarks in his biography of Coriolanus, Shakespeare's principal source for his play: "Now in those days valiantness was honored in Rome above all other virtues: which they call *virtūs*, by the name of virtue itself, as including in that general name, all other special virtues besides. So that *virtūs* in the Latin, was as much as valiantness."

Writing *Coriolanus* in 1608, Shakespeare considers the extent to which excellence in battle translates into other forms of meritoriousness. He works in an ageless tradition, still vital in the twenty-first century, of exalting great fighters: the mythically dauntless Hercules and Theseus, the fierce battle chieftains of classical Greek and Roman epic, the indomitable knights of medieval chivalric romance, the superheroes of modern films and comic books. Yet Shakespeare also deviates from that tradition. Caius Martius Coriolanus performs astonishing, almost superhuman, acts of strength and bravery in battle, fighting on behalf of a society that seems to venerate war. His aggressiveness ought to mesh perfectly with the needs of the community. If successful belligerence is the highest, or only, form of excellence, then Coriolanus, the preeminent soldier, is a natural candidate for Rome's top leadership positions.

In fact, however, Coriolanus's career is disastrous. Despite his phenomenal military successes and Rome's esteem for warriors, Coriolanus not only fails to win election as consul (leader) of Rome but barely escapes the death penalty. He is banished from the city and eventually killed while in the employ of Rome's enemies. The connection between "valiantness" and other forms of virtue seems anything but straightforward. Likewise the relationship between the supposedly exemplary individual and the community from which he springs seems profoundly troubled. The "hero" does not operate in a vacuum: if he is to be victorious, someone must be defeated; if he is to be a leader, he must have followers.

Coriolanus is not merely about a heroic individual but about the community from which he springs and how it is to be governed. It is a play, in other words, about politics, and it poses a number of fundamental political questions. What ought to be the relationship between the common people and the elite? Who is entitled to a voice in the running of the state, and on what basis is that voice granted: class status? personal merit? place of residence? Does citizenship, as Coriolanus argues, primarily entail duties such as military service? Or is citizenship, as many of the common people assume, essentially a set of entitlements or privileges? How does the state determine its domestic and military priorities? These are not merely questions for ancient Rome, but recur in any political community. Since the eighteenth century, *Coriolanus* has often been adapted to reflect contemporary politics. In 1930s Germany, the Nazis applauded the play's depiction of a strong military leader; in several famous productions in England during and after World War II, Laurence Olivier likewise associated Coriolanus's militarism and contempt for common people with modern fascism. Yet in postwar East Germany, the Communist playwright Berthold Brecht's adaptation emphasized instead the struggles of the working class against their aristocratic oppressors. In recent years *Coriolanus* has been successfully performed in modern dress, in settings evocative of the Balkans, Afghanistan, or Iraq.

In *Coriolanus*, Shakespeare suggests that his hero brings many of his problems upon his own head. Coriolanus succeeds as a warrior by channeling overpowering anger into feats of extraordinary strength, by refusing to calculate possible harm to himself or to others, and by preferring action to words. In the political domain, by contrast, relative goods are often more important than absolutes, negotiated compromises preferable to flat conquest. The ability to control oneself in the interest of manipulating others is crucial; so, too, is the capacity to predict the effects of one's own and other people's words and actions. Coriolanus's phenomenal forcefulness— such a superb advantage on the battlefield—cripples his effectiveness for other enterprises. His initial lack of political ambitions together with his hopeless awkwardness as a candidate suggest that his military prowess is not merely irrelevant to peacetime employment, but indeed renders him politically incompetent or even dangerous.

Like most of Shakespeare's tragic heroes after Richard II, then, Coriolanus is betrayed not so much by his vices or shortcomings as by what, in different circumstances, would be his best traits. Shakespeare alters his source material in order to make this pattern more distinct. For instance, Shakespeare entirely omits Plutarch's account of the historical Coriolanus's considerable political savvy. Plutarch's Coriolanus had already played several influential political roles before he made his bid for the consulship. He underwent without apparent compunction the traditional rituals required of all seekers after office; the plebeians later repudiated him on the grounds of a long political record that, in Shakespeare, does not exist. After his exile, Plutarch's Coriolanus cleverly exacerbated class strife in Rome by selectively refraining from burning patrician estates as he approached the city with his Volscian army. Shakespeare's relentless but hotheaded character would hardly be capable of such a calculated act.

The effect of Shakespeare's changes is to open up a chasm that does not exist in his sources between military and civic values. The general Cominius, praising Coriolanus in the Senate house, seems superficially to be echoing Plutarch's comment that "*virtūs* in the Latin, was as much as valiantness":

> It is held
> That valor is the chiefest virtue and
> Most dignifies the haver; if it be,
> The man I speak of cannot in the world
> Be singly counterpoised.
>
> (2.2.80–84)

But even in the process of making his argument, Cominius appears, in his evasive passive constructions and his conditional "if," to be partly disowning it.

Coriolanus's tragedy is not, however, merely a matter of personal idiosyncrasy and self-destructiveness; it takes place, as we have seen, in a political context. During Coriolanus's lifetime in the fifth century B.C.E., Rome had already embarked on the expansionist course that would culminate in its domination of Europe, North Africa, and the Middle East 400 years later, in the time of Julius Caesar, Marcus Brutus, and Mark Antony. But in these early years, dreams of world rule were far in the future: Coriolanus's Rome was still battling the nearby Volscians. Roman bellicosity was a cultural tendency, not yet a clear pathway to empire. At home, Rome was struggling to devise a new form of government. In Coriolanus's youth, King Tarquin and his family were expelled from Rome on the grounds that they had been abusing their power (an episode upon which Shakespeare based his narrative poem *The Rape of Lucrece*). The monarchy was replaced by a Senate composed of patricians (aristocrats). For military and civic matters requiring executive authority, the Senate elected "consuls" for short terms. Soon, however, this system proved inadequate, as the large plebeian, or working, class clamored for a say in the city's rule. In the aftermath of the uprising depicted in *Coriolanus* 1.1, the plebeians were granted the right to elect their own representatives, called tribunes.

In its eventual form, therefore, the Roman Republic was a "mixed" form of government that attempted to distribute rather than to concentrate power, as well as to balance the rights and privileges of various constituencies. Inventing republican institutions entailed addressing important questions about the relations between the social classes, questions that were not merely of antiquarian interest to Shakespeare and his contemporaries. *Coriolanus* considers, as we have seen, issues fundamental to any polity, but the question of how power was to be distributed was an especially sensitive one in the early seventeenth century. Most premodern states, including classical republics and Shakespeare's England, consisted of a relatively small, property-owning, politically empowered class and a large subpolitical population that was supposed to submit to the laws but had no voting rights. How small ought to be the privileged group, how large the disempowered group, and how distinct the differences between the two? These were matters of hot debate in Jacobean England. King James I and his son Charles, who liked to associate themselves with the imagery of imperial Rome, were attracted by absolutist models of government in which the monarch exercised virtually unlimited sway. By contrast, their opponents in Parliament often invoked the Roman Republic, which dispersed power over consuls, Senate, and tribunes, as an analogue to the English commonwealth with its monarch, House of Lords, and House of Commons.

Given the contemporary resonances of his story, Shakespeare's extensive alterations of Plutarch's account are fascinating. *Coriolanus* opens with an uprising among Rome's common people. According to Plutarch, the plebeians revolted because the moneyed patricians had promised easier terms on loans if the plebeians would agree to fight the nearby Sabines. After the plebeians acquitted themselves bravely in battle, the patricians reneged on the agreement and sold into slavery those debtors—many of them war veterans—who were bankrupted by high interest rates. Shakespeare's plebeians, by contrast, make only fleeting references to usury. Their main complaint is simple hunger, a familiar grievance to an English audience in 1608. Barely a year before *Coriolanus*'s first performance, food shortages precipitated serious rioting by the rural poor in the Midland counties west of London, near Shakespeare's hometown, Stratford-upon-Avon. The rioters accused the rich of hoarding foodstuffs in hopes of higher prices, and of having created a dearth by replacing the traditional cultivation of cereal grains with lucrative sheep farming. The rich countered that bad weather was to blame.

In updating the motives of his lower-class characters, Shakespeare translates Roman class conflicts into terms more immediate for his contemporaries. But his revision has other consequences, too: it minimizes the plebeians' political sophistication, their military indispensability, and much of the justification for their outrage. The famine might well be a natural rather than a political calamity: there is no hint of any prior betrayed agreement and no suggestion of unrewarded plebeian military service. Unlike Plutarch's plebeians, Shakespeare's are mediocre soldiers or worse: in *Coriolanus*, Shakespeare's Rome fails to appreciate Coriolanus's *virtūs* simply because the society is not, as Plutarch had claimed it to be, fully a warrior culture at all.

In Shakespeare's rendering, valor in battle seems less a "Roman" than a distinctively aristocratic trait, exercised and uniquely cherished by the patrician class. The difficulties Coriolanus experiences in trying to translate that valor into a civilian context reflect a persistent problem in defining the male aristocrat's proper role. Just as the equation of "valiantness" and "virtue" could fail in early republican Rome, it could also be seen to be failing in early modern England. In medieval times, noblemen had been feudally obliged to serve as battle captains over troops of their own vassals; the aristocrat's military function was his raison d'être, although proficiency in war was supposed to carry over into the management of civic affairs. In Shakespeare's time, the aristocrat's function was theoretically unchanged, but altered social circumstances placed it under increasing pressure. Throughout the late sixteenth and early seventeenth centuries, bureaucrats and policy makers like William Cecil, Robert Cecil, and Francis Bacon were sharply at odds with swashbuckling militarists like Walter Ralegh, King James's son Prince Henry, and Shakespeare's erstwhile patron the Earl of Essex. In these conflicts, the bureaucrats almost always had the advantage. Their skill at such tasks as overhauling the taxation system was hardly glamorous but proved indispensable for the newly powerful nation-state. By the early seventeenth century, the notion that the aristocrat rendered his most important service to his king on the battlefield seemed a remnant of a simpler age.

Coriolanus then, like Hotspur in Shakespeare's *1 Henry IV,* seems to embody a conception of aristocratic excellence whose historical moment, for better or worse, has already passed. A sense of the archaic quality of mighty warriors seems almost universal. Homer's epic heroes were already beginning to specialize their functions during the siege of Troy. For Plutarch, writing in the time of the Roman Empire, the original identification of aristocrat and warrior seems to have shattered in the long-ago days of the Roman Republic. Medieval writers locate both the flowering of knightly service and the beginning of its breakdown in the legendary fourth-century Arthurian court. Many Hollywood Westerns look back to a time in the nineteenth century when the older, rougher codes of the Indian fighter or nomadic frontiersman were being displaced by the values of permanent white settlers, including women and professional-caste men. From time immemorial, glorifying warriors has been tied up with nostalgia—not merely for the mighty soldier himself, but for a simpler, "manly" alternative to civilized complexities, an alternative always already lost.

In the tense dramatic milieu of *Coriolanus,* compounded from Shakespeare's own experience and what his sources provided him, the nature of his protagonist's heroism thus seems more intelligible and its failure less surprising. Since the heterogeneous Roman population has difficulty coming to any consensus about what it values, no single individual could possibly exemplify its ideals. Rather, Coriolanus possesses a narrow subset of traits more appealing to some groups (the patricians) than others (the plebeians) and more useful in some situations (war) than in others (peace). Coriolanus's mother, Volumnia, describing her son's education, suggests how his "heroism" has been developed by rigorously selecting for desired traits and just as sternly suppressing others.

> When yet he was but tender-bodied and the only son of my womb, when youth with comeliness plucked all gaze his way, when—for a day of kings' entreaties—a mother should not sell him an hour from her beholding, I—considering how honor would become such a person . . . was pleased to let him seek danger where he was like to find fame. To a cruel war I sent him, from whence he returned, his brows bound with oak. I tell thee, daughter, I sprang not more in joy at first hearing he was a man-child than now in first seeing he had proved himself a man.
>
> (1.3.5–15)

Volumnia's own shrewdness and ferocity seem to belie the "naturalness" of a system that excludes women from politics and combat. Unlike Coriolanus's wife, Virgilia, Volumnia hardly seems content to stay home and do the sewing. But the incongruity between her personality and her prescribed social role does not render her skeptical of that role. Instead, she embraces her gendered destiny with characteristic zeal. In maternity she finds an improbable outlet for her own aggressiveness:

> The breasts of Hecuba
> When she did suckle Hector looked not lovelier
> Than Hector's forehead when it spit forth blood
> At Grecian sword contemning.
>
> (1.3.37–40)

Symbolically equating milk and blood, the lactating mother with her wounded son, Volumnia both identifies vicariously with her war hero and wishes suffering upon him, delighting not merely in his triumphs but in his pain. Virgilia's conventionally feminine recoil from Volumnia's gory fantasies makes their aberrancy clear for the audience. In Volumnia, the discipline required to submit to rules of Roman womanliness seems to have generated a complicated sadomasochistic adaptation. She displaces her own forbidden aggressiveness onto a dream of exaggerated masculinity and then attempts to realize that dream in her son.

Volumnia's ruthless mothering produces a man whose characteristic gesture is violently to resist whatever he perceives to be outside himself. Battle is Coriolanus's model for identity formation, and his ideal self is like an impermeably walled city. Overstated *differences*—between patrician and plebeian, Roman and Volscian, male and female, man and boy—are the principles upon which Coriolanus has established his own sense of identity. Pride, contempt, and anger, like aggression, reinforce and clarify the boundaries of the self, marking it vividly off from those whom one despises or conquers. Coriolanus does not merely happen to be inflexible and narrow-minded; too much tolerance, too much sensitivity, would endanger him to the core. So would introspection, which might reveal an unwelcome complexity within. Coriolanus is hardly a taciturn character, but he is perhaps Shakespeare's most opaque tragic protagonist, for he is not inclined to reflect upon his own motives either in conversation or alone (indeed, he has only a single short soliloquy in the entire play). The great moments of Coriolanus's life are moments of embattled solitude: fighting by himself inside Corioles, standing alone for consul or separated from the Roman people after his exile, reflecting in an unaccompanied moment in Aufidius's hall, isolated in Corioles again at the end of the play, shouting at his old (and new) enemy: "Alone I did it" (5.6.115). He is thrilled by fantasies of absolute independence: "As if a man were author of himself / And knew no other kin" (5.3.36–37). With some justice, the hostile tribunes accuse him of wanting to be the only man left in Rome and of considering himself a god superior to ordinary mortals.

In his defiant self-sufficiency, however, Coriolanus is far needier than he acknowledges. When he allies himself with Aufidius, his former enemy, Aufidius's elated speech of welcome clarifies their shared dilemma.

> I loved the maid I married; never man
> Sighed truer breath. But that I see thee here,
> Thou noble thing, more dances my rapt heart
> Than when I first my wedded mistress saw
> Bestride my threshold. . . .
> . . . .
> . . . Thou hast beat me out
> Twelve several times, and I have nightly since
> Dreamt of encounters twixt thyself and me—
> We have been down together in my sleep,
> Unbuckling helms, fisting each other's throat—
> And waked half dead with nothing.
> (4.5.113–25)

The combination of pain and pleasure to which Aufidius bears witness is strikingly reminiscent of Volumnia's maternal feelings, in which aggressiveness toward the beloved seems to loom so large. It is impossible here to distinguish hostility from attraction, competition from dependency, combat from homosexual embrace. The warrior loves his adversary because he needs a manly competitor against whom to establish his own identity. The striving for autonomy depends on the existence of something set off against, beside, or below it.

To distinguish oneself from other people, then, one must rely on them. "Thy valiantness was mine: thou suck'st it from me," Volumnia informs her son (3.2.129).

Coriolanus and the attack on Corioles. Jost Amman, from *Icones Livianae* (1572).

Coriolanus wants to imagine his courage and honor as intrinsically his own, rather than conferred by others. But "our virtues," as Aufidius claims, "lie in th'interpretation of the time" (4.7.49–50). Roman merit, inextricable from social goals and needs, demands an admiring audience. Even while he professes to despise flattery, Coriolanus takes pride in such apparently trivial honorific gestures as the surname that commemorates his victory at Corioles, or the oaken garlands conferred upon him for valor in battle. Insignificant in themselves, such symbols acquire meaning from the way they are regarded by the group. The exiled Coriolanus defiantly insists that "there is a world elsewhere" (3.3.132), but it is impossible for him to retire to a quiet corner of Italy and live out his life in obscurity. He needs to prove himself against an enemy, but now that enemy, Rome, is the place from which his life has drawn its meaning. Threatening to annihilate the community that bore him, he puts himself in a painfully contradictory position.

Thus the superior is always dependent on the inferior, the inside on the outside, the civilized on the barbarian, the patrician on the plebeian, the performer on the audience, the man on the woman and on the boy, even while the "upper" term prides itself on its difference from its subordinate. Just as important, the dependency works in both directions, as the action of *Coriolanus* shows. If Coriolanus depends on the Roman populace in ways he refuses to recognize, so does the populace depend on him. When the tribunes shamelessly manipulate their constituency to orchestrate Coriolanus's exile, they leave the city open to its enemies and come close to bringing destruction upon it.

Since we hear an unusual amount about Coriolanus's boyhood, it is easy to see his conflicted desire for autonomy in terms of his simultaneous flight from and dependence on Volumnia. But that is an oversimplification: Coriolanus is not merely the product of a uniquely bad upbringing. His anxieties about autonomy and dependence, competitiveness and cooperation are shared, in some form, by almost everyone in the play: they are aspects of social and political dilemmas, not merely individual neuroses. Early in the first scene, the First Citizen notes—perhaps envi-

Volumnia entreating Coriolanus. Jost Amman, from *Icones Livianae* (1572).

ously, but also accurately—that the patricians enjoy seeing the lower classes suffer, because that suffering enhances their sense of comparative privilege. Who depends on whom, how far ought that dependency to extend, what forms ought it to take?

These concerns are powerfully evoked in the imagery of *Coriolanus*. It was a cliché already old in Plutarch's time, and still current in Shakespeare's, that human communities were modeled on individual bodies. In the optimistic version of this analogy, the state is a collection of harmoniously interrelated organs, each selflessly performing its own distinctive function in the service of the whole. Interconnectedness is the apparent moral of Menenius's "pretty tale" (1.1.83) of the belly in the opening scene. But even in Menenius's version, the analogy veers toward grotesquerie, the body-state becoming an apparently headless entity equipped with an unnaturally smiling belly. Elsewhere in *Coriolanus*, the body is less a marvel of smooth interaction than a site of disintegration: Coriolanus imagines the plebeians as "fragments" and "voices" (1.1.213, 2.3.118–24); Menenius rebukes a malcontent whom he calls "the great toe of this assembly" (1.1.146). The mutilations of the battlefield begin to seem corporeal equivalents for a profound crisis of the body politic. The shared needs of embodied, vulnerable human beings for food, shelter, and defense provide an obvious material basis for societies. But individual bodies tend to be selfish, unwilling to forgo their own urgent requirements in the interests of a collective good, reluctant to admit their reliance on one another lest that reliance be made a pretext for exploitation. Once again, dependence and autonomy seem simultaneously antithetical and inextricable.

Because the body in *Coriolanus* is so often imagined in negative terms—as starving, wounded, or cut to pieces—attempts to escape corporeal limitation seem understandable, even laudable. In fact, Coriolanus's battlefield heroism seems largely a matter of refusing to acknowledge physical constraints: he is inexhaustible, undaunted by wounds or danger. Late in the play, Menenius describes him as a kind of robot: "When he walks, he moves like an engine, and the ground shrinks before his treading" (5.4.17–18). But within a few lines, Menenius is proven wrong: blood relationships, the ties of the body, prove impossible for Coriolanus to disown. Volumnia, Virgilia, and young Martius come to the Volscian camp to plead for their city and their people; and, in a capitulation that he knows to be virtually suicidal, Coriolanus grasps his mother's hand.

Coriolanus is not only the last of Shakespeare's tragedies but the last of a series of plays about ancient Rome. It seems to look back upon, and anatomize, social and individual pathologies that in Julius Caesar and even Antony and Cleopatra were merely hinted at: the way "Roman" valor on the battlefield, for instance, becomes both a flight from and a replacement for heterosexuality; the way aggression and repression undergird the psyches of Roman men and women; the way both sexes deform their personalities in order to conform to highly restrictive patterns of masculinity or femininity. While in Julius Caesar class tensions serve mainly to exalt the patrician class, here the plebeians' grievances, and their different priorities, are understandable. Coriolanus's inability to comprehend the plebeians is a telling sign of both his personal rigidity and the alienation of rich from poor. Coriolanus has seemed to many audiences a relentlessly bleak play, and no wonder. Subjecting both its formidable but unpleasant hero and his society to intense critical scrutiny, Coriolanus implies that no political arrangement could possibly satisfy human needs, portrayed here as incorrigibly self-contradictory.

KATHARINE EISAMAN MAUS

SELECTED BIBLIOGRAPHY

Adelman, Janet. "'Anger's My Meat': Feeding, Dependency, and Aggression in Coriolanus." Representing Shakespeare: New Psychoanalytic Essays. Ed. Murray M. Schwartz and Coppélia Kahn. Baltimore, MD: Johns Hopkins UP, 1980. 129–49. Argues that the play's political and psychological anxieties crystallize around the figure of the mother who does not feed her children.

Barton, Anne. "Livy, Machiavelli, and Shakespeare's Coriolanus." Shakespeare Survey 38 (1985): 115–29. Looks at the Roman historian Livy and Machiavelli's commentary on Livy as sources of inspiration for Coriolanus.

Bloom, Harold, ed. William Shakespeare's "Coriolanus." New York: Chelsea House, 1988. Anthology of critical essays.

Cavell, Stanley. "Who Does the Wolf Love?" Disowning Knowledge in Six Plays by Shakespeare. Cambridge: Harvard UP, 1987. 143–78. Examines Coriolanus's affinity with sacrificial feasts, especially the Christian ritual of Communion.

Fish, Stanley. "How to Do Things with Austin and Searle: Speech-Act Theory and Literary Criticism." Is There a Text in This Class?: The Authority of Interpretive Communities. Cambridge: Harvard UP, 1980. 197–245. Analyzes Coriolanus's problems with speech-acts.

Goldberg, Jonathan. "The Anus in Coriolanus." Historicism, Psychoanalysis, and Early Modern Culture. Ed. Carla Mazzio and Doug Trevor. New York: Routledge, 2000. 260–71. Assesses the anal imagery and homoeroticism in the play.

Kerrigan, John. "Coriolanus Fidiussed." Essays in Criticism 42 (2012): 319–52. Looks at oaths, good faith, and the breaking of promises in Coriolanus.

Patterson, Annabel. "Speak, Speak! The Popular Voice and the Jacobean State." Shakespeare and the Popular Voice. Cambridge, MA: Blackwood, 1989. Analyzes the connection between Coriolanus and disenfranchised groups in Shakespeare's England.

Sanders, Eve Rachel. "The Body of the Actor in Coriolanus." Shakespeare Quarterly 57 (2006): 382–412. Looks at acting and theatrical display in Coriolanus.

Wheeler, David, ed. "Coriolanus": Critical Essays. New York: Garland, 1995. An anthology of essays and reviews of theatrical productions.

FILMS

Coriolanus. 1951. Dir. Paul Nickell. USA. 60 min. This Westinghouse Studio One black-and-white abridged television version, interspersed with occasional ads for refrigerators and laundry appliances, is performed in modern dress and strongly marked by the recent traumas of fascism and World War II. Richard Greene is handsome but inexpressive in the role of Coriolanus.

Coriolanus. 1984. Dir. Elijah Moshinsky. UK. 145 min. BBC-TV's spare, gripping production featuring Alan Howard as a tightly wound Coriolanus, Mike Gwilym as a canny Aufidius, and Irene Worth as a terrifying Volumnia.

Coriolanus. 2011. Dir. Ralph Fiennes (who also plays the title role). UK. 123 min. Vanessa Redgrave is Volumnia in this modern-dress version, largely filmed in Serbia and evoking contemporary theaters of war.

TEXTUAL INTRODUCTION

The 1623 Folio (F) is the sole surviving authority for *Coriolanus*. F is probably based on an authorial manuscript that has been annotated for performance, since it contains a number of detailed stage directions, such as those that indicate how an exit or entrance might be performed (e.g., "*Citizens steal away*," 1.1.241 SD; "*Enter Martius and Aufidius at several doors*," 1.8.0 SD), or what variety of instruments is required—cornetts, hautboys, trumpets, or drums (see 1.9.65 SD, 1.10.0 SD, 5.6.48 SD). Moreover, no entrances and very few exits are missing. That F's immediate source is likely to be authorial is indicated by certain stage directions containing information that is extraneous to performance (e.g., 1.3.0, where Volumnia and Virgilia are described as "*mother and wife to Martius*"); that exceeds what can readily be shown on the early modern stage (e.g., 1.8.15 SD: "*Martius fights till they be driven in breathless*"); or that acknowledges the illusion of performance, as in 2.2.0 (where officers enter "*to lay cushions, as it were in the Capitol*"). Some of these stage directions anticipate the action they describe; in such cases, in accordance with editorial tradition, *The Norton Shakespeare* moves F's stage directions to their logical location in the text.

F contains act divisions, which have been followed here. Scene divisions have been added, following standard editorial practice by ending a scene when the stage has been emptied, although during the battle scenes of act 1 (particularly during what is in this, and in many editions, designated 1.4) such divisions are not clear-cut.

The punctuation in F sometimes impedes sense, with periods placed in midsentence (e.g., 3.3.66) or no strong punctuation mark where one is obviously needed (e.g., 1.1.153). For the most part, punctuation has been silently modernized; points at which F's punctuation requires radical intervention have been noted in textual variants.

Following the principle of single-text editing, this edition has retained F's designation of characters in stage directions and (where it does not overly hinder the reader) speech prefixes; any changes made are noted in textual variants. Hence, the play's protagonist is known as "*Martius*" until the end of act 1; from act 2 onward—until the moment of his death—he is dubbed "*Coriolanus*" in both speech prefixes and stage directions. Names of individual characters in F's speech prefixes and stage directions are otherwise stable, apart from Lartius, who is variously "*Latius*" and "*Titus*." However, the terms used for different groups of characters are much more fluid. The non-elite of Rome are labeled both "*Citizens*" and "*Plebeians*": the former classification implies political enfranchisement, along with a civic role and civil responsibilities; the latter categorizes the group by their low social status. That F uses *"citizen"* and *"plebeian"* interchangeably is evident from 2.3, where the stage direction at 2.3.146 denotes the entrance of *"plebeians,"* but the speech prefixes that follow allocate the speeches to the *"first," "second,"* and *"Third Citizen"* (2.3.148, 150, 152). Rome's social elite are also known by a variety of terms: senators are a subset of patricians (legally, only patricians could be senators); however, in Shakespeare's Rome we also have lords, nobles, and gentry named in stage directions, speech prefixes, and the dialogue itself. Although historically the "gentry" could equate to the class of *equites* in ancient Rome, "nobles" and "lords" would seem to be synonymous with the patricians, and have been treated as such in the list of the persons of the play, particularly as the sliding nature of F's use of sociopolitical terms is evident from its treatment of the labels *"plebeian"* and *"citizen."* Nonetheless, Aufidius's speech at 4.7.29–30 complicates this pragmatic solution, since at this point he seems to distinguish between "the nobility of Rome" and the "senators and patricians."

By far the greatest editorial problem is lineation. Shakespeare's late style tested the boundaries of the iambic pentameter line, and *Coriolanus*—like other plays at the latter end of his writing career—has lines that run to twelve syllables, have feminine endings, or rely on clipped or syncopated forms, or where the syntax strains against the lineation (e.g., when lines end with a word such as "and" or "but"). There are also a number of short-line exchanges where it is unclear whether verse or prose is intended, and the same characters can slip between prose and verse within the same scene (e.g., the citizens in 1.1, Virgilia and Volumnia in 1.3, Menenius and the Watchmen in 5.2). Some of these problems may arise from the manuscript lying behind *Coriolanus*. If Hand D in the manuscript of *Sir Thomas More* is, as many scholars now believe, that of Shakespeare, then the authorial manuscript may have contributed to the confusion regarding lineation. Like many writers trained in the mid-sixteenth century, the Hand D writer did not automatically capitalize the initial letter in a line of verse; he also tended to cram the ends of overrunning lines into the preceding line in order to save space. The printing process and the need to squeeze the often long lines of *Coriolanus* into two columns in F—particularly problematic where the line includes a speech prefix—may further have exacerbated the lack of clarity of lineation in the manuscript.

CATHY SHRANK

PERFORMANCE NOTE

The foremost challenge for companies staging *Coriolanus* may be finding a demigod to play the lead, who conquers one city single-handedly and then brings Rome to its knees. The character is built on several paradoxes: he is Rome's loyal son and its scourge; an experienced soldier and a naïve boy; physically invulnerable and emotionally brittle; a callous anti-hero and a tragic victim. Actors must reconcile these contradictions while creating sympathy for a protagonist commonly considered unsympathetic. Directors often address the problem by shifting the focus of the tragedy from military to political or domestic conflicts. Productions may, for instance, emphasize the cunning and underhandedness of the tribunes, the homoeroticism underlying Coriolanus's rivalry with Aufidius, or the monumentality of Volumnia's personality and the psychological complexity of the relationship between mother and son.

Directors are often interested in *Coriolanus*'s representations of class division, and their productions can argue the contemporary relevance of plebeian complaints by setting the play in such places as occupied Palestine or Wall Street. Whatever a production's politics, it must decide whether Menenius is a shifty politician or a gracious steward; whether the tribunes are humble advocates for the people or self-serving intriguers; whether the citizens are hostile or conciliatory, irrational or fair-minded. Each choice will affect the audience's reception of Coriolanus and his tragic status. In addition, productions must decide whether Volumnia should clash with Virgilia or treat her with indifference; whether Virgilia's silence arises out of natural shyness or a serene confidence in her position and power; and whether Coriolanus understands or even welcomes Aufidius's sexually suggestive images and dreams (see Digital Edition PC 2). Other staging questions include how Coriolanus is to be shut within Corioles' walls (1.3) and whether Coriolanus or Virgilia initiates the kiss in 5.3.

BRETT GAMBOA

The Tragedy of Coriolanus

[THE PERSONS OF THE PLAY

Romans:
Caius MARTIUS, later surnamed CORIOLANUS
MENENIUS Agrippa
Titus LARTIUS
COMINIUS } generals
VOLUMNIA, mother to Martius
VIRGILIA, wife to Martius
YOUNG MARTIUS, son to Martius
VALERIA, a Roman noblewoman
GENTLEWOMAN, attending on Virgilia } patricians
SICINIUS Velutus
Junius BRUTUS } tribunes
PATRICIANS, including SENATORS, LORDS, and NOBLES
AEDILES
OFFICERS
LIEUTENANT
PLEBEIANS / CITIZENS
SOLDIERS
Nicanor, a ROMAN
HERALD
MESSENGERS
Other ROMANS
Usher, Scout, Captains, Trumpeters, Drummers, Lictors, Attendants

Volscians:
Tullus AUFIDIUS, general of the Volscians
Adrian, a VOLSCE
Aufidius's LIEUTENANT
Aufidius's SERVINGMEN
CONSPIRATORS with Aufidius
SOLDIERS
WATCHMEN
LORDS including SENATORS
CITIZENS / COMMONERS]

1.1

Enter a company of mutinous CITIZENS, with staves,
clubs, and other weapons.

FIRST CITIZEN Before we proceed any further, hear me speak.

ALL Speak, speak.

FIRST CITIZEN You are all resolved rather to die than to
famish?

5 ALL Resolved, resolved.

FIRST CITIZEN First, you know Caius Martius is chief enemy
to the people.

1.1 Location: A street in Rome.

ALL We know't, we know't.

FIRST CITIZEN Let us kill him, and we'll have corn° at our
10   own price. Is't a verdict?°   *grain* / *Do we agree*

ALL No more talking on't. Let it be done. Away, away!

SECOND CITIZEN One word, good citizens.

FIRST CITIZEN We are accounted poor citizens, the patricians
    good.° What authority[1] surfeits on would relieve us. If they   *noble; well off*
15   would yield us but the superfluity° while it were wholesome,° *excess / still edible*
    we might guess they relieved us humanely, but they think we
    are too dear.[2] The leanness that afflicts us, the object° of our   *visible fact*
    misery, is as an inventory to particularize their abundance;[3]
    our sufferance° is a gain to them. Let us revenge this with   *distress*
20   our pikes,° ere we become rakes;[4] for the gods know I speak *spears; pitchforks*
    this in hunger for bread, not in thirst for revenge.

SECOND CITIZEN Would you proceed especially against Caius
    Martius?

ALL Against him first: he's a very dog to° the commonalty.[5]   *persecutor of*

25 SECOND CITIZEN Consider you what services he has done for
    his country?

FIRST CITIZEN Very well, and could be content to give him
    good report for't, but that he pays himself with being proud.

ALL Nay, but speak not maliciously.

30 FIRST CITIZEN I say unto you, what he hath done famously,° *that has won fame*
    he did it to that end.° Though soft-conscienced men can be *(to advance his pride)*
    content to say it was for his country, he did it to please his
    mother and to be partly proud,° which he is, even to the *partly out of pride*
    altitude of his virtue.[6]

35 SECOND CITIZEN What he cannot help in his nature you
    account a vice in him. You must in no way say he is
    covetous.

FIRST CITIZEN If I must not, I need not be barren of accusa-
    tions. He hath faults, with surplus, to tire in repetition.
       Shouts within.
40   What shouts are these? The other side o'th' city is risen.
    Why stay we prating° here? To th' Capitol!   *chattering*

ALL Come, come!

FIRST CITIZEN Soft,° who comes here?   *Wait*
       Enter MENENIUS *Agrippa.*

SECOND CITIZEN Worthy Menenius Agrippa, one that hath
45   always loved the people.

FIRST CITIZEN He's one honest enough. Would all the rest
    were so!

MENENIUS What work's, my countrymen, in hand? Where go
    you
    With bats° and clubs? The matter speak, I pray you.   *cudgels*

50 SECOND CITIZEN Our business is not unknown to th' Senate.
    They have had inkling this fortnight what we intend to do,
    which now we'll show 'em in deeds. They say poor suitors° *petitioners*
    have strong[7] breaths; they shall know we have strong arms,
    too.

---

1. The nobility.
2. We cost too much to preserve; we are too rich.
3. To make their prosperity stand out by comparison.
4. Rakes are proverbially thin; playing on "pikes."

5. Common people.
6. That is, his pride is equal to his valor.
7. Strong-smelling, from eating onions, the food of
the poor.

55	MENENIUS Why, masters,° my good friends, mine honest neighbors,	*(artisans' title)*
	Will you undo° yourselves?	*destroy*
	SECOND CITIZEN We cannot, sir; we are undone already.	
	MENENIUS I tell you, friends, most charitable care	
	Have the patricians of you. For° your wants,	*As for*
60	Your suffering in this dearth,° you may as well	*famine*
	Strike at the heaven with your staves as lift them	
	Against the Roman state, whose course will on	
	The way it takes, cracking ten thousand curbs[8]	
	Of more strong link asunder than can ever	
65	Appear in your impediment.[9] For the dearth,	
	The gods, not the patricians, make it, and	
	Your knees° to them, not arms, must help. Alack,	*kneeling (in prayer)*
	You are transported by calamity	
	Thither where more attends° you, and you slander	*awaits*
70	The helms° o'th' state, who care for you like fathers,	*helmsmen*
	When you curse them as enemies.[1]	
	SECOND CITIZEN Care for us? True indeed! They ne'er cared	
	for us yet. Suffer us to famish, and their storehouses crammed	
	with grain; make edicts for usury[2] to support usurers; repeal	
75	daily any wholesome act established against the rich; and	
	provide more piercing° statutes daily to chain up and restrain	*severe*
	the poor. If the wars eat us not up, they will; and there's all	
	the love they bear us.	
	MENENIUS Either you must	
80	Confess yourselves wondrous malicious	
	Or be accused of folly. I shall tell you	
	A pretty tale. It may be you have heard it,	
	But since it serves my purpose, I will venture	
	To stale't a little more.°	*To make it more familiar*
	SECOND CITIZEN Well, I'll hear it, sir.[3]	
85	Yet you must not think to fob off our disgrace[4]	
	With a tale. But, an't° please you, deliver.	*if it*
	MENENIUS There was a time when all the body's members	
	Rebelled against the belly, thus accused it:	
	That only like a gulf° it did remain	*abyss*
90	I'th' midst o'th' body, idle and unactive,	
	Still cupboarding the viand,[5] never bearing	
	Like° labor with the rest; where th'other instruments°	*Equal / organs*
	Did see and hear, devise, instruct, walk, feel,	
	And, mutually participate,° did minister	*participating*
95	Unto the appetite and affection° common	*desire*
	Of the whole body. The belly answered—	
	SECOND CITIZEN Well, sir, what answer made the belly?	
	MENENIUS Sir, I shall tell you. With a kind of smile,	

8. Chain bits used to restrain unruly horses.
9. *than . . . impediment*: than you can ever offer in opposition.
1. PERFORMANCE COMMENT Productions vary in how sympathetically they present the plebian concerns and Menenius's response to them—and more generally, they vary in how much they emphasize the play's class politics. For a fuller discussion, see Digital Edition PC 1.
2. Permitting the lending of money at interest (widely considered immoral, because it enriched wealthy

lenders at the expense of poor borrowers).
3. TEXTUAL COMMENT In *Coriolanus*, upper-class characters typically speak in blank verse and lower-class characters in prose, but the distinction is not always consistently maintained, nor is it always reliably indicated in the Folio text. For the political significance of the Second Citizen's move to blank verse, see Digital Edition TC 1.
4. Dismiss our hardship.
5. Always hoarding the food.

Which ne'er came from the lungs,° but even thus—   *(organs of laughter)*
100 For, look you, I may make the belly smile
As well as speak—it tauntingly replied
To th' discontented members, the mutinous parts
That envied his receipt;° even so most fitly[6]   *what it received*
As you malign our senators for that°   *because*
They are not such as you.
105 SECOND CITIZEN   Your belly's answer, what?
The kingly crownèd head, the vigilant eye,
The counselor heart, the arm our soldier,
Our steed the leg, the tongue our trumpeter,
With other muniments° and petty helps   *supports*
In this our fabric,° if that they—   *body*
110 MENENIUS   What then?
Fore me,° this fellow speaks! What then? What then?   *(an oath)*
SECOND CITIZEN   —Should by the cormorant° belly be   *rapacious*
restrained,
Who is the sink° o'th' body—   *cesspool*
MENENIUS   Well, what then?
SECOND CITIZEN   The former agents, if they did complain,
What could the belly answer?
115 MENENIUS   I will tell you.
If you'll bestow a small°—of what you have little—   *small amount of*
Patience awhile, you'st° hear the belly's answer.   *you would*
SECOND CITIZEN   You're long about it.
MENENIUS   Note me this, good friend:
Your° most grave belly was deliberate,   *This*
120 Not rash like his accusers, and thus answered:
"True is it, my incorporate° friends," quoth he,   *united in one body*
"That I receive the general food at first
Which you do live upon; and fit it is,
Because I am the storehouse and the shop
125 Of the whole body. But, if you do remember,
I send it through the rivers of your blood
Even to the court, the heart, to th' seat° o'th' brain;   *throne*
And through the cranks and offices[7] of man
The strongest nerves° and small inferior veins   *muscles*
130 From me receive that natural competency°   *sustenance*
Whereby they live. And though that all at once"—
You, my good friends, this says the belly, mark me—
SECOND CITIZEN   Ay, sir, well, well.
MENENIUS   "Though all at once cannot
See what I do deliver out to each,
135 Yet I can make my audit up[8] that all
From me do back receive the flour[9] of all
And leave me but the bran." What say you to't?
SECOND CITIZEN   It was an answer. How apply you this?
MENENIUS   The senators of Rome are this good belly,
140 And you the mutinous members. For examine
Their counsels and their cares, digest[1] things rightly

---

6. In just the way.
7. Through the winding passages and workrooms.
8. Show on my balance sheet.

9. Nourishment (punning on "flower," or choicest part).
1. Interpret (playing on the belly's function).

Touching the weal o'th' common,[2] you shall find
No public benefit which you receive
But it proceeds or comes from them to you
145 And no way from yourselves. What do you think,
You, the great toe of this assembly?
SECOND CITIZEN   I, the great toe? Why the great toe?
MENENIUS   For that being one o'th' lowest, basest, poorest
Of this most wise rebellion, thou goest foremost.
150 Thou rascal, that art worst in blood[3] to run,
Lead'st first to win some vantage.°   *benefit*
But make you ready your stiff bats and clubs:
Rome and her rats are at the point of battle;
The one side must have bale.°   *injury*
        Enter Caius MARTIUS.
                    —Hail, noble Martius!
155 MARTIUS   Thanks. —What's the matter, you dissentious° rogues,   *rebelling*
That, rubbing the poor itch of your opinion,
Make yourselves scabs?
SECOND CITIZEN   We have ever your good word.
MARTIUS   He that will give good words to thee will flatter
Beneath abhorring. What would you have, you curs
160 That like nor° peace nor war? The one affrights you,   *neither*
The other makes you proud.° He that trusts to you,   *rebellious*
Where he should find you lions, finds you hares;
Where foxes, geese. You are no surer, no,
Than is the coal of fire upon the ice,
165 Or hailstone in the sun. Your virtue° is   *characteristic skill*
To make him worthy whose offense subdues him[4]
And curse that justice did it. Who deserves greatness
Deserves° your hate, and your affections° are   *Incurs / propensities*
A sick man's appetite, who desires most that
170 Which would increase his evil.° He that depends   *illness*
Upon your favors swims with fins of lead
And hews down oaks with rushes. Hang ye! Trust ye?
With every minute you do change a mind
And call him noble that was now° your hate,   *just now*
175 Him vile that was your garland.[5] What's the matter,
That in these several° places of the city   *various*
You cry against the noble Senate, who,
Under the gods, keep you in awe, which else°   *who otherwise*
Would feed on one another? [*to* MENENIUS] What's their seeking?
180 MENENIUS   For corn at their own rates,° whereof they say   *prices*
The city is well stored.
MARTIUS   Hang 'em! "They say"?
They'll sit by th' fire and presume to know
What's done i'th' Capitol,[6] who's like to rise,
Who thrives and who declines; side° factions and give out°   *side with / announce*
185 Conjectural marriages, making parties strong

2. Concerning the public good.
3. Most desperate; lowest born. *rascal:* wretch; inferior deer or dog.
4. *To make . . . subdues him:* To extol the man whose

wrongdoing makes him liable to punishment.
5. Hero (traditionally wreathed with laurel or oak leaves).
6. The temple of Jupiter and hub of the Roman state.

And feebling such as stand not in their liking
Below their cobbled° shoes. They say there's grain enough?   *patched*
Would the nobility lay aside their ruth°   *compassion*
And let me use my sword, I'd make a quarry[7]
190 With thousands of these quartered[8] slaves as high
As I could pitch my lance.
MENENIUS   Nay, these are almost thoroughly persuaded,°   *appeased*
For though abundantly they lack discretion,
Yet are they passing° cowardly. But I beseech you,   *exceedingly*
What says the other troop?
195 MARTIUS   They are dissolved, hang 'em.
They said they were an-hungry,° sighed forth proverbs: *very hungry*
That hunger broke stone walls, that dogs° must eat,   *(even dogs)*
That meat was made for mouths, that the gods sent not
Corn for the rich men only. With these shreds
200 They vented° their complainings, which being answered   *spoke; excreted*
And a petition granted them—a strange one,
To break the heart of generosity°   *the nobility*
And make bold power look pale—they threw their caps
As they would hang them on the horns o'th' moon,
Shouting their emulation.[9]
205 MENENIUS   What is granted them?
MARTIUS   Five tribunes° to defend their vulgar wisdoms,   *representatives*
Of their own choice. One's Junius Brutus,
Sicinius Velutus, and I know not. 'Sdeath,°   *God's death (an oath)*
The rabble should have first unroofed the city
210 Ere so prevailed with me. It will in time
Win upon power° and throw forth greater themes   *Prevail upon authority*
For insurrection's arguing.
MENENIUS   This is strange.
MARTIUS [*to the* CITIZENS]   Go, get you home, you fragments.°   *scraps of uneaten food*
        Enter a MESSENGER, *hastily.*
MESSENGER   Where's Caius Martius?
MARTIUS   Here. What's the matter?
215 MESSENGER   The news is, sir, the Volsces are in arms.
MARTIUS   I am glad on't; then we shall ha' means to vent
Our musty superfluity.°   *moldy excess*
        Enter SICINIUS *Velutus, Junius* BRUTUS, COMINIUS,
        Titus LARTIUS, *with other* SENATORS.
                      See, our best elders.
FIRST SENATOR   Martius, 'tis true that you have lately told us:
The Volsces are in arms.
MARTIUS   They have a leader,
220 Tullus Aufidius, that will put you to't.°   *to the test*
I sin in envying his nobility,
And were I anything but what I am,
I would wish me only he.
COMINIUS   You have fought together?
MARTIUS   Were half to half the world by th'ears[1] and he
225 Upon my party,° I'd revolt to make   *side*

---

7. A pile of animals killed in hunting.
8. Hacked to pieces (a punishment for treason).
9. Rivalry (either to shout loudest or to defy

the nobility).
1. If one-half of the world were fighting the other.

Only my wars with him. He is a lion
That I am proud to hunt.
FIRST SENATOR   Then, worthy Martius,
Attend upon° Cominius to these wars.   *Serve under*
COMINIUS [*to* MARTIUS]   It is your former promise.
MARTIUS   Sir, it is,
230   And I am constant. —Titus Lartius, thou
Shalt see me once more strike at Tullus' face.
What, art thou stiff?² Stand'st out?
LARTIUS   No, Caius Martius,
I'll lean upon one crutch and fight with t'other
Ere stay behind this business.
MENENIUS   O true bred!
235   FIRST SENATOR   Your company to th' Capitol, where I know
Our greatest friends attend us.
LARTIUS [*to* COMINIUS]   Lead you on.
     [*to* MARTIUS] Follow Cominius; we must follow you,
Right worthy° your priority.   *Who well deserve*
COMINIUS   Noble Martius.
FIRST SENATOR [*to the* CITIZENS]   Hence to your homes, be gone!
MARTIUS   Nay, let them follow.
240   The Volsces have much corn: take these rats thither
To gnaw their garners.°   CITIZENS *steal away.*   *storehouses*
Worshipful mutineers,
Your valor puts well forth.³ [*to the* SENATORS] Pray follow.
          Exeunt all but SICINIUS *and* BRUTUS.
SICINIUS   Was ever man so proud as is this Martius?
BRUTUS   He has no equal.
245   SICINIUS   When we were chosen tribunes for the people—
BRUTUS   Marked you his lip and eyes?
SICINIUS   Nay, but his taunts.
BRUTUS   Being moved,° he will not spare to gird⁴ the gods.   *angry*
SICINIUS   Bemock the modest moon.
BRUTUS   The present wars devour him! He is grown
Too proud to be so valiant.
250   SICINIUS   Such a nature,
Tickled° with good success, disdains the shadow   *Excited; flattered*
Which he treads on at noon. But I do wonder
His insolence can brook° to be commanded   *endure*
Under Cominius.
BRUTUS   Fame, at the which he aims,
255   In whom already he's well graced, cannot
Better be held nor more attained than by
A place below the first; for what miscarries
Shall be the general's fault, though he perform
To th'utmost of a man, and giddy censure°   *rash opinion*
260   Will then cry out of Martius, "Oh, if he
Had borne the business!"
SICINIUS   Besides, if things go well,
Opinion, that so sticks on° Martius, shall   *clings to*
Of his demerits° rob Cominius.   *Of Cominius's deserts*

---

2. Obstinate (but Lartius understands "stiff with age").   3. Promises well, like a budding plant (ironic).
4. He will not refrain from sneering at.

BRUTUS   Come,
Half all Cominius' honors are to Martius,
265 Though Martius earned them not; and all his faults
To Martius shall be honors, though indeed
In aught he merit not.
SICINIUS   Let's hence and hear
How the dispatch is made,° and in what fashion,   *business is executed*
More than his singularity,⁵ he goes
Upon this present action.
270 BRUTUS   Let's along.   *Exeunt.*

1.2

Enter Tullus AUFIDIUS *with* SENATORS *of Corioles.*

FIRST SENATOR   So, your opinion is, Aufidius,
That they of Rome are entered° in our counsels   *instructed*
And know how we proceed?
AUFIDIUS   Is it not yours?
Whatever have been thought on in this state
5   That could be brought to bodily act ere Rome
Had circumvention?° 'Tis not four days gone   *means to circumvent it*
Since I heard thence.° These are the words—I think   *from there*
I have the letter here—yes, here it is:
[*reading*] "They have pressed a power,° but it is not known   *conscripted an army*
10   Whether for east or west. The dearth is great,
The people mutinous, and it is rumored
Cominius, Martius—your old enemy,
Who is of Rome worse hated than of you—
And Titus Lartius, a most valiant Roman,
15   These three lead on this preparation
Whither 'tis bent;° most likely 'tis for you.   *Wherever it is bound*
Consider of it."
FIRST SENATOR   Our army's in the field;
We never yet made doubt but Rome was ready
To answer us.
AUFIDIUS   Nor did you think it folly
20   To keep your great pretenses° veiled till when   *aims*
They needs must show themselves, which in the hatching,
It seemed, appeared° to Rome. By the discovery   *became known*
We shall be shortened in our aim,° which was   *have to lower our sights*
To take in° many towns ere, almost, Rome   *seize*
25   Should know we were afoot.
SECOND SENATOR   Noble Aufidius,
Take your commission, hie° you to your bands;°   *haste / troops*
Let us alone to guard Corioles.
If they set down° before's, for the remove°   *encamp / to raise the siege*
Bring up your army, but I think you'll find
They've not prepared for us.
30   AUFIDIUS   Oh, doubt not that;
I speak from certainties. Nay, more,
Some parcels° of their power are forth already,   *parts*
And only hitherward.° I leave your honors.   *marching toward us*

---

5. Apart from his idiosyncrasies.   1.2 Location: Corioles, chief city of the Volscians.

If we and Caius Martius chance to meet,
35 'Tis sworn between us we shall ever strike°   *keep fighting*
Till one can do no more.
ALL   The gods assist you!
AUFIDIUS   And keep your honors safe.
FIRST SENATOR   Farewell.
SECOND SENATOR   Farewell.
ALL   Farewell.   *Exeunt all.*

1.3

Enter VOLUMNIA *and* VIRGILIA, *mother and wife to*
MARTIUS. *They set them down on two low stools*
and sew.

VOLUMNIA   I pray you, daughter, sing, or express yourself in a
more comfortable sort.° If my son were my husband, I should   *cheerful manner*
freelier rejoice in that absence wherein he won honor than
in the embracements of his bed where he would show most
5   love. When yet he was but tender-bodied and the only son of
my womb, when youth with comeliness plucked all gaze his
way, when—for a day of kings' entreaties—a mother should
not sell him an hour from her beholding, I—considering
how honor would become such a person,° that it was no bet-   *handsome figure*
10   ter than picture-like to hang by th' wall, if renown made it
not stir[1]—was pleased to let him seek danger where he was
like to find fame. To a cruel war I sent him, from whence he
returned, his brows bound with oak.[2] I tell thee, daughter, I
sprang not more in joy at first hearing he was a man-child
15   than now in first seeing he had proved himself a man.
VIRGILIA   But had he died in the business, madam, how then?
VOLUMNIA   Then his good report should have been my son; I
therein would have found issue. Hear me profess sincerely:
had I a dozen sons, each in my love alike, and none less
20   dear than thine and my good Martius, I had rather had
eleven die nobly for their country than one voluptuously
surfeit out of action.[3]
         Enter a GENTLEWOMAN.
GENTLEWOMAN   Madam, the Lady Valeria is come to visit you.
VIRGILIA   Beseech you give me leave to retire myself.°   *to go in*
25   VOLUMNIA   Indeed you shall not.
Methinks I hear hither your husband's drum;
See him pluck Aufidius down by th' hair;
As children from a bear, the Volsces shunning° him.   *fleeing*
Methinks I see him stamp thus and call thus,
30   "Come on, you cowards! You were got° in fear,   *begotten*
Though you were born in Rome!" His bloody brow
With his mailed° hand then wiping, forth he goes,   *armored*
Like to a harvest-man that's tasked° to mow   *ordered*
Or° all or lose his hire.°   *Either / pay*
35   VIRGILIA   His bloody brow? O Jupiter, no blood!
VOLUMNIA   Away, you fool! It more becomes a man

1.3 Location: Caius Martius's house, in Rome.
1. If desire for fame did not move it to action.
2. A garland of oak leaves (awarded to one who saved

the life of a Roman citizen in battle).
3. Indulge himself to excess away from the
battlefield.

Than gilt° his trophy. The breasts of Hecuba[4]   *gold leaf*
When she did suckle Hector[5] looked not lovelier
Than Hector's forehead when it spit forth blood
40   At Grecian sword contemning.° —Tell Valeria   *expressing contempt*
We are fit° to bid her welcome.   *Exit* GENTLEWOMAN.   *ready*
VIRGILIA   Heavens bless my lord from fell° Aufidius!   *fierce*
VOLUMNIA   He'll beat Aufidius' head below his knee
And tread upon his neck.
       Enter VALERIA *with an Usher and* [*the*] GENTLEWOMAN.
45   VALERIA   My ladies both, good day to you.
VOLUMNIA   Sweet madam.
VIRGILIA   I am glad to see your ladyship.
VALERIA   How do you both? You are manifest housekeepers.[6]
What are you sewing here? A fine spot,° in good faith. [*to*   *embroidered design*
50   VIRGILIA] How does your little son?
VIRGILIA   I thank your ladyship; well, good madam.
VOLUMNIA   He had rather see the swords and hear a drum
than look upon his schoolmaster.
VALERIA   O'my word, the father's son. I'll swear 'tis a very
55   pretty boy. O'my troth, I looked upon him o'Wednesday half
an hour together. He's such a confirmed° countenance. I   *determined*
saw him run after a gilded butterfly, and when he caught it,
he let it go again, and after it again, and over and over° he   *head over heels*
comes, and up again, catched it again. Or whether his fall
60   enraged him, or how 'twas, he did so set° his teeth and tear   *clench*
it. Oh, I warrant, how he mammocked° it!   *shredded*
VOLUMNIA   One on 's ° father's moods.   *of his*
VALERIA   Indeed, la, 'tis a noble child.
VIRGILIA   A crack,° madam.   *lively lad*
65   VALERIA   Come, lay aside your stitchery. I must have you play
the idle housewife° with me this afternoon.   *hussy*
VIRGILIA   No, good madam. I will not out of doors.
VALERIA   Not out of doors?
VOLUMNIA   She shall, she shall.
70   VIRGILIA   Indeed, no, by your patience. I'll not over the
threshold till my lord return from the wars.
VALERIA   Fie, you confine yourself most unreasonably. Come,
you must go visit the good lady that lies in.°   *is confined with child*
VIRGILIA   I will wish her speedy strength and visit her with my
75   prayers, but I cannot go thither.
VOLUMNIA   Why, I pray you?
VIRGILIA   'Tis not to save labor, nor that I want love.°   *lack affection for her*
VALERIA   You would be another Penelope.[7] Yet they say all the
yarn she spun in Ulysses' absence did but fill Ithaca full of
80   moths. Come, I would your cambric° were sensible° as your   *fine white linen/sensitive*
finger, that you might leave pricking it for pity. Come, you
shall go with us.
VIRGILIA   No, good madam, pardon me; indeed I will not
forth.

---

4. Trojan queen, mother of many sons.
5. The greatest Trojan warrior, killed by the Greek
Achilles (see *Troilus and Cressida*).
6. You are clearly being stay-at-homes.

7. In Homer's *Odyssey*, Ulysses' wife, Penelope, pretends during his protracted absence that she cannot remarry until she finishes her weaving, which she secretly unravels each night.

85 VALERIA In truth, la, go with me, and I'll tell you excellent
news of your husband.
VIRGILIA O good madam, there can be none yet.
VALERIA Verily, I do not jest with you: there came news from
him last night.
90 VIRGILIA Indeed, madam?
VALERIA In earnest, it's true. I heard a senator speak it. Thus
it is: the Volsces have an army forth, against whom Cominius
the general is gone with one part of our Roman power. Your
lord and Titus Lartius are set down before their city Corioles;
95 they nothing doubt prevailing[8] and to make it brief wars.
This is true, on mine honor, and so I pray, go with us.
VIRGILIA Give me excuse,° good madam. I will obey you in   Pardon me
everything hereafter.
VOLUMNIA Let her alone, lady. As she is now she will but
100 disease° our better mirth.   trouble
VALERIA In troth, I think she would. [to VIRGILIA] Fare you
well, then. [to VOLUMNIA] Come, good sweet lady. —Prithee,
Virgilia, turn thy solemnness out-o'-door, and go along with
us.
105 VIRGILIA No, at a word, madam; indeed I must not. I wish
you much mirth.
VALERIA Well, then, farewell.   *Exeunt.*

1.4

Enter MARTIUS, *Titus* LARTIUS, *with* [*a Trumpeter,*]
drum and colors,° *with Captains and* SOLDIERS [*with*   drummer and flag bearer
scaling ladders], *as before the city Corioles;*[1] *to them a*
MESSENGER.

MARTIUS Yonder comes news. A wager they have met.
LARTIUS My horse to yours, no?
MARTIUS   'Tis done.
LARTIUS   Agreed.
MARTIUS [*to* MESSENGER] Say, has our general met the enemy?
MESSENGER They lie in view, but have not spoke° as yet.   encountered
LARTIUS So, the good horse is mine.
5 MARTIUS   I'll buy him of you.
LARTIUS No, I'll nor° sell nor give him; lend you him I will   neither
For half a hundred years. [*to Trumpeter*] Summon the town.
MARTIUS [*to* MESSENGER] How far off lie these armies?
MESSENGER Within this mile and half.
10 MARTIUS Then shall we hear their larum,° and they ours.   call to arms
Now Mars,° I prithee, make us quick in work,   Roman god of war
That we with smoking° swords may march from hence   steaming (with blood)
To help our fielded friends.[2] [*to Trumpeter*] Come, blow thy blast.
They sound a parley.[3] *Enter two* SENATORS *with others*
on the walls of Corioles.
—Tullus Aufidius, is he within your walls?

---

8. They don't at all doubt that they will prevail.
1.4 Location: Before the walls of Corioles.
1. The rear of the stage represented the city walls,
the tiring-house door at the back of the stage the
gate, and the balcony the ramparts.
2. Our comrades in the battlefield.
3. Trumpet call for conference with the enemy.

15 FIRST SENATOR   No, nor a man that fears you less than he:
That's lesser than a little. (*Drum afar off.*) Hark, our drums
Are bringing forth our youth. We'll break our walls
Rather than they shall pound us up;° our gates,   *confine us*
Which yet seem shut, we have but pinned with rushes;°   *hollow reeds*
20 They'll open of themselves. (*Alarum far off.*) Hark you, far off!
There is Aufidius. List what work he makes
Amongst your cloven° army.   *divided; cut to pieces*
MARTIUS   Oh, they are at it!
LARTIUS   Their noise be our instruction. —Ladders ho!
        Enter the army of the Volsces.
MARTIUS   They fear us not, but issue forth° their city.   *rush from*
25 Now put your shields before your hearts and fight
With hearts more proof° than shields. —Advance, brave Titus.   *impenetrable*
They do disdain us much beyond our thoughts,[4]
Which makes me sweat with wrath. —Come on, my fellows!
He that retires, I'll take him for a Volsce,
30 And he shall feel mine edge.°   [*Exit.*]   *(sword edge)*
        Alarum. The Romans are beat back to their trenches.
        Enter MARTIUS, cursing.
MARTIUS   All the contagion of the south[5] light on you,
You shames of Rome! You herd of— Boils and plagues
Plaster you o'er,[6] that you may be abhorred°   *(by your smell)*
Farther than seen, and one infect another
35 Against the wind a mile!° You souls of geese   *Even a mile upwind*
That bear the shapes of men, how have you run
From slaves that apes would beat! Pluto° and hell!   *god of the underworld*
All hurt behind,[7] backs red, and faces pale
With flight and agued° fear! Mend and charge home,[8]   *shivering*
40 Or, by the fires of heaven,° I'll leave the foe   *the stars*
And make my wars on you. Look to't. Come on.
If you'll stand fast, we'll beat them to their wives,
As they us to our trenches. Follow's!
        Another alarum. [Volsces enter, attacking.] MARTIUS
        [*beats them back and*] *follows them to* [*the*] *gates.*
So, now the gates are ope. Now prove good seconds.°   *supporters*
45 'Tis for the followers fortune widens° them,   *opens*
Not for the fliers. Mark me, and do the like.
        [*He*] *enters the gates.*
FIRST SOLDIER   Foolhardiness! Not I.
SECOND SOLDIER   Nor I.
        [*The gates close;* MARTIUS] *is shut in.*[9]
FIRST SOLDIER   See,
They have shut him in.
        Alarum continues.
ALL   To th' pot,° I warrant him.   *cooking pot*
        Enter Titus LARTIUS.
LARTIUS   What is become of Martius?
ALL   Slain, sir, doubtless.

---

4. More than we had imagined.
5. South wind (thought to carry disease).
6. TEXTUAL COMMENT The Folio text is repunctuated
by modern editors; for the rationale, see Digital Edition TC 2.
7. An injury taken in flight was a disgrace.

8. Charge to the heart of their defenses.
9. TEXTUAL COMMENT The placement of the Folio
stage directions is often imprecise; here modern editors rearrange them to make sense of the action. For
a detailed account of this reordering, see Digital Edition TC 3.

50 FIRST SOLDIER   Following the fliers at the very heels,
With them he enters, who upon the sudden
Clapped-to° their gates. He is himself alone   *Shut*
To answer° all the city.   *confront*
LARTIUS   O noble fellow,
Who sensibly° outdares his senseless sword   *though having sensation*
55 And, when it bows, stand'st up! —Thou art lost, Martius.
A carbuncle entire,° as big as thou art,   *flawless ruby*
Were not so rich a jewel. Thou wast a soldier
Even to Cato's[1] wish, not fierce and terrible
Only in strokes, but with thy grim looks and
60 The thunder-like percussion of thy sounds
Thou mad'st thine enemies shake as if the world
Were feverous and did tremble.
        Enter MARTIUS, *bleeding, assaulted by the enemy.*
FIRST SOLDIER   Look, sir.
LARTIUS   Oh, 'tis Martius!
Let's fetch him off, or make remain alike.[2]
        They fight and all enter the city. [*Exeunt.*]

1.5
        Enter certain ROMANS *with spoils.*
FIRST ROMAN   This will I carry to Rome.
SECOND ROMAN   And I this.
FIRST ROMAN   A murrain° on't; I took this for silver.   *plague*
        Alarum continues still afar off. Enter MARTIUS, *and*
        Titus [LARTIUS] *with a Trumpet*[er].
                        Exeunt [ROMANS *with spoils*].
MARTIUS   See here these movers[1] that do prize their hours
At a cracked drachma!° Cushions, leaden spoons,   *Greek coin*
5 Irons of a doit,[2] doublets that hangmen would
Bury with those that wore them,[3] these base slaves,
Ere yet the fight be done, pack up. Down with them!
And hark, what noise the general makes. To him!
There is the man of my soul's hate, Aufidius,
10 Piercing our Romans. Then, valiant Titus, take
Convenient numbers to make good° the city,   *secure*
Whilst I, with those that have the spirit, will haste
To help Cominius.
LARTIUS   Worthy sir, thou bleed'st.
Thy exercise hath been too violent
For a second course° of fight.   *bout*
15 MARTIUS   Sir, praise me not:
My work hath yet not warmed me. Fare you well.
The blood I drop is rather physical[4]
Than dangerous to me. To Aufidius thus
I will appear and fight.
LARTIUS   Now the fair goddess Fortune
20 Fall deep in love with thee, and her great charms

---

1. Cato the Censor, Roman general and moralist.
2. Let's rescue him, or share his fate.
1.5 Location: Corioles.
1. Active persons (ironic); plunderers.
2. Worthless swords (a "doit" was a very small coin).
doublets: close-fitting jackets (common male attire in

Jacobean England).
3. That is, even a hangman, whose wage is his victim's clothing, would spurn these garments.
4. Curative (bloodletting was a common medical practice).

Misguide thy opposers' swords! Bold gentleman,
Prosperity be thy page.°   *Success attend you*
MARTIUS   Thy friend° no less   *(Prosperity)*
Than those she placeth highest. So farewell.   [*Exit.*]
LARTIUS   Thou worthiest Martius!
25   [*to Trumpeter*] Go sound thy trumpet in the market-place.
Call thither all the officers o'th' town,
Where they shall know our mind. Away.   *Exit.*

1.6

Enter COMINIUS, *as it were in retire,*° *with* SOLDIERS.   *controlled, strategic retreat*
COMINIUS   Breathe you,° my friends. Well fought! We are   *Get your breath back*
   come off¹
Like Romans, neither foolish in our stands
Nor cowardly in retire. Believe me, sirs,
We shall be charged again. Whiles we have struck,°   *we were fighting*
5   By interims and conveying gusts² we have heard
The charges of our friends. Ye Roman gods,³
Lead their successes as we wish our own,
That both our powers, with smiling fronts° encount'ring,   *faces; front ranks*
May give you° thankful sacrifice!   *(the gods)*
   Enter a MESSENGER.
                              —Thy news?
10   MESSENGER   The citizens of Corioles have issued°   *(from the gates)*
And given to Lartius and to Martius battle.
I saw our party to their trenches driven,
And then I came away.
COMINIUS   Though thou speakest truth,
Methinks thou speak'st not well. How long is't since?
15   MESSENGER   Above an hour, my lord.
COMINIUS   'Tis not a mile; briefly° we heard their drums.   *a short time ago*
How couldst thou in a mile confound° an hour   *waste*
And bring thy news so late?
MESSENGER   Spies of the Volsces
Held me in chase, that I was forced to wheel°   *detour*
20   Three or four miles about, else had I, sir,
Half an hour since brought my report.
   Enter MARTIUS.
COMINIUS   Who's yonder,
That does appear as he were flayed? O gods,
He has the stamp° of Martius, and I have   *form*
Before-time° seen him thus.   *Previously*
MARTIUS   Come I too late?
25   COMINIUS   The shepherd knows not thunder from a tabor°   *small drum*
More than I know the sound of Martius' tongue
From every meaner° man.   *lesser*
MARTIUS   Come I too late?
COMINIUS   Ay, if you come not in the blood of others,
But mantled in your own.

1.6 Location: The battlefield.
1. We have retreated.
2. *By interims . . . gusts:* At intervals, conveyed by the wind.
3. TEXTUAL COMMENT The Folio text has "The

Roman Gods," a misreading of the "y" that was frequently used to indicate "th" in Shakespeare's time (and is sometimes used today to convey an old-timey flavor: "ye olde shoppe"). See Digital Edition TC 4 for a fuller rationale of the emendation.

MARTIUS   Oh, let me clip° ye   *clasp*
30   In arms as sound as when I wooed, in heart
     As merry as when our nuptial day was done,
     And tapers burnt to bedward!
        [*They embrace.*]

COMINIUS   Flower of warriors,
     How is't with Titus Lartius?

MARTIUS   As with a man busied about decrees,
35   Condemning some to death, and some to exile,
     Ransoming him or pitying, threat'ning th'other;
     Holding Corioles in the name of Rome
     Even like a fawning greyhound in the leash,
     To let him slip° at will.   *off the leash*

COMINIUS   Where is that slave
40   Which told me they had beat you to your trenches?
     Where is he? Call him hither.

MARTIUS   Let him alone:
     He did inform° the truth. But for our gentlemen,°   *report / (sarcastic)*
     The common file°—a plague! Tribunes for them!—   *sort*
     The mouse ne'er shunned the cat as they did budge°   *flinch*
     From rascals worse than they.

45 COMINIUS   But how prevailed you?

MARTIUS   Will the time serve to tell? I do not think.
     Where is the enemy? Are you lords o'th' field?
     If not, why cease you till you are so?

COMINIUS   Martius, we have at disadvantage fought,
50   And did retire to win our purpose.°   *for tactical reasons*

MARTIUS   How lies their battle?° Know you on which side   *army*
     They have placed their men of trust?

COMINIUS   As I guess, Martius,
     Their bands i'th' vaward° are the Antiates   *front*
     Of their best trust, o'er them Aufidius,
     Their very heart of hope.

55 MARTIUS   I do beseech you
     By all the battles wherein we have fought,
     By th' blood we have shed together, by th' vows
     We have made to endure° friends, that you directly   *remain*
     Set me against Aufidius and his Antiates,
60   And that you not delay the present,° but,   *matter at hand*
     Filling the air with swords advanced and darts,
     We prove° this very hour.   *try*

COMINIUS   Though I could wish
     You were conducted to a gentle bath
     And balms applied to you, yet dare I never
65   Deny your asking. Take your choice of those
     That best can aid your action.

MARTIUS   Those are they
     That most are willing.—If any such be here—
     As it were sin to doubt—that love this painting°   *(blood)*
     Wherein you see me smeared; if any fear
70   Lesser his person than an ill report;[4]
     If any think brave death outweighs bad life

---

4. *Lesser . . . report:* Less for his body than for his reputation.

And that his country's dearer than himself,
Let him alone, or so many so minded,
Wave thus [*waving his sword*] to express his disposition,
75 And follow Martius.
    They all shout and wave their swords, take him up in
    their arms, and cast up their caps.
Oh, me alone! Make you a sword of me?
If these shows be not outward,° which of you   *superficial*
But is four Volsces? None of you but is
Able to bear against the great Aufidius
80 A shield as hard as his. A certain number—
Though thanks to all—must I select from all:
The rest shall bear the business in some other fight
As cause will be obeyed.° Please you to march,   *the situation requires*
And four shall quickly draw out my command,⁵
Which men are best inclined.
85 COMINIUS   March on, my fellows.
Make good this ostentation,° and you shall   *show of enthusiasm*
Divide in all⁶ with us.   *Exeunt.*

1.7

Titus LARTIUS, *having set a guard upon Corioles,*
going with drum and trumpet toward COMINIUS *and*
Caius MARTIUS, *enters with a* LIEUTENANT, *other*
SOLDIERS, *and a Scout.*
LARTIUS   So, let the ports° be guarded; keep your duties   *gates*
As I have set them down. If I do send, dispatch
Those centuries¹ to our aid; the rest will serve
For a short holding.° If we lose the field,   *brief occupation*
We cannot keep the town.
5 LIEUTENANT   Fear not our care, sir.
LARTIUS   Hence, and shut your gates upon's.
  [*to the Scout*] Our guider, come: to th' Roman camp conduct us.
                            Exeunt.

1.8

Alarum, as in battle. Enter MARTIUS *and* AUFIDIUS *at*
several° doors.   *separate*
MARTIUS   I'll fight with none but thee, for I do hate thee
Worse than a promise-breaker.
AUFIDIUS   We hate alike:
Not Afric owns° a serpent I abhor   *Africa doesn't contain*
More than thy fame and envy.° Fix thy foot.   *enviable reputation*
5 MARTIUS   Let the first budger die the other's slave,
And the gods doom him after.
AUFIDIUS   If I fly, Martius,
Holla° me like a hare.   *Shout in pursuit of*
MARTIUS   Within these three hours, Tullus,
Alone I fought in your Corioles' walls,
And made what work I pleased. 'Tis not my blood
10 Wherein thou seest me masked. For thy revenge,
Wrench up thy power to th' highest.

---

5. Select those I will command.
6. Share the honor and winnings.
1.7 Location: The gates of Corioles.

1. Companies of 100 men.
1.8 Location: The battlefield.

AUFIDIUS   Wert thou the Hector
That was the whip of your bragged progeny,[1]
Thou shouldst not scape me here.
    Here they fight, and certain Volsces come in the aid of
    AUFIDIUS.
[*to Volsces*] Officious° and not valiant, you have shamed me   *Meddling*
15   In your condemnèd seconds.[2]
    MARTIUS *fights till they be driven in breathless.* [*Exeunt.*]

1.9

    Flourish.[1] Alarum. A retreat is sounded. Enter at one
    door COMINIUS *with the* ROMANS; *at another door*
    MARTIUS, *with his arm in a scarf.°*   *sling*
COMINIUS   If I should tell thee o'er this thy day's work,
Thout° not believe thy deeds, but I'll report it   *Thou would'st*
Where senators shall mingle tears with smiles,
Where great patricians shall attend and shrug,°   *(with incredulity)*
5   I'th' end admire;° where ladies shall be frighted   *marvel*
And, gladly quaked,° hear more; where the dull° tribunes,   *made to tremble / sullen*
That with the fusty° plebeians hate thine honors,   *moldy; stinking*
Shall say against their hearts,° "We thank the gods   *despite themselves*
Our Rome hath such a soldier."
10   Yet cam'st thou to a morsel of this feast,
    Having fully dined before.[2]
    Enter Titus [LARTIUS], *with his power,° from the pursuit.*   *troops*
LARTIUS   O general,
Here is the steed, we the caparison.[3]
Hadst thou beheld—
MARTIUS   Pray now, no more. My mother,
Who has a charter° to extol her blood,°   *right / offspring*
15   When she does praise me grieves me. I have done
As you have done, that's what I can, induced
As you have been, that's for my country.
He that has but effected his good will[4]
Hath overta'en mine act.
COMINIUS   You shall not be
20   The grave of your deserving. Rome must know
The value of her own. 'Twere a concealment
Worse than a theft, no less than a traducement,°   *slander*
To hide your doings, and to silence that
Which to the spire and top of praises vouched°   *declared*
25   Would seem but modest.° Therefore I beseech you—   *inadequate*
In sign° of what you are, not to reward   *As a token*
What you have done—before our army, hear me.
MARTIUS   I have some wounds upon me, and they smart
To hear themselves remembered.
COMINIUS   Should they not,
30   Well might they fester gainst ingratitude

---

1. Romans claimed descent from the Trojans; Hector, the finest Trojan soldier, was the scourge ("whip") of the Greeks.
2. Contemptible assistance.
1.9 Location: The battlefield.
1. Trumpet call for the entry of the victorious Romans. *retreat:* signal to cease pursuit.
2. *Yet . . . before:* either "The feast of description is a morsel compared with the full dinner of your deeds," or "Your final onslaught was a mere morsel in addition to your earlier fighting."
3. That is, here is he who really did the work (Coriolanus, the horse); we are only the horse's trappings ("caparison").
4. Carried out his resolution.

And tent[5] themselves with death. Of all the horses—
Whereof we have ta'en good, and good store[6]—of all
The treasure in this field achieved and city,
We render you the° tenth to be ta'en forth ° *one*
35 Before the common distribution,
At your only° choice. ° *sole*

MARTIUS   I thank you, general,
But cannot make my heart consent to take
A bribe to pay my sword: I do refuse it
And stand° upon my common part with those ° *insist*
40 That have beheld the doing.

> *A long flourish. They all cry, "Martius, Martius," cast*
> *up their caps and lances.* COMINIUS *and* [Titus]
> LARTIUS *stand bare.°* ° *with hats removed*

May these same instruments, which you profane,
Never sound more. When drums and trumpets shall
I'th' field prove flatterers, let courts and cities be
Made all of false-faced soothing;[7] when steel grows
45 Soft as the parasite's° silk, let him be made ° *flatterer's*
An overture for th' wars.[8] No more, I say.
For that I have not washed my nose that bled,
Or foiled some debile° wretch—which, without note, ° *feeble*
Here's many else° have done—you shout me forth ° *others*
50 In acclamations hyperbolical,° ° *In exaggerated praise*
As if I loved my little should be dieted
In praises sauced with lies.[9]

COMINIUS   Too modest are you,
More cruel to your good report than grateful
To us that give° you truly. By your patience, ° *describe*
55 If gainst yourself you be incensed, we'll put you,
Like one that means his proper harm,° in manacles, ° *harm to himself*
Then reason safely with you. Therefore be it known,
As to us, to all the world, that Caius Martius
Wears this war's garland, in token of the which,
60 My noble steed, known to the camp, I give him,
With all his trim belonging;° and from this time, ° *fine trappings*
For what he did before Corioles, call him,
With all th'applause and clamor of the host,
Martius Caius Coriolanus.
65 Bear th'addition° nobly ever! ° *title*

> *Flourish. Trumpets sound, and drums.*

ALL   Martius Caius Coriolanus!

MARTIUS   I will go wash,
And when my face is fair,° you shall perceive ° *clean*
Whether I blush or no. Howbeit, I thank you.
I mean to stride° your steed, and at all times ° *bestride; ride on*
70 To undercrest° your good addition ° *uphold*
To th' fairness° of my power. ° *best*

COMINIUS   So, to our tent,
Where, ere we do repose us, we will write

---

5. Heal (a "tent" was a probe that cleansed a wound).
6. We have captured good quality and quantity.
7. Hypocritical compliments.
8. *let . . . wars:* a debated and perhaps corrupt pas-

sage; perhaps "let the parasite call soldiers to war."
9. *As if . . . lies:* As if I enjoyed having my small
achievements bulked up by lying flattery.

To Rome of our success. —You, Titus Lartius,
Must to Corioles back; send us to Rome
75 The best,¹ with whom we may articulate,°   *make terms*
For their own good and ours.
LARTIUS   I shall, my lord.
MARTIUS   The gods begin to mock me. I, that now
Refused most princely gifts, am bound to beg
Of my lord general.
COMINIUS   Take't, 'tis yours: what is't?
80 MARTIUS   I sometime lay here in Corioles
At a poor man's house; he used° me kindly.   *treated*
He cried° to me; I saw him prisoner,   *appealed*
But then Aufidius was within my view,
And wrath o'erwhelmed my pity. I request you
To give my poor host freedom.
85 COMINIUS   Oh, well begged!
Were he the butcher of my son, he should
Be free as is the wind. —Deliver° him, Titus.   *Free*
LARTIUS   Martius, his name?
MARTIUS   By Jupiter, forgot!
I am weary; yea, my memory is tired.
Have we no wine here?
90 COMINIUS   Go we to our tent.
The blood upon your visage dries: 'tis time
It should be looked to. Come.   *Exeunt.*

1.10

A flourish. Cornetts. Enter Tullus AUFIDIUS, *bloody,*
with two or three SOLDIERS.
AUFIDIUS   The town is ta'en.
FIRST SOLDIER   'Twill be delivered back
On good condition.¹
AUFIDIUS   Condition?
I would I were a Roman, for I cannot,
Being a Volsce, be that I am.° Condition?   *what I am (proud)*
5 What good condition can a treaty find
I'th' part that is at mercy?° Five times, Martius,   *For the conquered side*
I have fought with thee; so often hast thou beat me,
And wouldst do so, I think, should we encounter
As often as we eat. By th'elements,
10 If e'er again I meet him beard to beard,
He's mine, or I am his. Mine emulation°   *rivalry*
Hath not that honor in't it had, for where°   *whereas*
I thought to crush him in an equal force,
True sword to sword, I'll potch° at him some way: *thrust*
Or° wrath or craft may get him.   *Either*
15 FIRST SOLDIER   He's the devil.
AUFIDIUS   Bolder, though not so subtle. My valor's poisoned
With only suff'ring stain° by him; for him   *disgrace*
Shall fly out of itself. Nor sleep nor sanctuary,²
Being naked, sick; nor fane,° nor Capitol,   *temple*

---

1. The most noble Volscians.
1.10 Location: Outside Corioles.
1. Terms (Aufidius takes the meaning "state of being").

2. In early modern England, those who sought sanctuary in a church were protected from attack or legal
prosecution. *fly out of itself*: deviate from its nature.

20 The prayers of priests, nor times of sacrifice,
Embarquements° all of fury, shall lift up   *Impediments*
Their rotten° privilege and custom gainst   *worn-out*
My hate to Martius. Where I find him, were it
At home, upon° my brother's guard,° even there   *under / protection*
25 Against the hospitable canon,° would I   *rule of hospitality*
Wash my fierce hand in 's heart. Go you to th' city;
Learn how 'tis held, and what they are that must
Be hostages for Rome.
FIRST SOLDIER   Will not you go?
AUFIDIUS   I am attended° at the cypress grove. I pray you— *expected*
30 'Tis south the city mills—bring me word thither
How the world goes, that to the pace of it[3]
I may spur on my journey.
FIRST SOLDIER   I shall, sir.   [*Exeunt.*]

2.1

Enter MENENIUS *with the two tribunes of the people,*
SICINIUS *and* BRUTUS.

MENENIUS   The augurer[1] tells me we shall have news tonight.
BRUTUS   Good or bad?
MENENIUS   Not according to the prayer of the people, for they
love not Martius.
5 SICINIUS   Nature teaches beasts to know their friends.
MENENIUS   Pray you, who does the wolf love?
SICINIUS   The lamb.
MENENIUS   Ay, to devour him, as the hungry plebeians would
the noble Martius.
10 BRUTUS   He's a lamb indeed, that baas like a bear.
MENENIUS   He's a bear indeed, that lives like a lamb.[2] You two
are old men; tell me one thing that I shall ask you.
BOTH   Well, sir?
MENENIUS   In what enormity is Martius poor in that you two
15 have not in abundance?
BRUTUS   He's poor in no one fault but stored° with all.   *well stocked*
SICINIUS   Especially in pride.
BRUTUS   And topping all others in boasting.
MENENIUS   This is strange now. Do you two know how you
20 are censured° here in the city, I mean of us o'th' right-hand   *judged*
file?[3] Do you?
BOTH   Why? How are we censured?
MENENIUS   Because you talk of pride now—will you not be
angry?
25 BOTH   Well, well, sir, well.
MENENIUS   Why, 'tis no great matter, for a very little thief of
occasion will rob you of a great deal of patience.[4] Give your
dispositions the reins and be angry at your pleasures, at the
least, if you take it as a pleasure to you in being so. You
30 blame Martius for being proud?

---

3. In accordance with the situation.
2.1 Location: Rome.
1. Religious official who interpreted omens.
2. That is, how can you accuse him of being a bear

when he lives an innocent life?
3. Patrician class (who made up the right-hand "file,"
or line, in battle).
4. The least pretext will make you lose your temper.

BRUTUS   We do it not alone, sir.

MENENIUS   I know you can do very little alone, for your helps
are many, or else your actions would grow wondrous single.°   *solitary; trivial*
Your abilities are too infant-like for doing much alone. You
35   talk of pride. Oh, that you could turn your eyes toward the
napes of your necks and make but an interior survey of your
good selves! Oh, that you could!

BOTH   What then, sir?

MENENIUS   Why, then you should discover a brace° of unmer-   *pair*
40   iting, proud, violent, testy magistrates—alias fools—as any in
Rome.

SICINIUS   Menenius, you are known well enough, too.

MENENIUS   I am known to be a humorous° patrician, and one   *whimsical*
that loves a cup of hot wine with not a drop of allaying
45   Tiber° in't; said to be something imperfect in favoring the   *water*
first complaint,[5] hasty and tinder-like upon too trivial motion;°   *provocation*
one that converses more with the buttock of the night than
with the forehead of the morning.[6] What I think, I utter,
and spend my malice in my breath. Meeting two such weals-
50   men° as you are—I cannot call you Lycurguses[7]—if the drink   *statesmen*
you give me touch my palate adversely, I make a crooked
face at it. I cannot say your worships have delivered the matter well when I find the ass in compound with the major part
of your syllables;[8] and though I must be content to bear with
55   those that say you are reverend grave men, yet they lie
deadly° that tell you have good faces. If you see this in the   *extremely*
map of my microcosm,[9] follows it that I am known well
enough too? What harm can your bisson conspectuities°   *dim vision*
glean out of this character,[1] if I be known well enough too?

60 BRUTUS   Come, sir, come; we know you well enough.

MENENIUS   You know neither me, yourselves, nor anything.
You are ambitious for poor knaves' caps and legs.[2] You wear
out a good wholesome forenoon in hearing a cause between
an orange-wife and a faucet-seller,[3] and then rejourn° the   *adjourn*
65   controversy of threepence to a second day of audience.°   *hearing*
When you are hearing a matter between party and party, if
you chance to be pinched with the colic,° you make faces   *intestinal gas*
like mummers,[4] set up the bloody flag° against all patience   *declare war*
and, in roaring for a chamberpot, dismiss the controversy
70   bleeding,° the more entangled by your hearing. All the peace   *unhealed*
you make in their cause is calling both the parties knaves.
You are a pair of strange ones.

BRUTUS   Come, come, you are well understood to be a perfecter giber for the table than a necessary bencher in the
75   Capitol.[5]

5. *favoring the first complaint:* accepting the first version of a dispute I hear before considering the other
side.
6. That experiences more late nights than early
mornings.
7. Lycurgus was a famous Spartan lawgiver of the
ninth century B.C.E.
8. *I find the ass . . . syllables:* I find stupidity mixed in
most of what you say.
9. My face (thought to map the "little world" of the

human body).
1. Verbal description.
2. For deferentially doffed caps and bent legs.
3. Between a woman fruit vendor and someone who
sells taps for liquor barrels.
4. Dumb-show actors (who use exaggerated facial
expressions).
5. *perfecter giber . . . Capitol:* better at dinner jests
than at serving in the Senate.

MENENIUS Our very priests must become mockers if they
shall encounter such ridiculous subjects° as you are. When   *objects; citizens*
you speak best unto the purpose, it is not worth the wagging
of your beards, and your beards deserve not so honorable a
80   grave as to stuff a botcher's° cushion or to be entombed in   *clothes mender's*
an ass's pack-saddle.[6] Yet you must be saying Martius is
proud, who in a cheap estimation° is worth all your prede-   *low estimate*
cessors since Deucalion,[7] though peradventure some of the
best of 'em were hereditary hangmen.[8] Good e'en to your
85   worships; more of your conversation would infect my brain,
being° the herdsmen of the beastly plebeians. I will be bold   *you two being*
to take my leave of you.

> BRUTUS *and* SICINIUS [*stand*] *aside. Enter* VOLUMNIA,
> VIRGILIA, *and* VALERIA.

How now, my as fair as noble ladies—and the moon,[9] were she
earthly, no nobler—whither do you follow your eyes so fast?
90 VOLUMNIA Honorable Menenius, my boy Martius approaches.
For the love of Juno, let's go.
MENENIUS Ha! Martius coming home?
VOLUMNIA Ay, worthy Menenius, and with most prosperous
approbation.[1]
95 MENENIUS [*throwing up his cap*] Take my cap, Jupiter, and
I thank thee. Hoo! Martius coming home?
VIRGILIA *and* VALERIA Nay, 'tis true.
VOLUMNIA Look, here's a letter from him; the state hath
another; his wife another, and I think there's one at home
100   for you.
MENENIUS I will make my very house reel tonight. A letter for
me?
VIRGILIA Yes, certain, there's a letter for you: I saw't.
MENENIUS A letter for me? It gives me an estate° of seven   *endowment; condition*
105   years' health, in which time I will make a lip° at the physi-   *sneer*
cian. The most sovereign° prescription in Galen[2] is but   *effective*
empiricutic° and, to° this preservative, of no better report   *quackish / compared with*
than a horse-drench.[3] Is he not wounded? He was wont° to   *accustomed*
come home wounded!
110 VIRGILIA Oh, no, no, no.
VOLUMNIA Oh, he is wounded, I thank the gods for't.
MENENIUS So do I too, if it be not too much. Brings he° vic-   *Does he bring*
tory in his pocket? The wounds become him.
VOLUMNIA On 's brows. Menenius, he comes the third time
115   home with the oaken garland.
MENENIUS Has he disciplined Aufidius soundly?
VOLUMNIA Titus Lartius writes they fought together, but
Aufidius got off.
MENENIUS And 'twas time for him too, I'll warrant him that;
120   an° he had stayed by him, I would not have been so 'fidi-   *If*
ussed[4] for all the chests in Corioles and the gold that's in
them. Is the Senate possessed° of this?   *informed*

---

6. Hair from cut beards was used as stuffing.
7. Deucalion and his wife were sole survivors of a
great flood; their son was the ancestor of the Greeks.
8. A very base occupation.
9. Diana, goddess of chastity.
1. Rich praise; happy success.

2. Ancient medical authority still standard in the
Renaissance (Galen actually lived six centuries after
Coriolanus).
3. Horse medicine.
4. "Aufidiussed," Menenius's coinage for "beaten."

VOLUMNIA   Good ladies, let's go. [*to* MENENIUS] Yes, yes, yes:
the Senate has letters from the general wherein he gives my
125 son the whole name° of the war. He hath in this action out-   *credit*
done his former deeds doubly.
VALERIA   In troth, there's wondrous things spoke of him.
MENENIUS   Wondrous? Ay, I warrant you, and not without his
true purchasing.°   *truly earning it*
130 VIRGILIA   The gods grant them true.
VOLUMNIA   True? Pow waw!
MENENIUS   True? I'll be sworn they are true. Where is he
wounded? [*to* BRUTUS *and* SICINIUS] God save your good worships! Martius is coming home. He has more cause to be
135 proud. [*to* VOLUMNIA] Where is he wounded?
VOLUMNIA   I'th' shoulder and i'th' left arm. There will be large
cicatrices° to show the people when he shall stand for his   *scars*
place.[5] He received in the repulse of Tarquin[6] seven hurts
i'th' body.
140 MENENIUS   One i'th' neck and two i'th' thigh; there's nine
that I know.
VOLUMNIA   He had, before this last expedition, twenty-five
wounds upon him.
MENENIUS   Now it's twenty-seven. Every gash was an enemy's
145 grave.
            A shout and flourish.
Hark, the trumpets.
VOLUMNIA   These are the ushers of Martius: before him
He carries noise, and behind him he leaves tears.
Death, that dark spirit, in 's nervy° arm doth lie,   *muscular*
150 Which, being advanced, declines,° and then men die.   *being raised, descends*
            A sennet.° Trumpets sound. Enter COMINIUS *the general*   *ceremonial flourish*
            and Titus LARTIUS; *between them* CORIOLANUS,[7]
            crowned with an oaken garland, with Captains and
            SOLDIERS *and a* HERALD.
HERALD   Know, Rome, that all alone Martius did fight
Within Corioles' gates, where he hath won,
With fame, a name to° Martius Caius; these   *in addition to*
In honor follows "Coriolanus."
155 —Welcome to Rome, renownèd Coriolanus!
            Sound flourish.
ALL   Welcome to Rome, renownèd Coriolanus!
CORIOLANUS   No more of this; it does offend my heart.
Pray now, no more.
COMINIUS   Look, sir, your mother.
CORIOLANUS   Oh!
You have, I know, petitioned all the gods
For my prosperity.°   *success*
            [*He*] *kneels.*
160 VOLUMNIA   Nay, my good soldier, up.
My gentle Martius, worthy Caius, and

---

5. Will offer himself as a candidate for consul,
republican Rome's highest office.
6. Martius's first military experience was in the war
against the former King Tarquin.
7. TEXTUAL COMMENT From this point forward the

Folio uses the honorific name "*Coriolanus*" in speech
prefixes and stage directions. At 5.6.129, the moment
of his death, he once again becomes "*Martius*." See
Digital Edition TC 5 for the implications of this name
change.

By deed-achieving honor newly named—
What is it?—"Coriolanus" must I call thee?—
But, oh, thy wife!
CORIOLANUS [*to* VIRGILIA]   My gracious silence, hail!
165   Wouldst thou have laughed had I come coffined home,
That weep'st to see me triumph? Ah, my dear,
Such eyes the widows in Corioles wear,
And mothers that lack sons.
MENENIUS   Now the gods crown thee!
CORIOLANUS   And live you yet? [*to* VALERIA] O my sweet lady, pardon.
170   VOLUMNIA   I know not where to turn. Oh, welcome home;
—And welcome, General, and you're welcome all.
MENENIUS   A hundred thousand welcomes! I could weep
And I could laugh; I am light and heavy.° Welcome!   (*of heart*)
A curse begin at very root on 's heart
175   That is not glad to see thee! You are three
That Rome should dote on; yet, by the faith of men,
We have some old crab-trees° here at home that will not   (*gnarled, sour men*)
Be grafted to your relish.° Yet welcome, warriors!   *liking*
We call a nettle but a nettle and
The faults of fools but folly.
180   COMINIUS   Ever right.
CORIOLANUS   Menenius, ever, ever.
HERALD   Give way there, and go on!
CORIOLANUS [*to* VOLUMNIA *and* VIRGILIA]   Your hand, and yours!
Ere in our own house I do shade my head,
The good patricians must be visited,
185   From whom I have received not only greetings,
But with them change of honors.°   *a new set of honors*
VOLUMNIA   I have lived
To see inherited° my very wishes   *realized*
And the buildings of my fancy. Only
There's one thing wanting, which I doubt not but
Our Rome will cast upon thee.
190   CORIOLANUS   Know, good mother,
I had rather be their servant in my way
Than sway[8] with them in theirs.
COMINIUS   On, to the Capitol.
            Flourish cornetts.
            Exeunt in state, as before, [*all except*] BRUTUS *and*
                        SICINIUS[, *who come forward*].
BRUTUS   All tongues speak of him, and the bleared sights°   *dim-sighted people*
Are spectacled to see him. Your prattling nurse
195   Into a rapture° lets her baby cry   *fit*
While she chats him.[9] The kitchen malkin° pins   *wench*
Her richest lockram° 'bout her reechy° neck,   *linen / filthy*
Clamb'ring the walls to eye him. Stalls, bulks,[1] windows
Are smothered up, leads filled, and ridges horsed
200   With variable complexions,[2] all agreeing
In earnestness to see him. Seld-shown flamens°   *Seldom-seen priests*
Do press among the popular° throngs and puff°   *plebeian / pant*

8. Rule; prevail; deviate from a straight course.
9. Discusses Coriolanus.
1. Framework projecting from shopfronts ("stalls").

2. *leads . . . complexions:* lead roofs filled and roof-
tops bestridden by all types of people.

To win a vulgar station.° Our veiled dames   *a place in the crowd*
Commit the war of white and damask³ in
205 Their nicely gauded⁴ cheeks to th' wanton spoil
Of Phoebus'° burning kisses. Such a pother°   *the sun's / commotion*
As if that whatsoever god who leads him°   *(Coriolanus)*
Were slyly crept into his human powers
And gave him graceful posture.

SICINIUS   On the sudden°   *At once*
I warrant him consul.

210 BRUTUS   Then our office may,
During his power,° go sleep.   *term of authority*

SICINIUS   He cannot temp'rately transport° his honors   *convey*
From where he should begin and end,° but will   *to where he should end*
Lose those he hath won.

BRUTUS   In that there's comfort.

SICINIUS   Doubt not
215 The commoners, for whom we stand, but they
Upon their ancient malice⁵ will forget
With the least cause these his new honors, which°   *(which cause)*
That he will give them, make I as little question
As⁶ he is proud to do't.

BRUTUS   I heard him swear,
220 Were he to stand for consul, never would he
Appear i'th' marketplace, nor on him put
The napless vesture° of humility,   *threadbare garment*
Nor showing, as the manner is, his wounds
To th' people, beg their stinking breaths.°   *votes*

SICINIUS   'Tis right.
225 BRUTUS   It was his word. Oh, he would miss it° rather   *forgo the consulship*
Than carry° it but by the suit of the gentry to him   *go through with*
And the desire of the nobles.

SICINIUS   I wish no better
Than have him hold that purpose and to put it
In execution.

BRUTUS   'Tis most like he will.

230 SICINIUS   It shall be to him then as our good wills:°   *as our benefit requires*
A sure destruction.

BRUTUS   So it must fall out
To him, or our authority's for an end.
We must suggest° the people in what hatred   *insinuate to*
He still° hath held them; that to 's power he would   *always*
235 Have made them mules, silenced their pleaders,° and   *representatives*
Dispropertied° their freedoms, holding them   *Taken away*
In human action and capacity
Of no more soul nor fitness for the world
Than camels in their war, who have their provand°   *food*
240 Only for bearing burdens, and sore blows
For sinking under them.

---

3. The conflict between white and pink in delicate skin ("damask" refers to the dark-pink damask rose). 4. Fastidiously made up. TEXTUAL COMMENT "Gawded" in the Folio is from the verb "gaud," meaning "to ornament." Although the Norton edition retains the Folio wording, some editors emend to "guarded."

For the significance of the difference, see Digital Edition TC 6.
5. *Upon . . . malice:* Because of their long-standing hostility.
6. *make I as . . . as:* I have as little doubt as that.

SICINIUS   This, as you say, suggested
At some time when his soaring insolence
Shall touch° the people—which time shall not want°   *kindle / be lacking*
If he be put upon't, and that's as easy
245   As to set dogs on sheep—will be his fire
To kindle their dry stubble[7] and their blaze
Shall darken him for ever.
        Enter a MESSENGER.
BRUTUS   What's the matter?
MESSENGER   You are sent for to the Capitol. 'Tis thought
That Martius shall be consul. I have seen
250   The dumb men throng to see him, and the blind
To hear him speak. Matrons flung gloves,
Ladies and maids their scarves and handkerchiefs,
Upon him as he passed. The nobles bended
As to Jove's statue, and the commons made
255   A shower and thunder with their caps and shouts.
I never saw the like.
BRUTUS   Let's to the Capitol,
And carry with us ears and eyes for th' time,°   *present occasion*
But hearts for the event.°   *outcome*
SICINIUS   Have with you.°   *Exeunt.*   *Let's go; I'm with you.*

2.2

Enter two OFFICERS *to lay cushions, as it were in the
        Capitol.*
FIRST OFFICER   Come, come, they are almost here. How many
        stand for consulships?
SECOND OFFICER   Three, they say, but 'tis thought of everyone
        Coriolanus will carry it.
5   FIRST OFFICER   That's a brave fellow, but he's vengeance°   *intensely*
        proud and loves not the common people.
SECOND OFFICER   Faith, there hath been many great men that
        have flattered the people who ne'er loved them, and there be
        many that they° have loved they know not wherefore;° so   *(the people) / why*
10   that, if they love they know not why, they hate upon no better
        a ground. Therefore, for Coriolanus neither to care whether
        they love or hate him manifests the true knowledge he has
        in° their disposition, and out of his noble carelessness lets   *of*
        them plainly see't.
15   FIRST OFFICER   If he did not care whether he had their love or
        no, he waved indifferently[1] twixt doing them neither good
        nor harm; but he seeks their hate with greater devotion than
        they can render it him and leaves nothing undone that
        may fully discover° him their opposite.° Now to seem to   *reveal / adversary*
20   affect° the malice and displeasure of the people is as bad   *desire*
        as that which he dislikes, to flatter them for their love.
SECOND OFFICER   He hath deserved worthily of his country,
        and his ascent is not by such easy degrees as those who,

---

7. That is, Coriolanus's fiery insolence will kindle   2.2 Location: The Capitol, Rome.
the dry fuel of the plebeians' resentment.   1. He would waver without caring.

having been supple and courteous to the people, bonneted[2]
25 without any further deed to have them at all into their esti-
mation and report.° But he hath so planted his honors in   *good opinion*
their eyes and his actions in their hearts that for their
tongues to be silent and not confess so much were a kind of
ingrateful injury. To report otherwise were a malice that,
30 giving itself the lie,[3] would pluck reproof and rebuke from
every ear that heard it.
FIRST OFFICER   No more of him; he's a worthy man. Make
way; they are coming.

> *A sennet. Enter the* PATRICIANS *and* [SICINIUS *and*
> BRUTUS] *the tribunes of the people, Lictors[4] before
> them;* CORIOLANUS, MENENIUS, COMINIUS *the consul.*
> [*The* SENATORS *sit;*] SICINIUS *and* BRUTUS *take their
> places by themselves;* CORIOLANUS *stands.*

MENENIUS   Having determined of° the Volsces and   *made a decision about*
35 To send for Titus Lartius, it remains
As the main point of this our after-meeting
To gratify° his noble service that   *reward*
Hath thus stood for his country. Therefore please you,
Most reverend and grave elders, to desire
40 The present consul and last° general   *recent*
In our well-found° successes to report   *happily encountered*
A little of that worthy work performed
By Martius Caius Coriolanus, whom
We met here both to thank and to remember
With honors like° himself.   *befitting*
> [CORIOLANUS *sits.*]
45 FIRST SENATOR   Speak, good Cominius.
Leave nothing out for° length, and make us think   *on account of*
Rather our state's defective for requital
Than we to stretch it out.[5] [*to the tribunes*] Masters o'th' people,
We do request your kindest ears and, after,
50 Your loving motion toward° the common body   *persuasion of*
To yield° what passes here.   *agree to*
SICINIUS   We are convented°   *met together*
Upon a pleasing treaty,° and have hearts   *subject for discussion*
Inclinable to honor and advance
The theme of our assembly.
BRUTUS   Which the rather
55 We shall be blessed° to do if he remember   *happy*
A kinder value of the people than
He hath hereto prized them at.
MENENIUS   That's off, that's off.°   *irrelevant*
I would you rather had been silent. Please you
To hear Cominius speak?
BRUTUS   Most willingly,
60 But yet my caution was more pertinent
Than the rebuke you give it.

---

2. Put their bonnets back on (after doffing them as a
gesture of respect).
3. Showing itself to be false.
4. Officers who attended upon magistrates.

5. *Rather our . . . out:* We lack resources for adequate reward, rather than the will to reward him to
the utmost.

MENENIUS　　　　　　　　　He loves your people,
　　But tie him not to be their bedfellow.
　　—Worthy Cominius, speak.
　　　　CORIOLANUS *rises and offers° to go away.*　　　　*begins*
　　　　　　　　　　　　—Nay, keep your place.
FIRST SENATOR　　Sit, Coriolanus: never shame to hear
　　What you have nobly done.
65　CORIOLANUS　　　　　　　Your honors' pardon,
　　I had rather have my wounds to heal again
　　Than hear say how I got them.
　　BRUTUS　　　　　　　　　Sir, I hope
　　My words disbenched° you not?　　　　　　*unseated*
　　CORIOLANUS　　　　　　　No, sir. Yet oft,
　　When blows have made me stay, I fled from words.
70　You soothed° not, therefore hurt not; but your people,　　*flattered*
　　I love them as they weigh°—　　　　　　　　*deserve*
　　MENENIUS　　　　　　　Pray now, sit down.
　　CORIOLANUS　　I had rather have one scratch my head i'th' sun
　　When the alarum° were struck than idly sit　　*battle summons*
　　To hear my nothings monstered.[6]　　*Exit* CORIOLANUS.
　　MENENIUS　　　　　　　Masters of the people,
75　Your multiplying spawn° how can he flatter—　　*fast-breeding plebeians*
　　That's thousand to one good one—when you now see
　　He had rather venture all his limbs for honor
　　Than one on 's° ears to hear it? —Proceed, Cominius.　　*of his*
　　COMINIUS　　I shall lack voice; the deeds of Coriolanus
80　Should not be uttered feebly. It is held
　　That valor is the chiefest virtue and
　　Most dignifies the haver; if it be,
　　The man I speak of cannot in the world
　　Be singly counterpoised.° At sixteen years,　　*equaled by anyone*
85　When Tarquin made a head for° Rome, he fought　　*raised an army against*
　　Beyond the mark° of others. Our then dictator,[7]　　*reach*
　　Whom with all praise I point at, saw him fight
　　When with his Amazonian[8] chin he drove
　　The bristled lips° before him. He bestrid　　*bearded soldiers*
90　An o'erpressed° Roman and i'th' consul's view　　*overwhelmed*
　　Slew three opposers. Tarquin's self he met
　　And struck him on his knee. In that day's feats,
　　When he might act the woman in the scene,[9]
　　He proved best man i'th' field, and for his meed°　　*reward*
95　Was brow-bound with the oak. His pupil age
　　Man-entered thus, he waxèd like a sea,
　　And in the brunt° of seventeen battles since　　*violence*
　　He lurched° all swords of the garland. For this last,　　*cheated*
　　Before and in Corioles, let me say
100　I cannot speak him home.° He stopped the fliers　　*praise him enough*
　　And by his rare example made the coward
　　Turn terror into sport. As weeds before
　　A vessel under sail, so men obeyed
　　And fell below his stem.° His sword, death's stamp,　　*prow*

---

6. My trivial actions treated as marvels.
7. Roman magistrate with absolute authority, elected during emergencies.
8. Beardless (like a female Amazon warrior).
9. Might be expected to be cowardly (with an allusion to boys acting women's parts in the theater).

105 Where it did mark, it took;[1] from face to foot
He was a thing of blood whose every motion
Was timed[2] with dying cries. Alone he entered
The mortal° gate of th' city, which he painted   *fatal*
With shunless destiny;[3] aidless came off,
110 And with a sudden reinforcement struck
Corioles like a planet.[4] Now all's his,
When by and by the din of war gan° pierce   *began to*
His ready° sense; then straight his doubled spirit   *alert*
Requickened° what in flesh was fatigate,°   *Reanimated / exhausted*
115 And to the battle came he, where he did
Run reeking[5] o'er the lives of men as if
'Twere perpetual spoil;° and till we called   *slaughter*
Both field and city ours, he never stood
To ease his breast with panting.
MENENIUS   Worthy man.
120 FIRST SENATOR   He cannot but with measure° fit the honors   *exactly*
Which we devise him.
COMINIUS   Our spoils he kicked at°   *spurned*
And looked upon things precious as° they were   *as if*
The common muck of the world. He covets less
Than misery° itself would give, rewards   *poverty*
125 His deeds with doing them, and is content
To spend the time to° end it.   *merely in order to*
MENENIUS   He's right noble.
Let him be called for.
FIRST SENATOR   Call Coriolanus.
FIRST OFFICER   He doth appear.
              Enter CORIOLANUS.
MENENIUS   The Senate, Coriolanus, are well pleased
To make thee consul.
130 CORIOLANUS   I do owe them still°   *always*
My life and services.
MENENIUS   It then remains
That you do speak to the people.
CORIOLANUS   I do beseech you
Let me o'erleap that custom, for I cannot
Put on the gown, stand naked,° and entreat them   *exposed*
135 For my wounds' sake to give their suffrage.° Please you   *vote*
That I may pass this doing.
SICINIUS   Sir, the people
Must have their voices;° neither will they bate°   *votes / forgo*
One jot of ceremony.
MENENIUS   Put them not to't.°   *Do not defy them*
Pray you, go fit you° to the custom and   *adapt yourself*
140 Take to you, as your predecessors have,
Your honor with your form.°   *the custom prescribed you*
CORIOLANUS   It is a part
That I shall blush in acting, and might well
Be taken from the people.

---

1. It made a clear imprint (of death).
2. Rhythmically accompanied.
3. *painted . . . destiny:* covered with the blood of his
victims; unable to avoid their fate.

4. Planets were believed to have the power to afflict,
or blast, people and places.
5. Steaming (with blood and sweat).

BRUTUS [*to* SICINIUS] Mark you that?

CORIOLANUS To brag unto them, "Thus I did, and thus,"
145 Show them th'unaching scars which I should hide,
As if I had received them for the hire
Of their breath° only. *voice*

MENENIUS Do not stand° upon't. *insist*
—We recommend° to you, tribunes of the people, *commit*
Our purpose° to them, and to our noble consul *proposal*
150 Wish we all joy and honor.

SENATORS To Coriolanus come all joy and honor!
Flourish cornetts, then exeunt [all except] SICINIUS
and BRUTUS.

BRUTUS You see how he intends to use the people.

SICINIUS May they perceive 's intent! He will require° them *ask from*
As if he did contemn° what he requested *scorn that*
Should be in them to give.

155 BRUTUS Come, we'll inform them
Of our proceedings here on th' marketplace;
I know they do attend° us. [*Exeunt.*] *await*

2.3

Enter seven or eight CITIZENS.

FIRST CITIZEN Once° if he do require our voices, we ought *In short*
not to deny him.

SECOND CITIZEN We may, sir, if we will.

THIRD CITIZEN We have power in ourselves to do it, but it is a
5 power that we have no power to do,° for if he show us his *no justification to use*
wounds and tell us his deeds, we are to put our tongues into
those wounds[1] and speak for them. So if he tell us his noble
deeds, we must also tell him our noble acceptance of them.
Ingratitude is monstrous, and for the multitude to be ingrate-
10 ful were to make a monster of the multitude, of the which
we, being members, should bring ourselves to be monstrous
members.

FIRST CITIZEN And to make us no better thought of, a little
help will serve;° for once we stood up about the corn, he *it won't take much*
15 himself stuck° not to call us the many-headed multitude. *hesitated*

THIRD CITIZEN We have been called so of many, not that our
heads are some brown, some black, some abram,° some *auburn*
bald, but that our wits are so diversely colored. And, truly, I
think if all our wits were to issue out of one skull, they would
20 fly east, west, north, south, and their consent of° one direct *agreement to go*
way should be at once to all the points o'th' compass.

SECOND CITIZEN Think you so? Which way do you judge my
wit would fly?

THIRD CITIZEN Nay, your wit will not so soon out as another
25 man's will: 'tis strongly wedged up in a blockhead. But if it
were at liberty, 'twould sure southward.[2]

SECOND CITIZEN Why that way?

THIRD CITIZEN To lose itself in a fog where, being three parts
melted away with rotten° dews, the fourth would return for *unwholesome*
30 conscience' sake to help to get thee a wife.

2.3 Location: The marketplace in Rome. 2. The South is associated with plague.
1. That is, let those wounds inspire our voices.

SECOND CITIZEN   You are never without your tricks. You may,
you may.°   *(have your joke)*

THIRD CITIZEN   Are you all resolved to give your voices? But
that's no matter; the greater part carries it,° I say. If he would   *majority decides*
35   incline to° the people, there was never a worthier man.   *support*

    Enter CORIOLANUS *in a gown of humility*[3] *[and a hat],*
    with MENENIUS.

Here he comes, and in the gown of humility. Mark his
behavior. We are not to stay all together, but to come by him
where he stands, by ones, by twos, and by threes. He's to
make his requests by particulars,° wherein every one of us   *to individuals*
40   has a single honor in giving him our own voices with our
own tongues. Therefore follow me, and I'll direct you how
you shall go by him.

ALL CITIZENS   Content, content.   *[Exeunt* CITIZENS.]

MENENIUS   O sir, you are not right. Have you not known
The worthiest men have done't?

45   CORIOLANUS   What must I say?
"I pray, sir?" Plague upon't, I cannot bring
My tongue to such a pace. "Look, sir, my wounds:
I got them in my country's service, when
Some certain of your brethren roared and ran
From th' noise of our own drums."

50   MENENIUS   O me, the gods!
You must not speak of that. You must desire them
To think upon you.

CORIOLANUS   Think upon me? Hang 'em!
I would they would forget me, like the virtues
Which our divines lose by 'em.[4]

MENENIUS   You'll mar all.
55   I'll leave you. Pray you speak to 'em, I pray you,
In wholesome[5] manner.   *Exit.*

CORIOLANUS   Bid them wash their faces
And keep their teeth clean.

    Enter three of the CITIZENS.

                    So, here comes a brace.
—You know the cause, sir, of my standing here.

THIRD CITIZEN   We do, sir. Tell us what hath brought you to't.

60   CORIOLANUS   Mine own desert.

SECOND CITIZEN   Your own desert?

CORIOLANUS   Ay, but not mine own desire.

THIRD CITIZEN   How not your own desire?

CORIOLANUS   No, sir, 'twas never my desire yet to trouble the
65   poor with begging.

THIRD CITIZEN   You must think if we give you anything, we
hope to gain by you.

CORIOLANUS   Well, then, I pray, your price o'th' consulship?

FIRST CITIZEN   The price is to ask it kindly.

70   CORIOLANUS   Kindly, sir, I pray let me ha't. I have wounds to
show you, which shall be yours° in private. *[to* SECOND CITI-   *yours to see*
ZEN] Your good voice, sir, what say you?

---

3. Candidates for public office in Rome wore plain
white togas (the word "candidate" derives from Latin
candidus, white).

4. Our priests vainly try to instill in them.
5. Proper (but Coriolanus takes it as "healthy").

SECOND CITIZEN You shall ha't, worthy sir.

CORIOLANUS A match,° sir. There's in all two worthy voices   *agreement*
75   begged. I have your alms. Adieu.

THIRD CITIZEN [*to the other* CITIZENS] But this is something
    odd.

SECOND CITIZEN An° 'twere to give again—but 'tis no matter.   *If*
                            Exeunt [CITIZENS].
        Enter two other CITIZENS.

CORIOLANUS Pray you now, if it may stand° with the tune of   *accord*
80   your voices that I may be consul, I have here the customary
    gown.

FOURTH CITIZEN You have deserved nobly of your country,
    and you have not deserved nobly.

CORIOLANUS Your enigma?

85 FOURTH CITIZEN You have been a scourge to her enemies; you
    have been a rod to her friends: you have not indeed loved
    the common people.

CORIOLANUS You should account me the more virtuous that
    I have not been common° in my love. I will, sir, flatter my   *indiscriminate*
90   sworn brother, the people, to earn a dearer estimation of
    them; 'tis° a condition they account gentle.° And since the   *(Flattery) is / noble*
    wisdom of their choice is rather to have my hat than my
    heart, I will practice the insinuating nod and be off° to them   *take my hat off*
    most counterfeitly; that is, sir, I will counterfeit the bewitch-
95   ment° of some popular man° and give it bountiful to the   *charisma / demagogue*
    desirers. Therefore beseech you I may be consul.

FIFTH CITIZEN We hope to find you our friend and therefore
    give you our voices heartily.

FOURTH CITIZEN You have received many wounds for your
100   country.

CORIOLANUS I will not seal° your knowledge with showing   *confirm*
    them. I will make much of your voices and so trouble you no
    farther.

BOTH CITIZENS The gods give you joy, sir, heartily!
                            [*Exeunt* CITIZENS.]

105 CORIOLANUS Most sweet voices!
    Better it is to die, better to starve,
    Than crave the hire which first we do deserve.[6]
    Why in this wolvish toge[7] should I stand here
    To beg of Hob and Dick[8] that does appear
110   Their needless vouches?° Custom calls me to't.   *votes*
    What custom wills, in all things should we do't,
    The dust on antique time would lie unswept
    And mountainous error be too highly heaped
    For truth to o'erpeer.[9] Rather than fool it° so,   *act the fool*
115   Let the high office and the honor go
    To one that would do thus. I am half through;
    The one part suffered, the other will I do.
        Enter three CITIZENS *more.*
    Here come more voices.

---

6. Than beg for the wages we have already earned.   humility).
7. F has "woolvish toge"; some editors read "wolvish"   8. Any Tom, Dick, or Harry.
or "wool-less." The "toge" is the toga (gown of   9. To look over the top.

Your voices? For your voices I have fought,
120 Watched° for your voices; for your voices bear   *Gone sleepless*
Of wounds two dozen odd. Battles thrice six
I have seen and heard of. For your voices
Have done many things, some less, some more.
Your voices? Indeed I would be consul.
125 SIXTH CITIZEN   He has done nobly and cannot go without any
honest man's voice.
SEVENTH CITIZEN   Therefore let him be consul. The gods give
him joy and make him good friend to the people!
ALL CITIZENS   Amen, amen. God save thee, noble consul!
                          [*Exeunt* CITIZENS.]
130 CORIOLANUS   Worthy voices.
          Enter MENENIUS, *with* BRUTUS *and* SICINIUS.
MENENIUS   You have stood your limitation,° and the tribunes   *allotted time*
Endue° you with the people's voice. Remains   *Invest*
That, in th'official marks° invested, you   *insignia*
Anon° do meet the Senate.   *Immediately*
CORIOLANUS   Is this done?
135 SICINIUS   The custom of request° you have discharged: *requesting votes*
The people do admit you and are summoned
To meet anon upon your approbation.[1]
CORIOLANUS   Where? At the Senate-house?
SICINIUS   There, Coriolanus.
CORIOLANUS   May I change these garments?
SICINIUS   You may, sir.
140 CORIOLANUS   That I'll straight do and, knowing myself again,
Repair to th' Senate-house.
MENENIUS   I'll keep you company. [*to the tribunes*] Will you along?
BRUTUS   We stay here for the people.
SICINIUS   Fare you well.
          Exeunt. CORIOLANUS *and* MENENIUS.
He has it now, and by his looks methinks
'Tis warm at 's heart.[2]
145 BRUTUS   With a proud heart he wore
His humble weeds.° Will you dismiss the people?   *garments*
          Enter the PLEBEIANS.[3]
SICINIUS   How now, my masters, have you chose this man?
FIRST CITIZEN   He has our voices, sir.
BRUTUS   We pray the gods he may deserve your loves.
150 SECOND CITIZEN   Amen, sir. To my poor unworthy notice
He mocked us when he begged our voices.
THIRD CITIZEN   Certainly he flouted us downright.
FIRST CITIZEN   No, 'tis his kind of speech; he did not mock us.
SECOND CITIZEN   Not one amongst us, save yourself, but says
155 He used us scornfully. He should have showed us
His marks of merit: wounds received for 's country.
SICINIUS   Why, so he did, I am sure.
ALL CITIZENS   No, no. No man saw 'em.
THIRD CITIZEN   He said he had wounds which he could show in private
And with his hat, thus waving it in scorn,

1. For your ratification as consul.
2. That is, he's well pleased.
3. TEXTUAL COMMENT The Folio has *"Plebeians,"* not

"*Citizens*"; the terms used for the upper and lower
classes in *Coriolanus* are inconsistent. For the connotations of the different terms, see Digital Edition TC 7.

160 "I would be consul," says he: "Agèd custom,
But by your voices, will not so permit me.
Your voices therefore." When we granted that,
Here was, "I thank you for your voices. Thank you,
Your most sweet voices. Now you have left your voices,
165 I have no further° with you." Was not this mockery?   *(to do)*

SICINIUS   Why either were you ignorant° to see't,   *were you either unable*
Or, seeing it, of such childish friendliness
To yield your voices?

BRUTUS   Could you not have told him
As you were lessoned? When he had no power,
170 But was a petty servant to the state,
He was your enemy, ever spake against
Your liberties and the charters that you bear
I'th' body of the weal;° and now, arriving°   *state / reaching*
A place of potency and sway o'th' state,
175 If he should still malignantly remain
Fast foe to th' plebeii,° your voices might   *common people*
Be curses to yourselves. You should have said
That as his worthy deeds did claim no less
Than what he stood for,° so his gracious nature   *the office he sought*
180 Would think upon you for your voices and
Translate° his malice towards you into love,   *Change*
Standing your friendly lord.

SICINIUS   Thus to have said,
As you were fore-advised, had touched° his spirit   *tested*
And tried his inclination; from him plucked
185 Either his gracious promise, which you might—
As cause had called you up—have held him to,
Or else it would have galled his surly nature,
Which easily endures not article,°   *stipulation*
Tying him to aught. So putting him to rage,
190 You should have ta'en th'advantage of his choler°   *wrath*
And passed him unelected.

BRUTUS   Did you perceive
He did solicit you in free contempt
When he did need your loves, and do you think
That his contempt shall not be bruising to you
195 When he hath power to crush? Why, had your bodies
No heart among you? Or had you tongues to cry
Against the rectorship of judgment?°   *rule of common sense*

SICINIUS   Have you
Ere now denied the asker, and now again,
Of him that did not ask but mock, bestow
Your sued-for tongues?

200 THIRD CITIZEN   He's not confirmed. We may
Deny him yet.

SECOND CITIZEN   And will deny him:
I'll have five hundred voices of that sound.

FIRST CITIZEN   I twice five hundred, and their friends to piece° 'em.   *add to*

BRUTUS   Get you hence instantly, and tell those friends
205 They have chose a consul that will from them take
Their liberties, make them of no more voice
Than dogs that are as often beat for barking

As therefore kept to do so.
SICINIUS   Let them assemble,
And on a safer° judgment all revoke   *sounder*
210 Your ignorant election. Enforce° his pride   *Emphasize*
And his old hate unto you. Besides, forget not
With what contempt he wore the humble weed,
How in his suit° he scorned you; but your loves,   *petition; apparel*
Thinking upon his services, took from you
215 Th'apprehension° of his present portance,°   *perception / demeanor*
Which most gibingly,° ungravely, he did fashion   *mockingly*
After the inveterate hate he bears you.
BRUTUS   Lay
A fault on us, your tribunes, that we labored,
No impediment between,[4] but that you must
Cast your election on him.
220 SICINIUS   Say you chose him
More after our commandment than as guided
By your own true affections, and that your minds,
Preoccupied with what you rather must do
Than what you should, made you against the grain
225 To voice him consul. Lay the fault on us.
BRUTUS   Ay, spare us not. Say we read lectures to you
How youngly he began to serve his country,
How long continued, and what stock he springs of,
The noble house o'th' Martians, from whence came
230 That Ancus Martius, Numa's daughter's son,
Who after great Hostilius here was king;
Of the same house Publius and Quintus were,
That our best water brought by conduits hither,
And Censorinus that was so surnamed,[5]
235 And nobly naméd so, twice being censor,[6]
Was his great ancestor.
SICINIUS   One thus descended,
That hath beside well in his person wrought
To be set high in place, we did commend
To your remembrances; but you have found,
240 Scaling° his present bearing with his past,   *Weighing*
That he's your fixèd enemy, and revoke
Your sudden° approbation.   *hasty*
BRUTUS   Say you ne'er had done't—
Harp on that still—but by our putting on,°   *instigation*
And presently, when you have drawn° your number,   *gathered*
Repair to th' Capitol.
245 ALL CITIZENS   We will so: almost all
Repent in their election.   *Exeunt* PLEBEIANS.
BRUTUS   Let them go on:
This mutiny were better put in hazard°   *risked*
Than stay,° past doubt, for greater.   *await*
If, as his nature is, he fall in rage

---

4. *we . . . between:* we refused to allow anything to
stand in the way.
5. TEXTUAL COMMENT A line is missing in F; for a sug-

gestion of what it might be, see Digital Edition TC 8.
6. Roman magistrate who supervised public morals
and drew up the census.

250   With their refusal, both observe and answer
     The vantage of[7] his anger.
SICINIUS   To th' Capitol, come.
     We will be there before the stream o'th' people;
     And this shall seem, as partly 'tis, their own,
     Which we have goaded onward.   *Exeunt.*

3.1

     Cornetts. Enter CORIOLANUS, MENENIUS, *all*
     the gentry,° COMINIUS, *Titus* LARTIUS, *and other*   *patricians*
     SENATORS.
CORIOLANUS   Tullus Aufidius then had made new head?°   *raised a new army*
LARTIUS   He had, my lord, and that it was which caused
     Our swifter composition.[1]
CORIOLANUS   So then the Volsces stand but as at first,
5   Ready when time shall prompt them to make road
     Upon's again.
COMINIUS   They are worn,° Lord Consul, so   *exhausted*
     That we shall hardly in our ages see
     Their banners wave again.
CORIOLANUS   Saw you Aufidius?
LARTIUS   On safeguard° he came to me, and did curse   *Under safe-conduct*
10   Against the Volsces for they had so vilely
     Yielded the town. He is retired to Antium.
CORIOLANUS   Spoke he of me?
LARTIUS   He did, my lord.
CORIOLANUS   How? What?
LARTIUS   How often he had met you sword to sword;
     That of all things upon the earth he hated
15   Your person most; that he would pawn his fortunes
     To hopeless restitution,[2] so he might
     Be called your vanquisher.
CORIOLANUS   At Antium lives he?
LARTIUS   At Antium.
CORIOLANUS   I wish I had a cause to seek him there,
20   To oppose his hatred fully. Welcome home.
       Enter SICINIUS *and* BRUTUS.
     Behold, these are the tribunes of the people,
     The tongues o'th' common mouth. I do despise them,
     For they do prank them° in authority   *adorn themselves*
     Against all noble sufferance.[3]
SICINIUS   Pass no further.
CORIOLANUS   Ha? What is that?
25 BRUTUS   It will be dangerous to go on.
     No further.
CORIOLANUS   What makes this change?
MENENIUS   The matter?
COMINIUS   Hath he not passed° the noble and the common?   *been accepted by*
BRUTUS   Cominius, no.
CORIOLANUS   Have I had children's voices?

---

7. *answer the vantage of*: seize the opportunity provided by.
3.1 Location: A street in Rome.
1. Agreement (about returning Corioles to the
Volscians).
2. Without hope of recovery.
3. Beyond what the nobility can endure.

FIRST SENATOR   Tribunes, give way. He shall to th' marketplace.
BRUTUS   The people are incensed against him.
30 SICINIUS   Stop,
Or all will fall in broil.°   turmoil
CORIOLANUS   Are these your herd?
Must these have voices, that can yield them now
And straight° disclaim their tongues? What are your offices?   immediately
You being their mouths, why rule you not their teeth?
Have you not set them on?
35 MENENIUS   Be calm, be calm.
CORIOLANUS   It is a purposed° thing and grows by plot   deliberate
To curb the will of the nobility.
Suffer't, and live with such as cannot rule
Nor ever will be ruled.
BRUTUS   Call't not a plot.
40 The people cry you mocked them, and of late,
When corn was given them gratis, you repined,
Scandaled° the suppliants for the people, called them   Defamed
Time-pleasers, flatterers, foes to nobleness.
CORIOLANUS   Why, this was known before.
BRUTUS   Not to them all.
CORIOLANUS   Have you informed them sithence?°   since
45 BRUTUS   How? I inform them?
COMINIUS   You are like to do such business.
BRUTUS   Not unlike each way to better yours.[4]
CORIOLANUS   Why then should I be consul? By yond clouds,
Let me deserve so ill as you, and make me
Your fellow tribune.
50 SICINIUS   You show too much of that°   (quality)
For which the people stir.° If you will pass   are aroused
To where you are bound,[5] you must enquire your way,
Which you are out of,° with a gentler spirit,   strayed from
Or never be so noble as a consul,
Nor yoke with him° for tribune.   (Brutus)
55 MENENIUS   Let's be calm.
COMINIUS   The people are abused, set on. This palt'ring°   trifling
Becomes not Rome, nor has Coriolanus
Deserved this so dishonored rub,° laid falsely   shameful obstruction
I'th' plain way of his merit.
CORIOLANUS   Tell me of corn!
60 This was my speech, and I will speak't again—
MENENIUS   Not now, not now.
FIRST SENATOR   Not in this heat, sir, now.
CORIOLANUS   Now as I live, I will. My nobler friends,
I crave their pardons. For the mutable,
Rank-scented meinie,° let them regard me   multitude
65 As I do not flatter and therein behold
Themselves. I say again, in soothing them,
We nourish gainst our Senate the cockle°   weed
Of rebellion, insolence, sedition,

---

4. *Not unlike . . . yours:* Not unlikely in every respect   5. That is, the marketplace; the consulship.
to do better than you.

Which we ourselves have plowed for, sowed, and scattered,
70 By mingling them with us, the honored number,
Who lack not virtue, no, nor power, but that
Which they have given to beggars.

MENENIUS   Well, no more.

FIRST SENATOR   No more words, we beseech you.

CORIOLANUS   How? No more?
As for my country I have shed my blood,
75 Not fearing outward force, so shall my lungs
Coin words till their decay against those measles°   *skin eruptions*
Which we disdain should tetter° us, yet sought   *infect*
The very way to catch them.

BRUTUS   You speak o'th' people
As if you were a god to punish, not
A man of their infirmity.°   *with the same frailty*

80 SICINIUS   'Twere well
We let the people know't.

MENENIUS   What, what? His choler?

CORIOLANUS   Choler? Were I as patient as the midnight sleep,
By Jove, 'twould be my mind.°   *opinion*

SICINIUS   It is a mind
That shall remain a poison where it is,
Not poison any further.

85 CORIOLANUS   "Shall remain"?
Hear you this Triton[6] of the minnows? Mark you
His absolute "shall"?

COMINIUS   'Twas from the canon.°   *out of order*

CORIOLANUS   "Shall"?
O good but most unwise patricians, why—
You grave but reckless senators—have you thus
90 Given Hydra[7] here to choose an officer
That with his peremptory "shall," being but
The horn and noise° o'th' monster's, wants not spirit   *noisy horn*
To say he'll turn your current° in a ditch   *stream of power*
And make your channel his? If he have power,
95 Then vail° your ignorance; if none, awake°   *bow down / awake from*
Your dangerous lenity.° If you are learned,   *forbearance*
Be not as common fools; if you are not,
Let them have cushions by° you. You are plebeians   *Senate seats beside*
If they be senators; and they are no less
100 When, both your voices blended, the great'st taste
Most palates theirs.[8] They choose their magistrate,
And such a one as he, who puts his "shall,"
His popular° "shall," against a graver bench[9]   *plebeian*
Than ever frowned in Greece. By Jove himself,
105 It makes the consuls base, and my soul aches
To know, when two authorities are up°—   *established*
Neither supreme—how soon confusion°   *chaos*
May enter twixt the gap of both and take°   *overthrow*
The one by th'other.

COMINIUS   Well, on to th' marketplace.

---

6. Neptune's trumpeter, a minor sea god.
7. Mythical many-headed snake, a common figure for the multitude.

8. *the great'st . . . theirs:* the result tastes more like (or appeals more to) them than you.
9. A more respected body.

110 CORIOLANUS Whoever gave that counsel to give forth
  The corn o'th' storehouse gratis, as 'twas used
  Sometime in Greece—
 MENENIUS   Well, well, no more of that.
 CORIOLANUS Though there the people had more absolute power—
  I say they nourished disobedience, fed
  The ruin of the state.
115 BRUTUS   Why shall the people give
  One that speaks thus their voice?
 CORIOLANUS   I'll give my reasons,
  More worthier than their voices. They know the corn
  Was not our recompense,° resting well assured   *a payment from us*
  They ne'er did service for't: being pressed° to th' war,   *conscripted*
120 Even when the navel° of the state was touched,°   *center / threatened*
  They would not thread° the gates. This kind of service *go through*
  Did not deserve corn gratis. Being i'th' war,
  Their mutinies and revolts, wherein they showed
  Most valor, spoke not° for them. Th'accusation   *did not speak well*
125 Which they have often made against the Senate,
  All cause unborn,° could never be the native° *Without any cause / source*
  Of our so frank° donation. Well, what then?   *liberal*
  How shall this bosom multiplied[1] digest
  The Senate's courtesy? Let deeds express
130 What's like to be their words: "We did request it;
  We are the greater poll,° and in true fear   *number*
  They gave us our demands." Thus we debase
  The nature of our seats° and make the rabble   *senatorial positions*
  Call our cares "fears," which will in time
135 Break ope the locks o'th' Senate and bring in
  The crows to peck the eagles.[2]
 MENENIUS   Come, enough.
 BRUTUS Enough, with over-measure.
 CORIOLANUS   No, take more!
  What may be sworn by, both divine and human,
  Seal° what I end withal!° This double worship,[3] *Authorize / with*
140 Where one part does disdain with cause, the other
  Insult° without all reason; where gentry, title, wisdom *Behave insolently*
  Cannot conclude but by the yea and no
  Of general ignorance, it must omit°   *neglect*
  Real necessities and give way the while
145 To unstable slightness.° Purpose° so barred, it follows *trifling / Purposefulness*
  Nothing is done to purpose.° Therefore, beseech you— *any effect*
  You that will be less fearful than discreet,°   *judicious*
  That love the fundamental part of state
  More than you doubt the change on't,[4] that prefer
150 A noble life before a long, and wish
  To jump° a body with a dangerous physic°   *risk / medicine*
  That's sure of death without it—at once pluck out
  The multitudinous tongue;[5] let them not lick

---

1. *bosom multiplied*: multifarious belly (of the many-headed multitude).
2. The eagle not only is associated with courage and nobility but is the symbol of Roman power.
3. Divided magistracy.

4. You fear changing it (by repudiating the tribunes).
5. The tongue of the multitude, as represented by the tribunes.

The sweet which is their poison. Your dishonor
155 Mangles true judgment and bereaves the state
Of that integrity which should become't,
Not having the power to do the good it would
For° th'ill which doth control't.[6]   *Because of*

BRUTUS   He's said enough.
SICINIUS   He's spoken like a traitor and shall answer
As traitors do.
160 CORIOLANUS   Thou wretch, despite° o'erwhelm thee!   *contempt*
What should the people do with these bald° tribunes,   *paltry*
On whom depending, their obedience fails
To th' greater bench?° In a rebellion,   *(of the Senate)*
When what's not meet but what must be was law,[7]
165 Then were they chosen. In a better hour,
Let what is meet be said it must be meet[8]
And throw their power i'th' dust.
BRUTUS   Manifest treason.
SICINIUS   This a consul? No.
BRUTUS   The aediles,° ho!   *tribune's officers*
Enter an AEDILE.
                         Let him be apprehended.
SICINIUS   Go call the people,   [*Exit* AEDILE.]
170 [*to* CORIOLANUS]   in whose name myself
Attach° thee as a traitorous innovator,°   *Arrest / revolutionary*
A foe to th' public weal. Obey, I charge thee,
And follow to thine answer.°   *trial*
[*He lays hold of* CORIOLANUS.]
CORIOLANUS   Hence, old goat!
ALL PATRICIANS   We'll surety him.°   *ensure his compliance*
COMINIUS [*to* SICINIUS]   Aged sir, hands off.
175 CORIOLANUS   Hence, rotten thing, or I shall shake thy bones
Out of thy garments.
SICINIUS   Help, ye citizens!
Enter a rabble of PLEBEIANS *with the* AEDILES.
MENENIUS   On both sides more respect.
SICINIUS   Here's he that would
Take from you all your power.
BRUTUS   Seize him, aediles!
ALL CITIZENS   Down with him, down with him!
SECOND SENATOR   Weapons, weapons, weapons!
They all bustle about CORIOLANUS.
180 ALL [*variously*]   —Tribunes! —Patricians! —Citizens! —What ho!
—Sicinius! —Brutus! —Coriolanus! —Citizens!
—Peace, peace, peace! —Stay, hold, peace!
MENENIUS   What is about to be? I am out of breath.
Confusion's° near; I cannot speak. —You, tribunes   *Chaos is*
185 To th' people! —Coriolanus, patience!
—Speak, good Sicinius.
SICINIUS   Hear me, people. Peace!
ALL CITIZENS   Let's hear our tribune. Peace! Speak, speak, speak!
SICINIUS   You are at point° to lose your liberties: *about*

---

6. Overpower it.
7. *When . . . law:* When necessity rather than propriety prevailed. *meet:* proper.
8. Let what is proper be declared necessary.

Martius would have all from you—Martius,
Whom late you have named for consul.
190 MENENIUS   Fie, fie, fie,
This is the way to kindle, not to quench.
FIRST SENATOR   To unbuild the city and to lay all flat.
SICINIUS   What is the city but the people?
ALL CITIZENS   True, the people are the city.
195 BRUTUS   By the consent of all, we were established
The people's magistrates.
ALL CITIZENS   You so remain.
MENENIUS   And so are like to do.
COMINIUS   That is the way to lay the city flat,
To bring the roof to the foundation
200 And bury all, which yet distinctly ranges[9]
In heaps and piles of ruin.
SICINIUS   This deserves death.
BRUTUS   Or° let us stand to our authority,   *Either*
Or let us lose it. We do here pronounce,
Upon the part o'th' people, in whose power
205 We were elected theirs, Martius is worthy
Of present° death.   *immediate*
SICINIUS   Therefore lay hold of him.
Bear him to th' Rock Tarpeian,[1] and from thence
Into destruction cast him.
BRUTUS   Aediles, seize him.
ALL CITIZENS   Yield, Martius, yield!
MENENIUS   Hear me one word; beseech
You, tribunes, hear me but a word.
210 AEDILES   Peace, peace.
MENENIUS [*to* BRUTUS]   Be that you seem, truly your country's friend,
And temp'rately proceed to what you would
Thus violently redress.
BRUTUS   Sir, those cold ways,
That seem like prudent helps, are very poisonous
215 Where the disease is violent. —Lay hands upon him
And bear him to the Rock.
          CORIOLANUS *draws his sword.*
CORIOLANUS   No, I'll die here.
There's some among you have beheld me fighting;
Come try upon yourselves what you have seen me.
MENENIUS   Down with that sword. —Tribunes, withdraw
awhile.
BRUTUS   Lay hands upon him.
220 MENENIUS   Help Martius, help!
You that be noble, help him, young and old!
ALL CITIZENS   Down with him! Down with him!
          In this mutiny, the tribunes, the AEDILES, *and the*
          people are beat in° [*and*] *exeunt.*   *forced offstage*
MENENIUS [*to* CORIOLANUS]   Go, get you to our house; be
gone, away.
All will be naught else.

9. Extends in orderly ranks.
1. The cliff from which murderers and traitors were hurled to their deaths.

SECOND SENATOR   Get you gone.

CORIOLANUS   Stand fast.

225   We have as many friends as enemies.

MENENIUS   Shall it be put to that?

FIRST SENATOR   The gods forbid!

    —I prithee,° noble friend, home to thy house.   *pray thee (to go)*

    Leave us to cure this cause.°   *disease*

MENENIUS   For 'tis a sore upon us

    You cannot tent° yourself. Be gone, beseech you.   *treat*

230 COMINIUS   Come, sir, along with us.[2]

CORIOLANUS   I would they were barbarians, as they are,

    Though in Rome littered;° not Romans, as they are not,   *born (like animals)*

    Though calved i'th' porch o'th' Capitol.

MENENIUS   Be gone!

    Put not your worthy° rage into your tongue.   *justifiable*

    One time will owe° another.   *occasion will compensate*

235 CORIOLANUS   On fair ground

    I could beat forty of them.

MENENIUS   I could myself

    Take up a brace o'th' best of them—yea, the two tribunes.

COMINIUS   But now 'tis odds beyond arithmetic,°   *calculation*

    And manhood° is called foolery when it stands   *courage*

240   Against a falling fabric.° Will you hence   *building*

    Before the tag° return, whose rage doth rend   *rabble*

    Like interrupted° waters and o'erbear   *overflowing*

    What they are used to bear?[3]

MENENIUS   Pray you, be gone.

    I'll try whether my old wit be in request

245   With those that have but little. This must be patched

    With cloth of any color.[4]

COMINIUS   Nay, come away.

        Exeunt CORIOLANUS *and* COMINIUS [*with other*

                    PATRICIANS].

A PATRICIAN   This man has marred his fortune.

MENENIUS   His nature is too noble for the world.

    He would not flatter Neptune for his trident

250   Or Jove for 's power to thunder. His heart's his mouth:

    What his breast forges, that his tongue must vent,

    And, being angry, does forget that ever

    He heard the name of death.

        A noise within.

    Here's goodly work.

A PATRICIAN   I would they were abed.

255 MENENIUS   I would they were in Tiber! What the vengeance,

    Could he not speak 'em fair?°   *speak to them politely*

        Enter BRUTUS *and* SICINIUS *with the rabble* [*of*

        CITIZENS] *again.*

SICINIUS   Where is this viper

    That would depopulate the city and

    Be every man himself?

---

2. TEXTUAL COMMENT The speech prefixes in the next several lines are confused in F; Digital Edition TC 9 explains how the editor has sorted them out.
3. *o'erbear . . . bear:* overpower that to which they ordinarily submit.
4. *patched . . . color:* mended by whatever means possible.

MENENIUS You worthy tribunes—
SICINIUS He shall be thrown down the Tarpeian Rock
260 With rigorous hands. He hath resisted law,
And therefore law shall scorn° him further trial   *deny*
Than the severity of the public° power   *commoners'*
Which he so sets at naught.
FIRST CITIZEN He shall well know
The noble tribunes are the people's mouths,
And we their hands.
ALL CITIZENS He shall sure on't.
MENENIUS Sir, sir—
265 SICINIUS Peace!
MENENIUS Do not cry havoc⁵ where you should but hunt
With modest warrant.
SICINIUS Sir, how com'st that you
Have help to make this rescue?⁶
MENENIUS Hear me speak.
As I do know the consul's worthiness,
So can I name his faults.
270 SICINIUS Consul? What consul?
MENENIUS The consul Coriolanus.
BRUTUS He consul?
ALL CITIZENS No, no, no, no, no!
MENENIUS If, by the tribunes' leave and yours, good people,
I may be heard, I would crave a word or two,
275 The which shall turn° you to no further harm   *bring*
Than so much loss of time.
SICINIUS Speak briefly, then,
For we are peremptory to dispatch
This viperous traitor. To eject him hence
Were but one danger, and to keep him here
280 Our certain death. Therefore it is decreed
He dies tonight.
MENENIUS Now the good gods forbid
That our renownèd Rome, whose gratitude
Towards her deservèd° children is enrolled   *deserving*
In Jove's own book, like an unnatural dam°   *mother*
285 Should now eat up her own!
SICINIUS He's a disease that must be cut away.
MENENIUS Oh, he's a limb that has but a disease:
Mortal to cut it off; to cure it easy.
What has he done to Rome that's worthy death?
290 Killing our enemies, the blood he hath lost—
Which I dare vouch is more than that he hath
By many an ounce—he dropped it for his country;
And what is left, to lose it by his country
Were to us all that do't and suffer° it   *allow*
A brand° to th'end o'th' world.   *stigma*
295 SICINIUS This is clean cam.°   *completely perverse*
BRUTUS Merely° awry. When he did love his country,   *Absolutely*
It honored him.

---

5. "Havoc" was the signal to an army to pillage.
6. Have helped to remove this prisoner from custody ("make rescue" is a legal term).

SICINIUS   The service of the foot,
  Being once gangrened, is not then respected
  For what before it was.
    BRUTUS   We'll hear no more.
300 Pursue him to his house and pluck him thence,
  Lest his infection, being of catching nature,
  Spread further.
    MENENIUS   One word more, one word!
  This tiger-footed rage, when it shall find
  The harm of unscanned° swiftness, will, too late,   heedless
305 Tie leaden pounds° to 's heels. Proceed by process,°   weights / due process
  Lest parties°—as he is beloved—break out   factions
  And sack great Rome with Romans.
    BRUTUS   If it were so—
    SICINIUS   What do ye talk?
  Have we not had a taste of his obedience?
310 Our aediles smote, ourselves resisted? Come.
    MENENIUS   Consider this: he has been bred i'th' wars
  Since 'a could draw a sword and is ill-schooled
  In bolted⁷ language; meal and bran° together   flour and husks
  He throws without distinction. Give me leave,
315 I'll go to him and undertake to bring him
  Where he shall answer by a lawful form,
  In peace, to his utmost peril.⁸
    FIRST SENATOR   Noble tribunes,
  It is the humane way. The other course
  Will prove too bloody, and the end of it
  Unknown to the beginning.
320 SICINIUS   Noble Menenius,
  Be you then as the people's officer.
  [to the CITIZENS] Masters, lay down your weapons.
    BRUTUS   Go not home.
    SICINIUS   Meet on the marketplace. [to MENENIUS] We'll
    attend° you there,   await
  Where, if you bring not Martius, we'll proceed
  In our first way.
325 MENENIUS   I'll bring him to you.
  [to the SENATORS]   Let me desire your company. He must come,
  Or what is worst will follow.
    FIRST SENATOR   Pray you, let's to him. *Exeunt.*

3.2

Enter CORIOLANUS *with* NOBLES.
  CORIOLANUS   Let them pull all about mine ears, present me
  Death on the wheel or at wild horses' heels,
  Or pile ten hills on the Tarpeian Rock,
  That the precipitation° might down stretch   steepness
5 Below the beam of sight, yet will I still
  Be thus to them.
      Enter VOLUMNIA.
    A NOBLE   You do the nobler.
    CORIOLANUS   I muse° my mother   wonder that

---

7. Sifted; that is, carefully considered.   3.2 Location: Coriolanus's house.
8. Even at peril of his life.

Does not approve me further, who was wont
To call them woolen° vassals, things created   coarsely clad
10   To buy and sell with groats,° to show bare heads   fourpenny pieces
In congregations, to yawn, be still, and wonder
When one but of my ordinance° stood up   rank
To speak of peace or war. [to VOLUMNIA] I talk of you.
Why did you wish me milder? Would you have me
15   False to my nature? Rather say I play
The man I am.
VOLUMNIA   O sir, sir, sir,
I would have had you put your power well on
Before you had worn it out.
CORIOLANUS   Let go.°   Stop
VOLUMNIA   You might have been enough the man you are
20   With striving less to be so. Lesser had been
The taxings° of your dispositions if   challenging
You had not showed them how ye were disposed
Ere they lacked° power to cross you.   Before they lost
CORIOLANUS   Let them hang.
VOLUMNIA   Ay, and burn too.
                Enter MENENIUS with the SENATORS.
25   MENENIUS   Come, come, you have been too rough, something
        too rough.
You must return and mend it.
FIRST SENATOR   There's no remedy,
Unless, by not so doing, our good city
Cleave in the midst and perish.
VOLUMNIA   Pray be counseled.
I have a heart as little apt as yours,
30   But yet a brain that leads my use of anger
To better vantage.
MENENIUS   Well said, noble woman.
Before he should thus stoop to th' herd, but that
The violent fit o'th' time craves it as physic°   medicine
For the whole state, I would put mine armor on,
Which I can scarcely bear.
35   CORIOLANUS   What must I do?
MENENIUS   Return to th' tribunes.
CORIOLANUS   Well, what then? What then?
MENENIUS   Repent what you have spoke.
CORIOLANUS   For them? I cannot do it to the gods;
Must I then do't to them?
VOLUMNIA   You are too absolute,°   inflexible
40   Though therein you can never be too noble,
But when extremities° speak. I have heard you say   extreme situations
Honor and policy,° like unsevered friends,   tactical shrewdness
I'th' war do grow together. Grant that, and tell me
In peace what each of them by th'other lose
That they combine not there?
CORIOLANUS   Tush, tush.
45   MENENIUS   A good demand.°   question
VOLUMNIA   If it be honor in your wars to seem
The same° you are not, which for your best ends   That which
You adopt your policy, how is it less or worse
That it° shall hold companionship in peace   (dissimulation)

50	With honor as in war, since that to both	
	It stands in like request?°	*need*
	CORIOLANUS Why force° you this?	*urge*
	VOLUMNIA Because that now it lies you on to speak	
	To th' people, not by your own instruction,°	*conviction*
	Nor by th' matter which your heart prompts you,	
55	But with such words that are but roted° in	*memorized*
	Your tongue, though but bastards and syllables	
	Of no allowance to¹ your bosom's truth.	
	Now, this no more dishonors you at all	
	Than to take in° a town with gentle words,	*capture*
60	Which else would put you to your fortune² and	
	The hazard of much blood.	
	I would dissemble with my nature where	
	My fortunes and my friends at stake required	
	I should do so in honor. I am in this°	*I speak in this for*
65	Your wife, your son, these senators, the nobles;	
	And you will rather show our general° louts	*common*
	How you can frown than spend a fawn° upon 'em	*cringing courtesy*
	For the inheritance° of their loves and safeguard	*acquisition*
	Of what that want° might ruin.	*lack (of their loves)*
	MENENIUS Noble lady!	
70	[*to* CORIOLANUS] Come, go with us. Speak fair.	
	You may salve° so,	*smooth over*
	Not what is dangerous present, but the loss	
	Of what is past.³	
	VOLUMNIA I prithee now, my son,	
	Go to them with this bonnet° in thy hand,	*hat*
	And thus far having stretched it—here be with them,	
75	Thy knee bussing° the stones; for in such business	*kissing*
	Action is eloquence, and the eyes of th'ignorant	
	More learnèd than the ears—waving° thy head,	*repeatedly bowing*
	Which often thus correcting thy stout heart,	
	Now humble⁴ as the ripest mulberry	
80	That will not hold the handling; or say to them	
	Thou art their soldier and, being bred in broils,°	*tumults*
	Hast not the soft way which, thou dost confess,	
	Were fit for thee to use as they to claim°	*for them to expect*
	In asking their good loves, but thou wilt frame	
85	Thyself, forsooth, hereafter theirs so far	
	As thou hast power and person.°	*ability and authority*
	MENENIUS This but done,	
	Even as she speaks, why, their hearts were yours,	
	For they have pardons, being asked, as free	
	As words to little purpose.	
	VOLUMNIA Prithee now,	
90	Go, and be ruled, although I know thou hadst rather	
	Follow thine enemy in a fiery gulf	
	Than flatter him in a bower.°	*arbor*
	Enter COMINIUS.	
	Here is Cominius.	

---

1. *bastards . . . to:* illegitimate words not acknowledged by.
2. *put . . . fortune:* force you to take your chances (in battle).
3. *Not . . . past:* Not only the present danger, but what was lost before.
4. Malleable (or possibly a verb, "let droop").

COMINIUS   I have been i'th' marketplace, and, sir, 'tis fit
   You make strong party,° or defend yourself   *gather strong support*
95   By calmness or by absence. All's in anger.
MENENIUS   Only fair speech.
COMINIUS   I think 'twill serve, if he
   Can thereto frame his spirit.
VOLUMNIA   He must, and will.
   —Prithee now, say you will and go about it.
CORIOLANUS   Must I go show them my unbarbed sconce?°   *unhelmeted head*
   Must I
100   With my base tongue give to my noble heart
   A lie that it must bear? Well, I will do't.
   Yet were there but this single plot° to lose,   *(Coriolanus's body)*
   This mold° of Martius, they to dust should grind it   *form; earth*
   And throw't against the wind. To th' marketplace.
105   You have put me now to such a part which never
   I shall discharge to th' life.°   *perform convincingly*
COMINIUS   Come, come, we'll prompt you.
VOLUMNIA   I prithee now, sweet son, as thou hast said
   My praises made thee first a soldier, so
   To have my praise for this, perform a part
   Thou hast not done before.
110   CORIOLANUS   Well, I must do't.
   Away, my disposition, and possess me
   Some harlot's⁵ spirit. My throat of war be turned,
   Which choired° with my drum, into a pipe   *harmonized*
   Small as an eunuch or the virgin voice
115   That babies lull asleep. The smiles of knaves
   Tent° in my cheeks, and schoolboys' tears take up   *Encamp*
   The glasses° of my sight. A beggar's tongue   *windows*
   Make motion through my lips, and my armed knees,
   Who bowed but in my stirrup, bend like his
120   That hath received an alms. I will not do't,
   Lest I surcease° to honor mine own truth   *cease*
   And by my body's action teach my mind
   A most inherent° baseness.   *fixed*
VOLUMNIA   At thy choice, then.
   To beg of thee, it is my more dishonor
125   Than thou of them. Come all to ruin. Let
   Thy mother rather feel° thy pride than fear   *suffer*
   Thy dangerous stoutness,° for I mock at death   *stubbornness*
   With as big heart as thou. Do as thou list.°   *wish*
   Thy valiantness was mine: thou suck'st it from me.
   But owe° thy pride thyself.   *own*
130   CORIOLANUS   Pray be content.
   Mother, I am going to the marketplace.
   Chide me no more. I'll mountebank⁶ their loves,
   Cog° their hearts from them, and come home beloved   *Wheedle*
   Of all the trades in Rome. Look, I am going.
135   Commend me to my wife. I'll return consul
   Or never trust to what my tongue can do
   I'th' way of flattery further.

5. Vagabond; buffoon; prostitute.
6. Cajole (a mountebank was an itinerant quack who sold his cures from an improvised platform).

VOLUMNIA	Do your will. *Exit* VOLUMNIA.	
COMINIUS	Away! The tribunes do attend you. Arm yourself	

COMINIUS   Away! The tribunes do attend you. Arm yourself
    To answer mildly, for they are prepared
140   With accusations, as I hear, more strong
    Than are upon you yet.
CORIOLANUS   The word is "mildly." Pray you, let us go.
    Let them accuse me by invention,° I   *with invented charges*
    Will answer in mine honor.
MENENIUS   Ay, but mildly.
145 CORIOLANUS   Well, mildly be it, then, mildly.   *Exeunt.*

3.3

Enter SICINIUS *and* BRUTUS.

BRUTUS   In this point charge him home,[1] that he affects°   *desires*
    Tyrannical power. If he evade us there,
    Enforce° him with his envy° to the people,   *Urge against / malice*
    And that the spoil got on° the Antiates   *booty taken from*
    Was ne'er distributed.

Enter an AEDILE.

5   —What, will he come?
AEDILE   He's coming.
BRUTUS   How accompanied?
AEDILE   With old Menenius and those senators
    That always favored him.
SICINIUS   Have you a catalog
    Of all the voices° that we have procured,   *votes*
    Set down by th' poll?°   *individually*
10 AEDILE   I have; 'tis ready.
SICINIUS   Have you collected them by tribes?[2]
AEDILE   I have.
SICINIUS   Assemble presently the people hither,
    And when they hear me say, "It shall be so
    I'th' right and strength o'th' commons," be it either
15   For death, for fine, or banishment, then let them,
    If I say "Fine," cry "Fine!", if "Death," cry "Death!",
    Insisting on the old prerogative
    And power i'th' truth o'th' cause.[3]
AEDILE   I shall inform them.
BRUTUS   And when such time they have begun to cry,
20   Let them not cease, but with a din confused
    Enforce the present execution[4]
    Of what we chance to sentence.
AEDILE   Very well.
SICINIUS   Make them be strong and ready for this hint
    When we shall hap° to give't them.   *chance*
BRUTUS   Go about it. [*Exit* AEDILE.]
25   Put him to choler straight.° He hath been used   *anger at once*
    Ever to conquer and to have his worth[5]
    Of contradiction. Being once chafed,° he cannot   *excited*
    Be reined again to temperance; then he speaks

3.3 Location: The marketplace.
1. Press charges against him forcefully.
2. Romans voted by tribes (districts) or by social class; the former method favored the plebeians.

3. *old prerogative . . . cause:* traditional right to determine the truth of the case.
4. Insist upon the immediate performance.
5. Enjoy his fill; establish his reputation from.

What's in his heart, and that is there which looks
With us[6] to break his neck.

Enter CORIOLANUS, MENENIUS, *and* COMINIUS, *with*
other [SENATORS].

30 SICINIUS   Well, here he comes.
MENENIUS [*to* CORIOLANUS]   Calmly, I do beseech you.
CORIOLANUS   Ay, as an hostler,° that for th' poorest piece°   *stable keeper / coin*
    Will bear the knave by th' volume.[7] —Th'honored gods
    Keep Rome in safety and the chairs of justice
35 Supplied with worthy men; plant love among's;
    Throng our large temples with the shows° of peace   *ceremonies*
    And not our streets with war!
FIRST SENATOR   Amen, amen.
MENENIUS   A noble wish.

Enter the AEDILE *with the* PLEBEIANS.

SICINIUS   Draw near, ye people.
AEDILE   List to your tribunes. Audience! Peace, I say.
CORIOLANUS   First, hear me speak.
40 BOTH TRIBUNES   Well, say. —Peace, ho!
CORIOLANUS   Shall I be charged no further than this present?°   *at this present time*
    Must all determine° here?   *be determined*
SICINIUS   I do demand
    If you submit you to the people's voices,
    Allow° their officers, and are content   *Acknowledge*
45 To suffer lawful censure for such faults
    As shall be proved upon you.
CORIOLANUS   I am content.
MENENIUS   Lo, citizens, he says he is content.
    The warlike service he has done, consider. Think
    Upon the wounds his body bears, which show
    Like graves i'th' holy churchyard.
50 CORIOLANUS   Scratches with briers,
    Scars to move laughter only.
MENENIUS   Consider further
    That when he speaks not like a citizen,
    You find him like a soldier. Do not take
    His rougher accents for malicious sounds,
55 But, as I say, such as become a soldier
    Rather than envy° you.   *show hatred to*
COMINIUS   Well, well, no more.
CORIOLANUS   What is the matter that, being passed for consul
    With full voice, I am so dishonored that
    The very hour you take it off again?
SICINIUS   Answer to us.
60 CORIOLANUS   Say, then. 'Tis true, I ought so.
SICINIUS   We charge you that you have contrived to take
    From Rome all seasoned° office and to wind°   *time-honored / insinuate*
    Yourself into a power tyrannical,
    For which you are a traitor to the people.
CORIOLANUS   How? "Traitor"?
65 MENENIUS   Nay, temperately. Your promise.

6. *looks with us*: promises with our help.
7. Will endure being called knave any number of times.

CORIOLANUS The fires i'th' lowest hell fold in° the people! *enfold*
Call me their traitor, thou injurious° tribune? *insulting*
Within° thine eyes sat twenty thousand deaths, *If within*
In thy hands clutched as many millions, in
70 Thy lying tongue both numbers, I would say,
"Thou liest" unto thee with a voice as free
As I do pray the gods.
SICINIUS   Mark you this, people?
ALL CITIZENS To th' Rock, to th' Rock with him!
SICINIUS   Peace!
We need not put new matter to his charge.
75 What you have seen him do and heard him speak—
Beating your officers, cursing yourselves,
Opposing laws with strokes, and here defying
Those whose great power must try him—even this,
So criminal and in such capital kind,[8]
Deserves th'extremest death.
80 BRUTUS   But since he hath
Served well for Rome—
CORIOLANUS   What? Do you prate° of service? *babble*
BRUTUS I talk of that that know it.
CORIOLANUS   You?
MENENIUS Is this the promise that you made your mother?
COMINIUS Know, I pray you—
CORIOLANUS   I'll know no further.
85 Let them pronounce the steep Tarpeian death,
Vagabond exile, flaying, pent° to linger *imprisoned*
But with a grain a day, I would not buy
Their mercy at the price of one fair word,
Nor check my courage° for what they can give, *restrain my spirit*
To have't with saying "Good morrow."
90 SICINIUS   For that° he has, *Because*
As much as in him lies, from time to time
Inveighed against the people, seeking means
To pluck away their power, as now at last
Given hostile strokes, and that not in the presence
95 Of dreaded justice, but on the ministers
That doth distribute it, in the name o'th' people
And in the power of us the tribunes, we,
E'en from this instant, banish him our city,
In peril of precipitation
100 From off the Rock Tarpeian, never more
To enter our Rome gates. I'th' people's name
I say it shall be so.
ALL CITIZENS   It shall be so,
It shall be so. Let him away. He's banished,
And it shall be so.
105 COMINIUS Hear me, my masters and my common friends—
SICINIUS He's sentenced; no more hearing.
COMINIUS   Let me speak.
I have been consul and can show for Rome
Her enemies' marks upon me. I do love

___

8. Important; deserving death.

My country's good with a respect more tender,
110 More holy and profound, than mine own life,
My dear wife's estimate,° her womb's increase   *reputation*
And treasure of my loins.° Then if I would   *(that is, children)*
Speak that—
SICINIUS   We know your drift. Speak what?
BRUTUS   There's no more to be said, but he is banished
115 As enemy to the people and his country.
It shall be so.
ALL CITIZENS   It shall be so, it shall be so!
CORIOLANUS   You common cry° of curs, whose breath I hate   *yelping pack*
As reek° o'th' rotten fens,° whose loves I prize   *vapor / swamps*
As the dead carcasses of unburied men
120 That do corrupt my air: I banish you,
And here remain with your uncertainty!
Let every feeble rumor shake your hearts;
Your enemies, with nodding of their plumes,°   *(helmet plumes)*
Fan you into despair! Have the power still
125 To banish your defenders, till at length
Your ignorance—which finds not till it feels,⁹
Making but reservation of° yourselves,   *Seeking only to preserve*
Still your own foes—deliver you as most
Abated° captives to some nation   *Debased*
130 That won you without blows! Despising
For° you the city, thus I turn my back.   *On account of*
There is a world elsewhere.
        Exeunt CORIOLANUS, COMINIUS, *with* [MENENIUS *and*
                                other SENATORS].
AEDILE   The people's enemy is gone, is gone!
ALL CITIZENS   Our enemy is banished! He is gone! Hoo-oo!
        They all shout and throw up their caps.
135 SICINIUS   Go see him out at gates and follow him
As he hath followed you, with all despite.°   *contempt*
Give him deserved vexation. Let a guard
Attend us through the city.
ALL CITIZENS   Come, come, let's see him out at gates, come.
140 The gods preserve our noble tribunes! Come.   *Exeunt.*

4.1

        Enter CORIOLANUS, VOLUMNIA, VIRGILIA, MENENIUS,
        COMINIUS, *with the young nobility of Rome.*
CORIOLANUS   Come, leave your tears. A brief farewell. The beast
With many heads butts me away. Nay, mother,
Where is your ancient° courage? You were used   *former*
To say extremities was the trier of spirits;
5 That common chances common men could bear;
That when the sea was calm, all boats alike
Showed mastership in floating; fortune's blows
When most struck home, being gentle wounded craves
A noble cunning.¹ You were used to load me

---

9. Which does not learn until it suffers.   1. *being . . . cunning:* to suffer nobly requires a gen-
4.1 Location: Near the city gates of Rome.   tleman's skill.

10 With precepts that would make invincible
The heart that conned° them.   *learned*

VIRGILIA   O heavens! O heavens!

CORIOLANUS   Nay, I prithee, woman—

VOLUMNIA   Now the red pestilence² strike all trades in Rome,
And occupations° perish.   *handicrafts*

CORIOLANUS   What, what, what?

15 I shall be loved when I am lacked. Nay, mother,
Resume that spirit when you were wont to say,
If you had been the wife of Hercules,³
Six of his labors you'd have done and saved
Your husband so much sweat. —Cominius,

20 Droop not. Adieu. —Farewell, my wife, my mother.
I'll do well yet. —Thou old and true Menenius,
Thy tears are salter than a younger man's
And venomous to thine eyes. —My sometime⁴ general,
I have seen thee stern, and thou hast oft beheld

25 Heart-hard'ning spectacles. Tell these sad women
'Tis fond° to wail inevitable strokes   *as foolish*
As 'tis to laugh at 'em. —My mother, you wot° well   *know*
My hazards still° have been your solace, and   *always*
Believe't not lightly: though I go alone

30 Like to a lonely dragon that his fen
Makes feared° and talked of more than seen, your son   *fearful*
Will or° exceed the common° or be caught   *either / usual standard*
With cautelous° baits and practice.   *deceitful*

VOLUMNIA   My first son,
Whither will thou go? Take good Cominius

35 With thee a while. Determine on some course
More than a wild exposure to each chance
That starts° i'th' way before thee.   *leaps up*

CORIOLANUS   O the gods!

COMINIUS   I'll follow thee a month, devise with thee
Where thou shalt rest that thou mayst hear of us,

40 And we of thee, so if the time thrust forth
A cause for thy repeal,° we shall not send   *recall from banishment*
O'er the vast world to seek a single man
And lose advantage,° which doth ever cool   *favorable occasion*
I'th' absence of the needer.

CORIOLANUS   Fare ye well.

45 Thou hast years upon thee, and thou art too full
Of the wars' surfeits to go rove with one
That's yet unbruised. Bring me but out at gate.
—Come, my sweet wife, my dearest mother, and
My friends of noble touch;° when I am forth,   *proven nobility*

50 Bid me farewell and smile. I pray you, come.
While I remain above the ground, you shall
Hear from me still, and never of me aught
But what is like me formerly.

MENENIUS   That's worthily
As any ear can hear. Come, let's not weep.

55 If I could shake off but one seven years

---

2. Bubonic plague or typhoid.
3. Mythical hero of great strength who was assigned
twelve near-impossible labors.
4. Former (addressing Cominius).

From these old arms and legs, by the good gods
I'd with thee, every foot.
CORIOLANUS   Give me thy hand. Come. *Exeunt.*

4.2

Enter the two tribunes, SICINIUS *and* BRUTUS, *with the*
AEDILE.

SICINIUS [*to* AEDILE]   Bid them all home. He's gone, and we'll no further.
—The nobility are vexed, whom we see have
Sided in his behalf.
BRUTUS   Now we have shown our power,
Let us seem humbler after it is done
Than when it was a-doing.
5 SICINIUS [*to* AEDILE]   Bid them home.
Say their great enemy is gone, and they
Stand in their ancient strength.
BRUTUS   Dismiss them home.
                                                      [*Exit* AEDILE.]
—Here comes his mother.
                    Enter VOLUMNIA, VIRGILIA, *and* MENENIUS.
SICINIUS   Let's not meet her.
BRUTUS   Why?
SICINIUS   They say she's mad.
10 BRUTUS   They have ta'en note of us. Keep on your way.
VOLUMNIA   Oh, you're well met. Th' hoarded plague o'th' gods
Requite° your love!   *Repay*
MENENIUS   Peace, peace, be not so loud.
VOLUMNIA   If that I could for weeping, you should hear—
Nay, and you shall hear some. Will you be gone?
15 VIRGILIA   You shall stay too. I would I had the power
To say so to my husband.
SICINIUS [*to* VOLUMNIA]   Are you mankind?[1]
VOLUMNIA   Ay, fool, is that a shame? Note but this, fool,
Was not a man my father? Hadst thou foxship°   *slyness*
To banish him that struck more blows for Rome
Than thou hast spoken words?
20 SICINIUS   O blessed heavens!
VOLUMNIA   More noble blows than ever thou wise words,
And for Rome's good. I'll tell thee what—yet go.
Nay, but thou shalt stay too. I would my son
Were in Arabia[2] and thy tribe before him,
His good sword in his hand.
SICINIUS   What then?
25 VIRGILIA   What then?
He'd make an end of thy posterity.
VOLUMNIA   Bastards and all!
Good man, the wounds that he does bear for Rome!
MENENIUS   Come, come, peace.
30 SICINIUS   I would he had continued to his country
As he began and not unknit° himself   *untied*
The noble knot he made.

4.2 Location: Scene continues.   2. That is, in a desert without political institutions
1. Male (thus to speak in public); Volumnia takes the   or places to hide.
word to mean "human."

BRUTUS   I would he had.

VOLUMNIA   "I would he had"! 'Twas you incensed the rabble,
    Cats that can judge as fitly of his worth

35   As I can of those mysteries which heaven
    Will not have earth to know.

BRUTUS [*to* SICINIUS]   Pray, let's go.

VOLUMNIA   Now pray, sir, get you gone.
    You have done a brave deed. Ere you go, hear this:
    As far as doth the Capitol exceed

40   The meanest house in Rome, so far my son—
    This lady's husband here, this, do you see?—
    Whom you have banished, does exceed you all.

BRUTUS   Well, well, we'll leave you.

SICINIUS   Why stay we to be baited
    With one that wants° her wits?   *Exeunt tribunes.*   lacks

VOLUMNIA   Take my prayers with you.

45   I would the gods had nothing else to do
    But to confirm my curses. Could I meet 'em
    But once a day, it would unclog° my heart   unburden
    Of what lies heavy to't.

MENENIUS   You have told them home,[3]
    And, by my troth, you have cause. You'll sup° with me?   dine

50 VOLUMNIA   Anger's my meat. I sup upon myself
    And so shall starve with feeding. [*to* VIRGILIA] Come, let's go.
    Leave this faint puling and lament as I do,
    In anger, Juno-like.[4] Come, come, come.
                       Exeunt [VOLUMNIA *and* VIRGILIA].

MENENIUS   Fie, fie, fie.   *Exit.*

4.3

Enter [*Nicanor,*] *a* ROMAN, *and* [*Adrian,*] *a* VOLSCE.

ROMAN   I know you well, sir, and you know me. Your name,
I think, is Adrian.

VOLSCE   It is so, sir. Truly, I have forgot you.

ROMAN   I am a Roman, and my services are, as you are, against

5   'em.° Know you me yet?   (the Romans)

VOLSCE   Nicanor, no?

ROMAN   The same, sir.

VOLSCE   You had more beard when I last saw you, but your
favor° is well appeared° by your tongue. What's the news in   face / attested

10   Rome? I have a note° from the Volscian state to find you out   instruction
there. You have well saved me a day's journey.

ROMAN   There hath been in Rome strange insurrections: the
people against the senators, patricians, and nobles.

VOLSCE   Hath been? Is it ended, then? Our state thinks not

15   so. They are in a most warlike preparation and hope to come
upon them in the heat of their division.

ROMAN   The main blaze of it is past, but a small thing would
make it flame again, for the nobles receive so to heart the
banishment of that worthy Coriolanus that they are in a ripe

20   aptness to take all power from the people and to pluck from

---

3. Scolded them thoroughly.
4. Goddess of marriage and childbirth (and frequently infuriated by the infidelities of her husband,

Jupiter, king of the gods).
4.3 Location: A road between Rome and Antium.

them their tribunes forever. This lies glowing,° I can tell   *smoldering*
you, and is almost mature for the violent breaking out.

VOLSCE Coriolanus banished?

ROMAN Banished, sir.

25 VOLSCE You will be welcome with this intelligence, Nicanor.

ROMAN The day° serves well for them° now. I have heard it   *moment / (the Volscians)*
said the fittest time to corrupt a man's wife is when she's
fallen out with her husband. Your noble Tullus Aufidius will
appear well in these wars, his great opposer Coriolanus

30 being now in no request of° his country.   *unvalued by*

VOLSCE He cannot choose.° I am most fortunate thus acci-   *He is bound to*
dentally to encounter you. You have ended my business, and
I will merrily accompany you home.

ROMAN I shall between this and supper tell you most strange

35 things from Rome, all tending to the good of their adversaries. Have you an army ready, say you?

VOLSCE A most royal one: the centurions and their charges
distinctly billeted, already in th'entertainment,¹ and to be
on foot at an hour's warning.

40 ROMAN I am joyful to hear of their readiness and am the
man, I think, that shall set them in present° action. So, sir,   *immediate*
heartily well met, and most glad of your company.

VOLSCE You take my part° from me, sir. I have the most cause   *lines*
to be glad of yours.

45 ROMAN Well, let us go together.   *Exeunt.*

4.4

Enter CORIOLANUS *in mean apparel, disguised and*
muffled.

CORIOLANUS A goodly city is this Antium. City,
'Tis I that made thy widows; many an heir
Of these fair edifices fore my wars°   *before my onslaught*
Have I heard groan and drop. Then know me not,

5 Lest that thy wives with spits and boys with stones
In puny battle slay me.

Enter a CITIZEN.

                    Save° you, sir.   *God save*

CITIZEN And you.

CORIOLANUS   Direct me, if it be your will,
Where great Aufidius lies. Is he in Antium?

CITIZEN He is, and feasts the nobles of the state
At his house this night.

10 CORIOLANUS   Which is his house, beseech you?

CITIZEN This here before you.

CORIOLANUS   Thank you, sir. Farewell.

                    Exit CITIZEN.

O world, thy slippery turns! Friends now fast sworn,
Whose double bosoms seem to wear one heart,
Whose hours, whose bed, whose meal and exercise

15 Are still together, who twin, as 'twere, in love
Unseparable, shall within this hour,

---

1. *their . . . entertainment:* the men under their com-   4.4 Location: Before Aufidius's house in Antium.
mand already listed unit by unit on the payroll.

On a dissension of a doit,° break out   *trivial quarrel*
To bitterest enmity. So fellest° foes,   *fiercest*
Whose passions and whose plots have broke their sleep
20 To take the one the other,[1] by some chance,
Some trick° not worth an egg, shall grow dear friends   *trifle*
And interjoin their issues.[2] So with me.
My birthplace hate I, and my love's upon
This enemy town. I'll enter. If he slay me,
25 He does fair justice; if he give me way,°   *allows me to proceed*
I'll do his country service.   *Exit.*

4.5

Music plays. Enter a SERVINGMAN.
FIRST SERVINGMAN Wine, wine, wine! What service is here?
I think our fellows° are asleep.   [*Exit.*]   *fellow servants*
Enter another SERVINGMAN.
SECOND SERVINGMAN Where's Cotus? My master calls for
him. Cotus!   *Exit.*
Enter CORIOLANUS.
5 CORIOLANUS A goodly house. The feast smells well, but I
Appear not like a guest.
Enter the FIRST SERVINGMAN.
FIRST SERVINGMAN What would you have, friend? Whence are
you? Here's no place for you. Pray go to the door.   *Exit.*
CORIOLANUS I have deserved no better entertainment
10 In being Coriolanus.
Enter SECOND SERVINGMAN.
SECOND SERVINGMAN Whence are you, sir? Has the porter his
eyes in his head that he gives entrance to such companions?°   *low persons*
Pray get you out.
CORIOLANUS Away!
15 SECOND SERVINGMAN Away? Get you away!
CORIOLANUS Now thou'rt troublesome.
SECOND SERVINGMAN Are you so brave?° I'll have you talked   *insolent*
with anon.°   *right away*
Enter THIRD SERVINGMAN; *the* FIRST[*, entering,*] *meets
him.*
THIRD SERVINGMAN What fellow's this?
20 FIRST SERVINGMAN A strange one as ever I looked on. I can-
not get him out o'th' house. Prithee call my master to him.
THIRD SERVINGMAN What have you to do° here, fellow? Pray   *are you doing*
you, avoid° the house.   *leave*
CORIOLANUS Let me but stand. I will not hurt your hearth.
25 THIRD SERVINGMAN What are you?
CORIOLANUS A gentleman.
THIRD SERVINGMAN A marvelous poor one.
CORIOLANUS True, so I am.
THIRD SERVINGMAN Pray you, poor gentleman, take up some
30 other station.[1] Here's no place for you. Pray you, avoid. Come.
CORIOLANUS Follow your function.[2] Go and batten° on cold   *gorge*
bits.

1. *whose plots . . . the other:* whose plots to capture
one another have kept them awake.
2. Unite their causes; marry their children to one
another.

4.5 Location: Inside Aufidius's house.
1. Place to stand (punning on "social rank").
2. Perform your servant's tasks.

    [He] pushes him away from him.
THIRD SERVINGMAN What? You will not? —Prithee, tell my
   master what a strange guest he has here.
35 SECOND SERVINGMAN And I shall.
                          Exit SECOND SERVINGMAN.
THIRD SERVINGMAN Where dwell'st thou?
CORIOLANUS Under the canopy.°   *(of the sky)*
THIRD SERVINGMAN Under the canopy?
CORIOLANUS Ay.
40 THIRD SERVINGMAN Where's that?
CORIOLANUS I'th' city of kites and crows.°   *(carrion birds)*
THIRD SERVINGMAN I'th' city of kites and crows? What an ass
   it is. Then thou dwell'st with daws³ too?
CORIOLANUS No, I serve not thy master.
45 THIRD SERVINGMAN How, sir? Do you meddle⁴ with my master?
CORIOLANUS Ay, 'tis an honester service than to meddle with
   thy mistress. Thou prat'st and prat'st. Serve with thy trencher.° *wooden plate*
   Hence!
        [He] beats him away. [Exit THIRD SERVINGMAN.*]*
      Enter AUFIDIUS *with the* [SECOND] SERVINGMAN.
AUFIDIUS Where is this fellow?
50 SECOND SERVINGMAN Here, sir. I'd have beaten him like a dog
   but for disturbing the lords within.
        *[*FIRST *and* SECOND SERVINGMEN *stand aside.]*
AUFIDIUS Whence com'st thou? What wouldst thou? Thy name?
   Why speak'st not? Speak, man! What's thy name?
CORIOLANUS *[unmuffling his head]*   If, Tullus,
   Not yet thou know'st me and, seeing me, dost not
55   Think me for the man I am, necessity
   Commands me name myself.
AUFIDIUS   What is thy name?
CORIOLANUS A name unmusical to the Volscians' ears
   And harsh in sound to thine.
AUFIDIUS   Say, what's thy name?
   Thou hast a grim appearance, and thy face
60   Bears a command in't. Though thy tackle's torn,
   Thou show'st° a noble vessel. What's thy name?   *appear to be*
CORIOLANUS Prepare thy brow to frown. Know'st thou me yet?
AUFIDIUS I know thee not. Thy name?
CORIOLANUS My name is Caius Martius, who hath done
65   To thee particularly and to all the Volsces
   Great hurt and mischief; thereto witness may
   My surname, Coriolanus. The painful service,
   The extreme dangers, and the drops of blood
   Shed for my thankless country are requited
70   But with that surname, a good memory°   *reminder*
   And witness of the malice and displeasure
   Which thou shouldst bear me. Only that name remains.
   The cruelty and envy of the people,
   Permitted by our dastard nobles, who
75   Have all forsook me, hath devoured the rest
   And suffered me by th' voice of slaves to be

---

3. Jackdaws (proverbially foolish).
4. Busy yourself; but Coriolanus plays on the sense "have sexual intercourse."

Whooped out of Rome. Now this extremity
Hath brought me to thy hearth, not out of hope—
Mistake me not—to save my life, for if
80 I had feared death, of all the men i'th' world
I would have 'voided thee, but in mere° spite   *utter*
To be full quit of° those my banishers,   *revenged upon; rid of*
Stand I before thee here. Then, if thou hast
A heart of wreak° in thee that wilt revenge   *vengeance*
85 Thine own particular wrongs and stop those maims°   *injuries*
Of shame seen through thy country, speed° thee straight   *hasten*
And make my misery serve thy turn. So use it
That my revengeful services may prove
As benefits to thee, for I will fight
90 Against my cankered° country with the spleen°   *infected / wrath*
Of all the under-fiends.° But if so be   *underworld fiends*
Thou dar'st not this, and that to prove° more fortunes   *try*
Thou'rt tired, then, in a word, I also am
Longer to live most weary, and present
95 My throat to thee and to thy ancient° malice,   *longstanding*
Which not to cut would show thee but a fool,
Since I have ever followed thee with hate,
Drawn tuns° of blood out of thy country's breast,   *huge casks*
And cannot live but to thy shame, unless
It be to do thee service.
100 AUFIDIUS   O Martius, Martius!
Each word thou hast spoke hath weeded from my heart
A root of ancient envy. If Jupiter
Should from yond cloud speak divine things
And say, "'Tis true," I'd not believe them more
105 Than thee, all-noble Martius. Let me twine
Mine arms about that body, where against
My grainèd ash[5] an hundred times hath broke
And scarred the moon with splinters.
       [*He embraces* CORIOLANUS.][6]
                          Here I clip°   *embrace*
The anvil[7] of my sword, and do contest
110 As hotly and as nobly with thy love
As ever in ambitious strength I did
Contend against thy valor. Know thou first,
I loved the maid I married; never man
Sighed truer breath. But that I see thee here,
115 Thou noble thing, more dances my rapt heart
Than when I first my wedded mistress saw
Bestride my threshold. Why, thou Mars, I tell thee,
We have a power on foot,° and I had purpose   *an army in the field*
Once more to hew thy target° from thy brawn°   *shield / arm*
120 Or lose mine arm for't. Thou hast beat me out°   *outright*
Twelve several° times, and I have nightly since   *separate*
Dreamt of encounters twixt thyself and me—
We have been down° together in my sleep,   *(on the ground)*
Unbuckling helms, fisting° each other's throat—   *clutching*

5. Close-grained ashwood spear.
6. PERFORMANCE COMMENT In many productions,
the relationship between Coriolanus and Aufidius
has a homoerotic intensity. See Digital Edition PC 2

for some performance options.
7. Coriolanus's body, on which Aufidius has beaten
his sword.

125　And waked half dead with nothing. Worthy Martius,
　　Had we no other quarrel else to Rome but that
　　Thou art thence banished, we would muster all°　　　　　*enlist everyone*
　　From twelve to seventy° and, pouring war　　　　　　　*(years old)*
　　Into the bowels of ungrateful Rome,
130　Like a bold flood o'erbeat. Oh, come, go in,
　　And take our friendly senators by th' hands
　　Who now are here, taking their leaves of me,
　　Who am prepared against your territories,
　　Though not for Rome itself.
　　CORIOLANUS　　　　　　　　You bless me, gods.
135　AUFIDIUS　Therefore, most absolute° sir, if thou wilt have　　　*perfect*
　　The leading of thine own revenges, take
　　Th'one half of my commission° and set down°—　　　　*force / determine*
　　As best thou art experienced, since thou know'st
　　Thy country's strength and weakness—thine own ways:
140　Whether to knock against the gates of Rome,
　　Or rudely visit° them in parts remote　　　　　　　　*afflict*
　　To fright them ere destroy. But come in,
　　Let me commend thee first to those that shall
　　Say yea to thy desires. A thousand welcomes!
145　And more a friend than e'er an enemy;
　　Yet, Martius, that was much. Your hand. Most welcome!
　　　　　　　　Exeunt [AUFIDIUS *and* CORIOLANUS].
　　　　　[*The*] *two* SERVINGMEN [*come forward*].
　　FIRST SERVINGMAN　Here's a strange alteration!
　　SECOND SERVINGMAN　By my hand, I had thought to have
　　　strucken him with a cudgel, and yet my mind gave me° his　　*suggested to me that*
150　　clothes made a false report of him.
　　FIRST SERVINGMAN　What an arm he has! He turned me about
　　　with his finger and his thumb as one would set up a top.
　　SECOND SERVINGMAN　Nay, I knew by his face that there was
　　　something in him. He had, sir, a kind of face, methought—I
155　　cannot tell how to term it.
　　FIRST SERVINGMAN　He had so, looking as it were—would I
　　　were hanged but I thought there was more in him than
　　　I could think.
　　SECOND SERVINGMAN　So did I, I'll be sworn. He is simply the
160　　rarest man i'th' world.
　　FIRST SERVINGMAN　I think he is, but a greater soldier than
　　　he, you wot one.°　　　　　　　　　　　　　　　*know of*
　　SECOND SERVINGMAN　Who, my master?
　　FIRST SERVINGMAN　Nay, it's no matter for° that.　　　　*no doubt about*
165　SECOND SERVINGMAN　Worth six on him.
　　FIRST SERVINGMAN　Nay, not so neither, but I take him to be
　　　the greater soldier.
　　SECOND SERVINGMAN　Faith, look you, one cannot tell how
　　　to say[8] that. For the defense of a town, our general is
170　　excellent.
　　FIRST SERVINGMAN　Ay, and for an assault too.
　　　　　　Enter the THIRD SERVINGMAN.
　　THIRD SERVINGMAN　O slaves, I can tell you news! News, you
　　　rascals!

---

8. There's no basis for saying.

FIRST *and* SECOND SERVINGMEN What, what, what? Let's
175 partake.
THIRD SERVINGMAN I would not be a Roman of all nations. I
had as lief° be a condemned man.   *gladly*
FIRST *and* SECOND SERVINGMEN Wherefore? Wherefore?
THIRD SERVINGMAN Why, here's he that was wont to thwack
180 our general, Caius Martius.
FIRST SERVINGMAN Why do you say "thwack our general"?
THIRD SERVINGMAN I do not say "thwack our general," but he
was always good enough for him.
SECOND SERVINGMAN Come, we are fellows and friends. He
185 was ever too hard for him; I have heard him say so himself.
FIRST SERVINGMAN He was too hard for him; directly° to say   *simply*
the truth on't, before Corioles he scotched° him and notched   *scored*
him like a carbonado.[9]
SECOND SERVINGMAN An° he had been cannibally given, he   *If*
190 might have boiled and eaten him too.
FIRST SERVINGMAN But more of thy news.
THIRD SERVINGMAN Why, he is so made on° here within as if   *made so much of*
he were son and heir to Mars, set at upper end o'th' table, no
question asked him by any of the senators but they stand
195 bald° before him. Our general himself makes a mistress   *hatless*
of° him, sanctifies himself with 's hand[1] and turns up the   *woos*
white o'th' eye° to his discourse. But the bottom° of the news   *(in pious devotion) / gist*
is our general is cut i'th' middle and but one half of what
he was yesterday, for the other° has half by the entreaty   *(Coriolanus)*
200 and grant of the whole table. He'll go, he says, and sowl° the   *drag*
porter of Rome gates by th'ears. He will mow all down
before him and leave his passage polled.°   *stripped*
SECOND SERVINGMAN And he's as like to do't as any man I can
imagine.
205 THIRD SERVINGMAN Do't? He will do't, for look you, sir, he
has as many friends as enemies, which friends, sir, as it were,
durst not—look you, sir—show themselves, as we term it,
his friends whilst he's in directitude.°   *disgraced*
FIRST SERVINGMAN "Directitude"? What's that?
210 THIRD SERVINGMAN But when they shall see, sir, his crest up
again and the man in blood,[2] they will out of their burrows,
like conies° after rain, and revel all with him.   *rabbits*
FIRST SERVINGMAN But when goes this forward?
THIRD SERVINGMAN Tomorrow, today, presently.° You shall   *at once*
215 have the drum struck up this afternoon. 'Tis, as it were, a
parcel° of their feast, and to be executed ere they wipe their   *part*
lips.
SECOND SERVINGMAN Why, then, we shall have a stirring°   *busy*
world again. This peace is nothing but to rust iron, increase
220 tailors, and breed ballad-makers.[3]
FIRST SERVINGMAN Let me have war, say I. It exceeds peace
as far as day does night. It's sprightly walking, audible, and
full of vent.[4] Peace is a very apoplexy, lethargy, mulled,° deaf,   *stupefied*

---

9. Piece of meat for broiling.
1. Treats the touch of his hand as holy.
2. In full vigor (usually refers to hounds).
3. That is, fashionable dress and idle songs flourish

in peacetime while weapons rust.
4. *audible . . . vent:* either loud and full of action, or
quick of hearing and scent (like a hunting dog).

sleepy, insensible, a getter of more bastard children than
225 war's a destroyer of men.
SECOND SERVINGMAN 'Tis so, and as wars in some sort may be
said to be a ravisher, so it cannot be denied but peace is a
great maker of cuckolds.
FIRST SERVINGMAN Ay, and it makes men hate one another.
230 THIRD SERVINGMAN Reason: because they then less need one
another. The wars for my money. I hope to see Romans as
cheap as Volscians.
　　　　　[*A sound within.*]
They are rising; they are rising.°　　　　　　　　　　　　　　*(from dinner)*
FIRST *and* SECOND SERVINGMEN In, in, in, in!　　　*Exeunt.*

4.6

Enter the two tribunes, SICINIUS *and* BRUTUS.
SICINIUS We hear not of him, neither need we fear him.
His remedies are tame:[1] the present peace
And quietness of the people, which before
Were in wild hurry.° Here do we make his friends　　　　　*tumult*
5 Blush that the world goes well, who rather had,
Though they themselves did suffer by't, behold
Dissentious numbers pest'ring° streets than see　　　　*obstructing*
Our tradesmen singing in their shops and going
About their functions friendly.
　　　　　Enter MENENIUS.
10 BRUTUS We stood to't° in good time. Is this Menenius?　*acted resolutely*
SICINIUS 'Tis he, 'tis he. Oh, he is grown most kind of late.
　—Hail, sir.
MENENIUS Hail to you both.
SICINIUS Your Coriolanus is not much missed,
15 But with° his friends. The commonwealth doth stand,　　　*by*
And so would do were he more angry at it.
MENENIUS All's well, and might have been much better, if
He could have temporized.
SICINIUS　　　　　　　　　　Where is he, hear you?
MENENIUS Nay, I hear nothing.
20 His mother and his wife hear nothing from him.
　　　　　Enter three or four CITIZENS.
ALL CITIZENS [*to the tribunes*] The gods preserve you both.
SICINIUS　　　　　　　　　　　　　　Good
　e'en,° our neighbors.　　　　　　　　　　　　　　　　*evening*
BRUTUS Good e'en to you all, good e'en to you all.
FIRST CITIZEN Ourselves, our wives and children, on our knees
Are bound to pray for you both.
SICINIUS　　　　　　　　　　Live and thrive!
25 BRUTUS Farewell, kind neighbors.
We wished Coriolanus had loved you as we did.
ALL CITIZENS Now the gods keep you.
BOTH TRIBUNES　　　　　　　　　　Farewell, farewell.
　　　　　　　　　　　　　Exeunt CITIZENS.
SICINIUS This is a happier and more comely time

4.6 Location: A public place in Rome.
1. Those who favor him are unable to act; curing ourselves of him is without violent effects.

Than when these fellows ran about the streets
Crying confusion.
30 BRUTUS   Caius Martius was
A worthy officer i'th' war, but insolent,
O'ercome with pride, ambitious past all thinking,°   *beyond imagination*
Self-loving—
SICINIUS   And affecting one sole throne°   *aspiring to rule alone*
Without assistance.
MENENIUS   I think not so.
35 SICINIUS   We should by this,° to all our lamentation,   *now*
If he had gone forth consul, found it so.
BRUTUS   The gods have well prevented it, and Rome
Sits safe and still without him.
            Enter an AEDILE.
AEDILE   Worthy tribunes,
There is a slave, whom we have put in prison,
40 Reports the Volsces with two several powers°   *separate armies*
Are entered in the Roman territories
And with the deepest malice of the war
Destroy what lies before 'em.
MENENIUS   'Tis Aufidius
Who, hearing of our Martius' banishment,
45 Thrusts forth his horns again into the world,
Which were inshelled° when Martius stood for Rome   *(like a snail's)*
And durst not once peep out.
SICINIUS   Come, what talk you of Martius?
BRUTUS   Go see this rumorer whipped. It cannot be
The Volsces dare break° with us.   *(their treaty)*
MENENIUS   Cannot be?
50 We have record that very well it can,
And three examples of the like hath been
Within my age. But reason° with the fellow,   *discuss*
Before you punish him, where he heard this,
Lest you shall chance to whip your information
55 And beat the messenger who bids beware
Of what is to be dreaded.
SICINIUS   Tell not me.
I know this cannot be.
BRUTUS   Not possible.
          Enter a MESSENGER.
MESSENGER   The nobles in great earnestness are going
All to the Senate-house. Some news is come in
That turns° their countenances.   *changes*
60 SICINIUS   'Tis this slave.
[*to* AEDILE] Go whip him fore the people's eyes: his raising,°   *incitement*
Nothing but his report.
MESSENGER   Yes, worthy sir,
The slave's report is seconded, and more,
More fearful, is delivered.
SICINIUS   What more fearful?
65 MESSENGER   It is spoke freely out of many mouths—
How probable I do not know—that Martius,
Joined with Aufidius, leads a power gainst Rome
And vows revenge as spacious as between
The young'st and oldest thing.

SICINIUS   This is most likely!°   (sarcastic)
70 BRUTUS Raised only that the weaker sort may wish
 Good Martius home again.
SICINIUS   The very trick on't.°   Exactly
MENENIUS This is unlikely. He and Aufidius
 Can no more atone° than violent'st contrariety.   reconcile
   Enter [a SECOND] MESSENGER.
SECOND MESSENGER You are sent for to the Senate.
75 A fearful army, led by Caius Martius,
 Associated with Aufidius, rages
 Upon our territories and have already
 O'erborne their way, consumed with fire, and took
 What lay before them.
   Enter COMINIUS.
80 COMINIUS [to the tribunes] Oh, you have made good work!
MENENIUS   What news? What news?
COMINIUS You have holp° to ravish your own daughters and helped
 To melt the city leads° upon your pates,°   roof lead / heads
 To see your wives dishonored to° your noses— in front of
MENENIUS What's the news? What's the news?
85 COMINIUS Your temples burned in their cement,° and to their foundations
 Your franchises,° whereon you stood,° confined freedoms / insisted
 Into an auger's bore.[2]
MENENIUS   Pray now, your news.
 [to the tribunes] You have made fair work, I fear me.
  —Pray, your news?
 If Martius should be joined wi'th' Volscians—
COMINIUS   If?
90 He is their god. He leads them like a thing
 Made by some other deity than nature,
 That shapes man better, and they follow him
 Against us brats° with no less confidence   mere children
 Than boys pursuing summer butterflies
 Or butchers killing flies.
95 MENENIUS [to the tribunes] You have made good work,
 You and your apron-men,° you that stood so much (artisans wore aprons)
 Upon the voice of occupation° and   opinion of tradesmen
 The breath of garlic-eaters.
COMINIUS   He'll shake
 Your Rome about your ears.
MENENIUS   As Hercules
100 Did shake down mellow fruit.[3] You have made fair work!
BRUTUS But is this true, sir?
COMINIUS   Ay, and you'll look pale
 Before you find it other.° All the regions   otherwise
 Do smilingly° revolt, and who resists   gladly
 Are mocked for valiant° ignorance   steadfast
105 And perish constant° fools. Who is't can blame him? obstinate
 Your enemies and his[4] find something in him.
MENENIUS We are all undone unless
 The noble man have mercy.

2. A drill hole (that is, a narrow space).
3. Hercules' twelfth labor was to gather the apples of
 the Hesperides.
4. The patricians and the Volscians.

COMINIUS   Who shall ask it?
  The tribunes cannot do't for shame; the people
110 Deserve such pity of° him as the wolf   *from*
  Does of the shepherds. For his best friends, if they
  Should say, "Be good to Rome," they charged° him even   *would direct*
  As those should do that had deserved his hate
  And therein showed° like enemies.   *would behave*
MENENIUS   'Tis true;
115 If he were putting to my house the brand°   *fire*
  That should consume it, I have not the face°   *shamelessness*
  To say, "Beseech you, cease." [*to the tribunes*] You have made
    fair hands,°   *done well*
  You and your crafts. You have crafted fair!
COMINIUS   You have brought
  A trembling upon Rome such as was never
120 S'incapable of help.
BOTH TRIBUNES   Say not we brought it.
MENENIUS   How? Was't we? We loved him, but, like beasts
  And cowardly nobles, gave way unto your clusters,°   *crowds*
  Who did hoot him out o'th' city.
COMINIUS   But I fear
  They'll roar° him in again. Tullus Aufidius,   *(in fear)*
125 The second name of men,[5] obeys his points°   *directions*
  As if he were his officer. Desperation
  Is all the policy, strength, and defense
  That Rome can make against them.
              Enter a troop of CITIZENS.
MENENIUS   Here come the clusters.
  And is Aufidius with him? You are they
130 That made the air unwholesome when you cast
  Your stinking greasy caps in hooting
  At Coriolanus' exile. Now he's coming,
  And not a hair upon a soldier's head
  Which will not prove a whip. As many coxcombs°   *fools*
135 As you threw caps up will he tumble down
  And pay you for your voices. 'Tis no matter.
  If he could burn us all into one coal,
  We have deserved it.
ALL CITIZENS   Faith, we hear fearful news.
FIRST CITIZEN   For mine own part,
140 When I said banish him, I said 'twas pity.
SECOND CITIZEN   And so did I.
THIRD CITIZEN   And so did I, and to say the truth, so did very
    many of us. That° we did, we did for the best, and though we   *What*
    willingly consented to his banishment, yet it was against our
145 will.
COMINIUS   You're goodly things, you voices.
MENENIUS   You have made good work
  You and your cry. —Shall's to the Capitol?
COMINIUS   Oh, ay, what else?
              Exeunt both [COMINIUS *and* MENENIUS].

---

5. The second in reputation only to Coriolanus.

SICINIUS Go, masters, get you home. Be not dismayed.
150 These are a side° that would be glad to have   *faction*
    This true which they so seem to fear. Go home
    And show no sign of fear.
FIRST CITIZEN The gods be good to us! Come, masters, let's
    home. I ever said we were i'th' wrong when we banished
155 him.
SECOND CITIZEN So did we all. But come, let's home.

                          Exeunt CITIZENS.

BRUTUS I do not like this news.
SICINIUS Nor I.
BRUTUS Let's to the Capitol. Would half my wealth
160 Would buy this for a lie.
SICINIUS   Pray, let's go.   *Exeunt tribunes.*

4.7

Enter AUFIDIUS *with his* LIEUTENANT.

AUFIDIUS Do they still fly to th' Roman?
LIEUTENANT I do not know what witchcraft's in him, but
    Your soldiers use him as the grace fore meat,
    Their talk at table, and their thanks at end;
5 And you are darkened° in this action, sir,   *overshadowed*
    Even by your own.°   *(followers)*
AUFIDIUS   I cannot help it now,
    Unless by using means° I lame the foot   *stratagems*
    Of our design. He bears himself more proudlier,
    Even to my person, than I thought he would
10 When first I did embrace him. Yet his nature
    In that's no changeling,° and I must excuse   *waverer*
    What cannot be amended.
LIEUTENANT   Yet I wish, sir—
    I mean for your particular°—you had not   *own sake*
    Joined in commission° with him, but either   *command*
15 Have borne the action of yourself
    Or else to him had left it solely.
AUFIDIUS I understand thee well, and be thou sure,
    When he shall come to his account,[1] he knows not
    What I can urge against him, although it seems,
20 And so he thinks, and is no less apparent
    To th' vulgar eye, that he bears all things fairly
    And shows good husbandry for the Volscian state,
    Fights dragon-like, and does achieve as soon
    As draw his sword, yet he hath left undone
25 That which shall break his neck or hazard mine
    Whene'er we come to our account.
LIEUTENANT Sir, I beseech you, think you he'll carry° Rome?   *defeat*
AUFIDIUS All places yield to him ere he sits down,°   *lays siege*
    And the nobility of Rome are his.
30 The senators and patricians love him too.
    The tribunes are no soldiers, and their people
    Will be as rash in the repeal° as hasty   *recall from exile*
    To expel him thence. I think he'll be to Rome

4.7 Location: The Volscian camp near Rome.   1. That is, with the Volscian state.

As is the osprey to the fish, who takes it
35   By sovereignty of nature.[2] First he was
A noble servant to them, but he could not
Carry his honors even.° Whether 'twas pride,   *equably*
Which out of daily fortune[3] ever taints
The happy° man; whether defect of judgment,   *fortunate*
40   To fail in the disposing of those chances
Which he was lord of; or whether nature,
Not to be other than one thing, not moving
From th' casque° to th' cushion,° but commanding peace   *helmet / Senate seat*
Even with the same austerity and garb°   *stern demeanor*
45   As he controlled the war; but one of these—
As he hath spices° of them all, not all,   *touches*
For I dare so far free him[4]—made him feared,
So hated, and so banished. But he has a merit
To choke it in the utt'rance.[5] So our virtues
50   Lie in th'interpretation of the time,°   *contemporary observers*
And power, unto itself most commendable,
Hath not a tomb so evident as a chair
T'extol what it hath done.[6]
One fire drives out one fire; one nail, one nail;
55   Rights by rights falter, strengths by strengths do fail.
Come, let's away. When, Caius, Rome is thine,
Thou art poor'st of all; then shortly art thou mine.   *Exeunt.*

5.1

Enter MENENIUS, COMINIUS, SICINIUS [*and*] BRUTUS,
the two tribunes, with others.

MENENIUS   No, I'll not go. You hear what he hath said
Which was sometime his general,° who loved him   *(Cominius)*
In a most dear particular.° He called me "Father,"   *affectionate regard*
But what o'that? Go, you that banished him;
5   A mile before his tent fall down and knee°   *crawl*
The way into his mercy. Nay, if he coyed°   *was reluctant*
To hear Cominius speak, I'll keep at home.
COMINIUS   He would not seem° to know me.   *pretended not*
MENENIUS [*to the tribunes*]   Do you hear?
COMINIUS   Yet one time he did call me by my name.
10   I urged our old acquaintance and the drops
That we have bled together. "Coriolanus"
He would not answer to; forbade all names.
He was a kind of nothing, titleless,
Till he had forged himself a name o'th' fire
Of burning Rome.
15   MENENIUS [*to the tribunes*]   Why, so; you have made good work!
A pair of tribunes, that have wrecked° fair Rome   *destroyed*
To make coals cheap. A noble memory!°   *memorial*

---

2. Fish were imagined to surrender to ospreys without a struggle.
3. As a result of repeated successes.
4. For I'm sure he's not guilty of all these vices.
5. *he has . . . utt'rance:* his merit is so great that it overwhelms the recital of his faults; alternatively, his merit is of a kind that impedes attempts to praise it.

6. *Hath not . . . done:* a confusing passage, perhaps meaning, Will fall into certain oblivion unless it receives praise from the public rostrum; alternatively, is clearly ruined by public praise. In the first case, power requires reputation; in the second, reputation threatens power.
5.1 Location: A public place in Rome.

COMINIUS   I minded him how royal 'twas to pardon
          When it was less expected. He replied

20   It was a bare° petition of a state   worthless; barefaced
          To one whom they had punished.

MENENIUS   Very well.
          Could he say less?

COMINIUS   I offered° to awaken his regard   tried
          For 's private friends. His answer to me was
          He could not stay to pick them in° a pile   pick them out from

25   Of noisome musty chaff. He said 'twas folly
          For one poor grain or two to leave unburnt
          And still to nose° th'offense.   smell

MENENIUS   For one poor grain or two?
          I am one of those; his mother, wife, his child,
          And this brave fellow too: we are the grains;

30   [to the tribunes] You are the musty chaff, and you are smelt
          Above the moon. We must be burnt for you.

SICINIUS   Nay, pray be patient. If you refuse your aid
          In this so never-needed help, yet do not
          Upbraid's with our distress. But sure if you

35   Would be your country's pleader, your good tongue,
          More than the instant army we can make,[1]
          Might stop our countryman.

MENENIUS   No, I'll not meddle.

SICINIUS   Pray you, go to him.

MENENIUS   What should I do?

BRUTUS   Only make trial what your love can do

40   For Rome towards Martius.

MENENIUS   Well, and say that Martius return me
          As Cominius is returned, unheard: what then?
          But as a discontented friend, grief-shot°   grief-stricken
          With his unkindness? Say't be so?

SICINIUS   Yet your good will

45   Must have that thanks from Rome after the measure
          As° you intended well.   To the extent that

MENENIUS   I'll undertake't.
          I think he'll hear me. Yet to bite his lip°   (in anger)
          And hum at good Cominius much unhearts me.
          He was not taken well;[2] he had not dined.

50   The veins unfilled, our blood is cold, and then
          We pout upon the morning, are unapt
          To give or to forgive; but when we have stuffed
          These pipes and these conveyances° of our blood   channels
          With wine and feeding, we have suppler souls

55   Than in our priest-like fasts. Therefore I'll watch him
          Till he be dieted° to my request,   made amenable by food
          And then I'll set upon him.

BRUTUS   You know the very road into his kindness
          And cannot lose your way.

MENENIUS   Good faith, I'll prove° him,   try

60   Speed° how it will. I shall ere long have knowledge   Turn out
          Of my success.°   whether I succeed
                                                          Exit.

---

1. The army we can raise right now.   2. Not tackled at the right time.

COMINIUS He'll never hear him.

SICINIUS Not?

COMINIUS I tell you, he does sit in gold, his eye
Red as 'twould burn Rome, and his injury[3]
The jailer to his pity. I kneeled before him;
65 'Twas very faintly he said "Rise," dismissed me
Thus with his speechless hand. What he would do
He sent in writing after me; what he would not,
Bound with an oath to yield to his conditions.
So that all hope is vain,
70 Unless his noble mother and his wife
Who, as I hear, mean to solicit him
For mercy to his country. Therefore let's hence,
And with our fair entreaties haste them on.   *Exeunt.*

5.2

Enter MENENIUS *to the* WATCH *or* Guard.

FIRST WATCHMAN Stay. Whence are you?

SECOND WATCHMAN   Stand, and go back.

MENENIUS You guard like men; 'tis well. But, by your leave,
I am an officer of state and come
To speak with Coriolanus.

FIRST WATCHMAN   From whence?

MENENIUS   From Rome.

5 FIRST WATCHMAN You may not pass; you must return. Our general
Will no more hear from thence.

SECOND WATCHMAN You'll see your Rome embraced with fire before
You'll speak with Coriolanus.

MENENIUS   Good my friends,
If you have heard your general talk of Rome
10 And of his friends there, it is lots to blanks°   *the odds are*
My name hath touched your ears: it is Menenius.

FIRST WATCHMAN Be it so, go back. The virtue° of your name   *power*
Is not here passable.[1]

MENENIUS   I tell thee, fellow,
Thy general is my lover.° I have been   *friend*
15 The book° of his good acts whence men have read   *recorder*
His fame unparalleled happily amplified,
For I have ever verified[2] my friends,
Of whom he's chief, with all the size° that verity   *amplitude*
Would without lapsing suffer.° Nay, sometimes,   *erring allow*
20 Like to a bowl upon a subtle° ground,   *misleading*
I have tumbled past the throw,[3] and in his praise
Have almost stamped the leasing.[4] Therefore, fellow,
I must have leave to pass.

FIRST WATCHMAN Faith, sir, if you had told as many lies in his
25 behalf as you have uttered words in your own, you should
not pass here, no, though it were as virtuous to lie as to live
chastely.[5] Therefore go back.

---

3. The wrong inflicted on him.
5.2 Location: The Volscian camp near Rome.
1. Current (like a coin); effective (as a password).
2. Testified to the character of.

3. Overshot the mark (from the game of bowls).
4. Authenticated falsehood.
5. Honestly (but playing on "lies with a sexual partner").

MENENIUS   Prithee, fellow, remember my name is Menenius,
   always factionary on° the party of your general.   *adherent to*
30   SECOND WATCHMAN   Howsoever you have been his liar, as you
   say you have, I am one that, telling true under him, must say
   you cannot pass. Therefore go back.
MENENIUS   Has he dined, canst thou tell? For I would not
   speak with him till after dinner.
35   FIRST WATCHMAN   You are a Roman, are you?
MENENIUS   I am, as thy general is.
FIRST WATCHMAN   Then you should hate Rome, as he does.
   Can you, when you have pushed out your gates the very
   defender of them and—in a violent popular ignorance—
40   given your enemy your shield, think to front° his revenges   *confront*
   with the easy[6] groans of old women, the virginal palms of
   your daughters, or with the palsied intercession of such a
   decayed dotant° as you seem to be? Can you think to blow   *old fool*
   out the intended fire your city is ready to flame in with such
45   weak breath as this? No, you are deceived. Therefore back to
   Rome and prepare for your execution. You are condemned;
   our general has sworn you out of reprieve and pardon.
MENENIUS   Sirrah,° if thy captain knew I were here,   *(addressed to an inferior)*
   He would use me with estimation.°   *esteem*
50   FIRST WATCHMAN   Come, my captain knows you not.
MENENIUS   I mean thy general.
FIRST WATCHMAN   My general cares not for you. Back, I say,
   go, lest I let forth your half-pint of blood. Back, that's the
   utmost of your having.° Back!   *the most you'll get*
55   MENENIUS   Nay, but fellow, fellow—
        Enter CORIOLANUS *with* AUFIDIUS.
CORIOLANUS   What's the matter?
MENENIUS   Now, you companion,° I'll say an errand° for you.   *knave / deliver a message*
   You shall know now that I am in estimation; you shall per-
   ceive that a jack guardant° cannot office[7] me from my son   *uncouth guard*
60   Coriolanus, guess but my entertainment with him. If thou
   stand'st not i'th' state of hanging or of some death more long in
   spectatorship and crueller in suffering, behold now presently
   and swoon for what's to come upon thee. [*to* CORIOLANUS]
   The glorious gods sit in hourly synod° about thy particular   *council*
65   prosperity and love thee no worse than thy old father Menenius does. [*Weeping*] O my son, my son! Thou art preparing
   fire for us. Look thee, here's water to quench it. I was hardly°   *with difficulty*
   moved to come to thee, but being assured none but myself
   could move thee, I have been blown out of your gates with
70   sighs and conjure thee to pardon Rome and thy petitionary°   *suppliant*
   countrymen. The good gods assuage thy wrath and turn the
   dregs of it upon this varlet here, this, who like a block° hath   *blockhead; obstruction*
   denied my access to thee.
CORIOLANUS   Away!
75   MENENIUS   How? Away?
CORIOLANUS   Wife, mother, child, I know not. My affairs
   Are servanted° to others. Though I owe   *subjected*

---

6. Easily obtained; insignificant.   7. Officiously keep.

My revenge properly,[8] my remission° lies
In Volscian breasts. That we have been familiar,
80 Ingrate forgetfulness shall poison rather
Than pity note how much.[9] Therefore be gone.
Mine ears against your suits are stronger than
Your gates against my force. Yet, for° I loved thee,
 [*He gives him a letter.*]
Take this along. I writ it for thy sake
85 And would have sent it. Another word, Menenius,
I will not hear thee speak. —This man, Aufidius,
Was my beloved in Rome, yet thou behold'st.
AUFIDIUS   You keep a constant temper.
                    Exeunt [CORIOLANUS *and* AUFIDIUS].
         The Guard and MENENIUS *remain.*
FIRST WATCHMAN   Now, sir, is your name Menenius?
90 SECOND WATCHMAN   'Tis a spell, you see, of much power. You
   know the way home again.
FIRST WATCHMAN   Do you hear how we are shent° for keeping
   your greatness back?
SECOND WATCHMAN   What cause do you think I have to
95 swoon?
MENENIUS   I neither care for th' world nor your general. For
   such things as you, I can scarce think there's any, you're so
   slight. He that hath a will to die by himself° fears it not from
   another. Let your general do his worst. For you, be that you
100 are, long,[1] and your misery increase with your age. I say to
   you, as I was said to, "Away!"   *Exit.*
FIRST WATCHMAN   A noble fellow, I warrant him.
SECOND WATCHMAN   The worthy fellow is our general.
   He's the rock, the oak not to be wind-shaken.
                                  Exeunt WATCH.

5.3

Enter CORIOLANUS *and* AUFIDIUS [*with others*].
CORIOLANUS   We will before the walls of Rome tomorrow
Set down our host.° My partner in this action,
You must report to th' Volscian lords how plainly
I have borne this business.
AUFIDIUS   Only their ends
5 You have respected, stopped your ears against
The general suit of Rome, never admitted
A private whisper, no, not with such friends
That thought them sure of you.
CORIOLANUS   This last old man,
Whom with a cracked heart I have sent to Rome,
10 Loved me above the measure of a father,
Nay, godded° me indeed. Their latest refuge°
Was to send him, for whose old love I have—
Though I showed sourly to him—once more offered

forgiveness

because

scolded

at his own hand

Lay siege with our forces

deified / last hope

---

8. *owe . . . properly:* possess my own power of revenge.
9. *That we . . . much:* The memory of our friendship shall be poisoned by Rome's (alternatively, my own) ungrateful forgetfulness, rather than compassion be awakened by my awareness of how intimate we were.
1. *be that you are, long:* remain (as bad) as you are for a long time.
5.3 Location: Scene continues.

The first conditions, which they did refuse
15 And cannot now accept, to grace him only
That thought he could do more. A very little
I have yielded to. Fresh embassies and suits,
Nor from the state nor private friends, hereafter
Will I lend ear to.
          Shout within.
                    Ha? What shout is this?
20 Shall I be tempted to infringe my vow
In the same time 'tis made? I will not.
          Enter VIRGILIA, VOLUMNIA, VALERIA, YOUNG MARTIUS,
            with Attendants.
My wife comes foremost, then the honored mould
Wherein this trunk° was framed, and in her hand   body
The grandchild to her blood. But out, affection;
25 All bond and privilege of nature break!
Let it be virtuous to be obstinate.
          [VIRGILIA *curtsies.*]
What is that curtsy worth? Or those doves' eyes
Which can make gods forsworn? I melt, and am not
Of stronger earth than others. My mother bows,
30 As if Olympus to a molehill should
In supplication nod, and my young boy
Hath an aspect of intercession,° which   pleading look
Great Nature cries, "Deny not!" Let the Volsces
Plow Rome and harrow Italy, I'll never
35 Be such a gosling° to obey instinct, but stand   (foolish) baby goose
As if a man were author of himself
And knew no other kin.
VIRGILIA   My lord and husband.
CORIOLANUS   These eyes are not the same I wore in Rome.
VIRGILIA   The sorrow that delivers° us thus changed   presents
Makes you think so.
40 CORIOLANUS   Like a dull actor now
I have forgot my part and I am out,°   at a loss
Even to a full disgrace. Best of my flesh,
Forgive my tyranny, but do not say
For that, "Forgive our Romans."
          [*They kiss.*][1]
                    Oh, a kiss
45 Long as my exile, sweet as my revenge!
Now, by the jealous queen of heaven,[2] that kiss
I carried from thee, dear, and my true lip
Hath virgined it e'er since. —You gods, I prate,
And the most noble mother of the world
50 Leave unsaluted. Sink, my knee, i'th' earth;
          [*He*] *kneels.*
Of thy deep duty, more impression° show   indentation; effect
Than that of common sons.
VOLUMNIA   Oh, stand up blessed,
          [*He rises.*]

1. TEXTUAL COMMENT It is not clear from the Folio   2. Juno, queen of the gods and guardian of
SD who initiates the kiss; for the significance of the   marriage.
ambiguity, see Digital Edition TC 10.

Whilst with no softer cushion than the flint
I kneel before thee,
    [*She kneels.*]
           and unproperly°   *against propriety*
55   Show duty as mistaken all this while
Between the child and parent.
CORIOLANUS   What's this?
Your knees to me? To your corrected[3] son?
    [*He raises her to her feet.*]
Then let the pebbles on the hungry beach
Fillip° the stars; then let the mutinous winds   *Strike against*
60   Strike the proud cedars gainst the fiery sun,
Murd'ring[4] impossibility, to make
What cannot be slight work.[5]
VOLUMNIA   Thou art my warrior;
I holp to frame° thee. [*indicating* VALERIA] Do you know this   *helped to make*
  lady?
CORIOLANUS   The noble sister of Publicola,
65   The moon° of Rome, chaste as the icicle   *(emblem of chastity)*
That's curdied° by the frost from purest snow   *crystallized*
And hangs on Dian's[6] temple. Dear Valeria!
VOLUMNIA [*indicating* YOUNG MARTIUS]   This is a poor epitome°   *short version*
  of yours,
Which by th'interpretation of full time[7]
May show like all yourself.
70   CORIOLANUS   The god of soldiers,
With the consent of supreme Jove, inform
Thy thoughts with nobleness, that thou mayst prove
To shame unvulnerable and stick° i'th' wars   *stand firm*
Like a great sea-mark, standing every flaw[8]
And saving those that eye thee.
75   VOLUMNIA [*to* YOUNG MARTIUS]   Your knee, sirrah.
    [YOUNG MARTIUS *kneels.*]
CORIOLANUS   That's my brave boy!
VOLUMNIA   Even he, your wife, this lady, and myself
Are suitors to you.
CORIOLANUS   I beseech you, peace;
Or if you'd ask, remember this before:
80   The thing I have forsworn to grant may never
Be held by you denials.[9] Do not bid me
Dismiss my soldiers or capitulate°   *come to terms*
Again with Rome's mechanics.° Tell me not   *workmen*
Wherein I seem unnatural. Desire not
85   T'allay my rages and revenges with
Your colder reasons.
VOLUMNIA   Oh, no more, no more.
You have said you will not grant us anything,
For we have nothing else to ask but that
Which you deny already. Yet we will ask,

---

3. Rebuked (by Volumnia's irony).
4. Putting an end to the idea of.
5. An easy task of what cannot be.
6. Diana, goddess of the moon and chastity.

7. When time has clarified its full meaning.
8. Like a landmark at sea, withstanding every gust.
9. Be regarded by you as refusals.

90   That, if you fail in our request, the blame
        May hang upon your hardness. Therefore hear us.
     CORIOLANUS   Aufidius and you Volsces, mark, for we'll
        Hear naught from Rome in private.
            [*He sits.*]
                                        Your request?
     VOLUMNIA   Should we be silent and not speak, our raiment
95   And state of bodies would bewray° what life   *divulge*
        We have led since thy exile. Think with thyself
        How more unfortunate than all living women
        Are we come hither, since that thy sight, which should
        Make our eyes flow with joy, hearts dance with comforts,
100   Constrains them weep and shake with fear and sorrow,
        Making the mother, wife, and child to see
        The son, the husband, and the father tearing
        His country's bowels out; and to poor we
        Thine enmity's most capital.° Thou barr'st us   *fatal*
105   Our prayers to the gods, which is a comfort
        That all but we enjoy. For how can we,
        Alas, how can we for our country pray,
        Whereto we are bound, together with thy victory,
        Whereto we are bound? Alack, or° we must lose   *either*
110   The country, our dear nurse, or else thy person,
        Our comfort in the country. We must find
        An evident° calamity, though we had   *A certain*
        Our wish which side should win. For either thou
        Must as a foreign recreant° be led   *traitor*
115   With manacles through our streets, or else
        Triumphantly tread on thy country's ruin
        And bear the palm for having bravely shed
        Thy wife and children's blood. For myself, son,
        I purpose not to wait on fortune till
120   These wars determine.° If I cannot persuade thee   *conclude*
        Rather to show a noble grace to both parts°   *sides*
        Than seek the end of one, thou shalt no sooner
        March to assault thy country than to tread—
        Trust to't, thou shalt not—on thy mother's womb
        That brought thee to this world.
125 VIRGILIA   Ay, and mine,
        That brought you forth this boy to keep your name
        Living to time.
     YOUNG MARTIUS   'A° shall not tread on me.   *He*
        I'll run away till I am bigger, but then I'll fight.
     CORIOLANUS   Not of a woman's tenderness to be
130   Requires nor child nor woman's face to see.[1]
        I have sat too long.
            [*He rises.*]
     VOLUMNIA   Nay, go not from us thus.
        If it were so that our request did tend
        To save the Romans, thereby to destroy
        The Volsces whom you serve, you might condemn us
135   As poisonous of your honor. No, our suit

---

1. *Not . . . see:* To avoid having a woman's tenderness, a man must not see a child's or woman's face.

Is that you reconcile them, while the Volsces
May say, "This mercy we have showed," the Romans,
"This we received," and each in either side
Give the all-hail to thee and cry, "Be blessed
140 For making up this peace!" Thou know'st, great son,
The end of war's uncertain, but this certain,
That if thou conquer Rome, the benefit
Which thou shalt thereby reap is such a name
Whose repetition will be dogged with curses,
145 Whose chronicle thus writ:[2] "The man was noble,
But with his last attempt he wiped it out,
Destroyed his country, and his name remains
To th'ensuing age abhorred." Speak to me, son.
Thou hast affected° the fine strains° of honor,   *cherished / qualities*
150 To imitate the graces of the gods,
To tear with thunder the wide cheeks o'th' air,
And yet to charge thy sulfur[3] with a bolt
That should but rive[4] an oak. Why dost not speak?
Think'st thou it honorable for a noble man
155 Still° to remember wrongs? —Daughter, speak you;   *Perpetually*
He cares not for your weeping. —Speak thou, boy;
Perhaps thy childishness will move him more
Than can our reasons. There's no man in the world
More bound to 's mother, yet here he lets me prate
160 Like one i'th' stocks.[5] —Thou hast never in thy life
Showed thy dear mother any courtesy,
When she, poor hen, fond of° no second brood,   *desiring*
Has clucked thee to the wars and safely home,
Loaden with honor. Say my request's unjust
165 And spurn me back, but if it be not so,
Thou art not honest, and the gods will plague thee
That thou restrain'st° from me the duty which   *withhold'st*
To a mother's part belongs. —He turns away.
Down, ladies. Let us shame him with our knees.
170 To his surname Coriolanus 'longs° more pride   *belongs*
Than pity to our prayers.[6] Down! An end;
          [*They kneel.*]
This is the last. So, we will home to Rome
And die among our neighbors. [*to* CORIOLANUS] Nay, behold's.
This boy, that cannot tell what he would have
175 But kneels and holds up hands for fellowship,
Does reason our petition with more strength
Than thou hast to deny't. —Come, let us go.
          [*They rise.*]
This fellow had a Volscian to his mother;
His wife is in Corioles, and his child
180 Like him by chance. —Yet give us our dispatch.[7]
I am hushed until our city be afire,
And then I'll speak a little.

---

2. Whose biography will thus be written.
3. To discharge thy thunder (like Jupiter, king of the gods, whose tree was the oak).
4. Tear (destroy a tree, not human beings).
5. *prate . . . stocks*: rail pointlessly like a prisoner sentenced to public humiliation in the stocks.
6. Volumnia reinterprets the name as a sign of allegiance to Corioles.
7. Dismissal (with wordplay on "deathblow").

[He] holds her by the hand, silent.

CORIOLANUS   O mother, mother!
What have you done?[8] Behold, the heavens do ope,
The gods look down, and this unnatural scene
185   They laugh at. O my mother, mother! O!
You have won a happy victory to Rome;
But for your son—believe it, oh, believe it—
Most dangerously you have with him prevailed,
If not most mortal to him. But let it come.
190   —Aufidius, though I cannot make true° wars,   (as I vowed)
I'll frame convenient° peace. Now, good Aufidius,   suitable
Were you in my stead, would you have heard
A mother less? Or granted less, Aufidius?
AUFIDIUS   I was moved withal.°   as well
CORIOLANUS   I dare be sworn you were,
195   And, sir, it is no little thing to make
Mine eyes to sweat compassion. But, good sir,
What peace you'll make, advise me. For my part,
I'll not to Rome; I'll back with you, and pray you
Stand to° me in this cause. —O mother! Wife!   by
200   AUFIDIUS *[aside]*   I am glad thou hast set thy mercy and thy honor
At difference in thee. Out of that I'll work
Myself a former fortune.[9]
CORIOLANUS *[to the ladies]*   Ay, by and by;
But we will drink together, and you shall bear
A better witness back than words, which we,
205   On like conditions, will have counter-sealed.
Come, enter with us. Ladies, you deserve
To have a temple built you. All the swords
In Italy and her confederate arms
Could not have made this peace.   *Exeunt.*

5.4

Enter MENENIUS *and* SICINIUS.

MENENIUS   See you yond quoin° o'th' Capitol, yond
    cornerstone?   corner
SICINIUS   Why, what of that?
MENENIUS   If it be possible for you to displace it with your little
5   finger, there is some hope the ladies of Rome, especially his
    mother, may prevail with him. But I say there is no hope in't.
    Our throats are sentenced and stay upon° execution.   wait for
SICINIUS   Is't possible that so short a time can alter the condi-
    tion° of a man?   character
10   MENENIUS   There is differency between a grub and a butter-
    fly, yet your butterfly was a grub. This Martius is grown from
    man to dragon. He has wings; he's more than a creeping
    thing.
SICINIUS   He loved his mother dearly.
15   MENENIUS   So did he me, and he no more remembers his
    mother now than° an eight-year-old horse. The tartness of   than does
    his face sours ripe grapes. When he walks, he moves like an

---

8. PERFORMANCE COMMENT The dramatic confrontation between Volumnia and Coriolanus may be
variously staged; see Digital Edition PC 3 for some of

the possibilities.
9. *work . . . fortune:* regain my former preeminence.
5.4 Location: A public place in Rome.

engine,° and the ground shrinks before his treading. He is
able to pierce a corslet° with his eye, talks like a knell, and

20 his hum is a battery.° He sits in his state as a thing made for
Alexander.¹ What he bids be done is finished with his bidding. He wants° nothing of a god but eternity and a heaven
to throne in.

SICINIUS Yes, mercy, if you report him truly.

25 MENENIUS I paint him in the character.° Mark what mercy
his mother shall bring from him. There is no more mercy in
him than there is milk in a male tiger. That shall our poor
city find, and all this is 'long° of you.

SICINIUS The gods be good unto us!

30 MENENIUS No, in such a case the gods will not be good unto
us. When we banished him, we respected not them; and, he
returning to break our necks, they respect not us.

Enter a MESSENGER.

MESSENGER [*to* SICINIUS] Sir, if you'd save your life, fly to your
house.

The plebeians have got your fellow tribune

35 And hale° him up and down, all swearing if
The Roman ladies bring not comfort home,
They'll give him death by inches.°

Enter another MESSENGER.

SICINIUS   What's the news?

SECOND MESSENGER Good news, good news! The ladies have
prevailed,

The Volscians are dislodged,° and Martius gone.

40 A merrier day did never yet greet Rome,
No, not th'expulsion of the Tarquins.

SICINIUS   Friend,
Art thou certain this is true? Is't most certain?

SECOND MESSENGER As certain as I know the sun is fire.
Where have you lurked that you make doubt of it?

45 Ne'er through an arch so hurried the blown° tide
As the recomforted° through th' gates.

Trumpets, hautboys,° drums beat, all together.

                                  Why, hark you!

The trumpets, sackbuts, psalteries,° and fifes,
Tabors° and cymbals and the shouting Romans
Make the sun dance.

A shout within.

                        Hark you!

MENENIUS   This is good news.

50 I will go meet the ladies. This Volumnia
Is worth of consuls, senators, patricians,
A city full; of tribunes such as you,
A sea and land full. You have prayed well today.
This morning for ten thousand of your throats
I'd not have given a doit.°

Sound still with the shouts.

55   Hark how they joy!

SICINIUS [*to* SECOND MESSENGER] First, the gods bless you for
your tidings; next
Accept my thankfulness.

---

1. Sits on his throne like a statue of Alexander the Great (who actually lived after Coriolanus).

SECOND MESSENGER   Sir, we have all great cause to give great
    thanks.
SICINIUS   They are near the city?
SECOND MESSENGER   Almost at point to enter.
60   SICINIUS   We'll meet them and help the joy.   *Exeunt.*

5.5

Enter two SENATORS, *with [the] ladies [*VOLUMNIA,
VIRGILIA, *and* VALERIA], *passing over the stage, with
other* LORDS.

FIRST SENATOR   Behold our patroness, the life of Rome.
    Call all your tribes together, praise the gods,
    And make triumphant fires.° Strew flowers before them,   *(of sacrifice)*
    Unshout the noise that banished Martius;
5   Repeal[1] him with the welcome of his mother.
    Cry, "Welcome, ladies, welcome!"
ALL   Welcome, ladies, welcome!
    A flourish with drums and trumpets. [Exeunt.]

5.6

Enter Tullus AUFIDIUS, *with Attendants.*
AUFIDIUS   Go, tell the lords o'th' city I am here.
    Deliver them this paper. Having read it,
    Bid them repair to th' market-place, where I,
    Even in theirs and in the commons' ears,
5   Will vouch the truth of it. Him I accuse
    The city ports° by this° hath entered and   *gates / this time*
    Intends t'appear before the people, hoping
    To purge himself with words. Dispatch. *[Exeunt Attendants.]*
    Enter three or four CONSPIRATORS *of Aufidius' faction.*
                      Most welcome!
FIRST CONSPIRATOR   How is it with our general?
AUFIDIUS   Even so,
10   As with a man by his own alms empoisoned
    And with his charity slain.
SECOND CONSPIRATOR   Most noble sir,
    If you do hold the same intent wherein
    You wished us parties,° we'll deliver you   *allies*
    Of° your great danger.   *From*
AUFIDIUS   Sir, I cannot tell.
15   We must proceed as we do find the people.
THIRD CONSPIRATOR   The people will remain uncertain whilst
    Twixt you there's difference,° but the fall of either   *disagreement*
    Makes the survivor heir of all.
AUFIDIUS   I know it,
    And my pretext to strike at him admits
20   A good construction.° I raised him, and I pawned   *interpretation*
    Mine honor for his truth, who being so heightened,
    He watered his new plants[1] with dews of flattery,
    Seducing so my friends; and to this end

5.5 Location: Near the city gates of Rome.
1. Recall him from banishment.

5.6 Location: Corioles.
1. Followers (formerly Aufidius's adherents).

He bowed his nature, never known before
25 But to be rough, unswayable, and free.
THIRD CONSPIRATOR   Sir, his stoutness°   *stubbornness*
When he did stand for consul, which he lost
By lack of stooping—
AUFIDIUS   That I would have spoke of.
Being banished for't, he came unto my hearth,
30 Presented to my knife his throat. I took him,
Made him joint-servant° with me, gave him way   *partner*
In all his own desires; nay, let him choose
Out of my files,° his projects to accomplish,   *troops*
My best and freshest men; served his designments°   *plans*
35 In mine own person; holp to reap the fame
Which he did end all his,[2] and took some pride
To do myself this wrong, till at the last
I seemed his follower, not partner, and
He waged° me with his countenance° as if   *paid / appearance*
I had been mercenary.
40 FIRST CONSPIRATOR   So he did, my lord.
The army marveled at it, and in the last,
When he had carried° Rome and that we looked   *was about to vanquish*
For no less spoil than glory—
AUFIDIUS   There was it,
For which my sinews shall be stretched upon him.
45 At a few drops of women's rheum,° which are   *tears*
As cheap as lies, he sold the blood and labor
Of our great action. Therefore shall he die,
And I'll renew me in his fall.
                Drums and trumpets sound, with great shouts of the
                people.
                          But hark!
FIRST CONSPIRATOR   Your native town you entered like a post[3]
50 And had no welcomes home, but he returns
Splitting the air with noise.
SECOND CONSPIRATOR   And patient fools,
Whose children he hath slain, their base throats tear
With giving him glory.
THIRD CONSPIRATOR   Therefore, at your vantage,°   *best opportunity*
Ere he express himself or move the people
55 With what he would say, let him feel your sword,
Which we will second. When he lies along,°   *prostrate*
After your way° his tale pronounced shall bury   *In your version*
His reasons with his body.
AUFIDIUS   Say no more.
Here come the lords.
                Enter the LORDS *of the city.*
ALL LORDS   You are most welcome home.
60 AUFIDIUS   I have not deserved it.
But, worthy lords, have you with heed perused
What I have written to you?
ALL LORDS   We have.

---

2. Which he did conclude was (or did finally make)   3. Messenger (bearing news of Coriolanus).
entirely his own.

FIRST LORD   And grieve to hear't.
What faults he made before the last, I think
Might have found easy fines;° but there to end   *light penalties*
65   Where he was to begin and give away
The benefit of our levies,° answering us   *levied troops*
With our own charge,[4] making a treaty where
There was a yielding, this admits no excuse.
AUFIDIUS   He approaches; you shall hear him.
Enter CORIOLANUS *marching with drum and colors,*
the COMMONERS *being with him.*
70   CORIOLANUS   Hail, lords! I am returned your soldier,
No more infected with my country's love
Than when I parted hence, but still subsisting
Under your great command. You are to know
That prosperously[5] I have attempted and
75   With bloody passage led your wars even to
The gates of Rome. Our spoils we have brought home
Doth more than counterpoise a full third part
The charges of the action.[6] We have made peace
With no less honor to the Antiates
80   Than shame to th' Romans; and we here deliver,
Subscribed by th' consuls and patricians,
Together with the seal o'th' Senate, what
We have compounded° on.   *agreed*
AUFIDIUS   Read it not, noble lords,
But tell the traitor in the highest degree
He hath abused your powers.
85   CORIOLANUS   "Traitor"? How now?
AUFIDIUS   Ay, traitor, Martius.
CORIOLANUS   "Martius"?
AUFIDIUS   Ay, Martius, Caius Martius. Dost thou think
I'll grace thee with that robbery, thy stol'n name,
"Coriolanus," in Corioles?
90   —You lords and heads o'th' state, perfidiously
He has betrayed your business and given up
For certain drops of salt° your city Rome—   *(tears)*
I say "your city"—to his wife and mother,
Breaking his oath and resolution like
95   A twist° of rotten silk, never admitting   *thread*
Counsel o'th' war;[7] but at his nurse's tears
He whined and roared away your victory,
That pages[8] blushed at him and men of heart°   *courage*
Looked wond'ring each at others.
CORIOLANUS   Hear'st thou, Mars?
AUFIDIUS   Name not the god, thou boy of tears.
CORIOLANUS   Ha?
100   AUFIDIUS   No more.
CORIOLANUS   Measureless liar, thou hast made my heart

4. *answering . . . charge:* rewarding us with our own
costs (of mounting the campaign); answering accusations by saying that he acted on our authority.
5. Successfully; with gain of wealth.
6. *Our spoils . . . action:* The value of our plunder

outweighs by more than a third the costs of the war.
7. *admitting . . . war:* taking any advice about the
war.
8. Youthful servants.

Too great for what contains it. "Boy"? O slave!
—Pardon me, lords, 'tis the first time that ever
I was forced to scold. Your judgments, my grave lords,
105 Must give this cur the lie, and his own notion°—   *awareness of the truth*
Who wears my stripes° impressed upon him, that   *wounds*
Must bear my beating to his grave—shall join
To thrust° the lie unto him.   *turn the accusation of*
FIRST LORD   Peace, both, and hear me speak.
110 CORIOLANUS   Cut me to pieces, Volsces; men and lads,
Stain all your edges° on me. "Boy"! False hound!   *sword blades*
If you have writ your annals true, 'tis there
That, like an eagle in a dovecote,° I   *pigeon house*
Fluttered your Volscians in Corioles.
Alone I did it. "Boy"!
115 AUFIDIUS   Why, noble lords,
Will you be put in mind of his blind[9] fortune,
Which was your shame, by this unholy braggart,
Fore your own eyes and ears?
ALL CONSPIRATORS   Let him die for't.
COMMONERS [*variously*]   Tear him to pieces! Do it presently!°   *immediately*
120 —He killed my son! —My daughter! —He killed my cousin
Marcus! —He killed my father!
SECOND LORD   Peace, ho! No outrage.° Peace!   *violence*
The man is noble, and his fame folds in°   *envelops*
This orb o'th' earth. His last offenses to us
125 Shall have judicious hearing. —Stand,° Aufidius,   *Hold off*
And trouble not the peace.
CORIOLANUS   Oh, that I had him,
With six Aufidiuses, or more, his tribe,
To use my lawful sword.
AUFIDIUS   Insolent villain.
ALL CONSPIRATORS   Kill, kill, kill, kill, kill him!
      The CONSPIRATORS *draw [their swords] and kill*
      MARTIUS, *who falls;* AUFIDIUS *stands on him.*
LORDS   Hold, hold, hold, hold!
AUFIDIUS   My noble masters, hear me speak.
130 FIRST LORD   O Tullus.
SECOND LORD   Thou hast done a deed whereat valor will weep.
THIRD LORD   Tread not upon him. Masters all, be quiet.
Put up your swords.
AUFIDIUS   My lords, when you shall know—as in this rage
135 Provoked by him you cannot—the great danger
Which this man's life did owe° you, you'll rejoice   *hold in store for*
That he is thus cut off. Please it your honors
To call me to your senate, I'll deliver°   *show*
Myself your loyal servant or endure
Your heaviest censure.
140 FIRST LORD   Bear from hence his body
And mourn you for him. Let him be regarded
As the most noble corpse that ever herald
Did follow to his urn.

---

9. Random (fortune was commonly personified as blind).

SECOND LORD   His own impatience
Takes from Aufidius a great part of blame.
Let's make the best of it.
145   AUFIDIUS   My rage is gone,
And I am struck with sorrow. —Take him up.
Help, three o'th' chiefest soldiers; I'll be one.
Beat thou the drum that it speak mournfully;
Trail your steel pikes. Though in this city he
150   Hath widowed and unchilded many a one,
Which to this hour bewail the injury,
Yet he shall have a noble memory.° Assist.   memorial

                    Exeunt, bearing the body of MARTIUS,
                          a dead march sounded.

APPENDICES

APPENDICES

Early Modern Map Culture

In the early modern period, maps were often considered rare and precious objects, and seeing a map could be an important and life-changing event. This was so for Richard Hakluyt, whose book *The Principal Navigations, Voyages, Traffics and Discoveries of the English Nation* (1598–1600) was the first major collection of narratives describing England's overseas trading ventures. Hakluyt tells how, as a boy still at school in London, he visited his uncle's law chambers and saw a book of cosmography lying open there. Perceiving his nephew's interest in the maps, the uncle turned to a modern map and "pointed with his wand to all the knowen Seas, Gulfs, Bayes, Straights, Capes, Rivers, Empires, Kingdomes, Dukedomes, and Territories of ech part, with declaration also of their speciall commodities and particular wants, which by the benefit of traffike, and entercourse of merchants, are plentifully supplied. From the Mappe he brought me to the Bible, and turning to the 107 Psalme, directed mee to the 23 and 24 verses, where I read, that they which go downe to the sea in ships, and occupy [work] by the great waters, they see the works of the Lord, and his woonders in the deepe." This event, Hakluyt records, made so deep an impression on him that he vowed he would devote his life to the study of this kind of knowledge. *The Principal Navigations* was the result, a book that mixes a concern with the profit to be made from trade and from geographical knowledge with praise for the Christian god who made the "great waters" and, in Hakluyt's view, looked with special favor on the English merchants and sailors who voyaged over them.

In the early modern period, access to maps was far less easy than it is today. Before the advent of printing in the late fifteenth century, maps were drawn and decorated by hand. Because they were rare and expensive, these medieval maps were for the most part owned by the wealthy and the powerful. Sometimes adorned with pictures of fabulous sea monsters and exotic creatures, maps often revealed the Christian worldview of those who composed them. Jerusalem appeared squarely in the middle of many maps (called T and O maps), with Asia, Africa, and Europe, representing the rest of the known world, arranged symmetrically around the Holy City. Because they had not yet been discovered by Europeans, North and South America were not depicted.

Mapping practices changed markedly during the late fifteenth and sixteenth centuries both because of the advent of print and also because European nations such as Portugal and Spain began sending ships on long sea voyages to open new trade routes to the East and, eventually, to the Americas. During this period, monarchs competed to have the best cartographers supply them with accurate maps of their realms and especially of lands in Africa, Asia, or the Americas, where they hoped to trade or plant settlements. Such knowledge was precious and jealously guarded. The value of such maps and the secrecy that surrounded them are indicated by a story in Hakluyt's *Principal Navigations*. An English ship had captured a Portuguese vessel in the Azores, and a map was discovered among the ship's valuable cargo, which included spices, silks, carpets, porcelain, and other exotic commercial objects. The map was "inclosed in a case of sweete Cedar wood, and lapped up almost an hundred fold in fine calicut-cloth, as though it had been some incomparable jewell." The value of the map and an explanation for the careful way in which it was packed lay in the particular information it afforded the English about Portuguese trading routes. More than beautiful objects, maps like this one were crucial to the international race to find safe sea routes to the most profitable trading centers in the East.

In the sixteenth century, books of maps began to be printed, making them more affordable for ordinary people, though some of these books, published as big folio volumes, remained too dear for any but wealthy patrons to buy. Yet maps were increasingly a part of daily life, and printing made many of them more accessible. Playgoers in Shakespeare's audiences must have understood in general the value and uses of maps, for they appear as props in a number of his plays. Most famously, at the beginning of *King Lear*, the old king has a map brought onstage showing the extent of his kingdom. He then points on the map to the three separate parts into which he intends to divide his realm to share among his daughters. The map, often unfurled with a flourish on a table or held up for view by members of Lear's retinue, signals the crucial relationship of the land to the monarch. He is his domains, and the map signifies his possession of them. To divide the kingdom, in essence to tear apart the map, would have been judged foolish and destructive by early modern political theorists. Similarly, in *1 Henry IV*, when rebels against the sitting monarch, Henry IV, plot to overthrow him, they bring a map onstage in order to decide what part of the kingdom will be given to each rebel leader. Their proposed dismemberment of the realm signifies the danger they pose. Treasonously, they would rend in pieces the body of the commonwealth.

Maps, of course, had other uses besides signifying royal domains. In some instances, they were used pragmatically to help people find their way from one place to another. A very common kind of map, a portolan chart, depicted in minute detail the coastline of a particular body of water. Used by sailors, these maps frequently were made by people native to the region they described. Many world or regional maps, because they were beautifully decorated and embellished with vivid colors, were used for decorative purposes. John Dee, a learned adviser to Queen Elizabeth and a great book collector, wrote that some people used maps "to beautifie their Halls, Parlers, Chambers, Galeries, Studies, or Libraries." He also spoke of more scholarly uses for these objects. They could, for example, be useful aids in the study of history or geography, enabling people to locate "thinges past, as battels fought, earthquakes, heavenly fyringes, and such occurents in histories mentioned." Today we make similar use of maps, like those included in this volume, when, in reading Shakespeare's plays, we resort to a map to find out where the Battle of Agincourt took place or where Othello sailed when he left Venice for Cyprus.

The print edition of *The Norton Shakespeare* includes five maps; the Digital Edition seven. Four of these maps, found in both editions, are modern ones drawn specifically to show the location of places important to Shakespeare's plays. They depict the British Isles and western France, London, and the Mediterranean world, in addition to a map of England showing the typical routes the Chamberlain's Men followed when they went on tour outside of London. The print and digital editions also both contain a period map of the Christian Holy Lands at the eastern tip of the Mediterranean Sea. This map was included in what was known as the Bishops' Bible, first printed in London in 1568. Put together under the leadership of the Archbishop of Canterbury, Matthew Parker, working with a committee of Anglican bishops, the 1568 edition featured beautiful typography and illustrations. The text continued to undergo revisions, and twenty editions of it were published between 1568 and 1602.

This last map shows places mentioned in the first four Gospels (Matthew, Mark, Luke, and John), which collectively tell of the life and deeds of Jesus. It indicates, for example, the location of Bethlehem, where he was born; Nazareth, where he spent his youth; and Cana of Galilee, where he turned water into wine at a marriage. It suggests that, to the English reader, this particular territory was overwritten by and completely intertwined with Christian history. Yet in the Mediterranean Sea, on the left of the map, several large ships are visible, reminders of another fact about this region: it was a vigorous trading arena where European Christian merchants did business with local merchants—Christian, Jew, and Muslim—and with traders bringing luxury goods by overland routes from the East. A number of Shakespeare's plays are set in this complex eastern Mediterranean region where several religious traditions laid claim to territory and many commercial powers competed for preeminence. *Pericles*, for example, has a hero who is the ruler of Tyre, a city on the upper right side of the map. In the course of his wanderings, Pericles visits many cities along the eastern coasts of the Mediterranean. The conclusion of the play, in which the hero is reunited both with his long-lost daughter and with the wife he believes dead, has seemed to many critics to share in a sense of Christian miracle, despite its ostensibly pagan setting. *The Comedy of Errors* and parts of *Othello* and of *Antony and Cleopatra* are also set in the Eastern Mediterranean. One of Shakespeare's earliest plays, *The Comedy of Errors*, is an urban comedy in which the protagonists are merchants deeply involved in commercial transactions. It is also the first play in which Shakespeare mentions the Americas, which he does in an extended joke in which he compares parts of a serving woman's body to the countries on a map including Ireland, France, and the Americas. In *Othello*, the eastern Mediterranean island of Cyprus is represented as a tense Christian outpost defending Venetian interests against the Muslim Turks. In *Antony and Cleopatra*, Egypt figures as the site of Eastern luxury and also of imperial conquest, an extension of the Roman Empire. Clearly, this region was to Shakespeare and his audiences one of the most complex and highly charged areas of the world: a site of religious, commercial, and imperial significance.

Two other maps occur only in the Digital Edition, where their colors and their details can be appreciated. The first is a map of London that appeared in a 1574 edition of a famous German atlas, *Civitates Orbis Terrarum* (*Cities of the World*), compiled by George Braun with engravings by Franz Hogenberg. This remarkable atlas includes maps and information on cities throughout Europe, Asia, and North Africa; the first of its six volumes appeared in 1572, the last in 1617. Being included in the volume indicated a city's status as a recognized metropolitan center. In a charming touch, Braun added to his city maps pictures of figures in local dress. At the bottom of the map of London, for example, there are four figures who appear to represent the city's prosperous citizens. In the center, a man in a long robe holds the hand of a soberly dressed matron. On either side of them are younger and more ornately dressed figures. The young man sports a long sword and a short cloak, the woman a dress with elaborate skirts. In the atlas, the map is colored, and the clothes of the two young people echo one another in shades of green and red.

At the time the map was made, London was a rapidly expanding metropolis. In 1550, it contained about 55,000 people; by 1600, it would contain nearly 200,000. The map shows the densely populated old walled city north of the Thames River, in the middle of which was Eastcheap, the commercial district where, in Shakespeare's plays about the reign of Henry IV, Falstaff holds court in a tavern. The map also shows that by 1570 London was spreading westward beyond the wall toward Westminster Palace. This medieval structure, which appears on the extreme left side of the map, was where English monarchs resided when in London and where, at the end of *2 Henry IV*, the king dies in the fabled Jerusalem Chamber of the Westminster complex. On the far right of the map, one can see the Tower of London, where Edward IV's young sons were imprisoned by Richard III, an event depicted in Shakespeare's *The Tragedy of King Richard the Third*. The map also indicates the centrality of the Thames to London's commercial life. It shows the river full of boats; some of those on the east side of London Bridge are large oceangoing vessels with several masts. South of the river, where many of the most famous London theaters, including Shakespeare's Globe, were to be constructed in the 1590s, there are relatively few buildings. By 1600, this would change, as Southwark, as it was known, came to be an increasingly busy entertainment, residential, and commercial district.

The final map, of Great Britain and Ireland, comes from a 1612 edition of John Speed's *The Theatre of the Empire of Great Britain*, an innovative atlas containing individual maps of counties and towns in England and Wales, as well as larger maps that include Scotland and Ireland. Speed was by trade a tailor who increasingly devoted his time to the study of history and cartography. Befriended by the antiquarian scholar William Camden, he eventually won patronage from Sir Fulke Greville, who gave him a pension that allowed him to devote himself full-time to his scholarly endeavors. *The Theatre* was one product of this newfound freedom. The map included here, one of his most ambitious, shows the entire British Isles, nominated by Speed as "The Kingdome of Great Britaine and Ireland," though at this time Ireland was far from under the control of the English crown and Scotland was still an independent kingdom. James I, a Scot by birth, had unsuccessfully tried to forge a formal union between England and Scotland. This problem of the relationship of the parts of the British Isles to one another, and England's assertion of power over the others, is treated in *Henry V*, in which officers from Wales, Ireland, and Scotland are sharply delineated yet all depicted as loyal subjects of the English king.

One striking aspect of Speed's map is the balance it strikes between the two capital cities, London on the left, prominently featuring the Thames and London Bridge, and Edinburgh on the right. This would have pleased James, whose interest in his native country Shakespeare played to in his writing of *Macbeth*, which is based on material from Scottish history. Speed's map acknowledges the claims of the monarch to the territory it depicts. In the upper left corner, the British lion and the Scottish unicorn support a roundel topped with a crown. When James became king of England in 1603, he created this merged symbol of Scottish-English unity. The motto of the Royal Order of the Garter, "*Honi soit qui mal y pense*" (Shamed be he who thinks ill of it), is inscribed around the circumference. In the bottom left corner of the map, another locus of authority is established. Two cherubs, one holding a compass, the other a globe, sit beneath a banner on which is inscribed "Performed by John Speed." If the territory is the monarch's, the craft that depicts it belongs to the tailor turned cartographer.

Today, maps are readily available from shops or on the Internet, but in early modern England they were rare and valuable objects that could generate great excitement in those who owned or beheld them. Along with other precious items, maps were sometimes put on display in libraries and sitting rooms, but they had functions beyond the ornamental. They helped to explain and order the world, indicating who claimed certain domains, showing where the familiar stories of the Bible or of English history occurred, helping merchants find their way to distant markets. As John Dee, the early modern map enthusiast concluded, "Some, for one purpose: and some, for an other, liketh, loveth, getteth, and useth, Mappes, Chartes, and Geographicall Globes."

JEAN E. HOWARD

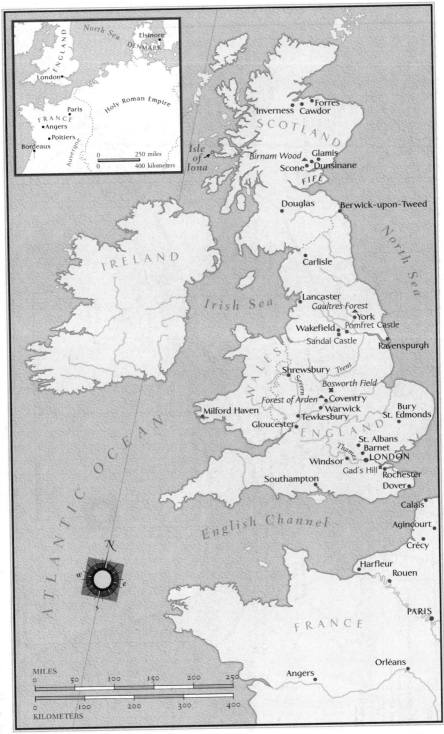

Ireland, Scotland, Wales, England, and Western France: Places Important to Shakespeare's Plays

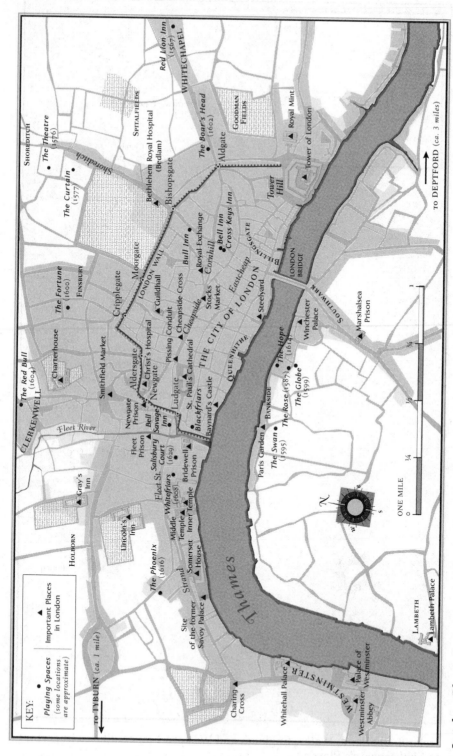

London: Places Important to Shakespeare's Plays and London Playgoing

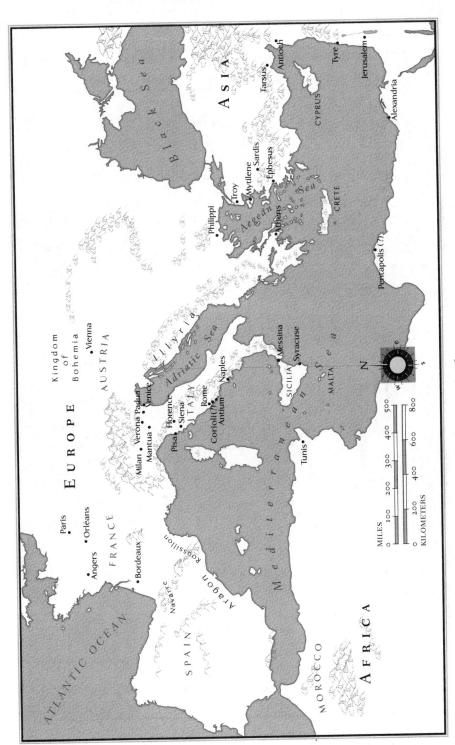

The Mediterranean World: Places Important to Shakespeare's Plays

The Chamberlain's Men and King's Men on Tour (adapted from a map first published by Sally-Beth MacLean in "Tour Routes: 'Provincial Wanderings' or 'Traditional Circuits'?" *Medieval and Renaissance Drama in England 6* [1992]: 1–14).

Map of the Holy Land, from the Bishops' Bible, printed in London, 1568

Documents

The documents in this section provide some early perspectives on Shakespeare's reputation and the works included in this volume. A much more extensive selection of documents can be found in the Digital Edition of *The Norton Shakespeare*, which offers a broad range of contemporary testimony about Shakespeare's character, his art, and the social and institutional conditions under which his art was produced. The first digital section, "Shakespeare and His Works," contains traces of Shakespeare's life and career, evidence of his reputation in the literary community, and a variety of reactions to his plays and poems. The second section, "The Theater Scene," takes a wider view of Shakespeare's professional world with playhouse documents that offer a behind-the-scenes glimpse of companies acquiring scripts and properties, actors rehearsing their parts, and new theaters being constructed, while government documents show dramatic patronage, regulation, and censorship in action.

MISHA TERAMURA

Francis Meres on Shakespeare (1598)

[Francis Meres (1565–1647) was educated at Cambridge and was active in London literary circles in 1597–98, after which he became a rector and schoolmaster in the country. The descriptions of Shakespeare are taken from a section on poetry in *Palladis Tamia. Wits Treasury*, a work largely consisting of translated classical quotations and *exempla*. Unlike the main body of the work, the subsections on poetry, painting, and music include comparisons of English artists to figures of antiquity. Meres goes on after the extract below to list Shakespeare among the best English writers of lyric, tragedy, comedy, and love poetry. The text is modernized from the first edition of *Palladis Tamia* (London, 1598).]

As the Greek tongue is made famous and eloquent by Homer, Hesiod, Euripides, Aeschylus, Sophocles, Pindarus, Phocylides, and Aristophanes, and the Latin tongue by Virgil, Ovid, Horace, Silius Italicus, Lucanus, Lucretius, Ausonius, and Claudianus, so the English tongue is mightily enriched and gorgeously invested in rare ornaments and resplendent habiliments[1] by Sir Philip Sidney, Spenser, Daniel, Drayton, Warner, Shakespeare, Marlowe, and Chapman. . . .

As the soul of Euphorbus was thought to live in Pythagoras, so the sweet witty soul of Ovid lives in mellifluous and honey-tongued Shakespeare. Witness his *Venus and Adonis*, his *Lucrece*, his sugared sonnets among his private friends, etc.

As Plautus and Seneca are accounted the best for comedy and tragedy among the Latins, so Shakespeare among the English is the most excellent in both kinds for the stage. For comedy, witness his *Gentlemen of Verona*, his *Errors*, his *Love Labor's Lost*, his *Love Labor's Won*,[2] his *Midsummer's Night Dream*, and his *Merchant of Venice*; for tragedy, his *Richard the 2*, *Richard the 3*, *Henry the 4*, *King John*, *Titus Andronicus*, and his *Romeo and Juliet*.

---

1. Sumptuous clothing.
2. Either the play has not survived, or it is now known by a different name. However, this title is recorded elsewhere, in a bookseller's jottings of 1603, where it again appears following *Lover's Labor's Lost*.

As Epius Stolo said that the Muses would speak with Plautus' tongue if they would speak Latin, so I say that the Muses would speak with Shakespeare's fine-filed phrase if they would speak English.

Thomas Platter on *Julius Caesar* (September 21, 1599)

[Thomas Platter (1574–1628), a Swiss traveler, recorded his experience at the Globe playhouse in an account of his travels. The German text is printed in E. K. Chambers, *William Shakespeare: A Study of Facts and Problems*, 2 vols. (Oxford: Clarendon, 1930), vol. 2.]

Den 21 Septembris nach dem Imbissessen, etwan umb zwey vhren, bin ich mitt meiner geselschaft vber daz wasser gefahren, haben in dem streüwinen Dachhaus die Tragedy vom ersten Keyser Julio Caesare mitt ohngefahr 15 personen sehen gar artlich agieren; zu endt der Comedien dantzeten sie ihrem gebraucht nach gar vberausz zierlich, ye zwen in mannes vndt 2 in weiber kleideren angethan, wunderbahrlich mitt einanderen.

On the 21st of September after lunch, about two o'clock, I crossed the water [the Thames] with my party, and we saw the tragedy of the first emperor Julius Caesar acted very prettily in the house with the thatched roof, with about fifteen characters; at the end of the comedy, according to their custom, they danced with exceeding elegance, two each in men's and two in women's clothes, wonderfully together.

[Translated by Noah Heringman]

Simon Forman on *Macbeth* (1611)

[Simon Forman (1552–1611) was a largely self-educated physician and astrologer who rose from humble beginnings to establish a successful London practice. A large parcel of his manuscripts, including scientific and autobiographical material as well as the diary from which this account of the plays is taken, has survived, making his life one of the best-documented Elizabethan lives. These manuscripts provide detailed information about Forman's many sidelines, such as the manufacture of talismans, alchemy, and necromancy, as well as about his sex life. *Macbeth* was one of four plays described in Forman's "Book of Plays"; the others were *Cymbeline, The Winter's Tale,* and a non-Shakespearean play based on the life of Richard II. The text is modernized from E. K. Chambers, *William Shakespeare: A Study of Facts and Problems*, 2 vols. (Oxford: Clarendon, 1930), vol. 2.]

The Book of Plays and Notes thereof, per Forman for Common Policy[1]

In *Macbeth* at the Globe, 1610,[2] the 20 of April, ♄ [Saturday], there was to be observed, first, how Macbeth and Banquo, 2 noblemen of Scotland, riding through a wood, the[re] stood before them 3 women fairies or nymphs, and saluted Macbeth, saying 3 times unto him, "Hail, Macbeth, King of Codon,[3] for thou shalt be a king, but shalt beget no kings," etc. Then said Banquo, "What, all to Macbeth and nothing to me?" "Yes," said the nymphs. "Hail to thee, Banquo, thou shalt beget kings, yet be no king." And so they departed and came to the

---

1. *Common Policy:* practical use. Forman's title for his notes on plays is not printed in Chambers, but is interpolated here from G. Blakemore Evans's transcription in the *Riverside Shakespeare*.
2. 1611 (New Style).
3. Cawdor.

court of Scotland to Duncan, King of Scots, and it was in the days of Edward the Confessor. And Duncan bad them both kindly welcome, and made Macbeth forthwith Prince of Northumberland,[4] and sent him home to his own castle, and appointed Macbeth to provide for him, for he would sup with him the next day at night, and did so. And Macbeth contrived to kill Duncan, and through the persuasion of his wife, did that night murder the King in his own castle, being his guest. And there were many prodigies seen that night and the day before. And when Macbeth had murdered the King, the blood on his hands could not be washed off by any means, nor from his wife's hands, which handled the bloody daggers in hiding them, by which means they became both much amazed and affronted. The murder being known, Duncan's 2 sons fled, the one to England, the [other to] Wales, to save themselves. They being fled, they were supposed guilty of the murder of their father, which was nothing so. Then was Macbeth crowned King, and then he for fear of Banquo, his old companion, that he should beget kings but be no king himself, he contrived the death of Banquo, and caused him to be murdered on the way as he rode. The next night, being at supper with his noblemen whom he had bid to a feast, to the which also Banquo should have come, he began to speak of noble Banquo, and to wish that he were there. And as he thus did, standing up to drink a carouse to him, the ghost of Banquo came and sat down in his chair behind him. And he, turning about to sit down again, saw the ghost of Banquo, which fronted him so that he fell into a great passion of fear and fury, uttering many words about his murder, by which, when they heard that Banquo was murdered, they suspected Macbeth.

Then Macduff fled to England to the King's son, and so they raised an army and came into Scotland, and at Dunston Anyse[5] overthrew Macbeth. In the meantime, while Macduff was in England, Macbeth slew Macduff's wife and children, and after, in the battle, Macduff slew Macbeth.

Observe also how Macbeth's queen did rise in the night in her sleep, and walk, and talked, and confessed all, and the doctor noted her words.

Elegy on Richard Burbage (1619?)

[As the leading actor of the Chamberlain's Men and the King's Men, Richard Burbage (1568–1619) was the player for whom Shakespeare wrote many of his greatest roles. The tributes that appeared following Burbage's death on March 13, 1619, reflect his widespread celebrity and the feeling that an unparalleled talent had been lost. William Herbert, Earl of Pembroke, was so grieved that, months later, he could not bring himself to attend a play "so soon after the loss of my old acquaintance Burbage." The anonymous elegy below is the most extensive of the poetic responses and cites Burbage's performances as some important Shakespearean characters. The text is modernized from the transcription in C. M. Ingleby, *Shakespeare, The Man and the Book*, 2 vols. (London, 1877–81), 2:180–82, with some emendations provided from another manuscript copy of the same poem.]

A Funeral Elegy on the Death of the Famous Actor Richard Burbage, who died on Saturday in Lent, the 13 of March 1618[1]

> Some skillful limner help me, if not so,
> Some sad tragedian help t'express my woe.
> But oh, he's gone that could both best—both limn

---

4. Probably Forman's error; Duncan gives Macbeth the title Thane of Cawdor. Duncan's son Malcolm is the Prince of Northumberland.

5. Dunsinane.
1. 1619 (New Style).

And act my grief,[2] and 'tis for only him
That I invoke this strange assistance to it
And on the point invoke himself to do it.
For none but Tully Tully's praise can tell,[3]
And, as he could, no man could act so well
This part of sorrow for him, no man draw
So truly to the life this map of woe,
That grief's true picture, which his loss hath bred.
He's gone and, with him, what a world are dead,
Which he revived, to be revivèd so
No more: young Hamlet, old Hieronimo,
Kind Lear, the grievèd Moor, and more beside
That lived in him have now for ever died.
Oft have I seen him leap into the grave,
S[u]iting the person, which he seemed to have,
Of a sad[4] lover, with so true an eye
That there, I would have sworn, he meant to die.
Oft have I seen him play this part in jest
So lively that spectators and the rest
Of his sad crew, whilst he but seemed to bleed,
Amazed, thought even then he died indeed.
Oh, let not me be checked and I shall swear,
Even yet, it is a false report I hear,
And think that he, that did so truly feign,
Is still but dead in jest, to live again.
But now this part he acts, not plays, 'tis known;
Other he played, but acted hath his own.
England's great Roscius,[5] for what Roscius
Was unto Rome, that Burbage was to us.
How did his speech become him, and his pace
Suit with his speech, and every action grace
Them both alike, whilst not a word did fall
Without just weight to ballast it withal.
Hadst thou but spoke to Death and used thy power
Of thy enchanting tongue at that first hour
Of his assault, he had let fall his dart
And quite been charmed by thy all-charm[in]g art.
This he well knew, and to prevent this wrong,
He therefore first made seizure on [thy] tongue,[6]
Then on the rest 'twas easy by degrees:
The slender ivy tops the [t]allest trees.
Poets, whose glory whilom[7] 'twas to hear
Your lines so well expressed, henceforth forebear
And write no more. Or, if you do, let 't be
In comic scenes, since tragic parts you see
Die all with him. Nay, rather sluice your eyes
And henceforth write naught else but tragedies,
Or dirges, or sad elegies, or those
Mournful laments that not accord with prose.
Blur all your leaves with blots, that all you writ

2. Burbage was known as both a celebrated actor and a talented painter ("limner").
3. No one but Cicero ("Tully") can adequately praise Cicero.
4. Another manuscript reads "mad."
5. A celebrated actor in ancient Rome.
6. Burbage spoke his final words the day before he died.
7. Formerly.

May be but one sad black, and [upon] it
Draw marble lines that may outlast the sun
And stand like trophies when the world is done.
Turn all your ink to blood, your pens to spears
To pierce and wound the hearers' hearts and ears.
Enraged, write stabbing lines, that every word
May be as apt for murder as a sword,
That no man may survive after this fact
Of ruthless death, either to hear or act.
And you, his sad companions, to whom Lent
Becomes more Lenten by this accident,
Henceforth your waving flag no more hang out:
Play now no more at all, when round about
We look and miss the Atlas of your sphere.[8]
What comfort have we, think you, to be there,
And how can you delight in playing when
Such mourning so affecteth other men?
Or if you will still put't out, let it wear
No more light colors, but death livery there.
Hang all your house with black, the hue it bears,
With icicles of ever-melting tears,
And if you ever chance to play again,
May naught but tragedies afflict your scene.
And thou, dear earth, that must enshrine that dust
By heaven now committed to thy trust,
Keep it as precious as the richest mine
That lies entombed in that rich womb of thine,
That aftertimes may know that much-loved mold
From other dust, and cherish it as gold;
On it be laid some soft but lasting stone
With this short epitaph endorsed thereon,
That every eye may read and, reading, weep:
'Tis England's Roscius, Burbage, that I keep.

Front Matter from the First Folio
of Shakespeare's Plays (1623)

After Shakespeare's death in 1616, his friends and colleagues John Heminges and Henry Condell organized this first publication of his collected (thirty-six) plays. Eighteen of the plays had not appeared in print before, and for these the First Folio is the sole surviving source. Only *Pericles, The Two Noble Kinsmen, Sir Thomas More,* and *Edward III* are not included in the volume. Reproduced below in reduced facsimile are the title page (which includes Droeshout's famous portrait of Shakespeare), Heminges and Condell's prefatory address "To the great Variety of Readers," the book's table of contents, and the first page of text from *The Tempest.* Following the facsimile images is a commendatory poem by Shakespeare's great contemporary Ben Jonson (1572–1637), which was also published in the First Folio's front matter.

8. Burbage is compared to the mythological Atlas, supporting the Globe (theater).

Mr. WILLIAM
SHAKESPEARES
COMEDIES,
HISTORIES, &
TRAGEDIES.

Publiſhed according to the True Originall Copies.

Martin Droeshout ſculpsit London.

LONDON
Printed by Iſaac Iaggard, and Ed. Blount. 1623.

To the great Variety of Readers.

Rom the moſt able, to him that can but ſpell: There you are number'd. We had rather you were weighd. Eſpecially, when the fate of all Bookes depends vpon your capacities : and not of your heads alone, but of your purſes. Well ! It is now publique, & you wil ſtand for your priuiledges wee know : to read, and cenſure. Do ſo, but buy it firſt. That doth beſt commend a Booke, the Stationer ſaies. Then, how odde ſoeuer your braines be, or your wiſedomes, make your licence the ſame, and ſpare not. Iudge your ſixe-pen'orth, your ſhillings worth, your fiue ſhillings worth at a time, or higher, ſo you riſe to the iuſt rates, and welcome. But, what euer you do, Buy. Cenſure will not driue a Trade, or make the Iacke go. And though you be a Magiſtrate of wit, and ſit on the Stage at *Black-Friers*, or the *Cock-pit*, to arraigne Playes dailie, know, theſe Playes haue had their triall alreadie, and ſtood out all Appeales ; and do now come forth quitted rather by a Decree of Court, then any purchas'd Letters of commendation.

It had bene a thing, we confeſſe, worthie to haue bene wiſhed, that the Author him ſelfe had liu'd to haue ſet forth, and ouerſeen his owne writings ; But ſince it hath bin ordain'd otherwiſe, and he by death departed from that right, we pray you do not envie his Friends, the office of their care, and paine, to haue collected & publiſh'd them ; and ſo to haue publiſh'd them, as where (before) you were abus'd with diuerſe ſtolne, and ſurreptitious copies, maimed, and deformed by the frauds and ſtealthes of iniurious impoſtors, that expos'd them : euen thoſe, are now offer'd to your view cur'd, and perfect of their limbes ; and all the reſt, abſolute in their numbers, as he conceiued thē. Who, as he was a happie imitator of Nature, was a moſt gentle expreſſer of it. His mind and hand went together : And what he thought, he vttered with that eaſineſſe, that wee haue ſcarſe receiued from him a blot in his papers. But it is not our prouince, who onely gather his works, and giue them you, to praiſe him. It is yours that reade him. And there we hope, to your diuers capacities, you will finde enough, both to draw, and hold you : for his wit can no more lie hid, then it could be loſt. Reade him, therefore ; and againe, and againe : And if then you doe not like him, ſurely you are in ſome manifeſt danger, not to vnderſtand him. And ſo we leaue you to other of his Friends, whom if you need, can bee your guides : if you neede them not, you can leade your ſelues, and others . And ſuch Readers we wiſh him.

A 3

Iohn Heminge.
Henrie Condell.

Line 8. *Stationer:* bookseller.
Line 13. *Iacke:* machine.
Lines 13–14. *And though . . . dailie:* addressed in particular to men of fashion who occupied seats onstage so they could be seen while watching the play.
Lines 15–17. *these Playes . . . commendation:* The legal puns that began with "Magistrate of wit" (fashionable playgoer) in line 13 continue here. The "purchas'd Letters of commendation" refer to escaping the consequences of a crime by means of bribery or other undue influence; Shakespeare's plays, by contrast, have been acquitted after a proper and rigorous trial (approved by theater audiences and not insinuated into the public favor by some outside influence).
Line 27. *absolute in their numbers:* correct in their versification. *thē:* them.
Line 28. *a happie:* an apt; a successful.

A CATALOGVE

of the seuerall Comedies, Histories, and Tragedies contained in this Volume.

COMEDIES.

He Tempest.	Folio 1.
The two Gentlemen of Verona.	20
The Merry Wiues of Windsor.	38
Measure for Measure.	61
The Comedy of Errours.	85
Much adoo about Nothing.	101
Loues Labour lost.	122
Midsommer Nights Dreame.	145
The Merchant of Venice.	163
As you Like it.	185
The Taming of the Shrew.	208
All is well, that Ends well.	230
Twelfe-Night, or what you will.	255
The Winters Tale.	304

HISTORIES.

The Life and Death of King John.	Fol. 1.
The Life & death of Richard the second.	23
The First part of King Henry the fow t'h.	46
The Second part of K. Henry the fourth.	74
The Life of King Henry the Fift.	69
The First part of King Henry the Sixt.	96
The Second part of King Hen. the Sixt.	120
The Third part of King Henry the Sixt.	147
The Life & Death of Richard the Third.	173
The Life of King Henry the Eight.	205

TRAGEDIES.

The Tragedy of Coriolanus.	Fol. 1.
Titus Andronicus.	31
Romeo and Juliet.	53
Timon of Athens.	80
The Life and death of Julius Cæsar.	109
The Tragedy of Macbeth.	131
The Tragedy of Hamlet.	152
King Lear.	283
Othello, the Moore of Venice.	310
Anthony and Cleopater.	346
Cymbeline King of Britaine.	369

Troilus and Cressida, despite its absence from the "Catalogue," was in fact printed in the First Folio. Due to negotiations over printing rights, it was included only at the last minute and placed between the histories and tragedies.

THE TEMPEST.

❧ Actus primus, Scena prima.

A tempestuous noise of Thunder and Lightning heard: Enter a Ship-master, and a Botefwaine.

Mafter.

BOte-fwaine.

Botef. Heere Maſter : What cheere ?

Maſt. Good : Speake to th'Mariners : fall too't, yarely, or we run our felues a ground, beſtirre, beſtirre. *Exit.*

Enter Mariners.

Botef. Heigh my hearts, cheerely, cheerely my harts : yare, yare : Take in the toppe-ſale : Tend to th'Maſters whiſtle : Blow till thou burſt thy winde , if roome e-nough.

Enter Alonfo, Sebaſtian, Anthonio, Ferdinando,
Gonzalo, and others.

Alon. Good Boteſwaine haue care : where's the Maſter ? Play the men.

Botef. I pray now keepe below.

Anth. Where is the Maſter, Boſon ?

Botef. Do you not heare him ? you marre our labour, Keepe your Cabines : you do aſſiſt the ſtorme.

Gonz. Nay, good be patient.

Botef. When the Sea is : hence, what cares theſe roarers for the name of King ? to Cabine ; ſilence : trouble vs not.

Gon. Good, yet remember whom thou haſt aboord.

Botef. None that I more loue then my ſelfe. You are a Counfellor, if you can command theſe Elements to ſilence, and worke the peace of the preſent, wee will not hand a rope more, vſe your authoritie : If you cannot, giue thankes you haue liu'd ſo long , and make your ſelfe readie in your Cabine for the miſchance of the houre, if it ſo hap. Cheerely good hearts : out of our way I ſay. *Exit.*

Gon. I haue great comfort from this fellow : methinks he hath no drowning marke vpon him, his complexion is perfect Gallowes : ſtand faſt good Fate to his hanging, make the rope of his deſtiny our cable, for our owne doth little aduantage : If he be not borne to bee hang'd, our caſe is miſerable. *Exit.*

Enter Botefwaine.

Botef. Downe with the top-Maſt : yare, lower, lower, bring her to Try with Maine-courſe. A plague——

A cry within. *Enter Sebaſtian, Anthonio & Gonzalo.*

vpon this howling : they are lowder then the weather, or our office : yet againe ? What do you heere ? Shal we giue ore and drowne, haue you a minde to ſinke ?

Sebaf. A poxe o'your throat, you bawling, blafphemous incharitable Dog.

Botef. Worke you then.

Anth. Hang cur, hang, you whoreſon inſolent Noyſemaker, we are leſſe afraid to be drownde, then thou art.

Gonz. I'le warrant him for drowning, though the Ship were no ſtronger then a Nutt-ſhell, and as leaky as an vnſtanched wench.

Botef. Lay her a hold, a hold , ſet her two courſes off to Sea againe, lay her off,

Enter Mariners wet.

Mari. All loſt, to prayers, to prayers, all loſt.

Botef. What muſt our mouths be cold ?

Gonz. The King, and Prince, at prayers, let's aſſiſt them, for our caſe is as theirs.

Sebaf. I'am out of patience.

An. We are meerly cheated of our liues by drunkards, This wide-chopt-rafcall, would thou mighteſt lye drowning the waſhing of ten Tides.

Gonz. Hee'l be hang'd yet, Though euery drop of water ſweare againſt it, And gape at widſt to glut him. *A confuſed noyſe within.* Mercy on vs. We ſplit, we ſplit , Farewell my wife, and children, Farewell brother : we ſplit, we ſplit, we ſplit.

Anth. Let's all finke with' King

Seb. Let's take leaue of him. *Exit.*

Gonz. Now would I giue a thouſand furlongs of Sea, for an Acre of barren ground : Long heath, Browne firrs, any thing ; the wills aboue be done, but I would faine dye a dry death. *Exit.*

Scena Secunda.

Enter Profpero and Miranda.

Mira. If by your Art (my deereſt father) you haue Put the wild waters in this Rore ; alay them : The skye it ſeemes would powre down ſtinking pitch, But that the Sea, mounting to th' welkins cheeke, Dafhes the fire out. Oh ! I haue ſuffered With thoſe that I ſaw ſuffer : A braue veſſell

A   (Who

To the memory of my beloved,
The AUTHOR
Mr. William Shakespeare:
And
what he hath left us.*

To draw no envy, Shakespeare, on thy name,
  Am I thus ample to° thy book and fame,   *copious in praising*
While I confess thy writings to be such
  As neither man nor muse can praise too much:
5 'Tis true, and all men's suffrage.° But these ways   *agreement*
  Were not the paths I meant° unto thy praise,   *(to take)*
For seeliest¹ ignorance on these may light,
  Which, when it sounds, at best, but° echoes right;   *merely*
Or blind affection, which doth ne'er advance
10   The truth, but gropes, and urgeth all by chance;
Or crafty malice might pretend this praise,
  And think° to ruin, where it seemed to raise.   *intend*
These are as° some infamous bawd or whore   *as though*
  Should praise a matron: what could hurt her more?
15 But thou art proof against° them, and indeed   *impervious to*
  Above th' ill fortune of them, or the need.
I therefore will begin. Soul of the age!
  The applause, delight, the wonder of our stage!
My Shakespeare, rise! I will not lodge thee by
20   Chaucer or Spenser, or bid Beaumont lie
A little further to make thee a room;²
  Thou art a monument without a tomb
And art alive still while thy book doth live,
  And we have wits to read and praise to give.
25 That I not mix thee so, my brain excuses,
  I mean with great but disproportioned° muses.   *not comparable*
For if I thought my judgment were of years°   *mature*
  I should commit° thee surely with thy peers,   *compare*
And tell how far thou didst our Lyly outshine,
30   Or sporting Kyd, or Marlowe's mighty line.³
And though thou hadst small Latin and less Greek,⁴
  From thence to honor thee I would not seek°   *lack*

---

* By Ben Jonson.
1. Silliest; blindest (falcons' eyelids were "seeled," or stitched shut, while they were being tamed).
2. Geoffrey Chaucer, Edmund Spenser, and Francis Beaumont were all buried near each other in Westminster Abbey (known today as the "Poets' Corner"), while Shakespeare was buried in Stratford-upon-Avon. An earlier elegy for Shakespeare had begun: "Renownèd Spenser, lie a thought more nigh / To learned Chaucer, and, rare Beaumont, lie / A little nearer Spenser to make room / For Shakespeare . . ."
3. John Lyly, Thomas Kyd, and Christopher Marlowe were all celebrated Elizabethan playwrights. *sporting*: gamesome; frolicking (like a young goat, or "kid").
4. The underrating of Shakespeare's Latin was likely influenced by Jonson's pride in his own impressive classical learning.

For names, but call forth thund'ring Aeschylus,
   Euripides, and Sophocles to us,
35 Pacuvius, Accius, him of Cordova dead,[5]
   To life again, to hear thy buskin tread
And shake a stage; or, when thy socks were on,[6]
   Leave thee alone for the comparison
Of all that insolent Greece or haughty Rome
40   Sent forth, or since did from their ashes come.
Triumph, my Britain; thou hast one to show
   To whom all scenes° of Europe homage owe.   *stages*
He was not of an age, but for all time!
   And all the Muses still were in their prime
45 When like Apollo° he came forth to warm   *god of poetry*
   Our ears, or like a Mercury° to charm!   *god of eloquence*
Nature herself was proud of his designs,
   And joyed to wear the dressing of his lines,
Which were so richly spun and woven so fit
50   As, since, she will vouchsafe° no other wit.   *grant*
The merry Greek, tart Aristophanes,
   Neat Terence, witty Plautus[7] now not please,
But antiquated and deserted lie,
   As they were not of Nature's family.
55 Yet must I not give Nature all; thy art,
   My gentle Shakespeare, must enjoy a part.
For though the poet's matter° nature be,   *raw material*
   His art doth give the fashion.° And that he°   *form / that he=he*
Who casts° to write a living line must sweat   *intends*
60   (Such as thine are) and strike the second heat
Upon the Muses' anvil, turn the same,
   And himself with it, that he thinks to frame,
Or for the laurel he may gain a scorn;[8]
   For a good poet's made as well as born,
65 And such wert thou. Look how the father's face
   Lives in his issue;° even so, the race   *offspring*
Of Shakespeare's mind and manners brightly shines
   In his well-turnèd and true-filèd° lines,   *truly polished*
In each of which he seems to shake a lance,[9]
70   As brandished at the eyes of ignorance.
Sweet swan of Avon, what a sight it were
   To see thee in our waters yet appear,
And make those flights upon the banks of Thames
   That so did take° Eliza and our James![1]   *transport*
75 But stay; I see thee in the hemisphere
   Advanced and made a constellation there.[2]

---

5. While the Latin tragedians Marcus Pacuvius and Lucius Accius were known to Jonson only by reputation, Seneca the Younger ("him of Cordova") was a major influence on Renaissance revenge tragedies.
6. The boots ("buskins") and shoes ("socks") worn by classical actors were symbolic of tragedy and comedy, respectively.
7. Aristophanes was a Greek writer of satirical comedies; Terence and Plautus were Roman comic dramatists.
8. Or else, instead of the laurel (the symbol of poetic accomplishment), he may gain derision.
9. Punning on Shakespeare's name.
1. Queen Elizabeth and King James.
2. It was a commonplace in classical literature that those who lived glorious lives became constellations after death.

Shine forth, thou star of poets, and with rage
  Or influence,[3] chide or cheer the drooping° stage,   *dejected*
Which, since thy flight from hence, hath mourned like night,
80   And despairs day, but for thy volume's light.

                              BEN: JONSON.

---

3. Stars and planets were thought to affect human affairs. "Rage" suggests poetic inspiration.

Timeline

Dates for plays by Shakespeare and others are conjectural dates of composition, based on current understanding of the evidence. Works of poetry and prose are listed by date of publication.

TEXT	CONTEXT
	1558 Queen Mary I, a Roman Catholic, dies; her sister, Elizabeth, raised Protestant, is proclaimed queen.
	1559 Church of England is reestablished under the authority of the sovereign with the passage of the Act of Uniformity and the Act of Supremacy.
1562 *The Tragedy of Gorboduc*, by Thomas Norton and Thomas Sackville; the first English play in blank verse.	**1563** The Church of England adopts the Thirty-nine Articles of Religion, detailing its points of doctrine and clarifying its differences both from Roman Catholicism and from more radical forms of Protestantism.
	1564 William Shakespeare is born in Stratford to John and Mary Arden Shakespeare; he is christened a few days later, on April 26.
	1565 John Shakespeare is made an alderman of Stratford.
	1567 Mary Queen of Scots is imprisoned on suspicion of the murder of her husband, Lord Darnley. Their infant son, Charles James, is crowned James VI of Scotland. John Brayne builds the first English professional theater in the garden of a farmhouse called the Red Lion on the outskirts of London.
	1568 John Shakespeare is elected Bailiff of Stratford, the town's highest office. Performances in Stratford by the Queen's Players and the Earl of Worcester's men.
	1572 An act is passed that severely punishes vagrants and wanderers, including actors not affiliated with a patron. Performances in Stratford by the Earl of Leicester's men.

TEXT	CONTEXT
	1574 The Earl of Warwick's and Earl of Worcester's men perform in Stratford.
	1576 James Burbage, father of Richard, later the leading actor in Shakespeare's company, builds The Theatre in Shoreditch, a suburb of London.
1577 First edition of Holinshed's *Chronicles*.	**1577** The Curtain Theater opens in Shoreditch.
	1577–80 Sir Francis Drake circumnavigates the globe.
	1578 Mary Shakespeare pawns her lands, suggesting that the family is in financial distress. Lord Strange's Men and Lord Essex's Men perform at Stratford.
1579 Sir Thomas North's English translation of Plutarch's *Lives*.	**1580** A Jesuit mission is established in England with the aim of reconverting the nation to Roman Catholicism. Francis Drake returns from circumnavigation of globe.
	1582 Shakespeare marries Anne Hathaway.
	1583 The birth of Shakespeare's older daughter, Susanna.
	1584 Sir Walter Ralegh establishes the first English colony in the New World at Roanoke Island in modern North Carolina; the colony fails.
	1585 The birth of Shakespeare's twin son and daughter, Hamnet and Judith. John Shakespeare is fined for not going to church.
	1586 Sir Philip Sidney dies from battle wounds.
1587 Thomas Kyd, *The Spanish Tragedy;* Christopher Marlowe, *Tamburlaine*.	**1587** Mary Queen of Scots is executed for treason against Elizabeth I. Francis Drake, leading a daring raid at Cádiz, destroys many Spanish naval vessels and materiel. John Shakespeare loses his position as an alderman. Philip Henslowe builds the Rose theater at Bank-side, on the Thames.
	1588 The Spanish Armada attempts an invasion of England but is defeated.

TEXT	CONTEXT
1589 Robert Greene, *Friar Bacon and Friar Bungay.* Thomas Kyd(?), *Hamlet* (not extant; perhaps a source for Shakespeare's *Hamlet*). Christopher Marlowe, *The Jew of Malta.* Anonymous, *The True Chronicle History of King Leir, and His Three Daughters.*	**1589** Shakespeare is possibly affiliated with Strange's men, Pembroke's men, or both between this time and 1594.
1590 Edmund Spenser, *The Faerie Queene* (1st edition, Books 1–3). Sir Philip Sidney, *Arcadia.*	**1590** James VI of Scotland marries Anne of Denmark. James believes that witches raised a magical storm in an attempt to sink the ship carrying him home with his bride. Witch trials in Scotland.
1591–92 *Two Gentlemen of Verona.* *2 and 3 Henry VI.* *The Taming of the Shrew.* *I Henry VI.*	**1592** The theatrical entrepreneur and financial manager of the Admiral's Men, Philip Henslowe, begins a diary—an important source for theater historians—recording his business transactions; continued until 1604.
1592–93 *Titus Andronicus.* *Richard III.* *Edward III.* *Venus and Adonis.*	From June 1592 to June 1594, London theaters are frequently shut down because of the plague; acting companies tour the provinces.
1594 *The Rape of Lucrece.* *The Comedy of Errors.*	**1594** Roderigo Lopez, a Christian physician of Portuguese Jewish descent, is executed on slight evidence for having plotted to poison Elizabeth I. The birth of James VI's first son, Henry.
1594–96 *Love's Labor's Lost.* *Richard II.* *Romeo and Juliet.* *A Midsummer Night's Dream.* *King John.*	**1595** Shakespeare lives in St. Helen's Parish, Bishopsgate, London. Shakespeare apparently becomes a sharer in (provides capital for) the newly formed Lord Chamberlain's Men. The Swan Theater is built in Bankside. Hugh O'Neill, Earl of Tyrone, rebels against English rule in Ireland. Walter Ralegh explores Guiana, on the north coast of South America.
1596 Edmund Spenser, *The Faerie Queene* (2nd edition, with Books 4–6). **1596–97** *I Henry IV.* *The Merchant of Venice.*	**1596** John Shakespeare is granted a coat of arms; hence the title of "gentleman." William Shakespeare's son Hamnet dies. James Burbage buys a medieval hall in the former Blackfriars monastery and transforms it into an indoor theater. **1597** The landlord refuses to renew the lease on the land under The Theatre in Shoreditch.

TEXT	CONTEXT
1598 *2 Henry IV.* *Much Ado About Nothing.* George Chapman begins to publish his translation of Homer. Ben Jonson, *Every Man in His Humor,* which lists Shakespeare as one of the actors.	**1598** Unable to renew the lease, the Chamberlain's Men move from The Theatre to the nearby Curtain Theater. The Edict of Nantes ends the French civil wars, granting toleration to Protestants. Materials from the demolished Theatre in Shoreditch are transported across the Thames to be used in building the Globe Theater, which opens in the following year.
1599 *The Merry Wives of Windsor.* *Henry V.* *As You Like It.* *Julius Caesar.* *The Passionate Pilgrim,* attributed entirely to Shakespeare. Michael Drayton and several collaborators, who object to Shakespeare's depiction of Oldcastle-Falstaff in the *Henry IV* plays, write *The First Part of the True and Honorable History of the Life of Sir John Oldcastle, the Good Lord Cobham.*	**1599** The Queen's favorite, Robert Devereux, Earl of Essex, leads an expedition to Ireland in March, but returning home without royal permission in September, is rebuked by the Queen and imprisoned. Satires and other offensive books are prohibited by ecclesiastical order. Extant copies are gathered and burned. Two notorious satirists, Thomas Nashe and Gabriel Harvey, are forbidden to publish.
1600–1601 *Hamlet.* *Twelfth Night.*	**1600** The Earl of Essex is suspended from some of his offices and confined to house arrest. The birth of James VI's second son, Charles. The founding of the East India Company. Edward Alleyn and Philip Henslowe build the Fortune Theater for the Lord Admiral's Men.
1601 "The Phoenix and Turtle" published in Robert Chester's *Love's Martyr.* In the "War of the Theaters," Ben Jonson, John Marston, and Thomas Dekker write a series of satiric plays mocking one another.	**1601** The Earl of Essex leads a rebellion against the principal adviser to Elizabeth I and possibly against the Queen herself. The previous afternoon, hoping to enlist support, some of the rebels pay for a performance of *Richard II.* Implicated in the uprising, which is quickly quelled, Shakespeare's patron, the Earl of Southampton, is imprisoned. The Earl of Essex is convicted of treason and beheaded, along with several of his chief supporters. Shakespeare's father dies.
1601–02 *Troilus and Cressida.*	**1602** Shakespeare makes substantial real-estate purchases in Stratford. The opening of the Bodleian Library in Oxford.

TEXT	CONTEXT
1601–03 *Othello.*	
1603 John Florio's translation of Montaigne's *Essays.* Ben Jonson, *Sejanus,* which lists Shakespeare as one of the actors.	**1603** Queen Elizabeth dies; she is succeeded by her cousin, James VI of Scotland (now James I of England).
1603–04 *Sir Thomas More* (revised version).	
	Plague closes the London theaters from mid-1603 to April 1604. Hugh O'Neill surrenders in Ireland.
1604 *Measure for Measure.*	**1604** The conclusion of a peace with Spain makes travel across the Atlantic safer, encouraging plans for English colonies in the Americas.
1605 *The History of King Lear.*	**1605** The discovery of the Gunpowder Plot by some radical Catholics to blow up the Houses of Parliament during its opening ceremonies, when the royal family, Lords, and Commons are assembled in one place. The Red Bull Theater built.
1606–07 *Timon of Athens.* *All's Well That Ends Well.* *Macbeth.* *Antony and Cleopatra.* Middleton(?), *The Revenger's Tragedy.*	**1606** The London and Plymouth Companies receive charters to colonize Virginia. Parliament passes "An Act to Restrain Abuses of Players," prohibiting oaths or blasphemy onstage.
1607–08 *Pericles.*	**1607** An English colony is established in Jamestown, Virginia. Shakespeare's daughter Susanna marries John Hall. Shakespeare's brother Edmund (described as a player) dies.
1608 *Coriolanus.*	
1609 *Shakespeare's Sonnets.*	
1610 *Cymbeline.* Ben Jonson, *The Alchemist.*	**1610** Henry is made Prince of Wales. Shakespeare probably returns to Stratford and settles there. The King's Men begin using Blackfriars Theater as a second, indoor venue.

TEXT	CONTEXT
1611 *The Winter's Tale.* *The Tempest.* Francis Beaumont and John Fletcher, *A King and No King.* Publication of the Authorized (King James) Bible.	**1611** Plantation of Ulster in Ireland, a colony of English and Scottish Protestants settled on land confiscated from Irish rebels.
1612–13 *Cardenio*, with John Fletcher (not extant). *Henry VIII*, with John Fletcher. John Webster, *The White Devil.*	**1612** Prince Henry dies.
1613–14 *The Two Noble Kinsmen*, with John Fletcher.	**1613** Princess Elizabeth marries Frederick V, Elector Palatine. The Globe Theater burns down during a performance of *Henry VIII.*
1614 Ben Jonson, *Bartholomew Fair.* John Webster, *The Duchess of Malfi.*	**1614** Philip Henslowe and Jacob Meade build the Hope Theater, used both for play performances and as a bearbaiting arena. The Globe Theater reopens.
1616 Ben Jonson publishes his *Works*, including the first collection of plays by a commercial English dramatist.	**1616** William Harvey describes the circulation of the blood. Shakespeare's daughter Judith marries. Shakespeare dies on April 23.
1623 Members of the King's Men publish the First Folio of Shakespeare's plays.	

Glossary

STAGE TERMS

"above"   The gallery on the upper level of the stage's back wall (see *frons scenae*). In open-air theaters, such as the Globe, this space may have included the lords' rooms. The central section of the gallery was sometimes used by the players for short scenes. Indoor theaters such as Blackfriars featured a curtained alcove for musicians above the stage.

"aloft"   See *"above."*

amphitheater   An open-air theater, such as the Globe.

arras   See *curtain.*

cellarage   See *trap.*

chorus   In the works of Shakespeare and other Elizabethan playwrights, a single individual (not, as in Greek tragedy, a group) who speaks before the play (and sometimes before each act or, in *Pericles*, at other times), describing events not shown on stage as well as commenting on the action witnessed by the audience.

curtain   Curtains, or arras (hanging tapestries), probably covered a part of the stage's back wall (see *frons scenae*), thus concealing the discovery space, and may also have been draped around the edge of the stage to conceal the open area underneath.

discovery space   A central opening or alcove concealed behind a curtain in the center of the stage's back wall (see *frons scenae*). The curtain could be drawn aside to "discover" tableaux such as Portia's caskets, the body of Polonius, or the statue of Hermione. Shakespeare appears to have used this stage device only sparingly.

doubling   The common practice of having one actor play multiple roles, so that a play with a large cast of characters might be performed by a relatively small company.

dumb shows   Mimed scenes performed before a play or as part of the play itself, summarizing or foreshadowing the plot. Dumb shows were popular in early Elizabethan drama; although they already seemed old-fashioned in Shakespeare's time, they were employed by writers up to the 1640s.

epilogue   A brief speech or poem addressed to the audience by an actor after the play. In some cases, as in *2 Henry IV*, the epilogue could be combined with, or could merge into, the jig.

frons scenae   The wall at the back of the stage, behind which lay the players' tiring house. The *frons scenae* of the Globe featured two doors flanking the central discovery space, with a gallery "above."

gallery   Covered seating area surrounding the open yard of the public amphitheater. There were three levels of galleries at the Globe; admission to these seats cost an extra penny (in addition to the basic admission fee of one penny to the yard), and seating in the higher galleries another penny yet.

gatherers   Persons employed by the playing company to take money at the entrances to the theater.

groundlings   Audience members who paid the minimum price of admission (one penny) to stand in the yard of the open-air theaters; also referred to as "understanders." "Groundling" is an unusual word, possibly coined by Shakespeare; it is unclear whether it was in common usage at the time.

heavens   The canopied roof over the stage in the open-air theaters, protecting the players and their costumes from rain. The "heavens" may have been brightly decorated with sun, moon, and stars, and perhaps the signs of the zodiac.

jig   A song-and-dance performance by the clown and other members of the company at the conclusion of a play. These performances were frequently bawdy and were officially banned in 1612.

lords' rooms   Partitioned sections of the gallery above the stage, or just to the left and right of the stage, where the most prestigious and expensive seats in the public playhouses were located. These rooms did not provide the best view of the action on the stage below. They were designed to make their privileged occupants conspicuous to the rest of the audience.

open-air theaters   Unroofed public playhouses in the suburbs of London, such as The Theatre, the Rose, and the Globe.

part   The character played by an actor. In Shakespeare's theater, actors were given a roll of paper called a "part" containing all of the speeches and all of the cues belonging to their character. The term "role," synonymous with "part," is derived from such rolls of paper.

patrons   Important nobles and members of the royal family under whose protection the theatrical companies of London operated; players not in the service of patrons were punishable as vagabonds. The companies were referred to as their patrons' "Men" or "Servants." Thus the company to which Shakespeare belonged for most of his career was first known as the Lord Chamberlain's Servants, then became the King's Men in 1603, when James I became their patron.

pillars   The "heavens" were supported by two tall painted pillars or posts near the front of the stage. These occasionally played a role in stage action, allowing a character to "hide" while remaining in full view of the audience.

pit   The area in front of the stage in indoor theaters such as Blackfriars; unlike an open-air playhouse's yard, the pit was designed for a seated audience.

posts   See *pillars*.

proscenium   The arch that divides the stage, scenery, and backstage area from the auditorium in many theaters built in and after the eighteenth century. It also separates actors and audiences, potentially creating the so-called fourth wall. The stages on which Shakespeare's plays were first performed had no proscenium.

repertory   The stock of plays a company had ready for performance at a given time. Companies generally performed a different play each day, often more than a dozen plays in a month and more than thirty in the course of the season.

role   See *part*.

sharers   Senior actors holding shares in a joint-stock theatrical company; they paid for costumes, hired hands, and new plays, and they shared profits and losses equally. Shakespeare was not only a longtime "sharer" of the Lord Chamberlain's Men but, from 1599, a "housekeeper," the holder of a one-eighth share in the Globe playhouse.

tiring house   The players' dressing (attiring) room, a structure located at the back of the stage and connected to the stage by two or more doors in the *frons scenae*.

trap   A trapdoor near the front of the stage that allowed access to the cellarage beneath and was frequently associated with hell's mouth. Another trapdoor in the heavens opened for the descent of gods to the stage below.

"within"   The tiring house, from which offstage sound effects such as shouts, drums, and trumpets were produced.

yard   The central space in open-air theaters such as the Globe, into which the stage projected and in which audience members stood. Admission to the yard in the public theaters cost a penny, the cheapest admission available.

TEXTUAL TERMS

aside   See *stage direction*.

autograph   Text written in the author's own hand. With the possible exception of a few pages of the collaborative play *Sir Thomas More*, no dramatic works or poems written in Shakespeare's hand are known to survive.

"bad quartos"   A polemical term for a group of Shakespeare quartos that are different from and often demonstrably inferior to other versions of the plays in question as they are found in later quartos or in the First Folio. Some of these texts are very short; others include notable distortions of language. Explanations for the "bad quartos" (or, more neutrally, "short quartos") include the possibility that they were Shakespeare's early drafts, abbreviated scripts prepared for performance under circumstances such as touring, or "memorial reconstructions."

base text   The early text upon which a modern edition is based, also known as a "control text."

canonical   Of an author, the writings generally accepted as authentic. In the case of Shakespeare's dramatic works, only two plays that are not among the thirty-six plays contained in the First Folio, *Pericles* and *The Two Noble Kinsmen,* have won widespread acceptance into the Shakespearean canon, but recent scholarship suggests that he wrote parts of a number of others, including *Edward III* and *Sir Thomas More.*

casting off   The practice of dividing up a manuscript to anticipate the number of pages needed to contain it in print. Errors in casting off sometimes led compositors to crowd lines, abbreviate spellings, and print verse as prose. If on the contrary a compositor found he had too much space remaining, he might leave spaces around stage directions, add ornaments, or break prose up into short "verse" lines.

catchword   A word printed below the text at the bottom of a page, matching the first word on the following page. The catchword enabled the printer to keep the pages in their proper sequence. Where the catchword fails to match the word at the top of the next page, there is reason to suspect that something has been lost or misplaced.

collaboration   The practice of two or more writers working together to create a play (or other literature). More than half of the plays in Shakespeare's period were collaborative. Shakespeare collaborated with John Fletcher on *Henry VIII, The Two Noble Kinsmen,* and the missing *Cardenio*; with George Wilkins on *Pericles*; and with Thomas Middleton on *Timon of Athens*. Shakespeare plays that probably have sections composed by others include *Titus Andronicus, 1 Henry VI,* and *Macbeth*; in turn, Shakespeare seems to have contributed a section to *Sir Thomas More*.

compositor   A person employed in a print shop to set type. To speed the printing process, most of Shakespeare's plays were set by more than one compositor. Compositors were expected to adjust spelling and provide punctuation and can often be identified by their different habits and preferences (e.g., *been/beene* or *O/Oh* and speech prefixes such as *Que./Queene*). They invariably introduced errors into the texts—for instance, by selecting the wrong letter from the type case or by setting the correct letter upside down.

conflation   A version of a play created by combining readings from more than one substantive text. Since the early eighteenth century, for example, most versions of *King Lear* and of several other plays by Shakespeare have been conflations of quarto and First Folio texts.

deus ex machina   Literally, "god from a machine," the term can refer to any plot device introduced to resolve a seemingly insurmountable problem.

dramatis personae (or The Persons of the Play)   A list of the characters that appear in the play. In the First Folio such lists, called "The Names of the Actors," were printed at the end of some but not all of the plays. In 1709 the editor Nicholas Rowe first provided lists of dramatis personae for all of Shakespeare's dramatic works.

emendation   A correction made in a text by an editor where he or she believes on the basis of evidence and/or inference that it has been corrupted in transmission and needs to be altered for coherence or sense.

exeunt / exit   See *stage direction*.

fair copy   A transcript of the "foul papers" made either by a scribe or by the playwright.

folio   A bookmaking format in which each large sheet of paper is folded once, making two leaves (a leaf is part of a folded sheet of paper with a page on each side). This format produced large volumes, generally handsome and expensive. The First Folio of Shakespeare's plays was printed in 1623.

forme   A body of type secured in a chase, or wooden frame, ready for printing. The forme would be placed into the press and inked and a sheet of paper lowered onto it for imprinting.

foul papers   A term for a playwright's working draft of a play, which is presumed to have contained "false starts," blotted-out passages, ghost characters, and revisions. To judge by apparent errors in the printed texts, several of Shakespeare's plays appear to have been printed from foul papers rather than fair copy; however, no clearcut instance of his foul papers survives, though certain pages in the manuscript of *Sir Thomas More* may represent this stage of the writing process.

ghost characters   Characters named in a stage direction who have no lines during the ensuing action. They may represent a "false start" as the author composed the play, and may not have actually appeared onstage in performance.

licensing By an order of 1581, new plays could not be performed until they had received a license from the Master of the Revels. A separate license, granted by the Court of High Commission, was required for publication, though in practice plays were often printed without license. From 1610, the Master of the Revels had the authority to license plays for publication as well as for performance.

manent / manet See *stage direction.*

massed entry The grouping of all characters who will appear at any point in a scene into a single opening direction. Playwrights such as Ben Jonson preferred this style because of its conformity with classical practice, and it was followed by certain scribes. Modern editors write entry directions to show the point in the scene at which each character enters.

memorial reconstruction The theory that some texts may have been reconstructed from memory by one or more actors, either because a promptbook had been destroyed or because it was not available—for example, while touring. It has been proposed that memorial reconstruction might explain the existence of "bad" or inferior quartos of some of Shakespeare's plays, though this is no longer universally accepted.

octavo A bookmaking format in which each large sheet of paper is folded three times, making eight leaves (sixteen pages front and back). Only one of Shakespeare's plays, *3 Henry VI* (1595), was published in octavo format.

playbook See *promptbook.*

press variants Minor textual variations among pages in books of the same edition, resulting from corrections made in the course of printing or from damaged or slipped type.

promptbook A manuscript of a play (either foul papers or fair copy) annotated and adapted for performance by the theatrical company. The promptbook incorporated stage directions, notes on properties and special effects, and revisions, sometimes including those required by the Master of the Revels. Promptbooks may be identifiable by the replacement of characters' names with actors' names.

quarto A bookmaking format in which each large sheet of paper is folded twice, making four leaves (eight pages front and back). Quarto volumes were smaller and less expensive than books printed in the folio format.

recto Literally, the right-hand page; in a quarto volume, each signature consisted of four leaves each of which had a recto and a verso; the pages were then numbered 1r[ecto], 1v[erso], 2r, 2v, 3r, 3v, 4r, 4v.

scribal copy A transcript of a play produced by a professional scribe (or "scrivener"). Scribes tended to employ their own preferred spellings, abbreviations, and punctuation and could be responsible for introducing a variety of errors.

signature A section of an early book consisting of one group of folded pages (e.g., in a quarto, four leaves or eight pages). Early modern printers indicated each signature by a letter (e.g., A) to assist them in keeping track of the parts of the book to bind together.

single-text editing Editing a work by staying as close as possible to a single early authoritative base text, emending only where necessary for sense and without either conflating by incorporating words or passages from other cognate texts or by reconstructing passages from source materials or other forms of inference.

speech prefix (SP)   The indication of the identity of the speaker of the following line or lines. Early editions of Shakespeare's plays often use different prefixes at different points to designate the same person. On occasion, the name of the actor who was to play the role appears in place of the name of the character.

stage direction (SD)   The part of the text that is not spoken by any character but that indicates actions to be performed onstage. Stage directions in the earliest editions of Shakespeare's plays are sparse; some necessary directions, most notably exits, are missing, and others may appear earlier or later than the plot requires. Directions for action (e.g., "Pray you, undo this button") may be implied in the dialogue but are not necessarily followed in a given production. By convention, the most basic stage directions were written in Latin. "Exit" indicates the departure of a single actor from the stage, "exeunt" the departure of more than one. "Manet" indicates that a single actor remains onstage, "manent" that more than one remains. Lines accompanied by the stage direction "aside" are spoken so as not to be heard by the others onstage. This stage direction appeared in some early editions of Shakespeare plays, but other means were also used to indicate such speech (such as placing the words within parentheses), and sometimes no indication was provided.

Stationers' Register   The account books of the Company of Stationers (the guild of printers, publishers, and booksellers that controlled the London book trade), recording the fees paid by publishers to secure their rights to certain texts, as well as the transfer of these rights between publishers. The Stationers' Register thus provides a valuable if incomplete record of publication in England.

substantive text   The text of an edition based upon access to a manuscript, as opposed to a derivative text based only on an earlier edition.

typecase   The compartmentalized box in which movable type (metal letters, punctuation, etc.) was stored; capital, or "upper-case," letters were traditionally stored at the top of the typecase, "lower-case" letters at the bottom. Compositors drew individual type from the typecase for placing into a "compositor's stick" that held one line of type; from there the type would be transferred to a chase and secured to create a forme. Mistakes in sorting used type back into the typecase may account for some textual errors.

variorum editions   Comprehensive editions of a work or works in which the various views of previous editors and commentators are compiled.

verso   See *recto*

Essential Reference Books

Bate, Jonathan, and Russell Jackson, eds. *Shakespeare: An Illustrated Stage History.* New York: Oxford UP, 1996.

Bullough, Geoffrey, ed. *Narrative and Dramatic Sources of Shakespeare.* 8 vols. New York: Columbia UP, 1957–75.

Chambers, E. K. *The Elizabethan Stage.* 4 vols. Oxford: Clarendon, 1923.

———. *William Shakespeare: A Study of Facts and Problems.* 2 vols. Oxford: Clarendon, 1930.

Crystal, David. *Pronouncing Shakespeare: The Globe Experiment.* Cambridge: Cambridge UP, 2005.

Dent, R. W. *Shakespeare's Proverbial Language: An Index.* Berkeley: U of California P, 1981.

Dessen, Alan C., and Leslie Thomson. *A Dictionary of Stage Directions in English Drama, 1580–1642.* New York: Cambridge UP, 1999.

Dobson, E. J. *English Pronunciation, 1500–1700.* 2nd ed. 2 vols. Oxford: Clarendon, 1968.

Dobson, Michael, and Stanley Wells, eds. *The Oxford Companion to Shakespeare.* Oxford: Oxford UP, 2001.

Duffin, Ross W. *Shakespeare's Songbook.* New York: Norton, 2004.

Foakes, R. A. *Illustrations of the English Stage, 1580–1642.* Stanford: Stanford UP, 1985.

Greenblatt, Stephen, and Peter G. Platt, eds. *Shakespeare's Montaigne: The Florio Translation of the Essays, a Selection.* New York: New York Review Books, 2014.

Greg, W. W., ed. *Dramatic Documents from the Elizabethan Playhouses: Stage Plots: Actors' Parts: Prompt Books.* 2 vols. Oxford: Clarendon, 1931.

Gurr, Andrew. *Playgoing in Shakespeare's London.* 3rd ed. New York: Cambridge UP, 2004.

———. *The Shakespearean Stage, 1574–1642.* 4th ed. New York: Cambridge UP, 2009.

Henslowe, Philip. *Henslowe's Diary.* Ed. R. A. Foakes. 2nd ed. New York: Cambridge UP, 2002.

Hosley, Richard, ed. *Shakespeare's Holinshed: An Edition of Holinshed's Chronicles, 1587.* New York: Putnam, 1968.

Murphy, Andrew. *Shakespeare in Print: A History and Chronology of Shakespeare Publishing.* New York: Cambridge UP, 2003.

Oxford Dictionary of National Biography. Oxford: Oxford UP, 2004. www.oxforddnb.com/

Oxford English Dictionary. Oxford: Clarendon, 1989. www.oed.com/

Partridge, A. C. *Orthography in Shakespeare and Elizabethan Drama.* London: E. Arnold, 1964.

Partridge, Eric. *Shakespeare's Bawdy: A Literary and Psychological Essay and a Comprehensive Glossary.* 3rd ed. New York: Routledge, 2001.

Schoenbaum, Samuel. *William Shakespeare: A Documentary Life.* New York: Oxford UP, 1975.

Spevack, Marvin. *A Complete and Systematic Concordance to the Works of Shakespeare.* 9 vols. Hildesheim: George Olms, 1968–80.

Stern, Tiffany. *Documents of Performance in Early Modern England.* Cambridge: Cambridge UP, 2009

Tilley, Morris Palmer. *A Dictionary of the Proverbs in England in the Sixteenth and Seventeenth Centuries*. Ann Arbor: U of Michigan P, 1950.

Wells, Stanley. *A Dictionary of Shakespeare*. 2nd ed. New York: Oxford UP, 2005.

———. *Re-Editing Shakespeare for the Modern Reader*. New York: Oxford UP, 1984.

Wickham, Glynne. *Early English Stages, 1300 to 1660*. 4 vols. New York: Routledge, 2002.

Williams, Gordon. *A Dictionary of Sexual Language and Imagery in Shakespearean and Stuart Literature*. 3 vols. London: Athlone, 1994.

For a much fuller bibliography, including critical and historical works bearing on the study of Shakespeare, see the Digital Edition of *The Norton Shakespeare*.

ILLUSTRATION ACKNOWLEDGMENTS

THE HOUSE OF YORK

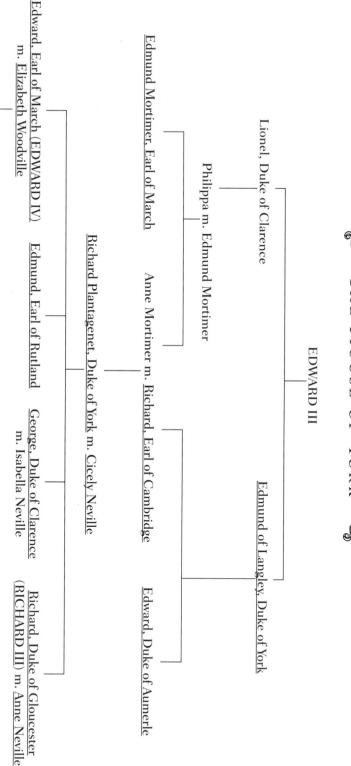

EDWARD III

Lionel, Duke of Clarence

Edmund of Langley, Duke of York

Philippa m. Edmund Mortimer

Edmund Mortimer, Earl of March

Anne Mortimer m. Richard, Earl of Cambridge

Edward, Duke of Aumerle

Richard Plantagenet, Duke of York m. Cicely Neville

Edward, Earl of March (EDWARD IV)
m. Elizabeth Woodville

Edmund, Earl of Rutland

George, Duke of Clarence
m. Isabella Neville

Richard, Duke of Gloucester
(RICHARD III) m. Anne Neville

Edward, Prince of Wales
(EDWARD V)

Richard, Duke of York

Elizabeth m. HENRY VII

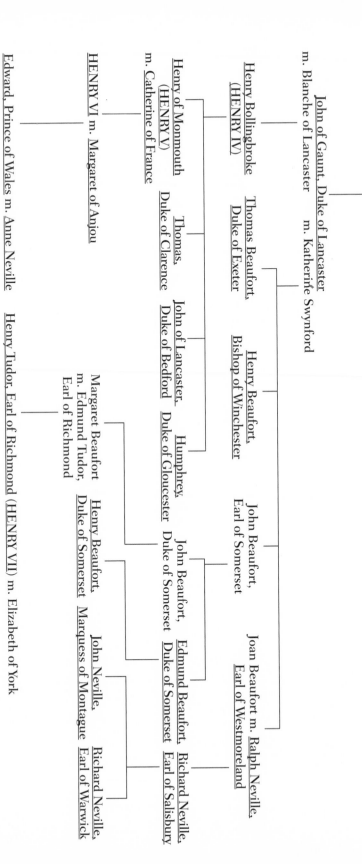

THE HOUSE OF LANCASTER

EDWARD III

John of Gaunt, Duke of Lancaster
m. Blanche of Lancaster   m. Katherine Swynford

Henry Bollingbroke (HENRY IV)

Thomas Beaufort, Duke of Exeter

Joan Beaufort m. Ralph Neville, Earl of Westmoreland

Henry of Monmouth (HENRY V)
m. Catherine of France

Thomas, Duke of Clarence

John of Lancaster, Duke of Bedford

Henry Beaufort, Bishop of Winchester

John Beaufort, Earl of Somerset

HENRY VI m. Margaret of Anjou

Humphrey, Duke of Gloucester

John Beaufort, Duke of Somerset

Edmund Beaufort, Duke of Somerset

Richard Neville, Earl of Salisbury

Margaret Beaufort
m. Edmund Tudor, Earl of Richmond

Henry Beaufort, Duke of Somerset

John Neville, Marquess of Montague

Richard Neville, Earl of Warwick

Edward, Prince of Wales m. Anne Neville

Henry Tudor, Earl of Richmond (HENRY VII) m. Elizabeth of York

TUDORS (1485–1603) AND STUARTS (1603–1714)

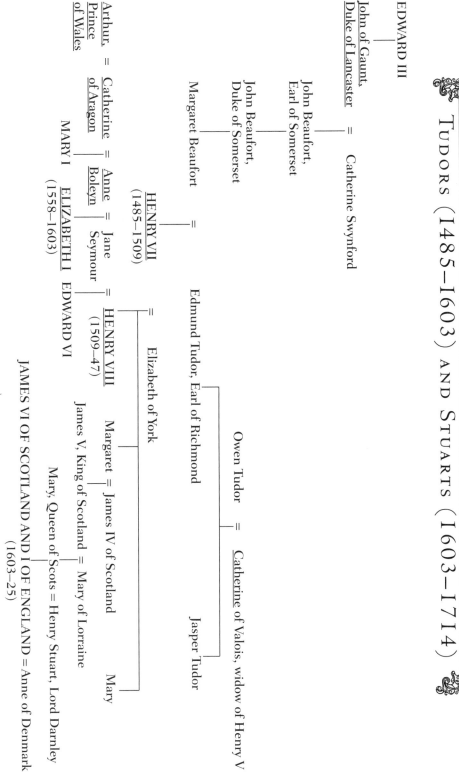

EDWARD III

John of Gaunt, Duke of Lancaster = Catherine Swynford

John Beaufort, Earl of Somerset

John Beaufort, Duke of Somerset

Margaret Beaufort = Edmund Tudor, Earl of Richmond

Owen Tudor = Catherine of Valois, widow of Henry V

Jasper Tudor

Arthur, Prince of Wales = Catherine of Aragon

HENRY VII (1485–1509) = Elizabeth of York

MARY I = Anne Boleyn = Jane Seymour

HENRY VIII (1509–47)

Margaret = James IV of Scotland

Mary

ELIZABETH I (1558–1603) EDWARD VI

James V, King of Scotland = Mary of Lorraine

JAMES VI OF SCOTLAND AND I OF ENGLAND (1603–25) = Anne of Denmark

Mary, Queen of Scots = Henry Stuart, Lord Darnley

An equal sign (=) stands for marriage. Underlined names indicate characters in the plays. Capitals note reigning Kings and Queens.